PERSONAL FINANCE

PERSONAL FINANCE

THIRD EDITION

E. Thomas Garman
Virginia Polytechnic Institute and State University

Raymond E. Forgue
University of Kentucky

HOUGHTON MIFFLIN COMPANY   Boston

Dallas   Geneva, Illinois
Palo Alto   Princeton, New Jersey

Cover photo by Robert Schoen Photography. Waltham, Massachusetts.

Library of Congress Catalog Number: 90–83020

ISBN: 0–395–43329–0

BCDEFGHIJ–RM–987654321

Contents

Preface

The 1990s have brought individuals the benefits of many new savings, credit, insurance, and investment options; but making financial decisions has become quite complex. It is much more difficult to manage finances today and avoid financial pitfalls than it was just 10 or 15 years ago. A solid understanding of the concepts and principles of personal finance is therefore absolutely vital. Accordingly, we believe it is essential to provide more than a simplistic approach to personal finance.

We have approached the subject of *Personal Finance* from the perspective of a prudent person who will apply specific personal finance concepts and principles to setting financial goals, choosing a career, budgeting and cash-flow management, managing cash, using credit, reducing income taxes, planning major expenditures, protecting income and assets, making investments, and making intelligent decisions about retirement and estate planning. We present the material in a way that will encourage readers to learn more about personal finance and managing finances effectively and successfully.

You probably have your own definition of "financial success," and the task of this book is to help you attain it. To do so will require that you practice effective personal financial management. You must plan, analyze, and control financial resources to successfully meet your personal financial goals. This involves using financial knowledge, skills, and tools in a confident manner to take advantage of favorable financial opportunities, to resolve personal financial problems, to achieve self-satisfaction, and to strive toward personal or family financial security.

Two broad goals underlay our efforts in writing *Personal Finance:* to help readers develop competence and to help them develop confidence. To *develop competence* in the subject of personal finance, the reader must be provided wide scope. We have worked to make this the most comprehensive textbook available, including all traditional topics and some of particular importance (such as speculative investments and investing in real estate). In addition, virtually all data in tables and illustrations are current through the summer of 1990. To help the reader become a lifelong competent manager of personal finances, we take a "how-to" approach, explaining, for example, how to select a career, manage cash, determine personal credit limits, reduce income taxes, buy a car, calculate how large a home mortgage loan can be afforded, select an insurance agent, choose a life insurance policy, select a stockbroker, compare mutual fund investments, project the anticipated return on any investment, and precisely determine retirement needs. We outline step-by-step procedures for the more complex financial activities, such as developing a total personal financial plan, planning and reconciling a 12-month budget, calculating income taxes, and determining how much life insurance is needed. Moreover, we aim to help the reader plan for a prosperous financial future—which is an increasingly complex task in a continually evolving financial marketplace—and we aim to help the reader actually become successful in personal financial matters for the rest of his or her life.

To *develop confidence* in the subject of personal finance, the reader needs to be led *through*, not simply *to*, the material. We aim to acquaint the reader with the subject matter logically and to offer no unanticipated "surprises." Assuming that most students in personal finance have little background in finance, economics, and mathematics, we have provided the supporting knowledge when necessary. Numerical examples are always explained parenthetically, and we have endeavored to discuss the benefits and costs of different personal finance decisions. Key words and concepts—which are printed in boldface type—are clearly and completely defined when they first occur and often again in later chapters, in case the chapters are read out of sequence.

There are over 200 tables, charts, and illustrations throughout the text, including many facsimiles of forms that are used in personal finance, such as checks, cash-management account statements, credit and insurance applications, and up-to-date income tax schedules. Both beginning- and end-of-chapter pedagogical materials are designed to develop confidence in the subject of personal finance.

Major Changes in the Third Edition

We have thoroughly enjoyed the challenge of updating and revising *Personal Finance*. The second edition became a best-selling book in the field. It was popular with students because of the informal writing style and with instructors because it was so readable that the students came to class prepared. We have again aimed to keep the narrative conversational and yet clear and concise. Responding to the comments and suggestions of both users and nonusers, we made revisions in central focus, topical treatment, organization, boxed inserts, tables and figures, and pedagogy.

Central Focus Most importantly, we have taken a personal finance perspective. This emphasizes how to develop and implement long-range plans to achieve financial objectives. This approach requires not a single plan, but a coordinated series of plans covering various parts of a person's overall financial affairs. Such financial planning is customized because it takes into consideration all financial aspects as an individual or family moves through life, making adjustments as they become appropriate, planning for changing financial needs in life, and dealing with each new situation as it occurs. This approach necessitates a completely integrated text to fully permit the reader to develop and implement his or her long-range plans to achieve financial success.

Topical Treatment   To keep pace with changes in the financial services industry and provide a complete perspective on personal finance, we have added emphasis on a number of current topics, such as using financial ratios to assess and guide financial progress, talking with your spouse about money matters, "cafeteria" fringe-benefit insurance plans offered by employers, no-fault automobile insurance, creative home mortgage financing, using a home-equity credit-line loan, employee stock ownership plans, new Securities and Exchange Commission requirements on advertising of yields, using arbitration to settle disputes with stockbrokers, investing using the asset-allocation technique, stocks with dividend reinvestment plans, using beta to estimate a rate of return, convertible securities, zero-coupon bonds, collateralized mortgage obligations, why people fail financially, what it takes to succeed financially, choosing between a rebate or a low-interest automobile loan, and employer-sponsored retirement plans.

Organization   We have held close to the successful format of the second edition, with three major changes. We have a new Chapter 2, Careers and Other Key Factors That Affect Income. In addition, we have resequenced the investments so that the discussion on buying and selling securities and managing your portfolio immediately follows material on investing in stocks, bonds, and mutual funds. Also, we provide a new appendix, entitled Careers in Personal Financial Planning and Counseling (Appendix E).

Boxed Inserts   We have added 13 new boxed inserts that highlight topics of special interest, such as What Does It Take for You to Reach Financial Success and Happiness, A Sample Resume, Cafeteria Plan Insurance Benefits: You Choose, Some Helpful Sources of Financial Planning Advice, Relative Interest Rates for Cash-Management Opportunities, Average First-Year Life Insurance Sales Commissions, and How to Invest: A Twelve-Step Process.

Tables and Figures   We have added 15 new tables and figures, such as Steps and Goals in Personal Finance Management, The Building Blocks of Financial Success, How Your Income Is Really Taxed, Automobile Liability Insurance Policy Limits, Illustrative Disability Income Insurance Premiums, What Is a Fair Price for Term Life Insurance? The Risk Pyramid in Investments, Illustrative Investment Portfolios, Techniques of Asset Allocation, Bond Prices Move When Interest Rates Change, Best and Worst Investments of the 1980s, and Typical Monthly Benefits from Company Pension Plans.

Pedagogy   Some new learning aids have been added, and substantial revisions to other pedagogy have been made. Most chapters have a new feature that responds to the big "what if" questions—key hypothetical questions so frequently asked by students, such as "What if you choose country living over life in the big city?" "What if you want to become more marketable?" "What if you and your spouse have conflicting personal spending styles?"

To emphasize key concepts, we have provided more than 600 marginal notes that highlight the material discussed in the text. We have also substantially updated the glossary at the end of the text.

Another new feature appearing in most chapters is "Advice for the Conservative . . . ." Each segment provides useful and practical advice (not esoteric recommendations) for spending, saving, and investing.

Case Problems   We have completely rewritten all the end-of-chapter case problems to improve clarity. A computer disk symbol marks those questions that can be answered both mathematically *and* with our revised software, *Personal Finance Cookbook* (free to adopters). The new cases also attempt to represent a variety of lifestyle stages as well as gender, racial, ethnic, and occupational groups. All cases require the student to carefully apply the concepts covered in the particular chapter.

Modern Money Management   This continuing case study has been updated to incorporate questions that can be answered using our revised software.

Suggested Readings   We have updated the Suggested Readings at the end of each chapter. All entries are from current periodicals such as *Money* and *Changing Times*.

Organization and Topical Coverage

As can be seen in the table of contents, we have approached topical coverage in a manner that provides a full explanation of the fundamentals of a topic before commencing further study. For example, chapters on the fundamentals of insurance (Chapter 11) and the fundamentals of investments (Chapter 15) precede chapters on specific types of insurance and investments. In addition, each chapter has a place in an overall sequence, but each is also a complete whole. Thus the chapters can be rearranged to be read in another developmental sequence with minimal loss of comprehension.

Part One provides an introduction to financial planning. Chapter 1 discusses what you will gain from the study of personal finance, describes the goals of financial planning, and helps you understand the economic environment so you can succeed financially by forecasting inflation, interest rates, and the state of the economy. Chapter 2 examines careers and other key factors that affect income, including some of the new "wild cards" available for people in the changing future workplace. In Chapter 3 we explain how to do financial planning over your life and review the types of financial records and statements that are pertinent to success in effective personal financial management, such as tax records and documents, balance sheets, and income and expense statements. Chapter 4 discusses how people can better understand how to talk about money; presents an overview of the financial tasks, problems, and challenges over various periods of the life cycle; and then illustrates a complete financial plan before examining the specifics of budgeting and cash-flow management (goal setting, planning, decision making, implementing, controlling, and evaluating).

Part Two, comprising four chapters, discusses the specifics of managing money. Chapter 5 examines the new concept of "cash management," which involves making effective use of today's changing financial services industry to earn maximum interest on your checking account, savings account, money market account, and other low-risk savings instruments. Chapter 6 discusses credit use and credit cards, including the new legal protections that are available, and Chapter 7 treats the subjects of the planned use of credit, non-credit-card borrowing, and what happens should you become overextended using credit. In Chapter 8 we take the student through all phases of personal income taxation—especially how to legally avoid taxes—and we give advice on how to successfully win an audit with the IRS. (To emphasize our view that reducing personal taxes can be crucial to obtaining funds for spending, saving, or investing—and improving one's lifestyle—we also discuss taxation wherever it is appropriate to do so in other chapters.)

In Part Three we focus on expenditure management. We cover automobiles and other major expenditures in Chapter 9, discussing several ways to save money when purchasing goods and services and detailing the several steps in the planned buying process, with emphasis on automobile purchases. Chapter 10 focuses on the housing expenditure, covering all aspects in the home-buying process, including new methods of financing, as well as renting (especially since renting is sometimes the wiser choice), and we provide information on selling a home.

Income and asset protection is the topic of Part Four. No text on personal finance is complete without a chapter, such as we have in Chapter 11, that thoroughly explains the concepts fundamental to understanding risk management, insurance, and how to purchase insurance coverage. Chapter 12 examines property and liability insurance (emphasizing automobile and home-related property and liability coverage). Chapter 13 details health and disability insurance and shows how such policies interface with Social Security coverage. Chapter 14 covers all the key concepts in term and cash-value life insurance (including single-premium life insurance and universal life insurance).

Because the topic of investments is too complex to treat superficially, Part Five, Investment Planning, contains seven separate chapters on investment fundamentals, stocks, bonds, mutual funds, buying and selling securities, real estate as an investment, and speculative investments. This breakdown of the topic into numerous chapters will offer instructors more flexibility in deciding which topics to teach. In all these chapters, we provide enough details for the reader to decide which investment alternatives are most suitable. Also, we provide specific guidelines on when each investment should be sold. Importantly, we offer a lengthy discussion (Chapter 19) on how to manage your long-term investments.

The text concludes with two valuable chapters in Part Six on financial planning for the future: Chapter 22 examines developing and implementing a plan for a secure retirement, and Chapter 23 reviews the essentials of estate planning, including wills and the importance of trusts in estate planning.

We also have provided six appendixes. Appendix A has over two dozen key illustrations of how to use the present and future value tables. Appendix B thoroughly explicates how to use the indexing method to calculate Social Security benefits. Appendix C provides details on how to use a computer to aid personal financial management. Appendix D offers a summary list of all the major concepts in *Personal Finance* (perhaps to be used by instructors on the last day of teaching a class in personal finance). Appendix E is on careers in personal financial planning and counseling. Appendix F provides instructions on how to use the *Personal Finance Cookbook* computer software.

Supplements to Text

Six supplements are available with the *Personal Finance* text: an *Instructor's Resource Manual with Test Bank*, a student *Study Guide*, a computerized version of the *Study Guide* called *Microstudy*, a computerized version of the test bank called *Microtest* (which allows the instructor to make up examinations), a professionally prepared set of 50 transparencies, and a revised computer software program called *Personal Finance Cookbook*.

The *Instructor's Resource Manual with Test Bank*, written by Professor Vicki Hampton of the University of Texas, has six components: suggested course outlines to emphasize a general approach to personal finance, insurance, or an investments approach to the subject; detailed outlines for each chapter; outside research class projects and assignments (and illustrative answers); and answers and solutions to all end-of-chapter Modern Money Management questions, review questions, and case problems. The manual also includes a test bank of over 2,000 questions, with the correct answers identified and the numbers of the pages in the textbook on which the responses to the questions can be found. Nearly 200 transparency masters are also included which illustrate most text tables and figures as well as some boxed inserts and formulas.

A comprehensive *Study Guide*, written by the authors, has the following components: detailed chapter summaries of all key ideas, lists of objectives, lists of Key Words and Concepts, completion exercises with correct responses printed alongside for programmed learning, true-false and multiple-choice questions to provide a self-check learning (all key terms are covered), and answers and solutions to *Study Guide* questions and problems. Additional case problems and applications are also included, giving students the opportunity to practice their analytical and decision-making skills utilizing personal finance concepts and principles as well as mathematical computations.

Approximately 50 professional-quality transparencies also are free to adopters of 50 copies or more of *Personal Finance*. These transparencies—

which include selected tables, figures, formulas, and boxed inserts from the text—illustrate the most commonly taught concepts in personal finance.

Microstudy and *Microtest* are computerized versions of the *Study Guide* and of the test bank portion of the *Instructor's Resource Manual with Test Bank*.

The *Personal Finance Cookbook (PFC)* is a computer software program provided free to adopters, who may make copies for students. The free version of PFC requires a spreadsheet program, such as LOTUS, to operate. The *Personal Finance Cookbook* software can be used with the text, or the programs could be used in one's own personal financial planning.

Acknowledgments

An instructional package of this breadth and depth could not be created without the assistance of many people. We should, of course, mention our reviewers, who offered helpful suggestions and criticisms of the first and second editions of the text. We especially appreciate the assistance of Hal Babson, Columbus Technical Institute; Rosella Bannister, Eastern Michigan University; Robert Blatchford, Tulsa Junior College; Jeffrey Born, University of Kentucky; Andrew Cao, American University; Charlotte Churaman, University of Maryland; Patricia Cowley, Scott & Stringfellow, Inc.; Joel J. Dauten, Arizona State University; Elizabeth Dolan, University of New Hampshire; Sidney W. Eckert, Appalachian State University; Mary Ellen Edmondson, University of Kentucky; Elizabeth Goldsmith, Florida State University; Hilda Hall, Surry Community College; Roger P. Hill, University of North Carolina, Wilmington; Jagdish R. Kapoor, College of DuPage; Naheel Jeries, Iowa State University; Eloise J. Law, State University of New York at Plattsburgh; Ruth H. Lytton, Virginia Polytechnic Institute and State University; Kenneth Marin, Aquinas College; Julia Marlowe, University of Georgia; Jerald W. Mason, International Association of Financial Planning; Randolph J. Mullis, University of Wisconsin (Madison); Steven J. Muck, El Camino College; Donald Neuhart, Central Missouri State University; William S. Phillips, Memphis State University; Carl H. Pollock, Jr., Portland State University; Thomas R. Pope, University of Kentucky; Eloise Lorch Rippie, Iowa State University; Michael Rupured, University of Kentucky; Wilmer E. Seago, Virginia Polytechnic Institute and State University; Horacio Soberon-Ferrer, University of Maryland at College Park; Mary Stephenson, University of Maryland at College Park; Jerry A. Viscione, Boston College; Grant J. Wells, Ball State University; Dorothy West, Michigan State University; and Tony Campolo, Columbus State Community College.

A survey of hundreds of personal finance instructors gave us additional insights into what teachers wanted in the overall instructional package. Indepth questionnaires were completed by a number of users and nonusers. In addition, we wish to thank Ruth H. Lytton (Virginia Polytechnic Institute and State University), who rewrote many of the end-of-chapter case problems and Modern Money Management narratives; Keisha Lamb (University of Kentucky), who served as a research assistant; Donna Brewer (Virginia Polytechnic Institute and State University), who also served as a research assistant; and the many students who had the opportunity to read, critique, and provide research inputs for various components of the *Personal Finance* project. The text has been unquestionably strengthened by all these contributions. We are deeply appreciative of the generous assistance given by all.

A project of this dimension would never have been completed without the patience, support, understanding, and sacrifices of our friends and families during the book's development, revision, and production. Thanks are also offered to those who have meant so much through the years: for Tom: Lucy Garman, Ron West, William Boast, and John Binnion; for Ray: Mary Ellen Edmondson, Gary Forgue, and Irene Leech.

Finally, we wish to thank the hundreds of instructors of personal finance around the country who have been generous enough to share their views on what should and should not be included in a high-quality textbook with ancillary materials. We have attempted to meet those needs in every way possible not only in the text, but also in the *Study Guide*, the *Personal Finance Cookbook*, and the *Instructor's Resource Manual with Test Bank*. We hope we have succeeded because we share the strong bias that students need to study personal finance concepts thoroughly and learn them well so that they may apply them effectively and successfully in their personal lives.

E. Thomas Garman
Raymond E. Forgue

P.S. Dear Students: If you are going to save any of your college textbooks, be certain to save this one. The principles of lifetime financial success remain the same forever. Also, you may wish to present the book as a gift to a spouse or a parent.

PERSONAL FINANCE

PART ONE

Financial Planning

1 The Importance of Personal Finance

OBJECTIVES

After reading this chapter, you should be able to

1. Discuss what you will gain from the study of personal finance.
2. Describe the five goals of effective personal financial management.
3. Understand the economic environment of personal finance so you can forecast inflation, interest rates, and the state of the economy.
4. Recognize fundamental economic considerations that affect financial decision making.
5. Describe the six key steps to successfully achieve your personal financial goals.

· · · · · · · · ·

Whether you are age 20, 31, or 58, you are lucky to be reading this book, because few people have the opportunity to study personal finance formally. Americans usually spend 12 to 16 years in school, where they become capable of earning an income without learning how to manage it.

Typically, people finish school, get a job, and start spending their earnings. And in that spending, they often make many mistakes. For example, they might choose a bank that has high costs for checking services, use credit cards that charge ridiculously high interest rates, or buy a seriously overpriced life insurance policy. They might finance an automobile for more in interest per year than necessary, rent an apartment that turns out to be too expensive, or buy a home in January and, because of a career change, move to another community in August and be forced to sell quickly at a financial loss. Also, they might invest in the stock of a company on the recommendation of a friend, only to find its value sharply declining, or pay an additional $400 in income taxes because they neglected to put some funds into a qualified retirement program. We suggest that money is easier to earn than it is to manage.

This textbook will thoroughly introduce you to the hows and whys of personal finance. You, too, will make mistakes in financial matters, because we all do. But studying this text will help you to make fewer mistakes in personal finance and will help you to become an effective and successful personal financial manager for the rest of your life.

This chapter begins by examining what you will gain by studying the subject of personal finance and the five goals of effective personal financial management so that you can begin to reflect on your personal financial values and goals. To be successful in financial matters also requires an understanding of the economic environment of personal finance so that you can forecast inflation, interest rates, and the state of the economy. It is also useful to recognize some fundamental economic considerations in financial decision making, such as opportunity costs, marginal analysis, income taxes, and the time value of money. Finally, we provide an overview of the six key steps to successfully achieve your personal financial goals.

What Will You Gain from Studying Personal Finance?

You probably recognize that life and the living process sometimes can be difficult and will get more involved as you grow older. You will make

Objective
To be able to discuss
what you will gain from
the study of personal
finance.

many complex decisions throughout your life, some related to your education, your career, and your personal lifestyle and many that affect your financial success. Although making these kinds of decisions may be accompanied by some anxious and uncomfortable moments, as you gain experience and become better educated, you will be better prepared to choose wisely.

Handling your personal finances with proficiency will help make your life more enjoyable. Unfortunately, many people do not learn about personal finance matters until they become mired in financial problems—they "learn from bad experience." Studying personal finance will help you avoid such difficulties and show you how to take advantage of financial opportunities. **Personal finance** is the study of personal and family resources considered important in achieving financial success; thus it has to do with how people spend, save, protect, and invest their money. Topics typically include budgeting, cash management, using credit cards, borrowing, tax management, major expenditures, risk management, investments, retirement planning, and estate planning. Successful study of personal finance topics will help you face the financial challenges, responsibilities, and opportunities of life successfully by helping you to (1) acquire financial knowledge, (2) develop your ability to effectively use financial skills and tools, (3) clarify your financial values and goals, and (4) identify specific needs and wants that can be satisfied with your financial resources.

Personal finance has to do with spending, saving, and investing.

Closely associated is the topic of **personal financial planning.** This is the process of developing and implementing long-range plans to achieve financial success. Making personal financial plans is a useful exercise and is instrumental in achieving success. Time will tell whether the efforts that you put into your personal financial matters lead to success or failure. To do well, you need to practice **effective personal financial management.** This is the process of planning, analyzing, and controlling financial resources to successfully meet personal financial goals by using financial knowledge, skills, and tools in a confident manner to take advantage of favorable financial opportunities, to resolve personal financial problems, to achieve self-satisfaction, and to strive toward personal or family financial security. Hence the focus of this book is to provide you with all of the "nuts and bolts"—knowledge, skills, tools, strategies, and tactics—necessary for you to plan and achieve personal financial success.

Acquiring Financial Knowledge

Acquiring financial knowledge is crucial to success.

Most of us seek a life of quality and financial security. We want to be able to make intelligent decisions about how to spend or invest our money and to eventually acquire some degree of wealth. A practical approach toward achieving these goals involves learning about the specific financial activities we will encounter: recordkeeping and budgeting, cash management, credit use, borrowing, paying taxes, making major expenditures (such as housing and an automobile), buying insurance, selecting investments, and making plans for retirement. In order to handle your personal finances both systematically and successfully, you must acquire knowledge about these topics.

Developing Financial Skills and Tools

Developing your ability to use financial skills and tools helps too.

As you acquire financial knowledge, you will develop financial skills and learn to use financial tools. **Financial skills** are techniques of decision making in effective personal financial management. Preparing a useful budget, establishing appropriate criteria to select investments, choosing an inexpensive insurance plan, and using credit wisely are examples of financial skills. **Financial tools** are the forms, charts, and other instruments used in making effective personal financial management decisions. Examples of financial tools are checks, credit cards, debit cards, insurance policies, investment prospectuses, and financial charts and tables.

Clarifying Financial Values and Goals

Clarifying financial values and goals makes for satisfaction.

A basic understanding of how you feel about money is important to effective personal financial management. In fact, studying personal finance gives you the opportunity to clarify your financial values and goals. For example, do you value a dollar more for the security it represents (a conservative and traditional viewpoint), for the expected return it might provide if prudently invested in a strong company (a more moderate viewpoint), or for the potential return it might provide if invested in the volatile commodities market (a risk-taking perspective with greater possibility of either gain or loss of money invested)? There is no single correct choice, because different people have different financial values.

Gaining a better understanding of your financial values (which remain rather consistent throughout life) will help clarify your financial goals as well. For example, Page Russell, a computer programmer and single mother of one child from Prescott, Arizona, wants to own a sporty-looking automobile. An $18,000 Ford Mustang might fulfill her goal, or it might take a $48,000 Porsche. Page is quite conservative in money matters, so she decides on the Mustang for three reasons: (1) she expects a relatively low and safe return on her present investments, which would not provide much extra money to be spent on car payments; (2) she probably would never seriously consider spending as much money on a car as a Porsche costs, because she believes that would be too much money going out for transportation; and (3) she would not feel comfortable having so much money tied up in an automobile when she could invest the funds elsewhere for her child's education. Page's conservative nature wins out.

Your financial values and goals are interrelated, and you will probably need to clarify them; this topic is examined in Chapter 2, Careers and Other Key Factors That Affect Income. How people value issues of money and learn to discuss financial matters with "significant others" is thoroughly examined in Chapter 4, Budgeting and Cash-Flow Management.

Identifying Specific Needs and Wants

Identifying specific needs and wants helps create success.

We all have many needs, and sometimes too many wants. **Needs** are those items which people find necessary to have to survive and live in society. Examples of basic needs are food, shelter, clothing, and medical services.

Wants are items that people would like to have to improve their comfort and satisfaction. Your individual wants will largely depend on your interests, tastes, lifestyle, and financial resources.

You will be able to satisfy more of your wants as you increase your knowledge of personal finance. You also will learn to apply this knowledge to help you distinguish between your needs and wants and to help you set priorities. If your personal financial management is ineffective, you may have to spend most of your income on needs. If you become proficient in handling your personal finances, however, you can acquire all your needs as well as numerous wants.

The Five Goals of Effective Personal Financial Management

Financial success is achievement of financial aspirations that are desired, planned, or attempted. It is defined by the individual or family that seeks it. For some people, financial success may be a financially secure retirement. Others may want vast wealth by the age of 50, and some may just want enough money to educate their children. Most people probably simply want a comfortable lifestyle. To be successful each individual must establish his or her own long-term personal financial objectives.

The broad goals of effective personal financial management are (1) to maximize earnings and wealth, (2) to practice efficient consumption, (3) to find life satisfaction, (4) to reach financial security, and (5) to accumulate wealth for retirement and a financial estate to leave to heirs. These goals are very much related; in fact, to achieve one, you probably need to achieve the others. The following sections describe these goals of effective personal financial management.

Maximizing Earnings and Wealth

A key step is to maximize earnings.

Wealth is an abundance of money, property, investments, and other resources. In order to attain the goal of maximizing wealth, you must first seek to maximize earnings. Whether you choose to maximize earnings primarily through employment or through investments will depend on your tastes, interests, and **lifestyle** (the way of living that reflects the attitudes and values of an individual or group).

Practicing Efficient Consumption

We use money for two purposes: consumption and savings. Since consumption spending, or buying goods and services, uses up the largest portion of income, it is important to practice it efficiently. Practicing efficient consumption requires developing effective personal financial management skills and techniques, such as keeping sound financial records and using credit and checking accounts inexpensively. Failure to practice efficient consumption is often the result of the careless use of money on

Advice for the Conservative College Athlete (and Most Everyone Else): Learn About Personal Finance

Many college athletes who are good enough to get a scholarship want to become good enough to become professionals. While in school they have little free time beyond training and maintaining a minimum grade point average. Football, baseball, basketball, hockey, and other professional sports pay substantial salaries for rookies, often $250,000 or more.

Yet, throughout their school years, college athletes live protected lives, and most are totally unprepared to handle personal financial management problems and opportunities. Many coaches are wonderfully supportive of their athletes but do little to help them understand personal finance. The National Collegiate Athletic Association (NCAA) requires athletes to forfeit their college eligibility if they sign a contract with an agent before their school careers are completed. Thus most college athletes live on limited budgets (instead of getting bonuses for signing professional contracts), while scholarships pay for some food, lodging, and book expenses. The nurturing

process continues for the successful athlete who later signs a professional contract, because agents typically negotiate the contract, obtain endorsements, provide the athlete with a spending allowance, offer advice on financial decisions, and draw up a will. Professional rookies are ill-prepared to handle their huge salaries.

Most colleges do nothing to help future professional athletes prepare for the world of high finance. Schools also do little to help the 11,999 of 12,000 players who do not get the opportunity to sign professional contracts and instead must face the challenges of getting a job and living on a regular income of $15,000, or perhaps $25,000, like many other college graduates. While college athletes are balancing academics and athletics, they ought to be encouraged to take a course or two in personal finance to enhance self-esteem, psychological security, and personal power as an effective and mature manager of money. Everybody else in college should be so encouraged.

nonessentials, abuse of credit, and/or poor judgment on purchases. Obtaining a 10 percent savings through efficient consumption is equivalent to a 10 percent increase in income, or more because this income is not taxed. Thorough study of unfamiliar areas of consumption can help you achieve the goal of efficient consumption, and you will have more money available to spend on other products and services or to save or invest.

Finding Life Satisfaction

Most people generally strive for quality and satisfaction in their lives. Some very important goals associated with **quality of life** are love, self-esteem, good health, achievement, and a general feeling of security. Many Americans find additional life satisfaction in owning material goods and enjoying investment income.

What kinds of things will help give you satisfaction in your life? Having a challenging job and earning a good living? Having warm personal relationships? Achieving a comfortable lifestyle? You may feel that accu-

What Does It Take for You to Reach Financial Success and Happiness?

We suggest throughout this book that for *you* to reach financial success and happiness, you should

1. Set some specific long-term financial goals and develop a plan to achieve them (Chapters 3 and 4).
2. Organize your financial records (Chapter 3).
3. Save regularly (Chapters 3 and 4).
4. Develop and use some kind of realistic budget where income usually exceeds expenses (Chapter 4).
5. Be able to discuss personal financial problems, concerns, and goals with significant others (Chapter 4).
6. Be in a career path that provides emotional satisfaction and a reasonable income (Chapter 2).
7. Be financially capable of paying for most unexpected expenses (Chapter 4).
8. Have an interest-earning checking account (Chapter 5).
9. Have more than one type of cash-management account, such as checking, savings, money market, certificates of deposit, and savings bonds that earn the best interest rates (Chapter 5).
10. Have access to revolving credit accounts and know how to efficiently use them (Chapter 6).
11. Have access to relatively inexpensive installment credit sources (Chapter 7).
12. Set your own appropriate personal debt limits (Chapter 7).
13. Know how to pay the lowest possible annual percentage rates for credit (Chapter 7).
14. Take advantage of legal ways to reduce income taxes (Chapter 8).
15. Not pay too much in income taxes (Chapter 8).
16. Know how to comparison shop when buying goods and services (Chapter 9).
17. Adequately manage transportation expenses (Chapter 9).
18. Plan when and how to make major expenditures (Chapter 9).
19. Know how to effectively complain to obtain redress when appropriate (Chapter 9).
20. Efficiently manage current housing expenditures (Chapter 10).
21. Properly apply the principles of risk management (Chapter 11).

(continued)

mulating many costly material goods is one measure of quality of life. Or you may value good health or strong friendships more than material goods. In order to reach the life satisfaction you seek, you must make decisions related to your personal financial management, such as which career to choose, what to buy, how much to save, whether to invest, and where to live. Financial success is a means to a better quality of life, whether you intend on living well or donating most of your income to charity.

Reaching Financial Security

What are your indicators of financial security?

Financial security is the comfortable feeling that your financial resources will be enough to fulfill any needs you have as well as most of your wants. People enjoying financial security have confidence in their money matters

What Does It Take for You to Reach Financial Success and Happiness? *(continued)*

22. Understand how to minimize the cost of buying insurance (Chapter 11).
23. Know how to properly select and utilize employee fringe benefits in the areas of health, life, dental, and long-term disability (Chapters 11 through 14).
24. Purchase adequate property and casualty insurance coverage at fair prices (Chapter 12).
25. Purchase adequate and fairly priced health insurance coverage (Chapter 13).
26. Understand how the disability benefit portion of Social Security coverage can have a positive impact on your disability insurance needs (Chapter 13).
27. Purchase fairly priced and adequate long-term disability insurance coverage (Chapter 13).
28. Understand how the survivor's benefit portion of Social Security coverage can have a positive impact on your life insurance needs (Chapter 14).
29. Select the proper type of life insurance to fit your needs based on coverage and costs (Chapter 14).
30. Be adequately but not overly protected by life insurance coverage purchased at fair prices (Chapter 14).
31. Possess knowledge about how to buy and sell investments appropriate to your needs (Chapters 15 through 21).
32. Have investments that match your investment philosophy (Chapter 15).
33. Be making progress in your current investments (Chapter 15).
34. Be able to wisely consider alternative investments other than savings (Chapters 15 through 21).
35. Understand how the retirement benefit portion of Social Security can have a positive impact on your retirement income needs (Chapter 22).
36. Utilize employer and private tax-sheltered savings, investment, and retirement programs (Chapter 22).
37. Have a valid will and some understanding of the techniques of proper estate planning to minimize taxes and adequately provide for heirs (Chapter 23).

and are largely free from doubt, anxiety, or fear about financial concerns. Indicators of financial security include a steady income to provide a basic lifestyle, a career with potential for advancement (or retirement from such a career), an adequate emergency savings fund, a home with affordable mortgage debt, adequate insurance coverage, investments in real estate other than a primary residence, a long-term investment program that likely includes corporate and government securities, a tax-sheltered retirement plan, an estate plan, and a will.

To reach financial security, first you need to set and prioritize your long- and short-term goals. This, of course, will give direction to your spending, credit use, saving, and investing. For example, if you spend most or all of your earnings on recreation or entertainment, you will have little money left for saving and investing. Chapter 3, Financial Planning over Your Life, goes into detail on how to set and achieve financial goals.

Accumulating Wealth for Retirement and an Estate

Retirement is a state of life that people either look forward to or cringe from with apprehension. It is the number one reason why people save money. A popular goal is having a retirement income sufficient to live in a style that is "comfortable." People typically seek to accumulate wealth to (1) provide income at retirement and (2) build a financial estate that can be passed on to their survivors upon their death. Retirement and estate accumulation are essential goals to work toward during your lifetime, and these topics are thoroughly examined in Chapters 22 and 23.

Understanding the Economic Environment of Personal Finance

Your success as an effective personal financial manager depends in part on how well you understand and utilize information to cope with the economic environment. **Forecasting** is the ability to predict, estimate, or calculate in advance. You should easily be able to forecast your income, income taxes, and living expenses. But you also need to be able to forecast inflation, interest rates, and the state of the economy so that you can have advance warning of the economic trends affecting your personal finances. Armed with such insight you can take some *planning* actions that reduce risks to exposure to conditions in the economy beyond your control. Planning involves working out beforehand a detailed scheme, program, or method for the accomplishment of an objective given certain assumptions.

Effects of Inflation on Income and Consumption

Inflation can dramatically affect your income and consumption.

When prices are rising, income also must rise in order to maintain its **purchasing power,** which is how much in goods and services one's income will buy. **Inflation** is a steady rise in the general level of prices, and it is measured by the changing cost over time of a market basket of goods and services. Inflation occurs when the supply of money (or credit) rises faster than the supply of goods and services available for purchases because of excessive demand and/or because of sharply increasing costs of production. Inflation also can be self-perpetuating. Workers will ask for higher wages, thereby adding to the cost of production. Manufacturers will charge more for their products in response to the increases in the costs of labor and raw materials. Lenders will require higher interest rates to offset the lost purchasing power of the loaned funds. Consumers will lessen their resistance to price increases because they fear prices will be even higher in the future. In times of inflation, buying power declines and those on fixed incomes suffer the most.

From an income point of view, the impact of inflation is significant. Consider the case of Scott Marshall of Chicago, a single man who left the

FIGURE 1.1

Inflation and the Half-Life of a Dollar
Source: Used by permission of The Conference Board, 845 Third Avenue, New York, NY, 10022.

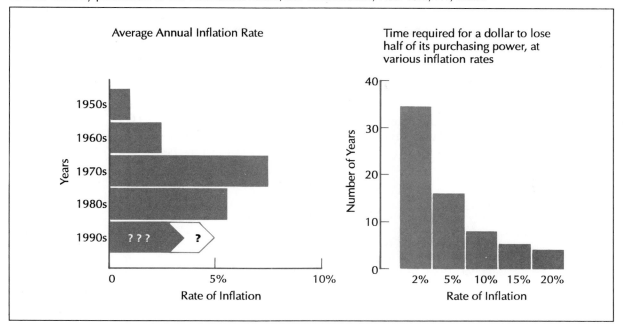

military and took a civilian job 3 years ago at $22,000 per year. Since that time, Scott has had annual raises of $1100, $1200, and $1300, but he still cannot make ends meet. The reason? Suppose the inflation rate was 6 percent each year. Even though Scott received raises, his new income ($22,000 + $1100 + $1200 + $1300 = $25,600) did not keep up with an annual inflation rate of 6 percent ($22,000 × 1.06 = $23,320 × 1.06 + $24,719 × 1.06 = $26,202). Scott lost purchasing power in the amount of $602 ($26,202 − $25,600) if his costs went up the same as the general price level.

Your **real income** (income measured in constant prices relative to some base time period) is the number that is important. It reflects the actual buying power of the current dollars (or **money income** or **nominal income**) that you have to spend. Rising money income during times of inflation gives the illusion that you are making more money, when in reality you may not be. Figure 1.1 illustrates inflation rates of recent decades and the half-life of a dollar, or the time required to lose half its purchasing power. If inflation in the 1990s slows somewhat from that of the 1980s, the purchasing power of a dollar will last longer. In any event, it is important to calculate your own real income to ascertain whether or not you personally are losing the battle against inflation. Personal incomes rarely keep up in times of high inflation.

Here is how to measure the effect of inflation on your raise.

To correctly make the comparison of your annual wage increase against the rate of inflation for the same time period, you must first convert your dollar raise into a percentage, as shown in Equation (1.1):

$$\frac{\text{Nominal income after the raise}}{\text{Nominal income last year}} = \text{percentage change in nominal income} - 1 \quad (1.1)$$

For example, if Luis Melendez, a single parent and assistant manager of a convenience store in Austin, Texas, received an $1800 raise to push his annual salary to $27,000 after a year during which inflation was 6.0 percent, he did better than the inflation rate because his raise amounted to 7.1 percent:

$$\frac{\$27,000}{\$25,200} = 1.071 - 1 = 7.1\%$$

Measured in real terms, Luis' raise was 1.1 percent (7.1 − 6.0). In dollars, Luis' real income after the raise can be calculated using Equation (1.2) by dividing his new nominal income by 1.0 plus the previous year's inflation rate:

$$\frac{\text{Nominal income after the raise}}{1.0 + \text{previous inflation rate}} = \text{real income} \quad (1.2)$$

$$\frac{\$27,000}{1 + 0.06} = \$25,472$$

It is clear that a good part of the $1800 raise Luis received was eaten up by inflation. To Luis, only $272 ($25,472 − $25,200) represents real economic progress, while $1528 ($1800 − $272) goes for inflated prices on goods and services. Note that the $272 real raise is equivalent to 1.1 percent (272/$25,200) of his previous income, reflecting the difference between his percentage raise in nominal dollars and the inflation rate.

Consumption is affected by inflation too. The **consumer price index (CPI)** is a broad measure of prices, or the cost of living for consumers, and is published monthly by the U.S. Bureau of Labor Statistics (BLS). The BLS, announces the CPI during the fourth week of every month. More than 400 prices of various goods and services sold across the country are tracked, recorded, weighted for importance in a hypothetical budget, and totaled. The index has a base time period, or starting reference point, from which to make comparisons. If 1982–1984 is the base period of 100 and the CPI is 134 in 1990, the cost of living has risen 34 percent since the base period [(134 − 100)/100]. Similarly, if in 1991 the index rises from 134 to 140, the cost of living has gone up. This time the increase has been 4.5 percent over 1 year (140 − 134 = 6; 6/134 = 4.5).

When prices rise, the purchasing power of the dollar declines.

When prices rise, the purchasing power of the dollar declines, but not by the same percentage. It falls the reciprocal amount of the price increase.

In the preceding example, prices rose 34 percent over 6 years and the purchasing power of the dollar declined 25.4 percent. [The base-year index of 100 divided by the 1990 index of 134 equals 0.746; the reciprocal is 25.4 (1 − 0.746), or 25.4 percent.] Similarly, in the preceding case in which prices rose 4.5 percent, the purchasing power declined 4.3 percent (134/140 = 0.957; the reciprocal is 0.043).

Inflation pushes up the costs of the products and services we consume. Rising prices for consumer products, such as new automobiles, provide an example. If automobile prices rose 25 percent over the past 5 years, then it will take $15,000 now to buy a car that used to sell for $12,000. Conversely, the purchasing power of the car-buying dollar has fallen to 80 percent of its original power ($12,000 ÷ $15,000) 5 years ago.

Effects of Inflation on Borrowing, Savings, and Investments

Inflation also affects your borrowing, savings, and investments —negatively.

Low inflation is good for the economy because it tends to keep interest rates down, which also makes money easily accessible for borrowers. **Interest rates** represent the price of money. Low inflation tends to increase real investment returns and make long-term personal financial management easier, because it is more predictable.

A high and/or rising inflation rate is bad news for stock and bond investors, whereas a falling inflation rate is good news. Lenders of money are negatively affected by high inflation. This is because dollars paid back by borrowers during inflationary times have less value than the amount originally borrowed. You are not making a penny if the inflation rate is 5¼ percent or more, and you are earning only 5¼ percent interest income on funds placed in a savings account (money actually loaned by you to a financial institution). Actually, you are losing money even when the inflation rate is the same as the interest rate because you must pay some of that interest income to the government in income taxes.

Inflation drives up both the real and the nominal costs of lending money. Interest rates on home mortgages and automobile loans always rise during times of high inflation. This leads to higher monthly repayments for home and automobile loans. High inflation rates negatively affect stock market prices because they reduce the value of future corporate earnings. In addition, high inflation rates can play havoc with long-term financial planning for retirement. Some people will have to postpone retirement during high inflationary times; those already retired will be financially squeezed as their buying power drops.

Investors who lend their money should make careful estimates of the future inflation rate so as to avoid losing purchasing power with the funds being returned in the future. Professional lenders, such as commercial banks and savings and loan associations, seek to earn a total return on monies they loan out sufficient to cover their costs, what they paid to get the funds they loan, estimated bad debts, an amount to compensate for inflation, and their hoped for net profit. You should do likewise.

Estimating Future Inflation

You should make your own estimates of future inflation so you can make sound financial decisions.

Inflation during the late 1980s was between 3 and 6 percent. Inflation was between 6 and 8 percent during the early 1980s following the highly inflationary times of the late 1970s, when it was between 9 and 13 percent. In the 1950s and early 1960s, inflation was between 1 and 3 percent. As you can see, inflation can vary considerably, and this makes forecasting inflation hazardous.

Projections about future inflation rates are made by the federal government's Office of Management and Budget (OMB), as well as by a number of economists and private organizations (such as Wharton, Data Resources, First Fidelity, and Merrill Lynch), and they are reported in popular newspapers and magazines, such as the *Wall Street Journal, U.S. News and World Report, Business Week, Money,* and *Changing Times.* In order to make sound financial decisions in the future, you need to make your own inflation estimates, both for the near term and for several years to come.

Your views on future inflation might be affected by how successful you think the U.S. Congress, the President, and the Federal Reserve Board will be in attempting to hold down inflation. Some people believe that the amount of inflation is directly related to the amount of overspending by the federal government. Anticipated world events also may affect inflation estimates, such as outbreaks of war, growth of peace, and supply cutbacks by the oil-producing OPEC countries. You should have little difficulty projecting inflation somewhat accurately over the near term, perhaps 1 or 2 years. Accurate long-term projections are more difficult to make, but they still must be made because many of your financial decisions will be significantly affected by inflation. You should be cautious in your estimates, perhaps erring slightly on the high side of inflation (because that will harm you the most), and you also need to retain some flexibility in your alternatives too in case long-term inflation estimates are off because of fundamental changes in the economy.

Projecting Future Interest Rates

You need to personally project future interest rates too.

Knowledge about interest rates gives you insight into what it will cost you to borrow and what rates you might earn on investments. When the rate of inflation is rising, things will cost more in the future; it will cost more to borrow also. Of course, the rate of inflation also eats into, and reduces, the value of future interest income. Accordingly, investors demand a much higher interest rate during times of high inflation. The degree of risk in a lending situation is higher for longer-term investments because there is a greater likelihood of error in the lender's inflation estimate when more time is involved. Thus long-term interest rates are generally higher than short-term interest rates because long-term investments are riskier.

You also should know how changing interest rates affect major investment areas. Rising interest rates depress stock prices because (1) businesses will have to pay more when they borrow, which will reduce profits, (2) future earnings will not be worth as much as today, and (3) stock investors are lured away to interest-paying investments that pay high rates, such as money-market funds and bonds.

You can forecast interest rates in the future by focusing on four key interest rates: (1) the **prime rate,** which is the short-term interest rate on loans that banks charge their large business customers with the highest credit rating, (2) the **three-month Treasury bill rate,** which is the rate the U.S. government sells its securities that mature and are payable in 91 days, (3) the **discount rate,** which is the rate financial institutions are charged when they borrow funds from Federal Reserve banks, and (4) the **mortgage rate,** which is the amount paid by individuals when they borrow to pay for home loans. These interest rates are regularly printed in the financial pages of daily newspapers and weekly and monthly magazines.

Since interest rates and the inflation rate often move in the same direction together, your estimates of future interest rates (both near term and longer) should be consistent with your estimates of inflation. As a generalization, short-term interest rates on conservative- and moderate-risk investments are 2 to 4 percent higher than the inflation rate, while long-term interest rates are 4 to 6 percent higher.

The State of the Economy

You need to know the state of the economy now and where is it headed.

An **economy** is a system of managing the productive and employment resources of a country, community, or business. Government attempts to regulate the American economy to maintain stable prices (low inflation) and stable levels of employment (low unemployment). The goal is steady **economic growth.** This is a condition of increasing production and consumption in the economy—and hence increasing national income.

Growth in the American economy varies over time. A **business cycle** (also called an **economic cycle**) is a wavelike pattern of economic activity that includes four phases that undulate from boom to bust: expansion, recession, depression, and recovery (Figure 1.2).

The economic cycle begins when inflation and interest rates are low or falling. This makes it easy for consumers to buy homes, cars, and expensive goods on credit; it also encourages businesses to borrow to expand production to meet the increased demand. The stock market also rises because investors expect greater profits. As the demand for credit increases, interest rates rise because more borrowers want money. As consumers and businesses purchase more goods, this exerts inflationary pressure on prices. Eventually, interest rates and inflation climb high enough to stifle consumer and business borrowing, send stock prices down, and choke off the expansion. The result is flat economic growth or even a decline. In such situations, the economy often moves toward a **recession,** where levels of production, employment, retail sales, and price increases mildly slow down, typically for a time period of 6 months or longer, and consumers become pessimistic about their future buying plans. The nation's worst recent recession was during 1973–1975, when unemployment soared to over 10 percent and there was widespread decline (averaging nearly 5 percent) in many sectors of the economy; the decline in the 1981–1982 recession was 3 percent.

FIGURE 1.2

Phases of the Economic
Cycle

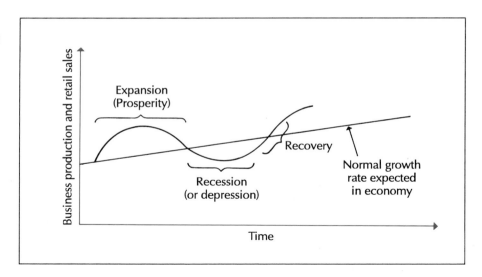

A **depression** is a severe downward phase of the economic cycle where unemployment is very high, prices are very low, purchasing power has decreased sharply, and economic activity has virtually ceased. Fortunately, depressions are very rare in American history, the last one occurring during the 1930s and into the early 1940s. Recovery from a depression or recession typically begins when inflation and interest rates are low or falling. This makes it easy for consumers to buy homes, cars, and expensive goods on credit; it also encourages businesses to borrow to expand production to meet anticipated increased demand. **Recovery** is a phase of the economic cycle in which levels of production, employment, and retail sales are rapidly improving, allowing the overall economy to experience some growth from its previously weakened state. The stock market also rises as investors expect greater profits and buy more stocks. As the demand for credit increases, interest rates rise because more borrowers want money. Prices are often pushed up a little during the recovery stage of the economic cycle. The economy may then move into the **expansion** phase, where production is at high capacity, there is little unemployment, and retail sales are high, to complete its cycle, which normally takes 3 to 4 years from start to finish. Obviously, expansion is the preferred phase of the economic cycle.

Tracking two statistics will tell you where the economy is going.

You should track at least two statistics to help you understand the direction of the economy: the nation's gross national product (GNP) and the index of leading indicators. The government regularly announces the annual rate at which the GNP has grown over the previous 3 months. **Gross national product** (GNP) is the value of all goods and services produced and bought for final use in the United States, and it is the broadest measure of how much economic activity is occurring. Less than 2 percent is considered low growth; more than 4 percent is considered vigorous growth. The **index of leading economic indicators** is a composite index reported monthly as a percentage by the U.S. Commerce Department and the average of 11 components of economic growth from different segments of the economy, such as new building permits for housing, orders for new machinery, length of the average work week, claims for initial unemployment insurance, and growth of money supply, which taken together suggest the future direction of the cyclical U.S. economy. A falling index for 3 or more consecutive months is a signal that growth will slow in the months ahead.

You need to know where the American economy is today and where it is headed in the next few years in order to make good financial decisions. For example, when the economy is headed toward a recession, it may be the time to invest in fixed-interest securities because interest rates are sure to fall during a recession as the government lowers its rates to help boost the economy. Further, when the economy is in the trough of a recession, it may be an excellent time to invest in stocks because the economy is soon to expand into the recovery stage. Also, a good time to sell stocks may be during the prosperity of an expansion phase of the economic cycle when most investors are probably incorrectly considering buying in the hope that prices will continue to climb. Information on the economic projections of government and private economists can be obtained in the publications cited earlier; after considering their views, you need to make your own projections and then make financial decisions accordingly.

In summary, to effectively manage your personal finances, you need to make personal projections about the near-term and long-term future regarding three economic events: (1) inflation, (2) interest rates, and (3) where the economic cycle is headed.

Useful Economic Considerations That Affect Financial Decision Making

Objective
To recognize economic considerations that affect financial decision making.

How well you understand a number of economic considerations will certainly affect your financial success in life. Important among these are (1) opportunity costs, (2) marginal costs, (3) income taxes, and (4) the time value of money.

Opportunity Costs

Opportunity costs occur when choices are made.

An **opportunity cost** (also known as an **alternative cost** or a **tradeoff**) is the cost of a decision measured in terms of the value of its foregone alternatives, and it is reflected by the highest value alternative cost of what one has to do without or what one could have done instead of spending, saving, or investing. By deciding to purchase 100 shares of General Motors stock, for example, you give up having those funds remain in a savings account, or buying a new automobile, or making a down payment on a home. Also, if you travel across town to look at a possible real estate investment opportunity, the opportunity cost is comprised of other things you could have done with the money you paid for gasoline to drive there and back plus the time spent traveling. People can use opportunity costs to help in making financial decisions.

It should be clear that most opportunity costs involve personal tastes and preferences that are difficult to quantify. You may have to choose between spending $20 on a concert ticket or spending the same amount on a compact disc recording (which you can hear again and again). If you choose the compact disc, you have to miss hearing the concert and participating in the experience with others in the audience. The real cost to you is missing the opportunity to hear the concert. Some opportunity costs involve money figures and should be considered carefully in decision making.

People use the principle of opportunity costs either consciously or unconsciously in their decision making. When understood and used consciously, the concept of opportunity costs helps people prioritize their decisions because they must make choices based on the best value that will provide maximum satisfaction among alternative opportunities. It is challenging to do, but effective personal financial managers need to carefully calculate some of the dollar costs in their decision making. A significant opportunity-cost decision facing some people, for example, is what the alternative costs are of quitting a job to go back to college to complete a graduate degree. Another difficult decision facing many people is what the opportunity costs are of renting an apartment versus buying a home.

Marginal Analysis

Marginal analysis can help us when there are a lot of variables to consider in decision making because it reminds us to compare only important variables. **Marginal cost** is the additional (marginal) cost of something. When known, it can be compared with additional (marginal) value received. Since **utility** is the ability of a good or service to satisfy a human want, a key task is to find out how much utility you will gain from a particular decision. For example, if you decide to spend $20 on a concert ticket, you can begin by thinking about what you might gain from the expenditure? (Perhaps a nice evening, good music, etc.) The marginal-cost situation arises when you consider spending $25 instead of $20 (an additional $5) to obtain a front-row seat at the concert. What will you gain from that decision? (Perhaps an ability to see and hear more, the satisfaction of having the best seat in the theater, etc.) The concept of **marginal utility** helps provide the answer. This is the extra satisfaction derived from having one more incremental unit of a product or service. Marginal analysis suggests that people always attempt to maximize dollar satisfaction when choosing between products using cold logic.

For example, two new automobiles were available on a dealership lot in Norfolk, Nebraska, where retired engineer Curtis Douglas and his wife Mary were trying to make a decision. Both vehicles were similar models, although one was a Mercury and the other a Ford. The Mercury, with a sticker price of $13,100, had a moderate number of options, while the Ford, with a sticker price of $14,800, had numerous options. Marginal analysis suggests that it is unnecessary for Curtis and Mary to consider all the options when comparing both vehicles. The concept of marginal cost says to compare the additional costs, $1700 in this instance ($14,800 − $13,100), with the additional options. Curtis and Mary need only decide if all the additional options are worth $1700.

In practice, however, human emotions often get in the way of making such logical decisions. When people choose between products, they typically consider such nonmonetary factors as beauty, comfort, or uniqueness. Sometimes people do not even compare, but instead simply say "I want that" and act on that emotion. In the real world, a number of other personal and environmental factors also affect consumer decision making.

Income Taxes

Income taxes affect financial decision making too.

Effective personal financial managers should regularly consider the economic effects of paying income taxes when making decisions. Of particular importance is the **marginal tax rate.** This is the tax rate at which your last dollar earned is taxed. As income rises, taxpayers pay progressively higher marginal income tax rates. Most financially successful taxpayers have to pay federal income taxes at the 28 percent marginal tax rate. For example, if Jane Hernandez, an unmarried office manager working in Fairfax, Virginia, has a taxable income of $32,000 and receives a $1,000 bonus from her employer, she must pay an extra $280 in taxes on the bonus income ($1000 × 0.28 = $280). Also, Jane has to pay state income taxes of another 6 percent, or $60 ($1000 × 0.06 = $60), and Social Security taxes of 7.65 percent, or $76.50 ($1000 × 0.0765 = $76.50). Thus Jane pays an effective marginal tax rate of almost 42 percent (28% + 6% + 7.65% = 41.65%), or $416.50, on the extra $1000 of earned income. Income taxes are discussed in detail in Chapter 8, Managing Taxes.

Taxpayers who have to pay high marginal tax rates often can gain by considering tax-free investments, such as tax-exempt bonds issued by various agencies of states and municipalities. For example, Dana Conway, a married chiropractor with two children from Mount Prospect, Illinois, currently has $5000 in savings earning 9 percent, or $450, annually. She pays $126 in federal income tax on that income at her 28 percent marginal tax rate. A tax-exempt $5000 state bond paying 7 percent will provide Dana with a better *after-tax* return. She would receive $350 tax free from the state bond compared with $324 ($450 − $126) after taxes on the income from savings. Investing in tax-free alternatives is discussed in Chapter 17, Investing in Bonds.

Tax free money is the best kind of income.

This discussion implies that the very best kind of income—from an effective personal financial management perspective—is that which is totally free of taxes. This is correct. For example, you are way ahead if you can legally receive $1000 and not have to pay taxes on that amount. For starters, if your situation is like that of Jane Hernandez above, you save $416.50 on the $1000 in earned income. The impact of opportunity costs is more dramatic. By paying an extra dollar in income taxes, first you lose the dollar paid. Second, you also lose the alternative use for that dollar. And third, you lose the value of another dollar that must be earned to take the place of the dollar paid.

The Time Value of Money

The time value of money may be the most important concept in personal finance.

One of the most important concepts in personal finance is the **time value of money.** The time value of money is not an incomprehensible notion, rather it is simple. The idea is to figure out "whether a bird in the hand is worth more than two in the bush." In modern times, the question might be "whether a lottery winner would prefer $1,000,000 now or $50,000 for each of the next 20 years." **Present value** is the current value of an asset that is to be received in the future. **Future value** is the valuation of an asset projected to the end of a particular time period in the future. Given assumed rates of return for a number of years, these values can be calculated.

For example, Dave Hollin, an unmarried automobile salesman from Jackson, Tennessee, was interested in two investments that paid certain sums of money in the future. First, his bank was offering a $5000 savings certificate of deposit for 3 years paying 7 percent annual interest. Second, a friend wanted to borrow the same sum for 3 years and pay Dave back $6000 in a lump sum. There are four ways to determine which is the best action for Dave to take, and each method gives the same answer.

Basic Math Method First, let's use basic mathematics for future value (*FV*). Assuming a rate of interest of 7 percent, the *FV* at the end of 1 year would be $5350 [$5,000 + (0.07 × $5000)]. The *FV* after 2 years would be $5724.50 [$5350 + (0.07 × $5350)]. The *FV* after 3 years would be $6125.22 [$5724.50 + (0.07 × $5724.50)]. Therefore, Dave would earn more by not lending the money to his friend because the bank will give him $125.22 more ($6125.22 − $6000). This method works fine, but it can become cumbersome.

Basic Calculation Method Using Equation (1.3) results in the same answer, where *i* represents the interest rate:

$$\begin{aligned} FV &= (\text{sum of money})(i + 1.0)(i + 1.0)(i + 1.0)\cdots \\ &= (\$5000)(1.07)(1.07)(1.07) \\ &= \$6125.22 \end{aligned} \tag{1.3}$$

Calculator Method Using any type of calculator will provide the same answer employing Equation (1.4), where *i* represents the interest rate and *n* represents the number of years:

$$\begin{aligned} FV &= (\text{sum of money})(1.0 + i)^n \\ &= (5000)(1.07)^3 \\ &= (\$5000)(1.225043) \\ &= \$6125.22 \end{aligned} \tag{1.4}$$

The Table Method can be performed using Appendix A.

Table Method Using Table 1.1 permits determination of the future dollar value of an investment. For the same illustration as above, use the table in the following manner: Go across the top row to the 7 percent column.

TABLE 1.1
Future Value of $1 after a Given Number of Periods (Portion of Full Table Shown in Appendix A-1)

Periods	1%	2%	3%	4%	5%	6%	7%	8%	9%	10%
1	1.010	1.020	1.030	1.040	1.050	1.060	1.070	1.080	1.090	1.100
2	1.020	1.040	1.061	1.082	1.103	1.124	1.145	1.166	1.188	1.210
3	1.030	1.061	1.093	1.125	1.158	1.191	1.225	1.260	1.295	1.331
4	1.041	1.082	1.126	1.170	1.216	1.262	1.311	1.360	1.412	1.464
5	1.051	1.104	1.159	1.217	1.276	1.338	1.403	1.469	1.539	1.611
6	1.062	1.126	1.194	1.265	1.340	1.419	1.501	1.587	1.677	1.772
7	1.072	1.149	1.230	1.316	1.407	1.504	1.606	1.714	1.828	1.949
8	1.083	1.172	1.267	1.369	1.477	1.594	1.718	1.851	1.993	2.144
9	1.094	1.195	1.305	1.423	1.551	1.689	1.838	1.999	2.172	2.358
10	1.105	1.219	1.344	1.480	1.629	1.791	1.967	2.159	2.367	2.594

Read down the 7 percent column and across the row for 3 years to locate the factor 1.225. Multiply by the present value of the cash asset ($5000) to arrive at a future value ($6125). (Note that this figure is off $.22 from the precise calculation because of rounding.)

Appendix A provides a more complete explanation of the time value of money and its applications. Realize that all the calculations assume that the interest earned was not withdrawn but left to be reinvested. This is known as **compound interest**, which is simply the calculation of interest on interest (because it is reinvested) *as well as* interest on the original amount invested.

An appreciation of compounding can be seen when funds are left to grow over a long period of time. Figure 1.3 demonstrates the impact of a $5000 investment earning 7 percent using compound interest. The $5000 grew to $74,850 in 40 years. If, instead, the interest earned each period was withdrawn and not itself invested to earn interest, the procedure would be called **simple interest**. The formula for simple interest is shown in Equation (1.5). For this example, the simple interest calculates to $14,000.

$$\begin{aligned} \text{Simple interest} &= \text{(principal)(rate)(time)} \\ &= (\$5000)(0.07)(40) \\ &= \$14,000 \end{aligned} \qquad (1.5)$$

This $14,000 in simple interest when added to the $5000 invested would total $19,000, which is $55,850 less than the $74,850 that compounding would yield. With compounding, the asset seems to grow slowly at first and then grows dramatically—this is the power of compound interest.

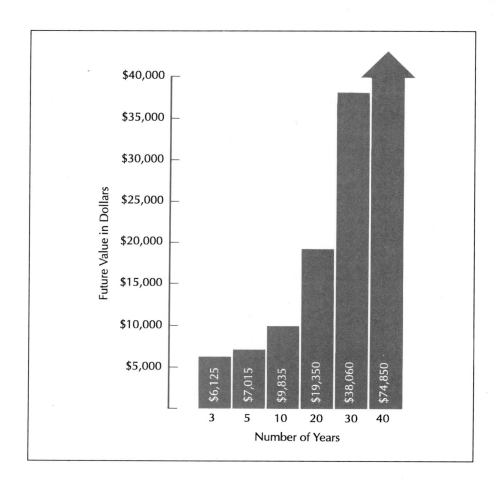

The Key Steps to Achieving Your Personal Financial Goals

Objective
To be able to describe
the six key steps to suc-
cessfully achieve your
personal financial goals.

There are six major steps in successfully achieving your personal financial goals. This text is divided into six parts to guide you through each of these steps: (1) financial planning, (2) money management, (3) managing expenditures, (4) income and asset protection, (5) investment planning, and (6) retirement and estate planning. Figure 1.4 shows how these steps are related to the goals of effective personal financial management discussed earlier in this chapter. Figure 1.5 illustrates how all the building blocks of a financially successful life fit together, and all these factors are examined in the remainder of the text.

Thorough Financial Planning

It is important for financial planning to be as thorough as possible and for the plan to be properly carried out. Problems can result if some aspects of your plan are neglected, as you can see in the situation described below.

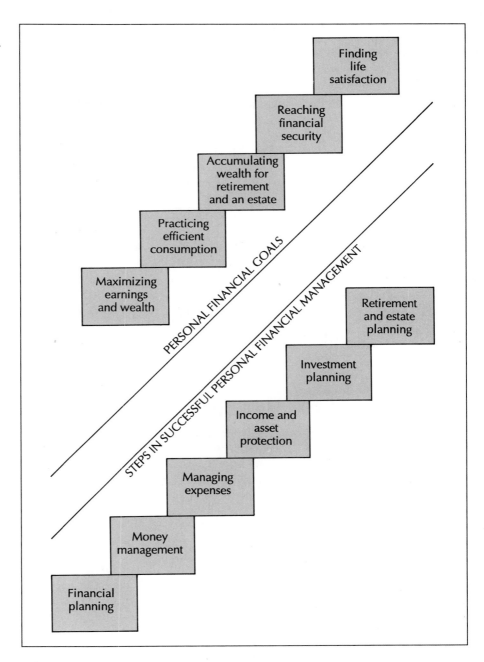

John Babson, of Columbus, Ohio, aspired to financial success like that of his parents, both of whom were physicians. He enjoyed an affluent lifestyle when growing up and wanted to lead a similar life of his own. He enjoyed being a liberal arts major, but it did not permit him the opportunity to take many science classes. Premed students, of course, must have a very strong background in science. Consequently, John did not

FIGURE 1.5
The Building Blocks of Financial Success[1]

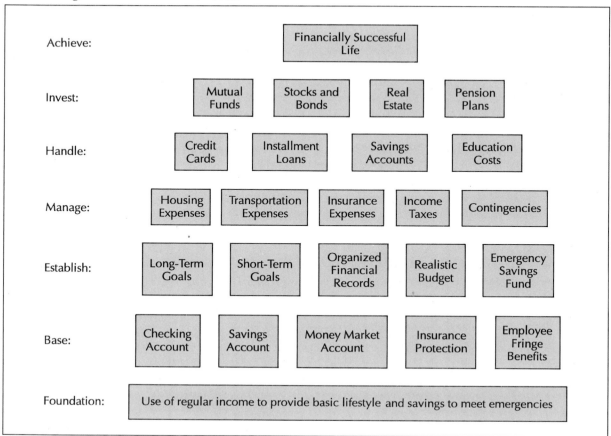

Achieve:	Financially Successful Life
Invest:	Mutual Funds / Stocks and Bonds / Real Estate / Pension Plans
Handle:	Credit Cards / Installment Loans / Savings Accounts / Education Costs
Manage:	Housing Expenses / Transportation Expenses / Insurance Expenses / Income Taxes / Contingencies
Establish:	Long-Term Goals / Short-Term Goals / Organized Financial Records / Realistic Budget / Emergency Savings Fund
Base:	Checking Account / Savings Account / Money Market Account / Insurance Protection / Employee Fringe Benefits
Foundation:	Use of regular income to provide basic lifestyle and savings to meet emergencies

score well on the national medical school entrance examination. His decision to get married during his senior year of college did not help him advance his plan either. Financial strains and increasing time constraints made it difficult for him to take the necessary science classes before he could retake the medical school entrance examination. Working as a salesperson for 2 years enabled him to take the science courses at night, pass the medical school examination, and finally begin his way toward medical practice and financial success.

The topics discussed in Part One of this text should help you avoid making decisions that might impede your progress toward financial goals. In addition to this chapter, they include Chapter 2, Careers and Other Key Factors That Affect Income; Chapter 3, Financial Planning over Your Life; and Chapter 4, Budgeting and Cash-Flow Management.

---

[1] These terms are defined in the glossary as well as in subsequent chapters.

Good Money-Management Practices

Another major step in effective personal financial management is learning efficient ways to manage money and money substitutes. Let's try to determine the primary reason Helen Daniel has been having difficulty managing money. Upon the death of her husband, she moved to LaFayette, Louisiana, and opened a floral shop.

Helen saw a beautiful living room suite displayed in a local furniture store window. She went inside the store to look it over. Then she decided to buy it. Helen used her VISA card to buy the suite, which cost $899.95 plus tax. About a month later her VISA bill came in the mail. The following statement was printed on her bill: "If you choose to pay a portion (but a minimum of $50), you may do so, but a finance charge of 1.75 percent per month will be assessed on the average daily balance. To avoid a finance charge, pay the full amount by the 25th of the month." Helen chose to pay only $50, since she also had her automobile insurance payment to make and was almost broke.

Because Helen did not pay the full amount due, she had to pay a finance charge. This decision would cost her about 21 percent per year (1.75 percent × 12 months) in finance charges if she continued the payment plan of sending in $50 a month. Helen did not practice efficient money management with her payment choice, since she could have borrowed the money from her company credit union at 12 percent annual interest.

Analysis shows that Helen's method of payment was not the best choice to make. What appears to be an easy purchase with a credit card sometimes can turn out to be otherwise when you end up paying the extra credit charges with each payment. However, a student of personal finance can learn to reduce, if not eliminate, such problems by mastering the topics in Part Two of this text: Chapter 5, Managing Your Cash; Chapter 6, Credit Use and Credit Cards; Chapter 7, Planned Borrowing; and Chapter 8, Managing Taxes.

Adequately Managing Your Expenditures

Managing expenditures is another step in effective personal financial management. This entails gathering information and making decisions about buying goods and services. It is likely that over the next few years you will need to make important decisions related to your financial well-being, such as buying a new car, shopping for additional home furnishings, and purchasing more insurance. Thus you must learn to make efficient decisions regularly as you deal with financial opportunities. The first personal financial decisions young people make may not be the best, but skill at making them improves as they read, discuss, and practice.

To illustrate the problem of managing expenditures, let's study the financial situation of a young couple just out of college. Ellen and Bill Frasier of St. Louis, Missouri, finished college together after being married for 2 years. Both decided to work, but Ellen became pregnant and had a difficult pregnancy. She had to quit working for money income. Before learning of the pregnancy, the couple had decided to buy a house rather than continue to rent for $675 per month. Living in their new home, a single-family dwelling, required paying $886 per month on a loan. The house was about 20 years old and needed some repair. During the first year, repair costs amounted to more than the Frasiers had planned. Also, after the baby was born, numerous hospital and baby bills had to be paid.

Essentially, Bill and Ellen did not clearly anticipate overall housing costs (including repairs and rising utility costs) in addition to the new baby costs. They may have made a more prudent decision—perhaps continuing to rent for another year or two—had they practiced more effective personal financial management. Knowing more about home ownership and its related costs probably would have altered their purchase decision, at least until they had additional money available for the expenses.

Predicting the future is no easy task. To prepare you to make better financial decisions, Part Three includes Chapter 9, Automobiles and Other Major Expenditures; and Chapter 10, The Housing Expenditure.

Protecting Your Income and Assets

Individuals obtain insurance to financially protect themselves, their survivors, and things of value that they own. The following case shows some of the pitfalls of buying insurance protection.

The "hard sell" for life insurance was put on Randy Mullis, of Madison, Wisconsin, as he was completing the second year of graduate school. The sales pitch made the need for insurance protection seem enormous, and Randy bought a $50,000 whole-life type of life insurance policy. It would cost him $1096 each year, and although the insurance started immediately, the payments did not begin until 1 year after his graduation.

Randy could have made a wiser decision on his insurance protection had he studied life insurance more carefully. His decision to buy $50,000 of coverage was unjustified; he had little need for this amount because he was single and his parents were both employed and did not depend on his income. Buying whole-life insurance also seems unwise because term life insurance may have been a better choice (whole-life policies have a savings account feature that makes them much more expensive than term policies). And Randy neglected to find out to what extent his future employer would pay for his insurance. Many employers provide substantial life insurance coverage for employees at little or no cost to the employees.

To protect yourself from financial loss and manage your risks, you need to develop the skills required to buy protection through insurance. Part Four introduces you to several areas of income and asset protection: Chapter 11, Insurance Fundamentals; Chapter 12, Property and Liability Insurance; Chapter 13, Health and Disability Income Insurance; and Chapter 14, Life Insurance.

Planning Your Investments

To achieve the goal of maximizing earnings and wealth, you must of necessity look to the future. Investing in the future in order to obtain a reasonable return on money is no small task—it requires skill and knowhow. Let's consider the case of Jane Ridnour, a married mother of two from North Platte, Nebraska, to examine some of the decisions to be faced in investment planning.

"Should I save in a regular savings account or invest in government or corporate securities?" Jane had pondered this question ever since receiving $40,000 from the estate of her late uncle. She knew that the regular passbook savings account would provide Federal Deposit Insurance Corporation (FDIC) protection for this $40,000. Consequently, she put the money in a regular savings account that earned her a return of 5.5 percent interest, paid quarterly.

Using a regular savings account, however, is not the only way to put money to work and still maintain a high degree of security. If Jane had known more about saving and investing, she probably would have invested her money differently. She would have discovered, for example, that her $40,000 could have given her about an 8 percent return if she had invested in short-term government securities. It would have given her the same protection as the regular savings account, with the same speed and ease of conversion into cash (**liquidity**), and yet have given her an additional $1000 annual return on investment.

Jane's situation is not unique, and it points up an important lesson: You must investigate before you invest. You must learn the hows, the whys, the wheres, the whens, and the whats of investing. The chapters in Part Five will provide you with the skills and tools to make intelligent investment choices: Chapter 15, Investment Fundamentals; Chapter 16, Investing in Stocks; Chapter 17, Investing in Bonds; Chapter 18, Investing in Mutual Funds; Chapter 19, Buying and Selling Securities and Managing Your Portfolio; Chapter 20, Investing in Real Estate; and Chapter 21, Speculative Investments.

Preparing for Retirement and Estate Planning

Sooner or later you must think about what to do when you retire from the workaday world. If you plan intelligently, you can have a comfortable retirement income to draw on during those years and a substantial financial estate to pass on. Your estate also can be your legacy to surviving loved ones after your death. Even though retirement and estate planning seems premature to most people, it is one of the major steps in effective personal financial management.

Retirement planning is a process that develops throughout your life. It is not something hastily done a year or two before retirement. One disadvantage of careless estate planning is the difficulty of correcting the effects of decisions made years ago. This is illustrated by the estate planning of Jane Waterson of Dallas, Texas.

Jane thought she had planned everything very thoroughly as she was growing older. She had earned the highest educational degree she could, taken all the right courses, planned her finances carefully, saved and invested frugally, secured a sound insurance program, and kept a reasonable amount of money in her checking account ready for current expenditures and/or emergencies. Jane had worked almost all her career as a credit manager for a small company that had a good, but not the best, retirement plan. Jane never married and regularly provided financial help for her mother and sister. She had a limited amount of savings, stock and bond investments, and life insurance in case of her death. Fortunately, Jane was always in good health, and she came from parents who lived well beyond the usual life expectancy.

For the first 3 years of retirement, Jane did fairly well on her Social Security income, the small company pension, and limited earnings from savings and investments. But Jane began to feel the pinch as these income sources could not keep up with the **personal inflation rate** (the rate of increase in prices of items purchased by a person or household). Jane used more and more money and got less and less for her dollar. A substantial part of her retirement income—the company pension—was fixed at about $1150 per month, but inflation was 6.7 percent per year. Consequently, Jane's purchasing power decreased. In 1 year, her fixed income of $1150 per month decreased to about $1078 in purchasing power: $100.0/106.7 = 0.937$; reciprocal is 0.063; $\$1150 - (\$1150 \times 0.063) = \$1077.55$, or $1078.

Jane could have avoided this problem of a declining purchasing power by arranging to have a greater retirement income beyond her company pension to offset inflation. It is important that this kind of long-range planning be done carefully. The chapters in Part Six will provide you with information about how and when to make such efforts: Chapter 22, Developing and Implementing a Plan for a Secure Retirement; and Chapter 23, Planning and Protecting Your Estate.

Summary

1. Effective personal financial management will enable you to face success-fully the financial challenges, responsibilities, and opportunities of life by helping you to acquire financial knowledge, develop your ability to effectively use financial skills and tools, clarify your financial values and goals, and identify specific needs and wants that can be satisfied with your financial resources.

2. There are five goals of effective personal financial management. The first goal is to maximize earnings and wealth. The second goal is to practice efficient consumption. The third goal is to find satisfaction in life. The fourth goal is to reach financial security. And the fifth goal is to accumulate wealth for retirement and an estate.

3. Your success in personal finance depends in part on how well you understand and utilize information to cope with the economic environment, including data about inflation, interest rates, and the state of the economy.

4. Four useful economic considerations that affect financial decision making are opportunity costs, marginal analysis, income taxes, and the time value of money.

5. The six steps in effective personal financial management are financial planning, money management, managing expenditures, income and asset protection, investment planning, and retirement and estate planning. Success in these steps is related to the specific goal(s) of personal financial management being sought.

Key Words and Concepts

alternative cost, 17
basic calculation method, 20
basic math method, 20
business cycle, 15
calculator method, 20
compound interest, 21
consumer price index (CPI), 12
depression, 16
discount rate, 15
economic cycle, 15
economic growth, 15
economy, 15
effective personal financial
   management, 4
expansion, 16
financial security, 8
financial skills, 5
financial success, 6
financial tools, 5
forecasting, 10
future value, 20
gross national product (GNP), 16
inflation, 10
index of leading economic
   indicators, 16
interest rates, 13
lifestyle, 6

liquidity, 27
marginal cost, 18
marginal tax rate, 19
marginal utility, 18
money income, 11
mortgage rate, 15
needs, 5
nominal income, 11
opportunity costs, 17
personal finance, 4
personal financial planning, 4
personal inflation rate, 28
present value, 20
prime rate, 15
purchasing power, 10
quality of life, 7
real income, 11
recession, 15
recovery, 16
simple interest, 21
table method, 20
three-month Treasury bill rate, 15
time value of money, 20
tradeoff, 17
utility, 18
wants, 6
wealth, 6

Review Questions

1. Cite four things that you will gain from the study of personal finance.
2. Differentiate between financial skills and financial tools.
3. Give an example of clarifying financial values and goals.
4. Differentiate between needs and wants.
5. List the five broad goals of effective personal financial management.
6. Summarize what it takes to reach financial success and happiness.

7. Explain how inflation can dramatically affect your income, consumption, savings, and investments.

8. Distinguish between real income and money income.

9. Why is it important to forecast interest rates?

10. Summarize the phases in the economic cycle.

11. Give an example of how opportunity costs affect financial decision making.

12. Explain how marginal utility analysis makes some financial decisions easier.

13. Describe how income taxes affect financial decision making.

14. Give an illustration of the importance of the time value of money.

15. Identify the six key steps in successful personal financial management.

Case Problems

1. Bill Gustafson of Lubbock, Texas, is a senior in college, majoring in sociology. He anticipates getting married a year or so after graduation. He has only one elective course remaining and must choose between another advanced class in sociology and one in personal finance. As Bill's friend, you want to persuade him to take personal finance. For each of the items listed, give one example of how Bill might benefit from the study of personal finance.
   a. Acquire financial knowledge.
   b. Develop financial skills and use financial tools.
   c. Clarify financial values and goals.
   d. Identify needs and wants.

2. You have been asked to give a brief speech on the goals of effective personal financial management. Since you have only 5 minutes for the presentation, it will be impossible to discuss all five broad goals. Therefore, you have decided to simply mention the five and focus in detail on only one. Choose one of the broad goals and describe what it means to you. Be sure to show how that one goal relates to overall financial success.

3. As a graduating senior, Kelly Jones of Urbana, Illinois, is anxious to enter the job market at an anticipated annual salary of $24,000. Assuming an average inflation rate of 5 percent and an equal cost-of-living raise, what will Kelly's salary be in 10 years? In 20 years? (Hint: Use Appendix A1.) To make real economic progress, how much of a raise in dollars must Kelly receive annually?

4. Vickie Frampton, a freshman nutrition major at the University of Texas at Austin, has some financial questions for the next three years of school and a little beyond. Answers can be obtained by using Appendix A *or* the appropriate worksheet in the Personal Finance Cookbook computer software program.

a. If Vickie's tuition, fees, and books this year total $5000, what will they be during her senior year (three years from now), assuming costs rise 6 percent annually? (Hint: Use Appendix A1 or the Personal Finance cookbook FVSUM worksheet.)

b. A scholarship Vickie is applying for is currently valued at $3000. If she is awarded it at the end of next year, how much is it worth in today's dollars, assuming inflation of 5 percent? (Hint: Use Appendix A2 or the Personal Finance Cookbook PVSUM worksheet.)

c. Vickie is already looking toward graduation and a job, and she wants to buy a new car sometime not too long after graduation. If after graduation she begins a savings program of $2400 a year in an investment yielding 6 percent, what will be the value of the fund after three years? (Hint: Use Appendix A3 or the Personal Finance Cookbook FVANNUIT worksheet.)

d. Vickie's Aunt Karroll told her that she would give her $1000 at the end of each year for the next three years to help with college expenses. Assuming an annual rate of interest of 6 percent, what is the present value of that stream of payments? (Hint: Use Appendix A4 or the Personal Finance Cookbook PVANNUIT worksheet.)

Suggested Readings

"A Spike in the Consumer Price Index Can Send Us into a Panic: What Is Behind This Number?" *Changing Times,* August 1990, p. 22. Analysis of why the CPI seems to jump around so much.

"Economics for the '90's." *Newsweek,* November 27, 1989, pp. 58–60. A primer on the business cycle for the last decade of the twentieth century.

"How TV Sees the Economy." *Changing Times,* December 1989, pp. 89–93. Suggestions on how to use economic information provided on television.

"Is Inflation Getting Better or Worse?" *Newsweek,* April 3, 1989, p. 44. Compares the meaning of the two measures of inflation: the Consumer Price Index (CPI) and the Producer Price Index (PPI).

"Laying Bets on the 1990's." *Newsweek,* January 15, 1990, p. 53. Jane Bryant Quinn's predictions for loans, earnings, taxes, spending, and investing in the 1990s.

"Mastering the Math Behind Your Money." *Money,* May 1989, pp. 129–138. Using a calculator to know how to figure out answers to several key personal finance computation questions.

"Outlook: Economy." *Changing Times,* January 1989, pp. 32–39. Economic forecasts for the 1990s.

"Outlook: Your Inflation Rate." *Changing Times,* January 1989, pp. 61–66. Forecasts for inflation in the 1990s.

"Prospering in the Coming Downturn." *U.S. News & World Report,* September 24, 1990, pp. 80–82. A recession or "recessionette" is a threat but also an opportunity.

"Questions You're Asking About Your Money." *Changing Times,* September 1989, pp. 86–91. Responses to a number of fundamental personal finance questions.

"Some Bold Forecasts for 1990." *Money,* December 1989, pp. 116–121. Economic forecasts of a panel of experts.

"Status Report on the American Dream." *Changing Times,* March 1990, pp. 41–50. *Changing Times'* annual "Personal Prosperity Index" shows an America that grew wealthier over the past decade, but not everyone shares equally in that wealth.

"The Millionaire Mindset: The Real Truth About Millionaires: You Can Be One." *Working Woman,* May 1989, pp. 93–103. How to think like a millionaire.

"33 Great Ways to Simplify Your Life." *Changing Times,* June 1989, pp. 22–28. The complexities of personal finance can be simplified.

"Test Your Economic I.Q." *Changing Times,* March 1989, pp. 89–91. Results of a nationwide economics test given to high school students.

"Upside Down Interest." *Business Week,* January 16, 1990, p. 86. How the federal government's war on inflation affects short-term interest rates.

"When Numbers Make You Numb." *Changing Times,* August 1990, pp. 77–80. The "rough, numerical horse sense" needed to function in personal finance.

"Will Our Kids Live As Well As We Do?" *Changing Times,* March 1989, p. 38. College graduates should outearn their parents.

"Your Best Ways to Beat Inflation." *Money,* May 1989, pp. 58–81. A series of articles providing advice on techniques in investments and lending to help you succeed in times of slow economic growth and rising prices.

2 Careers and Other Key Factors That Affect Income

OBJECTIVES

After reading this chapter, you should be able to

1. Explain how several key factors—such as career choice, education, place of residence, gender and race, marital status, age, and stage in the life cycle—affect income.

2. Appreciate the importance of getting to know yourself as a prerequisite to successful career planning.

3. Discuss the several steps in successfully setting and achieving career goals.

4. Appreciate that certain types of people, such as dual-career couples, single working parents, and those over age 35, need to use specific strategies to have successful careers.

5. Recognize that there are three "wild card" career possibilities available for people in the changing future workplace.

. . . .

You can come into money by finding a hidden treasure, inheriting, marrying, winning a lottery, triumphing in a lawsuit, or receiving an insurance settlement. Also, you can create money by using your talents, earning, saving, and investing. However, before you can properly consider how to achieve your personal financial goals (which is the subject of Chapter 3, Financial Planning over Your Life), it might be wise if you gave some thought to how you will earn a living, since your income is likely the primary source of funds to be used to achieve your financial goals. The subject of careers is the focus of this chapter.

We begin by examining several key factors that affect income: career choice, education, where you live, gender and race, marital status, age, and stage in the life cycle. Then we provide an overview of the complete process of career planning, which is divided into two phases: (1) a section on getting to know yourself and (2) a section on setting and achieving career goals. Special sections are also included that provide specific career suggestions for dual-career couples, single working parents, and those over age 35. The chapter closes with a discussion of three "wild cards" of new career possibilities in the changing future workplace.

Factors That Affect Income

Objective
To be able to explain how several key factors—such as career choice, education, place of residence, gender and race, marital status, age, and stage in the life cycle—affect income.

Personal income is affected by some factors that are controllable and some that are not. Your choices in life *will* make a difference in the amount of your income. *Controllable* factors include the career you choose, the amount of education you obtain, the geographic region in which you live, and your decision to marry or remain single. *Noncontrollable* factors that can affect income are gender and race, age, and stage in the life cycle.

Career Choice

Career choice is a primary determinant of financial success.

Whether you decide to become a computer programmer, a medical doctor, a schoolteacher, or something else depends on your interests and aptitudes. Finding areas of employment in which you are interested—as well as good at—is a difficult yet important task. Working at a job that is interesting can be enjoyable and personally rewarding. Also, having a high aptitude for a certain career will likely result in your excelling at that job, which will bring future promotions and raises.

Career planning is a process involving self-evaluation of aptitudes and interests, gathering information about occupations in various career areas, setting career goals, and developing a plan to achieve those goals. You may want to visit your college placement office to inquire about taking interest inventory and aptitude tests to help you discover more about yourself and your interests. These are often administered for little or no fee. It may be helpful to review such test results with a placement counselor.

In the information-gathering process, you can examine many publications that discuss careers, such as the *Occupational Outlook Handbook,* which is in the reference department of most libraries. Also, you can choose from a wide variety of credit and noncredit courses that might stimulate your career interests. Many college students change their majors several times; this illustrates the sampling process people go through in trying to decide which occupational areas best match their interests and aptitudes. Avoid specializing in college until you are confident that you have selected the best career path for you.

Table 2.1 illustrates both the starting salary and the salary for experienced individuals for various careers requiring a minimum of a bachelor's degree. In some fields, the starting salary is close to the salary for more experienced workers, as in the case of librarians and social workers. In other careers, such as airline pilots or security sales, the experienced people enjoy much higher salaries.

Be aware of income differences before settling on a career.

As you go about selecting a career or changing careers, be aware of these differences as well as your interests and aptitudes, because such factors definitely affect the amount of income you will earn. You should choose a career that matches your interests, aptitudes, and enthusiasms. While the nation's labor force is growing slowly because of early retirements and a lowering birth rate, there are an increasing number of employment positions available for skilled and educated workers, particularly in service businesses such as health care, real estate, education, insurance, financial services, and other nonretailing areas.

The **job search** involves preparing a resume, creating a list of potential employers, writing sample letters of application, practicing interviewing skills, filling out employment applications, taking employer tests, going on job interviews, and negotiating salary and fringe benefits. The job search process can be time-consuming, exhausting, and frustrating as well as exhilarating. The services of a good placement office can be invaluable.

Until recently, you could count on a career for life within one organization. Now, plant closings, downsizing, mergers, and other disasters for individual workers are commonplace. Thus you must keep your employment contacts and resumé up to date. This changing information age suggests that you need to train and retrain as new jobs are created and new technologies are developed. Then you must package and repackage yourself to fit employers' demands. Be adaptable, and keep your employment options open. Many people starting out in a career today will probably end up doing something entirely different than originally planned. On average, people work for six different employers during their career.

Occupation	Average Starting Salary	Average Salary of Experienced Individuals
Accountant	$25,400	$ 40,500
Actuary	26,000	56,600
Airline pilot	21,800	100,600
Architect	25,400	35,000
Chemical engineer	35,300	51,400
Chiropractor	24,200	66,500
Economist	27,100	44,300
Geologist	23,700	43,700
Librarian	25,300	35,000
Metallurgical engineer	33,700	51,400
Physician	55,900	128,600
Professor	33,700	43,000
Public relations	21,000	50,800
Securities sales	20,300	110,100
Social worker	20,200	33,000
Teacher, Secondary School	21,000	32,100
Underwriter	23,200	39,900
Veterinarian	26,600	52,000

Source: U.S. Department of Labor, Bureau of Labor Statistics, *Occupational Outlook Handbook* (Washington, D.C., April 1990); authors' extrapolations to January 1991.

Note: A growing number of people are retiring in their fifties, which further reduces the average income data.

Education

Education affects income and net worth in a positive way.

More than one-half of today's high school graduates go on to some form of higher education. A recent study by the American Council on Education reveals that 72 percent of freshmen reported that "making more money" was a very important factor in their decision to go to college. Whatever their reasons for going to college, the result is a personal investment. Data from the Bureau of Census show that educational investment pays off in higher incomes. The higher the educational level of the head of a household, the higher are both average annual family income and average lifetime family income. In a recent year, the annual income of households headed with a person with less than a high school education was $12,800; it was $18,900 for those with a high school diploma, $22,600 for those with 1 to 3 years of college, $29,700 for those with 4 years of college, and $35,200 for those with 5 years or more of college. The Bureau of Labor Statistics further reports that the real incomes of more highly educated people hold or gain during times of high inflation, while others lose.

Completion of a college bachelor's degree is a significant educational achievement. The educational attainments of the adults in the work force are as follows: 26 percent have 4 or more years of college, 23 percent have 1 to 3 years of college, 40 percent have 4 years of high school, and 11 percent have less than 4 years of high school. Such education and training increase people's **human capital,** the abilities, skills, and knowledge that permit them to perform work or services. Employers generally want to hire a person with a college degree, since it is evidence of training in selected areas. The Bureau of Labor Statistics predicts that through 1995, eight of every nine college graduates will find college-level jobs instead of lower-level jobs. Table 2.2 shows the average salary offered to bachelor's degree candidates, and Table 2.3 shows the starting salaries for various technical career positions that do not require a bachelor's degree.

There are lots of good paying jobs for people with a bachelor's degree.

Completing a 4-year college degree program is not a prerequisite for many high-paying and emotionally satisfying careers. However, additional education helps develop the kind of expertise that employers demand and is clearly associated with higher incomes. It also should be noted that education yields many benefits beyond higher income, such as enjoyment of work and more understanding of people and the world in which we live. Data from the U.S. Department of Labor show the relationship between education and unemployment. In a recent year, the unemployment rate for those with 4 or more years of college was 2.5 percent; it was 5.3 percent for those with 1 to 3 years of college, 8.1 percent for those with a high school diploma, and 14.4 percent for those with less than a high school education. The lower the level of formal education, the higher is the level of unemployment. Thus people with greater amounts of education are less likely to be unemployed, and, consequently, they can worry less about next week's paycheck and enjoy a more carefree lifestyle. This occurs partly because college graduates tend to work in industries less susceptible to swings in the economic cycle, such as professional services.

Geographic Region and Community Size

Geographic region and community size also affect income.

Data from the U.S. Department of Commerce show that incomes are highest in the Northeast. In a recent year, median household income was $25,100 in the South, $27,900 in the Midwest, $29,800 in the West, and $30,500 in the Northeast. This is the result of less unionization of employees in the South, lower living costs, and other factors. The growing desire of many people to live in the sunbelt states is causing more people to move to that region, bringing more industry, increased living costs, and eventually higher incomes. Employers in metropolitan areas pay higher wages than those in more rural areas, largely because they must compete with many other employers for persons with good skills. In a recent year, median household income was $21,900 for people living outside metropolitan areas, $27,900 in metropolitan areas under 1 million population, and $31,900 in metropolitan areas of more than 1 million population. Data Resources Incorporated forecasts that job growth through the year 2000 will be the fastest in the West, from Colorado to California and Washington to Alaska and Hawaii.

TABLE 2.2
Average Salary Offers for Bachelor's Degree Candidates by Curriculum by All Types of Employers (Data Combined for Men and Women)

Occupation	Average Salary Offer
Business	
Accountants	$26,300
Business administration	22,600
Economics and finance	24,300
Hotel/restaurant management	20,100
Human resources (including banking)	24,300
Management information systems	27,000
Marketing/marketing management	22,900
Engineering	
Aerospace and aeronautical	30,800
Chemical	35,400
Civil	27,800
Electrical	31,800
Engineering technology	30,100
Industrial	31,100
Mechanical	32,200
Other occupations	
Agribusiness	22,600
Architecture and environmental design	23,400
Allied health	26,700
Biological science	21,900
Chemical science	28,200
Communications	20,300
Computer science	29,200
Elementary education	19,200
Human ecology/home economics	19,000
Humanities	25,200
Information sciences and systems	28,800
Journalism	17,500
Letters	19,100
Mathematics (including statistics)	24,000
Nursing	26,900
Political science	21,400
Psychology	19,600
Telecommunications/broadcasting	18,200
Textiles and clothing	20,600
Visual and performing arts	19,000

Source: Original data from *The College Placement Council Salary Survey* (Bethlehem, PA: The College Placement Council, March 1990), p. 3; authors' extrapolations to January 1991.

TABLE 2.3
Technical Careers and Income (Careers That Generally Do Not Require a Bachelor's Degree)

Occupation	Average Starting Salary	Average Salary of Experienced Individuals
Accounting clerk	$17,300	$21,500
Aircraft mechanic	26,600	31,400
Dental hygienist	15,100	27,200
Drafter	15,800	30,600
Electrocardiograph technician	17,700	25,000
Flight attendant	15,100	29,000
Photographer	19,000	30,000
Regulatory inspector	17,900	29,900
Respiratory therapist	21,500	27,000
State police officer	22,900	32,300
Surveying technician	13,100	29,800

Source: U.S. Department of Labor, Bureau of Labor Statistics, *Occupational Outlook Handbook* (Washington, D.C., April 1990); authors' extrapolations to January 1991.

Marital Status

Married people have higher incomes and greater net worth.

Many, but not all, single men and women want to get married and have families. Only 58 percent of all adults are married. A growing proportion of individuals are deciding to remain single, and those who do marry are waiting even longer to tie the knot. Recent census data reveal that the median age for men to marry is 25.9 years, whereas women marry at a median age of 23.6 years. Today, approximately 69 percent of the males and 51 percent of the females between the ages of 20 and 24 are single.

Marriage is an important factor that affects net worth. **Net worth** is the amount left when you subtract what you owe from what you own. Census data extrapolated to 1991 indicate that households headed by married couples had a net worth of $65,151; it dropped to $18,051 for households headed by unmarried females and to $12,848 for those headed by unmarried males. Staying married also makes a difference in net worth—probably because two people can earn, save, invest, and create more net worth than a single person.

According to census data, more than 2.6 million single persons have chosen to live together without a legal wedding ceremony. A far greater number of young people have decided to marry and to postpone having children. Both groups join the growing number of **dual-earner households,** in which both spouses work for income. The old adage "two can live as cheaply as one" should probably be updated to read "the income of two increases the consumption level of one." Decision making may be more difficult with two income earners, but having two incomes greatly increases the resources available for financial planning and spending. Recent data on average annual income from the Bureau of Census indicate that single

What If You Choose Country Living over Life in the Big City?

Below are hypothetical but reasonably accurate annual estimates of selected costs experienced by a typical dual-income couple with one child living in a large metropolitan area with a population of 500,000 or more in contrast with living in a smaller community of fewer than 60,000. Clearly, life in the "big city" is more expensive than small-town living, but it is likely that community services are also more extensive in metropolitan areas and the lifestyle is different.

Large City		Small Community
$ 9,600	Rent for a three-bedroom apartment	$ 7,800
13,200	Mortgage loan for standard home	10,800
140	Renter's insurance	130
400	Homeowner's insurance	300
2,100	Real estate property taxes	800
400	Property tax on new automobile	60
2,640	Food at home	2,280
1,680	Food away from home	1,320
2,400	Entertainment	2,160
900	City income taxes	0
700	Gasoline costs	730
280	Automobile maintenance and repairs	240
5,200	Child care	4,160
700	Transportation to/from work	350
250	Visits to physicians	200
900	Clothing purchases	850
300	Cable television	240
360	Haircuts/hairdressers	300

female householders earn $21,800, single male householders earn $29,000, married couples with the wife not in the money-income labor force earn $32,600, and married couples with the wife working earn $40,600.

Gender and Race

Gender and race matter less and less.

Data from the Bureau of Census show that, on average, females earn only 70 percent as much as males. One reason for this discrimination in earnings is that the overall labor force remains sharply segregated by sex, with women typically concentrated in many low-paying careers. Women make up 90 percent or more of employed bookkeepers, bank tellers, nurses, and secretaries. These fields have been dominated by women for decades; many employers continue to label them as "female" jobs and pay low wages to

TABLE 2.4
Income and Age of Householder

Age in Years	Number of Households (Thousands)	Median Income
15–24	5,415	$18,700
25–34	20,924	31,200
35–44	19,952	40,300
45–54	14,018	42,000
55–64	12,805	31,800
65 and over	19,716	16,400

Source: Bureau of the Census, *Current Population Reports,* Series P.60, No. 166 (Washington, D.C., August 1989); authors' extrapolations on income to January 1991.

those people who perform them. The future looks brighter in that the Census Bureau reports that women in their early twenties already earn 86 percent of what their male counterparts make.

Similar discrimination in earnings occurs among races. In a recent year, household income for Hispanic families was 73 percent of that for white families and household income for black families was only 41 percent. Some employers also discriminate against women and minorities in opportunities for continuing education, promotions, and employment itself.

After extrapolating recent data from the Bureau of Census to 1991, the median net worth of white households was $50,876; of Hispanic households, $6387; and of black households, $4416. Some revealing insights follow about factors related to net worth after ignoring race. Households headed by college graduates had a median net worth of $78,542; it slipped to $4246 for those headed by high school graduates and to $3048 for those headed by someone with less than a high school education. Education clearly makes a difference in net worth.

Individuals are now helping to raise the aggregate income and net worth for women and minorities by entering managerial and professional specialty occupations, such as business management, medicine, military service, law, and engineering—and by postponing marriage. Society gains from the rising incomes and successes of women and minorities.

Age and Stage in the Life Cycle

Age and stage in the life cycle affect income.

Employers do not pay their youngest employees the highest wages because those employees lack experience. Table 2.4 reveals that an increasing average income is paid to workers over their lives, that is, until the age of 55 and older. Because many of the oldest members of the population do not have as much formal education as younger workers, they are generally not employed in the higher-paying jobs and thus, as a group, earn less income. Age is also an income-determining factor for some types of jobs requiring physical labor; older workers often lack the strength of younger ones.

The Complete Process of Career Planning: Phase One—Getting to Know Yourself

The career planning sequence is as follows: First, discover what you want out of life; second, decide on a career that is likely to permit you to lead such a satisfying life; and third, seek a job or series of jobs that serve as the means by which you achieve your career and life goals. If you are going to take charge of choosing your career, you must begin by examining your values, beliefs, and attitudes, which will help you analyze your work values, work style, and lifestyle. Then you can more carefully begin to assess your interests, abilities, and skills.

Discover Your Values

Career planning requires that you discover your values.

A systematic approach to the job hunt and a career change involves knowing what skills you enjoy using, determining where you want to use those skills, and finding the person who has the power to hire you. Prerequisite to the job search is understanding yourself. Knowing yourself better will enable you to select a career path that suits your interests, abilities, and skills. Your career progress must be considered a high-priority, do-it-yourself project. *You* must accept responsibility for who you are and where you are going, as well as how you are going to get there.

As we contemplate major choices in life, we need to be aware of what is important to us personally. We need to be aware of our values, attitudes, and beliefs that influence such choices. Many are consciously held concerns, while others are unconscious. **Values** are the principles, standards, or qualities considered worthwhile or desirable that provide criteria for goals, thereby giving continuity to decisions. Values provide a base for decisions about how to live because they serve as guides to future action and as standards or criteria by which our actions can be directed. In order for something to be a value, it must be prized, publicly affirmed, chosen from alternatives, and acted on repeatedly and consistently. Values are not right or wrong, or true or false—they are personal preferences.

Values, Beliefs, and Attitudes

Values change very little over time.

As people go through life, their fundamental values change little. For example, a police officer might personally value honesty. Note, though, that attitudes and beliefs are frequently changed and/or modified through the experiences we undergo. A **belief** is the mental acceptance of or conviction about the truth or actuality of some statement or some thing based on what one implicitly considers adequate grounds. An **attitude** is a persistent, learned predisposition to behave in a consistent way toward a given object or set of objects, not necessarily as they are, but as they are conceived to be. A police officer, after a number of years on the job, might come to believe that all people are anything but honest. The officer might further maintain an attitude that causes him or her to immediately suspect dishonesty when confronting criminal suspects. Attitudes are often reflected as evaluative beliefs by which we express our likes and dislikes. Together, our values, attitudes, and beliefs help us make sense of the world, and they determine how we think, feel, and act.

Most of us are unclear about or not even aware of what our values actually are. The better we understand our values, the better we can plan our lives to be consistent with them. By developing a greater awareness of your own values, you can become more aware of the unseen forces that guide you and, at the same time, you can make conscious decisions about alternative directions you want to pursue.

Following are some values: family, friends, helping others, religious commitment, security, honesty, pleasure, good health, material possessions, financial achievement, and a satisfying career. Some examples of confusion and conflict centering around values include family versus friends, love versus sex, religious beliefs versus actions, and work versus leisure. Conflicts such as these constantly require us to make choices, and the choices can be difficult unless we know what is most important to us. Of course, many decisions are based on value judgments determined in the past, thus allowing us to conserve time, energy, and often money.

When you make important decisions, you might be wise to think carefully to clarify your values before taking action. **Values clarification** is the process of determining values by searching and selecting one over another. The process of values clarification commences as individuals begin to rate their values. You should realize, too, that when used as guidelines for action, your values, attitudes, and beliefs tell you what to do.

Work Values and Work Style

A full examination of values clarification is beyond the scope of this book, and there are many books available in bookstores to assist you in this endeavor.[1] However, it would be useful for you to consider a number of work values critical to the process of career selection, particularly in the areas of work conditions, work purposes, and work relationships. A person's **work style** is the unique set of ways that a person works with and responds to his or her job surroundings and associates. Since your work style influences your career in important ways, it is wise to better understand the whos, wheres, and hows of your preferred occupation. A suggestion in that direction is offered in Table 2.5.

Values clarification can help you assess what is important in your life.

You can more clearly decide on careers that are most suitable for you as you assess what is important in your life through the process of values clarification. This is one of the most important means to achieving greater happiness, satisfaction, and success in life. Once you determine your most important values and have some idea of the priorities in your life, you will be better able to make decisions and will feel more control in your life. You also will feel more comfortable with decisions after you have made them. Self-understanding is essential to effective career decision making.

[1] A classic book on values clarification for teachers and students is *Values Clarification*, by Sidney B. Simon, Leland W. Howe, and Howard Kirschenbaum (New York: Hart Publishing Company, 1972).

TABLE 2.5
Rate Your Work Values

You might begin the process of selecting a career by rating how you value the following work values as either "very important in my choice of career," "somewhat important in my choice of career," or "unimportant in my choice of career."

1. *Work conditions*—independence/autonomy, time flexibility, change/variety, change/risk, stability/security, physical challenge, physical demands, mental challenge, pressure/time deadlines, precise work, and decision making
2. *Work purposes*—truth/knowledge, expertise/authority, aesthetic appreciation, social conditions, material gain, achievement/recognition, ethical/moral, and spiritual/transpersonal
3. *Work relationships*—work alone, public contact, close friendships, group membership, helping others, influencing others, supervising others, and controlling others

Now, consider going back to the list and circling the activities that you want to do more often.

Source: D. C. Borchard, J. J. Kelly, and N. P. K. Weaver, *Your Career: Choices, Chances, Changes.* Dubuque, Iowa: Kendall/Hunt Publishing Company, 1990, Chapter 11.

Lifestyle Considerations

When considering any career goals, you need to think about what lifestyle factors are important to you because this can help in decision making. For example, if access to big-name entertainment and cultural activities is important to you, then working and living in a rural area may not be appropriate. If you like to travel, you may choose a career that involves frequent travel. Consider the following lifestyle considerations in your decision making: urban/rural setting, close/far from work, own/rent housing, city/suburban life, warm/cold climate, near/far from relatives, and constant/variable climate.

Assessing Your Interests, Abilities, and Skills

Your **interests** are expressions of feelings of curiosity or concern about something, and they reflect the things that you like to do. Interests, including occupational interests, are likely to be stable over a long period of time. Your **abilities** are the things that you are capable of performing either physically, mentally, artistically, mechanically, financially, or legally. Most of us think of a **skill** as a proficiency, dexterity, or technique, particularly one requiring use of the hands or body, that results in getting a job done. For example, you might be interested in working with people, have the ability to easily meet the public, and be skilled in persuading people to buy a product or service. We need to better understand our interests, abilities, and skills in career planning because every occupation requires a worker to function in relation to data, people, and things in varying degrees.

Here is an exercise to help you identify your interests.

How to Find Out More About Your Interests You might consider taking out a sheet of paper and quickly listing 10 things that you enjoy doing. On that list there are probably some things that you enjoy but have not done recently. Because of conflicting interests and alternative claims on your time, you cannot do all of them. Therefore, it is important to evaluate your interests in terms of your values, your abilities, and your opportunities, because interests should be an influential part of your career planning. In this way, you will increase the likelihood of career satisfaction.

Fortunately, career planning and guidance offices are located at most universities, colleges, community and junior colleges, technical schools, and secondary schools, as well as state-operated career counseling facilities. Here they offer adults the opportunity to take **interest inventories,** such as the Strong Campbell Interest Inventory (SCII). These are pencil-and-paper psychological examinations that assist people in assessing and profiling their overall interest trends by indicating which personality types enter certain occupations. Interest inventories help identify within each occupation those interests which are similar but different from other occupations. The results of such examinations, usually offered free or at a nominal cost, provide scaling scores by which you can compare the similarities or dissimilarities between yourself and successful people in occupations that interest you.

How to Analyze Your Abilities and Skills How well you perform a task depends not only on your ability and skill level, but also on the particular situation. In addition, performance is evaluated in relation to others. A person might have played first violin in the high school orchestra but be too inexperienced to play for his or her university orchestra. To improve your chances of successfully applying your abilities and skills, therefore, you must understand the demands of the situation in which you will compete and work.

Your ability to function effectively is conceptually based on four factors: genetic makeup, past experiences, situational opportunities and constraints, and motivation. If, when analyzing your strengths and weaknesses, you find that you are not performing well in a given situation and you have ruled out the effects of genes, experiences, and constraints, it is likely that you are being held back by a lack of motivation. Thus success in a given task may be highly dependent on your trying harder, more frequently, or more consistently.

Here is an exercise to help you better understand your abilities and skills.

A useful experience to help you better understand your abilities and skills is to make some lists of three items each in response to the following statements: personal qualities you recognize as strengths, weaknesses you would like to improve on, academic abilities and strengths, and academic weaknesses you would like to improve on.

The Complete Process of Career Planning: Phase Two—Setting and Achieving Career Goals

Objective
To be able to discuss the several steps in success-fully setting and achieving career goals.

Setting and achieving career goals require an effort that will bring you lifelong satisfaction if done properly. This section includes discussions on how to think about setting your career goals, developing a personal marketing strategy, avoiding the resume trap, writing a letter that gets you a face-to-face meeting, understanding the employment industry, how to succeed in an interview, dealing with rejection, and how to get the salary you want.

Setting Your Career Goals

Some people set specific career goals, such as "to become a veterinarian," while others describe their goals in general terms, such as "to lead a giving life." It is probably best to have a general idea of where you want to go and a clear idea of where you do *not* want to go.

In thinking about setting long-term career goals, people need to consider appropriate general goals in terms of their own values, beliefs, interests, abilities, and skills (Figure 2.1). This is not easy to do. Besides understanding themselves, people also must seek out a great amount of information that is typically acquired only through the pursuit of educational opportunities. In addition, people gain experiences in life that affect their attitudes toward career goals.

Do not be too specific in your career goal too early in life.

One danger in setting career goals is to declare a specific choice too prematurely. This may result in locking into a choice before enough information has been collected about that occupation. An individual in this situation may find it difficult to change career goals selected earlier because of self-expectations and the expectations of others, even when the individual later realizes that the choice may be inappropriate.

People need to be flexible in planning their futures. One approach is to identify the choices that you intend to make in the future, but to wait until then to make the decisions. This keeps you free to gather more information and experiences before making any actual commitment. An exercise that might help you make a flexible career plan is to list five choices (perhaps related to schooling, marriage, other employment, and financial expenditures) that cover any aspect of your life but which relate to your career plans that you will have to make in the next 5 to 10 years. As time goes on and you make decisions in these areas, you will be gathering information and experiences to help you eventually make an actual career choice.

All states have a Career Information Delivery System (CIDS) to assist people in making career plans and finding rewarding jobs. For help, look in the telephone book under government listings for "Career."

FIGURE 2.1
Setting Long-Term
Career Goals

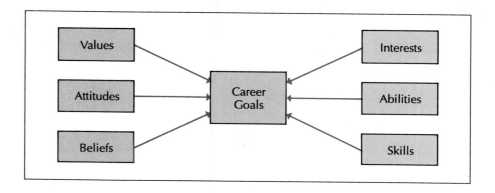

Developing a Personal Marketing Strategy for Careers

Finding the right job takes time, lots of time.

Getting a job is not easy, and it is usually not done quickly. Instead, it is a process that takes much effort over many months. Remember first and foremost that the best way to obtain a desirable employment position is to utilize your social contacts, maximize opportunities provided through casual meetings, and take advantage of personal referrals. The experts all say that "the greater the number of auxiliary avenues used by the job hunter, the greater the job hunting success."[2] Whether you are a graduating senior, an executive, or a person returning to the labor force, the following suggestions may be useful in your development of a personal marketing strategy for careers:

1. Visit a nearby college or university placement office. Such offices have an enormous amount of resources to assist people looking for career opportunities. You do not have to be a graduate to receive help, although such offices focus on assisting their job-hunting graduates throughout their lives.

2. Go to the office of student counseling services and take interest inventories to help you determine which types of occupations are most suitable for you. Are you interested in an organization that makes products, provides services, or processes information?

3. Ask parents, relatives, friends, and acquaintances about how they got into their present work, what they do in their job, what they like about their occupation, what they like least, and who else do they know who does the same kind of work who you could talk to. If appropriate, ask them for referrals to others who may be able to help you (not necessarily hire you) in your job search. Then telephone and go visit the people they suggest.

[2] An informative and best-selling book published annually on the subject of careers is *A Practical Manual for Job-Hunters and Career-Changers,* by Richard Nelson Bolles (Berkeley, Calif.: Ten Speed Press, 1990).

4. Get to know lots of people in the field and, if necessary, do so by telephone contact. Call textbook authors, key researchers, and officers in professional organizations to obtain information and get acquainted.

5. Ask the same questions and more specific questions of employed former students who graduated in previous years.

6. Go to the local office of your state employment service to seek their advice on where it would be best to locate employment positions in your field.

7. Go to the library and study such volumes as *Occupational Outlook Handbook* and *Dictionary of Occupational Titles.*

8. Locate key reference books in the library, such as those published by *Moody's* and *Standard and Poors,* that describe industries where your career is practiced. Learn about the industries, and assess future directions.

9. As you learn more about certain industries where your career is practiced, you also need to find out about the types of companies in the field. Look up particular companies in similar reference books in the same section of the library.

10. Write all companies that interest you as career choices informing them about your attributes and potential and telling them why you want to work for their wonderful organization.

11. Answer newspaper advertisements, and consider placing newspaper ads to describe your abilities and employment needs.

12. Attend meetings of professionals in the field, which sometimes have scheduled job interview opportunities, and make contacts with people who might be able to assist you.

13. Go to a private employment agency, an executive counseling service, or some other type of employment clearinghouse for advice and assistance.

Avoiding the Resume Trap

A **resume** is a summary record of one's personal history and experience submitted with a job application. Its primary function is to provide a basis for screening people *out* of consideration for jobs. When you supply a resume, you are providing documentation for some kind of subjective evaluation against unknown criteria, usually by someone whom you do not know. While it may be wise to look good on a resume, it is far more important to look good in reality. Thus you should prepare a resume after you have taken all kinds of steps in the employment process. When it is necessary to technically fulfill a requirement in the employment process, then tailor a special edition of your resume to fit this special set of circumstances.

A personal letter may let you "get acquainted" and help you avoid rejection.

A carefully crafted personal letter is the instrument of choice over a resume. The letter should be designed to get you a face-to-face, casual meeting in order to get acquainted. This way you avoid being screened

What If You Want to Become More Marketable?

If you are still in school, you can work on becoming more marketable well before you graduate. To do so requires that you have more knowledge and experience in the career field. Suggestions include:

- Attending club meetings in the field of your academic major.
- Getting to know names of as many people in the field as possible.
- Starting to attend statewide meetings of career professionals when you are a sophomore so that you get to know many practitioners over the years.
- Actively seeking out "people who count" in your career field and arrange for those persons to get to know you and your work.

- Becoming involved in the research projects of faculty as a volunteer.
- Obtaining part-time jobs in your career field to gain a variety of experiences.
- If your major is one that typically does not lead directly to employment (psychology, anthropology, history, English, literature, etc.), taking some courses that will help teach you marketable skills. Employers want to hire people with skills in computers, accounting, and marketing research.
- Obtaining an internship (paid if possible, free if necessary) in your career field.

out on paper or getting involved in a screening interview. Being screened out by the key decision maker is one thing; being rejected by some underling scanning your resume is a psychological downer. It is ridiculous to be rejected because your resume fails to fit some hypothetical profile or because of some background anomaly. People actually do sit around all day looking for "red flags" and other "knockout" factors to be found on resumes; then they pile them or file them. You want to avoid low-level screening.

A successful job search results in an evaluation not based on paper documentation, but rather based on a personal interview. In this manner, you can provide the future employer with an overall impression based on all senses.

Writing an Effective Cover Letter

A **cover letter** is a letter to a prospective employer designed to express your interest in obtaining an interview. It should be written on your own high-quality stationary. Address it to the key person and request a brief meeting. State as few qualifications as possible, and hit one reason very hard. Make it your strongest point, being certain that it is important to the position. Do not aim to be considered directly for a position, but

▌ A Sample Resume

The resume generally should be no longer than one or two pages because it usually serves as an introduction about a person. People usually list their experiences and accomplishments in an organized and attractive manner, often using logical categories such as education, experience, professional activities and leadership, and special talents. It is usually best to list the most current information first. However, note that most resumes leave room for the employment objective near the top of the first page.

In general, you should organize your resume in a way that best shows off and emphasizes your strengths. For example, if your educational background is strongest, show it first. Others might start with job experience first. You might want to have more than one resume to send to different prospective employers.

Jane Gordon Cathey-Rojas

SCHOOL ADDRESS:
1234 Ellis Street, Apt. 2
Ames, Iowa 50010
712-222-1111

HOME ADDRESS:
3055 Vallejo Street
Denver, Colorado 80211
303-111-7777

JOB OBJECTIVE: AN ENTRY LEVEL POSITION AS A METALLURGICAL ENGINEER

EDUCATION	Bachelor of Science in Metallurgical Engineering, Iowa State University, Ames, Iowa, May 1991
	Associate of Arts Degree, Northern Virginia Community College, Falls Church, Virginia, May 1989
EXPERIENCE	General Motors Locomotive Division, Metallurgical Engineering Department, Internship during summers of 1989 and 1990
	Iowa State University, Research Assistant to Professor John Binnion on projects on metals and plastics, August 1990—May 1991
	Dog and Suds Restaurant, Springfield, Virginia, Night Shift Manager, Summer of 1988
	Volunteer, Village Nursing Home, Springfield, Virginia, 1987
CAMPUS ACTIVITIES	Associate newspaper editor, Iowa State Progress
	Vice President, ISU Student Metallurgical Society
	Singer, University Choral
	Tutor for computer laboratory
	Attended two national meetings of American Metallurgical Society
HONORS	Most Valuable Club Member, ISU Metallurgical Society
	Academic Scholarship
REFERENCES	Furnished upon request

Sample Cover Letter to Seek Employment

1234 Ellis Street, Apt. 2
Ames, Iowa 50010
Today's date

Mr. Ted Ake, Department Head
Metallurgical Division
Ford Motor Company
Dearborn, Michigan 43210

Dear Mr. Ake:

Recently I learned from Dr. John Binnion of Iowa State University that the Metallurgical Division at Ford Motor Company might be adding a new position. I would appreciate having a brief face-to-face meeting with you to learn more about Ford Motor Company and to exchange impressions.

As indicated on my enclosed resume, I already possess some professional work experience as a metallurgical engineer. Most of my laboratory work as a summer intern at General Motors Locomotive Division was in metals; however, I also have had two courses in plastics at Iowa State and I worked on a "Star Wars" plastics research project with Dr. Binnion. One of my strengths is the ability to carefully follow directions and procedures, which I demonstrated in my school work and summer employment. I also enjoy meeting new people and helping to make them feel at ease.

I look forward to the opportunity to meet with you.

Sincerely,

Jane Gordon Cathey-Rojas

Enclosure

instead, try to gain a face-to-face meeting to exchange preliminary information and to gather impressions.

Understanding the Employment Industry

The employment industry includes everything from prestigious executive search companies to private employment firms and outplacement businesses. Keep in mind that such firms are client-driven, and normally, you are not the client. They typically are paid by the organizations that hire them to find people. During industry downturns, they also sell outplacement services to advise current employees about employment opportunities

What If You Want to Work for the Government?

Federal, state, and local governments fill hundreds of thousands of administrative, professional, and technical positions each year. In fact, the U.S. government is the nation's largest employer. Since the hiring practices of state and local governments vary so much, what follows is only about the federal government.

To secure a job as a civilian working for the federal government, look under "U.S. Government—Office of Personnel Management" in the blue pages of the telephone book for nearly 50 U.S. Federal Job Information Centers (FJIC) located across the country. Most positions are competitive in that people who apply for them compete with other applicants and must be evaluated by the Office of Personnel Management (OPM). However, a number of agencies (including the U.S. Postal Service, the U.S. Foreign Service, and the Veterans Administration) are exempted from OPM procedures, and should be contacted directly for employment. A complete list of agencies with independent hiring authority can be obtained through any FJIC. Eighty-five percent of the federal jobs are located outside of Washington, D.C.

You cannot get a job with the federal government without *first* getting **on a register**. This means that the Office of Personnel Management has on file your completed application and a satisfactory test score on an appropriate examination in a particular geographic area of the country where certain types of positions might become available in an occupational line of specialization. Once you are on a register, the OPM has certified that you are eligible for one type of occupation in a particular geographic area.

To apply for work for the federal government, you must complete an application, using Standard Form 171, and take an examination. After you complete and forward the employment application and take the examination appropriate for your career interest, OPM examiners evaluate your experience and abilities for the type of job you want and score it accordingly. If you are qualified, your name is listed on a register along with other qualified people. When an agency has an opening, it contacts OPM for the names of qualified people.

You should realize that veterans are given preferential treatment in that they are awarded an extra 5 or 10 points on their examination scores. The examinations are given only a couple

(continued)

elsewhere. The quality of these operations and the people in them vary. Almost all are working for a commission paid by the client; therefore, their priorities in descending order are themselves, their clients, and people looking for employment.

If you are looking for work, then you are the "product" in the employment industry. **Private employment agencies** are firms that specialize in locating employment positions for certain types of employees, such as executives, secretaries, computer personnel, and salespersons. Most private employment agencies are paid fees by organizations that hire them. Sometimes the job-hunter must pay a fee, which could amount to several hundred dollars or more, but only when the person is hired. An application and contract are filled out at the private employment agency, and the agency tries to find you suitable employment. Sometimes a fee must still be paid even though you find a job independently of them.

What If You Want to Work for the Government? *(continued)*

of times a year, and you must sign up in advance with a FJIC. There are no examination fees.

Most jobs with the federal government, particularly those requiring some amount of college education, require applicants to score successfully on a three-hour written test in one particular area of career interest. Six different tests (covering over 100 occupations) are given nationally for persons interested in the government's Administration Careers With America (ACWA) register: (1) health, safety, and environment, (2) writing and public information, (3) business, finance, and management, (4) personnel administration and computers, (5) benefits review, taxes, and legal, and (6) law enforcement and investigations. Five other entry-level examinations for various registers in addition to ACWA exist: (1) accounting/auditing, (2) biological sciences, (3) physical sciences, (4) professional engineering, and (5) mathematics and related occupations.

Note that for certain grade levels there is one nationwide register. Furthermore, some of the thirty local registers may contain a number of positions not available in other parts of the country. Since hiring needs vary from time to time and from place to place, you must file a different application in each location for positions that might become available. After your name has been on a register for one year, it is automatically removed; thus you must reapply to be put on the register again.

Persons about to graduate from college can telephone OPM's Career America College Hotline (1-900-990-9200) for advice on appropriate opportunities or telephone a local FJIC office for similar information. Those interested in mid-level careers can telephone FJIC to determine what nationwide and local registers are open and how to apply for particular positions.

There are some useful sources of information about federal jobs. The *Commerce and Business Daily*, published by the U.S. Government Printing Office, tells about which firms have been awarded government contracts and likely will be hiring new people. The *Federal Times*, a privately owned newspaper, reports on which agencies are hiring and where. It often takes 6 months to a year to land a job with the government. Federal salaries usually are very good and are competitive with private industry.

Employment registers list resume information about job seekers in a computer-based information-sharing system in an effort to facilitate employment. They charge job seekers for their service, and the lists may contain thousands of names. These are also known as **job clearinghouse operations** or **job banks.** For a fee of $50 to $100, some employment registers list the names and brief resumes of job seekers along with future projected openings and/or employers' vacancies. **Executive search firms** are firms that attempt to recruit personnel, especially executive personnel, for vacant positions in corporations. These are also known as **headhunters.** They are retained by employers to hire away good employees, such as executives, salespersons, and technicians, from where they are presently working. You might consider contacting some of them to see if they are looking for someone with your qualifications. The reference sections of libraries contain directories of executive search companies that might specialize in particular jobs or fields of work. While conceptually these businesses are a nice idea, most employers prefer to fill jobs paying above $15,000 using their own personnel departments or in more personal and informal ways.

How to Succeed in a Job Interview

Employment interviews are designed to finally find the match between an employer with a job opening and a job seeker possessing the appropriate skills. Each hopes a match will be made. Before an interview, you need to read *everything* you can lay your hands on about the organization, its goals, its recent activities, and the job itself. Find out the good and the bad because you intend on being part of the solution if they hire you. You must have a positive and confident attitude (not arrogant) about how you can help with their "needs"; otherwise, go do some more research. Since most job hunters fail to take this approach, they do not get the best jobs.

Know the employing organization well and you may very well get the job.

Potential employers are interested in finding out who you are, why you came to them, what you can do for them, whether you have a personality they will enjoy working with, and whether or not they can afford your services. Let them ask questions and you talk, and you ask questions and let them talk. For you to find out if a match exists between their needs and your desires, you need to ask some questions during the interview. Specifically, ask them what the job really involves and how well they think your skills fit their needs. While talking, you need to assess whether these are the kinds of people (and personalities) you really want to work with in the future. If so, you need to take actions during the interview to persuade them to hire you. Therefore, back your claims that you can help them by presenting them with evidence that you possess the necessary skills, interests, values, and attitudes to satisfy their needs. And at night, after every interview, always send a thank-you note to each person you saw that day.

Dealing with Rejection

The job hunting process is filled with rejections. Before you land a job, you might have 50, 100, or even more potential employers say "No!" Most of us have learned to hate rejection, but for some people it just rolls off them like water off a duck's back. For those of us who respond with anger or disillusionment, the next step must be to forget the disappointment and hurt and move on with our lives. Do not let employment rejections strip you of your self-esteem or you will begin to think falsely that there is something wrong with you.

How to Get the Salary You Want

Name your own salary.

Every job has its salary range. It is important to do some research to find out how wide that salary range usually is for this and for similar jobs. Your objective should be to get a salary near the top of the range, not the bottom. This will only occur if the prospective employer thinks that they must have you. Therefore, do not talk about salary prematurely. If successful

Advice for the Conservative Personal Financial Manager: Save Money by Working for an Employer Who Offers Lots of Fringe Benefits

Good advice for those who want to get ahead financially is to work for an employer who has a substantial fringe benefit program. A **fringe benefit** is any payment for employment that is not in the form of wages, commissions, or other taxable income. If needed benefits are provided by an employer, you do not have to purchase them privately yourself, and you can instead use those funds elsewhere for spending, saving, or investing.

The cost of employee benefit programs often amounts to about 25 percent more than salaries. Almost all firms offer sick leave and vacation time to employees.

About 95 percent of the employees in medium-sized and large U.S. firms are provided valuable fringe benefits as a condition of employment. Many smaller firms offer similar benefits. Employers commonly provide health and life insurance as a fringe benefit. If purchased privately, a good health insurance policy covering the costs of hospitals, physicians, prescription drugs, and major medical expenses for a single person would cost at least $130 a month, and for a couple with

or without children, it would amount to $200 or more per month. Life insurance coverage equal to twice your annual salary would cost at least $100 a year if purchased privately.

Many employers also offer dental insurance as a fringe benefit, probably worth $100 a year to a single person and twice that to a family. Long-term disability insurance can easily cost $1200 a year if purchased privately. Many employers also offer savings, pension, and profit-sharing plans as fringe benefits, and these plans often amount to 6 to 8 percent of a person's salary. A minority of firms offer employees free group legal services, marriage and family counseling, and financial counseling.

A growing number of employers also offer **cafeteria plans**, where employees are given a choice of health, dental, life, retirement, and disability insurance coverages, each with different levels of cost. The company usually will pay the entire premium for the basic benefits coverage, but not for broader coverage. The employee pays, with paycheck deductions, for the cost of all additional selected coverages.

applicants must have three interviews, wait until toward the end of the last interview and ask them for the highest amount they are able to pay for a person of your obvious suitability. After all, by now they really want *you*. Therefore, when the topic is brought up, by you or by the interviewer, tell the interviewer the salary range that you think exists for the position (because of your research) and name a figure near the top.

Objective
To appreciate that certain types of people, such as dual-career couples, single working parents, and those over 35, need to use specific strategies to have successful careers.

Strategies for Specific Types of People

Certain types of people, such as dual-career couples, single working parents, and those over age 35, need to use specific strategies to have successful careers because they have unique problems, challenges, and opportunities.

Dual-Career Couples

Dual-career couples always have to consider the impact of career decisions on at least one other person. While couplehood brings many desirable personal rewards and obligations, when both people are employed for money income, more obligations become apparent.

Dual-career families need formal planning. Dual-career planning requires that the couple take extra time to spend the energy and effort to maintain smoothly running dual careers. Particular efforts are needed to maintain the household and keep up with weekly and seasonal activities that define family life. In some instances, family schedules and routines have to be greatly disrupted in order to accommodate the needs of others. This is often true in managing child-care schedules, because getting up at 4:30 A.M. to begin a day may seem impossible, but it will be done if necessary. Such complications sometimes cause conflicts in the schedules and activities of other family members. Dual-career families typically have to do a lot of juggling to meet the needs of all involved.

In the broad sense, dual-career planning is not just for two adults, rather it is for two people who have career goals and plans. When there are children, each worker wants to have time for his or her own career and for family responsibilities while also attending to the needs and life plans of the children.

Dual-career couples, therefore, must be sensitive to each other's needs. They must find the time in their busy schedules to spot and resolve potential problems. This is especially important before commitment, resources, and patience wear thin. Many adults in dual-career families have been discouraged from even thinking about new career opportunities because of the seemingly overwhelming press of everyday work schedules, recreation plans, household responsibilities, school activities, social events, and vacation plans.

Joint planning discussions about careers can be helpful.

There is no one best way for dual-career couples to lead fulfilling lives while they are pursuing successful careers. However, the one key to success is to honestly communicate with each other about career plans and options. There is no substitute for joint planning discussions, perhaps done in casual conversations, perhaps done in more formal sit-down meetings every 6 months or so. Each person must try to be honest in giving advice and providing cooperation to the other adult. To be successful, each might benefit by writing down individual career goals and subgoals before coming together to discuss common career goals and needs. With frank and sensitive discussion, particularly with an eye toward spotting potential problems, dual-career couples can proceed to plan, modify if necessary, and reach agreement on their long-term common career goals. Couples should try to develop workable approaches to solutions rather than specific solutions. This will help them maintain flexibility to accommodate the inevitable changes and challenges that will occur in the future.

Single Working Parents

Single working parents share many of the same concerns of dual-career couples. However, single working parents typically are concerned about meeting family obligations and personal commitments without having another adult to consult. The whole burden of decision making falls solely on the single working parent.

Single working parents do not usually have backup systems of financial support and advice to depend on when needed, or those systems are weaker than for couples and families. The need for careful budgeting and emergency funds is usually critical for single working parents, and these topics may need to receive as much attention as career planning. There is little benefit in thinking about career plans when a single working parent is burdened by a ton of worries about bill paying, an automobile needing repairs, keeping up the morale of children, and trying to keep up his or her own morale. Having a significant other in one's life may complicate career planning even more for the single working parent.

Career planning is vital to success.

Clearly, each single working parent needs to plan his or her career while also considering the plans of others. He or she has a responsibility toward his or her children to assist them in learning and maturing toward their life plans and career choices. Good career moves may happen, but they can only occur when the single working parent has found the time and taken the opportunity to carefully assess all the factors in making career decisions. Good planning lessens the chance of mistakes and increases the chance of successful career moves.

Those over Age 35

After your first decade of employment experiences, it is wise to occasionally review where you have been and what you have done and evaluate why you have been successful or not so successful. The task is to focus your thinking forward to benefit your career planning in the years ahead.[3]

By your midthirties, you should have no difficulty being able to identify your strengths as well as what areas to avoid. You probably also recognize that those who really get ahead are not "superpeople" but folks much like you, possibly a few steps ahead of you in their careers. Experts suggest that the one thing that slows up career progress is the failure to set goals and objectives. Yet many people over age 35 are often fond of saying, "I don't know what I want to do" and "I just want to be happy."

Career planning requires careful thinking.

Career planning is not static. You just do not do it once and forget about it. Career planning is a vibrant process that you must become involved in throughout your life. Therefore, every now and then, perhaps every 5 or 10 years, it is wise to stop and carefully review your career situation. Remember that you always have the freedom to change your life and career objectives as you learn more about yourself and the environment in which you work. You can either make no choices at all and continue along the way you have been going, or you can look inside yourself and consider the possibilities. This requires thinking hard about who you are and where you are going. It requires taking charge of one's life and perhaps changing careers to move onto bigger and better things.

[3] An excellent book to assess and evaluate career choices after you have worked a few years is *What's Next? Career Strategies After 35*, by Jack Falvey (Charlotte, Vt.: Williamson Publishing, 1987).

Avoid serious career discussions with close associates at work.

Besides the traditional sources of help in career planning discussed earlier, the person over age 35 might be wise to consider discussing career thinking with professional friends. However, avoid career discussions with close associates at work because their feedback and advice to you may be biased and confidentiality is almost impossible at a workplace.

Instead, favor some higher-level professional friends in other organizations. These senior-advisor types can be more objective and their advice sage. They can provide you with advice, ideas, and a career overview from a perspective that you cannot develop on your own. They also can give you job leads if desired. It is smart to develop and maintain an informal list of senior-advisor types who you know and respect and who you are in contact with once or twice a year, perhaps at lunches or professional meetings. Your objectives are to avoid operating in a vacuum and to keep a realistic eye on future possibilities. Such people can help you evaluate alternatives.

"Wild Card" Career Possibilities in the Future

Objective
To recognize that there are three "wild card" career possibilities available for people in the changing future workplace.

Predictions about the future workplace abound. Some forecasters, such as futurists John Naisbitt and Alvin Toffler, anticipate that advances in technology will bring about a flourishing "high tech" American society with revolutionary and dramatic changes in the world of work. The U.S. Bureau of Labor Statistics offers moderate forecasts of a future not dramatically different from the present, and it identifies occupations and industries that are likely to evolve and grow. Labor organizations expect that the decline in American manufacturing industries will bring about large geographic pockets of unemployment, downscaling of jobs, and limited opportunities.

Author Carl McDaniels suggests that there are three "wild cards" in the changing workplace because there are three career possibilities where many people will be employed in the future.[4] First is the lure of entrepreneurship that stimulates the creation of new jobs. **Entrepreneurs** are people who organize, operate, and assume the risk for a business venture. They enjoy benefits such as increased commitment and satisfaction and a chance to demonstrate creativity and innovation. Second is the growth of small businesses. Most new jobs are being created by businesses with under 250 employees, often in firms that employ less than 100 people. Workers enjoy benefits, such as working outside the rigid organizational structures of big businesses. **Franchising** is one of these entrepreneurship opportunities, because it grants authorization by a manufacturer to a distributor or dealer to sell products. Third is the work-at-home trend, where people can apply leisure interests in developing more satisfying careers. An estimated 10

---

[4] Carl McDaniels, *The Changing Workplace: Career Counseling Strategies for the 1990s and Beyond* (San Francisco: Jossey-Bass, 1989).

million people currently work at home, including many in the fabled "electronic cottage" industry who have network connections to a mainframe computer, such as crafts people, direct salespersons (Amway, Mary Kay), and service people (accountants, copy editors, piano tuners, locksmiths).

Those considering future employment in one of the "wild card" areas would be wise to thoroughly discuss possibilities with many people, including professional employment counselors employed by schools, colleges, and universities, private employment/outplacement firms, and government. Such people can help you find satisfaction and challenge in tomorrow's workplace.

Modern Money Management: Continuing Narratives

Throughout this book we will present a continuing narrative about Harry and Belinda Johnson, a fictitious young couple who illustrate many of the important concepts in personal finance. Financial details and narrative about the Johnsons will appear within each chapter when the material is (1) self-explanatory and (2) useful to understanding the personal finance concept being presented. If fuller discussion is necessary, it will appear only at the end of a chapter. Therefore, we suggest you turn to Modern Money Management at the end of this chapter to "meet" the Johnsons.

Summary

1. Career choice greatly affects income because whether one has a bachelor's degree or technical degree, there is a wide range of salaries for people with different backgrounds.

2. Controllable factors beside career choice that generally affect personal income include the amount of education you obtain, the geographic region in which you live, and whether you decide to marry or remain single.

3. Individuals are now helping to raise the aggregate income for women and minorities by entering managerial and professional specialty occupations.

4. The career planning sequence is, first, discover what you want out of life; second, decide on a career that is likely to permit you to lead such a satisfying life; and third, seek a job or series of jobs that serve as the means by which you achieve your career and life goals.

5. Career planning requires that you discover and clarify your values, beliefs, and attitudes and try to match your interests, abilities, and skills with a career that offers a suitable lifestyle and work style.

6. The process of setting and achieving career goals includes how to think about setting career goals, developing a personal marketing strategy, avoiding the resume trap, writing a letter that gets you a face-to-face meeting, understanding the employment industry, knowing how to succeed in an interview, dealing with rejection, and how to negotiate and get the salary you want.

7. Certain types of people, such as dual-career couples, single working parents, and those over age 35, need to use specific strategies to have successful careers because they have unique problems, challenges, and opportunities.

8. There are three "wild cards" in the changing workplace of the future: entrepreneurship, small businesses, and working at home. Many people will be employed in these areas in the future.

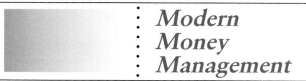

Modern
Money
Management

Harry and Belinda Do Some Career Planning

Harry Johnson graduated with a bachelor's degree in interior design last spring from a large state-supported university in the Midwest. He attended a community college in his home town before transferring to the university. Belinda graduated last year from an excellent business program at a mid-size college near where she grew up on the west coast. Belinda thinks she is interested in working with investments. She and Harry met at a conference for student leaders when they were juniors, and their relationship continued to develop, culminating in their marriage in June.

The Johnsons live in an apartment on the east side of the city. They own one car but often use public transportation.

1. What controllable and uncontrollable factors are likely to affect Harry and Belinda's future income?

2. What interests, abilities, and skills would you expect of Harry? How might Harry most effectively communicate these to a potential employer?

3. What steps should Belinda take to focus her career objectives and to develop a personal marketing strategy?

Key Words and Concepts

Review Questions

1. Personal income over your lifetime is affected by a variety of factors. Which are controllable?

2. Explain what is involved in career planning.

3. Discuss how education is related to both income and net worth.

4. Tell how geographic region and community size are related to personal income.

5. Comment on how income is affected by gender and race.

6. Contrast the income situation of single and married people.

7. Explain how income is affected by age and stage in the life cycle.

8. Distinguish between values and attitudes.

9. Give reasons why people need to better understand their values.

10. Explain what is meant by work values and work style.

11. Distinguish between abilities and skills.

12. How can you rather easily find out more about your career interests?

13. Name some suggestions on how to think about setting your career goals.

14. Identify three valuable ideas that people could use in developing a personal marketing strategy for careers.

15. Why do people, both employers and potential employees, use resumes?

16. Distinguish between a private employment agency and an employment register.

17. Give two key suggestions on how to achieve success in a job interview.

18. What is a good technique for dealing with rejection after a job application?

19. Describe some of the unique challenges facing dual-career couples in their career planning.

20. What is unique about single working parents in their decision making?

21. Give a couple of good career-oriented suggestions to people over age 35.

22. Describe one of the three "wild card" career possibilities in the future job marketplace.

Case Problems

1. After completing his associate of arts degree 4 months ago from a community college in Birmingham, Alabama, Jimmy Jackson has answered over a dozen advertisements and interviewed several times in his effort to get a sales job, but he has had no success. Jimmy never did sales work before, but he did take some business classes in college, including a course called "Personal Selling." After some of the interviews, Jimmy telephoned the potential employers only to find that even though they liked him, they hired people with previous sales experience.
   a. If Jimmy actually was suited for a position in sales, which work values and work-style factors do you think he would rate as "very important"?
   b. What would you recommend to Jimmy regarding how to find out about the depth of his interest in sales jobs?
   c. Assuming Jimmy has appropriate personal qualities and academic strengths to be successful in a sales career, what additional strategies should he consider doing to better market himself?

2. Nina and Ting Guo, of Des Plaines, Illinois, have been together for 8 years, having married just after completing college. Nina has been working as an insurance salesperson ever since. Ting began working as a family counselor for the state of Illinois last year after completing his Ph.D. degree. Recently, Nina's boss commented confidentially that he thought that Nina was likely to be the next salesperson to be promoted and relocated to the home office in St. Louis, Missouri. Nina thinks that if she is offered the opportunity, she would like to take it, even if it means that Ting will have to resign his new job.
   a. What suggestions can you offer Nina when she gets home from work and wants to discuss possible career changes with her husband?
   b. Which of the three wild cards in the changing future workplace might affect Ting's decision about relocating?

Suggested Readings

"Answers That Get You Hired." *Changing Times,* April 1989, pp. 53–55. Instead of giving canned responses to anticipated questions, successful job seekers need to show individuality.

"Career Workshop: How to Manage Your Career for Life-long Success." *Working Woman,* November 1989, pp. 101–119. Career planning tips for women, but men can use them too.

"Company Plans: The Tax Break You Shouldn't Ignore." *Money,* November 1989, pp. 127–132. How to use a flexible spending account effectively.

"Fighting to Have It All." *Money,* January 1990, pp. 130–134. How can you have a family and a career at the same time.

"Getting Your Name on Everyone's Lips." *Working Woman,* August 1989, pp. 68–70. How you can network so that you are the one an employer thinks of when that perfect job opens up.

"How to Change Your Life and Achieve Financial Security." *Money,* March 1990, pp. 74–86. Series of articles on changing careers.

"How to Walk the Benefits Wire." *Money,* September 1990, pp. 130–131. Avoiding taxation on employer-offered flexible spending accounts.

"Jobs with a Bright Future." *Changing Times,* January 1990, pp. 44–48. The best prospects for employment in the decade of the 1990s.

"Kissing the Big City Goodbye." *Changing Times,* August 1990, pp. 27–34. Five families tell their stories about leaving the rat race to live in a place where life is unhurried.

"Make the Most of Your Fringe Benefits." *Changing Times,* September 1989, pp. 93–98. How to make good selections of fringe benefits from among the choices offered by employers.

"Race and Money." *Money,* December 1989, pp. 152–172. How discrimination is eroding the wealth of the black middle class.

"Take Charge of Your Career." *Changing Times,* October 1990, pp. 93–95. Tips on how best to research the company you would like to work for.

"The Best Places to Live in America." *Money,* September 1989, pp. 125–141. The top 300 communities where life is good.

"The Eleventh Annual Salary Survey." *Working Woman,* January 1990, pp. 105–115. What women are earning in various jobs and careers and how to get more for yourself. Updated annually.

"The Elusive Affordable Franchise." *Changing Times,* October 1989, pp. 60–68. The hottest areas for franchising in the next decade likely will be office temps, travel help, and home maintenance programs.

"The Twenty-five Hottest Careers." *Working Woman,* July 1989, pp. 67–79. Trends affecting careers in the 1990s; for women and men.

"Write a Resume That Works." *Changing Times,* June 1990, pp. 91–95. How to write an effective resume and employment cover letter.

3 Financial Planning over Your Life

OBJECTIVES

After reading this chapter, you should be able to

1. Explain the concept of financial planning, its components, and its value.

2. Illustrate the impact of life-cycle periods and stages on the financial tasks, problems, and challenges facing people today.

3. State the purpose, value, and components of key financial statements, particularly the balance sheet and the income and expense statement.

4. Understand how your financial activities can affect your financial statements.

5. Know how to use financial ratios to help you evaluate your financial strength and progress.

6. Explain how to choose a financial planner.

7. Describe the purposes and uses of organized and complete financial records.

....

Most people develop a financial lifestyle that is consistent with their financial means, whether by trial and error or by design. Today's affluent society offers a bewildering and complex array of financial alternatives in banking services, savings options, housing accommodations, investment choices, insurance coverages, tax-savings devices, credit sources, and retirement plans. Because information about these financial opportunities usually is obtained piecemeal from different sources, decision making becomes even more difficult.

For these reasons, most people need financial planning. They have the idea that they want to succeed financially but lack clear goals, which makes it difficult to choose correctly among alternatives. People generally have financial records, but too often the records are poorly organized and some cannot be located easily. Such an approach to personal finance may result in failure rather than success.

This chapter begins with an explanation of financial planning: what it is and how it can be important to you. We also examine the life-cycle periods, stages, and pathways as well as the financial tasks, problems, and challenges confronting people today. Then we discuss financial statements and provide several examples to illustrate the personal finances of single persons, young married couples, and established families. For those who are interested, we also discuss how to choose a financial planner. An innovative section follows which explains how to use financial ratios to help you evaluate your financial strength and progress. The chapter concludes with an overview of financial recordkeeping presented in enough detail perhaps to inspire you to consider reorganizing your own financial records.

Successful Financial Planning

Objective
To be able to explain the concept of financial planning, its components, and its value.

Financial planning is the process of developing and implementing long-range plans to achieve financial objectives. It is not a single plan; rather, it is a coordinated series of plans covering various parts of a person's overall financial affairs.[1]

[1] Limited scope or single-subject financial planning advice is also available on numerous topics, such as how to invest in a lump-sum early retirement benefit distribution, how to allocate assets within a retirement savings plan, and how to establish a specific college fund for a child.

Successful financial planning is achievable.

Financial planning is customized because it takes into consideration all aspects of a coordinated plan as an individual or family moves through life, making necessary adjustments as they become appropriate, planning for changing financial needs in life, and dealing with each new situation as it occurs. Financial planning generally requires **diversification** of one's assets by putting money in a variety of investments (such as real estate, stocks, bonds, and mutual funds) so that if one does not perform well, a sufficient number of others are available to maintain the value of all.

Financial planning begins by recording in writing the financial objectives and goals that reflect your values, attitudes, life-cycle circumstances, wants, and needs. Success in financial planning requires (1) explicitly stated financial goals, (2) certain assumptions made about the economy, (3) logical and consistent financial strategies, and (4) consideration of resources available to meet the objectives. Then you start to take actions to achieve the goals.

Setting Financial Goals[2]

You will need to set financial goals.

Financial goals are the long-term objectives that your financial planning and management efforts are intended to attain. You should state explicitly your financial objectives in order to help you make choices and to serve as a rational basis for your financial actions. Setting financial goals helps you better visualize the gap between where you are now financially and where you want to be in the future—it is motivating.

You should make financial plans with appropriate objectives and goals in three broad areas: (1) *plans for spending,* (2) *plans against risks,* and (3) *plans for capital accumulation.* Figure 3.1 provides an overview of effective personal financial management.

An example of a financial goal in planning against risk is provided by Francine Mason of Radford, Virginia. Francine is a single parent with little extra money. Still she was concerned about the risk of being legally liable if she caused an accident with her automobile. After consideration of the risks and costs involved, Francine decided that one financial objective was to protect herself against automobile-related lawsuits. Her short-term goal was to spend the least amount of money on necessary insurance coverage. After telephoning three insurance agents to compare premium costs, Francine bought a policy with the minimum coverages allowed by Virginia law—instead of higher optional coverage available—and paid $276 annually, a good price because she lives in a rural area.

Another example of goal setting is provided by Ellen Law of Plattsburgh, New York, who got a new job as a marketing specialist and decided that one of her financial goals was to plan for capital accumulation. She wanted an emergency fund equal to 3 months' take-home pay that she could use for unexpected medical or automobile expenses not covered by insurance and that would provide a financial cushion if she should lose her job. Accordingly, Ellen began to put $300 a month into a bank savings account.

[2] Goal setting is examined in considerable detail in Chapter 4, Budgeting and Cash-Flow Management.

FIGURE 3.1

Overview of Effective Personal Financial Management Resulting in Financial Well-Being or Satisfaction

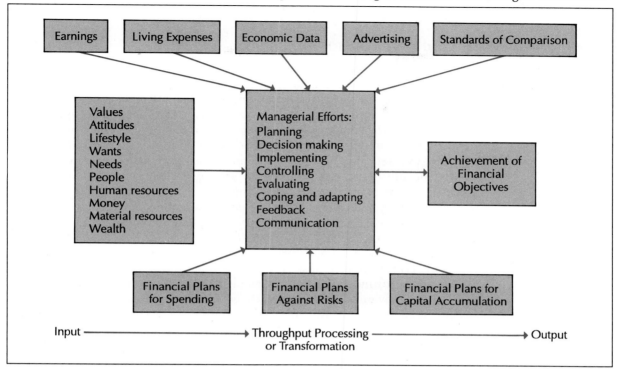

Economic Assumptions

You will need to make assumptions about the economy.

Financial planning requires that you make certain assumptions about the economy before taking appropriate action. People often do this subconsciously; for instance, they may assume that inflation "will be about the same for the next few years" or "the cost of credit—interest rates—will probably remain steady for some time." People who make conscious and explicit assumptions about the economy are often rewarded with favorable financial opportunities. For example, Laurie Wesswick of Laramie, Wyoming, correctly assumed that interest rates were going to decline during the last economic recession, so she put some of her funds into savings certificates of deposit (CDs) before rates declined and locked in the greater return for 2 years.

Financial Strategies

Strategies will help guide your financial behavior.

In order to be successful, financial plans must have logical and consistent **financial strategies.** These are plans of action to be taken in specific situations that help guide your actions. For example, a conservative investor, Wilma Hall of Dobson, North Carolina, decided that her strategy would be to sell most of her corporate stocks during times of prosperity close to when the stock market peaked and buy stock when prices were low during economic slumps. This permitted Wilma to make respectable profits when they were available and restricted her losses.

Employing Resources

Resources will help you meet your financial goals.

Successful financial planning also considers the variety of resources available to meet a person's financial goals. One of the most important resources is the employee benefits package provided as a fringe benefit by many employers. This often provides a range of benefits to an employee, many of which affect financial planning. Larger companies often provide (1) *compensation for time not worked,* such as paid holiday and vacation time, excused absences, sick pay, and other time away from work, such as paid lunch and rest periods, (2) *employee services,* such as social and recreational activities, day care and health care spending accounts, free legal services, educational reimbursement, and merchandise discounts, and (3) *employee security and health benefits,* such as life insurance, supplemental life insurance, dependent life insurance coverage for spouse and children, workers' compensation, Social Security, unemployment insurance, short-term disability insurance, long-term disability insurance, health insurance for individuals and dependents, dental insurance, a savings plan with tax advantages and matching contributions from the employer, and a supplemental investment/retirement plan. Successful financial managers understand their employee benefits package and utilize it effectively.

Table 3.1 lists 15 areas of financial planning, and Table 3.2 provides an illustration of a financial plan. Most people do not make written financial plans in all these areas. Many people ignore certain areas (retirement and liability losses, for example) and act with only partial knowledge in others (relying solely on employer-provided life insurance, for example). Success in financial matters is a result of effective financial planning in most if not all 15 areas. All subsequent chapters will examine personal finance topics in enough detail that you will feel comfortable and confident with the subject to the extent that you will be able to make an effective financial plan and follow it through with effective financial management.

TABLE 3.1
Fifteen Areas of Financial Planning

Plans for spending	Plans for capital accumulation
1. Plan major financial purchases	8. Tax fund
2. Manage debt	9. Revolving savings fund
	10. Emergency fund
Plans against risks	11. Education
	12. Savings
3. Medical costs	13. Investments
4. Property and casualty losses	14. Retirement
5. Liability losses	15. Estate planning
6. Premature death	
7. Income loss from disability	

Cafeteria Plan Insurance Benefits: You Choose

The company in the following illustration provides a contribution of $1460 to each employee to be used to purchase insurance benefits. Instead of providing workers who have diverse needs a slate of fixed benefits, many companies offer a menu of various benefits and allow employees to select their benefits—thus the term **cafeteria plan**. Employees typically are given a set sum of "credits," which are then expended by employee choices on a variety of fringe benefits, each with different levels of cost. The company will pick up and pay for the entire premium for the core plan, often providing limited coverage, but employees who desire more benefits than the company will pay for must pay for extra amounts themselves with paycheck deductions. If you were single, 30 years old, and earned $25,000 a year, what benefits might you choose if these were your choices?

1 Medical	Cost		
1. No coverage	$ 0		$
2. Low coverage	950	Medical Option	Medical Cost
3. Medium coverage	1,100	Number	
4. High coverage	1,230		

2 Dental	Cost		
1. No coverage	$ 0		$
2. Low coverage	70	Dental Option	Dental Cost
3. Medium coverage	100	Number	
4. High coverage	150		

3 Long-Term Disability	Cost		
1. No coverage	$ 0		$
2. Medium coverage	70	LTD Option	LTD Cost
3. High coverage	130	Number	

4 Life Insurance	Cost		
1. No coverage	$ 0		$
2. Low coverage	40	Life Option	Life Cost
3. Medium coverage	70	Number	
4. High coverage	100		

5 The Totals

Enter the total cost on this line. . .   Total Cost $
Compare the total cost to $1,460:
• If the total cost is *greater* than $1,460, this is the additional cost   Your Cost $
  you pay. . .
• If the total cost is *less* than $1,460, this is the extra pay you receive. . .Your Extra Pay $

TABLE 3.2

Financial Plans, Goals, and Objectives for Harry (Age 23) and Belinda (Age 22) Johnson (Prepared in January 1991)

Financial Plan Areas	Long-Term Goals and Objectives	Short-Term Goals
For spending		
1. Evaluate and plan major purchases	Purchase new car.	Begin saving up down payment for new car.
2. Manage debt	Besides a home, never have more installment debt than 10 percent of take-home pay.	Pay off charge cards at end of each month and do not finance any purchases of appliances or other similar products.
Against risks		
3. Medical costs	Avoid large medical costs.	Maintain employer-subsidized medical insurance policy by paying $65 monthly premium.
4. Property and casualty losses	Always have renter's or homeowner's insurance. Always have maximum automobile insurance coverage.	Make quarterly premium payments of $160 on automobile insurance policy. Make annual premium payment of $110 on renter's insurance policy.
5. Liability losses	Eventually buy liability insurance.	Hope for the best.
6. Premature death	Have adequate life insurance coverage for both as well as lots of financial investments so the survivor would not have any financial worries.	Maintain employer-subsidized life insurance of $34,200 on Belinda. Buy some life insurance for Harry. Start some investments.
7. Income loss from disability	Eventually buy disability insurance or have sufficient investment income not to worry.	Hope for the best.
For capital accumulation		
8. Tax fund	Have enough money for taxes (but not too much) withheld from monthly salaries by both employers to cover eventual tax liabilities.	Reconfirm that employer withholding of taxes is sufficient. Have some extra money withheld to cover additional tax liability because of income on trust from deceased father.
9. Revolving savings fund	Always have sufficient cash in local accounts to meet monthly and annual anticipated budget expense needs.	Develop cash-flow calendar to ascertain needs. Put money into revolving savings fund to build it up quickly to the proper balance. Keep all funds in interest-earning accounts.

(continued)

TABLE 3.2 (continued)

Financial Plan Areas	Long-Term Goals and Objectives	Short-Term Goals
10. Emergency fund	Build up monetary assets equivalent to 3 months' take-home pay.	Put $200 a month into emergency fund until it gets at least up to one month's take-home pay.
11. Education	Maintain educational skills and credentials to successfully compete with co-workers. Have employer assist in paying for Belinda to earn a master's in business administration (M.B.A.) degree. Eventually have Harry complete a master's of fine arts (MFA) degree and perhaps even a doctor of philosophy (Ph.D.) degree in interior design.	Both take one graduate class per term.
12. Savings	Always have a nice-sized savings balance. Regularly save to achieve goals. Save some portion of any extra income or gifts. Save $15,000 for a down payment on a home to be bought within 5 years.	Save enough to pay cash for a good quality video cassette recorder (VCR). Pay off VISA credit card balance of $390 soon.
13. Investments	Own substantial shares of a conservative mutual fund that will pay dividends equivalent to about 10 percent of family income at age 45. Own some real estate and common stocks.	Start investing in a mutual fund before next year.
14. Retirement	Retire at age 60 or earlier on an income that is the same as the take-home pay earned just before retirement.	Establish individual retirement accounts (IRAs) for Harry and Belinda before next year. Select the best retirement benefit plan offered by employer to meet long-term needs.
15. Estate planning	Provide a substantial sum of money for surviving spouse.	Each spouse makes a will.

Understanding Financial Activities over the Life Cycle

Objective
To be able to illustrate the impact of life-cycle periods and stages on the financial tasks, problems, and challenges facing people today.

Financial activities vary somewhat when you choose singlehood or couplehood.

A **life cycle** is a description of the progress of human life along a continuous sequence of family-status periods and stages. It includes three life-cycle periods—childhood, singlehood, and couplehood—and numerous stages, as shown in Figure 3.2.

Singlehood Versus Couplehood

Upon becoming adults, people enter into a time of predominant economic self-sufficiency. At that point, individuals move into either the singlehood or couplehood life-cycle period. Then they remain in either the singlehood or couplehood period or move back and forth between the periods while going through certain stages. For example, an individual in early singlehood could follow the traditional pathway (4, 5, 6, 7, 8, 9, and 10 in Figure 3.2). Or perhaps an individual could choose to follow stages 1, 2, 3, 11, and 12, the single adult's pathway.

What is important to point out is that earnings and consumption are sharply affected by an individual's changes in periods and stages in the life cycle. Numerous factors affect an individual's movement through periods of the life cycle, including values, attitudes, abilities, education, emotional makeup, jobs, careers, procreation inclinations, religion, marital stability, spouse's lifespan, life goals, opportunities, and luck. Many of these factors are controllable and, therefore, we can assume, within the destiny of the individual.

Financial Tasks, Problems, and Challenges

We all go through a series of life-cycle financial tasks, problems, and challenges.

Changes in the life cycle bring about numerous financial tasks, problems, and challenges, as depicted in Table 3.3. The resources each person brings to financial management problems also vary. Importantly, therefore, the remainder of this book addresses *each and every* task, problem, and

FIGURE 3.2
Life-Cycle Periods, Stages, and Pathways

Source: Adapted from Ronald W. Stampfl, *Journal of Home Economics,* Spring 1979. Copyright © 1979, American Home Economics Association, Alexandria, VA. Reprinted with permission.

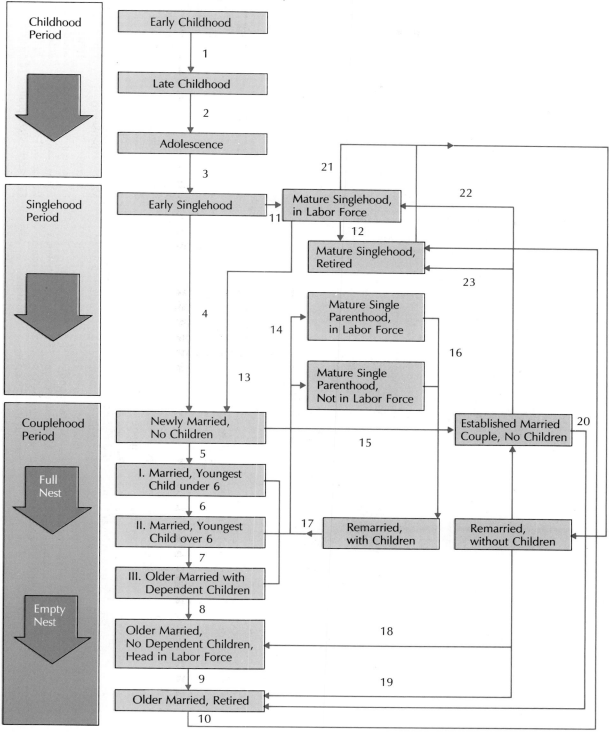

TABLE 3.3
Financial Tasks, Problems, and Challenges over Various Periods of the Life Cycle

	Singlehood, Transitional	Singlehood, Mature	Couplehood, Childless	Couplehood, Full Nest, First Stage	Couplehood, Full Nest, Second Stage
Characteristics	Views current status as traditional. May have unclear values. Highly mobile in housing and career. Possesses few assets. Income probably at lowest point, but rising.	Makes commitment to lifestyle and career. Possesses clear values and is goal oriented. Earns higher income. Enjoys quality vacations.	Makes commitment to relationship. Clarifies values and goals. Highly mobile. Possesses few assets. Both spouses earn money income.	First stage, youngest child under age 6. Decreased mobility. Some assets have been accumulated. Material needs seem to increase. Income does not rise much, may drop.	Second stage, youngest child over age six. Income continues to rise. Increased mobility. Have many assets. Both spouses may earn money income.
Financial management tasks, problems, and challenges	Use credit for the first time. Purchase first automobile, basic furniture, stereos, etc. Learn to control a budget. Establish a record-keeping system. Make a spending plan. Start a savings plan. Overspend budget. Rent an apartment. Buy automobile insurance. Establish financial goals and plans. Pay income tax.	Effectively handle increasing income. Need a more complex budget. Expand savings program. Start to make growth investments. Need financial planning. Buy a home or rent a dwelling. Purchase life and health insurance. Buy renter's and/or homeowner's insurance. Should itemize on income taxes.	Discuss and resolve disagreements over money. Resolve value and lifestyle differences. Buy life insurance. Consider opportunity costs of having children. Need a more complex budget. Avoid paying too much in income taxes. Write a will. Consider buying a house or condominium. Establish an individ-	Discuss and resolve spending styles. Buy renters and/or homeowner's insurance. Additional costs of child. Need a more complex budget. Potential unemployment of one parent. Match expenses to income. Frustrated with slow financial progress. Revise will. Consider estate planning.	Desire to replace assets with better quality. Higher expenses for children. Increased budget demands. Income tax return audited. Purchase a second home. Increase savings for children's education. Consider debt consolidation to pay bills. Consider disability insurance.

Resolve computer billing errors.
Pay medical bills.
Cover education costs.

Plan income tax strategies.
Write a will.
Build an emergency cash reserve.
Establish an individual retirement account (IRA).
Open a money market account.
Consider disability and liability insurance.
Consider tax-exempt investments.
Consider professional financial planning.
Develop an effective recordkeeping system.
Maintain credit standing.
Assess progress toward financial objectives.

ual retirement account (IRA).
Build an emergency cash reserve.
Open a money market account.
File claims for medical insurance reimbursements.
Potential overuse of credit.

Start an education savings plan for children.
Potential credit misuse as needs increase.
Purchase a second automobile.
Increase/change life and health insurance.
Start saving for down payment on a home.
Establish a spousal individual retirement account (IRA).
Consider life insurance for dependents.
First home purchase.
Itemization of income taxes.
Use tax breaks for working parents.
Consider 401(k) or 403(b) plans.
Appoint guardian for children.
Set up bypass trusts to minimize estate taxes.
Reexamine family/personal goals.

Consider opportunity costs of returning to school.
Have spouse return to earning money income.
Involve children in financial matters.

(continued)

TABLE 3.3 (continued)

	Couplehood, Full Nest, Third Stage	Couplehood, Empty Nest, Fourth Stage	Single Parenthood	Retirement
Characteristics	Third stage, all children have reached adolescence or left home. Values clear. Improving financial situation. Less mobile. Possess many assets. Both spouses may earn money income.	Empty nest, no children at home. Strong financial position. Values clear. Mobility possibility increases. Both spouses may earn money income.	Income limited. Reclarifying values. Mobility increases. Some assets have been accumulated.	Values clear. Financial condition sound. Less mobile. Possess many assets.
Financial management tasks, problems, and challenges	High educational costs for children. Money available for nonessential items (appliances, new furniture, boat). Tax shelter planning. Plan for retirement. Estate planning.	Desire to replace assets with better quality. Children need occasional financial aid. Pay for extended travel, home improvements. Increase emergency	Potential sharp drop in income. Compensate for or buy skills of a partner, such as housekeeping and day care. Income not rising much.	Decrease in income. Living on fixed income. Concern about outliving income. Increase in medical costs. Reduce life insurance.

Increasing recreational expenses.
Automobile insurance for teenager.
Make conservative investments.
Open a money market account.
Consider disability and liability insurance.
Update homeowner's insurance.
Consider tax-exempt investments.
Consider tax-free gifts and loans to children.
Consider professional financial planning.
Increased childrearing costs.
Consider changing housing after children leave home.
Evaluate dependents' future financial needs.

cash reserve.
Purchase other housing to accommodate changing needs.
Set up trusts for children.
Update will.
Consider tax-free gifts for children.
Consider tax-exempt investments.
Consider professional financial planning.
Reduce life insurance.
Analyze future retirement income and sources.

Consider opportunity costs of returning to school.
Need to acquire more assets.
Consider renter's/homeowner's insurance.
Need to match expenses to income.
Frustration with slow financial progress.
Make a will.
Start education savings plan for children.
Buy life insurance.
Potential credit misuse.
Involve children in financial matters.
Cope with increasing child care costs.
Need to establish short- and long-term goals.

Buy Medicare.
Purchase supplemental health insurance.
Update will.
Consider part-time job.
Use up part of investments without outliving funds.
Sell home/buy a retirement home.
Switch to lower-risk investments.
Establish trusts to reduce taxes.
Update letter of last instructions.
Finance leisure activities.

challenge thus identified to help you become successful in personal financial matters. Consequently, we hope that this book becomes a valuable resource for your effective financial management.

Financial Statements

Objective
To be able to state the purpose, value, and components of key financial statements, particularly the balance sheet and the income and expense statement.

Financial statements provide basic financial data.

Financial statements are compilations of personal financial data designed to communicate information on money matters. They are used, often along with other financial data, to provide indicators of the financial condition of an individual or family. The two most useful statements are (1) the balance sheet and (2) the income and expense statement. Keep in mind that the nuances and shadings of information in financial statements are open to interpretation by the creator and users of such statements.

Both types of financial statements are designed to allow a thorough review of a person's financial condition. A **balance sheet** describes an individual's or family's financial condition at a particular time, showing assets, liabilities, and net worth. The balance sheet gives a status report as of a certain date as well as a starting point for progressing financially. For example, if your balance sheet shows that you have a large cash balance, you can take action to achieve goals that require ready cash.

An **income and expense statement** relates an individual's or family's income and expenses by listing and summarizing the income and expense transactions that have taken place over a specific period of time, such as a month or a year. For example, if your weekly income was $500, an income and expense statement prepared on a monthly basis would show an income of $2000. Likewise, if weekly food costs were $80, a monthly statement would show food costs of $320.

The Balance Sheet

The balance sheet provides a snapshot of one's financial status.

It is useful to determine your financial assets and liabilities at least once a year. The information on the balance sheet can then be compared with that on previous balance sheets to help calculate how much financial progress you are making and provide directions for future planning. If you are serious about increasing your wealth, and most people are, then you need to sit down with pencil and paper and figure out your present financial position—the sum of what you own less what you owe. Note that applications for personal loans and home mortgages will ask for the same information.

Three Components of the Balance Sheet   There are three parts to any balance sheet: assets, liabilities, and net worth. Your **assets** are the current worth of anything you own that has commercial or exchange value. Your **liabilities** are the dollar value of the items you owe. Your **net worth** is the dollar value left when what is owed is subtracted from what is owned, or when liabilities are subtracted from assets.

What Is Owned—Assets As noted, the asset section identifies things that are valued at their current market prices, not amounts originally paid. It is useful to classify assets as monetary, tangible, or investment assets. **Monetary assets** (also known as **liquid assets**) are cash and near-cash items that can be readily converted to cash, since they are primarily used for maintenance of living expenses, emergencies, savings, and payment of bills. **Tangible assets** are physical items that have fairly long life spans and could be sold to raise cash but whose primary purpose is to provide maintenance of a lifestyle. People generally do not plan on selling their tangible assets, and to do so would take considerable time and effort. Tangible assets generally depreciate in value. **Investment assets** (also known as **capital assets**) are tangible and intangible items acquired for the monetary benefits they provide, such as generating additional income and increasing in value. Investment assets generally appreciate and are dedicated to the maintenance of one's future standard of living. Here are some examples of each kind of asset.

Investment assets are to maintain your future standard of living.

Monetary Assets

- Cash (including cash on hand, checking accounts, savings accounts, savings bonds, certificates of deposit, insurance cash value, and money-market accounts)
- Tax refunds due
- Money owed to you by others

Tangible Assets

- Automobiles, motorcycles, boats, bicycles
- House, mobile home, condominium
- Household furnishings and appliances
- Personal property (jewelry, furs, tools, clothing)
- Other "big ticket" items

Investment Assets

- Stocks, bonds, mutual funds, gold, partnerships, art, IRAs
- Life insurance and annuities (cash value only)
- Real estate and tax-sheltered investments
- Company pension and thrift plans

What Is Owed—Liabilities The liabilities section includes any items that reflect debts owed. It would include both personal debts (money borrowed from a friend) and business debts (money owed to a store or a bank). Also, the type of debt owed could be **short-term** (or **current**) **liabilities** (an obligation to be paid off within 1 year) or **long-term liabilities** (perhaps a 4-year debt on a car or a 25-year debt on a home). As you construct the liabilities section of your balance sheet, be sure to include all debt

What If You Use a Computer to Help Manage Personal Finances?

Using a computer to help you manage personal finances may be a good idea, depending on your circumstances. It is not expensive if you already own a computer. Most commercially available software programs for personal finance cost from $100 to $250. (Popular programs include Andrew Tobias's *Managing Your Money,* available from MECA, 285 Riverside Avenue, Westport, CT 06880, and *Dollars and Sense,* from Monogram, 8295 S. La Cienega Blvd., Ingleside, CA 90301.) Before making a purchase, however, realize that you must have the self-discipline to input data regularly or you will have simply wasted your money on software that is not functional because your financial management data base is outdated.

Benefits of using a computer in personal finance are many: Laborious calculations are reduced to a minimum, comparisons of data are simple to perform, budgets can be created easily with many revisions, income taxes can be prepared, investments can be analyzed, banking transactions can be performed, shopping can be done, financial statements can be prepared, and financial plans can be developed.

Finding a software program to fit your needs requires some investigation. After talking to friends and conducting some research on the topic, you may want to visit local libraries, schools, and colleges and try out the programs that are available. You should consider software that has a **data base** (an electronic filing cabinet suitable for checkbook and budgeting information) and **spreadsheet** capability (permits calculating the effects of a variety of transactions).

Appendix C, Personal Computers in Finance, provides many details on what types of personal finance software you might want to purchase and how to go about buying it. Readers also should know that a computer software program disk accompanies this textbook, called *Personal Finance Cookbook.* The easy-to-use software performs a number of calculations, solves several common financial problems, and utilizes spreadsheets to allow you to do your budgeting on the computer and prepare financial statements. The teacher's copy of the *Personal Finance Cookbook* software may be copied for student use and/or put on the hard disk of a computer.

obligations; otherwise, your financial condition will not be accurate. Examples of items to include in the liabilities section of a balance sheet, with some suggested subheadings, are

Short-Term Liabilities

- Personal loans (owed to other persons)
- Credit card and charge accounts (owed to stores)
- Check overdraft line-of-credit debt outstanding
- Bank credit cards (VISA, Discover, MasterCard)
- Travel and entertainment credit cards (American Express, Diners Club, Carte Blanche)
- Insurance premiums
- Professional services (doctors, dentists, chiropracters, lawyers)

- Utilities unpaid
- Repair services unpaid
- Rent unpaid
- Taxes unpaid

Long-Term Liabilities

- Automobile or other transportation loans
- Household furnishings loans
- Home mortgage
- Education loans

What Is Left—Net Worth Net worth is determined mathematically by subtracting liabilities from assets. It is calculated as follows:

$$
\begin{array}{ll}
\text{(What is owned)} - \text{(what is owed)} = \text{(what is left)} \\
\text{Assets} - \text{liabilities} \quad = \text{net worth}
\end{array}
$$

or

The assumption made in determining the net worth section is that if you were to convert all assets to cash and pay all liabilities, the remaining cash would be your net worth. You may determine which terminology to use. The terms are not as important as your understanding of the purpose of each section of the balance sheet.

Sample Balance Sheets The balance sheet serves as a statement of the assets and liabilities of a business, family, or individual at a specified date. The total assets on a balance sheet equals the totals of both the liabilities

▌ Key Factors Affect the Net Worth of Americans

Census data provide insights into the financial net worth of Americans. After extrapolating the data to 1991, the median net worth of white households was $50,876; Hispanic households, $6387; and black households, $4416.

Some revealing insights about the factors related to net worth after ignoring race follow. Households headed by college graduates had a median net worth of $78,542; it slipped to $4246 for those headed by high school graduates and to $3048 for those headed by someone with less than a high school education. Education clearly makes a difference in net worth.

Marriage is another factor. Households headed by married couples had a *net worth* (the amount left when you subtract what you owe from what you own) of $65,151; it dropped to $18,051 for households headed by unmarried females and to $12,848 for those headed by unmarried males. Staying married also makes a difference in net worth—probably because two people can earn, save, invest, and create more net worth than a single person.

TABLE 3.4
Balance Sheet for a College Student (Bill Soshnik), January 1, 1991

Assets

Cash on hand	$ 85.00	
Checking account	335.00	
Savings account	800.00	
Personal property*	1,240.00	
Automobile	3,600.00	
Total assets		$6,060.00

Liabilities

Utilities	$ 30.00	
Telephone	70.00	
Bank loan—automobile	3,100.00	
College loan	1,000.00	
Government educational loan	2,500.00	
Total liabilities		$6,700.00
Net worth		($640.00)
Total liabilities and net worth		$6,060.00

* Schedule includes clothes, $800; dresser, $50; television, $150; chair, $30; table, $40; desk, $120; and dishes/tableware, $50.

You decide how much detail you want and need.

and the net worth. Since both sides of a balance sheet must balance, this is the derivation of the term *balance sheet*. The amount of detail shown on a balance sheet depends on the person or family for whom it is prepared. Some balance sheets are more detailed than others; you must decide how much to include to accurately show your financial condition on a given date.

Tables 3.4, 3.5, and 3.6 show balance sheets reflecting the degree of detail that may be included for a college student, a young married couple, and a couple with two children. Notice that Table 3.4 includes very few items. This is typical of single persons who have not acquired many things of value. Observe also the excess of liabilities over assets. This is not unusual for young college students, for whom debts seem to rise much faster than assets. In such an example, the person is technically **insolvent** because he or she has a negative net worth. When students graduate and take on full-time jobs, their balance sheets typically change. Tables 3.5 and 3.6 show balance sheets with greater detail and more items, reflecting the increasing financial complexity that occurs at later stages in a person's life.

Information Sources for the Balance Sheet   To construct a balance sheet, you need to compile dollar values for your assets and liabilities. Your checkbook, savings account records, and receipts of various payments

Assets

Monetary assets

Cash on hand	$ 65	
Savings account	550	
Checking account	360	
Total monetary assets		$ 975

Tangible assets

Automobile	$4,300	
Personal property	2,800	
Total tangible assets		$ 7,100

Investment assets

Stocks	$ 260	
Bonds	500	
Mutual fund	1,200	
Total investment assets		$ 1,960
Total assets		$10,035

Liabilities

Short-term liabilities

Utilities	$ 68	
Credit cards	225	
Rent due	425	
Total short-term liabilities		$ 718

Long-term liabilities

Education loan	$2,200	
Bank personal loan	275	
Auto loan—GMAC	3,200	
Total long-term liabilities		$ 5,675
Total liabilities		$ 6,393

Net worth	$ 3,642
Total liabilities and net worth	$10,035

Value your assets at their fair market values.

or investments will be good sources from which to begin. You may have to estimate approximate dollar values for household furnishings, jewelry, and personal belongings. Remember to value such items at their **fair market value,** or what a willing buyer would pay a willing seller. The dollar values of homes, automobiles, investments, life insurance, and other cash items will be more precise. The degree of precision used to determine the values of assets depend on the purpose and use of a balance sheet. In most cases, your judgment will suffice and detailed estimates are unnecessary. Many people find it useful to make a detailed list or schedule of items summarized on the balance sheet, as illustrated in the footnote to

Assets

Monetary assets			
Cash on hand	$ 260		
Savings accounts	1,500		
Rick's checking account	600		
Sue's checking account	700		
Tax refund due	700		
Rent receivable	660		
Total monetary assets		$ 4,420	
Tangible assets			
Home	$76,000 82,000		
Personal property	9,000		
Automobile	11,500 2,500		
Total tangible assets		$ 96,500	
Investment assets			
Fidelity mutual fund	$ 4,500		
Scudder mutual fund	5,000		
General Motors stock	2,800		
New York 2006 bonds	1,000		
Life insurance cash value	5,400		
IRA	6,300		
Real estate investment	84,000		
Total investment assets		$109,000	
Total assets			$209,920

Liabilities

Short-term liabilities			
Utilities	$ 120		
Credit cards	1,545		
Total short-term liabilities		$ 1,665	
Long-term liabilities			
Sales finance company—automobile	$ 7,700		
Savings and loan—real estate	72,000		
Total long-term liabilities		$ 79,700	
Total liabilities			$ 81,365
Net worth			$128,555
Total liabilities and net worth			$209,920

Table 3.4 and in Figure 3.3, because it helps identify the proper fair market value (Figure 3.3).

A list of suggested sources for providing the fair market dollar values of assets follows:

1. *Cash items:* from your personal or bank records.
2. *Home:* from the agency where your home is financed or from any real estate broker.

FIGURE 3.3

Lists or Schedules of
Balance Sheet Items

Automobiles

Description	Date of Purchase	Cost	Market Value and Date
Toyota Tercel Wagon – 1987 model	*July 1987*	$12,520	$11,000 Dec. – '90
Chevy Impala 4 door – 1971 model	*June 1986*	$600	$500 Dec. – '90

Jewelry and Art

Description	Date of Purchase	Cost	Market Value and Date
⅓ carat solitaire diamond setting	*June 1986*	$1,600	$1,400 Dec. – '90
Remington print	*March 1985*	$400	$600 Dec. – '90
Oriental vase – 12" blue	*August 1986*	$550	$650 Dec. – '90
Oriental vase – 16" blue	*November 1986*	$900	$1,100 Dec. – '90

3. *Automobile:* from the lender who financed your automobile or from any lender.

4. *Cash value of insurance policy:* from the policy cash surrender table in your policy or from your insurance company.

5. *Investments:* from financial publications or from an investment broker.

6. *Other items of value:* from professional appraisers (for jewelry or collectibles, such as valuable coins or stamps).

Below are some suggested sources that provide the dollar values of liabilities:

1. *Personal debts:* from those to whom the debts are owed.

2. *Charge accounts, credit card accounts, loans from banks, and other unpaid bills:* from the lenders in the form of statements or bills.

3. *Other debts:* from the debt repayment record or the lender.

The Income and Expense Statement

The income and expense statement summarizes financial transactions over time.

The income and expense statement is very different from a balance sheet. The balance sheet shows your financial condition at a single point in time; the income and expense statement summarizes financial transactions over a period of time, such as the previous year. The purpose of the income and expense statement is to show the total amounts that have been earned and spent over a time period. Thus, rather than having to refer to each checkbook entry to know how much you have spent on food during a month or a year, you refer only to the food category of the income and expense statement.

The income and expense statement allows you to review how well you have done financially in the past period. It shows whether you were able to live within your income. If your expenditures were greater than your income for a given period, for example, you would need to make some spending and/or income adjustments.

The income and expense statement provides a look backwards.

Three Components of the Income and Expense Statement An income and expense statement consists of three sections: **income** (total income received), **expenses** (total expenditures made), and **net income** or **net loss** (the difference between total income and total expenses).

Income You may think that income is only what is earned from salaries or wages. However, there are many other types of income that you should include on an income and expense statement, such as the following:

- Wages and salaries
- Bonuses and commissions
- Allowances
- Child support and alimony
- Public assistance
- Social Security
- Pensions and profit-sharing
- Scholarships and grants
- Loans
- Interest received (from savings accounts, bonds, or loans to others)
- Dividends received (from investments)
- Gains and/or losses (from securities or other property)
- Tax refunds
- Other items (gifts, rent income, pensions, royalties, temporary jobs)

Expenses All expenditures made during the period covered by the income and expense statement are included in this section. The number and type of expenses shown will vary with each individual and family. Many people separate the expenses by whether they are fixed or variable. **Fixed expenses** are expenditures usually in the same amount each time period; they are often contractual. Examples are rent payments and automobile installment loans. It is usually difficult, but not impossible, to reduce a fixed expense.

Variable expenses can be controlled.

Variable expenses are expenditures over which an individual has considerable control. Food, entertainment, and clothing are variable expenses. Note that some items, such as savings, can be listed twice, as both fixed and variable expenses. Below are several categories of expenses that you could include in a typical income and expense statement.

Fixed Expenses

- Housing (rent, mortgage loan payment)
- Automobile (installment payment, lease)
- Insurance (life, health, liability, disability, renter's, homeowner's, automobile)
- Contributions (church)
- Loans (appliances, furniture)
- Cable television
- Savings (Christmas club, regular plan)
- Investments (monthly investment plan)
- Pension contributions (employer's plan, IRA)
- Taxes (federal income, state income, local income, real estate, Social Security, and personal property)

Variable Expenses

- Food (at home and away)
- Utilities (electric, water, gas, telephone)
- Transportation (gasoline and maintenance, licenses, registration, public transportation)
- Medical (physicians, dentists, hospitals, medicines)
- Child care (nursery, baby sitting)
- Clothing and accessories (jewelry, shoes, handbags, briefcases)
- Cigarettes and tobacco
- Lotteries and gambling
- Alcoholic beverages
- Education (tuition, fees, books, supplies)
- Household furnishings (furniture, appliances, curtains)
- Personal care (beauty/barbershop, cosmetics, dry cleaner)
- Entertainment and recreation (hobbies, recreational equipment, health club, records/tapes/discs, videotape rentals, movies)
- Contributions (gifts, Christmas, church, school, charity)
- Vacations/long weekends
- Credit cards
- Savings (variable amounts)
- Investments (variable amounts)
- Miscellaneous (postage, books, magazines, personal allowances, domestic help, membership fees)

There is no set list of categories to be used in the expense section, but you need to classify all expenditures in some way. The more specific the

TABLE 3.7
Income and Expense Statement for a College Student (Bill Soshnik), January 1–December 31, 1991

Income

Wages (after withholding)	$4,650
Scholarship	1,750
Government grant	2,500
Government loan	2,600
Tax refund	110
Loan from parents	100
Total income	$11,710

Expenses

Room rent (includes utilities)	$1,500
Laundry	216
Food	1,346
Automobile loan payments	1,392
Automobile insurance	422
Books and supplies	1,032
Tuition	3,260
Telephone	282
Clothing	475
Gifts	300
Automobile expenses	656
Health insurance	102
Recreation and entertainment	260
Spring break	100
Personal expenses	300
Total expenses	$11,643
Net gain (available to spend, save, and invest):	$ 67

categories are that you select, the more specific will be the information you show in the income and expense statement.

Net Gain (Loss) The next gain (loss) section is an important part of the income and expense statement because it shows the amount remaining after you have itemized income and subtracted expenditures from income. The sample figures below illustrate this calculation. (A business would call this figure "net profit" or "net loss.")

$$(\text{Total income}) - (\text{total expenses}) = (\text{net gain or loss})$$

$$\$12,500 - \$11,400 = \$1,100 \text{ net income}$$

$$\$14,900 - \$15,700 = (\$800) \text{ net loss}$$

It is important to strive to have **net gain** (total income minus total expenses where income exceeds expenses) rather than **net loss** (total income

TABLE 3.8
Income and Expense Statement for a Young Married Couple (Roy and Mary Als), January 1–December 31, 1991

Income

Husband's gross income	$18,500	
Wife's gross income	26,000	
Interest and dividends	300	
Total income		$44,800

Expenses

Fixed expenses

Home rent	$ 5,100	
Renter's insurance	260	
Automobile loan payments	1,975	
Automobile insurance, registration, and taxes	876	
Life insurance	240	
Bank personal loan	275	
Education loan payments	500	
Federal income taxes	11,964	
State income taxes	1,412	
Social Security taxes	2,686	
Total fixed expenses		$25,288

Variable expenses

Food	$ 6,132	
Utilities	2,800	
Gasoline, oil, and repairs	2,250	
Medical expenses	460	
Clothing and upkeep	2,628	
Church	300	
Gifts	340	
Personal allowances	925	
Miscellaneous	240	
Total variable expenses		$16,075
Total expenses		$41,363
Net gain (available to spend, save, and invest):		$ 3,437

minus total expenses where expenses exceed income). This shows that you are successful in managing your financial resources and do not have to use savings or borrow to make financial ends meet. When the subtraction shows a net income, that amount is then available (in your checking and savings accounts) to spend, save, or invest.

Sample Income and Expense Statements   Income and expense statements vary in detail depending on who is preparing the statement. Tables 3.7, 3.8, and 3.9 show income and expense statements for a college

TABLE 3.9
Income and Expense Statement for a Couple with Two Children (Rick and Sue Hira), January 1–December 31, 1991

Income

Husband's gross salary	$33,180	
Wife's salary (part time)	8,500	
Interest and dividends	1,800	
Bonus	600	
Tax refunds	200	
Rental income	7,720	
Total income		$52,000

Expenses

Fixed expenses

Mortgage loan payments	$10,800	
Homeowner's insurance	460	
Automobile loan payments	2,400	
Automobile insurance and registration	891	
Life insurance	1,200	
Hospitalization insurance	680	
Savings at credit union	360	
Federal income taxes	10,200	
State income taxes	1,400	
City income taxes	220	
Social Security taxes	2,686	
Real estate and personal property taxes	950	
Total fixed expenses		$32,247

Variable expenses

Food	$ 5,900	
Utilities	1,800	
Gasoline, oil, and repairs	1,700	
Medical expenses	1,425	
Medicines	165	
Clothing and upkeep	2,160	
Church	600	
Gifts	600	
Personal allowances	1,160	
Children's allowances	480	
Miscellaneous	270	
Total variable expenses		$16,260
Total expenses		$48,507
Net gain (available to spend, save, and invest):		$ 3,493

student, a young married couple, and a couple with two children. The last statement vividly illustrates the additional income needed to rear children and shows the increased variety of expenditures that reflect a family's life-cycle changes. Generally, as a person earns more income, the income and expense statement becomes more detailed or involved.

Information Sources for the Income and Expense Statement   Every check written, every receipt received, every payment made, and every earnings payment received provides a source of information to be included in the income and expense statement. Since the statement is a financial summary, the transaction data are taken from many sources. Some original sources from which information can be gathered include the following:

- Checks received
- Pay records
- Canceled checks
- Receipts
- Invoices
- Statements
- Bills marked paid
- Payment books or records

Poor records will result in inaccurate financial statements.

Of course, if you keep poor records and save few documents, it will be difficult to prepare a sufficiently detailed income and expense statement. Several helpful examples of keeping detailed and accurate income and expense information appear in the section entitled Financial Recordkeeping.

The Effect of Financial Activities

Objective
To understand how your financial activities can affect your financial statements.

Financial activities can affect financial statements. First, changes in market value affect the asset and net worth sections of your balance sheet. An antique vase valued at $900 last year with a current market value of $1100 increases net worth by $200. Similarly, an automobile valued at $12,520 last year may have depreciated to $11,000, decreasing net worth by $1520. Second, your liabilities can increase as you acquire more debts or decrease because you make payments. Third, the net gain (or loss) from the income and expense statement may be reflected as an increase (or decrease) in the assets and net worth on your balance sheet. You might take the net gain, for instance, and place it in a savings account, which increases net worth. Fourth, funds can be shifted among categories. For example, assume you make an automobile installment payment of $300 to the finance company by using money from your checking account. Your net worth would not change because your assets were reduced by $300 and your liability for the automobile loan was reduced by the same amount. If you take the $300 from your current earnings, net worth would increase because you are using income, instead of an asset, to reduce the debt, since only the liability changed.

When attempting to redeploy your assets to achieve particular goals, you generally focus on manipulating the balance sheet, and the income and expense statement will reflect how the manipulations affect your income stream. Try to rearrange both your assets and liabilities in various ways to test what brings you closer to your goal(s).

Financial Ratios

Objective
To know how to use financial ratios to help you evaluate your financial strength and progress.

Financial ratios are objective yardsticks designed to simplify making judgmental analytical measurements of financial strength and change over time. A number of objective criteria can be used to help to assess your financial condition and progress so that you can better manage financial resources and develop spending and credit-use patterns consistent with your goals. The first two ratios below pertain to a person's liquidity, the next four add insight into the burden of debt undertaken, and the last two are illustrative of a number of ratios that tell of progress toward meeting financial goals.[3] Since standards for these ratios do not exist, it is best to subjectively evaluate each ratio in light of the peculiarities of each individual and family circumstance, considering such factors as stage in the life cycle, marital status, income, and financial goals.

Basic Liquidity Ratio

For how long can you meet your living expenses?

Liquidity is the speed and ease with which an asset can be converted to cash. One useful financial yardstick is the **basic liquidity ratio,** which reveals the number of months the household could continue to meet its expenses after a total loss of income resulting from illness, disability, or unemployment. Look at the monetary assets on the balance sheet for Rick and Sue Hira in Table 3.6 ($4420) and compare it using Equation (3.1) with their monthly expenses in Table 3.9 ($48,507/12 = $4042):

$$\text{Basic liquidity ratio} = \frac{\text{liquid assets}}{\text{monthly expenses}}$$

$$= \frac{\$4420}{\$4042} = 1.09 \qquad (3.1)$$

This financial ratio suggests that the Hiras only have sufficient assets to live for 1.09 months; their liquid assets could support them for just over one month if they were facing a family crisis. Many experts recommend

---

[3] For additional suggestions, see J. W. Mason and R. Griffith, "New Ratios for Analyzing and Interpreting Personal Financial Statements," *Journal of the Institute of Certified Financial Planners,* Spring 1988, pp. 71–85; C. G. Prather, "The Ratio Technique Applied to Personal Finance Statements: Development of Household Norms," *Financial Counseling and Planning,* Volume 1, Number 1, 1990, pp. 53–69; and R. H. Lytton, E. T. Garman, and N. M. Porter, "How to Use Financial Ratios When Advising Clients," *Financial Counseling and Planning* (in press).

that people should have monetary assets equal to 2 to 6 months' expenses in emergency cash reserves to protect against unemployment. Of course, such an amount of monetary assets is dependent on your family situation and your job. A smaller amount may be sufficient if you have adequate loss of income protection through an employee fringe benefit program or a union, are employed in a job that is definitely not subject to layoffs, have an employed spouse, or have a ready source of ample credit. Households dependent on the income from a self-employed person may need a larger emergency cash reserve.

Expanded Liquidity Ratio

For how long can you continue if you sell all your investment assets too?

An **expanded liquidity ratio** compares the dollar amount of liquid assets and investment assets with monthly expenses and reveals how long the household could continue to meet its financial needs. As shown in Equation (3.2), it measures one's ability to repay debts recognizing that other investment assets might be called on if needed. As shown in Table 3.6, the Hiras have $4420 in monetary assets and $109,000 in investment assets, totaling $113,420.[4] The Hiras' expanded liquidity ratio is 28.1, suggesting that if they had to, they could live over 2 years (28.1 months) if they counted their monetary and financial assets. Of course, the advisability of using such assets for living expenses is questionable.

$$\text{Expanded liquidity ratio} = \frac{\text{liquid assets and investment assets}}{\text{monthly expenses}}$$

$$= \frac{\$113,420}{\$4042} = 28.1 \qquad (3.2)$$

Solvency Ratio

A **solvency ratio** is a broad measure of a household's financial liquidity as it compares one's total assets with total debts. It provides a measure of solvency, as shown in Equation (3.3). Using the figures in Table 3.6 shows that the Hiras have ample assets compared with debts because they own more than 2½ times what they owe. (Reversing the figures shows that they owe 0.38 times what they own.)

$$\text{Solvency ratio} = \frac{\text{total assets}}{\text{total debt}}$$

$$= \frac{\$209,920}{\$81,365} = 2.58 \qquad (3.3)$$

If you owe more than you own, then you are excessively in debt and technically insolvent. While you may have enough current income to pay your current bills, you still do not have enough money to pay all your

---

[4] Do not count tangible assets in this calculation because it is most unlikely that these assets will be sold to pay monthly living expenses.

bills. Many people in such situations seek credit counseling, and some eventually declare bankruptcy. (These topics are discussed in Chapter 7, Planned Borrowing.)

Liquid Assets to Total Debt Ratio

A **liquid assets to total debt ratio** reveals the relationship between a person or family's liquid assets and the total debt position in case a situation arises where such assets must be used to repay debts. Equation (3.4) uses figures from Table 3.9 (monetary assets are $4420, while debts total $81,365) and reveals a ratio of 0.054, or only about 5 percent. This ratio seems very low, even though most of the Hiras debt is long term, suggesting that they are heavily relying on income to repay debts and have very few liquid assets to call on to repay debts if needed. The ratio probably should be 15 to 20 percent.

$$\text{Liquid assets to total debt ratio} = \frac{\text{liquid assets}}{\text{total debts}}$$

$$= \frac{\$4420}{\$81,365} = 0.054 \qquad (3.4)$$

Debt-to-Income Ratio

A debt-to-income ratio of 0.30 or lower shows financial strength.

A **debt-to-income ratio** provides an incisive view of the total debt burden of an individual or family by comparing the dollars spent on gross annual debt repayments, including mortgages, to gross annual income. Using data in Table 3.9 in Equation (3.5) shows that the Hiras $13,200 in annual loan repayments ($10,800 for the mortgage loan and $2400 for the automobile loan) amount to 25.4 percent of their $52,000 annual income. A ratio of 0.30 or lower indicates adequate gross income to easily make debt repayments, and it implies that one has some flexibility in budgeting for other expenses. This ratio should decrease as one grows older.

$$\text{Debt-to-income ratio} = \frac{\text{annual debt repayments}}{\text{gross income}}$$

$$= \frac{\$13,200}{\$52,000} = 0.254 \qquad (3.5)$$

Debt Service Ratio

How much take-home pay is used to repay debts?

A **debt service ratio** compares the annual debt repayments for interest and principal to *service* (or repay) all consumer and mortgage debts with one's annual take-home pay. It provides a measure of how much income is required and committed to repay debts, as shown in Equation (3.6). Using the figures in Table 3.9 and the $37,494 take-home income ($52,000 in income less $14,506 in taxes withheld from their salaries, including $10,200 for federal income taxes, $1400 for state income taxes, $220 for city income taxes, and $2686 for Social Security taxes) shows that the Hiras have sufficient take-home income to easily make monthly loan repayments totaling $13,200 ($10,800 for the mortgage loan and $2400 for the automobile loan). The Hiras have a debt service ratio of 0.35; thus they have 35 cents committed to repaying interest and principal credit repayments for every dollar they have in take-home pay. A ratio of 0.40 or lower indicates adequate current take-home pay to easily make debt repayments, and it implies that one has some flexibility in budgeting for other expenses.

$$\text{Debt service ratio} = \frac{\text{annual debt repayments}}{\text{annual take-home pay}}$$

$$= \frac{\$13,200}{\$37,494} = 0.35 \tag{3.6}$$

Savings Ratio

A **savings ratio** provides an indicator of progress in achieving financial goals by measuring the percentage of disposable income (take-home pay) that is being saved annually. This is done by dividing one's net financial gain by the take-home pay. It provides a measure of how much you are able to save. (Realize, too, that people who pay off debts, instead of saving, are also "saving.") Using the figures in Table 3.9 and Equation (3.7), the take-home income from above shows that the Hiras have had a good year, since they have a net gain of $3493 for the year, or 9.3 percent of their take-home pay, which is a lot more than the American average of 4 to 6 percent.

$$\text{Savings ratio} = \frac{\text{net financial gain}}{\text{take-home pay}}$$

$$= \frac{\$3,493}{\$37,494} = 0.093 \tag{3.7}$$

Investment Assets to Net Worth Ratio

You should strive to have a high proportion of your net worth made up of investment assets.

An **investment assets to net worth ratio** reveals how well an individual or family is advancing toward financial goals other than home ownership as it compares the value of actual investment assets accumulated to net worth. Using the data in Table 3.6 and Equation (3.8), the Hiras have a ratio of 0.85. This means that 85 percent of their net worth is made up of investment assets, an excellent proportion for this stage in their lives. Younger people often have a net worth to investment assets ratio of less than 20 percent, primarily because they have few investments and have little or no equity in their homes.

$$\text{Investment assets to net worth ratio} = \frac{\text{investment assets}}{\text{net worth}}$$

$$= \frac{\$109,000}{\$128,555} = 0.85 \tag{3.8}$$

Other Data to Assess Your Financial Progress

In addition to calculating financial ratios, you can use figures from your balance sheets and income and expense statements independently or together to assist in analyzing your finances. Look over the assets on the balance sheet for Rick and Sue Hira in Table 3.6. Do they have too few monetary assets compared with tangible and investment assets? Many experts recommend that 15 to 20 percent of your assets be monetary, higher as you near retirement. Do you have too much invested in one asset, or have you diversified, as the Hiras have? Also, have your balance sheet figures changed in a favorable direction since last year? And, of course, are you making progress toward achieving your financial goals?

Look over your income figures to see what proportion comes from labor compared with what proportion comes from investments. Like the Hiras in Table 3.9, most people desire to have a growing proportion of income from investments. Twenty percent is an achievable goal for many persons. In the expense area, it is vital to ask, "Am I spending money where I really want to?" In which categories could you reduce expenses? In which categories could you increase income? The Hiras, for example, might consider increasing their savings and investments.

You also can use financial statements to assist in providing answers to such questions as, "What proportion of my assets earn income for me, such as interest, dividends, and rent?" "Is my consumption efficient?" "Do some expense items need justification?" "Can I take on more credit payments?" "Can I afford to buy a luxury item?" "How would a big purchase, such as a car or a vacation to Europe, change both sides of the balance sheet?" "Do I have enough net worth to risk some of it through investing?" "Should I save more?" "Do I have enough funds to increase my investments?" "In which areas can I reduce expenses to have money for an alternative purpose?" "Is my present homeowner's or renter's insurance coverage sufficient?" "Am I achieving my financial objectives?" Clear answers to these questions come from using financial statements; they help you assess your financial condition and progress and help you to achieve your financial goals.

Analysis of your financial statements reveals your financial progress.

How to Choose a Financial Planner

Objective
To be able to explain how to choose a financial planner.

Financial planning advice is information and counseling you can receive about taxation, credit, money management, insurance, savings, housing, economics, preservation of purchasing power, income from investments, growth in the value of investments, and estate planning. This advice may come from financial publications, nonprofessional advisors, and professional financial planners.

You may be able to get solid financial advice from friends, relatives, and co-workers. Professionals, such as the family lawyer, town banker, real estate agent, local accountant or tax preparer, insurance agent, credit counselor, and stockbroker, can help you draw up a will, set up an individual retirement account, buy and sell real estate, prepare taxes, buy life insurance, revise your budget to reduce your credit obligations, and purchase stock. These people may be specialists in one specific field, but they usually do not have the high-level expertise required to develop a thorough financial plan. For example, some investment firms designate their staffers as "financial consultants" or "financial planners" when they have completed company-sponsored educational programs, even though the subjects studied are only on investments.

Many professional people lack the expertise for proper financial planning.

Most of us have evolved ways of handling financial affairs that seem adequate in helping us to get along and/or get ahead. However, if you have an annual income of $35,000 or more, you should consider utilizing the expertise of a professional financial planner—a tax attorney, investment manager, or financial planner with appropriate professional certifications. Of course, you yourself should have a knowledge of the fundamentals of personal finance. A recent survey by the *National Underwriter* revealed that four-fifths of Americans have a formal financial plan and fully half see such a plan as important to achieving their goals. The study further indicated that 80 percent of Americans want to pay little or nothing for a formal financial plan. When asked how much they would pay for a plan, 41 percent said zero and 38 percent said less than $500.

Tax attorneys are specialists in income tax laws and regulations, and they should be up to date on complex tax laws and regulations. A young tax attorney with access to older and more experienced legal partners might be especially helpful. Interview some prospects and choose someone with whom you feel comfortable. **Investment managers** take almost complete charge of your investment portfolio and give you periodic reports on the results of their efforts. Rock stars and movie personalities frequently use such services.

Anyone may call himself or herself a "financial planner."

The meaning of the term **financial planner** is so broad that it covers any person who calls himself or herself by that title. It is also important to realize that most financial planners are biased because they sell something. The financial advice obtained from a banker, broker, or financial planner is always slanted toward the transactions and/or products sold by the firm he or she represents. This is because it is in the economic interest of the financial planner working for a brokerage firm to sell you stocks, bonds, or some other service from which a commission will be earned. In a similar way, both mutual fund and insurance salespersons earn commissions, and bankers get a year-end bonus for successfully promoting their products.

In the face of this inherent bias, you must be well armed with a knowledgeable background in personal finance. Then you can decide whether the economic interests of the financial planner coincide with your self-interest.

Estimates indicate that about 500,000 people call themselves financial planners. Many people who call themselves financial planners are really nothing more than salespersons for insurance, stocks, tax shelters, income tax preparation services, and other investments. A financial planner should be able to analyze a family's total needs in such areas as investments, taxes, insurance, education goals, and retirement and put all the information together into a cohesive plan. This may require helping a client select and prioritize goals and then rearranging assets and liabilities to fit the client's changed goals, lifestyle, and stage in the life cycle. Financial planners should be problem solvers and coordinators, because they often work with a group of outside advisers, such as attorneys, accountants, trust officers, real estate brokers, stockbrokers, and insurance agents.

Financial planning is a rapidly growing career field that one day might require that all persons calling themselves "financial planners" have to meet the same set of accredited educational standards, pass certification examinations, have prior work experience, and be licensed by a government regulatory agency. As the field becomes more professional, financial planning will become more altruistic. The public believes that a career, to be considered a profession, must involve a significant degree of helping others. Financial planners provide a useful support system for people in our increasingly complex financial world.

Professional Designations and Credentials

Many financial planners have voluntarily undergone training and have met various qualifications for particular professional certifications. Perhaps the best known is the **certified financial planner (CFP)**. This is a person who has been approved by the International Board of Standards and Practices for Certified Financial Planners (IBCFP). About 9,000 CFPs are certified as having completed a program of study in the following areas: introduction to financial planning, risk management, investments, tax planning and management, retirement planning and employee benefits, and estate planning. Persons interested in obtaining the CFP designation can take a university-based program at any one of more than 30 IBCFP-approved institutions or take correspondence courses from the proprietary College for Financial Planning in Denver (9725 East Hampden Avenue, Denver, CO 80231). CFPs must pass rigorous examinations, have 3 years of work experience in the field, agree to adhere to the IBCFP Code of Ethics, and continuously update their financial planning knowledge. Their professional association is the Institute of Certified Financial Planners (ICFP). A **chartered financial consultant (ChFC)** takes correspondence courses in investments, real estate, and tax shelters given by American College in Bryn Mawr, Pennsylvania. About 15,000 people have the ChFC designation, which is an outgrowth of American College's long-standing chartered life underwriter (CLU) program. The National Association of Personal Financial Advisors (NAPFA) is the largest nationwide organization of fee-only financial planners, and they are prohibited from receiving any type of product-related compensation, such as sales commissions.

The **Registry of Financial Planners** is a designation by the International Association for Financial Planning (IAFP) indicating that a person has passed a day-long case-problem examination. The approximately 1000 members must have 3 years of full-time financial planning experience; have their financial plans reviewed by a national committee; and have either a CFP, ChFC, or CPA (certified public accountant) designation or an academic degree in law or business. The address for the IAFP is Two Concourse Parkway, Suite 800, Atlanta, GA 30328.

Key professional designations include CFP and ChFC.

A **registered financial planner** is a person who meets the qualifications of the International Association of Registered Financial Planners: 3 years of full-time financial planning experience; CFP, ChFC, or CPA designation or an academic degree in law or business; a securities license; an insurance license; and a record absent of professional suspensions or revocations. No examinations are required.

A **registered investment advisor (RIA)** is a person required by the federal Investment Advisor Act to register with the Securities and Exchange Commission because he or she gives investment advice to more than five people a year. The RIA designation means that the person has paid the $150 application fee; no government professional standards must be met or tests passed. About 15,000 people are registered investment advisors. By contrast, about 60,000 people listed themselves as "financial planners" in the Yellow Pages in California alone. Many states also require registration of investment advisors, who generally are then allowed to call themselves "registered investment advisers."

Undergraduate and Graduate Education Programs

A **master's of science in financial services** is a graduate degree offered by the American College evidencing specialization in financial planning. A number of other colleges and universities also offer undergraduate and graduate degrees with similar titles. A growing number of people have earned academic credentials in addition to the various professional designations.

What Fees Do Financial Planners Charge?

Fee-only financial planners tend to offer unbiased advice.

Financial planners may or may not sell services other than their own advice. Some earn no commissions and work solely on a **fee-only basis.** These planners charge a fixed fee for their services, regardless of what those services involve. They typically charge $50 to $200 an hour or between 1 and 1½ percent of the client's assets, and they usually need 3 to 4 hours to analyze a client's financial situation thoroughly. Fee-only planners do not promote products of their own, such as stocks, insurance, real estate partnerships, or tax preparation; thus they can claim to not be burdened by any potential conflicts of interest in making recommendations. **Commission-only** financial planners live on the commissions they charge from the investments they sell to their clients. For example, if you invest $10,000 in a mutual fund recommended by a commission-only planner, it is likely that you will have put only $9150 of it to work because the remainder went to pay the 8½ percent commission. A **fee and commission** financial planner receives commissions on what his or her clients buy plus a per-hour fee or percentage of assets. Of course, it does not matter if you pay commissions for financial planning advice as long as you know what you are paying for and what you are getting.

Relatively few financial planners work on a fee-only basis. You can locate a financial planner by using the Yellow Pages or by asking for a referral. If desired, for about $100 you can obtain a direct-mail computer analysis printout of "personalized" financial planning advice that may provide you with a starting point. One of the largest firms that does this is Consumer Financial Institute (430 Lexington St., Newton, MA 02166).

Questions to Ask Financial Planners

You need unbiased advice.

You can locate financial planners by contacting several of the organizations that accredit financial planners. Also, you can ask friends, relatives, and colleagues for referrals. You need to determine whether the person is offering sound advice or is just trying to sell you something. Keep in mind that you need the most unbiased advice possible. Also, any financial plan will have to be monitored, because it will need to be changed as market and investment opportunities vary, as you move through the various stages of life, and as tax laws change.

When considering a financial planner, you might ask the following questions:

1. What is your professional background?
2. How long have you been in financial planning and related fields?
3. How long have you been in the community, and who can vouch for your professional reputation?
4. Will you provide references from three or more clients you have counseled for at least 2 years?
5. Will I be dealing with you or an associate?
6. May I see examples of plans and monitoring reports you have drawn up for other investors?
7. What financial planning trade organizations do you belong to?
8. If you earn commissions, from whom?

Financial Recordkeeping

Objective
To be able to describe the purposes and uses of organized and complete financial records.

Financial recordkeeping is important to financial success.

Records and documents of all types follow us throughout our lives. For example, a birth certificate records your entry into the world, report cards show your progress through school, and employment evaluations detail your working life. The Internal Revenue Service (IRS) expects people to maintain financial records for tax reporting, and banks encourage customers to keep a record of check writing. Having accessible, organized, and complete financial records is typically a prerequisite for effective financial management.

Your financial records will help determine where you are, where you have been, and something about where you are going, financially. There are advantages to keeping good records besides saving money. Documents are unlikely to get lost, and this can help you avoid penalties for overlooking financial obligations and running up needless credit charges. Also, you are likely to maintain the records that the government requires for tax purposes, such as property tax receipts, to support deductions. Organized records

100 *Part One / Financial Planning*

permit easier fact gathering when it is time to file income taxes. They enable you to review the results of financial transactions as well as permit other family members to find them in your absence. A good recordkeeping system also gives you more time for other things, since it takes little time to update and maintain records.

Original source records are formal documents that record personal financial activities. Purchase receipts, credit receipts, canceled checks returned from the banking institution, receipts from deposits, stock certificates, deeds, mortgages, records of capital improvements, papers from Social Security, individual retirement account (IRA) documents, military or government pension entitlements, insurance policies, correspondence with insurers, records of insurance claims, photocopies of filed income tax returns, and correspondence with tax collectors are all examples of original source records. You can use original financial records as backups for previous financial transactions: to prove a purchase, verify a price, or prove ownership. Thus you can show the IRS, for example, that claims for a tax-deductible expenditure are justified, document the price of a product purchased, or demonstrate ownership of an automobile by displaying the title. The primary reason for keeping records of any kind is to be able to use the information for some future purpose.

Use whatever record keeping system works for you.

Both original and other types of financial records are useful in financial management. Table 3.10 shows some categories for all types of financial records and what contents might be included. You might store them in two sections: one for active records and one for inactive. Use whatever recordkeeping system works for you, being sure that you can quickly locate the records you need and can easily keep them up to date.

Many people maintain written logs or records of financial activities and keep them filed with their original source records. Figures 3.4 and 3.5 illustrate two valuable records. The **housing ownership record** (Figure 3.4) shows the dates and amounts spent to improve and maintain the home. This record tells you at a glance how much you have spent on housing through the years. Importantly, a housing ownership record should be kept for tax purposes because the expenditures on improvements, not for maintenance, help reduce income taxes when the home is sold. (This is discussed in Chapter 8, Managing Taxes.) The **tax-deductible expenditure record** (Figure 3.5) serves as a written record of all income tax-deductible expenditures for a given year by date, amount paid and to whom, and tax classification. Such a system, although perhaps tedious to maintain, can help taxpayers reduce their final tax liability because they are less likely to overlook tax-deductible items. A good filing system can serve the same purpose.

Ways of Safeguarding Financial Records

Since some effort goes into developing and maintaining records, it makes sense to keep records safe. It does little good to keep records and then run the risk that they will be misplaced, stolen, or lost through fire or other causes owing to faulty safeguards. Storage places can vary from a cardboard

TABLE 3.10
Financial Records: Categories and Contents

Category	Contents In Home File	In Safe-Deposit Box
Financial plans	Copy of written financial plans and revisions Balance sheets and income statements List of safe-deposit box contents Names and addresses of all financial advisers and institutions where you have accounts	Names and addresses of your financial planner and all financial institutions Copy of financial plans
Financial services	Checkbook Unused checks Bank statements Savings passbooks Location information and number of safe-deposit box Deposit, withdrawal, and transfer slips	List of checking and savings account numbers Savings certificates
Budgeting	Annual budget Deadlines and expiration dates for such things as certificates of deposit Annual cash-flow statement Current budget control sheet Old budget control sheets List of short- and medium-term budget goals	Copy of annual budget
Insurance	Original insurance policies List of insurance premium amounts and due dates Calculation of life insurance needs Automobile insurance policy Health insurance booklet explaining coverage Health insurance claim forms Historical medical information on family members Receipts for payment of premiums	List of insurance policy numbers Photographs of all personal property
Housing	Copies of legal documents (lease, mortgage, deed, title insurance, termite inspections, etc.) Current receipts for home improvements	Mortgage papers, deed, lease Old receipts for home improvements
Contributions	Receipts and canceled checks Correspondence Log of any volunteer expenses	Papers pertaining to expensive gifts
Taxes	Numerous receipts for tax deductible costs, such as medical, real estate and personal property taxes, charitable contributions, and miscellaneous expenses Copies of income tax forms filed for last 3 years W-2 forms and 1099 forms Canceled checks for current year Income tax estimates for next year Payroll records	Copies of income tax forms and documentation for last 6 years Recordkeeping related to home improvements Records of nondeductible IRA contributions

(continued)

TABLE 3.10 (continued)

Category	Contents	
	In Home File	*In Safe-Deposit Box*
Credit	Payment books and receipts Charge slips for credit transactions Monthly credit statements Credit card company numbers and addresses Credit contracts List of account and telephone numbers for lost/stolen credit cards	Credit contracts Duplicate list of account numbers for credit and debit cards and their telephone numbers
Investments	Log of all savings and investment transactions, interest, and dividends Written record of investments	Stock and bond certificates Perhaps small collectibles Purchase and sales receipts Annual statements
Automobile	Title and ownership identification (unless required by law to be kept in the automobile) Log for costs of maintenance and repairs	Automobile title
Warranties, operating instructions, and receipts	Warranties, operating instructions, and service contracts for expensive items (such as television, VCR, stereo, and appliances) Receipts for major purchases Receipts for major repairs	Serial numbers of expensive products Photographs of valuable items and dates of purchase
Personal/legal	Copies of personal resume Employee policies handbook Fringe benefit and retirement information List of items placed in safe-deposit box Copy of will and letter of last instructions (original should be in your lawyer's safe) Information about locks, keys, and security systems Log of information on employee business expenses (bills/receipts on amounts above $25)	Copy of will and notes on location of original Pre- or post-nuptial agreement Birth, marriage, and death certificates Citizenship papers Military, custody, and adoption papers Copies of diplomas and certificates Social Security number and earnings record Passport Education records Driver's license number Trust information

FIGURE 3.4
Housing Ownership
Record

Date	Description of Improvement	Who Paid	Amount	Accumulative Cost of Home
1-6-90	Purchased new condo	Brown + Smith, Builders	$88,000	$88,000
1-30-90	Carpeted bathroom	Clifton Flooring	330	88,330
2-4-91	Installed storm door	Sears	140	88,470
8-6-91	Built-in wall cabinets	ETG Remodeling	2,400	90,870

box to a file cabinet in your home to a safe-deposit box located in a bank. Methods used to safeguard records need not be elaborate or expensive. Storage facilities should be expandable—because the volume is likely to grow over time—and preferably fire-resistant. Note that you can soon be overwhelmed if you save everything; therefore, don't save something if you do not need the record for tax purposes or if you are sure it can easily be replaced.

Safeguarding Records in the Home Most people maintain their own financial records someplace in their home. A desk drawer, a ring binder, a box, a portable file, an expandable paper or cardboard file, or an inexpensive paperboard file box are examples of places to maintain records. More elaborate record-safeguarding equipment, such as a fire-resistant file cabinet or a safe, can be used to ensure a higher degree of safety.

Safeguarding Records Outside the Home People correctly feel that some records are more valuable than others. Examples include investment documents, insurance policies, birth certificates, school records, marriage licenses, and other items proving ownership. Commercial safekeeping devices are available to protect them. **Safe-deposit boxes** are secured lock boxes available for rent in banks. Safe-deposit boxes are very safe, not only from theft, but also from fire and other catastrophes. By design, two keys must be used to open the box, so that no one can open the safe-deposit box independently. The customer has one key and bank personnel hold the other. Also, a signature comparison is made for each request to open a box. This almost eliminates the possibility of someone finding or stealing your key and gaining access to your private documents. You can make arrangements for a safe-deposit box by requesting one from a bank official, completing the required signature cards, and paying a small annual fee ($15 to $60).

Another way to store papers or records is to use a secure spot at your place of employment. Many people keep copies of key records at their workplace, since the possibility of records at home and in the office being stolen or destroyed simultaneously is slight. In any case, it is important to safeguard records, papers, or valuables either inside or outside the home

FIGURE 3.5
Tax-Deductible Expenditure Record

Date	To Whom/For	Deductible Category					
		Medical	Taxes	Interest	Charitable	Casualty	Miscellaneous
1-10	Giles County–property tax		135.00				
1-14	Methodist Church–pledge				25.00		
1-20	Giles Hospital–wrist	240.00					
1-20	ASID professional dues						100.00

because they are useful financial evidence. Because your records are personal, you must make decisions about how and where best to safeguard them.

Summary

1. Most people need to do some financial planning to achieve their financial objectives. Financial planning should reflect an individual's values, attitudes, and life-cycle circumstances and have appropriate objectives in three broad areas: plans for spending, plans against risks, and plans for capital accumulation.

2. Success in financial planning requires explicitly stated financial objectives, certain assumptions made about the economy, logical and consistent financial strategies, and consideration of resources available to meet the objectives. There are 15 areas of financial planning.

3. Life-cycle financial activities of singlehood and couplehood include a variety of financial tasks, problems, and challenges. Both earnings and consumption are sharply affected by an individual's changes in periods and stages in the life cycle.

4. Financial statements are compilations of personal financial data designed to furnish information about how money has been used and about the financial condition of the individual or family involved. The balance sheet describes an individual's or family's financial condition at a particular point in time. Its purpose is to show the present financial position.

5. The income and expense statement lists and summarizes an individual's or family's income and expense transactions over a specific period of time, such as the previous year. It summarizes recent financial history.

6. There are several ratios that can be used to help assess your financial condition and progress so that you can better manage financial resources and develop spending and credit-use patterns consistent with your goals.

7. Financial statements, such as a balance sheet and an income and expense statement, can be used effectively independently or together to assist in financial decision making.

8. When choosing a financial planner, you should recognize that many professional designations are meaningful, such as CFP and ChFC. Charges might be on a basis of fee-only, commission-only, or fee and commission.

9. Having accessible, organized, and complete financial records is a prerequisite to effective financial management. Many people also maintain written logs and records of financial activities, including their original source records. Your financial records are useful in preparing financial statements that can help you to evaluate where you are, where you have been, and something about where you are going.

Modern Money Management

The Johnsons' Financial Statements

Harry and Belinda both found jobs in the same city. Harry works at a small interior design firm and earns a gross salary of $1450 per month. He also receives $3000 in interest income per year from a trust fund set up by his deceased father's estate, which will pay that amount until 1998. Belinda works as a salesperson for a regional stock brokerage firm; when she finishes her training program in another month, her gross salary will increase $200 a month to $2100. She has many job-related benefits, including life insurance, health insurance, and a credit union.

The Johnsons live in an apartment about halfway between each place of employment. Harry drives about 10 minutes to his job, and Belinda gets downtown to work on public transportation in about 15 minutes. Their apartment is very nice, but small, and is furnished mostly with old furniture given to them by their families.

Soon after starting their first jobs, Harry and Belinda decided to begin their financial planning. Each had taken a college course in personal finance, so after initial discussion, they worked together for two evenings to develop the two financial statements presented here.

Balance Sheet for Harry and Belinda Johnson, January 31, 1991

Assets

Monetary assets

Cash on hand	$ 570	
Savings—First Federal Bank	190	
Savings—Far West Savings and Loan	70	
Savings—Smith Brokerage Credit Union	60	
Checking account—First Interstate Bank	310	
Total monetary assets		$ 1,200

Tangible assets

Automobile—1988 Toyota Supra	11,000	
Personal property	1,200	
Furniture	800	
Total tangible assets		$13,000
Total assets		$14,200

Liabilities

Short-term liabilities

Electricity	$ 65	
VISA credit card	390	
Sears	45	
Rent due	400	
Total short-term liabilities		$ 900

Long-term liabilities

Education loan—Belinda	3,800	
Automobile loan—First Federal Bank	8,200	
Total long-term liabilities		$12,000
Total liabilities		$12,900

Net worth		$ 1,300
Total liabilities and net worth		$14,200

1. Using the data from the balance sheet that Harry and Belinda have developed, enter the data in the Personal Finance Cookbook (PFC) BALANCE program. The program will calculate the totals and compute the net worth. Print the balance sheet. Compare the results with the text for accuracy.

2. Now briefly describe how Harry and Belinda probably determined the fair market prices for each of the tangible and investment assets.

3. Using the data from the income and expense statement developed by Harry and Belinda, calculate an annual debt-service ratio and the debt-to-income ratio. What do these two ratios tell you about the Johnsons' financial situation? Should Harry and Belinda incur more debt?

Income and Expense Statement (First 6 Months of Marriage) for Harry and Belinda Johnson, August 1, 1990–January 31, 1991

Income

Harry's gross income ($1,450 × 6)	$ 8,700	
Belinda's gross income ($1,900 × 6)	11,400	
Interest on savings accounts	15	
Harry's trust fund	3,000	
Total income		$23,115

Expenses

Fixed expenses

Rent	$ 2,400	
Renter's insurance	110	
Automobile loan payments	1,200	
Automobile insurance	320	
Medical insurance (withheld from salary)	390	
Student loan payments	720	
Life insurance (withheld from salary)	54	
Cable television	120	
Health club	300	
Savings (withheld from salary)	60	
Federal income taxes (withheld)	4,080	
State income taxes (withheld)	700	
Social Security (withheld)	1,400	
Automobile registration	40	
Total fixed expenses		$11,894

Variable expenses

Food	$ 2,300	
Electricity	450	
Telephone	420	
Gasoline, oil, and maintenance	400	
Doctors' and dentists' bills	310	
Medicines	40	
Clothing and upkeep	1,300	
Church and charity	800	
Gifts	480	
Christmas gifts	350	
Public transportation	580	
Personal allowances	1,040	
Entertainment	780	
Vacation (Christmas)	700	
Vacation (summer)	600	
Miscellaneous	440	
Total variable expenses		$10,990
Total expenses		$22,884
Net gain (available to spend, save, and invest):		$ 231

Key Words and Concepts

Review Questions

1. Cite some reasons why most people need financial planning.
2. What is financial planning, and in what three broad areas does it occur?
3. What four things need to be done to help assure success at financial planning?

4. List the 15 areas of financial planning.

5. What is a life cycle?

6. Describe a traditional pathway through life for a single person.

7. Give some examples of financial tasks, problems, and challenges for one period of the life cycle.

8. Why are financial statements prepared?

9. How can you use a balance sheet?

10. Explain how to derive net worth, and give an example.

11. Differentiate between monetary, tangible, and investment assets.

12. Explain the difference between short- and long-term liabilities.

13. Why must assets be listed on a balance sheet at their fair market value?

14. What does an income and expense statement show the person who prepares it?

15. Differentiate between fixed and variable expenses.

16. Explain what net gain can be used for.

17. Identify three ways of rearranging your financial statements.

18. Explain and give two examples of how you can use financial ratios to help to evaluate your financial progress.

19. Why do many people need a financial planner?

20. What do financial planners do for clients?

21. Explain the three methods that financial planners use to charge for their services?

22. Give a few examples of important questions to ask financial planners.

23. What are the values of keeping good financial records?

24. List some appropriate categories for organizing financial records.

25. Why do many people maintain additional written logs or records of financial activities?

26. Give examples of which financial records you should maintain in the home and which you should put in a safe-deposit box.

27. Explain how a safe-deposit box works.

Case Problems

1. Bernard Gitman of Dayton, Ohio, thinks his two sons, who live at home, need budgeting advice. Ralph is 19, works as a sales representative for an electronics manufacturer, and regularly spends his entire $1400 monthly income. Wilfred, 24, is a midlevel manager in a psychological testing company. He has completed three evening classes toward a master's degree and usually saves about 10 percent of his monthly salary of $2400. Wilfred is contemplating marriage. Bernard is looking to you to offer suggestions to his sons in financial management.

a. What advice would you offer Ralph regarding life's financial tasks, challenges, and opportunities?

b. Realizing that Wilfred is contemplating marriage, what advice would you offer him regarding life's financial tasks, challenges, and opportunities?

2. Using the data from the income and expense statement developed by Bill Soshnik (see Table 3.7), enter the data in the Personal Finance Cookbook (PFC) INCOME program. The program will calculate the totals.

a. Print the income and expense statement and compare the results with the text for accuracy.

b. What original source records might Bill have used to develop the income and expense statement?

3. Rick and Sue Hira of Des Moines, Iowa, spent some time making up their first balance sheet, which is shown in Table 3.6. Using the figures in their balance sheet, complete the following calculations and interpret the results.

a. Rick and Sue are a bit confused, though, about how various financial activities can affect their net worth. Assume that their home is appraised at $82,000 and the value of their automobile drops to $9,500. Calculate and characterize the impact of this situation on their net worth. How would this change the solvency ratio or its interpretation? [*Hint:* See Equation (3.3).]

b. If Rick and Sue take out a bank loan for $1545 and pay off their debts of $1545 on credit cards, what impact would this have on their net worth? on the solvency ratio?

c. If Rick and Sue take $300 from their earnings and put it into their savings account, what impact would this have on their net worth?

4. Review the financial statements of Roy and Mary Als (Tables 3.5 and 3.8), and respond to the following questions:

a. Using the data in the Alses' balance sheet, calculate an investment assets-to-net-worth ratio. How would you interpret the ratio? The Alses appear to have too few monetary assets compared with tangible and investment assets. What do you recommend they do over the next few years to remedy that situation?

b. Comment on their diversification of investment assets.

c. Calculate a liquid assets-to-total-debt ratio for Roy and Mary. How does this information help you understand their financial situation? How does their net worth compare to their total liabilities?

d. The Alses seem to have almost all their income coming from labor versus investments. What do you recommend they do over the next few years to remedy that imbalance?

e. The Alses want to take a 2-week vacation next summer, and they have only 8 months to save the necessary $1200. What reasonable changes in expenses *and* income should they consider to increase net income the needed $150 a month?

Suggested Readings

"Avoiding Fraud and Abuse by Financial Planners." *Consumer's Research Magazine,* February 1989, pp. 25–29. Advice on how to select a reputable financial planner and avoid the less reputable.

"Best of the Almost-Free Software." *Changing Times,* May 1989, pp. 41–44. Lots of computer programs that can help you with your personal finances.

"Celebrating a Bright Financial Future." *Working Woman,* February 1989, pp. 63–66. Financial records track the progress of your dual-career family.

"Figuring Out Your Net Worth," *U.S. News & World Report,* July 30, 1990, p. 76. Suggests format for you to follow.

"Get Your Act Together." *Money,* February 1989, pp. 67–89. A complete overview about what you should do to get your financial matters into shape.

"Here's a Hot Tip with a Guaranteed Payoff: Keep Good Records." *Money,* January 1989, p. 145. Explains the necessity of maintaining accurate financial records.

"How to Get Financial Advice You Can Really Trust." *Money,* November 1989, pp. 80–96. Series of articles on how to choose a stockbroker, financial planner, money manager, insurance agent, accountant, and real estate broker.

"Playing It Safe." *Changing Times,* June 1990, pp. 26–33. Feeling comfortable in your investments, home, job, taxes, etc.

"10 Tough Money Tasks Made Easy." *Changing Times,* May 1989, pp. 25–30. An overview of key financial tasks that may need your attention.

"The Art of the (Marriage) Deal." *U.S. News & World Report,* March 5, 1990, p. 68. Tips on writing and negotiating pre- and post-nuptial agreements.

"The Key to the Dream: Prosperity." *Changing Times,* March 1989, pp. 42–45. Hard work and investment will pay off in the future.

"The New Gospel of Financial Planning." *Money,* March 1989, pp. 56–94. Several articles on financial planning for marrieds, single parents, DINKS, singles, blended families, traditionals, those living together, and sandwich families.

"The Ten Mistakes Financial Planners Most Often Spot." *Glamour,* January 1989, p. 94. Explains common mistakes made by those who do their own financial planning.

"33 Great Ways to Simplify Your Life." *Changing Times,* June 1989, pp. 22–28. Explores how to save time while effectively managing your finances.

"When Having Everything Isn't Enough." *Psychology Today,* April 1989, pp. 27–30. Explores the psychological aspects of compulsive spending and acquisitiveness.

4 Budgeting and Cash-Flow Management

....

OBJECTIVES

After reading this chapter, you should be able to

1. Better understand how to talk about money.
2. Comprehend the relationships among key concepts in personal finance.
3. Understand how to set and achieve both long- and short-term goals as part of the financial goal-setting phase of budgeting.
4. Describe structural and mechanical aspects appropriate for one's personalized budget as part of the planning phase of budgeting.
5. Discuss how to resolve conflicting financial needs and wants.
6. Describe the key aspects of the implementing phase of budgeting.
7. Illustrate the methods and techniques used during the controlling phase of budgeting to help keep income and expenditures within planned budget totals.
8. Discuss the fundamental aspects of the evaluating phase of budgeting.

. . . .

"Plan the work and work the plan," say good organizers. Once you have taken stock of your financial position, you must take actions in the area of cash-flow management and budgeting. Here the focus is on the doing and implementing of financial planning.

We begin this chapter with a discussion of how to talk about money, a topic that most people shy away from discussing. Next is an examination of the relationships among the concepts of personal financial planning, family financial management, cash-flow management, and budgeting. All this is preparatory to a fuller understanding of the process of budgeting: establishing financial goals and objectives, planning, decision making, implementing, controlling, and evaluating.

Talking about Money

Objective
To understand better how to talk about money.

The primary cause of most marital problems frequently is money. Couples often disagree about what to spend their money on and how much to spend. Sometimes one person in a relationship will make a crucial financial decision without even consulting the other person. At the same time, many couples seem unable to perform the fundamental tasks of managing money, such as reconciling the checkbook balance with the bank statement, creating a workable budget, and paying bills on time. Many people get into financial trouble because they use too much credit, and they eventually begin to miss credit payments. Arguments about money matters often result in marital discord.

Each year over 1 million people seek credit and budget counseling advice at the more than 450 nonprofit Consumer Credit Counseling Service (CCCS) agencies across the country.[1] There they learn about how to better handle their personal finances. Last year over 900,000 people declared personal bankruptcy, thus admitting their ultimate failure and inability to manage personal and family finances. Most of these financial calamities could be avoided if couples only practiced communicating about money matters.

Reading this information will not ensure financial success, but it will explain how people manage money and make financial decisions, why couples should be cautious in money matters, how dual-earner households manage their money, and how remarried couples face additional compli-

[1] To locate the office nearest you, write to the National Foundation on Consumer Credit, 8701 Georgia Avenue, Suite 507, Silver Spring, MD 20910.

cations. Financial mistakes that many couples make, as well as the potentially serious consequences of those mistakes, are identified. Next is a section that will help you discover your personal spending style and identify problems that may occur should you and your spouse have conflicting personal spending styles. Understanding how people value money and what they argue about most may provide insight into your situation. Finally, concrete suggestions on how to talk with others about financial matters are provided. Mutual trust in money matters can be developed—and it must be—in order to have a successful marriage and be financially successful.

How Couples Manage Their Money and Make Decisions about Finances

Managing money and making decisions about money matters are two different things. In most homes, women rather than men handle the family finances, since women typically handle the household checkbook and oversee the budget. While "managing" family money is an important responsibility, it is also vital to know who in the family *makes* the financial decisions, because this is the area where disagreements typically arise.

Who "manages" the money and who "makes" financial decisions may differ.

Decision making can be unilateral, shared, or divided. In many traditional families, one person, usually the money earner, makes all financial decisions. Reasons for this approach include knowledge, interest, experience, culture, and temperament. In these families, one person decides how much money will be spent on food, entertainment, clothing, and personal allowances, as well as what new home appliances and automobiles will be purchased. While the spouse may be consulted on a few purchases, final decisions remain with one person.

Most couples today share decision making. They talk with each other and decide how much to spend on big purchasing decisions, perhaps concerning appliances, sports equipment, clothing, jewelry, and recreation activities. They additionally share decision making on more expensive planned financial outlays, such as buying automobiles and housing, as well as on such key topics as estate planning and investments.

Couples share, divide, or split decision making.

Many families also divide financial decision making, sometimes equally and sometimes according to mutually approved specifications, such as delegating particular jobs to the partner determined to be best suited to perform them. For example, the woman may shop for food and clothing and make all the minor daily financial decisions affecting herself and the children, while the man may take responsibility for automobile maintenance and investment decisions. Often the person with the most interest in an area makes decisions in that realm.

Some couples also split the recordkeeping chores. For example, one spouse might handle the checkbook(s) and bill paying, while the other might keep track of the budget, complete forms for health insurance claims, and fill out income tax returns. In many families, recordkeeping is the responsibility of one partner, and for a variety of reasons, the other partner is not involved.

Caution in Money Matters

All couples should be cautious in money matters.

Jointly owned assets are legally controlled by both partners and are available to either to use as needed. This arrangement is potentially dangerous in that jointly owned bank accounts can be emptied by one partner without the other's consent. Similarly, a home-equity credit-line loan can be borrowed to the maximum by either spouse unless both signatures are required for withdrawals. A lackadaisical attitude by one spouse about prompt payment of jointly owed bills can undermine the credit rating of both. Further, if one spouse is sued on a credit account in both names, the other can be in jeopardy.

Generally, dual-earner couples should own some property together and some separately. If you own a business and default on a loan, your creditors usually cannot attach your home if it is in your spouse's name. On the other hand, a nonworking spouse should get his or her name on all deeds and investments because divorce courts typically award property to the person(s) who legally owns it. In **community property states**—where all money and property acquired during a marriage is legally considered the joint property of both spouses—the rights of both husbands and wives are equally protected. (These include Arizona, California, Idaho, Louisiana, Nebraska, New Mexico, Texas, Washington, and Wisconsin.) Moreover, it is imperative that couples communicate with each other about money matters—exchanging information about various financial transactions can help keep you both out of trouble.

Complications for Dual-Earner Households

Money decisions are more complicated for dual-earner households.

In the United States today, the Census Bureau reports that 43 percent of all married households have two incomes. The financial tasks facing people in dual-earner households can be more complicated than for single-earners. Note also that some men exhibit jealousy when their wives earn the higher income, and this can complicate discussions about financial matters. While having dual earners can mean more income, expenses typically increase because of work-related costs such as child care, clothing, eating out, income taxes, and transportation. A financial danger facing dual-earner households is that they would likely experience an unexpected decline in joint income should one partner take time off from work to raise children, make a career change, decide to return to school, or lose a job. Therefore, it is important that dual-earner households limit their financial commitments that rely heavily on their dual income because their situation may change.

Difficult questions facing dual-earner households include: Shall we pool all our income and pay expenses out of one financial "pot" or keep accounts in two separate "pots"? Which partner should pay what household expenses? Should the proportion each pays for expenses represent the proportionate share of income contributed by each? Shall we put our money into a single joint checking account or open two accounts? Should we pool our savings? Should automobiles be registered in both names? Should homes and investments be put in joint names? Should each maintain a separate financial identity to build credit histories? Who should make purchasing decisions for various goods and services? Who should prepare the income tax return(s)? How should the joint income tax refund be spent? Who should manage the checkbook(s), recordkeeping, budgeting, investments, and retirement and estate planning? What criteria should be used to make difficult financial decisions that will satisfy both partners? How shall we resolve money matters upon which we disagree?

Furthermore, experts agree that no matter how it is accomplished, it is important for each person in a couple relationship to have money of his or her own. Dual-earner households are advised to make such a decision because research suggests that people generally seem more satisfied and in control of their lives when they have some money that they can call "mine." These feelings of autonomy encourage independence and self-control in a relationship rather than dependency on the other person.

Many couples may need three checking accounts.

Many experts recommend three checking accounts for most couples: a discretionary account for each individual (two "pots") and a joint account (a third "pot"). Then each partner can feel that he or she has access to money the other partner does not solely control. Sensible couples discuss the pros and cons of various financial arrangements and then make their decisions.

Remarriage Complications

People who remarry have additional complications.

People often remarry after divorcing or losing a spouse to death. Of the 5 million Americans who will marry this year, just over half will do so for the second or third time. Most commonly in the new marriage, both spouses work for money income and children are brought to the relationship as well. The result is a reconstituted family making efforts to combine two fully developed, complicated financial lives.

Some remarried couples have two substantial incomes bolstered by child-support payments from an ex-spouse. Just as often, however, at least one of the spouses may be paying (instead of receiving) alimony and child support. When there are "his," "hers," and "our" children, living expenses of such "blended" families can be quite steep.

Special concerns of blended families include who will assume financial responsibility for various progeny, how to protect each biological offspring without neglecting or offending spouses and stepchildren, possible resentment of alimony and support payments, and how to manage unequal assets, incomes, responsibilities, and debts. Even gift giving can become a quandary.

Many remarried people split household expenses fifty-fifty; others split according to the proportion of income they contribute to the total. Still others use "his" and "hers" funds along with requiring the legally responsible parent owing financial support to a previous spouse to make such payments out of his or her own money. Jean Lown, Professor of Home Economics at Utah State University, suggests that "what is best is what the couple can agree on." Regardless of the system, the effort should be designed to preserve peace in the relationship.

Many remarried people are nervous about financial matters and may even bring a sense of distrust, guilt, or illusions about financial matters into the relationship, especially when they are bringing substantial assets or debts to the new relationship. Therefore, some remarried couples sign a **prenuptial agreement,** which is a contract specifying what, if any, share of each person's assets the other will be entitled to during marriage and should they divorce. Another useful device is a **postnuptial agreement,** which is a contractual agreement signed after marriage to spell out each spouse's financial responsibilities. Such precautions may forestall grief later because courts generally uphold such agreements.

Serious Financial Mistakes

Couples often make a number of common money mistakes, but four areas exist where the financial consequences are extremely serious. First, spouses often argue over who will manage a large inheritance, as well as if and how it might be spent. Second, many couples do not purchase enough life or health insurance coverage and remain dangerously underinsured. Third, some employed spouses unwisely elect a straight retirement annuity with benefits paid to the retired person as long as he or she lives, but not to survivors. This action cuts the other out of expected pension benefits. Federal law gives "approval" power to each spouse over the other spouse's decisions on how employer pension benefits will be distributed. Unless a spouse waives this authority in writing, pension benefits are automatically in the form of a **joint and survivor annuity,** which means that when either spouse dies, the other continues to receive a reduced level of benefits for as long as he or she lives. Fourth, some people undercut the goals they expressed in their wills because they carelessly choose, or fail to update as family situations change, the beneficiaries of life insurance policies, company benefits, and funds in IRA and Keogh retirement plans when signing beneficiary forms. When you sign beneficiary forms, the proceeds of such assets are distributed by those legal contracts, not by your will, unless you designate as your beneficiary "my estate as per my will." The only way to avoid such problems is for couples to discuss financial goals and reach agreements.

Couples should be sure to update their financial plans or outdated ones will be carried out when one spouse dies.

Discovering Your Personal Spending Style

Personal attitudes about financial matters are based on our fundamental values and are influenced by one's innate personality traits, attitudes, emotions, childhood experiences, family history, parental behaviors, cultural norms, media, religious background, upbringing, education, and other factors shaped through the experiences of life. We each have developed our own personal spending style, and such styles differ greatly among people. **Personal spending styles** are the different ways that people spend or deal with their money. People's personal spending styles are usually quite well entrenched because we grow up learning more about spending than about saving and investing.

What If You and Your Spouse Have Conflicting Personal Spending Styles?

Some couples do have conflicting spending styles. If two people with sharply different spending styles commit to a relationship, some problems will probably arise. The conflict of "his" and "her" money may come into play—whoever earns the larger or only salary may want to tell the other how to spend. During disagreements over money, one person may think or say, "I earned it and I'll spend it."

For others, one member of the couple may try to control the relationship by controlling decisions on the spending of money. In such situations, one person usually handles all the family finances and is extremely reluctant to share responsibility. That person usually tries to maintain power by doling out money at his or her own discretion. These people may be reluctant to discuss money matters because of selfishness, vanity, and a desire for power and control.

In addition, one person (or both people) may resort to "retaliatory spending." For example, the wife might spend money on something expensive for herself. The husband then wants to do the same thing—spend money on himself—whether or not the funds are available. Another problem facing couples with different spending styles may be **impulsive buying**. This is an emotional, almost reckless buying of goods and services with little regard to planning or need. Impulsive buying can cause serious financial stress in relationships. As a couple, you may have to experiment with new behaviors by trying some of the exercises in this section of the book which are designed to break through any polarization in styles.

What kind of spending style do you have?

It is crucial in interpersonal relationships to have an understanding about each person's personal spending style. Many heartaches will be avoided by couples who discuss their philosophies on money matters in advance. In this way, you can establish methods to deal with differences.

Five personal spending styles are apparent among people. Can you recognize them? First are *tightwads*, who save so much that they do so compulsively and little is left even for essentials. Second are the *givers*, who are generous to a fault. Whether they have the money or not, they always seem to be giving gifts or other financial kindnesses. Third are the *me-spenders*, who love to spend money on themselves. They enjoy leading the materialistic lifestyle. Fourth are the *big spenders,* who simply like to spend money on themselves and others and enjoy it more if other people notice. They often reach for the bill when at a restaurant with a group. Buying status-symbol automobiles is common with both me-spenders and big spenders. The fifth group is composed of *normal* people. They do not have a pattern of excessive behavior, as do the previous four groups, but they usually have some degree of normal spending faults.

How People Value Issues of Money

Besides the economic goods and services that money can provide, people often ascribe a number of emotions to money, such as status, success, freedom, independence, autonomy, trust, self-esteem, materialism, guilt, indifference, envy, desire, jealousy, security, comfort, authority, power, and control. When talking to others, particularly in family relationships, it is useful to recognize how money is valued emotionally by each person.

Here is an exercise to help you understand your own views about money.

As individuals, we all have different values and attitudes about money, the things it can buy, and how to use it. Thus the first step in learning how to talk with others about financial matters is to better understand your own views. Perhaps you could get out a piece of paper and make a list of what money means to you. (Look at the list of emotions in the preceding paragraph to help get you started in your thinking.) Then make another list by noting which expressions are most important and least important to you. Finally, make a short enumeration of your financial fears, or "what would happen if. . . ." After the other significant person in your relationship separately makes such lists, there will be much to discuss together.

What People Argue about Most

Regardless of income, age, and education, arguments about money are a common problem among members of families. Sometimes inadequate income is the cause of such arguments; others are caused by families who are anxious and panicked about having too much money. Most often arguments about financial matters are caused by a lack of communication on the topic of money. Disagreements over finances are almost always cited as the number one or two reason for divorce.

Here is an exercise to help couples identify concerns and shared visions about money.

Clearly, it is in the interest of all couples to talk with each other about money matters. Early in a relationship, and later as needed, it would be wise for couples to share with each other their individual financial goals as well as financial fears. If necessary, get out two sheets of paper, one for him and one for her, and write down your financial worries and dreams. This effort will help identify conflicting concerns and shared visions. Then the spirit of open communication and compromise can contribute to effective and successful family financial management.

Money is a very powerful tool in family relationships. Many people have emotionally charged arguments over money, and sometimes the subject can bring out the worst in people. Family finances are occasionally a battleground for disputes over responsibility and commitment, even a forum for expressing doubts about self-worth. Fights over money are often a symptom of something else wrong in a relationship. For example, some people incorrectly equate money with love and demand that their spouse provide for them as proof of affection.

How People Should Talk about Financial Matters

Some couples communicate so little about financial matters that some spouses do not even know where important records are kept, such as life insurance policies, wills, loan agreements, or even the bank where the safe-deposit box is maintained. Others do not know the names of the family lawyer, accountant, or financial planner. Such a lack of communication invites problems.

Most people consider their way of handling money a deeply private and personal matter. They want to hold on to their fiscal autonomy as long as possible, and they are embarrassed to inquire about how much others, even loved ones, spend, earn, or owe. For many people, money is a dark little area of self-suspected incompetence, and it is a difficult subject to talk about. Judith Viorst, author of *Necessary Losses*, suggests that becoming responsible and adept at managing one's financial matters represents a true passage into adulthood—and for a lot of people, that is scary. Yet learning to talk about money with each other may be a precursor to reaching family financial security.

Talk about money matters is not always easy because it often reflects deeply held values that are difficult to change. Some people who are entirely rational about most things in life can be unpredictable or even careless in money matters. While unrealistic values need to be identified and discussed, adults need to accept that there are honest differences among people whom they love and that these must be respected.

Conflicts over money matters will arise, so instead of avoiding them, learn to manage financial disagreements. Give all family members time to express their views. Avoid blaming phrases such as "You always . . . ," "You never . . . ," "You are acting like . . . ," "You should forget that idea . . . ," and "If you don't, I will. . . ." These statements have a high probability of putting the other person down, making him or her feel guilty, and making him or her feel that his or her needs and wants are not important.

Instead, use phrases such as "I think" and "I feel." Messages focusing on "I" describe the behavior in question, the feelings you experienced because of the behavior, and any tangible effect on you. For example, a wife might say, "When you make all those credit purchases, I feel upset because I do not know where we will get the money to pay the bills at the end of the month." "I" messages simply say three things: when (the behavior), I feel (feelings), and because (reason).[2] Using "I" messages helps build stronger relationships because they tell the other person that "I trust you to decide what change in behavior is necessary."

Important also is that each family member listen to what the others are saying and feeling. If talking is too difficult, have each person separately write down his or her concerns. By swapping lists, you can share each other's ideas and concerns.

Communicating successfully about money requires that the effort be aimed toward agreeing on common goals and getting a consensus of opinion without substantially compromising the views of family members. This requires that each person be honest when talking about money matters; it further demands that family members regularly talk about

---

[2] "The 'I' Message" is a useful publication of the Cooperative Extension Service, prepared by Glenn Klein, Extension Education, Oregon State University.

finances, particularly when money decisions are not pressing. Schedule the time and place for financial talks, decide on agenda items, leave other conflicts outside the door, and agree to disagree or postpone difficult decisions until a later time. When talking, try not to blame the other person. Also try to avoid acting helpless. Recognize too that it is important to practice talking about money matters in an unemotional manner. Be prepared to listen to the other person—really listen. Be prepared to compromise. When you make decisions together, act on them.[3]

Here is an exercise to help couples discuss values and attitudes in nine key areas.

Another useful exercise for couples is to discuss each person's values and attitudes in several areas that significantly affect a family's finances:

1. *Childrearing.* How many children do you want to have? How soon?
2. *Employment.* Are you satisfied with your career(s)? Are you earning enough money? Are you willing to move for your spouse's advancement?
3. *Clothing.* How important is clothing to you? Are you satisfied with the amount, quality, and price of clothing that you have?
4. *Food.* Is the food you are eating at home the quality you really want? Do you want to eat out more often? Where?
5. *Housing.* How much do you want to spend on home furnishings? Do you really want to buy a home or is renting okay, or vice versa?
6. *Transportation.* Could you get along using mass transportation or by having just one automobile? Could one car be an inexpensive vehicle that gets high mileage? If so, who would drive it?
7. *Recreation.* Would you be satisfied spending less (or more) money on recreational activities?
8. *Vacations.* What do you really want to do on vacation? Should you consider separate vacations?
9. *Future security.* How comfortable are you using credit to buy now, thus committing future earnings? How important is savings? Will your retirement plan actually provide you with a decent (or high) level of living? What would happen financially if you became disabled or died?[4]

People learning to talk with each other about money matters often focus their attention on current financial needs to the exclusion of long-term financial planning. Therefore, you also should try to use these occasions to forge overall strategies for dealing with your family finances. Thus talking about money matters with family members, setting financial goals, and constructing a budget are investments in time that are likely to reap important rewards.

Going through life with a person you love can be so much more rewarding for all when you have fewer arguments. You can give the love in your relationship a chance to really blossom by getting rid of disagree-

[3] An excellent book on the subject is *How to Stop Fighting About Money: A Couple's Guide to Financial Success,* by Adriane G. Berg (New York: New Market Press, 1988).
[4] A useful publication on this topic is Cooperative Extension Service publication Number 768, "Family Communications About Money," by Cindy Darden and Mary Jane Shumard, available from the University of Georgia, Athens, Georgia.

FIGURE 4.1

Interrelationships of Financial Planning and Budgeting (Financial Plans Drive Budgets, which Affect Financial Statements, and Both Provide Feedback on Financial Progress)

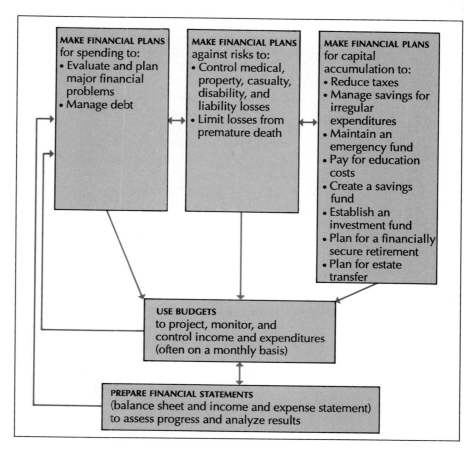

MAKE FINANCIAL PLANS for spending to:
• Evaluate and plan major financial problems
• Manage debt

MAKE FINANCIAL PLANS against risks to:
• Control medical, property, casualty, disability, and liability losses
• Limit losses from premature death

MAKE FINANCIAL PLANS for capital accumulation to:
• Reduce taxes
• Manage savings for irregular expenditures
• Maintain an emergency fund
• Pay for education costs
• Create a savings fund
• Establish an investment fund
• Plan for a financially secure retirement
• Plan for estate transfer

USE BUDGETS to project, monitor, and control income and expenditures (often on a monthly basis)

PREPARE FINANCIAL STATEMENTS (balance sheet and income and expense statement) to assess progress and analyze results

ments about money matters. These arguments can be eliminated if you practice communicating about finances with the person in the family who means the most to you. Sharing your confidentialities about financial matters also strengthens the bonds of love. Learning to talk about money matters is not that difficult—you only need to get started. Use the suggestions here and start talking today!

Interrelationships among Concepts

Objective
To comprehend the relationships among key concepts in personal finance.

The interrelationships of financial planning and budgeting are shown in Figure 4.1. We identified **financial planning** in Chapter 2 as the process of developing and implementing a coordinated series of plans and strategies covering various parts of a person's or family's financial affairs in an effort to achieve financial objectives. Financial plans drive the creation of budgets, which affect financial statements, and both provide feedback on financial progress.

Family Financial Management

Family financial management is a dynamic and active process performed to allocate income and wealth.

Successful financial plans are implemented by individuals and families through their efforts at **family financial management.** This is the dynamic and active process of planning, implementing, and evaluating done by individuals and family members involved in the allocation of their current flow of family income *and* their stock of wealth toward the end of meeting the family's implicit and explicit goals.[5] The tasks involve observable behaviors and unobservable mental activities and cognitive processes. Effective family financial management should address interrelated needs and decisions in the areas of recordkeeping, spending, cash flow, debt, savings, tax planning, insurance, investments, retirement planning, and estate planning, as well as analysis of all these types of decisions. Such efforts are focused on both short- and long-term goals and performed with varying degrees of frequency and success.

Cash-Flow Management

Cash-flow management is a set of activities performed by individuals and family members focused on allocating the family's flow of income toward the immediate goal of meeting their tacit or explicit financial needs.[6] Cash-flow management has a relatively short time horizon, often a week, a month, or a year. Cash-flow management decisions are made by all individuals and families, and they are made frequently, often weekly or daily. Cash-flow management is much broader than budgeting because "in addition to including the tasks which typically comprise *budgeting* (e.g., projecting future income, projecting anticipated future expenditures, and reconciling the two), family cash-flow management also includes other tasks, such as using financial statements to assess the current financial status of the family, planning financial goals . . . and evaluating family decisions about spending, borrowing, and savings."[7]

Cash-flow management is broader than budgeting.

Cash-flow management begins by using the financial statements discussed in Chapter 3, Financial Planning over Your Life, to assess a family's current financial position (using the balance sheet) and its past financial behavior (using the income and expense statement). Cash-flow management then continues with many of the steps associated with budgeting, such as projecting and prioritizing long- and short-term goals that the family would like to achieve, attaching time horizons and dollar values on the prioritized goals, projecting income and expenditures over a future period (often a year), adjusting income and expenditures to bring them into

[5] Deborah D. Godwin, "Toward a Theory of Family Cash Flow Management," unpublished paper, University of Georgia, Department of Housing and Consumer Economics, Athens, GA 30602. Also see Deborah D. Godwin, "Family Financial Management," *Family Relations*, Volume 39, April 1990, pp. 221-228.
[6] Godwin, "Toward a Theory." *Ibid.*
[7] *Ibid.*

balance, planning savings to meet irregular expenditures as they occur, recording and monitoring income and expenditures as they occur, adjusting expenditures when needed, analyzing and evaluating how well the plan was implemented, and beginning the process all over again for the next time period. Cash-flow management behaviors evolve over time as individuals and families adjust to and cope with life events.

Budgeting

A **budget** is a document or set of documents used to record both future and actual income and expenditures for a period of time. **Budgeting** is a process of projecting, monitoring, and controlling future income and expenditures (including cash and credit purchases as well as savings) and reconciling the two by planning and controlling efforts that involve using budgeting records to set and achieve short-term goals that are in harmony with long-term goals. Success in meeting life's financial tasks, problems, and challenges is likely to be greater if you have a good understanding of the process of budgeting.

Budgeting provides a detailed financial forecast that can be used to monitor and control expenditures, and the budgeting process provides the major mechanism through which financial plans are carried out. Budgeting is narrower in scope than cash-flow management because it is primarily concerned with the projecting future income and expenditures and reconciling the two. A fundamental purpose of budgeting is to help you achieve long- and short-term goals that are consistent with your overall financial plans.

The frequency and formality of performing budgeting tasks are a matter of personal preference. Budgeting for many people is comprised of mostly mental activities; others maintain extensive and formal written records. Either approach is acceptable as long as it is effective in achieving family financial goals, improving financial status (such as net worth, higher levels of liquid assets, and a lower debt/asset ratio), and/or increasing the subjective level of satisfaction of a family with its current financial situation. Successful budgeting requires an ability to manage financial resources as well as a willingness to do so.

Budgeting forces you to think about what is important in your life, what things you want to own, what it will take to obtain them, and more generally, what you want to achieve in life. Budgeting gives you control over your finances by providing the necessary information and insight that cannot be obtained in any other manner. Budgeting empowers you to achieve your financial goals while simultaneously and successfully confronting any intervening events. As you hopefully shall see, budgeting is an *exciting* endeavor, even though many people associate budgeting with such words as *tedious, nervousness, recordkeeping, time-consuming, self-denial, frustrating, details,* and *failure.* The six-phase budgeting process illustrated in Figure 4.2 can be adapted to suit your needs while giving you the competence and confidence to manage your financial affairs successfully—forever.

FIGURE 4.2
Phases in the Budgeting Process

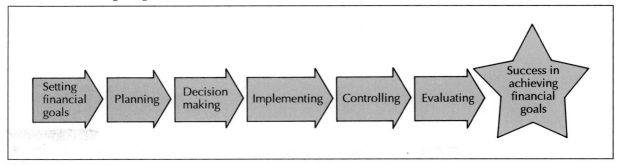

The Financial Goal-Setting Phase of Budgeting

Objective
To understand how to set and achieve both long- and short-term goals as part of the financial goal-setting phase of budgeting.

Financial goals are based on your values.

Setting financial goals is not an exercise in wishful thinking. It demands that you be realistic about the anticipated future income. Setting financial goals requires careful and reasoned thinking.

Financial Goals and Values

No two people spend their money in exactly the same way because personal values influence financial decisions. Our values shape our standard of what we want our lives to be. Each of us is different from others in the ways we value income, health, employment, credit use, family life, lifestyle, and many other factors. One's stage in the life cycle is important too because values, needs, wants, and resources change throughout our lives. Certain financial constraints, such as providing economic help for elderly parents or paying for a child's educational costs, also affect people's values and goals. Personal financial goals grow out of our values because we consider some things more important or desirable than others. We express our values, in part, by the ways in which we spend our money. Thus our personal values and attitudes dictate our financial goals.

Written financial plans to achieve goals and objectives to reflect your values can be made in three broad groups: (1) plans for spending, (2) plans for protection against financial risks, and (3) plans for capital accumulation. The key to developing financial plans is to identify your long- and short-term goals. You can do this during the financial goal-setting phase of budgeting. (This was illustrated in Figure 3.2 on page 70.)

Examples of goals include finishing a college education, paying off debts (including education loans), taking a vacation, returning to school to complete a graduate degree, starting a new career, owning a new automobile, owning a home, buying disability insurance, remodeling a home, traveling abroad, owning vacation property, giving money to a favorite charity, building a substantial stock portfolio, accumulating funds to send children through college, possessing a valuable antique collection, being the major stockholder in your own business, and having financial independence at retirement.

Family Goal Setting

Success in budgeting is more easily achieved when all members of a household have a part in establishing and achieving goals. Involving all members of the family gives each person a feeling of ownership as well as a sense of commitment to the overall budgeting process. Thinking and talking together about personal and mutual goals helps each family member prioritize and identify his or her most important goals. Each participant also feels a sense of belonging and importance. Once children reach the age of understanding, they too can participate in the process. Here they can learn to think and act in terms of priorities, goals, and objectives and become better able to set up their own plans in the future. Each informed family member can then be more understanding and more willing to cooperate, and perhaps compromise, with revised spending plans if income later becomes irregular or if a financial setback occurs. Talking together also helps avoid a tendency for a family member to subtly undermine the attainment of agreed-upon financial goals.

Setting Long-Term Goals or Objectives

Long-term goals or objectives are generally targets or ends that an individual or family desires to achieve using financial resources more than 1 year in the future, perhaps 2, 5, or even 30 years. Long-term goals and objectives provide direction for overall financial planning and for shorter-term budgeting. One long-term goal might be to save $15,000 within 5 years for a down payment on a home. Others could be more general, such as to have substantial shares of common stock investments that would pay dividends equivalent to 5 percent of an individual's salary income.

If you have a small income and/or large debts, it may be unrealistic to think of long-term goals until current difficulties are resolved. You may be unable to do much more than take care of immediate necessities, such as housing payments, food, and electric bills. In such instances, the focus needs to be on making short-term efforts to improve the financial situation.

How to Achieve Your Financial Goals

One effective goal-setting process includes eight steps:

1. Identify the goal.
2. Set a deadline to reach it (and, if necessary, intermediate checkpoints to assess progress).
3. List obstacles to its achievement.
4. Estimate appropriate costs.
5. Identify people and other factors that might help.

6. List your skills and knowledge that will help you reach the goal.

7. Develop a plan to succeed.

8. List the benefits to yourself that will occur when you reach the goal.

You are most likely to achieve a goal when you are convinced that it really is "your goal," when you can commit emotionally to the goal, and when you can visualize yourself achieving it.

How to Put Dollar Values on Goals

When placing dollar values on goals up to 5 years in the future, it is generally fair to assume that interest earned on savings will offset inflationary increases. Use the table in Appendix A-1 to make precise estimates. Note that estimated costs for long-term goals may need to be revised from time to time should market conditions and prices change.

A handy formula for figuring the number of years it takes to double principal using compound interest is the **Rule of 72.** You simply divide the interest rate the money will earn into the number 72. For example, if interest is compounded at 7 percent per year, your principal will double in 10.3 years; if the rate is 6 percent, it will take 12 years.

Target Dates

Putting target dates on goals is important, even though you may need to revise them.

Target dates may serve as checkpoints in your progress toward reaching goals or as deadlines by which time something should be achieved. Still, long-term goals and objectives need to be somewhat flexible given the length of time involved in achieving them. Also, you should recognize that thinking about and writing down goals as part of an overall financial plan does not mean that your life's goals are set forever. Some goals may need changing because they were too unrealistic. As circumstances change, you will want to review and make adjustments or deletions and/or add new goals to your overall financial plans as desired financial outcomes are achieved or changed. An annual review is appropriate.

Putting target dates on long-term goals is very important because this leads to the creation of short-term goals. You cannot reach long-term goals without first achieving short-term goals.

How to Establish Short-Term Goals or Objectives

Short-term goals or objectives are needs and wants requiring financial resources that can be satisfied in a year or less. These goals should be consistent with the general direction of long-term goals and objectives. One short-term objective might be to pay off an outstanding VISA credit card balance within 6 months. Another might be to save $1200 by July so you can go to Europe on vacation. Often, short-term goals represent partial steps toward achieving long-term goals. For example, to achieve a long-term goal of saving $15,000 for a down payment on a home within 5 years, your first-year goal may be to save $3000.

FIGURE 4.3
Goals Worksheet for Harry and Belinda Johnson

Date worksheet prepared _January 20, 1991_

LONG-TERM GOALS WORKSHEET

1 Goals	2 Approximate Amount Needed	3 Month and Year Needed*	4 Number of Months to Save	5 Date Start Saving	6 Monthly Amount to Save (2÷4)
European vacation	$ 3,000	August 1993	30	2-91	$ 100
Down payment on new auto	5,000	October 1994	45	1-91	111
Down payment on home	15,000	January 1996	48	1-92	312

*Goals requiring more than 5 years to achieve require consideration of investment return and after-tax yield, which will be presented in later chapters.

Date worksheet prepared _January 20, 1991_

SHORT-TERM GOALS WORKSHEET

1 Goals	2 Approximate Amount Needed	3 Month and Year Needed*	4 Number of Months to Save	5 Date Start Saving	6 Monthly Amount to Save (2÷4)
Part of down payment on new auto	$ 1,332	12-91	12	1-91	$ 111
Part of European vacation	1,100	12-91	11	2-91	100
Christmas vacation	700	12-91	12	1-91	58
Summer vacation	600	8-91	6	2-91	100
Anniversary party	250	6-91	5	1-91	50

Short-term goals are the key input in making a budget. You must try to avoid the tendency to overemphasize current consumption as opposed to preparing for consumption in the distant future. The task is to design a budget (perhaps covering 1 month at a time) that projects future income and anticipates future expenditures which, if followed, is likely to permit you to reach your short-term goals. One's effectiveness in reaching short-term goals greatly affects the likelihood of reaching long-term goals.

Clearly record your goals.

You should explicitly express both long- and short-term goals when possible. Figure 4.3 provides worksheet examples of how much must be saved to reach short- and long-term goals. Short-term goals in particular must be stated clearly or you will never know when you have achieved them. "To save enough for a down payment on an automobile" is not as clear as "to save $2400 by December of this year for a down payment on a new Honda Prelude."

Prioritizing Goals

You must prioritize both your long-term and short-term goals.

It makes sense to put the most important financial goals first, since all goals will probably not be achievable at once. You will have to balance your priorities between providing for your future goals without giving up all the good things today.

The Planning Phase of Budgeting

Objective
To describe structural and mechanical aspects appropriate for one's personalized budget as part of the planning phase of budgeting.

Budget planning is a developmental phase in budgeting in which people decide on the structural and mechanical aspects appropriate for their personalized budgets. You should plan to have a positive attitude toward budgeting, maintain flexibility, recognize the value of recordkeeping, plan the recording format, plan to use the cash or accrual basis of budgeting, plan to use various budgeting classifications, and plan to budget over a certain time period.

Your Budgeting Attitude

A positive attitude is very helpful.

Developing a positive attitude toward budgeting is important because effective family financial management cannot be done without it. If you enjoy recordkeeping and desire a very detailed budget, then you can easily spend 5 hours a week on appropriate tasks. If you do not particularly enjoy numbers, accept the fact—with a smile on your face—that you may need to spend 1 hour a week on budgeting efforts—then do it. Recognize, too, that it is your financial life that you are managing and only you will ever know what will satisfy you.

The Importance of Flexibility

Allowing for the unknown or for unexpected financial activities is part of the budgeting process. Bear in mind that budgeting is a process, a working tool, and that its use should be flexible. Do not treat a budget as if it were engraved in marble. Make and use a budget to fulfill your changing needs, wants, and goals.

For example, Mary Langley, a 66-year-old retired single person, earmarked $60 a month for medical expenses. Suddenly, she needed emergency medical service to treat a severe stomach ulcer. Common sense told her to treat the problem even though the cost would be quite high. Such occurrences typically mean that other expenditures will have to be reduced or eliminated. On the other hand, do not be overly flexible. To purposefully overspend on recreational activities because you feel constrained on a $100-per-month allowance may not be prudent.

Another aspect of financial flexibility is to plan your budget so that you will have substantial **discretionary income.** This is the money people have left over once they pay for the necessities of living. Most people prefer not to have too many debts and other claims on income, usually considered fixed expenses, because this allows them to use a good part of their spending for whatever suits them.

The Value of Recordkeeping

Recordkeeping, the process of recording the sources and amount of dollars earned and spent, is an integral part of the budgeting process. Its primary value lies in providing detailed information as to what happened financially during any given period of time. Recording both the *estimated* and the *actual* amounts for income and expenditures will help you keep track of money flow.

If you do not record data, such as $49.22 spent for food during the week, your alternatives are to trust the amount to memory or to keep a receipt of the expenditure. You could keep receipts for all expenditures and payroll check stubs for all income received and memorize estimates for all projected earning and spending, but such a practice would likely be inaccurate and cumbersome. Keeping track of all income and expenses may be one of the more uninteresting tasks in the budget process, but it is the only way to collect sufficient information to later evaluate how close you are to achieving your financial objectives.

Effective recordkeeping will help you be successful financially.

Select a Recording Format

People sometimes become frustrated with the budgeting process because of the recordkeeping it requires. For your budget to work, you probably will have to keep records. Therefore, you should select a recording format that suits your needs by choosing from among self-prepared, commercial, or computer budget records.

Commercially Prepared Budget Records Are Available   Numerous types of commercially prepared recordkeeping forms and booklets are available. They range in price from a few dollars for some forms to perhaps $100 for an elaborately prepared kit. A disadvantage of these kinds of records is that they reflect another person's ideas about how your budgetary data should be recorded. It is not essential to use an expensive format; you should simply pay for the kinds of forms that satisfy your needs.

Self-Prepared Budget Records Are Probably Best   Many people decide that commercially prepared records are inflexible, and they prefer to design a budget record suited to their own needs. Figure 4.4 shows four samples of self-prepared budget records that range in complexity. In the next section of this chapter you will learn how budget data are recorded.

Computer Budget Records Are Good Too   The use of personal computers and word processors in the budgeting process is becoming commonplace. Tandy, Apple, IBM, Lanier, and Wang are just a few brands of electronic recordkeeping equipment that are widely used. You can either purchase computer budget programs from these companies, purchase other software programs, or design your own budget programs.

FIGURE 4.4
Budget Forms

(a) Simple Form for Each Budget Classification

Food Budget—$90			
Date	Activity	Amount	Balance
2-6	Groceries	$20	$70
2-9	Dinner out	8	62
2-14	Groceries	11	51

(b) More Complex Form for Each Budget Classification

Date	Activity	Amount Budgeted	Expenditures	Balance
2-1	Budget estimate	$90		$90
2-6	Groceries		$20	70
2-9	Dinner out		8	62
2-14	Groceries		11	51
2-20	Groceries		25	26
2-26	Dinner out		10	16
2-28	Groceries		9	7
2-28	February totals	90	$83	$7

(c) Simple Form for All Expense Classifications

Date	Activity	Expenditures						Total Exp. Bud—$680	Remarks
		Food Bud—$90	Clothing Bud—$30	Auto Bud—$60	Rent Bud—$275	Savings Bud—$60	Utilities Bud—$40		
2-1	Gasoline			10				10	
2-6	Groceries	20						20	Had friends over
2-8	Gasoline			7				7	Good price
2-9	Dinner out	8						8	
2-14	Groceries	11						11	Pepsi on sale
2-15	Subtotals	/39		/17				/56	
2-16	Telephone						41	41	
2-17	Tire			64				64	Emergency

Computerized recordkeeping has many advantages. The data stored in a computer's memory can be displayed on a screen for analysis almost instantaneously, in most cases by the pressing of a button. In most systems, printed documents can be generated. The price of computer recordkeeping equipment is well within reach of many individuals and families and will probably become more accessible as costs go down and home computer use expands.[8]

[8] *Personal Finance Cookbook,* a computer software program capable of performing some budget estimating tasks, as well as more powerful financial tasks, is available free to instructors who adopt this book.

FIGURE 4.4 (continued)

(d) More Complex Form for All Income and Expenditure Classifications

			Income			Expenditures								
			Salary	Other income	Total income	Food	Cloth.	Auto Expend.	Rent	Savings		Util.	Total Expend.	Remarks
Estimates			700	40	740	90	30	60	275	60		40	680	
Balance forwarded (from January)			–	–	–	6	–	14	–	–		2	28	
Sum			700	40	740	96	30	74	275	60		42	708	
Date	Activity	Cash In												
2-1	Paycheck	700	700											
2-1	Texaco–gasoline							10					10	
2-6	Safeway–groceries					20							20	Had friends over
2-8	7/11 – gasoline							7					7	Good price
2-9	Dinner out–Pizza					8							8	
2-14	Giant–groceries					11							11	Pepsi on sale
2-15	Subtotals	/700				/39		/17					/56	
2-16	AT&T–telephone											41	41	
2-17	Goodyear–tire							64					64	Emergency
2-28	Totals	700		40	740	83	28	57	275	60		39	660	Good month

Using the Cash or Accrual Basis

You can use either of two systems of financial recording in your budgeting process. **Cash-basis budgeting** recognizes earnings and expenditures when money is actually received or paid out. **Accrual-basis budgeting** recognizes earnings and expenditures when the money is earned and expenditures are incurred, regardless of when money is actually received or paid. Most people follow the cash basis in the budgeting process because it is easier to use. Thus most people use what is called a *cash budget*.

Most people use a "cash budget."

To illustrate both practices for recording financial transactions, suppose you are paid on the twentieth of the month for work done the first through the fifteenth and on the fifth for work done the sixteenth through the end of the month. Using the cash basis, you would recognize and record income on the fifth and the twentieth, when it is paid. Using the accrual basis, you would recognize and record income on the fifteenth and at the end of the month, when it has been earned. Likewise, if you record a VISA purchase at the time of the purchase, you are using the accrual basis, when the expenditure is incurred. If you record the purchase when you actually make the VISA payment, however, you are using the cash basis.

Either basis will work as long as you use it consistently. Once you decide on a basis, stick with it. Otherwise your cash position will shift constantly and budget accuracy will be difficult to maintain.

Budgeting Classifications

People who use only a checkbook for budgeting purposes have only two broad budgeting classifications: income (deposits to the checking account) and expenditures (checks written). Although this provides useful data, there is much to be gained by having more detailed classifications.

Table 4.1 shows some simple as well as complex budget classifications for income and expenses. The simple budgeting classifications illustrated in the table number only 12 expense items, and this is a suitable format for many people. One danger exists: Too many expenditures may be classified under "miscellaneous," which will take away from the information value of the classification. Should this occur, perhaps when the miscellaneous classification amounts to more than 5 percent of the total expenditures, simply review this expenditure category carefully and create other classifications. For example, you might need to create a new classification called "contributions" or "vices." You can break any such broad categories into more detailed classifications when the need for more specificity warrants. Some computer programs offer more than 100 budget classifications. Should you need additional ideas, recall that Chapter 3 presented other suggestions.

There are four main ways to save money.

It is important in planning budget classifications to note the four different ways that savings can be categorized: (1) savings withheld from income and deposited directly to a savings account, (2) savings as a fixed expenditure (paying yourself a set amount each period), (3) savings as a variable expenditure (paying yourself an undetermined amount each period), and (4) savings that may be available after all other expenditures are paid. The problem with the last two methods is that you might not save at all.

Selecting Time Periods

People who budget usually plan a budget to cover income and expenses for a 12-month period. They also develop monthly budgets because they receive their paychecks on a monthly or semimonthly basis. Using a limited time frame, such as a month, enables you to identify and control your financial activities and to maintain accurate records.

The Decision-Making Phase of Budgeting

Objective
To be able to discuss how to resolve conflicting financial needs and wants.

The decision-making phase of budgeting focuses on the financial aspects of budgeting and the decisions about where the funds will come from as well as where they should go. The financial manager should begin by examining the anticipated impact of inflation and economic conditions on the budget. He or she should next make realistic budget estimates for income and expenditures and then resolve conflicting needs and wants by revising estimates as needed.

Inflation and Economic Factors

Inflation is perhaps the single most influential factor affecting budgets because the rate of inflation at any given time will affect your purchasing

TABLE 4.1
Sample Budgeting Classifications and Expense Guidelines

Simple	Complex

Income

Salary
Nonsalary

Expenses*

Food (12%–30%)†
Housing and utilities (20%–45%)
Transportation (5%–20%)
Insurance (2%–10%)
Clothing (1%–10%)
Medical (2%–8%)
Entertainment/vacations (2%–5%)
Savings and investments (0%–10%)
Personal/miscellaneous (2%–5%)
Credit payments (0%–15%)
Gifts and contributions (1%–10%)
Taxes (8%–20%)

Salary
Rent
Interest
Dividends

Fixed expenses
  Home mortgage loan
  Life insurance
  Health insurance
  Disability insurance
  Homeowner's insurance
  Automobile insurance
  Church
  Other contributions
  Christmas gifts
  Other gifts
  Automobile loan or lease
  Loan 1
  Loan 2
  Dues and club memberships
  Savings (withheld from salary)
  Federal income taxes
  State income taxes
  Social Security taxes
  Real estate property taxes
  Personal property taxes
  Mutual fund investment
  Monthly investment plan
  Child support and alimony
  Pension contributions
  Individual retirement account

Income

Capital gains
Tax refunds
Loans
Other

Expenses

Variable expenses
  Revolving budget savings fund
  Other savings
  Food at home
  Food away from home
  Electric and gas
  Water
  Telephone
  Cable television
  Gasoline and oil
  Automobile maintenance and repairs
  Automobile license renewal
  Home maintenance and additions
  Gifts
  Auto registration
  Public transportation
  Doctors
  Dentists
  Medicines and drugs
  Hospital bills
  Veterinary costs
  Legal advice
  Child care
  Domestic help
  Clothing and accessories
  Hobby supplies
  Sports equipment
  CDs, DATs, tapes, and records
  Books
  Newspaper and magazine subscriptions
  Tobacco products
  Alcoholic beverages
  Education and tuition
  School books and supplies
  Furnishings and appliances
  Personal care
  Entertainment
  Recreation
  Vacations and travel
  Long weekends
  Credit card 1
  Credit card 2
  Savings—other
  Investments—other
  Miscellaneous

---

* The percentages represent the range of expenses of various family units.
† The U.S. Department of Agriculture reports that more than half of all meals are eaten outside the home.

TABLE 4.2
Sample Monthly Budgeted Expenses for Various Family Units

Classifications	College Student	Single Working Person	Married Couple	Married Couple with Two Young Children	Married Couple with Two College-Age Children
Income					
Salary	$ 300	$1700	$1600	$2000	$2200
Salary	—	—	1400	160	600
Interest and dividends	5	15	15	15	80
Loans/scholarships	200	—	—	—	—
Savings withdrawals	570	—	—	—	500
Total income	$1075	$1715	$3015	$2175	$3380
Expenses—fixed					
Housing	$ 250	$ 250	$ 400	$ 400	$ 600
Health insurance	—	—*	60*	70*	70*
Life and disability insurance	—	—*	10*	15*	15*
Homeowner's/renter's insurance	—	—	10	10	15
Automobile insurance	—	40	60	40	60
Automobile loan repayments	—	230	200	150	—
Loan 1 (TV/stereo)	—	80	80	40	—
Loan 2 (other)	—	40	40	—	50
Savings (withheld)	—	20	20	10	100
Federal/state taxes	30	290	520	320	480
Social Security taxes	20	130	230	165	210
Real estate taxes	—	—	—	—	40
Personal property taxes	—	5	10	10	10
Investments	—	—	60	5	50
Pension contributions	—	20	40	0	100
Individual retirement account	—	20	160	0	105
Total fixed expenses	$ 300	$1125	$1900	$1235	$1905

(*continued*)

power. For example, Juan Hernandez, a widowed father with two children, has an income of $23,000. He wonders what would be the effect of an annual inflation rate of 6.5 percent on his purchasing power? Juan's purchasing power of $23,000 would drop in 1 year to $21,597 (100.0/106.5 = 0.939; the reciprocal is 0.061; $23,000 × 0.061 = $1403; $23,000 − $1403 = $21,597).

Serious unemployment in the general economy also may influence your budget. For example, a loss of income caused by a temporary layoff from a job most certainly affects your budgeting. A significant increase or decrease in government taxes also will alter the amount of money available to spend, save, and invest. A decrease in taxes may increase the amount of money you have available to spend; an increase in taxes would decrease it.

An increase in interest rates can have a serious effect on budgeting because the amount allocated for credit purchases may need to be increased.

TABLE 4.2 (continued)

Classifications	College Student	Single Working Person	Married Couple	Married Couple with Two Young Children	Married Couple with Two College-Age Children
Expenses—variable					
Revolving budget savings fund	$ —	$ 40	$ 50	$ 50	$ 45
Other savings	—	—	150	—	—
Food	190	120	280	240	200
Utilities	20	50	60	70	90
Automobile gas, oil, maintenance	—	60	60	60	100
Medical	10	30	40	70	50
Child care	—	—	—	60	—
Clothing	20	50	60	50	40
Gifts and contributions	10	20	40	60	80
Vices	20	40	60	40	40
Education	400	—	—	—	500
Furnishings/appliances	10	10	30	20	20
Personal care	10	15	25	30	30
Entertainment	40	60	100	60	120
Vacations	15	30	40	30	60
Credit card 1	—	20	20	20	20
Credit card 2	—	—	20	20	—
Miscellaneous/personal	30	45	80	60	80
Total variable expenses	$ 775	$ 585	$1115	$ 940	$1475
Total expenses	$1075	$1715	$3055	$2175	$3380

* Over and above amount subsidized or provided by employer.

Rising interest is one factor that may prevent you from buying a home.

Suppose it is June and you are planning to buy a $92,000 home with a $12,000 down payment; you will then obtain a 30-year mortgage loan at 9 percent for the balance. By July the interest rates may have risen (or fallen). If, for some reason, you must wait until July to buy the home, you may have a monthly mortgage payment of $702 instead of $644, only because interest rates have increased by one percentage point. Moreover, you must consider inflation, interest rates, and general economic conditions in your budget planning.

How to Make Realistic Budget Estimates

Budget estimates are the recorded amounts in a budget that are planned and expected to be received or spent during a certain period of time. Most people begin by estimating their total gross income from all sources. Some people use a figure for disposable income instead. **Disposable income** is income received after taxes and all other employer withholdings. It is the money available for spending, saving, and investing.

Everyone's budgeted expenditures are different because people vary. Yet it is useful in planning your own budget to review how other people allocate their money. Table 4.2 illustrates the budget estimates for a college student, a single working person, a married couple, a married couple with two young children, and a married couple with two college-age children.

Note that in Table 4.2 the college student's budget requires monthly withdrawals of previously deposited savings to make ends meet; the budget is also quite inflexible. The single working person's budget allows for an automobile loan but not much else. The married couple's budget permits one automobile loan, an investment program, contributions to individual retirement accounts, and significant spending on food and entertainment; having two incomes helps. The budget of the married couple with two young children allows only for an inexpensive automobile loan payment; note that one spouse has a part-time job to help with the finances. The budget of the married couple with two college-age children permits a home mortgage payment, ownership of two paid-for automobiles, savings and investment programs, and a substantial contribution for college expenses. This budget has income meeting expenses because one spouse works part time and there are monthly withdrawals of previously deposited savings.

Reliable estimates of income and expenses make budgeting more valuable.

To make realistic budget estimates of income and expenses, you need reliable financial information. The more accurate the estimates, the more valuable is the budget. Most people begin by making budget estimates for one pay period and then multiply by the number of pay periods per year to obtain annual budget figures. Although accuracy is important, it is sufficient to round figures to the nearest dollar (or sometimes even $5.00).

Information from your financial records can be used to set up a budget. For income data, look at your copies of last year's income tax forms. Review payroll stubs for gross income information as well as what amounts were withheld for taxes, insurance, and the like. Talk to your employer to obtain similar information for next year, and perhaps ask about a possible salary increase as well. Interest income probably can be estimated closely by looking at statements and passbooks from the previous year.

For fixed expenses, such as rent and automobile insurance premiums, use payment stubs and information from your checkbook. This information can be highly accurate because the payments do not change often. Variable expenses are more difficult to estimate, particularly if you have never prepared a budget before. It should be helpful to review the sample budgets of others, as illustrated in Table 4.2, and the expense guidelines in Table 4.1. If you use a checkbook, review the checkbook register for the previous year. Perhaps you have a box or drawer where you keep receipts. Lacking any previous financial records, you might find it useful to keep a detailed log of expenses for 1 or 2 months and then make your initial budget estimates.

Reasonable estimates of expenses are acceptable too.

You need to make reasonable estimates for things you know you want to do. If you have seven Christmas gifts to buy and estimate spending about $50 for each, it's easy to estimate $350. If you want to go out to dinner once a week at $15 per meal, you might estimate $60 a month. What you want to avoid in estimating expenses is writing down unrealistically low figures. This can be very frustrating when higher expenditures do occur. Simply be fair in your estimates. The next step is to add up your total budget estimates for monthly or annual income and expenses.

Resolving Conflicts in Your Budget

The shock for most people in setting up and using a budget comes when their estimated expenses far exceed their estimated income. Three choices are available: earn more income, cut back expenses, or try a combination of more income and less expenses.

Extra income, of course, is usually hard to find.[9] Therefore, the immediate task is to decide what is really important in the budget. You have to reconcile conflicting needs and wants as you revise your budget until total expenses do not exceed income. This is known as **reconciling budget estimates.** Review the fixed expenditures to see if they are accurate and are all truly necessary. Look through each of the variable expenditures and change some "must haves" to "maybe next year." Perhaps keep some quality items but reduce the quantity. For example, instead of $60 for four meals out per month consider dining out twice a month at $20 for each meal. Table 4.3 illustrates the annual budget for Harry and Belinda Johnson. It reflects their efforts to revise estimates until total planned expenses were less than total planned income.

The sometimes uncomfortable process of reconciling needs and wants is healthy. It helps identify your priorities by telling you what is important to you in life now. It suggests what you need to sacrifice to have something else. In short, the process of reconciling your financial wants and needs in making and revising budget estimates is crucial in developing what it takes to achieve your financial goals.

The Implementing Phase of Budgeting

In the implementing phase of budgeting, you proceed to put the budget into effect primarily by recording day-to-day financial activities. Specifically, you record expenditures made and income received during the budget time period, manage cash-flow problems, determine totals for the time period, and prepare financial statements.

Recording Actual Income and Expenditures

An **expenditure** is an amount of money that has been spent. You may plan a budgetary *expense,* but when the money has been spent, it is an actual expenditure. It is important to keep an accurate and up-to-date

---

[9] Purdue University Professor A. C. Sullivan reports that approximately 40 percent of married couples nationwide receive income from overtime or extra jobs and that the income was considered "very important to the family budget." This suggests that many families could be in serious financial trouble should the economy go into a recession because when economic times are difficult companies quickly reduce overtime employment and lay off part-time employees. You also should know that with any second-income situation it is wise to be really careful in calculating how much the job actually pays. As one disgruntled worker said, "I had the feeling that all my second-income money was going to panty hose for me and day care for my daughter."

TABLE 4.3
Annual Budget Estimates for 1991 for Harry and Belinda Johnson (Prepared January 15, 1991)

	January	February	March	April	May	June	July	August	September	October	November	December	Yearly Total	Average per Month
Income														
Harry's salary	$1450	$1450	$1450	$1450	$1450	$1450	$1525	$1525	$1525	$1525	$1525	$1525	$17850	$1487.50
Belinda's salary	1900	1900	2100	2100	2100	2100	2100	2100	2100	2100	2100	2100	24800	2066.67
Interest	15	20	20	30	30	35	35	35	35	40	40	20	355	29.58
Trust	—	—	—	—	—	—	—	—	3000	—	—	—	3000	250.00
Total income	$3365	$3370	$3570	$3580	$3580	$3585	$3660	$3660	$6660	$3665	$3665	$3645	$46005	$3833.75
Expenses—fixed														
Rent	$ 400	$ 400	$ 400	$ 400	$ 400	$ 400	$ 425	$ 425	$ 425	$ 425	$ 425	$ 425	$ 4950	$ 412.50
Health insurance	65	65	65	65	65	65	65	65	65	65	65	65	780	65.00
Life insurance	9	9	9	9	9	9	9	9	9	9	9	9	108	9.00
Renter's insurance	—	—	—	—	—	110	—	—	—	—	—	—	110	9.17
Automobile insurance	—	—	—	—	—	320	—	—	—	—	—	320	640	53.33
Automobile loan payments	200	200	200	200	200	200	200	200	200	200	200	200	2400	200.00
Student loan	120	120	120	120	120	120	120	120	120	120	120	120	1440	120.00
Savings	60	60	60	60	60	60	60	60	60	60	60	60	720	60.00
Health club	50	50	50	50	50	50	50	50	50	50	50	50	600	50.00
Cable television	20	20	20	20	20	20	20	20	20	20	20	20	240	20.00
Federal income taxes	680	680	680	680	680	680	680	680	680	680	680	680	8160	680.00
State income taxes	117	117	117	117	117	117	117	117	117	117	117	117	1404	117.00
Social Security taxes	233	233	233	233	233	233	233	233	233	233	233	233	2796	233.00

Expenses—variable

Savings/investment/long-term	—	—	—	—	—	—	—	—	—	—	—	—	—	—
Revolving savings fund	220	220	220	220	220	(80)	70	(530)	70	70	70	(700)	0	—
Food	380	380	380	380	380	380	380	380	380	380	380	380	4560	380.00
Utilities	100	100	100	100	50	50	50	50	50	75	75	100	900	75.00
Telephone	70	70	70	70	70	70	70	70	50	70	70	90	840	70.00
Automobile gas/maintenance	45	45	265	45	45	45	45	45	45	45	45	45	760	63.33
Medical	60	60	60	60	60	60	60	60	60	60	60	60	720	60.00
Clothing	210	210	210	210	210	210	210	210	210	210	210	210	2520	210.00
Church and charity	125	125	125	125	200	125	125	125	125	125	125	125	1575	131.25
Gifts	80	80	120	80	160	40	40	80	80	80	80	40	960	80.00
Christmas gifts	—	—	—	—	—	—	—	—	—	—	—	—	—	—
Public transportation	50	50	50	50	50	50	50	50	50	50	50	50	600	50.00
Personal allowances	175	175	175	175	175	175	175	175	175	175	175	175	2100	175.00
Entertainment	130	130	130	130	130	130	130	130	130	130	130	130	1560	130.00
Automobile license	—	—	—	—	—	40	—	—	—	—	—	—	40	3.33
Miscellaneous	75	75	75	75	75	75	75	75	75	75	75	75	900	75.00
Vacation—Christmas*	—	—	—	—	—	—	—	—	—	—	—	—	—	—
Vacation—summer*	—	—	—	—	—	250	—	600	—	—	—	—	—	—
Anniversary party*	—	—	—	—	—	—	—	—	—	—	—	700	—	—
Total expenses	$3674	$3674	$3934	$3674	$3779	$4004	$3459	$3499	$3479	$3524	$3454	$3779	$43933	$3661.08
Difference (available for spending, saving, and investing)	($309)	($304)	($364)	($94)	($199)	($419)	$201	$161	$3,181	$141	$211	($134)	$2,072	$172.67

* Provided for in revolving savings fund.

TABLE 4.4
Cash-Flow Calendar for Harry and Belinda Johnson

Month	1 Estimated Income	2 Estimated Expenses	3 Surplus/Deficit (1 − 2)	4 Cumulative Surplus/Deficit
January	$3365	$3674	−$309	−$309
February	3370	3674	−304	−613
March	3570	3934	−364	−977
April	3580	3674	−94	−1071
May	3580	3779	−199	−1270
June	3585	4004	−419	−1689
July	3660	3459	+201	−1488
August	3660	3499	+161	−1327
September	6660	3479	+3181	+1854
October	3665	3524	+141	+1995
November	3665	3454	+211	+2206
December	3645	3779	−134	+2072
Totals	$46005	$43933	—	+$2072

record of expenditures. You may wish to place your budgeting records in the kitchen or family room where they are easy to locate. This will remind you to record expenditures daily. If you have a good memory or keep a notepad in your pocket or purse for that purpose, expenditures can be formally recorded every few days. When recording in the "activity" column, be descriptive, such as shown in Figure 4.4, since you may need such information later. Many people also write comments in a "remarks" column in their records for the same reason, as shown in parts (c) and (d) of the figure. Use a pencil so that mistakes or revisions are easier to correct.

Cash-Flow Calendar

A cash-flow calendar identifies problems before they are problems.

For most people, income remains somewhat constant month after month, but planned expenses can rise and fall sharply. This is a major reason why people occasionally complain that they are "broke, out of money, and hate budgeting." As you will soon see, this problem can be foreseen by the creation of a cash-flow calendar and eliminated by using a revolving savings fund.

The budget estimates for monthly income and expenses in Table 4.3 have been placed in summary form in Table 4.4, providing a **cash-flow calendar** for the Johnsons. This is a budgeting device upon which annual estimated income and expenses are recorded for each budgeting time period in an effort to ascertain surplus or deficit situations. As has been observed, even though the Johnsons' planned annual income exceeds expenses, they start out the year with too many expenses, resulting in deficits for 6 months straight. In later months, income usually exceeds expenses, resulting in a planned surplus at the end of the year.

TABLE 4.5
Revolving Savings Fund for Harry and Belinda Johnson

Month	Contributions	Withdrawals	Balance
Beginning balance			—
January	$220		$ 220
February	220		440
March	220		660
April	220		880
May	220		1100
June	170	$250	1020
July	70		1090
August	70	600	560
September	70		630
October	70		700
November	—		700
December	—	700	—

Effective management of cash flow can involve curtailing expenses during months with financial deficits, increasing income, using savings, or borrowing. If you borrow money and have to pay finance charges, the credit costs further push up monthly expenses. It is better to borrow from yourself using a revolving savings fund.

The Revolving Savings Fund

The revolving savings fund solves budgeting problems.

In its simplest form, a **revolving savings fund** is a variable expense classification in budgeting into which funds are allocated in an effort to create a savings amount that can be used to balance the budget in later budget periods so as to prohibit the individual or family from running out of money. It involves planning ahead—as a college student does who saves money all summer (creating a revolving savings fund) to draw on during the school months. Most people need to establish a revolving savings fund to use in a planned way for two purposes: (1) to accumulate funds for large irregular expenses, such as automobile insurance premiums, medical costs, Christmas gifts, and vacations, and (2) to meet occasional deficits.

The Johnsons' revolving savings fund is shown in Table 4.5. It provides only enough savings to cover expenses for their planned vacations and anniversary party. As designed their revolving savings fund, however, does not contain enough money to cover their frequent monthly deficits in cash flow. The revolving savings fund concept works wonderfully only if enough money is in the fund to cover the largest cumulative deficit. Thus the Johnsons need $1689, the June figure in Table 4.4. Lacking that sum of money to start a revolving savings fund, they have two alternatives: (1) to borrow money to cover deficits during the first several months of the year or (2) to cut back on expenses enough to create surpluses during these months, or both. Note also in Table 4.4 that at the end of December the Johnsons have a planned surplus of $2072. This should be more than enough to put in their revolving savings fund to begin the new year so they will not be faced with planned deficits again.

Time Period Totals

After the budgeting period has ended—usually at the beginning of a new month—add up the actual income received and expenditures made during that period. You can do this on a form for each budget classification [as shown in parts (*a*) and (*b*) of Figure 4.4] or on a form with all income and expenditure classifications [parts (*c*) and (*d*) of Figure 4.4]. Such calculations indicate whether you have overspent in any of your budget classifications. If you are new at budgeting, do not be too concerned about this; overspending occurs almost always in some classifications, while underspending happens in others. Use such information to refine your budget estimates in the future, and in 3 or 4 months you will be able to estimate more accurately.

Financial Statements

Once all financial activities for a time period are completed and the figures are recorded and totaled, it is easy to summarize them. You can prepare miscellaneous financial statements for budget classifications as illustrated in Table 4.6. Sometimes such summaries can be insightful, as part 2 of Table 4.6 shows. In this case, the actual expenditures for the telephone are regularly running below budget estimates (see Table 4.3), suggesting that future estimates for the Johnsons should be lowered. Also, you can use budget data to develop a balance sheet and an income and expense statement. We discussed these two comprehensive financial statements in Chapter 3.

The Controlling Phase of Budgeting

Objective
To be able to illustrate the methods and techniques used during the controlling phase of budgeting to help keep income and expenditures within planned budget totals.

In the controlling phase of the budgeting process, an individual or family uses various methods and techniques to help keep income and expenditures within the planned budget totals. The controlling phase occurs simultaneously with the implementing phase, since the best time to control spending is *during* the budget time period.

What Are the Purposes of Budget Controls?

Budget controls let you know if you are on target and how well you are progressing as well as alert you to such problems as errors, overexpenditures, items considered as emergencies, and exceptions or omissions. For example, when semiretired Postal Service employee Hyuncha Choe, a

TABLE 4.6
Miscellaneous Summary Statements for Harry and Belinda Johnson

1. *Income and savings statement:*

   Income:

January	$3371	
February	3379	
March	3590	
Total quarter income		$10340

   Savings:

January	$520	
February	450	
March	550	
Total quarter savings		$ 1520

2. *Variable expenditure statement—housing-related items:*

	January	February	March	Total
Food	$360	$390	$370	$1120
Utilities	106	111	97	314
Telephone	60	58	62	180

graduate student at Eastern Michigan University, examined her budget figures for the month of May, she discovered that the total of her "cash out" column was equal to $876 and the total of all other expenditure columns was equal only to $832. The two figures should be the same if she had recorded all transactions and added all figures correctly, and this serves as a built-in control. On the other hand, it is nearly futile to try to account for every single dollar because some cash is bound to "slip away" every month. However, a $44 difference ($876 − $832) indicates that something is wrong. More than likely Hyuncha omitted some expenditure item. This is a valuable control check built into the recording process.

The controls used are not, of course, to be treated as absolute mandates with penalties should there be errors. They simply inform you that something needs to be looked at further and remedied for the budgeting process to be properly completed.

Eight Budget Control Measures

Eight methods of controlling a budget are (1) using a checking account, (2) using a credit controlsheet, (3) checking accuracy, (4) monitoring unexpended balances, (5) justifying exceptions, (6) using the envelope system, (7) coding expenses, and (8) using subordinate budgets.

Using a Checking Account   If you use cash frequently instead of checks, you have to keep track of the amount you spend, which can be difficult to control. You must hold onto many receipts and write the purpose of

Using checks provides a useful budget control.

each expense on the back of its receipt as well as keep a daily log that includes expenditures for which you obtained no receipt. Using checks provides a record of the business or person to whom you wrote a check, and each check contains a space to record the purpose, as shown in Figure 4.5. It is also good control to deposit all checks received to your checking account without receiving a portion in cash; if you need cash, write a check.

It is easy to write a check in haste without recording its purpose on the front of the check. The check stub or register (also shown in Figure 4.5) then becomes a handy place to record explanations of expenditures.[10]

Using a Credit Controlsheet   Figure 4.6 shows a sample **credit controlsheet** that can be used to monitor the use of credit, amounts owed, and to whom they are owed. This form can keep you abreast of outstanding credit obligations. A crosscheck can easily be made between the credit-flow checksheet and credit statements received in the mail.

People who keep budgets on a cash basis sometimes do not keep track of credit transactions until they receive a statement noting what amount is due. For some this system works well. But there are many people who continue to buy on credit and who seem to be completely unaware of the detail and amount of their indebtedness until they receive a statement. Those who make credit purchases also need to keep the receipts for future reference so charges listed on a statement can be verified. By using a credit controlsheet (see Figure 4.6), you can record each credit transaction when it occurs, and if you misplace a receipt, some record is available for verification.

Checking Accuracy   Another way to control a budget is to double-check the accuracy of financial records. Many people increase the accuracy of their records by using a computer, a word processor, or a calculator. Accuracy in recordkeeping builds confidence in handling financial affairs.

The best method to control overspending is to monitor unexpended balances.

Monitoring Unexpended Balances   The best method to control overspending is to **monitor unexpended balances** in each budget classification. You can accomplish this by using a budget design that keeps a declining balance, as illustrated by parts (*a*) and (*b*) of Figure 4.4. Other budget designs, such as those shown in parts (*c*) and (*d*) of Figure 4.4, need to be monitored differently. As illustrated in parts (*c*) and (*d*), simply run subtotals every week or so, or as needed, during a monthly budgeting period.

Justifying Exceptions   Budget exceptions occur when there is a difference between budget estimates in various classifications and the actual expenditures. These are usually in the form of overexpenditures. There also may

[10] You can use a check register as a management technique to show exactly how much you have spent for each living category by following the suggestions in Cooperative Extension Service publication no. MT 8703, "Using a Check Register to Track Your Expenses," by Martha A. Goetting and Judith G. Ward, available free from Montana State University, Bozeman, Montana 59715.

Figure 4.5
Check with Explanation Space, Check Stub, and Register
Courtesy of Bank of Lexington & Trust Company.

Check

JAMES R. JONES SSN 123-45-6789 1910 ROSE LANE 555-1289 LEXINGTON, KY 40509	102

April 4, 19 *91*   73-114 / 421

PAY TO THE ORDER OF ___ *K-Mart* ___ $ *11 40*

Eleven + _____ *40/100* ___ DOLLARS

Bank of Lexington & Trust Company
LEXINGTON, KY 40509   5-84

MEMO *SCHOOL SUPPLIES*   *James R. Jones*

⑈04210114⑈5⑈ 9116038411⑈ 0102

Check Stub

IF TAX DEDUCTIBLE CHECK HERE ☐	BAL. FOR'D	380	71	Date *April 4*, 19 *91* $ *11.40* 102
	DEPOSIT			
	TOTAL	380	71	To *Pens and Pads*
	THIS ITEM	11	40	
	OTHER DED. (IF ANY)			For *school supplies*
	BAL. FOR'D	369	31	

Check Register

RECORD ALL CHARGES OR CREDITS THAT AFFECT YOUR ACCOUNT

NUMBER	DATE	DESCRIPTION OF TRANSACTION	PAYMENT/DEBIT (-)	√ T	FEE (IF ANY) (-)	DEPOSIT/CREDIT (+)	BALANCE
							$ 290 51
101	4-2	Angelo's Pizza supper	$ 9 80		$	$	9 80
							280 71
—	4-3	Deposit birthday from Aunt Lin				100 00	1 00 00
							380 71
102	4-4	K-Mart school supplies	11 40				11 40
							369 31

FIGURE 4.6
Credit-Flow Checksheet

CREDIT FLOW FOR Jan– Mar   19–

Date 19--	Purpose for Credit	VISA Chg (Pay)	VISA Balance	MASTERCARD Chg (Pay)	MASTERCARD Balance	SEARS Chg (Pay)	SEARS Balance	AMES Department Store Chg (Pay)	AMES Balance	Summary: All Creditors Chgs	Paid	Balance
1-2	Has for Car	14.95	14.95							14.95		14.95
1-2	Clothing							32.00	32.00	32.00		46.95
1-15	Paid Visa	(14.95)	-0-								14.95	32.00
1-27	New Desk			320.00	320.00					320.00		352.00
2-12	Gas for car	20.00	20.00							20.00		372.00
2-15	Bought Tools					75.00	75.00			75.00		447.00
2-28	Paid Ames							(32.00)	-0-		32.00	415.00

148

be exceptions in the over- or underreceipt of earnings. Allowing for exceptions is a way of keeping your budget flexible, but you still need to monitor them. For good control, set a limit on exceptions by type, number allowed, or amount spent. For example, an exception of $200 for sudden medical services need not be questioned. But $200 used to take a spontaneous weekend trip may be subject to question. You should record a written justification for going over budget. You will probably find that the more justifications you have to come up with to cover overages, the more *unlikely* they are to occur, since your "justifications" may be proof enough that certain expenditures were unwarranted. Of course, to stay within your budget allocations, you must balance, or offset, overexpenditures with extra earnings received or with a reduction of spending elsewhere.

The envelope system offers the strictest control.

Using the Envelope System   The **envelope system** of budgeting gets its name from the fact that exact amounts of money are placed into envelopes for purposes of strict budgetary control. If you wish to use the envelope system, at the start of a budgeting period, place in an envelope money equal to the budget estimate for each expenditure classification. Write the classification name and the budget amount on the outside of the envelope. As expenditures are made, simply record them on the appropriate envelope and remove the proper amounts of cash. When an envelope is empty, funds are exhausted for that classification. This technique works well in controlling expenditures for variable expenses, such as entertainment, personal allowances, and food. It may be a good way for younger children to learn to budget allowances. Of course, the envelopes must be safeguarded to prevent theft.

Coding Expenses   For a sophisticated system of budget control, you may want to consider coding all income and expense classifications. For example, expenditures for food could be marked "1"; clothing, "2"; gasoline, "3"; and so on. As you pay a bill, write a check, or make a bank deposit, you can record the appropriate code. This enables you to sum up all budget classifications quickly and accurately.

Using Subordinate Budgets   A very useful method of budget control is to use **subordinate budgets**. These require putting explicit details in particular expense categories within the budget that should result in improved control over expenditures. For example, a monthly estimate of $70 for gas, oil, and automobile maintenance could be estimated in detail at the beginning: gasoline, $38; oil, $6; tune-up, $26. Similarly, an allocation of $700 for a week-long summer vacation might last only 4 or 5 days if you lack subordinate budget estimate details for the vacation.

Objective
To be able to discuss the fundamental aspects of the evaluating phase of budgeting.

The Evaluating Phase of Budgeting

Evaluation is of extreme importance to the budgeting process. Indeed, evaluation provides feedback for reexamining achievement of short-term goals and, if needed, for reclarifying long-term goals. Your basic financial-planning values may then be reaffirmed or reorganized to fit your or your family's needs. More specifically, the purpose of evaluation is to determine whether the earlier steps in the budgeting process have worked.

Although evaluation is a continuous process, an important evaluation phase occurs at the end of a budgeting time period. It includes comparing actual with budgeted amounts, deciding whether the budget objectives have been achieved, and judging whether the overall process of budgeting has worked.

Comparing Estimated and Actual Amounts (Variance Analysis)

The "remarks" column in your budget should explain any variances.

It is practical to compare actual expenditures with the budget estimates. This is sometimes called **variance analysis**, as illustrated in Figure 4.7. In some budget expenditure classifications, the budget estimates rarely agree with the actual expenditures, particularly in variable expenses. Making comparisons is important if you want to understand why expenditures were higher or lower than you estimated. The "remarks" column, as illustrated earlier by parts (*c*) and (*d*) of Figure 4.4, can be of help here.

What Do You Do with Balances?

At the end of the budgeting time period, some budget classifications may still have a positive balance. For example, perhaps you estimated the electric bill at $50 and it was only $45. You may then ask, "What do I do with the balance?" You also may ask, "What happens to budget classifications that were overspent?"

You can save, spend, or carry forward last month's budget balances.

Some people deposit the **net surplus** (the amount remaining after all budget classification deficits are subtracted from those with surpluses) in a savings account, such as their revolving savings fund account. Many spend it like "mad money." Others leave the funds in their checking account and carry the surpluses forward, which provides larger budget estimates for the following month. The budgeting form in part (*d*) of Figure 4.4 allows for **carrying forward balances** to the next period. Some people carry forward deficits, hoping that having less available in a budgeted classification the following month will motivate them to try harder to keep expenditures low. Because variable expense estimates are usually averages, it is best not to change the estimate on the basis of a variation up or down over just 1 or 2 months. If the estimate is too high or low for a longer period, however, you will want to make an adjustment.

Be aware of any over- or underestimates of the amounts actually recorded for earnings or expenditures. Overages on a few expenditures may be of little concern. Perhaps the estimates were too low, and perhaps the total overage was not very much. Or perhaps earnings were more than estimated. Such findings should not be alarming. Essentially, these observations will tell you how well you followed the budget. They also may mean that some minor changes need to be made in estimates during the next budgeting time period. If excessive variances have occurred, preventing

FIGURE 4.7

Quarterly Budget Variance Analysis for Harry and Belinda Johnson

	January				February				March			
	Budget	Actual	Variance	Cumulative Variance	Budget	Actual	Variance	Cumulative Variance	Budget	Actual	Variance	Cumulative Variance
Income												
Harry's salary	1,450	1,450	—	—	1,450	1,450	—	—	1,450	1,450	—	—
Belinda's salary	1,900	1,900	—	—	1,900	1,900	—	—	2,100	2,100	—	—
Interest	15	5	(10)	(10)	20	5	(15)	(25)	20	5	(15)	(40)
Trust	—	—	—	—	—	—	—	—	—	—	—	—
Total income												
Expenses												
Fixed:												
Rent	400	400	—	—	400	400	—	—	400	400	—	—
Health insurance	65	65	—	—	65	65	—	—	65	65	—	—
Variable												
Food	380	390	(10)	(10)	380	400	(20)	(30)	380	390	(10)	(40)
Utilities	100	110	(10)	(10)	100	120	(20)	(30)	100	95	5	(25)
Telephone	70	60	10	(10)	70	55	15	25	70	45	25	50
Auto gas/maint.	45	48	(3)	(3)	45	46	(1)	(4)	265	268	(3)	(7)

you from achieving objectives or making the budget balance, do something about it. New controls might have to be instituted, or present controls might have to be tightened. Reflective thinking in this type of evaluation will ensure an improved budgeting process in the future.

Did You Stay Within the Budget?

Experience in budgeting will bring about greater success.

You may feel quite critical of yourself if you did not stay within the budget estimates. On the other hand, pat yourself on the back if you deserve it. If your objective was to stay within both the overall budget and the specific estimates for each classification and you did not, make adjustments. Your next budgeting time periods then will be more workable, and your objective more attainable. Experience and practice in the budgeting process will bring about greater success.

Did You Achieve Your Budget Objectives?

Whatever your goals and objectives, it is exciting to know that some or all of them have been achieved and/or that progress has been made toward those ends. A successful budget reflects on the person who developed it and made it work. Even though achieving such objectives as staying within the budget estimates, or paying off a small debt, or saving a few hundred dollars within the budget period may seem unimpressive to some, you can say, "I achieved my goals because I made the plan and worked the plan successfully."

If you did not achieve some of your objectives, you can use the evaluation process to determine why and to adjust your budget and/or objectives accordingly. Suppose your objective was to save enough money to make a down payment on a new car, but you could not achieve it during the budgeting time period planned. By evaluating your budget, you realize that because of some unexpected medical expenses and a cross-country trip to visit a sick relative, you had to dip into savings. Under these circumstances you can easily understand why the objective was not achieved. You can still set your sights on it during the next budgeting time period.

Did the Budget Work?

Only you can judge whether or not your budget "worked."

A final aspect of the evaluation process involves asking yourself some questions: "Did the budget, as put into practice, work?" "Did the budget give me enough information to refer to?" "Was I able to accomplish my objectives?" "Was the backup information detailed enough to prove my deductible expenditures when I filed my income tax forms?" If your answers are a resounding "Yes!" you can be confident that your budget did work. Keep up the good work!

Remember, though, that if all these questions cannot be answered with a "Yes," the entire evaluation or budgeting process should not be considered negative. This would merely illustrate that some part of the budgeting process did not work as intended. If your evaluation is negative in some way, accept it, and find out why. Then correct the problem so that you will have a positive evaluation the next time.

Summary

1. Many people, particularly couples and remarried families, find it difficult to talk about money and the tough financial decisions they have to make. There are many exercises to resolve people's conflicting spending styles and improve communications about money matters.

2. While financial plans can be developed by professional planners or competent adults, the actual family financial management must be done by the people themselves. Cash-flow management and budgeting are key in this effort.

3. Budgeting is a process of projecting, monitoring, and controlling future income and expenditures (including cash and credit purchases as well as savings) and reconciling the two by planning and controlling efforts that involve using budgeting records to set and achieve short-term goals that are in harmony with long-term goals.

4. Our personal values dictate our financial goals and objectives in budgeting. Success in budgeting is more easily achieved when all members of a household have a part in establishing and achieving both long- and short-term goals.

5. In the planning phase of budgeting—which focuses on the structural and mechanical aspects of budgeting—you choose a recording format, select either the cash or accrual basis, choose various budget classifications, and select the time period for the budget. Throughout, it is important to have a positive attitude toward budgeting and to maintain flexibility.

6. The decision-making phase of budgeting focuses on the financial aspects of budgeting and the decisions about where funds will come from as well as where they should go. It requires you to make realistic budget estimates for income and expenditures as well as to resolve conflicting needs and wants by revising estimates as needed.

7. In the implementing phase of budgeting, you proceed to put the budget into effect primarily by recording day-to-day financial activities. Then you manage cash-flow problems, determine totals for the time period, and prepare financial statements.

8. The controlling phase of budgeting includes the potential use of eight different means of control. Using a checking account, checking accuracy, and monitoring unexpended balances are popular controls. Stricter budgeting controls include the credit controlsheet and the envelope system.

9. The evaluating phase of budgeting includes comparing actual with budgeted amounts, deciding whether the budget objectives have been met, and judging whether the overall process of budgeting has worked or needs modification during the next budget time period.

<table>
<tr>
<td>

</td>
<td>

Modern
Money
Management

</td>
</tr>
</table>

The Johnsons'
Budget Problems

The Johnsons enjoy a high income because they both work. They cannot believe that less than a year ago they were both living the difficult financial lives of college students. Times have changed for the better.

The Johnsons spent parts of three evenings over the past several days discussing their financial values and goals together. As shown in the upper portion of Figure 4.3, they have established three long-term goals: $3000 for a European vacation to be taken in 2½ years, $5000 needed in October 1994 for a down payment on a new automobile, and $15,000 for a down payment on a home to be purchased in January 1996. As shown in the lower portion of Figure 4.3, the Johnsons did some math calculations to determine how much they had to save up for each goal—over the short term—in order to stay on schedule to reach the long-term goals they established as well as pay for two vacations and an anniversary party.

After developing their balance sheet and income and expense statements (shown at the end of Chapter 3), they made a budget for the year (shown in Table 4.3). They then reconciled various conflicting needs and wants until they found that total annual income exceeded expenses. Next they created a revolving savings fund (Table 4.5) into which they were careful to include enough money each month to meet all their short-term goals. However, when developing their cash-flow calendar for the year (Table 4.4), they noticed a problem: a series of substantial cash deficits over the first several months of the year. In fact, despite their projected high income and anticipated substantial surplus at the end of the year, it is now January and the Johnsons are broke!

Harry and Belinda have very little money in savings to cover planned deficits. However, to meet this problem they do not anticipate increasing their income, using savings, or borrowing. They are considering modifying their needs and wants to reduce their budget estimates to the point where they would have zero or positive balances during the first six months of the year.

1. Using the data from Harry and Belinda's budget estimates (Table 4.3), enter the data in the Personal Finance Cookbook (PFC) BUDGET program. Compare the results with the text for accuracy. Print the budget.

2. Make specific recommendations to the Johnsons on how they could make reductions in their budget estimates. Do not offer suggestions that would alter their new lifestyle drastically; they would reject these.

Key Words and Concepts

accrual-basis budgeting, 133
budget, 125
budget controls, 144
budget estimates, 137
budget exceptions, 146
budgeting, 125
carrying forward balances, 150
cash-basis budgeting, 133
cash-flow calendar, 142
cash-flow management, 124
community property states, 116
credit controlsheet, 146
discretionary income, 130
disposable income, 137
envelope system, 149
expenditure, 139
family financial management, 124

financial planning, 123
impulsive buying, 119
joint and survivor annuity, 118
long-term goals or objectives, 127
monitoring unexpended
    balances, 146
net surplus, 150
personal spending styles, 118
postnuptial agreement, 118
prenuptial agreement, 118
reconciling budget estimates, 139
recordkeeping, 131
revolving savings fund, 143
Rule of 72, 128
short-term goals or objectives, 128
subordinate budgets, 149
variance analysis, 150

Review Questions

1. Briefly describe how financial matters are handled in most American families.
2. What kinds of financial questions do couples and remarried families face?
3. Describe two types of spending styles other than "normal."
4. Give five suggestions on how people can talk about money matters.
5. List and describe briefly the six phases of budgeting.
6. Concisely describe the relationships among the following terms: *personal financial planning, family financial management, cash-flow management,* and *budgeting.*
7. What are some advantages to family goal setting?
8. What does it take to achieve your financial goals?
9. Give some suggestions on how to establish short-term goals or objectives.
10. Why are a positive attitude and flexibility important in budgeting?
11. Why do people often prefer to design their own budgeting record formats rather than purchase them commercially?
12. Differentiate between cash- and accrual-basis budgeting.
13. Describe two of the four ways that savings can be categorized in a budget.

14. Briefly explain how inflation and economic factors affect budgeting.
15. Cite some examples of where to obtain information to make realistic budget estimates.
16. How can you go about resolving conflicting needs and wants in budgeting?
17. Explain the purpose of a cash-flow calendar.
18. How can you use a revolving savings fund?
19. What are the purposes of budget controls?
20. How can you use a checking account as a budget control?
21. Explain how the envelope system of budget control works.
22. How can a subordinate budget be used on a vacation?
23. What is the purpose of the evaluating phase of budgeting?
24. When someone says their budget "works" and that it is a "success," what do they probably mean?

Case Problems

1. Penny and Dick Stratton of Boston, Massachusetts, have just about decided to start a family next year, so they are looking over their budget (illustrated in Table 4.2 as the "married couple"). Penny figures that she can go on half salary ($800 instead of $1600 per month) for about 18 months and then return to full-time work.
   a. Looking at the Strattons' current monthly budget, identify categories and amounts in their $3015 budget where they realistically might cut back $800. (*Hint*: Federal and state taxes should drop about $250 as their income drops.)
   b. Assume that Penny and Dick could be persuaded not to begin a family for another 2 to 3 years. What specific budgeting recommendations would you give them for handling (i) their fixed expenses and (ii) their variable expenses to help them prepare financially for an anticipated $800 loss of income for 18 months, as well as the expenses for the new baby.

   c. If the Strattons' gross income of $3015 rises 6 percent regularly in the future, what will their income be after five years? (*Hint*: See Appendix A-1 or the Personal Finance Cookbook (PFC) software worksheet titled FVSUM.

2. Claude and Anne Marcus of Santa Ana, California, have two young children and have been living on a tight budget. Their monthly budget is illustrated in Table 4.2 as the "married couple with two young children." Claude and Anne have been nervous about not having started an educational savings plan for their children. Therefore, Anne just started to work part time at a local accounting firm, earning about $160 a month, and this amount is reflected in their budget. They have decided that they need to save $200 a month for the children's education, but Anne does not want to work any more hours away from home.

a. Review their budget and make suggestions to modify various budget estimates to point out how they could save $200 a month for the education fund.

b. Briefly describe the impact of your recommended changes on their lifestyle.

c. What factors should they remember as they attempt to discuss and resolve this important financial issue for their family?

3. Ron Fernandes of Dover, Delaware, graduated from college 8 months ago and is having a terrible time with his budget. Ron has a regular monthly income from his job and no really big bills, but he likes to spend. He goes over his budget every month, and his credit-card balances are increasing. Choose three budget control methods that you could recommend to Ron, and explain why each one will probably help him gain control of his finances.

Suggested Readings

"Figuring Out Your Cash Flow." *U.S. News & World Report,* July 30, 1990, p. 77. A useful format to follow.

"5 Crucial Financial Crossroads." *Changing Times,* April 1990, pp. 31–41. What to do financially when key life events occur, including marriage, birth of a child, mid-life, retirement, and death of a spouse.

"How to Pay a $150,000 Tuition Bill." *Changing Times,* October 1989, pp. 88–98. Making a plan to pay tuition bills in the future after costs rise.

"How to Stay Ahead of Your Paycheck." *Working Woman,* April 1989, pp. 91–94. The basics of budgeting for the young professional.

"Money Matters of the Mind." *U.S. News & World Report,* July 30, 1990, p. 53. Irrational financial behaviors lead to dissatisfaction.

"Teaching Your Kids About Money." *Money,* March 1990, pp. 126–135. Some good suggestions on how to give children money and how to discuss financial matters.

"To Free Money for What Matters Most, Analyze Expenses." *Money,* February 1989, pp. 68–70. How to find money in your budget for your most important goals.

"To Make a Harvest Honeymoon Last, First Decide What's Yours, Mine, and Ours." *Money,* September 1989, pp. 145–146. Many key financial decisions need to be made by couples early in their relationship.

Fred E. Waddell. *Financial Counseling Training Manual* (Auburn, AL: Genesis Press, 1031 Sanders Street, 1990), 120 pp. Self-instructional manual emphasizing communication skills.

"When a Spender Marries a Saver: One Family's Finances." *Money,* November 1989, pp. 114–124. Case analysis of two people with differing approaches to money and tips to resolve the differences.

Flora L. Williams. *Theories and Techniques in Financial Counseling and Planning for Middle Income and Low Income Clients* (West Lafayette, IN: Purdue University, Purdue Research Foundation, 1990), 309 pp. Step-by-step processes, forms, and client/student activities.

PART TWO

Money Management

5 Managing Your Cash

OBJECTIVES

After reading this chapter, you should be able to

1. Explain the importance of effective cash management and list the four tools of cash management.

2. Describe today's complex financial services industry.

3. Understand the many uses of electronic funds transfer and the legal protections available.

4. Recognize the differences among the primary providers of cash management opportunities in today's financial services.

5. Understand criteria for choosing a checking institution as well as why it is important to have an interest-bearing checking account.

6. Recognize the potential benefits of opening a savings account at a nearby financial institution as well as key factors to consider in comparing savings accounts.

7. Realize the importance of placing excess funds in a money-market account.

8. Recognize the potential benefits of putting money into low-risk, longer-term savings investments.

· · · · · · · · ·

This chapter begins with a discussion of the meaning of cash management and what you can do to properly manage your money. Next we provide an overview of today's financial services industry so you can better understand where to do your checking, savings, borrowing, insuring, investing, and other financial activities. The complex and complicated financial services industry is all possible because of the availability of electronic funds transfer, a topic you need to understand so you can use it to your financial advantage. Next we discuss the four primary providers of cash management services: banks, money market accounts, stock brokerage firms, and financial services companies. The remainder of the chapter focuses on details about the four tools of cash management: interest-bearing checking accounts, savings accounts, money-market accounts, and various low-risk, longer-term savings instruments.

What Is Cash Management?

Objective
To be able to explain the importance of effective cash management and list the four tools of cash management.

As your income increases, you will have more and more cash to manage, and the challenge is to do it properly. This requires that you strategize about how much cash to keep on hand, in what forms, and in which financial institutions. You also need to maintain an adequate amount of liquidity and safety. **Liquidity** is the speed and ease with which an asset can be converted to cash. **Safety** is freedom from financial risk. Cash management has to do with effectively managing all your monetary assets (as described in Chapter 3, Financial Planning over Your Life), such as cash on hand, savings accounts, checking accounts, tax refunds due, money-market accounts, other short-term investment vehicles, and various longer-term savings instruments. These monetary assets are also known as *cash-equivalent investments*.

Cash management is the task of earning maximum interest on all your funds, regardless of the type of account in which they are kept, while having sufficient funds available for living expenses, recurring household expenses, emergencies, and savings and investment opportunities. Effective cash management results in developing and arranging the resources to have sufficient funds for everyday living expenses, for unplanned expenditures (such as emergencies), and for savings to reach future financial goals. Proper cash management also encourages you to keep cash and credit purchases in line with your planned budgetary limits.

All of us need a certain amount of **pocket money**. This is a sum of coins and paper currency used daily and weekly to pay for marketplace transactions that generally require cash. This would include purchases from vending machines and expenditures for newspapers, buses, taxis, and lunches. People generally keep enough cash around to last for a week or two of anticipated pocket-money expenses. In deciding how much pocket money to have on hand, you need to balance your desire to maintain an adequate supply of cash against any tendency you might have to "spend what is in your pocket" and particular concerns about theft.

Most people use pocket money and a checking account for their everyday cash management needs.

Expenditures above and beyond pocket-money needs can then be met by using a checking account, perhaps in conjunction with credit and debit cards. A **checking account** is a bank account in which checks may be written against amounts on deposit. Checking accounts are also known as *transaction accounts,* and they let you transfer funds from your account to merchants and service providers. Nine out of ten American adults pay bills and make purchases using checking accounts. Typically, people can access their checking accounts by writing checks, using an automated teller machine (ATM), making electronic transfers (such as point-of-sale machines and direct deposits), sending materials by mail, giving instruction on the telephone, and talking with a teller inside the financial institution.

People pay for more than half their personal consumption expenditures with checks; therefore, the most basic need people have in cash management is to have a checking account, preferably one that pays interest. Since checking accounts often pay little or no interest, wise financial managers place excess funds not needed for everyday living expenses into other types of cash management accounts. This allows them to earn more money in the form of interest or dividends while at the same time still providing reasonable liquidity.

The four tools of cash management are illustrated in Figure 5.1. First, you need to have an *interest-bearing checking account* from which to pay for monthly living expenses. Second, you might want to have a small *savings account in a local financial institution* that can assure you of a source of ready emergency cash. Third, when income begins to exceed expenses regularly, you can consider opening a *money-market account* so you can earn the highest interest rates on excess funds while considering other savings and investment options. Fourth, your cash management plan is complete when you transfer some funds into *various low-risk, longer-term savings instruments,* such as certificates of deposit and government savings bonds because you want to earn even higher interest rates. Here you are committing the amounts for longer time periods, thus allowing you to build up amounts to be used for later spending, saving, or investing. These concepts are discussed in depth later in this chapter.

Today's Financial Marketplace

Objective
To be able to describe today's complex financial services industry.

Until just a few years ago, people practiced cash management primarily by using the banking industry. They maintained a checking account at a local bank because it was free, and they deposited their savings money in a nearby savings and loan association because it paid a higher rate of interest on passbook savings. Not so now!

FIGURE 5.1

Four Tools of Cash
Management and the
Options Available (with
Illustrative Interest
Rates Earned on Funds)

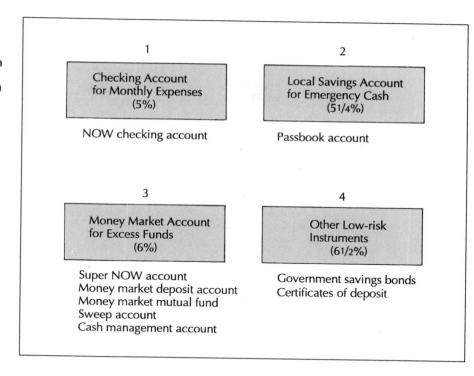

Wider use of computers, improved communications technology, deregulation of the traditional banking industry, and greater competition have brought about revolutionary changes in banking. In fact, the entire **financial services industry** (institutions and individuals offering one or more of the following services: checking, banking, savings, traveler's checks, credit, insurance, stocks, real estate, credit counseling, financial planning, or advice on accounting, taxes, and legal matters) has been transformed in the past decade. Effective cash management now requires a careful understanding of these transactions and the opportunities and perils they have brought.

Today's financial market-place is complex and changing.

Financial Services in the Past

Yesterday's financial services industry was heavily regulated.

The stock market crash of 1929 and the subsequent decade of economic depression brought an end to the carefree, competitive, laissez-faire banking era of the 1920s. More than 10,000 banks closed during the Great Depression years between 1929 and 1933, and 600 banks failed per year in the 1920s before the depression. Elected officials at that time decided that if competition could not prevent a depression, then government regulation would be the new order of the times.

Congress wanted to keep savings, checking, real estate, and securities services separated because the prevailing philosophy was that "unfettered competition in the past had resulted in excesses and abuses in banking as well as other industries." The 1930s saw the creation of the Federal Reserve System, including the Federal Reserve Board and the Comptroller of the Currency, to oversee approximately 25,000 federally chartered banks. The Federal Deposit Insurance Commission was established to guarantee small savers against financial losses in banks. The Federal Home Loan Bank Board was created to oversee the thrift industry (the savings and loans), and the Federal Savings and Loan Insurance Corporation guaranteed small savers against losses in these institutions. Banking commissions were established in all states to monitor the nearly 5000 banks chartered at the state level. Congress also established the Securities and Exchange Commission, which was to regulate stock and bond transactions. Federal laws were passed to prohibit banks from engaging in stock or insurance transactions. States then established insurance and securities commissions to regulate those industries. In short, government regulators heavily influenced which financial services could be sold, how, by whom, and at what prices.

Financial Services Today

Today's financial services industry is quite complicated.

The financial services industry, comprised of banking, brokerage, and insurance services, continued to be heavily regulated through the 1960s and 1970s by both the federal and state governments. The traditional concept of consumer banking, however, started to change in the late 1970s. Deregulation efforts increased in the early 1980s with passage of the Depository Institutions and Monetary Control Act of 1980. New groups of players in the industry, an expanding redefinition of the term *banking*, the availability of new products and services, rapid technological developments, and continued deregulation into the 1990s promise one thing for Americans—an increasingly complex financial marketplace. Thus people have had no alternative but to deal with the deregulated changes, learn about the new financial marketplace, and reap the benefits of higher interest rates on savings and new conveniences in the world of finance.

The deregulation issue is one of choice: Banks want more freedom to compete in the industry (to underwrite and sell stocks and bonds as well as to sell insurance and real estate), and outsiders (Gulf and Western, American Express, J. C. Penney, Sears, General Electric, Ford, and Merrill Lynch) want the freedom to enter the banking business. In today's increasingly competitive financial marketplace, many firms not traditionally thought of as banks offer a variety of financial services to consumers. A diverse range of institutions has moved into the traditional banking business. These outsiders are called **nonbank banks,** which are a new kind of financial institution offering many services including either granting commercial loans or accepting consumer deposits, but not both. This allows them to escape being defined as banks and thus not be subject to a number of banking laws and controls. Thus such institutions may be able to sell insurance and securities, depending on state laws. The Congress, regulatory agencies, and the courts generally have been supportive of continued deregulation of the financial services industry.

With further banking deregulation, it is expected that soon you will be able to make a deposit at your local bank (or, perhaps more appropriately, your financial service institution), go on vacation several states away, and make deposits, withdrawals, and electronic transfers at banks, supermarkets, discount outlets, and department stores while you are traveling. Networks of interlinked systems, such as MAC, CIRRUS, or TYME, are leaders in providing access to ATM machines across the country, and the machines are technically capable of processing purchases of stocks, mutual funds, and insurance policies. The result of all these changes has been an increasingly complex financial marketplace.

Electronic Funds Transfer (EFT)

Objective
To understand the many uses of electronic funds transfer and the legal protections available.

Electronic funds transfers make effective cash management possible.

The most noteworthy feature of today's financial services industry is the advent of a wide variety of electronically assisted transactions available to consumers. **Electronic funds transfer (EFT)** is a method of directly transferring funds by electronic means from or to a consumer's account at a financial institution to or from another account using data-processing computers and/or telecommunications.

You can use electronic funds transfer to

1. Authorize your financial institution to automatically pay your monthly automobile loan and home mortgage installments.
2. Have your employer deposit paychecks directly into your account.
3. Make a telephone call to your credit union to transfer funds from a share savings account to a share draft account.
4. Allow a daily sweep transaction of funds out of a savings account into an interest-bearing NOW account (discussed later in this chapter).
5. Obtain a $50 loan at midnight from a shopping mall terminal to pay for automobile repairs in an unfamiliar city.
6. Pay for groceries by punching a check-verification machine before giving the grocery clerk a personal check.
7. Obtain a computer-chip card with "$100 of use on it" with which to make purchases, get cash, or use a vending machine.
8. Purchase items at a local store and have your funds instantly transferred from your account to that of the store.
9. Make a deposit to your bank even when you are 1500 miles away.
10. Call up bank account information on your home computer.
11. Buy goods advertised on television from home by means of an interactive or cable system.
12. Transfer money from your checking account to your savings account.
13. Punch payment orders on a home computer, directing your bank to pay all the monthly bills as shown on the videoscreen.
14. Have money automatically transferred from your paycheck to a mutual fund retirement account.

15. Purchase life insurance, stocks, or real estate through a financial institution offering a cash management account.

16. Purchase a savings certificate of deposit (CD) and get a car loan at a branch bank in a K Mart discount store or in a supermarket.

17. Cash a check at an ATM machine and get both currency and coins to the penny.

The most recognized forms of EFT are the use of debit cards, computer-chip cards, preauthorized payments and deposits, and computer money management through a home computer or telephone. Important in discussing this topic is how electronic funds transfers are regulated by government to protect consumers.

Debit Cards

A **debit card** is a plastic card for use in automated teller machines (ATMs) and electronic funds transfer point of sale systems (EFTPOS) that authorize payment directly from or to the consumer's account. Consumers can make immediate deductions from or additions to their accounts through an automatic teller machine (ATM). An **automated teller machine (ATM)** is a computer terminal provided by a financial institution enabling funds to be withdrawn or deposited by consumers. This is done by putting a debit card into the terminal and entering your personal identification number (PIN) and the amount of cash involved. With some machines it is possible to get details of your account balance and carry out other banking functions, such as paying bills. A **personal identification number (PIN)** is a four- to seven-digit access number issued to each customer by a financial institution for use with a particular debit or credit card when using ATMs or **electronic funds transfer point of sale systems (EFTPOS).** EFTPOS are used to directly transfer funds by electronic means from a customer's bank account to a retailer's bank account. The transfer is triggered by use of the customer's plastic debit card and PIN in a retailer's terminal. Debit and credit cards are expected to replace most check usage at some point in the future.

Debit cards are expected to replace most checks in the future.

The PIN is used to verify that the person using the debit card is authorized to do so. The PIN must be punched into the ATM whenever the card is used. The ATM verifies that the account balance can cover the amount of the transaction (purchase or withdrawal). Personal identification numbers should not be written or stored near the debit card because if lost or stolen together they can "unlock" the account. Debit cards can be obtained from your local bank, savings and loan association, and credit union or such companies as VISA, MasterCard, and American Express.

Computer-Chip Cards

Some banks now issue **"smart" cards** (or **memory cards**), which are plastic cards with an embedded microchip or magnetic strip containing information that is changed when the card is used. For example, the card can be "charged" with a certain amount of money value that decreases every time it is used. A PIN must be used with a "smart" card to confirm the user's identity.

Preauthorized Deposits and Payments

You, or anyone else you so authorize, can make regular deposits, such as a paycheck, stock dividends, or Social Security benefits, to your account electronically. You also can authorize your financial institution to pay recurring bills in both regular amounts (such as a mortgage or automobile loan) and irregular amounts (such as electric or telephone bills).

Computer Money Management

A growing number of people do their banking by linking a home computer by means of the telephone (using a modem) to their financial institution. This is called **computer money management.** Customers can summon an electronic checkbook to their computer monitor, double-check calculations and earlier payments, and push a few buttons to order payment of monthly bills. A printer attached to the computer can provide a hard-copy receipt for each transaction.

The monthly service charge for computer money management is around $25. Included in this service may be price quotations on stocks and bonds, current interest rates paid on government securities, comparative cost information on life insurance policies, investment advice from specialists, weather reports, access to white and yellow pages of telephone books, retail-store catalogs, information for local theatrical events, and updated tax information. Such a service would allow you to apply for a loan, order traveler's checks, book airline reservations, reserve theater tickets, and purchase products and services. A home computer is not entirely necessary to computer money management because technology is yielding the "intelligent" telephone, which can function much like a home computer.

EFT Regulations

Both state and federal regulations have been adopted to provide protection for EFT users. The 1978 Electronic Funds Transfer Act established guidelines on EFT-card liability. A valid card can be sent only to a consumer who has requested it. Unsolicited cards can be issued only if the card cannot be used until validated and the user is informed of liability for unauthorized use as well as of other terms and conditions.

You can have unlimited liability if you lose an EFT card.

Regarding lost cards, cardholders are liable for only the first $50 of unauthorized use if they notify the issuing company within 2 business days after the loss or theft of their card or code. After 2 days, cardholder liability for unauthorized use rises to $500. You risk *unlimited* loss if, within 60 days after your financial statement is mailed to you, you do not report an unauthorized transfer or withdrawal. The logic is that if cardholders examine their monthly statements, they will note unauthorized use of the account. These regulations are for specific EFT cards or for

What If You Want to Send Cash in a Flash?

There is an emergency and you must send cash fast. First, find out the amount needed, when it must be there, and a telephone number of where to reach the person. This information will be necessary to call back the person so he or she will know where to pick the money up and how to identify himself or herself. A photo ID of the person being sent the funds is usually required, but something can usually be worked out when necessary. Sending money overseas is more complicated, but it can be done too. There are four methods of sending cash.

1. Visa and MasterCard holders can call Western Union (its toll-free number is in the telephone book) and use their Money Transfer Service, which operates 24 hours a day using 11,000 agents. Everything can be handled by telephone.

2. American Express cardholders may call 800-543-4080 to locate the agent nearest to you. Then you pay them with cash, MasterCard, or Visa, because American Express does not give cash advances.

3. The U.S. Postal Service can send a postal money order by means of Express Mail, and overnight delivery is guaranteed 7 days a week. You must pay by cash or check.

4. Any bank can wire the money to a designated bank; however, the transaction can only be completed during banking hours.

other cards (such as a VISA credit card) *used as* an EFT card to transfer funds.

Realize that it is difficult for consumers to dispute an item with a merchant (for faulty goods, for example) if the merchant has already been paid by means of EFT. Because the merchant already has the money, the consumer's only recourse to correct or reverse EFT transactions is to ask for a refund. Stop-payment orders for EFT transactions also may be difficult to manage because funds transfer very quickly.

A number of states have laws that provide additional protections for consumers in EFT transactions. For preauthorized deposits, one such law requires that the customer receive written notification that the deposit has been made. Another requires that if financial institutions receive a request for payment in an amount different from that authorized, they cannot pay the bill unless the customer has signed an agreement permitting payment of irregular amounts. Individual financial institutions may offer more rights or state laws may require them. For preauthorized payments, most states require that financial institutions set a maximum 3-day notification period to stop a payment. Some states require that all EFT machines capable of providing cash also provide a written receipt.

General protection of customers' accounts exists in the form of periodic statements that financial institutions regularly send out. Some state regulations also provide that when a customer suspects an EFT error and notifies the financial institution within 10 days, the account holder must have use of the funds in question until the matter is examined and resolved. If the institution is correct in its analysis, the sum is later deducted from the account. For all EFT transactions, your best protection is to carefully use and safeguard your PIN; writing your number on a piece of paper you keep in your wallet along with your EFT card is not a good practice.

Who Are the Providers of Today's Financial Services?

Objective
To recognize the differences among the primary providers of cash management opportunities in today's financial services.

The providers of today's financial services include banks, money market mutual funds, financial services companies, financial planners, brokerage firms, insurance companies, and others. Table 5.1 lists these along with what financial products and services they sell. We discuss these providers in this and in following chapters. Also, at appropriate points, we offer suggestions about who might best use the various providers of financial services. The following examines the four primary providers of cash management services: banks and banklike institutions, money market mutual funds, stock brokerage firms, and financial services companies.

Banks and Banklike Institutions

There are four types of financial institutions that offer various forms of both checking and savings accounts: commercial banks, mutual savings banks, savings and loan associations, and credit unions. Although each is a distinct type of institution and their characteristics will be detailed below, people often call them all **banks** or **banking institutions**.

Commercial Banks   **Commercial banks** are corporations chartered under federal and state regulations. Historically, they have offered the widest variety of financial services. Modern commercial banks offer numerous consumer services, such as checking, savings, loans, safe-deposit boxes, investment services, financial counseling, and automatic payment of bills. There are approximately 14,000 commercial banks nationwide, with another 50,000 branch offices of banks in states that allow branch banking. Each account in a federally chartered bank is insured against loss up to $100,000 in principal and interest per account by the Bank Insurance Fund (BIF) of the **Federal Deposit Insurance Corporation (FDIC),** an agency of the federal government. Accounts in state-chartered banks are usually insured by the FDIC's BIF program or sometimes through a state-approved insurance program.

Savings and Loan Associations   The original purpose of **savings and loan associations (S&Ls)** was to accept savings and provide home loans. This remains a focus today, and S&Ls are still called "thrift" institutions. Most of the approximately 2400 associations, with 15,000 branches, also give loans for consumer products, such as automobiles and appliances.

TABLE 5.1
Today's Providers of Financial Services

Providers	What They Sell
1. *Banks* Banks Savings and loan associations Mutual savings banks Credit unions	Checking, savings, lending, credit cards, investments, and trust advice
2. *Financial services company* Merrill Lynch Sears American Express Company Prudential Bache	Checking, savings, lending, credit cards, real estate, investments, insurance, tax shelters, accounting and legal advice, and financial planning
3. *Stock brokerage firms* Stock brokerage firms Discount stock brokerage firms	Stocks, bonds, unit investment trusts, real estate investment trusts, and tax shelters
4. *Mutual funds* Kemper Twentieth Century Fund Fidelity	Money-market mutual funds, tax-exempt funds, bond funds, and stock funds
5. *Insurance companies*	Policies to protect against risks, tax shelters, annuities, and retirement plans
6. *Accountants*	Income tax preparation and maintenance of the financial records for businesses
7. *Lawyers*	Income and estate tax planning, wills, bankruptcy, and other legal matters
8. *Real estate firms*	Buying and selling of real estate as well as management of rental properties
9. *Tax preparation services*	Preparation of income tax returns and tax advice
10. *Financial planners*	Various financial products and/or financial advice
11. *Credit counselors*	Suggestions on ways to reduce spending, balance personal and family budgets, and reduce indebtedness

S&Ls are not permitted to provide demand deposits (such as checks drawn on a commercial bank); however, they can offer interest-bearing NOW accounts to depositors, which are basically the same thing (these topics are discussed later in the chapter). The FDIC insures accounts in all federally chartered S&Ls (up to $100,000 in principal and interest per account) through its Savings Association Insurance Fund (SAIF), as well as some state-chartered institutions.

The two kinds of savings and loan associations are mutual and corporate. In the more common *mutual savings and loan association,* depositors are the actual owners of the association, or share owners. A mutual S&L operation usually allows one vote per share (for example, for each $100 on deposit) when electing its board of directors. Alternatively, *corporate savings and loan associations,* located primarily in the Midwest and West, operate as corporations and issue stock to denote ownership.

In recent years, more than 100 federally chartered savings and loan associations have changed their names to *bank* even though they are still S&Ls. Apparently they think there is a perception among the public that banks are better than S&Ls (since over 800 S&Ls have gone bankrupt since 1986) even though they each offer consumers virtually the same services. You can still recognize the renamed S&Ls because by law they must have the word *savings* in their title (for example, National Savings Bank of Missouri) or use the letters *FSB* for *federal savings bank* (such as Montgomery FSB Bank).

Mutual Savings Banks   A **mutual savings bank (MSB)** is quite similar to a savings and loan association. Historically, MSBs accepted deposits in order to make housing loans. They are called *mutual* because technically the depositors of savings are the owners of the institution. MSBs are state-chartered and have either FIDC's Bank Insurance Fund (BIF) insurance or a state-approved insurance program up to $100,000 per account. MSBs are legally permitted in 17 states, although most are located in the states of Connecticut, Maine, Massachusetts, New Hampshire, New Jersey, and New York. Like S&Ls, mutual savings banks compete for consumer loans and offer interest-bearing NOW accounts (discussed later in this chapter) to checking customers.

Credit Unions   **Credit unions (CUs)** are not-for-profit cooperative ventures, largely run by volunteers, developed to pool the deposits of members, which are then used to invest or lend to members/owners. Members usually have some common bond, such as the same employer, church, union, or fraternal association. Regulations make it possible for people to remain members of a credit union after the common bond has been severed. Over 32 million people belong to the nation's 9400 federally chartered and 6700 state-chartered credit unions. Those with federal charters have their accounts insured up to $100,000 through the National Credit Union Share Insurance Fund (NCUSIF), administered by the National Credit Union Administration (NCUA), which provides the same safety as deposits insured by the FDIC. State-chartered credit unions are often insured by NCUSIF for $100,000 per account, and most of the others participate in state-approved insurance programs.

About 32 million adults belong to credit unions.

Credit unions accept deposits and make loans for consumer products, although a few have the financial resources to make home loans. They typically make use of payroll deductions for deposits and loan repayments, often offer free term life insurance up to certain limits, and usually offer free insurance to pay off a loan in the event of death or disability. Many offer free budget and credit counseling.

Money Market Mutual Funds

A **mutual fund** is an investment company that raises money by selling shares to the public and invests those monies in a diversified portfolio of securities offered by other corporations or governments. The investments are then professionally managed, with securities bought and sold at the discretion of the manager. Many mutual fund companies have created money market mutual funds, which serve as money market accounts that can be used for purposes of cash management. A **money market mutual fund** (**MMMF**) is a mutual fund that pools the cash of thousands of investors and specializes in earning a relatively safe and high return by buying securities that have very short-term maturities, always less than 1 year. The average maturity for the portfolio of investments cannot, by law, exceed 120 days. This reduces price swings so that the money funds maintain a constant share value. The securities are bought and sold almost daily in money markets, and this results in payment of the highest daily rates available to small investors.

MMMFs are not federally insured but are still extremely safe.

Money deposited in mutual funds is not insured by the federal government. However, because of the high quality of the securities, MMMFs are considered extremely safe, and no modern money-market mutual fund has ever lost its shareholders money. Some mutual fund companies also purchase private insurance in an attempt to cover potential losses. Accounts in money-market mutual funds provide a convenient and safe place to keep money while awaiting alternative investment opportunities. Your principal is really not at risk, and you can easily get hold of your money. Chapter 18, Investing in Mutual Funds, includes more details.

Stock Brokerage Firms

A **stock brokerage firm** is a licensed financial institution that specializes in selling and buying securities. Such firms usually receive a commission for the advice and assistance they provide, and the commission is based on the buy/sell orders they execute. One of the services stock brokerage firms usually offer is a money-market mutual fund account into which clients may place monies while waiting to make investments in stocks and bonds. Money held in a money-market mutual fund at a stock brokerage firm is not insured against loss by any government agency; however, most brokerage firms purchase private insurance against such losses. Chapter 19, Buying and Selling Securities and Managing Your Portfolio, examines stock brokerage firms in detail.

Financial Services Companies

Continued government deregulation of the financial industry has not only eroded the traditional lines of business, but also has created opportunities for establishment of **financial services companies.** These are national or regional corporations that offer a great number of financial services to consumers, including the traditional checking, savings, lending, and credit cards, as well as accounts in money-market mutual funds and advice on investments, insurance, real estate, and general financial planning. These financial service institutions are also referred to as *quasi-banks* or *nonbank banks* because they provide limited traditional banking services, either accepting deposits or making commercial loans, but not both. The firm Merrill Lynch became a pioneer in the nonbank area by offering its usual brokerage services in conjunction with other financial services that it either

Financial service companies are nonbank banks.

bought outright (real estate), established a corporate relationship with (banking), or developed itself in (money market mutual funds and financial planning). The large corporations in the business are Sears, Prudential Bache, and Fidelity. Money held in a money-market mutual fund or another account at a financial services company probably is not insured against loss by the FDIC, but companies that are not insured by FDIC generally purchase private insurance against such losses.

Cash Management Tool 1: Interest-Bearing Checking Accounts

Objective
To understand criteria for choosing a checking institution as well as why it is important to have an interest-bearing checking account.

This section of the chapter focuses on having an interest-bearing checking account from which to pay for monthly living expenses. We examine the types of checking accounts, criteria to use in choosing a checking account, and how to use a checking account. Keep in mind that in addition to having an account for writing checks, you want to establish a working relationship with a financial institution so that, when appropriate, its staff can best fulfill your personal financial needs.

Types of Checking Accounts

Traditional checking accounts are technically known as **demand deposits.** This is because a financial institution must withdraw funds and make payments whenever demanded by the depositor, most often by writing a check. Current law still permits only banks to offer demand deposits, sometimes called *regular checking,* and while these accounts permit unlimited checking, they pay no interest. The Federal Reserve Board notes that about 12 percent of all bank and thrift deposits are in non-interest-bearing accounts.

There are various types of non-interest-bearing checking accounts. A **special checking account** is one that requires no minimum balance to open, does not earn interest, requires a monthly service charge and/or assesses fees for each check or transaction, and carries restrictions as to the maximum number of transactions allowed each month without additional fees. This type of account is meant for people who write few checks and keep low balances. A **regular checking account** is an account that does not pay interest and will not assess monthly and transaction fees as long as a minimum balance is maintained (it may have to be a minimum average daily balance), although it may assess charges for deposits and transactions made through an automated teller machine (ATM). (This is sometimes called a **single-balance, single-fee checking account.**)

Commercial banks, savings and loan associations, mutual savings banks, and credit unions also can offer depositors another kind of checking account, called a *negotiable order of withdrawal (NOW) account.* Monies deposited in a NOW account earn interest. When the financial institution receives a negotiable order of withdrawal—which looks just like a check—

The concept of **lifeline banking** (also called **lifeline financial services** or **basic banking**) is that banking institutions would be required to offer universal access to certain minimal financial services that every consumer must have, regardless of income, in order to function in society, such as cashing government checks without charge and offering low-cost checking accounts to low- and moderate-income consumers in their neighborhoods. To be qualified for acceptance in a lifeline program, an income and asset check would be run and how much one is able to afford would be determined. Since college students are often financially dependent on their parents, whose assets and income would be considered by a financial institution as part of the resources of the student, most do not qualify. The cost of lifeline banking accounts is extremely low, often less than $3 per month.

the funds on deposit are used to make the payment. NOW accounts are often called *interest-bearing checking accounts,* because users earn interest on their balances. Technically, NOW accounts are not demand deposits.

A **negotiable order of withdrawal,** or **NOW, account** is a checking account at a depository institution that pays interest as long as minimum-balance requirements are maintained, either consistently or as monthly or quarterly averages. NOW accounts usually pay about the same interest as passbook savings accounts, often 5 percent. Sometimes, NOW accounts pay higher interest rates on higher balances (such as $1000), but the amount up to the minimum earns only the base interest rate. This is called **tiered interest.** Rules usually specify that the NOW account will not earn interest during any month when a certain minimum balance is not maintained; plus service and maintenance fees are usually assessed. A *super NOW account* (discussed later) works the same way NOW accounts do but requires a higher minimum balance for which they pay higher tiered interest rates. A *money-market deposit account (MMDA)* (discussed later) is a government-insured money-market account offered through a depository institution, such as a bank, credit union, or savings and loan association, that pays higher interest rates but has a number of restrictions on the number of transactions. A **share draft** is the credit-union version of an interest-bearing check and it functions as a NOW account. It is called a share draft because members of a credit union technically own the organization and their deposits are called shares; accordingly, instead of earning interest, share draft accounts earn dividends. Fees for share drafts are typically lower than for checks at banks and savings and loan associations. When you write share drafts, you automatically make a carbonless copy instead of having canceled checks returned to you. Of course, you can always obtain a legal photocopy of the original, if necessary, to prove payment.

What Criteria Should You Use in Choosing a Checking Institution?

We will use the traditional term *checking* from this point on to include demand deposits, negotiable orders of withdrawal, and share drafts. The term *banking* will include commercial banks, mutual savings banks, savings and loan associations, and credit unions. In addition, you should know that the person who opens the checking account and writes the check is known as the **drawer** or **payer.** The name of the financial institution at which the account is held is the **drawee,** and the person or firm to whom the check is made out is the **payee.**

The Depository Institutions Deregulation Act of 1980 made it legal for each kind of depository institution to offer a variety of traditional banking services and compete for the business of the 88 percent of Americans who have checking accounts (writing 25 checks per month on average) and write billions of dollars worth of checks annually. With this blurring of differences, it is now more difficult for depositors to choose the best institution for their needs. For most people, five criteria can be applied: cost, safety, convenience, treatment of customers, and range of services.

Charges, Fees, and Penalties For many years, banks offered free checking, covering their expenses with other activities, such as lending. Most importantly, they also made money on their customers' checking account deposits, since, by law, interest was not paid on checking accounts. Today free checking is offered as a promotional device to bring in new customers, hoping that new customers will also want other, paid services. Many that offer free accounts have only the name of the customer preprinted on the checks even though most merchants require that the full address appear on the check. This disadvantage of some free accounts encourages customers to open another account that has all the personal information preprinted on the checks.

Banks now assess charges for each service rendered.

The trend in banking now is to assess charges for each service rendered, such as monthly service fees, per-check charges, fees to use the bank's own ATM machines, and higher fees to use other ATMs on its network. Thus institutions usually charge customers an average of just over $10 a month to maintain a checking account. Many so-called low-cost, high-interest accounts actually wind up costing consumers money because of a variety of fees, penalties, and charges, and many of these kick in if a customer does not maintain a certain minimum balance in an account. Note that three-quarters of all financial institutions do have minimum-balance requirements. Also, customers frequently have to pay for **account exceptions.** These are charges and penalties assessed on checking accounts for what the financial institution considers unusual transactions. People interested in getting their money's worth in banking would be wise to avoid as many as possible of the account exception charges shown in Table 5.2.

TABLE 5.2
Costs and Penalties on Checking (and Savings) Accounts

Account Exception	Criteria for Assessing Costs or Penalties	Assessed on Checking or Savings
Minimum account balance	A depositor's account balance falls below a set minimum balance. A set fee of $5 to $15 a month is often charged. An account could be reduced to zero.	Checking
Average account balance	A customer's average account balance falls below a set amount, such as $300. The cost varies but is usually based on a set fee, a scaled amount (the more the account falls below the average, the greater the cost), or a percentage of the amount the account falls below the average. An account could be reduced to zero.	Checking
Tiered balance	Accounts earn varying interest rates depending on the amount on deposit, such as 4.5 percent on the first $500, 5 percent on amounts above $500 to $1000, and 5.25 percent above $1000. Some institutions charge a monthly maintenance fee of $5 to $15 if the balance drops below $500.	Checking/savings
Bounced check	Costs of $10 to $20 are assessed for each check written or deposited to your account marked "insufficient funds."	Checking
Early account closing	Charges are sometimes assessed if a customer closes an account within a month or quarter of opening it. Charges range from $5 to $10.	Checking/savings
Delayed use of funds	Amounts deposited by check cannot be withdrawn until rules specify.	Checking/savings

(continued)

Table 5.3 shows typical costs for different types of checking accounts. You can pay very little for checking services with a non-interest-bearing account, and you can probably earn some interest income above the cost of checking with some type of NOW account. The task is to select the correct account for you.

Decision making gets difficult when the institution offers a NOW account in combination with either a minimum- or average-balance requirement. Check users have to consider the amount of interest the account will earn and how much of it will be offset by any occasional imposition of fees. A NOW account with no balance requirement is preferable, but rare. Realize that with a **minimum-balance account** the customer must keep a certain amount (perhaps $400) in the account throughout the time period (usually a month or a quarter) to avoid a flat service charge or fee (usually $5 to $15). With an **average-balance account,**

TABLE 5.2 (continued)

Account Exception	Criteria for Assessing Costs or Penalties	Assessed on Checking or Savings
Telephone, computer, or teller information	Costs are assessed to those who request account information by telephone, by computer, or from the teller. Typically the assessment would come after a certain number of requests have been made. This is generally set at three per month, with a cost of $.50 per telephone or teller contact. The cost of computer information would be higher, often assessed at $1 or more per request.	Checking/savings
Inactive accounts	A penalty may be assessed for inactive accounts. Usually there must be no activity for 6 months to a year before a penalty is assessed. The penalty varies, but typically it is $2 to $3 per set period. An account can be liquidated completely through these penalties.	Checking/savings
Excessive withdrawals	To discourage too many withdrawals, some savings institutions assess a penalty (ranging from $1 to $3 on those accounts where withdrawals exceed a certain number in a quarterly period.	Savings
Early withdrawal	Amounts withdrawn before the end of a quarter earn no interest for that quarter.	Savings
Deposit penalty	Deposits made during the present quarter earn no interest until the beginning of the next quarter.	Savings

a service fee is assessed only if the average daily balance of funds in the account drops below a certain amount (perhaps $300) during the time period, usually a month or a quarter. Note that some financial institutions are bundling a variety of banking services into a package for a set fee per month that permits unlimited checking in addition to a few thousand dollars of accidental death insurance, limited use of a photocopying machine, free overdraft protection, free traveler's checks, a free safe-deposit box, a no-fee bank credit card, and perhaps a few more services. Such an account may or may not be a good deal. The effective cash manager should definitely have a checking account that pays interest and that earns some net income after various fees and charges are levied.

Safety Accounts with financial institutions that are chartered by the federal government are always insured for up to $100,000. Most of the remaining state-chartered institutions are either insured for a like amount through the same federal insurance program or through a state-approved

TABLE 5.3
Types and Costs of Checking Accounts

Type of Account	Balance Required to Avoid Fees	Monthly Fees	Who Should Use It
Non-interest-bearing special account	$0	$.15–$.50 per check or deposit	People with a small amount of funds to leave on deposit and who use fewer than 10 checks a month
Non-interest-bearing regular account	$300–$500	None*	People with a sufficient amount of funds to leave on deposit but who never heard of NOW accounts
NOW account—minimum balance	$300–$1500 minimum balance on every day of the month	None*†	One who knows they will never have their balance drop below a certain minimum amount
NOW account—average balance	$300–$1500 daily average during month	None*†	One whose balance may vary throughout the month but will average a certain substantial amount

* Usually charge fees for deposits and withdrawals from ATM machines.
† Usually $5 to $15 if correct balance is not maintained.

program. However, there are still some institutions that are uninsured and should be avoided. If an uninsured institution becomes insolvent, depositors will lose part or all of their money.

In recent years, more than 200 insured financial institutions annually have been either forced out of business or permitted to merge with a financially stronger institution. Some have just gone bankrupt. Depositors with $100,000 or less per account in these failing institutions received all their money within 48 hours of closing. When the federal government assumes an institution's assets and liabilities, depositors are paid all monies due them plus previously promised interest as of the date of the closing, but they may get little or no interest during the liquidation period. When several of their state-insured financial institutions went bankrupt, the state insurance programs in Ohio and Maryland had difficulty in the mid-1980s repaying depositors. As a result, most state financial institutions now are required by state laws to purchase FDIC insurance.

The most important feature to most people is convenience.

Convenience   Convenience is often the most important factor in deciding where to open a checking account. Ask if payroll deduction and direct deposit are available. Find out if the main office, or at least a branch office, is located nearby. Does the bank have walk-up and drive-up services? Are the business hours set so that customers can make transactions before and after work and on Saturdays? Are there nearby automated teller machines (ATMs) available 24 hours a day? And, are the ATMs safe to use? Can you bank by mail? Does the institution give you immediate credit and interest on deposited checks?

Treatment of Customers   Research studies by financial institutions show that lack of courtesy is a major reason why they lose customers to competitors. Most checking account customers expect courteous service both in person and over the telephone. You need to find out the institution's reputation for providing prompt personal service, for answering questions, and for handling problems. If a financial emergency arose and you needed a few thousand dollars, would you expect your financial institution to lend it to you? When you are comparing checking institutions, ask them about how loyal they are to preferred customers. When credit is hard to get, your institution may give you priority or even a lower rate of interest (by perhaps ½ percent) on a loan.

Range of Services   Financial institutions offer a variety of services, and you should consider these in deciding where to open a checking account.

Short or No Waiting Periods for Use of Deposited Funds   All financial institutions require checking account customers to wait for certain deposited checks to clear before writing checks against those funds. **Check clearing** is the process of transferring funds from the bank, savings and loan association, or credit union upon which the check was drawn to the financial institution that accepted the deposit. Checks most likely to be subject to check-clearing delays include those written for large sums, from out-of-state, and used for an initial deposit when opening an account.

The Federal Reserve Board regulates how long banks may hold checks.

The Federal Reserve Board issued rules effective in 1988 requiring banks, savings institutions, and credit unions to meet strict deadlines in making funds from check deposits available to consumers. The law limits how long the institution can "hold" a check before crediting an account. Many institutions let their long-term customers have access to deposited funds right away, but the rules establish the following schedule: (1) funds from cash, the first $100 of any deposit of checks, cashier's check, certified check, government check, a check written on another account at the same institution, and direct deposit and other electronic credits must be made available by 9 A.M. the next business day after the day of the deposit; (2) funds from checks written on local institutions must be available the second business day after the deposit; and (3) funds from checks written on nonlocal institutions and deposits made at an automated teller machine not belonging to your institution must be available by the fifth business day after the day of the deposit. *Business days* include all days except Saturdays, Sundays, and federal holidays. These rules do not apply, however, to accounts less than 30 days old. This information must be placed at teller windows and on information available at ATMs.

Inexpensive Stop-Payment Orders   If you write a check in payment for a product you find is faulty, you may wish to issue a **stop-payment order** on the check. This ensures that the check will not be honored when presented to your financial institution. Almost all stop-payment orders do in fact stop checks from being cashed if they are issued soon enough. However, realize also that most financial institutions probably have a contract clause relieving them of responsibility in case of an oversight.

The cost for issuing a stop-payment order usually ranges from $5 to $15, and the order can last up to 6 months.

Protections Should You Write an Overdraft Some people have difficulty keeping track of how much money is in their checking account and occasionally write a **bad check,** that is, a check for which there are insufficient funds in the account. Less than 1 percent of all checks "bounce," and 60 percent of such bad checks are for amounts under $100. If you write a bad check, your financial institution can take one of four actions. First, your bank may stamp the check "insufficient funds" and return it to the payee. Your bank will charge you a fee of $5 to $30, and the payee also will probably charge a similar fee. Second, if the check amount is not too large and/or if you are a good customer, your bank might honor the check by paying it and telephoning to remind you to put the funds in the account as soon as possible. Some smaller institutions still have this policy. Third, if you have arranged for **automatic funds transfer** (**AFT**) with your bank, the necessary amount to cover the check will be transferred from your savings to your checking account. Fourth, if you have an **automatic overdraft loan** agreement with your bank (often called *check plus, check guarantee,* or *overdraft protection*), needed funds are automatically borrowed from your VISA or MasterCard account. Be careful, though, because at some institutions the loan is for more than enough to cover the overdraft. The loan may be advanced in fixed increments, say $100 or $500, when perhaps you only need $10, and you wind up paying interest on amounts not needed. You also should know that several states now allow merchants to sue bad-check writers for the amount of the original check plus a penalty of three times that sum, up to a maximum of $500.

It does help your credit rating to avoid writing bad checks. However using an automatic overdraft loan can be expensive. Suppose, for example, that a $10 charge was assessed on a check that overdrew an account by $50. A $10 fee on a $50 check is 20 percent ($10 divided by $50) for only a few days of credit. Practicing better cash management and using AFT will eliminate this problem completely.

Certified Checks to Guarantee Payment of Your Check Occasionally a merchant will take your check only if there is a guarantee that the check is good. A **certified check** is a personal check on which your financial institution imprints the word *certified,* ensuring that the account has proper funds to cover the check. In practice, the financial institution freezes that amount in the account when the check is certified and then waits for the check itself to come back before subtracting the funds. This way the institution is absolutely sure that the payer will not draw the balance in the account down below the amount certified. People who purchase certified checks, which are initialed by an officer of the financial institution, generally must pay a service charge of $2 to $5.

Cashier's Check to Guarantee a Bank's Check To be even more certain that a check is good, some merchants insist on receiving payment in the form of a **cashier's check.** This is a check drawn on the financial institution

Writing a bad check— having a check returned for insufficient funds— need never happen again.

itself and thus is backed by the drawee's finances. It is made out to a specific payee. To obtain a cashier's check, you would pay the financial institution the amount of the check and have an officer prepare and sign the check. Generally, a fee of $1 to $5 is charged.

Money Orders   Many financial institutions and the U.S. Postal Service sell money orders. A **money order** is a form of cash bought for a particular amount and signed over by the purchaser to the payee. The drawee thus guarantees payment to the payee. Money orders are usually for amounts smaller than cashier's checks, and the fee charged, usually from $.35 to $3.50, is based on the amount of the order. If you find yourself using more than two or three money orders a month, you should probably open a checking account.

Traveler's Checks   Cashing a personal check in a distant city is usually most difficult. **Traveler's checks** are checks that are issued by large financial institutions (such as American Express, VISA, and Carte Blanche) and sold through various institutions such as local banks or credit unions. Traveler's checks are accepted almost everywhere. Purchasers pay a typical fee of 1 percent of the amount of the traveler's checks, or $1 per $100. Sometimes this fee is waived by the seller if you are a regular customer. The checks come in selected denominations ($10, $20, $50, and $100) and should be immediately signed once by the purchaser. To cash a traveler's check, the purchaser need only fill in the name of the payee, date the check, and sign it for a second time. All traveler's check companies guarantee replacement if the serial numbers of lost checks are identified.

Automatic Payment of Bills   You can direct your financial institution to pay certain recurring bills, such as mortgage payments, local taxes, and utilities, by telling the bank to transfer funds electronically. Some institutions permit customers to telephone directly into their own bank accounts to direct that payments be made by computer.

Safe-Deposit Boxes to Safeguard Valuables   Most commercial banks have **safe-deposit boxes,** which are metal boxes that are locked inside the bank vault and can be rented for $10 to $150 annually. You can safely store jewelry, stocks, bonds, copies of wills, insurance policies, and other valuables in a safe-deposit box. It is extremely rare for burglars to get into a bank's safe deposit boxes. In such instances, the bank is not liable unless there was gross negligence. A married couple should put their safe-deposit box in both names, so that in case of the death of one person, the other will have access to its contents. Otherwise, the box contents become part of the estate of the deceased, which sometimes cannot be touched for several days or even months.

Be sure your safe-deposit box is in both names if you are married.

Trust Services When Needed   A **trustee** manages the financial assets of another. The will of a deceased person might establish a particular bank as a trustee to carefully distribute the estate to the heirs. Occasionally, trusts are established to oversee the finances of a minor. Fees for these services range widely, and the trust departments of large banks often manage many millions of dollars of other people's assets.

How to Use a Checking Account to Your Advantage

There are numerous benefits to having a checking account. There is no need to carry much cash, and it is more convenient and less expensive to pay bills by mailing a check rather than traveling all over town to make payments. Some people prefer to use checks rather than credit, since the check represents an immediate cash payment. Having a checking account also helps in budgeting because a written record of each check may be kept in an accompanying check register. Similarly, the canceled check provides proof of payment and a tax record. Use of a checking account through an ATM machine typically provides a printed receipt; however, these are easier to lose than canceled checks.

Open the Best Account for You: Individual or Joint   The process of opening a checking (or savings) account requires that you fill out forms giving the financial institution certain required personal information, complete some signature cards, and make your first deposit. After filling out some personal information forms, the next step in opening an account is completing a **signature card,** which provides verification of the saver's signature and which can be compared against withdrawal slips in the future. Once you make an initial deposit, you will be assigned an account number.

You also have to decide whether to open a separate or joint account. An **individual account** has one owner who is solely responsible for the account and its activity. A **joint account** or **joint tenancy account with right of survivorship** may be opened by two or more people, whether related or not. It lets each owner have access to the account, and both are responsible separately and collectively for deposits and withdrawals. Both must sign the signature card, and the financial institution will honor checks or withdrawal slips with *either* signature. An advantage of a joint account is that in the case of death, and regardless of provisions in a will, the funds automatically transfer by contract to the surviving account holder, who can have immediate access to the funds. It might take several months for an estate to be settled and the monies in an individual account released to the deceased person's spouse. A joint account is particularly attractive for married couples sharing a checking or savings account.

A disadvantage of a joint account is that one person can withdraw all the money in the account without the other knowing; therefore, some couples decide to have individual accounts. For the tightest control, a couple can open an account where both signatures are required for withdrawals. This **tenancy in common account** requires that both owners sign a withdrawal slip or check before it can be honored by the savings institution, thus preventing withdrawals by one owner without the knowledge of the other. Funds in this account do not pass automatically to the

Not one but two signatures can be required for the tightest control over spending.

surviving joint account holder after the death of one owner and may be disposed of by a will.

Note further that a **minor's account** can be opened with the permission of a parent or guardian when a child is not old enough to sign his or her name. In this type of account, the minor is the owner of the account and is the legal earner of the interest or dividends paid on the account. A **trustee account** may be set up by an adult for a child, and with this the child is restricted from withdrawing money from the account without the adult's signature. Many parents set up trustee accounts for their children; however, the adult is responsible for the account's activity, and any earnings generated from the account are income for the adult.

Make Safe Endorsements   **Endorsement** is the process of writing on the back of a check as evidence of the legal transfer of its ownership, especially in return for the amount on the face of the check. When you sign, or endorse, the back of a check written to you, it can then be either cashed or deposited. A check with a **blank endorsement** simply has the payee's signature on the back. Since such a check becomes a *bearer instrument* permitting anyone to cash it if it is lost or stolen, you should be wise by not making a blank endorsement prior to depositing or cashing a check. A **special endorsement** can be used to limit who can cash a check by writing "Pay to the order of [name]" on the back along with your signature. A special endorsement can easily be put on a check you receive that you want to sign over to another. Of course, this becomes a *two-party check*, which is difficult to cash except by depositing it in an account at a financial institution. A **restrictive endorsement** uses the phrase "For deposit only" written on the back along with the signature, and it authorizes the financial institution only to accept the check as a deposit to an account. Checks deposited by mail should always be endorsed this way.

Under authorization from the Expedited Funds Availability Act, the Federal Reserve Board issued strict guidelines in 1988 on where endorsements may be placed. The regulations require that all payee endorsements must be within 1½ inch of the **trailing edge** of the check. This is the left edge as you look at the front of the check. Consumers are to use that edge to determine the maximum amount for the endorsement area. This endorsement area must be used for all information, such as identification information and subsequent endorsements. If anything is put outside the 1½-inch limit, it may cause the check to be returned and fees to be assessed.

Use Float to Your Advantage   For an out-of-state payment, it could take from 4 to 12 days for the check to clear the original check writer's bank. The amount of time involved, called **float,** is the time the check writer actually has the funds in his or her local account until the check finally clears. Float is valuable, because it earns money in the form of interest for check writers who have their funds in an interest-bearing account. For a check written to a local business, the float is reduced to perhaps 1 to 2 days, since the check clearing is handled by a local check-clearing company or bank serving in that capacity.

What If You Want to Reconcile Your Checking Account?

The task in account reconciliation is to compare the financial institution's records with the check writer's. Most checking account holders receive, as shown in the following figure, monthly statements that itemize their checking transactions. Typically, the financial institution also returns checks and deposit slips. (To reduce costs, some financial institutions practice **check truncation**, which means they do not return actual checks, or even deposit slips, unless they are specifically requested and a fee is paid by the check writer.) It is important to reconcile the account soon after you receive your monthly statement to avoid the extra mathematics of having numerous **outstanding checks** (checks written but presented for payment too late to appear on the statement). Research suggests that only about half the population balances their checkbooks every month, and another one-quarter never balance them.

Most errors in account reconciliation come from two sources: (1) failure of the check writer to add and subtract correctly and (2) failure of the check writer to subtract from the check register certain charges of the financial institution (such as account activity fees, stop-payment charges, and costs for printing checks) or to add interest earned (on interest-bearing accounts).

Follow these steps in reconciling your checking account:

1. Place the checks in order by check number or issue date. Many financial institutions arrange the checks on the monthly statement in sequence as well. See the accompanying figure for an example of this.

2. Compare the canceled checks with the information in your check register to look for any recording errors. Place a checkmark by each correct amount in the check register.

3. In the check register, subtract any charges that appear on the monthly statement; also, add any interest earned.

4. List all outstanding checks, those which have been written but which were not presented for payment in time to appear on the statement. Total the amount.

5. Compare your deposit slips with the deposits listed on the statement and with deposit amounts noted in the check register. List **outstanding deposits** (amounts deposited too late to be included on the statement). Total the amount.

6. Finally, the moment of truth. Take the balance of the account as shown on the statement, add any outstanding deposits (from step 5), and subtract any outstanding checks (from step 4). The resulting amount should be the same as the amount in the check register. If not, first find out if you have committed the common error of reconciliation—*transposing digits,* such as 786 for 876. This will show up if the difference between your balance and the bank's is divisible by 9. If so, seek and locate the transposition. If not, recheck the arithmetic and carefully follow these six steps again. As a last resort, an officer at the financial institution can, usually for a fee, assist you in balancing your account.

(continued)

What If You Want to Reconcile
Your Checking Account? *(continued)*

Sample Monthly Statement
Courtesy of Bank of Lexington & Trust Company.

BANK OF LEXINGTON
& TRUST COMPANY

251 WEST VINE STREET • LEXINGTON, KENTUCKY 40507-1613
MEMBER FDIC

John J. Johnson
1 Smith Street
Lexington, Kentucky 43211

16 ENC

DIRECT INQUIRIES ON ELECTRONIC DEBITS AND CREDITS
TO (606) 253-0511 OR WRITE TO ABOVE ADDRESS
NOTICE: SEE REVERSE SIDE FOR IMPORTANT INFORMATION.

STATEMENT OF ACCOUNTS

CUSTOMER NUMBER	PAGE NUMBER
12–345–67	PAGE 1

STATEMENT PERIOD	
FROM	TO
8–15–90	9–12–90

ACCOUNT NUMBER BALANCE FORWARD	NUMBER OF CREDITS	TOTAL CREDITS	NUMBER OF DEBITS	TOTAL DEBITS	FEE	CLOSING BALANCE
01 INT. BEARING						
8,575.86	2	534.17	15	1,250.33	.00	7,859.70

01   INT. BEARING

DATE	DESCRIPTION				AMOUNT	DAILY BALANCE	
8-31	DEPOSIT				500.00	8-20	8,279.37
9-12	INTEREST PAID THRU DATE INDICATED				34.17	8-21	8,191.69
						8-22	7,912.69

CHECK NO.	DATE	AMOUNT	CHECK NO.	DATE	AMOUNT		
	8-28	28.44	5630	8-21	46.58	8-28	7,884.25
5631	8-20	12.53	5632	8-21	41.10	8-29	7,855.25
5633	8-20	283.96	5634	8-22	79.00	8-30	7,815.25
5635	8-31	60.82	5636	8-22	200.00	8-31	8,254.43
* 5638	9-04	7.00	5639	8-29	29.00	9-04	8,247.43
5640	8-30	40.00	5641	9-06	100.00	9-06	8,147.43
* 5643	9-10	79.00	5644	9-10	42.90	9-07	7,947.43
5645	9-07	200.00				9-10	7,825.53
						9-12	7,859.70

Cash Management Tool 2: Savings Accounts

After you have established an interest-bearing checking account to assist in payment of your monthly living expenses, the next phase of cash management is to consider opening a savings account. The major benefits of opening a savings account at a nearby financial institution are that it will provide you with a local source of emergency cash and will serve as a personal financial reference if ever needed.

Savings are considered time deposits rather than demand deposits. **Time deposits** are savings that are expected to remain on deposit in a financial institution for an extended period, and they are legal debts upon which the institution must pay interest as specified. (Technically, commercial banks pay interest on savings deposits, while other financial institutions pay dividends.) Institutions usually have a rule requiring that savings account holders give 30 to 60 days' notice for withdrawals, although this is seldom enforced. Some time deposits, however, are **fixed-time deposits**, which specify a period that the savings must be left on deposit, such as 6 months or 3 years; this is the case with certificates of deposit (CDs), discussed later in this chapter. In contrast, money in the form of demand deposits, such as checking accounts, must by law be paid immediately when demanded by the account holder. The types of local financial institutions that generally handle time deposits are banks, savings and loan associations, mutual savings banks, and credit unions. Below we examine how much to save, types of savings accounts, and techniques to calculate and compare the rate of return on savings accounts.

How Much Money Should You Save?

Personal savings in the United States averages about 4 to 6 percent of disposable personal income or take-home pay. Those with higher incomes generally save a greater proportion of income than those with lower incomes. People in many other countries save more. The British save about 11 percent; the French, about 15 percent; and the Japanese, about 18 percent. Reasons why Americans do not save much include a propensity to spend, easy access to credit, having to spend such a large proportion of income on housing (including its financing costs), shortage of government incentives to save, lack of personal discipline to save, and the extreme difficulty or impossibility to save when starting a household.

Americans do not save as much as people in many other countries.

Traditionally, many financial advisors have advocated that people should have two and one-half to three times their monthly take-home pay set aside as savings in readily accessible demand or time deposits. This is to serve as an emergency fund in case of job layoff, long illness, or other serious financial calamity. If your take-home pay is $1700 a month and you follow this suggestion, you would need to have $4250 to $5100 in savings.

Most people do not find it appropriate to keep such an amount in a local financial institution for four reasons. First, regular accounts usually have such a low interest rate (typically 5 percent) that they provide poor protection against inflation. (A study by *Consumer Reports* magazine revealed that banks and savings and loan associations pay an interest rate of about 5¼ percent on regular savings accounts, while credit unions pay about 6 percent.) Second, higher rates of interest generally can be obtained by placing such substantial savings amounts in long-term, fixed-time deposits or in nonlocal financial institutions. Third, people usually have ready access to credit when needed for emergencies. Fourth, people today typically feel that they have adequate job security as well as sufficient medical and disability insurance coverages to eliminate or greatly cushion the financial impact of such calamities.

Individual circumstances vary, of course, and some people definitely need to have a substantial emergency fund. Employed people with good job security and fringe benefits need to determine for themselves how much money they should set aside for emergencies in a local financial institution.

Types of Savings Accounts

Financial institutions offer various savings accounts to meet people's individual wants and needs. The process for opening a savings account is similar to that for a checking account. A regular savings account costs nothing to open and is offered in two forms: regular and club accounts.

Regular Account   A **regular savings account** is an account in a depository institution that permits frequent deposit or withdrawal of funds and assesses no fees as long as a low minimum balance ($1 to $50) is maintained. It has the fewest restrictions and is the simplest for most savers to use. A regular savings account is sometimes called a *passbook savings account* or a *statement account.*

Regular savings accounts include passbook and statement accounts.

The term *passbook* refers to the bank book in which the customer records transactions. Historically, the bank entered the balance and interest payments in the saver's record, a small booklet or passbook, hence the name *passbook savings account.* Not all banks issue passbooks today, even if they offer what they call passbook accounts. Today, many banks have substituted the *statement account,* which provides a printed monthly or quarterly financial statement from the bank. Statement account holders are provided printed receipts to indicate the account transactions, and transactions usually can be accessed through 24-hour ATMs.

Club Account   The **club account,** a form of regular savings account, is used to deposit money for a special purpose, such as saving for vacations, holidays, school, gift buying, or other reasons. For example, many people save in a Christmas club account. The amount deposited is generally quite small, ranging from $2 to $10 per week. The club account is offered in part to help discipline many heretofore nonsavers. It encourages saving on a regular basis because the amount to be saved is not large. Unfortunately, most club accounts do not pay much interest. A club account is usually not needed after a saver has launched a sound financial plan and budget.

Techniques to Calculate and Compare Rates of Return on Savings Accounts

You would think that if a savings institution advertises an interest rate of 6 percent, you would earn more interest income there than at another financial institution advertising a rate of 5.75 percent. This may or may not be true. The difficult task for wise money managers is to calculate the **yield,** the rate of return on an investment, reported as a percentage and stated in an annualized basis. The yield is what you shop for, not the simple interest rate. The percentage yield is higher because it includes the result of compounding the interest left on deposit over a specified time period.

There are literally thousands of ways to calculate interest yields, and the industry is sometimes embarrassed by the complexity. In fact, many financial institutions now support a proposed Truth-in-Savings Act in which the "cents per $100 per day" or other standardized periodic percentage rate is reported. The right question to ask is, "If I give you this much money today, how much will I have in the account at the end of the term, that is, after all penalties and fees?" Even bankers have trouble answering this question, so until clarifications in the law occur, you must examine the major factors affecting the return on savings deposits (how interest is calculated, method of determining the savings balance, grace periods, and costs and penalties) to obtain meaningful disclosure of factors affecting interest earned.

The **nominal rate of interest** (or **stated rate of interest**) is the apparent interest rate that is applied to deposits before consideration of the time period, method of determining the savings balance, grace periods, and other costs and penalties. This is often the advertised interest rate. What you actually earn on your deposits is an **effective rate of interest,** which is the actual rate at which deposits earn interest after consideration of all interest calculation variables, costs, and penalties. Comparison shopping could earn you an extra $15 to $30 a year on a $1500 account balance.

What is really important is the effective rate of interest on savings.

How Interest Is Calculated   The calculation of interest to be paid on deposits in financial institutions is primarily based on four variables: how much money is on deposit (the balance), the interest rate applied (the nominal rate), the method of determining the balance, and the frequency of compounding (annually, semiannually, quarterly, weekly, daily). With annual compounding, the amount of interest income earned on $1000 left on deposit in a savings account paying 6 percent annual nominal interest is calculated as follows for the first year: $1000 × 1.06 × 1 = $1060. After 2 years, the savings would be worth $1123.60 ($1000 × 1.06 first year = $1060; $1060 × 1.06 second year = $1123.60). The compounding process would continue for each annual interest period. This example illustrates the discussion presented in Chapter 1 on the time value of money. The future value *FV* formula is shown here, where *i* represents the nominal interest rate for each interest period (expressed as a decimal) and n represents the number of compounding periods.

$$FV = (\text{sum of money})(1.0 + i)^n \qquad (5.1)$$

Substituting the data in the illustration in Equation (5.1) reveals the same answer:

$$\$1123.60 = (\$1000)(1.0 + 0.06)^2$$

If the amount were compounded *quarterly* (every 3 months) for the 2 years, the substitutions in the equation would be (1) i is 0.015 because the 6 percent rate is paid quarterly and therefore must be divided by four annual quarters, and (2) n is 8 because over 2 years there are 8 quarters of time. The equation is

$$\$1126.49 = (\$1000)(1.0 + 0.015)^8$$

Table 5.4 uses the same data and provides an illustration of quarterly versus annual compound interest. You should note four points: (1) you earn more interest on your deposited funds when compounding is used, (2) the effective rate is the same as the nominal rate when interest is compounded annually, (3) the more frequent the compounding, the greater is the effective return, and (4) the fullest value of compounding is realized over longer time periods, since phenomenal differences occur. This is further depicted in Table 5.5.

Method of Determining Savings Account Balance   Financial institutions calculate earnings on the balances in depositors' accounts in four different ways: FIFO (first in, first out), LIFO (last in, first out), low-balance, and day of deposit to day of withdrawal (DDDW). Each method has advantages and disadvantages to a depositor.

FIFO   Under the **FIFO (first-in, first-out) method,** withdrawals are first deducted from the balance at the start of the interest period and then, if this balance is not sufficient, from later deposits. This erodes the base on which the interest is figured. It means automatically losing interest on money on deposit early in the interest period if it is withdrawn. Few institutions still use this method.

Table 5.6 illustrates a hypothetical case of a savings account with various deposits and withdrawals over the quarter from July 1 to September 30. Below the example are shown the interest calculations for each of the four methods used. The FIFO method would earn only $39.29 for this saver.

LIFO   Under the **LIFO (last-in, first-out) method,** withdrawals are first deducted from the most recent deposits and then from the less recent ones, and so on. The LIFO method does not penalize savers as much as the FIFO method does. In the case cited in Table 5.6, a total of $50.22 would be earned under the LIFO method. Few institutions still use this method.

TABLE 5.4
Illustration of Quarterly versus Annual Compound Interest ($1000 Deposit at 6 Percent Rate)

	Quarterly	Annually
First year		
First quarter	$1000.00 earns $15.00, totaling $1015.00	
Second quarter	$1015.00 earns $15.23, totaling $1030.23	
Third quarter	$1030.23 earns $15.45, totaling $1045.68	
Fourth quarter	$1045.68 earns $15.69, totaling $1061.37	
End of first year	$1000.00 earns $61.37, totaling $1061.37	$1000.00 earns $60.00, totaling $1060.00
Second year		
Fifth quarter	$1061.37 earns $15.92, totaling $1077.29	
Sixth quarter	$1077.29 earns $16.16, totaling $1093.45	
Seventh quarter	$1093.45 earns $16.40, totaling $1109.85	
Eighth quarter	$1109.85 earns $16.64, totaling $1126.49	
End of second year	$1061.37 earns $65.12, totaling $1126.49	$1060.00 earns $63.60, totaling $1123.60

TABLE 5.5
Effects of Compounding of Future Value of $1000 at 6 Percent Interest

Years	Annually	Compounding Period		
		Quarterly	*Weekly*	*Daily*
1	$1060	$1061.37	$1061.80	$1061.83
2	1124	1126.49	1127.42	1127.49
3	1191	1195.62	1197.09	1197.20
4	1262	1268.99	1271.07	1271.22
5	1338	1346.85	1349.62	1349.83
10	1791	1814.02	1821.49	1822.03
15	2397	2443.22	2458.33	2459.43
20	3207	3290.66	3317.82	3319.80
25	4292	4432.04	4477.81	4481.15

TABLE 5.6
Methods of Determining Savings Account Balances for Interest Calculations

| Date | Savings Account Activity | | |
	Deposits	Withdrawals	Balance
July 1	$2000		$2000
July 12	2500		4500
Aug. 8	1000		5500
Aug. 15	500		6000
Sept. 5		$1000	5000
Sept. 15		500	4500
Sept. 30		1000	3500

Methods of Determining Balance for Interest Calculation*

FIFO (first-in, first-out) method

$2000 × 0.06 × 81/365 = $26.63
1000 × 0.06 × 54/365 = 8.88
500 × 0.06 × 46/365 = 3.78

Total interest, FIFO: $39.29

LIFO (last-in, first-out) method

$2000 × 0.06 × 92/365 = $30.25
1500 × 0.06 × 81/365 = 19.97

Total interest, LIFO: $50.22

Low-balance method

$2000 × 0.06 × 92/365 = $30.25

Total interest, low balance: $30.25

Day of deposit to day of withdrawal (DDDW) method

$2000 × 0.06 × 92/365 = $30.25
2500 × 0.06 × 81/365 = 33.29
1000 × 0.06 × 54/365 = 8.88
500 × 0.06 × 46/365 = 3.78
−1000 × 0.06 × 26/365 = −4.27
−500 × 0.06 × 16/365 = −1.32
−1000 × 0.06 × 1/365 = −0.16

Total interest, DDDW: $70.45

* Using 6 percent and 365 days, with earnings including the day of deposit.

Low-Balance   Under the **low-balance method,** interest is paid only on the least amount of money that was in the account during the interest period. This method, which discourages withdrawals, is the most unprofitable for the saver. It provides earnings of only $30.25 for the saver in our hypothetical case. Low-balance methods are rarely used by banks but often used by credit unions.

The DDDW method is best for savers.

DDDW   The **day of deposit to day of withdrawal (DDDW) method** is a way of determining and calculating account balances daily. The majority of banks and savings and loan associations now use it. Each deposit earns interest for the total number of days it was actually in the institution. When withdrawals occur, interest is earned for the number of days the money remained before the day of withdrawal.

This method is costlier for the institutions, but it is the fairest for savers. In our hypothetical case, the saver would earn $70.45 under the DDDW method. With daily compounding, it provides the highest return of any of the methods used. Given the same nominal interest rates, savers should choose an institution using daily interest calculation methods.

Grace Periods   A **grace period** is the time period in days in which deposits or withdrawals can be made and still earn interest on savings from a given day of the interest period. Generally, a 10- to 15-day grace period is allowed for deposits. This means, for example, that if deposits are made by the tenth day of the month, interest will be earned from the first of the month.

For withdrawals, the grace period is more limited but generally ranges from 3 to 5 days. A saver might withdraw money from an account within 3 to 5 days of the end of the interest period and yet earn interest as if the money were in the account for the entire period. Wisely using a grace period increases a saver's real return. To illustrate, suppose you deposited $600 at 6 percent per year in a savings account on June 10. Normally, without a grace period, you would earn monthly interest of $2 ($600 $\times$ 0.06 $\times$ 20/360). With a grace period (deposits made by the tenth will earn from the first), you would earn $3 ($600 $\times$ 0.06 $\times$ 30/360). It is important to check with a savings institution to see if such a grace period is available. However, as more institutions adopt daily account balance and compounding procedures, the use of grace periods will diminish.

Savings Account Charges, Fees, and Penalties   Many charges, fees, and penalties are triggered when the customer fails to maintain a certain minimum balance in a savings account. Some institutions advertise high interest rates and then require depositors to keep an average daily balance of $1000 before crediting a dime's worth of interest. Other institutions pay 5 or 6 percent on that part of the balance over $1000 but zero on the other portion of the balance from $0 to $1000. And some hit depositors with a $10-a-month maintenance fee whenever the account balance drops below $1000. Since the Federal Reserve Board reports that 60 percent of regular savings accounts have less than $500 on deposit, it appears that the banking industry is interested in discouraging small savers from saving.

The wise money manager tries to avoid charges, fees, and penalties.

Costs and penalties frequently assessed on savings accounts are what savings institutions categorize as account exceptions. The wise money manager tries to be alert and avoid them. Table 5.2, presented earlier, lists these account exceptions along with the generally accepted criteria for assessing the costs or penalties. The costs and penalties noted here can be excessive and may be more important than small differences in interest rates. They are crucial factors that you need to examine when you are choosing a place to save money. If you can find a savings institution that charges low costs and penalties, it may be a suitable place to have a savings account. Follow these rules on where to open your savings account: (1) get interest calculated using the day of deposit to day of withdrawal method, (2) get daily compounding, (3) get the highest stated interest rate, and (4) choose an account that has account exceptions you can avoid.

What If You Are Considering Opening a Savings Account?

Recognizing that there is a wide choice of financial institutions with which to deposit money and that the proliferation of savings options has made it confusing for consumers, the Consumer Federation of America has created a list of seven factors to consider in assessing savings options:

1. *Yield:* How much do I earn on my deposit? Is the yield set at a fixed rate, or does it change with market rates?

2. *Liquidity:* To what extent are my funds available for withdrawal? Is there a penalty for early withdrawal? Am I limited as to the amount or number of times I can make withdrawals?

3. *Safety:* How safe is my deposit? Is it insured by an agency of the federal government, or by some other agency?

4. *Minimum deposit:* What is the minimum deposit required to open and maintain the account? What is the minimum required to earn to maximum yield and avoid charges?

5. *Convenience:* How much trouble is it to open, maintain, and close the account? Can this be done by phone, correspondence, or bank machine?

6. *Charges:* Are there one-time or periodic service charges? Am I charged for each deposit or withdrawal?

7. *Other services:* Does the account provide additional benefits such as check writing privileges or the ability to transfer funds between accounts?

Cash Management Tool 3: Money Market Accounts

Objective
To realize the importance of placing excess funds in a money-market account.

Most people establish their checking and savings accounts at local financial institutions as the cornerstones of their cash management efforts. They earn interest on both accounts. When income begins to exceed expenses regularly, perhaps by $200 or $300 a month, a substantial amount of excess funds can quickly build up. This is a comfortable situation to be sure; however, it is also wise from a cash management point of view to move excess funds to an account that pays the highest possible interest rate. Why earn only 5½ percent on your money when 7 or 8 percent or more might be earned simply by opening a money market account?

Money market account is a generic term describing a variety of high-interest-earning accounts (compared with regular savings accounts) that offer some limited check-writing privileges. Such accounts usually have daily compounding and are offered by banks, savings and loan associations, credit unions, stock brokerage firms, financial services companies, mutual funds, and other financial institutions. The types of money market accounts include super NOW accounts, money market deposit accounts, money market mutual funds, sweep accounts, and cash management accounts.

Super NOW Accounts

A **super NOW account** is a government-insured type of money market account offered through depository institutions as a high-interest NOW account with unlimited checking privileges. The initial minimum deposit ranges from $1000 to $2500, and yields are calculated weekly or monthly. If the average balance falls below a set amount, such as $1000, the account reverts to earning interest at the lower rate offered on a regular NOW account. Depositors can withdraw their funds (using checks, ATM machines, or electronic transfers) at any time without penalty. Rates are typically 1 to 1½ percent higher than those paid on interest-bearing NOW checking accounts and passbook savings accounts.

Money Market Deposit Accounts

MMDAs are insured by the federal government.

A **money market deposit account** (**MMDA**) is a government-insured money market account offered through a depository institution, such as a bank, credit union, or savings and loan association, that has minimum-balance requirements and tiered interest rates that vary with the size of the account balance and pays higher interest rates than other bank accounts. Account holders typically are limited to six transactions per month, three checks and three automatic transfers, before withdrawal fees are assessed. Transactions can be in any amount. Institutions are allowed to establish fees for transactions and maintenance. Each account is insured by the appropriate federal agency (FDIC or NCUSIF) for $100,000. Depositors can withdraw their cash at any time using checks, ATM machines, or electronic transfers. Often $500 to $1000 must be deposited to open an account, with no minimums on additional deposits.

Should the average monthly balance in an MMDA fall below a certain sum, such as $1000 or the norm of $2500, the entire account earns interest at the rate of a regular NOW account, which is likely to be about 5 percent. For this reason, money market deposit accounts are sometimes called *tiered-interest accounts.*

Depositors consider placing cash reserves in this type of fund for the high rate of return and the convenience of local transactions.[1] The interest rates paid may be 1¼ to 2 percent higher than passbook savings rates and perhaps ½ to 2 percent less than the best-managed money market mutual funds (discussed below), but many depositors like the extra margin of safety offered by these government-insured accounts.

Money Market Mutual Funds

A *money market mutual fund (MMMF)* is a money market account in a mutual fund (rather than a bank) that pools the cash of thousands of investors and specializes in earning a relatively safe and high return by buying securities that have very short-term maturities, always less than 1

[1] American Express has introduced its "Membership Savings" program for its members. This encourages cardholders to designate a portion of their payment for savings in the company's associated FDIC insured money market deposit account.

year. These securities are bought and sold almost daily in money markets. A *money market* is an auction at which borrowers and lenders bid over the price of cash-equivalent assets by buying and selling short-term debt instruments in million dollar denominations, including U.S. Treasury bills, commercial paper (corporate debt obligations), other credit agreements issued by financially top-rated companies, and bank certificates of deposit. By staggering the maturities of these large denomination securities, individual accounts in the money market mutual fund can earn the current cost of money on invested funds. Most money managers keep the average maturity of their holdings (the point at which the debts become due) to less than 60 days. Interest is paid at a rate that varies daily, there are usually no restrictions on check writing, and usually there are no restrictions on or penalties for withdrawals. This results in payment of the highest daily rates available to small investors.

Money market mutual funds typically pay the highest rate of return that can be earned on a daily basis, often 1 to 2 percent more than money market deposit accounts. An investor who keeps $4000 in a regular account at a local financial institution might earn $240 interest annually, while the person with that amount in a money market mutual fund could well earn $360, for a difference of $120 ($360 − $240). Interest fluctuates daily and in recent years has ranged from 6 to 11 percent. Money market mutual funds are convenient to use for special financial needs because checks can be drawn on the account. The minimum check limit is often $200, which discourages use of a money market mutual fund as a normal checking account. Electronic transfers are permitted too, but ATM machines cannot be used because MMMF are not depository institutions.

Some money market mutual funds buy only U.S. government securities and therefore are virtually risk-free, paying a return slightly lower than the other MMMFs. Another group of MMMFs invests only in tax-free securities, which earn lower yields but pay tax-free returns to depositors. MMMFs require a minimum deposit of from $500 to $1000, and a service fee is charged (for management, advertising, and postage costs), which averages .007 of the value of the account per year. To open a money market mutual fund account, you only need to contact a mutual fund company; details are provided in Chapter 18, Investing in Mutual Funds.

Sweep Accounts

Interest in a sweep account comes from a NOW account and a MMMF.

A **sweep account** is a money market account that automatically sweeps any deposits, interest, or dividends into either a regular NOW account or a money market mutual fund so that they will immediately begin to generate more interest. Banks, credit unions, savings and loan associations, credit-card companies (such as American Express and MasterCard), brokerage firms, and a few insurance companies provide variations of sweep accounts. The essence of sweep accounts is that an investor's money flows between a NOW checking account and a money market mutual fund, depending on the balance in the NOW account, and earns interest accordingly. For example, assume that the institution requires an initial deposit of $3500. A target amount, perhaps $2500, goes into the NOW checking account, where it earns perhaps 5 percent. The remaining portion, $1000, goes into a money market mutual fund, where it earns current market rates, which might be 8 percent. Thus it is a tiered account.

Account rules vary among institutions, but a sweep occurs whenever the balance goes above or below specific minimum or maximum amounts. On an account with a $2500 target, the minimum might be $2400 and the maximum $2600. A **sweep** is an automatic transfer of funds into or out of the sweep account's money market mutual fund. This may occur daily or twice a week. If the investor above makes a deposit of $75, it will bring the NOW account balance to $2575, which is not enough to trigger a sweep. With a subsequent deposit of $300, the balance rises to $2875. Then the institution sweeps all the funds in excess of the $2500 target ($375) into the money market mutual fund.

Checks written are drawn from the NOW account. If the account is drawn down to less than the minimum, sufficient funds are taken from the money market mutual fund to bring the balance back up to the target amount. For example, a sweep account with a balance of $4000 would have $2500 in the NOW account and $1500 in the money market mutual fund. A $500 check would draw the NOW account down to $2000 ($2500 target minus the $500 check), and the institution would sweep $500 from the money market mutual fund into the NOW account to maintain the target balance. The result of the transaction would be $2500 in the NOW checking account and $1000 in the money market mutual fund, for a sweep account balance of $3500.

Charges vary on sweep accounts. Some have a monthly and/or annual fee, and others have a one-time initiation fee. Most institutions charge a transaction fee for each sweep. In such instances, the fees and transaction charges may offset the gains of having this type of account.

Cash Management Accounts

A **cash management account** (CMA) is a multiple-purpose money-market account that provides the same services as sweep accounts and more as it gathers most of your financial transactions into a unified account and reports them on a single statement. It offers a checking account, money-market mutual fund, stock brokerage account, a credit card, and a debit card in one coordinated package. CMAs (also known as *central asset accounts*) are offered through brokerage firms, financial institutions, retailers, and mutual funds. A CMA offered through one of the financial services companies allows you to conduct all your financial business under one roof. The required minimum to open an account is $1000 or more. One monthly statement conveniently serves as a written record of all transactions, as Figure 5.2 illustrates.

The CMA rules usually determine what happens when deposits and withdrawals occur.

A computer program monitors and manages each account according to a predetermined set of rules. For example, say you open a CMA with $2000 in cash and $8000 in securities (stocks and bonds). The $8000 amount goes to the securities account, and the cash is swept into a money-market mutual fund to earn current high market rates. Cash from stock dividends or from sales of stock go into the money-market mutual fund

FIGURE 5.2
Cash Management Account Statement

CASH MANAGEMENT ACCOUNT

Kathy Amos
123 Main Street
Anytown, USA 01234

Date of Statement: March 1, 1991

Account Number: 01234567891

ACTIVITY IN ACCOUNT DURING MONTH OF FEBRUARY

Date	Activity	Description	Price	Amount	Cash Balance
1-31	OPENING BALANCE		-	-	11,481.40
2-03	Bought	Cash Mgt Acct	1.00	1,000.00	12,481.40
2-06	VISA	Sheraton-Miami	-	310.00	12,171.40
2-09	Bought	ATT shares	77.50	7,750.00	4,421.40
2-13	Bought	Cash Mgt Acct	1.00	1,000.00	5,421.40
2-17	VISA	Gourmet Rest	-	90.00	5,331.40
2-22	Sold	ATT shares	84.50	8,450.00	13,781.40
2-22	Cash Div	Cash Mgt Acct	-	71.80	13,853.20
2-22	Check	Bandy Chevrolet	-	240.00	13,613.20
2-26	Cash Div	Aetna shares	-	60.00	13,673.20
2-26	Bought	Kraft shares	48.50	4,850.00	8,823.20
2-27	Check	VISA	-	1,200.00	7,623.20
2-28	Cash Div	Cash Mgt Acct	-	13.60	7,636.80
2-28	CLOSING BALANCE		-	-	7,636.80

SUMMARY OF PORTFOLIO

Quantity Long	Quantity Short	Description	Month End Price	Est Value	Est Ann Yield	Est Ann Income
200		IBM	46.00	9,200	2.10	193
100		Kraft	48.50	4,850	3.10	150
300		Aetna	33.00	9,900	2.40	238
CLOSING BALANCE FOR SECURITIES				23,950		481

SUMMARY OF SECURITY TRANSACTIONS IN FEBRUARY

Date	Activity	Description	Price	Amount
2-09	Bought	ATT shares	77.50	7,750
2-22	Sold	ATT shares	84.50	8,450 CR
2-26	Bought	Kraft shares	48.50	4,850

automatically. Large withdrawals of cash come first from any money in the money-market mutual fund, then from selling the contents of the securities account or from the line of credit. Any deposit reduces a loan balance automatically even if the investor wants to keep the loan balance outstanding while adding to the money-market mutual fund. Note that CMAs may be swept daily or weekly; in the latter case, recently deposited money may not earn interest for several days. Some CMAs can code checks for budgeting purposes, as discussed in Chapter 4, Budgeting and Cash-Flow Management.

Relative Interest Rates for Cash Management Opportunities

If you want to put your money in a safe "parking" place, consider these alternatives. The interest rates are relative to each other during a time of moderate inflation, 5 to 6 percent.

Type of Account	Interest Rate (percent)
Savings accounts	5.20
NOW accounts	5.40
Super NOW accounts	5.90
Money-market deposit accounts (MMDA)	6.10
Sweep accounts	6.50
Cash management accounts	6.70
Money-market mutual funds (MMMF)	6.80
Series EE government savings bonds	7.00
Three-month bank certificates of deposit (CDs)	7.00
Three-month brokered bank certificates of deposit (CDs)	7.30
Six-month bank certificates of deposit (CDs)	7.40
Six-month brokered bank certificates of deposit (CDs)	7.60
One-year bank certificates of deposit (CDs)	7.80
One-year brokered bank certificates of deposit (CDs)	8.00

Initial fees for cash management accounts range from $25 to $100, usually with a monthly charge of $2 to $12. Most CMA firms offer several free features to attract investors: a credit and/or debit card, a rebate of 1 percent on card purchases, traveler's checks, term life insurance, and various advisory newsletters.

Cash Management Tool 4: Low-Risk, Longer-Term Savings Instruments

Objective
To recognize the potential benefits of putting money into low-risk, longer-term savings opportunities.

If you are a good manager of your personal finances, you have established an interest-bearing NOW checking account, a savings account, and a money-market account, and you are earning interest on all monies until they are expended. You have maximized your economic self-interest. After all, *someone* is going to earn a good return on deposited idle funds, and it might as well be you.

At this point in managing your ample cash flow, you might consider making investments in the stock market or real estate or something else; these are covered in later chapters. Depending on your situation, these investments may be appropriate. However, you might decide instead to transfer some funds into various longer-term, low-risk savings instruments, such as government savings bonds and certificates of deposit,[2] because you are interested in earning even higher interest rates. Here you are committing the amounts for longer time periods, thus allowing you to build up amounts to be used for later spending, saving, or investing.

This is the fourth phase of cash management. Funds for this part of cash management primarily come from your money market account and savings account. This occurs because you are interested in committing some of these funds for longer time periods, perhaps 6 months, perhaps 2 or 3 years, or more, in an effort to earn a higher rate of return and to do so safely.

U.S. Government Savings Bonds

Series EE and Series HH savings bonds have been offered since 1980, and they replace the older Series E and H bonds. The bonds are backed with the full faith and credit of the United States government.

Series EE savings bonds are U.S. government bonds that are purchased for 50 percent of their face value. They are very popular and are often purchased through employer payroll deduction plans. The actual maturity date on Series EE savings bonds is not specified, since they may pay a variable rate of interest. How long savings bonds have to be held to double in value depends on the interest rate set by the federal government. Interest earned on Series EE savings bonds is accumulated in the bond and is exempt from all state and local taxes, and federal income tax may be deferred until the bonds are *redeemed* (cashed in).

Interest on EE bonds is exempt from state and local income taxes.

Savings bonds can be purchased from any federally insured financial institution without any fees, charges, or commissions. The bonds carry a minimum guaranteed rate of interest that earns interest at a fixed, graduated scale that increases the longer the bonds are held. Bonds held more than 5 years are eligible to pay a market rate if it is higher than the guaranteed minimum rate that the bond is already earning. The **market rate for savings bonds** is 85 percent of the latest 6-month average rate on 5-year Treasury securities. For example, in 1990 EE bonds paid 6.0 percent. If the market rate rises to 7.81 percent before the bond is redeemed, the higher rate then in effect will apply. The rate changes twice a year on May 1 and November 1. Thus holding savings bonds past 5 years generally offers some protection against inflation.

Series EE bonds pay no periodic interest, since the interest earned is the difference between the purchase price and the bond's value at maturity. For example, a Series EE $100 bond can be purchased for $50 and redeemed at maturity for $100. Series EE bonds can be purchased in denominations from $25 to $5000, with a maximum purchase limit of

[2] Funds also could be placed into high-yielding, short-term Treasury bills (discussed in Chapter 17, Investing in Bonds), which are backed with the full faith and credit of the U.S. Treasury, although the minimum sized purchase is $10,000. Certificates of deposit, however, tend to yield ¼ to ¾ of a percentage point more than Treasury issues of comparable maturity.

$15,000 annually. Series EE bonds cashed in early are penalized with a lower interest rate than stated on the bond; they pay rates that are fixed and graduated based on how long the bond has been held. For example, a 6 percent Series EE bond might pay only 5.5 percent if redeemed (cashed in) after 4 years instead of at maturity. EE bonds will continue to grow in value until the Treasury specifies that they stop accruing interest, which is 30 years after the issue date.

Federal income taxes on EE bonds may be deferred or reported, whichever is better for the taxpayer.

Federal income taxes can be deferred on interest earned on Series EE bonds until the money is actually received. However, if desired, interest can be reported annually, such as when bonds are held in the name of a child who has no other reportable income, and this action could result in a zero tax liability. In addition, the interest on Series EE bonds can be further deferred when a bondholder trades in the Series EE bonds for Series HH savings bonds.[3]

Series HH savings bonds are U.S. government bonds that are purchased at face value, and they can be bought only by exchanging Series EE bonds (or their predecessor E bonds); they may not be purchased with cash. Series HH savings bonds pay interest semiannually until maturity 5 years later. For example, a $10,000 Series HH bond paying 7.5 percent interest annually will yield semiannual interest payments of $375 ($10,000 × 0.075/2 = $375). That income must be reported for federal income tax purposes. Bonds redeemed early are cashed in at slightly less than face value, a penalty that in effect adjusts and reduces the interest rates paid earlier. For example, a $10,000 Series HH bond paying 7.5 percent at maturity will yield less than $10,000 if redeemed after 4½ years to reflect an overall interest rate of perhaps only 6.8 percent.

The interest income earned from both Series EE and Series HH bonds is exempt from state and local income taxes but is reportable on federal income taxes unless deferred. Note further that accrued interest amounts on a Series EE savings bond exchanged for a Series HH bond and included in its issue price is reportable for federal income tax purposes in the year of redemption, disposition, or final maturity, whichever is earlier. If U.S. savings bond certificates are ever lost, stolen, or destroyed, they can be replaced.

Certificates of Deposit

A **certificate of deposit (CD)** is an interest-bearing savings instrument that requires people to deposit money for a fixed amount of time, commonly

---

[3] There is a new education bond program that permits taxpayers who meet certain income limits to exclude from their gross income the interest earned on Series EE bonds. Series EE bonds purchased after 1990 by persons age 24 or older other than college students are forever exempt from income tax on the interest if the bond is redeemed and the principal and interest are used to pay tuition, fees, and other college expenses of a dependent or, in the case of adult education, for your spouse or yourself. The bonds must be in the taxpayer's name, not in a dependent child's name. Proprietary institutions, such as beautician or secretarial schools, sometimes do not qualify. The bonds lose their tax-free nature if family income at the time the bond is redeemed rises from $60,000 to $90,000 for parents who file a joint return and from $40,000 to $55,000 for single taxpayers. Starting in 1991, the income limits are indexed to inflation.

ranging from 7 days to 8 years, with no fees charged by the institution. CDs are insured by the issuing banks and savings and loan associations up to $100,000 through the FDIC, and they may be purchased by mail or in person. The interest rate existing when the CD is purchased typically is locked in for the entire term of the deposit. The depositor collects his or her principal and interest at the end of the time period. In return for a higher interest rate on savings, you sacrifice free access to your money. Deposits can range from $500 to $100,000.

By giving up ready access when you buy a CD, you get very high yields.

CDs pay much greater interest rates than regular savings accounts because financial institutions can count on having deposits for a specific time and can make investments accordingly. Short-term CDs (less than 2½ years) have higher yields than standard savings accounts.

Interest rates on CDs usually go higher as your time commitment lengthens because the longer you are locked into a CD, the greater the risk that interest rates will rise, and you should be rewarded for accepting that risk. If interest rates fall, you will benefit from the excellent return; if interest rates rise, you will have missed out on earning even greater returns.

Note that **variable** (or **adjustable**) **rate certificates of deposit** are increasingly available. These instruments pay an interest rate that is adjusted periodically but also allows savers to "lock in" or fix the rate at any point in time before their CD matures. Of course, this detracts from the main virtue of the fixed-rate CD—predictability. The best variable rate CDs have an interest-rate floor or a guaranteed minimum rate.

The cash-flow manager with modest sums would do well to consider **small certificates of deposit**, which are fixed-time deposits in minimum denominations of no less than $100. People often purchase small CDs for $500. Interest is compounded daily, providing a yield higher than normal savings accounts but slightly less than large certificates of deposit, which are sold in denominations of $1000, $5000, $10,000, and $100,000. CDs can be purchased through banks, savings and loan associations, and credit unions.

If money is withdrawn from a CD before the time limit is up, there are usually interest penalties, so before putting money into a CD be certain that it is appropriate to tie up your funds. The federal government no longer heavily regulates the interest rates, penalties, and maturities on CDs. On certificates held less than 1 year, the depositor may lose a minimum of 1 month's interest; on certificates held more than 1 year, the depositor may lose a minimum of 3 months' interest. Note that if the penalty is greater than the interest, you will get back less than you deposited.

Since you do not make deposits and withdrawals after initially investing in a CD, there is good reason to look beyond nearby banks for the highest yields. An extra 1 percent yield amounts to $100 on a $10,000 CD every year! Every Thursday, national newspapers, such as the *New York Times*, the *Wall Street Journal*, and *USA Today*, print a list of banks paying high yields. Yields around the country are published monthly by *Changing Times* and *Money*. Also, you should check with a stockbroker for high yields, since stockbrokers buy CDs in volume and resell to individuals. These are called **brokered certificates of deposit**. CDs are an excellent cash management tool, and as bona fide banking deposits, CDs enjoy the protection of federal deposit insurance up to $100,000.

Summary

1. Cash management is the task of earning maximum interest on all your funds, regardless of the type of account in which they are kept, while having sufficient funds available for living expenses, recurring household expenses, emergencies, and savings and investment opportunities. The tools of cash management include an interest-bearing checking account, a savings account at a local financial institution, a money-market account, and various lower-risk, longer-term savings instruments.

2. Today's somewhat deregulated financial services industry is somewhat competitive and increasingly complex. It is made up of banks, mutual funds, stock brokerage firms, insurance companies, financial services companies, and others.

3. The most recognized forms of electronic funds transfer (EFT) are debit cards, computer-chip cards, preauthorized payments and deposits, and computer money management. The Electronic Funds Transfer Act protects consumers.

4. The four primary providers of cash management services are banks and banklike institutions, mutual funds, stock brokerage firms, and financial services companies.

5. Rather than paying money out for checking services, it is important to have the first tool of cash management, an interest-bearing checking account from which to pay monthly living expenses. In choosing a financial institution, one should consider such criteria as cost, safety, convenience, treatment of customers, and range of services.

6. The second tool of cash management is a local savings account. Employed people with good job security and fringe benefits need to determine for themselves how much money they should set aside for emergencies in a local financial institution. A regular account using the day of deposit to day of withdrawal method of determining the savings account balance will pay the highest effective interest rate.

7. The third tool of cash management is a money market account, which offers a higher interest rate than checking and savings accounts. Money market accounts include super NOW accounts, money market deposit accounts, money market mutual funds, sweep accounts, and cash management accounts.

8. The fourth tool of cash management is to transfer some funds to various low-risk, longer-term savings, such as government savings bonds and certificates of deposit. These types of fixed-time deposits pay higher interest rates than savings accounts but also tie up your money for several months or longer.

Modern
Money
Management

How Should the Johnsons Manage Their Cash?

In January Harry and Belinda Johnson had $1200 in monetary assets (see page 107): $570 in cash on hand, $190 in a passbook savings account at First Federal Bank earning 5 percent interest compounded daily, $70 in a passbook account at the Far West Savings and Loan earning 5.25 percent interest compounded semiannually, $60 in a share account at the Smith Brokerage Credit Union earning a dividend of 6 percent compounded quarterly, and $310 in their non-interest-bearing regular checking account at First Interstate.

1. What specific recommendations do you have for the Johnsons for selecting a checking account and savings account that will enable them to use effectively the first and second tools of cash management?

2. Their cash-flow calendar (see Table 4.4) indicates that by September they will have an extra $1854 available. They also expect continued surpluses of more than $200 a month from that point on because of anticipated salary raises, which are not reflected in their current financial statements. Surely you have some recommendations for the Johnsons on using the third and fourth tools of cash management. Specifically, what low-risk long-term savings instrument would you recommend for their savings, given the objective of saving enough to purchase a new car in five years? Support your answers.

3. If the Johnsons could put all their monetary assets, $1200, into a savings account earning 5½ percent, how much would they have in the account after one year? (*Hint:* Use Appendix A1 or the Personal Finance Cookbook FVSUM worksheet.)

Key Words and Concepts

account exceptions, 175
adjustable rate certificates of deposit, 201
automated teller machine (ATM), 166
automatic funds transfer (AFT), 180
automatic overdraft loan, 180
average-balance account, 176
bad check, 180
banking institutions, 169
banks, 169
basic banking, 174
blank endorsement, 183
brokered certificates of deposit, 201
cash management, 161

cash management account (CMA), 196
cashier's check, 180
certificate of deposit (CD), 200
certified check, 180
check clearing, 179
checking account, 162
check truncation, 184
club account, 187
commercial banks, 169
computer-chip card, 166
computer money management, 167
credit unions (CUs), 171
day of deposit to day of withdrawal (DDDW) method, 191

Review Questions

1. What is cash management?

2. Why is cash management important?

3. List the four tools of cash management.

4. Describe the importance of deregulation to the financial services industry.

5. Give several examples of electronic funds transfers.

6. What is a PIN? Explain how PINs work.

7. What are the provisions for lost EFT cards?

8. Describe briefly the providers of financial services and the products they sell.

9. Differentiate among the banklike institutions: commercial banks, savings and loan associations, mutual savings banks, and credit unions.

10. Explain how a money-market mutual fund works.

11. What do stock brokerage firms and financial services companies have to do with cash management?

12. Tell why having an interest-bearing checking account is important.

13. Distinguish between a NOW checking account and non-interest-bearing checking accounts.

14. Summarize the criteria used in choosing a checking account.

15. Distinguish between a minimum-balance and an average-balance requirement of a checking account.

16. What protections are available against writing a check with insufficient funds?

17. Distinguish between a certified check, a cashier's check, a money order, and a traveler's check.

18. Why would people want to open a checking or savings account using a tenancy in common account?

19. Distinguish among the three different types of endorsements: blank, special, and restrictive.

20. Explain the check-clearing process, including float.

21. What kinds of errors do people make when attempting to reconcile their bank statements with their check register?

22. Differentiate between time deposits and demand deposits.

23. How much money should a person save if he or she is employed at a good job and enjoys a number of fringe benefits?

24. What major factors are involved in calculating and comparing rates of return on savings accounts?

25. Explain the difference between the nominal and effective rates of interest.

26. Summarize how the day of deposit to day of withdrawal method of determining and calculating savings balances works.

27. Summarize three account exceptions.

28. Who needs a money-market account and why?

29. Differentiate between a money-market mutual fund and a money-market deposit account.

30. Summarize how a sweep account works.

31. Differentiate between the two types of government savings bonds.

32. Explain what a certificate of deposit is and who might want to purchase one.

Case Problems

1. Estelle Paradiso of Upper Montclair, New Jersey, has had a checking account at a commercial bank for 3 years. The bank has always required a minimum balance of $100 to avoid an account charge, and Estelle has always maintained this balance. Recently, Estelle heard that a nearby savings and loan association is offering NOW accounts paying 5 percent interest on the average daily balance of the account. This institution requires a minimum balance of only $300, but a forfeiture of monthly interest is assessed if the account falls below this minimum. With her past habits at the commercial bank, Estelle feels the $300 minimum would not be too hard to maintain. She is seriously thinking about moving her money to the NOW account.

   a. What is the main reason Estelle should move her money-market account?
   b. Tell Estelle about the differences among NOW accounts offered at various financial institutions.

   c. If Estelle maintained an average balance of $350 in a NOW checking account earning 5 percent, how much interest would she have earned on her money after one year? (*Hints:* Use Appendix A-1 or the Personal Finance Cookbook (PFC) FVSUM worksheet and do not forget to subtract her initial lump sum from the derived answer.)

   d. How much more would Estelle have earned in one year if she decided instead to maintain a money-market mutual fund paying 6½ percent interest instead of the NOW account? (*Hint:* Use Appendix A-1 or the Personal Finance Cookbook (PFC) FVSUM worksheet and make some subtractions.)

2. Celie Pollock of Portland, Oregon, pays a $25 fee every month for a computer money management service. Her friend Valerie feels Celie is wasting her money. Celie has a net income of $3000 a month, plus other earnings from some good investments. In addition, she is part owner of an apartment complex, which earns her approximately $1000 a month. She always tries to put her reserve money into solid investments so that they might bring her future earnings and security.

   a. What specific services offered by computer money management would help a person such as Celie?
   b. Justify Celie's paying the $25 monthly fee for computer money management.
   c. Recommend to Celie a combination of the four tools of cash management that will offer some alternative money management services. Defend your answer to Celie; be sure to consider factors such as convenience, cost, services, and safety.

Suggested Readings

"Advice from the Experts." *U.S. News & World Report,* July 30, 1990. pp. 54–57. Tips from the pros on how to get the most out of your savings.

"An End to the Fast Talk in Bank Ads?" *Business Week,* July 3, 1989, p. 97. Touts the benefits of the proposed truth-in-savings act.

"Automatic Ways to Save and Invest." *Consumer Reports,* February 1989, p. 78. How to use savings bonds, retirement plans, automatic bank transfers, and mutual-fund transfers.

"Banks Discover the Consumer." *Fortune,* February 12, 1990, pp. 96–104. A survey of the range of new services being offered by commercial banks.

"Check Fraud." *Consumer Research Magazine,* December 1989, p. 2. Points up the risks of letting retailers know your credit card number when writing a check.

"College Costs: The Pizza Factors." *Changing Times,* January 1990, pp. 73–74. Choosing cash and credit accounts to meet college needs.

"How to Choose and Use Money-Market Funds." *Consumer Reports,* May 1989, p. 316. What the differences are among money-market funds and how to open an account.

"How to Shop for CDs." *Consumer Reports,* June 1989, p. 392. How to get the best rate and invest in a safe institution.

"Joint Bank Accounts: The Hidden Dangers." *Consumer Reports,* July 1989, p. 458. How to set up the types of bank accounts to correctly meet your needs.

"Money Market Funds: The Banker Versus the Broker." *Business Week,* March 5, 1990, p. 96. Discusses which is the best source for money market funds.

"Nine Great Savings Moves." *Changing Times,* September 1990, pp. 70–78. Well thought out suggestions for the cash manager.

"Supercharge Your Savings." *Changing Times,* October 1990, pp. 28–33. Your money can earn almost 9 percent safely on any number of several alternatives.

"The Era of Debit Cards." *Newsweek,* January 2, 1989, p. 51. How to choose and use debit cards.

"The Savings Decade." *U.S. News & World Report,* July 30, 1990, pp. 46–48. Smart savers of the 1990s are using the reliable approaches of yesteryear.

"Today's Best Moves to Make Your Savings Grow." *Money,* February 1990, pp. 78–92. What alternatives are best for earning the highest safe yields.

"Where to Keep Your Cash." *Consumer Reports,* March 1989, p. 153. Putting your money in demand-deposit accounts, bank certificates of deposit, and money-market mutual funds.

"Where to Keep Your Cash—Part 2." *Consumer Reports,* April 1989, p. 260. Putting your money into Treasury bills and long-term Treasuries.

"Why Settle for 6.5% Instead of 9.5%?" *Money,* October 1989, pp. 76–77. How to safely earn a much higher return than what you might be getting on passbook savings accounts.

6

Credit Use and Credit Cards

OBJECTIVES

After reading this chapter, you should be able to

1. Compare and contrast installment and noninstallment credit and discuss the uses, pitfalls, and costs of credit.

2. List and describe the types of charge accounts.

3. Describe the process of opening a credit account and the procedures lenders use to evaluate credit applicants.

4. Describe the features of credit statements and explain how finance charges are computed.

5. Discuss the protection available to credit users under the major federal credit laws.

. . . .

Many people have strong feelings about the use of credit. On the one hand, you may be attracted to the ease of using a credit card to pay for gasoline on a cross-country trip or to finance the purchase of a home entertainment system with monthly payments. On the other hand, you may have vivid memories of a friend or relative who got too deeply into debt by overusing credit cards and ended up bankrupt. A recent survey revealed that one out of three households truly fears becoming overextended on credit.

The purpose of this chapter is to show you how to use charge accounts and credit cards wisely. We will first explore a number of positive reasons for using credit as well as some negative aspects of credit. Then the discussion will turn toward the types of charge accounts available today, along with how to open such accounts. The chapter continues with information on how finance charges are calculated and reported and concludes with a discussion of various federal laws that protect credit users.

Managing Your Use of Credit

Credit is a broad term used to describe any situation in which goods, services, or money are received with payment to be made in the future. It is a form of trust established between a lender and a borrower. If the lender believes that a prospective borrower has both the ability and the willingness to repay money, then credit will be granted. The borrower will hopefully live up to that trust and repay the lender.

Ten Reasons for Using Credit

Credit is widely used in the United States by governments, businesses, and consumers. Many local governments finance the construction of high schools and community colleges by borrowing, and the federal government often borrows to meet its responsibilities for such things as building highways and providing social services. Businesses that need to expand their production facilities to fulfill customer demand frequently borrow funds to build new plants.

Consumers establish and use credit for a variety of reasons, as the following list shows:

1. *Emergencies.* Consumers use credit to pay for such unexpected expenses as emergency medical services or automobile repairs.

2. *Early consumption.* Buying a color television on credit allows the consumer immediate use of the product.

3. *Convenience.* Using credit, and credit cards in particular, simplifies making many purchases. It provides a record of purchases, and it can be used as leverage in disputes over purchases.

4. *The good life.* Increasing numbers of people use credit as a way to raise their level of living in anticipation of higher incomes in the future.

5. *Education.* The rising costs of higher education forces many to borrow.

6. *To offset inflation.* Many people borrow money to buy a product before inflation causes the price of the product to rise, realizing that dollars to be repaid in the future will be worth less.

7. *Debt consolidation.* Many consumers who have difficulty making credit repayments turn to a **debt-consolidation loan.** Here the borrower exchanges several smaller debts with varying due dates and interest rates for one monthly payment, which is usually lower in amount than the payments on the other debts combined. For the privilege of consolidating all debts into one, the consumer is charged a substantial interest rate (probably 24 to 28 percent) and the term of the loan is lengthened—which, despite higher interest charges, allows for lower monthly payments.

8. *To take advantage of free credit.* Credit card users may be provided free credit for short periods of time, up to 50 to 55 days, depending on the timing of a purchase.

9. *Identification.* For many activities, such as renting an automobile or cashing a check, consumers often need to show one or two credit cards for identification.

10. *Making reservations.* Most motels and hotels require some form of deposit in order to hold a reservation for arrivals past 6 P.M. Providing a credit card number usually will serve as such a deposit, allowing guaranteed reservations to be made over the phone. (If you decide to cancel the reservation, generally you must do so by 6 P.M. in order to avoid credit card charges.)

Installment and Noninstallment Credit

Installment and non-installment credit are the two types of consumer credit.

Consumer credit is nonbusiness debt used by consumers for purposes other than home mortgages. (Borrowing for housing is considered an investment rather than an expenditure.) There are two types of consumer credit: installment credit and noninstallment credit. With **installment credit,** the consumer must, according to contract, repay the amount owed in a specific number of equal payments, usually monthly. Making monthly automobile loan payments is an example. **Noninstallment credit** includes single-payment loans (such as a loan of $2000 at 12 percent interest with a single payment of $2240 [$2000 plus ($2000 × 0.12) due at the end of 1 year] and open-ended credit. With **open-ended credit,** sometimes called a *charge account,* the consumer need not reapply each time credit is desired and may be required to repay the entire debt monthly or be allowed to make a series of equal or unequal payments. Most credit cards operate in this manner. This chapter is concerned mainly with open-ended credit; installment credit will be discussed in Chapter 7.

Consumer Credit and Modern Life

Consumer credit is a facet of modern life that has been expanding rapidly in recent years.

Families headed by younger persons use consumer credit more than families headed by older persons. Similarly, higher-income groups use more credit than do lower-income groups. This may result partially from the unwillingness of lenders to make loans to lower-income families. Not surprisingly, young families with children have the greatest credit use.

Attitudes toward the use of consumer credit have changed dramatically in the United States over the past 40 years. Historically, people who needed funds borrowed only from members of their own family. As the extended family began to be replaced by the nuclear family after World War II, those in need of money had to look to banks and other financial institutions for loans.

The economic expansion following World War II provided greater income for many Americans and a growing number of dual-earner households. The typical family has had increasing amounts of money income to spend on items beyond necessities. The per capita level of outstanding consumer credit (excluding home mortgages) has risen from about $680 in 1970 to over $3100 today. Over half of this debt consists of the amounts owed on automobiles and credit cards. Table 6.1 illustrates the growth of credit usage in recent years.

Problems with Credit Use

Credit use reduces future buying power.

Perhaps the greatest disadvantage of credit use is the loss of financial flexibility in personal money management. For example, if you have installment debts taking 10 percent of your after-tax income, you have lost the opportunity to spend those dollars for something else. Credit use also reduces your future buying power, since the money you pay out on a loan includes a **finance charge,** which is the total dollar amount the lender charges you for the use of the borrowed funds.

Credit use often leads to overspending. Buying some new clothes on a charge account for $25 a month for 20 months seems a lot easier than paying a full purchase price of $425. It is easier still to buy more clothes on credit the next month, especially if you have six credit cards; the average family does. Worse yet might be buying meals and entertainment on credit without paying the bill in full when the statement is received. Items purchased on credit should last longer than the time it takes to repay the debt.

Overindebtedness also can be a real problem for credit users. If a consumer has installment debts amounting to 20 percent of take-home pay, he or she is seriously in debt. Instead of working at a job and spending the income, the consumer slaves at a job to pay the bills. Misusing credit

TABLE 6.1
Consumer Credit Outstanding (Billions of Dollars)

| At End of | Non-installment Credit† | Installment Credit* | | | | | Total Consumer Credit |
		Total	Automobile	Revolving‡	Mobile Home	Other	
1950	$ 8.1	$ 15.1	$ 6.0	$ —	$ —	$ 9.1	$ 23.3
1955	12.1	29.8	13.5	$ —	$ —	16.3	41.9
1960	15.7	44.3	18.1	$ —	$ —	26.2	60.0
1965	23.1	72.8	29.4	$ —	$ —	43.4	95.9
1970	27.7	103.9	36.4	4.9	2.4	60.2	131.6
1975	37.9	167.0	57.0	14.5	15.3	80.2	205.0
1980	51.8	297.6	111.9	54.9	18.7	112.1	349.4
1985	74.7	517.8	209.7	122.0	26.8	159.3	592.4
1989**	64.7	711.8	289.3	199.2	22.5	200.8	776.5
1995§	75.0	928.0	380.0	275.0	18.0	255.0	990.0

Source: Economic Report of the President, 1990 (Washington, D.C., 1990), p. 382.

* Installment credit covers most short- and intermediate-term credit extended to individuals through regular business channels, usually to finance the purchase of consumer goods and services or to refinance debts incurred for such purposes, and scheduled to be repaid (or with the option of repayment) in two or more installments. Credit secured by real estate is generally excluded.

† Noninstallment credit is credit scheduled to be repaid in a lump sum, including single-payment loans, charge accounts, and service credit. Because of inconsistencies in the data and infrequent benchmarking, the series is no longer published by the Federal Reserve Board on a regular basis. Data are shown here as a general indication of trends.

‡ Consists of credit cards at retailers, gasoline companies, and commercial banks, and check credit at commercial banks. Excludes 30-day charge credit held by travel and entertainment companies. Prior to 1968, it was included in "other," except for gasoline companies, which were included in noninstallment credit before 1971. Since 1977 it has included open-ended credit at retailers, previously included in "other." Also beginning in 1977 some retail credit was reclassified from commercial to consumer credit.

** At end of November 1989.

§ Authors' estimates.

and not paying bills on time can give consumers a poor credit reputation or even result in the loss of items purchased.

Annual Percentage Rate (APR) and the Cost of Credit

The annual percentage rate (APR) is the best measure of the true cost of credit.

For virtually all types of consumer credit, the federal Consumer Credit Protection Act of 1968 (also known as the Truth-in-Lending Law) requires standardization of credit figures. Lenders must report both the total finance charge in dollars and the annual percentage rate of interest. The **annual percentage rate (APR)** is a measure of the cost of credit as a yearly rate expressed as a percentage. For example, a $1000 single-payment 1-year loan at 14 percent APR carries a finance charge of $140. Another lending source offering the same loan at 16 percent APR would require a $160 finance charge. Interest and all other loan charges *required* by the lender (such as those for a credit investigation or credit life insurance) must be included in both the calculation of the APR and the total finance charge in dollars. The annual percentage rate is a close approximation of the true cost of credit and can be used to compare credit contracts with different time periods, finance charges, repayment schedules, and amounts borrowed. The lower the APR, the lower is the true cost of credit.

Types of Charge Accounts

Charge accounts allow repeated borrowings without having to reapply each time. This is why they are also referred to as open-ended credit. Most of these accounts have a **credit limit**—the maximum outstanding debt on a credit account—and a flexible repayment schedule. Charge accounts generally make use of a credit card. A **credit card** is a plastic card identifying the holder as a participant in the charge account plan of a lender, such as a department store, oil company, or bank. Charge account holders can make merchandise purchases and, in some cases, obtain cash advances (loans). There are several types of charge accounts available to consumers. All allow multiple uses without reapplication, but some require that the entire balance be repaid each month. Each is described in the following sections.

Revolving Charge Accounts

A **revolving charge account** is any charge account for which the user has the option to either pay the bill in full or spread repayment over several months. More than two-thirds of all cardholders maintain balances, and the average customer takes more than 15 months to pay for the charges. The user may continue to make charges against the account as long as the total debt is below the credit limit. Many revolving charge accounts now assess a fee if the account is charged above the credit limit. Revolving charge accounts include option accounts, budget accounts, bank credit card accounts, and personal lines of credit.

Option Accounts An **option account** permits either payment in full when the bill arrives (with no credit cost) or partial payment spread over several months (at a typical interest rate of 1.5 percent per month, or an 18 percent APR). A fixed dollar minimum or percentage of the bill outstanding each month must be repaid.

Option accounts are exemplified by credit cards issued by local retail businesses, local shopping malls, national retail stores, and other major companies. Credit cards issued by a local retail business generally can be used only at that store, whereas cards from national retail chains (such as Sears Roebuck, Montgomery Ward, and J. C. Penney) and major companies (such as American Express Optima, Exxon, and Chevron) can be used almost everywhere. More than 60 percent of families use this type of credit card. The importance of option accounts to retailers can be illustrated by the fact that more than 50 percent of J. C. Penney Company sales are on credit.

Budget Accounts   A **budget account** is a somewhat limited revolving account, typically offered by local department stores and specialty shops carrying a relatively low credit limit (e.g., $300). Users must repay a specific portion of the charged amount (usually one-fourth to one-third) within 30 days and then pay the remainder over a period of just a few months. Lower credit limits and shorter repayment periods are allowed as compared with an option account. Again, an interest rate of 1.5 percent per month (18 percent APR) on the unpaid balance is commonly charged. Of course, early repayment of all charges will reduce the finance costs.

Bank Credit Card Accounts   **Bank credit card accounts,** such as VISA, MasterCard, and Discover, are a form of revolving charge account and are used by more than 60 percent of all households. They can be used to make purchases or to obtain a cash advance. A **cash advance** is a cash loan from a bank credit card account. Cash advances can be obtained at any financial institution that issues the type of card being used, as well as through 24-hour automated teller machines (ATMs).

Bank credit cards can be used worldwide.

Bank cards are honored nationally (some internationally) in hundreds of thousands of retail outlets and thus offer the widest selection of goods and services of any credit card account. Again, the user has the option of paying the bill in full when it arrives or repaying over several months. At any time during the repayment schedule the cardholder can pay the total balance due. There are more than 200 million VISA cards, 140 million MasterCards, and 30 million Discover cards held by consumers worldwide.

Bank cards are offered through a system of affiliated banks, savings and loan associations, and credit unions across the country. The consumer applies to the local financial institution, which then issues and services the card. An upper credit limit is established upon acceptance, commonly $500 to $10,000. Any time a cardholder requests a reasonable increase in the limit, it is usually given. In most states, banks are permitted to charge a card membership fee of $15 to $35 annually in addition to the finance charges. For $50 or more, users can have a "gold" or premium card, which has a higher spending ceiling and some added frills (travel insurance, for example). *Affinity cards* are sometimes available, too. Issued only to members of certain groups, such as the Sierra Club or a university, affinity cards are standard bank cards with the addition of the organization's logo; the bank pays a small fee to the organization based on members' usage, perhaps ½ of 1 percent of the charges. Revenues for bank credit cards are generated from membership fees, finance charges paid by those who do not pay their accounts in full, and assessments on merchants of from 2 to 8 percent on the purchases billed through them.

Personal Lines of Credit   A **personal line of credit** is a lending arrangement that allows the borrower access to loans much like the cash advance on a bank credit card. The loans are usually obtainable through special checks provided by the lender. These checks can be used to make purchases or can be deposited into your regular checking account. It is sometimes even possible to borrow against the credit line by telephone. Credit cards are not used with these accounts. Like all revolving accounts, there is a credit limit and a flexible repayment schedule.

Travel and Entertainment Accounts

T&E accounts require full repayment each month.

The major **travel and entertainment account** (T&E) credit cards are American Express, Diners Club, and Carte Blanche. Typically, the entire balance charged must be repaid within 30 days. T&E cards are used primarily by businesspeople for food and lodging expenses while traveling. The cards are somewhat difficult to obtain (less than 15 percent of families have one), since applicants must have higher than average incomes to qualify and must pay an annual membership fee of $35 or more. However, T&E cards are not accepted at as many outlets as are bank credit cards. T&E accounts are considered by some to be prestige cards; American Express has over 35 million cards outstanding.

Thirty-Day Accounts and Service Credit

Creditors expect debts incurred on a **thirty-day account** to be paid in full within 30 days. Consumers generally have such accounts with neighborhood businesses. Credit costs are not assessed because the companies expect full payment soon after mailing customers their bills. People with little or no credit experience can often open 30-day charge accounts.

Service credit is the credit granted to consumers by public utilities, physicians, dentists, and other service providers who do not require payment in full when services are rendered. For example, your local electric company allows you to use electricity all month and then sends you a bill that may not be due for 15 days. Service credit usually carries no interest charges, although there may be late fees if payments are slow; future service may be cut off for continued slow payment or for nonpayment.

How to Open a Charge Account

Obtaining credit is a three-step process. You must first fill out a credit application and then have your credit history investigated. The final step is credit scoring of your application.

Objective
To be able to describe the process of opening a credit account and the procedures lenders use to evaluate credit applicants.

The Credit Application

Figure 6.1 shows a sample **credit application,** which requests information about your (1) ability to repay and (2) willingness to repay. Lenders must make educated decisions about whether they will be repaid. A department store, for example, may desire to keep their losses below 1 percent of all credit sales. Even though a major purpose of extending credit is to build sales through loyal customers, it is important for lenders to keep bad debts to a minimum.

The Five C's of Credit Are Used to Evaluate You as a Credit Risk

In evaluating a credit application, lenders consider the five C's of credit:

1. *Character* involves your honesty and reliability in meeting financial responsibilities. Your previous credit history indicates how highly you value paying bills on time.

2. *Capital* is a measure of your financial net worth. Questions about assets (home ownership, stocks, savings accounts) and liabilities (balance due on present credit accounts) reveal whether your net worth is positive or negative (owing more than is owned).

3. *Capacity* is the income available to make repayment. Having a substantial income, having the same job for a number of years, and not having a lot of other debts suggest a strong financial capacity to repay.

4. *Collateral* generally includes all the assets you possess that could be available to meet liabilities. Specific collateral could be a named asset pledged to guarantee the loan repayment should you default. It makes good sense for a lender to rely more on an automobile put up as collateral than on the smiling face of a credit applicant. Should the debtor later default, the automobile would be sold and the proceeds applied against the loan.

5. *Conditions* are the general credit economy. When government and/or market conditions result in a restriction in the supply of money, less money is available for lending. In such cases, many applicants would be rejected who would normally have been approved for credit. Conversely, when large quantities of money are available, especially at low interest rates, it is much easier to obtain credit.

The credit application process may or may not include a brief interview with the lender to review or clarify the information you provided on the form or to obtain additional information. Answering questions completely and honestly both on the application form and during an interview is important. If there are inconsistencies, the lender could refuse your request for credit.

The Credit Investigation

If you have ever used credit, it is likely that a credit bureau has a file on you.

Upon receiving your completed credit application, the lender generally conducts a **credit investigation** of your financial history and compares that information with your application. Lenders usually obtain information about you from a credit bureau. **Credit bureaus** provide lenders with financial information on millions of Americans, compiling information primarily from court records, various merchants, and creditors. More than 2000 local credit bureaus belong to national groups, such as TRW Information Services and Credit Bureau, Inc., which have access to credit histories of over 80 million people. Members (lenders who provide data

Figure 6.1

Sample Bank Card Application

Courtesy of Bank of Lexington & Trust Company.

THIS BANK CARD APPLICATION/UPDATE IS FOR: ☐ INDIVIDUAL ACCOUNT ☐ VISA ACCOUNT ☐ UPDATE ACCOUNT
Please complete the following about: YOURSELF ☐ JOINT ACCOUNT ☐ M/C ACCOUNT ☐ INCREASE LIMIT TO_____

FIRST NAME	INITIAL	LAST NAME	PREVIOUS ADDRESS				
SOCIAL SECURITY NO.	BIRTHDATE MO. DAY YR.	TELEPHONE NO. ( )	CITY	STATE	ZIP CODE	YRS. THERE	
HOME ADDRESS		NO. OF DEPENDENTS	CHECKING ACCOUNT NUMBER		NAME OF FINANCIAL INSTITUTION		
CITY	STATE	ZIP CODE	YRS. THERE	SAVINGS ACCOUNT NUMBER	NAME OF FINANCIAL INSTITUTION		
☐ OWN ☐ RENT ☐ LIVE WITH PARENTS	MONTHLY PAYMENTS	MTG BAL.	MTG ACCT. #	NAME OF NEAREST RELATIVE NOT LIVING WITH YOU	(RELATIONSHIP)	TELEPHONE NO. ( )	
NAME & ADDRESS OF LANDLORD OR MORTGAGE COMPANY				ADDRESS OF NEAREST RELATIVE	CITY	STATE	ZIP CODE

YOUR JOB IF APPLICANT IS SELF-EMPLOYED, ATTACH CURRENT FINANCIAL STATEMENT AND/OR LATEST INCOME TAX RETURN

PRESENT EMPLOYER	OCCUPATION	YRS. THERE	Income from alimony, child support or separate maintenance payments need not be revealed if you do not choose to have it considered as a basis for repaying this obligation.
STREET ADDRESS	CITY	STATE	ZIP CODE	
BUSINESS PHONE NUMBER ( )	NET MONTHLY INCOME	OTHER INCOME $_____ PER _____
		SOURCE OF OTHER INCOME
LAST EMPLOYER	YRS. THERE	ALIMONY, CHILD SUPPORT, SEPARATE MAINTENANCE RECEIVED UNDER: ☐ COURT ORDER ☐ WRITTEN AGREEMENT ☐ VERBAL UNDERSTANDING

COMPLETE INFORMATION ON JOINT ACCOUNT ONLY IF JOINT ACCOUNT DESIRED (CO-APPLICANT'S SIGNATURE REQUIRED ON APPLICATION).

FIRST NAME	INITIAL	LAST NAME	PREVIOUS ADDRESS			
SOCIAL SECURITY NO.	BIRTHDATE MO. DAY YR.	TELEPHONE NO. ( )	CITY	STATE	ZIP CODE	YRS. THERE
HOME ADDRESS			CHECKING ACCOUNT NUMBER	NAME OF FINANCIAL INSTITUTION		
CITY	STATE	ZIP CODE	YRS. THERE	SAVINGS ACCOUNT NUMBER	NAME OF FINANCIAL INSTITUTION	
PRESENT EMPLOYER	OCCUPATION	YRS. THERE	Income from alimony, child support or separate maintenance payments need not be revealed if you do not choose to have it considered as a basis for repaying this obligation.			
STREET ADDRESS	CITY	STATE	ZIP CODE	OTHER INCOME $_____ PER _____		
BUSINESS PHONE NUMBER ( )	NET MONTHLY INCOME		SOURCE OF OTHER INCOME			
LAST EMPLOYER		YRS. THERE	ALIMONY, CHILD SUPPORT, SEPARATE MAINTENANCE RECEIVED UNDER: ☐ COURT ORDER ☐ WRITTEN AGREEMENT ☐ VERBAL UNDERSTANDING			

COMPLETE FOLLOWING INFORMATION FOR ALL APPLICANTS.

CREDIT REFERENCES CREDIT REFERENCES (CREDIT CARD, DEPT. STORES, BANKS, FINANCE CO., ETC.) & COMPLETE LIST OF ALL DEBTS NOW OWING OR PAID. ATTACH ADDITIONAL SHEETS IF NECESSARY

NAME OF CREDIT REFERENCE	STREET ADDRESS AND CITY	DATE OPENED	ACCOUNT NO.	MONTHLY PAYMENT	BALANCE DUE

CREDIT STATEMENT:

This statement is submitted to obtain credit and I (We) certify that all information herein is true and complete. I (We) also authorize the issuer to verify or obtain further information the issuer may deem necessary concerning My (Our) credit standing. I (We) authorize the issuer to retain this application as its property and agree to the terms and conditions accompanying the Bank Card(s) for which I (We) hereby apply. Also accompanying the terms and conditions will be a copy of the Right to Dispute Billing Errors.

By signing this application, I (We) agree, if this application is approved, to be contractually liable for all charges and transactions made on the account, including repayment of all amounts due and owing by virtue of the use of the Bank Card(s). I (We) hereby agree to be bound by the terms and conditions accompanying the Bank Card(s), including any amendments thereto.

If I (We) have checking and/or savings account(s) with the bank from whom I (We) received this application, I (We) request that a personal identification number related to such card(s) be issued to me (us) and agree to be bound by the terms and regulations applicable to the checking and/or savings account(s) as amended from time to time.

I (We) understand and agree that the Bank Card(s) will be issued by Bank of Lexington & Trust Company; that my (our) credit account will be owned and administered by Bank of Lexington & Trust Company; and that Bank of Lexington and Trust Company may collect all amounts owed by me (us) on such account.

SIGNATURE OF APPLICANT	DATE	DRIVER'S LICENSE NO.
SIGNATURE OF CO-APPLICANT (if applicable)	DATE	DRIVER'S LICENSE NO.
SIGNATURE OF AUTHORIZED USER OF THIS ACCOUNT		

BANK USE ONLY		
VISA ACCOUNT NO.	CREDIT LINE	NO. CARDS
APP'D BY		DATE
MASTERCARD ACCOUNT NO.	CREDIT LINE	NO. CARDS

REDDI RESERV SERVICE ☐ CHECK BLOCK IF THIS SERVICE IS ALSO DESIRED

(1) I (We) request and agree that, if a Bank Card Account is established for me (us) and if my (our) checking account(s) described below has (have) insufficient funds to cover any checks or charges presented against it (them) for payment, my (our) bank may on my (our) behalf request, receive and deposit into my (our) checking account(s) such funds in fifty dollar ($50.00) increments, as are required to pay such checks or charges. Each such transfer of funds shall constitute a Cash Advance under the Bank Card Account for which this application is made, and shall be governed by the Terms & Conditions thereof. (2) Cash Advances may not be made for this purpose if the Bank Card Account is closed, past due or over-limit, or if the transfer would cause the Bank Card Account to be over-limit. I (We) release Bank of Lexington & Trust Co. and the bank named below from liability for checks which are returned without payment because a Cash Advance on my (our) Bank Card Account is not approved for any of these reasons at the time a request is made for this purpose, or because the Reddi Reserv Service has been terminated. (3) This agreement shall be terminated automatically when the checking account(s) described below has (have) been closed, or when my (our) Bank Card Account is cancelled or otherwise terminated for any cause. Either my (our) bank named below or Bank of Lexington & Trust Co. may cancel this Reddi Reserv Service by a written notice mailed to me (us) at an address shown for me (us) on either bank's records, and such cancellation shall be effective five (5) days after such notice has been mailed. I (We) may cancel this agreement by written notice to Bank of Lexington & Trust Co., Post Office Box 2010, Lexington, Kentucky 40594, or to my (our) bank at the address shown below, shall be effective five (5) days after such notice has been mailed. (4) This agreement shall not be effective until I (we) have received written notification of approval from the bank named below:

Bank of Lexington & Trust Co., Post Office Box 2010, Lexington, Kentucky 40594-2010

CHECKING ACCT. NO. _____ CHECKING ACCT. NO. _____

AUTHORIZED SIGNATURE _____

AUTHORIZED SIGNATURE _____

AUTHORIZED SIGNATURE _____

**ALL AUTHORIZED SIGNATURES ON A JOINT ACCOUNT MUST SIGN THIS APPLICATION

After examining a credit-scoring chart, most people who are new to the world of credit wonder if they will ever get credit when they need it. There are five ways to prove, to a limited extent, that you have the ability to manage credit.

1. *Act on some factors you can control.* Establish both a checking and a savings account. Avoiding overdrafts on a checking account and making regular deposits to a savings account may be good financial management, but the lender wants only to know that you *have* a checking and a savings account.

2. *Visit a local retail establishment.* Tell them that your intention is to establish a credit rating, and request an account. A local retailer is more likely to open a limited account if you visit the store in person and dress neatly. Once the account is open, use it to make a few purchases for which you typically use cash. When the bill arrives, pay it promptly and in full. Presto, a credit history is established.

3. *Request and acquire an oil-company credit card.* Although more difficult to obtain than a local retail credit account, these are not impossible to get. Should one company refuse, apply at another, since scoring systems differ. Again, use the credit sparingly once obtained and repay promptly.

4. *Apply for a bank credit card.* Most bank card issuers have a program of test credit for people without an extensive credit history. The limit on credit purchases may be low (e.g., $300), but once again, the opportunity then exists to establish a credit rating. Later you can request an increase in the credit limit.

5. *Ask a bank for a small short-term cash loan.* Putting these funds into a savings account at the bank will almost guarantee that you will make the required three or four monthly payments. Also, the interest charges on the loan would be partially offset by the interest earned on the savings.

6. *Pay off student loans.* Many people have their first exposure to credit through the student loan they use to attend college. Paying off these loans quickly through a series of regular monthly payments can show prospective lenders that you are a responsible borrower.

to a credit bureau) pay both an annual charge and a specific fee for each credit report requested. The cost can vary from $1.50 for a telephone inquiry to $10 for a copy of the file on hand to $25 or more for an updated comprehensive report. Nonmembers must pay higher fees for these reports.

Credit Scoring

The lender, not the credit bureau, decides on your **credit rating,** which determines whether credit is granted to you. Scoring systems developed by most lenders help reduce subjectivity in decision making, avoid unfair discrimination, and improve the likelihood of making correct decisions. Some risk is involved, of course, since at any time about 3 percent of consumer loans are past due. If lenders approved applications of only those who would repay with 100 percent certainty, few people would

How Would You Score on a Credit Application?

In the table below are 12 questions typical of those often asked of credit applicants. Each response carries, in parentheses, a hypothetical point score that may or may not illustrate the relative weight given to that characteristic in a particular credit-scoring scheme. Circle your response to each question and insert the point value in the blank at the right. Total the number of points you scored.

While we can't establish a real "approve/reject" cutoff score in this example, people with higher scores are likely to be better credit risks than those with lower scores. Note that you may gain or lose points because a creditor takes into account your credit bureau report. Several accounts paid on time would increase your point total, while overdue accounts, a tax lien, or a bankruptcy would decrease it. The scores needed for approval vary from lender to lender and depend on economic conditions, a lender's profit target, and its tolerance of risk. One lender, for example, might accept a 5.1 percent bad-debt ratio on our hypothetical scorecard below and approve everyone who scored more than 75 points; another might be more conservative and approve only those who were able to score more than 125.

A Hypothetical Credit-Scoring Scheme

1. What is your age?
   Under 25 (8)   25–29 (12)   30–34 (10)   35–39 (6)   40–44 (14)
   45–49 (18)   50 or more (25)   _____

2. How many years have you lived at your current address?
   Less than 1 (−10) 1–2 (−3) 2–3 (0) 3–5 (4) 5–9 (14) 10 or more (26) _____

3. Do you own your home or do you rent?
   Own (30)   Rent (−32)   Other (0)   _____

4. How many years have you held your current job?
   Less than 1 (−14)   1–3 (0)   3–6 (5)   6–8 (9)   9 or more (16) _____

5. What bank accounts do you have?
   Checking and savings (24)   Savings only (11)   Checking only (6)   Neither (0) _____

6. Do you have a current bank loan?
   Yes (3)   No (0)   _____

7. Do you have a phone?
   Yes (9)   No (0)   _____

8. How many bank and travel and entertainment cards do you have?
   0 (0)   1 (12)   2 or more (21)   _____

9. How many major department store credit cards do you have?
   0 (0)   1–2 (5)   3 or more (8)   _____

10. How many loans from a small-loan company do you have?*
    0 (0)   1 (−4)   2 or more (−12)   _____

11. How many marginal credit references would you have to use?†
    0 (0)   1 or more (−6)   _____

12. What is your annual family income?
    0–$10,000 (−7) $10,000–$15,000 (0) $15,000–$19,000 (5)
    $19,000–$25,000 (8) $25,000 or more (13)   _____

---

* Do not include loans from automobile-finance companies such as GMAC.
† In filling out an application form, a certain number of credit references are required. If you have to use small stores without an organized credit-reporting system, you'll lose points.

(continued)

receive credit. Since types of credit and credit applicants vary, each lender uses different scoring techniques. Lenders typically use computers to analyze credit files and determine credit scores. A recent study revealed that about 12 percent of those applying for credit are denied. About half the turndowns had no established credit history or their credit report contained adverse information. The box that begins on page 219 shows a hypothetical credit-scoring chart combined with estimates of the probability of repayment.

Managing a Charge Account

Objective
To be able to describe the features of credit statements and explain how finance charges are computed.

To manage your charge account properly, you must become familiar with the details of credit statements and with how finance charges are computed.

Credit Statements

Each month charge account holders receive a **credit statement** (also called a *periodic statement*) that summarizes the charges, payments, finance charges, and other activity on the account. The significant features of most credit statements are the billing date, due date, grace period, payment schedule, and merchandise credit given. Figure 6.2 shows a monthly statement for a credit card.

Billing Date The **billing date** (sometimes called *statement date* or *closing date*) is the last day of the month on which any transactions are reported; in Figure 6.2 it is 5/22/91. Any purchases or credits after this date will be

FIGURE 6.2

Sample Statement for a
Revolving Charge
Account

Courtesy of Bank of
Lexington & Trust Company.

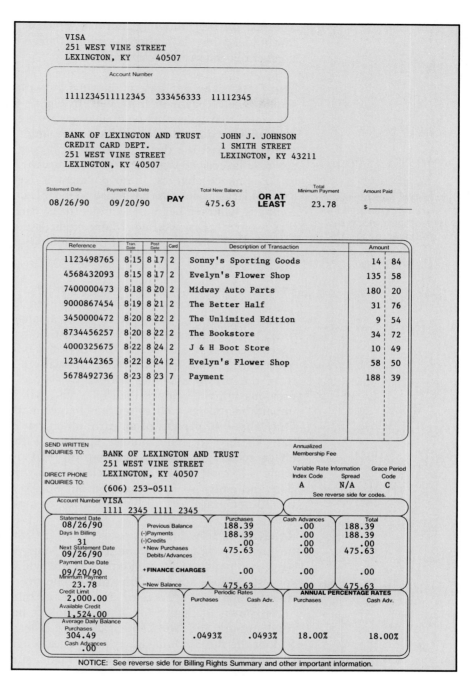

VISA					
251 WEST VINE STREET					
LEXINGTON, KY 40507					

Account Number

1111234511112345 333456333 11112345

BANK OF LEXINGTON AND TRUST
CREDIT CARD DEPT.
251 WEST VINE STREET
LEXINGTON, KY 40507

JOHN J. JOHNSON
1 SMITH STREET
LEXINGTON, KY 43211

Statement Date	Payment Due Date		Total New Balance		Total Minimum Payment	Amount Paid
08/26/90	09/20/90	PAY	475.63	OR AT LEAST	23.78	$ _____

Reference	Tran. Date	Post Date	Card	Description of Transaction	Amount
1123498765	8 15	8 17	2	Sonny's Sporting Goods	14 84
4568432093	8 15	8 17	2	Evelyn's Flower Shop	135 58
7400000473	8 18	8 20	2	Midway Auto Parts	180 20
9000867454	8 19	8 21	2	The Better Half	31 76
3450000472	8 20	8 22	2	The Unlimited Edition	9 54
8734456257	8 20	8 22	2	The Bookstore	34 72
4000325675	8 22	8 24	2	J & H Boot Store	10 49
1234442365	8 22	8 24	2	Evelyn's Flower Shop	58 50
5678492736	8 23	8 23	7	Payment	188 39

SEND WRITTEN
INQUIRIES TO:

BANK OF LEXINGTON AND TRUST
251 WEST VINE STREET
LEXINGTON, KY 40507

DIRECT PHONE
INQUIRIES TO:

(606) 253-0511

Annualized
Membership Fee

Variable Rate Information		Grace Period
Index Code	Spread	Code
A	N/A	C

See reverse side for codes.

Account Number VISA
1111 2345 1111 2345

Statement Date 08/26/90		Purchases	Cash Advances	Total
Days In Billing 31	Previous Balance	188.39	.00	188.39
	(-)Payments	188.39	.00	188.39
Next Statement Date 09/26/90	(-)Credits	.00	.00	.00
	+ New Purchases Debits/Advances	475.63	.00	475.63
Payment Due Date 09/20/90	+FINANCE CHARGES	.00	.00	.00
Minimum Payment 23.78	=New Balance	475.63	.00	475.63

Credit Limit 2,000.00	Periodic Rates		ANNUAL PERCENTAGE RATES	
Available Credit 1,524.00	Purchases	Cash Adv.	Purchases	Cash Adv.
Average Daily Balance Purchases 304.49				
Cash Advances .00	.0493%	.0493%	18.00%	18.00%

NOTICE: See reverse side for Billing Rights Summary and other important information.

recorded on the following month's bill. The statement is mailed to the cardholder a few days after the billing date. The date of the billing period is generally the same each month.

Due Date The **due date** is the time by which the credit card company should receive payment from you. In Figure 6.2, this is 6/17/91. Federal law states that bills must be mailed to cardholders at least 14 days before payments are due. Most credit card companies permit payment to be made a few days past the due date, since mail is sometimes slow. However, if payment is received later than the due date, the customer is legally obligated to pay finance charges. If no payment is received by the due date, the cardholder is in **default** (has failed to meet legal financial obligations). The company will then begin collection efforts, usually by first mailing a notice that a payment is overdue. Many credit issuers assess late payment fees (usually $10, but up to $50) if the minimum payment is not made by the due date.

Grace Period The days between the billing date and the due date, usually 20 to 25 in number, represent time allowed for bills and payments to be mailed and for the borrower to make arrangements to pay. During this time, finance charges may or may not be assessed on *new* credit card purchases. If they are not, the time period is referred to as the **grace period.** Most cards have a grace period, especially if there is no unpaid balance from the previous billing period. In Figure 6.2, the cardholder has a previous unpaid balance, $228.39, and will be charged interest on the unpaid balance as well as on the charges made within the billing period. Only about 40 percent of all cardholders pay their bills in full by the due date, thereby avoiding finance charges. With the grace period they, in effect, receive an interest-free loan on their purchases for 1 month. One tactic is to make credit card purchases a day or two after the usual billing date and enjoy 50 to 55 days (about 30 days until the next billing plus the 20-day grace period) before having to make a payment.

Repayment Schedule Borrowers can get into severe financial difficulty through unwise charge account usage. Many lenders require as little as 5 percent repayment each month and are willing to raise credit limits on request. It does not take long to become overburdened if you have more than the national average of six charge accounts.

As shown in Figure 6.2, the cardholder has two options: to pay the total amount due ($684.55) or to make at least the minimum payment of $35. If the full amount due is paid, finance charges in future months can be avoided. If a partial payment is made, such as $35, the amount due next month and the finance charges based on that amount will be assesed.

Merchandise Credit If you want to return merchandise you bought on credit, the merchant will issue you a **credit receipt,** written evidence of the item(s) returned and the transaction amount. This will be shown on your

TABLE 6.2
Sample Repayment Schedule

If new balance is:					
Less than $25	$25–100	$101–200	$201–300	$301–500	Over $500
Your minimum monthly payment is:					
Balance amount	$10	$20	$30	$50	1/10 balance amount rounded to next highest $5 increment

next monthly statement as a reduction of the total owed. The credit statement in Figure 6.2 shows a $16.37 merchandise credit.

Computation of Finance Charges

Lenders want to charge whatever interest rates they need to ensure a profit from credit card operations. However, many states have **usury laws** (legal interest-rate maximums that can be charged by lenders) that govern the charges assessed. In states with usury laws, people may pay lower interest rates than in other states. Merchandise purchases may be assessed at one rate (for example, 15 percent APR) and cash advances at another rate (perhaps 18 percent APR). Note also that a fee is usually assessed each time a cash advance is taken. Lenders issue credit cards with **fixed** or **variable interest rates.** Most cards have fixed (constant) rates; for some, however, the interest rate is variable—that is, it moves up or down monthly according to changes in some index of the lender's cost of funds.

Companies that issue credit cards must tell consumers the annual percentage rate applied as well as what method they use to compute the finance charges. They also will disclose the **periodic rate,** which is the APR for a charge account divided by the number of billing periods per year, usually 12. Typically, the finance charge is calculated by first computing the **average daily balance.** This is the sum of the outstanding balances owed each day during the billing period divided by the number of days in the period. Then the periodic rate is applied against that balance.

Finance charges are usually assessed on the average daily balance.

The method of computing the account balance is a critical feature of charge accounts, and can be confusing, as Table 6.3 illustrates. Descriptions of the five methods of computing account balances (*average daily balance*—including or excluding new purchases—*two-cycle average daily balance*—including or excluding new purchases—*previous balance, adjusted-balance,* and *ending balance*) are shown. With the adjusted balance method, new purchases are not added to the balance until they first appear on the credit statement and the grace period has expired without repayment in full, yet payments made are subtracted. The adjusted-balance method is the most favorable to borrowers, though fewer and fewer bank card issuers are using this method. If you can't find a card that uses the adjusted-balance method, at least find a card that uses an average daily balance method

The key element in determining the finance charge on credit cards is the method used to calculate the balance of the account which is then multiplied by the periodic interest rate. The five methods described below are most often used.

1. Average Daily Balance (including or excluding new purchases)

   Your balance is calculated each day. The balances for each day in the billing cycle are added together and divided by the number of days in the cycle. In all cases, payments are subtracted from the balance when posted to your account. New purchases may or may not be added to your balance when they are posted to your account. Most commonly new purchases are added when you have an outstanding balance from the previous billing period. Some creditors include new purchases in your balance even when you have paid your account in full.

2. Two-cycle average daily balance (including or excluding new purchases)

   This method is similar to the average daily balance method except that the average daily balance is calculated over the previous two billing periods rather than one.

3. Previous balance

   Your balance is simply the balance at the beginning of the billing cycle. New purchases are not added but neither are payments subtracted.

4. Adjusted balance

   Your balance at the beginning of the billing cycle is adjusted for payments made during the billing cycle. Thus the balance is reduced for payments made and not increased for new purchases. Further, the timing of the payment does not affect the balance, because a payment made at the end of the cycle reduces the adjusted balance by the same magnitude as one made at the beginning.

5. Ending balance

   Your balance is simply the balance at the end of the billing cycle. The timing of the pattern of payments and purchases is not a factor as it is in the average daily balance methods.

that excludes new purchases. However, many creditors use an average daily balance method that includes new purchases in the balance immediately when the creditor is notified of the transaction (the post date in Figure 6.2), even if you had paid your bill in full during the previous billing period. It is no wonder that a recent survey revealed that 60 percent of the public is not aware of the wide variations in interest costs on credit cards.

Federal Credit Laws

The original Truth-in-Lending (TIL) of 1968 requires lenders to disclose both the annual percentage rate and the finance charge in dollars, to advertise credit information truthfully, to refrain from issuing unrequested credit cards, and to protect credit users who use their homes as security. Since then, amendments to TIL and other laws have added to these protections.

Illegal Discrimination

Discrimination in lending against women, the elderly, and religious and racial minorities resulted in the passage of the Equal Credit Opportunity Act of 1975, which prohibits certain types of discrimination when granting credit. Rejecting a credit application due to poor credit history is legal, but rejecting a person on the basis of sex, race, age, or religion is not. In addition, credit applications cannot probe for information that could be used in a biased manner. The act requires creditors to provide to the applicant a written statement, if requested, of the reasons for refusing credit. Should discrimination be proven in court, the lender may be liable for up to $10,000 in fines.

To avoid discriminating illegally, lenders must use the same criteria to judge applications from single and married persons. Credit granted in both the husband's and wife's name must build a credit history for each. A married man or woman applying for credit need not disclose marital status or a spouse's income unless he or she wants that information used as a basis for granting credit. Some states take exception to this, considering any property or debts acquired by either the husband or the wife as jointly owned/owed and equally shared.

Credit Card Liability

You should notify lenders immediately when credit cards are lost or stolen.

Unauthorized use of your credit card (including telephone credit cards) results in a maximum legal liability of $50 per card. This **credit card liability** occurs only if you receive notification of your potential liability, you accepted the card when it was first mailed to you, the company provided you with a self-addressed form with which to notify them if the card was lost, and the card was used illegally before you notified them of the loss. Although your financial liability is low, some companies specialize in selling lost credit card insurance; it is profitable for them and an unnecessary expense for you. As a gesture of good will, most companies waive the $50 fee for unauthorized use of credit cards when notified promptly of the unauthorized use. Note also that homeowner's and renter's insurance policies (see Chapter 12) generally pay for such losses.

The Fair Credit Reporting Act

The objective of the Fair Credit Reporting Act is to place certain restrictions on credit-reporting agencies to reduce errors. If you are denied credit because of a poor credit bureau report, the law requires disclosure to you of the name and address of any credit-reporting agency that supplied information about you. You then have 30 days to request a free summary of the contents of your file from the credit-reporting agency. Even if you have not been denied credit or if you waited more than 30 days after a credit denial, upon your request, you must be told the contents of your file at a credit bureau, although a small fee ($10 to $25) may be charged. Many credit bureaus will provide a copy of the same report they would send to a lender. However, medical information is withheld. If you dispute an item, it must be reinvestigated. If the information was in error, it must be corrected. If the credit bureau refuses to make a correction, you also may wish to provide your version of the disputed information (in 100 words or less). All new information (corrections and/or your side of the story) must be sent to anyone who received a credit report on you in the previous 6 months.

Negative information in your file is generally not reportable after a period of 7 years (except for data on bankruptcy, for which the time limit is 10 years). If you have applied for life insurance or certain employment, your file may include comments from neighbors and friends about your morals, living habits, and the like. For these kinds of investigations, you must be informed when a report is being compiled.

The Fair Credit Billing Act

The Fair Credit Billing Act went into effect in 1975 to help people who wish to dispute credit card billing errors. In the past, complaining about a bill often resulted in delays and in harmful information going into a consumer's credit file. Now, consumers can legally withhold payment for a billing error under the act. You must make a billing error complaint within 60 days after the first bill containing the error was mailed to you. The lender then has 30 days to acknowledge your notification and, within 90 days, must either correct the error or explain why it believes the bill to be correct. This law applies to errors on charges made in your state or within 100 miles of your home, whichever is farthest. Notification to the credit card issuer must be in writing. During the time of the dispute, creditors cannot assess interest on or penalties for nonpayment of the disputed amount, send **dunning letters** (notices that make insistent demands for repayment) to you, or send negative information about your account to a credit bureau without stating additionally that "some items are in dispute." Note that any back interest and penalties will be owed if it turns out that the disputed item is legitimately owed.

Charge-Backs

Regulations now permit **charge-backs,** which are the withholding of payments to third-party lenders such as credit card companies for defective products or services. This is true for credit card and non-credit card purchases. The ruling applies to credit card purchases if the product or service cost over $50 and was purchased within your home state or within

What If You Discover an Error on Your Credit Card Statement

Billing errors can occur on credit card statements. Numbers can be transposed. Charges can be made against the wrong account number. Items can be posted twice. When such errors occur, quick action is advised.

1. Notify the credit card issuer by phone that you have found an error.
2. Withhold payment for the disputed item(s). If possible, pay the remaining amount owed in full in order to isolate the disputed item.
3. Send a written notice of the error to the credit card issuer. The notice must be in writing to qualify for the protections provided under the Fair Credit Billing Act. (Items 1 through 3 should all be done the same day.)
4. Provide photocopies (not originals) of any necessary documentation, and explain fully why you feel there has been an error.
5. After the dispute is settled, it might be wise to review your file at the local credit bureau to ensure that no information regarding your refusal to repay the disputed amount was included.

100 miles of your home (whichever is farther). You can withhold payment until the problem has been remedied. Be sure to fully document your case in your written notification to the lender. Both the seller and the holder (the credit card company) are legally responsible should the consumer sue for replacement of the product or for payments already made. For a defective product, however, it may well be the manufacturer that is finally legally liable.

This protection does not apply when the borrower independently makes the lending arrangements directly with a creditor. However, in the great majority of cases, the ruling does apply, since only the seller and the lender cooperate in arranging the financing. In the typical credit card transaction, this provision means that you can question any item on your bill and the company must investigate and provide you with either a credit or evidence (such as a copy of a charge slip you signed) that the charge is valid. Most lenders apply the spirit of the Fair Credit Billing Act to any complaints about credit card charges.

Holder-in-Due-Course Doctrine

The **holder-in-due-course doctrine** once held that if a merchant sold a product on credit to a consumer and then sold the credit contract to a sales finance company (the holder), a legally binding contract existed between the consumer and the finance company. If the merchant went out of business or simply refused to repair a defective product, the consumer still had to pay off the full amount owed to the holder. The only other recourse was to find the merchant and sue, but payments to the finance

You may have the right to refuse credit payments for defective goods and services.

company had to continue. A 1976 Federal Trade Commission ruling resulted in the virtual elimination of this practice.

The Fair Debt Collection Practices Act

The Fair Debt Collection Practices Act of 1977 is aimed at improving the ethical practices of third-party debt-collection agencies. Banks, dentists, lawyers, and others who do their own dunning are exempt. Collection agencies attempt to make collections that could not be obtained by the original lender. In some cases they are assisting (for a fee) the original lender, and in others they have actually taken over (bought) the debt and have become the creditor. By law, collection agencies cannot telephone at unusual hours, make numerous repeated telephone calls during the day, use deceptive practices (such as claiming they are attorneys, unless they are), make threats, or use abusive language. They also cannot spread rumors that you are a "deadbeat." Even with these limitations, realize that collection agencies can be irritatingly persistent in collecting past-due accounts. If they are not successful, they take the consumer to court as the last resort.

Cost Information Disclosure

The 1988 Fair Credit and Charge Card Disclosure Act has made it easier to shop around for the best credit card. The law requires that key pieces of information must be disclosed in direct-mail advertising and on applications for credit cards (see Figure 6.2). Such information includes the annual percentage rate (APR) and how it is calculated if it is a variable rate, any and all fees (including late fees), the length of the grace period, and the method used to calculate the account balance against which the periodic rate is applied.

Summary

1. People borrow for financial emergencies, to have things immediately, and to try to offset inflation. Perhaps the greatest disadvantage of credit use is the loss of financial flexibility in personal money management. The annual percentage rate (APR) is the best approximation of the true cost of credit.

2. Open-ended credit, or charge accounts, permits repeated access to credit without a new application each time. The consumer may choose to repay the debt in a single payment or to make a series of payments of varying amounts. Revolving charge accounts and travel and entertainment accounts are the most commonly used charge accounts.

3. In the process of opening a credit account, the lender generally conducts an investigation into your credit history and assigns a credit rating accordingly.

▌ Advice for the Conservative Credit Card Holder

Credit cards are virtually essential in modern financial management, yet they carry a potential for misuse. How can you take advantage of the benefits and avoid the disadvantages of credit cards? Keeping in mind and applying a few basic rules can help overcome the pitfalls of credit card usage.

1. Seek out cards with the lowest APRs and no or low additional fees. Bank credit cards can be obtained from banks in states with low usury limits and where annual fees are disallowed. Certain bank card issuers focus on segments of the market that are likely to be very good credit risks. Thus they can afford to charge lower interest rates.

2. Sign up for just a few cards. One bank card, one oil-company card, and one or two cards from specific retail outlets should be sufficient for most people. VISA and MasterCard are honored at so many outlets that one such card may be all that is necessary.

3. Avoid using credit cards for major purchases. Credit cards are difficult to manage because a repayment plan is unspecified. Buying major appliances, furniture, and so on in this way quickly builds up debt with no plan for repayment. If you are going to need more than 6 months to repay on a purchase, consider an installment loan for its lower APR and fixed repayment plan. (Installment loans are the subject of the next chapter.)

4. Do not use credit cards for day-to-day expenses. Many grocery stores, restaurants, fast-food outlets, and gas stations accept credit cards, but you should use cash for such purchases.

5. Leave your cards at home. Credit usage should be planned, not impulsive. Keeping your credit cards at home takes away the opportunity for an impulsive purchase. Carry only one multipurpose card such as a bank card for emergencies.

6. Protect yourself from unauthorized use of your account. Like a debit card, a credit card is an opening into your finances. Watch what salespeople do with your card to make sure they do not use it on a fraudulent second charge slip. Protect your account number by tearing charge slip carbons in half and keeping your receipts. Never give your account number to someone over the telephone unless you have made the call and know with whom you are dealing. Review your statements each month and compare them with your receipts. Promptly report any discrepancies.

7. Do not consolidate your debts. Debt-consolidation loans are often used by people who have reached the credit limit on their cards and wish to pay off the balance. If it is necessary to pay off your cards through debt consolidation, your credit cards should be destroyed and the accounts closed to avoid charging anew.

8. Pay your credit card bills in full each month.

4. Credit statements provide a monthly summary of your credit transactions and the calculation of the finance charges assessed. Most credit card issuers compute finance charges by multiplying the average daily balance by the periodic interest rate.

5. Major federal credit protection laws prohibit unfair discrimination in the granting of credit, require that finance charges be disclosed, limit liability

on lost credit cards, force credit-reporting agencies to correct errors, provide guidelines on billing disputes for regular credit transactions as well as sales through third-party lenders, and govern collection methods used by third-party credit collectors.

Modern
Money
Management

**The Johnsons'
Credit and Cash
Flow**

Harry and Belinda have a substantial annual joint income, over $46,000. Yet they also have some cash-flow deficits planned for the first months of the year (see Tables 4.3 and 4.4).

To resolve this difficulty, they opened two VISA accounts and one MasterCard account at different banks and then obtained cash advances at interest rates above 19 percent. When they are supposed to pay on one account, they just get the needed money from another bank credit card. They now owe over $1200, and it will be some months until Harry's trust income arrives in September.

1. What are the advantages and disadvantages of the Johnsons opening more than one bank credit card account?

2. Comment on the costs involved in continually getting cash advances from one bank card to pay amounts due on the others.

3. Harry and Belinda have thought about applying for additional installment credit to start replacing the old furniture given to them by their families. Regardless of the methods used for judging credit potential, the five C's of credit (on page 216) will continue to be factors considered carefully in any credit approval. Using the five C's of credit, write a paragraph evaluating the Johnsons' application. Be sure to review their financial statements in Chapter 3 on pages 107 and 108.

Key Words and Concepts

annual percentage rate (APR), 212
average daily balance, 223
bank credit card account, 214
billing date, 220
budget account, 214
cash advance, 214
charge-backs, 226
consumer credit, 210
credit, 209
credit application, 215

credit bureaus, 216
credit card, 213
credit card liability, 225
credit investigation, 216
credit limit, 213
credit rating, 218
credit receipt, 222
credit statement, 220
debt-consolidation loan, 210
default, 222

Review Questions

1. Describe the relationship between a lender and borrower that is vital for successful credit use.

2. Give 10 reasons to justify using consumer credit.

3. Distinguish between installment credit and open-ended credit.

4. Identify the greatest disadvantage of using consumer credit, and explain how it is a disadvantage.

5. What two items of credit-cost information must lenders report according to the Consumer Credit Protection Act (Truth-in-Lending Law)?

6. Give one advantage of using a credit card account as compared with other types of credit accounts.

7. Distinguish among the following types of charge accounts: the revolving charge account, travel and entertainment account, and thirty-day account.

8. Describe the four types of revolving charge accounts.

9. Describe how a bank credit card works.

10. Identify the five C's of credit, and give an example of each.

11. What types of information are requested on a credit application?

12. Explain what is involved in a credit investigation.

13. Describe the type of credit-rating system called credit scoring. Why do lenders employ this system?

14. Name and describe briefly courses of action you can take to prove you can manage credit effectively.

15. What information is provided on a credit statement?

16. What advantages accrue to the credit user from the availability of a grace period?

17. What are usury laws?

18. How is an average daily balance determined for a credit account?

19. Describe the purpose of the Equal Credit Opportunity Act of 1975.

20. Identify the conditions that must exist before a credit card holder can be liable for $50 for charges on a lost credit card.

21. Describe the rights and procedures outlined by the Fair Credit Reporting Act.

22. Explain how should one go about disputing credit card billing errors?

23. Describe the holder-in-due-course doctrine and its applicability today.

24. What is a charge-back, and how can it be used to protect a borrower from defective products?

25. List practices of debt collectors that are illegal under the Fair Debt Collection Practices Act.

Case Problems

1. The use of credit has expanded greatly over the last several decades. This has been particularly true for consumer debt. Some people still advocate the old Ben Franklin adage, "Neither a lender nor borrower be." Examine this saying for a moment. Taken literally, and in view of the use and growth of credit, this adage seems somewhat outmoded today.
   a. What impact would the preceding adage have on our modern economy?
   b. If you were unable to use credit of any kind, what sorts of changes would you have to make in your money-management goals? Explain.
   c. Justify the use of credit as a positive financial tool for consumers and for businesses.

2. Bill and Mary Smith are tired of their old furniture. A local store offers credit at an annual interest rate of 16 percent, with a maximum loan length of 4 years. The furniture they wish to purchase costs $2800 with no down payment required. Using the Personal Finance Cookbook (PFC) program INSTALL, compute the following. Print your results.
   a. What is the amount of their monthly payment for 4 years?
   b. How would the payment change if they reduced the loan to 3 years.
   c. How would the payment change if they could afford a down payment of $500 with 4 years financing?
   d. How would the payment change if they could afford a down payment of $500 with 3 years financing?

3. Geoff Dalrymple of Thibodaux, Louisiana, is the menswear buyer for a regional chain of department stores. His good credit rating has secured him a total of five credit cards, which he regularly uses for personal expenditures and business travel. Geoff makes it a policy to pay off the outstanding balance on each card every month.

   Recently Geoff received an offer to purchase lost credit card insurance, the premium for which would be billed on one of the cards. With Geoff's travel schedule a lost card could be anywhere. He is seriously considering this offer.

a. Write a paragraph to help Geoff consider the advantages and disadvantages of this insurance.
b. What other alternatives might he consider?

Suggested Readings

"Looking Behind AT&T's Hot New Credit Card." *Changing Times*, September 1990, pp. 98 and 99. Some pluses and minuses about AT&T's new bank card.

"Smart Cards: Pocket Power." *Newsweek*, July 31, 1989, pp. 53–55. An interesting coverage of the new technology in credit cards that are electronically readable.

"The Cheapest Credit Cards." *Consumer's Research Magazine*, March 1989, pp. 18–19. Provides information on how and where to get low-cost credit cards.

"The New World of Debit Cards." *Consumer Reports*, June 1990, p. 422. The benefits and costs of using debit cards.

"The Right Credit Card for the Road." *U.S. News & World Report*, June 26, 1989, p. 68. Explores the pros and cons and how to choose among travel and entertainment cards.

"Those $*&*!!#% Credit Cards." *Money*, February 1989, pp. 120–121. How to understand the details of your credit card statements.

"Welcome to the 1990's." *Newsweek*, May 21, 1990, p. 72. Tips on how to get low-cost credit in the tight-credit market of the early 1990s.

"With Credit Cards, As Ever, If You See Bait, Look for a Trap." *Money*, May 1989, p. 15. Advises that consumer be wary when credit card offers promise too much.

"Your Credit Muscle." *Changing Times*, June 1989, p. 90. Explains your rights to withhold payment for ripoffs purchased with a credit card.

7 Planned Borrowing

OBJECTIVES

After reading this chapter, you should be able to

1. Discuss the planned use of credit and explain the role of inflation and taxes in the decision to borrow or wait and pay cash.

2. Speak the language of consumer loans.

3. Describe the sources of consumer loans.

4. Calculate the APR and finance charges on both single-payment and installment loans.

5. Explain the components of a credit agreement.

6. Identify and describe eight signals of overextension of credit, list places to obtain credit counseling, and distinguish between two types of bankruptcy.

As mentioned in the last chapter, more people use installment debt than open-ended credit. This chapter examines the hows and whys of planned borrowing, sometimes called *installment debt* or *consumer loans*. First we discuss planned credit usage, including the issue of whether to save or use credit considering the impact of inflation and taxes. Then we examine some of the important terminology of consumer loans and where to get them. This is followed by an explanation of how finance charges on consumer loans are computed and a description of the features of a credit agreement. The chapter ends with the topics of credit overextension and bankruptcy.

Planning Credit Use

Using credit requires deliberate action and thinking. To use credit intelligently, you should learn when it is best to borrow and how to establish your own debt limits. Setting debt limits for dual-earner households may be a special problem.

When Should You Use Credit?

People use credit for four primary reasons: convenience, emergencies, planned expenditures for major purchases, and investments. It may be convenient to use credit cards to purchase gasoline, to take advantage of a sale price on clothing, or to enjoy an expensive meal. It is important to pay these credit bills in full when they are due because it will be difficult to get ahead financially and achieve your goals if month after month you commit dollars to repayments for convenience borrowing. Borrowing for emergencies is warranted, because emergencies cannot be completely planned for in the budgeting process. If you have only $500 in savings and emergency automobile repairs cost $1600, your choice is twofold: Either don't drive the vehicle or borrow funds to pay for the repairs. Again, your financial management objective should be to pay off such debts as quickly as possible. This then frees funds for savings, investments, and/or other spending.

Planned borrowing typically is for homes, automobiles, computers, furniture, and major appliances. For many people, these items are too expensive to purchase without using credit. The financial management task is to determine when and how often to use credit for these purchases and how much credit to use. Your decisions will be based on your needs and wants as well as how effectively you personally handle debt. Sometimes it is advantageous to borrow funds in order to make investments. This is especially true when the cost of borrowing is exceeded by the return on the investment.

Should You Borrow to Buy Now or Save Up to Pay Cash?

Your conscience may tell you never to use consumer credit because you want to avoid getting into debt, and about half the population agrees with you. There are times, however, when it may be wiser to use credit. Let's consider the comparative costs of buying on credit versus saving the money to later pay cash.

Suppose you want to buy a $2000 stereo system. A loan of $2000 that must be repaid in 12 monthly installments could have payments of $182 each, including interest. The dollar cost of credit would be $184 (12 months × $182 = $2184; $2184 − $2000 = $184). Your alternative is to save $162 for 12 months at 6 percent interest. At the end of the year, you would withdraw the $1944 deposited, plus $56 in interest, a total of $2000, to make the purchase. At first glance it seems that the better course of action is to save, thereby avoiding the $184 cost of credit. But is it? Only if you ignore two important factors—inflation and taxes—in your decision.

Inflation and taxes affect the choice between using credit or saving up to pay cash.

Using the preceding example, let's assume inflation is at 10 percent. The stereo system will then cost $200 more at the end of the year than it did at the beginning, or $2200. You also must consider taxes. Interest income earned on savings deposits is taxable on your federal tax return. Assuming that you pay a marginal tax rate of 28 percent on income (discussed further in Chapter 8), you will need to save $178 per month, and the tax on the interest income will be $18. Thus the final dollar cost for the product in 1 year, after inflation and taxes, is $2218 ($2200 + $18). Yet, as shown earlier, the cost to make the $2000 purchase immediately on credit is $2184. Thus it costs $34 less ($2218 − 2184) to buy on credit now than it would if you waited and bought later, after prices rose. Does this mean you should seriously consider buying most items on credit? No, but it should certainly demonstrate that buying on credit may be wise when inflation is high, the cost of credit is not prohibitive, and interest rates on savings are low.

Establishing Debt Limits

Smart people establish their own debt limits.

A debt limit may be set for you if you go to a bank and try to borrow $45,000 to purchase a fancy sports car. Based on what the lender feels is manageable for you, you might be allowed to borrow $15,000. People who succeed financially generally establish their own **debt limit,** which is the maximum *they* feel they should borrow based on their ability to meet the repayment obligations. When setting a realistic debt level, do not include convenience debts that you will pay in full when the bill arrives. Also do not include first mortgage loans on homes; these will be handled

TABLE 7.1

Debt Limits as a Percentage of Disposable Personal Income

Percent	For Current Debt*	Take on Additional Debt?
10 or less	Safe limit; borrower feels little debt pressure.	Could be undertaken cautiously.
11 to 15	Possibly safe limit; borrower feels some pressure.	Should not be undertaken.
16 to 20	Fully extended; borrower hopes that no emergency arises.	Only the fearless and/or foolhardy ask for more.
21 to 25	Overextended; borrower worries about debts.	No, borrower should see a credit counselor.
26 or more	Disastrous; borrower may feel desperate.	Impossible; borrower will probably declare bankruptcy.

* Excluding home mortgage loans and convenience purchases to be repaid in full when the bill arrives.

separately when making an estimate of the mortgage you would qualify for (see Chapter 10). There are three ways to determine debt limits: the disposable-income method, the ratio of debts to equity method, and the continuous-debt method.

Disposable-Income Method   Here you must decide what percentage of your disposable personal income can be spent for regular debt payments. Your **disposable personal income** is the amount of your take-home pay left after all deductions are withheld for taxes, insurance, union dues, and the like.

Table 7.1 shows some monthly debt-payment limits expressed as a percentage of disposable personal income. As illustrated, having to make payments of 16 to 20 percent of disposable personal income means that a borrower is fully extended and that taking on additional debt probably would not be wise. (As mentioned, current debt excludes the first mortgage loan on a home.)

Table 7.2 demonstrates the impact of increasing debts on a budget. After deductions, disposable monthly personal income is $1800. Current budgeted expenses (totaling the full $1800) are allocated in a sample distribution throughout the various categories.

You can see how assuming debt payments of $180 to $450 per month (to buy on credit a new automobile, television set, or stereo system, for example) affects this budget. The financial manager must make decisions about where to make cutbacks so that monthly credit payments can be met. Notice as the debt increases by each 5 percent how much more difficult it is to "find the money" and make the cutbacks. This person reduced expenditures on savings and investments immediately and then finally eliminated all allocations in the category. Food was cut back, but only so much. Utilities, automobile insurance, and rent are relatively fixed; it is hard to reduce these amounts without moving or getting a cheaper

TABLE 7.2
Impact of Increasing Debts on the Budget*
(One Person's Decisions on Where to Cut Back Expenses to Make Increasing Monthly Debt Payments)

Gross income		$26,000	
Deductions for taxes, retirement, insurance		4,400	
Disposable personal income		$21,600	
Monthly		$ 1,800	

	No Debt	10% Debt	15% Debt	20% Debt	25% Debt
Rent	$ 400	$ 400	$ 400	$ 400	$ 400
Savings and investments	200	100	100	60	0
Food	180	160	160	150	150
Utilities (telephone, electricity, heat)	150	150	150	150	150
Insurance (automobile and life)	90	90	90	90	90
Transportation expenses	210	210	180	180	180
Charitable contributions	50	30	20	0	0
Entertainment	200	180	160	150	150
Clothing	50	40	30	30	0
Vacations and long weekends	25	25	20	15	15
Medical and dental expenses	20	20	20	20	20
Newspapers and magazines	10	10	10	10	10
Vices	40	40	35	35	35
Cable TV	15	15	15	15	15
Personal care	25	25	25	25	25
Gifts and holidays	25	25	25	20	20
Health club	40	40	40	40	40
Miscellaneous	70	60	50	50	50
Debt repayments	0	180	270	360	450
TOTAL	$1800	$1800	$1800	$1800	$1800

* Amounts in color are the changes—cutbacks—made in order to make the increasingly larger debt payments.

High debts will severely reduce disposable income.

car. Entertainment was steadily reduced, and charitable contributions were eliminated. Further reductions in other areas would seriously affect the person's quality of life.

Are you curious as to where you would have made the reductions? Perhaps spending a few minutes right now changing the figures in Table 7.2 will give you a feel both for your priorities and for how large a debt limit you might establish. Understand also that the disposable-income method focuses on the debt payments and not the debts themselves. You can get lower payments by taking out a longer-term loan, but the total repayment goes up because of the higher finance charge on longer-term loans.

Ratio of Debts to Equity Method Another method of determining whether you have too much debt is to calculate the ratio of your debts (not including a first mortgage) to your net worth (excluding the value of a first home). Most people have more in assets than in liabilities, resulting in a positive net worth. For example, a person with $42,000 in assets who owes $14,000 has a debt-to-equity ratio of 1:2 ($42,000 − $14,000 = $28,000/$14,000). This method gives a quick idea of your financial solvency. If debts equal or exceed equity (1:1 or 1.1:1), you are probably at your maximum debt limit. Exceptions would be recent graduates, who often accumulate large education loans. They would have a poor ratio of debt to equity, but their substantial earning power offsets the ratio. However, if 5 years later the situation has not changed, then a problem likely exists.

Continuous-Debt Method   A final method to use in determining when debts are too large is the continuous-debt method. If you are unable to get completely out of debt every 3 years (except for mortgage and education loans), you probably lean too heavily on debt. You could be developing a credit lifestyle, in which you are never out of debt and continuously pay out income for finance charges.

Debt Limits for Dual-Earner Households

Aside from the companionship and other emotional benefits, it can be wonderful to double your income by joining incomes with another. Two people earning $26,000 a year each will gross $52,000! The net disposable personal income from this total may be around $39,000, or $3250 monthly. Such an amount means a couple can afford a much higher level of living than before combining incomes.

After joining incomes, couples will find it wise to mutually decide on a debt limit, remembering to include any unpaid student loans in their calculations. The guidelines given in Table 7.1 are realistic, but they would allow a doubling of debt payments if the addition of a second earner doubled household earnings. Since it is likely that one of the earners will see a reduction in earnings as family responsibilities grow, debts that were manageable with two incomes may become burdensome and possibly overwhelming. Also, it is likely that a dual-earner couple will never have a better opportunity to seriously expand an investment program than shortly after beginning couplehood. Taking on substantial debt payments will seriously constrain investment opportunities. Although some new debts are probably desirable and unavoidable, couples would be wise to pay early attention to making investments that will ensure future financial security.

Speaking the Language of Consumer Loans

Consumer loans are usually classified as installment or noninstallment credit. As discussed in the preceding chapter, **installment credit**, requires that the consumer must, by contract, repay the amount owed in a specific

TABLE 7.3
Monthly Installment Payment (Principal and Interest) Required to Repay $1000*

Terms of Installments	Annual Percentage Rate								
	4%	*6%*	*8%*	*10%*	*12%*	*14%*	*16%*	*18%*	*20%*
1 year (12 months)	85.15	86.07	86.99	87.92	88.85	89.79	90.73	91.68	92.63
2 years (24 months)	43.42	44.32	45.23	46.14	47.07	48.01	48.96	49.92	50.90
3 years (36 months)	29.52	30.42	31.34	32.27	33.21	34.18	35.16	36.15	37.16
4 years (48 months)	22.58	23.49	24.41	25.36	26.33	27.33	28.34	29.37	30.43
5 years (60 months)	18.42	19.33	20.28	21.25	22.24	23.27	24.32	25.39	26.49

* To illustrate, assume you want to know how much the monthly payments would be to finance an automobile loan of $9000 at 10 percent for 3 years. To repay $1000, the figure is $32.27; therefore, multiply by 9 (for $9000) to determine that $290.43 is required for 36 months of payments. When using amounts greater or less than $1000, convert using decimals. For example, a loan of $950 at 10 percent for 3 years would be calculated as follows: $32.27 × .95 = $30.66.

Source: This table was derived from the INSTALL program of the Personal Finance Cookbook software package.

number of equal payments, usually monthly. An example is an automobile loan to be repaid in 48 equal monthly payments. Most installment loans involve a *loan book.* This is a coupon booklet with perforated, tear-out pages that are to be sent to the lender along with each payment. Each coupon gives details of each payment, such as the date and amount due. To help you figure out the monthly payment for various loan amounts, Table 7.3 illustrates various monthly installment payments to repay a $1000 loan at common interest rates and time periods. For loans of other dollar amounts, divide the amount by 1000 and multiply the result by the appropriate figure from the table. **Noninstallment credit** (covered in Chapter 6) is debt that is repaid in a single payment or repaid as open-ended credit.

Loans are made on the assumption that they will be repaid. To help ensure repayment, **creditors** (persons or institutions to whom money is due) frequently prefer to offer secured loans. A **secured loan** requires **collateral,** which is a certain asset that the borrower pledges to back up the debt, or a **cosigner,** another person who will agree to pay the loan should the borrower fail to do so. Cosigners have the same legal obligations for repayment as the original borrower. Hence being a cosigner is a major responsibility. A loan secured with collateral means that the lender has a **security interest** in that collateral. Thus the creditor can go to court in the event that the borrower defaults to seize the property through the process of **repossession.** Generally, the repossessed item is sold by the lender and the proceeds received (minus expenses) are applied to the debt owed. Then the borrower is sued for any remaining balance due. By having a secure interest in the property, the lender can be fairly confident that most, if not all, of the loan eventually will be repaid. A common type of secured loan is a **second mortgage** loan, which is a loan over and above a first mortgage with the borrower's home as the collateral. An **unsecured loan** has neither the assurance of collateral nor a cosigner. It is a loan given primarily on the good character of the borrower. Since there is a greater risk with unsecured loans compared with secured debts, the interest rate charged is usually higher. Most single-payment loans are unsecured debts.

Consumers typically obtain installment credit in the form of cash loans and purchase loans. A **cash loan** means that a person borrows cash and then uses it to make purchases, to pay off other debts, or to make investments. A **purchase loan** (sometimes called **sales credit**) means that a consumer makes a purchase on credit with no cash transferring from the lender to the borrower. Cash flows from the lender to the seller, or the seller may be the lender. For example, a buyer may obtain a purchase loan from General Motors Acceptance Corporation (GMAC) to buy a new Chevrolet.

Sources of Consumer Loans

Objective
To be able to describe the sources of consumer loans.

Table 7.4 summarizes the features of the four major sources of typical consumer loans: banks/S&Ls, credit unions, consumer finance companies, and sales finance companies. These are also discussed below, along with several other sources of consumer loans, including friends and relatives, life insurance companies, industrial banks, loans by mail, second mortgages and home-equity credit-line loans, education loans, and pawnbrokers.

Banks and S&Ls

Banks and S&Ls are in business to make loans.

The term *bank* technically refers to commercial banks and mutual savings banks (described in Chapter 5) because they accept checking deposits *and* make commercial loans. However, from the consumer-borrower perspective, deregulation has made savings and loan associations (S&Ls) very similar to commercial banks and mutual savings banks. Thus all will be described as one source of consumer loans—"banks."

Banks are full-service institutions offering a variety of loans—secured, unsecured, installment, and noninstallment—to consumers and businesses. Many banks allow customers to use their savings accounts for collateral and charge a lower interest rate, since this almost guarantees repayment. Banks associated with a bank card company (such as VISA or MasterCard) prefer to offer very small loans ($100 to $300) as cash advances on a credit card, since recordkeeping costs can exceed interest earned on installment loans of less than $500.

Banks tend to make loans to their own customers and to others who are good financial risks. However, research indicates that many people who go elsewhere for loans actually do meet the qualifications for bank lending. For most loans, banks are quite competitive in their rates; this is partially because funds loaned are obtained primarily from depositors. Commonly, the APR is 10 to 18 percent.

Credit Unions

Credit unions can be a low-cost source of consumer loans.

Credit unions are cooperative thrift and loan associations that serve members only. People who wish to borrow or save at a credit union and who qualify for membership can easily join by purchasing a **credit union share** by making an interest-earning deposit of as little as $5 or $10. Most

TABLE 7.4

Major Sources of Consumer Loans

		Credit Source		
	Banks/S&Ls	*Credit Unions*	*Consumer Finance Companies*	*Sales Finance Companies*
Types of loans	Single-payment loans Installment loans Passbook loans Credit card loans Second mortgages Home-equity credit-line loans Automatic overdrafts	Installment loans Credit card loans Automatic overdrafts Home-equity credit-line loans	Installment loans Second mortgages	Installment loans
Lending policies	Loans to average and better credit-risk people Often requires collateral Makes secured and unsecured loans Rates vary according to type of loan and security Lower rates to their own customers	Lend to members only Average credit risk people approved Requires repayment by payroll deductions Makes secured and unsecured loans Provide free credit life and disability insurance for the amount of the loan Often have lowest interest rates available	Most credit risks acceptable Collateral often required Rates are high and vary according to risk, type of loan, and security	Loans to average and better credit-risk people Loans for collateral purchases only Loans tied in to seller (Sears, GMAC, etc.) who approves application Rates are usually competitive with banks/S&Ls; special promotion rates are lower

credit union loans are installment loans, and payments are typically withheld from the borrower's paycheck through an arrangement with the employer. This convenience for employees also lowers collection costs for credit unions. They prefer to make loans to good risks and will require collateral or a cosigner for large or higher-risk loans. Since some members of credit unions donate their time to the organization (the elected officers) and office space is inexpensive (sometimes provided by the employer), costs are kept down. Also, because the funds lent almost always come from deposits made by members, credit unions do not have to borrow money at high rates to then lend to applicants. Commonly, the APR is 9 to 18 percent, which is quite competitive. Credit unions usually offer free **credit life insurance** (where the loan is paid in full should the borrower die) on all loans.

Consumer Finance Companies

Consumer finance companies specialize in small loans and are therefore also known as small-loan companies. They range from the well-recognized Household Finance Corporation and Beneficial Finance Corporation to a local neighborhood lender. Such companies make secured and unsecured loans on an installment basis. All states have small-loan laws that regulate consumer finance companies. These limit the maximum amount that can be lent (commonly $2000 to $5000) and the maximum interest rate that can be charged (perhaps 48 percent on loans of less than $500, 36 percent on amounts from $500 to $2000, and 24 percent on amounts above $2000).

Rates are higher because consumer finance companies make higher-risk loans that have higher default rates. Higher rates also result because these companies accept no deposits; they borrow from commercial banks to obtain funds to lend to customers. Also, small loans are generally more expensive in terms of recordkeeping. Approximately one-fifth of the loans granted by consumer finance companies are for the purpose of debt consolidation. Other common purposes of such loans are for travel, vacations, education, automobiles, and home furnishings.

Sales Finance Companies

Sales finance companies are business-related lenders (such as General Motors Acceptance Corporation, Ford Motor Credit, and J. C. Penney Credit Corporation) that are primarily engaged in financing the sales of their parent companies. They specialize in making purchase loans, with the item being purchased as collateral. The seller of the item has the customer fill out a credit application. Then, because the seller often works in association with the sales finance company, credit can be approved almost immediately.

Since sales finance companies require collateral and deal only with customers that are medium to good risks, their interest rates are competitive. Sales finance companies' rates are usually 1 or 2 percentage points higher than a bank's or a credit union's but are lower than the rate of interest on most credit cards. However, the rates may be much lower if the seller subsidizes the rate to encourage sales, as exemplified by periodic special financing deals on new cars.

Friends and Relatives

Friends and relatives were a typical source of loans in the past before banks began offering consumer loans in addition to their traditional commercial loans to businesses. People borrow from friends and relatives when the purpose of the borrowed funds is too risky for conventional lenders or if the borrower has a poor or nonexistent credit history. Two things are important when borrowing from friends and relatives. First, make out a *promissory note* (a written loan contract), since it is more businesslike. In case of default, the lender will need such a document to take an income tax loss. Second, establish a specific repayment schedule. Failure to follow these suggestions may result in the borrower deciding that the loan was actually a gift with ill feelings developing in the lender. One advantage of these loans is the generally low or nonexistent interest rate.

Life Insurance Companies

You are actually borrowing your own money when you borrow against a life insurance policy.

Policyholders can obtain loans from their life insurance companies *if* their policies have an accumulated cash value. *Term* policies have no cash value, and the policies that do have cash value take many years to build up to an amount sufficient to borrow. (This is discussed in detail in Chapter 14.) A significant advantage to borrowing on a life insurance policy is that the interest rate ranges from 5 to 8 percent, which is extremely low. However, it is *your* money that you are borrowing. Also, it may become difficult to pay back the loan, because there is no fixed schedule of repayment and no dunning letters are sent to remind the borrower to pay off the debt. Of course, there is no risk for the lender because the policy is 100 percent security. If the insured dies before repaying the loan, the insurance company pays the beneficiaries the value of the policy minus the debt and any outstanding interest.

Industrial Banks

The term *industrial* in the name *industrial bank* comes from the early twentieth-century emphasis of these banks on making small loans to industrial workers. Although they have been largely replaced today by consumer finance companies, these typically small thrift and loan institutions are legally authorized in almost half the states. They make small installment loans, and their interest rates are governed by state small-loan laws and are similar to rates charged by consumer finance companies. Industrial banks make loans to higher-risk customers and frequently require collateral or a cosigner.

Loans by Mail

Small-loan companies, such as industrial banks and consumer finance companies, sometimes specialize in making loans by mail. They advertise in magazines to attract borrowers, who complete a credit application and receive an approval by mail.

Higher-risk people are more apt to want to borrow by mail, especially those who have been turned down by other sources. Accordingly, the interest rate charged is higher than for a typical loan from a consumer finance company (perhaps 6 to 10 percent more). Such lenders also have the added expense and risk of having to collect a debt from out of state. The rates charged are based on the usury or small-loan laws of the state in which the lender is incorporated. Collateral and cosigners are often required to help ensure repayment.

Second Mortgages and Home-Equity Credit-Line Loans

Banks, savings and loan associations, credit unions, bank credit card companies, and financial services companies make second mortgage loans on an installment basis. The home serves as collateral for the loan, although the holder of the first mortgage would have first right to the home in the event of default. In recent years, lenders also have begun offering **home-equity credit-line loans,** which are a form of second mortgage setup much like a revolving charge account. The credit limit is set at perhaps 75 percent of the home's appraised value minus what might be owed on the first mortgage. Once such a line of credit has been established, for a fee of $50 to $1500 or more, it can be used for years, usually by check or debit or credit card. Interest rates are variable, but they tend to be lower than for other types of consumer credit. Failure to repay a second mortgage or home-equity credit-line loan may result in the forced sale of the home even if the first mortgage is not in default. Second mortgage loans and home-equity credit-line loans are discussed more fully in Chapter 10.

Education Loans

Several types of education loans are available.

Education loans are available directly from the federal government and from private sources, such as banks, savings and loan associations, and credit unions. Before applying for such loans, a student should check into obtaining an educational grant that does not have to be repaid. There are two main grant programs. Pell grants, also known as Basic Educational Opportunity Grants (BEOG), are the largest government educational grant program. Pell grant money is granted on the basis of financial need, with maximum amounts varying from college to college up to $22,000 per year. Supplemental Educational Opportunity Grants (SEOG) are available to students attending higher-cost schools. Again, the amounts vary but can be as high as $4000 per year.

There are three federal loan programs for students. Both the Perkins loan (formerly the National Direct Student Loan) and the Stafford loan (formerly the Guaranteed Student Loan) programs are for needy students, while the Parent Loans for Undergraduate Students (PLUS) and Supplemental Loans for Students (SLS) have no income restrictions. These loans have relatively low interest rates (Perkins loans may be as low as 5 percent), and repayment usually must begin 6 months after graduation. Education loans are also available from almost all state governments, and these are often not based on need. Loan limits are usually $10,000 or more a year rather than the more restrictive federal loans. Many colleges also have special loan programs, and a limited number of financial institutions offer reduced-interest education loans. You can get more information about these loan programs from college financial aid offices and state offices of higher education. Those who fail to repay their federal loans face the likelihood that the government will keep their income tax refunds and probably sue them to collect the debt.

| What If You Need to Borrow $1000 in a Hurry?

Your 5-year-old car has just suffered a cracked engine block. The car is in otherwise good condition and should provide several more years of service. You decide to go ahead with the $1000 repair. Perhaps you are thinking of charging the repairs to a bank credit card or an oil-company card. Or you are thinking of applying for a loan through your credit union or local bank. Where can you get the funds for a good price? The following table shows the cost of borrowing $1000 over 2 years from various sources. Obviously, the life insurance option is best, but it is only available if you have a cash-value policy. It may be worthwhile to join a credit union and apply for a loan. If these options take more time than the repair shop will allow, using a credit card may be necessary initially. But then you can go ahead and apply for a credit union or bank loan to pay off the credit card bill. As an aside, some consumer advisors recommend always using a credit card initially for automobile repairs because it is possible to obtain a charge-back if the repairs are faulty.

Relative Costs to Borrow $1000 as an Unsecured Loan for 2 Years and Repay in Monthly Installments

Lender	Annual Percentage Rate	Monthly Payment	Total Finance Charge
Life insurance company	8%	$45.23	$ 85.82
Credit union	12	47.07	129.68
Commercial bank	16	48.96	175.04
Mutual savings bank	16	48.96	175.04
Savings and loan association	16	48.96	175.04
Bank credit card	18	49.92	198.08
Oil-company credit card	20	50.90	221.60
Consumer finance company	24	52.87	268.88

Pawnbrokers

Pawnbrokers are the lenders of last resort.

Pawnbrokers offer single-payment loans (typically for 6 months or less) based on the value of items of personal property of the borrower that are turned over to the pawnbroker. The pawnbroker can legally sell the item if the borrower fails to redeem the property by turning in the pawn ticket along with the amount due, plus interest, during the time period specified. The interest rate charged can go as high as 100 percent, depending on state laws and the item being pawned. Clearly, a pawnbroker is a lender of last resort for borrowers. On the plus side, loans are made immediately when the item of personal property is turned over to the pawnbroker.

Know How Finance Charges and Annual Percentage Rates Are Calculated

Objective
To be able to calculate the APR and finance charges on both single-payment and installment notes.

The federal Truth-in-Lending law (Consumer Credit Protection Act of 1968) requires lenders to disclose to credit applicants the interest rate expressed as an annual percentage rate (APR) as well as the finance charge in dollars. Borrowers can then compare rates for the best deal. When a borrower inquires about the interest rate that will be charged, the lender will respond with a **stated rate** of interest (simply any verbal interest rate quoted by a lender). By law, this rate must be the same rate as the APR. In practice, this may not be the case. Some lenders are ignorant of the law, and others may attempt to hide the annual percentage rate. In some cases, such as in open-ended credit, the APR will not be known until all the specifics of the transaction have been decided.

The finance charge for a loan must include all mandatory charges to be paid by the borrower. In addition to interest, lenders may charge fees for a credit investigation, a loan application, or credit or disability life insurance (to pay the lender in case the borrower dies or becomes seriously disabled before completing repayment). When these fees are *required,* the lender must include them in the finance charge in dollars as part of the APR calculations. When the borrower elects them voluntarily, the fees are not part of the finance charge and APR calculations but do raise the cost of borrowing.

Interest costs make up the greatest portion of finance charges. There are three methods used to calculate interest on installment and noninstallment credit: the simple-interest method, the add-on interest method, and the discount method. Equation (7.1) is a *simple-interest formula* that is often used to calculate the dollar amount of interest.

$$I = PRT \tag{7.1}$$

where

$I = $ *interest* or finance charges
$P = $ *principal* amount borrowed
$R = $ *rate* of interest (simple, add-on, or discount rate)
$T = $ *time* of loan in years

Always use the APR to compare the cost of credit from various sources.

Borrowers should check that they are being verbally quoted the annual percentage rate (APR) and that the same APR is the rate in the written credit contract. What follows is a discussion of the way the annual percentage rate is calculated for various types of loans.

APR Calculations for Single-Payment Loans

There are two methods of calculating interest on single-payment loans: the simple-interest method and the discount method. The APR reveals the difference in the effective cost of credit for each.

The Simple-Interest Method With the *simple-interest method,* interest is calculated by applying an interest rate to the unpaid balance of the debt. Suppose you took out a single-payment loan of $500 for 2 years at a simple interest rate of 12 percent. Your interest charges would be $120 ($500 × 12 percent × 2 years), which would be added on to the debt, and you would make one payment of $620 at the end of 2 years. To calculate the APR, divide the average outstanding loan balance ($500, since the full amount was owed the entire time) into the average *annual* finance charge ($60, since $120 is the total for 2 years).

$$APR = \frac{\text{average annual finance charge}}{\text{average outstanding loan balance}}$$

$$= \frac{\$60}{\$500} = 12 \text{ percent} \tag{7.2}$$

As you can see, the APR is 12 percent. When the simple-interest method is used, the simple rate of interest and the APR are always equivalent for single-payment loans.

The Discount Method Banks and consumer finance companies often use the *discount method* when making loans. With this method, interest is calculated and then *subtracted* from the amount of the loan. The difference is the actual cash given to the borrower. Essentially, the finance charges are prepaid by the borrower.

If we use the same figures as in the last example to illustrate, only the denominator changes in Equation (7.2). The average outstanding loan balance, or principal, is $380 [$500 − ($500 × 0.12 × 2)], because that is the actual amount of money received from the lending institution 2 years ago. Thus $380 divided into the average annual finance charge of $60 gives an APR of 15.8 percent, as compared with the discount rate of 12 percent. It should be clear that if a borrower does not have full use of the money borrowed, the annual percentage rate must be higher. The discount method always gives a higher APR than the simple-interest method for single-payment loans at the same interest rates.

APR Calculations for Installment Loans

The simple-interest, add-on, and discount methods are all used to determine the interest on installment loans. The simple-interest method is widely used to calculate interest by credit unions. The add-on method predominates at banks, S&Ls, and finance companies in installment loans for automobiles, furniture, and other credit requiring collateral.

A simple-interest rate is equivalent to the APR.

The Simple-Interest Method Again, with the simple-interest method, the interest assessed each payment period (usually each month) is based on the outstanding balance of the installment loan. The lender initially designs a schedule to have the balance repaid in full after a certain number of months, such as in Table 7.5. The borrower is free to vary the rate of

TABLE 7.5
Sample Repayment Schedule for $1000 Principal plus Simple Interest (1.5 Percent per Month)

Month	Outstanding Balance	Payment	Interest	Principal	Ending Balance
1	$1,000.00	$91.68	$15.00	$76.68	$923.32
2	923.32	91.68	13.85	77.83	845.49
3	845.49	91.68	12.68	79.00	766.49
4	766.49	91.68	11.50	80.18	686.31
5	686.31	91.68	10.29	81.39	604.92
6	604.92	91.68	9.07	82.61	522.31
7	522.31	91.68	7.83	83.85	438.46
8	438.46	91.68	6.58	85.10	353.36
9	353.36	91.68	5.30	86.38	266.98
10	266.98	91.68	4.00	87.68	179.30
11	179.30	91.68	2.69	88.99	90.31
12	90.31	91.66	1.35	90.31	0

repayment by making payments larger than those scheduled or to repay in full at any time. Thus Equations (7.1) and (7.2) are not useful with simple-interest installment loans because the finance charges are not known in advance owing to possible variations in the repayment schedule.

It is easy to illustrate the simple-interest method applied to an installment loan. As shown in Table 7.5, at the end of the first month, a periodic interest rate of 1.5 percent (18 percent annually divided by 12) is applied to the beginning balance of $1000 for an interest charge of $15. Of the first monthly installment of $91.68, $76.68 goes toward payment of the principal and $15 goes toward the simple interest. For the second month, the interest portion of the payment drops to $13.85, since the outstanding balance after the first month is $923.32 ($1000 minus $76.68). Since the simple-interest method of calculating interest on installment loans applies the rate to the outstanding loan balance, the APR and the simple interest rate are the same. (This method of paying off a loan, called *amortization*, is discussed further in Chapter 10.)

The Add-On Method The add-on method is a traditional and widely used technique for computing finance charges on installment loans. Once again, Equation (7.1) is used to calculate the finance charge or dollar cost of credit. [The interest rate used in Equation (7.1) for the add-on method is an add-on rate and is not to be confused with the APR.]

For example, assume that Lillian Mohr of Tallahassee, Florida, obtained a $2000 loan for 2 years at 9 percent add-on interest. Using Equation (7.1), the finance charge is $360 ($2000 × 0.09 × 2). The finance charge ($360) is *added* to the principal ($2000) for a total of $2360, which is divided by the number of payments (24) for a monthly payment of $98.33. However, we know that the APR must be higher than the add-on rate of 9 percent because the monthly payments mean that Lillian does not have full use of the principal for the 2 years. Equations (7.3) or (7.4) in Table

What If You Are Offered a Variable-Rate Loan?

It is becoming increasingly common for lenders to offer variable-rate loans as one of the alternatives available to borrowers. Should you consider this type of loan? And just what is a variable-rate loan anyway? A **variable-rate loan** is one for which the periodic rate fluctuates according to some measure of interest rates in the economy as a whole. Variable-rate loans are typically simple-interest loans. They can be structured such that the payment increases or decreases with changes in the interest rate applied to the unpaid balance. Or, more commonly, the payment stays the same, but the payments will last beyond the scheduled final payment or there will be a final balloon payment. The advantage of variable-rate loans is that they usually have a slightly lower (1 to 3 percentage points) initial APR than an equivalent fixed-rate loan. The lender is willing to do this because the lender can pass the negative effects of inflation on to the borrower, since interest rates generally go up when inflation is accelerating. However, interest rates also can decline, and the borrower will benefit. The disadvantage is the obvious potential for a higher rate to be applied in the future. If you think that interest rates in the economy will likely decrease over the life of the loan, a variable rate might be a wise choice. However, of course, the opposite is also true.

TABLE 7.6
Calculating the Annual Percentage Rate (APR)*

Constant-Ratio Formula [Equation (7.3)]	N-Ratio Formula [Equation (7.4)]

$$\text{APR} = \frac{2YF}{D(P+1)}$$

$$\text{APR} = \frac{Y(95P + 9)F}{12P(P+1)(4D+F)}$$

$$= \frac{2(12 \times \$280)}{\$2000(12+1)}$$

$$= \frac{12[(95 \times 12) + 9]\$280}{12(12)(12+1)[(4 \times \$2000) + \$280]}$$

$$= \frac{\$6720}{\$26,000}$$

$$= \frac{3,860,640}{15,500,160}$$

$$= 25.8 \text{ percent}$$

$$= 24.9 \text{ percent}$$

where

$\text{APR} =$ *annual percentage rate*
$Y =$ number of payment periods in 1 *year*
$F =$ *finance* charges in dollars (dollar cost of credit)
$D =$ *debt* (amount borrowed or proceeds)
$P =$ total number of scheduled *payments*

---

* For a $2000 loan for 1 year at 14 percent, add-on interest with equal monthly payments of $190.

The conservative borrower shops for credit (yet only one person in three does) and verifies the accuracy of the APR that is quoted when looking for a loan. If you use the methods illustrated in this chapter, be sure to include any mandatory charges other than interest in the finance charge you use. Or, you could total the fees and the monthly payments to be made and substract the actual dollar amount received to determine the finance charge. The formulas in Table 7.6 are roughly equivalent, although the N-ratio formula is more precise than the constant-ratio formula, since the latter often slightly overstates the correct rate. These formulas can be used to determine the APR for all add-on loans that require regular payments of equal amounts.

7.6 can be used to calculate the APR. Using Equation (7.3), the APR is 17.28 percent $[(2 \times 12 \times \$360)/(\$2000 \times 25)]$. Note that the APR is approximately double the add-on rate because, on average, Lillian only has use of half the borrowed money during the loan period.

The Discount Method   Occasionally, the discount method may be used for an installment loan. In the preceding example, Lillian would only receive \$1640 at the beginning of the loan period. Using Equation (7.3) again, the APR would be 21.07 percent $[(2 \times 12 \times \$360)/(\$1640 \times 25)]$.

The Credit Agreement

Objective
To be able to explain the components of a credit agreement.

The credit agreement is the contract between the creditor and you.

When you obtain an installment loan, you will sign a contract between you and the lender called a **credit agreement**. A **retail installment contract** is the type of credit agreement used to finance an automobile or a color television set, for example, through the seller or a sales finance company. A retail installment contract contains all the elements of credit agreements and will serve as an example here. It includes a sales contract, a security agreement, a note, an insurance agreement, and some credit clauses to safeguard the lender in case of default. Figure 7.1 shows a retail installment contract form that complies with the Truth-in-Lending Act.

Two kinds of retail installment contracts are used. With an **installment purchase agreement** (also known as a *collateral installment loan* or *chattel mortgage*), the title of the property passes to the buyer when the document is signed. With a **conditional sales contract** (also known as a *financing lease*), the title does not pass to the buyer until the last installment payment has been paid. The installment purchase agreement provides full protection for the buyer, since the seller must follow all state-prescribed legal procedures when repossessing the property and suing for any balance of

Figure 7.1
Retail Installment Contract

Source: Copyright 1989 Bankers Systems, Inc., St. Cloud, MN. Used with permission.

RETAIL INSTALLMENT CONTRACT AND SECURITY AGREEMENT

© BANKERS SYSTEMS, INC., 1982, ST. CLOUD, MN 56301 FORM RS-PI-KY 1/23/84

Date _____
Number _____

Buyer(s) Name and Address _____ (A)

Seller(s) Name and Address _____

SALE: In this contract the words I, me, and my refer to the Buyer(s) listed above, jointly and severally. The words you and your refer to the Seller(s) identified above, and anyone to whom this contract is assigned. I have been given an opportunity to purchase the property described below for the cash price or the total sale price, which is the total price of the property if I buy it over time. I agree to buy this property from you at the total sale price stated below.

I agree to pay you the total of payments of _____

Dollars ($ _____) as specified below:

☐ a. in _____ installments of _____ each, beginning _____ , 19 _____ and on the same day of each ☐ month

Payment Schedule ☐ _____ thereafter until paid in full.

☐ b. _____ (D)

PAYMENTS: This is a precomputed contract, which means the sum I have agreed to pay already includes the finance charges payable hereafter to the maturity date.

PREPAYMENT: I may prepay this contract in full or in part at any time. Any partial prepayment will not excuse any later scheduled payments until this contract is paid in full.

Upon prepayment in full, or acceleration of the balance upon my default, I will receive a refund credit of the finance charge based on the rule of 78's. No refund less than $1.00 will be made.

☐ If checked, an acquisition fee of $ _____ will be deducted from the finance charge before application of the rebate formula. No part of this fee will be refunded.

DELINQUENCY: I agree to pay a late charge of 5% of the amount of a payment which is late by more than 10 days after it is due, but not less than $1.00 or more than $5.00.

I agree to pay the court costs you incur to collect this contract, if I default, and attorney's fees not exceeding 15% of the amount due and payable under the contract, if referred to an attorney, not a salaried employee of yours.

SECURITY: I give you a security interest in the property described below, including all accessions, attachments, accessories, equipment and all proceeds from the property.

DESCRIPTION	NEW OR USED	UNIT NO. OR SERIAL NO.	CABINET OR MOTOR NO.	SALE PRICE OF EACH
(C)				

If Motor vehicle, including: ☐ radio ☐ power seats ☐ automatic transmission ☐ power brakes ☐ power windows
☐ no. of cylinders ☐ air conditioning ☐ power steering ☐ _____

WARRANTIES: ANY WARRANTIES FOR THE PROPERTY DESCRIBED IN THE SECURITY SECTION ARE ATTACHED TO THIS CONTRACT, AND MADE A PART OF THIS CONTRACT BY REFERENCE. ALL IMPLIED WARRANTIES OF MERCHANTABILITY AND FITNESS FOR A PARTICULAR PURPOSE ARE DISCLAIMED BY THE SELLER AND EXCLUDED FROM THIS AGREEMENT. SELLER SHALL NOT BE LIABLE FOR CONSEQUENTIAL DAMAGES.

USE: This property will be used for ☐ personal, family or household ☐ farming ☐ business purposes.

LOCATION: The property will be located at my address stated above, or _____

If this property is to be attached to real estate, the legal description of the real estate is: _____ and the record owner (if not me) is: _____

I will furnish to you, at your request, a disclaimer signed by all persons having an interest in the above described real estate of any right, title or interest in or lien upon this property prior to the security interest created by this contract.

ANNUAL PERCENTAGE RATE The cost of my credit as a yearly rate.	FINANCE CHARGE The dollar amount the credit will cost me.	AMOUNT FINANCED The amount of credit provided to me or on my behalf.	TOTAL OF PAYMENTS The amount I will have paid when I have made all scheduled payments.	TOTAL SALE PRICE The total cost of my purchase on credit, including my down payment of $ _____
___ %	$	$	$	$

My Payment Schedule will be:	Number of Payments	Amount of Payments	When Payments Are Due
		$	(B)
		$	
		$	

Security: I am giving a security interest in: ☐ (brief description of other property) _____
☐ the goods or property being purchased.

Late Charge: I will be charged 5% of the amount of a payment that is late by more than 10 days after it is due, but not less than $1.00 or more than $5.00.

Prepayment: If I pay off this contract early, I ☐ may ☐ will not be entitled to a refund of part of the Finance Charge.

Filing fees $ _____ Non-filing Insurance $ _____ If the letter "e" is used, it means an estimate. I can see my contract documents for any additional information about nonpayment, default, any required repayment before the scheduled date, and prepayment refunds and penalties.

---

money due on the credit contract. With a conditional sales contract, the lender can repossess the property much more easily. In fact, in some states the lender can take the property back as soon as the buyer falls behind in payments, possibly by taking a car right out of your driveway.

The Sales Contract

The sales contract identifies the parties and the terms of the loan.

The **sales contract** discloses pertinent information about the borrower or lender, the merchandise being purchased, and the mathematical details of

FIGURE 7.1 (continued)

ITEMIZED FINANCE CHARGE OF	$ _____

1. Time price differential .... $ _____
2. _____ $ _____

Credit Insurance: Credit life insurance and credit disability insurance are not required to obtain credit, and will not be provided unless I sign and agree to pay the additional costs.

Type	Premium	Term
Credit Life	(E)	
Credit Disability		
Joint Credit Life		

I ☐ do ☐ do not want credit life insurance.
X _____

I ☐ do ☐ do not want credit disability insurance.
X _____

I ☐ do ☐ do not want joint credit life insurance.
X _____ XX _____

Property Insurance: I may obtain property insurance from anyone that is acceptable to you. If I get the insurance from or through you, I will pay $ _____ for _____ of coverage. The property insurance premium is calculated as follows:

☐ Fire-Theft and Comb. Add'l. Cov. $ _____
☐ $ _____ Deductible Com. Cov. $ _____
☐ $ _____ Deductible Col. Cov. $ _____
☐ _____ $ _____
☐ _____ $ _____

Single Interest Insurance: I may obtain single interest insurance from anyone I want that is acceptable to you. If I get the insurance from or through you I will pay $ _____ for _____ of coverage.

The above insurance does not include liability insurance coverage for bodily injury and property damage unless such insurance is specifically described above.

SALES TAX

1. Sale Price .... $ _____
2. Less: Gross Trade-In Allowance .... – $ _____
3. Taxable Amount .... $ _____
   Sales Tax Percent X _____ %
4. Sales Tax .... $ _____

ITEMIZATION OF AMOUNT FINANCED

1. Cash Price (excluding Sales Tax) .... $ _____
2. Down Payment Computation
   Description of Trade-In

   a) Gross Trade-In Allowance $ _____
   b) Pay-Off (if any) $ _____
   c) Net Trade-In (a - b) $ _____
   d) Cash Down Payment $ _____
   e) Total Down Payment (c + d) $ _____
3. Unpaid Balance of Cash Price (1 - 2) .... $ _____

4. Other Charges | Paid in Cash | Being Financed

   a) To Property Insurance Company $ _____ $ _____
   b) To Credit Life Insurance Company $ _____ $ _____
   c) To Disability Insurance Company $ _____ $ _____
   d) To Public Officials $ _____ $ _____
   e) _____ $ _____ $ _____
   f) _____ $ _____ $ _____
   g) _____ $ _____ $ _____
   h) _____ $ _____ $ _____
   i) _____ $ _____ $ _____
   j) _____ $ _____ $ _____
   k) _____ $ _____ $ _____
5. Principal Balance (3 + 4(a) through 4(k) if financed) ... $ _____
6. Prepaid Finance Charges .... $ _____
7. Amount Financed (5 - 6) .... $ _____

NOTICE TO THE BUYER: (1) Do not sign this contract before you read it or if it contains blank spaces. (2) You are entitled to a copy of the contract you sign. (3) Under the law you have the right, among others, to pay in advance the full amount due, and to obtain under certain conditions a partial refund of the finance charge. (4) This contract shall become effective only when signed and executed by the buyer and seller, and shall apply to and inure to the benefit of and bind the heirs, executors, administrators, successors and assigns of both parties to this contract.

Signed _____ Title _____
For Seller

Assignment

Seller assigns this contract on _____, 19 ____
to _____
_____ in accordance with the
Seller's Assignment appearing on the reverse side. The assignment is 1. ☐ Without Recourse 2. ☐ With Recourse 3. ☐ Subject to a Separate Agreement.
(Seller)
By _____ Title _____

I AGREE TO THE TERMS SET OUT ON THE FRONT AND BACK OF THIS CONTRACT. I have received a copy of this document on today's date.

1. Signed _____ Buyer
2. Signed _____ Buyer
3. Signed _____ Buyer

Any person who signs within this enclosure does so to give you a security interest in the collateral described above, but assumes no personal obligation to pay this contract.
Name _____
X _____ Date _____

White First Copy - Original   Canary Second Copy - Seller/Assignee's Copy   Pink Third Copy - Buyer's Copy   Goldenrod Fourth Copy - Seller's Copy

---

the contract. In Figure 7.1, the sales contract is the section marked "A" and the section marked "B." The Truth-in-Lending Act requires that items in the section marked "B" be written in a consistent manner, including in bold print the terms *finance charge* in dollars and the *annual percentage rate* in numbers.

The Security Agreement

The security agreement identifies the collateral.

The security agreement is the portion of the contract that indicates whether the sales contract is an installment purchase agreement or a conditional sales contract. It is marked "C" in Figure 7.1. (This is an installment purchase agreement.) The **security agreement** gives the lender a legally secure interest in the item being financed. The lender files a **lien** (legal right to hold property or to sell it for payment of a claim) in court in order to make the security interest known to the public. When the contract is paid, the lien is removed.

The Note

The note contains the promise to repay.

The **note** is the formal promise of the borrower to repay the lender as detailed in the contract. It specifies what happens if the borrower defaults, who pays attorney fees in that event, and what credit clauses are considered part of the terms of the note. The note is in the section marked "D" in Figure 7.1.

The Insurance Agreement

The insurance agreement protects the lender should the borrower die or become disabled.

The **insurance agreement** is the section marked "E" in Figure 7.1. It is used to indicate whether the borrower agrees to purchase credit life and/ or disability insurance that would pay the lender the balance of the loan in full should the borrower die or become seriously disabled. In some cases, purchase of such insurance is required as a condition for getting the loan. Usually, it is optional. Most people do not need the coverage because their existing insurance already covers potential financial losses. The monthly premium for such insurance coverage purchased through the lender might seem nominal, but similar coverage can be purchased through a traditional insurance agency for perhaps one-sixth the cost. If insurance is required by the lender, be sure to buy it yourself through a reputable insurance agent. A full discussion of disability and life insurance appears in Chapters 13 and 14.

Other Important Credit Clauses

A variety of credit clauses are included in contracts. Some of these you should avoid, if possible. Most clauses necessarily protect the lender from credit users who might otherwise try to skip town with the collateral property.

1. *Acceleration clauses can be triggered by one missed payment.* The **acceleration clause,** which appears in almost all contracts, states requires that after one payment is late (defaulted), all remaining installments are due and payable at once or on the demand of the lender.

2. *Repossession can result in losing more than the collateral.* In some states, repossession can occur quite easily under a conditional sales contract. In most states where an installment purchase agreement is the contract, the lender must first get a court judgment of default and then follow legally prescribed procedures to regain possession of the goods. The latter method provides more protection for the borrower.

In either case, the creditor will sell the repossessed items(s), usually at auction. If the sale brings in less than the debt, the creditor can take court action to collect the remainder of the debt.

3. *A balloon clause refers to a higher final payment.* The **balloon clause** permits the last payment to be abnormally large in comparison with the other installment payments. The Truth-in-Lending law requires any payment more than twice the size of others to be identified as a balloon payment.

4. *A prepayment penalty is common with add-on loans.* The **rule of 78s,** sometimes called the *sum of the digits method,* is a commonly used method of calculating rebates of finance charges and the prepayment penalty charged the borrower who pays off an installment loan early. It takes into consideration that you pay more in interest in the beginning of a loan when you have the use of more money and that you pay less and less interest as the debt is reduced. To illustrate, suppose on a $500 loan for 12 months, $80 in finance charges were scheduled to be paid. If the loan is paid off after only 6 months, the borrower will not have the interest reduced $40. To calculate the reduction, first add together all the numbers between 1 and 12 (1 + 2 + 3 + 4 + 5 + 6 + 7 + 8 + 9 + 10 + 11 + 12 = 78). If the loan is paid off after 1 month, the amount of interest paid is assumed to be 12/78 of the total, with a reduction of 66/78 due the borrower. For a loan paid in full after 2 months, the amount of interest paid is assumed to be 23/78 of the total (12/78 for month 1 and 11/78 for month 2). In this example, after 6 months the lender assumes that $58.46 (57/78) has been paid in interest, and the interest is reduced $21.54 (21/78). Thus the borrower does not get 50 percent of the interest as a reduction for paying the loan off in half the time, but only 27 percent ($21.54/$80). To avoid prepayment penalties obtain simple-interest loans.

Signals of Credit Overextension

Many people in today's credit-oriented economy find themselves using more credit than they would like to. Such uncomfortable feelings may propel credit users to reexamine their own debt limits, as discussed earlier in this chapter. **Credit overextension,** in which excessive personal debts make repayment difficult, is a more serious matter. Perhaps not surprisingly, numerous research studies have found that a primary reason for divorce is money problems. Eight signals of credit overextension are discussed below.

1. *Exceeding debt limits.* The debt limits established in Table 7.1 are only guidelines. Generally, however, spending more than 20 percent of disposable personal income on debt repayments (excluding mortgage loans) is a clear sign of difficulty ahead.

2. *Out of money.* We all have emergencies and sometimes simply run out of money. But if you are running out of money on a month-to-month

basis because a good portion of earnings goes to debt repayments, you may be overextended. Are you using credit cards where you previously used cash? Or are you using credit card cash advances and checking account credit lines to pay bills?

3. *Paying only the minimum amount due.* When the revolving credit card bills come in, are you paying the minimum payment—or less—instead of the full balance owed?

4. *Requesting increases in credit limits.* Department stores and bank credit card companies are usually pleased when customers request increases in their approved credit limits because it usually means more income for them. Raising your limit from $500 to $1000 may make sense if you just graduated from school. However, if you request a raise of another $1000 because you *need* the higher limit, it may be time to think. Of course, some people have credit limits that are simply too low to permit much flexibility. Note that many people get deeper into debt after obtaining an increase in their credit limit. Adding new credit card accounts also increases your potential debt load, perhaps in excess of any realistic debt limit.

5. *Missing credit payments.* By the time you have missed a credit payment, you may have noticed some of the danger signals noted above. Of course, you can simply forget to mail a check, and the only penalty is the probable late payment fee. However, when money is not available to pay your bills, real trouble has arrived. Maybe you have lost track of how much you owe and are avoiding adding up the total.

6. *Add-on loans.* **Flipping,** or taking **add-on loans,** occurs when you take out a second loan for a larger amount before you repay your first loan. Say your original loan of $1000 has been repaid down to $400. You decide to refinance the debt balance of $400 and borrow an additional $300 from the same lending source. While it may be a wise course of action to increase an existing note, perhaps at a lower interest rate, it may also be a sign of both increasing debt and an inability to handle the repayments.

7. *Debt-consolidation loans.* Many people who are in debt owe several creditors different amounts at varying interest rates. People in such situations often obtain a debt-consolidation loan to pay off all the bills and to make one payment that is less in amount than all the others combined. The payment is less because the time period for repayment is lengthened. Such action reduces pressure on the budget. It is also a sign that the credit user was simply using too much credit.

Garnishment gives a creditor a portion of your pay.

8. *Garnishment.* **Garnishment** is a legal attachment to your wages directed by a court. Fortunately, the Truth-in-Lending Law offers some protections for credit users. Your wages cannot have more than two garnishments attached. Also, the total amount garnished cannot be more than 25 percent of your disposable income for the pay period *or* more than the amount by which your weekly disposable income exceeds 30 times the federal minimum wage (whichever is less). Also, the law prohibits garnishments as grounds for employment discharge.

What If You Become Overextended

Even the most well-meaning credit user can become overextended as a result of illness, unemployment, or simple inattention to credit usage. Reviewing the checklist of signals of credit overextension can sound the alarm and motivate you to consider a "debt diet" before creditors begin collection procedures. But what should you do if you realize that you are overextended?

1. Determine exactly how much is owed, to whom, and the payment amounts needed to pay off each revolving credit account in 2 years and any installment loans in accordance with the payment plan in the contracts.
2. Develop and stick to a balanced budget. The budget should include making all the payments determined above.
3. Seek an extension of the repayment period for one or two debts if it is clear that your budget cannot handle the new repayment schedule you have developed. Realize, however, that the lower payments resulting from a longer payback will come at the expense of higher finance charges and a longer period of difficulty.
4. Take on no new credit. Credit cards should be destroyed or locked up so they cannot be used. Avoid debt-consolidation loans because they pave the way for new borrowing, especially on credit cards.
5. Seek help if you see no progress in 6 months. Disciplined action to reduce debt should show results in a few months. If not, seek professional help. Many large employers offer budget

counseling through their personnel offices. You also may be able to find free credit counseling at your credit union or labor union. Another place to turn is to your creditor(s). Many creditors, such as banks and consumer finance companies, provide budgeting advice that helps debtors get out of financial trouble. Finally, excellent assistance is offered through the nationwide offices of the Consumer Credit Counseling Service, a nonprofit organization. You can locate a local office by writing the National Foundation for Consumer Credit, 8701 Georgia Avenue, Silver Spring, MD 20910. All the preceding services are provided at virtually no cost.

6. Avoid "credit clinics" that charge for their service. Some profit-making credit clinics advertise that they will negotiate with your creditors to get repayment schedules changed so you can make smaller payments. Be aware that nonprofit counseling groups also can do this, and they won't charge you $250 to $1000 to get you back on your feet. Some credit clinics offer people new loans on the theory that an additional debt taken out and repaid on schedule will help rebuild a poor credit history. This theory is tempting but dead wrong, since the negative information will remain in credit bureau files for years. Contrary to advertised claims, no credit clinic will be able to remove accurate but negative information in anyone's credit history.

Bankruptcy

Bankruptcy should only be sought when all else has failed.

When things are really bleak, you might seek the advice of an attorney and consider bankruptcy. Bankruptcy is a constitutionally guaranteed right of Americans and is available in two forms. Chapter 13 of the Bankruptcy Act (also known as the **wage-earner plan**) is designed for persons with regular incomes and debts less than $450,000 who might be able to pay off their debts given certain protections of the court. Chapter 13 is designed for rehabilitation. Under this plan, the court notifies all creditors of the petition for bankruptcy. At a scheduled hearing and with the help of a bankruptcy trustee, a repayment plan is designed to repay as much of the debts as possible, typically in 36 months. Interest charges and collection efforts by creditors generally stop at this point. Should the person make all the scheduled payments, he or she is judged free and clear of any remaining amounts due that could not be repaid within the period. Many responsible people choose this option to repay a portion, if not all, of what they owe.

Straight bankruptcy is available through Chapter 7 of the Bankruptcy Act. Chapter 7 is designed for liquidation of assets. Many consumers choose this option once the bankruptcy trustee has listed the debts and determined that it would be highly unlikely that substantial repayment could ever be made. Upon petition, the bankruptcy judge can rule that the person is immediately judged free and clear of all debts. Once a person has declared bankruptcy, he or she cannot be legally discharged from debts again for 6 years. Realize that most of the bankrupt person's assets are given to the trustee and sold. Legally, bankrupt people are allowed to keep a small equity in their homes, an inexpensive automobile, and limited personal property. State or federal laws govern what can be kept, and some debts can never be excused, including education loans, fines, alimony, child support, and income taxes. Bankruptcy is the court of last resort for those overextended in debt and should be avoided if at all possible.

Summary

1. Inflation and taxes both have an impact on the decision to use credit, as does a person's debt limit, which can be established using three techniques: the disposable-income method, the ratio of debts to equity method, and the continuous-debt method.

2. Consumer loans are classified as either installment or noninstallment credit. Borrowers also must distinguish between secured loans, which make use of collateral or a cosigner, and unsecured loans, which are riskier for the lender and therefore carry higher finance charges.

3. Four major sources of consumer loans are banks, credit unions, consumer finance companies, and sales finance companies, with the latter specializing in secured loans, often at competitive interest rates, with the items sold serving as the collateral.

4. Both the simple-interest and add-on methods are used with installment loans, but the annual percentage rate formula gives the correct rate in all cases. The simple-interest method allows early repayment of the loan without a prepayment penalty.

5. A credit agreement (also known as a retail installment contract) has all the components necessary to effect a contract: a sales contract, a security

agreement, a note, an insurance agreement, and some credit clauses to safeguard the lender in case of default. Borrowers need to be wary of some of these clauses.

6. There are several signals of credit overextension, and some of the early ones are exceeding credit-limit guidelines, running out of money too often, and requesting increases in credit limits.

7. People with serious financial difficulties can obtain professional assistance through credit counseling and/or by using Chapters 7 or 13 of the Bankruptcy Act.

13,000

Modern
Money
Management

**The Johnsons'
Credit Questions**

Harry and Belinda need some questions resolved regarding credit. Their 3-year-old car has been having mechanical problems lately. So instead of buying a new set of tires, as planned for in March (see Table 4.3), they are considering trading it in for a new vehicle so Harry can have a dependable car for commuting to work. They still owe $3,600 to the bank for their present car, or $200 a month for the remaining eighteen months of the 48-month loan. The trade-in value of the car and $1,000 that Harry earned from a freelance interior design job should pay off the auto loan and leave $1250 for a down payment on the new car. They have agreed on a sales price for the new car of $14,250. The money planned for tires will be spent for other incidental fees associated with the purchase.

1. Make recommendations to Harry and Belinda regarding where to finance and what APR to expect.

2. Using Personal Finance Cookbook (PFC) program INSTALL or the information in Table 7.3, calculate the monthly payment for a loan period of 3, 4, and 5 years at 14 percent APR. Describe the relationship between the loan period and the payment amount.

3. Harry and Belinda have a cash flow deficit projected for several months this year (see Tables 4.3 and 4.4). Suggest how, when, and where they might finance the shortages by borrowing.

Key Words and Concepts

acceleration clause, 254
add-on loan, 256
balloon clause, 255
cash loan, 241

collateral, 240
conditional sales contract, 251
cosigner, 240
credit agreement, 251

Review Questions

1. Explain how taxes and inflation can affect your decision to borrow rather than pay cash for products.
2. List the four primary reasons why people borrow.
3. How does setting a debt limit help the borrower?
4. Describe three methods for establishing debt limits.
5. Distinguish between noninstallment credit and installment credit.
6. Distinguish between a secured loan and an unsecured loan.
7. Explain how a borrower can lose two ways when a lender resorts to repossession of property used to secure a debt.
8. Describe the type of loans available and the lending policies of banks/S&Ls, credit unions, consumer finance companies, and sales finance companies.
9. Distinguish between a consumer finance company and a sales finance company.
10. Since life insurance companies are not noted for lending money to consumers, explain why they can be identified as a source for borrowing money.
11. What is the process followed by pawnbrokers in lending money to consumers?
12. What fees must be included in the finance charge when calculating the APR on a loan?
13. Explain why using the discount method of interest calculation results in a higher APR than the add-on method.
14. Explain why the APR is always larger than the add-on rate of interest.
15. How is interest calculated under the simple-interest method?

16. Distinguish between variable-rate and fixed-rate loans.

17. According to the Truth-in-Lending Law, what two items must be shown in bold print in the disclosure section of an installment contract?

18. Distinguish between an installment purchase agreement and a conditional sales contract.

19. Why is the rule of 78s clause considered a prepayment penalty?

20. List and identify the sections of a retail installment contract.

21. What requirement is described in an acceleration clause?

22. Name four of the eight signals of credit overextension and briefly describe each.

23. Distinguish between the wage-earner plan and straight bankruptcy.

Case Problems

1. Ricardo Millender of Santa Barbara, California, needs money to purchase a new refrigerator. One store will finance his purchase of $1000 at a 12.0 add-on rate, with 12 monthly payments of $93.33. This, of course, would mean paying an APR considerably greater than 10.0 percent. However, Ricardo desperately needs the new refrigerator.
   a. Calculate the APR using Equation (7.3) in Table 7.6. Can Ricardo justify borrowing $1000 at this rate? Why or why not?
   b. What other alternatives are available to Ricardo that may not be as costly?

2. Peter Nishi of Carson City, Nevada, had an old car that was operating fairly well but needed repairs to the extent of $800 per year. He recently saw new cars advertised at several hundred dollars less than those advertised previously. A particular model was priced at $1700 below the regular selling price of $13,200. Peter gathered all the information and realized that to buy this car he would have to borrow $2000 from his bank at an APR of 11.5 percent. Peter also would have to withdraw $2000 from a savings account paying 7.5 percent interest annually. He is in the 28 percent tax bracket (meaning that 28 cents of each additional dollar earned goes to taxes), and inflation for the economy is projected to be 5 percent each year for the next 2 years. Peter is still undecided about what to do.
   a. What are some of the questions and concerns Peter must consider before making a decision?
   b. How does inflation enter into a decision of this type?
   c. What action would you recommend for Peter? Justify.

3. Nola Okimoto of Pearl City, Hawaii, recently entered into a sales contract to buy a new automobile. After signing the contract to finance $12,000, she hurriedly left the office of the sales finance company with her copy of the contract. Later that evening Nola reread the contract and noticed several clauses—an acceleration clause, a repossession clause, a

balloon clause for $900, and a rule of 78s clause. She was in a hurry when she signed the contract and was told these were standard clauses that should not concern her.

    a. Should Nola be concerned about these clauses? Why or why not?

    b. What are some fair warnings for Nola regarding the balloon clause?

    c. Considering the rule of 78s clause, what should Nola realize if she pays off the loan before the regular due date?

    d. If Nola had financed the $12,000 for 4 years at 12 percent APR, what would her monthly payment be using the Personal Finance Cookbook (PFC) program INSTALL or the information in Table 7.3?

4. Keith Shildt of Indiana, Pennsylvania, had an unusual amount of debt. He owed $1800 to one bank, $600 to a clothing store, $900 to his credit union, and several hundred dollars to other stores and persons. Keith was paying over $450 a month on the three major obligations and $425 a month for an apartment. He realized that with take-home pay of just over $1200 a month he didn't have much excess cash. He discussed an alternative way of handling his major payments with his credit union officer. The officer suggested he pool all his debts and take out a debt consolidation loan at a lower interest rate. As a result, he would pay only $230 a month for all his debts. Keith seemed ecstatic over the idea.

    a. Is Keith's enthusiasm over the idea of a debt-consolidation loan justified? Why or why not?

    b. How is it possible for the credit union to offer such a "good deal" to Keith?

    c. To make payments of only $230 as compared with $450, what compromise would Keith make?

    d. If you assume that the consolidation loan will cost more in total interest, what would be a justification for this added cost?

Suggested Readings

"A Banker Tells the Secrets of the Vault." *Money,* June 1989, pp. 95–98. Tips to help you get the loan you want on the most favorable terms.

"Are We in over Our Heads?" *Changing Times,* March 1989, p. 36. Debts are up but so is our ability to handle it.

B. H. Nunnally, Jr. and D. A. Plath, "Lending Versus Borrowing: Evaluating Alternative Forms of Consumer Credit." *The Journal of Consumer Affairs,* Volume 22, Number 2, Winter 1989, pp. 383–392.

"Credit Doctors Can Hurt." *Changing Times,* August 1989, p. 78. Cautions against believing advertisements for credit repair and rebuilding services.

"Cheap Credit." *Changing Times,* April 1990, pp. 85–89. How to find the best deals when borrowing.

"Going for the Broke." *Newsweek,* April 2, 1990, pp. 40–41. Discusses the impacts of the increasing numbers of Americans who are choosing bankruptcy.

"Good Rates for Good Risks." *Changing Times,* May 1989, p. 47. New automobile financing plans available for good risks.

"How to Cope with Lending Rate Gloom." *Money,* May 1989, pp. 70–81. Clear ideas on how to beat today's high cost of money, including suggestions on home mortgage loans.

"How to Find the Best Home-Equity Loan." *Changing Times,* November 1989, pp. 37–42. How to correctly lower your tax bill and borrow at reasonable rates.

"Learning to Kick the Debt Habit." *Business Week,* March 12, 1990, pp. 112–113. How to get out and stay out of debt.

"The Mad Rush to Refinance." *Changing Times,* October 1989, pp. 41–45. The facts you need to determine whether or not to refinance a home mortgage loan.

V. B. Langrehr and F. W. Langrehr, "Measuring the Ability to Repay: The Residual Income Ratio." *The Journal of Consumer Affairs,* Volume 22, Number 2, Winter 1989, pp. 393–406.

8 Managing Taxes

OBJECTIVES

After reading this chapter, you should be able to

1. Explain how taxes are administered and classified.

2. Describe how tax rates affect your income.

3. Determine whether you should file an income tax return and recognize the proper filing status.

4. Describe the two ways of paying taxes: payroll withholding and estimated taxes.

5. Identify the nine steps of calculating income taxes.

6. Calculate illustrative tax liabilities for different types of taxpayers.

7. Understand strategies and tactics to legally avoid overpayment of income taxes.

8. Determine which method of preparing tax returns is best and why.

9. Explain the effect of numerous types of federal, state, and local taxes on income available to spend, save, and invest.

Besides banking, using credit cards, and borrowing, money management includes the crucial area of taxation. Taxation is of utmost importance in the study of personal finance for two reasons. First, taxes often take up 20 to 40 percent, or more, of your income—a considerable amount of money. Second, if through poor financial management you send more money in taxes to the government than is necessary, you will have less money available to spend, save, or invest.

This chapter examines the principles of taxation and the impact of tax rates on your income. It then discusses who must pay taxes and the ways of paying them, including both payroll withholding and estimated tax payments. Next, nine steps detail the entire process of paying taxes from the determination of gross income through the final computation of taxes due. We also provide examples of calculating tax liability. Finally, we examine the respectable and desirable financial management practice of legal tax avoidance as well as who should prepare your income tax returns, discuss how to successfully survive an income tax audit, and note the effects of the variety of federal, state, and local taxes on income.

How Income Taxes Are Administered and Classified

Objective
To be able to explain how taxes are administered and classified.

Taxes are compulsory charges imposed by a government on citizens and property. To learn how to manage taxes effectively, you should know how taxes are administered and classified.

Federal Tax Laws

The federal tax laws are administered through IRS regulations.

Taxes are administered at all levels of government. Because the largest amount of tax you pay is on your income, this chapter focuses on the personal income tax and on the Internal Revenue Service (IRS). Many other taxes are discussed at the end of this chapter. The IRS is the agency charged with the responsibility of collecting federal income taxes based on the legal provisions in the Internal Revenue Service Code. The code represents the major tax laws written by Congress.

The IRS issues various **IRS regulations,** which are its interpretations of the laws passed by Congress. These have the force and effect of law and are contained in numerous thick volumes in large libraries. Dozens of **IRS rulings** are issued each year; these are Internal Revenue Service decisions based on its interpretations of both the tax laws and the IRS regulations.

Tax rulings provide guidance to how the IRS will act in certain general situations. **IRS private letter rulings** are issued to several hundred individuals and corporations each year, giving the IRS advisory opinions on individual tax-management inquiries. When these opinions are made public, all taxpayers gain some insight into IRS policy; IRS rulings often eventually follow issuance of several private letters on similar topics. In addition to the preceding, the tax courts issue many decisions each year giving the judicial interpretation of tax laws that Congress passes and the regulations and decisions of the Internal Revenue Service.

Progressive or Regressive Taxes

A tax is either progressive or regressive.

Taxes can be classified according to a taxpayer's ability to pay as progressive or regressive. A **progressive tax** demands a higher percentage of a person's income as income increases. In this country, the federal personal income tax is a progressive tax because the tax rate increases as a taxpayer's income (or implied ability to pay) increases. Table 8.1 shows that under the federal income tax, upper segments of a taxpayer's income are taxed at increasingly higher rates.

A **regressive tax** operates in the opposite way. As income rises, the tax rate remains the same or decreases, and so the tax demands a decreasing proportion of a person's income as income increases. Such taxes are not based on ability to pay. State sales tax is an example of a regressive tax. Assume that a stereo system costs $500, plus a 5 percent sales tax. Taxpayer A, with a monthly income of $1000, and taxpayer B, with a monthly income of $5000, each buy one. The sales tax would be $25 for both, yet it would represent 2.5 percent of A's monthly income and only 0.5 percent of B's income. Since the sales tax rate remains the same, 5 percent, it might appear that the tax is proportional, or fair to all. But, as shown here, one person may pay proportionately fives times as much as another. Thus the tax is regressive. The Social Security tax is also regressive because its flat rate of 7.65 percent is only applied to all incomes up to $51,300 (in 1990).

How Tax Rates Affect Your Income

Objective
To be able to describe how tax rates affect your income.

Taxes have a major effect on your income. This section provides an understanding of marginal, effective marginal, and average tax rates. Realize first, however, that all income is not subject to the federal income tax. You pay personal income taxes only on your **taxable income.** You determine taxable income by subtracting your allowable exclusions, adjustments, exemptions, and deductions from your total income, with the result being the income upon which the tax is actually calculated. Details are provided later, but the key personal finance idea in successfully managing your income tax liability is to reduce taxable income as much as possible. The marginal tax rate is then applied to your taxable income.

266   *Part Two / Money Management*

TABLE 8.1
The Progressive Nature of the Federal Income Tax*

Segment of Taxable Income	Taxed Rate (percent)
First $19,450	15
$19,450 to $47,050	28
$47,050 to $97,620	33†

* Rates quoted are for a single taxpayer in the 1990 tax year.
† Drops to 31 percent for the 1991 tax year.

You must understand your marginal tax rate to be successful in personal finance.

Perhaps the single most important concept in personal finance is the **marginal tax rate.** This is the tax rate on your last dollar of earnings. It tells you how much of any extra earnings—from a raise, investment income, or moonlighting—you get to keep after paying income taxes; it also measures the tax savings benefits of a deductible expense. This concept is illustrated in Figure 8.1.

A **marginal tax bracket (MTB)** is each income-range couplet shown in the tax-rate schedules (as shown in Tables 8.1 and 8.2). Each year the tax brackets are modified to reduce the effects of inflation, and this is called **indexing.** In 1991, the 28 percent tax bracket for 1990 taxable income begins at $19,450 for singles, $26,050 for heads of households, and $32,450 for joint filers; projections for 1992 and 1993 are shown in Table 8.2.

To illustrate, Judy Van Name, a postal employee from Newark, Delaware, is a single person with a gross income of $26,000 and after certain subtractions has a taxable income of $22,000. The upper portion of Table 8.2 indicates that she is in the 28 percent marginal tax bracket because of her $22,000 taxable income, as are all single taxpayers with taxable incomes between $19,450 and $47,050. They will pay taxes at the 28 percent marginal tax rate. (In fact, most taxpayers are in the 28 percent MTB, so if they earn another $100, $28 of it goes to federal income taxes.) Taxpayers have three federal income marginal tax rates: 15 percent, 28 percent, and 33 percent.

For an example of how changes in income can affect taxes paid, assume that Jane Hernandez, a single person who is a pharmaceutical sales representative from San Jose, California, has a total income of $52,000 and after certain subtractions a taxable income of $46,000. Her employer gives her a $1000 year-end bonus to recognize the quality of her work. Table 8.3 shows that Jane pays an extra $280 in taxes on the fully taxable $1000 bonus income; thus she pays a marginal tax rate of 28 percent on the last income earned.

For another example, assume that Jane receives a bonus of $4000 instead of $1000, which pushes up her taxable income from $46,000 to $50,000. The upper portion of Table 8.2 shows that the marginal tax rate for a taxable income of $47,050 is 33 percent. Thus a small portion of

FIGURE 8.1

How Your Income Is Really Taxed (Example: Susan Bassett with a $30,000 Gross Income)

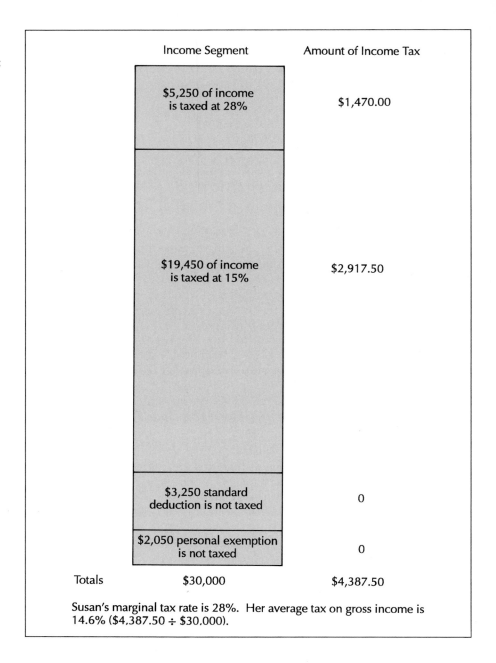

Income Segment	Amount of Income Tax
$5,250 of income is taxed at 28%	$1,470.00
$19,450 of income is taxed at 15%	$2,917.50
$3,250 standard deduction is not taxed	0
$2,050 personal exemption is not taxed	0
Totals $30,000	$4,387.50

Susan's marginal tax rate is 28%. Her average tax on gross income is 14.6% ($4,387.50 ÷ $30,000).

the $4000 bonus will be taxed at a rate of 28 percent, and a greater portion of the *last* dollars earned will be taxed at a marginal rate of 33 percent. Jane's bonus pushes her from the 28 percent to the 33 percent marginal tax bracket.

Our discussion so far has focused on the tax-rate schedules (Table 8.2), but most people use the tax tables instead (a portion of which is illustrated in Table 8.4) because the tax tables cover incomes up to $50,000, are

TABLE 8.2
Tax-Rate Schedules

1991 tax-rate schedules (for 1990 tax-year income):

If Taxable Income Is

Over	But not Over	The Tax Is	Plus the Following Percent	Of Amount Over
Single Return				
$ 0	$ 19,450	$ 0	+15	$ 0
19,450	47,050	2,917.50	+28	19,450
47,050	97,620	10,645.50	+33*	47,050
97,620	. . .	†	+28	0
Joint Return				
$ 0	$ 32,450	$ 0	+15	$ 0
32,450	78,400	4,867.50	+28	32,450
78,400	162,770	17,733.50	+33*	78,400
162,770	. . .	†	+28	0
Head of Household				
$ 0	$ 26,050	$ 0	+15	$ 0
26,050	67,200	3,907.50	+28	26,050
67,200	134,930	15,429.50	+33*	67,200
134,930	. . .	†	+28	0

1992 tax-rate schedules (for 1991 tax-year income):‡

If Taxable Income Is

Over	But not Over	The Tax Is	Plus the Following Percent	Of Amount Over
Single Return				
$ 0	$ 20,300	$ 0	+15	$ 0
20,300	49,150	3,045.00	+28	20,300
49,150	. . .	11,123.00	+31§	49,150
Joint Return				
$ 0	$ 33,900	0	+15	0
33,900	81,900	5,085.00	+28	33,900
81,900	. . .	18,525.00	+31§	81,900
Head of Household				
$ 0	$ 27,200	$ 0	+15	$ 0
27,200	70,200	4,080.00	+28	27,200
70,200	. . .	16,120.00	+31§	70,200

(*continued*)

TABLE 8.2 (continued)

1993 tax-rate schedules (for 1992 tax-year income):‡

If Taxable Income Is		The Tax Is	Plus the Following Percent	Of Amount Over
Over	But not Over			
Single Return				
$ 0	$ 21,200	$ 0	+15	$ 0
21,200	51,350	3,180.00	+28	21,200
51,350	. . .	11,622.00	+31§	51,350
Joint Return				
$ 0	$ 35,400	$ 0	+15	$ 0
35,400	85,550	5,310.00	+28	35,400
85,550	. . .	19,352.00	+31§	85,550
Head of Household				
$ 0	$ 28,400	$ 0	+15	$ 0
28,400	73,350	4,260.00	+28	28,400
73,350	. . .	16,846.00	+31§	73,350

Source: Internal Revenue Service.

* The value of paying only a 15 percent rate on the first part of taxable income is phased out for higher-income taxpayers with this 5 percent surtax on a portion of income.

† The value of personal exemptions is phased out for higher-income taxpayers. To calculate your tax liability, (1) multiply your taxable income by 28 percent, (2) subtract the phaseout amount for your filing status ($97,620, $162,770, or $134,930) from taxable income, (3) multiply the number of your exemptions times $10,250, (4) multiply the lessor of step 2 or 3 by 5 percent, and (5) add step 1 and step 4. Assumes exemption value of $2050.

‡ Cost of living adjustments are made annually to the tax schedules and tables because the IRS is required by law to prevent hikes in inflationary prices from resulting in a tax increase. The 1992 and 1993 schedules here are not official IRS tax schedules. They are the authors' estimates based on assumed increases in the consumer price index of 4.5 percent from the previous year; such adjustments for inflation have the effect of widening the tax brackets slightly.

§ The value of the personal exemption begins to be phased out for singles with an adjusted gross income of $100,000 and marrieds earning $150,000, thus losing $17.50 of every personal exemption for each $1000 of income. Also, they lose $300 in deductions for each $10,000 of income above those threshold amounts. Therefore, high-income taxpayers pay an effective marginal rate of 32 to 34 percent.

convenient to use, and do not require math calculations. You can calculate someone's marginal tax rate from the tax tables in the following way, assuming the person's taxable income can be found in the income brackets illustrated:

1. Assuming the person is single and has a taxable income of $46,000, find in the tables the amount of tax on that income ($10,359).
2. Add $100 to that income for a total of $46,100, and find the tax on that amount ($10,387).

TABLE 8.3
Marginal Tax Rate Illustrated

Taxable Income	Tax*
$46,000	$2,917.50 + $7,434 ($46,000 − $19,450 = $26,550 × 0.28) = $10,351.50
$47,000	$2,917.50 + $7,714 ($47,000 − $19,450 = $23,050 × 0.28) = $10,631.50

Marginal Tax Rate with Bonus

$ 47,000	$ 10,631.50
− 46,000	− 10,351.50
$ 1,000 additional income results in . . .	$ 280 additional tax

* From upper portion of Table 8.2.

3. Calculate the difference between the two tax amounts ($10,387 − $10,359 = $28) and divide by 100 (28/100 = 28 percent). Thus the $28 higher tax resulting from an increase in taxable income of $100 reflects a marginal tax rate of 28 percent.

The marginal tax rate can have a great effect on tax deductions as well as savings and investment decisions. Consider someone with a 28 percent marginal tax rate who wants to make a $100 tax-deductible contribution to a charity. The charity receives the $100 and the taxpayer may deduct $100 from taxable income. This results in a $28 reduction in income tax ($100 × 28 percent), and the taxpayer is really only out $72 ($100 − $28 = $72). In effect, the taxpayer gives $72 and the government "gives" $28 to the charity.

Effective Marginal Tax Rate

Your effective marginal tax rate is even higher.

The truth is that most of us pay tax marginal rates higher than 15, 28, or 33 percent; this is especially true for those who have an income of $51,300 or less. The **effective marginal tax rate** on income is even *higher* than that given in the preceding discussion because it includes all tax claims against a specific income. This is because often there are three other taxes that must be subtracted from increases in income. Most workers pay 7.65 percent of income in Social Security taxes, 6 percent or more in state income taxes, and perhaps an additional city income tax of 3 to 5 percent.

To determine the effective marginal tax rate on increases in income, you must add these other taxes to the federal marginal tax rate. A single person with a taxable income of $22,000 would have a federal marginal income tax rate of 28 percent, a Social Security tax of 7.65 percent, perhaps a state marginal income tax of 6 percent, and perhaps a city marginal income tax of 4 percent. On an increase in income of $100, these taxes result in an effective marginal tax rate of 45 percent (28 percent + 7.65 percent + 6 percent + 4 percent = 45.65 percent). Thus many employed taxpayers pay an effective marginal income tax rate of 35 to 45 percent. People with

TABLE 8.4
Illustration of a Portion of the Tax Tables*

If Taxable Income Is		Single	Joint Return	Head of Household
		And You Are Filing		
At Least	But Less Than	Your Tax Is		
$ 5,000	$ 5,050	$ 754	$ 754	$ 754
5,050	5,100	761	761	761
5,100	5,150	769	769	769
5,150	5,200	776	776	776
8,500	8,550	1,279	1,279	1,279
8,550	8,600	1,286	1,286	1,286
8,600	8,650	1,294	1,294	1,294
8,650	8,700	1,301	1,301	1,301
19,200	19,250	2,884	2,884	2,884
19,250	19,300	2,891	2,891	2,891
19,300	19,350	2,899	2,899	2,899
19,350	19,400	2,906	2,906	2,906
20,000	20,050	3,079	3,004	3,004
20,050	20,100	3,093	3,011	3,011
20,100	20,150	3,107	3,019	3,019
20,150	20,200	3,121	3,026	3,026
21,900	21,950	3,611	3,289	3,289
22,100	22,150	3,667	3,319	3,319
22,150	22,200	3,681	3,326	3,326
22,200	22,250	3,695	3,334	3,334
22,250	22,300	3,709	3,341	3,341
24,100	24,150	4,227	3,619	3,619
24,150	24,200	4,241	3,626	3,626
24,200	24,250	4,255	3,634	3,634
24,250	24,300	4,269	3,641	3,641
30,200	30,250	5,935	4,534	5,077
30,250	30,300	5,949	4,541	5,091
30,300	30,350	5,963	4,549	5,105
30,350	30,400	5,977	4,556	5,119
30,400	30,450	5,991	4,564	5,133
30,450	30,500	6,005	4,571	5,147
30,500	30,550	6,019	4,579	5,161
30,550	30,600	6,033	4,586	5,175
46,000	46,050	10,359	8,669	9,501
46,050	46,100	10,373	8,683	9,515
46,100	46,150	10,387	8,697	9,529
46,150	46,200	10,401	8,711	9,543

* Derived from the tax schedules in the upper portion of Table 8.2.

incomes above the maximum income that can be assessed the Social Security tax ($54,300 in 1991) also must pay an extra 1.45 percent Medicare tax on wages in excess of $54,300 up to $125,000 (which historically had been lumped in with the Social Security tax), and this may push their effective marginal tax rate up to 35 or 36 percent.

Average Tax Rate

The **average tax rate** is a calculated figure showing your tax liability as a percentage of total income. People often confuse their marginal tax bracket with such a percentage. Realize that your total income is not fully taxed by the federal government. It can be reduced by exclusions, adjustments, exemptions, deductions, and credits; this all will be explained later in the chapter.

For example, Holly Bender, a part-time college student and full-time grocery cashier from Summit, Mississippi, has a total income of $21,000 and, after certain subtractions, a taxable income of $16,000. She can calculate her tax liability by using the tax rate schedules shown in the upper portion of Table 8.2. Holly is single, so her tax liability is $2400 ($16,000 × 0.15). A look at Table 8.2 reveals a marginal tax bracket of 15 percent. The average tax rate based on a total income of $21,000 is only 11.4 percent $2400/$21,000).

Therefore, Holly pays an average tax rate of 11.4 percent on her total income even though she is in the 15.0 percent marginal tax bracket. If she were to earn an additional $1000, it would be taxed at the 15 percent marginal tax rate and the federal government would get another $150 from her. Meanwhile, her average tax rate would rise slightly to 11.6 percent [$2400 + $150 = $2550/($21,000 + $1000) = 11.6].

Who Should File a Tax Return?

Most people who earn an income should file a tax return. It is fairly easy to determine whether you should file and what your filing status is. "To file" simply means to report formally to the IRS any amounts owed.

Should You File?

U.S. citizens and residents of the United States or Puerto Rico must file a federal income tax return if they have earned sufficient income (except income derived from Puerto Rican sources, unless earned as an employee of the United States). This includes U.S. citizens living abroad. Table 8.5 shows who is required to file.

Students often wonder whether they should file. The regulations require that if someone (such as your parent) can claim you as a dependent and you have unearned income greater than $500, as opposed to earned income, or you have an earned income greater than the value of the

TABLE 8.5
Persons Required to File an Income Tax Return*

Taxpayer	Must File If Gross Income Exceeds
Single, under 65 and not blind	$ 5,300
Single, under 65 and blind	6,100
Single, elderly (age 65 or older) or blind	6,100
Head of household, under 65 with 1 dependent	6,800
Head of household, elderly (65 and older) or blind with 1 dependent	7,600
Married couple	9,550
Married couple, one elderly (age 65 or older) or blind	10,200
Married couple, both spouses elderly (over age 65) and blind	10,850

* Income amounts for the tax forms filed in 1991 on 1990 tax-year income before allowances for the standard deduction, personal exemption, and amounts for being elderly or blind. These numbers are updated for inflation each year by the IRS.

standard deduction ($3250), you must file a return.[1] **Earned income** includes salaries, wages, fringe benefits, and income from sole proprietorships. **Unearned income** includes rents, dividends, capital gains, interest, and royalties. **Transfer payments** include payments by governments and individuals for which no goods or services are expected in return, such as welfare payments.

There are two other cases in which it is wise to file a tax return:

The IRS will not return money withheld from your paycheck unless you file a return and ask for a refund.

1. *To get a refund of any federal income taxes withheld.* People who have had federal income taxes withheld but did not have enough income to be required to file a return should file to obtain a refund of those monies. (Remember, the IRS keeps your money without even sending you a thank you note if you fail to file an income tax return to obtain money withheld from salaries and wages to pay for anticipated income taxes.) If you have neglected to file for refunds in the past, you can complete **Tax Form 1040-X,** Amended U.S. Individual Tax Return, to obtain deserved refunds for the previous three years.)

2. *To get a refund if you can take the earned income credit.* If your adjusted gross income is less than $19,340 and a child lives with you more than half the year, filing an income tax return might qualify you for a refund of up to $910. (This is known as the *earned income credit,* which is discussed later in the chapter.)

[1] However, an exception may occur for a child under age 14 if the child's income was only from interest and dividends and amounted to less than $5000. In order for such a child not to file a return, the parent must report the child's income on his or her income tax return.

What Is Your Filing Status?

The amount of tax people pay on their taxable income is determined partially by their tax status. Your tax status will be either single, married, or head of household.

Singles pay the highest income tax rates for a given level of income.

Single   Taxpayers who are not married on December 31 are considered single for the entire year and must file a separate return if their income exceeds the minimum income threshold. Partially as a result of IRS efforts to construct a truly fair tax system, single taxpayers pay at rates higher than most others at the same level of taxable income because it is felt that single taxpayers have a higher ability to pay than a married couple or a head of household.

Married   For given levels of income, the lowest tax liabilities are paid by married taxpayers who file a joint return. In this case, one income or two combined incomes represent the income of the married couple. Married couples can file either separately or jointly. For most couples, filing jointly results in paying a lower tax. A couple need only be married on December 31 to qualify for this tax status. A surviving widow or widower with a dependent child may qualify for married status for 2 years after the death of a spouse. Realize also that filing jointly means that the IRS can pursue either spouse for payments and can even attach assets held separately.

Head of Household   This special category is used most commonly by taxpayers with low to moderate incomes who are single and who pay the majority of expenses for a tax-qualifying relative, such as a child, parent, or sibling, who lives with them. People who are separated from a spouse for at least the last 6 months of the tax year also may qualify. The tax rate for heads of households is higher than for married persons filing jointly but less than that for singles.

Two Ways of Paying Income Taxes

Objective
To be able to describe the two ways of paying taxes: payroll withholding and estimated taxes.

When taxpayers complete their tax returns for mailing to the Internal Revenue Service by the April 15 deadline, they determine their exact **tax liability,** the actual tax owed on income earned during the previous year.[2] However, the federal income tax is a pay-as-you-go tax, and taxpayers are required to use one of two methods to gradually discharge their tax liability during the year: payroll withholding or estimating taxes.

---

[2] If you are unable to file your tax return on time, you may file a special IRS form and get an automatic extension for 4 months. To do so, you must send in Form 4868 (or a letter containing the same information) by the due date and pay the full amount of tax you estimate that you will owe. This way you avoid a penalty for late filing. About 5 percent of all taxpayers ask for extensions.

Payroll Withholding

Payroll withholding is a method of prepaying taxes through which your employer withholds a portion of each of your paychecks as an estimate of the tax you owe and forwards those funds to the government. The amount withheld is based on income earned, the number of exemptions reported by the employee on the W-4 form, called the Employee's Withholding Allowance Certificate, and other factors. An **exemption** is the legally permitted reduction in the taxpayer's income based on the number of persons supported by that income. Taxpayers can count as *personal* exemptions themselves and their spouses (if filing jointly), and this reduces amounts withheld. Those who are blind or over age 65 get reduced amounts withheld. *Dependent* exemptions may be claimed for any qualifying dependents, such as children or parents. A Social Security Number is required for those age 2 and older claimed as dependents.

You can be exempt from withholding (perhaps you are a student who works only summers) if you meet three tests: (1) you had no income tax liability last year and were entitled to a full refund of any tax withheld, (2) you expect to owe no tax in the current year on an income of $500 or less, and (3) you are not being claimed as an exemption on another person's tax return. If appropriate, request a W-4 form from your employer and write in the word *exempt* in the appropriate place; if not, file a tax return after the end of the year to obtain a refund of money withheld. Withholding for Social Security taxes occurs regardless of whether you are exempt from income taxes.

If your tax liability is anticipated to be lower than the federal government's withholding schedule, you are allowed to refigure your withholding allowances to lower the amount withheld. Those who deliberately have their taxes substantially underwithheld will be assessed a penalty.

Overwithholding occurs when employees have employers withhold more in estimated federal withholding taxes than the tax liability due the government. Approximately two-thirds of all taxpayers practice overwithholding, actually a form of forced savings. This way they get a refund (averaging over $800 in a recent year) approximately 6 weeks after filing their income tax return. However, the IRS does not pay interest on such refunded monies. You should take the necessary time to calculate estimated income tax liability and attempt to have the proper amount withheld. This way your money can be spent, saved, or invested as it is earned.

Overwithholding gives the government a free loan of your money

Estimated Taxes

Many people are self-employed or have substantial income from an employer who does not practice payroll withholding. Lawyers, accountants, consultants, movie stars, and owners of rental property are examples. According to the pay-as-you-go requirements, the IRS directs such taxpayers to estimate their tax liability and pay it in quarterly installments during the year on the 15th of April, June, September, and the following January. **Tax Form 1040-ES,** Declaration of Estimated Tax for Individuals, must be filed if the estimated tax is $500 or more. No penalties are assessed for failure to file the form and pay the taxes unless the estimated tax underpaid the actual amount owed by more than 10 percent.

Taxpayers who earn income in addition to that from an employer can avoid having to pay estimated taxes by amending their W-4 form to increase the payroll withholding to cover the anticipated extra liability. This directs the employer to overwithhold taxes so the taxpayer then has sufficiently prepaid the taxes on the other income.

Nine Steps in Calculating Your Income Taxes

Objective
To be able to identify the nine steps of calculating income taxes.

There are nine basic steps in calculating federal income taxes:

1. Determine your gross income (by identifying taxable sources as well as tax-exempt sources, since the latter can reduce taxable income).
2. Determine adjustments to your income (since these can lower taxable income).
3. Identify the IRS's standard deduction amount for your tax status (since this reduces taxable income).
4. Or list your itemized deductions (since this reduces taxable income).
5. Claim your personal exemptions (since this reduces taxable income).
6. Determine whether you should use the tax tables or the tax-rate schedules.
7. Determine your tax liability (by finding out how much you probably owe).
8. Subtract appropriate tax credits to find your final tax liability (since this also can reduce taxable income).
9. Calculate the balance you owe the IRS or the amount of your refund.

Our discussion of the nine steps in calculating income taxes will be general. Even though we provide a number of details, limitations, and qualifications, we do not examine them in depth. The wise financial manager will write the IRS to obtain Publication 17, *Your Federal Income Tax: For Individuals*. This booklet is less than 200 pages long and is revised annually. Since it represents IRS interpretation of tax policies, it is a most important publication to have when preparing your income taxes. It also includes a listing of the nearly 100 other detailed IRS publications on specific tax topics. A visit to a bookstore also will give you an opportunity to purchase privately produced tax guides that offer advice on how to reduce income taxes.[3] The overall process of federal income tax is illustrated in Figure 8.2; details are discussed throughout the chapter.

[3] One of the best is the authoritative and popular *J. K. Lasser's Your Income Tax* (New York: Simon and Schuster), a 500-plus page annual publication purchased by over 1 million people each year.

FIGURE 8.2
The Process of Income
Taxation

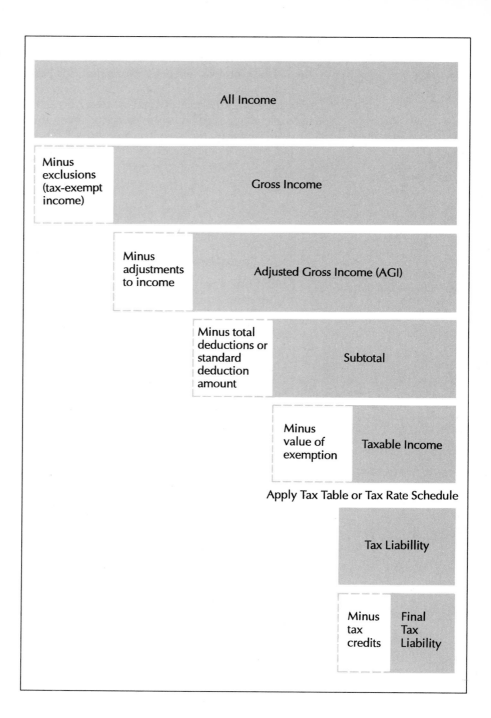

All Income

Minus exclusions (tax-exempt income)

Gross Income

Minus adjustments to income

Adjusted Gross Income (AGI)

Minus total deductions or standard deduction amount

Subtotal

Minus value of exemption

Taxable Income

Apply Tax Table or Tax Rate Schedule

Tax Liabillity

Minus tax credits

Final Tax Liability

1. Determine Your Gross Income

You do not pay income taxes on your total gross income.

On the tax form, **gross income** is all income received in the form of money, goods, services, and property on which you must pay tax; it does not include nontaxable income. To determine the gross income, you need to examine which kinds of income are excluded from the gross income and which kinds are included. Recall that all income is not subject to the federal income tax. You calculate and pay personal income taxes only on your taxable income. The steps in determining taxable income require subtractions for all allowable exclusions, deductions, adjustments, exemptions, and credits from total income. Your objective in effective tax management is to legally reduce your gross income to the lowest possible taxable income.

What to Include   Most people have their income reported to them annually on a W-2 form, Wage and Tax Statement, sent by their employer by January 31. If you also receive income from interest or dividends or other sources, those sources may send you a **Form 1099**, Miscellaneous Income, statement that is also furnished to the IRS. Types of taxable income include the following:

- Wages and salaries
- Commissions
- Bonuses
- Professional fees earned
- Interest income (including dividends from credit unions and any interest on federal income tax refunds)
- Dividends (including capital gains distributions from mutual funds)
- Tips earned
- Alimony received
- Scholarship and fellowship income spent on room, board, and other living expenses
- Grants and the value of tuition reductions that pay for teaching or other services
- Annuity and pension income received (portions excluded)
- Military retirement income
- Social Security income (a portion is taxed above certain income thresholds)
- Disability payments received
- Punitive (not compensatory) damages in a lawsuit that do not compensate for physical injury or sickness
- Value of personal use of employer-provided car
- Withdrawals and disbursements from retirement accounts (such as from an IRA, 401(k), or Keogh account; discussed in Chapter 22)
- State and local income tax refunds (only if the taxpayer itemized the previous year)

- Fair value of anything received in a barter arrangement
- The gain element on a tuition prepayment plan (such as offered in Michigan and other states) obtained by a dependent going to college
- Employer-provided amounts for education expenses (but they also may be deducted as an adjustment to income)
- Employee productivity awards
- Awards for artistic, scientific, and charitable achievements unless assigned to a charity
- Prizes and contest winnings
- Gambling and lottery winnings
- Rewards
- Any kind of illegal income
- Fees for serving as a juror or election worker
- Unemployment benefits received
- Partnership income or share of profits
- Net rental income
- Royalties
- Business and farm profits and losses
- Capital gains or losses on sales or exchanges of property

What to Exclude   Exclusions are sources of income that are not considered legally as income for federal tax purposes; thus such income is tax-exempt. Some of the more common exclusions are

- Interest received on municipal bonds (issued by states, counties, cities, and districts)
- Interest received on Series EE bonds used for college tuition and fees (this is discussed in Chapter 5)
- Income from a car pool
- Income from items sold at a garage sale that sold for less than what you originally paid
- Cash rebates on purchases of new cars and other products
- Scholarship and fellowship income spent on course-required tuition, fees, books, supplies, and equipment (degree candidates only)
- Federal income tax refunds
- Child-support payments received
- Marriage settlements, lump sum received
- Return of money loaned
- Proceeds from health and accident insurance policies
- Earnings accumulating in annuities, single-payment life insurance policies, Series EE bonds, IRAs and other pensions
- Life insurance death benefits

- Compensatory damage payments from lawsuits for personal injuries, illnesses, or accidents
- Gifts and inheritances
- Veterans benefits
- Welfare, black lung, and worker's compensation benefits
- Value of food stamps
- Portion of strike benefits (food and rent)
- First $125,000 of the capital gain on the sale of one residence (only for persons who are 55 years of age or older)
- Income earned from overseas employment (subject to limits)
- Social Security benefits (subject to limits)
- Rental income from vacation home (subject to limits)
- Dividends paid by your insurance company to reduce your premiums
- Tuition reduction if not for compensation for teaching or service
- The first $5000 of death benefits paid by an employer to a worker's beneficiary
- Amounts paid by employers for premiums for medical insurance, worker's compensation, and Social Security
- Employer-provided insurance for group legal services (up to $70 in value)
- Employer-provided seminars for financial and retirement planning and programs to stop smoking and lose weight, provided the sessions are open to rank-and-file employees
- Employer-paid health and accident insurance and the first $50,000 worth of group term insurance
- Employed-subsidized or paid-for meals during working hours to keep you available for emergencies
- Employer-provided tuition assistance (up to $5250) for any type of undergraduate education and job-related graduate education
- Employer-provided costs for dependent care assistance (for children and elderly parents) as well as set-aside salary-reduction plans for dependent care
- Employer-provided "cafeteria plan" fringe benefits to pay for such things as medical and life insurance
- Costs for "flexible benefits accounts" (paid with employee tax-free salary reductions) used for dependent care and medical costs not covered by a health benefits program

Capital Gains and Losses   A **capital gain** is income received from the sale of a capital asset above the costs incurred to purchase and sell the asset. It is taxed at the same rate as other income. A **capital loss** results when the sale of a capital asset brings less income than the costs of purchasing the asset. A **capital asset** is property owned by a taxpayer for pleasure or as an investment. Examples of capital assets are stocks, bonds, real estate, household furnishings, jewelry, automobiles, and coin collections. Gains and losses on investment properties must be reported. Gains from the sale or exchange of property held for *personal use* must be reported as income, but losses are *not* deductible.

The federal government requires that gains and losses be identified as short or long term. A **long-term capital gain (or loss)** occurs when the asset was held for more than 1 year. A **short-term capital gain (or loss)** occurs when the asset was held for 1 year or less. In an effort to encourage investments, beginning with the 1991 tax year, long-term capital gains are taxed at your marginal tax rate or 28 percent, whichever is lower.

It is important for taxpayers to realize that not all investments are profitable, so capital losses are deductible first against capital gains (a tax break that encourages venturesome investments) and then against up to $3000 of other income. Any remaining loss is carried forward to successive years, each with a $3000 maximum. **Tax swaps** allow investors to sell securities for a tax loss by maintaining their same investment strategy. This occurs when the investor sells one depressed security to register a tax loss and then immediately purchases another security for approximately the same price that is similar but not identical. Tax swaps permit investors to take their capital losses while also upgrading the quality of their portfolio. In a similar manner, the tax code also permits **tax-free exchanges,** where capital gains of up to $100,000 in real estate can be "exchanged solely for property of a like kind to be held either for productive use and trade or business or for investment."

Selling your home results in a capital gain that receives special tax consideration. The cost of your home includes its price, the broker's commission, and any money spent to improve the value of the property. If you bought an $80,000 home 5 years ago and sold it for $140,000 today, less $10,000 in selling costs, you would have a capital gain of $50,000 ($140,000 − $80,000 − $10,000). That much additional income could push you into a higher tax bracket.

The capital gain on a home can be completely avoided if another, more expensive home is purchased within 24 months. Also, for persons age 55 or over, a once-in-a-lifetime capital gains exclusion of $125,000 is permitted, providing they have lived in the home as their principal residence for 3 of the previous 5 years. The tax aspects of housing are examined in more detail in Chapter 10, The Housing Expenditure, and in Chapter 20, Investing in Real Estate.

2. Determine Adjustments to Your Income, If Any

It is important to reduce total income as much as possible to bring your final tax liability to its minimum legal amount. **Adjustments to income** are a selected group of legal reductions to gross income generally related to employment. They are called *above-the-line deductions* because they are permitted whether or not you itemize deductions or take the standard deduction amount (procedures explained next in this section). Adjustments are subtracted from gross income to give **adjusted gross income (AGI)**. Adjustments help reduce your AGI and are also valuable because they help you qualify for other AGI-based write-offs, such as itemized deductions for medical and miscellaneous expenses (deductible only to the extent they exceed 7.5 and 2.0 percent of AGI, respectively).

Adjustments to income include (1) business expenses for self-employed persons, such as depreciation and operating expenses for a vehicle and costs to buy a computer and office equipment, (2) related entertainment (limited to 80 percent) and gift expenses (limited to $25 per person), (3) travel costs, (4) up to 80 percent of the cost of club dues if used more than 50 percent of the time for business, (5) contributions to retirement plans, (6) possible home office expenses, (7) 25 percent of the cost of health insurance premiums, (8) interest penalties for early withdrawal of savings certificates of deposit, (9) alimony paid, and (10) all or a portion (depending on income level) of contributions to a qualified retirement program (such as Keogh plans for the self-employed and individual retirement accounts for others). To illustrate, for a person with a gross income of $24,000 who contributes $1500 to an individual retirement account (IRA), the adjustment reduces gross income to $22,500 in adjusted gross income. Contributions to retirement plans (such as an IRA, 401(k), or a Keogh account) are covered in Chapter 22, Developing and Implementing a Plan for a Secure Retirement.

You should deduct reimbursed employee expenses as an adjustment to income if your employer reimburses you for job-related expenses and then reports the reimbursement as income to you. Similarly, should employer payments and reimbursements for your education expenses be included as part of your income, all expenses up to the amount paid or reimbursed may be taken as an adjustment to income. Jury pay surrendered to an employer and included as gross income may be recorded as an adjustment to income to eliminate the effects of taxation of the income not received.

A sideline business can provide tax deductions as adjustments to income.

Some people start a sideline business to take advantage of significant tax deductions as adjustments to income, but a simple hobby will not qualify if all you do is try to take tax losses every year. You may deduct expenses and even take deductible losses if you can show that your business activity is profit-oriented. The IRS says that the best way is to earn a profit in at least 3 of 5 consecutive years, although that is not a firm requirement.

3. Identify the IRS's Standard Deduction Amount

The **standard deduction** is the amount all taxpayers who do not itemize deductions (except some dependents) may deduct from adjusted gross income whenever they file an income tax return, since it is the government's legally permissible estimate of any likely tax-deductible expenses such taxpayers might have. The amount of the standard deduction is the dollar threshold, or floor, for determining whether or not the taxpayer may itemize deductions. For example, the standard deduction amounts in tax forms filed in 1991 for income in the 1990 tax year were $3250 for singles, $5450 for married people filing jointly, and $4750 for heads of households. We estimate that the amounts for singles will be $3400 for 1992 and

Single people get a standard deduction of $3250 even if they cannot itemize.

$3550 for 1993, the amounts for married people filing jointly will be $5700 for 1992 and $5950 for 1993, and the amounts for heads of households will be $4950 in 1992 and $5200 in 1993, assuming inflation rates of 4.5 percent annually. For those age 65 or over or blind, an extra standard deduction of $650 is allowed on tax forms filed in 1991 for each qualifying married individual or $800 if single. Those taxpayers who do not have itemized deductions totaling in excess of the amount permitted for the standard deduction use the appropriate standard deduction figure when calculating their income tax liability.

4. Or, List Your Itemized Deductions

Taxpayers who have tax-deductible expenses in *excess* of the standard deduction amount may forgo the standard deduction and list their itemized deductions. **Itemized deductions** are specific expenses that can be subtracted from adjusted gross income to reduce taxable income. About one-half of all taxpayers have itemized deductions that total more than the standard deduction amount for their filing status. For example, a single person might list all possible tax deductions and find that they total $4000, which is more than the standard deduction amount of $3250 permitted for single taxpayers. The following classifications of itemized deductions are listed on the tax form: (1) medical, dental, and hospital expenses, (2) taxes, (3) interest expenses, (4) charitable contributions, (5) casualty or theft losses, and (6) miscellaneous expenses. Examples of deductions in each of these categories follow.

Medical, Dental, and Hospital Expenses (Not Paid by Insurance) in Excess of 7.5 Percent of Adjusted Gross Income

- Medicine and drugs
- Medical insurance premiums (including contact lens insurance)
- Medical portion of automobile insurance policy
- Medical services (doctors, dentists, nurses, hospitals) and medical equipment (hearing aids, eyeglasses, etc.)
- Home improvements made for the physically handicapped
- Transportation costs to and from obtaining medical services, using a standard flat mileage allowance

Taxes

- Real property taxes (such as on a home or land)
- Personal property taxes (such as on an automobile when any part of the tax is based on the value of the car)
- State, local, and foreign income taxes

Interest Expenses

- Interest paid on first and second home mortgage loans (up to $1,000,000 debt)

- Interest for "points" paid to purchase a home or secure a home mortgage loan for improvements of a principal residence (discussed in Chapter 10)
- Interest paid on home equity loans for amounts up to $100,000 debt
- Interest paid on loans used for investments (up to the amount of investment income)

Charitable Contributions

- Cash contributions to qualified organizations (churches, schools, and other nonprofit groups)
- Noncash contributions (such as personal property) at fair market value
- Travel expenses incurred while performing volunteer services for a charitable organization, usually using a standard flat mileage allowance

Casualty or Theft Losses in Excess of 10 Percent of Adjusted Gross Income

- Casualty losses (such as from storms, vandalism, and fires) in excess of $100 not reimbursed by insurance
- Theft of money or property in excess of $100 not reimbursed by insurance (a copy of the police report provides good substantiation)
- Mislaid or lost property if loss results from an identifiable event that is sudden, unexpected, or unusual (such as catching a diamond ring in a car door and losing the stone)

Miscellaneous Expenses in Excess of 2 Percent of Adjusted Gross Income (Partial Listing Only)

- Union or professional association dues and membership fees
- Safe-deposit box fees for a box used to store papers related to income-producing stocks, bonds, or other investments
- Individual retirement account (IRA) custodial fees
- Purchase and maintenance of specialized clothing that is not suitable for off-the-job use (such as protective shoes, hats, and gloves), including uniforms for those in the armed forces reserves
- Unreimbursed employee business expenses (but only 80 percent of the cost of meals and entertainment), including long-distance telephone calls
- Tax counsel and tax preparation fees
- Investment advisory and management fees
- Tools and supplies used in profession
- Books and periodicals used in profession
- Expenses for investment publications if you have investment income
- Custodial fees for stock and mutual fund dividend reinvestment plans
- Business use of a personal residence or home office (subject to limits)

- Fees paid to obtain employment through an agency
- Travel costs between two jobs, using a flat mileage allowance
- Job-related car expenses (but not for commuting to work) using a flat mileage allowance
- Commuting costs that qualify as a business or education expense
- Medical examinations required (but not paid for) by an employer to get or keep a job
- Appraisal fees on taxable types of items
- Education expenses for employees required by their employer to maintain and improve skills to advance one's career, but generally not if the training readies one for a new career
- Travel and living expenses for job hunting (which does not have to be successful) in one's present career
- Expenses for typing, printing, career counseling, and mailing resumes for seeking a job in one's present career field

Miscellaneous Expenses Allowed as 100 Percent Deductions

- Moving expenses to a new job location, including house-hunting costs (must be at least 35 miles from old home and you must work 39 of the next 52 weeks)
- Gambling losses (but only to offset reported gambling income)
- Business expenses for handicapped workers and performing artists

Given the considerable list of deductions noted here and numerous others for which you might qualify, it makes sense to develop an estimate of your possible deductions. If the total estimates exceed the standard deduction amount or are even close, go back and itemize deductions more carefully. You get no tax benefit from the expenses you pile up if you take the standard deduction instead of deducting the actual costs.

5. Claim the Proper Number of Exemptions

A single person's exemption is worth $2050.

As noted earlier, an exemption is a legally permitted deduction of a taxpayer's income based on the number of persons supported by that income. Each exemption you may claim on tax forms filed in 1991 reduces 1990 taxable income by $2050. The amounts for personal exemptions are estimated to be $2150 in 1992 and $2250 in 1993, assuming inflation rates of 4.5 percent annually. You may claim an exemption for yourself, a spouse, and for other dependents. The personal exemption is phased out for higher-income taxpayers. (This is explained in a footnote to Table 8.2.)

The number of exemptions you claim on your tax return may be different from what you claimed on your W-4 form filed with your employer. For example, you may have chosen to claim fewer exemptions on your W-4 form so that your employer would withhold more in taxes and you would get a refund.

To claim someone else as a dependent for tax purposes and claim their exemption value, the dependent must meet five criteria:

1. More than one-half the dependent's total support must have been provided by you. (Exceptions include children of divorced parents, who generally can be claimed only by the custodial parent.)

2. The dependent must have received less in income for the year than the amount of the personal exemption (excluding tax-exempt income such as Social Security and welfare), unless the person is a child under age 19 or a full-time student younger than age 24.

3. The dependent must be a relative or, if unrelated, must have resided in your home as a member of your household.

4. The dependent must not have filed a joint return with his or her spouse.

5. The dependent must be a U.S. citizen or a legal resident of the United States, Canada, or Mexico.

If you are claimed as a dependent on a parent's return or are *eligible* to be claimed, you cannot claim a personal exemption for yourself, since only the parent gets the exemption. If a parent's exemption claim for a child is disallowed, the child may declare an exemption on his or her own tax return.

For those dependents who are claimed as an exemption by another person, the standard deduction is limited to whichever is greater—$500 or the amount of income earned on a job, up to the amount of the standard deduction ($3250). Parents may no longer claim a personal exemption for dependent children who are full-time students (at least 5 calendar months during the tax year) if they are age 24 as of the end of the year unless they earn less than the exemption amount. Thus, if your child is a full-time student over age 23 and earned $2050 or more (in 1990), you may not claim the child as a dependent; if the child is under age 24, you may claim the child as a dependent regardless of his or her income.

6. Determine Whether You Should Use the Tax Tables or Tax-Rate Schedules

You will use *either* the tax tables or one of the tax-rate schedules to find your tax liability. For taxable incomes up to $50,000, the IRS provides tax tables that you must use to determine your tax liability. Table 8.4 shows segments from the tax tables.

Most taxpayers use the tax tables.

If your taxable income exceeds $50,000, you must use the tax-rate schedules (shown in Table 8.2). Although the IRS rules do not allow you to choose whether you use the tax tables or tax-rate schedule, in fact they are equivalent and will yield nearly equal tax liabilities (differing only a few dollars because of rounding) if used for the same taxable income. The tax schedules and tax tables are adjusted each year to reduce the efforts of inflation.[4]

---

[4] Taxpayers with extremely high incomes and/or substantial income from tax-exempt sources and those who have certain "preference items" equal to 33 percent of adjusted gross income also may have to use a special formula in addition to the tax-rate schedules to pay an *alternative minimum tax (AMT)*. You may owe the flat 21 percent AMT if it exceeds your regular tax bill; this rises to 24 percent in the 1991 tax year.

7. Determine Your Tax Liability

Taxpayers using the tax tables need only find their taxable income in the tables to find their correct tax liability. For example, according to the segment of the tax tables found in Table 8.4, a married couple filing jointly with a taxable income of $46,120 would have a tax liability of $8697. A single taxpayer with the same taxable income would have a tax liability of $10,387.

Taxpayers who must use the tax-rate schedules are required to do some basic calculations once their taxable income has been determined. To prove the equivalence of the tax tables and the tax-rate schedules, we will consider the previous examples of the married couple filing jointly and the single taxpayer, both with taxable incomes of $46,120. For the married couple, refer to the tax schedules in upper portion of Table 8.2. Their tax liability would be calculated as follows: Find the income bracket in the first two columns that contains their taxable income. A taxable income of $46,120 for those filing a joint return falls between the limits of $32,450 and $78,400, as shown in the table. The tax liability is $4867.50 plus 28 percent of the taxable income that exceeds $32,450, or $13,670 ($46,120 − $32,450). Since 28 percent of $13,670 is $3827.60, the tax liability would be $8695.10 ($4867.50 + $3827.60), or almost exactly the tax liability drawn from the tax tables ($8697).

The tax tables and tax rate schedules are equivalent.

To determine your tax liability, you must determine your taxable income. To summarize, taxable income is calculated by taking the taxpayer's gross income, subtracting adjustments to income, subtracting either the standard deduction or total itemized deductions, and subtracting the amount permitted for the number of exemptions allowed. The taxable-income figure is used to determine the taxpayer's tax liability by using the tax tables or tax-rate schedules. You can calculate taxable income by following the step-by-step, line-by-line instructions on the tax return. The process is similar whether you itemize deductions or not.

For taxpayers who take the standard deduction, calculating the tax liability is a straightforward process: Determine gross income; subtract adjustments to income, which leaves adjusted gross income; subtract the $3250 value of the standard deduction for singles; subtract $2050 for each exemption claimed, which results in taxable income; and find the liability by using the tax tables based on the taxable income and filing status.

The following examples show how to determine tax liability.

1. A married couple filing jointly has a gross income of $45,000, $5150 in adjustments, $3200 in itemized deductions, and two exemptions. They take the standard deductions of $5450 because their itemized deductions do not exceed that amount.

Gross income	$ 45,000
Less adjustments to income	− 5,150
Adjusted gross income	39,850
Less standard deduction for married couple	− 5,450
Subtotal	34,400

Less value of two exemptions	− 4,100
Taxable income	30,300
Tax liability (from Table 8.4)	$ 4,549

2. A single person has a gross income of $37,000, $1300 in adjustments, $2600 in itemized deductions, and one exemption. The standard deduction of $3250 is taken because itemized deductions do not exceed that amount.

Gross income	$ 37,000
Less adjustments to income	− 1,300
Adjusted gross income	35,700
Less standard deduction for single person	− 3,250
Subtotal	32,450
Less value of one exemption	− 2,050
Taxable income	30,400
Tax liability (from Table 8.4)	$ 5,991

3. A married couple filing jointly has a gross income of $48,000, $5100 in adjustments, $8600 in itemized deductions, and two exemptions. They deduct their total itemized deductions because the amount is in excess of the $5450 permitted standard deduction value.

Gross income	$ 48,000
Less adjustments to income	− 5,100
Adjusted gross income	42,900
Less total itemized deductions	− 8,600
Subtotal	34,300
Less value of two exemptions	− 4,100
Taxable income	30,200
Tax liability (from Table 8.4)	$ 4,534

4. A single person with a gross income of $75,000 has $400 in adjustments, $3,800 in itemized deductions, and one exemption. The itemized deductions are taken because they exceed the standard deduction value of $3250 for singles.

Gross income	$ 75,000
Less adjustments to income	− 400
Adjusted gross income	74,600
Less total itemized deductions	− 3,800
Subtotal	70,800
Less value of one exemption	− 2,050
Taxable income	68,750
Tax liability, calculated from the tax-rate schedules in the upper portion of Table 8.2 because the taxable income is above $50,000, which is as high as the tax tables go. The tax liability is computed as follows: $10,645.50 + [0.33 × (68,750 − $47,050)] = $17,806.50.	$17,806.50

8. Subtract Any Tax Credits to Find Your Final Tax Liability

After all your diligent efforts to reduce taxable income and thus your tax liability, you may lower it even more through **tax credits.** These are a group of items that directly reduce tax liability on a dollar-for-dollar basis, as opposed to deductions that reduce the income subject to tax. You may take tax credits whether or not you itemize deductions. Subtracting tax credits directly reduces your tax liability to **final tax liability,** which is the amount you actually owe.

There are many special tax credits. Tax credits are available to businesspersons for payment of foreign taxes and employment of special targeted groups. The elderly are allowed a credit while receiving public disability benefits. Tax credits are also available to taxpayers for making payments to care for a child or a disabled dependent, and there is also a credit for some people with a low earned income.

The Child- and Dependent-Care Credit   A credit of up to 30 percent of the cost of caring for a child or disabled dependent younger than age 13 is available. The child- or dependent-care expenses must have been necessary because the taxpayer(s) was working, seeking work, or attending school full time. A maximum of $720 can be claimed as a credit on expenses totaling a maximum of $2400 ($2400 × 0.30 = $720). For taxpayers with two or more qualifying dependents, the credit is permitted on a maximum of $4800 in costs, resulting in a maximum $1440 credit ($4800 × 0.30 = $1440). The credit is 30 percent of child- or dependent-care expenses if adjusted gross income is $10,000 or less. The 30 percent is reduced by 1 percent for each $2000 of adjusted gross income, or part of $2000, above $10,000 until the percentage is reduced to 20 percent for income above $28,000.

Such expenses could include home upkeep, cooking, and general care, such as a nursery. The taxpayer must have earned some income during the year; income from part-time employment qualifies. To get the credit, married taxpayers must file a joint return (unless they are living apart) and must have worked during the year. A spouse is also classified as working if he or she was a full-time student or incapacitated during 5 months of the tax year. The IRS must be told the name and Social Security number of the babysitter or day-care provider.

Note that some employers offer **flexible spending accounts,** which are salary-reduction programs that set aside up to $5000 of an employee's pretax income for dependent-care expenses of children and/or elderly parents. Employee taxpayers who use flexible spending accounts, however, may then be ineligible for the child-care credit, since the credit limit is reduced by the amount of tax-free reimbursements. Still, flexible spending accounts are a good deal because taxpayers do not pay income or Social Security taxes on such salary reductions.

The Earned Income Credit   The **earned income credit** is a form of negative income tax. This credit is available for those whose earned income (wages, salaries, and so forth) and adjusted gross income are each less than $20,000 (even $0) and who have a child living with them for the whole year. The $20,000 of earned income excludes pensions or annuities (other than disability pensions), Social Security payments, worker's compensation, or unemployment compensation. A taxpayer filing as married or a qualifying widow or widower who seeks the credit must have a child who is a dependent (whether married or not); a taxpayer filing as head of household qualifies if there is a married child in the home even though the child is not a dependent. A person with two children who might not otherwise have to file an income tax return could, if qualified, file for the earned income credit and obtain a refund of up to $2005.

Low-income families are eligible for a tax refund even if the adult did not earn any income.

9. Finally, Calculate the Balance You Owe or the Amount of Your Refund

After subtracting your tax credits, you have your final tax liability. Now look at your W-2 form, Wage and Tax Statement, which summarizes your income and withholding for the year. The key figure is the federal income tax withheld. If the amount withheld plus any estimated tax payments is larger than your final tax liability, then you should receive a tax refund. If the amount withheld is less than your final tax liability, then you have a tax balance due. Before mailing your return, attach to it a check or money order made out to the IRS in the amount owed.

Taxpayers generally hear from the IRS within 3 weeks if they have failed to sign the tax return, neglected to attach a copy of the W-2 form, made an error in arithmetic, or used the wrong tax tables or tax-rate schedules. Refunds are usually received within 6 weeks.

Calculating Income Tax Liability: Some Examples

Objective
To be able to calculate illustrative tax liabilities for different types of taxpayers.

Below are examples of calculating tax liability for different types of taxpayers: college students, a single working person, and a married couple with two children and a dependent adult.

College Students

Joe Heisman, who attends Michigan State University, plays football and receives a partial grant-in-aid of $4800 ($2000 was for room and board). In a part-time job last summer, he earned $1600 ($290 was withheld for federal income taxes), and his savings account earned interest of $62. Joe owes no federal income taxes, since his total income totals $3662 ($2000 + $1600 + $62), which is less than the value of his standard deduction ($3250) and exemption ($2050) combined. (Also see the income thresholds in Table 8.5.) However, Joe still needs to file federal **Tax Form 1040-EZ** to obtain a refund of the $290 in income tax withheld by his summer employer. The IRS calls the 1040-EZ its "very short form," which is to be used by single people who have uncomplicated tax information to provide, such as interest income of no more than $400 and other income only from salary and wages.

Susan Blackstone graduated last year from California State University at Fresno, where she enjoyed a swimming scholarship in the amount of $1600. After graduating in June, she began full-time work and earned $11,100 last year for 7 months of full-time work ($1644 was withheld for federal income taxes). Susan also earned $600 in interest on her savings account, $520 in stock dividends, and $1200 by giving private swimming lessons. After adding up her possible tax-deductible expenses, they amounted to only $390. Susan should file **Tax Form 1040A** to obtain her refund, because it permits reporting of salaries, wages, nontraditional sources of income (up to $50,000), and tax credits for taxpayers who do not itemize deductions. Her adjusted gross income of $14,020 includes $11,100 in salary, $600 in interest, $520 in stock dividends, $1200 from swimming lessons, and $600 in scholarship money (the portion allocated for housing; the remaining $1000 was for fees and books and thus not considered taxable income). Susan subtracts $3450 for the standard deduction and $2050 for the value of a personal exemption to determine her taxable income of $8520. Using the tax tables in Table 8.4, she determines her tax liability to be $1279. Subtracting the $1644 from the $1279 withheld yields a refund due her of $365.

Single Working Person

Hanna Pallagrosi of Rome, New York, took a position at a small furniture manufacturing company in February 2 years ago. Last year she earned $28,400 and her employer withheld $3450 in income taxes. Hanna wisely made a $1000 contribution to her new individual retirement account (IRA). Her possible itemized expenses came to only $1800, so she took the standard deduction of $3250. After subtracting the $1000 adjustment to income, $3250 for the standard deduction, and $2050 for her personal exemption ($28,400 − $1000 − $3250 − $2050), her taxable income was $22,100. Her tax liability as shown in Table 8.4 was $3667. After filing Tax Form 1040-A, she was upset at both the magnitude of her tax liability and the fact that she had to mail a check to the government for an additional $217 ($3667 − $3450).

This year Hanna got a raise and earned $31,000. She asked her employer to withhold a little extra, and the total amounted to $4100. Hanna was determined to reduce her federal income taxes, so she increased her IRA contributions to $1600, which reduced her adjusted gross income, and she became a homeowner. She bought a condominium in January, and during the year she paid out $5800 in interest expenses and $420 in real estate taxes. Hanna had $1900 in other itemized deductions as well. Hanna should file **Tax Form 1040** (known as the "long form"), which allows the taxpayer to itemize deductions and utilize a number of other tax-saving deductions and credits. Her total itemizations amounted to $8120 ($5800 + $420 + $1900). Combining the $1600 adjustment to income, the

$8120 in deductions, and the $2050 value of an exemption reduced her gross income to a $19,230 taxable income ($31,000 − $1700 − $8120 − $2050). Using Table 8.4, the resulting tax liability was $2884, and Hanna received an income tax refund of $1216 ($4100 − $2884).

Hanna was pleased that her tax bill had gone down, and since she was curious, she recalculated it assuming that she had not purchased a home. With a gross income of $31,000 less a $1600 adjustment, a $3250 standard deduction (since she could not itemize without the housing deductions), and a $2050 personal exemption, she would have had a taxable income of $24,100 and her final tax liability would have been $4227. Hanna's actual tax bill of $2884 was $1343 less than what it would have been had she not bought the condominium. She correctly concluded that the IRS "paid" $1343 toward the purchase of her condominium and her living costs there, since she did not pay those dollars to the government.

Married Couple

Heinz and Rosetta Klingstead of Carbondale, Illinois, have a complex income tax return because they have both made it a habit to learn about possible tax deductions and to take advantage of them whenever possible. Table 8.6 shows the Klingsteads' income and various reductions.

The Klingsteads have two small children as well as Heinz's mother living at their home. By thinking hard about how to reduce taxes, they have taken advantage of many applicable adjustments, deductions, exemptions, and credits. Part of their income also comes from tax-exempt sources. Their deductions and tax credits, typical for a couple with two children, result in a final tax liability of only $2929.

TABLE 8.6
Income Tax Calculations for a Married Couple (Heinz and Rosetta Klingstead)

All income		
Heinz's salary	$27,700	
Rosetta's salary	15,000	
Capital gains (sales of stock)	450	
Rosetta's year-end bonus	1,000	
State income tax refund (itemized last year)	180	
Interest on savings account	350	
Dividends on stocks	120	
Interest on tax-exempt state bonds	2,000	
Gift from Rosetta's mother	2,500	
Car-pool income (Heinz's van pool)	250	
Total all income		$49,550
Minus tax-exempt income ($2000 + $2500 + $250 from above):		−4,750
Gross income		$44,800

(continued)

TABLE 8.6 (continued)

Adjustments to income		
Payment to Heinz's retirement account	$ 1,000	
Payment to Rosetta's retirement account	1,000	
Minus adjustments to income		− 2,000
Adjusted gross income (AGI)		$42,800
Deductions		
Medical expenses	$ 3,500	
Exclusion (7.5% of AGI)	3,210	
Total		$ 290
Taxes		
Real property	$ 1,800	
Personal property	210	
Total		$ 2,010
Interest expenses		
Home mortgage	$ 6,190	
Home equity loan	160	
Total		$ 6,350
Contributions		
Church	$ 1,200	
Other charities	240	
Goodwill	300	
Charitable travel	90	
Total		$ 1,830
Casualty or theft		
Loss—diamond ring	$ 4,500	
Insurance reimbursement	− 0	
Reduction	− 100	
Exclusion (10% of AGI)	− 4,280	
Total		$ 120
Miscellaneous		
Union dues (Heinz)	$ 280	
Safe-deposit box	30	
Investment publications	60	
Tax publications	20	
Subtotal	390	
Less 2% of AGI	− 856	
Total		0
Minus total itemized deductions		− 10,600
Minus exemptions (5 @ $2,050)		− 10,250
Taxable income		$21,950
Tax liability (from Table 8.4)		3,289
Tax credits		
Child care	$ 1,800	
80% exclusion	− 1,440	
Minus tax credits		360
Final tax liability		$ 2,929

The marginal tax rate for the Klingsteads is 15 percent. Their average tax rate compared with all income is 5.9 percent ($2929/$49,550); compared with gross income, it is 6.5 percent ($2929/$44,800); and compared with taxable income, it is 13.3 percent ($2929/$21,950). For a family with such a substantial income, they have been quite successful in lowering their final tax liability.

Avoiding Taxes

At the beginning of this chapter we defined *taxes* as compulsory charges imposed by a government on citizens and property. Although you must pay taxes, you do not have to pay more than is required. If you are knowledgeable about tax laws and regulations and assertive in your financial planning, you can avoid overpayment of taxes. The U.S. tax laws are strict and punitive about compliance, but neutral about whether the taxpayer should take advantage of every "break" and opportunity possible.

Avoiding taxes is both desirable and respectable.

This section discusses ways to avoid overpaying taxes by (1) understanding the difference between tax avoidance and tax evasion, (2) recognizing the opportunity cost of an extra dollar paid in taxes, (3) avoiding the inherent bias in taxation against some married couples, (4) bunching deductions and postponing income, (5) examining methods of reducing taxable income, and (6) increasing deductions. Using these techniques will enable you to accumulate more personal assets, to share those assets with family members in lower tax brackets, and eventually to pass the assets on to surviving relatives with a minimum of tax erosion.

Tax Avoidance Versus Tax Evasion

Tax evasion is illegal. It involves deliberately and willfully hiding income, falsely claiming deductions, or otherwise cheating the government out of taxes owed. A waiter who does not report tips received as income and a babysitter who does not report such wages as income are both guilty of tax evasion. So is a person who deducts $150 in church contributions but who has not contributed to a church in years. **Tax avoidance** is completely different. It is avoiding taxes by reducing tax liability through legal techniques. This involves applying knowledge of the tax code and regulations to personal income tax.

Tax avoidance is legal and will give you additional funds to spend, save, or invest.

The U.S. Supreme Court in 1945 upheld the "legal right of a taxpayer to decrease the amount of what otherwise would be his taxes, or to avoid them altogether, by means which the law permits." Judge Learned Hand wrote further that "nobody owes any public duty to pay more than the law demands; taxes are enforced extractions, not voluntary contributions. To demand more in the name of morals is mere cant."

Tax evasion results in penalties, fines, excess interest charges, and an occasional jail sentence. Tax avoidance, on the other hand, results in paying less in taxes and having more money for spending, saving, and investing. You need to devise and use effective tax strategies to be absolutely sure that you pay no more in taxes than you should.

A Dollar Saved Is Really Two Dollars—Or More!

Sufficient reason to avoid taxes can be illustrated in three ways. First, there is the concept of **opportunity cost.** This is the cost of a decision measured in terms of the value of forgone opportunities, and it is reflected by the cost of what one has to do without or what one could have bought instead. By deciding to watch television at home for 3 hours on a warm summer day, for example, you give up enjoying those same hours on a nearby beach, or playing a neighborhood game of volleyball, or sleeping. In financial matters, you should further recognize that giving up an extra dollar in taxes also has a cost. By paying a dollar in taxes, you lose not only the dollar paid, but also the alternative use (perhaps for spending, saving, or investing) for another dollar that must take the place of the dollar paid in taxes.

If you pay an extra dollar in taxes, you must earn more than one dollar to replace it.

A second illustration is that if you pay a dollar in taxes, you may have to go out and earn *another* dollar to replace it. Thus a dollar saved in taxes may amount to two dollars back in your pocket available for alternative uses. Third, a dollar also becomes more than two dollars when the concept of effective marginal tax rate is considered. A single person earning a taxable income of $48,000 has a marginal tax rate of 33 percent. Adding 7.65 percent in Social Security taxes, 6 percent for state income taxes, and 4 percent for city income taxes results in an effective marginal tax rate of 50.65 percent. Consequently, for every $2 earned, this person pays just over $1 ($2 $\times$ 0.5065 = $1.01) in taxes. Conversely, for every $1 saved in taxes, this high-paying taxpayer would have about 50 cents available for other purposes. Moreover, after considering opportunity costs plus one's effective marginal tax rate, a dollar saved in income taxes could amount to a $2.50 return to the taxpayer. This should be sufficient motivation to find legal ways to reduce your tax liability. Those in the highest tax brackets realize the largest proportional benefits.

Marriage Tax Penalty

We are not advocating divorce, but it could save money for some people, since marriage does not always mean lower tax rates than for singles. One of the inequities in our current progressive income tax system is that the tax rates contain a **marriage tax penalty.** The marriage tax penalty occurs because many two-earner married couples pay more in income taxes than they would if they were single because their pooled incomes boost them into a higher tax bracket than they would face individually as singles.

Here's how the system works. (These calculations are derived from the upper portion of Table 8.2.) A single person earning a taxable income of $25,000 pays income taxes in the amount of $4472. Should that person get married to a person who has no income and they file a joint return, the tax is reduced to $3750. The tax liability drops because by filing together they receive an extra exemption of $2050 and a standard deduction amount of $5450, instead of the $3250 for a single. The impression given is that marriage reduces tax liabilities. It does for some, but for many the marriage tax penalty means higher tax bills than for singles. The inequity

TABLE 8.7
Marriage Penalty Tax Illustration (Total Taxable Income for Couple, $50,000)

Income Split %		Income Split				
Spouse 1	Spouse 2	Spouse 1	Spouse 2	Unmarried Liability	Married Liability	Extra Tax Liability
70	30	$35,000	$15,000	$9,522	$9,782	$260
60	40	30,000	20,000	8,944	9,782	838
50	50	25,000	25,000	8,944	9,782	838

is serious. The marriage penalty generally exists when the spouse who earns less contributes approximately 30 percent or more toward total income.

To illustrate, Table 8.7 shows the final tax liabilities of married and unmarried couples earning a total taxable income of $50,000. Unmarried couples where one partner's taxable income is $35,000 and the other's is $15,000 have a $260 lower tax liability. As the income split nears $25,000 for each partner, the married couple must pay up to an additional $838 in taxes. Thus a married couple would pay 9.4 percent ($838/$8944) more taxes on precisely the same taxable income merely because they are married.

Avoid the marriage tax and let the IRS pay for part of a vacation.

For $838, a married couple may not be willing to get a divorce. But for some married couples, that may be enough difference in tax liability to partially finance a divorce in late December and a 1-week vacation at a resort. Then, upon their return in January, they could remarry, only to repeat the process the next year, in effect letting Uncle Sam pay for all their expenses. Note, however, that the IRS has ruled that such "quickie tax divorces" are a form of tax evasion. Meanwhile, the marriage tax penalty remains, and a growing number of married couples divorce but still live together to save tax dollars.

It would be tax wise for people earning similar incomes to wait until January to get married. The marriage tax penalty they save could help pay for the honeymoon. In the cases of divorce, if one spouse earns most of the income, a couple could save taxes by having the judge sign the divorce decree in January instead of December. Also, in divorce situations, if the former spouse with the higher income can claim the children as exemptions, he or she will save a substantial amount of money, assuming the custodial parent signs a waiver for the income tax exemption. (A $2050 exemption is worth only $308 to someone in the 15 percent bracket but $677 to someone in the 33 percent bracket.)

Bunching Deductions and Postponing Income

You have seen that considering the financial impact of taxation is important. The timing of tax decisions may be crucial. Bunching deductions and postponing income may help you lower your tax liability.

One problem confronting many people is not having enough itemized deductions to exceed the standard deduction amount. By shifting the payment dates of some deductible items, you can increase your deductions. For example, if you have about $3000 of deductible expenses each year, you could prepay some items in December of one year to push the total over the $3250 threshold and receive the tax advantage of having excess deductions. The next year you can simply take the standard deduction amount. This process is known as **bunching deductions.** Some items that can be prepaid are medical expenses, dental bills, real estate taxes, state and local income taxes, personal property taxes, dues in professional associations, and charitable contributions. You may mail the payments or charge them on credit cards by December 31.

Bunch deductions one year and take the standard deduction the next year.

By **postponing income** you can achieve the same result. Say you expect a year-end commission check of $3000; the extra income might be enough to push you into paying a higher marginal tax rate. If your employer is willing to date the commission check in January, the income need not be reported until the next year, when tax rates might not be as high. Your tax bracket might be lower next year because you anticipate lower sales commissions, know that you will not work full time (if you return to school, have a child, decide to travel, and so forth), or another reason. Retired people may be able to postpone voluntary distributions of income from retirement plans, and businesses may delay billing customers for work.

Reducing Taxable Income (Yes, Reducing Income!) to Lower Taxes

It may sound puzzling to suggest that to lower tax liability you should reduce taxable income. The key is to reduce taxable income, not total income. Although it is true, this advice is often ignored. The wise financial planner will reduce taxable income through tax-exempt income, income splitting (or shifting), and tax shelters. Also, because the personal income taxes collected by states and municipalities are usually based on one's federal taxable income, reducing federal taxable income through adjustments to income will reduce other tax liabilities as well. Three methods to reduce your taxable income are suggested below.

Use Tax-Exempt Income   Taxpayers in higher income brackets (28 percent or higher) often can gain by purchasing tax-exempt municipal bonds issued by various agencies of states and municipalities. (Bonds are the subject of Chapter 17.) For example, assume that Mary Ellen Rider of Johnson City, Texas, currently has $5000 in savings earning 9 percent, or $450 annually. She pays $126 in tax on this income at her 28 percent marginal tax rate. A tax-exempt $5000 state bond paying 7 percent will provide her with a better after-tax return. She would receive $350 tax free from the state bond compared with $324 ($450 − $126) after taxes on the income from savings. The increase in after-tax income is $26 ($350 − $324). Finding tax-exempt income is a strategy to reduce your tax liability, sometimes considerably.

Advice to the Conservative Taxpayer: Know How to Calculate and Compare Tax-Exempt and Taxable Yields

Conservative taxpayers, especially those in higher tax brackets, have the opportunity to lower income tax liabilities by investing in tax-exempt municipal bonds and/or tax-exempt money-market funds. To do so correctly, you first need to be able to calculate how well a **tax-exempt investment** (an investment free from federal taxation) compares with taxable alternatives. The **taxable-yield formula** calculates the federal **taxable yield** (**TY**). This is determined by subtracting one's federal marginal tax rate from 1.0:

$$TY = \frac{\text{tax-exempt yield}}{1.00 - \text{federal marginal tax rate}} \quad (8.1)$$

For example, assume that you are a taxpayer paying at the 28 percent federal marginal tax rate. This means that any extra income earned over a certain amount will be taxed at that rate. You are considering buying a tax-exempt bond yielding 7 percent. Substituting in the equation gives

$$TY = \frac{0.07}{1.00 - 0.28}$$
$$= \frac{0.07}{0.72}$$
$$= 9.7 \text{ percent}$$

Therefore, a 9.7 percent taxable yield is equivalent to a tax-exempt 7 percent yield. Thus you would have to earn a yield greater than 9.7 percent on a taxable bond (or any other taxable investment) in order to earn more than the tax-exempt yield of 7 percent. Restated in the opposite way, you would have to get a tax-exempt yield greater than 7 percent to do better than a taxable yield of 9.7 percent.

When you know the taxable yield, you can reverse the problem. For example, assume that you are a taxpayer paying at the 33 percent federal marginal tax rate and you are considering investing in a taxable corporate bond yielding 10.6 percent. How much of a **tax-exempt yield** (**TEY**) would you need to do better than you would with the taxable bond? The *TEY* is calculated by subtracting one's federal marginal tax rate from 1.0, which is simply reversing the preceding equation, as done in the **tax-exempt yield formula** below:

$$TEY = TY \times (1.00 - \text{federal marginal tax rate}) \quad (8.2)$$

Substituting figures, we have

$$TEY = 10.6 \times (1.00 - 0.33)$$
$$= 10.6 \times 0.67$$
$$= 7.1 \text{ percent}$$

Therefore, you would have to earn a tax-exempt yield above 7.1 percent to earn more after taxes than on a 10.6 percent taxable investment.

The effective marginal tax rate also includes the effect on an investment of both state and local taxes. Residents of New York City who buy municipal bonds, for example, enjoy exemption from federal taxation as well as from state and local income taxes on the earnings from these bonds, and the equivalent yields on their bonds rise accordingly. People living in high tax states, such as California, New York, Massachusetts, North Carolina, Ohio, and Minnesota, especially benefit from tax-exempt investments. Tax-exempt bonds are examined in Chapter 17.

Income Splitting (or Shifting)   **Income splitting** takes place when one person with a high marginal tax rate shifts income to another person who is in a lower tax bracket (or who pays no taxes at all). Today, children under age 14 pay no tax on $500 or less of unearned income (interest, dividends, and capital gains), and they are taxed at their own rate, typically 15 percent on the next $500. The IRS will not be completely beaten, however, and now there is something called the **kiddie tax,** which provides taxation on unearned income received by a child in excess of $1000. This provision of the IRS regulations taxes a child's yearly investment income in excess of $1000 at the parent's rate (probably 28 or 33 percent) until the child is age 14. At that time, taxes are figured at the teenagers' rate, probably 15 percent.

Children usually pay taxes at lower rates than their parents.

Here is another useful illustration of income splitting. Suppose a parent wants to create a college fund for a 2-year-old child and presently has $5000 in a savings account earning 7 percent interest income ($350 annually). If the parent gives the child the $5000, the parent will not have any interest income on which to pay taxes, perhaps at the 33 percent rate. To the parent, shifting income represents an immediate gain of $116 ($350 × 0.33), since that amount will not go to the government. Note also that people are allowed to make tax-free gifts of cash or property (which escapes estate taxes) of as much as $10,000 a year—$20,000 if the money is given jointly with a spouse—to anyone, including children. Chapter 23 discusses this in more detail.

Assuming that the child has no other source of taxable income, no taxes on the child's interest earnings on the $5000 will have to be paid. After 10 years with compound interest at 7 percent, the child's college fund will have grown to $9835, although the child would have owed some small tax liabilities through a few of the years when income went above $500. Note though that since a child with annual unearned income between $500 and $1000 pays tax on the amount over $500 at a 15 percent rate, this amounts to an average rate of only 7.5 percent given that the first $500 is tax exempt.

Also, in such circumstances, parents should consider putting Series EE government savings bonds in the name of a child, since $500 of interest income on these bonds can be reported on the child's annual tax return and avoid taxation. This is better than waiting until redemption and reporting all the accrued interest at once, unless the money is eventually used for education purposes. If so, all the income is tax exempt, as noted in Chapter 5.

Another income-shifting technique occurs when a parent chooses to give appreciated stocks and/or income property to a minor child instead of selling it. When the child sells it at age 14 or older, the gains will be taxed at his or her rate rather than the parent's.

Tax Shelters   Have you ever wished you could have a tax shelter like wealthy people do? People paying high tax rates have been known to easily be enticed into investing in some rather risky ventures that most of us would never consider. This is because investment losses are partially "paid for" by the government, since the high-income taxpayer reports these as tax deductions. If an investor in the 28 percent bracket puts $1000 into an investment that fails, that $1000 tax loss may be used to offset $1000 in other income. This means that the investor does not have to pay $280 in taxes, since the money was already lost in the investment, and in reality, the investor is out only $720. Examples of such tax-shelter investments not covered in this text are cattle-feeding operations, leasing of business assets, production of films, and oil- and gas-drilling programs. Sophisticated investment "opportunities" become available, in part, because of our high marginal tax rates.

Tax shelters sometimes provide tax losses.

Tax losses are paper losses, in the sense that they may not represent out-of-pocket losses, often created when deductions generated from an investment (such as depreciation) exceed the income from the investment. The IRS has tightened up on permitting tax losses in recent years, partially by limiting certain types of deductions, such as tax losses generated through passive activities. **Passive activities** include rental operations and all other businesses in which you do not materially participate (such as limited partnerships), although there are certain exceptions. Investors may not use passive-activity tax losses to offset ordinary taxable income, such as salary, interest, dividends, annuity, self-employment income, and stock market profits. Passive tax losses can be used only to offset income from passive investments. Of course, disallowed losses may be carried forward to the next taxable year, when they may be used to offset passive income.

However, there is one key IRS exception that does permit taxpayers to deduct passive losses against salary or self-employment earnings. Deductions are allowed for real estate investors who (1) have an adjusted gross income of $150,000 or less and (2) actively participate in the management of the property, and in such instances, they may deduct up to $25,000 of net losses from passive investments against regular income. For example, a residential real estate investment property could be generating an annual cash income $1000 greater than the out-of-pocket operating costs. The result could be a $1500 tax loss with depreciation expenses on the building taken as a tax deduction, and this amount can be used to offset other income. This useful tax shelter remains for most taxpayers because such tax losses may be taken for investments in various real estate investments, which are discussed in Chapter 20, Investing in Real Estate.

Owning rental property is a useful tax shelter for many taxpayers.

With few exceptions, a tax shelter does not permit an investor to avoid taxes forever. Rather, most **tax shelters** are methods of deferring taxes until a later date when the tax rate might be lower. During the interim period, the taxpayer gains an alternative use of the money not yet given the government as well as the time value of such funds. One shelter used by some investors is called *selling short against the box*. Here the investor sells borrowed stock equal to the number of shares that are owned. Any gain is not taxed until the short position is closed the following year with the original stock. (Selling short is explained in detail in Chapter 21.)

The tax shelters emphasized in this text are voluntary contributions to pension funds, such as individual retirement accounts (IRAs), salary-reduction plans, and Keogh accounts. They are aimed at putting money that would be taxed at today's high rates into qualified retirement programs that first of all grow tax-free and second will provide income during later years, presumably at lower tax rates. It is sufficient to point out at this time that putting $2000 into a qualified retirement account permits the taxpayer to use that amount immediately as an adjustment to income, thus lowering the tax liability for the current year. A $2000 contribution to a retirement plan immediately saves the taxpayer in the 28 percent tax bracket $560 because that amount does not have to be sent to the IRS. Most employees are allowed to contribute—and shelter—up to $7979 annually to a qualified retirement plan. These tax-sheltered programs are detailed in Chapter 22, Social Security and Other Retirement Plans.

Increasing Tax Deductions

A dollar given to charity may only cost you 72 cents.

Another way to reduce taxable income is to increase tax-deductible expenses. IRS Publication 17 and other tax-information publications describe what tax deductions you can take. An almost sure way to increase itemized deductions, for example, is to purchase a home with a mortgage loan. The large amounts of money homeowners pay out for interest and real property taxes are deductible. (The pros and cons of obtaining a mortgage are examined in detail in Chapter 10, The Housing Expenditure.) Remember that when you itemize, every dollar counts. If you are in the 28 percent bracket, an extra dollar in a found deduction puts 28 cents back in your pocket; $100 in deductions saves you $28.

Here are just a few examples on how to increase your taxable deductions and put more tax dollars back into your pocket. Assume you are in the 28 percent marginal tax bracket and itemize deductions. Cash contributions made to people collecting door to door or at a shopping center during holidays are deductible, even though receipts are not given. (The IRS reasonably expects people to make such contributions.) Fifty dollars in contributions deducted can save you $14 in taxes. Instead of throwing out an old television set, donate it. An $80 charitable contribution for a TV (get a receipt) will save you $22. Expenses for business-related trips can be a most fruitful area for tax deductions. If you take one business trip a year, perhaps incurring $400 in deductible expenses, you will save another $112 in taxes assuming your miscellaneous deductions already exceed 2 percent of your AGI. The IRS also permits tax deductions for the costs expended on job-hunting trips. In other words, Uncle Sam foots the bill for 28 percent of the cost of such trips and all other legitimate tax deductions.

How to Prepare Your Income Tax Return

Objective
To be able to determine which method of preparing tax returns is best and why.

It has been said that taxes are the price we pay for our free society. In reality, we pay even a little more by spending the time, and sometimes money, to prepare and send in income tax returns.

Superficially, the task seems easy enough. If you earn a moderate income and have no itemized deductions, you may complete Tax Form 1040-EZ or 1040-A and mail it to the IRS; alternatively, you may file *electronically*, using an income-tax preparation service. All others send in Tax Form 1040 with extra supporting forms. Often, however, it is not so easy, and as a result, 1 in 10 returns contains an error. Each year the directions for filling out tax forms are "simplified," but they can still be confusing. And the tax code is changed every year by Congress. Further, tax regulations and court rulings are published almost weekly. Completing your income tax return correctly *and* paying the lowest tax possible requires considerable effort. You have three options at tax preparation time. You can (1) let the IRS do it, (2) use a tax-preparation service, lawyer, or CPA, or (3) fill out the return yourself.

IRS Assistance

Aid from the Internal Revenue Service is available, but their advice may or may not be valid.

The IRS makes tax publications available, handles questions from taxpayers on a toll-free hotline (mostly a busy signal around tax time), and will complete a taxpayer's form to determine final tax liability. To have the IRS compute your tax liability, you must (1) have an adjusted gross income of $25,000 or less ($50,000 or less if filing jointly), (2) have income entirely from salaries, wages, tips, interest, dividends, pensions, or annuities, (3) have no itemized deductions, (4) complete the entire first page of the return, (5) complete all supporting schedules, and (6) mail the return by April 15. The IRS will look up your tax liability on the appropriate tax table and, if you qualify, calculate your earned-income credit.

IRS advice is often unreliable and not valid.

IRS advice received over the telephone, in person, or even from IRS publications is not final. In audits, which are discussed below, the IRS frequently overrules tax advice given out by its representatives. Unfortunately, not all IRS personnel are well-versed in all IRS policies. Research suggests that nearly half the tax advice given out by the IRS on the telephone is not accurate. Other studies have shown that about half the returns prepared by all types of tax specialists have an error, such as inaccurate math or an incorrect deduction. Your knowledge about tax regulations may be your best protection against occasional IRS and/or tax specialist incompetence.

Tax-Preparation Services, Lawyers, and CPAs

In a recent year, 47 percent of taxpayers hired professionals to prepare their returns. National **tax-preparation services** specialize in completing individual taxpayers' income tax returns and are affiliated with a nationally advertised tax service (such as H&R Block). Local tax-preparation services do not have such an affiliation but typically offer tax advice year round to business customers as well as individuals. Both can help you list appropriate deductions, compute accurately, and determine proper tax liability. National services are not necessarily better than local ones. Choose a tax-preparation service with a staff that asks lots of questions about possible deductions and searches for ways to legally reduce your liability.

Most taxpayers will not need the special services of a lawyer or a certified public accountant (CPA) to complete their tax forms. However, one reason to see a lawyer would be for a recommendation on alternative investments from a tax perspective. Help from a CPA, or any accountant who is certified to represent clients before the IRS, should again be reserved for complicated tax matters. Lawyers and accountants will complete your return just as accurately as a tax-preparation service but will charge more.

Use tax specialists for complicated tax matters.

When someone other than the taxpayer prepares an income tax return (such as a professional tax-preparation service, friend, or relative), the law requires the preparer to put his or her name and address at the bottom of the form. In spite of all the efforts by professionals and others, you may be surprised to hear that getting help does not substantially reduce math errors, nor does it always result in obtaining advice on deductions with which the IRS will agree. The solution may be to learn a lot about income taxes yourself and prepare your own tax returns.

Preparing Your Own Tax Returns

If you can read and follow simple directions, you can fill out Tax Form 1040-A or Tax Form 1040-EZ, neither of which permits itemized deductions. These are the tax forms filled out by most people. Taxpayers who have adjustments to income or who itemize deductions can fill out their own returns too if they have the patience to follow the directions detailed on the tax forms and in IRS instruction booklets.

If income taxes are something you definitely do not want to get involved with, then by all means find someone to properly complete your tax returns. If, on the other hand, the prospect challenges you, you can have fun at it. You yourself can be the one best prepared to reduce your tax liability. Study Publication 17, *Your Federal Income Tax,* to learn what is deductible and what is not. Only you know the personal quirks in your expenditures that could qualify for tax deductions. Only you can review other commercially available tax-preparation booklets (which are themselves tax deductible) to find overlooked areas for possible deductions. (Such publications do not give the narrow IRS perspective on deductions; they offer suggestions on what is probably deductible given certain circumstances.) Finally, only you have the assertiveness to take a deduction because you believe it is deductible. A tax adviser may give you guidance, but only you can make the decision.

We believe that taxpayers need to learn about taxes and complete the forms themselves to practice effective financial management. Of course, it is wise to seek professional assistance occasionally to find out if there is an area of tax reduction you might have overlooked or not taken advantage of fully or if dramatic changes have occurred in your life (such as marriage or divorce or a business opening or failure). With some study, in no time at all you can become the expert on your own taxes.

You can become your own expert on taxes.

What If You Are Audited?

A **tax audit** is a formal examination of a taxpayer's tax forms by the Internal Revenue Service for accuracy and completeness, generally limited to a 3-year period after you file. Audits are conducted to collect the proper amounts due. Audits also motivate others to complete their tax returns properly; if you are audited, you usually tell friends about it. People who are organized and prepared do not worry about audits because most audits cover only facts and documentation, so it may simply be a matter of supplying back-up material. Those who do worry have the legal right to choose to stay away from an audit and send a competent representative instead.

With over 110 million tax returns coming in annually, it is no wonder that the IRS can audit only a very small percentage. However, with computer assistance, the IRS does subject *every* return to a series of computer-based **reasonableness tests**. These tests are based on average amounts for each category of deductions, and they are revised each year. For example, for a married couple with two exemptions and an income of such and such, medical deductions usually amount to X and contributions amount to Y. Returns that exceed these averages are sorted for examination by IRS employees who decide whether or not particular taxpayers will be audited. To help avoid an audit, many taxpayers try to eliminate audit questions in advance. A police report attached to a return to document a large casualty loss or any other unusually large deduction (even though not required by the IRS) might convince the IRS person not to conduct an audit.

Other returns are audited on a random basis. Approximate chances of an audit are about less than 1 percent for those with an AGI of $10,000 to $25,000, 1 percent for AGIs of $25,000 to $50,000 and 2 percent for AGIs over $50,000. For those deducting losses from an unusual tax shelter, the chances rise to two out of every three. Five out of six people audited wind up paying more taxes.

All taxpayers should know that the "Taxpayer Bill of Rights" is finally law. In response to complaints of unfair treatment by IRS officials, Congress passed this 1989 law which requires clearer explanations of proposed actions (such as property seizures), relaxes certain audit and collection procedures, and explains IRS obligations. If you are audited, the IRS must tell you your rights, including appeal procedures, in non-technical language. In addition to using the normal appeals process, taxpayers or their representatives may make application for relief (to cease collection efforts or release property from an IRS seizure) through the IRS's new ombudsman when the government is about to take enforcement action that will impose a significant hardship, such as causing loss of employment, damage to credit rating, and threat of imminent bankruptcy. Installment repayment agreements will be granted if they will ensure collection.

Different Types of IRS Audits

The most common IRS notification received by taxpayers is a **document matching notice**. Here the IRS is solely interested in simple verification. This occurs when information in your return is electronically matched with other sources of information. For example, you may have failed to report income even though you were sent a **Form 1099** from a financial institution. This form reports income of all kinds (stock dividends, interest, consulting income, and so on) directly to IRS computers. Affected taxpayers need only respond to the notice by sending a letter of explanation and photocopies of requested documentation to the IRS. If the taxpayer is in error, he or she only needs to forward the extra amount owed as specified in the notice.

Official audits can be **complete**, **correspondence**, or **office**. Subjects for the complete audit are selected randomly. Every 3 years, the IRS selects a sample of 50,000 tax returns to help

(continued)

the government establish the range of numbers for their reasonableness tests. This effort is called their Taxpayer Compliance Measurement Program, the most grueling tax audit imaginable. In this complete audit, each deduction must be proven to the satisfaction of the auditor. Note, though, that the taxpayer need not have a receipt for every deduction because the IRS accepts estimates for many items.

Much more likely is a correspondence audit, in which the IRS questions a particular deduction and wants documentation. It could be a legitimate deduction that is out of line with what the IRS considers normal, perhaps a large amount for home mortgage loan interest or a single contribution of thousands of dollars. These audits are conducted entirely by mail. An office audit requires the taxpayer to visit the nearest IRS office to document all items in a particular section of the form (such as "miscellaneous" or "charitable contributions").

Good Advice If You Are Ever Audited

If you are ever audited, try to consider it a challenge. Be prepared, and enjoy the opportunity to see how the system works. Most auditors are well trained and courteous. They realize that you may be nervous and will attempt to put you at ease. But do not forget the purpose of the meeting: The IRS wants to get more dollars out of your pocket if possible. Therefore, do *not* (1) be overly chatty with the auditor, (2) offer a bribe (a federal marshal will arrest you even if you are kidding), (3) talk about other deductions that you took elsewhere on the form or took in an earlier year (the auditor can broaden the investigation if your comments cause suspicion and suggest other problem areas), (4) bring any records not asked for in the letter explaining the purpose of the audit, (5) volunteer any extra information, (6) concede immediate defeat even if you lack full documentation, or (7) compromise too quickly or allow yourself to be rushed, confused, intimidated, or insulted.

Do realize that if your judgment on the correctness of a deduction seems right, you do not have to accept the auditor's judgment. Most auditors (but not all) and the great majority of auditing supervisors and appeals officers will accept reasonable explanations of how you came up with figures, even if you lack full documentation, so pursue your rights, be logically persuasive, and you might save some money. Should you have too many problems with an auditor or experience a serious personality clash, you have the right to demand another one. If you believe you are right about an item or two that the auditor disagrees with, you may request an appeal with the auditor's supervisor; then read more on the topic and return in a few weeks to see the supervisor. If necessary, make a further appeal and ask to schedule an appointment with the regional appeals officer, who will give you a full opportunity to present your arguments. If still

(continued)

Other Types of Federal, State, and Local Taxes

Objective
To be able to explain the effect of numerous types of federal, state, and local taxes on income available to spend, save, and invest.

There are other types of taxes besides the federal income tax. The most important is the Social Security tax, which is discussed in detail in Chapter 22 and in Appendix B. This tax results from the Federal Insurance Contribution Act (FICA), which is a combination of 11 different programs designed to prevent people from becoming destitute. Two of the larger programs are the old-age benefits program and Medicare.

dissatisfied, for a nominal fee you may formally appeal an issue to the Tax Court's Small Case Division. This operates much like a small claims court, and in a recent year taxpayers won or partially won 54 percent of the time. Part of the reason for the success rate is that the court's decision on your case is legally binding for you but does not set a precedent for all other tax-payers, as does the expensive process of proving a case in the federal courts. Keep in mind that the IRS often advocates its own position and not necessarily the interpretation of the Internal Revenue Code as decided by the courts, thus when challenged you may need to vigorously assert your rights.

Only about 200 people a year go to jail for tax evasion. The IRS wants money, not jail sentences. If the IRS disagrees with your deductions and disallows something, you will owe them two or possibly three payments. First, you must pay the increased tax liability. For example, assume the IRS disallowed a $400 deduction and you are in the 28 percent bracket; your additional tax is $112 ($400 multiplied by 0.28). Second, interest on the additional tax liability is assessed from the date the tax "should have" been paid. If the audit takes place in April of the following year, the interest charge on the additional $112 might be $12. (The IRS interest rate has varied from 9 to 14 percent in recent years.) Third, you may owe a 20 percent penalty applied to the portion of any underpayment attributable to negligence, substantial understatement of income tax, overvaluation of property, or undervaluation of property on a gift tax or estate tax return. More serious penalties exist if you willfully failed to pay tax or filed a return (misdemeanor—up to $25,000 fine or 1 year in prison, or both), or willfully made and subscribed to a false return (felony—up to $100,000 fine or 3 years in prison, or both). Remember, though, having a deduction disallowed generally does not result in a penalty, so be confident and take it.

You should keep your tax records for at least 3 years, since this is the standard statute of limitations time period during which the IRS can audit you. (Sample formats to maintain tax records are illustrated in Figures 3.4 and 3.5) However, the IRS does have up to 6 years to conduct an audit if you have understated your income by at least 25 percent. There is no time limit if the IRS suspects fraud. You should never discard records relating to home purchases, contributions to IRA and Keogh accounts, and investments held for a number of years. Also remember that in an audit you have the burden of proving that the numbers you provided the IRS are accurate. When in doubt about any tax record, do not throw it out. Recordkeeping is fundamental in tax matters, and being able to prove your deductions is crucial to surviving an audit and keeping more of your money.

The Social Security tax is a tax on earnings, and equal amounts are paid by employers and employees. To increase revenues, Congress regularly raises both the tax rate and the base upon which the rate is applied. For example, in 1990 the Social Security tax was 7.65 percent applied on earned income up to a maximum of $51,300 (maximum tax $3924.45). The base amounts are estimated to be $53,600 in 1991, $56,000 in 1992, and $58,500 in 1993, assuming inflation rates of 4.5 percent annually. Reducing your Social Security tax is extremely difficult to do, since that tax rate is applied to earned income.

Taxpayers also pay a considerable amount in personal income taxes to

TABLE 8.8
Federal, State, and Local Taxes (for Robert Chong)

Gross income		$39,000
Taxes		
Federal income tax ($30,000 taxable income)	$6,080	
Social Security tax (assumed at 7.65%)	2,984	
State income tax (assumed at 6%)	1,800	
City or county income tax (assumed at 2%)	600	
Sales taxes (state/county/city assumed at 5% on $15,000 consumption)	750	
Use taxes (gasoline, cigarettes, liquor, assumed at various rates)	80	
Personal property taxes (assessed on 3-year-old automobile)	160	
Estate taxes (assumes taxpayer lived)	—	
Gift taxes (assumes taxpayer did not give large sums away)	—	
Total annual taxes		12,454
Money available to spend, save, and invest		$26,546

state and local governments. Reduction of these tax liabilities generally can be accomplished by reducing your federal adjusted gross income as much as possible (using adjustments to income) and by studying the state and local tax guidelines, since they often permit other special deductions not allowed on the federal form. For example, renter's credits are allowed in California and Hawaii, and several states permit tax reductions for installing energy-saving equipment. Most other federal, state, and local taxes are difficult to avoid.

U.S. citizens pay about 32 percent of their total income for all types of taxes.

Table 8.8 shows amounts of various taxes to be paid by Robert Chong of Brooklyn, New York, who earns $39,000 annually. Approximately 32 percent ($12,454/$39,000) of his income goes to pay various taxes—and this is the average for all Americans. Robert can probably reduce his federal income tax liability by finding more tax deductions. For instance, if he bought a home, both real property taxes and mortgage loan interest expenses would be deductions. By carefully analyzing the subject of income taxes and assertively filling out income tax returns, you can have more money available every year to spend, save, and invest—activities that are the focus of the rest of this book.

Summary

1. Taxes are compulsory charges imposed by a government on citizens and property. The Internal Revenue Service issues various IRS regulations, which are its interpretations of the laws passed by Congress, and these have the force and effect of law.

2. Perhaps the most important concept in personal finance is the marginal tax rate—the tax rate on your last dollar of earnings. Your effective marginal tax rate is even higher.

3. Those who should file an income tax return include children with unearned income greater than $500, as opposed to earned income, or with gross incomes greater than the value of the standard deduction.

4. To help ensure getting the tax liability due it, the government requires payroll withholding for most of us and estimated taxes for others.

5. A number of steps are involved in reducing gross income down to final tax liability using five legal techniques: exclusions from total income, adjustments to income, deductions, exemptions, and credits.

6. The final tax liability varies when one calculates the income tax liability for different types of taxpayers.

7. Avoiding taxes is both desirable and respectable. There are a number of ways to legally avoid income taxes, and these involve applying knowledge of the tax code and regulations to personal income tax preparation.

8. Four choices are available in preparing a tax return: let the IRS do it, use a tax-preparation service, have it done by a lawyer and/or CPA, and fill out the return yourself. The last technique allows the taxpayer to become the expert.

9. People who are organized and prepared do not worry about audits by the IRS. In addition, having a deduction disallowed generally does not necessarily result in a penalty, so it is recommended that you be confident and take the deduction.

10. Besides the federal income tax, there exists a variety of other taxes, with Social Security being the largest for most people.

Modern Money Management

The Johnsons Calculate Their Income Taxes

Harry and Belinda are both working hard and earning good salaries. However, they feel that they are paying too much in federal income taxes. Calculate their income taxes this year, and then give them some tax-planning advice.

The Johnsons' total income included Harry's salary of $17,850, Belinda's salary of $24,800, $355 interest on savings, $80 interest on checking, $3000 interest income from the trust, $90 refund from Belinda's health insurance claim, $210 state income tax refund (they did not itemize last year), $390 federal income tax refund, and a $400 cash gift from Harry's aunt. Note that the interest income from the trust is taxed the same way as the interest income from their checking and savings accounts.

1. What is the Johnsons' reportable gross income?

2. Harry put $500 into an individual retirement account last year, so what is their adjusted gross income?

3. Assuming that they file a joint federal income tax return, what is the total value of their exemptions?

4. How much is the allowable standard deduction permissible for the Johnsons?

5. They have $3600 in itemized deductions; should they itemize or take the standard deduction?

6. What is the Johnsons' taxable income?

7. Since the Johnsons have no tax credits, what is their final tax liability? Using the Personal Finance Cookbook (PFC) program TAXLIAB, calculate the Johnsons' tax liability. Compare your results.

8. Since they had $8160 in federal income taxes withheld, what will be their refund?

9. What is their marginal tax rate?

10. Based on gross income, what is their average tax rate?

11. List four or five things the Johnsons can do to reduce their tax liability for next year. Even though they are renters, assume the Johnsons had a home with monthly payments of nearly $800, or $9600 for the year. The sum of $8400 might go for interest and real estate property taxes, both of which are tax deductible. This would give them $12,000 ($8400 + $3600) in itemized deductions. Calculate their taxable income and final tax liability, assuming the $12,000 of itemized deductions instead of taking the standard deduction.

12. What is your advice to the Johnsons about the tax wisdom of purchasing a home instead of renting?

Key Words and Concepts

office audit, 305
opportunity cost, 296
overwithholding, 276
passive activities, 301
payroll withholding, 276
postponing income, 298
progressive tax, 266
reasonableness tests, 305
regressive tax, 266
short-term capital gain (or loss), 282
standard deduction, 283
taxable income, 266
taxable-yield formula, 299
taxable yield (TY), 299
tax audit, 305
tax avoidance, 295
tax credits, 290
taxes, 265

tax evasion, 295
tax-exempt investment, 299
tax-exempt yield formula, 299
tax-exempt yield (TEY), 299
Tax Form 1040, 292
Tax Form 1040-A, 292
Tax Form 1040-ES, 276
Tax Form 1040-EZ, 291
Tax Form 1040-X, 274
tax-free exchanges, 282
tax liability, 275
tax losses, 301
tax-preparation services, 303
tax shelters, 301
tax swaps, 282
transfer payments, 274
unearned income, 274

Review Questions

1. Summarize the importance of IRS regulations.
2. Distinguish between a progressive and a regressive tax.
3. Give an illustration showing how one's effective marginal tax rate is higher than one's marginal tax rate.
4. Explain and illustrate how one's marginal tax rate differs from one's average tax rate.
5. Name two special instances in which it would be wise to file a tax return if not required by law.
6. Summarize why the IRS has three different tax rates, for singles, marrieds, and heads of households.
7. Briefly describe the process of payroll withholding.
8. What does it take to be exempt from payroll withholding taxes?
9. What are the disadvantages to taxpayers of overwithholding taxes through payroll deduction?
10. List five examples of taxable income that must be reported to the IRS. (Perhaps note those you had not thought of before.)
11. List five examples of exclusions to income. (Perhaps note those you had not thought of before.)
12. What is a capital gain, and how do long- and short-term capital gains differ?
13. Differentiate between a tax swap and a tax-free exchange.
14. What are adjustments to income? Give two examples.

15. Distinguish between claiming a certain number of exemptions on your tax return and a different number of exemptions on your W-4 form.

16. Explain whether the parent or the child gets the personal exemption when the child is 21 and earned $1900 last year.

17. Tell what the term *standard deduction* means and who should use it.

18. List five examples of tax-deductible items, excluding the miscellaneous category. (Perhaps note those you had not thought of before.)

19. List five examples of miscellaneous deductions. (Perhaps note those you had not thought of before.)

20. What determines whether you use the tax tables or the tax-rate schedules?

21. List the subtractions in getting from gross income to taxable income and then finding the tax liability.

22. Briefly describe the value of one type of tax credit (choose either child and dependent care or the earned income credit) to a taxpayer earning a taxable income of $17,000.

23. What steps do you take to actually calculate the balance you owe or the amount of your tax refund?

24. Differentiate between tax evasion and tax avoidance.

25. Illustrate the concept of opportunity cost with income taxes using an example not from the text.

26. Explain why a married couple might consider divorce as a way of saving taxes.

27. Briefly describe two ways to lower your tax liability where timing is crucial.

28. Choose one of the three methods of reducing your taxable income to lower taxes and illustrate how it works.

29. Tell why it is useful from an income tax perspective for taxpayers to buy a home with a mortgage loan.

30. Give some reasons why taxpayers should prepare their own income tax returns.

31. List three guidelines to consider if the IRS cites you for a tax audit.

32. Name other types of taxes that are typically paid by taxpayers.

Case Problems

1. James Burton of Sacramento, California, is interested in the relationship between marginal tax rates and average tax rates.
   a. Given the information below, use Table 8.2 to calculate the tax liabilities and marginal tax rates based on the taxable incomes and appropriate filing status. Put the information in columns G and H of the following table. *Note:* Phil files a joint return; Jane files as head of household.

b. Calculate the average tax rates based on gross income, adjusted gross income, and taxable income. Put the information in columns B, D, and F of the following table.

	Gross Income A	Average Rate B	Adjusted Gross Income C	Average Rate D	Taxable Income E	Average Rate F	Tax Liability G	Marginal Tax Rate H
James, single	$23,000		$22,000		$16,700			
Maria, single	29,000		28,000		22,700			
Phil, married	71,000		69,000		59,450			
Jane, married	46,000		41,000		31,450			

c. Briefly describe the relationships between marginal tax rates and average tax rates.

2. Juanita Linzey lives with her daughter in Portland, Oregon, where she is a union organizer, and she needs your advice about her income taxes.
   a. Which of the following types of income of Juanita's must be included as total income for the IRS: $17,000 in salary, $10,000 in life insurance proceeds of deceased aunt, $140 in interest on savings, $4000 in alimony from ex-husband, $1200 in child support, $500 cash Christmas gift from parents, $90 from a friend who rides to work in Juanita's vehicle, $60 in lottery winnings, $420 state income tax refund (since she itemized last year), $570 federal income tax refund, $170 worth of dental services traded for a quilt she gave the dentist, and $1600 tuition scholarship she received to go to college part time last year?
   b. What is the total of Juanita's reportable gross income?
   c. Juanita put $800 into an individual retirement account (IRA) last year, so what is her adjusted gross income for tax purposes?
   d. How many exemptions can Juanita claim, and how much is the total value allowed the Linzey household?
   e. How much is the allowable standard deduction for the Linzey household?
   f. Juanita has listed her itemized deductions, which total $4000. Explain why she should itemize or take the standard deduction.
   g. What is Juanita's taxable income?
   h. What is her tax liability?
   i. Assuming she gets a credit of $140 for child care, what is Juanita's final tax liability?
   j. Using the Personal Finance Cookbook (PFC) TAXLIAB program, input the data for Juanita's taxes and compare the results with your calculations.
   k. If Juanita's employer withheld $2000 for income taxes, does she owe money to the government or does she get a refund? How much?

3. Bruce Williams, radio manager in Franklin Township, New Jersey, is in the 28 percent federal marginal tax bracket and pays an additional 8 percent to the state of New Jersey. Bruce currently has over $20,000

invested in various corporate bonds earning differing amounts of taxable interest: $10,000 in ABC earning 11.0 percent, $5,000 in DEF earning 10.2 percent, $3,000 in GHI earning 9.8 percent, and $2,000 in JKL earning 9.1 percent. His stockbroker is suggesting that Bruce consider investing these same sums into tax-exempt municipal bonds, which currently pay a tax-free yield of 6.3 percent. What is your advice? (*Hint:* Add the tax brackets together.) Use the Personal Finance Cookbook (PFC) software worksheet titled TAXEQUIV to calculate your answers or use the tax-equivalent formulas on page 299.

Suggested Readings

"But Those Coming Tax Hikes May Not Be So Bad After All," *Money,* August 1990, pp. 139–140. Effect of likely increases in personal income taxes.

"Checklist: What You Need to Collect." *Money,* January 1989, pp. 75–78. How to organize your papers for income tax preparation.

"18 Ways to Get on Top of the Feds." *Money,* January 1990, pp. 93–100. Tax-cutting moves.

"50 Ways to Save Time and Money on Your Taxes." *Changing Times,* February 1989, pp. 26–33. Brief descriptions of definite ways to reduce your income taxes.

"Finding Paydirt in the Tax Forms." *Changing Times,* February 1990, pp. 44–52. Line-by-line tips on how to save money on income taxes.

"Household Help: Avoiding the Tax Squeeze." *Changing Times,* August 1989, pp. 57–62. To enjoy the child care credit on your income tax return you must follow IRS regulations to the letter.

"How to Avoid a Tax Audit." *Working Woman,* March 1989, pp. 86–89. Advice on how to avoid this most unpleasant tax experience.

"How to Ease Your Total Tax Burden." *Money,* January 1990, pp. 74–77. State and local taxes are the fastest growing segment of your total tax bill.

"How to Pay $0 Taxes." *Money,* April 1989, pp. 163–170. How effective financial planning can actually reduce taxes to zero.

"How to Win When the IRS Demands More Money from You." *Money,* April 1990, pp. 84–96. How people can fight the IRS when its inefficiencies cause it to inadvertently ask millions of taxpayers to pay up when they really do not have to.

"How to Work with Your Tax Preparer." *Money,* January 1989, pp. 67–72. How to make sure your tax preparer does the best possible job with your return.

"How You Can Still Cut Your Taxes." *Money,* September 1989, pp. 84–103. Reducing all kinds of taxes.

"Keys to the Forms." *Money,* January 1989, pp. 90–99. Which form to use for which type of income tax deduction.

"Lining Up a First-Rate Preparer." *Money,* January 1989, pp. 64–65. Details on how to choose the best tax preparer.

"Personal Business." *Business Week,* March 19, 1990, pp. 134–142. This installment of the regular personal business section provides a series of articles on tax planning, including choosing tax preparation computer software.

"Presumed Guilt by the IRS." *Money,* October 1990, pp. 80–92. Horror stories of how the IRS continues to use abusive and draconian measures against so-called delinquent taxpayers.

"Ready, Set . . . Go!" *Money,* January 1989, pp. 54–58. Strategies for effective tax management.

"Taxes: Last-Minute Questions . . . Just-in-Time Answers." *Changing Times,* April 1990, pp. 58–61. Areas in which many taxpayers need knowledge to avoid mistakes and lower taxes.

"Tax-Proofing Your Home Office." *Changing Times,* June 1989, pp. 75–79. How to properly deduct the expenses of a home office.

"10 Errors to Avoid This Year." *Money,* January 1989, pp. 83–90. Suggestions on what not to do wrong in preparing your income tax return.

"The Pros Flub Our Third Annual Tax-Return Test." *Money,* March 1990, pp. 90–98. A national sample of income tax preparation specialists score poorly on accurately completing *Money*'s sample income tax return.

"The Taxes You Can No Longer Ignore." *Money,* January 1990, pp. 80–91. State-by-state analysis of tax burdens.

"Timely Answers to Taxing Questions." *Changing Times,* April 1989, pp. 48–51. Solutions to perplexing tax questions.

"Year-End Tax Savers." *Changing Times,* December 1989, pp. 94–98. Ideas to reduce your income taxes.

"Your Guide to the 1989 Tax Guides." *Money,* January 1989, pp. 101–105. Overview of the books and software programs on taxes.

PART THREE

Managing Expenditures

9

Automobiles and Other Major Expenditures

OBJECTIVES

After reading this chapter, you should be able to

1. Understand several ways to save money when purchasing goods and services.
2. Explain the concept of life-cycle planning for making major expenditures.
3. Discuss the seven steps in the planned buying process.
4. Identify the major consumer rights and responsibilities, and recent major pieces of consumer-protection legislation.

· · · · · · · · ·

The last eight chapters examined important topics in the areas of financial planning and money management. Now that you understand the key elements of budgeting and cash management, how to manage your credit card use, planned borrowing, and income taxes, we can get down to the enjoyable process of spending.

This chapter focuses first on ways to save money—simple steps that can save lots of money. We realize that many people would like to start out life with all the possessions it took their parents a lifetime to acquire. The section here on life-cycle planning will give you perspective on when to make major expenditures. The steps in the buying process are then examined and illustrated using a sample automobile purchase: determining needs and wants, fitting the budget, preshopping research, comparison shopping, negotiating, making the decision, and complimenting or complaining.

A Half-Dozen Simple Rules Can Help You Save Money

Objective
To be able to understand several ways to save money when purchasing goods and services.

Examples of ways that people waste money could fill the pages of dozens of books. Fortunately, a few simple rules can yield savings of 10 to 20 percent during a year, equivalent to a 10 to 20 percent raise. Six of these are discussed below.

Don't Buy on Impulse

Simple restraint will help you avoid impulse buying. Say, for example, you have done some careful comparison shopping and have gone to a discount store to pay $150 for a microwave oven. While at the store, you also pick up some microwave cookware that you really don't need. The extra $25 spent while in a "buying mood" ruined some of the benefits of the comparison shopping.

Avoid Buying on Credit

Once in a while you may feel the need to go out and buy on credit items that you really can't afford. As discussed in Chapters 6 and 7, overuse of credit can strangle you financially by taking away your financial flexibility. When using credit, you may pay 15, 20, or even 30 percent more for your purchases, because you pay that much more in interest.

Buy at the Right Time

If you pay attention to sales and look for the right time to buy, you will save money. As you probably know, you can save 30 to 60 percent on telephone charges just by making calls in the evenings and on weekends. Many items, such as sporting goods and clothing, are marked down near certain holidays and at the end of the season. Also, you can save $5 or $10 weekly on food simply by stocking up on advertised specials. Make sure that what you buy on sale is something you will really use, however.

Don't Pay Extra for a "Name"

Some people have an "Excedrin headache" for 30 cents a dosage or an "Anacin headache" for 25 cents a dosage, and others have a plain aspirin headache for 2 cents a dosage. Scientific research (not the advertiser's research) consistently shows that the effectiveness of all over-the-counter pain relievers is about the same. This is why the ads say "none better" rather than "we're the best." Gasoline, vitamins, laundry and other soaps, and soft drinks are all products with minor real quality differences.

Store brands are often made by brand-name manufacturers.

Buying generic products is a good way to save money. Many physicians will write prescriptions for generic-equivalent drugs, which cost you 20 to 60 percent less than prescriptions for brand-name drugs. Also note that many less expensive, store-brand appliances (such as those sold at Sears and J. C. Penney) are actually made by the brand-name manufacturers, such as RCA, Panasonic, Eureka, General Electric, and others.

Recognize That Convenience Costs Money

A bottle of ketchup or jar of peanut butter bought at a supermarket probably costs 50 cents less than at a nearby convenience store, whereas bread and milk may be priced about the same. Stopping daily at a convenience store to buy a few items rather than making a planned, weekly visit to a grocery store can raise your food bill up to 30 percent or more through higher prices and the temptation of impulse purchases. Also, although it may be convenient to shop for furniture and appliances in your local community, you may find better prices on the same items in larger, competitive shopping areas.

Question the Need to Go First Class

Many people feel they should always go first class. When taking vacations, they may stay at brand-name motels (Radisson, Hyatt, Sheraton) rather than save 40 to 50 percent at budget inns such as Motel 6 or Days Inn that have virtually the same accommodations. When going first class, people usually don't think about the extra that they are paying. While it is important to make informed financial decisions consistent with your personal values, and you can go first class if you truly want to, you should realize how much money is involved.

TABLE 9.1
Some Major-Expenditure Items Desired by Adults

Early years of singlehood

Television
Living and bedroom furniture
Stereo system
Used automobile
Home computer

Middle years of singlehood or early years of couplehood

Major appliances
New automobile
Better stereo system
Extra television set
Children's furniture
Washer and dryer

Later years of singlehood or middle years of couplehood

Better living room furniture
Home video/entertainment center
Luxury automobile
Antiques
Piano
Boat or motor home

Using Life-Cycle Planning for Major Expenditures

Objective
To be able to explain the concept of life-cycle planning for making major expenditures.

"You can't have everything," as the old saying goes, but many Americans certainly try. This is one of the reasons why the average household headed by someone under age 25 spends 17 percent more than its disposable income. They use credit! What is important to realize is that although you cannot have everything *right now,* planning will help you achieve your financial goals. Intelligently setting goals and recognizing your budget limitations will enable you to reach goals for major expenditures as soon as possible.

Table 9.1 lists some of the items many people want to own during their adult years categorized by life-cycle stage. This categorization has three major benefits. First, it helps you to plan expenditures by setting up an appropriate timetable. This makes it easier to delay some purchases, knowing that the delay is not permanent. Second, it is a first step in setting up a budget category for saving in preparation for the purchase. Third, it makes clear that many major purchases are really replacements for obsolete items. The replacement process is a good opportunity to upgrade the quality of a basic model purchased when funds were more limited.

FIGURE 9.1

Wants and Needs
Worksheet (for Betti
Sidwell)

Needs	Automobile Feature	Wants	Don't Care
✓	Power steering		
	Tinted windows	✓	
	Automatic windows	✓	
✓	Automatic transmission		
	Leather seats		✓
✓	AM-FM Radio		
	Cassette player	✓	
	Super sound system		✓
	Telescope and tilt steering wheel		✓
	Automatic light dimmer		✓
	Air conditioning	✓	
✓	Whitewall tires		
	Four-wheel drive		✓

Applying the Buying Process to Automobiles

Objective
To be able to discuss the
seven steps in the
planned buying process.

There are seven steps in the planned buying process: (1) distinguishing between needs and wants, (2) fitting the budget, (3) preshopping research, (4) comparison shopping, (5) negotiating, (6) making the decision, and (7) complimenting or complaining appropriately.

Distinguish Between Your Needs and Wants

In Chapter 1 we distinguished between needs and wants. A *need* is something that is thought to be a necessity; a *want* is unnecessary but desired. For example, most people need transportation to and from work, but they do not need a *new* automobile for this purpose.

The task of separating needs from wants becomes harder when there are many ways of satisfying a need. For example, assume that Betti Sidwell of Lynchburg, Virginia, finds that neither her 12-year-old compact car, public transportation, nor carpooling can reliably get her to her new job. She needs a new automobile. She likes Lincolns, Cadillacs, Nissans, Plymouths, and Fords. She may decide to meet her needs by purchasing an inexpensive Plymouth or Nissan. Or she may meet her needs *and* her wants by buying a Cadillac or a Lincoln. To make this decision, Betti used the worksheet in Figure 9.1. She found, to her surprise, that there were several features she did not want and that her wants were not as numerous as she had thought.

Preshopping Research

Preshopping research arms buyers with information.

Preshopping research is gathering information about products or services before you actually begin shopping for them. Manufacturers, sellers, and service providers are important sources of information on products and services during your preshopping research. Automobile manufacturers publish many brochures on their products and sponsor automobile shows that are used both to promote and to provide information on their cars. Two other sources of information are friends and consumer magazines. If someone you know drives an automobile you are thinking of buying, ask the person about his or her experience with the vehicle. You also could read about the car in a consumer magazine, such as *Consumer Reports,* which tests and reports on 10 to 20 products monthly. In addition, *Consumer Reports Buying Guide Issue,* published in December of each year, lists facts and figures on numerous products. Monthly issues of *Consumer Reports* generally provide a two- to five-page narrative analyzing the products and summarizing the information in chart form. Figure 9.2 is an example of such a chart. The April issue of *Consumer Reports* each year is devoted entirely to the buying of new and used cars.

You can find *Consumer Reports* in your library. When you are shopping for any product, it may help to review publications on a more specific topic, such as *Photography, Car and Driver,* and *Stereo Review,* or of general consumer interest, such as *Changing Times.* Realize, however, that trade magazines that accept advertising for the products they report on are not likely to be as unbiased as *Consumer Reports,* which accepts no advertising.

Preshopping research for new cars should focus on three special pieces of information: price, trade-in value, and financing. To obtain price information, you will need to visit a dealership. This is not a buying trip, and you should make this perfectly clear to the salesperson. You will want to gather information about the car's **sticker price,** which is the manufacturer's suggested retail price (MSRP) for a new car and its options as listed on the window sticker. This information will help you estimate the dealer's cost for the car and, therefore, the room you might have for negotiation. In addition, there are several sources of dealer cost information, such as Nationwide Auto Brokers and Consumers Union, publishers of *Consumer Reports* magazine. The $10 or so these services charge for a price report is a very wise investment. You also should know the true value of any car you will be trading in. Take the car to a couple of used car lots and ask them how much they would give for the car in cash. The highest offer is a good estimate of the car's value in trade. You also can determine the car's value by talking to someone at your bank or credit union who has access to the National Automobile Dealers Association (NADA) "red book" of used car prices. Generally, however, you can do better selling a car on your own rather than trading it in.

The sticker price on a new car is virtually meaningless.

Since over 70 percent of new cars are purchased on credit, it is important to gather information on the current APRs on car loans from various sources. An important source of loans for new cars is sales financing arranged through the car's manufacturer. In addition, you should get quotes from local banks and credit unions.

FIGURE 9.2

Consumer Reports Ratings on Power Hedge Trimmers

Source: Copyright 1990 by Consumers Union of United States, Inc., Mount Vernon, N.Y. 10553. Reprinted by permission from *Consumer Reports,* June 1990.

RATINGS

Better ◀————————————▶ Worse

Power hedge trimmers

Listed by types in order of estimated quality, based primarily on safety, performance, and convenience. Bracketed models were judged about equal in quality and are listed alphabetically.

1 Price. Manufacturer's list and what CU paid last year in NYC metropolitan area. + indicates shipping was extra.

2 Blade length. Measured to the nearest ¼-inch. This determines how wide a swath you can trim.

3 Cutting speed. How quickly a trimmer sliced through thick growth. The gasoline models needed just a single pass where the slowest electrics needed several.

4 Cleanness of cut. Our judgment of how cleanly a trimmer cut branches up to about ¼-inch thick. The highest-scoring models trimmed thick branches evenly while the poorest performers left a rough surface. All cut new growth cleanly.

5 Ease of handling. An overall judgment of comfort and convenience, including maneuverability, weight, and balance.

Brand and model	Price, list/paid **1**	Blade length **2**	Speed **3**	Cut **4**	Handling **5**	Advantages	Disadvantages	Comments
Electric models								
Aircap 519	$48/50	18 ¾ in.	◑	○	◑	C,G	—	—
Black & Decker HT-120	155/110	20	○	◑	○	B,D	g,k	D
Sears 79663 [1]	43/40+	18	○	◑	◑	—	a,b	—
Sears 79669	70/88	20	○	◑	○	B,D	g,k	D
Snap Cut 8718	87/69	16 ½	○	◑	◑	—	a,b	—
Sears 79662 [1]	35+/40+	16	◑	○	◑	—	a,b	—
Black & Decker 8134	78/55	18	◑	○	◑	—	b,g	L
Black & Decker 8124	68/40	16	◑	◔	◑	—	g	L
Paramount HT-1700	[2]/65	17	●	○	◑	C	b,j	A,C,L
■ The following model was downrated for having an excessive gap between its blade teeth and for lacking safety extensions.								
AEG HES 50	193/184	19	●	●	●	B,E,G,H,K	f	B,D,F,I,M
Not Acceptable								
■ The following model was Not Acceptable because it lacks a safety shield, in addition to having an excessive gap and lacking safety extensions.								
Little Wonder 1600DE	175/166	16 ½	○	◑	◑	E,G,H	a	D,J
Gasoline models								
Homelite HT-17 A Best Buy	160/150	17	◑	●	●	A,B,D,I,L	d,e	E
Sears 79667	200+/177+	18	●	●	○	I,J,L	—	—
■ The following models were downrated for having an excessive gap between their blade teeth and for lacking safety extensions.								
Homelite HT-18	270/260	17	●	●	○	I	—	—
Tanaka THT-200	270/280	18	●	●	○	F,I,J,K	a	H
Echo HC-1500	260/290	18	●	●	◑	F,J	a,b,h	K,O
John Deere 172	299/259	18	●	●	◑	F,J	a,b,h	K
Shindaiwa HT 20-20	330/300	20[3]	●	●	●	C,I,J	b,c,i,l	B
Little Wonder 1222E	269/270	16	●	●	●	D	c,h,i,l	B,G,N

[1] Discontinued; very limited availability.   [2] Not available from manufacturer.   [3] Safety shield near handle reduces swath of blade by 7 in.

Specifications and Features

All electric models: • Have double-edged blades that can trim left or right. • Weigh about 5-8 lb.
Except as noted, all electric models: • Have wraparound front handle. • Have safety shield between front handle and blade. • Are double-insulated. • Have short power cord. • Have stationary lower blade with safety extensions. • Have narrow gap between blade teeth (passed test with ¾-in. dia. probe). • Have power switch that can be locked On. • Should be used on growth no thicker than about ⅜ in., according to mfr. • Have 1-yr. warranty on parts and labor.
All gasoline models have: • 2-stroke engine that requires mixture of gasoline and oil. • Emergency Off switch within easy reach. • Safety shield between handle and blade.
Except as noted, all gasoline models: • Weigh 10-12 lb. • Have double-edged reciprocating blades that can trim left or right. • Have wraparound front handle. • Have wide gap between blade teeth (failed test with ¾-in. dia. probe). • Lack safety extensions. • Should be used on growth no thicker than about ⅜ in., according to mfr. • Have 2-yr. warranty on parts and labor.

Key to Advantages

A–Lightest weight of gasoline models, 8½ lb.
B–Quieter than most of its type.
C–Stopped more quickly than most when power switch was released.
D–Vibrated less than most of its type.
E–Vibration was virtually imperceptible.
F–Has throttle lockout, a safety feature.
G–Power switch does not have lock-on device.
H–Switches in both handles must be kept depressed to operate trimmer, a safety feature.
I–Throttle trigger can be locked in slightly open position for convenient starting.
J–Comes with tools for maintenance.
K–Comes with sheath for blade to protect hands when trimmer is not being used.
L–Unlike other gasoline models, has narrow gap between blade teeth, a safety advantage. **Homelite** also has safety extensions.

Key to Disadvantages

a–Noisier than most of its type.
b–Vibrated more than most of its type.
c–Blades have teeth on left side only.
d–Took longer than most to stop when power switch was released.
e–Has small, 5⅛-oz. fuel tank.
f–Lacks double insulation (see story).
g–For maintenance, trimmer must be returned to service center every few seasons.
h–Lacks grease fitting for lubricating gear case.
i–Foot can't steady trimmer during starting.
j–Inconvenient power switch must be locked on for comfortable use, a safety disadvantage.
k–Front-heavy design; trimmer tiring to use.
l–Handle design was judged unwieldy.

Key to Comments

A–Has 2 straight handles about 5 in. apart.
B–Front handle does not wrap around.
C–Original 17-in. blade can be replaced by 14-, 19-, or 22-in. blades. (The longer blades would probably reduce performance.)
D–Unlike most tested electric models, has 2 reciprocating blades.
E–Unlike other tested gasoline models, has a single reciprocating blade and a fixed blade.
F–Has 10-ft. power cord.
G–Maximum cut specified is 1 in.
H–Maximum cut specified is ¾-in.
I–Maximum cut specified is ⅝-in.
J–Maximum cut specified is ½-in.
K–Maximum cut specified is ¼-in.
L–Has no cord; plug is at rear of housing.
M–Has 6-mo. warranty.
N–Has 1-yr. warranty.
O–Electronic ignition module has lifetime warranty for parts, 5-yr. warranty for labor.

Fitting the Budget

How will the purchase fit into your budget?

Everybody asks themselves "Can I afford it?" when making a buying decision. When the purchase is a major one, this question is crucial. An unaffordable cash purchase can wreck a budget for one or more months, and an ill-advised credit purchase can have negative effects for years. One way to view the cost of a major purchase is to consider the cost per use of the product to be purchased. For example, Frank Lenz of Chicago is considering buying a camera. He has been looking at several autofocus SLR models in the $350 price range. He also knows that he could buy a basic 110 disk film camera at a discount store for $25. Frank figures that he uses a camera about 15 times per year and that most models will last about 10 years, giving him 150 uses. Dividing this figure into the cost of an SLR model yields a cost per use of $2.33 ($350 divided by 150) excluding the cost of film and developing. The 110 model would have a cost per use of 17 cents ($25 divided by 150).

Let's look at how Betti Sidwell might fit a new car into her budget. She estimates that the sticker price of the type of car she wants will be about $12,000. This includes the four items she checked as needs because she would not consider buying a car without them. The other options she wants will likely have sticker prices as follows:

Tinted windows	$ 300
Automatic windows	250
Cassette player	300
Air conditioning	750
	$1600

Fitting the budget might provide ways to afford wants as well as needs.

To buy a car that meets her needs and her four wants might cost Betti $14,300 ($12,000 + $1600 + $700 for sales tax and title registration). She can use $2300 in savings as a down payment and borrow the remaining $12,000. Yet the prices given above for the car and its options are Betti's estimates from her preshopping research. The actual price she will pay for the car will depend on how well she can negotiate the price down from the sticker price. She knows from her research that the dealer cost of new cars averages about 12 percent lower than the sticker price. By multiplying the sticker price by 12 percent, she can get a rough estimate of the room she has for bargaining. For example, by driving a hard bargain, Betti might get the price of the car with the wanted options and taxes reduced 10 percent to $12,870 [$14,300 − ($14,300 × 0.10)]. Or she could even use the 12 percent figure.

The monthly payment that Betti must fit into her budget will depend on five factors: the price she actually pays for the car, the down payment she can make, the time period for payback of the loan, the amount she gets in trade for her old car, and the interest rate on the loan. We will choose the down payment of $2300 and assume a 48-month time period because that is currently common. Betti figures that she can get no more than $500 for her old car. But what about the actual price and interest rate?

We will assume that Betti has done a good job of estimating the price she might pay for the car. If she can reduce the sticker price by 10 percent,

TABLE 9.2
Fitting an Automobile Payment into a Monthly Budget

	Budget Last Month	Possible Cutbacks	Budget with Automobile
Food	$180	$ − 20	$160
Clothing	100	− 25	75
Transportation	80	− 80	-0-
Auto Insurance	30		30
Gasoline	25		25
Housing	400		475
Utilities	65		65
Telephone	35		35
Entertainment	100	− 50	50
Gifts	50	− 25	25
Church & Charity	20		20
Beautician	25		25
Savings	60	− 10	50
Miscellaneous	60		60
Total	$1230	$ − 210	$1020
Car payment			255
Total with car payment			$1275

she will need to borrow $10,070 ($12,870 − $2300 − $500). However, she should realize that this is only an estimate that can vary by as much as $1000 depending on her negotiating skills. If the $10,070 is the loan amount, Betti would then need to use the likely APR figure from her preshopping research to determine a monthly payment. If she obtains a 10 percent annual percentage rate loan, she estimates her monthly payment would be $255.38 (10.07 × 25.36 from Table 7.3 on p. 240).

Table 9.2 shows Betti's monthly budget. Her monthly take-home pay of $1230 is totally committed. Let's see what she has to do to be able to pay for an automobile. To buy the automobile with options, she will need $255 per month and will have to change her budget drastically. To get to her former job, she has used public transportation at a cost of $80 per month; those dollars can go toward a car payment. To get the rest of the money, she could cut savings ($10 per month), cut entertainment and gifts in half ($50 and $25), cut back on food ($20), and cut back on clothing ($25). In all, these efforts would raise only $210 ($80 + $10 + $50 + $25 + $20 + $25), still $45 short of the amount she needs for the car. In addition, the gasoline, parking, and insurance costs on her new car would make the figure higher. Betti's alternatives are to make more cutbacks in her budget, to work overtime or get a part-time job, or to buy a cheaper or used car. Betti could reduce her payments to $214 per month by taking out a 60-month loan (10.07 × $21.25 from Table 7.3). However, she should be wary about continuing to make monthly car payments on a 5-year-old vehicle with 60,000 to 75,000 miles on it.

Comparison Shopping

Comparison shopping is designed to help you identify your best buy.

Comparison shopping is the process of comparing products or services to find what you think is the best buy. A **best buy** is a product or service that, in your opinion, represents acceptable quality at a fair or low price for that level of quality. Note that buying the product with a low price does not necessarily assure you of a best buy. In comparison shopping, you should visit different stores to compare dealer reputation and service, and warranty and credit terms.

Comparison shopping for cars does take time and effort, but when you are spending thousands of dollars, the payoff can be considerable. During the first three steps in the buying process you should narrow your choices to specific makes and models and the options that you desire. Then visit the various dealerships again. (You should have visited them earlier during your preshopping research.) This time you will be much closer to the decision to buy and will be ready to discuss details, but you will still not buy. Here you tell the salesperson exactly what you are interested in and ask about price, availability, warranties, financing currently available, and any manufacturer's incentives, such as **rebates** (refunds from the manufacturer) that apply. Your goal is to narrow the choice even further so that you can begin negotiating for the very best deal, which is the next step in the buying process. To do so, you begin by considering warranties, service contracts, and financing options.

Warranties   Warranties are an important consideration in comparison shopping. Virtually all products have **warranties** (assurances by sellers that goods are as promised) because they have implied warranties. An **implied warranty** provides that products sold are warranted to be suitable for sale and will work effectively whether there is a written warranty or not. The first implied warranty in that definition is a *warranty of merchantability*. The second is a *warranty of fitness for a particular purpose*. Implied warranties are required by state law; the only time they are not in effect is if the seller states in writing that the product is sold "as is" or specifically states that there is no implied warranty. This is often the case with used cars. If you buy a used car "as is," you have little legal recourse should the car fail to perform, even if the salesperson made verbal promises to take care of any problems.

Products purchased "as is" carry no warranties.

Written and oral warranties accompany many products and are offered by manufacturers on a voluntary basis to induce customers to buy. These are called **express warranties.** Companies that offer written express warranties must do so under the provisions of the federal Magnuson-Moss Warranty Act if the product costs more than $15. This 1975 law provides that if a written warranty is offered, it must be classified as either a full warranty or a limited warranty. A **full warranty** is a warranty that includes the stringent requirements that (1) a product will be fixed at no cost to the buyer within a reasonable time after the owner has complained, (2) the owner will not have to undertake an unreasonable task to return the product for repair (such as mail back a freezer), and (3) a defective product that cannot be fixed after a reasonable number of attempts will be replaced with a new one or the money will be returned. A **limited warranty** is a warranty that offers less than a full warranty. For example, a limited warranty may offer only free parts, not labor. Note that one part of a product could be covered by a full warranty, perhaps the engine on a lawn mower, and the rest of the unit by a limited warranty. It pays to read warranties carefully. Note also that both full and limited warranties are valid only for a specified period.

New cars generally come with a warranty on most major components for 12,000 miles or 1 year, whichever passes first. This warranty often will also cover the drive train (engine, transmission, drive shaft, and so forth) for up to 70,000 miles or 7 years.

Service contracts are a form of insurance and add to the cost of a product.

Service Contracts A **service contract** is an agreement between the contract seller (a dealer, manufacturer, or independent company) and the buyer of a product to provide free or nearly free repair services to covered components of the product for some specified time period. A service contract is generally purchased apart from the purchase of the product (such as an automobile, appliance, or electronics product). The cost is either paid in a lump sum or may require monthly payments by the purchaser. Service contracts are very similar to insurance. For example, a 25-inch television selling for $600 could have a service contract that promises to fix anything free for the first 2 years of ownership after the warranty expires. This contract might cost $60, or $5 per month for 1 year, even if no servicing is done. You may want to buy a service contract for peace of mind in case an expensive product breaks down, but it is unwise economically. Find out if you can take the product back for repair without a service contract and simply pay for the servicing.

Service contracts have become increasingly prevalent in the new and used car market. All the major automobile manufacturers and many dealers offer service-contract plans. Ford offers more than 25 variations for its new cars. In addition, there are a number of independent companies not traditionally associated with the automobile market that offer service contracts for new cars. Names such as "extended warranty" and "buyer protection plan" are sometimes used rather than service contract. All these plans tend to extend the coverage provided under the new car's warranty, perhaps by extending the mileage and/or covering more components. The cost can be $700 or more, and if the manufacturer or dealer offers the plan, it may be included with the purchase price of the vehicle and financed with the loan for the car. Of that $700, $500 may be dealer profit. A seller can afford to be generous on a car deal if he or she knows that he or she will make the money back on the service contract. Often there is a deductible of about $100 that must be paid each time the car is serviced. Preventive maintenance to covered components is not usually included. Used car service contracts can cost $200 to $600 per year and usually provide protection for no more than 2 years.

Explore All Financing Options Most people need to consider financing options when comparison shopping for a car. It may be possible to take advantage of a special low interest rate when you use seller financing. To do so, however, you may have a higher monthly payment because of

What If You Must Choose Between a Low APR and a Rebate on a New Car?

It is not uncommon to see ads for new cars offering low APRs for dealer-arranged loans. For those wishing to arrange their own financing or pay cash, a cash rebate of from $500 to $3000, or more, off the price of the car is offered. If you intend to pay cash, obviously the rebate is the better deal. But how about when you arrange your own financing? You can't simply compare the dealer APR to the APR through your bank or credit union because this leaves out an important cost of the dealer financing—the rebate. You can add this opportunity cost to the finance charge of the dealer financing to adjust the dealer APR to make it roughly comparable to the APR you have arranged on your own. Equation (7.3) can be used to illustrate such a comparison.

Suppose you have been offered 4.9 percent financing for 3 years with a $906 finance charge, or you can receive a $1500 rebate on a car that cost $14,000. Assuming you can make a $2000 down payment and that you can get a 10.5 percent loan on your own, apply Equation (7.3).

$$\text{APR} = \frac{2 \times 12 \times (\$906 + \$1500)}{\$12,000 \times (36 + 1)}$$
$$= 13 \text{ percent} \qquad (7.3)$$

Viewed in this way, the financing that you arrange on your own is more attractive. In fact, any loan you arrange that carries an APR lower than 13 percent compares favorably with the dealer-arranged financing in this case.

restrictions on the time period of the loan. Most low-interest specials run concurrently with some type of rebate plan for people who pay cash or arrange their own financing. Thus you might be able to get a standard-interest-rate loan for a longer period through your bank or credit union and use the rebate as compensation for the extra finance charges.

Leasing is a form of renting rather than buying.

Leasing is another "financing option" that is now routinely available. With a lease you are, in effect, renting the car with the title remaining with the lease grantor. Usually there is an initial outlay for the first month's lease payment and a security deposit. Your monthly payments are based on the price of the car (always negotiate a price before discussing a lease) minus its **residual value,** which is its projected value at the end of the lease time period. This difference represents the depreciation of the car. It pays to shop for and negotiate the residual value, since the difference is divided by the number of months in the contract in order to establish the base for the monthly lease payment. Monthly lease payments are lower than monthly loan payments for equivalent time periods because with a lease you are paying *only* for the reduction in the car's value—not its entire cost. Sometimes the cost of automobile insurance and a service contract are also included in the monthly lease payment.

Many bank lenders have had their demand for automobile loans slacken because of the popularity of automobile leasing. In response, they have developed balloon automobile loans. With a **balloon automobile loan,** the last monthly payment is equal to the projected residual value of the vehicle

What If You Want to Lease a Car?

Leasing a new car is becoming increasingly attractive with the rising prices of today's new cars. However, is leasing a better deal? The answer cannot be known until some basics of leasing are understood.

You can obtain an open-end lease or a closed-end lease. An **open-end lease** is a leasing arrangement in which you must pay any difference between the projected residual value of the car and its actual market value at the end of the lease period. In recent years, cars have depreciated faster than expected, meaning that many holders of open-end leases have had to come up with extra money when the lease expires. The Consumer Leasing Act of 1977 limits this end-of-lease payment to a maximum dollar amount equivalent to three times the monthly payment. A **closed-end lease** (also called a *walkaway lease*) is a leasing arrangement in which there is no charge if the end-of-lease market value of the vehicle is lower than the originally projected residual value. Closed-end leases may carry some end-of-lease charges if the car has had above normal wear or mileage, however. For example, a 4-year closed-end lease might require a 10 cents per mile charge for mileage in excess of 55,000 miles. If you actually drove the car 60,000 miles during the 4 years, you would be charged an extra $500 (.10 × 5000). With either open- or closed-end leases you may purchase the car for its actual market value at the end of the lease-period.

Other charges are possible with a lease. A *capital cost reduction* is equivalent to a down payment and is not refundable like the security deposit. A *disposition fee* is a charge assessed when you turn in the car at the end of the lease in order to pay for getting it ready for resale. A *termination fee* may be charged if you desire to get out of the lease early. This charge is justified on the grounds that the car depreciates most rapidly in the early years, yet the early monthly payments are the same as those later in the lease.

In the early years your lease may be financially "upside-down," which means that you owe more on the car than it is worth. (This is also likely to happen when you buy a car on credit.) Be wary of a lease with a termination fee, even if you plan to keep the lease until the end, because termination also occurs when a leased car is totally wrecked or stolen.

So how can you compare the cost of a lease with that of a loan? Remember that the real cost of credit is the finance charge. It is the extra that you pay because you borrowed. Leases also have costs, but they are hidden in the contract and some are unknown until the end of the lease period. The following calculation provides an example of one way to determine the cost of a lease arrangement. The dollar cost can be compared with the finance charge on a loan for the same time period.

36 monthly payments of $275	$ 9,900
Plus capital cost reduction (if any)	300
Disposition charge (if any)	300
Excess mileage/wear & tear (if any)	0
Projected residual value of the car at the end of the lease	4,500
Amount you are responsible for under the lease	15,000
Less the value of the car at the beginning of the lease period	12,600
Difference to be compared with a finance charge	$ 2,400

Notice that to make the comparison you must know the underlying price of the car. Often you are not told this in a lease arrangement, so you must negotiate a price for the car before mentioning the lease option. You also should shop for a lease through various car dealers and through independent leasing companies because the costs vary considerably.

at the end of the loan period. For example, you could have 47 monthly payments of $245 and a forty-eighth payment of $2350. This has the effect of lowering the other monthly payments to make them more competitive with lease payments. When the final balloon payment is due, you generally have three options: (1) pay the balloon payment and keep the car, (2) return the car to the lender, or (3) sell the car and pay the balloon payment with the proceeds.

Negotiating

The next step in the buying process is **negotiating**, which is the process of discussing the actual terms of an agreement with a seller. We skip this step in most of the purchases we make because there is little room for individualizing the sale. For many big-ticket items, however, especially appliances, furniture, automobiles, and real estate, it is expected that there will be offers and counteroffers before arriving at the exact price.

Negotiating is especially difficult in automobile buying because there are so many variables. There is the price of the car, the trade-in value, the possibility of a rebate, the interest rate, and possibly a service contract. The dealer can appear to be cooperative in one aspect and make up the difference elsewhere. Many times the car comes with a number of dealer-installed options such as special striping, undercoating, and fabric finish protection. Negotiate prices on these items as well, knowing that dealer profit on them can exceed 50 percent.

The key to success in negotiating a car purchase is to obtain a price for the car itself before discussing *any* other aspects of the deal. To do this, do not discuss anything about a loan or a trade-in until you have pinned the salesperson (and ideally the manager) down to a price. That price then can be taken to other dealers for comparisons and possibly to play one dealer off against the other. It also serves as a basis for negotiating the other aspects of the deal.

Dealers will like to talk in terms of a monthly payment instead of a total price because so much else is hidden. Consider, for example, the case of Gary Joseph of Canyon Country, California. Gary had narrowed his choice of cars down to one model and two dealerships. To the first dealer, Gary presented his list of desired options and was shown a suitable car on the lot. He had arranged his own financing and was interested only in price and whether the dealer could offer cheaper financing than Gary had arranged at his credit union. When Gary asked about price, the salesperson asked him what monthly payment he could afford. Gary responded that what he could afford was unimportant and that he wanted to know the price. When the salesperson responded that it was policy to get the affordable payment before answering Gary's questions, Gary left the dealership with the salesperson in pursuit, seeking to continue the sale. The salesperson even called Gary later at home saying he would lose his job if he quoted a price before getting an affordable monthly payment amount. But Gary had already bought his car at the other dealership. Had Gary responded to the salesperson's questions, the salesperson could have tailored the price to Gary's figure, which likely would not have been the lowest price the dealership would have accepted.

What If You Want to Buy a Used Car?

The average new car now sells for more than $14,000. For many people, these prices are simply more than they are able or willing to pay. For them, a good, reliable used car can do very nicely. However, you need to be careful when buying a used car. There are some basic steps you can follow to help ensure that you don't get a "lemon."

1. Decide on features and options. Your first step is to select the features you want, such as power steering, air conditioning, and stereo. In contrast with new cars, you do not need to be as careful about distinguishing between the options you need and want. If you want an option, you can usually obtain it without spending more simply by choosing an older model. Since there are many cars to choose from, this is not a difficult task.
2. Decide how much you can afford to spend. You can purchase a used car for as little as $200 and as much as $20,000 or $30,000. Decide in advance how much you can afford, and then search for cars in your price range.
3. Select several reliable makes and models in your price range. When you know what you

can afford, you can then select four or five makes and models that fit your price range. The National Automobile Dealers Association (NADA) publishes monthly reports on the average retail and wholesale prices of various makes and models of used cars. Your bank or credit union should have a copy of these reports, sometimes called the "black," "blue," or "red" books. The want ads in your local newspaper and used car advertising tabloids distributed at supermarkets, convenience stores, and so forth also can be a source of price information. In addition, you should consult the most recent April issue of *Consumer Reports* for its list of recommended used cars in various price ranges. The same issue also lists the frequency-of-repair histories for most makes and models as reported by its readers. While these histories and price-range recommendations only go back 6 years, you can consult the April issues from past years to get information back 10 to 12 years.
4. Start your search. Armed with your list of reliable makes and models in your price range,

(continued)

Making the Decision

The final decision whether or not to buy should be made at home.

Most people make buying decisions inside a store or dealer's showroom. This is not the best place because of pressures to buy that may be applied by the seller and/or by a customer's desire to get the process over with. This is especially true for big-ticket items such as cars. However, it is better to wait until you get home to make the decision. There, you can rationally retrace your steps through the buying process, making sure that your decision is based on the proper facts. Then you can return to the dealer's showroom and sign the necessary papers.

We should discuss one final problem: *lowballing*. If used, it occurs at the point of closure of the sale. At that point, the salesperson writes up the sale on the appropriate forms and, just before you sign, states that, as a formality, his or her superior's approval is necessary. While the salesperson is gone, you are envisioning driving away in your new car, but then he or she returns and indicates that there is some problem, a mistake, and that you can start looking for specific vehicles for sale. You may purchase a used car from a new car dealership, a used car dealership, a rental car company, a private individual, or even at a repossession auction. New car dealerships tend to offer the nicer, more reliable, and expensive cars. Trade-ins are their major source of cars, and dealers sell those which aren't in the best condition to wholesalers. Used car dealerships tend to have the widest range of choices and quality. Some used car dealerships deserve the image that they sometimes have, so be careful. Private individuals deserve your attention because they own the car and know its history. Used cars sold by rental agencies such as Hertz and Avis can be a good choice because they have been regularly maintained. Regardless of the source, immediately rule out any car that seems to have a problem or raises a question in your mind. Do the same for sellers who do not seem cooperative. There are too many cars available to waste time with cars of poor quality or uncooperative sellers.

5. Check your selections carefully. By now you should have narrowed your choice to two or three specific cars. Inspect them inside and out. Take along a friend who is knowledgeable about cars if you are not. Test drive the car, and check all its functions. Ask for maintenance records if the seller is an individual or a rental company. Ask the dealer for the name and address of the previous consumer owner and give that person a call. Before you agree to buy any car, have it examined by a mechanic whose $30 to $50 examination can save hundreds of dollars in repairs later.

6. Negotiate and decide. Never pay the asking price for a used car. Sellers expect to negotiate and set a price higher than required to give room for bargaining. Get *all* verbal promises and guarantees in writing. Verbal agreements are useless legally if problems come up later. If a seller will not put his or her words in writing, shop elsewhere. Return to the quiet of your home to consider your alternatives and to make your final decision.

the price has to be higher. Perhaps the trade-in value is too high, or the sticker price can't be discounted by quite as much as planned, or the price of a certain option has gone up. In reality, of course, the dealer wants to get more money out of you. If this technique is used on you, quickly leave without signing anything. Do not look back, and do not apologize.

Compliment or Complain Appropriately

"A warm word goes a long way, but a nasty one will not, unless you know how to communicate it." This philosophy overviews the following material: complimenting, complaining, and seeking legal redress.

Complimenting Is More Than Just Courtesy When a seller does an effective job of meeting your needs, it is clearly appropriate to give a word of thanks and a compliment. Your comment is justified because it was deserved. However, it is more. Such comments from customers provide

Advice for the Conservative Car Buyer

You will find yourself shopping for a car up to 20 times over your lifetime, so you might as well develop some skills. The following points are designed to help you get the most for your transportation dollar.

1. Buy used cars. New cars lose 20 to 40 percent of their value as a result of depreciation in the first 2 years. Let someone else pay for this.
2. Buy used cars from private owners. Why pay retail prices when you can get a price closer to wholesale. In addition, you will be dealing with someone closer to your level of expertise.
3. Visit a car dealer at least three times before actually signing a deal. The first trip is for preshopping research, the second is for comparison shopping, and the third is to negotiate. Even then, you should go home to make the final decision.

4. Negotiate price first. The bottom line in any car deal is the price of the vehicle itself. Never discuss your affordable monthly payment with a dealer. The price should be determined before even mentioning that you might have a trade-in, need a loan, desire a service contract, or are considering leasing. Then comparison shop and negotiate each of these items separately.
5. Consider the leasing option. Leasing is becoming increasingly attractive. This is especially so for the person who intends to buy a new car every 3 to 5 years.
6. Use your cars up. The best way to get full value out of a car is to keep it for its entire lifetime. Cars built today should last 12 years or up to 150,000 miles with proper maintenance. The repairs to an older car cost much less than the depreciation on a new car.

information to sellers as to what policies and procedures best serve customer needs. Some people offer compliments assuming that they will get even better service the next time. Whatever your motivation, try to provide a deserved compliment.

Complaining Helps Sellers Do Better   Most Americans simply refuse to accept shoddy products or services. When you have a negative purchasing experience, make sure your complaint does the most good. Decide on the objective of your complaint. If your objective is to be treated a little better while in a store, just ask to see the person in charge. This may be the store manager or an assistant manager. Simply report the quality of service you received and request that someone more capable be provided so you can spend your money in the store. If your objective is **redress,** that is, to right a wrong, more work is necessary.

Table 9.3 shows the four channels of complaining: to business, to self-regulatory groups, to consumer-action personnel, and to the private-action legal arena. You can follow these channels individually or simultaneously, but it is important to begin with the merchant before moving to other levels or channels. For example, a complaint not resolved satisfactorily with an auto dealer could be brought to the attention of the manufacturer's

TABLE 9.3
Complaint Procedure

Place to Bring Your Complaint	Channel for Complaint		
1. Particular business	Merchant	Manufacturer's consumer affairs department	Manufacturer's president or chief executive officer
2. Self-regulatory groups	Chamber of Commerce	Better Business Bureau	Trade association consumer panels
3. Consumer-action groups	Local consumer-action group	City or county consumer-protection office	State office of consumer affairs
4. Private-action legal arena	Small claims court	Regular civil court system	State attorney general

consumer affairs department before communicating with the manufacturer's president or to an AUTOCAP, a trade association consumer action panel. Note that federal agencies, such as the Food and Drug Administration, the Consumer Product Safety Commission, and the Federal Trade Commission, are not included in this table. These federal agencies can register consumer complaints but do not have the power to assist individual concerns. Seeking redress through the first three channels in the complaint procedure in Table 9.3 can rectify almost all consumer complaints.

You Have a Right to Seek Legal Redress Sometimes the forms of redress described above are not successful. As a result, the wronged person can then consider legal action against the business. Most people think that the costs for this are too high, but costs depend on the case and the type of court chosen.

A **civil court** is a state court in which numerous civil matters are resolved and a written record is made of the happenings; the proceedings are completed with the assistance of attorneys, witnesses, a judge, and often a jury. The wronged person generally must hire an attorney and pay additional fees. It is not unusual to spend $200 to $500 resolving an issue in this court.

Small claims courts are convenient and inexpensive.

A **small claims court** is a state court with no written record of testimony in which civil matters are often resolved without the assistance of attorneys (in some states attorneys are actually prohibited from representing clients in small claims courts). This court is also known as a **court not of record.** It is designed to litigate small civil claims with typical legal maximums of $500 to $2500. Claims above the small claims court maximum must be filed in a regular civil court.

To file a small claims court action, you would go to the courthouse and inquire as to which court hears small claims. A small fee, often $15 or less, is required, along with fees of normally $2.50 for each court summons (also called a *subpoena*) for each witness needed. When you complete the necessary forms, it is important to fill out the full legal name of the **defendant** (the person who allegedly committed the wrong deed and is the subject of the litigation) and to carefully describe the action with which the lawsuit is concerned. The court will subpoena all necessary witnesses and the defendant for the day of trial. The day the case is heard, you, the **plaintiff** (the person who has filed the small claims or civil court case and is suing the defendant), should be well prepared and have a clear understanding of the sequence of events that led up to the claim. Bring all relevant documentation. A written record of the court is not kept, and in most courts the decision of the judge can be appealed by the loser to a higher court (which, of course, results in considerable attorney fees and related costs). Most small claims court decisions are won by the plaintiff and are not appealed.

Our Consumer Rights Carry Responsibilities   In 1962, President Kennedy proclaimed four basic rights of consumers: (1) the right to safety, (2) the right to be informed, (3) the right to choose, and (4) the right to be heard. Like all rights, these consumer rights carry with them corresponding responsibilities.

1. *Regarding the right to safety, consumers should* examine merchandise for safety features before buying, read and follow care and use instructions carefully, assume personal responsibility for normal precautions when using a product, and inform retailers, manufacturers, trade organizations, and government agencies when a product does not perform safely.

2. *Regarding the right to be informed, consumers should* seek out accurate information about products and services, read advertisements and promotional materials carefully, ask questions of sellers about products and service when complete information is not available, and become more knowledgeable about the American marketplace and the consumer's role in it.

3. *Regarding the right to choose, consumers should* carefully select merchandise and services, carefully choose from whom to buy, compare products for both price and quality, continue to buy when products and services are satisfactory, and refuse to buy when products and services are unsatisfactory.

4. *Regarding the right to be heard, consumers should* seek redress when errors occur or when the quality of products or service is inferior, make suggestions for product and service improvements, report favorable products and incidents to retailers and manufacturers, and become informed and speak up about issues that affect consumers in general.

Consumer Protection Laws

There have been three notable eras of consumer activism at the federal level. The first spanned the 25 years preceding World War I, and the second took place during the 1930s. During these first two eras, the focus was primarily on the safety of foods and drugs and on antitrust laws. The third era began in the late 1950s and lasted until the late 1970s. During this period, over 40 major pieces of federal legislation focusing on consumer problems and concerns were passed. Today virtually every product and service offered in the marketplace is in some way covered by federal regulations. The following table describes the major laws enacted in recent years.

Law	Year	Synopsis
Fair Credit and Credit Card Disclosure Act	1988	Requires direct-mail applications and solicitations to reveal fees and interest rates.
FTC Used Car Rule	1985	Requires all used car dealers to place a large sticker, called a *Buyer's Guide,* in the window of each car they offer for sale.
NHTSA Tire Quality Grading Standard	1984	Requires that tires be labeled for traction, treadwear, and heat resistance.
Depository Institutions Deregulation and Monetary Control Act	1980	Allow banks and other depository institutions to offer interest on checking accounts and set up a mechanism to promote competition among such institutions.
Fair Debt Collection Practices Act	1977	Restricts unfair techniques used by third-party debt collectors.
Magnuson-Moss Warranty Act	1975	Authorizes the Federal Trade Commission to write rules governing warranties.
Fair Credit Billing Act	1974	Assists consumers in resolving disputes involving defective products purchased with a credit card.
Consumer Product Safety Act	1972	Created the Consumer Product Safety Commission, with responsibility for the safety of virtually all products except foods, drugs, cosmetics, medical devices, and motor vehicles, which are regulated by other agencies.
Poison Prevention Packaging Act	1970	Authorized the establishment of standards for child-resistant packaging of hazardous substances.
Truth-in-Lending Act	1968	Requires full disclosure of annual percentage rates and other information in credit contracts.
National Traffic and Motor Vehicle Safety Act	1966	Established programs for the setting of mandatory safety standards for new cars.
Kefauver-Harris Drug Amendment	1962	Requires that all new drugs be proven safe and effective.
Food Additives Amendment	1958	Requires that all new food additives be proven safe.

Summary

1. People can save money by following six basic rules of wise buying: don't buy on impulse, avoid buying on credit, buy at the right time, avoid paying extra simply for the name, recognize that convenience costs money, and question the need to go first class.

2. Although most people cannot have immediately all the expensive material possessions they may want, life-cycle planning for major purchases may help in achieving such goals.

3. The planned buying process includes distinguishing between needs and wants, obtaining information during preshopping research, fitting the planned purchase into the budget, comparison shopping to find the best buy, negotiating, making the decision, and complimenting or complaining as needed.

4. Consumers have four basic rights: to safety, to be informed, to choose, and to be heard. Each carries corresponding responsibilities to observe safety precautions, seek out consumer information, choose wisely, and speak out appropriately.

Modern Money Management

The Johnsons Decide to Buy a Car

It is now October and the Johnsons have decided that it is time to move out of their apartment and into some form of purchased housing. Although they have not decided on what type of housing they will buy, they do know that Belinda will no longer be able to ride the bus to work. Thus they are in the market for another car. They have decided not to buy a new car, and they think they have some room in their budget, given the raises each has received this year (see Table 4.3), for a car. They estimate that they could afford to spend about $3000 on a used car by making a downpayment of $600 and financing the remainder over 24 months at $120 per month.

1. Make suggestions about how the $120 might be integrated into their budget (Table 4.3) without changing the amount left over at the end of each month. Harry and Belinda want that extra money to help defray the added expenses of home ownership.

2. Which sources of used cars should they consider seriously? Why?

3. Assume that the Johnsons have narrowed their choices to two cars. Both have air conditioning, AM/FM radio, and automatic transmission. The first car is a 6-year-old Chevrolet Cavalier with 62,000 miles, being sold for $3100 by a private individual. The car has a six-cylinder engine and is a hatchback style. The seller has records of all repairs, tuneups, and

oil changes. The car will need new tires in about 6 months. The second car is a 5-year-old Ford Escort two-door with 66,000 miles, being sold by a used car dealership. It has a four-cylinder engine. Harry contacted the previous owner and found that the car was given in trade on a new car about 6 months ago. The previous owner cited no major mechanical problems but simply wanted a bigger car. There is a written 30-day warranty on parts only. The asking price is $3400. Which would you advise they buy? Why?

Key Words and Concepts

balloon automobile loan, 329
best buy, 327
civil court, 335
closed-end lease, 330
comparison shopping, 327
court not of record, 335
defendant, 336
express warranties, 327
full warranty, 327
implied warranty, 327
limited warranty, 327

negotiating, 331
open-end lease, 330
plaintiff, 336
preshopping research, 323
rebates, 327
redress, 334
residual value, 329
service contract, 328
small claims court, 335
sticker price, 323
warranties, 327

Review Questions

1. Identify six major ways people can save money on major expenditures.
2. How does your place in the life cycle affect your major expenditures? Give examples of changes in expenditures over the life cycle.
3. List the seven steps in the buying process.
4. Distinguish between needs and wants.
5. Explain how preshopping research can help you save money.
6. Explain why magazines that accept advertising of products they rate for quality are not always reliable for product information.
7. Why doesn't getting the lowest price for a product ensure that you are getting the best buy?
8. Explain the difference between an implied warranty and an express warranty.
9. Distinguish between full and limited warranties as defined by the Magnuson-Moss Warranty Act.
10. What is the value of having a service contract? What is a disadvantage?
11. Why are lease payments for a new car lower than loan payments for the same vehicle?

12. Explain the relative benefits of open-end versus closed-end leases.
13. Define a *balloon automobile loan*.
14. Describe three keys to success in negotiating the price of a new car.
15. Where should one make major buying decisions?
16. Explain how consumer complaints can benefit sellers.
17. Define the word *redress*.
18. How could you seek redress without going to court?

Case Problems

1. Martha Law of Plattsburgh, New York, is remodeling her kitchen. She has decided to replace her refrigerator with a newer model that has more conveniences. She has narrowed her decision down to a model that is 19.2 cubic feet in size and has a top freezer. Basic models in this size cost about $750. She also has drawn up a list of possible convenience options and their prices: automatic defrost—$125, ice maker—$50, textured enamel surface—$75, glass shelving—$30, and ice water port—$95. Martha's credit union will loan her the necessary funds for 1 year at 12 percent APR on the installment plan. Following is Martha's budget for her $1115 monthly take-home pay. She lives alone.

Food	$150	Entertainment	$75
Clothing	50	Gifts	50
Car payment	232	Personal care	40
Automobile expenses	75	Savings	75
Housing	325	Miscellaneous	43

   a. What preshopping research should Martha do to select the best brand refrigerator?
   b. Advise Martha on which convenience options you think she needs and which she should consider wants.

   c. Using the information in Table 7.3 or the Personal Finance Cookbook (PFC) program INSTALL, calculate Martha's monthly payment for (1) the basic model, (2) the basic model with needed options, and (3) the basic model with needed and wanted options?
   d. Fit each of the three monthly payments into Martha's budget.
   e. Advise Martha on her decision.

2. Ron McCord of Malibu, California, purchased a new automobile for $9800. He used the car often and in less than 9 months had put 14,000 miles on it. A 24,000-mile, 2-year warranty was still in effect for most of the power-train equipment, and Ron did have to pay the first $100 on each repair. At 16,500 miles and the eleventh month of driving, Ron had some severe problems with the transmission. He took the car to the dealer for repairs. A week later he picked the car up, but some transmission problems still remained. When he took the car back to the dealer, the dealer said no more problems could be identified. However, Ron was

sure the problem was still there, and he was amazed that the dealer would not correct it. The dealer told him he would do nothing more.

a. Was Ron within his rights to take the car back for repairs? Explain.

b. What would be some logical steps to follow if Ron continues to be dissatisfied with the dealer's unwillingness or inability to repair the car?

c. May Ron seek any help from the court system? If so, describe what he could do without spending money on attorney's fees.

Suggested Readings

"A Better Way to Buy a Car." *Consumer Reports,* September 1989, pp. 593–595. How to buy a car using an automobile broker.

"Airfares: Speak Up for a Discount." *Consumer Reports,* June 1989, pp. 363–366. Getting great airfare prices by using consolidators, which are listed state-by-state.

"Appliance Service Contracts: Why the Dealer Wins." *Changing Times,* January 1989, pp. 83–86. Exposé on the profit margins on service contracts and the small likelihood of product breakdowns.

"Best Deals in Auto Clubs." *Changing Times,* February 1989, pp. 41–49. Only a few auto clubs offer good value for both emergency road service and travel services.

"Best Ways to Get Around in Europe." *Changing Times,* July 1989, pp. 39–41. Suggestions on travel in Europe.

"Best Ways to Get Your Money Back." *Money,* April 1989, pp. 149–158. How to collect when things go wrong, including state-by-state details on small claims courts.

"Cars: Cheap Loans Vs. Rebates." *Changing Times,* March 1989, pp. 53–54. How to figure out whether a loan or rebate is the better deal.

"Car Options: Why You Should Kick the Tires—Hard." *Business Week,* July 10, 1989, p. 97. Advises against accepting new car dealer options such as rustproofing, paint and fabric protection, and extended warranties.

"Car Trouble." *Changing Times,* November 1989, pp. 63–68. Which cars consumers complain about the most and least to the government.

"Consumer Gripes: How to Get Results." *Changing Times,* November 1989, pp. 79–83. Getting satisfaction when complaining about a range of products and services.

"Do All Mono Monitors Support Herc Graphics." *Changing Times,* March 1990, pp. 75–82. All the basic information you need to go out and buy a personal computer system.

"Hold That Scalpel!" *Money,* February 1989, pp. 105–116. Sources of information, including financial data, on what you need to consider before deciding to undergo surgery.

"How to Buy a New Car You'll Love." *Changing Times,* December 1989, pp. 29–63. Annual car report on more than 500 makes and models.

"How to Buy Upholstered Furniture." *Consumer Reports,* January 1989, pp. 33–38. Step-by-step details on the process of buying upholstered furniture.

"How to Read the Fine Print in Contracts." *Money,* June 1990, p. 111–120. Most large expenditures involve contracts, and there are ways you can protect yourself in these situations.

"Leasing Your Wheels." *Newsweek,* May 22, 1989, p. 65. Explores the benefits of auto leasing and how it compares to buying on credit.

"Sorry, That's Out of Warranty." *Changing Times,* March 1990, pp. 53–57. How and why automakers will fix your car for free even when it is out of warranty.

"Surprising Cars You'll Drive Tomorrow." *Changing Times,* October 1989, pp. 79–83. Design aspects of tomorrow's smarter and safer automobiles.

"The 1990 Cars." *Consumer Reports,* April 1990, pp. 206–295. Issue devoted solely to new cars and how to buy them; includes frequency of repair records.

"To Buy or Lease a Car." *Working Woman,* January 1989, pp. 61–64. Pointers for making the lease-buy decision.

"Update on CD Players," *Changing Times,* July 1989, pp. 63–66. What you do and do not need when buying a CD player.

"What Your Bucks Will Buy Abroad This Summer." *Changing Times,* May 1989, pp. 74–78. Tips on traveling to Europe and beyond.

"World's Biggest Garage Sale." *Changing Times,* April 1989, pp. 65–67. How to make bids on goods auctioned by the federal government.

10 The Housing Expenditure

OBJECTIVES

After reading this chapter, you should be able to

1. Identify seven goals of housing that people seek in accordance with their values and goals.

2. Generalize as to whether renters or owners pay more for housing.

3. Describe ways to determine how much buyers can afford for housing.

4. Discuss the various aspects of renting a home or apartment. Describe the types of owned housing.

5. Discuss the various aspects of financing a home, including the traditional and alternative mortgage and home financing options.

6. Identify the numerous costs of buying a home, including principal, interest, and closing costs.

7. List and describe the steps in the home-buying process.

8. Identify some important concerns in the process of selling a home.

• • • • • • • • •

The four major areas of expenditure are housing, food, transportation, and insurance. Of these, the greatest expenditure is usually for housing, often requiring up to 40 percent of disposable income. Consequently, it is an extremely important component of personal financial planning.

This chapter begins with a discussion of values and goals related to housing, followed by sections on the questions of renting versus buying and how much you can afford for housing. We then will discuss choosing an apartment and will describe most everyone's dream: owned housing. Next we will discuss how to finance a home (with both traditional and alternative mortgages), examine how real estate taxes are assessed, and explain how to estimate total home-buying costs. The chapter ends with a look at the processes of buying and selling a home. The important topic of real estate as an investment is covered later, in Chapter 20.

Housing Provides More Than Just Space

Objective
To be able to identify seven goals of housing that people seek.

Our housing choices are based on our values and goals. In housing, Americans generally value large living quarters that provide opportunities for privacy, storage, and an absence of noise. Most people pursue their housing goals according to their values and personalities. Categories of housing goals include functionality, efficiency, internal ambience, external ambience, mobility, safety, and manageable cost.

1. *Functionality* of housing reflects the relationships among public, private, and work areas. Public space is normally for leisure activities. Private space is for sleeping, dressing, and bathing. Work space includes food preparation and storage areas, as well as a home office and workshop. Traffic patterns are important to functionality. For example, it is inconvenient to have the kitchen located too far from the dining area or to have to walk through a bedroom to get to the only bathroom.

2. *Efficiency* of the housing relates to the ease of housekeeping and maintenance of a dwelling and partly reflects the dweller's lifestyle. A person who travels a great deal and spends little time at home might not need much total space. Someone who eats most meals away from home might not need a large kitchen that requires considerable cleanup. Renters do not have to worry about such things as plumbing and lawn mowing.

3. *Internal ambience* relates to the comfort and attractiveness of the housing interior. Warm and cozy might fit some people. Bright and

airy is another popular goal. Most people consider their homes a haven. Returning after work or a business trip to an attractively decorated home can be very relaxing. Party-loving people should consider large open spaces in which to entertain.

4. *External ambience* relates to such things as the type of neighborhood, size of the lot, and proximity to work, play, and shopping. People generally want to avoid neighborhoods afflicted by water, air, land, and noise pollution. Some people like lots of trees. Others like more open surroundings. Realtors often say that there are three criteria in choosing housing: location, location, and location.

5. *Mobility* has to do with how easily you can change residences for such reasons as obtaining a new job, getting married, or simply wanting a change. Mobility is important to consider when making a rent-versus-buy decision.

6. *Safety* is important to many people. Some people feel safe knowing there are sufficient fire-escape ladders, and others require an environment where a guard checks all who enter and a security force patrols the area day and night. Some people say they will not live in the country because it feels unsafe; others say the same about big cities.

7. *Manageable costs* for *total* housing are a vital concern. Your rent or mortgage loan payment does not reflect total housing costs. You must also consider utility costs, maintenance costs, homeowners' association fees, and if there are special charges for storage and recreational areas.

Who Pays More, Renters or Owners?

Objective
To be able to generalize as to whether renters or owners pay more for housing.

According to research studies, home owners have an advantage over renters. This is a generalization and involves total housing costs over the years. Renters generally pay out less money in terms of cash flow, but owners usually see an increase in the value of their homes over time and have some income tax advantages which eventually make them financially better off. A key determinant in whether one rents or buys housing is the ability to come up with the significant up-front costs for down payment and closing costs when one buys. Thus it should come as no surprise that nearly 90 percent of the households headed by persons under age 25 are rental households compared with slightly less than 20 percent of those headed by persons aged 55 to 64.

Based on Cash Flow, Renters Win

To compare renting and buying fairly, we must use comparable forms of housing. Comparing a house with an apartment is not a fair comparison, since differences are likely to exist in privacy, square footage, and neighborhood. Table 10.1 illustrates a comparison for a small three-bedroom home that an owner is willing to sell or rent. The house would rent for $580 per month. Assume you could buy the house for $80,000

Advantages and Disadvantages of Renting versus Buying Housing (Renting May Look Better)

Advantages

Renting

Easy mobility

Apartment amenities (pool, tennis courts, party rooms, laundry facilities)

Lifestyle requires fewer responsibilities

No maintenance or repairs

No large down payment needed, only a security deposit

Fixed housing expenditure (rent) makes it easier to budget

No chance for financial loss (beyond the amount of the lease)

Proximity of neighbors gives sense of security

Opportunity to look over the community and move again

Low moving-in costs

Pride of occupancy

Buying

Pride of ownership

Higher status for home owners

Better credit rating

Monthly payment usually remains relatively constant for many years

Income tax deduction for mortgage interest and real estate property taxes

Potential for home to increase in value resulting in a significant gain

Owner is forced to save by making payments on an asset that grows in value

Owner can borrow against owner's equity as value of home increases against what is owed on it

More space available

Freedom to make home improvements and alterations

Disadvantages

Renting

No special tax deductions

No potential gain from the rising value of property

Usually less space for the money

Alterations cannot be made

Rent rises with inflation, except where there are many rental units available

Many restrictions on noise level, pet ownership, or children

No pride of ownership

Buying

Substantial down payment needed

A big commitment in time, emotions, and money must be made to the home

Possibility that the home will decrease in value if the neighborhood deteriorates or changes quickly

Limited liquidity, since owner's money is tied up in the home

Possibility of limited marketability for resale

Cost of repairs and maintenance

Time and effort required for repairs and maintenance

Difficulty in budgeting for repair, maintenance, and home improvements

Possibility that real estate property taxes could increase dramatically

Total housing costs might be more than the budget can handle

Higher moving-in costs, since new items may have to be purchased for a home

Possible feeling of less security if neighbors are not near

TABLE 10.1
Should You Buy or Rent?

	Calculating the Cost to:	
	Rent	*Buy*
Cash-flow considerations		
Annual rent ($580/month) or mortgage payments ($619/month)*	$6,960	$ 7,428
Property and liability insurance	270	425
Real estate taxes	0	2,000
Maintenance	0	800
Less interest on funds not used for down payment (at 8 percent)	− 1,245	0
Cash-flow cost for the year	$5,985	$10,653
Tax and appreciation considerations		
Less principal† repaid on the mortgage loan	—	−$ 293
Plus tax on interest of funds not used for down payment (28 percent tax bracket)	348	0
Less tax savings due to deductibility of mortgage interest‡ (28 percent tax bracket)	0	− 1,998
Less tax savings due to deductibility of real estate property tax (28 percent tax bracket)	0	− 560
Less appreciation on the dwelling (4 percent rate)	0	− 3,200
Net cost for the year	$6,333	$4,602

* Calculated from Table 10.6.
† Calculated according to the method used in Table 10.4.
‡ Mortgage interest tax savings equals total mortgage payments minus principal repaid multiplied by the marginal tax rate.

by using your $15,000 savings as a down payment and borrow the remaining $65,000 for 30 years at 11 percent interest. As the table shows, renting would have a cash-flow cost of $5985 after a reduction for the interest that could be earned on your savings. Buying requires several expenses beyond the monthly mortgage payment. In this illustration, the cash-flow cost of buying is $10,653, or $4668 more than renting.

Based on Tax Advantages and Appreciation, Owners Win

To make the comparison more accurate, we need to consider the tax and appreciation aspects of the two options. If you buy the home, $293 (see Table 10.4 for an example of this type of calculation) of the mortgage payments for the year will go toward the principal of the debt. Both mortgage interest and real estate property taxes qualify as income tax deductions. Assuming that you are in the 28 percent marginal tax bracket, you would lower your taxes $1998 [($7428 − $293) × 0.28] as a result of mortgage interest deductibility and $560 ($2000 × 0.28) for real estate tax deductibility. (These reductions would be greater if your state income tax laws allow such deductions.) Homes also carry the likelihood of

Advice for the Conservative Housing Consumer

The biggest tax break offered the average American taxpayer is deductibility of both mortgage interest and real estate taxes. As the following example illustrates, a middle-income individual or family can usually save $1000 or $2000 per year in taxes because of these deductions. In addition, these deductions usually exceed the standard deduction (see page 283 in Chapter 8), thereby making it advantageous to itemize your other deductions. This can open up the possibility of using even more of the deduction opportunities not available to those who do not itemize. Let's look at an example.

	Couple A (Renters)	Couple B (Home Buyers)
Adjusted gross income	$32,000	$32,000
Standard deduction	−5,450	Itemized instead
Mortgage interest	0	−7,500
Real estate taxes	0	−1,300
Other deductions	0	−4,200
Exemptions	−4,100	−4,100
Taxable income	$22,450	$14,900
Tax liability	$3,368	$2,235

Couple B saves $1,133 ($3,368 − 2,235) on their federal income taxes as a result of being able (1) to deduct housing-related interest and taxes and (2) to itemize other deductions, possibly for health care expenses, state and local income taxes, charitable contributions, and job and other miscellaneous deductions. Actually, the savings would be even greater for couple B because they also would likely be able to reduce their state income tax liability.

appreciation, or increase, in the home's value. Historically, in most areas of the country, the value of housing has risen faster than the general inflation rate. Let's be conservative and assume that the home will increase in value by 4 percent a year. The home valued at $80,000 would be worth $83,200 ($80,000 × 1.04) after 1 year, a gain of $3200. If you rent, however, you would have to pay $348 ($1245 × 0.28) in income taxes on the interest on your savings account. In this case, buying is financially better than renting by approximately $1731 ($6333 − $4602).

Note that the appreciation on a purchased home is not money in your pocket until the home is sold. Until then, it is only a "paper profit." When you sell a home, you will likely pay approximately 6 percent commission if a real estate agent handles the sale. Thus, in the first few years, a large percentage (if not all) of the appreciation will be eroded by the anticipated sales commission. It should be clear that the appreciation benefits of home ownership generally do not begin to be realized until 3 to 5 years after purchase. For those who are likely to move in a year or two, renting is probably the better option.

TABLE 10.2
Changes in the Median Price of Existing Homes In the Most and Least Expensive Metropolitan Areas

Metropolitan Area*	1987	1988	1989	1990†
Peoria, Illinois	$ 46,500	$ 45,000	$ 46,800	$ 47,100
Spokane, Washington	51,200	51,100	52,400	52,800
Oklahoma City, Oklahoma	62,300	56,200	53,500	54,100
Mobile, Alabama	55,600	53,000	56,700	57,900
Des Moines, Iowa	55,600	55,800	57,500	58,100
Louisville, Kentucky	51,700	54,500	58,400	59,900
National average	85,600	89,300	93,100	95,300
Boston, Massachusetts	177,200	181,200	181,900	180,200
New York, New York	185,300	183,800	183,200	181,400
Los Angeles, California	147,700	179,400	215,500	221,400
Orange County, California	167,300	206,900	245,300	253,500
San Francisco, California	171,300	212,600	260,600	261,200
Honolulu, Hawaii	186,000	215,100	267,600	281,600

Source: Home Sales, March 1990, (Vol. 4, No. 3), National Association of Realtors.

* Metropolitan area includes the named central city and surrounding areas.

† Authors' estimates.

How Much Can You Afford for Housing?

Objective
To be able to describe ways to determine how much buyers can afford for housing.

Your decision to spend a certain amount of money on either renting or buying housing should be based on a careful analysis. Too often people take the first reasonably priced apartment they can find or quickly accept an offer to share expenses with a friend, perhaps in a more expensive and larger home. Two important points to remember when deciding how much to spend on housing are (1) setting up a housing budget and (2) avoiding outdated rules of thumb.

Set Up a Housing Budget

Housing costs have and will likely continue to rise in most areas of the United States as indicated in Table 10.2 (although you might note the experience in Oklahoma City). Another perspective can be seen in Table 10.3 which provides indicators of the affordability of owned housing in recent years. You needn't become depressed about the high costs of housing, although affordability is still a problem for first time buyers as Table 10.2 shows. This chapter will provide valuable suggestions to help you. Your task is to figure your housing budget using some of the budgeting tactics described in Chapter 4. Add up your living expenses *other than* for housing to determine how much income is left to spend on housing. Families buying housing today may well spend 35 to 45 percent of their total income on the mortgage payment, taxes, insurance, and utilities.

TABLE 10.3
Housing Affordability in Recent Years

| Year | Affordability Indexes* | | | First-time Buyers |
	Composite†	Fixed Mortgage	ARM	
1984	89.1	84.6	92.1	64.9
1985	94.8	89.6	100.6	68.3
1986	108.9	105.7	116.3	75.6
1987	114.2	107.6	122.4	78.9
1988	113.5	103.6	122.0	79.0
1989	106.1	101.8	112.3	74.2
1990‡	105.1	102.5	112.0	N/A

Source: Home Sales, March 1990 (Vol. 4, No. 3), National Association of Realtors.

* The higher the index, the more likely that typical families would be able to afford or qualify for a mortgage on an existing (not new) single-family dwelling. Specifically, the index represents the median family income as a percentage of the income required to qualify for a mortgage with a 20 percent down payment on a median priced existing single-family home. For example, in 1990 the median family income was 105.1 percent of the income required to qualify for such a loan. An index of 100 would mean that a family at the median income level would likely qualify for a mortgage on a median priced home if they were able to put down 20 percent.

† The composite represents the index for various types of mortgages.

‡ For February 1990.

Note that such calculations give you a figure for the *maximum* amount available for housing, assuming that expenses other than housing costs will not go up, which they often do. It is good planning to initially pay less than the maximum amount available, if possible.

Avoid Overreliance on Outdated Rules of Thumb

"The purchase price of a home should not exceed $2\frac{1}{2}$ times gross income." "Monthly housing costs should not exceed 25 percent of gross income." "Housing expenses should not exceed 35 percent of take-home pay." Many of these rules of thumb have become outdated and provide only a ballpark figure for estimating affordable rent payments or borrowing capacity because housing costs have risen so dramatically. Let's look at a couple of examples.

Traditional guidelines on housing affordability do not always work in today's market.

The national median price of an existing home in 1991 is expected to be $96,000; the highest prices are in the far west. A three-bedroom home available in St. Louis for $100,000 might sell for $140,000 in Boston. To buy it, the "$2\frac{1}{2}$ times gross income" rule requires an income of $40,000 in St. Louis and $56,000 in Boston. Many people wish to buy housing before making this much income. In addition, after you make a down payment of $15,000, the monthly payment on a 25-year mortgage at 11 percent would be $833.09 (from Table 10.6) on the St. Louis home and

▮ Qualifying to Buy a Home

The following table will give you a quick idea of how much income you need to have to buy a certain price home according to qualification rules followed by most lenders. For each home price, the table shows the monthly payment for principal, interest, taxes, and insurance (PITI) for various interest rates. It also shows the required gross annual income to qualify for the loan. The *top* figure in each row shows the monthly PITI payment; the *bottom* figure shows the required gross annual income. For example, an 11 percent loan on an $80,000 home requires a monthly PITI payment of $676, plus an income of $27,046 to qualify. Loans are 80 percent of purchase price; term is 30 years. Taxes and insurance (TI) are calculated at 1 percent of the purchase price (divided by 12 months). Most lenders require that annual PITI (monthly figure multiplied by 12 months) cannot exceed 30 percent of gross annual income.

Interest Rate	Price of Home				
	$60,000	$80,000	$100,000	$120,000	$140,000
8.0%	$ 402	$ 536	$ 670	$ 804	$ 938
	$16,088	$21,451	$26,814	$32,177	$38,539
9.0%	$ 436	$ 582	$ 727	$ 872	$ 1,018
	$17,449	$23,265	$29,081	$34,898	$40,714
10.0%	$ 471	$ 628	$ 785	$ 942	$ 1,100
	$18,849	$25,132	$31,416	$37,699	$43,982
11.0%	$ 507	$ 676	$ 845	$ 1,014	$ 1,183
	$20,285	$27,046	$33,808	$40,569	$47,331
12.0%	$ 544	$ 725	$ 906	$ 1,087	$ 1,269
	$21,749	$28,999	$36,249	$43,499	$50,749
13.0%	$ 581	$ 775	$ 968	$ 1,162	$ 1,356
	$23,239	$30,985	$38,732	$46,478	$54,224
14.0%	$ 619	$ 825	$ 1,031	$ 1,237	$ 1,444
	$24,750	$32,999	$41,249	$49,499	$57,749
15.0%	$ 657	$ 876	$ 1,095	$ 1,314	$ 1,533
	$26,277	$35,036	$43,796	$52,555	$61,314
16.0%	$ 695	$ 927	$ 1,159	$ 1,391	$ 1,623
	$27,819	$37,092	$46,366	$55,639	$64,912

$1225.14 in Boston. Perhaps another $225 per month also must be paid out for real estate property taxes and home owner's insurance. Thus, even if a St. Louis buyer's income is $40,000 (approximately $2333 take-home pay per month), the St. Louis buyer would have expenses of about $1058 ($833 + $225), or 45 percent ($1058/$2333) of take-home pay, far in excess of the "35 percent of take-home pay" rule.

Choosing Housing That Can Truly Become Your Home

Objective
To be able to discuss the various aspects of renting a home or apartment and to describe the types of owned housing.

Many families' needs are met by rental housing.

You can choose from a wide variety of rented and owned housing, depending on your wants and needs and the amount available in your housing budget. Each type of housing has special features, which are discussed below.

Rented Housing

People who rent housing may not have the funds for a down payment and high mortgage payments on a home and may prefer the easy mobility of renting or may prefer to avoid altogether many of the responsibilities of buying. Prospective renters need to consider the amount of rent and related expenses, the lease agreement and restrictions, and tenant rights.

Rent, Deposit, and Related Expenses   Rent is the cost of using an apartment or other housing space and is usually due on a specific day each month. A late charge of perhaps an additional 5 percent of the rent payment may be assessed on tenants who are late in paying rent. A lost-key replacement fee of $10 is typically charged, as is a $15 fee to let in a tenant who has been locked out. Other fees could be for rental of a party room and the use of a pool, tennis courts, cable television, and space for storage and parking.

The **security deposit** is an amount paid in advance to a landlord to pay for repairing the unit beyond what would be expected from normal wear and tear; it is sometimes charged in addition to prepayment of the last month's rent. Thus to move into an apartment with a monthly rent of $500 might require prepayment of the first and last month's rent ($1000 total), as well as a security deposit (of perhaps $300). If you leave the rental unit clean and undamaged, you should obtain a refund of your security deposit. It is wise to make a list of all damages and defects in an apartment before moving in and have the landlord sign the list. Do the same upon moving out. This verifies the condition of the unit before and after your tenancy and can prevent you being charged for damages you did not cause.

Lease Agreement and Restrictions   If you rent a unit on a month-to-month basis without signing any legal contract, you have few protections. A **lease** is a legal contract specifying the legal responsibilities of both the tenant and the landlord. It identifies the amount of rent and security deposit, the length of the lease (sometimes 6 months to 2 or 3 years, but typically 1 year), who pays for utilities and repairs, penalties for late payment of rent, eviction procedures and costs for continued nonpayment of rent, and what happens when the term of the lease is up. Leases often state whether interest is paid on the security deposit, how soon after the tenant vacates must the unit be inspected for cleanliness, and how soon the security deposit (or the balance) is to be forwarded to the tenant.

Lease agreements also contain restrictions that are legally binding on tenants. Pets may or may not be permitted; when permitted, a larger security deposit is often required. Excessive noise from musical instruments, stereos, televisions, or parties also may be limited. To protect all other renters from overcrowding, a clause often places some restrictions on the number of overnight guests. A most important restriction is on **subleasing** (leasing the property from the original tenant to another tenant). A tenant who moves before the lease is up may have to get permission from the landlord to permit someone else to take over the rental unit. The new tenant may even have to be approved, and the original tenant may have some financial liability until the term of the original lease expires.

Tenant Rights   Many legal rights are available to tenants under laws in most states and many local communities. Some important ones are noted below.

1. Reporting building-code violations to a local government housing authority is not just cause for eviction or for harassment in the form of rent increases or utility shutoffs.

2. The habitability of the rental unit must meet some legally prescribed minimum standard (such as running water, heat, and a working stove), often in compliance with local housing codes. In most states, an implied warranty covers the availability of heat and the safety of access areas, such as stairs.

3. In many states, tenants can legally make minor repairs themselves and deduct those costs from their next rent payment. This is subject to certain restrictions, such as giving sufficient prior written notification to the landlord.

4. Security deposits must be returned, by law, in a timely manner in most states. Limits are placed on the kinds of deductions, and landlords must explain specific reasons for deductions. In some states, interest must be paid on security deposits.

5. Joining a tenant organization is not cause for eviction. These are groups whose aim is to improve the bargaining power of tenants.

6. Filling a lawsuit against a landlord for nonperformance is permitted in all states. This is usually done in a small claims court, where for a nominal filing fee (perhaps $15) lawsuits up to a certain dollar amount (perhaps $2500) can be pursued without an attorney.

Owned Housing

Americans have historically favored single-family dwellings to satisfy their owned-housing needs. However, because of rising construction and interest costs, other, less expensive alternatives such as condominiums and cooperatives and manufactured housing and mobile homes have been increasing in popularity.

Single-Family Dwellings   A housing unit detached from others is a **single-family dwelling.** It is traditionally located in a residential neighborhood.

The four basic styles available are (1) the one-floor ranch, which requires more land for construction than do other styles; (2) the two-story, which offers a lower cost per square foot and the privacy of upstairs bedrooms; (3) the split-level, which requires more land than the two-story because each floor level is about a half-story above or below adjacent floors (this style fits well in rolling terrain); and (4) the Cape Cod (one-and-a-half story), which has second-floor windows protruding through the roof, can be built on a small lot, and has sloped ceilings upstairs. There are many variations on these basic styles.

In addition to choice of style, there is the choice between newer and older homes. Many people prefer the modern kitchens and other features found in newer homes; others prefer the larger rooms, higher ceilings, bigger closets, and completed landscaping of older homes. Note, though, that some older homes have almost no closet space. Buyers considering an older residence should look for termite infestation and wood rot, as well as any sagging in the structure caused by a weak foundation. Additionally, check the wiring, heating and cooling system, insulation, plumbing, hot-water heater, roof and gutters, and the dryness of the basement.

Condominiums and Cooperatives The terms *condominium* and *cooperative* describe a form of ownership rather than a type of building. These "owned apartments" are located in high-rise multiunit structures and multiplex units, as well as in townhouses and row houses. Many people prefer these forms of ownership to single-family dwellings because of lower unit costs than for houses, the possibility of the value of the property increasing, availability of recreation facilities, reduced obligations for maintenance, and locations close to employment. More than half of all condominium purchasers are unmarried; 45 percent are women.

A **condominium** owner holds legal title to a specific housing unit within a multiunit building or project and a proportionate interest in the common grounds and facilities. The entire complex is run by the owners themselves through a homeowners' association they establish. Operation must be in accordance with the association's bylaws, which detail what can and cannot be done. For example, the association could be in charge of swimming pool maintenance and of setting swimming hours. Also, improvements purchased by individual home owners (such as screen doors and window shutters) may have to be approved by the association for consistency of design.

The condominium home owner's fee can add to the cost of such housing.

Besides making mortgage loan payments, the home owner also must pay a monthly **home owner's fee**, which is established by the home owners' association. This amount pays for maintenance of common areas and facilities, repairs to the outside of any unit, real estate taxes on common areas, liability insurance, and fire insurance covering the exterior of the buildings. Some areas of concern for the potential buyer include rapidly increasing home owner's fees (developer-subsidized costs may be transferred to the home owners' association after all units are sold), limited marketability for resale (especially when new units in the development are still for sale), excessive rental of unsold units by the developer (which reduces the value of owner-occupied units), and the possibility that the developer might retain the right to charge increasingly higher fees for use of common areas instead of allowing the home owners' association to set fees.

A **cooperative** is actually a corporation that owns and manages groups of housing units. Buyers of cooperative housing purchase shares of ownership in the corporation equivalent to the value of their particular unit and also hold a proportional interest in all common areas. The cooperative holds legal title to the apartments and leases specific units to each buyer. The shareholders have some say in the rules and regulations and usually can change management firms if they desire. The monthly assessment covers the same types of items as does a condominium fee, but also includes an amount for the professional management of the complex and payments on the cooperative's mortgage debt. (The pro rata share for interest and property taxes is deductible on an individual's tax return.)

A major concern for prospective buyers of cooperatives is the likelihood of rapidly increasing monthly fees due to numerous unexpected vacancies or nonpayment of fees by other owners. Typically, cooperatives have less marketability than single-family dwellings or condominiums. Also, shareholders in some cooperatives sometimes can legally prohibit the sale of shares to particular individuals they dislike. Purchasers of both cooperatives and condominiums should realize that operating costs might be much higher for older, remodeled, and converted apartment buildings than for newer complexes.

Manufactured Housing and Mobile Homes **Manufactured housing** consists of partially factory-assembled housing units designed to be transported (often in portions) to the home site. Final assembly and readying of the housing for occupancy usually require another 2 to 6 weeks. The quality of such homes is generally good to excellent, and many regional and national chains (for example, Jim Walter Homes, Inc.) are in this rapidly growing business. Costs on a per-square-foot basis are low compared with on-site construction methods. Further cost reductions are available to persons who purchase a partially completed home and finish it themselves. The manufacturer sometimes offers lower-than-market mortgage interest rates. Predesigned floor plans often can be modified. The wise buyer is encouraged to examine model homes to determine the quality of construction. More than one-fourth of all new single-family dwellings sold are manufactured units.

Buying manufactured housing can significantly reduce housing costs.

Mobile homes are fully factory-assembled housing units built to a certain size (for example, to a maximum of 14 feet by 70 feet) and designed to be towed on a frame with a trailer hitch. These homes are usually sold complete with appliances, furniture, carpeting, and curtains. Mobile home variations include a double-wide (two units connected side to side) and an expandable unit (an additional section perhaps attached to the living room area). Mobile homes are considered personal property, like automobiles, and are thus subject to lower taxes than those for real estate property. The building cost per square foot is about half that of a single-family dwelling. Although portable, today's mobile homes are generally sold rather than moved when the owners wish to move to a new location.

Of utmost importance is the quality of the mobile home park in which the home will be located and the protections offered to the person who leases the "pad" upon which the mobile home is placed. Mobile homes rarely appreciate in value like other forms of housing; in fact, they often depreciate. For this reason, purchasers are often limited to mortgage loans of no longer than 15 years.

Financing the Largest Expenditure You Will Likely Make: Your Home

Objective
To be able to discuss the various aspects of financing a home.

Buying a home probably represents the largest expenditure you will ever make. You should prepare for it thoroughly and become knowledgeable about traditional and alternative mortgage loans and how they work. It is also important to decide whether to buy now or to wait.

Advance Planning Is Required

Your decision to become a home owner rather than a renter is based not only on your values and goals, but also on your finances. The financial aspect of buying includes money for the down payment, other moving-in costs, and monthly mortgage payments.

You can use several strategies to get the needed finances. Many people establish a "home savings" fund while renting. Young persons often must rent for 5 years or more before they are able to save enough to purchase a home. Some couples decide to postpone beginning a family, and others cut back on entertainment and vacations and put off making major purchases.

Relatives can be an important source of funds for first-time home buyers.

A number of home buyers obtain gifts or loans from relatives. Anyone may give up to $10,000 per year to another person without having to pay gift taxes, and the receiver does not have to pay income taxes on the amount. Thus some younger persons ask more affluent relatives for a cash gift to help buy a home now rather than wait a number of years for an expected inheritance. (This topic is discussed further in Chapter 23).

You also can prepare for home ownership by renting a home with an option to buy. Some landlords give renters the chance to buy the home they rent after 1 or 2 years. Obviously, if you have lived in a home for some time, you are in a good position to judge its value.

In preparing for home ownership, you also should plan to have funds for moving-in costs and home repairs. Additional costs might include furniture, lamps, draperies, carpeting, shrubbery, and lawn and power tools. Also, you might want to establish a special cash reserve for repairing or replacing items such as a water heater, furnace, or air conditioner.

Mortgage Loans

A **mortgage loan** is a loan to purchase real estate, with the real estate itself serving as collateral for the loan. In exchange for the loan, the lender

TABLE 10.4
Amortization of Monthly Payment of $720.03 on a $70,000, 30-Year Mortgage Loan at 12 Percent

First month

$70,000 × 12% × 1/12 = $700.00	Interest payment
$720.03 − $700.00 = $20.03	Principal repayment
$70,000 − $20.03 = $69,979.97	Balance due

Second month

$69,979.97 × 12% × 1/12 = $699.80	Interest payment
$720.03 − $699.80 = $20.23	Principal repayment
$69,979.97 − $20.23 = $69,959.74	Balance due

Third month

$69,959.74 × 12% × 1/12 = $699.60	Interest payment
$720.03 − $699.60 = $20.43	Principal repayment
$69,959.74 − $20.43 = $69,939.31	Balance due

(*mortgagee*) has a **lien** on the real estate, which is the legal right (the security) to obtain the property in the event the borrower (*mortgagor*) defaults on the loan. **Foreclosure** is the process of suing the borrower to prove default and asking the court to order the sale of the property in order to pay the debt. Mortgage loans are available from savings and loan associations, mutual savings banks, commercial banks, and credit unions. (These institutions were described in Chapters 5 and 7).

Traditionally, lenders made loans to home buyers at a fixed rate and a fixed payment for a term of 15 to 30 years. For example, a $70,000 loan could be granted at a 12 percent interest rate over a period of 30 years with a monthly payment of $720.03. The process of gradually paying off a mortgage loan through a series of periodic payments to a lender is **amortization**. Each payment goes toward repayment of both the **principal** (the original amount borrowed) and the interest. As the principal is paid off, this amount plus any appreciation in the value of the home become the home owner's **equity** (dollar value of the home in excess of that owed on it).

Payment of interest and a portion of the principal is a feature of amortization.

Most of each monthly payment during the early years of a mortgage loan goes for interest. Table 10.4 shows the interest and principal payment amounts for the first 3 months of a $70,000, 30-year, 12 percent mortgage loan. For the first month, $700 goes for interest costs and only $20.03 goes toward retirement of the principal of the loan. The principal monthly payment increases very slowly over the life of a loan as the amortization schedule in Table 10.5 shows. Many years pass before much of the monthly payment begins to reduce the outstanding balance of the loan.

The amortization table illustrated in Table 10.6 gives the amount of monthly payment required for each $1000 of a mortgage loan at different interest rates. Using this table, you can calculate the monthly payment for

TABLE 10.5

Amortization Schedule for a $70,000, 30-year (360-Payment) Mortgage Loan at 12 Percent

Month	Monthly Payment	Total Principal Payment	Total Interest Payment	Total Paid	Outstanding Balance
1	$720.03	$ 20.03	$700.00	$ 720.03	$69,979.97
2	720.03	20.23	699.80	1,440.06	69,959.74
3	720.03	20.43	699.60	2,160.09	69,939.31
4	720.03	20.64	699.39	2,880.12	69,918.67
5	720.03	20.84	699.19	3,600.15	69,897.83
6	720.03	21.05	698.98	4,320.18	69,876.78
7	720.03	21.26	698.77	5,040.21	69,855.52
8	720.03	21.47	698.56	5,760.24	69,834.05
9	720.03	21.69	698.34	6,480.27	69,812.36
10	720.03	21.91	698.12	7,200.30	69,790.45
11	720.03	22.13	697.90	7,920.33	69,768.32
12	720.03	22.35	697.68	8,640.36	69,745.97
24	720.03	25.18	694.85	17,280.72	69,459.73
36	720.03	28.37	691.66	25,921.08	69,137.18
48	720.03	31.97	688.06	34,561.44	68,773.73
60	720.03	36.03	684.00	43,201.80	68,364.18
120	720.03	65.45	654.58	86,403.60	65,392.34
180	720.03	118.91	601.12	129,605.40	59,993.42
240	720.03	216.02	504.01	172,807.20	50,185.23
300	720.03	392.44	327.59	216,009.00	32,366.69
360	715.89	708.80	7.09	259,210.80	0

mortgage loans of different sizes. For example, a $70,000 mortgage loan at 12 percent for 30 years costs $10.2861 per $1000. Thus 70 × $10.2861 equals $720.03.

Down Payment   The down payment that a lender will require for a mortgage loan is based on the lender's desired loan-to-value ratio. Basically, the lender places a limit on how much it would want to risk on a loan for a property to ensure that if the loan went into default the lender would be able to recover the debt. The **loan-to-value ratio** is the maximum the lender will loan on a piece of property divided by its value. For example, a home with a value of $100,000 for which a lender will loan $85,000 will have a loan-to-value ratio of 85 percent ($85,000/$100,000). Thus the down payment required would be 15 percent, or $15,000.

Perhaps you think of a down payment as the maximum amount you would want to pay to obtain a mortgage and move into a home. For those with limited cash, this may be true, but for those with an extra $5000 or $10,000 available, the situation differs. Making a larger down payment than required lowers the amount of the total mortgage loan needed and the amount of the resulting monthly payments. A smaller loan also carries lower total interest costs.

TABLE 10.6

Estimate Your Mortgage Loan Payments (Monthly Payment on $1000 Debt)

Interest Rate	Payment Period (Years)			
	15	20	25	30
8	$ 9.5565	$ 8.3644	$ 7.7182	$ 7.3376
8.5	9.8474	8.6782	8.0528	7.6891
9	10.1427	8.9973	8.3920	8.0462
9.5	10.4422	9.3213	8.7370	8.4085
10	10.7461	9.6502	9.0870	8.7757
10.5	11.0539	9.9838	9.4418	9.1474
11	11.3660	10.3219	9.8011	9.5232
11.5	11.6819	10.6643	10.1647	9.9030
12	12.0017	11.0109	10.5322	10.2861
12.5	12.3252	11.3614	10.9035	10.6726
13	12.6524	11.7158	11.2784	11.0620
13.5	12.9832	12.0737	11.6564	11.4541
14	13.3174	12.4352	12.0376	11.8487
14.5	13.6550	12.8000	12.4216	12.2456
15	13.9959	13.1679	12.8083	12.6444
15.5	14.3399	13.5388	13.1975	13.0452
16	14.6870	13.9126	13.5889	13.4476

Note: Use this table to figure almost any monthly mortgage payment. For example, an $80,000, 20-year loan at 11 percent will require a monthly payment of $825.75 ($10.3219 × 80); over 30 years it will require a monthly payment of $761.86 ($9.5232 × 80).

Large down payments can lower monthly payments.

Table 10.7 shows the progressively smaller monthly payments resulting from increasing the amount of the down payment. At 12 percent interest, a 30-year loan of $75,000 costs $771.46 per month. Making an extra $5000 down payment reduces the monthly payment to $720.03, and an additional $5000 reduces it further to $668.60.

People often prefer to make a smaller down payment so they can keep some funds to pay for moving-in expenses or to maintain a savings account. Others consider the after-tax return that might be earned on alternative investments if the extra down payment money were placed elsewhere. (Chapters 15 through 21 explore this topic in detail.)

Length of Maturity The total amount of interest on a loan is based on both the interest rate charged and the length of the repayment period. For loans with the same interest rate, the longer the term of repayment, the smaller is the payment size. However, the longer the term of repayment, the more interest is charged. Table 10.8 illustrates the relationship among maturity length, monthly payment, and interest cost. The monthly payment goes up as the term of the loan becomes shorter. For example, the monthly payment on a 12 percent loan is $720 for 30 years and $771 for 20 years. Note also that when the loan is paid back sooner, perhaps in 20 instead of 30 years, the total interest costs are much lower ($115,000 rather than $189,000, for a savings of $74,000).

TABLE 10.7
Effect of Down Payment Size on Monthly Payment
(12 Percent Mortgage Loan for 30 Years)

Amount of Loan	Approximate Monthly Payment
$75,000	$771.46
70,000	720.03
65,000	668.60
60,000	617.17
55,000	565.74
50,000	514.31

TABLE 10.8
Monthly Payment and Total Interest to Repay a $70,000 Loan*

Length of Loan	Interest Rate					
	8%	10%	12%	14%	16%	18%
30 years	$ 514	$ 614	$ 720	$ 829	$ 941	$ 1,056
	$115,000	$151,000	$189,000	$229,000	$269,000	$310,000
25 years	$ 540	$ 636	$ 737	$ 843	$ 951	$ 1,063
	$ 92,000	$121,000	$151,000	$183,000	$215,000	$249,000
20 years	$ 586	$ 676	$ 771	$ 870	$ 974	$ 1,081
	$ 71,000	$ 92,000	$115,000	$139,000	$164,000	$189,000

Note: Figures are rounded.
* The top figure in each pair is the monthly payment, and the bottom figure is total interest paid.

Buyers who can afford to make higher monthly payments than required on longer loans often choose a shorter-term mortgage loan. However, some buyers with this capability choose a longer-term loan anyway and place extra money in savings or make alternative investments.

Three Traditional Types of Financing

There are three variations of traditional home financing that have been popular for more than 60 years: the conventional mortgage loan, the mortgage assumption, and seller financing.

Conventional Mortgage Loan   The most traditional home loan is the conventional mortgage loan. This is the fixed-rate, fixed-payment loan described earlier, which the home buyer obtains directly from a financial institution. Since a lender's only protection against possible loss is the home itself, most require a down payment of 20 to 30 percent of the loan amount. On a $100,000 home, for example, a savings and loan association would likely lend only $70,000 to $80,000. Then, should the borrower default, the lender probably could sell the home for at least the amount of the outstanding loan balance. Lenders feel more secure with substantial down payments and often give a slightly reduced interest rate with them. Thus, with a down payment of $30,000, a lender might offer an interest rate one-quarter or one-half of 1 percent lower than with a $20,000 down payment. Note, however, that lenders may accept as little as 5 percent down if the mortgage is insured. Mortgage insurance is discussed on pages 369–371.

In recent years, some borrowers have opted for a *15-year mortgage,* which is nothing more than a conventional mortgage loan for a comparatively short 15-year maturity. Advantages include a faster buildup of equity, less paid out for interest, and a quicker payoff. A disadvantage is the necessarily higher monthly payment. For example, an $80,000 loan at 11 percent would require a $909.28 monthly payment (from Table 10.6; 80×11.3660) over 15 years as opposed to $761.86 ($80 \times 9.5232$) over 30 years.

Assumable Mortgage (ASM)   When buying a home, it may be possible to assume, or take over, the mortgage of the seller. More than 1 million mortgage loans a year are assumed by new purchasers through a written agreement made between the lender and the new owner. When an agreement is executed, the new buyer often obtains the loan at either the original interest rate or a rate below current market rates (called a *preferred rate*). In order to pay off the seller's equity, the buyer usually must make a substantial down payment or obtain a second mortgage.

A **second mortgage** is an additional loan on a residence besides the original mortgage, and in case of default, what is owed on the original mortgage is paid first. With this additional risk, the interest rate on a second mortgage is often 2 to 5 percent higher than an original mortgage rate. Second mortgages are used primarily to help consumers purchase or remodel homes. Suppose Robert and Louise Bond, a dual-earner family from Van Nuys, California, wish to buy a $150,000 home from the Roget family. The Bonds want to assume the Rogets' remaining mortgage of $70,000, but they have only $50,000 available to pay the Rogets for their $80,000 ($150,000 − $70,000) equity. A lender that thinks the Bonds can afford to make two mortgage payments might give them a second mortgage loan of $30,000 to make up the difference. Second mortgages often run from 3 to 10 years in length, so the new home owner can look forward eventually to having only one mortgage payment. However, a new home owner paying off both first and second mortgages may feel considerable budget stress.

Second mortgages are often used with assumable mortgages.

Seller Financing (SELF)   Seller financing occurs whenever the seller of a home agrees to accept all or a portion of the purchase price in installments rather than a lump sum. The Bond family in the preceding example could have used seller financing if the Rogets would have agreed to installment payments on the $30,000 the Bonds were short for the equity. Other

What If You Are Considering a Home-Equity Credit-Line Loan*

Most second mortgages take the form of an installment loan. In recent years, however, many people have taken out second mortgages structured more like a revolving credit account. These arrangements are referred to as **home-equity credit-line loans**, with the credit limit equal to a figure based on the owner's equity in the home. Lenders often set the credit limit as high as 80 percent of the equity in the home. Thus, if you own a home valued at a $140,000 with a first mortgage of $100,000, you may borrow up to a credit limit of $32,000 ($40,000 × 0.80).

Funds can be withdrawn from a home-equity credit-line loan at any time as long as the total debt does not exceed the credit limit. It may be possible to withdraw funds by telephone, writing a special check against the account, or through a bank credit card. Thus it may be possible to charge a meal at a restaurant by borrowing against your home; of course, this is a very unwise use of credit. What factors should you consider when deciding whether to obtain a home-equity credit-line loan?

1. Realize that home-equity credit-line loans have low interest rates. Because your home is the collateral, the interest rate on a home-equity credit-line loan will likely be 2 to 7 percentage points lower than for an installment loan or credit card or other open-end credit arrangement.
2. Be wary of low, teaser rates. Many home-equity credit lines carry an adjustable rate,

and lenders may offer an artificially low initial rate to induce people to sign up. Once the credit line is established, it may be tempting to use, yet later on the interest rate will increase.
3. Shop for low closing costs and points. Like other forms of mortgages, home-equity credit-line loans often require payment of loan origination fees when established. The amount of these fees is not regulated and varies considerably among lenders. Obviously, a loan with no initial fees is best if the APR is competitive.
4. Home-equity credit-line loan interest is tax deductible. The interest on your loan is deductible on federal income taxes (whereas regular credit card interest is not). All the interest on amounts borrowed (including the first mortgage) up to $100,000 is deductible regardless of how you use the funds. Interest on amounts over $100,000 and up to $1,000,000 is also deductible if the loan funds are used for home improvements.
5. Your wealth is at risk. For most people, the equity in their home is the largest single component of their net worth. Using and abusing a home-equity credit-line loan exposes this wealth to considerable risk. In fact, since the outstanding balance on the credit line is a liability on the personal balance sheet, you are directly lowering your net worth when you use the line of credit for purchases that may add little or nothing on the asset side.

* Home-equity credit-line loans are governed by appropriate federal regulations.

variations also exist. A seller may be willing to finance the entire purchase price for 20 or 30 years with a 10 or 20 percent down payment, acting much like a mortgage lending institution. Usually these loans are shorter-term arrangements, however, with payments based on amortization over 20 years or more but with a balloon payment due after 5 or 10 years.

Thus all principal not paid up to that point would be due. This extremely large sum generally would require refinancing by means of a conventional mortgage, which should not be difficult to obtain because of the equity built up in the property. Note, though, that interest rates could have risen dramatically, making it difficult for the buyer to budget the larger mortgage payments.

In most seller financing, the buyer obtains the title to the property upon moving in. However, this is not the case with a contract sale, a land contract, or a contract for deed. These latter situations are more risky for the buyer because all terms in the contract must be satisfied before obtaining title. This means that if you choose or must move before paying off the contract in full, you forfeit all money paid in installments to the seller and any appreciation in the home's value. In other words, you build no equity until the contract is completed.

Alternative Mortgage Loans

Mortgage loan rates in recent years have ranged from a low of 4.5 percent in 1972 to more than 20 percent in 1980. Such enormous swings created havoc in the lending industry, since lenders found themselves with thousands of low-rate mortgage loans outstanding while having to offer high interest rates to savers. New borrowers also suffered because monthly payments soared as a result of high interest rates: A $70,000 loan for 30 years at 9 percent has a monthly payment of $563.23; at 16 percent, it is $941.33, or 67 percent more. Alternative mortgage approaches have come about in response to these interest-rate fluctuations and the high cost of the dwellings themselves. In general, most new alternative lending approaches replace the long-term, fixed-rate, equal-payment type of mortgage loan with techniques to keep the monthly payment as low as possible. The lower payments also permit borrowers to purchase larger, more expensive homes than they could afford with a traditional fixed-rate loan.

Alternative mortgage loans may result in negative amortization.

Some of the newer mortgage loans allow smaller monthly payments than are actually necessary to pay the interest. This causes *negative amortization,* in which the principal loan balance actually rises. In later years, the borrower repays the larger principal amount due. For example, Table 10.3 illustrates that a payment of $700 is needed to pay the first month's interest on a 30-year $70,000 mortgage at 12 percent. If the monthly payment in the early years was only $675, the principal balance owed would increase each month. Higher payments, perhaps of $750, $800, or $900, would be required later to amortize the larger total principal and interest amounts owed because of the earlier negative amortization.

The alternative mortgage loans described below are the adjustable-rate mortgage, graduated-payment and lender buy-down mortgage, renegotiable-rate mortgage, shared-appreciation mortgage, growing-equity mortgage, and reverse-annuity mortgage.

Adjustable-Rate Mortgage (ARM)   With the **adjustable-rate mortgage**— sometimes called a *variable-rate mortgage*—a borrower's interest rate can fluctuate up or down according to some index of interest rates. The monthly payment could increase or decrease, perhaps monthly or quarterly.

Or the payment could remain fixed while the principal increased, causing negative amortization. Or the payment could remain constant, but the term of the loan might increase by several years. Lenders may offer rates at 1 to 3 percent or more below conventional mortgage rates to induce usage or guarantee that the rate will not increase for perhaps a 1- or 2-year period. Sometimes the lender will offer a **teaser rate** for the first year or two that is perhaps 5 percentage points below conventional loan rates. Later increases in the rate make monthly payments greater and perhaps unaffordable, forcing some borrowers to sell. However, if rates drop, the costs would be lower than those of a conventional mortgage. *Interest-rate caps,* which place a limit on the amount an interest rate can increase (perhaps no more than 2 percent per year in one direction and no more than 5 percent in one direction over the life of the loan) are common. ARMs with interest rate caps have been the most popular alternative mortgage. *Payment caps* limit the amount that the payment can vary on an ARM. Having a loan with a payment cap but without an equivalent interest-rate cap is an invitation to negative amortization. When interest rates change, payments should be allowed to change accordingly.

Beware of teaser rates that cause ARM payments to increase dramatically later on.

Three recent innovations in ARMs have been developed. The first is the *convertible adjustable-rate mortgage,* which allows conversion of an ARM to a fixed-rate mortgage, usually during years 2 through 5 of the ARM. The fee for the conversion is around $500, as compared with several thousand dollars if the borrower wanted to pay off (refinance) the ARM with a fixed-rate loan. On the downside, the fixed interest rate after conversion is usually $\frac{1}{4}$ percentage point higher than a fixed-rate loan obtained through refinancing. The second innovation is the *reduction-option loan (ROL).* This arrangement begins as a fixed-rate loan that allows a one-time optional adjustment in the interest rate to current rates during years 2 through 6 of the original loan. If rates have dropped, you can take the option and reduce your payments. If rates do not drop, you simply choose not to exercise your option. The third innovation is a *price-level-adjusted mortgage.* The initial rate is extremely low, perhaps 4 percent, and amortization does occur. The rate is subsequently adjusted according to the inflation rate over the years. Payments go up to reflect the higher interest rates. Since prices could triple or quadruple over a 20-year period, so could the interest rate on the loan. Hopefully, income would keep up with inflation, maintaining the affordability of the loan payments. The risk is that income will not keep up.

Graduated-Payment Mortgage (GPM) and Lender Buy-Down Mortgage

Smaller-than-normal payments are required in the early years but gradually increase to larger-than-normal payments in later years with these two types of mortgages. The assumption that increased income will be available for the higher payments justifies taking on one of these mortgages. With the graduated-payment mortgage, the interest rate remains the same, but payments early in the mortgage are lower than necessary to pay even the interest. Then payments could increase 2.5 percent each year for 5 years and then level off. Or the payment could be level for 5 years and then rise 15 percent for the next 5 years, with another rise of 15 percent 5 years

Graduated-payment mortgages result in negative amortization during the first few years.

later, and so forth. Because payments in the beginning are less than the interest owed, the result is negative amortization.

With the lender buy-down mortgage, it is the interest rate that changes, triggering corresponding changes in the monthly payments. First-time home buyers often use buy-down mortgages to take advantage of lower monthly payments in early years of the loan. A base interest rate is set, usually 0.5 percentage points above current fixed rates. For the first year, you would pay a rate 2 percentage points below the base rate. In the second, you would pay a rate 1 point below the base. In the third and future years, the base rate would be changed. Unlike an adjustable-rate mortgage, these changes are known in advance and are contractual. Negative amortization does not occur with a buy-down mortgage.

A rollover mortgage is really a series of short-term loans.

Renegotiable-Rate, or Rollover, Mortgage (RRM) This mortgage is a series of short-term loans for 2 to 5 years, but with total amortization spread over the usual 25 to 30 years. The loan must be renewed each time period. If interest rates have increased, the borrower can increase the monthly payments, extend the term of the loan, or seek another mortgage loan from a different source. Rates usually cannot change more than one-half of 1 percent per year or more than a total of 5 percent.

Shared-Appreciation Mortgage (SAM) In this mortgage arrangement, the lender offers an interest rate about one-third less than the market rate in exchange for the right to receive perhaps one-third of any appreciation in the home's value when the home is sold or after 10 years. One question is, should the lender share in any increase as a result of home improvements made by the borrower? If so, how? Also, how does the borrower pay the lender's share of the appreciation after 10 years if the home has not been sold?

Growing-Equity Mortgage (GEM) The GEM is for people who design their loan in advance to reduce interest costs by paying off the mortgage loan early. The payments on the fixed-interest loan are scheduled to increase by a predetermined amount each year, perhaps 2 to 7 percent. The increase goes toward reducing the principal owed, so, for example, a 30-year mortgage may be paid off in 15 years.

Paying additional amounts on the principal reduces the time period of the debt.

One form of GEM is the *biweekly mortgage,* which calls for payments every 2 weeks of half the normal monthly payment. The result is 26 payments per year. For example, the loan in Table 10.3 requires a $720.03 monthly payment for a total of $8640.36 (12 × $720.03) paid in 1 year. On a biweekly basis with payments of $360.02, the total payments per year would be $9360.52. The difference of $720.16 ($9360.52 − $8640.36) is equivalent to an extra monthly payment per year and is applied to the principal of the loan. The biweekly repayment plan would result in the loan being repaid in approximately 19 years rather than 30 years under the monthly payment plan. Of course, almost all types of mortgage loans will permit payment of additional amounts toward principal without penalty.

Reverse-annuity mort-
gages allow borrowing
against the equity of a
paid-for home.

Reverse-Annuity Mortgage (RAM) A RAM allows a home owner to borrow against the equity in a home that is fully paid for and receive the proceeds in a series of monthly payments often over a period of from 5 to 10 years. The most likely prospects for such loans are the elderly who have paid off their mortgages but are strapped for income. No interest is charged during the time period of the loan, and the home is sold to pay the accrued interest and principal at the end of the loan period, which is usually set to be after the owner's death. An owner could sell his or her home to obtain income, but the RAM allows the person to continue living in the home. A sale would not. A risk of these loans is that the borrower might outlive the loan agreement, finding himself or herself with no home and no equity.

What Does It Cost to Buy a House?

Objective
To be able to identify the numerous costs of buying a home.

Some prospective home buyers look at homes that are too expensive but end up buying them anyway. Such a buyer will have a nice home but may also be what is called "home poor." This home owner will spend such a great proportion of income on housing costs that there will be very little money left over for other items. To avoid becoming home poor, the wise financial planner carefully estimates all initial and subsequent costs of housing and thus makes more knowledgeable decisions.

In the discussion that follows, we assume that the prospective home owner has the funds necessary for the down payment to buy an $80,000 home. We use an alternative mortgage approach, so the down payment is only 5 percent ($4000). All other costs are described below, and Table 10.9 shows a summary of estimated costs.

Choosing Between Buying Now or Waiting

If you think you can predict the future and know when home prices and interest rates will drop, you should wait before buying. If not, you should buy as soon as you are able. Even during an economic recession, home prices generally rise every year.

Table 10.10 shows the financial consequences of waiting instead of buying now. Assume you are considering waiting to buy a $90,000 home with a 30-year, 12 percent mortgage loan, hoping that interest rates will drop next year. If the rate does drop to 11 percent and the price of the home rises only 6 percent, you may gain a little. Instead of a down payment of $9000, you will pay $9540. Furthermore, the monthly payment on the current 12 percent, $81,000 mortgage loan is $833.17, but next year on the 11 percent, $85,860 loan it will be $817.66, a savings of $15.51 per month. If you guess wrong about next year's interest rates and they remain at 12 percent, the monthly payment on $85,860 will be $883.16. This is an extra $49.99 per month and $17,996.40 over the life of the loan.

TABLE 10.9

Estimated Buying and Closing Costs (Purchase Price of Home, $80,000; Closing on July 1)

Home Buying Costs	At Closing	Monthly
Down payment	$4,000	—
Points (2)	1,520	—
Principal and interest (30 years, 12 percent, $76,000; from Table 10.6)	—	$781.74
Taxes (for first half-year)	450	75.00
Insurance (home owner's policy)	480	40.00
Private mortgage insurance	—	31.67
Loan application fee	160	—
Loan origination fee	400	—
Title search	100	—
Title insurance (to protect lender)	190	—
Title insurance (to protect borrower)	190	—
Attorney's fee	200	—
Credit report	25	—
Recording fees	20	—
Appraisal fee	150	—
Real estate transfer tax (2 percent)	1,600	—
Termite and radon inspection fee	130	—
Survey fee	100	—
Notary fee		—
	$9,740	$928.41
Less amount provided by seller	450*	
Subtotal	$9,290	
Warranty insurance (optional)	240	20.00
Mortgage life insurance (optional)	312	26.00
Totals	$9,842	$974.41

* Funds from seller to pay taxes for first 6 months of the year.

Principal and Interest

The mortgage loan requires repayment of both principal (P) and interest (I). The monthly payment schedule shown earlier in Table 10.6 (page 359) gives the amount needed per month to repay each $1000 of mortgage loan at different interest rates. To estimate this amount, simply multiply the figures. For our 30-year, 12 percent loan, the amount in the table is $10.2861. In our example, the loan amount is $76,000 ($80,000 − $4000); multiplying 76 by $10.2861 gives a monthly payment of $781.74 to repay the principal and interest.

Taxes and Insurance

The acronym PITI stands for principal, interest, taxes, and insurance.

Taxes (T) and insurance (I) are the last part of the popular abbreviation **PITI**, which realtors and lenders often use to indicate a mortgage payment that includes principal, interest, taxes, and insurance. As discussed later

TABLE 10.10
Buy a House Now or Wait? (Assumes a 6 Percent Increase in the Price of a House in 1 Year)

Cost to buy now

Price	$90,000
Down payment (10 percent)	9,000
Mortgage loan	81,000

Fixed-rate mortgage over 30 years, monthly payment at

8%	$594.35
9%	651.74
10%	710.83
11%	771.38
12%	833.17
13%	896.02
14%	959.74
15%	1,024.20
16%	1,089.26

Cost to wait a year and buy with 6 percent increase

Price	$95,400
Down payment (10 percent)	9,540
Mortgage loan	85,860

Fixed-rate mortgage over 30 years, monthly payment at

8%	$630.01
9%	690.85
10%	753.48
11%	817.66
12%	883.16
13%	949.78
14%	1,017.33
15%	1,086.56
16%	1,154.61

in this chapter, real estate property taxes must be paid to local governments. The total amount, $900 in our example, is due once a year when the government sends out its tax bill. This amount varies by community, usually ranging from 1 to 4 percent of the cost of the home. Most lenders require that the borrower prepay a pro rata share (one-twelfth) of the estimated real estate taxes each month ($75 here) along with the monthly principal and interest. If a buyer takes possession at the midpoint of the tax year, the seller should make one-half ($450 here) of the taxes due available to the buyer on the day of **closing**. This is the day when the home is financially and legally transferred to the new buyer, which usually takes place in the office of the lender or an attorney.

Lenders always require home owners to insure the home itself in case of fire or other calamity. Insurance on the contents of the home is up to the home owner. Both the home and its contents can be covered in a typical home owner's insurance policy. (Chapter 12 covers this information

Understanding Real Estate Property Taxes

The major source of revenue for most communities, to provide for numerous community services and schools, is **real estate property taxes.** These are local (town, city, county, township, parish) taxes based on the determined value of buildings and land. Since a tax bill on a typical home could amount to $600, $3000, or even more, prospective home owners need to learn something about the process of such taxation and how to legally avoid some of those taxes, if possible.

The process of determining real estate tax liability begins when local government officials establish a **fair market value** for the owner's home and land. This value should be what "a willing buyer would pay a willing seller." Next the **assessed** (or *taxable*) **value** of the property is calculated. This value is established arbitrarily by the local tax assessor or by law as a fixed percentage of fair market value (perhaps 50, 60, or 100 percent). A home with a fair market value of $100,000, for example, might have an assessed value of $60,000. The real estate tax rate is the percentage then levied on assessed valuations of property. Property with a taxable value of $60,000 at a tax rate of 30 mills (each mill represents one one-thousandth of a dollar) would have a tax liability of $1800 ($60,000 × 0.030).

When you consider purchasing a home, find out how the property taxes are assessed, what the amount of the most recent tax liability was (by telephoning the tax assessor), and whether local officials expect the taxes to rise substantially in the next year or so. It is not enough to know that one community has a tax rate of 20 mills and a neighboring community has one of 25 mills. Although you can do little to affect the tax rate on real estate property, you can claim that the assessed valuation on your home is too high. If your appeal is successful, your tax bill will be lowered accordingly.

in detail.) The annual premium must be paid each year in advance. Most lenders require prepayment of a pro rata share (one-twelfth) each month ($40 here) of the next year's estimated insurance premium. Additionally, on closing day the purchaser must be prepared to prepay 1 year's premium ($480 here).

Funds deposited with a lender for taxes and insurance go into an **escrow account,** which is a special reserve account used to pay third parties. Most lenders pay interest on funds deposited for taxes and insurance until the bills arrive at the financial institution; these are then paid out of the escrow account by the lender, who acts as the borrower's agent.

Mortgage Insurance

When a buyer makes a minimum down payment, a lender almost always requires the purchase of mortgage insurance. In this example, assume a premium charge totaling one-half of 1 percent of the mortgage loan (0.005 × $76,000 = $380), which must be prepaid monthly ($31.67 here) to the lender, who forwards it to the mortgage insurance company. There are several sources of mortgage insurance.

Privately Insured Mortgage   A conventional loan can be obtained by people with a good income and credit rating but who are unable to make a substantial down payment. In such situations, the lender simply requires the borrower to purchase **private mortgage insurance,** which insures the first 20 percent of a loan in case of default. For example, a lender could loan a home buyer $95,000 for a $100,000 home with only a $5000 down payment. The mortgage insurance company would insure 20 percent, or $19,000 ($95,000 × 20 percent), of the debt, which would assure the lender payment of the loan balance if the home were later repossessed for default and sold for perhaps only $80,000.

Mortgage insurance protects the lender.

Private mortgage insurance for a borrower is typically arranged by the financial institution. The largest private mortgage insurer is the Mortgage Guaranty Insurance Corporation (MGIC, pronounced "magic"). On top of the mortgage payment for principal and interest, the cost is usually one-half of 1 percent of the mortgage loan for the first 5 years and one-quarter of 1 percent thereafter, or until the unpaid balance drops to 80 percent of the original loan. At that point it may be possible to cancel the insurance, but it is up to the borrower to request the cancellation.

FHA-Insured Mortgage   Because of the favorable lending terms, many borrowers seek government mortgage insurance and guarantees instead of private mortgage insurance. To encourage lending, the **Federal Housing Administration (FHA)** of the federal government's Department of Housing and Urban Development (HUD) insures loans that meet its standards. The borrower must be creditworthy, and the home must be approved. Most new homes meet the minimum-quality standards of the FHA and are approved.

The borrower goes to the usual lenders, and the FHA insures the mortgage so that the lender will not lose money if the borrower defaults. Like private mortgage insurers, the FHA charges borrowers a mortgage insurance premium. This premium is paid in total as an up-front, lump-sum payment or may be financed.

Usually, only very small down payments are required, since this is a federally backed loan. Down payment minimums are calculated as follows: 3 percent on the first $25,000 of appraised value and 5 percent on amounts above $25,000. FHA-insured mortgage loans can be made on homes that do not exceed FHA lending limits, which change frequently and vary across the country according to local housing market prices. Terms can be as long as 30 years, and the waiting time to process an application is often 60 to 90 days.

VA-Guaranteed Mortgage   The **Veterans Administration (VA)** promotes home ownership among veterans by providing the lender with a guarantee against buyer default. Mobile homes also qualify. In effect, the VA guarantee is much like that of the FHA or private insurers because the lender is protected for a portion of the value of the loan in the event the home must be repossessed and sold. Homes must meet VA standards of construction (most newer homes do), and only veterans qualify under this program. Little or no down payment is required on VA loans. Lending limits are set by the VA. Usually 60 to 90 days are needed to approve an application.

Points

A point is equal to 1 percent of the mortgage loan amount.

A **point** is a fee equal to 1 percent of the total loan amount, and it must be paid in full when the home is bought. For example, if a lender charges 2 points on a $60,000 loan, this amounts to a charge of $1200. Note that by law these points do not have to be included in calculating the annual percentage rate (APR). However, each point charged would increase the annual percentage rate approximately 0.125 percent. Most lenders charge points.

Lenders also charge points to increase the yield on FHA and VA mortgage loans to what market conditions demand. These government-regulated loans have interest rates that are always set lower than prevailing conventional mortgage interest rates. For example, if conventional mortgage loans average 12 percent, FHA and VA loans will probably be about 11 percent. Lenders must be encouraged to make such below-market-rate loans. Accordingly, the lender charges the seller or the buyer of a home 1 or more points. When sellers of FHA and VA homes pay points, most simply increase the sales price of the home by an equivalent amount when negotiating a price with a prospective purchaser who intends to use FHA or VA mortgage assistance. Home purchasers are protected to some extent from these inflated prices because the FHA and VA will not insure loans for more than the appraised value of the home.

Additionally, points are often used in connection with a **loan origination fee.** This is what the lender charges the borrower for doing all the paperwork and setting up the mortgage loan. This fee usually ranges from 1 to 2 percent of the amount of the loan, or 1 or 2 points.

Title Insurance

A deed transfers ownership of real estate.

The **title** to real property is the legal right of ownership interest. In real estate transactions, the title is transferred to a new owner through a **deed,** which is a written document used to convey real estate ownership. Usually with the assistance of an attorney at closing, the buyer reviews various documents to ensure having as clear a title as possible. Examples of claims against property include electrical work that a previous owner never paid for and the sale of mineral rights perhaps 75 years ago.

There are four types of deeds used: (1) a *warranty deed* is the safest, since it guarantees that the title is free of any previous mortgages; (2) a *special warranty deed* guarantees only that the current owner has not placed any mortgage encumbrances on the title; (3) a *quitclaim deed* transfers whatever title the current owner had in the property with no guarantee whatsoever; (4) a *deed of bargain and sale* conveys title with or without a guarantee with an assertion that the seller had an ownership interest.

If the quality of the deed is suspect, a title search and the purchase of title insurance can offer better protection. An attorney or title company can inspect court records and prepare a detailed written history of property ownership called an *abstract.* In a **title search,** an attorney examines the abstract and other documents and may issue a **certificate of title.** This is a legal opinion (not a guarantee) of the status of the title and is often provided when an abstract is unavailable or lost. The seller normally pays the fees for preparation of these documents.

A lender often requires a buyer to purchase **title insurance** because it protects the lender's interest if the title is later found faulty. A *separate* title insurance policy must be purchased by home owners if they wish to insure their own interest. Policies for home owners usually cover only the amount of the down payment (the beginning equity) rather than any appreciating equity occurring over the years. The premium for each title policy varies among title companies. The one-time charge at closing may amount to one-quarter of 1 percent of the amount of the loan for each policy ($190 here).

In areas where real estate transfers are frequent, the wise money manager might want to ask a title insurance company about a **reissue rate.** This is a policy with lower-rate premiums because the property history has been checked in recent years. Some home owners do not purchase title insurance for themselves, assuming that the title insurance company will successfully fight any claims; this may not be true, however.

Employing the Services of an Attorney

About half of all home buyers hire an attorney to represent them during closing to review all documents and provide advice. Fees are commonly one-half of 1 percent of the purchase price of the home, although some attorneys do this work for as low as one-quarter of 1 percent. (The attorney's fee is $200 in our example.)

Miscellaneous Costs

A credit report normally must be compiled before a home buyer can obtain a loan. The borrower pays the fee for this report too. Recording fees are charged to transfer ownership documents in the county courthouse. An **appraisal fee** may be required for a professionally prepared estimate of the value of the property by an objective party. A *survey* is sometimes required to certify the specific boundaries of the lot. Occasionally, fees are charged for termite and radon inspections. Many local communities have implemented *real estate transfer taxes* as a revenue-generating measure. Tax rates can be as high as 4 percent of the purchase price of a home. Finally, separate *notary fees* may be charged for the services of those legally qualified to certify (or notarize) signatures.

The costs for most home-buying expenses are set by tradition and are subject to negotiation. The wise financial manager shops for better prices whenever possible. (Table 10.9 shows sample fee amounts.)

The federal Real Estate Settlement Procedures Act requires that on or before closing day a "good faith estimate" of all specific closing costs be given to the borrower. Each borrower also must receive a settlement information booklet that explains many details of the closing process.

Depending on state laws, closing costs could vary from 1 percent of the mortgage loan up to 4 or 5 percent. Prospective home owners should visit a lender to get an idea of total closing costs in their community.

Warranty Insurance

All homes for sale carry some type of **implied warranty,** which is a legal doctrine in all states suggesting a promise of a certain level of quality that an ordinary buyer has a right to expect. Thus the heating unit and air conditioner should work at the time the buyer purchases the home. This does not mean, however, that they must still be working 2 years from purchase of the home. Nor does an implied warranty mean that the roof will not have a small leak or that water will not slowly seep into the basement. A seller who knowingly hides such serious defects might be liable, but the buyer will have to hire an attorney and sue.

It is possible to buy a warranty on your new home.

Warranty insurance provides another option for the home owner. Home protection warranty insurance is sold through real estate brokers for a one-time premium of perhaps $200 to $500. Buyers no longer need simply to trust the seller's assurances on the apparent good quality of the home. If the central air-conditioning unit fails at a cost of $1800, the home owner need pay only an insurance deductible of perhaps $250 and the insurance company will pay the rest. No inspection of the home is needed unless the policy also covers structural defects. The largest insurance company in the field is American Home Shield.

For new homes, the industry trade group the National Association of Home Builders (NAHB) has established a Home Owners Warranty Corporation (HOW), made up of more than 100 local councils of builders. Participating builders pay a beginning one-time insurance premium on all their homes, plus a service fee each of the years the warranty is in effect. These costs are built into the sale price of each home. The builder is responsible for repairs during the first 2 years and an insurance company is responsible for the remaining term, usually 8 more years. About 40 percent of new houses being sold today are protected by the HOW program.

A little-known benefit of having a mortgage loan insured by the FHA or guaranteed by the VA is that newly built homes have a 1-year warranty against the builder failing to meet specifications. Further, defects that seriously affect livability can be repaired at government expense during the first 4 years of ownership.

Special Considerations in the Home-Buying Process

Objective
To be able to list and describe the steps in the home-buying process.

A **realtor,** or **broker,** is a person licensed by a state to provide advice and assistance, usually for a fee, to both buyers and sellers of real estate. If you are unfamiliar with housing in an area or if you need special financing arrangements to pay for your housing, the services of a realtor could be invaluable. Realtors are also often a good source of information about rental housing.

Realtors typically earn a commission of 6 to 7 percent on the sale price of a home. Since the seller pays this commission, it is included in the sale price. A realtor can show you housing that is *listed* (under contract with the seller and the realtor) by the realty firm. In addition, many communities have a **multiple-listing service**, which is an information and referral network among real estate brokers allowing properties listed with a particular realtor to be shown by all other realtors as well. (This also may be called an *open listing*.) Although realtors primarily represent the seller in all transactions, by custom, the realtor is supposed to be fair to both buyer and seller. However, the realtor's legal obligation is to the party that will pay his or her fee/commission, generally the seller. Buyers should keep this in mind and hire their own broker if they need such services.

After you find the home you really want, the buying process can move rapidly. The steps in home buying are very similar to the planned buying steps outlined in Chapter 9. Special attention will need to be paid, however, to (1) fitting the cost of buying into your budget, (2) negotiating, (3) shopping for a mortgage loan, and (4) signing your name on closing day.

Fitting the Home to Your Budget

Lifestyle changes may be required to fit the home to your budget.

The wise financial manager adds a few more budget items when considering buying a home. For starters, some estimate ought to be made for maintenance. It could range from $15 to $20 monthly for a small owned apartment up to $40 to $50 for a single-family dwelling. Other budget items could be for moving-in costs and new furniture and tools. These expenses are likely to be much higher during the first year of ownership than in later years. Research shows that people spend in excess of $2500 on such items. It may be helpful to estimate the cost of utilities as well. The previous owner may agree to show you receipts of the past year with which to develop your estimates. Budgetary forms to help in estimating costs are shown in Chapter 4.

Negotiating

Sellers and buyers should expect to negotiate the price of a home.

It is essential that you be prepared to negotiate the terms of a home purchase. Sellers of homes generally put a sales price on the property 5 to 10 percent higher than what they expect to get for it. Therefore, you probably should make an offer to buy that is somewhat lower than the asking price. Perhaps $10,000 to $20,000 is at stake here.

Make an Offer to Buy   Once you have selected the home you wish to purchase, you will make an offer to the seller. The written offer to purchase real estate is called an **offer to purchase**. Of course, you will specify a price. However, other aspects of the sale also may be included in your offer. Examples of conditions you might want to list are seller-paid termite and radon inspections; certification of the plumbing, heating, cooling, and electrical systems; inclusion of the living room drapes and kitchen appliances in the purchase price; and financing terms approved by your lender.

At the time you make an offer, you will want to give the seller some **earnest money** as a deposit to ensure that the seller will not sell the house to someone else while you are negotiating. Make sure that your earnest money is protected by a **contingency clause** in the offer to purchase that stipulates that the money will be refunded by the seller if you cannot obtain satisfactory financing within a specified time period, usually 30 days. This protects you if lending conditions suddenly become unfavorable or if you are turned down for a loan. Earnest money is usually kept in an escrow account. Of course, if you simply change your mind about buying, you may forfeit your earnest money.

Respond to a Counteroffer   Most people who sell their homes do not accept the first offer. They assume that if a buyer is willing to make a formal offer of X amount of dollars, that buyer may be willing to pay X plus a few thousand dollars more. The seller might make you an official *counteroffer,* which is a legal offer to sell (or buy) a home at a different price and perhaps with different conditions. Realize that if a seller is willing to make you a counteroffer, he or she may be willing to sell even at a slightly lower price. Thus, if you then make a counteroffer between the two prices, a sale will usually result. However, if you push the seller too far, you risk having the seller back out of the negotiations altogether. Remember that while all this dickering is going on, the seller could be receiving (though not accepting) offers from other prospective buyers.

Sign a Purchase Contract   A **purchase contract** or **sales contract** is the formal legal document that outlines the actual agreement that results from the real estate negotiations. It includes the agreed-on price and a list of conditions you want that the seller has agreed to accept. It is wise to use preprinted forms available from real estate professionals and attorneys, since they often include protective clauses. A seller may request additional earnest money because he or she has agreed to take his home off the market and sell to you. All earnest money will be applied to the down payment on the home at closing.

Applying for a Mortgage Loan

Prior to actually negotiating with a seller, you should have talked with lenders to get a good idea of the mortgage terms available in your community. Only after you sign a purchase contract will you formally apply for a mortgage loan on the specific home you have selected. The financial institution usually approves or disapproves the loan within 10 days. Your exact interest rate may be the current rate at the time of application *or* the rate at the time of closing.

You formally apply for a mortgage loan after signing a purchase contract.

You may wish to obtain a mortgage lock-in if you expect rates to rise between the time you apply for the loan and the actual closing. A *mortgage lock-in* is a lender's promise to hold a certain interest rate (and possibly the number of points) for a specified period of time. It may be part of, but is not the same as a loan commitment. A *loan commitment* is a lender's promise to grant a loan.

Sign Your Name on Closing Day

Everybody and everything come together at the closing.

The buyer and seller and their representatives generally meet in the lender's office on closing day and sign all required documents. The buyer must be prepared to write several checks, including one for the purchase price itself. You might want to review the middle column of Table 10.9 for a list of all the items that are addressed during the closing. Closing costs in the illustration amounted to $9842.

The Real Estate Settlement Procedures Act (RESPA) governs the disclosure and procedures to be used during a closing on owner-occupied housing. The benefit of this law is that it provides buyers with information about closings. Lenders must provide borrowers with *Closing Costs and You: A HUD Guide for Homebuyers*. This booklet alerts buyers to the items that will be addressed and paid for during the closing. Buyers can use this information to shop around for the best deal on such items as appraisals, title insurance, home owner's insurance, and attorney services.

Selling a Home: A Lesson in Role Reversal

Objective
To be able to identify some important concerns in the process of selling a home.

Although most of this chapter deals with buying a home, there also are important considerations when selling a home. Generally it helps to do some minor painting, cleaning, and repairing before listing your home for sale. Let's examine the pros and cons of listing your home with a realtor, note some of the costs of selling, become aware of some dangers of seller financing, and consider some aspects of income taxes.

Should You List with a Realtor or Sell a Home Yourself?

Knowing that the sales commission to a realtor on a $100,000 home could easily be $6000 or $7000 is usually enough motivation for home owners to consider selling the home themselves. About one-third of home sales each year do not involve realtors. The key is to know what price to ask for your home. Asking too little could cost you much more than the commissions paid to a realtor.

Many home owners begin by contacting a few realtors to get their opinions on how much their home is worth. Realtors are often most willing to give their opinions, since the home owner might list the home with them if it does not sell quickly. A "For Sale" sign on your lawn and about $100 in advertising should keep your telephone ringing for a month or so with all types of inquiries. If your home does not sell by then, perhaps you should list with a realtor.

Realtors generally require that home owners sign a **listing agreement** permitting them to list the property exclusively and/or with a multiple-listing service. When there may be only a few prospective buyers, a multiple-listing service may work best, since every broker in the community can show and sell the home. Brokers are invaluable in "qualifying" (keeping people away who want to visit homes they simply cannot afford) prospective buyers and distinguishing between serious buyers and people who are just looking. If your broker cannot find a buyer within 60 days, you should consider signing an agreement with another broker who might be more aggressive in advertising and selling your property. A sale that occurs (or begins) during the time period of the listing agreement will result in a commission paid to the realtor even if you find the buyer on your own.

Selling Carries Its Own Costs

A realtor's commission is the largest selling cost, and sellers typically are unaware that many brokers will negotiate their commission. Most sellers also pay for the cost of updating the title with a title search. Some sellers get a professional appraisal as well.

Most mortgage loans have a prepayment fee if the home is sold before the mortgage has been fully paid off.

An often-overlooked selling cost is a **prepayment fee** charged by the mortgage lender. This fee is designed to discourage people from refinancing a mortgage every time interest rates drop. Most mortgage loans are paid off before maturity because people move and have to sell. Almost all mortgage loan contracts, therefore, include a clause that specifies a prepayment fee or penalty. This is often 1 to 3 percent of the original mortgage loan. On an $80,000 mortgage loan, for example, the charge would be from $800 to $2400.

Many home sellers have an existing loan with an interest rate well below current market rates. A low rate could make it much easier to sell a home through a loan assumption rather than making the buyer obtain his or her own mortgage, but only if no due-on-sale clause is in the original mortgage loan agreement. A **due-on-sale clause** requires that the mortgage loan be paid off if the home is sold. This clause can impose a heavy burden on the seller, since it generally prohibits a buyer from assuming the mortgage loan. The U.S. Supreme Court has upheld the constitutionality of such clauses whether expressly written in the loan agreement or implied by various state laws. Avoid this clause, if possible, when buying, since it eliminates one selling option. If you are unclear about your present mortgage loan clause, simply telephone your lender for clarification.

Be Wary of Seller Financing

Sellers having trouble marketing their homes have successfully resorted to many variations of seller financing, although serious difficulties can arise. Suppose you have a home worth $100,000 with a mortgage loan balance of $45,000 and equity of $55,000. The buyer assumes the existing mortgage loan, puts up $20,000 in cash, and takes out a second mortgage from you of $35,000 for 5 years. At closing, the broker gets $6000 in commission and you come away with only $14,000 cash. This is a small sum for you to use to make a down payment on another home. Also, think what could happen if the buyer cannot make the second mortgage payments to you and defaults on the loan.

Income Taxation Affects Selling Decisions

If you sell a home for more than you paid, you will have a taxable gain. Such gains may be taxed at the same rates as income from ordinary sources. A home bought for $80,000 and sold for $100,000, for example, would yield proceeds of $20,000. If your marginal tax rate is 28 percent, the tax on the $20,000 would be $5600.

IRS regulations permit deferring tax payment on capital gains from home sales if all the proceeds from one sale are invested in another home or in a newly constructed home within 24 months. You can defer taxable gains for years by buying another, higher-priced home within the IRS time limits each time you sell. At age 55, another more generous tax break becomes available: Home owners aged 55 and older who have lived in their last home for 3 of the past 5 years before selling it are allowed a once-in-a-lifetime capital gains exclusion amounting to the first $125,000 of accumulated gains. This might be a prize worth waiting for.

Remember too that your tax liability may be lowered if you maintained accurate records of home improvements you made over the years (such as constructing a new garage or adding shrubbery) that added to the value of your property. (See Chapter 3 for an example of such records.) These can be subtracted from any taxable gains resulting from the sale of a home. The IRS requires proof of tax-deductible expenses.

Summary

1. Most people have seven categories of goals in housing that reflect to some extent their values; these include functionality, efficiency, internal ambience, external ambience, mobility, safety, and manageable cost.

2. When we compare the pros and cons of renting versus buying housing, renting may look advantageous because of its low initial cost and ease of mobility.

3. Renters generally pay out less money in terms of cash flow, while owners/buyers have tax advantages and usually see an increase in the value of the home, permitting them to be financially better off in the long run.

4. The decision to spend a certain amount of money on housing should be based on careful budget analysis and an avoidance of overreliance on outdated rules of thumb.

5. Besides rent, other factors you should compare when considering rental units are security-deposit requirements, late charges, and restrictive subleasing clauses.

6. Tenants have several legal rights; in some states these include withhold-

ing rent for landlord noncompliance with the lease, as well as requiring that security deposits be returned in a timely manner.

7. Condominiums and cooperatives are increasing in popularity as apartment-style homes in part because they are less expensive than single-family dwellings.

8. Successful strategies to get needed financing to purchase a home include gifts from relatives and renting a home with an option to buy.

9. Traditional mortgage loans for homes are amortized. Amortization is the process of gradually paying off a mortgage through a series of periodic payments to a lender.

10. Numerous alternative types of mortgages are available that have reduced the importance of the long-term, fixed-rate mortgage loan in addition to providing ways to keep the monthly payment as low as possible.

11. Mathematics show that most people considering buying a home might be wise to buy it as soon as possible instead of waiting, even if interest rates are slowly declining.

12. The wise financial planner tries to avoid becoming "home poor" by carefully estimating all housing costs, such as principal and interest, taxes and insurance, title insurance, and closing costs.

13. The major source of revenue for local communities is often the real estate property tax, which is calculated on the basis of the assessed value of the property.

14. In addition to determining needs and wants and doing preshopping research, four steps that expedite the process of buying a home include (1) fitting the cost of buying into your budget, (2) negotiating, (3) shopping for a mortgage loan, and (4) signing your name on closing day.

15. When selling a home, it is wise to consider the pros and cons of listing with a real estate broker or selling the home itself, the extent of selling costs, the dangers of seller financing, and the impact of income taxes.

Modern
Money
Management

The Johnsons Decide to Buy a Condominium

Belinda Johnson's parents and maternal grandmother have combined their finances and presented Harry and Belinda with $15,000 for them to use to purchase a condominium. The Johnsons have shopped and found two that they like very much. The financial alternatives are presented in the following information, and the data for Condo 1 are summarized in the accompanying table.

Condo 1: Price, $85,000; Taxes, $600; Insurance, $240

	Loan Term and Type	Interest Rate	Down Payment	Loan Amount	Points	Other Closing Costs	Total Closing Costs	P&I Payment	PMI	Taxes	Insurance	Total Monthly Payments
Developer A	30, ARM	9%	$ 8,500	$76,500	$1530	—	$10,030	$615.53	$48	$50	$20	$733.53
Lender C	30, CON	12%	$17,000	$68,000	$ 680	—	$17,680	$699.45	$ 0	$50	$20	$769.45
Lender D	15, CON	11.5%	$17,000	$68,000	$ 680	—	$17,680	$794.37	$ 0	$50	$20	$864.37
Lender E	20, REN*	9.5%	$ 8,500	$76,500	$2295	—	$10,795	$713.08	$44	$50	$20	$827.08

* Renegotiable every 5 years.

1. Study the financial information for Condo 1 in the table and create a similar table for Condo 2 using the financial information given.
2. Which plan has the lowest total closing costs? Highest?
3. If the Johnsons had enough spare cash to make the 20 percent down payment (which they do not), would you recommend lender C or D? Why?
4. Assuming that the Johnsons will need about $2500 for moving-in costs (in addition to closing costs) and they have to choose between developer A or B, which would you recommend. Why?
5. Choose the best of the five options for the Johnsons and explain briefly why you recommend that developer or lender.
6. Use the information in Table 10.6 or the Personal Finance Cookbook (PFC) program MORTLOAN to calculate the monthly payment for the Johnsons if after 5 years the interest for their ARM has jumped to the maximum of 14 percent with a remaining balance of $74,500. What would the payment be if the rate dropped to 9.5 percent?

Financing Details on Two Condominiums Available to the Johnsons

Condo 1: Price: $85,000
Developer A will finance with a 10 percent down payment and a 9 percent ARM 30-year loan with 2 points as a loan origination fee. The initial monthly payment for principal and interest is $615.53 ($76,500 after the down payment results in 76.5 × $8.0462). After 1 year the rate goes to 10 percent, with a principal plus interest payment of $670.48. At that point, the rate can go up or down as much as 2 percent per year, depending on the cost of an index of mortgage funds. There is a cap of 5 percent over the life of the loan. Taxes are estimated to be about $600, and the home owner's insurance premium should be about $240 annually. A mortgage insurance premium of $48 a month must be paid monthly.

Condo 2: Price: $81,000
Developer B will finance with 5 percent down payment and an 11 percent GPM 30-year loan with 3 points as a loan origination fee. The initial monthly payment for principal and interest is $710. After 5 years, the monthly payment increases to $740; after 10 years, it goes to $768; after 15 years, $784; after 20 years, $806; and after 25 years, $829. Taxes are estimated to be about $552, and the home owner's insurance premium should be about $240 annually. A mortgage insurance premium of $3000 must be paid in full at the closing.

Other lenders

Lender *C* offers a conventional 30-year mortgage loan at 12 percent with a 20 percent down payment on either condo and a 1 point loan origination fee. On condo 1, the monthly payment for principal and interest will be $699.45. On condo 2, it amounts to $666.54. Lender *D* offers a 15-year mortgage loan at 11.5 percent with a 20 percent down payment on either condo and a 1 point loan origination fee. On condo 1, the monthly payment will be $794.37; on condo 2, it will be $756.99. Lender *E* offers a 20-year renegotiable-rate (every 5 years) mortgage at 9.5 percent with a 10 percent down payment on either condo and a 3 point loan origination fee. Initial monthly payments would be $713.08 on condo 1 and $679.52 on condo 2.

Key Words and Concepts

adjustable-rate mortgage, 363
amortization, 357
appraisal fee, 372
appreciation, 348
assessed value, 369
broker, 373
certificate of title, 372
closing, 368
condominium, 354
contingency clause, 375
cooperative, 355
deed, 371
due-on-sale clause, 377
earnest money, 375
equity, 357
escrow account, 369
fair market value, 369
Federal Housing Administration (FHA), 370
foreclosure, 357
home owner's fee, 354
implied warranty, 373
lease, 352
lien, 357
listing agreement, 377
loan origination fee, 371
loan-to-value ratio, 358

manufactured housing, 355
mobile homes, 355
mortgage loan, 356
multiple-listing service, 374
offer to purchase, 374
PITI, 367
point, 371
prepayment fee, 377
principal, 357
private mortgage insurance, 370
purchase contract, 375
real estate property taxes, 369
realtor, 373
reissue rate, 372
rent, 352
sales contract, 375
second mortgage, 361
security deposit, 352
seller financing, 361
single-family dwelling, 353
subleasing, 353
teaser rate, 364
title, 371
title insurance, 372
title search, 372
Veterans Administration (VA), 370
warranty insurance, 373

Review Questions

1. List four major areas of expenditure in housing and identify the largest one.

2. Identify the seven goals that most people pursue in acquiring housing.

3. Illustrate how housing buyers pay less than renters only after considering taxes and appreciation of housing values.

4. Give support for the statement, "Renters do better financially on a cash-flow basis than home buyers."

5. Why are the several so-called rules of thumb for housing affordability outdated today?

6. Identify one procedure to use in determining whether you can afford the housing you want.

7. Why do landlords require that renters pay a security deposit?

8. Explain the purpose and value of a lease.

9. List some tenant rights and explain how they work to the advantage of the tenant.

10. Distinguish among the several types of owned housing.

11. List the purposes of the home owner's fee associated with condominium ownership.

12. Distinguish between manufactured housing and mobile homes.

13. Define the term *amortization*.

14. Illustrate how home owners build equity in their home.

15. Explain the reduction of the principal of a home loan as a result of monthly payments over several years. Include what happens to principal and interest amounts with each subsequent payment.

16. Give one reason for and one reason against using a longer maturity period for a loan payback.

17. Describe the conventional mortgage.

18. Describe four factors to consider regarding home-equity credit lines.

19. What are the benefits and pitfalls of seller financing?

20. Specify the consequences of negative amortization.

21. Why have adjustable-rate mortgages become so popular?

22. Who might benefit most from a reverse-annuity mortgage?

23. Identify the components of the term *PITI*.

24. Who is protected by private mortgage insurance.

25. Explain the purpose for using points in home loans. Who is responsible for paying points?

26. Distinguish between the four types of deeds used to transfer the title to real property.

27. Explain the purpose of warranty insurance.

28. What is the benefit to a seller of using a multiple-listing service?

29. Besides the price, what other items should be included in an offer to purchase real estate.

30. Define a real estate purchase contract.

31. What occurs at a real estate closing?

32. Give one reason for and one reason against a home owner selling a home personally rather than through a real estate broker.

33. What is the once-in-a-lifetime capital gains exclusion?

Case Problems

1. Grant Higginbott and Richard Van Ness of Binghamton, New York, are trying to decide whether each should rent or purchase housing. Both men are single. Grant is in favor of buying, and Richard leans toward renting, and both seem able to justify their particular choice. Grant thinks that the tax advantage is a very good reason for buying. Richard, however, believes that cash flow is so much better when renting. See if you can help them decide by responding to the issues listed below.
   a. Is there a tax advantage for the home buyer? Explain.
   b. Discuss Richard's belief that cash flow is better with renting.
   c. Suggest some reasons why Grant should consider renting rather than purchasing housing.
   d. Suggest some reasons why Richard should consider buying rather than renting housing.
   e. Is there a clear-cut basis for deciding either to rent or to buy housing? Why or why not?

2. Sally Donelan of Boston, Massachusetts, has examined several options for new home financing. She has been favoring alternative mortgage plans because of the current high mortgage rates. She hopes that the market rate will drop in a couple of years.
   a. What broad concerns are there with alternative mortgages?
   b. What financing option would you suggest for Sally, assuming she is able to use any type available? Why?

3. Jeremy Jorgensen of Salt Lake City, Utah, is concerned about the costs involved in selling his home, so he has decided to sell his house himself rather than pay a broker to do it.
   a. What problems will Jeremy encounter, if any, when selling his own home?
   b. How would you advise Jeremy if he asked you whether he should sell the house himself or list with a broker? Explain your answer.
   c. Would Jeremy really save money by selling his home himself if he considers his time as a large part of his costs? Why or why not?
   d. Can you suggest any ways that Jeremy could use to reduce selling costs without doing the selling himself? Explain.

4. Walt and Mary Jensen of Atlanta, Georgia, a couple in their late twenties, currently are renting an unfurnished two-bedroom apartment for $550 per month, with an additional $62 for utilities and $10 for insurance. They have found a condominium they can buy for $80,000 with a 20 percent down payment and a 30-year, 11 percent mortgage. Principal and interest payments are estimated at $609 per month. Closing costs

are estimated at $2400, in addition to property taxes of $600 per year and a home owner's insurance premium of $200 per year. The monthly home owner's association fee is $35, and utility costs are estimated at $100. The Jensens have a combined income of $33,000 per year, with take-home pay of $1980 per month. They are in the 28 percent tax bracket, pay $225 per month on an installment contract (10 payments left), and have $19,000 in savings and investments.

a. Can the Jensens afford to buy the condo? Use the results from the Personal Finance Cookbook (PFC) program QUALIFY or the information on page 351 to support your answer. Also consider the effect of the purchase on their savings and monthly budget.

b. Walt and Mary think their monthly housing costs would be lower the first year if they bought the condo. Do you agree? Support your answer.

c. If they buy, how much will Walt and Mary have left in savings to pay for moving expenses?

d. Available financial information suggests that the mortgage rates might drop over the next few weeks. If the Jensens wait until the rates drop to 10.5 percent, how much will they save on their monthly mortgage payment? Use the information in Table 10.6 or the Personal Finance Cookbook (PFC) program MORTLOAN to calculate the payment.

Suggested Readings

"Do You Know Where Your Mortgage Is?" *Consumer Reports*, July 1989, p. 441. How to anticipate problems when your home mortgage loan is sold to another company.

"Homeownership: Who Can Afford It?" *Changing Times*, March 1989, p. 34. It is harder today for people to buy a home.

"House Rich and Cash Poor? Then Let the Bank Pay You." *Business Week*, January 22, 1990, p. 82. This article provides a primer on the what, how, and where of reverse annuity mortgages.

"How to Buy Your First House." *Money*, April 1989, pp. 137–144. Details on how to go about buying your first home.

"How to Pay for Your First Home." *Changing Times*, May 1989, pp. 49–58. Suggestions on where to buy a home and how to go about it creatively.

"IRS Traps for the Unwary Home Seller." *U.S. News & World Report*, May 22, 1989, p. 80. Explores the opportunities and shortcomings of the one-time tax deductibility of home ownership capital gains for those over age 55.

"It's Time to Rethink Your Biggest Investment." *Money*, June 1989, pp. 69–76. Home prices no longer always beat the rate of inflation, so you need new strategies to protect yourself.

"Living (Phew!) Through a Home Improvement." *Money,* April 1990, pp. 166–174. Survival tips, including financial considerations, on how to successfully complete a home improvement project.

"Outlook: Home Prices." *Changing Times,* January 1989, pp. 48–60. Forecasts for housing in the decade of the 1990s.

"Selling Your Home Yourself." *Changing Times,* April 1990, pp. 63–66. Step-by-step suggestions on selling your home without a broker.

"The Great Housing Bust." *Newsweek,* December 25, 1989, pp. 54–55. The affects of declining housing values in some areas of the country.

"Top Dollar for Your Home: The First Step." *Changing Times,* March 1990, pp. 35–39. The listing agreement is the first place to save money when you sell a home.

"What Is Your Home Worth Now?" *U.S. News & World Report,* April 9, 1990, pp. 55–65. Provides tips for both sellers and buyers of houses in today's market.

"When to Refinance and When to Stay Put." *Business Week,* August 28, 1989, p. 96. Tips on refinancing your mortgage loan to take advantage of lower interest rates.

PART FOUR

Income and Asset Protection

11 Insurance Fundamentals

OBJECTIVES

After reading this chapter, you should be able to

1. Define insurance by explaining the relationship between risk and insurance and how insurance serves to reduce risk.

2. Define the basic terms used to clarify the role of insurance in protecting us from financial losses.

3. Apply the four steps of the risk-management process to personal financial affairs.

4. Describe the contractual nature of an insurance policy and the purposes of its various sections and identify the major types of insurance.

5. Discuss the origins, goals, and methods of government regulation of the insurance industry.

6. Discuss the important aspects of the insurance marketplace and points to consider when buying insurance.

. . . .

So far this book has focused on ways to maximize financial resources and to use them to achieve personal goals. The next step is to protect the resources and assets you have attained, and plan to attain, from the possibility of financial loss. You can obtain some of this protection by locking doors, being careful with fire, and driving safely, but you need additional protection from the financial losses that can result from automobile accidents, fires, illness, disability, death, and many other events. Such protection can be provided by insurance.

This chapter begins by discussing the concept of insurance—what it is and what it can do for you. Central to this discussion is the relationship between risk and insurance. Next comes a discussion of the topic of risk management, of which insurance is one component. Sections on insurance as a product and on insurance regulation follow. The chapter closes with a discussion of how to buy insurance.

What Is Insurance?

Objective
To be able to define insurance by explaining the relationship between risk and insurance.

Insurance is a mechanism for reducing risk.

Insurance is a mechanism for reducing risk by having a large number of individuals share in the financial losses suffered by members of the group. Insurance protects each individual in the group by replacing an uncertain and possibly large financial loss with a certain but relatively small fee. This fee for insurance protection is called the **premium**. It includes the individual share of the group's losses, reserves set aside to pay future losses, a proportional share of the expenses of administering the insurance plan, and an allowance for profit if the plan is administered by a profit-seeking company.

The history of insurance can be traced to ancient civilization. Babylonian merchants found it necessary to protect themselves from losses resulting from theft by the distributors hired to transport and trade their wares. Thus began the form of insurance called *bonding*. In more recent times, casualty insurance was designed to protect shippers from the possibility that their cargoes might be lost at sea. The famous Lloyd's of London began as providers of this marine insurance. In the United States, the first fire insurance plan was established in Philadelphia by Benjamin Franklin.

Today insurance is a major component of the American economy. More than $280 billion is spent on insurance annually, and approximately 2 million people are employed by the over 6100 companies in the industry. According to the National Insurance Consumer Organization, the average family spends about 11 percent of its disposable income on insurance each year. This exceeds the percentages spent on clothing, gasoline, and entertainment.

Modern insurance provides a vast and complicated assortment of products designed to help us protect our assets and our income. Yet insurance is one of the least understood purchases we make. Many people buy too little insurance. Others buy too much. Most of us know too little about insurance to make the most of the protection it provides. This and the next three chapters will help you recognize the need to protect your financial well-being by acting as a risk manager who plans and organizes the mechanisms available for minimizing your financial losses.

Insurance Terminology

A sound understanding of insurance requires a knowledge of its basic terms and concepts. These meanings will bring insurance into a sharper focus and clarify its role as a protection from financial loss.

Perils

The protection that insurance provides is often associated with the occurrence of some event, such as a fire or automobile accident. Any event that causes a financial loss is called a **peril**. Fire, theft, illness, and accidents are among the many perils that could occur to you or your property. Insurance does not provide protection from perils, but it does protect you from the financial losses that result when they happen.

Hazards

Protection from the actual occurrence of a peril requires an elimination or reduction of hazards. A **hazard** is any condition that increases the probability that a peril will occur. Driving under the influence of alcohol is an example of an especially deadly hazard.

Three types of hazards are important in insurance. First, a *physical hazard* is a particular characteristic of the insured person or property that increases the chance of loss. An example of a physical hazard is high blood pressure in a person covered by health insurance. Second, a *morale hazard* exists when a person is indifferent or does not care if a peril occurs. For example, a morale hazard exists if the insured party, knowing that theft insurance will pay the loss, becomes careless about locking doors and windows. Third, a *moral hazard* exists when a person wants and causes a peril to occur. An example of a moral hazard would be the temptation to cause a loss intentionally in order to collect on an insurance policy. Insurance companies often limit or deny coverage if a loss occurs as a result of a morale or moral hazard.

Financial Loss

The major reason for buying insurance is to provide reimbursement for financial loss. A **financial loss** is any decline in value of income or assets in the present or future. Certain minimum requirements must be met for a loss to be insurable: the loss must be fortuitous, financial, and personal. *Fortuitous losses* are unexpected in terms of both their timing and their magnitude. A loss caused by lightning is fortuitous. A loss caused by a decline in the value of a corporate common stock is not fortuitous because it is reasonable to expect stock values to go up and down with the market. *Financial losses* can be measured in dollars and cents. When you are sick, you suffer as a result of the discomfort, inconvenience, lost wages, and medical bills. However, insurance will cover only the lost wages and medical bills, because these are the only losses that can be objectively measured. Finally, *personal losses* can be directly attributable to specific individuals or organizations. This means that losses occurring to society as a whole cannot be insured against.

Insurable Interest

Having an insurable interest means that you stand to suffer a loss if a peril occurs.

To buy insurance, an individual or organization must have an **insurable interest** in the property or person insured. This exists when a person or organization stands to suffer a financial loss resulting directly from a peril. You can buy fire insurance on your own home, but you cannot buy it on a friend's home. Nor could you purchase insurance on the life of a total stranger.

The requirement of insurable interest separates insurance from gambling. If you bought insurance on a friend's house, you would actually be gambling, since you would gain if your friend's home burned down. Insurance is not gambling because you can only buy it if you stand to suffer a loss.

The Principle of Indemnity

The **principle of indemnity** states that insurance will pay no more than the actual financial loss suffered. For example, an automobile insurance policy will pay only the actual cash value of a stolen automobile. This principle prevents a person from gaining financially from a loss. Thus, if a windstorm causes $500 worth of damage to a home, the amount paid to the home owner should not exceed $500.

It is difficult to apply the principle of indemnity in the case of life insurance. The financial losses suffered from an untimely death are very difficult to measure because they involve lost future income. As a result, life insurance policies are written for a specific **face amount,** which is the dollar value that the insurance company agrees to pay if the peril (the death of the insured in this case) occurs. The maximum face amount a life insurance company will write depends on the likely loss as well as the relationship between the person whose life is covered and the person who will receive the benefits.

Although the principle of indemnity states that insurance will pay no more than the loss suffered, it does not guarantee that insured losses will be totally reimbursed. Insurance policies are not open-ended agreements to pay. Every policy will have **policy limits,** which are the maximum dollar amounts that will be paid under the policy. Insurance purchasers must be careful that the policy limits are sufficient to cover losses they might suffer.

Risk

Risk is defined as uncertainty.

Insurance was defined earlier as a mechanism for reducing risk. In insurance, **risk** is the uncertainty about whether a financial loss will occur and how large the loss will be. There are two types of risk. **Speculative risk** exists whenever there is potential for gain as well as loss. Gambling is an example of speculative risk, as is buying corporate stock. **Pure risk** exists when there is no potential for gain but there is a possibility of loss. Fires, automobile accidents, illness, and theft are examples of events involving pure risk. Insurance can be bought to reduce pure risk but not speculative risk.

The definition of risk as uncertainty differs somewhat from the usual definition of risk as odds, chance, or probability. The difference is subtle but very important. A peril with a 95 percent chance of occurrence is highly certain to occur. Thus both uncertainty and risk are low. When the probability of financial loss is high, it is usually best to provide for loss in the household budget rather than pay the high insurance premiums that would be required. When a peril has a lower probability of occurrence, 10 percent, for example, the uncertainty and risk are relatively high, because it is difficult to predict the one person in ten to whom the loss will occur. In such cases, insurance is often a wise choice for reducing risk.

The Law of Large Numbers

The **law of large numbers** states that as the number of units in a group increases, predictions about the group become increasingly accurate. This increased accuracy decreases uncertainty and therefore risk. For example, consider a city of 100,000 households in which the probability of a fire striking a household is 1 in 1000, or 0.1 percent. If we focus on groups of 10 or even 100 households at a time, we cannot predict very accurately whether a fire will strike a house in a given group. Some groups might have two or three fires, and others might have none. However, if we combine all the households into one group, we can accurately predict that there will be 100 fires (100,000 × 0.1 percent). Even if there were 103 fires, our prediction would be in error only by a small percentage. Insurance companies, which may have millions of customers, can be even more accurate in their group predictions.

Insurance thus consists of just two basic elements: the reduction of risk and the sharing of losses. Risk is reduced for the insurance company by the application of the law of large numbers. Risk also is reduced for each insurance customer by trading the uncertainty of a potentially large financial loss for the certainty of a fixed insurance premium. Loss sharing occurs as the insurance company pools all the premiums into a fund for the payment of individual losses.

When viewed in this way, the key benefit of insurance becomes clear. Individual insurance purchasers benefit whether or not they suffer a loss. The reduction of risk is itself a benefit. Reduced risk provides the freedom to drive a car, own a home, and plan financially for the future knowing that some unforeseen event will not result in financial disaster. Society also benefits from insurance. No major business activity, whether it be the construction of a house, the drilling of an oil well, or the establishment of a law firm, is undertaken without insurance protection. Without insurance, the only sure way to handle risk is to avoid risky situations.

The Risk-Management Process

Objective
To be able to apply the four steps of the risk-management process to personal financial affairs.

People usually have one of three personal reactions to risk. Some people are **risk takers** who are not upset by uncertainty and may even enjoy risky situations. Others are **risk-neutral,** neither fearing nor enjoying risk. Still others are **risk-averse.** These people are very uncomfortable with risk and will avoid it whenever they can. These chapters on insurance will start you on your way to becoming a successful risk manager with a knowledgeable eye toward understanding the risks you face now and in the future.

The risk-management process helps you manage the risks you face.

You may view insurance as an effective way to handle risk. It is, however, only one of many ways, and it is not always the best choice. **Risk management** is the process of identifying and evaluating each risky situation you face to determine the best way to handle it. Risk management will enable you to choose among the many alternative ways of handling risk. The risk-management process involves four basic steps: (1) identify risk exposures and potential losses, (2) evaluate the potential losses that might result, (3) decide on the best way(s) to handle risk and losses, and (4) administer the risk-management program. Table 11.1 illustrates the steps in the risk-management process.

Identify the Risk Exposures That You Face

Sources of risk are the items you own and your activities that expose you to the risk of financial loss. These items and behaviors are called **exposures.** Consider, for example, the very common exposure of owning an automobile. One loss that could occur is the destruction of the automobile by fire or accident. There is additional exposure to loss when you drive the car, since you may cause an accident and be held liable for losses suffered by others. In risk management you should take an inventory of what you own and what you do to identify your exposures to loss.

TABLE 11.1
The Risk-Management Process Illustrated

Step 1: Identify your exposures to risks

Determine source of risk:

Possession	Activity	Accompanying Peril
Car	Driving	Accident
House	Smoking	Fire
Jewelry	Traveling	Theft

Step 2: Evaluate potential losses

A. Determine the likely frequency of losses associated with each exposure.
B. Determine the potential severity and magnitude of losses associated with each exposure.

Step 3: Choose among mechanisms for handling the risk exposures and losses

A. Avoid risk.
B. Retain risk.
C. Control losses.
D. Transfer risk.
E. Reduce risk.

Step 4: Implement and administer your overall risk-management plan

A. Refrain from certain activities.
B. Take extra precautions.
C. Buy insurance.
D. Evaluate the plan.

You also need to identify the perils that cause losses. Some perils are associated more with some exposures than with others. For example, the theft peril does not apply to a dwelling, but does apply to the contents of a dwelling. Similar kinds of financial losses may result from an accident and an illness, but the ways you handle the risks associated with these two perils may differ.

Evaluate the Potential Losses

Once you have identified your exposures to loss, you must evaluate each to assess the possible impact on your financial security. To do so, it is necessary to estimate both loss frequency and loss severity. *Loss frequency* refers to the likely number of times a loss might occur over a period of time. *Loss severity* refers to the potential magnitude of the loss that may occur. An important consideration when evaluating severity is the range or variation in potential losses. For example, the average automobile driver will be involved in an accident approximately once every 5 years. Yet the severity of these accidents can range from the small fender-bender to catastrophic, fatal accidents with losses in the hundreds of thousands of dollars. The maximum possible loss is an important figure, since you can use this figure to choose the policy limits.

Choose among the Mechanisms for Handling Risk

There are five major ways to handle risk of loss. Each has strengths and is appropriate given the risk exposure and potential losses faced. Each of these methods is described below.

Risk avoidance is not always practical.

Risk Avoidance   The first and simplest way to handle risk is to avoid it. To do this, you must refrain from owning items or engaging in activities that provide exposure to risk of financial loss. For example, choosing not to own an airplane or not to skydive limits your exposure. However, avoiding risk is not always practical. You can avoid some of the risk of home ownership by renting, for example, but then you will lose the benefits of owning a home.

Risk Retention   A second way to handle risk is to retain it, by recognizing and accepting certain risks and potential losses as part of everyday life. The breakage of glassware in your home is usually a retained risk, as is the risk that your shrubbery may die during a dry spell. Although this approach might seem somewhat fatalistic, risk retention has a role to play in risk management. Risk retention should be considered when no other method is available (risk avoidance also might be necessary here), when the worst possible loss is not serious, and when losses are highly predictable in both frequency and severity. For example, a person who races motorcycles will have a high probability of loss due to repair expenses and considers repairs a cost of the hobby and provides for them accordingly.

There are two cases in which risk retention is inappropriate. The first is risk retention because of ignorance. If people do not understand the risks they face, they take no action and engage in risk retention by default. The second is risk retention because of inaction. Many people retain the risk of loss associated with premature death by putting off the purchase of life insurance because they feel it is a morbid, unpleasant task. Such uses of risk retention are the opposite of effective risk management.

Loss control reduces the frequency and severity of losses.

Loss Control   Loss control is designed to reduce both the frequency and severity of losses. For example, installing heavy-duty locks and doors will reduce the frequency of theft. Installing fire alarms and smoke detectors will reduce the severity of fire losses. Insurance companies often require and/or give discounts for loss-control efforts.

Transferring Risk   A fourth way to handle risk is to transfer it. This is an arrangement by which another party agrees to reimburse you for a financial loss. Note that while insurance reduces risk by means of the law of large numbers, risk transfer does not use the law of large numbers. Instead, with risk transfer an insurance company simply assumes the risk the insured wishes to transfer. An example would be an insurance policy taken out on the legs of a football team's star running back. There is no combination of exposure units. In fact, there is only one exposure unit (or two, if you count each leg). The uncertainty is simply transferred (for a not-so-small fee) from the running back or his team to an insurance company or companies. We call such transfers insurance, but technically they are not.

Risk reduction is the essential feature of insurance.

Risk Reduction The fifth way to handle risk is to reduce it to more acceptable levels, or to reduce the uncertainty of financial loss. Risk reduction invariably entails the use of insurance, since risk is reduced for the individual insured and for the insurer through the law of large numbers. The greater the number of exposures, the easier it is to predict collective losses accurately. For example, a chain of retail stores will have a reduced level of fire loss risk (remember, risk is defined as uncertainty) as the number of stores increases. Ultimately the stores' fire losses may become so predictable that the owners will be able to set aside funds to pay fire losses as they occur. This type of risk reduction effort is called *self-insurance*. It is not risk retention because it involves a formal setting aside of funds. Households cannot reduce risk through self-insurance because they cannot make use of the law of large numbers. However, they can buy insurance individually to reduce their risk.

People sometimes think that they can obtain insurance whenever they want to reduce risk. There are, however, certain situations and types of losses for which insurance may *not* be obtainable. The following rules describe such situations:

1. *Too few exposure units.* When there are too few exposure units or people desiring coverage, the law of large numbers will not operate and uncertainty will not be reduced. Thus the major rationale for insurance will be lost.

2. *Inability to determine the probability of loss.* Without an accurate assessment of the probability of losses, it is impossible to determine the premium (the share of the total losses) to be paid by each policyholder. There may be too few exposure units or insufficient time to establish a loss history for a type of exposure. For some time after condominiums started becoming popular in this country, it was difficult to find insurance specifically for condominium owners. Such policies became available as more people bought condominiums and their losses became more predictable.

Insurance will not cover intentional losses caused by the policyholder.

3. *Intentional losses.* Insurance covers only unexpected or accidental losses. If this rule were not followed, insurance could be used to achieve financial gain.

4. *Small losses.* Insurance cannot be purchased for occurrences such as glassware breakage and other small losses. The reason is simply that the cost of providing the coverage would exceed the probable loss.

5. *Many losses occurring at the same time.* If the peril to be insured against is likely to occur to many policyholders at the same time, an insurance company may not be able to pay all the claims. To avoid

such situations, property insurance companies will not write policies on all the homes in a neighborhood for fear that a common disaster such as a hurricane or earthquake might generate unmanageable losses. It is sometimes difficult to obtain flood insurance for the same reason.

In deciding how to handle risk, you must weigh each source of risk with each risk-handling method to select the proper method(s) for each source. Remember that you cannot rely on any one method in all cases. The mix of risk avoidance, risk retention, loss control, risk transfer, and risk reduction that you choose will depend on the source of the risk, the size of the potential loss, your personal reactions to risk, and your financial resources available to pay for losses. The financial considerations are especially important when you choose insurance as a risk-handling method.

Administer the Risk-Management Program

Selecting a method of handling risk is not the final step in risk management. You must implement and administer the method you have chosen. For risk avoidance, this might mean refraining from a certain type of activity, such as drinking and driving. For risk retention, it might mean taking extra precautions to protect items that may not be insured, such as jewelry. For most households, the risk-handling method of most significance is risk reduction through insurance. The remainder of this chapter will address the general subject of insurance. The next three chapters will closely examine property and liability, health, and life insurance.

The Insurance Policy

Objective
To be able to describe the contractual nature of an insurance policy and to identify the major types of insurance.

When you buy insurance, you are buying an insurance policy. An **insurance policy** is a written agreement between a person buying insurance (the **insured**) and an insurance company (the **insurer**). The policy contains language that describes the rights and responsibilities of both the insured and the insurer. In order to understand the policy, you will need an understanding of its contractual nature and its various sections. Different types of losses will be covered by different types of insurance policies as well.

Insurance as a Contract

An insurance policy is a legally binding agreement.

Insurance policies are contracts. A **contract** is a legally binding agreement between two or more parties. *Legally binding* means that the provisions of the agreement can be enforced in a court of law. *Agreement* means that the two parties involved have had a meeting of the minds and promise to honor the provisions of the contract.

Contracts are formed when one party makes an offer that is accepted by another. In most selling situations, the seller offers and the buyer accepts. The process is reversed with insurance. The initial offer is made by the purchaser in the form of an application for coverage. The decision to accept or reject is then made by the insurance seller. Usually, the insurer gives temporary acceptance when an applicant submits full or partial payment of the initial premium. This temporary insurance contract, called a **binder,** is either replaced at a later date with a written contract (the policy) or allowed to expire.

Sections of an Insurance Policy

Each section of an insurance policy provides important information.

Few people read an entire insurance policy before or even after they purchase one, relying instead on the salesperson to describe the coverage for them. This often leads to misunderstandings when a loss occurs and is a major reason why insurance consistently ranks among the top ten sources of consumer complaints.

Insurance policies historically have been written in complex, unfamiliar language because precise legal definitions of the terminology have evolved over the years. Yet these meanings are often not fully understood by the public, and in recent years a number of states have enacted legislation requiring that insurance policies be written in plain English. This trend has helped make policies more understandable, but the responsibility still remains with the insured to read and understand their insurance policies.

You can best comprehend an insurance policy by separating it into its component parts and examining each part separately. Insurance policies have five basic components, each of which serves a specific purpose and provides specific information. These five, in order of their usual location in the policy, are as follows: declarations, insuring agreements, exclusions, conditions, and endorsements or riders.

Declarations   Declarations provide the basic descriptive information about the insured person and/or property, the premium to be paid, the time period of the coverage, and the policy limits. Also included may be promises by the insured to take steps to lessen the hazards associated with the peril insured against. For example, a home owner may promise to install a smoke alarm and maintain a fire extinguisher in exchange for paying a discounted premium. The information in the declarations is used to set the premium and for identification purposes.

Insuring Agreements   The **insuring agreements** are the broadly defined coverages provided under the policy. These are promises that the insurer makes in return for the premium paid by the insured. For example, in an automobile insurance policy, the insurer will promise to pay medical expenses to the driver and passengers in the event of an accident. The insuring agreements will often include definitions of *motor vehicle* or *insured premises* in order to specifically focus the promises made.

Exclusions   Exclusions narrow the focus and eliminate specific coverages broadly stated in the insuring agreements. These are exceptions and special circumstances for which the insurer will make no promise to pay. One exclusion might deny coverage under a family's automobile policy if the car is used primarily for business purposes. Another would deny coverage if the insured intentionally sets a fire. Exclusions eliminate unnecessary coverage, reduce moral hazards, lower the cost of the policy, and generally make the promises made by the insurer more specific. People who do not understand the exclusions in their policies often believe they are covered for a loss when in fact they are not.

Coverage may be denied if policy conditions are not met.

Conditions   Conditions impose obligations on both the insured and the insurer by establishing the ground rules of the agreement. This section contains information on how claims are to be made in the event of a loss and what procedures the insurer will follow when settling the claim. Other items might be the time limits for making a claim after a loss, rules for cancellation of the policy by either party, rules for obtaining estimates of damages, and procedures for changing the terms of the policy. The insured who fails to adhere to procedures or obligations described in the conditions risks being denied coverage when a loss occurs.

Endorsements   Endorsements (or **riders**) are amendments and additions to the basic insurance policy, which is itself almost always a preprinted form. The insured may wish to alter the form to suit specific needs, and endorsements and riders are the mechanisms for accomplishing the alterations. These can both expand and limit coverage provided in the body of the policy. Therefore, when the terms of an endorsement or rider differ from the terms of the basic policy, the endorsement will be considered valid. Endorsements may be added at any time during the life of the policy to expand coverage, raise the policy limits, and make many other changes.

Five Basic Types of Insurance

Insurance and insurance policies can be classified according to the type of loss they cover. The five main types of insurance are property, liability, health, life, and income insurance.

Property insurance protects against financial losses resulting from damage to or destruction of property or possessions. Property insurance can pay for repair or replacement of property and cover other expenses that might result from the occurrence of a peril. If a fire damages your home, property insurance can pay for repair of the structure and replacement of your home's contents and cover your temporary living expenses. People most commonly purchase property insurance to protect homes and automobiles.

Liability insurance protects the insured party who is found liable for another's losses.

Liability insurance protects against financial losses suffered by others for which you are responsible. Such responsibilities can arise when you are negligent or when a contract, a law, or court judgment requires you to pay for the losses of another. Automobile owners typically carry liability insurance to cover damage to another's property in the case of a car accident. Doctors, dentists, accountants, and other professionals usually purchase professional liability insurance.

Health insurance protects against financial losses resulting from illness, injury, and disability. Health insurance benefits pay hospital and doctor bills and can offset the expenses that must be paid as a result of an illness or accidental injury.

How to Make Sense of an Insurance Policy

Insurance policies do not invite casual reading. As a result, many people fail to read their policies until a loss occurs, only to find that they had misunderstood the terms of the agreement. Avoid these problems by carefully and systematically reading a policy before you purchase it. Although the language of the policy may not be entirely familiar to you, your understanding of the policy provisions can be enhanced if you focus on eight key points.

1. *Perils covered.* This information can be provided in two ways. Some policies will list only those perils which are covered. Other policies will cover all perils *except* those listed. This latter type of policy will provide more comprehensive coverage. Realize that the definition of a peril may differ from that used in everyday language. Such definitions are often provided in the policy itself; if not, consult the insurance seller.

2. *Property covered.* Like perils, the property covered under a policy may be listed individually, or only the excluded property may be listed. When the property is listed individually, any new acquisitions must be added to the policy.

3. *Types of losses covered.* When a piece of property is damaged or destroyed by a peril, three types of losses can result: (a) the loss of the property itself, (b) extra expenses that may arise because the property is unusable for a time, and (c) loss of income if the property was used in the insured's work. The extra expenses and the lost income may exceed the dollar loss of the property itself.

4. *People covered.* Insurance policies will often cover only certain individuals. This is especially true of automobile, life, and health insurance. This information is usually contained in the policy declarations but may be changed subsequently in the exclusions and endorsements.

5. *Locations covered.* Where the loss occurs may have a bearing on whether or not it will be covered. It is especially important to know what locations are not covered.

6. *Time period of coverage.* Policies are sometimes written to cover only specific time periods. These restrictions may exclude coverage during specific times of the day and/or during certain days of the week, month, or year.

7. *Hazards that nullify coverage.* Hazards increase the chances of a peril occurring. Insurance policies often stipulate that if a certain hazard exists, coverage will be suspended. For example, coverage on a restaurant may be denied if the owner fails to maintain an adequate fire-extinguishing system.

8. *Amount of coverage.* All insurance policies specify the maximum amount the insurer will pay for a loss. The amount specified will vary greatly from policy to policy and for the various types of losses covered under a policy.

Finally, note that the information on these eight points may be spread throughout a policy. In fact, coverage that appears to be provided in one location may be denied elsewhere. Study the entire policy to fully determine what protection it provides.

Income insurance protects against the loss of future income. Two kinds of income insurance are purchased by employers: *unemployment insurance,* which provides income for employees who are fired or who may be laid off when business is slow, and *workers' compensation insurance,* which provides medical care and replacement of lost income for employees who are injured on the job. In addition, individuals can purchase *disability* *income insurance* to provide income if they cannot work as a result of an injury or prolonged illness.

Life insurance protects against financial losses resulting from death. Such losses can include burial expenses, expenses for settlement of the estate, and lost future income needed to provide for the dependents of the deceased. People who financially support a family probably need to be covered by life insurance.

Insurance Regulation

Objective
To be able to discuss the origins, goals, and methods of government regulation of the insurance industry.

Insurance contracts hold high potential for problems and misunderstandings because they involve promises. Thus insurance is classified as a contract of "utmost good faith," meaning that all parties to the contract are held to higher-than-usual standards of honesty and good faith. The insurance industry is subject to considerable government regulation owing to the status of insurance as a contract of utmost good faith. This section discusses the history of insurance regulation, what is regulated, rate regulation, and insurance redress.

The Evolution of Insurance Regulation

The regulation of insurance dates back to the 1830s, when several states began chartering insurance companies and overseeing the financial solvency of insurers. Historically, the regulation of insurance was a state, rather than a federal, responsibility. This pattern was affirmed in 1869, when the U.S. Supreme Court ruled that insurance was not commerce and was therefore exempt from the power of the federal government to regulate interstate commerce. For 75 years the regulation of insurance remained a function of the individual states.

Then, in 1944, the U.S. Supreme Court reversed the earlier ruling and held that insurance was indeed commerce and that when such commerce was transacted *interstate* (across state lines) it was subject to federal control. This new ruling did not cancel the right of states to regulate insurance, and so the insurance industry was faced with the prospect of regulation on two levels. Of particular concern to some insurers was the prospect of being subject to federal antitrust laws. Insurance companies often share data on losses in an effort to jointly set rates based on large numbers of insureds, and many feared that federal antitrust laws would *Insurance is regulated by* forbid such sharing of information. To head off such an application of
each state. federal law, proposals were presented to Congress to establish the primacy of state regulation of insurance. In response, Congress passed the McCarran-Ferguson Act in 1945. This law exempted the insurance industry from federal regulation until July of 1948, at which time the exemption would expire unless states had acted to regulate insurance. By July of 1948, all states had moved to provide such regulation, and to this day the regulation of insurance remains a state function, although in the last few years there have been efforts to repeal McCarran-Ferguson.

What Areas of Insurance Activity Are Regulated?

State regulation of insurance focuses on four areas: (1) licensing of companies and agents, (2) financial solvency of insurance companies, (3) insurance policies and forms, and (4) insurance rates.

Companies and Agents Must Be Licensed In order to sell insurance in a state, insurance companies must be licensed by the state insurance commissioner or other officials responsible for regulating insurance. Such licensure is granted only to those companies which exhibit minimum standards of financial soundness and use approved insurance policies and forms.

Insurance agents sell, modify, and terminate contracts of insurance between the insured and insurers. Agents are legally permitted to act on behalf of an insurer and to establish contractual obligations that are binding on the insurance company. They must be licensed by each state in which they wish to operate. The license is granted only after the prospective agent passes a test covering knowledge of insurance products and procedures.

Insurance companies must be strong financially to be able to pay losses that will occur.

Insurance Companies Must Be Financially Strong Regulators monitor insurance companies' finances to ensure that the companies can pay the claims of the insureds as losses occur. Insurance companies do not keep the premiums of their policyholders until loss payments must be made; rather they invest these funds in real estate, stocks and bonds, and other forms of investment. Income from these investments is a primary source of revenue to insurance companies. Insurance regulators restrict the types of investments insurers can make and require that insurers keep some funds in reserve for the payment of losses. Every state requires that all insurance companies pay into state-administered funds to pay the claims of customers of insurance companies that fail.

Insurance Policies and Forms Must Be Approved Because insurance policies are very technical, the potential for misunderstanding or for the inclusion of policy provisions unfavorable to the insured is high. State regulators generally require approval of the policies and forms used by insurers in order to prevent the use of vague or deceptive policies. Some states require that standardized, identical policies be used by all companies selling certain types of coverage, such as basic fire insurance.[1]

Insurance Premiums Are Regulated In most forms of business activity in the United States prices are set through the mechanism of the marketplace and the workings of supply and demand. Historically, though, this has not been the case in insurance, especially property and liability insurance. Each state has enacted some type of rating law that establishes procedures for the submission and approval of proposed insurance rates.

[1] This does not mean, however, that every policy sold provides good value for the money. Some policies (such as some mail-order and supplemental health insurance policies) are designed not to provide much protection, yet they are perfectly legal.

An **insurance rate** is the cost to the insured for each unit of insurance coverage. Units are usually stated in dollars of coverage, but they also may apply to individual pieces of property to be covered. The price of insurance, the premium, is determined by multiplying the rate by the number of units purchased.

How Is Insurance Rate Regulation Achieved?

The insurance rating laws of all 50 states have the same objectives, but the mechanisms and procedures by which these objectives are reached vary from state to state.

Insurance rates should be adequate, not excessive, and not unfairly discriminatory.

Three Goals of Rate Regulation   The three goals of insurance rate regulation are (1) to ensure that rates are adequate, (2) to prevent excessive rates, and (3) to prevent unfair rate discrimination.

Adequate rates generate sufficient premium revenue to provide the funds necessary to pay losses that occur. The goal of adequacy benefits both those insureds and the insurers. Those insured benefit because they can be confident that funds will be available to pay for their losses. Insurers benefit because the requirement of adequacy prevents unfair competition from unscrupulous insurers who may attempt to cut the price of their coverage without concern for future loss payments. Such a company could steal customers from companies who take their promises to pay future losses more seriously.

Excessive rates generate premium revenues that exceed the amount needed for the payment of future losses, the expenses of providing coverage, and a fair rate of profit for the company. Overpriced policies are, of course, harmful to those insured.

Unfair rate discrimination exists when insurers charge different insureds different rates without sufficient statistical justification for the differences. People who own brick houses pay lower fire insurance rates than do owners of frame homes. Poor drivers pay higher automobile insurance rates than do careful drivers. Nonsmokers may pay lower life insurance premiums than do smokers. These types of discrimination are considered fair. Discrimination is considered unfair when it is not based on accurate and verifiable probabilities of loss or when it is based on unacceptable social criteria, such as race or religion.

Methods of Rate Regulation   States use two basic methods to achieve the three objectives of rate regulation. The first method requires *prior approval* of insurance rates. In the prior-approval states, insurance companies must file their proposed rates with the insurance regulatory body and must receive approval before putting the new rates into effect. A second method of rate regulation, called *competitive rating,* is used by a growing number of states. Competitive-rating laws allow companies to change their rates as needed without prior approval. The philosophy behind such laws is that the competitive marketplace will keep insurance rates under control. However, even when companies use competitive rating, they must have statistical evidence to support the rates they set. In competitive-rating states, monitoring of insurance company solvency is used to ensure that companies have the funds to pay future losses.

Solving Insurance Disputes

Insurance transactions sometimes result in disputes between the insured and the insurers. Disputes over policy language, premium levels, coverage, and the amount of reimbursement are typical disagreements that may arise. If you have a complaint in any of these or other areas, you have three places to turn. First, contact the insurer itself. This will usually entail making the problem known to the agent who sold you the policy or the agent to whom the policy is currently assigned. Many insurance disputes are simply the result of a misunderstanding that can be most easily handled this way. If the agent cannot or will not handle the dispute satisfactorily, you should contact the appropriate representative of the insurance company. Most large insurers maintain a staff of consumer representatives whose job it is to resolve disputes.

Inform your state's insurance regulator of unresolved insurance disputes.

If such a contact is unsuccessful, a second approach is to notify the state insurance regulatory office, which may be called the department of insurance or the office of the commissioner of insurance. One of the regulatory functions of these offices is to resolve disputes between insureds and insurers. In some states these offices offer toll-free telephone services. However, it is best to put a complaint in writing with full documentation and to keep copies of all correspondence.

Third, if necessary you can contact the state consumer protection office. Each state has consumer protection legislation that prohibits unfair and deceptive business practices and identifies a state agency for the resolution of consumer problems. This function is usually the responsibility of the state attorney general. Most state consumer protection offices provide toll-free telephone services. If you do phone, remember also to put a complaint in writing.

Buying Insurance

Objective
To be able to discuss the important aspects of the insurance marketplace and points to consider when buying insurance.

Buying insurance is much like shopping for other products and services.

Although insurance is not like a product that can be physically measured or a service where one person performs a task for another, it is certainly marketed like other products and services offered in the marketplace. It is designed, packaged, advertised, promoted, bought and sold, and consumed, and it becomes obsolete and often needs to be replaced. Buying insurance requires a knowledge of the types of insurers and the means by which insurance is sold and distributed. You also need to understand the procedures for creating an insurance contract, the concept of group insurance, and how to minimize the cost of insurance.

Types of Insurers

An insurer is any individual or organization that provides insurance coverage. The major function of insurers is to combine the premiums paid

FIGURE 11.1

Sources of Insurance
Company Profits

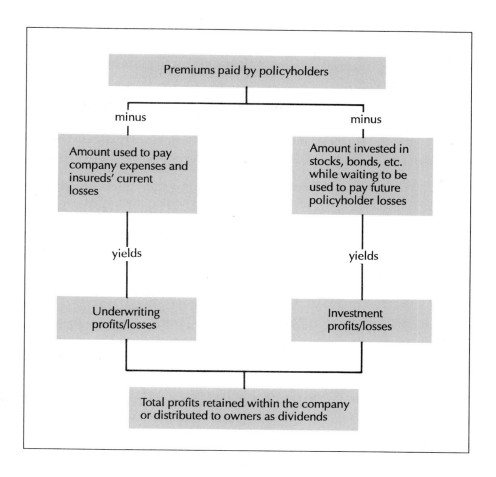

by the insureds into a fund for the payment of losses. Some insurers are in business to make a profit; others operate on a not-for-profit basis. The major types of insurers are stock companies, mutual companies, reciprocal exchanges, and producer cooperatives.

Stock insurance companies operate to earn a profit.

Stock Insurance Companies **Stock insurance companies** are owned by stockholders and provide insurance coverage in return for the opportunity to earn a profit for their owners. Like any other business, they sell stock to raise capital, use the proceeds to sell a product or service, and distribute any profits to the owners. These distributed profits are called *dividends*.

Like all insurers, stock insurance companies derive their earnings from underwriting profits and investment profits. Figure 11.1 diagrams the sources of insurance company profits. Underwriting profits result when the premiums collected exceed the expenses of providing coverage plus the losses paid by the company. Investment profits result when there is return on the investments made with premiums collected from the insureds. Insurers need not make an underwriting profit in order to be profitable. For example, automobile insurers often have underwriting losses that are more than offset by their investment profits.

Some stock insurance companies may make **insurance dividend** payments to their policyholders. These dividends differ from those paid to the owners of the company in that they are not a distribution of the company's profits. Instead, they are considered a partial refund of premiums paid by the policyholders. These refunds can result from a lower-than-anticipated level of losses for an entire group of policyholders or lower-than-expected losses for an individual policyholder or are simply one of the benefits written into the contract. Insurance policies with such provision for dividend payments are called **participating policies.** The Internal Revenue Service and most insurance experts view these insurance dividends not as profits but as refunds for overpayment. **Nonparticipating policies** do not pay dividends to policyholders. Many stock insurance companies offer both participating and nonparticipating policies, and participating policies often require higher premiums enabling the refund of overcharges.

Insurance dividends from participating policies are refunds for overpayment.

Mutual Insurance Companies **Mutual insurance companies** are owned by their policyholders and operate on a not-for-profit basis. Mutual insurance companies sell only participating policies. Any funds remaining after expenses and losses are paid are returned to the policyholders. In addition to receiving dividends, the policyholders of a mutual company maintain voting control of the company. In practice, however, most policyholders in mutual companies do not take active roles in the management of the company.

Mutual insurance companies are owned by their policyholders.

Reciprocal Exchanges **Reciprocal exchanges** are self-insurance mechanisms through which the insureds share in the provision of insurance. Assume, for example, that 1000 Fire Island property owners wish to obtain insurance coverage on their homes. Instead of buying insurance from a stock or mutual company, the members of the group agree to provide a proportional share of each group member's insurance needs. If a member's house is destroyed, all other members will contribute their share of the loss reimbursement. The automobile insurance provided through the American Automobile Association (AAA) is an example of a reciprocal exchange.

Producer Cooperatives **Producer cooperatives** are owned by individuals or organizations that have come together to provide insurance coverage. The best-known examples of producer cooperatives are many of the Blue Cross and Blue Shield health insurance plans. Under some Blue Cross plans, hospitals come together to provide insurance for their patients. Blue Shield is often a producer cooperative of physicians that provides insurance to patients to help pay medical bills.

Who Actually Sells Insurance?

Sellers of insurance, called *insurance agents,* act as representatives of one or more insurance companies. They have the power to enter into, change, and cancel insurance policies on behalf of the companies they represent. There are two types of insurance agents, independent agents and exclusive agents.

Independent insurance agents represent two or more insurance companies. They are independent businesspersons who act as a third-party link between insurers and insureds. Independent agents earn a commission from the companies they represent and will place each insurance customer with the company that they feel best meets the customer's needs. Legally, the agent represents the insurance companies, not the customer, but an insurance agent who neglects customers will not be successful for very long. Insurance companies that rely on a sales force of independent insurance agents are called *agency companies.*

Exclusive insurance agents represent only one insurance company. They are often employees of the insurance company they represent. Life insurance is usually sold through exclusive insurance agents. Since World War II, the proportion of insurance sold through exclusive agents has grown steadily, mainly because commissions paid to exclusive agents tend to be lower than those paid to independent agents. Because insurers using exclusive agents save on commissions and may be more selective in whom they insure, they can sometimes offer protection for a lower premium.

Not all insurance is sold and serviced through agents. Many companies are **direct sellers,** selling their policies through salaried employees, mail-order marketing, newspapers, and even vending machines. Although any type of insurance can be sold directly, the most common are supplemental health insurance, life insurance, and airplane accident life insurance.

The Insurance Contract

There are four steps in the creation of an insurance contract.

The procedure for the creation of an insurance contract involves four distinct, although sometimes nearly simultaneous, steps: the application, underwriting, premium determination, and issuance of the policy.

Complete the Application   The creation of the insurance contract begins with an offer by the purchaser in the form of a written or oral application for coverage. Generally, an oral application is followed later by a written application. The application provides the insurer with information about the persons or property to be insured, the perils insured against, the policy limits, the existence of hazards that may affect the premium, and other relevant matters. Figure 11.2 shows an application form for life insurance.

When the application is accepted by the agent or seller, a legally binding insurance contract is formed. Even when the application is oral or not directly accompanied by payment, a contract may be formed if the offer is accepted. Often the contract is a conditional and temporary binder and becomes permanent only after the insurance company underwrites and issues the policy.

Underwriting is the process of selecting among insurance applicants.

Next Comes Underwriting   Underwriting is the insurer's process of deciding which insurance applicants to accept. Some underwriting is done by agents when they decide to accept or reject an applicant. In general, however, most formal underwriting is done by the insurance company when it receives the written application. To best describe the process of underwriting, we must first discuss how insurance rates are set.

What If You Need to Buy Insurance?

There are literally hundreds of insurance companies and agents as sources of insurance. When the time comes to buy insurance, many people rely on the same company that has served their family in the past. While a tried and true performer should not be abandoned, it pays to shop around, since rates often vary 20, 50, 150, or even 300 percent. The wise insurance shopper will do the following:

1. *Gather Information.* Insurance companies spend millions of dollars a year on advertising, but these ads provide little useful information to insurance purchasers. This is especially true for cost information. One source of helpful information is the insurance regulatory agency in your state. Such agencies usually publish "insurance buyer's guides" that discuss how to buy specific types of insurance, provide comparisons of premiums, and rate the companies providing such insurance. Insurance regulatory agencies also may report on the reputation of a company for fairness and competent handling of complaints. Another source of useful information is *Consumer Reports* magazine, published by Consumers Union, which regularly includes articles on insurance, especially life insurance. It periodically publishes feature articles that rate various types of insurance policies on the basis of price. The book *Winning the Insurance Game* (Knightsbridge Publishing, 1990) by Ralph Nader and Wesley Smith is also useful.

2. *Obtain quotes from several sources.* Insurance premiums can vary 300 percent and more for essentially the same coverage. Most agents will provide quotes over the telephone, so don't hesitate to use the Yellow Pages when considering a new policy or renewal of an existing policy.

3. *Carefully select an agent.* Choosing among independent agents, exclusive agents, and direct sellers is not an easy task. Each seller has advantages and disadvantages. Independent agents may be able to provide more personalized service and can select one company among many that best fits your needs. Exclusive agents can provide personalized service too, but they are limited in what they may offer by the one company they represent. Nonetheless, premiums may be lower through exclusive agents. If you know what company you want, you may do better with an exclusive agent. Many agents have received training and have taken tests to receive professional designations such as *Chartered Life Underwriter (CLU)* in life insurance and *Chartered Property and Casualty Underwriter (CPCU)* in automobile and home owner's insurance. These designations can indicate a high level of expertise and professionalism.

4. *Carefully select a company.* The selection of an insurance company is tied to the selection of an insurance agent. Independent agents initially make the company selection, with final approval by the customer. With exclusive agents, the customer first chooses the company and then chooses among the agents who represent that company. Direct sellers, of course, have no agent. For information on specific companies, *Best's Key Rating Guide* is available in most public libraries. This book rates companies on the basis of financial strength. By consulting this guide, you can avoid the companies that have shaky finances. *Best's* rates companies only for financial soundness and avoids other important attributes such as price, service, and speedy payment of claims. You might want to write for the National Association of Insurance Commissioners' *watch list* of companies in financial difficulty. (Send $5 to *The Insurance Forum*, P.O. Box 245, Ellettsville, Indiana 47429.) Of course, you should not ignore service and convenience either. A good company and agent will be one that combines a low price with quick and efficient service when a loss occurs.

Figure 11.2
Life Insurance Application

Source: Reproduced courtesy of Teachers Insurance and Annuity Association of America. (TIAA).

TIAA

APPLICATION FOR INSURANCE/PART I
This Application form is for your use

PLEASE PRINT
Be sure to answer
every question;
go by question number.

1 First Name (Proposed Insured)   Middle Name / Initial   Last Name

2 Date of Birth   Mo. / Day / Yr.

3 Sex ☐ Male ☐ Female

4 Social Security Number

5 Addresses: State both; *mail will be sent to residence unless otherwise requested.*
Number / Street / Apt. No.   City/Town   State   Zip Code   Telephone
Residence: ( )
Business: ( )

6 Nonprofit Employer: *(If eligible through spouse, please indicate both employers.)*
(a) Proposed Insured's Employer   Title & Duties
(b) Spouse's Employer   Title & Duties
Please check appropriate box to indicate type of eligible institution: ☐ College or University ☐ Public School / School District ☐ Private School ☐ Other ____

7 State title of new policy you want (e.g., Annual Renewable Term, 20-Yr. Decreasing Term, etc.)   Amount of insurance

Policy will include the Disability Waiver of Premium Benefit provision if the issue age is below 56.

8 How are premiums to be paid?
☐ Annually   ☐ Semiannually   ☐ Quarterly

9 To whom shall the insurance benefits be paid at your death?

Primary beneficiary(ies) (Class I)	Date of birth	Relationship to you

Contingent beneficiary(ies) (class II) if any

The right to change beneficiaries is reserved to me unless TIAA is notified otherwise.
Note: If no primary beneficiary (class I) is living at time of insured's death, benefits are payable to the contingent beneficiary (class II). If a class includes more than one person, the benefits are divided equally among the living beneficiaries of the class.

10 List all insurance policies on your life *(if none, write none)*

Name of Company	Amount	Plan	Year Issued

11 Will this insurance replace or change any existing insurance or annuity? (If yes, state which and give name of company and policy number below.)   YES ☐   NO ☐

12 HAS THE PROPOSED INSURED: YES   NO
(a) other life insurance applications pending? ☐ ☐
(b) within the past 3 years had driver's license suspended, revoked or been convicted for driving under the influence of alcohol or drugs? (If yes, give driver identification number) ☐ ☐
(c) applied for life, health or disability insurance which was declined, postponed or rated substandard? ☐ ☐
(d) any intention of traveling or residing outside the U.S.A. or Canada within the next 12 months? ☐ ☐
(e) changed employers within the past 2 years or plan to do so? ☐ ☐
(f) smoked any cigarettes during the past 12 months? ☐ ☐

IF ANY OF THE ANSWERS TO 11 THROUGH 12 (f) ARE YES, GIVE FULL DETAILS IN "REMARKS".

REMARKS

The insurance applied for will not take effect unless and until, during the lifetime of the proposed insured, TIAA has both: (a) received the full first premium payment; and (b) approved the insurance applied for (TIAA will notify you in writing of the approval date).

I understand the above and I elect:

☐ To enclose a premium in the amount of $_____.
This payment will be returned to me if TIAA does not approve the insurance applied for.

or

☐ Not to enclose a premium. Please bill me when my insurance is approved.

I AUTHORIZE any physician, medical practitioner, psychiatrist, psychologist, hospital, Veterans Administration clinic or other medical or medically related facility, or mental health facility, insurance company, consumer reporting agency, other organization, institution or person, that has any records or knowledge of me or my health, to give to TIAA or its reinsurers, any such information. I further authorize a consumer reporting agency to make an investigative report on me if it is required by TIAA.

I UNDERSTAND the information obtained by use of the Authorization will be used by TIAA to determine my eligibility for insurance. Any information obtained will not be released by TIAA to any person or organization in an individually identifiable form EXCEPT to reinsuring companies, or other persons or organizations performing business or legal services in connection with my application for insurance, or as may be otherwise lawfully required or as I may further authorize.

To facilitate rapid submission of such information, I authorize all said sources to give such records or knowledge to any agency employed by TIAA to collect and transmit such information. A photographic copy of this Authorization shall be as valid as the original. I agree this Authorization shall be valid for two years from the date shown below, and that upon request I have a right to receive a copy of this Authorization. I also acknowledge receipt of written notice of my rights under state and federal Fair Credit Reporting Acts.

To the best of my knowledge and belief, each and all of the above answers are true and complete. These answers, together with those provided in Part II of the Application, are my Application. I understand TIAA will rely upon the information provided herein, and that such statements and answers are given as an inducement to TIAA to consider issuing the insurance applied for.

9008P

Signature of proposed insured   Date

Please be sure all questions are answered. TIAA will send you Part II upon receipt of your Application Part I.
18.29 (12/89) A   **Teachers Insurance and Annuity Association**—730 Third Avenue, New York, NY 10017, 1 800 842-2733   9006A

Insurance rates were previously defined as the price per unit of coverage. Rates represent the average cost of providing coverage to various groups of insureds. These groups, called *classes,* are made up of the insureds who share characteristics that are associated with the potential for suffering losses. For example, automobile insurance policyholders may be classified by age, sex, marital status, and driving record, as well as by the make and model of the car they drive. Insurance companies use statistical information about losses to establish rates for the various classes of insureds.

When underwriters receive an application for insurance, they assign the applicant to the appropriate class and then determine whether the rates established for that class are sufficient to provide coverage for that applicant. Remember that rates are averages for a class. Because some applicants will generate higher-than-average loss expectancies, and others lower-than-average loss expectancies for their class, underwriters divide insurance applicants into four groups. The first group, preferred applicants, have lower-than-average loss expectancies and may qualify for lower premiums. The second group consists of applicants with average loss expectancies for their class. These first two groups are accepted for coverage. The third group has loss expectancies projected to be slightly above average. These substandard applicants are accepted but may be charged higher premiums or have restrictions placed on the types or amounts of coverage they may purchase. The fourth group has loss expectancies that are much too high. These applicants are deemed ineligible for coverage and are rejected.

The Premium Is Determined   After underwriting, the premium is determined. The premium is equal to the rate multiplied by the number of units of coverage. Rates are sometimes stated as per $1000 of coverage. For example, the rate on a life insurance policy may be $2 per $1000 of coverage per year. Thus a $50,000 policy would require payment of a $100 premium per year ($2 $\times$ 50 units of $1000).

The Policy Is Issued   The final act in the formation of an insurance contract is the issuance of the policy. At least partial payment of the premium will be made at this point if this has not occurred previously. The policy then becomes a legally enforceable agreement between insured and insurer.

What Is Group Insurance?

Group insurance is usually less expensive than an individual policy.

The process just described for the creation of an insurance contract applies most directly when individuals seek insurance coverage on their own. Alternatively, **group insurance** is sold collectively to an entire group under one policy. The most common example of group insurance is the health insurance provided employees by their employers. Other types of insurance often available on a group basis are life and disability insurance.

Group insurance may be more desirable than individual insurance for two reasons. First, an insured may be able to obtain group insurance at

▌ Advice for the Conservative Insurance Buyer

A discussion of the process of buying insurance would be incomplete without a description of how to minimize insurance costs. As we mentioned earlier, you can save a good deal of money by shopping around whenever you buy insurance. There are also specific features of insurance policies that can lower premiums without significantly lowering protection. These features are deductibles, coinsurance, hazard reduction, and loss reduction.

Deductibles are requirements that you pay an initial portion of any loss. For example, automobile insurance is often written with a $100 deductible. The first $100 of loss to the car must be paid by you. The insurer then pays the remainder of the loss, up to the limits of the policy. Deductibles are also included in most health and property insurance policies. They are sometimes required and sometimes optional, and you usually have a choice of deductible amounts. The higher the deductible you choose, the lower your premiums will be. You should always choose the highest deductible that you can afford. The conservative insurance buyer obtains protection from large, infrequent losses not small, predictable losses.

Coinsurance is a method by which insured and insurer share proportionately in the payment for a loss. For example, it is common in health insurance for the insured to pay 20 percent of any loss and the insurer to pay the remaining 80 percent. Paying part of the costs yourself provides you with an incentive to keep losses down. Substantial premium reductions can be realized through coinsurance, but you must be prepared to pay your share of losses.

The following *deductible and coinsurance reimbursement formula* can be used to determine the amount of a loss that will be reimbursed when there is a deductible and a coinsurance clause:

$$R = (1 - CP)(L - D) \qquad (11.1)$$

where

R = *reimbursement* (i.e., the amount the insurance company will pay)
CP = *coinsurance percentage* required of the insured
L = *loss*
D = *deductible*

Assume a health insurance policy with a $100 deductible per hospital stay and a 20 percent coinsurance requirement. If the hospital bill is $1350, the reimbursement will be $1000, calculated as follows:

$$
\begin{aligned}
R &= (1.00 - 0.20)(\$1350 - \$100) \\
&= 0.80(\$1250) \\
&= \$1000
\end{aligned}
$$

Hazard reduction is action by the insured to reduce the probability of a loss occurring. Insurance companies will sometimes offer reduced premiums to insureds who practice hazard reduction. For example, some life insurance companies offer lower premiums to nonsmokers.

Loss reduction is action by insureds to lessen the severity of loss should a peril occur. Many property insurers offer reduced premiums to insureds who practice loss reduction. For example, premium discounts are often offered to home owners who install smoke alarms and fire extinguishers in their homes. These items will not prevent fires, but they may lessen the severity of the loss a fire would cause.

lower rates. Second, employers often provide group insurance as a fringe benefit for employees. Underwriting is done on the basis of the group, and individual employees are not parties to the contract. They simply participate as recipients of the benefits of the policy.

The policy itself is not provided to the individual group members. Instead, members are given booklets or pamphlets describing the coverage. If you are covered under a group policy, you should know what coverage the policy provides so that, if necessary, you can then purchase supplemental insurance.

Summary

1. Insurance is a mechanism for reducing risk by having a large number of individuals share in the losses suffered by members of the group.

2. Insurance is designed to provide reimbursement for financial losses. It cannot be used in a risky situation in which there is a potential for gain as well as loss. Nor can insurance be used to provide payment in excess of the actual financial loss suffered. Insurance basically consists of two elements: (a) the reduction of risk through application of the law of large numbers and (b) the sharing of losses.

3. Personal financial managers must practice risk management in order to protect their present and future assets and income. Risk management entails identifying the sources of risk, selecting the appropriate risk-handling method, and implementing the risk-management plan.

4. The purchase of insurance involves the establishment of a contract (the policy) between the insured and the insurer. There are five sections to an insurance policy: declarations, insuring agreements, exclusions, conditions, and endorsements or riders. The major types of insurance are property, liability, health, income, and life insurance.

5. Because an insurance policy is a contract of utmost good faith, the insurance industry is carefully regulated by the states. The principal focus of this regulation is on the rates charged for coverage. The goal is to ensure that the rates are adequate, not excessive, and not unfairly discriminatory.

6. There are four types of insurers: stock insurance companies, mutual insurance companies, reciprocal exchanges, and producer cooperatives. Most insurance is sold through either independent or exclusive agents. Two ways of reducing the cost of insurance are through the use of deductibles and through coinsurance.

**The Johnsons
Decide How to
Manage Their Risks**

The financial affairs of the Johnsons have become much more complicated since we began following them in Chapter 2. Both Harry ($75 per month) and Belinda ($200 per month) have been given raises at work. They have purchased an $85,000 condominium that has added about $400 per month to their cost of housing. They have purchased a $3000 used car, adding about $120 per month to their expenses. As a result of these changes, Harry and Belinda have begun to realize that they are facing more risks in their financial affairs. They have decided to step back and take a look at their situation with an eye toward managing their risks more effectively. Use Table 11.1, their net worth and income and expense statements at the end of Chapter 3, and other information in Chapter 11 to answer the following questions.

1. What are Harry and Belinda's major sources of risk from home and automobile ownership, and what is the potential magnitude of loss from each?
2. Given the choices listed in step 2 of Table 11.1, how would you advise they best handle the sources of risk listed in question 1?

Handwritten notes in margin:
Car $3000.00
Condo $85,000
Personal property $1200
Furniture $800.

Key Words and Concepts

binder, 398
coinsurance, 411
conditions, 399
contract, 397
declarations, 398
deductibles, 411
direct sellers, 407
endorsements, 399
exclusions, 398
exclusive insurance agents, 407
exposures, 393
face amount, 391
financial loss, 391
group insurance, 410
hazard, 390
hazard reduction, 411
health insurance, 399
income insurance, 400
independent insurance agents, 407

insurable interest, 391
insurance, 389
insurance agents, 402
insurance dividends, 406
insurance policy, 397
insurance rate, 403
insured, 397
insurer, 397
insuring agreements, 398
law of large numbers, 392
liability insurance, 399
life insurance, 400
loss control, 395
loss reduction, 411
mutual insurance companies, 406
nonparticipating policies, 406
participating policies, 406
peril, 390
policy limits, 392

premium, 389
principle of indemnity, 391
producer cooperatives, 406
property insurance, 399
pure risk, 392
reciprocal exchanges, 406
riders, 399
risk, 392

risk-averse, 393
risk management, 393
risk-neutral, 393
risk takers, 393
speculative risk, 392
stock insurance companies, 405
underwriting, 407

Review Questions

1. Define insurance.
2. Describe how insurance serves to reduce risk.
3. Distinguish between perils and hazards.
4. What are the three types of hazards?
5. Describe the types of losses covered by insurance.
6. How does the requirement of insurable interest affect your ability to buy insurance?
7. Why is the principle of indemnity so important to insurance sellers?
8. State the relationship among insurance, risk, and the law of large numbers.
9. Describe the four steps of risk management.
10. Define an insurance policy.
11. Distinguish among the components of an insurance policy.
12. Why are insurance contracts considered to be legally binding?
13. List the five main types of insurance typically offered for sale to individuals.
14. List the four aspects of insurance activity that are typically state-regulated?
15. Describe three goals of insurance rate regulation.
16. What three contacts can you use to get insurance redress? Describe each one.
17. What is the difference between a stock insurance company and a mutual insurance company?
18. Identify the parties that provide insurance protection under a reciprocal exchange.
19. Distinguish between the two types of insurance agents.
20. List and characterize the four steps in the procedure for creating an insurance contract.
21. What are two advantages of being covered by group insurance?
22. Specify four ways in which you can minimize the cost of insurance.

Case Problems

1. Carmen Telimen, age 27, of Mishawaka, Indiana, recently purchased her first new car. She called her automobile insurance agent to make the change in vehicles and was quoted a premium of $430 every 6 months. This was an increase of $115, which was a shock to Carmen. She wanted to take a hard look at her policy to see if she could cut back on some of the coverage to save some money, but she could not make sense of the policy.
   a. Advise Carmen on how an insurance policy is organized.
   b. What key points should she focus on to help her understand the policy.

2. Larry Larsen of Green Bay, Wisconsin, wanted to buy renters insurance after moving into a new apartment. He knew something about life insurance, but most other types of insurance were unfamiliar. He certainly didn't know how much insurance to buy or when to buy it. Nor did he know much about insurance agents, companies, or costs.
   a. Advise Larry about the basic purpose of insurance.
   b. What sources would you tell Larry to contact to learn more about insurance?
   c. What guidelines would you suggest to Larry concerning the selection of a company and agent?
   d. Assuming Larry decided to buy some renter's insurance, how could he keep his insurance costs low?

3. Assume that you have been talking to some friends about how much more you know about insurance. One young married couple in the group says that they believe insurance is really a waste of money in most cases. They argue that "the odds of most bad events occurring are so low that you needn't worry." Further, they say that "buying insurance is like pouring money down a hole; you rarely have anything to show for it in the end." Based on your reading in this chapter, how might you argue against this couple's point of view?

Suggested Readings

"A Buyer's Guide to Cheaper Rates." *Newsweek*, April 23, 1990, pp. 50–54. Tips on how to lower the cost of your automobile, home owner's, and health insurance coverage.

"Filing a Claim—A Pro Can Help." *Business Week*, October 2, 1989, p. 118. When and how to retain the services of an independent claims adjuster.

"If the Insurance Company Goes Before You Do." *Changing Times*, June 1990, pp. 57–63. A state-by-state review of guaranty laws and a listing of which insurers have invested heavily in junk bonds.

"Insurance Myths You Probably Believe." *Changing Times*, August 1989, pp. 31–33. Explodes the misconceptions many consumers have about insurance especially those related to cancellation and filing claims.

"Insurance Your Kids Won't Need." *Changing Times*, September 1989, pp. 111–115. An overview of the types of insurance that are unnecessary for children, even if the insurance industry suggests otherwise.

"The Insurance Hard Sell." *Consumer Reports*, June 1989, pp. 386–391. Exposes unfair insurance sales techniques.

12 Property and Liability Insurance

OBJECTIVES

After reading this chapter, you should be able to

1. Identify the types of losses that give rise to the need for property and liability insurance.

2. Design a home owner's insurance program to meet your needs and keep the cost of the plan to a minimum.

3. Design an automobile insurance program to meet your needs and keep the cost of the plan to a minimum.

4. Describe property and liability insurance policies designed to meet needs other than those related to housing and automobiles.

5. Specify the steps to take when making a claim against a property or liability insurance policy.

· · · · · · · · ·

On average, an automobile accident occurs once every second in the United States. Every 7 seconds someone is injured in an automobile accident. Every 49 seconds a residence is damaged by fire. And every 3 seconds a crime against property is committed. Each of these events results in a financial loss. Who pays for these losses? As a society, we all do, since these losses take away resources that could be put to more productive uses. On a more personal level, however, the victims of these events will pay the costs unless they have purchased property and liability insurance.

Property insurance protects you from financial losses resulting from the damage to or destruction of your property or possessions. **Liability insurance** protects you from financial losses suffered by others for which you are responsible. Individuals spend over $100 billion per year for property and liability protection, and businesses spend over $125 billion. Automobile insurance accounts for over 40 percent of these expenditures. The list of perils that could be covered by property and liability insurance is virtually endless. Fire, wind, flood, automobile accidents, falling objects, medical malpractice, and theft are covered perils that are familiar to most people.

This chapter will first discuss the need for property and liability insurance and then cover the two major types of property and liability insurance: home owner's insurance and automobile insurance. The next section will describe several other types of property and liability insurance. The final section examines the process of collecting from your insurance company when a property or liability loss occurs.

Why Do People Buy Property and Liability Insurance?

Objective
To be able to identify the types of losses that give rise to the need for property and liability insurance.

When you own property, you may suffer three kinds of losses. First, the property itself can be damaged or destroyed. When the financial risk (uncertainty) associated with this property damage is high, people commonly purchase insurance to reduce such risk. A second type of loss results from loss of the use of property. The need to rent a car because yours has been damaged in an accident is an example of this second type of loss. Third, a liability might arise from use of the property. For example, the owner of a car may be held liable if the driver of the car causes damage to others by destroying property or injuring individuals. Liability also can arise out of the various activities that people engage in at work or for enjoyment. Many professionals, such as doctors, dentists, accountants, and lawyers, buy professional liability insurance to provide payment for possible liability losses.

Home Owner's Insurance

Objective
To be able to design a home owner's insurance program to meet your needs.

Home owner's insurance combines property and liability insurance into one policy.

Whether you own a home or a condominium or rent an apartment, you face the possibility of suffering property and liability losses. **Home owner's insurance** combines liability and property insurance coverage needed by home owners and renters into a single-package policy. Today there are five types of home owner's insurance for those who own a house, one type for the owners of condominiums, and another type for those whose rent. All will be referred to here as *home owner's insurance*.

Policy Sections 1 and 2 Describe the Coverages

The standard home owner's insurance policy is divided into two sections. Section 1 provides protection from various types of property damage losses. Included are coverages for losses due to (1) damage to the dwelling, (2) damage to other structures on the property, (3) damage to personal property and dwelling contents, and (4) expenses arising out of loss of use of the dwelling (for example, food and lodging). Additional coverages are usually provided for such things as debris removal, trees and shrubs, and fire department service charges. An important variable related to Section 1 is the number of loss-causing perils that are covered. Most home owner's insurance policies are **named-perils policies** and cover only those losses caused by perils specifically named in the policy. Some are **all-risk policies,** which cover losses caused by *any* peril other than those specifically identified as *excluded*. This type of policy provides broader coverage because there are hundreds of perils that could cause property losses but only a few would be excluded. Table 12.1 summarizes the prominent types of home owner's polices and the coverages provided.

Section 2 is the liability insurance section. **Home owner's general liability protection** covers situations where you are legally liable for the losses of another. Such a loss might be a broken arm suffered by a visitor who trips on a broken sidewalk on your property. You may be liable because you have an obligation to keep sidewalks in good repair. Whenever you are negligent or otherwise do not exercise due caution in protecting visitors to your property, there is a potential for suffering a liability loss.

You may wish to take responsibility for the losses of another regardless of the legal liability. Say, for example, a guest of yours suffered burns from touching a hot barbecue grill even though you warn him that the grill was hot. **Home owner's no-fault medical payments protection** will pay for injuries to visitors regardless of who was at fault for the loss. Such coverage would help pay for the medical treatment of your guest's burns. Members of your immediate family are not covered under no-fault medical payments and should be covered by health insurance (see Chapter 13).

TABLE 12.1
Summary of Home Owner's Insurance Policies

	HO-1 (Basic Form)	HO-2 (Broad Form)	HO-3 (Special Form)
Perils covered (descriptions are given below)	Perils 1–11	Perils 1–18	All perils except those specifically excluded for buildings; perils 1–18 on personal property; except glass breakage
Property coverages/limits			
House and any other attached buildings	Amount based on replacement cost, minimum $15,000	Amount based on replacement cost, minimum $15,000	Amount based on replacement cost, minimum $20,000
Detached buildings	10 percent of insurance on the home	10 percent of insurance on the home	10 percent of insurance on the home
Trees, shrubs, plants, etc.	5 percent of insurance on the home, $500 maximum per item	5 percent of insurance on the home, $500 maximum per item	5 percent of insurance on the home, $500 maximum per item
Personal property	50 percent of insurance on the home	50 percent of insurance on the home	50 percent of insurance on the home
Loss of use and/or add'l living expense	10 percent of insurance on the home	20 percent of insurance on the home	20 percent of insurance on the home
Credit card, forgery, counterfeit money	$500	$500	$500
Liability coverages/limits			
Comprehensive personal liability	$25,000–$100,000	$25,000–$100,000	$25,000–$100,000
Damage to property of others	$250–$500	$250–$500	$250–$500
Medical payments	$500–$1000	$500–$1000	$500–$1000

Special limits of liability*

For the following classes of personal property, special limits apply on a per-occurrence basis (e.g., per fire or theft): money, coins, bank notes, precious metals (gold, silver, etc.), $100 to $200; securities, deeds, stocks, bonds, tickets, stamps, $500–$1000; watercraft and trailers, including furnishings, equipment, and outboard motors, $500–$1000; trailers other than for watercraft, $500–$1000; jewelry, watches, furs, $500–$1000; silverware, goldware, etc., $1000–$2500; guns, $1000–$2000.

List of perils covered

1. Fire, lightning
2. Loss of property from premises that are endangered by fire or other perils (has been discontinued by many companies)
3. Windstorm, hail
4. Explosion
5. Riots
6. Damage by aircraft
7. Damage by vehicles owned or operated by people not covered by the homeowner's policy
8. Damage from smoke
9. Vandalism, malicious mischief
10. Theft
11. Glass breakage
12. Falling objects
13. Weight of ice, snow, sleet

Note: This table describes the standard policies. Specific items differ from company to company and state to state.
* Where two figures are given, they represent the range of possibilities; most companies use one or the other as their standard limit. When you want a limit that exceeds the standard limit for your company, you usually can increase the limit by paying an additional premium.

HO-5 (Comprehensive Form)	HO-8 (For Older Homes)	HO-4 (Renter's Contents Broad Form)	HO-6 (For Condominium Owners)
All perils except those specifically excluded	Perils 1–11	Perils 1–18	Perils 1–18
Amount based on replacement cost, minimum $30,000	Amount based on actual cash value of the home	10 percent of personal property insurance on additions and alterations to the apartment	$1000 on owner's additions and alterations to the unit
10 percent of insurance on the home	10 percent of insurance on the home	Not covered	Not covered
5 percent of insurance on the home, $500 maximum per item	5 percent of insurance on the home, $500 maximum per item	10 percent of personal property insurance, $500 maximum per item	10 percent of personal property insurance, $500 maximum per item
50 percent of insurance on the home	50 percent of insurance on the home	Chosen by the tenant to reflect the value of the items, minimum $6000	Chosen by the home owner to reflect the value of the items, minimum $6000
20 percent of insurance on the home	20 percent of insurance on the home	20 percent of personal property insurance	40 percent of personal property insurance
$500	$500	$500	$500
$25,000–$100,000	$25,000–$100,000	$25,000–$100,000	$25,000–$100,000
$250–$500	$250–$500	$250–$500	$250–$500
$500–$1000	$500–$1000	$500–$1000	$500–$1000

14. Collapse of building or any part of building
15. Leakage or overflow of water or stream from a plumbing, heating, or air-conditioning system
16. Bursting, cracking, burning, or bulging of a steam or hot water heating system, or of appliances for heating water
17. Freezing of plumbing, heating, and air-conditioning systems and home appliances
18. Injury to electrical appliances and devices (excluding tubes, transistors, and similar electronic components) from short circuits or other accidentally generated currents

Types of Home Owner's Insurance

Home owner's insurance protects house and condominium owners plus renters.

There are seven distinct types of home owner's insurance policies: HO-1 through HO-6 plus HO-8. They are described in detail in Table 12.1 and more generally in the following text. The terms and numbers used to identify each are generally recognized, since they are used by most companies.

Basic Form (HO-1) The *basic form* home owner's policy is a named-perils policy that covers 11 major property-damage-causing perils and provides 3 liability-related protections: personal liability, property damage liability, and medical payments. Fire and lightning, explosion, windstorm, and smoke are the most common perils that can cause property damage. Each is covered in the basic home owner's policy.

Broad Form (HO-2) The *broad form* home owner's policy is a named-perils policy that covers 18 major property-damage-causing perils and provides protection from the 3 liability exposures.

Special Form (HO-3) The *special form* home owner's policy provides all-risk protection for four property coverages: losses to the dwelling, losses to other structures, landscaping losses, and losses for additional living expenses. Contents and personal property are covered on a named-perils basis for 17 of the 18 major home owner's perils. The exception is the peril of glass breakage. With liability protection and in all other respects, the coverage under HO-3 is the same as under HO-2.

Renter's Contents Broad Form (HO-4) The *renter's contents broad form* home owner's policy is a named-perils policy that protects from losses to the contents of a dwelling rather than the dwelling itself. It covers all 18 major perils and provides liability protection. HO-4 is ideal for renters in that it provides protection from losses to the contents and personal property and provides for additional living expenses if the dwelling is rendered uninhabitable by one of the covered perils. Only about one-fourth of all renters carry HO-4 protection.

Comprehensive Form (HO-5) The *comprehensive form* home owner's policy provides all-risk property protection. An HO-5 policy affords all-risk coverage on the dwelling, other structures, *and* personal property. Few companies will write the comprehensive form because they do not want to cover personal property on an all-risk basis and be obligated for such perils as breakage, ripping, tearing, and spilling.

HO-4 for renters and HO-6 for condominium owners are designed primarily to protect personal property.

Condominium Form (HO-6) The *condominium form* home owner's policy is a named-perils policy protecting condominium owners from the three principal losses they face: losses to contents and personal property, losses due to the additional living expenses that may arise if one of the covered perils occurs, and liability losses. Further, there are two additional coverages included that meet the specific needs of condominium owners.

The first is protection against losses to the alterations and additions that condominium owners sometimes make to their units. The second is supplemental coverage for the dwelling unit to protect the condominium owner if the owner of the building (usually the condominium association) is not sufficiently insured.

Older Home Form (HO-8) An older home may have a replacement value that is much higher than its market or actual cash value. The HO-8 named-perils policy provides actual-cash-value protection and does not provide that the dwelling be rebuilt to the same standards of style and quality, standards that may be prohibitively expensive today. Instead, the dwelling will be rebuilt to make it serviceable.

Buying Home Owner's Insurance

You can purchase home owner's insurance with varying coverage amounts, exclusions, and limitations. To do so, you must tailor protection to your needs and consider how home owner's insurance is priced.

Determining the Coverage Needed on Your Dwelling Both property and liability losses can occur to owners or renters of housing. The easiest way to identify the property losses is to make an inventory of the property and its contents and then determine the dwelling's replacement value. To determine the value of the dwelling, you could (1) use the services of a professional property appraiser, (2) use the value of the property employed to figure property taxes, or (3) consult with your insurance agent to assist in determining replacement value.

Home owner's insurance policies usually contain a replacement-cost requirement that stipulates that a home must be insured for 80 percent of its replacement value for the policy to pay the full reimbursement (after payment of the deductible) for any losses to the dwelling. The 80 percent figure is used because it is assumed that 20 percent of the value is associated with the foundation and land, which would rarely be destroyed. If you fail to meet the replacement-cost requirement, you will be using a form of coinsurance and the amount of reimbursement for any loss will be calculated using the **replacement-cost-requirement formula:**

$$R = L \times \frac{I}{(RV \times 0.80)} \qquad (12.1)$$

where

$R = reimbursement$ payable
$L = $ the *amount of loss* in excess of any deductible
$I = amount\ of\ insurance$ actually carried
$RV = replacement\ value$ of the dwelling

To protect people, many home owner's policies have a clause that automatically raises the policy coverage amount each year to keep up with inflationary increases in the cost of replacing the dwelling.

What If You Fail to Insure Your Home for Its Replacement Cost?

Consider the example of twin brothers, John and Jim Otto, of Independence, Missouri. Each owns a home with a replacement value of $100,000 and each home suffers a $40,000 fire loss over and above the deductible. John, who took a personal finance class in college, has insured his home for $80,000. Jim, in an attempt to save some money, has insured his home for $72,000. Applying Equation (12.1), each brother determines the amount he will be reimbursed for the loss to his dwelling. John's calculations are

$$R = \$40,000 \times \frac{\$80,000}{(\$100,000 \times .80)}$$
$$= \$40,000 \times \frac{\$80,000}{\$80,000}$$
$$= \$40,000$$

Thus, John will be fully covered for his loss. Jim's calculations are

$$R = \$40,000 \times \frac{\$72,000}{(\$100,000 \times .80)}$$
$$= \$40,000 \times \frac{\$72,000}{\$80,000}$$
$$= \$40,000 \times .90$$
$$= \$36,000$$

Thus, Jim will be reimbursed for only $36,000 of his loss. His failure to insure his house for 80 percent of its replacement cost, or $80,000 = ($100,000 × .80), means he will be covered for only 90 percent ($72,000 ÷ $80,000) and he must pay 10 percent of any loss; in this case, $4000.

Determining the Coverage Needed on Your Personal Property   Making an inventory of and placing a value on the contents of your home are time-consuming, but important tasks. Table 12.2 shows the inventory and valuation for the contents of and personal property in an average living room. Such an inventory should be conducted for each room, the basement, garage, shed, and yard possessions. The values are especially important, since when totaled they allow the selection of proper policy limits. Most home owner's policies will automatically cover contents and personal property for up to 50 percent of the coverage on the home. If your home is insured for $100,000 but contains $55,000 worth of personal property, you probably need to purchase an extra $5000 worth of contents coverage. Furthermore, some specified items of personal property may have specific policy limits. For example, a home owner's insurance policy might provide a maximum of $2200 theft coverage for precious metals (gold, silver, etc.). If your inventory reveals a higher valuation on such items, an endorsement providing extra coverage might be needed.

You can choose actual cash value or replacement cost protection on your personal property.

Notice that Table 12.2 lists three estimates for the value of the contents of a room: the purchase price, the actual cash value, and the replacement

TABLE 12.2
Personal Property Checklist: Living Room

| Item | Date Purchased | Valuation | | |
		Purchase Price	Actual Cash Value	Replacement Cost
Furniture				
Couch	8/86	$ 750	$ 375	$ 950
Chair	11/84	250	100	375
Lounger	12/87	575	300	695
Ottoman	12/87	100	50	120
Bookcase	4/89	275	225	300
End table (2)	7/90	300	250	300
Appliances				
TV	1/91	550	500	600
VCR	6/89	400	300	400
Wall clock	7/83	60	10	100
Furnishings				
Carpet	6/83	375	50	600
Painting	12/87	125	225	225
Pole lamp	4/85	150	50	225
Table lamp	4/85	75	40	100
Table lamp	5/90	125	100	135
Throw pillows	7/86	45	20	60
TOTAL		$4155	$2595	$5185

cost. Historically, property insurance policies paid only the **actual cash value** of an item of personal property, which represents the purchase price of the property less depreciation. The **actual-cash-value (ACV) formula** is

$$ACV = P - \left(CA \times \frac{P}{LE} \right) \qquad (12.2)$$

where

P = *purchase price* of the property
CA = *current age* of the property in years
LE = *life expectancy* of the property in years

As an example, consider the case of Reneé Jones, a single mother from Minneapolis, Minnesota, whose 8-year-old color television set was stolen.

The TV cost $500 new and had a total life expectancy of 10 years. Its actual cash value at the time it was stolen was

$$ACV = \$500 - \left(8 \times \frac{\$500}{10}\right)$$
$$= \$500 - (8 \times \$50)$$
$$= \$100$$

Contents replacement cost protection pays to-day's prices for losses.

Reneé would be hard pressed to replace the TV for $100. A more realistic replacement cost for the TV might be $600. **Contents replacement-cost protection** is an option now available in many home owner's insurance policies (including the renter's form) that pays the replacement cost of any personal property. Note that the standard limitation that applies to contents (50 percent of insured value of the dwelling) is still in effect if contents replacement-cost protection is purchased. This overall limit may need to be raised, since it is easier to reach the 50 percent figure when replacement-cost valuation is used.

Determining the need for liability loss coverage is not as complicated as that for property losses. For example, standard home owner's policies typically provide $100,000 of general liability coverage, $250 of no-fault property damage coverage, and $1000 of no-fault medical expense coverage. It is wise to increase the policy limits for all three liability coverages, since the extra cost is not high.

How Home Owner's Insurance Is Priced   Many factors affect the pricing of home owner's insurance. Most important are the amount and type of coverage and the number of perils insured against. In addition, the loss experience of the company affects the premium paid because the company must collect sufficient premiums to pay the loss claims made by its customers. Insurance companies vary their premiums by the adequacy of the firefighting system in a town or city; even the distance of a fire hydrant from the home can affect the premium. The type of construction used to build a house also affects the home owner's insurance premium. When all other factors are equal, it will cost more to insure a frame house than a brick house. Further, certain neighborhoods generate higher and more frequent losses than others. For example, city neighborhoods and extremely rural areas have higher home owner's insurance costs than do suburban neighborhoods.

Automobile Insurance

Objective
To be able to design an automobile insurance program to meet your needs.

Owning and driving an automobile expose you to the risk of devastating financial losses. A split-second error in driving judgment can result in a loss of thousands of dollars in property damage and personal injury. More than 35 million automobile accidents occur annually in the United States; that's one for every four drivers. These accidents result in injury to almost 6 million people, nearly 50,000 deaths, and economic losses approaching $100 billion. **Automobile insurance** combines liability and property insur-

TABLE 12.3
Summary of Family and Personal Automobile Policies

Section	Type of Coverage	Persons Covered	Property Covered	Recommended Limits
1	(a) Bodily injury liability	Nonexcluded relatives living in insured's household driving an owned or non-owned automobile	Not applicable	At least legally required minimums or $50,000/$100,000, whichever is greater
	(b) Property damage liability	Nonexcluded relatives living in insured's household driving an owned or non-owned automobile	Automobiles and other property damaged by insured driver while driving	At least legally required minimums or $25,000, whichever is greater
2	Medical payments	Passengers in insured automobile or non-owned automobile driven by insured family member	Not applicable	$50,000
3	Collision	Anyone driving insured car with permission	Insured automobile	Actual cash value
	Comprehensive	Not applicable	Insured automobile and its contents	Actual cash value
4	Uninsured motorists	Anyone driving insured car with permission and insured family members driving nonowned automobiles with permission	Not applicable	$10,000/$20,000

ance coverage needed by automobile owners and drivers into a single-package policy. More than 30 states require automobile owners to purchase automobile insurance, and the remainder require automobile owners to show in advance financial responsibility for any accident that might occur. This requirement is most commonly fulfilled through the purchase of automobile insurance.

Losses Covered

Automobile insurance is a package of four distinct types of coverage: (1) liability insurance, (2) medical payments insurance, (3) property damage insurance, and (4) protection against uninsured and sometimes underinsured motorists. Each has its own policy limits, conditions, and exclusions. Table 12.3 summarizes the coverage provided by automobile insurance policies.

TABLE 12.4
Average Automobile Insurance Liability Claims*

Year	Bodily Injury	Property Damage
1980	$4010	$ 787
1984	6163	1125
1985	6815	1217
1986	7396	1298
1987	7847	1410
1988	8736	1535
1989	9338	1646
1990†	9980	1765

Source: Used with permission of the Insurance Information Institute, 110 Williams St., New York, NY 10038.

* Dollar averages include all loss adjustment expenses and exclude data from Massachusetts and most states with no fault automobile insurance laws.

† Author's estimate.

Automobile liability insurance includes bodily injury and property damage liability protection.

Liability Insurance Covers Losses to Others That You Cause Two types of liability can arise out of the ownership and operation of an automobile. **Automobile bodily injury liability** occurs when a driver or car owner is legally responsible for bodily injury losses suffered by others. **Automobile property damage liability** occurs when a driver or car owner is legally responsible for damages to the property of others, such as another vehicle, a building, or roadside signs and poles. Table 12.4 lists the average automobile bodily injury liability and property damage liability claims in recent years. Note that the average bodily injury liability claim is more than five times the average property damage liability claim. Further, the cost of insurance claim settlements and court awards resulting from automobile accidents has risen steadily in recent years.

The policy limits for automobile liability insurance are usually quoted with three figures, such as 100/300/50, with each figure representing a multiple of $1000, as illustrated in Figure 12.1. The first of the three figures is the maximum that will be paid for *one* person's bodily injury losses resulting from an automobile accident, or $100,000 in our example. The middle figure represents the overall maximum that will be paid for bodily injury liability losses to *any number* of persons resulting from an automobile accident, or $300,000 in our example. The third figure represents the maximum that will be paid for property damage liability losses resulting from an accident, $50,000 in our example.

In some policies, the liability limits are stated as a single figure, such as $250,000. Under such policies, all property and bodily injury liability losses from an accident would be paid until the limit is reached. Note that liability insurance covers others. Thus it cannot be used to pay for losses the driver at fault or for property damage to that driver's car. Injured passengers of the at-fault driver may collect under his or her liability coverage, but usually only after exhausting the coverage provided under

FIGURE 12.1

Automobile Liability Insurance Policy Limits

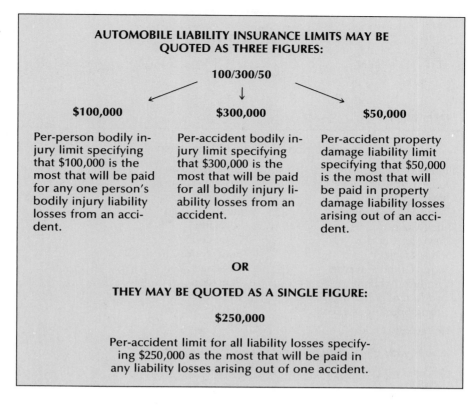

AUTOMOBILE LIABILITY INSURANCE LIMITS MAY BE QUOTED AS THREE FIGURES:

100/300/50

$100,000

Per-person bodily injury limit specifying that $100,000 is the most that will be paid for any one person's bodily injury liability losses from an accident.

$300,000

Per-accident bodily injury limit specifying that $300,000 is the most that will be paid for all bodily injury liability losses from an accident.

$50,000

Per-accident property damage liability limit specifying that $50,000 is the most that will be paid in property damage liability losses arising out of an accident.

OR

THEY MAY BE QUOTED AS A SINGLE FIGURE:

$250,000

Per-accident limit for all liability losses specifying $250,000 as the most that will be paid in any liability losses arising out of one accident.

medical payments (discussed below) and only after those injured in other vehicles or as pedestrians are reimbursed.

Medical Payments Insurance Covers You and Your Passengers   Automobile **medical payments insurance** will pay limited benefits toward the personal injury losses suffered by the driver of the insured vehicle and any passengers regardless of who is at fault. Medical losses occurring within 1 year and as a direct result of an accident will be reimbursed up to the limits of the policy. Automobile medical payments insurance also covers insured family members when injured as passengers in *any* car, as pedestrians, or while riding a bicycle. Medical payments coverage is subject to a single policy limit, usually $5000 to $10,000, which is applied per person per accident.

Medical payments limits are applied per person per accident.

In states that have adopted some type of no-fault automobile insurance mechanism (see below), the medical payments coverage is referred to as *personal injury protection (PIP),* and it covers driver and passengers for bodily injury losses as well as possibly lost wages and rehabilitation expenses. Under medical payments or PIP, drivers and their injured parties collect directly from the driver's insurer without regard to who was at fault for the accident. If the driver was not at fault, his or her insurer pays the claims and then exercises its subrogation rights from another party. **Subrogation rights** allow an insurer to take action against a negligent third

TABLE 12.5
Collision Claims for Passenger Cars During First Year of Purchase

Makes and Series	Body Style	Relative Average Loss Payment per Insurance Vehicle Year*	Average Loss Payment per Insurance Vehicle Year
Models with the best collision coverage loss experience			
Plymouth Grand Voyager	Passenger Van	48	$103.05
Dodge Caravan	Passenger Van	48	103.05
Chevrolet Caprice	Station Wagon	48	103.05
Chevrolet Astro Van	Passenger Van	49	105.20
Buick Century	Specialty	49	105.20
Chevrolet Caprice	Four-door	50	107.35
Dodge Spirit	Four-door	51	109.50
Dodge Grand Caravan	Passenger Van	52	111.64
Plymouth Acclaim	Four-door	52	111.64
Ford Extended Aerostar	Passenger Van	53	113.79
Oldsmobile Cutlas Ciera	Station Wagon	53	113.79
All Passenger Cars		**100**	**$214.70**
Models with the worst collision coverage loss experience			
Mercedes 300SE	Specialty	235	$504.55
BMW 3251 2D	Specialty	217	465.90
BMW 3251 Conv.	Specialty	200	429.40
BMW 3251 4D	Specialty	190	407.93
Ford Mustang	Sports	182	390.75
BMW 500 Series	Specialty	180	386.46
Nissan 240 SX	Two-door	169	362.84
Pontiac LeMans	Two-door	168	360.70
Saab 900	Two-door	167	358.55
Lincoln Mark VII	Specialty	162	347.81
Mercedes SEL Series	Specialty	160	343.52

Source: Highway Loss Data Institute, 1990. Used with permission.

* 100 represents $214.70, the average loss payment per insured vehicle year for all 1989 models in their first year.

party (and that party's insurance company) to obtain reimbursement for payments made to an insured. In no-fault states, the rights of subrogation may be limited.

Automobile property insurance provides protection for your car from collision, theft and other losses.

Property Insurance Covers Losses to Your Vehicle A number of perils can cause property losses to an insured automobile. The most common peril is, of course, a collision with another vehicle or an object. Table 12.5 gives the frequency and average loss payment per collision claim and the average loss payments for various car models. In general, the cars with the highest collision losses per vehicle tend to be the smaller, sportier models offered by foreign manufacturers. Other perils can cause property losses to automobiles. The most common of them is theft. About 1 out of every 160 automobiles is stolen each year. Again, sportier models have the highest frequencies of theft claims.

Collision insurance reimburses you for losses resulting from a collision with another car or object or from a rollover. It pays the cost of repairing or replacing your car when you are at fault for the accident or when fault cannot be determined. When the other driver is at fault, reimbursement should be obtained through that driver's property damage liability protection. Collision insurance is written with a deductible, usually $100 to $500. If you carry collision insurance coverage on your own car, you are generally covered when you drive someone else's car (including rental cars) with their permission. If you are going to rent a car, consult your agent beforehand to confirm coverage. Avoid buying a *collision damage waiver (CDW)* through the rental agency because it is extremely overpriced and unnecessary if you are covered through you own car's policy.

Collision insurance covers your car when you are at-fault.

Comprehensive automobile insurance provides payment for property damage losses caused by perils other than collision and rollover. [Thus it is sometimes referred to as *other than collision (OTC)* coverage.] Covered perils include fire, theft, hail, and wind, among many others. Usual problems paid for under comprehensive coverage include vandalism, such as broken windows, antennas, mirrors, and scratches. Comprehensive insurance is written on an all-risk basis. Comprehensive liability insurance is often written with a $50 to $250 deductible.

When you make a claim for payment under collision and comprehensive insurance, you must get an estimate of the repair cost. If the estimate exceeds the book value of the car, the lower of the two figures is paid, less any deductible. The **book value** of a car is based on the average current selling price of cars of the same make, model, and age. In the case of vintage, restored, or specialty cars, the book value may be much less than the true value of the particular car being insured. Thus the owners of such vehicles should obtain additional coverage in order to be adequately insured. Many automobile insurance purchasers forego collision insurance on cars that have lost much of their resale value owing to old age or high mileage.

Uninsured and Underinsured Motorist Insurance Sometimes the driver at fault in an automobile accident carries no or insufficient liability insurance despite laws to the contrary. To protect yourself from such losses, you can purchase uninsured and underinsured motorist insurance as part of your automobile insurance policy. **Uninsured motorist insurance** protects you and your passengers from bodily injury losses (and, in a few states, property damage losses) resulting from an automobile accident caused by an uninsured motorist. Uninsured motorist insurance provides protection above that provided by the automobile medical payments insurance. **Underinsured motorist insurance** protects you and your passengers from bodily injury losses (and, in some cases, property damage losses) when the at-fault driver carries insufficient liability insurance. The limits for uninsured motorist insurance are quoted in a manner similar to that for automobile liability insurance. For example, uninsured motorist pro-

Uninsured and under-insured motorist insurance protect you when the at-fault driver has inadequate or no insurance.

tection with limits of 50/100 would provide up to $50,000 for any one injured person and up to $100,000 for multiple bodily injury losses in one accident. Where available, uninsured and underinsured motorist insurance carries a very low premium, often under $25 per year.

Other Protections Two inexpensive but sometimes important coverages are also available to automobile insurance buyers. The first is towing coverage, which will pay the cost of having a disabled automobile transported for repairs. Towing coverage usually has a limit of between $25 and $50 per occurrence but will cover any towing need, not just one due to an accident. The second minor coverage will provide a rental car when the insured's vehicle is being repaired or has been stolen. Such rental reimbursement often has a daily limit of $10 or $20 and, therefore, provides only part of the funds needed to obtain a replacement.

Types of Automobile Insurance

There are variations of the standard automobile insurance policy; however, each provides coverage for essentially the same types of losses and is organized in nearly the same way. The **family automobile policy (FAP)** and the **personal automobile policy (PAP)** are the types of automobile insurance most commonly selected by individual consumers and households. As you might expect, the FAP is designed for automobiles owned by families in which there are several persons who might drive the car. The family automobile policy provides coverage for you, relatives living in your household unless specifically excluded, and persons who have your permission to operate the insured vehicle. If a friend loans you his or her car, your relatives living in your household and other persons acting on your permission also will be covered under *your* family automobile policy when driving that borrowed car. The PAP is designed for automobiles owned by an individual who is likely to be its only driver. Two other types of automobile insurance of interest are automobile insurance plans and no-fault automobile insurance.

Automobile Insurance Plans In more than 30 states it is illegal to operate a motor vehicle without being covered by automobile insurance. Even when insurance is optional, it is unwise to be uninsured because of the potentially devastating effects of automobile accidents. Nonetheless, insurance companies do not voluntarily accept every applicant for automobile insurance. Thus drivers with poor driving records may find it difficult, if not impossible, to obtain coverage at any price. Because automobile insurance is so vital, most states have established a mechanism to provide coverage for drivers who are otherwise uninsurable. These **automobile insurance plans (AIPs)** assign a proportional share of the uninsurable drivers to each company writing automobile insurance coverage in a state according to each company's share of the total automobile insurance premiums written in that state. As you might assume, the premiums for such coverage are extremely high. In addition, coverage is usually limited to liability insurance for the minimum legal policy limits.

Drivers assigned to one of these plans by an insurance company should check with various insurers to compare prices.

No-Fault Automobile Insurance   In recent years, several problems in the automobile insurance market provoked calls for reform. One problem is the long delay between an accident and the receipt of payment by the person who suffered the loss. A second problem is that a high proportion of the automobile insurance premium is allocated to costs of determining of who is at fault for accidents. A third problem is the rapidly increasing cost of automobile insurance. The most prominent reform suggested is based on the concept of no-fault automobile insurance. **No-fault automobile insurance** allows you to collect directly from your insurance company for losses resulting from an automobile accident without regard to who was at fault. Proponents of no-fault insurance argue that delays in the payment of claims and claims-handling expenses are greatly reduced, thereby lessening the pressure to increase premiums.

No-fault automobile insurance allows you to collect directly from your company when the other driver is at-fault.

Approximately half the states enacted some variation of the no-fault concept. The results have been mixed. Studies have shown that in states with strong no-fault automobile insurance laws, payment delays have been reduced, claims-handling expenses have come down as a proportion of the premiums collected, and premiums, although continuing to rise, have done so at a lower rate than in states without a no-fault system. In general, however, the benefits envisioned after the enactment of no-fault plans have not been fully realized because only two states (Michigan and Massachusetts) have fully implemented the no-fault concept by severely restricting lawsuits.

During the last few years, automobile insurance rates have increased dramatically in many states. These increases have been due to higher health care and automobile repair costs, an increase in the number and dollar amount of automobile liability lawsuits, and increased traffic congestion, especially in large urban areas. Voters in a few states have passed laws calling for mandatory rollbacks of automobile insurance prices, although the effect of these laws has been minimal to date.

Another reaction to high automobile insurance rates has been renewed interest in no-fault automobile insurance. The no-fault concept is being revised in the latest proposal that allows people to choose whether they would be insured under a no-fault system or an at-fault system. If this new proposal were adopted and you chose no-fault, you would collect directly from your own company for any losses you suffer. Who is at fault for the accident would not be an issue. You would be prohibited from suing an at-fault driver who caused your losses and you also would be protected from lawsuits if you cause an accident because you could not be sued. If you chose the at-fault system, you would retain your right to sue other drivers who have chosen this approach and make claims against their insurers. You also could be sued if you caused an accident. If your losses were caused by a driver who chose the no-fault approach, you would make a claim against your own company and have the right to use your own company for your losses, if necessary. Part of the appeal of this proposed approach is that people would have a choice. Proponents argue

What If You Cause a Serious Automobile Accident?

Just how the many provisions in an automobile insurance policy apply to a specific accident is a mystery to many people. The result is often considerable dissatisfaction with the claims process after an accident. The example illustrated here and in the following chart are intended to help clarify the application of the multiple coverages and limits.

In September of last year, Donna Redman, a college student from Lynchburg, Virginia, caused a serious accident when she failed to yield to an approaching vehicle while attempting to make a left turn. Donna suffered a broken arm and facial cuts resulting in medical costs of $1254. Her passenger, Phillip Windsor, was seriously injured, with head and neck wounds requiring surgery, a 2-week hospital stay, and rehabilitation. Phillip's injuries resulted in medical costs of $17,650. The driver of the other car, John Monk, suffered serious back and internal injuries and facial burns resulting in some disfigurement. His medical care costs were $22,948. His passenger, Annette Combs, suffered cuts and bruises requiring minor medical care at a cost of $423. Both cars were totally destroyed. Donna's 10-year-old Buick was valued at $2150. John's brand-new Mazda Miata was valued at $19,350. The force of the impact spun John's car around, causing it to destroy a traffic-signal control box (valued at $3,650) and catch fire. Fortunately, both Donna and John were covered by a family automobile policy.

In our example, both Donna's and John's automobile insurance policies had liability limits of $20,000/$50,000/$15,000 and medical payments limits of $5000 per person. Donna and Phillip Windsor were reimbursed for their medical losses by Donna's medical payments coverage. Because Phillip's losses ($17,650) exceeded Don-

na's medical payments policy limits, he also made a liability claim against her policy. John Monk's policy also comes into play here. Remember that medical payments insurance will pay regardless of who is at fault for an accident. Therefore, John and Annette Combs were initially reimbursed by John's FAP for $5000 (the policy limit) and $423, respectively. Then John made a claim against Donna's insurance company in order to be reimbursed for the remainder of his bodily injury losses. Also, John's insurer exercised its subrogation rights and made a claim against Donna's insurer in order to collect the $5000 it had paid John and the $423 it had paid Annette. Donna's policy paid $20,000 (the per-person policy limit) toward John's injuries ($15,000 to John and $5000 to his insurance company) and the $423 loss suffered by Annette Combs. Her policy also reimbursed Phillip Windsor for the $12,650 in bodily injury losses not covered by her medical payments protection. Donna's policy also paid a total of $15,000 in property damage liability losses, since that was the policy limit. Donna Redman collected $2050 for her car under her collision coverage, which carried a $100 deductible. In total, Donna had to pay $11,408 out of her own pocket, since the policy limits were exceeded by John Monk's injuries and the property damage. If she had a single-limit personal automobile policy for $65,000 (the total of her $50,000 per accident bodily injury liability and $15,000 per accident property damage liability), she would have had no out-of-pocket liability losses.

An additional point needs to be raised concerning situations in which an accident victim suffers serious, permanent injuries that are not

(continued)

What If You Cause a Serious Automobile Accident? *(continued)*

fully reimbursed by the insurance policy protecting the driver at fault. In our example, John Monk suffered very painful injuries resulting in permanent disfigurement. He may wish to sue Donna for his pain and suffering and his unpaid medical expenses. If he were to file such a suit, Donna would be provided legal assistance by her insurance company. However, any judgment that exceeds the policy limits (remember that Donna's per-person policy limit has already been reached) will be Donna's responsibility.

Donna Redman's Accident: Who Pays What?

Coverage	Donna's Automobile Policy	John's Automobile Policy
Liability (limits)	(20/50/15)	(20/50/15)
Bodily injury		
John Monk	$20,000	
Annette Combs	423	
Phillip Windsor	12,650	
Property damage		
John Monk's Car	15,000	
Medical payments (limits)	($5,000)	($5,000)
John Monk		$5,000*
Annette Combs		$5,000*
Donna Redman	$1,254	
Phillip Windsor	5,000	
Collision coverage (limits)	(ACV, $100 deductible)	(ACV, $100 deductible)
Donna's car	$2,050	
Donna's out-of-pocket expenses		
John Monk's bodily injury	$2,948	
John Monk's car	4,350	
Traffic signal control box	3,650	
Collision insurance deductible	100	
TOTAL	$11,048	

* Also included in Donna's liability column, since John's company filed a claim against Donna by exercising its subrogation rights.

that those choosing the no-fault approach would pay lower premiums because there would be faster, more direct payments without the cost of lawsuits. Those choosing an at-fault approach would retain their right to use the courts to settle who should pay and how much but would pay higher premiums as a result of the cost of litigating these cases.

Buying Automobile Insurance

The personal risk manager must shop carefully for automobile insurance because its cost can be as high as $1500 or more per year. The proper automobile insurance program must be selected while keeping premiums as low as possible. Several methods of reducing premiums are available and should be considered.

Determining Your Automobile Insurance Coverages and Policy Limits   The first step toward designing an adequate automobile insurance program involves identifying the losses that might occur. This is not a difficult task because the personal and family automobile policies cover most of the losses that you can reasonably expect to face as a result of owning and driving a car.

It is sometimes possible to eliminate some of the coverages provided in a policy to reduce the overall premium. However, the only way to obtain a substantial reduction is to eliminate collision coverage. The premium for collision coverage represents from 30 to 40 percent of the total automobile insurance bill. Cars with a book value under $1000 are candidates for collision insurance elimination. Other nonessential coverages, such as comprehensive, towing, or uninsured motorist insurance, would not yield significant savings if eliminated.

Choose high liability limits with the money saved by raising your collision deductible.

Next you must determine the amount of coverage you need. At a minimum, you must conform to the financial responsibility requirements in your state (see Table 12.6). Most automobile owners, even in states that do not require automobile insurance, will choose automobile insurance as the means to show the required financial responsibility. Because of high health care and automobile repair costs, it is wise to buy as much coverage as you can afford. Recommended insurance coverage would provide liability protection with limits of $100,000/$300,000/$50,000. And you can usually double these limits for under $100 per year. Similar policy limits for uninsured and underinsured motorist coverage are advisable, although in some states there is a legal maximum on such coverages. Recommended limits for automobile medical expense coverage are at least $50,000 per person.

How Automobile Insurance Is Priced   The premium charged for an automobile insurance policy is based on up to 52 different characteristics that describe the driver, the car itself, and the usage of the car. These characteristics are used to place the insured in one of 260 classes. Members of each class have a similar probability of loss. The same price per unit of insurance is assigned to each member of the class and is then adjusted for the individual driver's accident and traffic violation experience, as well as

TABLE 12.6
Automobile Financial Responsibility Limits

State	Liability Limits*	State	Liability Limits*
Alabama	20/40/10	Nebraska	25/50/25
Alaska	50/100/25	Nevada	15/30/10
Arizona	15/30/10	New Hampshire	25/50/25
Arkansas	25/50/15	New Jersey	15/30/5
California	15/30/5	New Mexico	25/50/10
Colorado	25/50/15	New York	10/20/5†
Connecticut	20/40/10	North Carolina	25/50/10
Delaware	15/30/10	North Dakota	25/50/25
Florida	10/20/5	Ohio	12.5/25/7.5
Georgia	15/30/10	Oklahoma	10/20/10
Hawaii	35/unlimited/10	Oregon	25/50/10
Idaho	25/50/15	Pennsylvania	15/30/5
Illinois	20/40/15	Rhode Island	25/50/25
Indiana	25/50/10	South Carolina	15/30/5
Iowa	20/40/15	South Dakota	25/50/25
Kansas	25/50/10	Tennessee	20/50/10
Kentucky	25/50/10	Texas	20/40/15
Louisiana	10/20/10	Utah	20/40/10
Maine	20/40/10	Vermont	20/40/10
Maryland	20/40/10	Virginia	25/50/20
Massachusetts	10/20/5	Washington	25/50/10
Michigan	20/40/10	Washington, D.C.	25/50/10
Minnesota	30/60/10	West Virginia	20/40/10
Mississippi	10/20/5	Wisconsin	25/50/10
Missouri	25/50/10	Wyoming	25/50/20
Montana	25/50/5		

Source: Used with permission of the Insurance Information Institute, 110 Williams St., New York, NY 10038.

* The first two figures refer to bodily injury liability limits, and the third figure refers to property damage liability. For example, 10/20/5 means coverage up to $20,000 for all persons injured in an accident, subject to a limit of $10,000 for one individual, and $5000 coverage for property damage.
† 50/100 in cases of wrongful death.

any discounts for which the driver qualifies. The resulting price per unit is then multiplied by the number of units to obtain the premium charged.

Most of the characteristics used to classify the insured generate little controversy. Some of these characteristics are the miles driven to work or per year, the make and model of car insured, whether the car is used for business or pleasure, and where the car is garaged (more congested city traffic generates more frequent accidents). Several of the characteristics have generated considerable controversy in recent years, however. These are the age, gender, and marital status of the driver.

Unmarried males under the age of 25 pay higher premiums than any other group. Insurance industry representatives argue the validity of the classifications being used. For instance, young drivers are involved in a

TABLE 12.7
Accidents by Age of Driver

Age Group (years)	Accident Involvement Rate	
	*All Accidents**	*Fatal Accidents†*
14–19	39	62
20–24	37	68
25–34	25	43
35–44	18	31
45–54	14	26
55–64	14	24
65–74	13	25
75 +	24	66
All drivers	22	39

Source: Data from National Safety Council.

* Drivers in all accidents per 100 drivers in each age group.
† Drivers in fatal accidents per 100,000 drivers in each age group.

disproportionate share of the automobile accidents in the United States (see Table 12.7), as are unmarried drivers and males. Opponents of these classifications point out that although the statistics used by the industry may be actuarially valid, the result is still discrimination based on age, gender, and marital status, which is prohibited in other commercial activities. Critics question why a young, male driver who operates a car safely should pay a higher premium solely because of his age and gender. Legislators and insurance regulators in many states have proposed abolishing the use of age, gender, and marital status as determinants of automobile insurance premiums, although fewer than 10 states have enacted such laws.

Other Property and Liability Loss Exposures

Objective
To be able to describe property and liability insurance policies designed to meet needs other than those related to housing and automobiles.

Many individuals need other types of protection against property and liability losses. This section will discuss some of the less well known but still important property and liability policies.

Floater Policies

Floater policies provide all-risk protection for accident and theft losses to movable personal property regardless of wherever in the world the loss occurs. Floater policies can be purchased as an addition to a home owner's policy or as a separate policy. Some of the personal property items commonly protected under a floater policy are stereo equipment, sporting goods, cameras, and gifts. *Scheduled floater policies* provide insurance protection for specifically identified items of personal property. *Unscheduled floater policies* provide insurance protection for certain classes of property or all movable property owned by the insured.

Antique and Specialty Cars

Antique and specialty cars are often worth more than their book value, but the collision and comprehensive coverages under a standard automobile insurance policy will pay only the book value when an automobile is destroyed. In order to avoid receiving inadequate payment after a loss to such a vehicle, you can purchase special coverage from an automobile insurance company. The amount of coverage should be based on a professional appraisal of the worth of the vehicle.

Government-Provided Property Insurance

Crop and flood insurance are the result of federal government programs.

Crop insurance and flood insurance are two types of property insurance provided through the federal government. **Crop insurance** provides all-risk protection from losses to crops between planting and harvest. The Federal Crop Insurance Corporation is the major source of such insurance. The policy limits for crop insurance are stated as a certain dollar amount per acre. **Flood insurance** protects property from losses caused by floods and mud slides provided that the property is located in areas eligible under the National Flood Insurance Act of 1968. The U.S. Department of Housing and Urban Development and the National Flood Insurers Association jointly administer the program. Eligibility is based on the existence of flood-control measures in the community and the proximity of the property to the flooding source.

Comprehensive Personal Liability Insurance

Owning a home and driving a car are not the only sources of potential liability you face. Consider, for example, the case of Michael Hunt, a pharmacist from Golden, Colorado. While climbing in a restricted area, Michael accidentally loosened some rocks, which fell down the slope and seriously injured hikers below. Because Michael had failed to warn the hikers that he was above them, he was held liable for their injuries and was ordered to pay a court judgment of $78,000. Fortunately for Michael and the injured hikers, he was protected by a **comprehensive personal liability insurance** policy, which provides protection from liability losses that might arise out of any activity.

Remember that the standard home owner's insurance policy includes a specified limit on personal liability coverage for losses associated with the insured dwelling. For those without such coverage or who wish higher limits, a separate comprehensive personal liability policy (also called an

The conservative buyer of property and liability insurance is careful to buy adequate coverage while keeping insurance expenditures to a minimum. There is no point in paying more for insurance than is absolutely necessary.

1. *Shop around for the lowest-cost coverage.* You may obtain quotes that differ by as much as $500 per year for essentially the same automobile insurance protection. While the range is not so great in home owner's insurance, savings still can be realized by seeking quotes from several agents. To obtain a quote, telephone an agent and provide some basic descriptive information. Most agents are happy to call back later with a quotation in the hope of obtaining a new customer. What else should the conservative buyer do?

2. *Select appropriate coverages and limits.* Each of the property insurance coverages provided under automobile and home owner's insurance policies is subject to specific policy limits. In home owner's insurance, people focus on the policy limit for the coverage on the dwelling itself, but although this limit is important, you also must select the proper limit for coverage on the contents, other structures, and general liability. Match each limit in your home owner's insurance policy as closely as possible with the potential for loss. If some of your assets (such as a coin or stamp collection) are worth more than the coverage provided in the standard policy, you may wish to raise the limits on these items. If a car is never driven for business or to work, make sure that this is reflected in the policy. Or if certain drivers in the family are the source of high premiums, it might be wise to exclude them from coverage and use of the car.

3. *Assume risks that you can afford.* Deductibles are a form or risk assumption. You could choose a $500 or even $1000 deductible. Raising the deductible can be an effective way of lowering automobile collision insurance. Doubling the deductible from $100 to $200 can lower the collision premium by 25 percent. Consider dropping collision coverage altogether for cars worth less than $1200.

If you wish to reduce the cost of your home owner's insurance policy, you can select a lower face amount than that required under the replacement-cost requirement (see page 423)—in effect, coinsuring any loss you suffer. Select such a premium-reduction technique cautiously, however. Lowering the face amount of the policy by as little as 10 percent may result in your paying thousands of dollars of unreimbursed losses.

(continued)

umbrella liability policy) is advisable. When such coverage is designed to pay for only the excess of that provided in an automobile or home owner's policy, the premiums are generally affordable.

Professional Liability Insurance

Professionals, such as surgeons, dental hygienists, and accountants, can be held legally liable for losses suffered by their patients or clients. Such losses can arise out of a breach-of-contract dispute or as a result of negligence on the part of the service provider. **Professional liability insurance** (sometimes called *malpractice insurance*) protects individuals and organizations that provide professional services when they are held liable for the losses

Many people assume risk by selecting low liability insurance limits. This is an inappropriate technique for most people, because choosing 50 percent lower policy limits for liability coverage will reduce the liability premium only by 10 to 15 percent. One should assume risks one can afford, by raising a deductible, for example, and insure against losses that would be unaffordable, such as a massive liability loss that might occur if you caused a major automobile accident. As a general rule, buy the highest liability limits (such as 250/500/100) and pay for them with the savings gained from choosing a high collision deductible (e.g., $500).

4. *Take advantage of discounts.* Many companies offer discounts to policyholders who reduce the probability and/or severity of a loss. For example, discounts are available if you install dead-bolt door locks and a fire extinguisher in your home. The locks reduce the probability of a theft loss, and the fire extinguisher can reduce the severity of small fire losses. Another discount is commonly offered for the installation of smoke alarms. You also can save on premiums by taking advantage of the discounts offered by automobile insurers. If your family owns more than one car,

they all might be insured with the same company, because most companies will insure two cars without doubling the premiums. Most automobile insurers provide discounts when a driver has attained a certain number of accident-free years. If you buy a car that has air bags or automatic seat belts, you may receive a discount. You also may receive a discount if you buy your automobile and home owner's insurance from the same company.

5. *Make sure you are properly classified.* You can save money by making sure you have been placed in the proper class for premium-determination purposes. Automobile insurers will classify a car driven just a few miles to work each day differently than one driven a greater distance. If a job change results in a shorter drive to work, you should notify your automobile insurance agent. Home improvements may affect the class you are placed in for home owner's insurance. Verifying that you are in the proper class is also important for obtaining the protection desired. If you use your car regularly in a manner not anticipated when the premium was determined, a claim may be denied if a loss occurs.

of their clients. Policy limits, deductibles, and other characteristics of such policies vary considerably depending on the profession involved. Generally, professional liability policies are written with policy limits of $1 million and more. The premiums for such policies vary considerably. A $1 million professional liability policy written for a dental hygienist may cost as low as $300 per year. Yet some surgeons pay in excess of $60,000 per year for professional liability insurance.

Group Legal Insurance

Personal liability insurance policies will provide reimbursement for legal expenses if you are sued or held liable for the losses of others. However, legal services are often needed in situations not involving a question of liability. In response to such needs, a **group legal insurance plan** provides reimbursement for legal expenses to eligible members of a group, such as a labor union or a credit union. Most group legal insurance plans currently in effect have been provided as an employee fringe benefit.

Collecting on Your Property and Liability Losses

For most people, the peace of mind and reduction of risk that insurance can provide are worth the cost. However, the real value of owning insurance becomes evident when a loss occurs and reimbursement is obtained. Collecting this reimbursement sometimes can be very frustrating, however, particularly if you do not understand the processes involved and are not prepared to present timely and accurate evidence of loss.

People often question whether they should file a claim out of fear that it will lead to higher insurance premiums. This feeling is especially common for minor automobile accidents. As a rule, it is always best to notify your agent. Ask if your rates will go up if you file an official claim. Then weigh the cost of paying a loss out of your pocket against the higher premiums. You should be aware, however, that paying out of your own pocket for minor property damage can be viewed as an admission of liability if you are later sued for bodily injury losses that were not evident at the time of the accident. Further, most companies will not raise premiums after an accident if you have been accident-free for the previous 3 to 5 years.

The first step in making an insurance claim is to contact your insurance agent or other company claims representative. Do this as soon as possible. Then keep the company informed of everything relevant to the loss. This may mean daily or weekly contact until the claim is settled. The tenacious claimant is most likely to collect fully on a loss.

Documenting Your Loss

You are responsible for documenting your loss.

The burden of proof is on you whenever a property or liability loss occurs. Adequate documentation of the circumstances and the amount of the loss is essential. In the absence of such documentation, the insurance company will interpret the situation in the manner most favorable to their interests. While essentially the same in principle, the documentation needed for home owner's and automobile insurance differs in detail.

How to Document Claims for Home Owner's Insurance   The best way to document a theft, fire, or other personal property loss is with pictures. Photograph or videotape all valuable property in your home when you purchase it or when you obtain insurance coverage. Write the date of purchase, price paid, description, model name and number, and serial number (if any) of the property on the back of the photograph or verbally record it on the videotape. Keep the documentation and a list of any unphotographed property (with a complete description) separate from the property itself. These items could be safely kept in a safe-deposit box or in a file cabinet at work or with a relative.

When a loss occurs, file a report with the police or fire department, and present a copy of this report and copies of the photographs and list to the agent or company when you file your claim for reimbursement. If your home has been damaged in a way that might allow for subsequent damage from rain or wind, the opening should be boarded up or otherwise secured. Often the insurance agent will arrange for these temporary repairs. No permanent repairs should be attempted until the insurance company has been notified and has inspected the premises.

Always file a police report when involved in an automobile accident.

How to Document Claims for Automobile Insurance   Always contact the police and file a report when involved in an automobile accident. The potential for misunderstanding or intentional deception between the drivers of the cars involved and their respective insurance companies is too great to rely solely on any verbal statements made by the drivers at the time of the mishap. Consider the case of Lisa Chen, a nurse from San Mateo, California, who was involved in an accident with a driver who had struck her car after attempting to pass on the right shoulder. Such a maneuver is illegal, and the other driver was clearly at fault and verbally admitted as much. Because the accident caused no bodily injury and both cars could be driven afterward, Lisa agreed to the other driver's request that the police not be contacted. Instead, Lisa and the other driver exchanged information. Later, Lisa found out that the other driver's insurance had been canceled and that he had given her a false address and telephone number. Because she had no collision insurance on her car, Lisa paid the $2638 repair bill herself. Had she filed a police report, her chances of collecting from the other driver would have been greatly increased, since she would have had the evidence of the circumstances of the accident and the police would have obtained valid and proper identification.

You also should prepare a written report of any automobile accident for your own records. This report should include a diagram of the accident scene showing the location of the vehicles before, at, and after the time of impact, plus the location of traffic lights and signs and any landmarks (for example, road construction or repairs). Also include a written description of the accident giving the time and place, the direction of travel and speed of the cars involved, road and weather conditions, and behavior of the parties involved. If possible, obtain the names and addresses of at least two witnesses. These notes will help you in the event of later litigation.

Filing the Claim

Your contact when filing an insurance claim is called a claims adjuster.

An **insurance claim** is a formal request to the insurance company for reimbursement for a covered loss. All the documentation and information will be requested by the insurance agent or **claims adjuster,** who is the person designated by the insurance company to assess whether the loss is covered and the dollar amount the company will pay. A claims adjuster can be an employee of the insurance company or an individual who provides these services to an insurance company for a fee. Generally, the insurance agent oversees the settlement process.

Insurance companies require that requests for payment be made in writing. Figure 12.2 shows a claim form similar to that used by many automobile insurance companies for an automobile insurance claim. Some companies will require you to fill out the forms, although most will complete the forms for you.

The most common problem occurring in the claims process is disagreement over the dollar amount of the loss. When property is damaged rather than destroyed or stolen, most companies request that you obtain repair estimates. Some companies, to speed up the settlement of claims, allow the claims adjuster to estimate the repair costs and issue a check to you to use for repairs. Although this process is faster, it may not be easy to find a source willing to make the repairs for the amount paid. Disputes over the dollar amount of a loss are most common when policies cover only the depreciated value of the property rather than its replacement cost. People often feel that their property had a greater value than that established by the insurance company. A solution to this dilemma is to purchase replacement-cost insurance, but this lesson is often learned too late.

Signing a Release

Sign a release only when satisfied with the loss settlement.

The final step in the claims-settlement process is the signing of the **release**, which is an insurance document affirming that you accept the dollar amount of the loss settlement as full and complete reimbursement and that you will make no further claims for the loss against the insurance company. The legal effect of signing the release is to absolve the insurance company of any further responsibility for the loss. Never sign a release prematurely, since the full extent of the loss may not manifest itself until some time after the loss occurs. This is especially true for bodily injury losses. Sometimes the insured is pressured into signing the release quickly in order to receive payment as soon as possible, but you should resist the temptation to give in to such pressure. When dealing with your insurance company, gently but firmly insist that adequate time elapse so that the full magnitude of the loss has a chance to become evident. You may face difficulties dealing with the insurance company of the at-fault driver, but most can be avoided by your insistence that the insurance company of the liable party negotiate through your agent. A qualified agent has the experience and expertise to resist undue pressure and best represent your interests.

Summary

1. The ownership of property exposes an individual to two types of losses. First, the property itself can be damaged or destroyed. Second, the use of the property can result in losses to another person for which the owner is legally liable.

FIGURE 12.2
Automobile Insurance Claim Form
Source: Used by permission of Acord Corporation.

ACORD. PROPERTY LOSS NOTICE

DATE (MM/DD/YY)

PRODUCER	PRODUCER PHONE (A/C, No., Ext.)	MISCELLANEOUS INFORMATION (Site & Location Code)		
	COMPANY	POLICY NUMBER		CAT. #
	POLICY EFF. DATE (MM/DD/YY)	POLICY EXP. DATE (MM/DD/YY)	DATE (MM/DD/YY) & TIME OF LOSS	PREVIOUSLY REPORTED
CODE SUB CODE			A.M.	YES
			P.M.	NO

INSURED

NAME AND ADDRESS	INSURED'S RESIDENCE PHONE (A/C, No.)	INSURED'S BUSINESS PHONE (A/C, No., Ext.)
	PERSON TO CONTACT	WHERE TO CONTACT
		WHEN
	CONTACT'S RESIDENCE PHONE (A/C, No.)	CONTACT'S BUSINESS PHONE (A/C, No., Ext.)

LOSS

LOCATION OF LOSS	POLICE OR FIRE DEPT. TO WHICH REPORTED
KIND OF LOSS (Fire, Wind, Explosion, Etc.)	PROBABLE AMOUNT ENTIRE LOSS

DESCRIPTION OF LOSS & DAMAGE (Use reverse side, if necessary)

POLICY INFORMATION

MORTGAGEE (If none so indicated)

HOMEOWNER POLICIES SECTION 1 ONLY (Complete for coverages A, B, C, D & additional coverages. For Homeowners Section II Liability Losses, use ACORD 3.)

COVERAGE A	COVERAGE B	COVERAGE C	COVERAGE D	DESCRIBE ADDITIONAL COVERAGES PROVIDED
DWELLING	APPURTENANT PRIVATE STRUCTURES	UNSCHEDULED PERSONAL PROPERTY	ADDITIONAL LIVING EXPENSES	ON
				ON

SUBJECT TO FORMS. (Insert form nos. & edition dates, special deductibles)	DEDUCTIBLES

FIRES, ALLIED LINES & MULTI-PERIL POLICIES (Complete only those items involved in loss)

ITEM	AMOUNT	BLDG.	CONTENTS	OTHER	%COINS	DEDUCTIBLE	COVERAGE AND / OR DESCRIPTION OF PROPERTY INSURED

SUBJECT TO FORMS. (Insert form nos. & edition dates, special deductibles)

MISCELLANEOUS INFORMATION

OTHER INSURANCE (List companies, policy numbers, coverages & policy amounts)

REMARKS

ADJUSTER ASSIGNED	DATE ASSIGNED (MM/DD/YY)

REPORTED BY	REPORTED TO	SIGNATURE OF PRODUCER OR INSURED

ACORD 1 (2/88)	NOTE: IMPORTANT STATE INFORMATION ON REVERSE SIDE	© ACORD CORPORATION 1988

2. Home owner's insurance is designed to protect home owners and renters from property and liability losses. There are seven different types of home owner's insurance. Home owner's policies can be purchased on a named-peril or all-risk basis.

3. Automobile insurance is designed to protect the insured from property and liability losses arising out of use of a motor vehicle. The typical policy will provide liability insurance (both bodily injury and property damage liability), medical payments or personal injury protection insurance, property insurance on your car, and underinsured and uninsured motorist insurance. The most commonly purchased type of automobile insurance is the family automobile policy. The premium for automobile insurance is based on the characteristics of the insured driver, including age, gender, marital status, and driving record.

4. Other important types of property and liability insurance include floater policies to protect personal property regardless of its location, flood insurance provided by the federal government, and professional liability insurance.

5. Responsibility for documenting and verifying a loss lies with the insured. Photographs or a videotape of the insured property is ideal for documenting losses under a home owner's insurance policy. A police report provides the best documentation for losses under an automobile insurance policy.

Modern Money Management

The Johnsons Change Their Insurance Policies

The recent purchase of a condominium and a used car have forced the Johnsons to change their home owner's and automobile insurance policies. Their personal property and furniture are now valued at about $12,000. Their used car is a 7-year-old Chevrolet Citation with 87,000 miles on the odometer. They currently carry a 30/60/20 family automobile policy with $200 deductible collision and $100 deductible comprehensive and a $10,000 medical expense protection on their Toyota.

1. What type of home owner's insurance policy will they need to buy? Would you recommend actual cash value contents coverage or contents replacement cost protection? Why?

2. What should be the face amount of the policy, and what major property and liability coverages should it provide?

3. In addition to adding their "new" car to their existing automobile

insurance policy, how might the Johnsons change Parts 1, 2, 3, and 4 of their policy?

4. Should the Johnsons buy collision insurance on the used car? Why or why not?

Key Words and Concepts

actual cash value, 425
actual-cash-value (ACV) formula, 425
all-risk policies, 419
automobile bodily injury liability, 428
automobile insurance, 426
automobile insurance plans (AIPs), 432
automobile medical payments insurance, 429
automobile property damage liability, 428
book value, 431
claims adjuster, 443
collision insurance, 431
comprehensive automobile insurance, 431
comprehensive personal liability insurance, 439
contents replacement-cost protection, 426
crop insurance, 439
family automobile policy (FAP), 432

floater policies, 438
flood insurance, 439
group legal insurance plan, 442
home owner's general liability protection, 419
home owner's insurance, 419
home owner's no-fault medical payments protection, 419
insurance claim, 443
liability insurance, 418
named-perils policies, 419
no-fault automobile insurance, 433
personal automobile policy (PAP), 432
professional liability insurance, 440
property insurance, 418
release, 444
replacement-cost-requirement formula, 423
subrogation rights, 429
underinsured motorist insurance, 431
uninsured motorist insurance, 431

Review Questions

1. Who pays for financial losses suffered from various kinds of accidents, such as automobile accidents and fire, and from crimes against property?

2. Distinguish between property and liability insurance.

3. Explain why you would purchase property and liability insurance?

4. Define home owner's insurance.

5. Name the five types of losses covered under the property insurance portion of a home owner's policy.

6. Identify two perils that are commonly excluded from home owner's policies.

7. Distinguish between a named-perils policy and an all-risk policy.

8. Give an example of a home owner's liability loss that could be covered under general liability insurance.

9. Briefly distinguish among the seven types of home owner's insurance policies identified as HO-1 through HO-6 and HO-8.

10. If you do not insure your home for the full amount of the coinsurance requirement, what would be the result in case of a loss?

11. In most home owner's insurance policies, contents and personal property are covered up to what percentage of the coverage on the dwelling itself?

12. Distinguish between actual cash value and contents replacement-cost policies.

13. Define automobile insurance.

14. Name and distinguish between the two types of losses covered by automobile insurance.

15. Identify the two automobile insurance policies most often purchased by individuals or families and name their four parts.

16. Many automobile insurance policies identify dollar coverage for the insured as $20,000/$50,000/$15,000. Explain what each amount means.

17. Explain the type of coverage provided under automobile medical payments insurance.

18. How do subrogation rights come into play as related to automobile insurance?

19. Distinguish between collision and comprehensive automobile insurance coverage.

20. What is the benefit to the insured of no-fault automobile insurance? What is the benefit to the insurer?

21. How many different characteristics do insurers use to classify the insured when determining the premium for an automobile insurance policy? Identify five of the most prominent of these characteristics.

22. Identify the three most controversial characteristics insurers use to assess an automobile insurance premium?

23. What type of property loss would be covered under a floater policy?

24. What is the best way to document a theft, fire, or other loss to personal property in the home? Also, identify the documentation process.

25. Describe what you should do to file a claim most effectively when involved in an automobile accident.

Case Problems

1. Joe and Pam Cleve of Buffalo, New York, recently suffered a fire in their home. The fire began in a crawl space at the back of the house, causing $24,000 of damage to the dwelling. The garage, valued at $8400, was

totally destroyed but did not contain a car at the time. The damage to their personal property in the home and garage came to $18,500 for replacement. Also, $350 in cash and a stamp collection valued at $3215 were destroyed. While the damage was being repaired, the Cleves spent 3 weeks in a motel and spent $1350 on food and lodging. The house had a value of $95,000 and was insured for $68,400 under an HO-5 comprehensive form home owner's policy with a $250 deductible. (Use Table 12.1 to answer this problem. Use the higher figure where two are given for the limits of coverage. Hint: You must first determine if they have adequate insurance, and if not what percentage of the necessary 80 percent coverage they do have. The resulting answer will determine the percentage of the loss to the dwelling covered, and consequently the amount to be reimbursed by the insurance company.)

a. Assuming that the deductible was applied to the damage to the dwelling, calculate the amount covered by insurance and the amount paid by the Cleves for each loss listed: the dwelling itself, the garage, the cash and stamp collection, and the extra living expenses.

b. How much of the amount of the personal property loss would be covered by the insurance? paid for by the Cleves?

c. Assuming contents replacement cost protection on the personal property, what amount and percentage of the total loss was paid by the Cleves?

d. What two things could the Cleves have done to prevent their having to pay anything more than the deductible?

2. Louise Miller of Denver, Colorado, drives a 3-year-old Plymouth Horizon valued at $5600. She has a $75,000 personal automobile policy with $10,000 per person medical payments coverage and both collision ($200 deductible) and comprehensive. David Smith of Fort Collins, Colorado, drives a 2-year-old Chevrolet Celebrity valued at $8500. He has a 25/50/15 family automobile policy with $20,000 in medical payments coverage and both collision ($100 deductible) and comprehensive. Late one evening, while he was driving back from Rocky Mountain National Park, David's car crossed the center line, striking Louise's car and forcing it into the ditch. David's car also left the road and did extensive damage to the front of a roadside store. The following table outlines the damages and the dollar amounts of each.

Item	Dollar Amount
Bodily injuries suffered by Louise	$ 6,800
Bodily injuries suffered by Fran, a passenger in Louise's car	28,634
Louise's car	5,600
Bodily injuries suffered by David	2,700
Bodily injuries suffered by Cecilia, a passenger in David's car	12,485
David's car	8,500
Damage to the roadside store	14,123

a. How much will Louise's policy pay Louise and Fran?

b. Will subrogation rights come into play? How?

c. How much will David's bodily injury liability protection pay?

d. To whom and how much will David's property damage liability protection pay?

e. To whom and how much will David's medical protection pay?

f. How much reimbursement will David receive for his car?

g. How much will David be required to pay out of his own pocket?

3. Donald Kriminshaw, of Burlington, Vermont, has frequently questioned the basis for setting the premium he pays for automobile insurance. He takes issue with three factors: his age (he is 20), his sex, and his marital status (he is single). He feels that being judged a greater financial risk on the basis of these factors is discriminatory, and he thinks that many other factors should be given overriding consideration.

a. Is Donald correct in his assessment of the use of age, sex, and marital status as being discriminatory? Explain.

b. Why do you think insurance companies consider these factors when determining premium rates for automobile insurance?

c. Describe other factors that could be used in addition to or instead of these three that would result in a more equitable premium charge.

d. Will Donald ever be able to overcome these three negative factors and pay lower insurance premiums? How?

Suggested Readings

"A Crash Course on When to Come Clean." *U.S. News & World Report*, November 6, 1989, p. 106. Explains the importance of keeping your automobile insurance company informed of your accidents and losses.

"Car Insurance: Dial Up a Better Deal." *Changing Times*, April 1990, pp. 43–48. How to shop quickly and efficiently for automobile insurance and get the cheapest rates.

"Getting What You Deserve on a Homeowner's or Auto Claim." *Money*, June 1989, pp. 147–150. Suggestions on preventing problems with your insurer and challenging them when necessary.

"How to Make Your Home Secure." *Consumer Reports*, February 1990, pp. 96–109. How to save on home owner's insurance premiums; includes ratings of locks, alarms, and alarm systems.

"Insuring Your Home." *Consumer Reports*, September 1989, pp. 572–578. Complete information on purchasing home owner's or renter's insurance.

"The Compelling Case for No-Fault Insurance." *Changing Times*, July 1989, pp. 49–52. Advocates say that auto insurance rates can be cut with no-fault coverage.

"When to Say No to Car Rental Insurance." *Money*, February 1990, pp. 21–22. Explores situations in which it is best to decline collision-damage waiver protection offered by car rental companies.

13 Health and Disability Income Insurance

OBJECTIVES

After reading this chapter, you should be able to

1. Describe potential health care losses and the process used to determine your health insurance needs.

2. Identify and describe the major types of health insurance available, and list the health care expenses covered by each.

3. Describe the purpose and major features of disability income insurance.

4. Explain the major provisions and exclusions contained in health insurance policies, and identify the benefits and negative aspects of each.

5. Identify the major sources of health insurance so you can select health insurance policy features to meet your health insurance needs.

Although the American population is healthier now than at any time in our history, illness and injury still strike frequently. By 1995, total expenditures for health care in the United States will approach $1 trillion per year. This will represent more than 11.5 percent of the gross national product and amount to more than $3600 each for every man, woman, and child in the country. Table 13.1 illustrates the rising expenditures for health care in the United States.

Health insurance provides protection against financial losses resulting from illness, injury, and disability. The development of health insurance is a relatively recent event. The first insurer that offered sickness insurance was organized in 1847, but not until the 1930s did health insurance begin to be widely established. In 1929, the first health maintenance organization (HMO) was established, as was the first Blue Cross plan. In 1935, passage of the Social Security Act brought the federal government onto the health insurance stage.

If you are among the 85 percent of Americans covered by some form of private or government health insurance, you can receive financial assistance when injury or illness strikes. However, will the assistance be sufficient to meet your needs? Do you have the correct type of coverage? Do you understand your policy? Are you getting the most for your premium dollar, and have you selected coverage from the best source? This chapter will help you answer these questions.

Health insurance helps pay for losses from illness, injury, and disability.

TABLE 13.1
Health Care Expenditures in the United States

Year	Health Care Expenditures (in Billions)	Health Care Expenditures as Percentage of GNP	Percentage Change in Health Care CPI (Over Previous Year)
1970	$ 75.0	7.4%	6.4%
1975	132.7	8.3%	12.0%
1980	248.1	9.1%	10.9%
1985	422.6	10.4%	6.2%
1988	553.0	11.3%	6.5%
1991*	680.0	11.4%	6.8%

Source: Source Book of Health Insurance Data, Health Insurance Association of America.
* Author's estimate.

Private health insurance and government programs now account for about 70 percent of the annual health care expenditures in this country. The remaining 30 percent represents people's out-of-pocket expenditures. In truth, however, the entire health care bill comes out of the pockets of individuals, since government expenditures are supported by taxes and insurer expenditures are supported by premium payments.

The decisions you make regarding health insurance can be complicated. This chapter is designed to remove some of the mystery surrounding the subject. The first section addresses the question of why you need health insurance. Then we discuss how to determine your health insurance needs. A thorough examination of the types of health insurance follows. The next section covers the important topic of disability income insurance. The final two sections of the chapter address key provisions in health insurance policies as well as guidelines for shopping for health insurance.

Determining Health Insurance Needs

Objective
To be able to describe potential health care losses and the process used to determine your health insurance needs.

The reason for buying any type of insurance is to reduce the risk of financial loss that might result from the occurrence of a peril. Health insurance reduces the risk of financial loss resulting from the perils of illness and injury. Insurance to reduce risk is only one way to handle health-related risk; risk also can be assumed. Most people assume the risk of small losses when they buy health insurance because most policies have a deductible. Likewise, people assume the risk of a very large health-related loss when they buy health insurance with low policy limits.

The task is to match your health insurance coverage to your needs. It is just as possible to be overinsured as it is to be underinsured. Thus, your first step is to assess the types and magnitude of losses that can occur. You can then match these against the resources available to cover the losses. The difference between the potential losses and the resources available can be taken care of through the purchase of insurance.

Health-Related Losses

There are four categories of losses that can result from an injury or illness. The most obvious is the expense for direct medical care. The other three are often overlooked, although they may result in larger dollar losses during a specific illness than direct medical care. They are losses resulting from the need for recuperative care, for rehabilitation, and for replacement of income lost while unable to work.

The bulk of health care losses are for direct medical care expenses.

Direct Medical Care Expenses When illness or injury strikes, little attention usually is paid to the cost of medical care. It is much more important to treat the problem and restore the health of the patient. Eventually, however, the bills come rolling in and are often met with disbelief. Not only are the amounts a shock, but there may be more people requesting payment than the patient had anticipated.

A quick look at health care expenditures shows why you need health insurance. The average American spends more than $350 on physician services per year. The bill for a 1-day hospital stay averages over $700, including physicians' charges, drugs, and the cost of any medical procedures performed. The bill for a 1-day stay in an intensive care unit can exceed $3000. The birth of a baby can cost $3200 even if there are no complications. None of these figures represents extraordinary medical treatment. On the other hand, an illness or injury that requires advanced medical science (such as CAT scans, nuclear medicine, or microsurgery) can quickly wipe out family savings or, worse, go untreated because of lack of funds.

Consider the case of Irma Hayenga, a court stenographer from Minneapolis, Minnesota, who fell while ice skating and suffered a compound fracture of her right arm. An ambulance transported her to the hospital, and she was admitted through the emergency room and seen by a physician. There will be separate charges for the ambulance and emergency room, and the admitting physician may send a separate bill. Irma's first stop was the x-ray department. There will be a charge for each x-ray, and any technologists or physicians needed to read the x-rays also will charge for their services. Irma then underwent a series of blood tests and other laboratory work, which will each carry a separate charge. For surgery and postoperative recovery, Irma will be charged for a variety of items: professional services of an anesthesiologist, a surgeon, and an assisting surgeon; intravenous fluid and drugs; 2 days' stay in a hospital room (with extra charged for a telephone and television); personal items such as tissues and a water jug; and possible follow-up complications.

As you can see from this example, the variety of direct medical expenses can seem endless. Irma would probably pay a total of around $5000. These costs increase dramatically with more complicated medical treatments.

Recuperative Care Expenses The need for health care may not end when a patient is discharged from the hospital. Sometimes there is a need for a period of confinement in a convalescent center or nursing home. Even after the patient returns home, there may be a need for home nursing care, possibly 24 hours per day.

Rehabilitation Expenses Some illnesses or injuries are so severe that they result in a total or partial disability. A **total disability** is an injury or illness that prevents you from performing any of the tasks of your previous occupation or of any other occupation. A **partial disability** is an injury or illness that prevents you from performing one or more functions of your regular occupation. **Rehabilitation** is the retraining of disabled persons for their previous, or a new, occupation. Although her cast was removed after 6 weeks, Irma Hayenga went through a 10-week program of physical therapy before returning to her job as a court stenographer.

Rehabilitation expenses pay for retraining disabled persons.

Lost Income The average worker in the United States misses 5 workdays per year because of illness or injury. An occasional workday lost will not put much of a strain on the family budget, but when an illness is severe or becomes chronic, serious budget disruptions can result. When a disability strikes, income may be lost because the victim may not be up to full-time work or may be forced to take a lower-paying, less-demanding position. It takes little imagination to visualize the hardships if such a disability is permanent. In Irma Hayenga's case, she was out of work for 4 months and lost almost $10,000 in income.

Health Insurance Coverage

You need not purchase health insurance if you have sufficient resources available to cover health-related losses. Three types of resources need to be considered: (1) monetary and other assets, (2) other insurance, and (3) skills and education. Assets such as savings and investments can lessen the need for health insurance. However, the assets that most families accumulate during a lifetime are often specifically intended to cover retirement expenses, not health-related losses. Some health-related losses may be reimbursed through other types of insurance, such as automobile insurance policies or workers' compensation insurance. These can be helpful, but they provide only limited coverage. They can only supplement, not replace, health insurance. A disabled person's skills and education will have a bearing on the amount of rehabilitation needed following a partial or total disability. A physical disability, such as paralysis, might not prevent an accountant from doing his or her job, but blindness might require a change of careers.

To determine the amount of health insurance you need, you must subtract the losses that can result from an injury or accident from the resources available to pay for such losses. The differences will be in terms of both the type of coverage and the dollar amount needed. Most people will need some health insurance. The next section will cover types of health insurance available, and a later section will discuss the dollar amounts of coverage.

Types of Health Insurance

The term *health insurance* is a general name for a wide variety of insurance policies and plans that cover financial losses resulting from illness, injury, or disability. No one policy or plan provides coverage for all types of losses that can occur. The health insurance purchaser faces a situation not unlike that of a diner who must choose from an à la carte menu. You must select coverages for medical expenses, recuperative care, rehabilitative care, and lost income. The following sections discuss the health insurance "menu."

Hospital Insurance

Hospital insurance pays all or a portion of your hospital charges.

Hospital insurance (also called *hospitalization insurance*) protects you from the costs arising out of a period of hospitalization, including room and board charges, routine laboratory expenses, general nursing services, basic supplies, and drugs. Approximately 80 percent of all Americans are covered by hospital insurance, but many are not adequately protected.

There are three types of hospital insurance: hospital expense insurance, hospital-service-incurred plans, and hospital indemnity insurance. *Hospital expense insurance* provides cash reimbursement for specific hospital expense items incurred during a hospital stay. These expenses include the per-day hospital room charges and miscellaneous hospital expenses (drugs, supplies, etc.). If the total charges for covered items during the first day of hospitalization are $410 and they are $390 for the second day, the reimbursement will be $800 (subject to deductible and coinsurance requirements). Such insurance may have a daily maximum reimbursement, an overall per-stay maximum, and a maximum number of days for which reimbursement will be provided. A *hospital-service-incurred plan* pays the hospital directly for the covered services rather than providing a cash reimbursement to the insured for hospitalization expenses. In all other respects such a plan is much like a hospital expense insurance plan.

Service-incurred plans pay the hospital directly.

Hospital indemnity insurance provides a cash payment of a specific amount per day of hospitalization, and often is very limited coverage. No attempt is made to match the payment to a specific item of expense. Such a plan might pay $200 per day of hospitalization up to a maximum number of days. Even if the charges for the first day are $410 and they are $390 for the second day, the reimbursement will be $200 per day, or $400, not $800.

Surgical Insurance

Surgical insurance protects you from the expenses of surgical procedures. *Surgical expense insurance* reimburses you directly for up to 50 or more listed surgical procedures. Dollar maximums are established for each procedure listed, and provision is made for determining the reimbursement to be made for unlisted procedures. A *surgical-service-incurred plan* pays the surgical service providers (surgeon, anesthesiologist, hospital, and others) directly for their services. Surgical-service-incurred plans usually do not have dollar maximums per procedure. Instead they pay the "usual, customary, and reasonable" charge, based on what most service providers are charging for like services in a specific geographic area.

Surgical insurance pays all or a portion of the costs of surgical procedures.

Medical Expense Insurance

Medical expense insurance provides reimbursement for physicians' and medical services other than those directly connected with surgery. Medical expense insurance may pay for doctors' visits, drugs, nonsurgical outpatient procedures, x-rays, and other bills. Such plans usually include a dollar maximum per year, as well as a coinsurance clause and a deductible clause. The deductible clause is often written on an item basis rather than in terms of an annual dollar amount. This means, for example, that the policy will not cover the first few dollars of office visits or x-rays. Like hospital and surgical insurance, medical expense insurance may be written on a service-incurred basis.

TABLE 13.2

Supplemental Major Medical Plan* Applied to Joe Preston's Stroke and Neurosurgery

	Total Expenses $200,000	
	Paid by Joe	Paid by Insurer
Items covered by "first-dollar" protection (hospital, surgical, and medical expense insurance)	$ 0	$ 23,400
Major medical deductible	500	
Portion of the loss subject to major medical coinsurance clause	2,000	8,000
Remainder covered by major medical insurance		142,000
Expenses beyond major medical policy limit	24,100	0
TOTALS	$26,600	$173,400

* $150,000 aggregate policy limits, $500 deductible, 20 percent/80 percent coinsurance requirement, $2000 out-of-pocket coinsurance cap.

Major Medical Expense Insurance

Major Medical expense insurance is designed to pay for very expensive health care losses

The three types of health insurance discussed thus far are sometimes referred to as providing "first dollar" protection. They will pay the first dollar, or nearly so, of a covered health care expense. As discussed, however, these plans do place limits on the amounts to be reimbursed. Expenses beyond these limits are your responsibility. In a sense, this violates one of the principles of buying insurance: Assume the risks that you can afford, and insure the risks you cannot. If you rely solely on hospital, surgical, and medical expense insurance, you may be reimbursed for small losses but could be wiped out by a serious illness with costs beyond the limits of your protection.

Major medical expense insurance provides reimbursement for a broad range of medical expenses (including hospital, surgical, and medical expenses) and has policy limits as high as $1 million and deductibles as high as $1000. Major medical insurance is often used as a supplement to hospital, surgical, and medical expense insurance. This means that major medical insurance will cover expenses beyond those covered by the more basic plans but only after the major medical deductible has been met.

Most major medical policies include a **health insurance coinsurance clause,** which requires you to pay a percentage of health care expenses once the deductible is paid. Usually, there is a **coinsurance cap** that limits the annual out-of-pocket payments of the insured when meeting the coinsurance requirement. Table 13.2 shows how a supplemental major medical plan might apply to the $200,000 health care emergency incurred by Joe Preston, of Bloomington, Indiana. Note that with even a $150,000 limit on the major medical policy and reimbursement from hospital, surgical, and medical expense insurance, Joe will still have out-of-pocket expenses of $26,600. With health care costs as high as they are today, a major medical policy with an overall limit of $500,000 may not be sufficient.

Comprehensive Health Insurance

A **comprehensive health insurance** plan combines the protection provided by hospital insurance, surgical insurance, medical expense insurance, and major medical expense insurance into one policy. It is simply a package of protections that provides the coverage of the basic plans and the broad, high-limit coverage of major medical insurance. Comprehensive health insurance plans usually have a $100 or $200 deductible and a 20 percent coinsurance requirement for all expenses up to the coinsurance cap. Policy limits of $1 million or more are common. A benefit of comprehensive policies is that there is no need to determine which policy applies to a given expense. Comprehensive health insurance plans are primarily available on a group basis, and many employers who wish to provide a full line of health insurance coverage to workers do so under one comprehensive policy.

Comprehensive health insurance is usually written on a group basis.

Dental Expense and Eye Care Insurance

Dental expense insurance provides reimbursement for dental care expenses. Dental expense insurance is similar to other forms of health insurance in that there are deductibles, coinsurance requirements, maximum payments for specific procedures, and overall policy limits. Oral surgery is often excluded because it is more appropriately covered under surgical expense insurance. Most dental expense insurance is written on a group basis as an employment benefit.

Eye care insurance provides reimbursement for the expenses related to the purchase of glasses and contact lenses. Such a policy would cover eye examinations, refraction tests, fitting of the lenses, and the cost of the lenses and frames. Most eye care insurance is written on a group basis as an employment benefit. For an individual, eye care insurance is probably not a good buy. The cost of glasses is not so high nor is the risk great enough to prevent such expenses from being paid out of the regular budget. Further, the greatest expense for eye care arises out of diseases and injuries to the eyes. These expenses would be covered under general health insurance plans.

Supplemental Health Insurance

Taken together, the health insurance plans discussed thus far would cover virtually all the anticipated health care expenses you might have. Each plan does, however, have limitations in terms of dollar amounts and procedures covered. **Supplemental health insurance** plans are designed to fill the gaps in coverage of the standard health insurance plans or to provide reimbursement in addition to that provided by the standard plans. Often supplemental health insurance is advertised directly through the

Supplemental health insurance plans often have severe coverage limitations.

mail or on television. Many of these plans are overpriced and not as generous as implied in their sales promotions. Typically you are covered for a narrow range of services and are paid only a small portion of the expenses supposedly "covered." Purchasers are often unaware of these limitations until they request reimbursement.

Accident Insurance   **Accident insurance** pays a specific amount per day (for example, $100) for a hospital stay arising out of an accident and/or a specific amount for the loss of certain limbs or body parts (for example, $2000 for the loss of a finger or an arm). The premium for such a policy is very low, and the benefits are not generous, perhaps $50 per day. Such per-day hospitalization benefits usually are too low to be helpful, and the benefits usually begin only after the hospitalization exceeds 7, 10, or 14 days. You should realize that the average cost of a semiprivate hospital room in the United States is more than $300 per day (room charges only) and the average hospital stay is 7 days.

Dread Disease Insurance   **Dread disease insurance** provides reimbursement for medical expenses arising out of the occurrence of a specific disease. Cancer is the disease most commonly addressed by this type of policy. The fear of cancer and the staggering costs of its treatment lead many people to consider buying cancer insurance. Yet this purchase, as of all dread disease insurance, is not a wise use of scarce funds. It is much wiser to buy a major medical policy with high limits.

Medicare Supplement (Medigap) Insurance   Closely associated with dread disease insurance is **Medicare supplement insurance** (sometimes called *medigap*), which is intended to broaden and supplement the protection provided by Medicare. **Medicare** is a federal government health insurance plan for the elderly that includes coverage for hospital, surgical, and medical expenses. Medicare does have certain limitations that make the purchase of a supplemental policy seem desirable. As changes in Medicare coverage have occurred, the volume of television and print ads for medigap insurance has increased dramatically. Unfortunately, many Medicare supplement policies fall far short of the benefits provided by major medical insurance, and the endorsement of a celebrity is far from a guarantee of quality. The best supplement to Medicare would be similar to a standard major medical policy.

The best Medicare supplement insurance is patterned after major medical expense insurance.

Disability Income Insurance

Objective
To be able to describe the purpose and major features of disability income insurance.

Disability income insurance replaces a portion of the income lost when you cannot work due to illness or injury. It is probably the most overlooked type of insurance, yet it is vitally important for all workers. For example, a 22-year-old man without dependents would probably need no life insurance. Yet he would likely need disability insurance to support himself during a period of disability. Further, at age 22, the chances of becoming disabled for at least 3 months are $7\frac{1}{2}$ times greater than the chances of death (the probability of death for a male age 22 is 18.9 per 10,000; the likelihood of disability is 142.8).

There are a number of sources of income protection during a period of disability. Many workers have sick pay benefits. These can help ease the burden of a short period of disability. Social Security disability benefits are available to many disabled workers and their families. See Appendix B for an illustration of how to estimate these benefits. Or you can write the Social Security Administration, Bethesda, Maryland, for an estimate of your benefits based on your history of Social Security earnings. Other government programs provide disability protection for veterans, railroad workers, and civil servants. Some employers offer group disability income insurance, although typically only for a short term (less than 2 years). In addition, many pension plans provide benefits to workers who become disabled. However, these plans often fall short of a worker's needs, and he or she may want to buy more protection.

Level of Need

The key question to ask is, "How much disability income insurance do I need?" One way to find out is to determine your current monthly after-tax income. From this figure, subtract the amounts you would receive from insurance currently in force, Social Security disability benefits, and other sources of disability income. As shown in Table 13.3, the resulting figure would provide an estimate of extra coverage needed.

However, there are problems with this method. First, some of the subtractions just listed may not actually be available for all disabilities. For example, Social Security disability benefits do not begin until 5 months after the disability occurs and are only payable if you are unable to perform any gainful employment. Fully 70 percent of all applicants are rejected. It is possible that a less severe disability that does not qualify for Social Security may result in the need for a larger income replacement than a more severe disability that does qualify for Social Security. A second problem is that some disability benefits may cover short-term but not long-term disability. Despite these reservations, it would be wise to complete the calculations in Table 13.3 using the figure obtained as a starting point in your shopping for disability income insurance protection. The dollar limits on disability income policies are either written in increments of $100 per month or as a percentage of monthly income. Most companies will not write policies for more than 60 to 80 percent of one's after-tax earnings. The major factors affecting premiums are the amount of coverage desired and your age, health status, occupation, and gender.

Important Policy Provisions

Once you have estimated your level of need, you can begin the search for a disability income insurance policy. The key is to look among the major policy provisions for those which meet your needs in terms of short-term

TABLE 13.3
Determining Disability Income Insurance Needs: An Example

Current monthly after-tax income		$2100
Minus previously established disability income protections		
Estimated monthly Social Security disability benefits	$ 750	
Monthly benefit from employer-provided disability insurance	600	
Monthly benefit from private disability insurance	—	
Monthly benefit from other government disability insurance	—	
Reduction of monthly life insurance premiums due to waiver of premium options	50	
Total subtractions		− 1400
Estimated monthly disability income insurance needs		$ 700

and long-term protection and in terms of full versus partial disability. This section includes a discussion of these important policy provisions.

Elimination Period   The **elimination period (waiting period)** in a disability income policy is the time period between the onset of the disability and the date the disability benefits begin. The longer the elimination period, the lower the premium will be. Increasing the disability period from 30 to 90 days can reduce the premium by one-third. If you have sick pay benefits from your employer, you can coordinate the elimination period in a policy with the number of sick days you have accrued. Or if you have some savings set aside as an emergency fund to carry you through several months without income, your elimination period can be lengthened. Note that because disability income benefits are paid monthly, the first check will not arrive until 30 days after the elimination period ends.

Choose a longer waiting period to be able to afford a long benefit period.

Benefit Period   The **benefit period** in a disability income policy is the maximum period of time for which benefits will be paid. It begins when the elimination period ends. The benefit period is usually stated in years and can be from 1 year to "to age 65." Most disability income policies will not pay past age 65.

Residual Clause   A *residual clause* allows for some reduced level of disability income benefits when a partial, rather than full, disability strikes. Consider the case of Shirley Whitaker, a criminal lawyer in Kansas City, Missouri, who had purchased a $3000-per-month disability policy. Shirley later suffered from extremely high blood pressure and was forced to cut back her workload by 50 percent, thereby taking a 50 percent pay cut. Her disability policy had a residual clause, so she received $1500 (50 percent × $3000) per month during her disability.

Social Security Rider   If you have figured your disability income insurance needs assuming that you would receive Social Security benefits, you will find yourself with inadequate protection if your application is denied. To provide an extra dollar amount of protection should you not qualify for Social Security disability benefits, a *Social Security rider* may be added to your policy. Consider the dilemma faced by Sharon Senn, a florist from New Orleans, Louisiana. Sharon determined her disability insurance needs to be $1400 after assuming that she would receive $1000 from Social Security if she were to become disabled. She could have purchased a $2400-per-month policy and removed all uncertainty, but the premium would be more than she could afford. Instead, she bought a $1400 policy with a $1000 Social Security rider for a premium savings of 30 percent.

Cost-of-Living Adjustments   You should insist on a *cost-of-living clause* in your policy, which will increase your benefit amount to keep up with inflation. Alternatively, you might consider buying a policy that uses a percentage of income as a limit on benefits rather than a specific dollar amount per month. This way, your potential monthly benefit would increase automatically with other increases.

Making Sense of Your Health Insurance Policy

Objective
To be able to explain the major provisions and exclusions contained in health insurance policies.

The most important source of information about health insurance benefits is the health insurance policy itself. The policy outlines the general benefits and, most important, includes the limitations and conditions that affect the amount reimbursed. You will find important information throughout a health insurance policy. When covered by group health insurance, you will receive a **certificate of insurance,** which is a document that outlines the benefits and policy provisions for individuals covered by group insurance. The official group policy will remain on file with your organization, and you should be allowed to consult it if you choose. This section describes important provisions, especially those that limit payment and coverage provided.

General Terms and Provisions of the Policy

The first section of a health insurance policy contains general terms and provisions that define the terminology used in the policy and outline its basic provisions. Important parts of this section are the application, the insuring agreements, the definitions, who is covered, and the time period of the protection.

Advice for the Conservative Disability Income Insurance Shopper

Fewer than one in four American workers is covered by *long-term disability insurance* (benefit period more than 2 years). Yet such a period of disability could destroy your financial security for life. How does the conservative purchaser of disability income insurance obtain such long-term coverage and still keep the premiums affordable? The answer lies in an analysis of the table below. Note that for each waiting period, the premium increases with the length of the benefit period such that the illustrated policy with a 7-day waiting period and benefits to age 65 would cost $1022 per year. This premium could be cut by more than one-half if a 60- or 90-day waiting period is chosen. Because of the catastrophic effects of being disabled for a period of several years or more, it is to your advantage to select a long benefit period. The extra premium required can be offset by choosing a longer waiting period. As illustrated below, it costs far less to buy a policy with a 90-day waiting period than a policy with a 7-day waiting period. Again we see an application of the rule that says "Insure the losses you cannot afford (in this case a long-term disability) and assume the losses that you can reasonably afford (the first few months of a disability)."

Illustrative Disability Income Insurance Premiums*

Waiting Period	Maximum Benefit Period			
	1 Year	*3 Years*	*5 Years*	*Age 65*
7 days	$586	$653	$709	$1022
14 days	463	553	608	910
30 days	269	334	378	604
60 days	184	242	285	498
90 days	—	194	237	446
1 year	—	—	207	370

* Illustrative annual premium for a $2000 per month disability income policy for a 35-year-old male in a white-collar occupation.

The Application   Your application for health insurance becomes part of your policy. The application contains specific information about you that is used to establish the premium to be charged, such as your health status and possibly the results of a medical examination. Also important are your age and occupation. Errors, omissions and false statements in an application can result in a denial of payment.

Insuring Agreements   As defined in Chapter 11, insuring agreements describe in general language the type of coverage being provided. This information is the first indication of whether the policy will meet your needs, but it is unwise to rely solely on the insuring agreements as a sign of appropriate coverage. Other policy information can greatly modify the terms of the agreement. Basically, the insuring agreements can be used to eliminate a policy from consideration, since benefits not outlined in the insuring agreements will not be available under the policy.

Policy definitions are an important concern in health insurance.

Definitions   Of vital importance are the definitions of the terms used in the policy. For example, a policy may promise to pay $100 for each day of a hospital stay. But what is a *hospital?* Would such a policy cover nursing home care? Probably not. Would it cover a stay in an osteopathic hospital? Maybe. Two of the more critical definitions in health insurance policies are those for *injury* and *sickness*. Expenses resulting from an injury may be covered to a greater or lesser degree than those resulting from a sickness.

Who Is Covered   Health insurance policies can be written to cover an individual, a family, or a group. When an individual is the focus of the coverage, there is little chance of a misunderstanding, but family policies can be more complex. Generally, a family is a husband, wife, and dependent children. But at what age are children no longer covered? Are children who are born while the policy is in effect automatically covered from the moment of birth? Each policy may answer these questions differently.

Consider carefully who is covered under a family policy.

The question of who is covered under a group policy is also very important. All group members are usually covered, but there may be a waiting period for new members. If the group consists of the employees of a business, there may be different protection for full-time and part-time employees. The family of the group member also may be covered, but again, the definition of *family* needs to be considered.

The Time Period   Individual and group health insurance policies are usually written on an annual basis. An annual policy beginning on January 1 will start at 12:01 A.M. that day and end at 12:01 A.M. on January 1 the following year. Any illness that begins during the year will be covered. But will coverage end if the policy expires while you are still in the hospital? The answer is usually no. Similarly, a surgical procedure performed after a policy expires but for an illness or injury for which treatment was sought during the policy period may be covered.

A time-period concern also may arise with accident insurance policies. Many of these policies are in effect only during specific hours of the day and in specific locations. For example, an accident policy may cover a child only while he or she is at school or traveling to or from school.

Payment Limitations

A health insurance policy will contain a number of provisions that limit the level of payments for covered expenses. These provisions include policy limits, deductibles, coinsurance/copayment requirements, and coordination of benefits requirements.

Policy Limits   *Policy limits* are the maximum amounts an insurance policy will pay to reimburse a covered loss. Health insurance policies may employ up to four types of policy limits. To illustrate these, we will consider the case of Jim Foulks, an electrician from Marquette, Michigan, who owns a 5-year hospitalization policy. **Item limits** specify the maximum reimbursement for a particular health care expense. Jim's policy contains a $500 maximum for x-rays. Jim suffered a heart attack and had x-ray expenses of $617. The policy will pay $500 of this expense, and Jim will pay the remainder. **Episode limits** specify the maximum payment for health care expenses arising from a single episode of illness or injury. Each episode is considered separately. Jim's policy contains an episode limit of $10,000 for hospitalization expenses. Jim was hospitalized for 2 weeks after his heart attack and incurred $11,223 in hospital charges. His policy will pay $10,000 of these charges. One month later, Jim suffered burns from a cooking accident at home and was hospitalized for 3 days, incurring hospital care costs of $1310. His policy will pay these expenses in full because the second hospitalization is considered a separate episode.

Time period limits specify the maximum payment to be made for covered expenses occurring within a specified time period, usually 1 year. Consider again Jim Foulks's heart attack and burn hospitalizations. If his policy contained a $10,000 annual time period limit rather than an episode limit, the hospital expenses from Jim's second hospitalization would not have been covered. **Aggregate limits** place an overall maximum on the total amount of reimbursement that can be made under a policy. Jim's policy might have an aggregate limit of $100,000. This means that during the life of the policy, no more than $100,000 will be reimbursed for hospitalization expenses he incurs.

The dollar amounts of these policy limits increase in the order in which they were discussed. Aggregate limits are always higher than time period limits, which are higher than episode limits. A policy with high aggregate limits may seem attractive, but if the episode limits are too low, the policy may not be a good buy. Analyze each limit separately to determine if it allows for sufficient protection.

Deductibles   *Deductibles* are clauses in insurance policies that require you to pay an initial portion of any loss before receiving insurance benefits. Deductibles may apply to specific types of expense items. For example, a medical expense plan may require you to pay the first $50 of any x-ray expense during a year. Deductibles also may apply to each episode of illness or injury. A hospitalization policy might require you to pay the first $500 of expenses from a hospital stay. If you are hospitalized three times during a year, you would have to pay the deductible each time, for a total of $1500. Deductibles also can apply per time period. Major medical policies often have annual deductibles requiring you to pay the first portion of expenses each year before collecting under the policy. Generally speaking, annual deductibles are best.

Family policies warrant special attention. Generally there will be a deductible for each family member, perhaps $200 per year, with a maximum family deductible, perhaps $500 per year. Once the deductible

Aggregate limits place a maximum on the reimbursement over the lifetime of the policy.

payments for individual family members reach the family deductible, in this example $500, further individual deductibles will be waived.

Coinsurance/Copayments   A *coinsurance clause* requires you to pay a proportion of any loss suffered. This share is usually 10, 20, or 25 percent. A variation of coinsurance, a **copayment clause,** requires you to pay a specific dollar portion of specific covered expense items. Copayment is often required for doctor's office visits and prescription drug coverage. You would pay a specific amount (for example, $5) for each prescription, and the insurer would pay the remainder. A copayment differs from a deductible in that a deductible might require that you pay the first $100 of x-ray expenses during a year, but a copayment clause might require that you pay the first $10 of each x-ray.

Coordination of Benefits   The principle of indemnity prevents you from collecting insurance benefits that exceed the loss suffered. This principle is maintained in health insurance through the inclusion of coordination-of-benefits clauses. A **coordination-of-benefits clause** prevents you from collecting more than 100 percent of a loss and designates the order in which policies will pay benefits if multiple policies are applicable to a loss. The primary policy is the insurance policy that will be first applied to any loss when more than one policy provides coverage for the loss. If the primary policy fails to reimburse 100 percent of the loss, secondary (or excess) policies, if any, will be applied in order until the loss is fully paid or benefits are exhausted, whichever occurs first.

When covered by more than one policy, note which is primary.

Coverage Limitations

In addition to limits on the dollar amounts reimbursed, health insurance policies may contain a number of provisions that limit the types of expenses covered by the policy. For purposes of discussion, these coverage limitations will be grouped in three categories: limitations based on timing of the loss, general exclusions, and maternity benefits.

Limitations Based on Timing of the Loss   For losses to be insurable, they must be unexpected. Say, for example, you develop a serious ulcer and are told by your doctor that surgery will be needed. You might be tempted to buy surgical insurance before having the surgery if you were not already insured. However, because the surgery is expected, it would not be covered under the new policy. Health insurance policies contain provisions that prohibit coverage for a **preexisting condition,** which is a medical condition that was diagnosed before issuance of the policy. Group policies exclude fewer preexisting conditions than individual policies.

Preexisting conditions are generally excluded from coverage under a health insurance plan.

Disputes sometimes arise as to whether or not a medical loss is the result of a preexisting condition. In order to clarify matters and prevent such disputes, insurance policies may contain waiting periods for specific types of expenses. The most common example is the 1-year wait that is generally required for maternity benefits to be covered under a new health insurance policy.

Disputes also arise when episode deductibles and limits are applicable under a policy. The dispute may center on whether a recurrence of an illness is or is not a separate episode. If the recurrence is considered a separate episode, the deductible will need to be paid, but reimbursement will be available up to the full episode limits. If the recurrence is considered a continuation of the original episode, the deductible will not apply, but the loss may exceed the episode limit. A **recurring clause** clarifies whether a recurrence of an illness is considered a continuation of the first episode or a separate episode. Recurring clauses often will stipulate a minimum number of days between hospital stays for a recurrence to be considered a separate episode. Usually, the best recurring clause is one that has a short waiting period before a recurrence is considered a separate episode. This is because it is usually less expensive to pay a deductible than to pay expenses exceeding the episode limit. Nonetheless, you should judge each policy individually in terms of the recurring clause, the amount of the deductible, and the amount of the episode limit.

General Exclusions   Exclusions narrow the focus of and eliminate specific coverages provided in a policy. Losses resulting from war, riot, and civil disturbance are generally excluded from health insurance policies, as are the expenses for voluntary cosmetic surgery. Many policies will deny coverage if the illness or injury occurs outside the United States. Expenses resulting from self-inflicted wounds are commonly nonreimbursable, especially in the first 2 years of the policy.

Maternity expenses should be handled no differently than other health care expenses.

Maternity Benefits   Maternity benefits are often considered separately from other benefits in a health insurance policy, and specific limits and exclusions may apply. The best coverage considers maternity care similar to any other health care episode. A common limitation on maternity benefits restricts payment for hospitalization of the newborn once the mother is discharged from the hospital.

Nonmedical Provisions

In addition to medical expense payment provisions, each health insurance policy contains important provisions that regulate the payment of premiums and the terms under which the policy may be renewed and canceled. These nonmedical provisions are continuation provisions, waiver-of-premium benefits, grace period, and convertibility.

Continuation Provisions   Health insurance and disability income insurance policies usually expire after 1 or 5 years, at which time they can be renewed, changed, or dropped. Even during the policy period they may be canceled. The following terms apply to the continuation of health insurance policies:

1. *Cancelable policies* may be canceled or changed at any time at the option of the insurer. Such policies are not as common now as they were in the past and should be avoided.

2. *Optionally renewable policies* may be canceled or changed by the insurer but only at the time of expiration.

3. *Guaranteed renewable policies* must be continued in force as long as the insured pays the required premium. Premiums may change, but only if the change applies to an entire class of the insured rather than to an individual insured. This prevents the company from raising the premium for a specific individual to force him or her to cancel. This is the most common and desirable type of health insurance policy.

4. *Noncancelable policies* must be continued in force without premium changes (up to age 65) as long as the insured pays the required premium. Noncancelable policies are recommended when buying disability income insurance.

Waiver of Premium   Health insurance policies can include a waiver-of-premium option. This allows the insured to stop making premium payments during a period of disability and have the policy remain in force.

Grace Period   Health insurance policies may contain provisions for a grace period, commonly 31 days. This prevents the lapse of a policy if a payment is late. The policy remains fully in force during the grace period, but only if the premium is paid before the end of the grace period.

Convertibility   Many people are covered by group health insurance through their employer. Federal law requires that employers with more than 20 employees who offer group health insurance continue to offer coverage for 18 months after an employee has quit or been laid off. The employee generally must pay the premiums plus a 2 percent fee. (Widows, widowers, divorced spouses, and their dependents must be provided this option for 36 months.) Eventually, however, eligibility to remain a member of the group will expire. A convertibility option allows conversion of the group coverage to an individual basis without proving insurability. The higher individual policy premium will have to be paid, but waiting periods and preexisting condition provisions will not apply.

Where and How to Shop for Health Insurance

Objective
To be able to identify the major sources of health insurance so that you can select health insurance policy features to meet your health insurance needs.

As a purchaser of health insurance, you should ask yourself a number of questions. Is group health insurance best? Where can I obtain individual health insurance? How are the premiums determined? How can I make good comparisons? What type of coverage should I buy, and how much protection do I need? The following section will help you answer these and other questions.

Employee Fringe Benefits (Choices of Harry and Belinda Johnson)

You may be understating your true income by thousands of dollars if you think only of your salary as your payment for employment. A **fringe benefit** is any payment for employment that is not provided in the form of wages, salary, or commissions. Many employees receive 40 to 50 percent over and above their salary in the form of fringe benefits. Some of the most common benefits are paid or subsidized group health insurance (about 75 percent of companies providing health insurance benefits require that employees pay some share of the cost of a family plan), group life insurance, retirement programs, savings programs, tuition subsidies, unemployment insurance, child care, clothing allowances, and employee discounts. The value of these benefits is even greater because the income they represent is often nontaxable or tax-deferred.

About 95 percent of the employees of medium-sized and large U.S. firms are covered by health insurance, according to a recent Labor Department survey. Ninety-six percent have life insurance, 89 percent have a retirement plan, 80 percent have protection against catastrophic medical expenses, 74 percent have dental benefits, and 49 percent also have some protection against long-term disability.

Employees have traditionally had little choice as to what fringe benefits they receive. For dual-income households this often resulted in duplication of some benefits. For example, both Harry and Belinda's employers provide partially subsidized family health insurance plans as fringe benefits. Harry and Belinda chose to be covered under Belinda's policy because it provides more protection and is less expensive. The net effect of this choice is that Harry may choose other benefits under his employer's "cafeteria style" fringe benefit plan.

Harry's employer offers a flexible approach toward providing fringe benefits. Employees are provided with a maximum dollar amount that can be used for benefits. They then choose from a "menu" of fringe benefits those which they desire the most. Harry has decided to continue to forgo his health insurance in order to receive master's degree tuition support and some additional life insurance protection.

Comparing Group Versus Individual Health Insurance

More than half of all Americans are covered by a group health insurance policy, mainly because group health insurance is so often a fringe benefit provided by employers. Employers benefit from offering group policies because the premiums are a tax-deductible business expense; employees benefit because the value of the policy is not subject to federal income taxation. Even if employers did not provide group coverage, it would still be popular because premiums are lower and underwriting criteria are less restrictive for group insurance than for individually purchased policies. This latter feature is especially attractive to anyone who has a negative medical history.

A problem with a group insurance policy is that it sometimes cannot be specifically tailored to the needs of an individual or family because there will be some limits on choices. However, many employers offer several group insurance policies from which to choose, so some individualization is possible. If you are eligible for group health coverage, do not overlook it.

Sources of Health Insurance

Health insurance protection is available from several different sources. You can choose from among Blue Cross/Blue Shield plans, private insurance companies, and health maintenance organizations. All of these may be available to you on a group basis. The federal government is also a source of health insurance protection, and this may lessen the need to obtain coverage elsewhere. Table 13.4 summarizes the sources of health care protection.

Blue Cross/Blue Shield   Blue Cross/Blue Shield plans are probably the best-known sources of health insurance protection. Technically, these plans are not insurance but are producer cooperatives that provide health care protection on a service-incurred basis. Originally, Blue Cross provided hospital insurance and Blue Shield provided surgical insurance. However, major medical and comprehensive insurance are now available through Blue Cross/Blue Shield. The "Blues," as they are sometimes called, also provide dental insurance through their Delta Dental Plan subsidiary.

The Blues provide group or individual health care protection. There are 74 individual Blue Cross and/or Blue Shield plans operating in the United States. Each is a separate nonprofit organization operating in a specific geographic area to provide health care protection on a service-incurred basis. *Participating* doctors and hospitals accept Blue Cross or Blue Shield reimbursement as payment in full. *Nonparticipating* doctors and hospitals do not accept Blue Cross or Blue Shield reimbursement as payment in full and require patients to pay the difference between the reimbursement and their higher fees for services.

Private Insurance Companies   The hundreds of individual private health insurance companies operating in the United States (Aetna and The Travelers are but two examples) provide protection for over half the people in this country. Because there are so many different companies, you may know little about the ability and willingness of a company to live up to its promises. Do not trust advertising to provide the necessary information. Ads will describe the coverage in the broadest terms and use ideal situations when discussing the benefits that could be paid. Ads never mention the serious exclusions that can reduce benefits.

HMO plans are not technically health insurance but provide prepaid health care.

Health Maintenance Organizations   Health maintenance organizations (**HMOs**) provide a broad range of health care services to members on a prepaid basis. Health maintenance organizations do not provide health insurance, they provide health care. HMOs provide their services to groups

TABLE 13.4
Summary of Health Insurance Plans

Type of Plan	Sources				Basis	
	Private Insurers	Service Incurred	Government	HMOs	Group	Individual
Basic plans						
Hospital	×	×	× *	× †	×	×
Surgical	×	×	× *	× †	×	×
Medical expense	×	×	× *	× †	×	×
Major medical	×	×		× †	×	×
Comprehensive	×	×		× †	×	×
Dental care	×	×	× ‡		×	×
Eye care	×			× †	×	×
Supplemental plans						
Dread disease	×					×
Accident	×				×	×
Medigap	×				×	×
Disability income insurance	×		×		×	×

* Medicare and Medicaid.
† Prepaid health care.
‡ Medicaid.

as well as individuals. For a specific monthly fee, HMO members will receive a wide range of health care services, including hospital, surgical, and preventive medical care. Many HMOs also provide eye examinations, psychiatric care, and ambulance service. If an HMO is not set up to provide certain types of care, it will contract with a local hospital or clinic that does. HMOs operate out of one building or cluster of buildings housing physicians' offices, treatment rooms, laboratories, and so forth. A variation is the *individual practice association,* with each physician maintaining his or her own office in various locations and using a local hospital to provide hospital and surgical services.

HMOs have grown to be a major force in the American health care system. There are more than 700 HMOs providing services to more than 50 million Americans. The reason for this popularity may lie in the emphasis HMOs place on preventive care and efficiency. Because HMOs do not charge for services over and above the monthly fee, patients are motivated to seek care whenever symptoms appear, or even before. (Some plans have a small, $5 to $10 copayment per office visit for those wishing to pay a lower monthly fee.) This means that problems tend to be prevented or at least caught early, thereby reducing the probability of a high-cost medical emergency. Also, because HMOs collect only the monthly fee, there is an incentive for the HMO to keep costs and unnecessary procedures to a minimum. Some critics of HMOs argue that cost-cutting measures lead to a reduction in the quality of services provided. Another common

Federal law requires that employers of more than 25 workers who provide group health insurance benefits to their employees offer HMO membership as an alternative, but only if an HMO in the area has solicited their business. It would certainly pay to investigate the HMO alternative if it is available to you either through a group or as an individual. Often the monthly HMO fee is slightly higher than the group or individual health insurance premiums, but the avoidance of deductibles and coinsurance costs can more than offset the extra monthly cost. When considering an HMO, ask questions about turnover rates among the physicians (high is bad, low is good), the level of satisfaction among current members, whether you will be reimbursed for all or just emergency medical expenses required when you are out of town, and the waiting time for a nonemergency appointment (10 to 14 days should be the maximum).

A growing number of employers have decided to offer an HMO as the only health care option for their employees in response to rising health insurance costs in recent years. HMO rates have risen as well, but employers feel they are better able to control health care costs with a single HMO. The principle applied is that of *managed care*, which involves establishing mechanisms to control the usage of and expenditures for health care by controlling access to services and procedures. An example might be a requirement that all nonemergency hospitalizations be approved prior to admission by an oversight panel of medical personnel if they are to be covered by the plan. By using an HMO for health care, the employer can exert more control and keep costs down than if employees were free to choose their insurance plan and health care providers. In some cases, a "dual option" plan is used allowing employees to go outside the HMO if they are willing to pay large deductibles and a higher proportion of the costs themselves.

criticism is the reduced freedom of choice among doctors. Members are assigned a primary-care physician, but they are seen by another physician if their primary-care physician is not on duty when they are seeking treatment.

You can save money with a PPO.

Preferred Provider Organizations   A **preferred provider organization (PPO)** is a group of medical care providers (doctors, hospitals, and other health care providers) who contract with a health insurance company to provide services at a discount to policyholders. The discount is then passed along to the policyholders in the form of reductions or elimination of deductibles and/or coinsurance requirements when they choose the PPO providers for their medical care. The discounts do not apply if the policyholders choose to be served by non-PPO members. In addition, if the nonmembers charge more than what the insurer feels is reasonable, policyholders must pay the excess as well as any deductible and coinsurance portions.

Employers who provide group health insurance to their employees as a fringe benefit of employment have become increasingly interested in PPOs in recent years. This is because they usually pay reduced premiums for PPO-associated health plans. Consider the case of Ralph Brite, who works for a large engineering firm in Memphis, Tennessee. His firm's health insurance plan has contracted with a PPO representing a local university's teaching hospital and its affiliated physicians. Because Ralph chose the university hospital for treatment of a broken ankle, he saved $150 on the $250 deductible and did not have to pay the usual 20 percent coinsurance share of the bill. Of course, he gave up the right to go to his family doctor, who is not a PPO member, but he could use that doctor for any further health care needs.

Government Health Care Insurance Since establishment of the Social Security program, the federal government has steadily expanded its role as a provider of health insurance protection. Federal, state, and local programs account for about 40 percent of health care expenditures each year. There are four major federal programs: (1) **Social Security disability income insurance** provides benefits that will help replace the lost income of eligible disabled workers, (2) **Medicare** is a program administered by the Social Security Administration that provides payment for hospital and medical expenses of persons aged 65 and over and some others, (3) **Medicaid** is a jointly financed program of the federal government and the states that pays some medical expenses of the poor (these programs will be discussed below), and finally, (4) many military veterans are eligible for free or low-cost health care provided at Veterans Administration hospitals around the country. **Veterans Administration hospitals** are medical care facilities designed exclusively to provide care to veterans.

Social Security disability income insurance provides eligible workers and their dependents with income during a period of disability expected to last 12 full months or until death. There is a 5-month waiting period after which benefits begin, and the disability must be total. This means that recipients must not be able to engage in any substantial, gainful activity. If they can do any work for pay, they will be ineligible for benefits. Social Security disability income protection may provide upward of $18,000 in tax-free income to the family of a fully insured disabled worker.

Medicare is a hospital and medical expense insurance program for the elderly and other eligible persons. It is funded by means of the Social Security payroll tax. Those eligible for Medicare include persons aged 65 and over who are eligible for Social Security retirement benefits, federal civilian employees aged 65 and over who retired after 1982, persons who are disabled and eligible for Social Security disability benefits, and individuals with kidney disorders that require kidney dialysis treatments.

Medicare is divided into two parts. Part A is the hospitalization portion of the program and requires no premium. Part B is the medical expense insurance portion of the program. It is optional and is open to all Part A recipients and anyone else age 65 or over upon payment of a monthly premium ($29.90 in 1991 and scheduled to increase).

Medicare Part A will pay benefits for up to 90 days of hospitalization per benefit period. A benefit period begins on the first day of any hospitalization and lasts until the patient goes 60 consecutive days without

Medicaid is a program for the poor.

Medicare has two parts: Part A for hospital charges and Part B for surgical and medical charges.

hospitalization. There are no limits on the number of benefit periods that a person may use.

For a longer hospital stay a patient may draw on a lifetime maximum of 60 reserve days of benefits. Part A also will pay benefits for up to 100 days of care in a nursing facility following a 3-day or longer episode of hospitalization. Additionally, it will provide benefits for home health care visits after a 3-day or longer period of hospitalization. As with other hospital insurance plans, Medicare Part A requires the payment of deductibles, which can result in substantial out-of-pocket expenses for the insured. In 1990, the hospitalization deductible was $592 for the first 60 days of a benefit period, $148 per day for each of days 61 through 90, and $296 per day for any reserve days used. Deductibles also apply to nursing facilities and home health care visit benefits.

Medicare Part B will pay benefits for surgical procedures and medical expenses for surgery, outpatient care, hospitalization, or certain other services. Part B requires the payment of an annual deductible ($150 in 1990) and has a 20 percent/80 percent coinsurance requirement. Part B will reimburse 80 percent of the reasonable approved charge for covered expenses. If the service provider will not accept the approved charge designated by the Social Security Administration, the insured must pay the difference. Part B also will pay a portion of the expenses for treatment of mental illness, chiropractic services, dental care, and physical therapy.

Medicaid is a program of health care for the poor that is jointly administered and funded by the federal and state governments. Eligibility for Medicaid is based on household income, and the program is generally available to those households receiving Aid to Families with Dependent Children (AFDC) benefits. Health services provided through Medicaid vary from state to state. Benefits generally include hospital, surgical, and some medical care, and in some states dental care for children may be covered.

Workers' Compensation If you are injured on the job or become ill as a direct result of employment, state law requires your employer to pay the medical costs that result. **Workers' compensation insurance** protects employers from liability for injury or disease suffered by employees that results from employment-related causes. The benefits to the employee include health care, recuperative care, replacement of lost income, and, if necessary, rehabilitation. Thus the full range of health-related losses is covered by workers' compensation insurance. However, because only those losses resulting from work-related accidents are covered and benefits are limited, workers' compensation can only supplement your total health insurance plan.

Shopping for Health Insurance

Shopping for health insurance requires careful comparison of the many options available. An extremely valuable resource was provided in the August and September 1990 issues of *Consumer Reports*. You should focus your attention on four areas: the cost, the company, the policy, and claims procedures.

The Cost It is very difficult to provide estimates of the cost of health insurance. There is such a wide variety of plans, limits, deductibles, and exclusions that there is no standardized pricing mechanism as there is for life insurance. Without doubt, however, health insurance is expensive and becoming increasingly so. The rapid price increases in the health care industry and the general aging of the population indicate that there is little prospect of substantial relief in the near future. A sound health insurance program for the typical family of four can easily cost more than $350 per month. There is little mystery as to why employer-paid group health care programs are so popular. For the individual purchaser of health insurance, careful comparisons of plans and policies are absolutely necessary in order to stretch the health care dollar.

When you apply for individual health insurance, the decision of whether to accept you is based on a number of underwriting factors, including your age, sex, occupation, family and personal health history, and physical condition. Each of these factors has a bearing on the likelihood of health-related losses. If you have a hazardous occupation or a history of heart disease, you may be required to pay higher-than-standard rates for any policy you select. Many applicants are simply denied coverage (recall that group plans accept all employees).

If you are accepted for coverage at the standard rates, the price you will pay for individual health insurance will be based on three factors: age, occupation, and gender. Generally, age will not affect the premium unless the applicant is a child or is over 40 years old. Occupation will be more of a factor for accident insurance coverage than for sickness coverage. If your occupation is hazardous, this will be factored in during the underwriting process. Women pay higher health insurance premiums than men because they generally suffer somewhat more frequent and more severe health losses.

The Company Many companies offer health insurance. As in the selection of a life insurance company (see Chapter 14), health insurers should be rated A+ or A by *Best's*. It is also a good idea to consult the insurance regulatory agency in your state to determine if there have been any problems with a company. Such agencies will not be able to recommend a company, but they may be helpful in eliminating those which engage in questionable practices. The company itself can be a source of information. *Choose a company with a high claims ratio.* Wise financial planners always ask about the company's **claims ratio,** which represents the percentage of premiums collected by an insurance company that is subsequently paid out to reimburse the losses of the insured. The **claims ratio formula** is

$$\text{Claims ratio} = \frac{\text{losses paid}}{\text{premiums collected}} \qquad (13.1)$$

Blue Cross/Blue Shield companies typically have claims ratios that exceed 90 percent. At the other extreme there are many companies, especially those that sell hospital indemnity and dread disease insurance by mail, over the phone, or through newspaper inserts, that have claims ratios of

TABLE 13.5
Recommended Health Insurance Criteria

Plan*	Policy Limits	Deductible	Coinsurance/ Copayment	Coordination of Benefits	Exclusions
Hospital insurance	Should pay usual, reasonable, and customary charges for a period of 180 days per episode; semiprivate room recommended	Small deductible ($100) can be used to lower premium; deductible should apply on an annual basis	None	Primary	Exclusions should be kept to a minimum; maternity benefits can be excluded, as can mental illness benefits and hospitalization for elective cosmetic surgery
Surgical insurance	Should pay usual, reasonable, and customary charges with no limit	None	None	Primary	Should be few exclusions; elective cosmetic surgery can be excluded; outpatient and doctor's office surgical procedures should not be excluded
Medical expense insurance					
Drugs	$500 annually	$100 annually	$1 or $2 copayment recommended	Primary	Drugs provided during hospitalization should be covered under hospital insurance; will not cover nonprescription drugs and medicines
Home nursing care	Full payment for 30 days per episode	None	None	Supplement to hospital insurance	None
X-rays	$500 annually	$50 annually	$5 copayment per x-ray may help lower premium	Supplement to hospital insurance	None
Maternity	Maternity protection should treat a maternity event like any other hospitalization episode and surgical procedure				
Major medical	$500,000 per episode	$500 annually	20 percent/80 percent with $5000 cap	Supplemental to basic plans	Very few exclusions recommended, such as cosmetic surgery
Comprehensive	Any comprehensive plan chosen should have at least the same features as the basic and major medical plans outlined above				
Dental	$3000 annually	$100 annually	10 percent or 20 percent coinsurance would help lower premium	Primary	Exclusion of orthodontic procedures may help reduce premiums; cleaning and other preventive care should not be excluded
Eye care	Not recommended				
Supplemental					
Dread disease	Not recommended				
Accident	Not recommended				
Medigap	See major medical recommendations				

* All policies should be written on a guaranteed renewable basis.

less than 25 percent. The lower the claims ratio, the lower is the return (the actual benefits) to the policyholder on the premium dollar paid.

The Policy   The variety of health insurance policies makes it difficult to make comparisons. The most effective way to compare health insurance policies is to set some criteria for judging whether a policy provides the needed coverage. Those policies which do provide the needed coverage can then be compared for price. Table 13.5 outlines a set of criteria to use in judging the merits of various types of policies. These criteria reflect the need to obtain adequate coverage and to keep premiums affordable. Many policies will greatly exceed the criteria in this table, but they will do so for a price you may not be willing to pay. Similarly, you may find lower-priced policies, but the lower price may be at the expense of adequate coverage.

Pay special attention to the purchase of any health insurance policy offered through the mail or in newspapers. The advertising for such policies cannot possibly detail what is covered and what is not. Further, many of these ads intentionally leave out important restrictions and exclusions. No insurance policy should be purchased sight unseen. If an agent or company will not allow you to study a policy for a few days, buy elsewhere.

Claims Procedures   An often-overlooked aspect when comparing health insurance policies is the procedure used to make a claim when a loss occurs. Service-incurred plans and HMOs have the advantage in that they require little or no paperwork on your part. Some other plans require you to submit the appropriate forms yourself.

Another important aspect of the claims procedure is the method of payment. Service-incurred plans, HMOs, and some other insurers do not require you to pay for your health care and then wait for reimbursement. Using an insurer who will reimburse only may cause you some financial hardship, especially if the health care provider wants payment soon after or even before services are rendered.

Summary

1. Health insurance is purchased to provide reimbursement for expenses arising out of injury, illness, and disability.
2. Health insurance needs are determined by balancing the medical losses likely to occur against the resources available to cover those losses. The medical losses most likely to occur include direct medical care expenses, recuperation expenses, rehabilitation expenses, and lost income. Resources that might be available to cover these losses include savings, other insurance, and education.
3. The major types of health insurance are hospital insurance, surgical insurance, medical expense insurance, major medical expense insurance, comprehensive health insurance plans, dental expense insurance, eye care insurance, and supplemental health insurance plans.

4. Disability income insurance replaces a portion of the income lost when you cannot work as a result of illness or injury. The amount you need is equal to your monthly after-tax income less any benefits such as Social Security to which you are entitled. By selecting among various policy provisions, you can tailor a policy to fill the gaps in your existing disability protection.

5. The health insurance policy outlines the general provisions of the coverage and, most important, includes the limitations and conditions that affect the amount reimbursed under the policy. Some of the more important policy provisions include who is covered under the policy and the time period for the coverage. Important limitations include the deductible, the coinsurance requirement, and limitations on the types of losses covered.

6. The decision to buy health insurance must be based on consideration of the sources of coverage, the premium to be paid, and the company, the policy, and the claims procedures. The ideal health insurance program provides protection from catastrophic losses and smaller losses that the insured may find unaffordable.

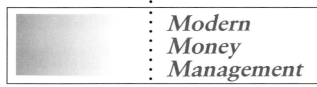

Modern Money Management

The Johnsons Consider Buying Disability Insurance

Although the employee benefit program Belinda receives is generous, it does not provide disability income protection other than 8 sick days per year that may accumulate to 30 days if she does not use them. Harry also has no disability income insurance. Although both have worked long enough under Social Security to qualify for disability benefits, Belinda has estimated that Harry would receive about $640 and she would receive about $800 per month. Harry and Belinda have come to realize that they could not live up to their current standards on one salary alone. Thus the need for some disability income insurance has become evident even though they probably cannot afford such protection at this time. In fact, they chose not to purchase the disability waiver of premium option when they purchased their life insurance. Advise them on the following points.

1. Use Table 13.3 to determine how much disability insurance Harry and Belinda each need. Use the December salary figures from Table 4.6. To determine the amount of taxes and Social Security paid by each, assume that Harry, whose salary represents approximately 42 percent of the total income, paid a comparable percentage of the taxes.

2. Use the information on pages 461, 462, 467, and 468 to advise them as to their selections related to the following major policy provisions: elimination period, benefit period, residual clause, continuation provisions, and cost-of-living adjustments.

Key Words and Concepts

accident insurance, 459
aggregate limits, 465
benefit period, 461
certificate of insurance, 462
claims ratio, 475
claims ratio formula, 475
coinsurance cap, 457
comprehensive health insurance, 458
coordination-of-benefits clause, 466
copayment clause, 466
dental expense insurance, 458
disability income insurance, 459
dread disease insurance, 459
episode limits, 465
eye care insurance, 458
elimination period (waiting period), 461
fringe benefit, 469
health insurance, 452
health insurance coinsurance clause, 457
health maintenance organization (HMO), 470
hospital insurance, 455

item limits, 465
major medical expense insurance, 457
Medicaid, 473
medical expense insurance, 456
Medicare, 459
Medicare supplement insurance, 459
partial disability, 454
preexisting condition, 466
preferred provider organization (PPO), 472
recurring clause, 467
rehabilitation, 454
Social Security disability income insurance, 473
supplemental health insurance, 458
surgical insurance, 456
time period limits, 465
total disability, 454
Veterans Administration hospitals, 473
workers' compensation insurance, 474

Review Questions

1. Describe the perils covered by health insurance.
2. Categorize the losses that can result from an injury or illness.
3. What resources might be available to cover losses due to injury or accident?
4. Explain the differences among the three types of hospital insurance.
5. Distinguish between surgical expense insurance and surgical service-incurred plans.
6. Define medical expense insurance.

7. How does major medical insurance differ from the three types of first-dollar health insurance?

8. Describe comprehensive health insurance.

9. List three supplemental health insurance plans, and give a positive and negative aspect of each.

10. Define disability income insurance and how one determines the level of need for such insurance.

11. Identify the major policy provisions to consider when purchasing disability income insurance.

12. Explain what a certificate of insurance is.

13. Distinguish among item limits, episode limits, time period limits, and aggregate limits as used in health insurance policies.

14. What are the usual coinsurance percentages used in health insurance policies, and how does a coinsurance cap apply to these percentages?

15. Explain the purpose of a coordination-of-benefits clause.

16. What is a preexisting condition, and what is its relationship with a recurring clause in an insurance policy?

17. Explain the various continuation provisions typically used in health insurance policies.

18. Distinguish between HMOs and PPOs.

19. Describe the four major federal health insurance-related programs.

20. Distinguish between Medicare and Medicaid.

21. What variables are used to determine health insurance premiums?

22. What three areas should you focus on when shopping for health insurance coverage?

23. What valuable piece of information is conveyed by an insurance company's claims ratio?

Case Problems

1. Bernard Goldhart of East Lansing, Michigan, aged 61, recently suffered a severe stroke. He was in intensive care for 12 days and was hospitalized for 18 more days. Then he was in a nursing home 45 days for medically necessary nursing and rehabilitative care. Bernard had hospital, surgical, and medical expense insurance through his employer. He had also purchased major medical insurance through a group with a $1000 deductible and $50,000 episode and $250,000 aggregate limits. The major medical policy had a 20 percent/80 percent coinsurance clause with a $20,000 coinsurance cap. All Bernard's policies covered medically necessary services performed in a nursing home setting. Bernard's total medical bill was $125,765. His insurance from his employer covered $42,814 of these charges.

a. Of the remainder, how much did the major medical policy pay?

b. How much did Bernard pay?

2. Jim Alford of Richmond, Kentucky, recently took a new job as a manufacturer's representative for an aluminum castings company. While looking over his employee benefits materials he discovered that his employer would provide 10 sick days per year that he could accumulate to a maximum of 60 days if any went unused in a given year. In addition, his employer provided a $1000 per month short-term (1 year) total disability policy. After calling the employee benefits office where he worked, Jim found that he probably would qualify for $400 per month in Social Security disability benefits. Jim also knew that he could cease paying $50 per month in life insurance premiums if he became disabled under a waiver-of-premium option in his life insurance policy. Jim earns a base salary of $1500 per month and expects to earn about that same amount in commissions, for an average after-tax income of $2100 per month. After considering this information, Jim became understandably concerned that a disability might destroy his financial future.

a. What is the level of Jim's short-term (1 year) disability insurance needs?

b. What is the level of Jim's long-term disability insurance needs?

c. Help Jim select from among the important disability insurance policy provisions to design a disability insurance program tailored to his needs.

3. Your good friend, Amy Short of Tulsa, Oklahoma, recently started a new job in a moderately sized CPA firm. Knowing that you were taking a personal finance course, she asked your advice about the selection of her health insurance plan. Her employer offered four options.

Option A: A package of hospital, surgical, and medical expense insurance plus a major medical policy. The first-dollar coverages provide for 45 days per year of hospitalization and otherwise would pay the usual, customary, and reasonable charges for most any event including maternity. The major medical policy has a $500 annual deductible and a 20 percent/80 percent coinsurance clause with a $20,000 coinsurance cap. The major medical policy has a $100,000 aggregate limit.

Option B: A comprehensive health insurance policy with a $250 per year annual deductible, a 20 percent/80 percent coinsurance clause with a $10,000 coinsurance cap, and a $250,000 aggregate limit.

Option C: Same as option B except that there is a PPO associated with the plan. If Amy agrees to have services provided by the PPO, her annual deductible drops to $100 and the coinsurance clause is waived. As an incentive to get employees to select option C, Amy's employer also will provide dental expense insurance worth about $20 per month.

Option D: Membership in an HMO. Amy would have to contribute $25 per month extra if she chose this option.

a. Explain to Amy why her employer requests her to pay extra if she joins the HMO.

b. Why might Amy's employer provide an incentive of dental insurance if she chooses option C?

c. To help her make a decision, Amy has asked you to make a list of three positive and three negative points about each plan. Prepare such a list.

Suggested Readings

"Accident-proofing Your Paycheck," *U.S. News and World Report*, July 30, 1990, p. 59. Describes how you may be shortchanged by the limited disability coverage available under Social Security.

"A Microscope on Nursing-home Plans," U.S. News & World Report, August 13, 1990, pp. 62–64. Explains which plans to avoid and which ones to buy.

"A Source List for Children Who Care." *Money*, October 1989, pp. 169–172. Recommended references for the financial aspects of caring for elderly parents.

"Beyond Medicare." *Consumer Reports*, June 1989, pp. 375–391. Series of articles on medical insurance needs for the elderly and how to get the best coverage for a fair or low price.

"Can You Afford to Get Sick Now?" *Newsweek*, January 3, 1989, pp. 45–51. Exposes the problems in health care and health insurance.

"Check That You Have the Coverage You Need Most." *Money*, February 1989, p. 77. Techniques for analyzing the sufficiency of your disability income insurance.

"Finding Health Care and Housing." *Money*, October 1989, pp. 158–166. Suggestions on obtaining appropriate health care housing, including elder-care communities and nursing homes.

"Medigap: Costs More, Covers Less." *Changing Times*, April 1989, pp. 57–62. Rising premiums for Medicare forces people to shop for supplementary private insurance.

"Nursing Home Insurance: Who Needs It?" *Changing Times*, July 1989, pp. 59–62. Late middle-age may be the best time to purchase nursing home insurance.

"Ouch! The Squeeze on Your Health Benefits." *Business Week*, November 20, 1989, pp. 110–122. A thorough discussion of the rapidly changing environment of employer provided health benefits.

"Paying for a Nursing Home." *Consumer Reports*, October 1989, pp. 664–667. How to choose a long-term health care policy that is not a ripoff.

"Plugging the Black Hole." *Newsweek*, September 11, 1989, p. 47. Explores newly developed policies that make disability income insurance more affordable for young workers.

"Policies for the Worst of Times." *Business Week,* May 14, 1990, pp. 158–159. Describes the nuts and bolts of long term care insurance and sources of further information on this increasingly important topic.

"The Crisis in Health Insurance, Part 1 and Part 2." *Consumer Reports,* August 1990, pp. 533–549 and September 1990, pp. 608–617. A must-read analysis of the problems in health care and health insurance affordability and availability. Includes ratings and premium information on over 75 policies from prominent companies.

"The Hard Sell." *Consumer Reports,* June 1989, pp. 386–391. Deceptive and misleading practices to avoid when buying health insurance policies.

"What If You Couldn't Work Anymore," *Changing Times,* August 1990, pp. 53–56. Ways to make disability insurance more affordable.

14 Life Insurance

After reading this chapter, you should be able to

1. State the purpose of life insurance and identify the reasons for buying it.
2. Understand the varying needs for life insurance over the life cycle.
3. Discuss the procedures used to calculate life insurance needs.
4. Define and distinguish among the various types of term and cash-value life insurance policies.
5. Describe the major provisions of life insurance policies and explain the value of each.
6. Discuss the important points to consider when choosing and buying life insurance.

The average life expectancy for people born between 1991 and 1994 will exceed 78 years for women and 72 years for men. Although no one knows how long he or she will live, people tend to think of every death as a premature death, as an unwanted interruption of life. With the uncertainty of when death will occur comes the uncertainty of the financial losses that will result from it. One way to reduce uncertainty or risk is to purchase insurance. **Life insurance** protects against financial losses resulting from death. Coverage begins the moment one pays for a policy. A **policy** is the written agreement between the company and the policyholder stating the terms of the insurance contract.

The first life insurance company in the United States, the Corporation for Relief of Poor and Distressed Widows and Children of Presbyterian Ministers, was established in 1759. Since then, life insurance has grown to be an immense industry, with today more than $7.5 trillion worth of life insurance in force in this country. Life insurance companies control assets of more than $950 billion. Seven out of eight U.S. families own some life insurance, and their coverage averages more than $75,000 per family.

This chapter will focus on the role of life insurance in your overall personal financial management plan. Topics to be covered include reasons for buying life insurance, understanding the varying needs for life insurance over the life cycle, how to determine your life insurance needs, the many types of life insurance, the life insurance policy and its major provisions, and how to buy life insurance.

Why Buy Life Insurance?

The term *life insurance* is in a sense a misnomer. Obviously, the person whose life is insured will not be protected from death, nor will he or she benefit financially from the proceeds of the policy paid after death. The **insured** is the person on whose life an insurance policy is issued. The primary reason for buying life insurance is to obtain financial protection from losses suffered by others when the insured party dies. Perhaps it should be called *death insurance*.

In another sense, however, life insurance is appropriately named. Life insurance can allow the survivors and heirs of the deceased to continue the financial aspects of their lives free from the financial burdens that death can cause. The death of a breadwinner is particularly devastating when there are young children in the home; life insurance can at least allow the family's financial needs to be satisfied. Home ownership can be safeguarded, and the surviving parent may be able to stay at home for a time rather than have to take or go back to a job immediately. College or other educational plans can remain intact, and retirement income can be available for the surviving spouse.

Insurance companies employ **actuaries,** who calculate the probabilities of death for individuals based on such characteristics as age, health, and lifestyle and then use these probabilities to establish the rates an individual must pay for life insurance. The **death rate** represents the probability that an individual will die at a given age. A **mortality table** is a statistical table showing the death rate at each age. Table 14.1 shows a mortality table for persons covered by life insurance. As you would expect, the death rate increases as a person grows older. In recent years, death rates for all age groups except one have declined owing to medical advances in the treatment of heart disease, stroke, and cancer. The exception is the 15- to 24-year-old age group. Death rates for this group have increased recently as a result of increased numbers of automobile accidents, suicides, and homicides.

The death rate for the population as a whole is expected to continue to decline. Table 14.2 ranks the top 10 causes of death and contains a clue to why the death rate should continue to decline. Note that the top three causes of death are those for which medical advances are taking place. As people survive these diseases, their prospects for longevity increase. Some actuaries believe that life expectancies of 90 to 100 years are not too far in the future.

Although most people live to retirement age, approximately 25 percent of today's adults will die during their working years. Life insurance purchased as part of an overall financial management plan will enable you to deal financially with this potential loss.

Life Insurance Needs over the Life Cycle

The whys behind life insurance vary over the life cycle. During childhood and singlehood, the need for life insurance is nonexistent or very small. This is because few, if any, other people are relying on the income of the person under consideration. With marriage comes the increased responsibility for another, although life insurance needs will probably remain low because each spouse usually has the potential of self-support if the other were to die. The arrival of children, though, triggers a sharp increase in life insurance needs unless other financial resources are available in sufficient amounts. Children often require up to 25 years of financial support with little ability to provide for themselves. As children grow older, the number of years of dependency declines. This may seem to suggest declining insurance needs, but the impact of inflation and higher income levels may keep insurance needs high. A married couple will see a much reduced need for life insurance once their children become independent. This is partly because their responsibility for others is reduced

TABLE 14.1
Commissioner's Standard Ordinary Mortality Table

Age	Male Mortality Rate per 1000	Male Expectancy, Years	Female Mortality Rate per 1000	Female Expectancy, Years	Age	Male Mortality Rate per 1000	Male Expectancy, Years	Female Mortality Rate per 1000	Female Expectancy, Years
0	4.18	70.83	2.89	75.83	50	6.71	25.36	4.96	29.53
1	1.07	70.13	0.87	75.04	51	7.30	24.52	5.31	28.67
2	0.99	69.20	0.81	74.11	52	7.96	23.70	5.70	27.82
3	0.98	68.27	0.79	73.17	53	8.71	22.89	6.15	26.98
4	0.95	67.34	0.77	72.23	54	9.56	22.08	6.61	26.14
5	0.90	66.40	0.76	71.28	55	10.47	21.29	7.09	25.31
6	0.85	65.46	0.73	70.34	56	11.46	20.51	7.57	24.49
7	0.80	64.52	0.72	69.39	57	12.49	19.74	8.03	23.67
8	0.76	63.57	0.70	68.44	58	13.59	18.99	8.47	22.86
9	0.74	62.62	0.69	67.48	59	14.77	18.24	8.94	22.05
10	0.73	61.66	0.68	66.53	60	16.08	17.51	9.47	21.25
11	0.77	60.71	0.69	65.58	61	17.54	16.79	10.13	20.44
12	0.85	59.75	0.72	64.62	62	19.19	16.08	10.96	19.65
13	0.99	58.80	0.75	63.67	63	21.06	15.38	12.02	18.86
14	1.15	57.86	0.80	62.71	64	23.14	14.70	13.25	18.08
15	1.33	56.93	0.85	61.76	65	25.42	14.04	14.59	17.32
16	1.51	56.00	0.90	60.82	66	27.85	13.39	16.00	16.57
17	1.67	55.09	0.95	59.87	67	30.44	12.76	17.43	15.83
18	1.78	54.18	0.98	58.93	68	33.19	12.14	18.84	15.10
19	1.86	53.27	1.02	57.98	69	36.17	11.54	20.36	14.38
20	1.90	52.37	1.05	57.04	70	39.51	10.96	22.11	13.67
21	1.91	51.47	1.07	56.10	71	43.30	10.39	24.23	12.97
22	1.89	50.57	1.09	55.16	72	47.65	9.84	26.87	12.28
23	1.86	49.66	1.11	54.22	73	52.64	9.30	30.11	11.60
24	1.82	48.75	1.14	53.28	74	58.19	8.79	33.93	10.95
25	1.77	47.84	1.16	52.34	75	64.19	8.31	38.24	10.32
26	1.73	46.93	1.19	51.40	76	70.53	7.84	42.96	9.71
27	1.71	46.01	1.22	50.46	77	77.12	7.40	48.04	9.12
28	1.70	45.09	1.26	49.52	78	83.90	6.97	53.45	8.55
29	1.71	44.16	1.30	48.59	79	91.05	6.57	59.35	8.01
30	1.73	43.24	1.35	47.65	80	98.84	6.18	65.99	7.48
31	1.78	42.31	1.40	46.71	81	107.48	5.80	73.60	6.98
32	1.83	41.38	1.45	45.78	82	117.25	5.44	82.40	6.49
33	1.91	40.46	1.50	44.84	83	128.26	5.09	92.53	6.03
34	2.00	39.54	1.58	43.91	84	140.25	4.77	103.81	5.59
35	2.11	38.61	1.65	42.98	85	152.95	4.46	116.10	5.18
36	2.24	37.69	1.76	42.05	86	166.09	4.18	129.29	4.80
37	2.40	36.78	1.89	41.12	87	179.55	3.91	143.32	4.43
38	2.58	35.87	2.04	40.20	88	193.27	3.66	158.18	4.09
39	2.79	34.96	2.22	39.28	89	207.29	3.41	173.94	3.77
40	3.02	34.05	2.42	38.36	90	221.77	3.18	190.75	3.45
41	3.29	33.16	2.64	37.46	91	236.98	2.94	208.87	3.15
42	3.56	32.26	2.87	36.55	92	253.45	2.70	228.81	2.85
43	3.87	31.38	3.09	35.66	93	272.11	2.44	251.51	2.55
44	4.19	30.50	3.32	34.77	94	295.90	2.17	279.31	2.24
45	4.55	29.62	3.56	33.88	95	329.96	1.87	317.32	1.91
46	4.92	28.76	3.80	33.00	96	384.55	1.54	375.74	1.56
47	5.32	27.90	4.05	32.12	97	480.20	1.20	474.97	1.21
48	5.74	27.04	4.33	31.25	98	657.98	.84	655.85	.84
49	6.21	26.20	4.63	30.39	99	1000.00	.50	1000.00	.50

Source: Used with permission of the National Association of Insurance Commissioners, 120 W. 12th St., Suite 1100, Kansas City, MO 64105. Developed by the Society of Actuaries.

TABLE 14.2
Leading Causes of Death in the United States

Cause of Death*	Death Rate†	Number of Deaths Per Year
Diseases of the heart	313.0	762,820
Cancer	196.0	477,190
Stroke	61.0	149,220
Accidents and their effects‡	38.2	94,723
Major lung diseases	27.0	69,511
Pneumonia and influenza	25.0	59,474
Motor vehicle accidents	20.1	47,380
All other causes	18.1	49,343
Diabetes	15.4	36,292
Chronic liver disease	11.0	26,208
Suicide	10.7	28,203
Hardening of the arteries	9.2	24,175

Source: U.S. Department of Health and Human Services, *Monthly Vital Statistics Reports* and 1990 press releases of the National Centers for Disease Control.
* As of 1991, AIDS was not one of the top 10 causes of death.
† Per 100,000 people.
‡ In a recent year, accidental deaths numbered 11,000 from falls, 5600 from drownings, 4800 from fire, 4000 from accidental poisonings, 3600 from inhaling food and other objects, 1800 from guns, 1200 on bicycles and 1000 from electrocution.

and partly because their investments will have matured and may be used for income. Retirement and the likelihood of another period of singlehood reduce the need for life insurance even further—if not eliminating it altogether.

How to Determine Your Life Insurance Needs

Objective
To be able to discuss the procedures used to calculate life insurance needs.

Life insurance needs are highly individualized and can vary from zero to more than $1 million. This section will cover the four areas to consider when determining your life insurance needs: (1) the types of losses that will occur, (2) the projected dollar amount of losses, (3) resources that may be available to cover losses, and (4) the amount of life insurance needed.

Estimating Losses Resulting from Premature Death

In addition to grief over the substantial personal loss in the death of a loved one, survivors may experience severe financial losses as well. These include lost income and such costs as final expenses, readjustment-period expenses, and debt-repayment expenses.

Lost Income for Household Expenses   The major financial loss resulting from premature death is the lost income of the deceased—the money used to pay for ongoing needs such as basic household expenses, child-care costs, and an emergency fund for such items as car repairs. Included in this lost income, especially that of the primary family breadwinner, should be the value of any essential employment fringe benefits, such as health insurance. Similarly, the contributions of a full- or part-time homemaker should not be overlooked. The dollar income of primary homemakers is not indicative of the full financial contributions they make to family life. The best way to allow for funds needed after the death of a family's homemaker is to estimate the annual cost of hiring the lost services. Realize too that in many dual-earner families both incomes are needed to maintain the desired level of living and may need to be replaced. Further, it may be necessary to use life insurance proceeds to pay college costs if previous plans called for using parental income for these expenses.

You may need to estimate the cost of hiring lost services.

Necessary Final Expenses   Final expenses are those one-time expenses occurring just prior to or after a death. Probably the greatest of these expenses is the cost of the funeral. It is not unusual for a modest funeral to cost more than $3000. Emergency travel expenses for family members during a terminal illness and to attend a funeral also can be quite high. Food and lodging expenses for mourners are often substantial. The severe and costly disruptions of family life can last 2 weeks, a month, or even longer. Inheritance and estate taxes (discussed in Chapter 23) also are often paid for with life insurance proceeds.

Another type of final expense includes the final health care expenses of the deceased. Although life insurance can provide funds for the payment of these charges, it is best to provide for them through health insurance. (Health insurance was covered in Chapter 13.) Unless otherwise provided for in some type of emergency fund, final expenses should be covered by life insurance.

Readjustment-Period Expenses   A period of readjustment is often necessary after the death of a loved one. This period may last for several years, and the readjustment may have financial aspects that may require substantial life insurance proceeds. For example, the death of a sole breadwinner with infant children may be such a shock that the surviving spouse must forgo seeking employment for a while. Similarly, a working spouse may need to take time off from a job, or a nonworking spouse may wish to obtain further education. Parents mourning the death of a child may need special counseling or travel to help heal the wounds.

Debt-Repayment Expenses   Many people feel that life insurance should cover installment loans, personal loans, and the outstanding balance on the mortgage should a breadwinner die. No doubt there will be a need to pay debts, and difficulties may arise, but a family that has provided adequately for the replacement of lost income will probably not need to make specific insurance provisions for the repayment of debts. Note, however, some lenders occasionally require borrowers to purchase life insurance as a condition for granting a loan; such insurance will help lessen the need for insuring for debt repayment.

Calculating the Actual Dollar Amount of Losses

Determining the magnitude of the possible losses resulting from a premature death can be difficult, since the amounts of final expenses and lost income are relatively unknown. At least three approaches can be used. A relatively unsophisticated and imprecise approach is to put a dollar value on the life to be insured based on some notion of the psychological loss that would be felt by survivors. This **value-of-life approach** is particularly hazardous because it carries so much potential for error. It should not be used.

The Multiple-Earnings Approach A great improvement over the value-of-life approach, the **multiple-earnings approach** involves estimating the funds needed to replace the lost income by multiplying the annual take-home pay of the person involved by the number of years the income will be needed. However, this will overestimate the needed funds for two reasons. First, approximately 25 percent of an individual's take-home pay is spent on his or her own personal expenditures. Thus only about 75 percent of the take-home pay of the deceased will need to be replaced. Second, if the funds needed to replace lost income are received shortly after death (as life insurance benefits are), they can be invested and earn interest. This interest also can be used to help replace lost income.

The Needs Approach The **needs approach** involves estimating the total dollar loss due to a premature death. It builds on the calculations of the multiple-earnings approach by including an accurate assessment of lost income and the dollar losses likely to result from final, readjustment-period, and debt-repayment expenses. It also takes into account government benefits that lessen the need to replace lost income.

Most families—widows or widowers with surviving children—may collect **Social Security survivors' benefits** if a breadwinner dies, with the level of benefits depending on the amount of Social Security taxes paid by the deceased. Details on estimating Social Security benefits are in Appendix B. If eligible, a family can receive up to about $20,000 per year, but these benefits will generally cease when the youngest child reaches age 18 and not begin again until the surviving spouse reaches retirement age. This period of ineligibility for Social Security benefits is called the **Social Security blackout period**. It ends when the surviving spouse reaches the age of 60. At age 62 the survivor may begin collecting Social Security benefits based on his or her own Social Security taxes or on the taxes paid by the deceased, whichever results in the higher payment.

The formula for the needs approach is

$$DL = (0.75AI - AGB)PVIFA + FE + RE + DR \qquad (14.1)$$

where

DL = *dollar loss* from premature death

AI = *annual income* of the person insured, including fringe benefits that survivors depend on and/or the cost of replacing their household services

AGB = *annual government benefits* available if insured dies (this estimate is derived from Appendix C)

PVIFA = the *present-value interest factor of an annuity* from Appendix A4, which incorporates the number of years the income will be needed and the interest rate (*after* taxes *and* inflation) earned by invested life insurance proceeds

FE = *final expenses*

RE = *readjustment expenses*

DR = *debt-repayment expenses*

To illustrate the application of the needs approach, consider the Martin family of Grand Rapids, Michigan. John Martin is a 33-year-old married father with two children, aged 7 and 4. John is a landscape architect. His annual salary is $52,000 before taxes and $40,000 after taxes, including fringe benefits. He has worked steadily for the past 12 years, received average pay raises, and contributed at or near the maximum in Social Security taxes. John applies Equation (14.1) to find the dollar loss from his premature death as follows:

AI = $40,000 (take-home pay)

AGB = $20,500 rounded (Social Security survivors' benefits while children are under the age of 18; see calculations in Appendix B)

PVIFA = 12.659 [income needed for 18 years (until the youngest child finishes college at age 22); 4 percent return, after taxes and inflation, on invested life insurance proceeds; see Appendix A4]

FE = $10,000 (assumed estimate)

RE = $40,000 (to replace lost income in the first year after death)

DR = $2000 (assumed estimate)

DL = [(0.75 × $40,000) − $20,500]12.659 + $10,000 + $40,000 + $2000

= ($30,000 − $20,500)12.659 + $52,000

= $172,261

Thus John estimates that his death would result in financial losses of $172,261 for his survivors. The level of potential losses will not, however, dictate the amount of life insurance needed. First, John must determine whether existing resources can meet the financial losses of his early death.

Identifying Resources Available to Cover Losses

There is no need to purchase life insurance if resources will be available to cover the losses resulting from a premature death, such as Social Security

Life Insurance for Young Professionals

When people graduate from college, their names and accomplishments may become known to many people through listings in hometown newspapers and other sources. Life insurance agents use such lists to obtain prospects for their sales efforts. Other prospects are solicited by mail or by phone for a life insurance "consultation." They key question is, "Do you really need life insurance?" Let's look at a typical example of a recent college graduate.

Nancy Jones of San Francisco, California, recently graduated with a degree in hotel management and has a position as night desk manager at a major resort hotel. She earns $24,000 per year in gross salary. Nancy is single and owes $7500 on a car loan as well as $11,800 in education loans. Among her fringe benefits are an employer-paid term insurance policy equal to her annual salary and an option to buy an additional $24,000 for $1.25 per year per thousand. Thus, for an additional $30 per year (24 × $1.25), Nancy can increase her employer-related life insurance coverage to $48,000.

Nancy has been approached by a life insurance agent whose calculations suggest that she needs a $120,000 policy. Does she? If we apply the needs approach formula to Nancy's situation, we see the following:

$$DL = (0.75AI - AGB)PVIFA \\ + FE + RE + DR$$

where

DL = *dollar loss* from premature death

AI = *annual income* required to support survivors dependent on that income. In Nancy's case, this would be $0.

AGB = *annual government benefits* to survivors. In Nancy's case, this would be $0. Since she has not qualified for Social Security benefits as yet and she has no qualifying survivors.

$PVIFA$ = *present-value interest factor,* which Nancy figures is irrelevant for her because there is no need to replace lost income.

FE = *final expenses.* Nancy figures that her burial would cost about $8,000.

RE = *readjustment expenses,* which Nancy has determined would be $0.

DR = *debt repayment.* Nancy would like to see her $7500 in automobile and $11,800 in education loans repaid in the event of her death. She feels better knowing that her college loans would be repaid and that her younger brother could inherit her car free and clear.

The resulting calculations show that Nancy has a likely dollar loss of $27,300 ($8000 + $11,800 + $7500), which can easily be met by the $48,000 in insurance available through her employer. Clearly, she does not need further insurance at this time. When her circumstances change, Nancy should reappraise her needs.

benefits and wealth assets. However, since government benefits typically provide limited financial assistance, various resources often must be utilized to provide for survivors. Savings accounts and investments are the most obvious resources, and others are existing insurance, education, and asset equity.

Existing Savings and Investments   As time passes, individuals and families usually acquire at least a minimal amount of savings and investments. These amounts in savings accounts, certificates of deposit, stocks, bonds, and mutual funds often are specifically intended to meet some special purpose, such as retirement, travel, or college for children. If necessary in the event of a premature death, these funds can be used to meet final and readjustment expenses as well as to replace lost income. Pension funds and profit-sharing plans of the deceased, such as 401(k), 403-b, and IRAs, also can be utilized as resources. As children grow older and leave the home, the potential losses that would result from the death of a parent typically lessen. At some point savings and investments may exceed potential losses and eliminate the need for life insurance.

Other Insurance   Life insurance is often a fringe benefit paid for employees by their employers. In addition, automobile insurance sometimes pays a specific small sum when death results from a traffic accident. This may be a consideration for young people, since automobile accidents are the leading cause of death for persons aged 24 and under. Also, it is likely that income from Social Security survivors' coverage could be depended on by families with children, since most workers have earned enough credits to qualify for survivor's benefits.

Skills and Education of Survivors   The level of skills and education attained by a surviving spouse will affect whether he or she can earn enough to replace the lost income of the deceased. A spouse who had been working part time outside the home could take a full-time position. A spouse who had not been working outside the home could begin or renew a career. In either case, the potential for extra income can reduce the need for life insurance. Spouses returning to work should increase their own life insurance coverage to reflect the income that would be lost if they were to die, assuming there are survivors dependent upon that income.

Amount of Equity in Assets   Over time, individuals and families acquire tangible assets that can provide services or funds after the death of a family member. **Equity** is that portion of the dollar value of an asset that is owned by an individual. For example, if you drive a car with a market value of $10,000 on which you still owe $4400, your equity is $5600. You can build up equity by paying cash for an asset, by repaying a loan used to purchase an asset, or through appreciation of an asset. For most families, the equity built up in their home represents their largest asset. When one spouse dies, the other may decide to sell the home and use part of the income to buy or rent less-expensive housing. The remainder of the equity could then be used for living expenses or other needs.

Determining the Amount of Life Insurance Needed

The death of any individual may result in some financial losses for family, friends, business associates, and others. This does not mean that every individual should have life insurance coverage, however. Figure 14.1 shows

FIGURE 14.1
Determining Life Insurance Needed

Losses Resulting from Premature Death: Lost income Final expenses Readjustment expenses Debt repayment expenses	−	Resources Available: Government benefits Savings and investments Existing insurance Education Asset equity	=	Amount of Life Insurance Needed

the calculation for determining the amount of life insurance needed. The resources available are subtracted from the losses resulting from premature death. If the result is a negative number, life insurance is probably not needed because assets can cover the losses. However, some people in this situation may wish to buy life insurance anyway so that they can pass substantive resources on to heirs.

If anticipated losses exceed resources available, life insurance is probably needed. The amount needed will depend on the magnitude of the losses, the resources available, and the individual's willingness to assume the risk of premature death. The amount of life insurance purchased will depend on all three of these factors, plus the funds available to buy life insurance. Once you determine how much life insurance you need, you must decide what type of life insurance is best and from whom to buy your policy. The remainder of this chapter covers these topics.

Types of Life Insurance Available

Objective
To be able to define and distinguish among the various types of terms and cash-value life insurance policies.

Many people are confused by the variety of life insurance policies. However, there are really just two types of life insurance: term life insurance and cash-value life insurance. *Term life insurance* is often described as "pure protection" because you make no investment and it pays benefits only if the insured person dies; the premiums rise as you grow older. *Cash-value life insurance,* which costs far more, also pays benefits at death and includes a savings element that may provide some benefit to the insured while alive; the premium level generally remains constant. Providing this savings element adds to the cost of cash-value life insurance and it should be evaluated separately from the death benefits provided under the policy. The **premium** is the fee for insurance protection. It is the payment, or one of the regular periodic payments, that a policyholder is required to make to keep an insurance policy in force.

A life insurance policy is more than just a contract between the purchaser and the company. Several other parties might be named in the policy. The **policyholder** (also called the **owner**) is the person who pays for the policy and retains all rights and privileges granted by the policy, including the right to amend the policy and the right to designate who shall receive theproceeds. The insured is the person whose life is insured. The **beneficiary** is the person or organization named in the policy that will be the recipient of the life insurance or other benefit payment in the event of the insured's death. The **contingent beneficiary** is the person or organization that will become the beneficiary if the original beneficiary dies before the insured does. The owner and the insured are often the same person, but it is possible for four different people to be named in a policy. For example, a father (the owner) might insure the life of his son (the insured) and name the boy's mother as beneficiary and sister as contingent beneficiary. This section will cover term and cash-value life insurance and their variations and briefly examine annuities.

Term Life Insurance

Term life insurance is a plan of insurance that covers the insured for only a certain period of time (the term), not for his or her entire lifetime. It pays death benefits only if the insured party dies within the term of the contract. If the insured survives the specified time period, the beneficiary receives no monetary benefits. Term insurance can be purchased in contracts with face amounts in multiples of $1000, usually with a minimum face amount of $25,000. The **face amount** is the dollar value that the insurance company agrees to pay in case of death or at maturity.

Term life insurance contracts are most often written for 1, 5, 10, or 20 years. A new contract is required to continue coverage past the end of the contract period. Unless otherwise stipulated in the original contract, this means that you must apply for a new contract and may be required to submit the results of a medical examination. If you have a health hazard, you may be denied a new policy or have to pay higher premiums. Even if your health status remains the same, the premium will increase, because you will be older and thus more likely to die while the new policy is in force. Thus term insurance premiums rise with each renewal, and a change in health status may disqualify an applicant for coverage. For example, a $50,000 five-year term policy for a man age 25 might have an annual premium of $180; at age 35 the policy will cost him $105, and at age 45 it will cost $200. Nonetheless, term policies are *less* expensive than cash-value policies, since there is no savings element in term insurance.

Guaranteed Renewable Term Policies   Term life insurance policies may be written with a **guaranteed renewability option,** which eliminates the need to prove insurability when you want to renew a policy. Proving insurability may be difficult if you developed a health problem during the period of the original policy. In a sense, the renewability option insures against the possibility of becoming uninsurable. Thus you can avoid the requirement for a medical examination at renewal if you include a guaranteed renewability option in a policy. There may be a limit to how many renewals you can make without proving insurability and a maximum age for these renewals. Unless you are positive you will not need a renewal, it is best to buy term life insurance with a guaranteed renewability option. Of course, the premium rates increase at each renewal as the age of the insured increases. Most people who purchase term life insurance buy it with a guaranteed renewability option. Thus, when shopping for term life insurance, many people ask for **annual renewable term (ART)**.

You can avoid premium increases as you grow older by purchasing a term policy with a long time period, say 20 or 30 years. Under such a policy, the premiums remain constant throughout the period, increasing only for a renewal after the policy expires. Such policies initially cost more than policies written for shorter time periods, but they cost less than shorter-term policies toward the end of the policy period. This is because premiums are higher than necessary in early years to balance out the higher premiums that would have been necessary in later years. To illustrate, consider two $100,000 term policies for a man aged 25, one on a 20-year basis and one on a 5-year basis. A typical annual premium for the 20-year policy would be $225 for each of the 20 years. The annual premium for the 5-year policy might be $150 for each of the first 5 years. After renewal, the premiums would increase to $200 for each of the second 5 years. Annual premiums for the third 5 years might be $250, and for the fourth 5 years $325. Thus the annual premiums for the 20-year policy remain constant and are higher in the early years and lower in the later years than those of four 5-year policies.

The premiums paid for the 20-year policy would total $4500, and premiums for the four 5-year policies would total $4625. There is a difference in total premiums because the insurance company (1) will save expenses by writing one policy rather than four and (2) will invest the excess premiums paid in the early years of the 20-year policy and use the income on these investments to reduce later premiums paid by the insured. Given the figures cited in this example, it appears that the 20-year policy is less expensive than four 5-year policies. However, a policyholder could buy the 5-year policies, invest the premium differences from the early years, and earn enough interest on the investments to more than offset higher premiums in later years. A method of comparing the price of insurance policies that takes into account the potential investment effects of policy price differences is discussed later in this chapter.

Decreasing Term Insurance   With **decreasing term insurance,** the face amount declines annually and the premiums remain constant. You can choose a face amount and a contract period, then the face amount of the policy gradually declines (usually each year) to some minimum, such as $5000, in the last year of the contract. As expected, the premiums for a decreasing term policy are lower than those for a comparable term policy with a fixed face amount. For example, a woman aged 25 could buy a 30-year $50,000 decreasing term policy for about $110 per year. A 30-year $50,000 term policy that does not decline would cost about $150 per year.

Typically, around the age of 45, people's insurance needs decrease. The major benefit of decreasing term policies is that they can more closely fit your changing insurance needs. It is important to realize, however, that decreasing term policies vary in the rate at which the face amount declines. Some decline at a constant rate, such as 5 percent per year for 20 years, and some have accelerating rates of reduction. The rate of reduction in the face amount must closely fit the rate at which your insurance needs decrease. Another caution concerning decreasing term insurance is that inflation may cause life insurance needs to *increase* even when your financial obligations for others might appear to decline as you age.

Convertible Term Insurance Convertible term insurance offers the policyholder the option of exchanging a term policy for a cash-value policy without evidence of insurability. Usually, this conversion is available only in the early years of the term policy. Some life insurance policies provide for an automatic conversion from term insurance to cash-value insurance after a specific number of years.

There are two ways to convert a term policy to a cash-value policy. One is to simply request the conversion and begin paying the higher premiums required for the cash-value policy. No proof of insurability is required to convert the policy. The savings element of the cash-value policy will begin accumulating as of the date of the conversion. A second conversion method entails paying the savings that would have built up had the policy originally been written on a cash-value basis. Although this lump sum may be a considerable amount, it does represent an asset to the policyholder. Furthermore, with this method the new premiums are based on your age at the time you bought the original term policy, which may result in substantially lower premiums than for comparable cash-value coverage available at the time of conversion.

Credit Term Life Insurance Credit term life insurance will pay the remaining balance of a loan if the insured dies before repaying the debt. Basically, credit life insurance is a decreasing term insurance policy with the creditor named as beneficiary. Some lenders will require credit life insurance as a condition of granting you a loan. If so, you may buy the insurance through the lender or obtain coverage elsewhere, often for lower premiums.

If the lender merely offers credit life insurance, you must decide whether insurance is really needed and if the premiums offered by the lender are competitive. Such coverage is not needed if you are otherwise adequately insured. Credit life insurance requires no proof of insurability. Individuals who have health problems that make life insurance expensive or difficult to obtain might use credit life insurance to help meet their overall life insurance needs. Generally, this type of insurance is overpriced.

Group Term Life Insurance Group life insurance is issued to people as a group rather than individually. The typical policy is written for a group of employees, regardless of their health, with premiums paid in full or in part by the employer. Group life insurance premiums are average rates and are sometimes lower for individuals than are premiums for individual policies. However, if you are a good risk, you might be able to do better buying life insurance on your own. If you are insured under a group plan, you need not prove your insurability, and if you leave the group, you may be able to convert the policy to an individual basis without proof of insurability. Most group life insurance is term insurance and has no savings element.

Cash-Value Life Insurance

Cash-value life insurance pays benefits upon the death of the insured and has a savings element that allows the payment of benefits prior to death. The **cash value** is the savings/investing element of cash-value life insurance policies. While the policyholder is alive, he or she may obtain the cash value by borrowing it from the company or by surrendering and canceling the policy; however, the cash value is not refunded when the insured dies. Cash-value life insurance is sometimes called **whole life insurance** or **permanent life insurance** because the time period of coverage under the policy is the entire life of the insured. You need never renew the policy nor prove your insurability again, and the annual premiums (payable for life) for cash-value policies usually remain constant.

The premiums for cash-value policies are always higher than those for term policies providing the same amount of coverage. This is because only a portion of the cash-value life insurance premium is for payment of a death benefit. The remainder is used to build cash value, the savings element. Figure 14.2 illustrates the premium differences between cash-value and term life insurance policies.

One way to describe cash-value insurance is that it is nothing more than a combination of decreasing term insurance and a savings/investment account arranged so that the face amount of the policy remains the same. Initially, for example, you might have $100,000 of insurance and no savings. Several years later you might have built up $5000 in savings within the policy. If you were to die, your beneficiary would collect $100,000, but $5000 of the payment would be your own money. If you lived long enough, the cash value would equal—and might surpass—the $100,000 figure, and, in effect, your beneficiary would collect your savings account rather than an insurance payment.

The rate at which the cash value accumulates in a policy will depend on the size of the premiums and the rate of return paid. Most cash-value policies have a guaranteed minimum interest rate. Policies written before 1978 may have guaranteed rates as low as 2 or 3 percent, but more recently issued policies have guaranteed rates of up to 6 percent. Some newer varieties of cash-value policies will pay even higher rates depending on prevailing interest rates in the economy. Table 14.3 shows the cash-value accumulations for a typical cash-value policy with a guaranteed rate of return of 4 percent.

At any time you may borrow your cash value or cancel the policy and take the cash.

Even though the cash value of a life insurance policy accumulates throughout your life, upon your death only the face amount of the policy will be paid. Prior to death you have the option of cashing in the policy for the accumulated cash value, which cancels your insurance coverage, or you may borrow all or part of the cash value. What you borrow you must repay with interest, and the amount owed will be subtracted from the face amount of the policy if you die while the debt is outstanding. The

FIGURE 14.2
Comparison of Premium Dollars for Life Insurance*

* For example, the annual premium for a $100,000 cash-value policy might be $850 for a 25-year-old female but only $150 for a $100,000 term policy.

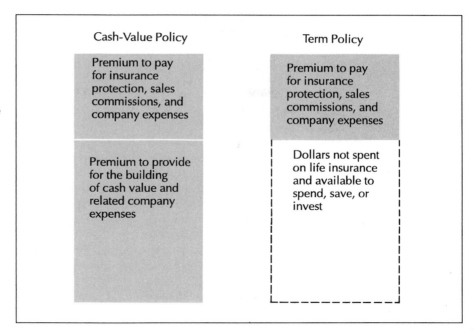

specifics of cashing in a policy and borrowing cash values will be discussed in more detail later. For now, remember that cash values represent a kind of forced savings that allows the buildup of funds while you buy life insurance.

There are several different types of cash-value life insurance. Each of the major types will be discussed.

TABLE 14.3
Illustrative Cash-Value Accumulations* (4 Percent Guaranteed Rate)

Policy Year	Cash Value
1	$ 0
2	0
3	585
4	1,280
5	1,993
10	5,816
15	10,089
20	14,738
25	17,492
30	22,197

* For a $50,000 whole life insurance policy for a male aged 35 with an annual premium of $658.

Whole Life Insurance   Whole life insurance is a form of cash-value life insurance that provides life insurance protection for your lifetime and requires you to pay premiums for life. In developing insurance rates, insurers assume that all insureds die at the age of 100. Therefore, the last premium is paid after your 99th birthday and the face amount of the policy is paid at age 100. *Straight life* and *ordinary life* are sometimes used interchangeably with *whole life.*

Modified Life Insurance   Modified life insurance is whole life insurance with reduced premiums in the early years and higher premiums thereafter because some of the protection during the early years is provided by term insurance. The period of reduced premiums can vary from 1 to 5 years. Modified life insurance is primarily designed for those whose life insurance needs are high but who cannot immediately afford the premiums required for a cash-value policy, such as a young family. Because of the lower premiums in early years, modified life insurance accumulates cash value more slowly than other cash-value policies.

Limited-Pay Life Insurance   Limited-pay life insurance is whole life insurance that allows premium payments to cease before you reach the age of 100. Two common examples are *twenty-pay life* policies, which allow premium payments to cease after 20 years, and *paid at 65* policies, which require payment of premiums only until the insured turns 65. An extreme version of limited-pay life insurance is the *single-premium* life insurance policy, which is fully paid for in a lump sum. As you might expect, the annual premiums for limited-pay policies are higher than for ordinary policies because the insurance company has fewer years to collect premiums. Although premiums need be paid only for the time period specified, insurance protection lasts your lifetime. Limited-pay policies are said to be **paid up** when all required premiums have been paid. Paid-up policies will continue to accumulate cash values because the insurer will continue to pay returns on the funds.

Endowment Life Insurance   Endowment life insurance provides for payment of the face amount either at your death *or* at some previously agreed-upon date, whichever occurs first. The date of payment, called the **endowment date,** is commonly some specified number of years after issuance of the policy (say, 20 or 30 years) or some specified age (such as 65). Many such policies name a child as beneficiary and endow when the child turns 18. Sometimes the beneficiary of the policy is a different person from the one who is to receive the endowment. For example, one spouse may name the other as beneficiary of the death benefit but designate the children as recipients of the endowment payout.

Endowment policies are the most expensive form of life insurance per dollar of coverage. This is because insurers have a limited time to collect premiums and also must pay the face amount by the endowment date. Furthermore, premiums must be large enough to provide the funds needed for a rapid accumulation of cash value.

Adjustable Life Insurance   The three cornerstones of cash-value life insurance are the premium, the face amount, and the rate of cash-value accumulation. **Adjustable life insurance** allows you to change any of the three with corresponding changes in the other two. Adjustable life insurance was created in response to policyholder demands for more flexibility in policies. Say, for example, you feel that inflation has increased your need for life insurance. Adjustable life insurance would allow you to increase the face amount. In response, your premiums could go up or the cash-value accumulation could slow, or both. With more traditional life insurance policies, these changes can be made only if you purchase a new policy and/or cash in an existing one. Adjustable life insurance policies allow changes with no added proof of insurability.

Interest-Sensitive Cash-Value Life Insurance   Traditionally, the cash-value life insurance policies discussed thus far have paid a fixed, guaranteed rate of return on the accumulated cash value. You will recall from earlier chapters that fixed interest rate arrangements in credit and savings often have been replaced by more flexible interest rate arrangements in response to variable inflation and interest rates in the economy. Life insurance has not been immune to these pressures, and several new forms of cash-value life insurance that employ variable rates of return that are sensitive to changing conditions in the economy have come on the market. A further pressure for such a change in life insurance has come from those who have criticized the low yields paid on cash-value life insurance and have advised buyers to "buy term and invest the money saved" in ways that pay a better rate of return. The more prominent among these new products are variable life insurance, universal life insurance, and a hybrid of the two known as variable-universal life.

Universal Life Insurance   **Universal life insurance** provides both the pure protection of term insurance and the cash-value buildup of whole life insurance but with variability in the face amount, rate of cash-value accumulation, premiums, and rate of return. Essentially, the purchase of universal life insurance represents combining the purchase of annual term insurance (allowing for annual variations in face amounts and premiums) with an investment program (allowing for variations in premiums, cash value, and other characteristics of the policy). Universal life policies are usually available only in initial face amounts of $100,000 or more. The rate of return is tied to some interest rate prevailing in the financial markets or is more commonly dictated by the company. In either case, the rates of return are higher than commonly available under other types of cash-value policies. With some universal life policies, the payment of a higher premium allows payment of both the face amount and the accumulated cash value at death of the insured party.

An examination of a universal life policy requires an understanding of four elements: the premium, the cost of the death benefit, the interest rate, and the company expense charges. Table 14.4 includes these four elements in a summary comparison of term, whole life, and universal life policies.

What If You Buy Term Life Insurance and Invest the Money Saved?

The principle underlying "buy term and invest the money saved" is simple: If you save or conservatively invest the difference between the cost of term insurance and that of another type of policy, you will *always* be ahead financially. For example, look at the first year of estate buildup in the following table for a 30-year-old. Instead of purchasing a $100,000 whole life policy with an annual premium of $870, the person pays $100 for the first year's premium of a $100,000 annual renewable term policy and puts the difference of $770 ($870 − $100) in a bank savings account. If the person dies tomorrow, the estate is already ahead because of the money just put into the bank; upon death, the beneficiary would collect the $100,000 in insurance and also receive the $770 in savings. If the person dies years into the future, the estate is even more ahead because of the growing principal and interest in the savings account. Note that after age 50 the cost of term insurance rises rapidly.

Estate Buildup If Term Life Insurance Buyer Saves/Invests the Difference

Age	Premium for Annual Renewable Term	Difference (Not Spent on Whole Life)	Total Savings and Earnings Put into Savings* at 5 Percent†	Total Estate‡
30	$ 160	$ 710	$ 746	$100,746
31	164	706	1,525	101,525
32	168	702	2,338	102,338
33	172	698	3,188	103,188
34	176	694	4,076	104,076
35	180	690	5,004	105,004
36	184	686	5,975	105,975
37	188	682	6,990	106,990
38	192	678	8,051	108,051
39	196	674	9,161	109,161
40	200	670	10,323	110,323
41	205	665	11,537	111,537
42	210	660	12,807	112,807
43	215	655	14,135	114,135
44	220	650	15,524	115,524

(*continued*)

There are literally thousands of variations among universal life policies, so comparisons are extremely difficult.

Initially, the purchaser selects a face amount, and an annual premium is quoted. The annual premium goes into the cash-value fund. From this fund the cost of providing the death benefit and charges for company expenses are deducted. As time goes by, the insured may reduce or increase the premium with corresponding changes in the death benefit or amount

What If You Buy Term Life Insurance and Invest the Money Saved? *(continued)*

Age	Premium for Annual Renewable Term	Difference (Not Spent on Whole Life)	Total Savings and Earnings Put into Savings* at 5 Percent†	Total Estate‡
45	$ 225	$ 645	$16,977	$116,977
46	230	640	18,498	118,498
47	235	635	20,090	120,090
48	240	630	21,756	121,756
49	245	625	23,500	123,500
50	250	620	25,326	125,326
51	300	570	27,191	127,191
52	370	500	29,076	129,076
53	450	420	30,971	130,971
54	540	330	32,866	132,866
55	640	230	34,751	134,751
56	750	120	36,615	136,615
57	870	0	38,446	138,446
58	1,000	− 130	40,232	140,232
59	1,150	− 280	41,950	141,950
60	1,320	− 450	43,575	143,575
61	1,510	− 640	45,082	145,082
62	1,740	− 870	46,423	146,423
63	2,000	− 1,130	47,558	147,558
64	2,310	− 1,440	48,424	148,424
65	2,700	− 1,830	48,924	148,924

* The whole life policy premium for the same $100,000 in coverage is assumed to be $870 every year.
† It is assumed that the buyer pays the annual renewable term premium at the beginning of each year and the difference is saved and placed on deposit instead. Those amounts stay in the savings account all year in addition to the previous year's ending balance. Savings are compounded annually at a 5 percent rate. To illustrate the calculations for 1 year, such as beginning at age 30, simply take the difference not spent on the whole life policy ($870 − $160 = $710) and multiply it times 1.05 (for 5 percent interest), which yields the total savings ($746 by the end of the year) including interest earned for the year.
‡ Upon death at a certain age, the beneficiary would receive the $100,000 face amount of the term life insurance policy plus the amount built up in the savings account earning 5 percent.

added to cash value. If premiums drop below that necessary to cover the death benefit and expenses, funds are removed from the cash-value account to cover the shortfall. Sometimes universal life policies are promoted as allowing the cessation of premium payments after 5, 7, or 10 years. While this may be possible, it should be clear that the funds to support these unpaid premiums come at the expense of cash-value accumulation.

The portion of the premium that is required to provide the death benefit

TABLE 14.4
Comparisons of Three Popular Life Insurance Policies

Feature	Term Insurance	Whole Life Insurance	Universal Life Insurance
Face amount	Fixed or declining during term of the policy; changeable at renewal	Fixed	Variable
Premiums	Low with increases at renewal	High and fixed	High but variable within limits
Cash-value accumulation	None	Fixed rate of accumulation	Variable accumulation as premium and interest rates vary
Rate of return paid on cash accumulations	Not applicable	Fixed	Variable with interest rates in the economy or as specified by company
Cost of the death benefit portion	Low, with interest at renewal	Unknown	Known but can vary and may hide some expense charges
Company expense charges	Low but unknown; hidden in premium	Unknown; hidden in premium	Known; may be high

is clearly disclosed in universal life insurance policies. This is not the case with whole life and other traditional cash-value policies. This disclosure is of great benefit because it allows the insured to compare the cost of protection with other universal life policies and, more important, a similar amount of term insurance. Most policies have two tables of charges for various death benefit amounts. One table lists the charges that are currently being assessed to purchasers. The second table lists the maximum that can be charged for various death benefit levels. Most companies charge less than the maximum, and the lower charge is the one emphasized by the agent, but the company is within its rights to raise the charges for death benefits up to the maximum in the contract.

Current rates of return on cash values are not guaranteed.

The rate of return applied to the cash-value balance and the amount of the premium paid are the two determinants of the rate of cash-value accumulation under a universal life policy. This rate is clearly disclosed, but usually two rates are quoted. One is the **guaranteed minimum rate** (the rate which by contract the company is legally obligated to pay) and the other is the **current rate** (the rate of return recently paid by the company to policyholders). It is the current rate that is emphasized by the agent, who will often present a table illustrating the rate of cash-value accumulation resulting from the two rates. Table 14.5 is an example of such a table. Note the differences in the two cash-value columns. It is easy to understand why the agent would emphasize the current rate. Note also that initial cash-value accumulations, often the first $500 or $5000, under some policies will earn only the guaranteed rate. A high current rate of

TABLE 14.5
Cash-Value Buildup: Guaranteed versus Current Rates

Policy Year	Guaranteed Cash-Surrender Value (4 Percent Rate)*	Cash-Surrender Value at Current Rates (11.2 Percent Rate)*
1	$ 0	$ 0
2	0	472
3	585	1,187
4	1,280	1,977
5	1,993	2,852
6	2,723	3,851
7	3,470	4,955
8	4,234	6,177
9	5,016	7,528
10	5,816	9,022
15	10,089	19,408
20	14,738	36,886

* Policy has a back-end load that reduces buildup of cash values in early years.

return that is not applied to the entire cash value is a misleading indicator of the approximate true annual rate of return.

The company expense charges are the last of the four elements necessary for an understanding of universal life insurance. Like the rate of return and the death benefit charges, the company expense charges are disclosed clearly in a universal life policy. The most typical of these involves a deduction of a fee of from 5 to 10 percent from each annual premium. Such charges are not the traditional sales commission but are referred to as a **front-end load** to pay for corporate marketing costs. Some companies also will charge a **back-end load**, which is a fee assessed if you wish to withdraw some or all of the cash value accumulated. This latter charge is often highest in the early years of the policy and is eliminated in later years. The policy illustrated in Table 14.5 has a back-end load in the first few years that accounts for the initially low cash values. Be wary of policies that have both front- and back-end loads.

Variable life insurance gives you control over how the cash values are invested.

Variable Life Insurance   **Variable life insurance** allows you to choose the investments made with your cash-value accumulations and to share in the gains and losses. The face amount of your policy and the policy's cash value may rise or fall as the rates of return on the invested funds vary. The face amount of the policy, however, usually will not drop below the originally agreed-upon amount. What will fluctuate is the cash value. Because you are continually paying premiums, the cash value will increase, but it may increase slowly if poor investments are made.

Holders of variable life insurance policies have some control over the types of investments made with their premiums. If you are unfamiliar with markets for corporate stocks and bonds and money-market securities, you should probably avoid variable life insurance. Another negative aspect of variable life insurance is that many policies contain provisions calling for the payment of fees and sales charges before the policyholders can share in investment returns. Variable life insurance policies require very careful reading and analysis before purchase.

Variable-Universal Life Insurance **Variable-universal life insurance** is a form of universal life insurance that allows the policyholder some choice in the investments made with the cash value accumulated by the policy. It is sometimes called *flexible-premium variable life insurance* or *universal life II*. It is probably the life insurance product that most closely embodies the philosophy of "buy term and invest the money saved." Because you select the investment vehicles (a combination of stocks, bonds, or money-market mutual funds), there is the potential for a higher rate of return than under a universal life policy. With this potential for a higher rate of return comes the risk of a lower rate of return. As a result, variable-universal life policies usually have no minimum guaranteed rate of return. It is possible that you might lose cash value and even be required to come up with a higher premium payment to keep the policy in effect. Prospective purchasers of variable-universal life insurance need to consider carefully how much risk they are willing to accept in their life insurance program.

What Is Really Contained in a Life Insurance Policy?

Objective
To be able to describe the major provisions of life insurance policies and explain the value of each.

A life insurance policy is the written contract between the insurer and the policyholder. The policy contains all the information relative to the agreement. Even though individual policies vary somewhat, most of them contain the following common provisions: (1) general terms and provisions, (2) living benefits, (3) optional living benefits, and (4) settlement options.

General Terms and Provisions

Life insurance policies define the terminology used in the policy and outline the basic provisions. The purpose of such information is to clarify the meaning of the policy and the protections afforded the insurer and the policyholder.

Death Benefit The **death benefit** of a life insurance policy is the amount that will be paid upon the death of the insured person. The amount of the death benefit will differ somewhat from the face amount. The face amount will be slightly adjusted up or down to allow for such items as any earned dividends accumulated but not yet paid the policyholder (on participating policies), outstanding cash-value loans, premiums paid in advance, or unpaid premiums. For example, consider a $100,000 participating whole life policy with annual premiums of $1380. If the insured

Annuities Are Not Life Insurance

An **annuity** is a contract (generally with a life insurance company) that provides income for a set period of time or for a person's lifetime in return for the payment of a premium or premiums. In a sense, an annuity is the opposite of a life insurance contract. Life insurance reduces the financial risk of the insured dying prematurely, whereas annuities reduce the financial risk that the insured will live too long, that is, longer than income will be available for support.

Annuities are not life insurance, but they are often sold by life insurance agents and companies as a way of investing life insurance or endowment proceeds. Because annuities provide income, they are investments and should be compared with the many investment options available in today's financial marketplace. Annuities will be covered more fully in Chapter 22, Developing and Implementing a Plan for a Secure Retirement.

were to die halfway through the policy year, with an outstanding cash-value loan of $5000 and earned but unpaid dividends of $11,000, the death benefit would be $106,690, calculated as follows:

$100,000	Face amount
11,000	Unpaid dividends
+ 690	Premiums paid in advance (one-half year)
$111,690	Subtotal
− 5,000	Outstanding cash-value loan
$106,690	Death benefit

Beneficiaries   Note that the proceeds from a life insurance policy are generally not subject to federal and state income taxes. In addition, life insurance benefits can be designated to be paid to a named beneficiary rather than to the estate of the deceased and thus avoid estate taxation as well as the reach of potential creditors. The policy also gives the procedure for payment of the death benefit if a named beneficiary dies before the insured does and the policyholder has not named a new beneficiary. Occasionally, as with married couples, there may be a dispute as to who died first, the beneficiary or the insured, such as may occur in an airplane accident. Procedures for settling this type of problem and for changing beneficiaries will be included in the policy.

Insurable Interest   As we discussed in Chapter 11, you have insurable interest if you stand to suffer a financial loss when a peril occurs. It is sometimes difficult to determine exactly who has an insurable interest in the life of an insured and what the dollar value of that interest is. Life insurance companies will question an application for life insurance that seems to request more coverage than warranted by the nature of the relationship among the policyholder, the beneficiary, and the insured. Sometimes policies will be issued and appear suspect only after a loss occurs. In such a case, the company may challenge a loss claim and may refuse to pay the death benefit (although they usually do return the premium). Policies contain general language giving the company the right to make such challenges.

The Application   The life insurance application is the policyholder's offer to purchase a policy. The application requests specific information and becomes part of the life insurance policy. Any errors or omissions in the application may allow the insurance company to deny a request for payment of the death benefit.

The Incontestability Clause   Life insurance policies generally have an **incontestability clause,** which places a time limit—usually 2 years after issuance of the policy—on the right of the insurance company to deny a claim. This clause applies to the problems arising out of questionable insurable interest and false statements in the application.

The Suicide Clause   Life insurance policies will generally have a **suicide clause,** allowing the life insurance company to deny coverage if the insured commits suicide within the first few years after issuance of the policy. If the specified number of years has elapsed (usually 2), the full death benefit will be paid. If not, only the premiums that had been paid will be payable to the beneficiary.

Living Benefits

Most life insurance policies include provisions for benefits to an insured prior to death.

Cash Dividends   Life insurance **dividends** are defined legally as a return of a portion of the premium paid for a life insurance policy. They represent the surplus earnings of the company that reflect the difference between the premium charged and the cost to the company of providing insurance. Dividends are paid when losses and/or company expenses are below the investment returns on the insurer's assets. Policies that pay dividends are called **participating policies,** and policies that do not pay dividends are called **nonparticipating policies.** Both term and cash-value policies may pay dividends. It is not unusual for an insurance company to charge higher-than-necessary premiums in order to pay high dividends. Carefully evaluate the premiums charged and the dividend likely to be paid when you compare participating and nonparticipating policies.

Owners of participating policies may receive dividends in one of several ways. One option is to receive the dividends as a cash payment at the end of each policy year. A second option is to have the dividends remain with the insurance company to accumulate and earn interest until retirement, when the funds may be used to purchase an annuity. A third option is to use the dividends for the purchase of small amounts of paid-up life insurance. With some policies, this paid-up insurance, plus accumulated cash values, grows to a sufficient level over the years to allow the insured to discontinue paying premiums and still maintain the same amount of coverage. Until the dividends are actually withdrawn from the policy, the policyholder is free to change the option chosen.

Grace Period Prompt payment of the premium is crucial to the continuation of coverage provided by any insurance policy. A **lapsed policy** is an insurance policy that has been terminated at the end of the grace period because of nonpayment of premiums. Most policies that lapse do so in the first two years.

If your life insurance policy lapses, you must prove insurability and pay any missed premiums plus interest in order to be reinstated. You will pay a higher premium for a new policy, reflecting your current age. In order to help prevent a lapse, state laws generally require that cash-value and multiyear term policies include a **grace period,** which is a period of time, usually 31 days following each premium due date, other than the first payment date, during which an overdue premium may be made without a lapse of the policy. During the grace period, all provisions of the policy remain intact, but only if payment is made before the grace period ends. For example, assume that payment was due but not paid on January 1. If the insured were to die on January 15, the policy could be reinstated as long as payment is made by January 31, given a 31-day grace period.

Nonforfeiture Values After paying premiums for a cash-value policy for a few years, you will have accumulated a **cash surrender value.** This is a savings amount within the policy that increases over the years and that the policyholder receives upon request if the policy is canceled because the insurance contract specifies certain nonforfeiture values. This amount received when a policy is canceled is the cash value minus any back-end load surrender charges. **Nonforfeiture values** are clauses in the insurance contract that protect the value, if any, either in cash or in another form of insurance, available to insureds upon failure to pay the required premium payments. Nonforfeiture values prevent you from immediately losing the accumulated cash value if your policy lapses or is cashed in.

Because of clauses in the insurance contract pertaining to nonforfeiture values, you can receive the accumulated cash-value funds in one of three ways. The first option is simply to surrender the policy and receive the funds as a cash payment. The second option is to continue the policy with the original face amount but for a time period shorter than the original policy. A third option is to continue the policy on a paid-up basis, and a new and lower face amount for the policy will be established based on the amount that can be purchased with the accumulated funds. Table 14.6 illustrates the year-to-year changes in the cash surrender value of the nonforfeiture options for a paid at 65 cash-value policy. Observe that unless you have had a cash-value policy for a number of years it has very little cash surrender value.

Inexpensive Policy Loans You may borrow against the accumulated cash value of your policy. The maximum amount you may borrow is the total cash value accumulated. Interest rates charged for the loan will range

TABLE 14.6
Table of Nonforfeiture Values* (3.5 Percent Guaranteed Rate)
(Policyholder Can Elect Choice A, B, or C)

Policy Year	A Cash or Loan Value†	B Period of $10,000 Term Insurance Years	Days	C Face Value of Term Insurance Paid Up for Life†
1	$ 0	0	0	$ 0
2	0	0	0	0
3	60	2	81	240
4	190	7	35	720
5	310	10	282	1,140
10	1,000	19	351	3,160
15	1,790	22	346	4,900
20	2,690	23	122	6,410
30	4,350	21	228	8,260
35	5,390	20	286	9,140
40	6,520	For life		10,000
45	7,110			10,000

* For a $10,000 paid at 65 limited-payment cash-value life insurance policy for a male aged 25. The annual premium is $180.
† Policy has a back-end load that reduces buildup of cash value in early years.

from 2 to 8 percent depending on the terms of the policy. Because interest rates in general have been high in recent years, policies issued since about 1980 have higher policy loan interest rates. In addition to paying interest on borrowed funds, you will lose the return that would have been earned had the funds remained in the policy.

The charging of interest on cash-value policy loans is controversial. Many people argue that the cash value in a policy really belongs to policyholders, who have merely deposited the funds with the insurance company, and that policyholders should not be required to pay interest on their own money. Insurers, unlike most lenders, do not require proof of creditworthiness prior to granting a policy loan and will not require any repayment schedule other than annual payment of the interest charges. The principal may remain outstanding indefinitely. However, any policy loan outstanding when the insured dies will reduce the death benefit. The deduction is actually from the face amount to arrive at the death benefit.

Optional Living Benefits

The living benefits discussed thus far are generally available on most policies. They are automatically included in the agreement and require no increased premiums. However, there are several other living benefits that you can obtain for slightly higher premiums. These optional benefits are multiple indemnity, waiver-of-premium, automatic premium loan, and guaranteed insurability.

Multiple Indemnity   A **multiple indemnity clause** provides for a doubling or tripling of the face amount if death results from certain specified causes. This type of clause is most often used to double the face amount if death is the result of an accident. A multiple indemnity clause is often included automatically as part of the policy at no extra cost; sometimes there is a charge for it. If you are adequately insured, a multiple indemnity clause will add little to your insurance protection and is probably not worth any extra premium. If you are not adequately insured, the money used to obtain a multiple indemnity clause would best be spent on raising the face amount of the policy.

Waiver-of-Premium   A **waiver-of-premium** is a provision that sets certain conditions under which an insurance policy would be kept in full force by the company without the payment of premiums. It usually will apply when a policyholder is totally and permanently disabled, but it may apply under other conditions depending on the policy provisions. In effect, the waiver-of-premium option is insurance against the risk of becoming disabled and unable to pay premiums.

Automatic Premium Loan   An **automatic premium loan** provision allows any premium not paid by the end of the grace period to be paid automatically with a policy loan if sufficient cash value or dividends have accumulated. In the first few years of a policy, this provision may not be of much benefit because cash value and dividends accumulate slowly. Eventually these funds may become sufficient to pay premiums for a considerable length of time and may effectively prevent the lapse of the policy.

Guaranteed Insurability   The **guaranteed insurability option** permits the cash-value policyholder to buy additional stated amounts of life insurance at stated times in the future without evidence of insurability. This option differs from the guaranteed renewability option for term insurance in that guaranteed insurability enables you to increase the face amount of the policy or to buy an additional policy.

There are usually limits to the number of times you may exercise the guaranteed insurability option. For example, consider the purchase of a $20,000 cash-value policy by a 22-year-old woman. Perhaps for $30 a year extra, the policy could include a guaranteed insurability option. The option would allow the purchase, for an additional premium, of an extra $20,000 in coverage on up to five subsequent occasions. The policy might allow the exercise of these options when the insured turns 25, 30, 35, or 40, or when she gets married or has children.

Settlement Options

Settlement options are the choices the life insurance beneficiary and/or the insured have concerning the form of payment of the death benefit of a life insurance policy. The option may be chosen by the insured before death or by the beneficiary after the insured's death. Upon receipt of the death certificate, the insurance company will pay the funds, usually within 2 weeks.[1] The five settlement options are to receive *lump sum, interest income, income for a specific period, income for life,* and *income of a specific amount.* Under the last four settlement options, the death benefit is left on deposit with the company to earn interest. The funds (death benefit and/or interest) are then paid to the beneficiary over time according to the settlement option chosen. If the beneficiary dies before the proceeds are fully exhausted, the remaining funds will be paid in a lump sum to the estate of the beneficiary. The rate of return is determined by the company at the time of death of the insured, although the policy will stipulate some minimum rate (for example, 4 percent).

Lump Sum   One option is simply to receive the death benefit in a lump sum cash settlement immediately after death.

Interest Income   Under this settlement option, the beneficiary will receive the annual interest earned from the death benefit. For example, the beneficiary would receive $7000 each year from a $100,000 death benefit earning 7 percent interest. Payments may be made monthly, quarterly, semiannually, or annually at the beneficiary's option. The $100,000 principal would remain intact to earn interest until the death of the beneficiary and then become part of his or her estate.

Income for a Specific Period   Under this option, the beneficiary will receive an income from the death benefit for a specific number of years. For example, a widow with small children may choose to receive an income for 18 years. The insurance company would calculate a level of income that would allow for equal proceeds each year, with all funds, including interest, being exhausted at the end of the eighteenth year.

Income for Life   Under this option, the beneficiary will receive an income for life. The insurance company would use the life expectancy of the beneficiary to calculate the level of income that would allow for equal annual payments so that funds would be exhausted by the expected date of the beneficiary's death. If the beneficiary lives longer than expected, the income payments will continue. This option is similar to the purchase of an annuity.

Income of a Specific Amount   Under this option, the beneficiary will receive a specific amount of income per year from the death benefit. Payments will cease when the death benefit and interest are exhausted.

---

[1] A growing number of life insurance companies now will make a policy's death benefit available to a living policyholder to cover medical expenses for terminal illnesses or long-term nursing home care. Of course, any sum received reduces the amount that may eventually go to a beneficiary. This approach is not a substitute for health insurance.

For example, a $100,000 death benefit earning 5 percent interest would provide a $15,000 annual income for approximately 8 years. (To find this, divide the death benefit by the desired annual income. Then find the factor in the 5 percent interest rate column in Appendix A4 that comes closest to the figure obtained. The year corresponding to that factor is the approximate number of years the death benefits will last.)

How Should You Go about Buying Life Insurance?

In a recent year, more than 18 million new individual life insurance policies were purchased. Did each individual really need to be covered by life insurance? Was the price paid too high? Was the policy purchased the right one, and was it purchased from a reputable company and agent? This section will help you, as an insurance purchaser, answer these questions.

Should Your Life Be Insured at All?

Anyone whose death will result in financial losses to others should be covered by life insurance unless there are sufficient resources to cover the losses. As a practical matter, obtaining insurance also depends on the financial resources available to pay the insurance premiums. Most American families do not own enough life insurance. On a more positive note, more than 90 percent of the male heads of households with children are covered by at least some life insurance. However, almost one-third of all female heads of households are not insured at all.

The bulk of any family's life insurance expenditures and protection should be concentrated on the primary income earner(s). If other workers are currently providing income that the family depends on, they too should be covered in order to protect that income. The remainder should be concentrated on persons who would become income earners should the other income earners die. People who do not need life insurance include (1) children, (2) singles with no dependents, and (3) people with no dependents, a sufficient income, and no desire to leave an estate.

Many families purchase life insurance for members who are not income earners. Most often these individuals are children. If income earners are sufficiently protected, buying a small amount of life insurance for the children is perhaps understandable. However, when the income earners are not sufficiently insured, the family would be much better off buying more term insurance for the income earners. Others who are sometimes unnecessarily insured are the elderly. Since life insurance premiums for those over the age of 60 are extremely high, such people would be better off by saving or by keeping only a small policy for funeral expenses.

College students nearing graduation and young, single, working persons are often approached by life insurance agents. The sales pitch is that it is

What If a College Student Is Approached by a Life Insurance Salesperson?

Students are often approached by life insurance agents. Here are some tips from consumer-minded insurance experts:

1. If you have no dependents, you probably don't need life insurance. Life insurance is essentially protection against loss of income for dependents.
2. There is no mathematical advantage to buying life insurance at an early age. Premiums increase at the same rate for everybody regardless of the age at which you start the policy.
3. If you need protection for your dependents, term insurance can do the job at the lowest cost.
4. Be wary of offers of "free" insurance or cash-value policies for only a few dollars the first year. Agents who make such claims are probably hiding vital details. A small initial premium may be only a down payment on a sizable loan for the rest of the first year's cost. This is called **deferred-premium life insurance,** where a modest amount of insurance is purchased with an interest-bearing loan that is repaid through a series of postponed payments. There are disadvantages to financing the first year's premium. Signing a promissory note binds you to a long-term debt and substantially raises the price of insurance because of the interest charges. If you cannot afford to pay the full first year's premium, you probably should not sign up.
5. If you fail to pay *any* premium (which legally is a note repayment) on time during the years when a promissory note is in force, the entire note becomes due immediately.
6. Before you buy life insurance, get the advice and approval of people you trust—such as your parents—and at least one insurance expert or knowledgeable professor other than the agent selling the policy.
7. Read everything carefully. If an agent does not allow you time to read, don't sign anything. Don't be afraid to ask questions or take a few days to think it over.
8. Bring a friend with you when you meet with an agent. Take notes on the sales presentation. An agent will be less likely to misrepresent the policy if he or she realizes you are paying close attention.
9. Don't be pressured into buying anything you do not want. If you think an agent is misleading or dishonest, report him or her to state insurance officials and to officials at your school.
10. If you buy a policy and then run into a problem that cannot be solved by the insurance company, call your state insurance department. Many companies will make adjustments in hardship cases referred to them by state insurance officials.

best to buy life insurance while you are young and healthy and while premiums are still low. The fact that life insurance needs are low or nonexistent at this time is not mentioned by many agents. Furthermore, young adults have a seven times greater chance of becoming disabled than of dying. If they buy insurance to protect their income, it probably should be disability income protection.

TABLE 14.7
Typical Premiums* for Various Types of Life Insurance (Face Amount $100,000)

Policy Type	Policy Year							
	1	2	3	5	10	11	20	Age 65
Annual renewable term (guaranteed renewability to age 70)	$ 100	$ 100	$ 100	$ 100	$ 140	$ 140	$ 190	$2700
Decreasing term (over 20 years)	170	170	170	170	170	170	170	0
Convertible term (within 5 years)	185	185	185	185	940	940	940	940
Whole life	870	870	870	870	870	870	870	870
Universal life	590	590	590	590	680	730	760	790
Limited-pay life (paid at age 65)	920	920	920	920	920	920	920	0
Endowment (at age 65)	1070	1070	1070	1070	1070	1070	1070	0

* Premiums quoted are for a 21-year-old male nonsmoker. Smokers pay 30 to 100 percent extra because they typically live 7 years less than nonsmokers, according to data from the State Mutual Life Assurance Company of America.

How Do You Make Cost Comparisons in Life Insurance?

The price people pay for life insurance depends on their age, their health, and their lifestyle. Age is important, of course, because the probability of dying increases with age. Health also affects mortality, and a person who has a health problem such as heart disease or diabetes may pay considerably higher life insurance rates or may not be able to obtain coverage at any price. People with extremely hazardous lifestyles or occupations (stunt pilots, grand prix racers) or who engage in hazardous hobbies (sky diving, hang gliding) historically have been required to pay higher life insurance premiums. Life insurance companies typically offer lower prices to applicants whose lifestyles suggest longevity, such as nonsmokers.

Premium per $1000 of Coverage Comparing life insurance prices is a difficult task because policies and plans vary from company to company. Life insurance premiums are usually quoted in dollars per $1000 of coverage. Generally, the higher the face amount of the policy, the lower will be the rate per $1000. For example, a company might sell term life insurance for $1 per $1000 per year when purchased in face amounts of $100,000 or more. You can see the problems involved in comparing this policy with, say, a cash-value policy with a different face value. Simply comparing the premium per $1000 of coverage will not tell you which policy is the better bargain. Table 14.7 lists annual premiums that are near the average required for various types of insurance policies.

There are several sources of information about the prices for life insurance policies. Popular magazines such as *Changing Times, Consumer Reports,*

TABLE 14.8
What Is a Fair Price for Term Life Insurance?

Age	Nonsmokers		Smokers	
	Male	*Female*	*Male*	*Female*
18 to 30	$0.76	$0.68	$1.05	$1.01
35	0.80	0.74	1.36	1.26
40	1.03	0.95	2.06	1.65
45	1.45	1.20	2.95	2.30
50	2.60	1.76	4.16	3.30

Source: National Insurance Consumer Organization, *Taking the Bite Out of Insurance, A Comprehensive Guide to Life Insurance,* available for $11.96, which is periodically updated, including tables. Reprinted by permission of the National Insurance Consumer Organization, 121 N. Payne St., Alexandria, VA 22314.

Note: The National Insurance Consumer Organization says to multiply the rate by each $1000 of coverage desired and then add $60 to cover estimated administrative fees.

and *Money* regularly feature articles that give average or typical premiums for different types of policies. In addition to providing excellent explanations of life insurance, articles in these magazines compare the actual premiums for policies offered by hundreds of insurance companies. Another source of information is your state department of insurance. Many such departments publish life insurance buyers' guides that provide price guidelines useful for evaluating quotes from agents.

It is easy to pay too much for term life insurance, especially if you do not comparison shop. The National Insurance Consumer Organization (NICO) suggests that the best way to judge a *term* life insurance policy is by the cost per $1000 of coverage. NICO says that the rates shown in Table 14.8 represent good values.

The Net Cost Method The most obvious source of information about the cost of life insurance is the agent selling the policy. An **agent** is an authorized representative of an insurance company who sells, modifies, terminates, and services insurance contracts. Agents will discuss the price of a life insurance policy in terms of the premium per $1000 of coverage and the annual premium. Regarding cash-value life insurance, many agents also will mention the net cost of the policy under consideration. The **net cost** of a life insurance policy is the total of all premiums to be paid minus any accumulated cash value and accrued dividends. The net cost is calculated for a specific point in time during the life of the policy, say, at the end of the tenth or twentieth year. The formula for calculating the net cost is

$$\text{Net cost} = \text{premiums paid} - \text{dividends accrued} - \text{cash value} \qquad (14.2)$$

Consider the following example of determining the net cost of a cash-value life insurance policy. Sarah Nelson of Dubuque, Iowa, is considering the purchase of a $100,000 participating cash-value life insurance policy.

Her annual premium will be $1444. Total dividends accumulated for the first 20 years will be $10,500. The policy also will have a cash value of $26,348 at the end of 20 years. The net cost of the policy after 20 years will be

$$\text{Net cost} = (\$1444 \times 20) - \$10,500 - \$26,348$$
$$= -\$7968$$

Because this net cost is a negative figure, it appears that the policy will pay for itself within 20 years. Many life insurance agents have been known to make this false claim for cash-value policies by using the net cost method.

The net cost method fails to consider the opportunity cost of the forgone interest Sarah could earn by investing the premiums rather than buying life insurance. This failure to consider the opportunity cost of the forgone interest is the basic flaw of the net cost method. You should ignore net cost calculations provided by a life insurance agent.

The Interest-Adjusted Cost Index Method A **cost index** is a numerical method to compare the costs of similar plans of life insurance where a smaller index number is generally a better buy than a comparable policy with a larger number. The **interest-adjusted cost index (IACI)** is a measure of the cost of life insurance that takes into account the interest that would have been earned had the premiums been invested rather than used to buy insurance. The lower the IACI, the lower is the cost of the policy. The interest rate usually used to calculate the IACI is 5 percent. This figure was chosen because a reasonably sophisticated investor would generally be able to invest funds to earn 5 percent after taxes. Like net cost, the IACI is calculated for a specific point in time, usually the twentieth year, during the life of the policy.

To illustrate the IACI, consider again Sarah Nelson's purchase of a $100,000 cash-value policy for $1444 per year. At 5 percent interest, she could invest $1444 per year for 20 years and accumulate $47,747. Total dividends of $10,500 also would be adjusted for 5 percent interest, to $14,719. Subtracting the interest-adjusted dividends of $14,719 and the cash value of $26,348 from $47,747 yields $6680. This figure represents the interest-adjusted cost of buying the policy. Because this cost is spread over 20 years, it must be divided by a constant, 34.719, to obtain the interest-adjusted cost index. The same constant would be used whenever calculating a 20-year IACI. The IACI for Sarah's policy is $192.40 or $1.92 per $1000 of coverage.

Sarah may use this figure to compare similar policies from other agents and companies. Interest-adjusted cost indexes vary considerably among policies and companies. IACIs as low as −3.00 are available. Yet some high-cost policies will have an IACI as high as +5.00. Certainly policies with a positive IACI should be avoided. Sarah need not make the IACI calculations herself. She needs only to ask the agent to provide the 20-year interest-adjusted cost index. She should receive a quick, accurate response.

Ask an insurance agent to provide the interest-adjusted cost index for the policy you are considering. Reputable agents should have this information at hand and are required in 38 states to disclose it if asked. However, in most of these states the disclosure need only be made after the sale is closed, and then the buyer has 10 days to cancel if he or she feels that the index is too high. You should insist on being told the index before you agree to buy a policy, and you should shop elsewhere if the agent refuses, resists, or tries to imply that the index will be of no help.

The Interest-Adjusted Net Payment Index Method   The IACI assumes that the policy will be cashed in and surrendered at the end of a certain period (usually 20 years) rather than remain in force until the death of the insured. If, however, the policy is to remain in force until death, the IACI will not be an accurate measure of the cost of the policy. To overcome this deficiency, you can use the **interest-adjusted net payment index (IANPI)** to measure the cost of cash-value insurance held until death. This method does not subtract the accumulated cash value, as the IACI does, because policies held for life do not pay cash value. Instead, the face amount is paid at death. Using the previous example as an illustration, the IANPI after 20 years for Sarah Nelson's $100,000 policy would be $9.51 per $1000 of coverage. This is obtained by subtracting the interest-adjusted dividends ($14,719) from the interest-adjusted premiums paid ($47,747) and dividing by the same constant (34.719) and then 100 (to obtain the IANPI per $1000 of coverage). Notice that the IANPI is about five times greater than the IACI. This higher figure reflects the fact that no cash value is paid if the policy is held until death.

Which Is the Preferred Method of Cost Comparison?   We have examined four measures of the cost of life insurance policies: (1) premium per $1000 of coverage, (2) net cost, (3) interest-adjusted cost index, and (4) interest-adjusted net payment index. Although none of these measures provides a means for comparing among all the different types of policies, the interest-adjusted cost index has been adopted by the National Association of Insurance Commissioners as the recommended measure to be used in the industry. However, some insurance companies have been accused of manipulating the timing of dividend payments and cash-value accumulation in order to make their policies appear less expensive at the 20-year point than they really are. Further, the IACI does not provide an accurate means of comparing among greatly different types of policies. It is totally inappropriate, for example, when comparing term insurance and cash-value insurance. It is best to decide beforehand which type of policy you need and then to use the IACI to compare policies of that type.

Linton Yields   Many people who buy cash-value life insurance want to know the rate of return they will earn on the cash value accumulated under the policy. With such knowledge, they can compare different policies and compare buying cash-value insurance with buying a term policy and investing the difference saved in some other investment vehicle. The most frequently used measure of the annual compound after-tax rate of return on cash-value insurance is the **Linton yield.** The mathematical formula for calculating Linton yields is complicated. The annual premium for an equivalent amount of low-priced term insurance is subtracted from the cash-value policy annual premium. The result is the "extra" premium that goes into the building of cash values. This figure is then compared to the cash value (plus dividends for participating policies) that would be accumulated after a given number of years (5, 10, 20, and so forth) to determine an annual rate of interest at the end of the given time period.

Agents are often unprepared to answer questions about rates of return and Linton yields, but it would not hurt to ask, being aware that the response may not be accurate. An even better idea would be to consult *Consumer Reports'* 1986 series of articles on life insurance. The Linton yields after 5, 10, and 20 years are given for the policies the magazine staff examined. Five-year Linton yields ranged from −100.0 percent to more than 7 percent, with most being negative. The reason for such low rates of return is the slow or nonexistent cash-value accumulation in the early years of most policies. Twenty-year Linton yields ranged from less than 5 percent to more than 12 percent. It should be obvious that when rates of return vary so widely, it pays to shop for policies that pay the better rates of return.

How to Choose the Best Type of Life Insurance Policy for You

A fundamental decision to make when buying life insurance is whether to buy term insurance or cash-value insurance. Cash-value policies are often recommended because the premiums usually stay the same and because they provide protection for life and have a savings element. They also can be a method of forced savings for people who lack the discipline to save for retirement. Life insurance companies and agents generally recommend cash-value life insurance. This is not too surprising, since cash-value policies are much more profitable for them than are term policies.

Historically, more people bought cash-value insurance than term insurance. Since the mid-1970s, however, term insurance has become more popular. Now the volume of term insurance sold each year is greater than that of cash-value insurance. This trend toward the purchase of term insurance seems to be slipping somewhat with the growth of universal life insurance. Such shifts in consumer choices have resulted partly because of changing inflation and interest rates. When inflation rates are high, life insurance needs increase rapidly, and buying term insurance is the least expensive way to increase life insurance protection. When interest rates are high, cash-value policies lose their attractiveness because many pay relatively low interest rates on their cash values. When inflation and interest rates moderate, cash-value insurance becomes more competitive.

People have become increasingly sophisticated life insurance purchasers and many people have come to agree with the adage "Buy term and invest the money saved." This means that you are better off buying term insurance to meet your life insurance needs and investing elsewhere the extra funds you would have spent on cash-value insurance. Most cash-value policies pay guaranteed interest rates below 6 percent. Careful investors can earn after-tax rates of return that exceed this percentage (see Chapters 8 and 17). Of course, the decision to buy term and invest the money saved

Advice for the Conservative Life Insurance Purchaser

A recommended life insurance and investment plan for the income-producing years in an individual's life cycle is diagramed in the following figure. The plan is built on two cornerstones. The first is the purchase of term insurance for the bulk of life insurance needs, since term insurance is more flexible than cash-value insurance and provides more protection for each premium dollar. The second is a systematic, regular investment program. Because the rates of return on cash-value policies are often low, it is wise to make other investments.

At the age of 20, as diagramed, the average person needs little or no life insurance. If desired, a small term or cash-value policy with guaranteed insurability is sufficient. Over time, however, an individual's responsibilities for the financial well-being of others may increase. These responsibilities will in turn increase the need for protection from the risk of premature death. Since the early years of an investment program will not yield enough protection, life insurance likely should be purchased. The amount purchased will depend on the individual's needs, and the amounts in the figure are only examples. At about the age of 45, the probable losses from a premature death will begin to diminish because the investment program

started at the age of 20 will have grown sufficiently to provide some of the resources to offer protection from a premature death. Thus, there will be a leveling off or decrease in the need for life insurance around the same time that term insurance premiums become somewhat expensive. By the age of 65, life insurance needs will be greatly reduced or eliminated and the investment program will have grown sufficiently to provide retirement income. (Investments are examined in detail in Chapters 15 to 21.)

Life insurance companies have begun to realize that a program such as the one described above is in the best interest of policyholders. In response, many companies now offer interest-sensitive life insurance (discussed earlier), which offers the flexibility of term insurance, the permanence of cash-value insurance, and the high rates of return available in the financial markets. Universal and variable life insurance policies are no panacea, however. You should still compare the term insurance component of interest-sensitive life insurance with term policies that can be purchased separately and evaluate the investment component against other alternative investments. Investments are covered in the next section of this book.   *(continued)*

requires some planning and action on your part. If you do not invest the funds systematically, you will lose the benefits of a higher rate of return and compounding. To make it easier, some investment plans will automatically deduct funds from your paycheck or checking account, and others will bill you monthly or annually (see Chapter 19).

Although term insurance provides more coverage for the same premium than does cash-value insurance, term policies do have some negative features. You can avoid these by purchasing guaranteed renewable and convertible term insurance. The guaranteed renewability option allows continuation of the same amount of term insurance without requiring you to prove insurability. The convertibility option allows you to convert to cash-value insurance if you wish. Make sure that convertibility is an option and not required at some future date. Neither of these options will prevent

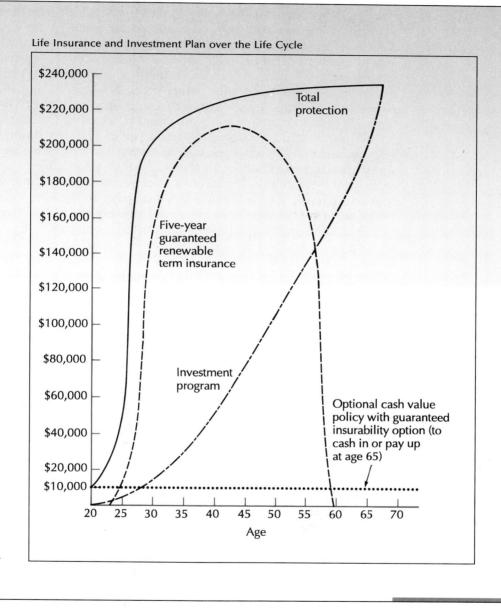

Life Insurance and Investment Plan over the Life Cycle

Total protection

Five-year guaranteed renewable term insurance

Investment program

Optional cash value policy with guaranteed insurability option (to cash in or pay up at age 65)

Age

the cost of term insurance from increasing at renewal, however. You can avoid a cost increase by purchasing decreasing term insurance or a 20- or 30-year term policy. Further, a person age 25 who buys a term policy would see the price of the term policy stay below that of a cash-value policy until he reached his late fifties.

How to Choose a Company and an Agent

The most important feature of a life insurance company is its ability to pay its obligations. The company must have the stability and financial strength to survive for the many years your policy will be in force. A. M. Best Company publishes *Best's Key Rating Guide,* which rates the financial strength of life insurance companies on a scale from A+ to C. A rating of A+ or A indicates that the financial strength of the company has been judged excellent. There is really no need to consider any company with less than an A+ rating, since this rating has been given to over 200 of the nation's 2000 companies. More than 200 other companies have received an A rating. It is important to your financial security to select a financially sound company and, when needed, a qualified, reputable agent.

Life insurance in the United States is commonly sold through agents who represent one company exclusively, although some agents are *brokers* who represent more than one company. For their efforts, agents commonly receive compensation in the form of sales commissions. Commissions, of course, are passed on by the insurance company to the salesperson.

Life insurance is also sometimes sold directly through the mail. The National Insurance Consumer Organization recommends the following no-load direct-mail life insurance companies: USAA Life (800-531-8000), Bankers National Life (800-631-0099, 201-267-2540 in New Jersey), and Amica Life (800-992-6422). **No-load insurance** does not involve payment of a commission by the insurer to the insurance agent. A recent trend in the insurance industry is to hide the sales commission in a bevy of annual fees and surrender charges that are difficult for buyers to figure out. No-load insurers market their products directly to consumers or through financial planners and fee-for-service insurance agents.

You may save a substantial amount on life insurance premiums by using a **premium-quote service.** Such services are offered by profit-oriented firms that make computer-aided comparisons among 20 to 80 companies and help you select the least expensive life insurance policies and companies. Insurance Information Corporation (800-472-5800) will refund its $50 fee if you do not save that much in premium charges the first year. Four other premium-quote services that do not charge a fee but which receive a commission if you buy from a recommended company are Insurance Quote (800-972-1104), LifeQuote (800-521-7873, 800-843-1768 in Florida), SelectQuote (800-343-1985), and TermQuote (800-444-8376).

Choosing an agent is somewhat more difficult than evaluating individual insurance companies. Your relationship with your life insurance agent is both professional and personal. The agent must be qualified to design a program tailored to your specific needs and must understand the dynamics of family relationships, which are the source of life insurance needs. The agent should have earned a professional designation, such as *chartered life underwriter (CLU).* To earn the CLU, an agent must have 3 years of experience and pass a rigorous 10-course program in life insurance counseling. Some agents also may have earned the *certified financial planner (CFP)* or *chartered financial consultant (ChFC)* designation. If possible, choose an agent with these qualifications. Also be sure the agent

▌ Average First-Year Life Insurance Sales Commissions

First-year commissions for people selling life insurance vary from 30 to 100 percent of the first-year premium, and here are some estimates for various types of policies: 35 percent on term insurance; 45 percent on modified life, adjustable life, and interest-sensitive policies; and 55 percent on limited pay and endowment life insurance policies. Commissions are paid every year the policy is in force, but commissions in succeeding years drop steadily. For example, the second-year commission usually drops to about 15 percent, the third year to 10 percent, the fourth year to 7 percent, the fifth year to 5 percent, and the remaining years to 3 percent.

is willing to take the time to provide personal service and answer all questions about the policy both before and after you purchase it. An agent who is a personal friend or relative is not necessarily the best choice.

Summary

1. Life insurance is designed to provide protection from the financial losses that result from a premature death.

2. The whys behind life insurance vary over the life cycle. During childhood and singlehood, the need for life insurance is nonexistent or very small.

3. Life insurance needs are calculated by subtracting the financial resources that will be available at death from the financial losses likely to result from the death. The losses likely to occur include lost income, final expenses, readjustment-period expenses, and debt-repayment needs. The resources available to cover these losses include savings, other insurance, skills and education, and asset equity.

4. There are basically only two types of life insurance, term life insurance and cash-value life insurance. Variations of term life insurance include decreasing term insurance, convertible term insurance, and credit life insurance. Variations of cash-value insurance include whole life insurance, limited-pay life insurance, endowment life insurance, and interest-sensitive life insurance.

5. A life insurance policy is a written contract between the insurance purchaser and the insurance company spelling out in detail the terms of the agreement. When buying life insurance, it is important to pay attention to the policy's general terms and conditions, living benefits, optional living benefits, and settlement options.

6. You should purchase life insurance only after you determine the actual dollar amount and type of policy you need and analyze comparative premiums. Term life insurance provides the most insurance protection for each premium dollar. The interest-adjusted cost index can provide a means of comparing similar policies, but its use is limited when comparing dissimilar policies.

Modern
Money
Management

The Johnsons Change Their Life Insurance Coverage

Harry and Belinda Johnson spend $9 per month on life insurance. This represents the premium on a $10,000 paid at 65 cash-value policy on Harry. Belinda receives a group term insurance policy from her employer with a face amount of $37,800 (1.5 × her annual salary). By choosing a group life insurance plan from his "menu" of fringe benefits, Harry now has $18,300 (his annual salary) worth of group term life insurance. Harry and Belinda have decided that since they have no children, they could reduce their life insurance needs by protecting each other's income for only 4 years, assuming the survivor would be able to fend for himself or herself after that time. They also realize that their savings fund is so low that it would have no bearing on their life insurance needs.

Harry and Belinda are basing their calculations on a projected 4 percent earnings after taxes and inflation. They also estimate the following expenses: $8000 for final expenses, $4000 readjustment expenses, and $5000 for repayment of short-term debts.

1. Should the $3000 interest earnings from Harry's trust fund be included in his annual income for the purposes of calculating the likely dollar loss if he were to die? (See the discussions about the Johnsons at the end of Chapter 3.) Explain your response.

2. Based on your response to question 1, how much more life insurance does Harry need? Use Equation (14.1) or the Personal Finance Cookbook (PFC) program INSURANC to arrive at your answer.

3. Repeat the calculations to arrive at the additional life insurance needed on Belinda's life.

4. How might the Johnsons most economically meet any additional life insurance needs you have determined they may have?

5. In addition to their life insurance planning, what might the Johnsons begin to do now to prepare for their retirement years? See the figure in the box entitled, Advice for the Conservative Life Insurance Purchaser, on page 520.

Key Words and Concepts

actuaries, 486
adjustable life insurance, 501
agent, 516
annual renewable term (ART), 496
annuity, 507
automatic premium loan, 511
back-end load, 505
beneficiary, 494
cash surrender value, 509
cash value, 498
cash-value life insurance, 498
contingent beneficiary, 495
convertible term insurance, 497
cost index, 517
credit term life insurance, 497
current rate, 504
death benefit, 506
death rate, 486
decreasing term insurance, 496
deferred-premium life insurance, 514
dividends, 508
endowment date, 500
endowment life insurance, 500
equity, 493
face amount, 495
final expenses, 489
front-end load, 505
grace period, 509
guaranteed insurability option, 511
guaranteed minimum rate, 504
guaranteed renewability option, 495
incontestability clause, 508
insured, 485
interest-adjusted cost index (IACI), 517

interest-adjusted net payment index (IANPI), 518
lapsed policy, 509
life insurance, 485
limited-pay life insurance, 500
Linton yield, 518
modified life insurance, 500
mortality table, 486
multiple-earnings approach, 490
multiple indemnity clause, 511
needs approach, 490
net cost, 516
no-load insurance, 522
nonforfeiture values, 509
nonparticipating policies, 508
owner, 494
paid up, 500
participating policies, 508
permanent life insurance, 498
policy, 485
policyholder, 494
premium, 494
premium-quote service, 522
settlement options, 511
Social Security blackout period, 490
Social Security survivors' benefits, 490
suicide clause, 508
term life insurance, 495
universal life insurance, 501
value-of-life approach, 490
variable life insurance, 505
variable-universal life insurance, 506
waiver-of-premium, 511
whole life insurance, 498

Review Questions

1. Briefly explain why the term *life insurance* may be considered a misnomer.

2. Identify the role actuaries play in the life insurance business.

3. What purpose does a mortality table serve in the life insurance industry?

4. What is considered to be the major financial loss suffered upon the death of a family's breadwinner?

5. Name three other types of losses resulting from the premature death of a family's primary wage earner.

6. What is the multiple-earnings approach toward estimating lost income for a family or individual?

7. What is the basic difference between the multiple-earnings approach and the needs approach in estimating income losses?

8. Identify four resources that may be available to cover the losses resulting from a premature death.

9. What is the calculation used to determine the amount of life insurance needed?

10. What is the basic difference between term life insurance and cash-value life insurance?

11. Why might you want to buy a decreasing term policy?

12. Why might you want to have a convertibility option on a term life policy?

13. What is the major reason for not buying credit life insurance?

14. Give two reasons why you might want to buy group life insurance.

15. Explain why endowment policies are the most expensive form of life insurance to buy.

16. What three things do universal life insurance purchasers know about their policies that purchasers of more traditional cash-value policies do not know?

17. How does variable-universal life insurance differ from variable life insurance?

18. Why is an annuity considered the opposite of a life insurance contract?

19. What are the general terms and provisions contained in a life insurance policy?

20. What benefit can you gain through a life insurance policy prior to your death?

21. What benefit does a grace period offer to life insurance policyholders?

22. Of what value is a guaranteed insurability option to life insurance policyholders?

23. What is meant by the term *settlement options*, and what options are available to life insurance beneficiaries?

24. Name several factors that influence the cost of life insurance.

25. Give the names of three publications that can provide information on the cost of life insurance.

26. What is the interest-adjusted cost index?

27. What is a Linton yield as it relates to cash-value life insurance?

28. What might you gain by "buying term and investing the money saved"?

29. What is the most important factor to consider when choosing a life insurance company?

Case Problems

1. Tracy and Clark Cristner of Savannah, Georgia, are a young married couple in their early thirties. They have two children, aged 5 and 3, and Tracy is pregnant with their third child. Tracy is an interior design consultant for medical and dental offices and last year earned $15,000. Because she does much of her work at home, it is unlikely she will need to curtail her work after the baby is born. Clark is a family therapist with a thriving practice; he earned $42,000 last year. Because both are self-employed, Tracy and Clark do not have access to group life insurance. They are covered by a $50,000 universal life policy they purchased 3 years ago. Clark is also covered by a $50,000 five-year renewable term policy, which will expire next year. They feel that now is a good time to reassess their life insurance program. As a preliminary step in this reassessment, they have determined that Tracy's account with Social Security would yield the family $802 per month, or an annual benefit of $9624 if she were to die. For Clark the figure would be $1799 per month, or an annual benefit of $21,588. (See Appendix B for the determination of these benefits.)

   Both agree that they would like to support each of their children to age 22, hoping that the children would be able to obtain the necessary extra college expense funds. They expect it would take about $6000 each for burial, and they would like to have a lump sum of life insurance clearly marked for paying off their $70,000 home mortgage. They also feel that each would want to take a 6-month leave from work if the other were to die.

   a. Calculate the amount of life insurance that Tracy needs using the information above. Use Equation (14.1) or the Personal Finance Cookbook (PFC) program INSURANC. Assume a 3 percent present value interest factor and an income need for 22 years since the unborn child will need financial support for that many years.

   b. Calculate the amount of life insurance that Clark needs using the information above. Use Equation (14.1) or the Personal Finance Cookbook (PFC) program INSURANC. Assume a 3 percent rate of return after taxes and inflation and an income need for 22 years since the unborn child will need financial support for that many years.

   c. If Tracy and Clark purchased term insurance to cover their additional needs, how much more would they each need to spend?

   d. How might the Cristners lower their need for more life insurance without greatly affecting their financial protection?

2. Just-married couples sometimes overindulge in the type and amount of life insurance they buy. Arnold and Jayne Tucker of Barberville, Kentucky, however, took a different approach. Both were working and had a small amount of life insurance provided through their respective employers—Arnold, $35,000, and Jayne, $15,000. During their discussion of life insurance needs and related costs, they decided that if Jayne completed her master's degree in industrial psychology, she would have

better employment opportunities. Consequently, they decided to take money they had available for more life insurance to help pay the costs for Jayne's education. They both feel, however, that they do not want to become "life insurance poor."

a. In what way does Jayne's returning to school alter the Tuckers' life insurance concerns?

b. Would you agree that the amount of life insurance provided by the Tuckers' respective employers is adequate while Jayne is in school? Explain your response.

c. How might the Tuckers' life insurance needs change over the life cycle?

3. Jim Howe is a college friend of yours from Santa Ana, California. Jim is about to graduate from college and was approached recently by a life insurance agent who set up a group meeting for about a dozen members of Jim's fraternity. During the meeting, the agent presented about six life insurance plans and was very persuasive about the benefits of a plan his company calls Affordable Life II. It allows the students to buy $100,000 of permanent life insurance for a very low premium during the first 5 years and then a higher premium later when their income presumably will be higher. Jim felt pretty confused after the meeting, as did his friends. Knowing that you were taking a personal finance course, they asked you to meet with them and answer some of their questions.

a. Do you think this Affordable Life II is a good deal for these young men? Why or why not?

b. How can they decide how much life insurance they need?

c. Is life insurance really as confusing as the agent made it seem? If not, what more simple explanation would you give?

d. What type of life insurance program would you advise for the fraternity brothers?

e. How do you know if a life insurance policy is offered at a fair price?

Suggested Readings

"A Primer on New Wrinkles in an Old Standby—Life Insurance." *Fortune*, September 25, 1989, pp. 25–26. Explains new developments in life insurance policy offerings.

"A Shopper's Guide to the Best Term Policy." *Money*, August 1989, pp. 137–138. How and where to buy basic life insurance protection.

"Choosing the Right Life Insurance Agent." *Black Enterprise*, February 1990, pp. 55–56. Pointers for finding a life insurance agent to meet your specific needs.

"Collect Now, Die Later." *Esquire*, January 1989, p. 54. Describes life insurance policies with long-term health care coverage riders.

"Get Your Life Insurance Wholesale and Save Big Bucks." *Money*, December 1989, pp. 189–190. Money saving tips on how to buy life insurance directly in order to save on agents commissions.

"Good Policies Are Sized Right and Fit Needs That Change." *U.S. News & World Report,* July 17, 1989, pp. 55–56. Tips on policies that tailor your life insurance program to your needs.

"Life Insurance after 40." *Changing Times,* May 1989, pp. 65–70. How to get the best buys in life insurance.

"Life Insurance That Pays Off While You're Still Around." *Business Week,* July 31, 1989, pp. 100–101. Explains the positives and negatives of life insurance policies that pay death benefits if you become incurably ill.

"Tapping Your Insurance for Cash." *Changing Times,* October 1989, pp. 85–86. How to get a cheap loan using your life insurance policy.

"The Money on Your Life." *Newsweek,* May 8, 1989, p. 46. The perils of cashing in cash-value life insurance policies in order to buy term.

PART FIVE

Investment Planning

15 Investment Fundamentals

OBJECTIVES

After reading this chapter, you should be able to

1. Summarize reasons why people start to invest, what is required before beginning, how returns are earned on investments, and some ways to obtain funds to invest.

2. Explain how to set and achieve investment goals.

3. Determine your own investment philosophy.

4. Recognize the variety of choices among the alternative investments available.

5. Identify the major factors that affect the return on investments.

6. Know what a good return is and be able to calculate the potential total return on an investment.

7. Understand how to achieve your investment goals.

8. Summarize descriptive characteristics of several common investment alternatives.

. . . .

Making investments might seem to be an activity that is too far in the future for you to consider now. However, if you understand the importance of practicing good financial management as well as protecting income and assets, you will also recognize the related benefits of investment planning. For starters, you need to do something today with the money you will be counting on tomorrow. Investments can increase your income and help maximize your enjoyment of life, whether you most enjoy reading a good book and taking long walks or dining in fine restaurants, taking exotic vacations, and driving expensive automobiles.

To begin the general study of investments, you must understand investment fundamentals. This chapter first examines why and how people start to invest and then discusses how to set *your* investment goals. Next is a section to help you identify *your* investment philosophy. Alternative investments are then introduced. The next section describes factors that affect return on investment, especially such factors as risk and yield, diversification, leverage, taxes, and inflation. Then we explain what a good return on an investment is and show you how to calculate the potential total return of any investment. The next section offers reasons why people fail to succeed financially as well as ideas on how to succeed. The chapter concludes with a detailed summary of characteristics of many of the investment alternatives examined in later chapters.

So You Are Thinking about Investing

Objective
To be able to summarize why people start to invest, what is required before beginning, how returns are earned on investments, and some ways to obtain funds to invest.

Before starting your investment plan, you need to know why people invest, some prerequisites for investing, how various types of investments earn returns, and how to go about getting money to invest in the first place.

Why People Invest

People invest for one or more of four general reasons: (1) to achieve financial goals (such as a new car, down payment on a home, child's education, and so forth), (2) to increase income, (3) to gain wealth and a feeling of financial security, and (4) to have funds available during retirement years. People report these kinds of specific motivations for investing:

- "I like the feeling of 'money in the bank.'"
- "I have too much money just 'wasting away' in the bank."

- "I want to get rich quickly."
- "I want to get rich slowly."
- "I want to buy a Mercedes-Benz automobile."
- "I hate paying money to the Internal Revenue Service."
- "I want to retire with a secure income."
- "My parents might have to depend on me financially after their retirement."
- "I want to protect my spouse's finances in case I die first."
- "My children should not have to support me in my old age."
- "My children should not have to suffer financially when I die."
- "The return on my current investments is not keeping up with the rate of inflation."
- "My investments should provide an income equal to one-quarter of my salary income by age 50."

Prerequisites to Investing

Before you embark on an investment program, make sure you do the following:

1. *Live within your means.* If you can live within your financial means, you will have financial control over your life. If you find yourself constantly running short of cash toward the end of the month, you may need better budget controls and probably won't have any money available for investments. On the other hand, if you are not overly indebted and generally have money available for unexpected automobile repairs, small gifts, and occasional self-indulgences, you can begin thinking about an investment program.

2. *Continue a savings program.* Good financial managers save regularly to acquire goods and services and/or to build an emergency fund. Investors also save so that they can make periodic investments with accrued savings as well as have cash reserves if they need additional investment funds in a hurry.

3. *Establish lines of credit.* Having a line of credit will help you meet personal financial emergencies and reduce the need to have large amounts of readily available savings. For example, you might have a line of credit of $3000 at a local bank, $5000 at a brokerage firm, and $4000 on a bank credit card.

4. *Carry adequate insurance protection.* Liability insurance will protect your assets and lifestyle in the event you are sued, and health insurance will help defray costs if you or a member of your family falls ill. Life insurance is frequently purchased in conjunction with investments to protect the lifestyle of dependents in the event of an investor's death.

Returns on Investments

Alternative investments offer the promise of higher returns than that on savings accounts.

Two broad types of investment are available. With **savings investments,** you would expect virtually no risk for either the **principal** (amount placed in the investment) or the *interest* (amount earned on the principal). Various types of savings accounts and cash management techniques were discussed in Chapter 5, Managing Your Cash. **Alternative investments** are riskier, since monies are placed in assets that guarantee neither return of the principal nor earnings, but they have the possibility of a greater return than savings investments.

The return on investment may come from two sources: current income and capital gains. In the field of investments, **current income** is money received from an investment, usually on a regular basis, in the form of interest, dividends, rent, or other such payment. **Interest** is the payment you receive for allowing a financial institution (or an individual) to use and invest your money. Banks, credit unions, and savings and loan associations typically take funds on deposit, invest them profitably, and pay interest to depositors. **Dividends** are distributions of profits you receive for holding stock in a corporation. Generally, corporations retain some profits to use for continued growth of the company and distribute the remainder as dividends. **Rent** is the payment received in return for someone's use of your property, such as land or a building.

A **capital gain** is income that results from an increase in the value of an investment, and it is calculated by subtracting the total amount paid for the investment (including commission costs) from the higher price at which it is sold, less any sales commissions and costs. Of course, a **capital loss** results if the selling price (plus expenses) is less than the original amount invested (plus commissions). The value of a small apartment building you own could increase over a few years from $200,000 to $275,000. The value of a common stock you own could increase from $80 to $100 a share in 6 months. You will realize a capital gain on each of these investments only when you sell the assets. For most investments, there is a tradeoff between capital gains and current income: investments with high capital gains potential often pay little current income, and investments that pay substantial current income generally have little or no capital gains potential.

The total return on an investment includes income and capital gains.

The **return** or **total return** is the total income from an investment, including current income plus capital gains or minus capital losses. The **rate of return** or **yield** is the return expressed as a percentage of the cost of the investment. It is usually stated on an annualized basis. Say, for example, that Geoffrey Heagney purchases $1000 of H&M stock, including broker's commissions, and receives $50 in cash dividends during the year. If he then sells the stock for $1100, minus $60 in broker's commissions, he will have a capital gain of $40 ($1100 − $1000 − $60). Adding this $40 to the $50 in cash dividends provides a total return of $90, or a 9 percent annual yield on the investment ($90/$1000). Similarly, if you buy a $10,000, three-month Treasury bill for $9857.90, you have a 1.44 percent yield on your investment ($10,000 − $9857.90 = $142.10/

A law requiring truth in advertising for investment yields does not exist. To understand an advertised yield well enough for you to compare it with another investment requires that you know the variables used in its calculation. You need to know whether the advertised yield takes compounding into consideration, and if so, the frequency of compounding, as well as the time period upon which the calculations are based.*

All money-market funds report a current

* This topic is discussed more thoroughly in Chapter 5, Managing Your Cash.

yield, and the Securities and Exchange Commission requires that the calculation be based on the fund's net earnings over the past 7 days and then annualized to project what it might earn for the next 12 months. Current yield is similar to simple interest, since no compounding occurs.

A **compound yield,** also known as **effective yield,** occurs when dividends are reinvested and accumulate additional earnings for the next payout date. Yields can be compounded daily, weekly, monthly, quarterly, semiannually, or annually. The effective yield increases as the frequency of compounding increases.

$9857.90), which translates into an annual yield of 5.76 percent (1.44 × 4 quarters).

Getting Money to Invest

Obtaining a return on an investment means earning money above and beyond your salary income. Instead of laboring for more money, your investment money works for you. This is an attractive idea, of course, but you must first have the funds to invest. Unless you inherit money or win a lottery, you must save to build up some principal. Some suggestions follow.

The most successful investors pay themselves first.

1. *Pay yourself first.* We recommend various ways to save in your budgeting (see Chapter 4). First, you should treat savings as a fixed expense and pay it regularly along with other dollar commitments. Second, when budgeted costs do not exceed income for a given time period, you should place the surplus (or part of it) in savings.

2. *Use forced savings plans.* When asked, most employers will direct a portion of your salary to a savings account at a bank, credit union, savings and loan association, or even a special company savings plan. This way you never "see" the money, since it is deposited automatically. Another form of forced savings is to have the IRS overwithhold money from your paycheck and to receive a larger tax refund (a disadvantage of this method is that the IRS does not pay interest on withheld funds). An advantage of forced savings plans is that you have to take forceful

action to *not* save, thus making it easier to continue saving. Forced saving is especially advantageous when you are saving for a specific goal.

3. *Save—don't spend—windfalls.* When unexpected money arrives, you may have the impulse to spend it quickly. However, if you save such windfalls rather than spend them, you will be able to add substantially to your savings account. Examples of extra money are a year-end bonus from an employer, the amount of a raise above your previous salary, money gifts, and an income tax refund.

4. *Keep making installment payments.* If you make installment repayments on a consumer debt, you have an unusual opportunity to save after making the last repayment on the debt. Simply continue to make payments—to your savings account. You will build up funds quickly over a few months.

5. *Scrimp one month per year.* If one month a year you make a concerted effort to scrimp on all expenses, you can accumulate a sizable amount of money for savings and investment. To do this, cut back on some planned expenditures and question every possible variable expense. Knowing that this level of frugality will end after 30 days will help motivate you toward success.

How to Set Investment Goals

Objective
To be able to explain how to set and achieve investment goals.

Investment goals are partially based on motivations, which are sometimes hard to pinpoint. For example, what exactly is a "feeling of security"? The goal of "being financially successful over a lifetime" is a laudable objective, but it is not specific enough. Investment goals need to be specific so you can prioritize them *and* know when you have achieved them. To achieve your investment goals, you need to determine the dollar amount of the goal and set the maturity date for the goal.

Dollar Amount of Goal

It is not too difficult to place a dollar value on a current goal of buying an automobile, a sailboat, or a home or even planning on a certain retirement income. However, it can be difficult to estimate the dollar value of future goals. To illustrate, assume that Elaine Arno of Columbus, Georgia, finds that the home she wants to buy currently costs $100,000, and she decides to make a 20 percent down payment. If she buys it today, she will need to put $20,000 down. What if she waits a year or more? If prices on homes rise 5 percent per year, she will need a larger amount for a down payment. In 1 year the price would rise to $105,000 ($100,000 × 1.05), requiring a 20 percent down payment of $21,000 ($105,000 × 0.20). In 2 years the price would be $110,250 ($105,000 × 1.05), and the down payment would be $22,050; in 3 years the price would be $115,763 ($110,250 × 1.05), and the down payment would be $23,153.

What If Your Child Needs Money to Go to College?*

The earlier you start saving money for your child's education, the better off you will be. The following table shows how much you need to save each year and month to pay for the entire cost of a college education, based on the current costs of tuition, room and board, and other expenses. The average annual costs are estimated at $20,000 for an Ivy League school, $15,000 for a private school, and $8000 for a public college. The figures assume that college costs will rise 6 percent per year and that your investment portfolio will earn 8 percent annually. The investment strategy section offers ideas on effective ways to invest saved funds.

| Current Age of Child | Amount to Save Each Year/Month | | | Investment Strategies |
	Public College	Private College	Ivy League College	
Infant	$ 2,439 $ 203	$ 4,140 $ 345	$ 5,520 $ 460	Buy growth stocks, zero-coupon bonds, and aggressive-growth mutual funds
Age 3	$ 2,825 $ 235	$ 5,297 $ 441	$ 7,063 $ 588	Buy growth stocks, zero-coupon bonds, and aggressive, growth mutual funds
Age 6	$ 3,392 $ 283	$ 6,360 $ 530	$ 8,481 $ 707	Buy growth stocks, zero-coupon bonds, income and growth mutual funds, and EE Savings Bonds
Age 9	$ 4,327 $ 361	$ 8,114 $ 676	$10,818 $ 902	Buy stocks paying high dividends, zero-coupon bonds, income and growth mutual funds
Age 12	$ 6,190 $ 516	$11,606 $ 967	$15,474 $ 1,290	Buy stocks paying high dividends, zero-coupon bonds, balanced mutual funds, and certificates of deposit
Age 15	$11,741 $ 978	$22,014 $ 1,835	$29,353 $ 2,446	Sell growth-oriented stocks and mutual funds; buy fixed-income investments so you will have money ready for college expenses

* Calculations are based on the figures in the table in Appendix A3.

In order to have the proper amount of funds available to reach her goal when she decides to buy, Elaine must try to estimate the dollar amount she needs.

Maturity Date for Goal

The preceding example shows that when prices rise, more money will be required the longer the time period for goal achievement. The task is to set maturity dates for goals far enough in the future to allow raising of sufficient funds but soon enough that one remains motivated and does not lose sight of the goal. If you set too long a maturity date for your goal, it could become too difficult to reach. You should set maturity dates that are not too unreasonably far in the future. Three years is probably enough time to save for an expensive automobile, and 5 years is enough time to set up a sizable fund to make a down payment on a home. If you cannot save enough within a certain time frame, you will have to set longer maturity dates to reach goals. (See Appendix A1 for illustrations of calculations for lump-sum investments and Appendix A3 for calculations for annual investments.)

Discovering Your Own Personal Investment Philosophy

Objective
To be able to determine your own investment goals.

Have you ever known someone who received a substantial inheritance and quickly lost it on poor investments? This happens when people forget to match their financial decisions with their usual manner of thinking, feeling, and acting. For example, many people are simply unwilling to take much risk and probably would lose sleep at night worrying about speculative investments such as in the commodities market (see Chapter 21).

How Do You Handle Risk?

Risk, and your ability to handle it, has much to do with determining your personal investment philosophy. **Risk** is the uncertainty that the yield on an investment will deviate from what is expected. Placing money in a federally insured savings account is virtually a no-risk situation, since the government guarantees both the principal and the yield. Buying stock in a corporation is riskier, since no one guarantees the future success of a company. For most investments, the greater the risk, the greater the possible yield, and the potential for gain is what motivates people to take increasingly greater risks.

As an investor trying to figure out your own investment philosophy, you first need to determine your ability to handle risk. Basically, you need to determine how much anxiety you can handle with your investments. We sometimes call this your "stomach and sleep quotient," or "SSQ." Ask yourself, "What is my basic temperament or natural disposition?"

"How strong is my stomach?" "How well do I sleep at night?" "Will my financial decisions cause loved ones to worry?" "Can I afford a 10, 20, or 30 percent loss on my investments?" "Will I take the time to investigate investment opportunities?" Answering these questions honestly will help you match investments to your temperament and investment philosophy.

Ultraconservative Investors Do Not Risk Their Money

Remember, there are many ways to save without risk and still get respectable, although limited, returns: federally insured savings accounts, certificates of deposit, EE and HH Savings Bonds, and various Treasury bills, notes and bonds. Ultraconservative investors, especially those who cannot sleep at night if they think any of their money is at risk, do not consider alternative investments because they stick with the 100 percent safe options backed by Uncle Sam. Long-term Treasury issues and federal agency offerings come with virtually the same protection. An ultraconservative investor with $1000 will not lose a penny and likely will gain $70 or more over a year.

Ultraconservative people tend to keep their money in savings accounts rather than consider alternative investments.

Is Your Investment Philosophy Conservative, Moderate, or Speculative?

If you decide to invest in an alternative investment, such as stocks, bonds, mutual funds, or real estate, you need to develop an **investment philosophy**—a personal investment strategy that anticipates specific returns and risks and contains tactics for accomplishing your investment goals. If you record your strategy and tactics in writing, you can avoid inconsistent investment decisions.

The financial goal of obtaining a specific potential rate of return is accompanied by varied degrees of risk. If you have a **conservative investment philosophy**, you accept very little risk and are generally rewarded with relatively low rates of return. You could be characterized as a "risk averter." Conservative investors are mainly concerned with inflation, which could lower the value of their investments. Conservative investors often protect themselves against losses with short maturities (perhaps 1 or 2 years) and try to ride gains for much longer time periods (frequently 5 or 10 years). Tactically, they might consider selling investments when the price has risen 15 percent, selling if values drop by 15 percent, and holding bonds until maturity or a 15 percent rise is realized. They also tend to spread their funds among several investment alternatives.

People seeking conservative returns consider investing in high-quality (blue-chip) corporate stocks, balanced mutual funds (which own both stocks and bonds), certificates of deposit, fixed annuities, high-quality corporate bonds, Treasury bills, notes and bonds, municipal bonds, and some real estate. A conservative investor with $1000 might lose $50 over a year or gain $85.

If your investment philosophy is **moderate investment philosophy**, you invite only a fair amount of risk. A moderate investor accepts the risk of a capital loss but not to a great degree. Tactics of moderate investors might include selling stocks when the price has risen 25 percent, selling if the price drops by 25 percent, and spreading investment funds among three or four choices.

People seeking moderate returns consider investing in dividend-paying common stocks, growth and income mutual funds, high-quality corporate bonds, government bonds, variable annuities, and real estate. A moderate investor with $1000 might lose $300 over a year or gain $200.

If your goal is to obtain a very high return and thus to accept a high degree of risk, your investment philosophy is **speculative investment philosophy**, and you could be characterized as a "risk seeker." Your tactics might be to place most of your investment funds in a single stock in the hope that it will rise 10 percent over 90 days, giving an annual yield of more than 40 percent. Then you would sell those shares, which would give you money to invest elsewhere. However, speculators must be willing to suffer substantial temporary losses, perhaps a downward swing in price of 30 percent over 90 days, with the expectation that an even stronger upswing in price might occur in the near future. There are many investment tactics for speculative investors that require short-term maneuvers, and these are discussed in Chapter 21, Speculative Investments. A speculative investor with $1000 might lose $800 over a year or gain $2500.

People seeking speculative returns consider investing in common stocks of new fast-growing companies, high-yielding junk bonds, aggressive-growth mutual funds, commodities, puts and calls, limited real estate partnerships, and undeveloped land.[1] Some speculative investors might consider putting money into precious metals, gems, commodity futures, stock-index futures, and collectibles of every stripe.

Speculators must be willing to suffer substantial temporary financial losses.

Choosing among Alternative Investments

Objective
To be able to recognize the variety of choices among the alternative investments available.

You have two key decisions to make when choosing alternative investments: (1) Do you want to lend your money or own an asset? and (2) Do you want to invest for the short or long term?

Do You Want to Lend or Own?

You can invest money in two ways, by lending and by owning. When you loan your money, what you get is an IOU and the promise of future income. You can earn income by depositing money in banks, credit unions, and savings and loan associations (with savings accounts and certificates of deposit) and by giving money to governments (Treasury notes and bonds as well as state and local tax-free securities), businesses (corporate bonds), mortgage-backed securities (Ginnie Maes), and life insurance companies (cash-value policies and annuities). Lending investments generally have both a fixed maturity and a fixed income. **Fixed maturity** means the borrower agrees to repay the principal to you on a specific date. **Fixed**

---

[1] These and other terms are defined in later chapters as well as in the Glossary.

income means the borrower agrees to pay you a specific rate of return for use of the principal. What people like most about lending investments is being confident that they will receive a certain amount of interest income for a specific period and that all the loaned funds will be returned to them.

The other way to invest money is through ownership. When you buy an investment asset, you hold title to it; thus these investments are often called *equities*. You can buy common or preferred corporate stock (to obtain part ownership in a corporation), purchase shares in a mutual fund company (which then invests in corporate stock and bonds), put money into your own business, buy investment property through a syndicate, purchase real estate, buy commodities (pork bellies and oranges), or buy investment quality collectibles (such as rare antiques, fine art, or stamps). Many people enjoy ownership investments, especially when the value of ownership increases.

Lending investors typically earn less than ownership investors.

For a lending investor, the return is somewhat assured. But no matter how much profit the borrower makes with your funds, you as an investing lender get only the fixed rate. On the other hand, as an investment owner, you face a greater possible return along with a greater risk. If your ownership is unsuccessful, you could lose your entire investment. Some forms of ownership (sole proprietorships and unlimited partnerships, for example) might even render you personally liable for ownership losses. During times of rising inflation, lending investors often lose because fixed maturities and fixed rates result in fixed values for investments. Ownership investors, however, may have a hedge against inflation, since the value of most assets increases during inflationary periods.

Do You Want to Make Short-Term or Long-Term Investments?

Most individual investors lack the expertise, time, and money to reap substantial short-term financial gains from investments (*short term* meaning less than 1 year). You may find it difficult to monitor an investment carefully and too expensive to get professional advice. Further, any short-term gains may be offset by payments of fees and commissions.

Most individual investors invest for the long term.

For these kinds of reasons, most individual investors make long-term investments, keeping funds working in the investment for 2, 5, or 10 or more years. Regardless of the length of the investment period, you should periodically reexamine your investments with an eye toward maximizing return. The value of making long-term investments and the time value of money was clearly illustrated in Chapter 1.

Now Choose

This chapter on investment fundamentals provides the tools of analysis to permit you to decide which types of investment alternatives probably suit your needs. Should you lend or own? Do you prefer short-term or long-term investments? Also, when you set your investment objectives, you must decide which you want the most—income or capital gains. You may want considerable current earnings or you may want substantial capital gains, but you cannot have lots of both from the same investment. The following six chapters examine the details of alternative investments to enable you to give appropriate thought to making investments consistent with your objectives and to making wise financial decisions.

You will observe that stocks and bonds are the most popular of all alternative investments, and each is examined separately in the next two chapters. Chapter 18 covers the important subject of mutual funds as an investment, and millions of Americans have been turning to this alternative in recent years. Chapter 19 delves into the complexities of buying and selling all types of securities and outlines many successful tactics of profitable investing. No textbook on personal finance would be complete without an examination of real estate from the point of view of real estate as an investment rather than for personal use (Chapter 20). Finally, the subject of speculative investments (such as precious metals, commodities, and options) is examined in Chapter 21. An overview of which types of investments match which investment goals is provided in Table 15.1.

Two important points should be noted. First, in *all* the investment chapters that follow, we will provide you with enough details to help you decide which alternatives are suitable for you. Second, we also provide specific guidelines for deciding when each investment should be sold. In sum, your goal should be to learn enough about alternative investments to make your own wise investment decisions.

You also need to know when to sell your investments.

Major Factors That Affect the Rate of Return on an Investment

Several factors affect the rate of return on an investment: the risk and yield relationship, various types of risks, diversification, leverage, taxes, and inflation. Each of these is discussed below.

Risk and Yield Relationships

On average, the greater the potential risk of an investment, the greater is the potential yield. Pure risk, concerning the uncertainty of events occurring with no potential for gain was discussed in Chapter 10. The risk referred to here, however, is **speculative risk,** which involves potential for gain as well as loss. Common stock, for example, may rise or fall in value; whether it will rise or fall is an unknown. Since this feeling of speculation surrounds most alternative investments, many people choose conservatively to keep their risk low; others who want higher yields accept greater unknowns and higher risk.

Figure 15.1 diagrams the relationship between risk and knowledge of the future. Where the curve intersects the vertical axis, there is total knowledge of the future and thus virtually no risk. An investment in U.S.

TABLE 15.1
Which Investments Match Your Goals?

Time	Investment Goals	Tradeoffs	Possible Investments
Less than 2 years	Easy access to funds Moderate yields Steady income Stable prices	Low returns Vulnerable to inflation	NOW checking account Savings account Money-market account Certificates of deposit Treasury issues and corporate bonds maturing within 2 years
2 to 5 years	Moderately high yields Steady income Narrow price movements	Less safety than for shorter-term investments Lower returns than for longer-term investments Some vulnerability to inflation	Corporate bonds maturing within 5 years Ginnie Mae bonds Stocks paying high dividends Balanced mutual funds
6 to 10 years	Moderately high yields Predictable price movements	Less safety than for shorter-term investments Lower returns than for longer-term investments	Stocks paying high dividends Ginnie Mae bonds Short-term bonds Long-term bonds Long-term certificates of deposit (CDs) Growth and income mutual funds Real estate
More than 10 years	Previous record of high long-term yields Potential for appreciation Returns that outpace inflation	Price volatility May have limited liquidity and marketability Patience required	Growth stocks Long-term bonds Precious metals Aggressive-growth mutual funds Real estate

There are specific trade-offs between risk and reward in investments.

Treasury bonds could be placed near this point, since they are loans from the people to the government and are guaranteed with the "full faith and credit of the U.S. government." A bond issued by a large corporation with a long history of financial stability would be slightly riskier because it carries no government guarantee. To make up for increased risk, the yield on the corporate bond must be higher. Figure 15.2 gives sample investments with increasing degrees of risk relative to yield. The government bond has virtually no risk, and the corporate bond has a slight risk. Most corporate common stock would be placed further along the risk curve, and ownership in a new business to convert coal to a liquid-burning state, a highly speculative investment, would be even further along the curve. Figure 15.3 presents the risk pyramid, which illustrates the tradeoff between risk and reward.

FIGURE 15.1
Risk and Knowledge
Relationship

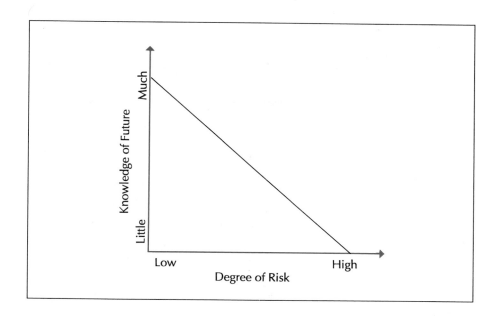

FIGURE 15.2
Investment Risk and
Yield Relationship

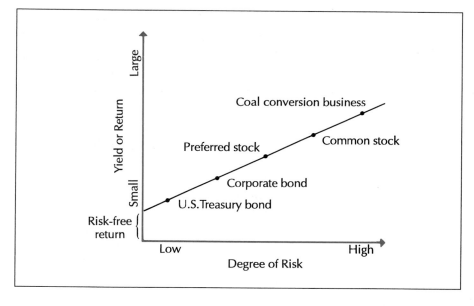

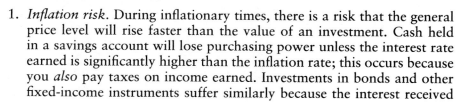

Types of Investment Risk

There are eight major types of risk in investments.

1. *Inflation risk.* During inflationary times, there is a risk that the general price level will rise faster than the value of an investment. Cash held in a savings account will lose purchasing power unless the interest rate earned is significantly higher than the inflation rate; this occurs because you *also* pay taxes on income earned. Investments in bonds and other fixed-income instruments suffer similarly because the interest received

FIGURE 15.3
The Risk Pyramid in Investments (The Tradeoffs Between Investment Rewards and Risks)

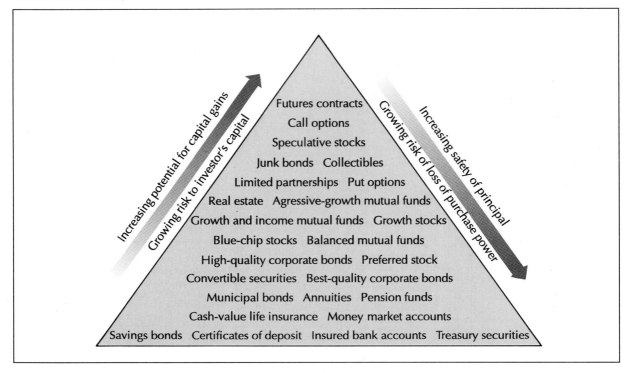

is paid in ever-cheaper dollars. The result is that you get less and less buying power from your investment's return.

2. *Deflation risk.* Should prices decline, as has happened a few times in U.S. history, the value of the dollar actually increases. Houses, real estate, and other ownership investments are subject to deflation risk, since their values might decline.

3. *Interest-rate risk.* Some investments will lose part of their value if they have to be sold because of fluctuations in the level of interest rates in the economy. This can occur with fixed-interest-rate obligations such as bonds and preferred stocks, investments that have an almost guaranteed current dollar income. For example, suppose that a corporation sells you a 20-year $1000 bond at 6 percent. This obligates the corporation to pay you $60 a year ($1000 × 0.06) and to repay the $1000 principal in 20 years. Should interest rates in the economy rise substantially, perhaps to 8 percent, the market value of the 6 percent bond will decline. Other investors could buy a new bond for $1000 that pays 8 percent or offer to buy your old bond for $750, which would raise their effective yield of 6 percent to 8 percent ($60/$750).

4. *Financial risk.* You might expect that most investments are profitable, but this is not the case. There is some financial risk that the investment

will be unable to pay a return to the investor. A corporation could experience difficult financial times and not be able to pay interest on corporate bonds or dividends on shares of stock. And there is always the financial risk that the company could go bankrupt. In contrast, an insured savings account carries almost no financial risk.

5. *Market-volatility risk*. Even in times of economic prosperity, the value of individual investments can change dramatically. Generally, prices on real estate do not fluctuate nearly as much as prices on corporate stocks do. Residential real estate in a suburban area is likely to increase steadily, whereas the value of stock in a food company could change sharply when a new product is successfully introduced to the public or when one fails.

6. *Liquidity risk*. **Liquidity** is the speed and ease with which an asset can be converted to cash. Cash is 100 percent liquid, a check slightly less. Liquidity needs vary among investors, particularly according to stage in the life cycle (long-term investors do not need much liquidity) and perceptions about the need to have quick access to cash. People choose somewhat liquid investments (such as most stocks and mutual funds) when they expect that they might soon need the money to buy some item or make another investment. Investors choose less liquid investments, such as real estate, for different goals.

7. *Marketability risk*. When you have to sell an asset quickly, a marketability risk may occur because there may be so few buyers that you have to accept a selling price lower than expected and thereby be unable to regain the amount of money originally invested or the value you anticipated. The **marketability risk** is the loss you might have to absorb if forced to sell an investment before you had planned. Selling real estate in a hurry often requires the seller to make price concessions. Coin and stamp collections also might be difficult to sell quickly for the right price too. An investment that is nonmarketable also is illiquid.

8. *Political risk*. The political environment can often sharply affect the value of investments. Imposition of wage and price controls, government efforts to settle labor strikes, and election of officials who change defense-spending and tariff policies as well as raise income taxes can all affect investments negatively or positively.

Table 15.2 summarizes the degrees of each type of risk for each type of investment. You may want to return to this table, as well as Table 15.1, as you read in more detail about these types of investments in the following chapters.

Diversification

Diversification is the process of reducing risk by spreading investment monies among several investment opportunities. It results in a potential rate of return on all the investments that is generally lower than the potential return on a single alternative. The idea is to spread your investment monies over several choices to reduce the **random risk** that any one

TABLE 15.2
Types of Investments and Degrees of Risk

Type of Investment	Type of Risk							
	Inflation	Deflation	Interest Rate	Financial	Market Volatility	Market-ability	Liquidity	Political
Savings account	High	Low	Low	Low	Low	Low	Low	Low
Money market funds	Medium	Low	Low	Low	Low	Low	Low	Low
Insurance (cash value)	Medium	Low	Low	Low	Low	Low	Low	Low
Insurance annuities	High	Low	Low	Low	Low	Low	Low	Low
Bonds (best quality)	High	Low	High	Low	Medium	Low	Low	Low
Bonds (high quality)	High	Low	High	Medium	Medium	Low	Low	Low
Common stocks	Medium	Medium	Medium	Medium	High	Low	Low	High
Mutual funds	Medium	Medium	Medium	Medium	High	Low	Low	High
Real estate	Low	Low	Medium	Low	Low	High	High	High
Precious metals, options, and commodities	Low	Low	Low	High	High	High	Low	High

By diversifying into five investments you cut your risk in half.

investment will go down in value because of chance. If you invest in only one stock, its value might rise or fall, but if you invest in two stocks, the odds are lessened that both will fall in price. Research suggests that you can eliminate random risk by holding 15 or more securities, and it can be cut in half by diversifying into as few as 5.

To illustrate, if you were absolutely sure that the interest rates would decline in future years, you might be wise to put $10,000 into high-yielding corporate bonds (perhaps paying 10 percent) before the interest rates slipped lower. If you were wrong and interest rates went up, pulling bond rates upward too, the value of your bonds would decline sharply. (If the rate of return on new bonds rose to 12 percent, the market value of a $10,000, 10-percent bond might drop to $8333). The first column in Table 15.2 shows that bonds have a high risk to inflation and that real estate has a low risk to inflation (real estate prices generally rise during inflationary times). By making investments in several areas, say, in both bonds and real estate, you can reduce your risk.

Other types of diversification will be discussed as appropriate in the following chapters. For example, when buying common stocks, you might want to purchase a speculative stock along with an income stock to reduce the possibility of losing everything with the speculative stock (see Chapter

TABLE 15.3

Illustration of Leverage (Buying Real Estate As an Investment)

	Pay Cash	Use Credit
Purchase price of office building	$ 100,000	$ 100,000
Amount borrowed	0	90,000
Amount invested	$ 100,000	$ 10,000
Rental income	$ 13,200	$ 13,200
Minus tax-deductible interest (12.5 percent 30-year loan on $90,000)	0	11,113
Net earnings before taxes	$ 13,200	$ 2,087
Minus income tax liability (28 percent bracket)	3,696	584
Rental earnings after taxes	$ 9,504	$ 1,503
	÷ 100,000	÷ 10,000
Percentage return on amount invested	9.5 percent	15.0 percent

16, Investing in Stocks). The potential return is reduced somewhat by diversification, since in this example some funds are invested in the lower-yield income stock rather than in the speculative stock. The lower return on investment is the opportunity cost of reducing the risk of loss.

At the same time, however, realize that diversification also may improve the odds for substantial gains. For example, instead of putting all your eggs into one basket—which could go down in value—you might spread your money over several alternatives hoping that the gain of one or two will pull up the average return of all.

Leverage

Another factor that can affect return on investment is **leverage.** This is using borrowed funds to make an investment with the goal of earning a rate of return in excess of the after-tax costs of borrowing. Investing in real estate for its rental income provides an illustration of leverage. Assume you can buy a small office building either by making a $10,000 down payment and financing the $90,000 remainder or by paying $100,000 cash. Assuming that rental income is $13,200 annually ($1100 per month) and your income tax bracket is 28 percent, it would be better to use credit to buy the building, as Table 15.3 shows.

Using other people's money (OPM) can greatly enhance your return.

There is a potentially negative side to using leverage too. In the preceding example, if you used credit, you would need a rental income of more than $11,000 to be able to pay the mortgage loan payments. A couple of vacant months and/or expensive repairs to the building could result in a losing situation. Even though some cash losses are tolerable for tax purposes (as shown in Chapter 20, Investing in Real Estate), you can become financially overextended by using leverage for investments, a risk that you should consider.

A plus for using leverage is that capital gains can occur, sharply boosting the return on the investment. Assume that at the end of 1 year the building has appreciated 10 percent and you could sell it for $110,000 (excluding commission costs). If you had purchased it for $100,000 cash and then sold it for $110,000, the capital gain on the sale would be 10 percent ($10,000 return ÷ $100,000 originally invested). However, if you had bought it using credit, the capital gain would be *100 percent* ($10,000 return ÷ $10,000 originally invested ignoring taxes and inflation). Other examples of leveraged investments appear in later chapters.

Taxes

You should analyze investments carefully in terms of (1) anticipated income, (2) possible capital gains, and (3) the after-tax effects of total investment income. Sending your investment income on a one-way trip to Washington guarantees a lower rate of return on investments than if you could keep some tax-free dollars. Increasing the after-tax return on your investments requires an understanding of your marginal tax rate and the concept of taxable versus tax-free income.

Marginal Tax Rate This concept was discussed in Chapters 1 and 8, but a reminder from the perspective of after-tax return is appropriate. In the example illustrated in Table 15.3, whether you pay $100,000 cash or make a down payment of $10,000 for the building, you expect to receive $13,200 in before-tax rental income. If you pay cash, you earn a before-tax rate of return of 13.2 percent ($13,200/$100,000). If you use credit, you have expenses of $11,113, which reduce before-tax income to $2087. On an investment of $10,000, this provides a before-tax rate of return of 20.9 percent ($2087/$10,000). In the example shown in Table 15.3, the rental income received is subject to a 28 percent marginal tax rate, which reduces the respective yields to 9.5 and 15.0 percent.

Taxable Versus Tax-Free Income Chapter 8 covered various techniques of legal tax avoidance, including tax-free investments. Many states and municipalities issue bonds that are exempt from federal and state income taxes. (Chapter 17, Investing in Bonds, will provide more details.)

Investors should consider the after-tax return of comparable taxable and tax-free alternatives. For example, Naheel Jeries, part of a dual-income family in Ames, Iowa, is comparing a $1000 corporate bond paying a 7.6 percent return with a municipal bond paying 5.9 percent. Since she is in the 28 percent marginal tax bracket, $21 of the $76 interest earned annually on the corporate bond would go to income taxes ($76 × 0.28). This provides Naheel with an after-tax return of 5.5 percent ($76 − $21 = $55/$1000). The municipal bond annual interest of $59 is exempt from federal income taxes. Naheel should choose the municipal bond because the after-tax return is 5.9 percent ($59/$1000), which is 0.4 percent higher than the corporate bond (5.9 percent − 5.5 percent). Whether you should invest in tax-free opportunities depends on the yields available and your

Taxpayers who are in the 28 percent marginal tax bracket may earn a better after-tax return with tax-free investments.

TABLE 15.4
Best and Worst Investments of the 1980s

Type of Asset	Total Return (%)	Annual Rate of Return (%)	Type of Asset	Total Return (%)	Annual Rate of Return (%)
Stocks	381	17.0	**CPI**	**74.1**	**5.7**
Coins	236	12.9	Housing	70.8	5.5
Bonds	181	10.9	Gold	31.8	2.8
Treasury bills	159	10.0	Oil	12.7	1.2
Old masters	150	9.6	Foreign exchange	− 9.4	0.9
Chinese ceramics	130	8.7	U.S. farmland	− 5.1	−0.5
Diamonds	122	8.3	Silver	−56.8	−4.6

Source: From *U.S. News & World Report,* December 4, 1989, p. 71. Reprinted with permission.
Note: Rates are compound annual rates of return for the period June 1, 1979, to June 1, 1989.

marginal tax rate. Formulas 8.1 and 8.2 (on page 299) show very simply how you can determine tax-equivalent yields on any type of investment.

Inflation

You should recognize by now that inflation reduces the purchasing power of the dollar. Inflation is an extremely important factor for investors to consider because it consistently takes from the unwise and gives to the wise. Consider Richard Belisle of Shepherdstown, West Virginia, who thought he had a hedge against inflation by depositing $10,000 in a bank account paying 5 percent interest. His account earned $500 interest during the year, but unfortunately, the inflation rate was 6 percent. Richard's bank won, since it wisely invested his deposit at rates somewhat above 6 percent. To beat inflation, Richard must invest his money and earn a substantially higher return.

To beat inflation, Richard must invest his money and earn a substantially higher return.

Most investors expect inflation to continue, and the only question is how quickly prices will rise. During periods of high inflation, the value of most assets declines and the value of some rises. Historically, common stocks and real estate rise with inflation over several years. Bonds lose value during inflationary times because they are fixed-dollar investments that offer the return of a certain number of dollars rather than dollars with their original purchasing power. The recent performance of a number of investment alternatives—and whether or not they beat inflation—is shown in Table 15.4.

The challenge to you is to analyze carefully the risks of making alternative investments to earn the highest possible **real return on investment** (the yield after subtracting the effects of taxes and inflation). This is difficult to accomplish during periods of high inflation, but it is important if you expect to stay ahead of inflation. Table 15.5 shows common investment choices and real returns for people with different investment philosophies.

TABLE 15.5
Common Investment Choices and Real Returns (after Taxes and Inflation) for People with Different Investment Philosophies*

Conservative (1 to 2 percent)	Moderate (3 to 4 percent)	Speculative (5 percent or more)
Fixed-dollar investments (Chapter 5)	Growth stocks (Chapter 16)	Speculative stocks (Chapter 16)
Blue-chip income stocks (Chapter 16)	Mutual funds (Chapter 18)	Options, rights, warrants and futures (Chapter 21)
Preferred stocks (Chapter 16)	Real estate (Chapter 20)	Raw land real estate (Chapter 20)
Treasury bonds (Chapter 17)	Corporate and municipal bonds (Chapter 17)	Junk bonds (Chapter 17)
Municipal bonds (Chapter 17)	Unit investment trusts (Chapter 18)	Precious metals (Chapter 21)
	Real estate investment trusts (Chapter 19)	
	Collectibles (Chapter 21)	

* For example, a moderate investor may invest in a well-known growth common stock, hoping to receive an annual total return of 11 percent (perhaps 2 percent from cash dividends and 9 percent in price appreciation), which might provide a real return of 2.9 percent after subtracting 3.1 percent for income taxes (11.0 percent × expected marginal tax bracket of 28 percent) and 5 percent for the effects of inflation.

What Is a Good Return and How Do You Calculate an Investment's Potential Total Return?

Objective
To be able to know what a good return is and be able to calculate the potential total return on an investment.

This section reviews why you must earn an investment return in excess of inflation and taxes, that you must decide on your desired rate of return, and the procedure to calculate an estimate for the desired potential rate of return on an investment alternative.

The Return Must Exceed Inflation and Taxes

All individual investors who consider alternative investments are interested in earning a return somewhat greater than the rate of inflation. Otherwise, the investor loses money because of inflation and the payment of income taxes. For example, assume that inflation is 4 percent and Jefferson Schwertly, a married manager of a day care canter in Norfolk, Nebraska, has invested $3000 in a stock paying a cash dividend of $130 per year. Just to stay even with a 4 percent inflation rate, Jefferson needs an annual return of $120 ($3000 × 0.04). Since he is in the 28 percent tax bracket, he also needs an additional return of $47 ($120/.72 = $167 − $120) to stay even with the federal Internal Revenue Service, which gets 28 percent of his earnings. Because he needs $167 ($167 × .28 = $47 + $120) just to break even with inflation and taxes and his current return is only $130,

Calculating the Real Return (after Taxes and Inflation) on Investments

Step 1. Identify anticipated total return. Perhaps you think that a stock is expected to pay a total return of 11 percent in 1 year, including current income and capital gain.

Step 2. Subtract the impact of your marginal tax rate on anticipated total return to get net return after taxes. You are in the 28 percent federal income tax bracket, so $(1 - 0.28) \times 0.11 = 0.0792$, or 7.9 percent.

Step 3. Subtract estimate of anticipated inflation from net return after taxes to get **real return on investment** *(after taxes and inflation).* You estimate annual inflation of 5 percent for the coming year; therefore, 7.9 percent − 5 percent = 2.9 percent. Thus your anticipated total return of 11 percent provides a real return of 2.9 percent after taxes and inflation.

actually he is losing. Jefferson will continue to lose unless the market price of the stock rises and he sells to realize a capital gain of $37 ($167 − $130) or more.

Decide on Your Desired Rate of Return

The rate earned on Treasury bills is usually slightly above the rate of inflation.

The return on the virtually risk-free short-term U.S. Treasury bills historically has been just slightly above the rate of inflation. For this reason, investors often use the yield on Treasury bills as a base number that provides a zero *real* rate of return, that is after inflation and income taxes. Since there is some risk in quality long-term corporate bonds, the rate of return on corporate securities must be a little higher than that for Treasury securities. If Treasury bills were yielding 7.5 percent, high-quality long-term bonds might be yielding 9.5 to 10 percent. Further, investors figure that to earn a positive real return on stocks, they must have a rate of return at least three percentage points above that available on quality long-term corporate bonds to compensate for the additional risks taken by investing in the stock market. Thus, if Treasury securities are yielding 7.5 percent and long-term bonds are paying 9.5 percent, you should expect a minimum potential total return of 12.5 percent if you invest in stocks; otherwise, why take the risk.

Procedure to Calculate an Estimate for the Desired Potential Rate of Return on an Investment Alternative

The **potential total return** for any investment can be determined by adding anticipated income (from interest, dividends, rents, or whatever) and price appreciation (or loss) over a period of years. As an investor, your task begins by applying an estimated growth rate (perhaps for 5 years) to the

TABLE 15.6
One Investor's Projections of the Potential Total Return for Running Paws Catfood Company

End of Year	Earnings	Income
1	$2.76	$0.76
2	3.17	0.87
3	3.65	1.00
4	4.20	1.15
5	4.83	1.33
Total Dividends		$5.12

Add projected income and projected price appreciation to determine the potential rate of return.

latest 12-month earnings (in the case of stocks, the figure is typically reported as earnings per share, or *EPS*). Then multiply the last year's earnings by a projected price/earnings (*P/E*) ratio for the same year, which relates the current market value of the investment to its earnings.[2] Estimate income by applying an estimated growth rate to the current cash income received. Finally, sum up the projected income and price appreciation. Table 15.6 provides an illustration.

Example: Running Paws Catfood Company   In looking for an investment that will provide a better return than inflation and income taxes, Jefferson Schwertly is considering Running Paws Catfood Company upon recommendation from his stock broker. Jefferson has determined the following information on this stock investment: It is currently priced at $30 per share, its latest 12-month earnings amounted to $2.40, and the most recent cash dividend was $0.66 per share. He calculated the price/earnings ratio to be 12.5 (30 ÷ 2.40).

Last year's annual report for Running Paws showed earnings per share of $2.40 and a cash dividend of $0.66. As shown in Table 15.6, Jefferson then estimated a 15 percent rate of growth for the earnings per share for each year ($2.40 × 1.15 = $2.76 × 1.15, and so forth) and a 15 percent growth rate in the cash dividend ($0.66 × 1.15 = $0.76 × 1.15, etc.)

Using a *P/E* ratio of 12.5 (the same as it is now), Jefferson estimated the market price at the end of the fifth year to be $60.38 (12.5 × $4.83). This gives a projected appreciation in stock price over 5 years of $30.38 ($60.38 minus the current price of $30). The **annual average dividend** computes to $1.02 by dividing the $5.12 in dividend income by 5 years. Combined with the sum of the estimated cash dividends of $5.12, the projected total return in dollars is $35.50 ($30.38 + $5.12).

Now the question is, "What is the percentage yield for this in return in dollars?" The **approximate compound yield** (*ACY*) formula provides a measure of the annualized compound growth of any long-term investment.

[2] *Earnings per share, price/earnings ratio,* and other key terms are defined in the chapters that follow as well as in the Glossary. This approach to determining the potential total return may be used for other investments, such as stocks, bonds, mutual funds, real estate, and speculative alternatives.

You can determine this by using Equation (15.1). If you substitute the data from Table 15.6, being certain to use the average annual dividend and not the specific projected dividends, you will obtain an approximate compound yield of 15 percent on the potential investment in Running Paws.

$$ACY = \frac{\text{average annual dividend} + \dfrac{\substack{\text{projected price} \\ \text{of stock}} - \substack{\text{current price} \\ \text{of stock}}}{\text{numbers of years projected}}}{\dfrac{\substack{\text{projected price} \\ \text{of stock}} + \substack{\text{current price} \\ \text{of stock}}}{2}}$$

$$= \frac{\$1.02 + \dfrac{\$60.38 - \$30.00}{5}}{\dfrac{\$60.38 + \$30.00}{2}}$$

$$= \frac{\$1.02 + \$6.08}{\$45.19}$$

$$= 15.7 \text{ percent} \tag{15.1}$$

The projected total 5-year return of $30.38 on a cost of $30 works out to an approximate compound yield of 16 percent (15.7 percent rounded). This compares favorably with high-quality long-term bonds, which may yield about 9.5 percent. Jefferson Schwertly estimated that the total projected return advantage for Running Paws would be 6.5 percentage points (16 percent − 9.5 percent), and this would make it a good buy at its price of $30 for a moderately speculative investment.

How to Achieve Your Investment Goals

Objective
To be able to understand how to achieve your investment goals.

Every investor has different investment goals. The likely investment goal of retired persons would be current income rather than potential long-term capital gains, since such people probably need additional money for living expenses. Younger persons might choose growth as an investment goal. Earning extra income is always nice, but for young people the possibility of long-term growth through capital gains would usually be more appealing and rewarding. Investing in a small company in the high-technology field, for example, could be an alternative that pays little or no dividends but has promising potential for growth. Below are some pitfalls to avoid in your financial behavior and some guidelines to follow toward successful investing.

How Not to Succeed Financially

There are 15 major reasons why people fail financially.

1. *Procrastination.* You will have a difficult time attaining financial success if you keep spending all your income and continually postpone planning and implementing specific savings and investments programs.

2. *Lack of specific goals.* Although saving may give you feelings of security and success, to provide yourself with a true incentive to save and invest, you must make specific short- and long-term financial goals and prioritize them.

3. *Lack of commitment to pursue goals.* You may be able to list your financial goals but lack the commitment or determination to reach them. For example, if you need to save $150 a month for a year to make a sufficient down payment on an automobile, then 12 months of saving are necessary, not 11 or 10 or 9. Although a financial emergency might prevent you from saving during a particular month, your commitment to your goal will enable you to make up the difference over the following months.

4. *Ignorance about investments.* With all the information available on different types of investments, there is no excuse for not learning as much as you can.

5. *Buying when prices are high.* As hard as it may be to believe, many investors fail to buy when prices are low, instead choosing to buy when everyone else is buying.

6. *Miscalculating.* Sometimes people miscalculate intentionally, such as when telling others their stocks went up 10 percent when they actually went up 7 percent. Others miscalculate by failing to consider the effects of commissions, such as an 8½ percent load on a mutual fund.

7. *Falling in love with an investment.* Don't get "married" to a particular stock, mutual fund, or other investment. An investment is not a member of your family, so don't be sentimental about selling it when weeding out the poor performers in your portfolio.

8. *Ignoring their investments.* Many people simply make an investment and wait until some years later to see if it has gained value. Such optimism is foolhardy. You need to keep track of the annual rate of return for each of your investments.

9. *Losing patience.* It is unwise to become overly impatient and sell an investment because it gains little in value or goes down. While mutual fund managers and other professional money managers feel pressure to perform this year and dump all their losers by the end of the year, small investors do not. Individuals should show a willingness to hold on to slow movers for 2 to 4 years, if possible, as long as the investment was bought for a valid reason, remains fundamentally sound, and has good prospects.

10. *Following ill-advised tips.* Every year there is a new investment fad. Following ill-advised tips, whims, and hunches can quickly deplete your investment funds, so investigate before you invest.

11. *Ignorance about taxes.* Failing to understand how your marginal tax bracket works and the impact of tax-free investments can prevent you from effectively reducing taxes in the years ahead and making the most of your wise investment decisions.

12. *Payment of high insurance premiums.* An overly insured person may not be able to afford to invest. You may determine that some insurance protection is a necessity, but make sure that you do not purchase too much insurance or pay exorbitant premiums for it.

13. *Failure to have a line of credit.* Investors often need a line of credit at a financial institution to occasionally provide them with needed funds instead of being forced by events to raise cash by selling investments.

14. *Lack of diversification.* People who put all or most of their funds into just one kind of investment will only do well in a world that does not change. Economic change is absolutely certain, however, and investors must establish strategies and tactics to control risk by diversifying into several high-performing areas. This shelters them from surprise swings in any one area and increases the likelihood of high yields. Wise investors review their holdings twice a year to make sure certain risks have not changed and take action accordingly.

15. *Lack of discipline in following investment tactics.* You should set and follow your own tactical guidelines for taking profits or cutting losses and for moving into and out of particular investments. Say you have decided on guidelines to sell an investment when its value rises by 25 percent, sell if its value slides 25 percent, and sell regardless of value during the late stages of a sharply rising market. If you fail to follow your guidelines, you invite considerably more risk and an increased likelihood of losses or smaller gains. For example, assume that your investment increased 30 percent in value and you didn't sell, hoping instead to see the value increase by 40 or even 50 percent. In reality, your gain could drop swiftly to perhaps 5 percent, or even a loss, as the market declines after peaking.

Succeeding in Investments

Getting ahead financially through investments requires willingness, ability, and discipline. *Willingness* involves understanding your own motivations. *Ability* has to do with knowing alternative investments, finding investment funds, and making intelligent investment decisions. And *discipline* describes the courage to act responsibly in financial matters. You will not accumulate savings very quickly without the discipline to budget expenses carefully; success in making proper investments also requires disciplined effort. To achieve your investment goals, follow the three steps described below.

1. *Prioritize your investment goals.* Your first task is to prioritize your goals. This requires making decisions on what is important and what is not. Figure 15.4 illustrates a list of goals for Ellen Campbell of Palos Verdes, California, who decided to stop her habit of "spend, spend, spend" because it was beginning to hurt her financially. Ellen has only $1000 in a money-market fund and no real investments. As shown in

FIGURE 15.4
Goals Worksheet for Ellen Campbell

Goals	(1) Current Amount Needed	(2) Years Before Funds Are Needed	(3) Assumed Rate of Inflation	(4) Inflation Factor[a]	(5) Inflated Amount Needed (1 × 4)	(6) Estimated Return on Investment	(7) Return Factor[b]	(8) Annual Investment Amount Needed (5 ÷ 7)
Save/Invest $1,200 a year	—	—	—	—	—	—	—	$1,200
New automobile $10,000, plus trade-in	$10,000	2	6%	1.124	$11,240	8%	2.080	$5,404
European vacation (two weeks)	$4,000	5	8%	1.469	$5,876	8%	5.867	$1,002

[a] See Appendix A1.
[b] See Appendix A3.

558

Figure 15.4, she recorded her three most important goals—savings or investment of $1200 per year, a new automobile, and a European vacation—and excluded others that were less important.

2. *Calculate the amount of investment money you need annually.* Ellen's next task is to calculate how much she will need to invest annually to achieve her goals. For her first goal, she simply records $1200 in the last column. For her second goal, she estimates that with a trade-in a new car would cost $10,000 today. Using Appendix A1 and assuming that inflation is 6 percent, Ellen finds the inflation factor 1.124 (at the intersection of 6 percent and 2 years) and multiplies it by the current amount needed ($10,000) to determine the inflated amount needed ($11,240) in 2 years. Ellen thinks that her money-market fund will continue to pay an estimated return of 8 percent. Using Appendix A3, she finds the factor 2.080 for 2 years; this factor divided into the inflated amount needed ($11,240) gives an annual investment amount of $5404. Ellen calculates her third goal in a similar manner. Assuming that vacation costs will rise 8 percent (faster than 6 percent inflation), Ellen figures, using Appendix A1, that a $4000 trip will cost $5876 in 5 years. Using Appendix A3, she finds the factor 5.867 (at 8 percent and 5 years); this factor divided into the inflated amount needed ($5876) gives an annual investment amount of $1002. Adding together the three annual amounts ($1200 + $5404 + $1002) gives a total of $7606. This will require Ellen to put $634 a month ($7606/12) into her money-market account.

3. *Reevaluate your investment goals when necessary.* Because of her habit of spending virtually all her income each month, it may be difficult for Ellen to save $634 a month. She may have to cut back on entertainment, food, clothing, or even vacations. She may have to find another source of funds, perhaps a part-time job. Ellen might also want to change her investment goals. For example, if she drops the idea of a vacation, she would need $1002 less annually, or about $84 less a month. Or if she drops the goal of an automobile and continues to plan for a vacation, she would need only $184 a month ($1200 + $1002 = $2202/12 months).

Summary of Characteristics of Common Investment Alternatives

Objective
To be able to summarize descriptive characteristics of several common investment alternatives.

The next six chapters will examine alternative investments available to most investors. Table 15.7 summarizes the characteristics of each investment. As you read later chapters you may want to look back at this table for perspective on the alternatives.

TABLE 15.7
Characteristics of Common Investment Alternatives

	Financial Risk	Protection Against Inflation	Yield Range in Recent Years	Yields Relative to Alternative Investments	Relative Yields during Economic Prosperity	Yields during Economic Decline
Savings accounts	Low	None	4½–5½%	5½%	5½%	4½%
Savings bonds (EE and HH)	Low	None	5½–7%	6½%	6½%	5%
Certificates of deposit	Low	None	6½–9%	7½%	10%	6½%
Money market funds	Low	Some	6½–9½%	7%	10%	6½%
Cash-value insurance	Low	None	4–8½%	6%	8%	4%
Annuities	Low	None	4½–9%	6%	8½%	4½%
Treasury bills and notes	Low	None	6½–9%	7½%	8½%	6½%
Treasury bonds	Low	None	7½–10½%	8%	10%	7½%
Municipal bonds (best quality)	Low	None	5½–8%	5%	7½%	5½%
Corporate bonds (best quality)	Low	None	6½–9½%	8½%	9%	6½%
Corporate bonds (high quality)	Medium	None	7–11%	9%	10%	7%
Corporate (junk) bonds (low quality)	Medium to high	None	8–14%	10%	13%	8%
Common stocks	Medium to high	Good	0–20%	10%	20%	4%
Preferred stocks	Low to medium	Good	5–9%	7%	7%	5%
Mutual funds	Medium	Good	0–16%	10%	14%	7%
Real estate	Medium to high	Good	4–20%	12%	16%	4%
Real estate investment trust	High	Good	0–20%	10%	12%	5%
Precious metals, options and commodities	High	Good	0–30%	14%	18%	10%

Minimum Initial Investment Required	Personal Management Time Required	Illiquidity/ Maturity	How Many Years You Plan to Leave the Money Untouched		
			2 Years or Less	5 Years	10 Years or More
$1	None	Immediate to 90 days	×		
$25	Some	Varies with interest rates		×	
$200–$500	Some	30 days to 8 years	×	×	
$500	None	Immediate	×		
$200–$400	None	14 days	×	×	×
$10,000	None	1 month to 10 years		×	×
$10,000	Some	Immediate to 1 year	×	×	
$1000	Some	Immediate to 30 years	×	×	×
$1000	Some	Immediate to 30 years	×	×	×
$1000	Some	Immediate to 30 years	×	×	×
$1000	Some	Immediate to 30 years	×	×	×
$1000	Some to much	Immediate to 30 years	×	×	×
$100 or less	Some to much	1 to 2 weeks	×	×	×
$100 or less	Some	1 to 2 weeks		×	×
$100 or less	Some to much	1 to 2 weeks		×	×
$2000–$10,000	Much	2 weeks to 2 years		×	×
$5000	Some	1 month to 1 year		×	×
$500 or less	Much	A few days	×	×	

Summary

1. Investing requires an understanding of why people invest, what they should have accomplished before beginning to invest, how to figure investment returns, and how to get money to initially invest.

2. To achieve your investment goals, you need to determine the dollar amount of the goal and set the maturity date for the goal.

3. It is important to understand how you personally handle risk so that you can discover your own investment philosophy, whether it is conservative, moderate, or speculative.

4. You have two key decisions to make when choosing alternative investments: (a) Do you want to lend your money or own an asset? and (b) Do you want to invest for the short or long term? Then you can go about the process of comparing and choosing among alternative investments.

5. The major factors affecting the rate of return on investments include risk and yield relationship, various types of investment risks, and the concepts of diversification, leverage, taxes, and inflation.

6. When considering an alternative investment, you need to be able to determine what is a good return and how to calculate an investment's potential total return, including its approximate compound yield.

7. Steps necessary to achieve investment goals include, first, understanding and avoiding a number of things that cause people to fail financially, and second, doing what it takes to succeed, such as prioritizing your investment goals, calculating the annual amount of investment money you need, and reevaluating your investment goals when necessary.

8. Numerous investment alternatives are available to most investors that typically differ on such characteristics as protection against inflation, recent yields, relative yields during economic prosperity and decline, minimum initial investment required, personal time management required, illiquidity, marketability, and how many years you plan to leave the money untouched.

Modern
Money
Management

The Johnsons Want to Start an Investment Program

Harry and Belinda's finances have improved in recent months, even though they have incurred new debts for an automobile loan and a condominium. This has come about because they also cut back a little in their spending on discretionary items (clothing, food, and entertainment) and because Harry recently got a sizable raise after changing employers. The new job is assistant head designer at Medical Facilities Incorporated, which pays $6000 more than his other job, and it is 1 mile closer to home, which reduces Harry's commuting time.

The Johnsons have decided to concentrate on getting a solid investment program underway while they have two incomes available. They are willing to accept a moderate amount of risk and expect to invest between $200 and $400 a month over the next 5 years. Assuming that they have an adequate savings program, respond to the following questions.

1. In what types of investments (choose only two) might they place the first $2000 for that purpose? (Review Figure 15.3 and Tables 15.1 and 15.2 for available options, and consider the types of investment risks apparent in the options.) Give reasons for your choices.

2. In what types of investments might they place the next $4000 for that purpose? Why?

3. What types of investments should they choose for the next $10,000? Why?

4. If inflation is 6 percent and the Johnsons are in the 35 percent marginal tax bracket (including both federal and state taxes), what would their real return be if they earn 15 percent on their investment? Calculate the projected real return using the information on page 553 or the Personal Finance Cookbook (PFC) program REALRATE.

Key Words and Concepts

alternative investments, 535
annual average dividend, 554
approximate compound yield
    (ACY), 554
capital gain, 535
capital loss, 535
compound yield, 536
conservative investment
    philosophy, 540
current income, 535
deflation risk, 546
diversification, 547
dividends, 535
effective yield, 536
financial risk, 546
fixed income, 541
fixed maturity, 541
inflation risk, 545
interest, 535
interest-rate risk, 546
investment philosophy, 540

leverage, 549
liquidity, 547
liquidity risk, 547
market-volatility risk, 547
marketability risk, 547
moderate investment philosophy, 540
political risk, 547
potential total return, 553
principal, 535
random risk, 547
rate of return, 535
real return on investment, 551
rent, 535
return, 535
risk, 539
savings investments, 535
speculative investment
    philosophy, 541
speculative risk, 543
total return, 535
yield, 535

Review Questions

1. Identify the four reasons why most people are motivated to invest.
2. Name four prerequisites to investing.
3. Distinguish between savings and alternative investments.
4. Distinguish between current income and capital gain.
5. Name five ways you can get money to invest.
6. Give reasons why investment goals need to be specific.
7. What is the difference between an ultraconservative investor and the other types of investors?
8. Compare and contrast the three primary types of investment philosophies.
9. Describe the difference between lending investments and owning investments, and give examples of each.
10. Why do more investors make long-term rather than short-term, investments?
11. Explain the relationship between risk and knowledge of the future.
12. Tell why the investment return must be greater on a share of common stock than on a government bond.
13. Explain interest-rate risk.
14. Distinguish between illiquidity risk and marketability risk.
15. Explain how diversification works, and give an example.
16. Identify the advantage of using leverage in the investment process.
17. Give an example of how your marginal tax rate affects return on investments, citing both before- and after-tax yields.
18. How is the real return on an investment calculated, and why is it important to know?
19. Summarize the logic in knowing what a good return is on a stock investment.
20. Summarize the essence of how to figure the potential total return on an investment.
21. Summarize four major reasons why people fail financially.
22. Explain what it takes to succeed in investments.
23. Cite two examples of alternative investments that offer little protection against inflation and two that offer ample protection against inflation.

Case Problems

1. Gerald Beardsley of San Luis Obispo, California, has worked for 4 years for a large accounting firm. He has earned a fairly good income and has had bonuses of more than $1000 every year. Gerald feels frustrated because he has not started to make any investments. He simply seems to spend too much every month and has less than $400 in savings. Often

he has to get cash advances on his VISA card. Gerald owes the credit union at work more than $2000, which he borrowed to pay off some bills last summer. Following the prerequisites for investing, how would you advise Gerald on these matters?

a. Living within his means
b. Having a savings program
c. Having a line of credit
d. Having insurance protection

2. Susan Hayenga of Galveston, Texas, is hoping to continue her savings and investment program for 3 more years before making a down payment on a condominium. The home that interests her is currently priced at $70,000.

a. If inflation is 5 percent for each of the next 3 years, how much will the condominium probably cost? See Appendix A1 or use the Personal Finance Cookbook (PFC) program FVSUM. (See the section on time value of money in Chapter 1 on page 20.)
b. If she wants to make a 20 percent down payment, how much money will she need given the projected value of the condominium?
c. Should Susan invest her money during the next 3 years by lending or owning? Why?

3. John Knox of Fennimore, Wisconsin, has a sister, Kate, who is dissatisfied with the low rate of return she is earning on the $4000 in her savings account, and she has asked John for advice. Kate says that she is a bit nervous about risky things and would not want to lose any of her money in some foolish venture. Further she says she views the $4000 as money for long-term investment, perhaps even to be used in her retirement years. She has been told by a friend at work to consider investing in bonds or common stocks. If you were John, explain how you would advise your sister about the following:

a. The financial risk of bonds and common stocks
b. Interest-rate risk
c. Liquidity risk
d. Kate thinks she can earn a total annual return of 18 percent with common stocks, 12 percent with corporate bonds, and 6 percent with her savings account. If inflation is 5 percent and Kate is in the 28 percent federal marginal tax bracket, what would her real return be? Calculate the projected real return using the information on page 553 or the Personal Finance Cookbook (PFC) program REALRATE. Are Kate's concerns realistic?

4. Richard Ellis, a family counselor in Charlotte, North Carolina, is thinking about investing the $2000 gift his uncle gave him. Perhaps you can help him with some questions about return.

a. How much will Richard's real return be (after taxes and inflation) if he earns a 14 percent total return on a stock investment this year, assuming inflation is 5 percent and he is in the 28 percent marginal tax bracket? Use the information on page 553 or the Personal Finance Cookbook (PFC) program REALRATE.

b. How much will Richard's real return be if he earns a 16 percent total return on the investment? Use the information on page 553 or the Personal Finance Cookbook (PFC) program REALRATE.

 c. If Richard invests the money in the stock earning a taxable return of 14 percent, how would the tax-exempt yield compare if instead he put the money into a tax-exempt government bond paying 9 percent. Use the information on page 299 or the Personal Finance Cookbook (PFC) program TAXEQUIV.

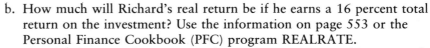 d. What would the tax-exempt yield on the 16 percent stock investment compare if instead Richard put the money into a tax-exempt government bond paying 10.5 percent? Use the information on page 299 or the Personal Finance Cookbook (PFC) program TAXEQUIV.

Suggested Readings

"Battling Your Broker Just Got Easier." *Business Week*, June 5, 1989, p. 142. Explains new SEC rules on conflict of interest for arbitrations between brokers and investors.

"Big Ideas for Your Small Business." *Changing Times*, November 1989, pp. 57–60. Growth of small companies will continue sharply upward.

"Building Your Own Portfolio." *Nation's Business*, April 1989, p. 30. How to build a diversified portfolio of investments to reduce risk and increase your overall return.

"Clubs Where Your Dues Can Pay Dividends." *Business Week*, September 21, 1989, pp. 102–103. Explores the benefits of investment clubs.

"How Are You Doing?" *Money*, October 1989, pp. 78–81. How to check your investment performance against other small investors and the professionals.

"Investing for the 1990s." *Business Week*, November 16, 1989, pp. 91–119. Cover story on the likely best investment strategies for the coming decade.

"Investing in Europe: The Time Is Now." *Changing Times*, January 1990, pp. 65–71. Bargains and niches are available now for good investments in European companies.

"Investments That Beat Inflation and Recession." *Money*, May 1990, pp. 104–114. Investment choices that will be successful in times of economic difficulty.

"Just How Safe Is That Guaranteed Investment?" *Money*, March 1990, pp. 123–132. Review of who, if anybody, really backs up the so-called guaranteed investments.

"Learning to Invest with Confidence." *Working Woman*, December 1989, pp. 61–65. How four women improved their investment skills.

"Low-Stress Investments for the Decade Ahead." *Changing Times*, November 1989, pp. 29–35. Investing in a healthy world economy in the 1990s whether you have $5000 or $100,000 to invest.

"No Pain, No Gain." *Working Woman,* June 1990, pp. 42–44. Investing tips from Wall Street wizards.

"Outlook: Investing." *Changing Times,* January 1989, pp. 40–47. Forecasts for investors in the decade of the 1990s.

"7 Deadly Investment Sins and How to Avoid Them." *Changing Times,* July 1989, pp. 54–58. The common errors and how to avoid them.

"30 Ways to Invest $1,000," *Changing Times,* August 1990, pp. 46–52. Brief descriptions and projected returns on numerous investment alternatives.

"Tips for Long-Term Savers," *U.S. News & World Report,* July 30, 1990, p. 50. How stocks and bonds outperform savings.

"Top Ways to Invest for Income Now." *Money,* April 1990, pp. 117–126. Alternatives to lock in high yields before rates drop.

"What to Do with a Windfall." *Changing Times,* November 1989, pp. 93–98. What to do with sums from lotteries, distributions from retirement plans, and legacies.

"Where to Invest Your Money Now." *Money,* July 1989, pp. 60–73. Series of articles on good investments for those with $1000, $10,000, or $25,000 or more.

"Where to Put Your Money." *Changing Times,* January 1990, pp. 32–37. Suggestions of alternative places to invest your money.

"Where to Put Your Money in 1990." *Money,* December 1989, pp. 70–121. Series of articles on where to invest your money during times of economic volatility and recession.

"Winning Investors Know Their Returns." *Money,* September 1989, pp. 149–150. How to calculate performance.

16

Investing in Stocks

OBJECTIVES

After reading this chapter, you should be able to

1. Explain what stocks are and how they are used by corporations and investors.

2. Understand the three primary concerns of stock investors: investment income, price appreciation, and total return.

3. Define more than a dozen everyday terms in the language of stock investing.

4. Classify stocks according to their basic descriptive categories.

5. Discuss the three primary theories about what affects the price of stocks: efficient-market theory, technical theory, and fundamental theory.

6. Describe advantages and disadvantages of owning common stock.

7. List guidelines for when investors should consider selling stocks.

8. Explain what kind of investor would want to invest in preferred stock.

After you have accumulated a certain amount of savings, your good feeling of financial security may be accompanied by a new sense of frustration. If inflation is higher than the after-tax rate of return on savings accounts, you will realize that you are losing ground. Even if inflation is just less than the after-tax yield on savings, you will be gaining by only a very small amount. Consequently, you may begin to think about increasing risk so as to increase yield. If you increase your knowledge about investments and choose investment alternatives with common sense, you can increase returns significantly while increasing risk only slightly.

Common stocks are investments that provide opportunities for conservative, moderate, and speculative investors. This chapter begins by examining what stocks are and how they are used. We then discuss the three primary concerns of stock investors: investment income, price appreciation, and total return. A review of important investment terms follows. Next we discuss the basic classifications of stocks (such as growth stocks) as well as some theories about what affects the price of stocks. Then a section on the advantages and disadvantages of common stocks is provided to help you discover whether they are for you. This is followed by some guidelines for selling stock. Finally, the chapter examines preferred stocks and the individual investor.

What Stocks Are and How They Are Used

Objective
To be able to explain what stocks are and how they are used by corporations and investors.

Stocks are shares of ownership in the assets and earnings of a business corporation. Stocks are sold to investors to finance corporate goals. Stocks represent potential income for investors, since stockholders own a piece of the future direction of the company. People who own stocks typically expect that (1) the corporation will be profitable enough to pay **dividends** (a share of profits distributed in cash) and that (2) there will be an increase in the **market value** (or **market price**) of the stock held, which is the current price that a buyer is willing to pay a willing seller.

Forms of Business Ownership

There are three forms of business ownership. The **sole proprietorship** is a business owned by one person who is responsible for and has control over all aspects of the operation. Net profits earned are taxed as ordinary income, and the owner's liability for business losses is unlimited. Most small businesses are run as sole proprietorships. Since the business could fail on the death of the proprietor, he or she should provide for future management of the firm in a legally executed will. This topic is examined in Chapter 23, Estate Planning.

A **partnership** is a business owned by two or more persons and operated in the interests of all partners. Net profits earned are normally taxed as ordinary income, and the owners' liability for business losses is usually unlimited. The benefits of having a partner include being able to obtain more capital to run the business, getting additional expertise, and a sharing of the business risks. A contract called the **articles of partnership** defines responsibilities and restrictions and how profits and losses are to be divided. A partnership may be dissolved upon the request of any partner to withdraw as well as for reasons of incapacitation or death.

A **corporation** is a state-chartered legal entity that can conduct business operations in its own name and be totally responsible for its actions as well as its debts. Net profits earned are taxed at corporate income tax rates. Corporations sell shares of ownership (stock) to investors and thus have the potential to raise large sums of money for expansion. An investor's liability is limited to the amount of stock purchased. Corporations continue to exist even as the shares of ownership change hands. Since a corporation may have a great number of investors, this form of business ownership offers a company the potential to develop into a firm of considerable size.

The corporate form of ownership can raise vast sums of capital by selling securities.

Types of Corporate Stocks Sold to Investors

A corporation's financial needs may differ from time to time. To begin business, a new corporation will need money for startup **capital** (funds invested in a business enterprise). During its life, a corporation may need additional monies to expand and grow. To raise capital and finance its goals, a corporation issues three different types of **securities** (negotiable instruments of ownership or debt): common stock, preferred stock, and bonds. Common stock and preferred stock are securities discussed in this chapter, whereas bonds are examined in the next chapter.

Common Stock **Common stock** is the most basic form of ownership of a corporation. The owner of common stock—called a **shareholder** or **stockholder**—has a residual claim on the assets of the firm after those made by bondholders and preferred stockholders (discussed later). Sale of common stock conveys legal ownership of such shares to the shareholder. With common stock, one share usually represents one part ownership of any earnings distributed as dividends. A corporation may have one owner/ shareholder or have millions of shares owned by numerous owners/ shareholders. Each shareholder has a proportionate interest in the ownership and therefore in the income of the corporation. For example, if you own 200 shares of a company that declares a $5 million dividend to be paid on 2 million outstanding shares, you will receive $2.50 per share, or $500 [($5,000,000/2,000,000) × 200].

Each shareholder may vote to elect a board of directors, which names the principal officers of the company to set policy and run the day-to-day business of the firm. The number of votes each shareholder has depends on the number of shares owned. A shareholder's liability for business losses is limited to the amount invested in the shares of stock owned. In the case of bankruptcy, the common stockholder's equity is what is left after the claims of all debtors are met. This risk of loss is offset by the potential to share in substantial profits when the corporation does well.

Common stockholders can only lose the amount of their investment— nothing more.

Preferred Stock   **Preferred stock** is a special type of fixed-income ownership security in a corporation. Preferred stockholders have the legal right to assets and earnings before the claims of common stockholders but after those of bondholders. Generally, preferred stock pays a fixed dividend per share that must be paid before any dividends are made to common stockholders. Usually, preferred stockholders have no voting privileges (unless preferred stock dividends are in default) and they do not share in any extraordinary profits made by a corporation.

The Three Primary Concerns of Stock Investors

Objective
To be able to understand the three primary concerns of stock investors.

Three factors are of particular concern to stock investors: (1) investment income, (2) price appreciation, and (3) total return. These are discussed below and then illustrated in an example.

Investment Income

The revenues of a profitable corporation generally are used to pay expenses, interest to bondholders, taxes, cash dividends to preferred stockholders, and cash dividends to common stockholders, in that order. The average corporation pays out 40 to 60 percent of its after-tax earnings in cash dividends to stockholders; the remainder, called **retained earnings,** is used by the company most often to facilitate growth.

Cash dividends to preferred stockholders are a set amount per share and often remain the same each year despite good or bad economic conditions. The common stockholder has no guarantee of dividends. Most profitable companies pay common stockholders a small regular dividend on a quarterly basis until increased earnings justify paying out a higher amount. On a $30 share of Greenfield Computer's common stock, for example, the dividend for several past years might have been 30 cents quarterly, or a total of $1.20 annually. If the company has higher profits this year, the dividend might be raised to $1.90 annually. It is this cash dividend, or more accurately, the anticipation of it, that is of interest to a potential investor. In recent years, the rate of return from cash dividends on common stocks that paid dividends has ranged from 3.5 to 5.0 percent.

Cash dividends average only 3.5 to 5.0 percent.

Price Appreciation

Given the low rate of return in cash dividends relative to savings accounts, you may wonder why people invest in stock. There are two reasons. First, as a company becomes more efficient and profitable, the cash dividend to common stockholders can rise. Second, the market value of the stock also can go up as more investors become interested in the profitable and growing company. Remember that stock is a share of ownership, so as the company grows, so grows the value or price of its stock.

Total Return

Total return includes both cash dividends and capital gains.

Many investors in common stocks look only at the amount of cash dividend that a corporation has paid in recent years rather than also at the potential for capital gains upon later sale of the stock. (Preferred stockholders rarely share in capital appreciation, since their stock pays a fixed dividend.) **Total return** is the combination of the dividend paid *and* the price appreciation. (The latter is also called *capital gains.*)

Let's see how dividends and price appreciation result in total return when combined. The **dividend yield** is the cash dividend return to an investor expressed as a percentage of the value of a security. It is determined by dividing the dollar amount of a recent annual dividend by the current market value of the stock or purchase price if the stock is already owned. Say that Greenfield Computer's preferred stock, currently selling at $104, has an annual dividend of $8, which is a preferred stock cash dividend yield of 7.69 percent ($8/$104). Greenfield's common stock is now selling for $30 and its recent quarterly cash dividend suggests an annual dividend of $1.90; this would provide a common stock cash dividend yield of 6.3 percent ($1.90/$30).

You do not have a real profit until you actually sell.

The **capital gain** or **price appreciation** (net income received from the sale of capital assets beyond the expenses incurred in the purchase and sale of those assets) is actually realized when the stock is sold. Until then, such gains are known as paper profits. A **paper profit** (or **paper loss**) is an unrealized profit or loss on an investment still held. Paper profits and losses become realized only when the investment is sold. If you purchased Greenfield common stock at $30 a share and sold it at $35 a share, you realized a capital gain of $5 a share. Assuming that you bought 200 shares for a commission of $60, your cost would have been $6060 ($30 × 200 + $60). If you sold at $35 per share and paid $70 sales commission, the proceeds would be $6930 ($35 × 200 − $70). Your capital gain is thus $870 ($6930 − $6060). Based on the invested amount of $6060, the capital gain of $870 represents a 14.4 percent yield ($870/$6060). Thus, if you sell your Greenfield common stock after 1 year, the return would include $870 in capital gains plus $380 in cash dividends (200 shares × $1.90) for a total return of $1250, or a 20.6 percent yield on $6060 invested.

An alternative would be to hold the shares in anticipation of a further increase in the market value of the stock. The price of Greenfield stock could rise to $38 in the next several months. Of course, the price could also drop to $31 and reduce your gain, or it could drop to $29 and result in a capital loss if you sold the stock. Suggestions on how to project an investment's total potential return are offered in Chapter 15; more details are provided in Chapter 19.

Example: Running Paws Catfood Company   To visualize better how a corporation finances corporate goals with common and preferred stock while achieving returns for stockholders, consider the following illustration. Running Paws Catfood Company, a small family business, was started in New Jersey by Linda Webtek. She developed a wonderful recipe for catfood and sold the product to the local grocery store. As sales increased, she decided to incorporate the business and to expand operations. Running Paws issued 10,000 shares of stock at $10 each. Three friends bought 2500 shares each, and Linda signed over the catfood formula and equipment to the corporation itself in exchange for the remaining 2500 shares. Running Paws then had $75,000 in working capital (7500 shares sold at $10 each), a four-person board of directors, and each person began working for the firm, although they paid themselves very low salaries.

Capacity quickly expanded, and sales increased. Soon more orders were coming in from New York City than the firm could handle. After 3 years, the owners of Running Paws decided to expand again. They needed an additional $100,000. They wanted to borrow it, but their business was so new and uncertain that lenders demanded an extremely high interest rate. They considered issuing bonds as debts of the corporation, but again they found that their new business was viewed as quite risky for investors to consider making a loan through the purchase of bonds. They then decided to issue 5000 shares of preferred stock at $20 a share, paying $1.20 a share annually. When they found that no one wanted to buy preferred shares with that yield ($1.20/$20 = 6 percent), they voted to increase the dividend to $1.80 annually, providing a 9 percent yield to investors. The preferred stock was sold to some outsider investors; however, the original investors retained control of the company with their common stock because the preferred stockholders could not vote for the board of directors.

Following its consistent philosophy of expanding into new markets, Running Paws soon developed new lines of catfood, which sold well. After a new plant in Los Angeles opened, sales picked up so much that the income of the 4-year-old business finally exceeded expenses. That year it earned $13,000. The board of directors declared a dividend payment of $9000 to the preferred stockholders, but none for the common stockholders. The following year, net profits after taxes amounted to $28,000. Again the board paid the preferred stockholders but retained the remainder to be reinvested in the firm for continued expansion and efficiency of operations.

One of the original partners wanted out of the business and needed to sell her 2500 shares of stock, for which she had paid $25,000 five years earlier. Fortunately, because Running Paws was beginning to show some profits as a corporation, two other private investors recommended by a local stockbroker made offers to purchase her shares. The shares were sold at $16 a share: 1500 to one investor and 1000 to another. Thus the original investor gained $15,000 in price appreciation ($16 × 2500 = $40,000 − $25,000) when she sold out. (Of course, the corporation did not profit from this transaction.) Now there were five owners of the common stock, including the two new ones, who voted for the board of directors.

During the following year, sales were up again and earnings amounted to $39,000. This time the board voted $9000 for the preferred stockholders and $5000 ($0.50 a share) for the common stockholders and retained the remaining $25,000. After all these years, the common stockholders finally began to receive some cash dividends.

With all its success, Running Paws faced another difficult decision. To distribute its products nationally would mean another $200,000 to $250,000 in expansion costs. After much discussion, the board voted to sell an additional 10,000 shares of common stock at $25 a share. This action diluted the owners' proportion of ownership by half, but the potential for profit was considered to be much higher with such an increased production capacity.

It took several months to sell all the new common stock at $25 a share, because so few people knew the company had stock available for sale. Various local stockbrokers also took selling commissions totaling $16,000, leaving $234,000 available to use for expansion. If things continue well for Running Paws, the board might work toward having its stock listed on a regional or national stock exchange to facilitate trading of shares and further enhance the image of the company.

It may take several years for a new corporation to begin paying dividends.

The Language of Stock Investing

Objective
To be able to define more than a dozen everyday terms in the language of stock investing.

Before you study stocks as an investment, you need to understand the everyday terms in the language of stock investing. Some of these terms describe ways of measuring investments, and others describe important concepts.

Earnings per Share (EPS)

EPS measures the profitability of a company.

Earnings per share (*EPS*) indicates the amount of income a company has, on a per-share basis, to pay dividends and reinvest in itself as retained earnings. *EPS* is a dollar figure determined by dividing the corporation's total after-tax annual earnings (before common stock cash dividends but after payment of dividends to preferred stockholders) by the total number of shares of common stock held by investors. It is a useful measure of the profitability of a firm on a common stock per-share basis because investors can compare the financial conditions of companies. Usually, companies calculate this figure and report it in the business section of many newspapers. For example, assume that after payment of dividends to preferred stockholders, Running Paws Catfood Company has a net profit of $34,000. With 20,000 shares of company stock, the *EPS* would be $1.70 ($34,000/20,000). Thus Running Paws has that amount available for common stockholders, although a portion is typically retained to finance growth of the business.

Price/Earnings Ratio (P/E Ratio)

The price/earnings ratio tells how much investors are willing to pay for future earnings.

The **price/earnings ratio** *(P/E ratio* or *P/E multiple*) is a popular way to compare stocks selling at various price levels. It is a ratio of the current market value (price) of a common stock to its earnings per share (*EPS*), which indicates how many times a stock's selling price is greater than its earnings per share. The *P/E* multiple shows in ratio form how the market is valuing the stock because it describes the amount of money investors are willing to pay for each dollar of a company's earnings. Further, it is a measure of investor confidence in a stock's future over the next 5 years or so. For example, if the market price of a share of Running Paws stock is currently $25 and its *EPS* is $1.70, the *P/E* ratio will be 15 ($25/$1.70 = 14.7, which is rounded up to 15). This also could be called a *15-to-1 ratio* or a *P/E multiple of 15*. The price/earnings ratio or multiple for many corporations is also widely reported as financial news. In general, low *P/E* stocks tend to have higher dividend yields, less risk, lower prices, and a slower earnings growth rate. To effectively use a company's *P/E* ratio, compare it with other *P/E* ratios for firms in the same industry.

The only valid reasons for buying stock in a company are to realize income from dividends, capital gains, or both. The company must have earnings out of which to pay cash dividends and/or the market value of the stock needs to rise over time. The *P/E* ratios for most corporations have ranged between 5 and 25. Financially successful companies that have been paying good dividends through the years might have a *P/E* ratio of 7 or 8. Firms that are expected to have strong earnings growth generally have a higher stock price and *P/E* ratio. Companies that are rapidly growing, such as Running Paws, would most likely have a much higher *P/E* ratio. Speculative companies might have *P/E* ratios of 40 or 50, since they have or are expected to have a much higher than average earnings growth rate. In general, a *P/E* ratio that is half the company's anticipated growth rate is quite positive, while one that is twice the company's anticipated growth rate may be a bad sign. This is because stocks with a high *P/E* ratio carry the risk of a quickly falling price if the company's earnings do not grow as vigorously as projected.

Cash Dividends per Share

Cash dividends are distributions in cash by a corporation usually paid out of earnings to holders of common stock. The board of directors of a firm usually declares a dividend on a quarterly basis according to the fiscal year, typically at the end of March, June, September, and December. Dividends are ordinarily paid out of current earnings. In the event of unprofitable times, the money could come from previous earnings. Occasionally, a company will borrow to pay the dividend in order to maintain a reputation of consistently paying dividends to its stockholders. Of course, later profits will be needed to repay any funds borrowed.

Dividends per share translate total cash dividends paid out by a company to common stockholders into a per-share figure. For example, Running Paws Catfood Company could declare a total cash dividend of $11,000 for the year. Thus cash dividends per share amount to $0.55 ($11,000/ 20,000 shares). The dividend yield also can be determined. For example, the $0.55 cash dividend of Running Paws Catfood Company divided by the current $25 market price reveals a dividend yield of 2.2 percent ($0.55/ $25). Growth and speculative companies typically pay little or no cash dividend.

Dividend Payout Ratio

Newer companies have low payout ratios.

The **dividend payout ratio** is a measure of the percentage of total earnings paid out to stockholders as cash dividends. For example, Running Paws Catfood Company earned $34,000 (after paying preferred stockholders), paid out a cash dividend of $11,000 to company stockholders, and retained the remaining $23,000 to facilitate growth of the company. This is a dividend payout ratio of 0.32 ($11,000/$34,000). For that year, Running Paws paid a dividend equal to 32 percent of earnings. The remaining $23,000 is called retained earnings. These are amounts of past and current earnings not paid to shareholders but instead left to accumulate and finance the goals of the company. Newer companies usually retain most if not all of their profits to facilitate growth. An investor interested in growth would want to invest in a company with a low payout ratio. The lower the payout ratio, the greater are the odds that the company's earnings will sustain future dividend payments.

Price/Sales Ratio

The price/sales ratio tells how good a buy a particular stock is at today's price.

The **price/sales ratio** (*PSR*) is a ratio obtained by dividing the total current market value of a stock (current market price multiplied by the number of shares outstanding) by the corporate revenue over the past year. It is a measure of how good a buy a particular stock is at its current market price. For example, if Running Paws Catfood Company common stock is selling for $25 per share and there are 20,000 shares outstanding, the total current market value is $500,000. If revenues of the company were $750,000 over the past year, the stock's *PSR* is 0.67 ($500,000/$750,000). The lower the ratio, the better is the marketability of the stock. Market analysts generally suggest that investors avoid companies with a ratio greater than 1.5 and stay with those which have *PSR*s of less than 0.75.

Book Value and Price-to-Book Ratio

Book value is the net worth of a company, determined by subtracting the total of a company's liabilities (including preferred stock) from its assets. It is also known as *shareholder's equity* because it theoretically indicates a company's worth if assets were sold, its debts paid off, and the net proceeds distributed to shareholders.

Book value per share is the book value of a company divided by the number of shares of common stock outstanding. For Running Paws, the net worth is $230,000, which when divided by 20,000 shares gives a book value per share of $11.50. This figure is particularly relevant in the case of bankruptcy, when the firm would be liquidated. Often there is little relationship between the book value of a company and its earnings or market price. Note, though, that the market price for a company's common stock is usually higher than its book value.

The **price-to-book ratio** is a ratio of the current price (market value) of a common stock to its book value per share. The current price-to-book ratio for most stocks is 2.1 to 1.0. If the ratio is less than one, something is wrong with the usefulness of the assets, and in such cases, an under-performing and undervalued company may become a target of a corporate takeover.

Par Value

Historically, **par value** meant the dollar amount assigned to a share of stock by the company's charter when it was issued by a corporation. Par value is sometimes printed on the front of a share of common stock. Many people have falsely assumed that this was a minimum price, but par value bears no relation to the current market value of common stock. Today, common stocks are issued at **no par** (zero par value) or at **low par** (usually $1 or $2). Many companies issue no-par common stock but give a stated value per share on the balance sheet for accounting purposes.

Par value on a common stock is meaningless.

In the case of preferred stocks, par value signifies the dollar value upon which dividends are paid. After issuance, the price of preferred stocks may rise or fall, but dividends paid are calculated on the original par value.

Market Value or Market Price

The market value or market price of an investment is the current price that a willing buyer would pay a willing seller for the asset. Sales commissions are not included. In stock transactions, the market value is the current price of a single share of stock. This may be estimated by looking at prices quoted in financial newspapers, as shown in Chapter 19, Buying and Selling Securities and Managing Your Portfolio. *True market value* is the price you actually receive when selling an investment or pay when buying an investment. For example, if Running Paws stock has recently been selling at $25 a share, this is its market value on paper. The true market value at the exact time you sell your Running Paws stock might be $24 a share.

Beta

An important aspect of a common stock is a characteristic called **beta,** which is a measure of an investment's price stability or volatility in relation to the market for similar investments as a whole. For stocks, this is a statistically determined measure of the relative risk of a common stock compared with the market for all stocks. The historical performance of each stock has been examined in relation to stock market averages. The average for all stocks in the market is +1.0. Betas can be positive or negative. Most are positive because most stocks move in the same direction as the general market.

Historically, all stocks combined have a beta of +1.0.

Most individual stocks have betas of between +0.5 and +2.0. A beta of zero suggests that the price of the stock is independent of the market, similar to a risk-free U.S. Treasury security. A beta of zero to +0.9 means that the stock price moves in the same direction as the general market but not quite to the same degree. A beta of +1.1 to +2.0 (or higher) indicates that the price of the security moves in the same direction as the market but by a greater percentage.

For an example, assume that you are willing to accept more risk than the general investor and you buy a stock with a beta of 1.5. If the average price of all stocks rises over time by 20 percent, it is probable that the price of the stock you chose will rise by 30 percent, which is the beta of 1.5 multiplied by the increase in the market (1.5 × 20 percent). Should the average market drop in value by 10 percent, the price of the stock you chose might drop by 15 percent (1.5 × 10 percent).

Note that the statistical averages used by brokerage firms, advisory services, and other investment companies to determine the betas for individual stocks assume that each stock is owned along with a well-diversified portfolio of other stocks. A **portfolio** is a collection of securities and other instruments. Also, the performance of just one particular stock with a certain beta may be in error compared with its historical activity. On the other hand, if you own several stocks, the betas as a group are more likely to be reliable estimates of price volatility. If you own 20 different stocks, for example, it is likely that the beta for the entire portfolio will be a good indicator of volatility. This would be even more likely for a large institutional investor than for an individual because the institution can own hundreds of different stocks.

Preemptive Rights

Most common stockholders have a **preemptive right** to purchase additional shares in the company, frequently at a discount from the market price and before shares are offered to the public, so that they can maintain their proportionate ownership interest. Thus new issues of common stock may have to be offered to the current stockholders before being sold to the public.

Stock Dividends

A **stock dividend** is a dividend paid in securities instead of cash. The dividend may be additional shares of the issuing company or shares of another company (usually a subsidiary) held by the issuing company. Shares are distributed to existing stockholders on the basis of current proportional ownership. For example, the board of directors of Running Paws could decide to declare a 10 percent stock dividend to stockholders who currently own the 20,000 shares outstanding. Thus, if you owned 2000 shares, the company would mail you an additional 200 shares. If you owned 55 shares, the company would mail you 5 shares and ask how you would like to handle the value of the remaining half share. You might have the option of either receiving the cash equivalent of the half share or paying for an additional half share so that you could receive 6 full shares.

Many people incorrectly assume that when they receive a stock dividend the value of their holdings increases. Although the price of the stock might rise for a day or so after a stock dividend is declared, it then corrects for the additional shares of stock now available and drops accordingly. Assume that the 20,000 shares of Running Paws stock are currently valued at $25 per share and last year paid a cash dividend of $0.55. With a stock dividend of 10 percent, there are now 22,000 shares of ownership. If you had owned 2000 shares of the 20,000 total, you would have owned 10 percent of the company. After the stock dividend, you own 2200 shares out of a total of 22,000. You still own exactly 10 percent.

Stock dividends do not change the value of each stockholder's investment.

The value of a company is not affected by a stock dividend, although the value of each share is. For example, suppose Running Paws continues to pay a $0.55 per share cash dividend the year following a 10 percent stock dividend. To do this will require greater earnings because the company will by paying out $12,100 rather than $11,000, a cash dividend 10 percent greater than the previous year. Alternatively, the company could have kept the number of shares at 20,000 and simply increased the cash dividend by 10 percent. Some companies offer stock dividends knowing that some stockholders will think they have gained something of value. The result of a stock dividend is to slightly dilute stock ownership and reduce the market price of the stock by a like percentage while not changing the actual value of each stockholder's investment.

Stock Splits

A **stock split** is a trade of a given number of old shares of stock for a certain number of newly issued shares. A two-for-one stock split usually results in a 100 percent increase in the number of shares outstanding and a 50 percent reduction in cash dividends per share. For example, in a two-for-one stock split at Running Paws, the owners of the 22,000 shares (remember the 10 percent stock dividend) would be issued 44,000 new shares. If the market price of the old stock was $22.50 per share, the new stock will be worth approximately $11.25, or 50 percent, since the number of shares was doubled. A three-for-one or a three-for-two stock split also might occur.

The net effect of a stock split is threefold: (1) no change in the proportion of ownership held by the original stockholders, (2) no change in the proportion of cash dividends per share, and (3) a sharp change in the market price of the stock.

A stock split may make the stock more attractive to investors.

A company whose stock is selling at $90 per share might want to have a stock split to reduce the market price to $45 (two for one) or even $30 (three for one) to encourage more investors to buy and sell stock. Stock splits, therefore, can have the effect of opening up trading to a greater number of investors. For this reason, stock splits ordinarily require the consent of the board of directors and a two-thirds approval by the current stockholders. A *reverse stock split* is opted for when a company wishes to increase the market price of its stock. For example, a company with stock selling at $10 per share could have a one-for-three or one-for-four reverse split to increase the price per share to $30 or $40. Because investors generally view a stock split as a sign of management's confidence in the company, the price of a stock often rises again after its initial adjustment for the split.

Voting Rights

Owners of common stock normally have **voting rights.** This is the proportionate authority to express an opinion or choice in matters affecting the company. Each share of common stock gives the holder one vote. (Very rarely does a company issue nonvoting common stock.) At the annual meeting of the company, the board of directors is elected (or reelected) and matters of special interest are voted on. Each stockholder gets an opportunity to take part in these activities by either attending the meeting or voting by **proxy.** This is written authorization given by a shareholder to someone else to represent him or her and to vote his or her shares at a stockholders meeting. (It is usually easier to vote by mail through a proxy than to attend the meeting in person.) In reality, most issues facing a corporation are foreseen by the board of directors, which then obtains control, by means of proxies, of a large voting bloc to ensure that its desires are met. On rare occasion, a *proxy battle* occurs, as two competing forces (often the existing board of directors and an outsider group perhaps seeking a merger or buyout) actively seek the individual voting rights (proxies) of each stockholder to gain control of the company. In such instances, the competing forces write letters to stockholders soliciting their proxies.

Most individual stock-holders cast their votes by proxy.

Four Basic Classifications of Common Stock

Objective
To be able to classify stocks according to their basic descriptive categories.

Although the terminology is imprecise, many investment brokers, securities analysts, and individual investors find it helpful to group certain stocks according to specific characteristics. This is an aid when matching an investor's preferences with stock investment options.

There are four basic classifications of stock: (1) income stocks, (2) growth stocks (well known), (3) growth stocks (lesser known), and (4) speculative stocks. In addition, other terms are used to characterize classifications.

Income Stocks

Income stocks pay higher than average dividends.

An **income stock** has a cash dividend that is higher than average year after year because the company has fairly high earnings and chooses to declare high cash dividends regularly and retain only a small portion of the earnings. This requires the company to have a steady stream of income, as do, for instance, utility companies. Stocks issued by telephone, electric, and gas companies are normally labeled income stocks. Investors in these companies usually are not too concerned with the P/E ratio or the growth potential of the value of the stock. Betas are often less than 1.0. Elderly or retired persons often are interested in income stocks.

Growth Stocks (Well Known)

Growth stocks (well known) emphasize growth over income.

Stock of a company with a record of growth in earnings at a relatively rapid rate is described as **growth stock**. The return to investors from growth stocks comes primarily from increases in share price. Such stocks typically pay little or no dividends because most of their earnings are used to keep the company growing.

Stocks of companies that are leaders in their fields and have several consecutive years of above-industry-average earnings are considered **growth stocks (well known)**. Such companies grow rapidly and retain most of their earnings (usually about 75 percent) to assist that growth. Investor awareness of such corporations is widespread, and expectations of continued growth are high. The P/E ratio is high, too. Many growth stocks have a glamorous reputation that improves or declines sharply with the market. Thus they often have betas of 1.5 or more. Investors generally seem to prefer growth stocks of well-known companies, since they typically offer some dividends and a good opportunity for price appreciation. In the past, well-known growth stocks were offered by such companies as Pepsico, Abbott Laboratories, Apple Computer, and Xerox.

Growth Stocks (Lesser Known)

Some excellent companies that are not necessarily the industry giants have had higher-than-industry-average earnings in recent years and have good

Growth stocks (lesser known) offer clear opportunities for profit.

prospects for the future. They are considered **growth stocks (lesser known).** Since they are not the most popular with investors, their *P/E* ratios are generally lower than those of the more glamorous, well-known growth stocks (although the *P/E* ratios are still high), such as MCI, Walmart, Tandy, and Activision. Often such firms are regional businesses with strong earnings, such as Popeye's Chicken in the South. Others may be the third- or fourth-leading firm in an industry or may have less name recognition, such as Wendy's, Cray Research, and The Limited, Inc. Their betas are usually 1.5 or more.

Speculative Stocks

Speculative stocks are for those who like risk.

A **speculative stock** may have a spotty earnings record or be so new that no pattern has emerged but has an apparent potential for substantial earnings at some time in the future, even though such earnings may never be realized. Investors in these types of firms take a bit of a chance, since the recent history of earnings and dividends is likely to be poor or very inconsistent. Investors in speculative stocks rank the safety of their principal as a secondary factor. With little or no dividends anticipated, the investor hopes that the company will make a new discovery or invent a new product or generate some type of valuable information that later may push up the price of the stock and result in substantial capital gains.

Examples of speculative companies include computer-graphics and videogame companies, small oil businesses, genetic engineering firms, and some drug manufacturers. The *P/E* ratio fluctuates widely along with the fortunes of the company, and a beta above 2.0 is common. For every speculative company that succeeds there are many others that do poorly or fail. The investor willing to accept little or no dividends and a high risk of financial loss might consider such an investment.

Other Characterizing Terms

A variety of other terms are used to better describe particular stocks within the four basic classifications. These include *blue-chip, cyclical,* and *countercyclical* or *defensive.* A **blue-chip stock** indicates a company with a well-regarded reputation, dominant in its industry, with a long history both of good earnings and consistent cash dividends, growing about the same rate as the economy, and whose shares are widely held by individual investors and institutions. The earnings of blue-chip companies (usually an income stock or well-known growth stock) are expected to grow at a consistent but unspectacular rate because these firms are the leaders in their industries and are usually the most stable of firms. Examples are J. C. Penney, Du Pont, and H. J. Heinz. Investing in such companies is considered much less risky than investing in other firms.

Cyclical stocks basically move with the general direction of the economy.

A **cyclical stock** is that issued by a company whose profits are greatly influenced by changes in the business cycle of the economy. For example, when the economy is strong, housing and automobile stocks do well. The market prices of cyclical stocks typically mirror the general state of the economy and the various phases of the business cycle. During times of prosperity and economic expansion, the company's earnings are high; during a recession, earnings decline sharply. Examples are stocks of firms in the basic industries: housing, automobiles, steel, and heavy machinery. Of course, many blue-chip, income, growth, and speculative stocks also can be described as cyclical stocks. Most cyclical stocks have a beta of about 1.0. Investors buying cyclical stocks should necessarily aim to buy at or near the bottom of a recession and sell at a high point during the expansionary days of prosperity before the price begins to slide downward again.

You should buy a cyclical stock during a recession and sell it when economic times are good.

Despite a general decline in economic activity, some companies maintain substantial earnings because their products are always in demand. These are considered **countercyclical (defensive) stocks** because they resist market declines. Most smokers, for example, do not quit during a recession, and people usually continue to go to movies, consume softdrinks, and buy groceries. Similarly, the earnings of utility companies generally hold up well during periods of economic decline. During rising markets, these stocks tend to rise less quickly than cyclical stocks. Countercyclical stocks, by definition, usually have a beta of less than 1 and sometimes even negative. Investors interested in consistent cash dividends through the years sometimes choose these stocks.

Some Theories on What Affects Stock Prices

Objective
To be able to discuss the three primary theories about what affects the price of stocks.

The prices of some stocks rise when others fall. The television news commentator tells us why the market acted the way it did or asks for the analytical commentary of a "Wall Street expert." Do these people know why stock prices rise or fall? Not really. They are simply offering their opinions or theories about what is occurring. If they actually knew what made stock prices rise or fall, they would be billionaires. There are three general areas of stock theory: efficient-market theory, technical theory, and fundamental theory.

Efficient-Market Theory

Many researchers have concluded that short-term stock price movements, such as over 1 year, are purely random. This idea has been called the **random-walk hypothesis** and has evolved into the **efficient-market theory,** which holds that knowledge of stock market investors as a group about a company's prospects and the direction of the economy is considered to be perfect and the price of each stock accurately reflects all available and anticipated information. Thus the market reacts swiftly to all unexpected information from news accounts, brokerage analysts, and disclosure documents filed with the Securities and Exchange Commission, and properly prices each stock. The data to back up this theory come from the large institutional investors, such as mutual funds, pension plans, and bank trusts, for which information about investment activities is publicly available. The conclusion is that no one can consistently do better than the average. Efficient-market theorists believe that some do better than average because of luck. In fact, they suggest that the traders—those who buy and sell their stocks frequently—do less well than the stock market averages by an amount equal to the commissions they pay.

Most investors reject the efficient-market theory.

Most investors reject the efficient-market theory as false because they know that people who are investors do not always act rationally. Further, many believe that the stock market is inefficient because prices are artificially pushed up by the dealmakers, big traders, and institutions involved in mergers and restructurings. Most investors use technical or fundamental theories (discussed below) to improve the likelihood of investment success and claim that such knowledge improves their investment expertise.

Technical Theory

Some people believe that stock prices vary because of technical factors in the stock market as a whole. **Technical theory** is an attempt to assess the possible effect of current market action on future supply and demand for securities and individual issues and then make buying and selling decisions accordingly. It is not based on forecasted earnings, and consequently, the intrinsic value of a stock is ignored. Technical information generally consists of charts and graphs that show broad market averages as well as trading in industry groups and individual stocks. Trading information may include volume of shares traded, buying versus selling trends, and comparison of price movements. Patterns are revealed by charting these factors.

Technical analysts carefully plot price movements in conjunction with various market indexes and other technical data that when combined into a theoretical model indicate when to buy or sell. Factors included in such a model could be the total volume of shares traded, the ratio of the number of stocks that rose compared with those that declined, published information on the amount of legal insider sales (to officers of companies), the ratio of *short sales* (sales of borrowed shares to be replaced later when the price may be lower) to other sales, high-low indexes, odd-lot trading, and moving average lines.

Technical theorists are generally unsuccessful.

The individual investor may find it valuable to do some charting, and more complex models are constructed by some professional investors. Also, a number of investment advisory services sell subscriptions to technical theory indicators. Different services weigh factors differently, hoping to offer more reliable advice. Given the difficulty of trying to outguess the market, it is not surprising that many technical theorists have been unsuccessful over the years.

Fundamental Theory

Fundamental theory assumes that a stock's price movement is determined by current and future earnings trends, industry outlook, and management's expertise. Further, because knowledge about the futures of companies is not perfect, some stocks are underpriced and others are overpriced. The investor's task is to study certain fundamental factors, such as the company's sales, assets, earnings, products or services, markets, and management, to determine a company's basic value. Many of these items can be found on the company's balance sheet and income statement. Such study may enable the investor to select undervalued stocks for purchase and sell overvalued stocks. Fundamental factors to be examined include the historical profitability of an industry, the leading companies in the industry, the economic outlook for the profitability of the industry as a whole, and the outlook for the general economy. The potential investor then estimates the value of one company by comparing the history and expected future profitability of this company with competing firms. Such comparisons are based on both objective and subjective information. The task is to seek out sound stocks, perhaps those that are unfashionable, that are priced well below the market's multiples of earnings, cash flow, and book value.

The premise of fundamental theory is that each particular stock has an intrinsic, or true, value based on its expected future earnings. If the company expects to be extremely profitable in coming years, this should be reflected in a high *P/E* ratio. If prospects look dismal and earnings are expected to be quite low, the price of a stock and the *P/E* ratio should be low. The *P/E* ratio is one piece of objective data that can be used in fundamental analysis. However, it may be too subjective when used to forecast the future. Fundamental investors often compare the expected *P/E* ratio of a firm with that of its competitors and the industry as a whole. In a growth industry, such as robotics, all such *P/E* ratios would be high. In a cyclical industry, such as automobiles, all such *P/E* ratios would be low. The task for the common stock investor is to analyze the fundamental factors at work and choose the best company. Most investors believe in fundamental theory.

When to Sell Stocks

It is hard for an investor to know exactly when to sell owned stocks, although the following guidelines should assist in the decision making. You should consider selling when:

1. Losses are moderate and before they become enormous.
2. It is unlikely that good profits will continue.
3. The stock reaches your target price.
4. The stock lags others in an industry group.
5. Favorable developments occur, which temporarily push up the price.
6. Company profits start to fall short of analysts' projections.
7. Industry and company prospects are deteriorating.
8. The stock's price/earnings ratios seems too high.
9. You have found a better place for the money.

Two final suggestions: Consider keeping a stock as long as it is reasonable that good profits will continue, and avoid the notion to wait to try to sell at the top of a price rise because it is almost impossible to predict when it will occur.

What If You Are Considering Investing in Common Stock?

People invest in common stock because they want to make money. For the possibility of earning a higher return, they assume more risk compared to putting their money in a savings account. There are several advantages and disadvantages of investing in common stock.

Advantages

The likelihood of cash dividends and price appreciation motivates most investors to consider common stocks. Many companies might declare relatively small cash dividends, perhaps with a yield of only 2 or 3 percent, but these companies also may offer a good chance for price appreciation over time. Historically, the combined annual cash dividend and price appreciation of all stocks has been between 8 and 9 percent; this includes times when inflation was 10 percent and when it was 1 percent. Common stocks historically have offered a good hedge against inflation, since the combined cash dividends and price appreciation has exceeded inflation over time, although certainly not in every year.

Another popular advantage of common stocks is the low minimum investment amount required. A share of stock could sell for as little as $5 or $10, although it is rare to buy one share at a

time. This can encourage savers to consider investing in common stocks. Two other advantages are limited liability (if the corporation goes bankrupt, all you lose is the price of the stock) and liquidity (stocks can generally be sold with considerable ease).

Disadvantages

Risks of various types are present with common stock investments. There is the financial risk that the company will go bankrupt. There is the market-volatility risk that the price of a stock might be quite low when you want to sell it. Inflation risk is also present, and during times of extremely high inflation, many common stock prices are depressed. As inflation rises, interest rates rise, which increases the costs of doing business (thus lowering profits) and provides much higher rates of return to savers. When inflation is high, interest rates are also high and common stockholders typically sell their somewhat riskier stocks and put their money in safer alternatives such as bonds or savings. This depresses stock prices. Low inflation is good news for the stock market because current corporate

(*continued*)

Preferred Stocks and the Individual Investor

Objective
To be able to explain what kind of investor would want to invest in preferred stock.

Corporations are the main buyers of preferred stock.

Probably 90 percent of all stocks outstanding today are common stocks, since they have a broader appeal to investors than preferred stocks. U.S. tax laws do not permit a corporation to deduct as an expense the dividends paid to common or preferred stockholders. However, because interest paid to bondholders is tax deductible, most corporations today find it less expensive to sell bonds to raise money than to sell preferred stock. Still, some corporations issue shares of preferred stock, and these may or may not fit the investment needs of individual investors. Corporations, instead of individuals, are the main buyers of preferred stocks because tax laws allow profits are not artificially distorted by general price increases.

A market in which stock prices are generally declining is called a **bear market.** In a **bull market,** average stock prices are increasing. (Similarly, a "bull" in the market is a person who is an optimist and who expects growth and prices that will go up; a "bear" is a pessimist who expects the general market to decline.) The origin of the terms is unknown, but some suggest that they refer to the ways the animals attack: bears thrust claws downward and bulls move horns upward.

A bear market of 2 or 3 years' duration can play havoc with your investment timing. For example, assume that your child's college fund is made up of common stock investments and a severe bear market exists when the child turns 18. At that point, the value of the investments could be sharply depressed, and it might not be wise to sell the stocks to pay tuition bills.

Uncertainty of yield is another disadvantage of common stocks. Even a company with an excellent record of paying cash dividends might have to skip one or two quarterly dividends during times of low profitability. Or such a company might declare dividends of varied amounts, say, quarterly dividends of $0.40, $0.45, $0.30, and $0.40, during a year. Investors who want to depend with high certainty on regular dividends as income should probably not own common stocks, except for income and blue-chip stocks.

Because many common stocks vary in price with certain news events, world happenings, and economic and political variables, they require a significant amount of time for personal management. Investors need to be alert to current happenings in order to know when to sell quickly in order to reap profits or reduce losses. Also, it is probably true that the riskier an investment is, the more attention it requires.

A final disadvantage relates to your risk disposition. If you are averse to much risk taking, then most common stocks are not suitable investments for you. You will sleep better with less risky investments. Also, if you cannot take the pressure of knowing that the price of your common stock could vary weekly and monthly up or down by 10 or 20 percent or more, then your disposition may not be suited to common stocks.

them to avoid taxes on 85 percent of the dividends they receive. This section describes some characteristics of preferred stocks.

Fixed Dividends

Preferred stocks pay fixed dividends.

As noted earlier, a preferred stock is a fixed-income ownership security with the right to assets and earnings of a corporation before the claims of common stockholders but after those of bondholders. The dividends to preferred stockholders are usually fixed and represent a financial obligation of the firm. When a company profits, first in line are the preferred stockholders, and any remaining profits may then be distributed to common stockholders. Since preferred stockholders are offered only a strong assurance, not a guarantee, that a specific cash dividend will be paid, there is still some risk involved.

Since the dividend yield is fixed, the price of preferred stocks generally will not increase as the company becomes more profitable and successful. Thus the typical preferred stockholder does not benefit from price appreciation, as would a common stockholder. Instead, the price, or market value, of preferred stocks is primarily based on prevailing interest rates. With the advantage of a priority claim on assets, the yields on preferred stocks generally will be slightly lower than those on investments with somewhat similar risks, such as long-term certificates of deposits and corporate bonds.

In times of rising interest rates, the market value of a preferred stock will drop so that the real yield will remain competitive with similar-risk investments. For example, a preferred stock that cost you $100 and paid an annual cash dividend of $7 would provide you with a 7 percent return. If returns on other investments of similar risk later climbed to around 9 percent, the market price others would be willing to pay for your preferred stock would have to drop to reflect the differences in return. After all, who would pay $100 for a preferred stock paying $7 when they could put their money into a similar investment and receive $9? With a cash dividend of $7, the market price of the preferred stock would have to drop to about $78 to increase the yield to approximately 9 percent ($7/ $78 = 0.089).

Participating or Nonparticipating Stock

Participating preferred stocks can share in corporate profits.

A few companies offer **participating preferred stock,** which allows the preferred stockholder to receive extra dividends above the stated amount after the common stockholders have received a certain level of dividends. This extra dividend is sometimes called a *bonus dividend.* The enticement of participating preferred stock is sometimes offered by firms experiencing difficulty in raising money through more conventional sources. However, most preferred stock is **nonparticipating preferred stock** and permits the owner to receive only the fixed dividend per share.

Cumulative or Noncumulative Stock

Preferred stocks can be cumulative or noncumulative.

Sometimes a corporation decides not to pay dividends to preferred stockholders because of a lack of profits or simply because of a desire to retain and reinvest all the earnings. **Cumulative preferred stock** provides that when the board of directors votes to skip (pass) making a cash dividend to preferred stockholders, the dividend must be paid before any future dividends are distributed to the common stockholders. For example, assume that a company passes on two quarterly dividends of $2.25 each to preferred stockholders, who are accustomed to receiving $9 a year. If in the third quarter the company profits and wants to give a cash dividend to its common stockholders, it must first pay the cumulative preferred stockholders their passed $4.50. Further, the usual cash dividend of $2.25 must be made to the preferred stockholders for the third quarter before any dividends can be paid to the common stockholders.

In the case of **noncumulative preferred stock,** the noncumulative preferred stockholder would have no claim to previously skipped dividends. However, in the preceding example, during the third quarter, preferred stockholders would still have preference over common stockholders. Thus preferred stockholders would receive the $2.25 but not the skipped $4.50 ($2.25 + $2.25). Most preferred stock is cumulative.

Callable Preferred Stock

Callable preferred stock may be bought back by the corporation.

Most preferred stock is **callable,** which refers to a preferred stock (or bond) that can be bought back from the investor by the issuer before the maturity date. This means that the company can repurchase it by paying a slight premium (often 5 percent above par value) if the price reaches a certain level. Precise call dates must be stated. The call price is stated in advance as either a specific amount or a proportion of the original par value. A company with preferred stock generally would like to call it in when interest rates have dropped substantially. For example, assume that a company issues preferred stock for $100 paying a $9 annual dividend. This presumably provides a good return to the investor and a high price for money for the corporation. Should interest rates drop to about 7 percent, the price of the preferred stock would rise to reflect a yield comparable with investments of similar risk. A price increase to $128 would result in a yield of 7.03 percent ($9/$128 = 7.03 percent).

The issuing company that calls in preferred stocks is not trying to cheat the preferred stockholders out of a nice capital gain (from $100 to $128, but the gain will be lost if the preferred stock is called), but rather is looking to keep its operating costs down. If it is currently paying preferred stockholders $9 per share, it may be prudent to pay a 5 percent penalty to retire the stock. Then it can issue new preferred stock or sell bonds at around 7 percent to regain use of the capital at a substantial savings.

Convertible Preferred Stock

Convertible preferred stock may be an alternative to some.

Preferred stocks that have a **convertibility privilege** can be exchanged for a certain number of shares of the issuing company's common stock during a specified time period. Thus they offer the investor the chance for both dividend income and equity participation if a stock ever moves up in price. A small but growing number of firms are offering convertible preferred stock and stipulating the conditions of the conversion feature. Because the idea is attractive to some investors, preferred stocks with a conversion privilege can be sold with a lower fixed dividend. For example, assume that one share of preferred convertible stock bought at $100 is convertible to two shares of common stock until October 1, 1997, and the current market price of the common stock is $30. Should the company prosper in coming years and the value of the common stock increase, at some point it may be profitable for preferred stockholders to convert. Thus the convertible preferred stockholder does have a chance to share in a part of the price appreciation of common stock. Note, though, that the conversion

Preferred stocks with their fixed cash dividends seem to attract investors who are interested in reliable and relatively high dividends, not in price appreciation. Because of the callability feature (all convertible preferred stocks are also callable), the potential for price appreciation is limited. Preferred stocks are also susceptible to the risks of rising inflation and interest rates, since the price of preferred stocks drops under such conditions. Thus, for most individual investors, preferred stocks are not the best alternative investment. In sum, preferred stocks have many of the disadvantages of common stocks without the same advantages.

ratio might be unrealistic. If only 2 years were left to convert the preceding stock, it might seem unlikely that a $30 common stock would rise to above $50 to make conversion profitable for the investor. In this instance, the conversion privilege is almost worthless.

Summary

1. Stocks are shares of ownership in the assets and earnings of a business corporation. Stocks are sold to investors to finance corporate goals. Stocks represent potential income for investors, since stockholders own a piece of the future direction of the company.

2. Investors in stocks have three primary concerns: investment income, price appreciation, and total return. Total return is the combination of the dividend yield and the price appreciation (the latter is also called capital gains).

3. In the study of stock investments, several important terms need to be understood, such as earnings per share, price/earnings ratio, market value, beta, and preemptive rights.

4. Stocks can be classified according to their characteristics, such as income stocks that pay higher than average dividends, growth stocks that emphasize growth over income, and speculative stocks that may have a spotty earnings record or be so new that no pattern has emerged but have an apparent potential for substantial earnings at some time in the future.

5. There are three general theories about why stock prices rise or fall: efficient-market theory, technical theory, and fundamental theory.

6. The likelihood of dividends and the potential for sharp price appreciation are perceived as major advantages of common stock investments, while disadvantages include financial risk, market-volatility risk, and the time required to personally manage your stock portfolio.

7. Preferred stocks with their fixed cash dividends seem to attract investors who are very interested in reliable and relatively high dividends and not in price appreciation.

Modern Money Management

The Johnsons Compare Investments for the Future

With their incomes increasing and having brought their spending under control, Harry and Belinda Johnson have decided to begin investing for the future. They intend to take about $3000 out of savings and then put an additional $200 to $400 a month into investments. They both have a moderate investment philosophy and seek some cash dividends as well as price appreciation.

1. Calculate the five-year return on the investment choices below. Put your calculations in tabular form like that of Table 15.6. (Hint: At the end of the first year the *EPS* for Running Paws will be $2.40 with a dividend of $0.66, while the *EPS* for Eagle Packaging will be $2.76 with a projected dividend of $0.86.)

	Running Paws	Eagle Packaging
Current price	$30	$48
Current earnings per share (*EPS*)	$ 2.00	$ 2.30
Current quarterly cash dividend	$ 0.15	$ 0.18
Current *P/E* ratio	15	21
Projected earnings annual growth rate	20 percent	20 percent
Projected cash dividend	10 percent	20 percent

2. Using the appropriate *P/E* ratios, what are the estimated market prices of Running Paws and Eagle after 5 years?

3. Show your calculations in determining the projected price appreciations for the two stocks over the 5 years.

4. Add the projected price appreciation of each stock to its projected cash dividends, and show the total 5-year percentage returns for the two stocks.

5. Determine the average annual dividend for each stock, and use these figures in calculating the approximate compound yields for each alternative.

6. Check your responses by entering the data in the Personal Finance Cookbook (PFC) program (RETURN). Which stock has the largest potential total return?

7. Assume that inflation is about 6 percent and the return on long-term quality bonds is 11 percent. Given the Johnsons' investment philosophy, explain why you would recommend (a) Running Paws, (b) Eagle, or (c) a long-term quality bond as a long-term growth investment. Support your answer by calculating the projected real return using the information on page 553, in Chapter 15, or the Personal Finance Cookbook (PFC) program REALRATE. The Johnsons are in the 28 percent marginal tax bracket.

Key Words and Concepts

articles of partnership, 570
bear market, 587
beta, 578
blue-chip stock, 582
book value, 577
book value per share, 577
bull market, 587
callable, 589
capital, 570
capital gain, 572
cash dividends, 576
common stock, 570
convertibility privilege, 589
corporation, 570
countercyclical (defensive) stocks, 583
cumulative preferred stock, 588
cyclical stock, 582
dividend payout ratio, 576
dividends, 569
dividends per share, 576
dividend yield, 572
earnings per share (*EPS*), 575
efficient-market theory, 583
fundamental theory, 584
growth stock, 581
growth stocks (lesser known), 582
growth stocks (well known), 581
income stock, 581
low par, 577
market price, 569

market value, 569
no par, 577
noncumulative preferred stock, 589
nonparticipating preferred stock, 588
paper profit (paper loss), 572
par value, 577
participating preferred stock, 588
partnership, 570
portfolio, 578
preemptive right, 579
preferred stock, 571
price appreciation, 572
price/earnings ratio (*P/E* ratio or *P/E* multiple), 575
price/sales ratio (*PSR*), 576
price-to-book ratio, 577
proxy, 580
random-walk hypothesis, 583
retained earnings, 571
securities, 570
shareholder, 570
sole proprietorship, 569
speculative stock, 582
stock dividend, 579
stockholder, 570
stocks, 569
stock split, 579
technical theory, 584
total return, 572
voting rights, 580

Review Questions

1. Explain what stocks are and how they are used.
2. Distinguish among the three forms of business ownership: sole proprietorship, partnership, and corporation.

3. Summarize the differences between common and preferred stock.

4. Explain and illustrate the two components that make up total return.

5. What does price/earnings ratio mean, and how would you interpret a P/E ratio of 8 to 1?

6. Explain why one company might have a dividend payout ratio of 0.65 and another a ratio of 0.30.

7. Explain the likely relationship of the market price of a stock with its par value and its book value per share.

8. What does beta mean, and how can it be used by an investor who hopes to select stocks that will go up much more than average during a rise in the stock market?

9. What is the effect of stock dividends on the individual investor who already owns shares of stock in a company?

10. Identify some reasons why some companies have stock splits.

11. Discuss the value of voting rights for a stockholder.

12. Differentiate between well-known growth stocks and speculative stocks.

13. Explain how a particular growth stock could also be called a cyclical stock.

14. What is the efficient-market theory, and why do most investors reject this approach?

15. Explain the basic differences between the fundamental and technical theories as to what affects stock prices.

16. List some advantages of buying common stock.

17. Distinguish between a bull and a bear market, and give an illustration of how a bear market can hurt your investment portfolio.

18. List three guidelines for when an investor should consider selling stocks.

19. Give reasons why most investors do not buy preferred stocks.

Case Problems

1. Robert Chisholm of Memphis, Tennessee, opened his successful food-service business as a sole proprietorship 3 years ago. Phyllis Stevens and her partner, William Pyeatt, recently opened their second retail toy store in Memphis after becoming partners 4 years ago.
   a. Justify opening a business as a sole proprietor and as a partnership.
   b. What are some arguments for Chisholm as well as Stevens and Pyeatt to change to a corporate form of ownership?

2. Richard Ford of Riverside, California, has $5000 that he wants to invest in the stock market. Richard is in college on a scholarship and does not plan on needing the $5000 or any dividend income for another 5 years, when he plans to buy a new automobile. Richard is currently considering

a stock selling for $25 with an EPS of $1.25. Last year, the company earned $900,000, of which $250,000 was paid out in dividends.

a. What classification of common stock would you recommend to Richard? Why?

b. Calculate the price/earnings ratio and the dividend payout ratio for this stock. Given this information and your recommendation, would this stock be an appropriate purchase for Richard? Why?

c. Identify the components of the total return Richard might expect, and estimate how much he might expect annually from each component.

Jean Maynard of Evanston, Illinois, graduated from college 3 years ago and is now a successful salesperson for a real estate firm. She bought a condominium to live in last year (primarily for the tax advantages) and is now considering the stock market as an area for investments. Jean has $6000 in cash to invest.

a. Give Jean some reasons why she should consider buying common stock as an investment.

b. Advise her also on major cautions she should recognize when investing in common stocks.

c. If Jean bought a stock with a market price of $50 and a beta value of 1.8, what would be the likely value of her $6000 investment after 1 year if the general market for stocks rose 20 percent?

d. What would the investment be worth if the general market for stocks dropped 20 percent?

Suggested Readings

"Biotech: Where to Invest Now." *Changing Times,* August 1990, pp. 69–75. Key companies that may do very well in the future.

"Buying on Bad News." *Changing Times,* August 1989, pp. 41–44. Bad news often forces prices of good stocks down, making them excellent buys for investors.

"5 Ways to Find Good Stocks Now." *Changing Times,* December 1989, pp. 64–72. Stocks with low *P/E* ratios are expected to rise sharply in the next 5 years.

"Great Stocks in Your Own Backyard." *Changing Times,* October 1989, pp. 28–38. A 50-state review of which are the best investments in your home area.

"How *P/E* Ratios Can Lead You to the Best Buys." *Money,* March 1990, pp. 159–160. Understanding how to use the price/earnings ratio to help you make better investment decisions.

"How to Beat the Pros." *Changing Times,* May 1989, pp. 32–39. Champion mutual funds manager Peter Lynch shares his secrets on how to select stocks.

"IPO's Are Back—And They're Still a Treacherous Lot." *Business Week,* August 14, 1989, pp. 134–135. Identifies the risks of initial public offerings of stocks that were previously privately traded.

"Making Money in *Un*mergers." *Changing Times,* June 1989, pp. 31–35. The spin-off pieces that companies sell off sometimes are good investments.

"One Up on Wall Street." *Money,* January 1989, pp. 128–143. In-depth interview with mutual funds manager Peter Lynch about his book on how amateur investors can and should do better than the professionals.

"Small Stocks with Big Ideas." *Changing Times,* March 1990, pp. 59–61. Research shows that small companies typically beat the S&P index for the first 10 years of existence.

"Stock Bargains That Wall Street Missed." *Changing Times,* September 1990, pp. 93–97. Fundamental factors reveal some underpriced stocks.

"Stocks That Pay and Pay and Pay." *Changing Times,* October 1990, pp. 44–45. List of the companies that have paid increasing dividends for the past fifteen years.

"The Message of the Market." *Newsweek,* October 30, 1989, pp. 64–68. A history of the hows and whys of the past 5 years' stock market fluctuations.

"The Stock Table Simplified." *Consumer Reports,* August 1989, p. 535. How to read the stock listings in the newspaper.

"Why You Should Hate the Mets." *Changing Times,* February 1990, pp. 41–43. What theories really affect stock market prices.

17 Investing in Bonds

OBJECTIVES

After reading this chapter, you should be able to

1. Distinguish among the three types of fixed-asset investments.

2. Describe the ten major characteristics of bonds.

3. Differentiate among the four general types of bonds: corporate bonds, U.S. government securities, municipal bonds, and specialty bonds.

4. Describe what you should consider before investing in bonds, particularly the current yield and yield to maturity.

5. List the advantages and disadvantages of investing in bonds.

6. Explain factors to consider when buying and selling bonds.

• • • • • • • • •

Many people who make investments in stocks often do not understand the important part bonds can play in their portfolios. Bonds are easier and less expensive to purchase now than they were some years ago, and they often provide a much better total return than savings accounts, certificates of deposit, and many stocks.

This chapter first discusses fixed-income investments in general and then details important terminology used in bond investing. After describing the three major types of bonds, we cover the advantages and disadvantages of owning bonds and what key factors the investor should consider before investing in bonds. The chapter ends with a section on how to buy and when to sell bonds.

What Are Fixed-Asset Investments?

Objective
To be able to distinguish among the three types of fixed-asset investments.

Fixed-asset investments require a specific amount of money to be invested for a certain amount of time. You can be reasonably certain of receiving periodic income (often interest received quarterly or semiannually) as well as getting back the amount you originally invested. For this small financial risk you usually earn a relatively low total yield, particularly when compared with the typically higher total returns earned on investments in common stocks and real estate. Examples of fixed-asset investments are savings accounts, certificates of deposit (both discussed in Chapter 5), government bonds, corporate bonds, and annuities. (Annuities are examined in Chapter 14 and are discussed in more detail in Chapter 22.) Fixed-asset investments can be classified according to whether the value and yield of the asset are variable or fixed.

Fixed Value and Fixed Yield

An asset has a fixed value and a fixed yield when its value (or price) and the yield do not change during the time period. For example, a 36-month $5000 certificate of deposit paying 8 percent that is purchased through a savings institution probably has a fixed value and yield guaranteed by the government. At any time during the 36 months the asset is always worth $5000, and no matter what happens to interest rates in the general economy, the yield is fixed at 8 percent, which provides an investor with $400 of annual income ($5000 $\times$ 0.08) on the original amount invested.

Fixed Value and Variable Yield

Government savings bonds (EE and HH) and funds deposited in savings accounts in banks, S&Ls, and credit unions are examples of fixed-asset investments with a fixed value but a variable yield. (These were examined in Chapter 5.) With these investments, the government guarantees the value of the asset. Over time, however, the yield can vary. For example, the interest rate on savings bonds was 8.5 percent in 1982 and 6.1 percent in 1990. The government offers a guaranteed yield on savings bonds even when interest rates decline. When the rate on newly issued savings bonds is higher than that on old government savings bonds, the rate on the older bonds is raised. The rate paid on savings accounts has fluctuated from 4 to 6.5 percent in recent years, too.

Variable Value and Fixed Yield

Bonds are interest-bearing negotiable certificates of long-term debt issued by a corporation, municipality (such as a city or state), or the federal government. The most common denomination for a bond is $1000. The issuer promises to pay back investors (lenders) the full loan amount (known as the **face** or **par value**) as specified on the certificate (excluding accrued interest) at a stated time (called the **maturity date**). In addition, the issuer pays lenders an annual fixed rate of interest (known as the **coupon rate** or **stated interest rate**) at regular intervals, usually every 6 months, which remains the same until maturity. This is the interest rate printed on the bond certificate. The coupon rate is determined by dividing the total annual interest (in dollars) by $1000 (assuming the face value of the bond is $1000).

The variable value of bonds results primarily because of interest-rate risk.

The value (or price) of bonds fluctuates with the interest rates in the general economy. This is known as **interest-rate risk,** which is the uncertainty of the market value of an asset that results from possible interest-rate changes. For example, assume that you buy a 20-year $1000 bond with a stated annual interest rate of 8 percent, or an annual return of $80 ($1000 × 0.08). If after 1 year interest rates in the general economy jump to 12 percent, no one will want to buy your bond for $1000 because it pays only $80 per year. Should you want to sell it at that time, the price of the bond will have to be lowered, perhaps to $700 or $750. On the other hand, if after 1 year interest rates slip to 6 percent, the value of your bond will increase sharply (perhaps to $1200 or $1300), because people are willing to pay a premium to own your bond paying 8 percent when other rates are 6 percent. Because of the possibility of capital gains, bonds offer a unique investment opportunity for the moderate and speculative investor as well as the conservative investor. It is important to realize that if the bond is held to maturity (19 more years in this example), no matter what happens to market value over the life of the bond, the issuer is obligated to repay the face value (the stated price or par value printed on the certificate) of $1000.

Bonds do offer the possibility of capital gains.

The Language of Bond Investing

Objective
To be able to describe
the ten major character-
istics of bonds.

It should be clearly understood that a bond represents a debt obligation of the bond issuer to the bondholder/investor. Bonds have 10 major characteristics: legal indenture, denomination of value, maturity date, sinking fund, being secured or unsecured, being senior or subordinated, being registered or bearer, callability, warrants, and convertibility. Each of these is discussed below.

Indenture

The indenture specifies debtor responsibilities.

An **indenture** is a written legal agreement between a group of bondholders (representing each bondholder) and the debtor as to the terms of the debt, setting forth maturity date, interest rate, and other factors. For corporate bonds, this lengthy document specifies many of the debtor's responsibilities regarding what the borrowed money will be used for, the date(s) the bond principal must be repaid (maturity date), and the dates interest payments must be made. A trustee, a bank or trust company, is normally appointed to represent the bondholders and ensure that the obligations of the indenture are completed. State laws require issuers of corporate bonds to pay interest due to bondholders even if the company is not profitable. Government bonds usually do not have indentures, since the authorizing statute typically details responsibilities of the public agency issuing the bond.

Denomination of Value

Denomination of value states the amount of the debt.

Bonds are usually issued in units of $1000. This amount is a bond's *face value, stated value,* or *par value.*

Maturity Date

Maturity date is the date the face amount is due.

Bonds are paid off, or **retired,** at the maturity date specified in the indenture. When bonds mature, the issuing agency is obligated to pay the face value to the bondholder. Most corporate bonds mature in 20 to 30 years; government bonds often mature in 10 to 20 years. The maturity time could be as short as 5 years on some government issues or as long as 40 years on a corporate bond.

Sinking Fund

A sinking fund sets money aside for repayment of the principal portion of the debt.

Investors in bonds want to be as confident as possible that interest payments will be made on time *and* that the principal will be repaid as scheduled. For this reason, many bonds have a **sinking fund,** which is a requirement in the indenture that monies be set aside each year to repay (or redeem) the bond. The trustee receives the funds and oversees this responsibility. The added assurance of a sinking fund reduces risk and permits the agency to issue bonds at interest rates lower than rates on similar bonds.

Occasionally, bonds are retired serially, whereby each bond is numbered consecutively and matures according to a prenumbered schedule at stated intervals. Such bonds are known as **serial bonds.**

Secured or Unsecured Bonds

Bonds are issued on the financial reputation of the issuing agency as either secured or unsecured. A corporation issuing a **secured bond** would pledge specific assets as collateral in the indenture or have the principal and interest guaranteed by another corporation or a government agency. In the event of default, the trustee could take legal action to seize and sell such assets. Three types of secured bonds are *mortgage bonds* (land and buildings as collateral), *collateral trust bonds* (stocks and perhaps other bonds as collateral), and *equipment bonds* (certain equipment, such as airplanes or railroad cars, as collateral). In the event of bankruptcy, the claims of secured creditors are paid first.

Unsecured bonds have no collateral backing them.

An **unsecured bond** has no collateral named as security for the debt and is backed only by the good faith and reputation of the issuing agency. All government bonds are unsecured. Any unsecured bond is called a **debenture,** which is backed by the general credit of the issuer and usually not secured by a mortgage or lien on any specific property. You may think that secured bonds are safer than unsecured bonds, but often this is not the case. U.S. government bonds are debentures that are backed by the "full faith, credit, and taxing power of the government." Also, the fine financial reputations of many large corporations enable them to offer unsecured bonds that are safer than the secured bonds of many other companies.

Senior Versus Subordinated Bonds

Senior debentures are repaid before subordinated bonds.

A corporation that issues bonds several times over the years must rank the bonds for repayment in the event of default. These details are spelled out in the indenture of each issuance of bonds. A **senior debenture** gives holders a right to all assets not pledged to secured bondholders. A **subordinated debenture** gives holders a lesser claim to assets, perhaps similar to that of the stockholders. Of course, the riskier a bond is, the higher the interest rate should be.

Registered or Bearer Bonds

All new bonds are registered.

Historically, all corporations issued **bearer bonds,** also called **coupon bonds.** The owners of such bonds are unknown to the corporation; a series of postdated coupons attached to the bond represents their ownership. When the interest payment is due, a bondholder detaches the proper coupon and presents it to the corporation, a paying agent, or a bank for payment. The principal is received in the same manner. By law, all bonds now issued are **registered bonds,** which provide for the recording of the bondholder's name so that checks or electronic funds transfers for interest and principal can be safely forwarded when due. The Internal Revenue Service is therefore notified as well. A registered bond can be transferred only when endorsed by the registered owner. Older issues of coupon bonds are still traded. The terms **coupon** and **coupon yield** refer to the interest rate printed on the certificate when it is issued.

To keep costs down, many corporations, state and municipal governments, and the federal government issue bonds in what is known as **book-entry form.** In this method of registry, records of transactions are held electronically by a depository and bonds are registered in the name of the brokerage firm that sold them to the customer or in the name of the customer. When interest is due, the depository pays each account electronically. The federal government no longer issues certificates, preferring the book-entry approach, and many stockbrokers hold their customers' certificates for them.

Callable Bonds

Bonds that are callable are less attractive investments.

It would be nice if you could buy a $1000 bond scheduled to pay 15 percent annually for a long time period, such as 20 years. During times of low interest rates, such a bond would be highly attractive. Often, however, bonds carry provisions requiring that they be sold back to the issuing agency if the agency so requests.

Probably 80 to 90 percent of long-term bonds are classified as **callable bonds.** This refers to bonds that can be bought back from the investor by the issuer before the maturity date. Precise call dates must be stated in the **prospectus.** This is a required written disclosure to the Securities and Exchange Commission and prospective investors of pertinent facts about a corporation, including the experience of its management, its financial status, any anticipated legal matters that could affect the company, and potential risks of investing in the corporation. It may even be to the issuer's advantage to pay a premium of perhaps 5 or 10 percent (as specified in the indenture) to pay off, for example, bonds paying 11 percent if rates have dropped to 8 percent. Bonds are most likely to be called when interest rates fall, because the issuer can then raise capital at the new, lower rates.

Bond investors consider the callable feature a negative one because they stand to lose their high interest rate returns if the bonds are called. As a result, callable bonds usually have a higher stated rate than similar bonds without such a feature. A good strategy is to purchase bonds that are not callable during the first 5 or 10 years of a new issue. (A **new issue** is a bond or stock sold by a corporation or government for the first time.) Also, all other things being equal, it is wise to choose the bond with the higher call premium.

Warrants

A warrant attached to a bond may make a bond more attractive.

A bond sold with a warrant attached gives some of the benefits of stock ownership to bondholders. A **warrant** is a type of security attached to a bond, a preferred stock, or some issues of common stock giving the holder the right to purchase a specific number of shares of stock at a stipulated price within a specified time limit or perpetually. It is also called a **purchase warrant.** A warrant is offered with securities as an inducement to buy.

To illustrate, assume that you have a Running Paws Catfood Company bond with a face value of $1000 and an 8 percent interest rate and it has an attached warrant. For the next 5 years the warrant gives you the privilege of buying 10 shares of common stock for $30 per share. If the price of the common stock rises above $30, the warrant will have substantial value. If the price rises to $36, say, you can purchase 10 shares at $30, for a total of $300 (saving $60 on the market price of $360). Thus, in this example, the warrant has a value of $60, and the value of the bond will rise by the same amount. If you do not want to use the warrant, you may sell it, assuming it is "detachable" from the bond. If the common stock price never rises above $30 per share, the warrant will be valueless. However, because the stock price has the potential to rise, the interest rate on bonds with warrants is a little lower than it would be otherwise.

Convertibility

A convertibility provision may make a bond attractive too.

A **convertible bond** can be exchanged by the owner before maturity for a specified number of shares of common stock or another security, usually of the same company, in accordance with the terms of the issue. Convertible securities include bonds, debentures, and preferred stocks. Bonds sold with a convertibility feature are an attempt to attach some of the benefits of stock ownership to bondholders. The coupon rate on a convertible bond is generally 4 to 6 percentage points higher than the current dividend yield on the same company's common stock.

Convertibles have priority over common shareholders in the event of bankruptcy. Because convertibles are safer than common stocks and their income yield is higher, they typically trade 5 to 30 percent above their exchange value of the underlying shares of the common stock. Investors get a bondlike cash return while they wait for the underlying common stock to appreciate; then they make their swap. Investors like convertibles because they have reduced volatility and greater safety than most stocks. Moreover, convertible securities give you a bond's steady yield unless and until you swap them for shares of stock.

To illustrate, assume you have a $1000 Running Paws Catfood Company convertible bond that is issued at 9 percent and it permits conversion to 30 shares of Running Paws common stock at any time during the next 20 years. During this time, you will receive interest from the bond and hope that the stock price will rise. The conversion feature starts to affect the value of the bond when Running Paws stock rises above $33.33 per share ($1000/30 shares). If the stock price rises to $36, for example, the bond value will rise to $1080 (30 shares × $36), regardless of general interest rates, which also affect the prices of bonds. As the common stock price continues to rise, so will the value of the bond. Of course, if the bond is also callable, the issuer may force the bondholder to convert to common stock equal to the par value of the bond by paying the bondholders a small penalty. If the common stock price stays below $33.33, the conversion privilege makes no difference. Note, however, that since the *possibility* exists that the price will rise, the inclusion of a convertibility option has value, and this permits the original bond to be issued at a slightly lower interest rate than it could be otherwise.

Note further that when the underlying stock price does poorly, the convertible's price also will drop slightly because its appeal to investors is marred. Of course, since convertibles generate a fixed income, their prices (like those of bonds) are sensitive to interest rates, tending to increase as rates fall and decline as rates rise. Prices on convertibles do horribly if interest rates jump while stocks take a dive, but interest payments should continue. There are over 600 convertible securities available today.

The Four General Types of Bonds

There are four general types of bonds: (1) corporate bonds, (2) U.S. government securities, (3) municipal bonds (also called state and local bonds), and (4) specialty bonds.

Corporate Bonds

Corporate bonds are an important source of funds for corporations as they are interest-bearing certificates of long-term debt of a company. Corporations can obtain long-term financing of projects (typically 20 to 30 years) through bonds at a relatively low cost compared with selling stock because of tax regulations. In fact, for every dollar of newly issued common stock there are three dollars of newly issued corporate bonds. Payments of dividends to common and preferred stockholders are not tax deductible for corporations, but interest to bondholders is. Because a corporation must by law make interest payments on time (usually semiannually), companies in financial difficulty usually pay bondholders before paying short-term creditors. Before buying corporate bonds, it is important for investors to size up the financial quality of the company, considering both current profitability and the likelihood of long-term profits. Recognize too that corporations are sometimes profitable and sometimes not; during the 1980s, hundreds of corporations that had issued bonds went bankrupt.

Bonds are sold in organized securities markets where investors (lenders) compare the risks and potential rewards of investments. To help you in appraising such risks, two major independent advisory services attempt to grade bonds for credit risk. Moody's Investors Service, Inc. and Standard & Poor's Corporation (S&P) publish unbiased ratings of the financial condition of corporations and municipalities that issue bonds. They examine each bond offering and assign it a quality rating according to the likelihood that the interest and principal will be repaid as detailed in the indenture. These are measures of the **default risk** (or **credit risk**), which is *Each bond issue is graded for its default risk.* the uncertainty of not receiving the promised periodic interest payments and the principal amount when due at maturity. Moody's and Standard & Poor's examine the financial strength of each bond issuer, the quality of its management, its prospects for the future, how strong it is compared

TABLE 17.1
Summary of Municipal and Corporate Bond Ratings

Moody's Rating	Standard & Poor's Rating	Interpretation of Rating
Aaa Aa A	AAA AA A	High investment quality suggests ability to repay principal and interest on time. Aaa and AAA bonds are generally referred to as "gilt-edged" because they have demonstrated profitability over the years and have paid their bondholders their interest without interruption; thus they carry the smallest risk.
Baa Ba	BBB BB B	Medium-quality investments that adequately provide security to principal and interest. They are neither highly protected nor poorly secured; thus they may have some speculative characteristics.
B Caa Ca	CCC CC C	Lack characteristics of a desirable investment, and investors have decreasing assurance of repayment as the rating declines. Elements of danger may be present regarding repayment of principal and interest.
C	DDD DD D	In default with little prospect of retaining any investment standing.

with competitors or other municipalities, future directions of the industry or region, and a variety of other factors.

Ratings for each bond issue are constantly reevaluated, and they are frequently changed after the original issue is sold to the public. Table 17.1 shows the rating scales used by Moody's and Standard & Poor's. The higher the rating, the greater is the probable safety of the bond. The lower

▌ Advice for the Conservative Bond Investor*

If interest rates are volatile, put money in a money market fund, short-term CDs, or Treasuries, and wait for a trend to develop.

If interest rates show little movement, put money in a money market fund, short-term CDs, or Treasuries to catch any upswings in rates.

* Especially if you have some well-reasoned opinions on the direction of interest rates, inflation, and the economy for the next year or more.

When interest rates are low, take profits by selling your bonds, and keep money in a money market fund, short-term CDs, or Treasuries.

When interest rates are rising, stay liquid; be alert for bargains, since falling bond prices and rising yields will create opportunities.

If interest rates are falling, move your money out of money market funds and into long-term CDs and Treasuries to lock in yields.

What If You Want to Invest in a Junk Bond?

So-called **junk bonds** (or **speculative bonds**) are high-risk, high-interest-rate corporate or municipal bonds rated BB or lower by Standard & Poor's or Ba or lower by Moody's. These are bonds whose ratings are below traditional investment grade. Junk bonds are issued by young companies with short track records or those with questionable financial strength.

Junk bond is also a term of denigration used to describe high-interest bonds often used to raise funds for corporate takeovers. In many takeovers and **leveraged buy-outs** (LBOs), the purchaser puts up very little money and borrows enormous amounts of cash to finance the purchase. (LBOs are takeovers of a company, usually by its officers and other private investors, financed with the assets of the corporation pledged as security for the debt.) LBOs saddle a corporation with a huge amount of debt, increasing the chance that the company might default in the future. More than 50 well-known corporations defaulted on junk bonds between 1986 and 1990. When growth in the economy slows, more overindebted companies default on their bonds.

The default rate on high-quality bonds is less than 1 percent; the default rate on junk bonds is over 3 percent. A recent study by Edward Altman, a New York University finance professor, shows that although only 2 percent of junk bond issuers defaulted in their first year, 11.5 percent of them defaulted within 5 years. Altman quantified the "cumulative adjusted mortality rate" 10 years after an original Standard & Poor's rating and found AA bonds at 0.23 percent, A bonds at 0.26 percent, BBB bonds at 2.51 percent, BB bonds at 5.83 percent, and B bonds at 36.18 percent. Data Resources, an economic consulting firm, projects that junk bonds will have a 13 percent default rate through 1993 under conditions ranging from moderate economic growth to a severe recession. Yet, since junk bonds pay 2 to 5 more interest points than quality bonds, large numbers of investors have purchased these bonds in recent years despite the higher risk in order to obtain the anticipated higher returns.

If you want to invest in a junk bond, you should carefully research and evaluate the bond issue on its own merits. Key questions include: How strong financially is the company? What are the company's prospects for financial success in both the near and long term? How strong is the company compared with its competitors? Where is the industry headed? What other bonds must be paid before this issue? Moreover, you must assess the likelihood of getting your principal back as well as receiving interest payments every 6 months.

If you do not want to select and invest in junk bonds directly, you can invest in a "high-yield income" bond mutual fund. These are also casually called "junk bond mutual funds." Your money will be safer in a mutual fund because risks will be reduced by the fund's diversification and professional management. Mutual funds are discussed in the next chapter.

the rating value of the bond, the higher is the stated interest rate or the effective interest rate when such bonds are reduced in price, since more risk is involved. Higher ratings denote confidence that the issuer will not default and, if necessary, that the bond can readily be sold before maturity. You can obtain the Moody's and Standard & Poor's ratings for specific bond issues from libraries, banks, and brokerage firms.

U.S. Government Securities

There are two general groups of U.S. government securities: (1) Treasury bills, notes, and bonds and (2) federal agency issue notes, bonds, and certificates.[1] The interest rates on federal government securities are usually lower than on corporate bonds because they are almost risk-free—the possibility of default is near zero. Conservative investors like the certainty of U.S. government securities. New issues of the U.S. Treasury cannot be called (redeemed early) if rates drop. You may invest in U.S. government securities by purchasing them directly though the government or through banks and stock brokerage firms.

Interest income on U.S. government securities is exempt from state and local income taxes.

Unlike Series EE and HH savings bonds, most government bonds are transferable and can be sold by one investor to another. This means that you may purchase a U.S. Treasury security directly from the government as well as in the securities markets. When buying U.S. government securities, you are required to provide the government with your Social Security number as well as the name of your financial institution so the latter can report correct tax information. You do not receive certificates; rather, purchases are recorded electronically, with all interest, principal, and other payments deposited with your local financial institution. One major advantage of federal government securities is that the interest income is exempt from state and local taxes.

Treasury Bills, Notes, and Bonds   Treasury bills, notes, and bonds—collectively known as **Treasury issues**—are debt instruments used by the federal government to finance the public debt (or national debt). After purchase, they can easily be sold in a secondary market prior to maturity. (A **secondary market** is also called an **aftermarket,** since this is the place where existing securities, which have already been sold to the public, are bought and sold; a stock exchange is an example.) Benefits of Treasury issues are that they are a safe source of current income, have excellent liquidity and safety, and are simple to acquire. U.S. Treasury notes and bonds pay interest semiannually; Treasury bills do not pay interest because they are sold at a discount.

The interest on a T-bill is the gain at maturity.

Treasury bills, also called **T-bills,** are U.S. government securities that mature in 13, 26, or 52 weeks. New issues are generally sold in $10,000 denominations with additional increments of $5000. The 13- and 26-week bills are sold every week, and the 52-week bills are sold every 4 weeks. No current interest income is paid on Treasury bills (as it is on notes and bonds) because they are sold on a discount basis, with the gain at maturity representing the interest for federal income tax purposes. The return on such investments is called a **discount yield.** For example, if you purchase a 52-week $10,000 T-bill for $9200, it will mature in a year and the U.S. Treasury Department will electronically forward you $10,000. The discount yield would be 8.7 percent ($10,000 − $9200 = $800/$9200) on your

---

[1] United States savings bonds (both Series EE and HH) represent another type of government security, and these are discussed from a cash-management perspective in Chapter 5, Managing Your Cash.

investment of $9200. Realize also that T-bills calculate interest based on a 360-day year but actually earn interest for 365 days, which increases the effective yield slightly.

You may purchase Treasury issues directly from any Federal Reserve Bank or branch office. Individuals buy new issues of T-bills on a noncompetitive bid basis. The price individuals pay for the bill will be the average of all the competitive offers made by large institutions that buy millions of dollars' worth of T-bills that week. Simply submit a certified or cashier's check for the face amount along with the proper form. A few days later you will receive notification that you own the T-bill and an electronically wired refund in the amount of the difference between the face value of the bill and the purchase price. You also can make the purchase through a securities broker or a bank, but there you must pay a $15 to $30 fee.

U.S. **Treasury notes** are U.S. government securities that have a maturity of 2 to 10 years and pay interest semiannually. Two- and three-year Treasury notes can be purchased only in $5000 denominations; 4- to 10-year notes are available in $1000 denominations. These notes are registered and sold with a fixed interest rate, and the rates are slightly higher than those of Treasury bills. **Treasury bonds** are U.S. government securities that have a maturity period of 11 to 30 years and are sold in $1000 denominations. Interest is paid semiannually on these registered bonds. The fixed interest rates are higher than on notes because they are longer-term issues.

Sales of Treasury issues are recorded on a *book-entry basis,* meaning that all interest earned is deposited directly into your account at a bank or another financial institution. The *Treasury Direct* plan requires that you open a Treasury Direct account. To do so, write your nearest Federal Reserve Bank and ask for Form PD 5182, or you can obtain it from the Treasury Department, Division of Customer Services, Washington, D.C. 20239. The form requires that you give information for a bank account to which the Federal Reserve can wire your twice-yearly interest earnings, because the FED no longer mails certificates or checks for interest. There are no commissions, charges, or fees when buying and redeeming Treasury issues directly with the government; there are fees when a bank or stock brokerage firm handles such transactions.

Federal Agency Bonds, Notes, and Certificates   More than 100 different bonds, notes, and certificates are issued by various federal agencies, such as the Government National Mortgage Association (Ginnie Mae), the Federal National Mortgage Association (Fannie Mae), the Federal Home Loan Mortgage Corporation (Freddie Mac), the Resolution Trust Corporation (RTC), and the Federal Farm Credit Banks Funding Corporation. They are often called **agency issues.** These certificates are backed by the assets and resources of the issuing agency instead of the full faith and credit of the U.S. government. For example, Ginnie Mae is a government corporation that buys and repackages mortgages for sale. Its GNMA certificates, backed by the association and representing interest in a pool of mortgages, are sold to institutions and investors in units of $25,000. As home owners make monthly mortgage payments, a part of the principal and interest is passed through to investors. Agency issues are not as popularly known as Treasury securities, and they often pay a yield that is 1 to 2 percentage points higher than comparable-term Treasury bonds.

The actual certificates that evidence ownership of agency issues are held in trust in a bank. Interest is electronically sent directly to your account at a bank or a brokerage firm. Redemption of government securities is not automatic at maturity. You must submit evidence of ownership (records of transactions) either to a financial institution or to a Federal Reserve Bank.

Municipal (State and Local) Bonds

Municipal bonds, also called **munies,** are long-term debts issued by local governments (cities, states, and various districts and political subdivisions) and their agencies, and they are used to finance public improvement projects, such as roads, bridges, and parks, or for ongoing expenses. Moody's *Bond Record* lists some 20,000 munies, and there are twice as many unrated issues. The range could be from Aaa rated state highway bonds to unrated issues by local parking authorities.

Among the dozen or more types of specialized municipal bonds, two are frequently issued: general obligation and revenue bonds. **General obligation bonds,** the more common, are backed by the full taxing authority of the issuing agency. Since the local government has a primary responsibility to repay these debts, such bonds usually have the highest safety rating and pay lower yields than other municipal bonds. Massachusetts and other states have recently offered general obligation bonds known as *minibonds* issued directly to the public in denominations as small as $100 and $500. **Revenue bonds** are backed by the revenues from the projects built or maintained by the bond's proceeds, such as dormitories, sewers, waterworks, and toll roads. Revenue bonds typically have yields about ½ percentage point higher than general obligation bonds of the same quality, because they are less safe.

To attract investors and to lower the cost of state and municipal borrowing, the federal government allows municipal bond *interest* to be exempted from federal income tax. Thus municipal bonds are known as *tax-free bonds.* Also, interest income is normally exempt from state and local taxes if the investor lives in the state that issued the bond. Municipal bonds almost always offer a lower stated return than other bonds. This is not a problem as shown in the following example. A single taxpayer in the 28 percent bracket would have to earn more than 10 percent on a taxable investment to equal the yield on a tax-free muni earning 7.2 percent [7.2 percent = $0.10 \times (1.00 - 0.28)$]. The two formulas for tax-equivalent yields are discussed in detail on page 299.

Note that *capital gains* on the sale of munies are taxable. Gains are possible because bonds may be bought at a discount and then sold at a higher price or redeemed for full value at maturity. In addition, bonds bought in the secondary market at a premium can further appreciate for a gain. (These concepts are discussed later in this chapter.)

In the 1970s and 1980s, numerous local governments and municipalities experienced financial difficulties and failed to pay their bond obligations on time. Examples include New York City, Cleveland, and the Washington Public Power Supply System (often known as the "Whoops" utility). Typically, over 100 municipal bond issues default every year. This is evidence that although municipal bonds are generally safer than corporate bonds, they are not as safe as U.S. government securities. Both Moody's and Standard & Poor's rate municipal bonds. Note further that more than one-fourth of all new municipal bonds being sold today have insurance that guarantees repayment of principal and interest. Since this insurance only reduces the return about 0.16 percent, it may be wise to ask about insured municipal bonds.

Specialty Issues

The types of bonds that interest most investors are those which simply pay interest regularly and are redeemed at maturity. Three newer variations issued by some corporations and municipalities are floating-rate bonds, collateralized mortgage obligations, and zero-coupon bonds. **Floating-rate bonds** (or **variable-rate bonds**) are long-term corporate or municipal bond issues with an interest rate fixed for only 6 to 18 months, after which it varies according to an index of government interest rates. These bonds are usually redeemable early at the option of the bondholder after 2 or 3 years. Since the investor shares in the risk of an interest-rate decline, floating-rate bonds are issued at higher rates than other corporate bonds.

Collateralized mortgage obligations (CMOs) are bonds secured by mortgage securities that pass interest and principal payments on to investors. CMOs are similar to Ginnie Maes, which bundle together mortgages, but repayment uncertainty is reduced with CMOs. Several classes of mortgage debt are grouped with different average lives: short (2 years), intermediate (5 years), medium to long (10 years), and long (20 years). Yields are higher than for Treasuries.

Zero-coupon bonds (also called **zeros** or **deep discount bonds**) are municipal, corporate, or Treasury issues[2] that pay no annual interest, are offered to investors at prices far lower than their face value, and are redeemed at full value upon maturity. They pay out no interest income to the investor (thus no coupons are cashed), and the return to the investor comes from redeeming them at their stated face value. In this manner, zeros operate much like Series EE savings bonds and U.S. Treasury bills. The interest, usually compounded semiannually, accumulates within the bond itself. When you buy a zero, you actually own a bond's interest coupon, reissued as a new security, that will be paid out in a lump sum at maturity.

The maturity date for a zero could be in a few months or as long as 30

---

[2] The Federal Reserve Board issues its own type of zeros, backed by Treasury bonds, called STRIPS (separate trading of registered interest and principal of securities) because they have been stripped of their interest coupons. The Treasury leaves the stripping to brokerages and other financial institutions, which then market the zeros under such names as TIGRs and CATs.

years. Investors in Treasury and corporate zeros must pay federal (but usually not state and local) income taxes on the "phantom" interest income every year, even though it isn't received until the bond matures. Municipal zeros issued in your own state are generally exempt from all taxes.

Zeros are good investments for tax-sheltered retirement plans.

Zeros are ideal for cautious investors because you know exactly how much you will receive upon maturity. For example, an investor might purchase a 10-year zero-coupon corporate bond for $250. As noted, the Internal Revenue Service requires that the assumed interest of $75 ($1000 − $250 = $750/10) per year be reported annually. Zero-coupon bonds are particularly advantageous to investors utilizing tax-sheltered investments (such as IRAs and 401-k plans) because federal income taxes are further deferred. (The uses of tax-sheltered investments for retirement planning are discussed in Chapter 22.) Realize also that with a regular bond, you must find a place to invest the semiannual interest checks, and at times you may only be able to find a lower rate. When you purchase a zero, the interest rate is locked in for the duration. Zeros may be purchased from stockbrokers.

What Should the Investor Consider before Investing in Bonds?

Objective
To be able to describe what the investor should consider before investing in bonds.

A bond's value is affected by a number of factors, including its type, current yield, the demand for the bond, its availability in the marketplace, and the underlying credit quality of the issuer. Both the price and yield of a bond are functions of current market interest rates, prices for similar bonds, the stated interest or coupon rate on the bond, and the number of years that must elapse before the bond matures. Transaction costs and taxes also affect yields significantly.

Market Interest Rates

The state of the economy and the supply and demand for credit affect **market interest rates.** These are the current interest rates paid on various types of corporate and government debts that have similar levels of risk. When the economy slumps, the federal government often lowers the interest rates on Treasury issues in an attempt to stimulate economic activity.

Market interest rates for various investments on a particular day might be Treasury bills providing a return of 7.0 percent; U.S. Treasury notes, 7.4 percent; U.S. Treasury bonds, 8.8 percent; federal agency issues, 9.2 percent; high-quality corporate bonds, 9.9 percent; long-term certificates of deposit, 9.0 percent; junk bonds, 13.2 percent; and high-quality municipal bonds, 7.1 percent. (Munies are lower because the income is tax-exempt.) These market interest rates usually change frequently. In order for a bond to be attractive to investors, it must return the market interest rate or better for debts with similar risks.

When a bond is first issued, it is sold in one of three ways: (1) at its face value (the value of the bond as stated on the certificate; it is also the amount the investor will receive when the bond matures), (2) at a **discount** below its face value, or (3) at a **premium** above its face value.[3] Since the stated interest rate on the bond is fixed, it is the price that changes to provide a competitive effective rate of return.

To illustrate, assume that Running Paws Catfood Company decided to issue 20-year bonds at 8.8 percent. In the time it took to print and prepare the bonds for sale, the market interest rate on comparable bonds might have risen to 9 percent. In this instance, Running Paws bonds will sell at a slight discount in order to provide a competitive return. Discounts and premiums are factors of market interest rates and the number of years to maturity.[4]

Current Yield

Recall that the coupon rate of a bond remains at a fixed rate of interest until maturity. This is the interest rate printed on the bond certificate. For example, Glenda Champion, a retired postal worker from Williamston, North Carolina, bought a 20-year $1000 Running Paws Catfood Company bond last week that is to pay her $70 in interest a year; thus it pays at a 7.0 percent coupon rate. (The coupon rate is determined by dividing the total annual interest, in dollars, by $1000.) While this is useful information, it does not tell an investor the actual rate of return (or yield) he or she is earning on the bond because it probably was purchased at a premium or discount rather than at precisely $1000. Such was the case for Glenda.

Bonds are most often bought at a discount or at a premium rather than for their face values.

The **current yield** of a bond is a measure of the current annual income (the total of both semiannual interest payments in dollars) expressed as a percentage when divided by the bond's current market price. For example, if Glenda Champion bought that $1000 bond paying $70 a year for $940, the bond's current yield is 7.45 percent, as shown below in the **current yield formula:**

$$\text{Current yield} = \frac{\text{current annual income}}{\text{current market value}}$$

$$= \frac{\$70}{\$940}$$

$$= 7.45 \text{ percent} \qquad (17.1)$$

Current yields of bonds are reported in newspapers.

Financial sections of larger newspapers publish the current yields for a great number of bonds. Note, however, that the total return on a bond investment is made up of the same components as stock or any other

---

[3] A taxpayer may elect to amortize a bond premium by deducting it over the life of the bond. For new bonds, investors may reduce interest income by the amount of the premium allocated to the taxable year.

[4] What you always want to avoid is purchasing a bond in the secondary market at a premium ($1200 for example) and soon afterward have it called by the issuer at a lower price (perhaps $1050). Therefore, you should always find out about the callability provisions of a bond before investing.

What If Interest Rates Change after You Purchase a Bond?

On any given day, the major determinant of bond prices is the prevailing level of interest rates in the economy. The following figure illustrates the price changes for bonds when interest rates rise or fall. In general, rising interest rates reduce bond values and falling rates increase bond values. In addition, the longer until maturity of a bond, the more sensitive is the price to changes in interest rates. Thus prices on long-term bonds fluctuate much more than those of short-term issues. When bonds prices change, the measurement of variation is referred to in **basis points**. One hundred basis points equal 1 percent.

Lenders usually require extra compensation (more basis points) for lending money over the long term because it is difficult to accurately project inflation and the future value of bond and interest payments. Also their money is exposed for many years to credit risks and other perils, such as early calls. Should interest rates rise, the investor will be locked into a lower rate of return for more years than with a shorter-term issue. As a result, bonds are priced to achieve current and future values and include an *inflation premium*. If the premium proves to be too low, the investor loses some or all of the profit, as well as perhaps some of the purchasing power of the initial investment. If inflation and interest rates fall instead, bond prices will increase to provide exceptional levels of return.

Bond Prices Move When Interest Rates Change

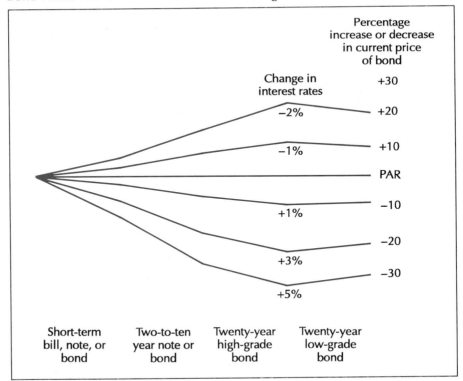

Source: Original data from Vanguard Group Press, Inc.

investment: current income *and* capital gains. In Glenda Champion's situation, she will receive $1000 at the maturity date (20 years from now) even though she only paid $940 for the bond; therefore, her anticipated total return (or effective yield) is going to be higher than the 7.45 percent current yield.

Yield to Maturity

Yield to maturity (*YTM*) is the total annual effective rate of return earned by a bondholder on a bond when it is held to maturity; it reflects *both* the current income *and* any difference if the bond was purchased at a price other than face value. Three generalizations exist: (1) if a bond is purchased at face value, the yield to maturity is the same as the coupon rate printed on the certificate; (2) if a bond is purchased at a premium, the *YTM* will be lower than the coupon rate; and (3) if a bond is purchased at a discount, the *YTM* will be higher than the coupon rate.

The YTM is the most accurate measure of the effective return earned by the investor.

For example, since Glenda Champion's 20-year bond with a coupon rate of 7 percent was bought at a discount for $940, her yield to maturity must be greater than the coupon rate because she will receive $60 more than she paid for the bond when she receives the $1000 at maturity. Exactly how much higher can be determined.

You can find exact *YTM*s in detailed bond tables available at large libraries or a broker's office. Large-circulation newspapers also publish yields to maturity, but only for Treasury issues. Also, you can calculate an approximate yield to maturity when contemplating a bond purchase, since seemingly comparable bonds may have different *YTM*s. The *YTM* varies for each bond at various prices. The **yield to maturity (*YTM*) formula** shown below factors in the approximate appreciation when a bond is bought at a discount or at a premium:

$$YTM = \frac{I + [(FV - CV)/N]}{(FV + CV)/2} \qquad (17.2)$$

where

$$I = \textit{interest} \text{ paid annually in dollars}$$
$$FV = \textit{face value}$$
$$CV = \textit{current value}$$
$$N = \textit{number} \text{ of years until maturity}$$

For example, Glenda Champion paid $940 for a 20-year 7 percent coupon rate bond, and a *YTM* of 7.53 percent for that bond is calculated as follows:

$$YTM = \frac{\$70 + [(\$1000 - \$940)/20]}{(\$1000 + \$940)/2}$$
$$= \frac{\$73}{\$970}$$
$$= 7.53 \text{ percent}$$

If you plan to buy and hold a bond until maturity, you should compare *YTMs* instead of current yields, because *YTMs* fairly represent all factors. The current yield on a bond is not an effective measure of the total annual return to the investor, and the fewer years until maturity, the worse an indicator it becomes. Using the preceding data, Glenda Champion's 20-year bond with a coupon rate of 7 percent and a current yield of 7.45 percent has a *YTM* of 7.53 percent. If it matured in 20 years, the *YTM* would be 7.53 percent; if it were purchased with only 10 years until maturity, the *YTM* becomes 7.84 percent; with 5 years, the *YTM* becomes 8.45 percent; and with 2 years, the *YTM* is 10.3 percent.

Transaction Costs

The purchase and sale of bonds often involve **transaction costs,** which include fees charged by the broker and the seller to pay for the expenses of transferring ownership of the certificate(s). You can avoid fees for U.S. securities only if you purchase the bonds directly from a government agency and later redeem them. Otherwise, bonds almost always have transaction costs.

The impact of transaction costs can be avoided or reduced.

Payment of transaction costs, of course, reduces the yield. Since such expenses are usually incurred at both the purchase and the sale of bonds (but not at retirement), they can cause sharp reductions in yield on a bond with a short maturity or in a small denomination. For example, the 10 percent coupon rate on a $1000 corporate bond would be quickly reduced to about 4 percent if the bondholder had to pay a $30 fee to purchase the bond and another $30 to sell it a year later. The wise investor will (1) avoid transaction costs when possible (by buying T-bills or buying directly from the issuer), (2) place a large amount of funds in bonds to reduce the effect of transaction costs (on 10 $1000 bonds the preceding $60 in fees would amount to only six-tenths of 1 percent), and (3) purchase bonds with a longer maturity to reduce the effect of the transaction costs ($60 in fees on a $1000 bond would be a reduction in yield of about 6 percent over 1 year, 3 percent over 2 years, and 2 percent over 3 years). Some banks charge maintenance fees of up to $5 a month to serve as custodian of bonds, and you can avoid this fee by locating a bank that does not charge it.

Tax-Equivalent Yields

In Chapter 8 we illustrated the impact of the effective marginal tax rate on your income. The less you pay in taxes, the more you have available for spending, saving, and investing. Because municipal bonds receive special tax treatment, many investors consider buying them. In general, the higher your federal tax bracket, the more favorable municipal bonds are as an investment compared with taxable bonds. Your task, as illustrated in Chapter 8, is to compare the taxable yield with the tax-exempt yield to determine the better after-tax return for you.

Advantages and Disadvantages of Bond Investments

Objective
To be able to list the advantages and disadvantages of investing in bonds.

The advantages and disadvantages of investing in bonds are explained below.

Advantages

1. *Higher interest rates than savings accounts.* You receive a higher current income yield than you do on savings accounts. When market interest rates are declining, many conservative investors purchase bonds with a 3- to 4-year remaining maturity to "lock in" the higher rates.

2. *Safe return of principal.* Choosing a highly rated bond provides excellent assurance that the principal will be returned when the maturity date arrives. There is less financial risk with bonds than with common stocks. A bond issued from a highly regarded company provides security to an investor who has almost a guarantee of return of principal.

3. *Less volatility than stocks.* Bonds perform with less volatility than stocks. They also do better than stocks during economic recessions. Temporary losses in a bond's market value show up only on paper, while the income that bonds pay continues to flow to the investor.

4. *Regular income.* The fixed interest payments of bonds represent a known amount of money that almost assuredly will come in on a regular basis.

5. *Diversification of investment portfolio.* The investor who wishes to spread out the risk of losing capital can choose among several different types of investments. Placing funds in common stocks, in real estate, and in four or five bonds provides diversification.

6. *Low purchase cost.* You may purchase most bonds in denominations of $1000, and some municipals are available for as little as $100.

7. *Ease of management.* Although you should never ignore your investments, bonds need less careful attention than most alternatives. If you choose government or other top-rated bonds and hold them to maturity, they will need minimal management.

8. *No taxes on municipal bonds.* Interest earned on municipal bonds is exempt from federal, and sometimes state and local, taxes. Thus persons in higher marginal tax brackets might find them attractive.

Disadvantages

1. *Interest-rate movements affect bond prices.* Bond prices are influenced partially by supply and demand and mostly by the cost of money. If you paid $1000 for a 20-year 7 percent bond and needed to sell it when current interest rates were at 9 percent, you might lose more

than $200. You can estimate the selling price of an existing bond (assuming it is not just a couple of years from maturity) with the following **bond-selling price formula:**

You can determine how much your existing bond will sell for today after interest rates change.

$$\text{Bond selling price} = \frac{\text{annual interest income in dollars}}{\text{current market interest rate}} \qquad (17.3)$$

Substituting figures, the selling price equals $70/0.09, or $777.78. If you bought the bond for $1000, you will lose $222.22 if you sell it for $777.78. (Keep it until maturity and the issuer will retire it for $1000.)

2. *Bond prices can be quite volatile.* Since market interest rates vary after a bond has been issued, bond prices can change rapidly on occasion. They are most volatile when (a) bonds are sold at less than face value when first issued, (b) the stated rate is low, and (c) the bond maturity time is long. The investor who holds a bond to maturity might ignore such information, but the person considering selling before maturity might be shocked to see price swings of 20 percent or more. The speculator might see such rapid price changes as opportunities.

3. *No hedge against inflation.* During inflationary times, market interest rates rise, which pushes bond interest rates up as well. Thus the bond investor earns a current return that may or may not stay even with a rising inflation rate.

4. *Principal does not appreciate.* Unlike common stocks, bonds do not increase in value with increased profitability of the firm or good expectations for the future. Bond prices are instead tied to general interest rates. Except for convertible bonds, price appreciation is unlikely to occur unless the financial rating rises or interest rates decline. And in such circumstances the investor must sell the bond to profit.

5. *Difficulty of compounding.* Unlike many stockholders, most bond-holders cannot reinvest dividends to receive the benefits of compounding (earning interest on principal and interest). They must instead hold interest payments in lower-yielding savings accounts or money-market accounts until they accumulate enough to purchase another bond.

6. *High taxes.* Except for tax-exempt bonds, the interest and capital gains on bonds are subject to an investor's effective marginal tax rate.

7. *Possible poor marketability.* A bond is liquid when it trades regularly and in quantity. Although most bonds are liquid, holding lots of five or fewer may make selling a bit expensive. Note also that a commission premium of as much as $50 might be charged for odd-lot sales (less than 10 bonds). Further, prices of bonds are not published daily except for the larger issues.

8. *Poor diversification.* Because most bond issues sell at $1000 each, it may be difficult for some small investors to diversify if all their investments are in bonds.

How to Buy and Sell Bonds

If you want to make money on bonds, the timing of their purchase and sale can be crucial. This section discusses the selection of bonds and when it is best to sell a bond.

Should You Invest in Bonds?

Deciding whether to buy bonds as an investment depends on your investment needs, the current returns of investment alternatives, and your estimate about the future of interest rates. Conservative and moderate bondholders typically desire income rather than the opportunity for appreciation. Also, most bonds held to maturity carry little financial risk as compared with common stocks and real estate.

The total return on bonds historically has been lower than stocks.

The total annual after-tax return on bonds is historically about one-half to two-thirds that of stocks. This is not true, however, during economic downturns. During an economic recession, declining profits reduce both dividends and prices of common stocks, while total returns on existing bonds tend to increase, likely equaling or even exceeding those on stocks.

How to Select a Bond in Which to Invest

The process of selecting a bond involves the following four decisions:

1. *Decide on risk level.* The level of financial risk is related to the likely rate of return; the safest bonds offer the lowest yields. U.S. government securities offer virtually no risk. For slightly more risk, consider the highest-rated corporate and municipal bonds. Lower-rated bonds, such as Baa or B, offer substantial risk as well as higher yields.

2. *Decide on maturity.* Consider the time schedule of your financial needs. Bonds with a short maturity generally have a lower current yield but greater price stability. For people who desire a maturity time of a year or less, a Treasury bill rather than a savings certificate of deposit often provides a better return. Remember too that since you buy T-bills at a discount, you need less cash.

3. *Decide on tax equivalents.* Carefully consider the impact of the return from bonds on the total income taxes to be paid. As shown in Equations (8.3) and (8.4), tax-exempt securities may be a better investment than taxable alternatives.

4. *Select the highest yield to maturity (YTM).* Given similar bond issues with comparable risks, maturity, and tax equivalency, investors should choose the one that offers the highest yield to maturity (*YTM*), which was illustrated in Equation (17.2).

When to Sell a Bond

In a few distinct instances, a bondholder should consider selling before a bond matures.

1. *When interest rates have dropped.* When interest rates drop, the price of a bond necessarily increases. If, for example, you have an 8 percent bond and interest rates decline to 6 percent, the price of your bond could rise to over $1333 [as determined by Equation (17.3)]. You may wish to take your profits by selling.

2. *When the bond rating has slipped.* Despite your efforts to choose a quality bond, unexpected events can cause a bond's rating to change. Perhaps the corporation suffered some economic setbacks; perhaps the municipality had a loss in taxing authority. Be alert to any changes in bond ratings. A decreased bond rating can mean greater financial risk and a lower market price.

3. *When shifts in interest rates are definitely expected.* Interest rates are constantly changing, but some events clearly suggest that substantial changes in interest rates are ahead. Perhaps a conservative (or liberal) government is elected; perhaps federal budget deficits are growing larger (or smaller) with corresponding forecasts of greater deficits (or surpluses) in the future. How you might react to a likely interest-rate shift depends on what bonds you own and the direction of the shift. Should interest rates be expected to rise, you could sell short-term bonds and reinvest the proceeds when the rates have gone up. In a market of falling interest rates, you can realize capital gains by selling bonds with higher coupon rates.

Summary

1. Fixed-asset investments are classified according to variability of value and yield, such as fixed value and fixed yield, fixed value and variable yield, and variable value and fixed yield. Bonds are in the last category.

2. As evidences of debt, bonds have 10 characteristics: legal indenture, denominations of value, maturity time, being secured or unsecured, senior or subordinated, and registered or bearer, sinking fund, callability, warrants, and convertibility.

3. There are four general types of bonds: corporate bonds, U.S. government securities, municipal bonds, and specialty bonds. Municipal bonds are exempt from federal income taxes.

4. Before investing in bonds, the investor should consider both the price and yield of a bond because they are functions of current market interest rates, prices for similar bonds, the stated interest or coupon rate, and the number of years until the bond matures.

5. The advantages of investing in bonds include higher interest rates than on savings accounts, safe return of principal, regular income, and ease of management. Some of the disadvantages are that interest-rate movements affect the market value of a bond before it reaches maturity, the principal does not appreciate, and interest is not compounded.

6. Four steps are involved in selecting a bond for investment: deciding on risk level, maturity, tax equivalents, and highest yield to maturity. A bondholder should consider selling when interest rates have dropped, when the bond rating has slipped, and when interest rate shifts are definitely expected.

Modern Money Management

The Johnsons Compare Some Investments

Harry and Belinda Johnson have saved $6,000 toward a down payment on a very expensive luxury automobile they hope to purchase in the next 3 to 5 years. Because they are not getting too high a return on their money market account, they seek the greater yields of bond investments. Examine the following table, which identifies eight investment alternatives; respond to the questions that follow.

Name of Issue	Bond Denomination	Coupon Rate %	Years Until Maturity	Moody's Rating	Market Price	Current Yield	YTM
Corporate ABC	$1000	9.0	4	Aa	$ 980		
Corporate DEF	1000	9.5	20	Aa	1020		
Corporate GHI	1000	8.4	12	Baa	735		
Corporate JKL	1000	8.8	5	Aaa	990		
Corporate MNO	1000	10.1	15	B	820		
Corporate PQR	1000	6.0	11	B	450		
Treasury note	1000	8.1	3	—	995		
Municipal bond	1000	6.6	20	Aa	960		

1. What is the current yield of each investment alternative? (Put your responses in the proper column in the table.)

2. What is the yield to maturity for each? (Put your responses in the proper column in the table.) You may calculate the *YTMs* using Equation (17.2) or use the Personal Finance Cookbook (PFC) program YTM.

3. Knowing that the Johnsons are moderate in investment philosophy, which one of the six corporate bonds would you recommend? Why?

4. Since the Johnsons are in the 28 percent federal marginal tax bracket, and given the one municipal bond choice, what is the tax-equivalent yield? Should they invest in your recommendation in question 3 or in the municipal bond? Why? You may calculate tax-equivalent yields using the formulas on page 299 or use the Personal Finance Cookbook (PFC) program TAXEQUIV.

5. What three of the eight alternatives would you recommend as a group so that the Johnsons would have some protection for their $6000 because of diversification? Why do you suggest that combination?

6. Assume that the Johnsons bought all three of your recommendations in question 5. If market interest rates drop by 2 percent in 2 years (for example, from 9.4 to 7.4 percent), what are your recommendations for buying or selling each alternative? Why? Support your answer by calculating the selling price for each bond using Equation (17.3).

Key Words and Concepts

aftermarket, 606
agency issues, 607
basis points, 612
bearer bonds, 600
bonds, 598
bond selling price formula, 618
book-entry form, 601
callable bonds, 601
collateralized mortgage obligations
    (CMOs), 609
convertible bond, 602
corporate bonds, 603
coupon, 601
coupon bonds, 600
coupon rate, 598
coupon yield, 601
credit risk, 603
current yield, 611
current yield formula, 611
debenture, 600
default risk, 603
discount, 611
discount yield, 606
face value, 598
fixed-asset investments, 597
floating-rate bonds, 609
general obligation bonds, 608
indenture, 599
interest-rate risk, 598
junk bonds, 605
leveraged buy-outs (LBOs), 605
market interest rates, 610

maturity date, 598
municipal bonds (munies), 608
new issue, 601
par value, 598
premium, 611
prospectus, 601
purchase warrant, 602
registered bonds, 600
retired, 599
revenue bonds, 608
secondary market, 606
secured bonds, 600
senior debenture, 600
serial bonds, 600
sinking fund, 599
speculative bond, 605
stated interest rate, 598
subordinated debenture, 600
transaction costs, 614
Treasury bills (T-bills), 606
Treasury bonds, 607
Treasury issues, 606
Treasury notes, 607
unsecured bonds, 600
variable rate bonds, 609
warrant, 601
yield to maturity (*YTM*), 613
yield to maturity (*YTM*) formula,
    613
zero coupon bonds (zeros or deep
    discount bonds), 609

Review Questions

1. Explain the general characteristics of a fixed-asset investment, and give an example of one.

2. Identify a type of fixed-asset investment that has a fixed value but a variable return.

3. Explain how bonds have a variable value and a fixed return.

4. Explain how an indenture works and why government bonds do not have indentures.

5. Explain how a sinking fund works.

6. Distinguish between secured and unsecured bonds.

7. Explain the difference between a senior debenture bond and a subordinated debenture bond.

8. What is the difference between coupon bonds and registered bonds?

9. Explain what the book-entry process means.

10. Describe a situation in which a bond issuer would exercise a bond's callable feature.

11. Explain why some bonds have warrants.

12. What is the value of having a convertible bond?

13. Name the four general types of bonds, and distinguish among them.

14. Summarize the differences among Treasury bills, notes, and bonds.

15. Why are U.S. government bonds the safest bonds to buy?

16. Distinguish between the two most popular types of municipal bonds.

17. What tax characteristic is unique to municipal bonds?

18. Explain how zero-coupon bonds work and which types of investors might like them.

19. Explain how changes in market interest rates cause bonds to be sold at a premium or at a discount.

20. Explain the difference between current yield and yield to maturity.

21. What are transaction costs, and how can they be reduced or avoided?

22. Illustrate how your effective marginal tax rate can influence your decision to invest in different types of bonds.

23. List some advantages and disadvantages of having bonds as an investment.

24. Summarize the four-step procedure of selecting bonds.

25. Describe three situations in which it may be wise to sell bonds.

Case Problems

1. Mary Ellen Boyer of Taos, New Mexico, has purchased several types of bonds over the years. Her total bond investment exceeds $40,000. She prefers a variable-value and fixed-yield investment. Her sister Margaret, on the other hand, has more than $50,000 invested in various blue-chip income common stocks in a variety of industries.
   a. Justify Mary Ellen's attitude toward bond investments.
   b. Justify Margaret's attitude toward stock investments.

2. Johnson Edwards of Henderson, Tennessee, is interested in investing $10,000 in bonds because he believes that market interest rates are going to decline during a business slowdown over the next 18 months or so. Johnson is in the 33 percent marginal tax bracket and is a conservative investor. Assuming that his conclusion is correct, give him appropriate advice in response to the following questions.

   a. Should Johnson buy corporate or government bonds? Why?

   b. Johnson has to choose between a corporate bond with a current yield of 10.0 percent and a municipal bond yielding 7.0 percent. Which would you recommend? Why? You may calculate tax-equivalent yields using Equations (8.3) and (8.4) or use the Personal Finance Cookbook (PFC) program (TAXEQUIV).

   c. If high-quality corporate bonds have a current yield of 10.0 percent, long-term government bonds have a current yield of 9.2 percent, and Treasury notes are yielding 8.4 percent, which type do you recommend to Johnson? Why?

   d. If Johnson were to purchase municipal bonds, would you recommend general obligation or revenue bonds? Why?

   e. Assume that Johnson bought a 20-year $1000 corporate bond with a coupon rate of 9 percent for $950. Calculate his current yield and also tell him what the selling price of his bond might be if interest rates drop 2 percent over the next year. [*Hint:* Use Equations (17.1) and (17.3) to determine your answer.]

   f. Calculate the yield to maturity of the bond in *e* above using Equation (17.2) or use the Personal Finance Cookbook (PFC) program (YTM).

3. Charlotte Chang of Martin, Tennessee, is a speculative investor who believes that interest rates will drop over the next year or two because of an economic slowdown. Charlotte wants to profit in the bond market by buying and selling during the next several months. She seeks your advice on how to invest her $15,000.

   a. If Charlotte buys corporate or municipal bonds, what rating should her selections have? Why?

   b. Assume that Charlotte has a choice between two comparable $1000 corporate bonds. One has a coupon rate of 7.4 percent. The other is a convertible bond with a coupon rate of 7 percent. The convertible right is for 30 shares of Running Paws common stock with a current market price of $30 over the next 5 years. Tell Charlotte which bond is the better choice, and give your assumptions about the market value of the stock.

   c. If Charlotte buys fifteen 30-year $1000 corporate bonds with a 9.8 coupon rate for $960 each, what is her current yield? [*Hint:* Use Equation (17.1).]

   d. If market interest rates drop 2 percent over the next 12 months (from 10.2 to 8.2 percent), what will be the approximate market value of each of Charlotte's bonds in part c? [*Hint:* Use Equation (17.3).]

   e. Assuming rates do go down 2 percent in 12 months, how much is Charlotte's capital gain on the $14,400 investment if she sells? How much was her current return for the two semiannual interest payments? How much was her total return both in dollars and as an annual yield? (Ignore transaction costs.)

f. If Charlotte is wrong about projecting the future and interest rates go up 1 percent over the year, what would be the probable market value of each of her bonds? [*Hint:* Use Equation (17.3).] Tell why you would advise her to sell or not to sell.

Suggested Readings

"A Word to the Muni-mad." *Newsweek,* September 25, 1989, p. 39. A warning on the need to be cautious when investing in municipal bonds.

"Bad Deals in High Yields." *Changing Times,* June 1989, pp. 63–67. High interest rates means higher risks for investors.

"Bond Ratings Are a Security Blanket That Sometimes Gets Ripped Away." *Changing Times,* June 1989, p. 18. Cautions against putting too much trust in bond rating and emphasizes the importance of other sources of information about bonds.

"Catching the Crest of Rising Yields." *Money,* April 1989, pp. 90–97. How to lock in long-term bond yields once it looks like rates are topping.

"Fixed Income with a Hedge." *Forbes,* June 26, 1989, p. 246. Explains the benefits of indexed bonds.

"Munis, State by State: Bargains That Beat the Tax Man." *Fortune,* April 9, 1990, pp. 29, 32. An analysis of various municipal bond offerings and techniques for investing.

"Pigging Out on Tax Shelters." *Changing Times,* June 1989, pp. 45–52. Tax-free munies and how various states tax them.

"Riding the Wave of Long Bond Yields." *Money,* April 1989, pp. 100–111. Precision timing helps the investor know when to get out of money market funds and into long-term bonds to earn high returns.

"The Basics of Bonds." *Consumer Reports,* September 1989, p. 579. Explanation of definitions and the risks of investments in bonds.

"Why Junk Bonds Face New Losses." *Money,* January 1990, pp. 109–117. The worst times for junk bond investors may be yet to come.

18 Investing in Mutual Funds

OBJECTIVES

After reading this chapter, you should be able to

1. Understand why people invest in mutual funds.
2. Explain the unusual tax status given to mutual funds and to investors in mutual funds.
3. Distinguish among the four major objectives of mutual funds.
4. Classify mutual funds by portfolio.
5. Recognize that the costs of investing in mutual funds may include various charges and fees.
6. List the unique benefits of mutual funds.
7. Describe the advantages and disadvantages of investing in mutual funds.
8. Explain how to select a mutual fund in which to invest.
9. Consider five factors that help determine when to sell a mutual fund.

• • • • • • • • •

The concept of mutual funds began more than 100 years ago in London with the Foreign and Colonial Government Trust, which was established to provide "the investor of moderate means the same advantages as the large capitalists in diminishing the risk of investing . . . by spreading the investment over a number of different stocks." In essence, the group formed an **investment company,** which is a corporation, trust, or partnership in which investors with similar financial goals pool their funds to utilize professional management and to achieve diversification of their investments in securities and other alternative investments. Mutual funds are the most common form of investment company in the United States. A **mutual fund** is an investment company that combines the funds of investors who have purchased shares of ownership in the investment company and invests those monies in a diversified portfolio of securities issued by other corporations or governments. Today there are more mutual funds (over 2400) than there are companies on the New York Stock Exchange (1450).

This chapter examines the appeal and logic of mutual funds as an investment. We first explain why people might want to invest in a mutual fund. Also examined are returns to the investor in view of the special tax status given mutual funds. We then distinguish among the four major objectives of mutual funds and classify them according to their portfolio holdings. Next we discuss the fact that the costs of investing in mutual funds may include various fees and charges. After this we discuss unique benefits of mutual funds that are usually appealing to the average investor and provide a summary of the advantages and disadvantages of mutual funds. Two sections then answer key questions about selecting and selling a mutual fund.

Why People Invest in an Open-End Mutual Fund

Objective
To be able to understand why people invest in mutual funds.

Currently, more than 25 percent of U.S. households own mutual funds, and the public is investing in mutual funds more than ever before. Some reasons for this growth are that newer and more attractive types of funds have been recently created, many funds carry little or no sales charges, some have performed much better than an average common stock, and aggressive marketing efforts have been used to promote mutual funds. Many people feel that investing in mutual funds can provide a better return

FIGURE 18.1
How a Mutual Fund Works

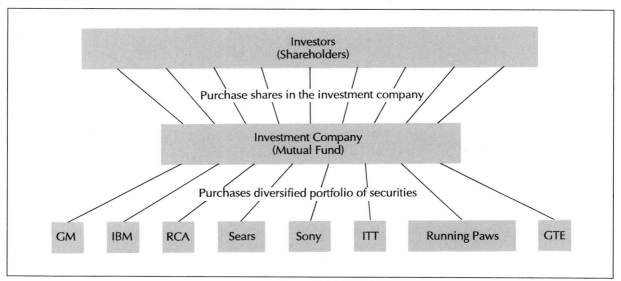

than investing in separate securities. The concept of mutual funds is illustrated in Figure 18.1.

All investment companies operate similarly. They pool funds obtained by selling shares to investors and make investments in particular areas to achieve the financial goal of income, growth, or both. Voting rights are generally retained by management, and investors pay a fee for the management service. Investment companies avoid most federal income taxation as long as they distribute 98 percent of their income to shareholders. These companies are guided by the federal Investment Company Act and regulations of the Securities and Exchange Commission (SEC).

An **open-end mutual fund** is always ready to sell new shares and to redeem old ones at a price called *net asset value*.[1] **Net asset value (*NAV*)** is a fund's total net assets (securities, cash, and any accrued earnings after deduction of liabilities) divided by the number of shares outstanding. For example, say the current market value of a fund's securities amounts to $75 million and the fund's liabilities amount to $4 million, leaving net assets of $71 million. If 10 million shares of the open-end fund are outstanding, the net asset value would be $7.10 ($71 million/10 million). The net asset value is calculated at least twice daily and represents the worth of each share of the open-end mutual fund. The *NAV* is similar to

---

[1] The other type of mutual fund is a **closed-end mutual fund,** which issues a limited and fixed number of shares of stock and does not buy them back (*redeem* them), so that after the original issue is sold, the price of a share is established by supply and demand in the secondary market. Thus closed-end shares are traded much like the common stock or bonds of a corporation. Of the more than 2400 mutual funds, only about 10 percent are closed-end funds.

a stock's market price. About 90 percent of all mutual funds are open-end funds, and these types of funds are the focus of this chapter. Shares can be purchased from the mutual fund itself, from a financial planner, or through a brokerage firm; shares can always be redeemed or sold back to the fund.

Taxes and Mutual Funds

Objective
To be able to explain the unusual tax status given to mutual funds and to investors in mutual funds.

The special tax status of mutual funds and of the returns earned by shareholders is examined below.

Income Taxes

Returns to investors in mutual funds take two forms: (1) income and (2) potential price appreciation. Investors in profitable mutual funds receive a quarterly or semiannual dividend check that represents both ordinary income dividend distributions and capital gains distributions. **Ordinary income dividend distributions** are made when the fund distributes dividend and/or interest income (plus some short-term capital gains) after operating expenses are deducted. These distributions to the fund shareholders may be made monthly, quarterly, or annually. A **capital gains distribution** represents net gains (capital gains reduced by capital losses) a fund realizes on its sale of securities during the year. Ordinarily, funds distribute net capital gains at least annually.[2] Because both these types of distributions represent investment income, mutual fund investors must pay income taxes on all such earnings paid to them by the company.

Investors must pay income taxes on profits from mutual funds.

Price appreciation is another form of return on mutual funds. You hope that the market price of the mutual fund, the NAV, will increase in value. If, for example, your mutual fund owns common stock in IBM and General Electric and the stocks of those two companies increase in value, the fund will have **capital growth.** This growth is an increase in the market value of a mutual fund's securities. As the value of the underlying securities increases, it is usually reflected in the net asset value of fund shares. Of course, price appreciation is only a paper profit until you sell the mutual fund shares and realize the profit.

Special Tax Status

Mutual funds have a special tax status.

A diversified investment company (including most mutual funds) that registers with the SEC qualifies under the Investment Company Act of 1940 and subsequent amendments for special tax status. Like any other registered security, such a regulated investment company must follow specific rules and regulations of the SEC designed to protect investors.

---

[2] Realize further that when a fund declares a capital gain distribution, the fund's net asset value (*NAV*) is reduced, making shareholders liable for taxes on the distribution. If there is no distribution, the *NAV* is not reduced, thus not causing shareholders to have an income tax liability.

The special tax treatment for mutual funds avoids double taxation on fund earnings of dividends and capital gains. Most of the earnings of mutual funds are not subject to the federal corporate income tax, since shareholders must report the same earnings on their own income tax forms. The law requires regulated investment companies to distribute 97 percent of ordinary income and 98 percent of capital gains prior to the end of the calendar year. This enables them to exempt up to 98 percent of their net earnings (excluding long-term capital gains that may be distributed or retained) from corporate taxes if they distribute those profits directly to shareholders. The remaining 2 percent (if any profits are kept) is taxed in the usual way. This law encourages a substantial flow of funds into regulated diversified investment companies, which must pay out almost all their profits to shareholders, who are eventually taxed on these profits as personal income.

Mutual Fund Objectives

Objective
To be able to distinguish between the four major objectives of mutual funds.

A mutual fund's objectives must be stated in its **prospectus**. This is a required written disclosure to the Securities and Exchange Commission and prospective investors of pertinent facts about a corporation, including the experience of its management, its financial status, any anticipated legal matters that could affect the company, and potential risks of investing in the corporation. Mutual funds have one of four major objectives: (1) growth, (2) income, (3) growth and income, and (4) balance.

Growth Objective

A mutual fund with a growth objective focuses on long-term growth or price appreciation of the value of the securities in its portfolio rather than a flow of dividends. The fund buys and holds the common stocks of growing companies, which tend not to declare cash dividends but to reinvest most of their earnings. Stocks of such companies generally increase in value over long periods of time, which pushes up the net asset value of the mutual fund. Such funds strive to provide a very good total return for the investor willing to accept some risk. The return probably will be in the form of small income dividends, some income from capital gains distribution, and a strong potential for price appreciation.

Income Objective

When a mutual fund has income as a primary focus, its almost exclusive aim is to earn a high level of interest and dividends. Capital gains are definitely a secondary consideration. Such a mutual fund would purchase bonds, preferred stocks, and blue-chip income stocks with a history of good earnings and high dividends. These funds provide the investor with a high income dividend, some income from capital gains distributions, and little likelihood of price appreciation.

Growth and Income Objective

A mutual fund with a combination of growth and income as an objective aims for a somewhat aggressive return, not as low as offered by funds with an income objective nor as high as offered by funds with a growth objective. The portfolio of such a fund would include a combination of securities with an emphasis on common stocks. These funds provide the investor with some income dividends, some income through capital gains distributions, and a good chance for price appreciation.

Balanced Objective

Mutual funds with a balanced objective typically emphasize preservation of capital along with moderate growth and income. The objectives of growth and income vary according to economic times, but stability remains paramount. In an economy that is expanding, the portfolio might include many blue-chip growth stocks. In an economy that is in a recession, the fund would purchase more bonds and blue-chip income stocks as a defensive action. These funds provide low financial risk with small income dividends, small income from capital gains distributions, and some opportunity for price appreciation.

Portfolio Classification of Mutual Funds

Objective
To be able to classify mutual funds by portfolio.

With the hundreds of different mutual funds available, there is something for just about every investor's needs. Each mutual fund chooses a variety of investments to achieve its specific investment objectives. The portfolios of mutual funds can concentrate on holdings ranging from risk-free government bonds and blue-chip income stocks to junk bonds to speculative **letter stocks,** which are securities that have not yet been registered with the SEC for sale to the public. Keep in mind that size is important too, since smaller funds (less than $100 million) have greater flexibility than the perhaps more stable, larger funds. Sometimes funds are classified according to their objectives (as described earlier), but just as often they are described by their portfolio as discussed below. Table 18.1 presents summary information.

Common Stock Funds

Some mutual funds include only common stocks in their portfolios. The objective of **common stock funds** is growth and payment of capital gains distributions from price appreciation, evidenced by the six basic types of common stock funds. The first type is the **maximum capital gains fund.** This fund places no emphasis on income dividends, relying primarily on price appreciation as the return for the investor. Holdings could be in little-known companies, firms exploring new technology, and other businesses with good long-term profit potential. Such funds use high-risk

TABLE 18.1
Classification of Mutual Funds by Type and Size

Type of Fund	Number of Funds	Combined Assets (in billions)	Percentage of Total
Common stock			
Maximum capital gain	95	40	2.7
Growth	376	73	0.4
Growth and income	153	80	11.6
Specialized			
Canadian & international	134	25	1.0
Gold and precious metals	31	4	0.4
Government securities	204	107	11.6
Industry funds	77	9	1.0
Tax-exempt bond funds	415	106	11.5
Other	14	3	0.3
Balanced	39	9	1.0
Income	92	27	2.9
Bond and preferred stock	246	51	5.6
Money market	356	326	35.4
Tax-free money market	167	63	6.9
TOTAL	2,399	922	100.0

Source: Reprinted by permission from the Wiesenberger Investment Companies Service, 50th Edition, Copyright 1990, Table 4, Warren Gorham & Lamont, Inc., One Penn Plaza, New York, NY 10019.

investment techniques, such as borrowing money for leverage, short selling, hedging, options, and warrants (see Chapter 21). Such funds are sometimes called performance, aggressive-growth, or "go-go" funds. Popular maximum capital gains funds include Integrated Equity-Aggressive Growth, Forty Four Wall Street Equity, and Babson Enterprise.

A second type is the **growth fund,** the most popular form of common stock fund. It takes a more conventional approach, buying stock in small and moderately well-known companies paying little or no dividends; again, price appreciation is expected. Popular growth funds include Fidelity Magellan, Weingarten Equity Fund, and Scudder Capital Growth. The third type is the **growth and income fund,** which also is quite popular. Its portfolio generally includes a variety of well-known common stocks paying reasonable dividends, along with stocks from some lesser-known firms with strong growth potential. Popular growth and income funds include Fidelity Growth and Income Fund, Vanguard Windsor, and Templeton World.

The fourth type of common stock fund is the **sector fund,** which specializes in common stocks from one particular industry or related group of industries. Of course, investing in only one sector increases risks as well as potential returns—even in a diversified portfolio. Popular sector funds include Vanguard Special Health Portfolio, Blanchard Precious Metals, and Financial Strategic-Leisure. The fifth type is the **diversified international fund,** which invests in stocks of companies listed on foreign exchanges and often focuses on one country or geographic region. Popular international funds include Sogen International, Vanguard World-International Growth, and Alliance International. The sixth type is the **index fund,** which is composed of a large number of the best-performing stocks that are part of a particular index, such as Standard & Poor's 500. The return is expected to be equal to that of all the stocks in the index, which is a benefit if the market is going up. Popular index funds include Colonial U.S. Equity Index, Rushmore Stock Market Index Fund, and Vanguard S&P Index-500.

Bond and Preferred Stock Funds

Bond and preferred stock funds concentrate their holdings on senior securities: bonds and preferred stocks. The emphasis is on safety of principal and income earned through interest and dividends. The bond portion of the portfolio is diversified by maturity date. Popular bonds and preferred stock funds include Financial Industrial Income, ISI Income, and Keystone Custodian Series K-1.

Balanced Funds

Balanced funds include various amounts of bonds, preferred stocks, and common stocks in their portfolios. Their investment policy is to maintain a balance of such holdings and vary them according to economic conditions, with the emphasis on conserving the investor's initial principal. Popular balanced objective funds include Century Shares Trust, United Continental Income, and Phoenix Balanced Series.

Income Funds

Income funds have a primary objective to earn current income and pay ordinary income dividend distributions. They usually seek a portfolio of bonds, preferred stocks, and some select blue-chip income stocks. Some income funds specialize in investing in high-yield bonds or junk bonds. Popular income funds include Fidelity Puritan, Vanguard Qualified Dividend Portfolio I, and Dreyfus Special Income. Table 18.2 gives a sample portfolio of an income fund.

Municipal Bond (Tax-Exempt) Funds

Investors in **municipal bond (tax-exempt) funds** seek to earn current tax-exempt income by investing solely in municipal bonds issued by cities, states, and various districts and political subdivisions. The interest income earned on these bonds is exempt from federal personal income taxes. Popular municipal bond funds include Boston Company Tax-Free Bond, T. Rowe Price Tax-Free High Yield, and Scudder Managed Municipal Bond.

TABLE 18.2
Sample Portfolio of an Income Fund

Holding	Percentage of Total Holdings
Common stock	13
Preferred stock	35
Municipal bonds (long term)	25
U.S. government securities (long term)	10
Corporate bonds	10
U.S. government securities (short term)	5
Liquid assets	2
TOTAL	100

Specialty Funds

Specialty funds can be created for just about any investment need that requires both concentration and diversification in a field. Popular specialty funds include Franklin Utilities, National Aviation and Technology, and Dean Witter Natural Resources Development. **Mutual fund funds** earn a return with money invested in the shares of other mutual funds, thereby diversifying extensively, such as the Vanguard Star, Rightime Fund, and FundTrust Aggressive Growth. **Socially conscious funds** have investments only in companies that meet their shareholders' ethical or moral standards. Dreyfus Third Century, New Alternatives, and Calvert Social Investment are mutual funds that do not have investments in companies that pollute the environment, have a history of poor labor relations, do business in South Africa, or manufacture weapons.

Money Market Funds

Money market funds are mutual funds that specialize in investments in securities that have very short-term maturities, always less than 1 year. (They are also called **money market mutual funds.**) These assets include Treasury bills and notes, certificates of deposit, commercial paper, and repurchase agreements. By staggering the maturities of these securities, the money market fund can earn the current cost of money on its investments. Some money market funds have investments only in tax-exempt securities, so the dividends to the investor avoid federal income taxes. Money market funds provide a convenient place to keep money while awaiting alternative investment opportunities. Many large mutual fund companies have money market funds, including Dreyfus, Lexington, and Twentieth Century. Money market funds are an important part of many investors' cash management plans, as discussed in Chapter 5.

The Special Costs of Investing in Mutual Funds

The costs of investing in mutual funds may include various charges and fees.

Sales Charges

Open-end mutual funds can be classified as to whether they have a **sales charge,** also called a **load** (which is a commission charged for buying into a mutual fund), collected by mutual fund sales personnel, financial planners, banks, or brokerage firms when some mutual funds are sold to an investor. A mutual fund that does not have a sales charge at purchase is generally called a **no-load fund.**

Load Funds   A **load fund** is a mutual fund sold to the public by a broker or salesperson that requires payment at purchase of a sales commission on the amount invested. The commission, typically 7.5 to 8.5 percent, is usually called a **front-end load** because it is paid at the time of initial purchase. The load pays the cost of selling the mutual fund.

For example, assume that you have discussed the investment potential of the Conglomerate Cat and Dog Food Mutual Fund with a salesperson. After examining the prospectus, you decide to invest $10,000. Since this is a load fund with a commission of 8.5 percent (the maximum permitted by the Securities and Exchange Commission), $850 ($10,000 × 0.085) goes to the salesperson. As a result, you have only $9150 working for you to earn dividends and capital gains. Note that this commission is much higher than stock transaction costs, which are usually about 2 percent.

The sales charge may be shown either as the stated commission or as a percentage of the amount invested. The stated commission (8.5 percent here) is always somewhat misleading. The percentage of the amount invested is a more accurate figure because it is based on the *actual* monies invested and working. A stated commission of 8.5 percent amounts to 9.3 percent of the amount actually invested: $10,000 − $9150 = $850/ $9150). If you want to invest a full $10,000, you would need to pay out $10,930 [$10,930 − ($10,930 × 8.5 percent) = $10,000]. Sales charges are lower on invested amounts of $40,000 or more. So-called **low-load funds** may have a 2 to 3 percent sales charge. They are often sold by mail, sometimes sold in shopping centers, and are advertised as having small commissions.

Low-load funds exist too.

No-Load Funds   No-load mutual funds sell their shares at net asset value without the addition of sales charges. Historically, no-loads charged no sales commissions on the amount initially invested, and they were bought directly from the fund by the investing public by mail or telephone. Traditionally, there were no sales personnel for no-load funds; interested investors simply sought out advertisements for these funds in financial newspapers and magazines. The situation is different now, as discussed below. Many excellent no-load funds are described and analyzed in publications such as *Forbes, Barron's, Business Week,* and *Money.*

Hidden Fees

Many no-load funds charge hidden fees.

More than half of all no-load mutual funds are charging hidden fees, or **hidden loads,** which, of course, reduce the anticipated total return to the investor. The negative impact of a number of hidden fees is illustrated in Figure 18.2. The most common hidden fee assessed on many *so-called* no-load mutual fund investments is called a 12b-1 fee. A **12b-1 fee,** named after the 1980 Securities and Exchange Commission (SEC) rule that permits it, is an annual charge assessed to shareholders that pays for advertising, marketing, and distribution costs of the fund. It also pays for **trailing commissions,** those paid to salespersons for months or years in the future. Typically, a 12b-1 fee ranges from 0.25 to 1.50 percent of a fund's net asset value; the industry average in a recent year was 0.61 percent.[3] A 12b-1 fee is actually a "perpetual sales load," since it is assessed on the investment, as well as on reinvested dividends, every year, forever. Such fees are quite costly for the shareholder over a period of years, and you would be better off investing in a load fund than paying 12b-1 assessments if you plan to own the fund for more than 10 years. Norman Fosback, president of the Institute for Econometric Research, in Fort Lauderdale, Florida, describes 12b-1 fees of more than 1 percent as "clearly abusive." A broker or financial planner may claim that a 12b-1 fund is no-load when in fact the fund pays delayed commissions to sellers.

Other hidden charges include back-end loads. A **back-end load** (or **rear-end load**) is a charge paid when a shareholder redeems fund shares (sells them back to the mutual fund company). Back-end loads, including contingent deferred sales charges and redemption fees, are becoming common on both load and no-load funds. **Contingent deferred sales charges** are sales commissions of 1 to 6 percent levied on the mutual fund investor if the shares are redeemed within a certain period after purchase. For example, a fund might charge a 5 percent fee if an investor redeems the shares within 1 year of purchase. Fees often decline for every year the investor owns the shares, perhaps reaching zero after 6 years. **Redemption charges** (also called **exit fees**) are charges levied when shares are redeemed (sold back to the fund) regardless of the length of time the investor has owned the shares. This increasingly common fee is usually 1 percent of the value of the shares redeemed.

To assist the investing public, the SEC requires that a standardized expense table be included in the first few pages of a stock or bond mutual fund's prospectus that describes and illustrates its fees. The data in the

---

[3] What this really means is that the mutual fund manager uses some of the fund's assets to pay for these expenses. Kathryn McGrath, the Securities and Exchange Commission's former director of Investment Management Division, says that she does not believe that "people know that they are paying for such costs." If they did, they might react differently, such as not want to pay any expenditures for advertising.

FIGURE 18.2
How the Anticipated Return in a No-Load Mutual Fund Investment May Be Reduced by Hidden Fees and Charges

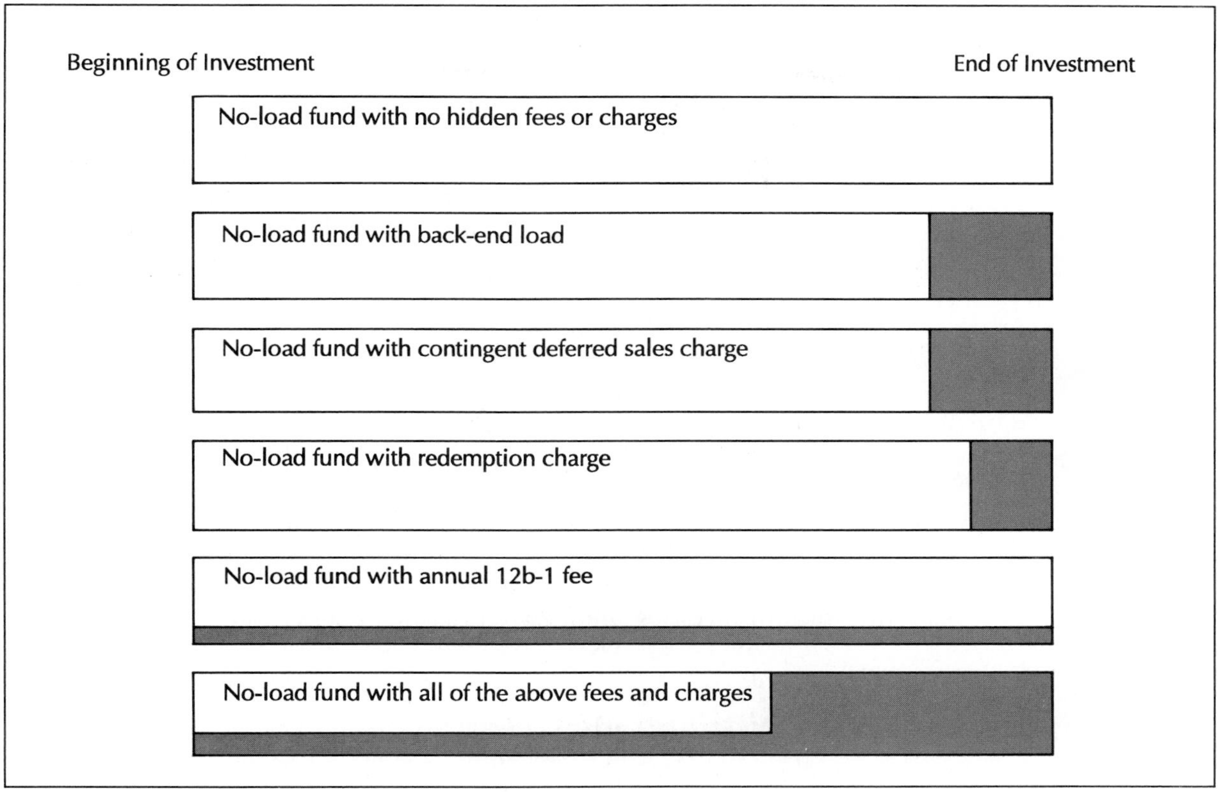

Beginning of Investment	End of Investment

No-load fund with no hidden fees or charges

No-load fund with back-end load

No-load fund with contingent deferred sales charge

No-load fund with redemption charge

No-load fund with annual 12b-1 fee

No-load fund with all of the above fees and charges

tables are not exact representations of past charges, but are designed to illustrate the effect of all sales costs (front- and back-end), management fees, and expenses that an investor would have to pay after meeting three assumptions over time: (1) a uniform 5.0 percent growth rate in return, (2) dividends and capital gains have been reinvested, and (3) the investment was not redeemed. Using a hypothetical example, the tables show how much the expenses and fees reduce a hypothetical $1000 investment for 1, 3, 5, and 10 years.

Clearly, it is important to read the fine print in the prospectus before investing in a mutual fund, including the heretofore no-load funds, because they detail information on how stiff a 12b-1 fee is as well as other costs. In general, the up-front charges are more costly to the investor in the short run, while the annual charges are more costly over the long run. Information in the prospectus helps you evaluate mutual fund choices, and fortunately, there are still plenty of true no-load funds available.[4] Of course, fees are

[4] A new trade organization was formed in 1989, the *100% No Load Mutual Fund Council,* which sells its membership directory to the public for $1.00. Write to 1501 Broadway, New York, NY 10036.

only one factor in a decision to invest in a mutual fund; appropriateness of the fund's investment objective, management, size of the fund, volatility, and past performance are important considerations too.

Management Fees

The professional managers who operate mutual funds are paid for their investment expertise and managerial abilities with a percentage of the investment company's assets as specified in the articles of incorporation. As the assets of the firm increase, the financial rewards for managers will increase as well. Depending on the size of the fund, management fees range from 0.35 to 1.5 percent of the fund's assets assessed annually; the industry average is about one-half of 1 percent. Management fees are deducted when calculating the net asset value.

Unique Benefits of Open-End Mutual Funds

Objective
To be able to list the unique benefits of mutual funds.

The professional management and diversified investments of open-end mutual funds make investing in them different than simply buying common stocks or corporate bonds. The distinct features of mutual funds that make this form of investing unique are discussed below.

Automatic Reinvestment of Dividends and Capital Gains Distributions

Most mutual funds permit (and some even require) **automatic income reinvestment.** This is a provision of a mutual fund voluntary or contractual agreement that allows for the automatic reinvestment of ordinary income dividend distributions and capital gains distributions to buy more shares of the fund. You can elect to have income dividends and/or income from capital gains distributions reinvested in additional shares. Fractional shares are purchased as needed. Over three-fourths of mutual fund shareholders have their income reinvested. The value of automatic income reinvestment is that it compounds share ownership; the number of your shares continues to grow. Figure 18.3 illustrates the concept.

With some funds you may reinvest dividend income at a price that includes a commission charge; with others you may reinvest at the current net asset value. Whether earnings are automatically reinvested or not, the investor owes income taxes on all distributions the year they are paid. The only exceptions are investors whose monies are invested in tax-deferred accounts, such as IRAs or Keoghs. (These are discussed in Chapter 22.)

Automatic EFT Transfers

Investors in mutual funds may have their periodic investment payments automatically forwarded to the mutual fund company using electronic funds transfer (EFT) from a checking or savings account. Your financial

FIGURE 18.3

The Value of Automatic Reinvestment of Income (Dividends and Capital Gains)

An initial investment of $9,150 ($10,000 − $850 commission) grew to $13,076 in 10 years (because the value of the underlying securities pushed up the net asset value) while the investor took dividends in cash (to save, spend or invest elsewhere). If instead all dividends were left to be reinvested automatically, the $9,150 would have grown to $40,831. Data based on over 1,000 stock and bond mutual funds in operation over the past 10 years.

Source: Basic data from the *1990 Mutual Fund Fact Book*, Investment Company Institute, Washington, DC. Reprinted with permission.

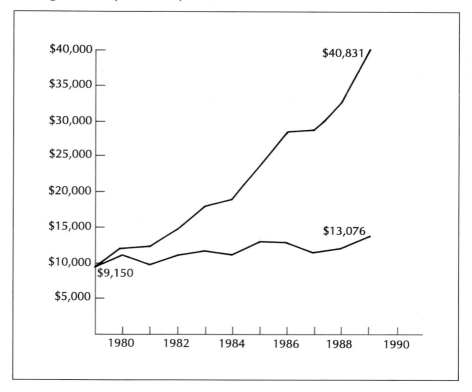

institution will send you written notification of each withdrawal, and you may stop automatic withdrawals at any time.

Check Writing

Most money market mutual fund companies permit you to withdraw money by writing special checks drawn on your account. This provides you with a high-yielding cash management account.

Note that many other funds also permit check writing. Usually, checks must be written in amounts no smaller than $100 or $500, and only a limited number may be written per year. The effect of writing a check on a mutual fund account is to redeem the number of shares necessary to honor the check. For example, if Conglomerate Cat and Dog Food Mutual Fund shares had a net asset value of $10 and you wrote a check for $500, the fund would redeem 50 shares ($10 × 50 = $500). You may usually repurchase a like number of shares without a sales charge.

Telephone Transactions

You can buy and sell shares by telephone after you have opened an account with a mutual fund company. When you call a toll-free number—where operators record your verbal instructions—the mutual fund company will electronically transfer funds from one account to another or to your local bank.

Switching (or Exchange) Privileges

A **switching** (or **exchange**) **privilege** permits mutual fund shareholders, if their needs or objectives change, to swap shares on a dollar-for-dollar basis for shares in another mutual fund managed by the same corporation. Switching often includes swaps among stock, bond, or money market funds. Switching is valuable, and it exists only for mutual fund shareholders in the same **family of funds.** This is a group of mutual funds under the same management company, such as American Funds, Dreyfus, Kemper, Merrill Lynch, and Putnam. To illustrate, the Vanguard group offers 50 funds, ranging from an aggressive-growth fund to a technology sector fund to a municipal bond fund; Fidelity offers over 147 funds. Since your investment objectives could change over time, the switching privilege is valuable. It allows transfer (by telephone or in writing) at no cost or for only a small fee, as little as $5. For example, at age 55 a person who has been investing in a growth fund for the past 20 years may want to convert the monies to an income fund to begin to prepare for early retirement.

Switching is also worthwhile for the investor shrewd enough to observe market trends. For example, assume that you have more than $8000 in your growth fund and have arranged for automatic dividend reinvestment. Fund performance for a couple of years has been around 7 percent, and you notice that interest costs are rising in the general economy. You switch to a bond fund yielding 10 percent. Money gets even tighter, so you switch again to a money-market fund, which increases up to 14 percent for a period of several months. As rates begin to decline, you switch back to a bond fund, locking in a yield of 12 percent for the next 2 years. As yields continue to decline and nearly reach bottom, you move the funds back to a growth and income fund, hoping for significant price appreciation. You can see how being alert to changing market trends can increase your investment returns. Note that if switching results in capital gains, these amounts are taxable events during the year of the exchange.

Systematic Withdrawal Plans

All mutual funds have various types of withdrawal plans available to shareholders. These are used by people who want a periodic income from their mutual fund investments. To be eligible, your investment must have a total net asset value of at least $5000. Each withdrawal must be no less than $50. The firm mails you checks at regular intervals according to one of the following four plans.

Fixed Dollar Amount   You receive a specified fixed amount per month or quarter until the fund is depleted. Income from dividends and capital gains distributions is used first to make the payments, and then shares are redeemed as needed.

Fixed Number of Shares   You receive varying amounts, as the net asset value of each share changes, until the fund is depleted. This plan always results in eventual liquidation of the fund after a certain number of periodic payments. For example, say you own 500 shares of a mutual fund and request that the proceeds of four shares per month be forwarded to you. Not counting any shares that might be acquired by reinvestment, the fund would run out in just over 10 years (500/4 = 125 months). If the net asset value per share is $40, your beginning monthly check would be $160 ($40 × 4). This value could easily increase to $60 over several years as the mutual fund becomes more profitable and perhaps provide monthly checks of $240 ($60 × 4) during later years.

Dividends and Capital Gains Distribution   You receive periodic payments of varying amounts that represent only the ordinary income dividend and capital gains distributions of the fund. This can continue indefinitely, since the principal remains untouched. For example, if your $20,000 fund declares income dividends of $200 and a capital gains distribution of $300 after 3 months, you would receive a check for $500. At the same time, the underlying portfolio of the mutual fund could have grown (because the value of unsold investments could have risen), pushing the net asset value up to perhaps $20,400; of course, the value also could drop. The point is that you can receive dividends and capital gains distributions while the value of your fund continues to increase.

Fixed Percentage of Asset Growth   You receive periodic payments amounting to a percentage of the growth in value of the mutual fund. For example, you might choose to receive 75 percent of the growth, to be paid quarterly. If your $10,000 fund increases in value to $10,400 during a 3-month period, you will receive a check for $300 ($400 × 0.75). If the assets do not grow, you will not receive a check. Note that this plan permits systematic withdrawals from the mutual fund account without depleting it. In fact, since the withdrawals are always a portion of the growth (less than 100 percent), the value of the fund will likely continue to increase.

Your choice of a withdrawal plan depends on your financial needs and investment goals, and you can change it at any time. For example, you could make withdrawals to help pay for a child's college expenses or to supplement a retirement income.

Collateral for Loans

An increasing number of mutual funds permit shareholders to use their investment as collateral for loans. Fund rules usually require that loans be in excess of $5000. The interest rate charged is competitive, since it is just a few points higher than the fund company's cost of borrowing. Often there are no repayment terms, which gives you increased flexibility.

IRS-Approved Retirement Plans

Most mutual funds have programs that "qualify" and are registered with the IRS as tax-free ways to invest money for retirement. Depending on eligibility qualifications, you can put thousands of dollars a year into a mutual fund, deduct the amount from your taxable income, watch the fund grow tax-free, paying no income taxes on the profits until funds are withdrawn during retirement. These programs include individual retirement accounts (IRAs), 401(k) plans, and Keogh retirement programs. (Chapter 22 discusses these mechanisms in retirement planning.[5])

How to Select a Mutual Fund

Objective
To be able to explain how to select a mutual fund in which to invest.

The task of selecting an open-end mutual fund involves examining important sources of information and comparing the performance of various funds.

Sources of Information

You can obtain information about mutual funds from sources such as local newspapers, *The Wall Street Journal,* and *Barron's.* The magazines *Business Week, Fortune, Forbes,* and *Money* are also useful. Of particular value are the late August issue of *Forbes,* the October issue of *Money,* and the late February issue of *Business Week,* which feature comprehensive examinations of the performance of numerous mutual funds.

Three popular specialized investment publications that examine mutual funds in considerable detail are often available in large libraries as well as in brokers' offices: *Investment Companies,* an annual publication of Wiesenberger Financial Services; *Johnson's Investment Company Charts,* published by Hugh A. Johnson and Company; and *Fundscope,* published by Fundscope, Inc. Standard & Poor's also rates the safety of some mutual funds using their familiar AAA, AA, A, and B symbols, which gauge a fund's ability to maintain its net asset value and avoid capital losses.

Comparing the Historical Performance of Mutual Funds As you consider mutual funds, recall the negative impact of inflation. Even if a

---

[5] Another unique benefit is that mutual funds offer a **beneficiary designation clause** when they are purchased as part of a retirement plan. This clause provides that the shareholder can name a beneficiary in a separate legal trust agreement; in the event of death, the proceeds go to the beneficiary without going through probate. (The delays and expenses of probate are discussed in Chapter 23.) Such a clause helps expedite the orderly transfer of assets to the beneficiary.

Advantages and Disadvantages of Open-End Mutual Funds

As you consider investing in open-end mutual funds, you should review their advantages and disadvantages. Some of these are described below.

Advantages

1. The variety of funds available makes it fairly easy to choose a fund that matches your investment objectives.

2. The switching privilege within a family of funds permits easy exchange if your investment objectives change.

3. Marketability and liquidity are good, since shares can always be redeemed for the net asset value.

4. The provision permitting automatic reinvestment of income permits reinvestment of small sums at minimum or no cost for further compounding of profits.

5. Systematic withdrawal income plans provide a convenient method of receiving income.

6. Since professional managers run the fund, your supervisory responsibilities are reduced.

7. Your recordkeeping requirements are minimal because mutual funds offer automatic confirmations and quarterly, semiannual, and annual reports.

8. No-load funds put all your money to work.

9. Your liability is limited to only the amount invested.

10. You need make only a minimum investment per month or quarter and/or a lump-sum investment.

11. Many funds earn returns that beat inflation.

12. You carry less financial risk because the fund is able to diversify investments widely.

Disadvantages

1. Many load funds carry high transaction costs, often above 8 percent; as a result, many people choose no-load funds.

2. Deferred sales charges and exit fees make it difficult to determine the better-performing companies.

3. Management costs generally amount to only a fraction of 1 percent of the assets of the funds annually, but hidden loads often further reduce the annual return to investors.

4. A fund that cannot be switched allows no flexibility should your objectives change.

5. No-load funds are not heavily advertised and thus must be sought out and researched by the investor.

6. Because many funds (including load and low-load funds as well as those with 12b-1 fees) are promoted by salespersons who want to earn commissions, the funds may be represented as promising more than they can likely deliver.

7. Because of diversification, the return on most mutual funds is 1 to 2 percent less than the total yield possible on most common stocks; of course, few individual investors have done as well as the consistently higher-performing funds.

What If You Are Trying to Compare Advertised Yields on Mutual Funds?

Regulations of the Securities and Exchange Commission now compel stock and bond mutual fund operators to present standardized performance calculations when computing such numbers as *annual yield* (the percentage rate earned on your investment), *tax-equivalent yield* (comparing taxable and tax-exempt investments), and *total return* (including such things as income from options and capital gains and losses).* Also, there is a minimum ad type-size requirement. The regulations apply to both advertising and sales literature.

Fund performance may be quoted in advertising in terms of yield or total return. Such data on performance are based on historical results and, of course, do not indicate future results. The SEC regulation says that the **yield of a mutual fund** must be expressed as the rate of income the fund earns on its investments as a percentage of the fund's share price. Yields must be calculated on a uniform 30-day basis.

Funds may no longer just cite a few hot months of performance but must include a uniformly computed annual compounded total return, after expenses, for the preceding 1, 5, and 10 years. The SEC regulation says that the **total return of a mutual fund** must show its overall change in value, including changes in share price and assuming all the fund's ordinary income dividend and capital gain distributions are reinvested. A fund less than a year old must disclose its total return since inception. Finally, all figures must be adjusted to reflect the impact of load charges. Every mutual fund investor benefits by the uniformity in mutual fund advertising because now we all can make meaningful comparison between funds.

* Money market funds have had a similar uniform yield computation requirement by the SEC since 1980.

---

fund's net asset value increased by 140 percent over a decade, inflation could have pushed prices up 125 percent during the same period. Also, the Dow Jones Industrial Average may have climbed 160 percent. Thus you should first compare the historical performance of a mutual fund with other broad indicators.

Use Comparative Performance Data   To compare the performance of mutual funds, you can use data from Wiesenberger, Johnson's, *Fundscope, Money, Barron's, Business Week, Forbes,* and other financial services and publications.[6] They generally rank funds according to 1- , 5- , and 10-

[6] The following newsletters can be used to compare the performance of mutual funds: *The Exchange Report* (1200 Westlake Ave. North, Seattle, WA 98109), *Donoghue's Mutual Fund Almanac* (Box 540, Holliston, MA 01746), *NoLoad Fund X* (235 Montgomery St., San Francisco, CA 94104), *Professional Tape Reader* (P.O. Box 2407, Hollywood, FL 33022), and *Switch Fund Advisory* (8943 Shady Grove Ct., Gaithersburg, MD 20877). You can obtain complimentary copies by writing to the addresses given.

FIGURE 18.4

The Risk/Return Tradeoff

Source: Basic data from Investment Company Institute, 1600 M Street, N.W., Washington, DC 20036. Used with permission.

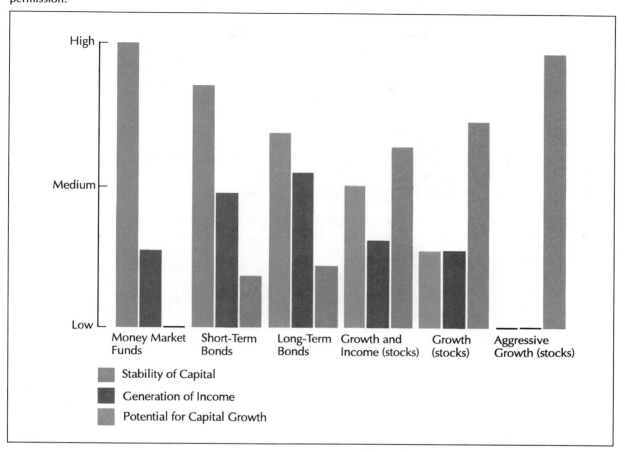

year performance; they also note the risk of each fund relative to performance.

Your task is to match your interpretation of performance data with your own investment philosophy. You might have one of four common objectives: maximum appreciation of capital, long-term growth of capital and future income, current income, or relative stability of capital. Figure 18.4 illustrates the risk/return tradeoff for various types of funds that have different objectives. If you want to realize one specific objective (such as stability of capital), you must usually sacrifice another objective (such as appreciation of capital). **Stability of capital** is akin to freedom from financial risk; it also can be defined in terms of relative performance when the value of your shares in a declining market does not decline as much as the values of other shares.

Another complication in comparing performance arises when you consider long- and short-term performance. Note that some funds have been in operation for less than a decade, whereas some older funds may have changed managers, grown substantially, and adopted a more aggressive (or conservative) investment philosophy. Should you choose a mutual fund that has done somewhat well over the past 10 years or one that has done very well during the past 12 months? Trading off return for risk, or vice versa, may be necessary.

There is also the question of choosing a load fund versus a no-load fund. About half of mutual funds are load funds. A load fund with an 8 percent commission must have an average yield of three-quarters of 1 percent more than a no-load fund to provide the same yield. Further, broad evidence indicates that over the long haul load and no-load funds provide the same yield. Sales commissions do not buy superior performance.

Use Published Performance Data   Several investment services publish performance data on mutual funds. Such calculations use a slightly different approach than the SEC method, and they provide useful comparisons. One of the largest services is Wiesenberger mutual fund indexes. Wiesenberger's fund performance is based on total return, assuming a fixed investment with income dividends reinvested and capital gains accepted in shares. Data such as Wiesenberger's are informative, particularly if you use them to compare the performance of individual mutual funds with others analyzed by Wiesenberger.

Use Mutual Funds Prospectuses   Annual reports and prospectuses provided either by the funds themselves or through brokerage firms detail the performance of individual mutual funds. The SEC requires mutual fund prospectuses to have standardization in presentation of yields, expenses, and returns. In addition, the SEC bars the use of false and misleading investment literature. For consistency in comparing funds, you might use the figures of just one of the reference investment publications. Figure 18.5 shows a sample description of a mutual fund company from Wiesenberger.

Compare Performance in Up and Down Markets   It is important to find a fund that has performed well over the past year or past 10 years. It is also useful to compare the performance of mutual funds in up (rising) and down (declining) markets. Table 18.3 contains fund data for three recent periods when the general market has declined and three periods when it has risen. For a fund to score highly, it "must perform consistently well in all three up or down periods." If a fund performs poorly, its rating is adjusted downward. The total yield excludes sales charges and assumes reinvestment of all distributions; it is reflected as a compound average annual return rate. Note that the Fidelity Magellan Fund is rated A+ in up markets and B in down markets, which illustrates the general difficulty of a growth fund that invests in common stocks during declining markets.

FIGURE 18.5
Wiesenberger's Description of a Mutual Fund

Source: Reprinted by permission from the Wiesenberger Investment Companies Service. 50th Edition. Copyright 1990 by Warren Gorham & Lamont, Inc., One Penn Plaza, New York, NY 10119.

FIDELITY EQUITY-INCOME FUND

The fund was initially offered on May 16, 1966, as Everest Income Fund. There was no wide distribution until May 1967. In 1969, the name was changed to Everest Fund and on July 25, 1975, the present name was adopted. At the same time, the investment policy was amended to place less emphasis on current income. On September 12, 1975, a merger with Fidelity Convertible & Senior Securities Fund was consummated, adding about $11 million of assets. Fidelity Equity Income Fund is designed for the investor who wants current income but also desires stock market participation for capital appreciation and growth. The fund invests in common and convertible preferred stocks both for current dividend yields and their potential for future earnings and capital growth.

At the close of calendar 1989, the fund had 74.7% of its assets in common stocks with 20.6% in bonds and preferred stock and 4.7% in net cash and equivalent. The common stock position included substantial representation in five industries: finance (27.3% of net assets), utilities (17.9%), energy (11%), basic industry (7.8%) and technology (5%). The five largest individual common stock holdings were Telefonica de Espana (2.2%), Phillips Gloeilampen (2.1%), Security Pacific (2%) and Bank of Montreal and RJR Holdings (each 1.8%). The rate of portfolio turnover during the latest fiscal year was 80% of average assets.

Statistical History

							% of Assets in							
Year	Total Net Assets ($)	Number of Share-holders	Net Asset Value Per Share ($)	Offering Price ($)	Yield (%)	Cash & Gov't	Bonds & Pre-ferreds	Com-mon Stocks	Income Div-idends ($)	Capital Gains Distribu-tion ($)	Expense Ratio (%)	Offering Price ($) High	Low
1989	5,037,692,573	199,805	26.90	27.45	6.1	5	20	75	1.75	1.16	0.68	30.58	25.58
1988	4,066,371,294	208,107	25.20	25.71	5.9	2	21	77	1.51	—	0.66	26.53	22.13
1987	3,476,014,528	230,399	21.85	22.30	5.8	5	24	71	1.51	3.92*	0.65	31.27	21.69
1986	3,360,021,586	208,362	27.29	27.85	5.5	6	34	60	0.65	3.08*	0.66	30.16	27.28
1985	2,238,618,884	121,946	27.51	28.07	6.0	9	40†	51	1.70	0.53*	0.72	27.10	23.70
1984	1,185,883,385	75,759	23.95	24.44	5.9	4	24†	72	1.63	3.12*	0.80	27.72	21.47
1983	743,584,092	66,996	26.53	27.07	5.6	4	34	62	1.70	1.42*	0.82	28.06	23.10
1982	355,616,555	34,493	23.23	††	6.8	3	32	65	1.68	1.49*	0.83	23.86	17.89
1981	187,458,264	23,904	20.32	—	6.9	7	28	65	1.57	2.59*	0.80	23.18	18.93
1980	147,706,088	18,049	22.59	—	5.8	6	26	68	1.42	1.84*	1.00	22.91	17.10
1979	87,983,494	11,609	20.07	—	5.9	7	27	66	1.19	—	0.90	20.87	16.40

† Includes a substantial proportion in convertible issues.
†† Sales charge initiated in 1983.

* Includes $0.52 short-term capital gains in 1980; $2.40 in 1981; $0.66 in 1982; $1.42 in 1983; $2.13 in 1984; $0.10 in 1985; $0.35 in 1986; $1.00 in 1987.

	1980	1981	1982	1983	1984	1985	1986	1987	1988	1989
Value of Shares Initially Acquired Through Investment of $10,000	$11,030	$9,922	$11,343	$12,954	$11,695	$13,433	$13,325	$10,669	$12,305	$13,135
Value of Shares Resulting From Reinvestment of Capital Gains and Income Dividends (Cumulative)	1,936	4,269	7,781	11,762	15,625	20,732	26,644	28,647	35,854	44,016*
Total Return	12,966	14,191	19,124	24,716	27,320	34,165	39,969	39,316	48,159	57,151

Dollar amounts of distributions reinvested:

	Capital Gains	Income Dividends
1980	$ 898	$ 768
1981	1,487	1,022
1982	1,060	1,295
1983	1,169	1,503
1984	2,907	1,733
1985	593	2,020
1986	3,989	2,305
1987	6,041	2,365
1988	—	2,777
1989	2,283	3,471
Total	$20,427	$19,259

Results Taking Capital Gains in SHARES and Income Dividends in CASH

Initial Investment At Offering Price, January 1, 1980 .... $10,000
Value as of 12/29/89 of Shares Initially Acquired $13,135
Value of Shares Accepted as Capital Gains Distributions $16,344#
Total Value as of December 29, 1989 .... $29,479
Total Dividends PAID From Investment Income $12,924

Dollar Amount of these distributions at the time shares were acquired: $14,160

Results Taking All Dividends and Distributions in CASH

Initial Investment At Offering Price, January 1, 1980 .... $10,000
Total Value as of December 29, 1989 .... $13,135
Distributions From Capital Gains .... $ 9,346
Dividends From Investment Income .... $ 7,896

TABLE 18.3
Comparing Mutual Fund Performance in Up and Down Markets

Market Up	Down	Fund	Total Return — Annual Average 11/80 to 6/90 (percent)	Total Return — Last 12 Months (percent)	Yield (percent)	Assets 6/30/89 (millions)	Assets — Percentage Change 1990 vs. 1989	Maximum Sales Charge	Annual Expenses per $100
		Standard & Poor's 500 stock average	14.9	16.4	3.2				
		Forbes stock fund composite	12.1	12.3	2.7				$1.44
B	C	Acorn Fund	14.5	12.3	1.3	953	29	none*	$0.73
C	A	American Capital Comstock	15.5	15.9	3.5	952	5	8.50	0.69
A	B	AMEV Capital Fund	15.2	18.4	1.6	159	26	4.75	1.16†
C	A	Fidelity Equity-Income Fund	16.0	−0.5	6.9	4,739	−1	2.00	0.71
A+	B	Fidelity Magellan Fund	23.1	16.7	2.4	14,039	31	3.00	1.03
A	B	Fundamental Investors	16.9	15.5	3.7	835	19	5.75	0.67†
A	B	Guardian Park Avenue Fund	17.0	6.1	4.6	253	24	4.50	0.68
B	A	Investment Company of America	16.7	15.0	3.8	5,874	22	5.75	0.52†
B	A	Janus Fund	17.4	23.5	1.2	1,246	152	none	1.00
A	B	Mutual Benefit Fund	17.0	7.3	2.3	38	24	4.75	1.45
A	B	New England Growth Fund	18.5	23.4	1.4	640	27	6.50	1.22†
A	A	United Income Fund	19.1	15.6	3.6	1,742	26	8.50	0.69

Source: Forbes, September 3, 1990. © Forbes, Inc., 1990.

* Distributor may impose redemption fee whose proceeds revert to the fund.
† Has shareholder-paid 12b-1 plan exceeding 0.1 percent (hidden load) pending or in force.

When to Sell a Mutual Fund

Objective
To be able to consider five factors that help determine when to sell a mutual fund.

Since people invest in mutual funds for different reasons, and because the objectives of the funds vary widely, it is impossible to generalize about when you should sell a mutual fund. However, we do suggest that you consider the following five factors before selling.

Substantial Changes in Net Asset Value

You must remember that all assets fluctuate in value over time. For example, the net asset value of many excellent growth funds can easily vary 25 percent during a 1-year period. Learn to determine why a particular holding is falling or rising in value. For example, you needn't panic if all common stock funds are declining, since it is difficult for any such fund to grow during economic recessions. Also, keep your investment goals in mind and relate them to the relative performance of the fund when there are substantial changes in the net asset value of your mutual fund. For example, over a year, a growth mutual fund should outperform the Dow Jones Industrial Average and the averages of other similar funds.

Poor Performance in Down Markets

To most mutual fund investors, a down market is not something that lasts only 30 or 40 days. (The exceptions are traders in high-performance funds and traders/switchers in families of funds.) A down market could last 3 months, 6 months, or longer than a year. An investor in a growth and income fund should expect down-market performance to be not more than 10 percent worse than the decline in the Dow Jones Industrial Average.

If the performance is sharply lower than comparable funds, it is the result of poor fund management. In this instance, you should consider selling.

Weak Performance in Up Markets

An up market is characterized by general market price increases for 3 months, 6 months, or longer than a year. If you have invested in a growth mutual fund, you should expect superior performance in up markets and generally should not settle for the average of similar funds. Being average for one up market is all right, but if a growth fund shows only mediocre performance during two up markets in succession, you should probably sell it. If you have invested in an income fund, you should expect performance in up markets about 2 percent above the current rate that could be earned on a corporate bond.

Market Trends Suggest Changes

Mutual funds investors need to remain alert to general conditions in the business cycle. When it is clear that peaks and valleys are being rounded, selling might be wise. As a rising stock market begins to peak, the growth fund investor will almost surely see the current high value of the investment begin to drop. Similarly, when the economy begins to pull up from a recession, it may be wise to sell an income fund, since interest rates are not likely to rise quickly. An advantage of investing in families of funds is that during such market shifts you can easily switch from one type of fund to another.

Sell When You Need Cash

You will probably not hesitate to sell mutual fund shares when you need money for a down payment on a home, for a child's college education, or to meet an emergency. But, there are ways to plan for these contingencies so that you can redeem mutual fund shares at the best possible prices. For example, if your child will need money for college 2 years from now, you should consider the prospects of selling the shares now instead of waiting 2 years. If your view of the economy over the next couple of years is uncertain or gloomy, then now is the time to sell shares in a growth fund because they may drop in value and be worth much less in 2 years. Conversely, you should hold shares in an income fund if the economy is expected to decline because interest rates likely will slide and probably push up the net asset value of your fund. In sum, try to anticipate cash needs and consider selling when it is most beneficial.

Summary

1. More than 25 percent of U.S. households own mutual funds, and the public is investing in mutual funds more than ever before.

2. Most mutual funds are taxed as a diversified investment company, which permits them to exempt 98 percent of their net earnings; returns to investors are in the form of income and potential price appreciation.

3. Mutual funds have one of four broad objectives, which a company must report in the prospectus: growth, income, growth and income, and balance.

4. Mutual funds can be classified according to their portfolio of investments, such as common stock funds, bond and preferred stock funds, balanced funds, income funds, municipal bond funds, specialty funds, and money market funds.

5. Investors in mutual funds may be confronted with sales charges (on load funds), deferred sales charges (on no-load funds), management fees, and hidden loads that reduce income from the funds.

6. As a specialized form of securities investment, mutual funds have several unique features, such as automatic dividend reinvestment, check writing, and switching privileges.

7. Mutual funds have numerous advantages (such as professional management and marketability), as well as some disadvantages (such as high transaction costs on load funds and management costs reducing returns).

8. Selection of a mutual fund involves examining important sources of information as well as comparing performance in both up and down markets.

9. Investors in mutual funds should think about selling when their investment is performing worse than the average of similar funds, as well as when peaks and valleys in the business cycle are approaching.

Modern
Money
Management

The Johnsons Decide to Invest in Mutual Funds

After learning about mutual funds, the Johnsons are convinced. They really like the concepts of diversification and professional management. Accordingly, they sell their stock and bond investments and now have a nest egg of $9500 to invest in mutual funds. In addition, they want to invest another $300 a month regularly.

Although not yet completely firm, Harry and Belinda's goals at this point are as follows: (1) they want to continue to build for retirement income, (2) they will need about $10,000 six to eight years from now to use as supplemental income if Belinda has a baby and does not work for 6 months, and (3) they might buy a superexpensive luxury automobile requiring a $10,000 down payment if they decide not to have a child or to adopt. Knowing that the Johnsons have a moderate investment philosophy, that they live on a reasonable budget, and that they have a well-established cash-management plan, advise them on their mutual fund investments by responding to the following questions:

1. Using Figure 18.4, if you could recommend two separate types of funds to meet the Johnsons' goals, what would they be? Why?

2. How would you divide the $9500 between the two types of funds? Why?

3. How much of the $300 monthly amount would you allocate to each type of fund? Why?

4. Some comparable mutual fund performance data on stock funds are shown in Table 18.3. Using only that information and assuming that you are recommending a stock fund for their retirement needs, why would you recommend the Fidelity Equity-Income Fund or the Fidelity Magellan Fund?

5. Assume that the Janus Fund performs above average for the next 10 years. Then there is a bear market and Janus Fund's *NAV* drops 25 percent from the previous year. What conditions must exist before you would recommend that the Johnsons sell their accumulated shares in the fund?

Key Words and Concepts

Review Questions

1. Explain how a mutual fund works and why someone would want to invest in one.
2. Distinguish between a load fund and a no-load mutual fund.
3. How can an 8.5 percent stated commission appear to be misleading?
4. List some hidden fees of no-load mutual funds, and tell when it is better to buy a load or a no-load fund with such fees.
5. Why do mutual funds charge management fees, and what is the typical amount?
6. Distinguish between ordinary income dividend distributions and capital gain distributions to the investor.
7. How do investment companies avoid paying income taxes on some of their profits?
8. Distinguish between a mutual fund with a growth and income objective and one with a balanced objective.
9. Describe two types of common stock funds.
10. Explain how automatic dividend reinvestment works.
11. How could a mutual fund shareholder benefit from switching privileges?
12. Identify two systematic withdrawal plans where the funds are not depleted over time.
13. Name and briefly explain three advantages of investing in open-end mutual funds.
14. Name and briefly explain two disadvantages of investing in open-end mutual funds.
15. How would you interpret a mutual fund with an A rating for performance in up markets and a C rating in down markets?
16. Summarize the Securities and Exchange Commission requirements on mutual fund advertising.
17. Describe two situations that would cause you to consider selling your mutual fund shares.

Case Problems

1. Glenn Sandler, a veterinarian for the past 10 years in Green Bay, Wisconsin, is interested in investing in mutual funds. He wants to put half of his $20,000 of accumulated savings into a stock mutual fund and then continue to invest $200 monthly for the forseeable future, perhaps using the money for retirement starting in about 25 years. Glenn has limited his choice to those mutual funds in Table 18.3.

a. Glenn wants to invest the full $10,000 now and diversify his holdings into two mutual funds. Glenn's personal economic projections for the next couple of years include low interest rates, moderate inflation, and medium-to-high economic growth. Given those assumptions, which two funds listed in Table 18.3 do you recommend for his $10,000? Why? (You may want to review the section on making economic projections in Chapter 1 before responding.)

b. If Glenn's short-term economic forecast had been high interest rates, moderate-to-high inflation, and sluggish economic growth (perhaps even with a recession), would you recommend that he put the $10,000 into mutual funds right now? If yes, explain why and suggest a fund from Table 18.3. If no, explain why not as well as suggest an alternative place for the $10,000.

c. Glenn also wants to invest $200 a month into one mutual fund over the next 25 years. Assuming favorable long-term economic projections, which of the funds listed in Table 18.3 would you recommend? Why?

2. Tina Fortunato works in a marketing firm in Newark, New Jersey, and is willing to invest $2000 to $3000 per year in a mutual fund. She wants the investment income to supplement her retirement pension starting in about 20 years. Her investment philosophy is moderate. Advise Tina by responding to the following questions.

a. Would you recommend that Tina invest in a mutual fund with growth as its objective or growth and income? Why?

b. Tina tells you that she wants to invest in a mutual fund that focuses on common stocks. Which two types of common stock funds would you recommend she avoid? Why?

c. Explain to Tina your reasons for having her invest in a load fund or a no-load fund.

d. After a few years, Tina's investments have been doing very well. In fact, she's considering a plan for periodically withdrawing income rather than automatically reinvesting. Advise her on the advantages and disadvantages of this plan given her long-term investment objective.

Suggested Readings

"By the Numbers." *Financial Planning,* May 1990, pp. 85–87. Here is a more accurate way to measure a fund's returns, because performance figures can be so misleading.

"Chasing the Foreign-Stock Jackpot." *Changing Times,* June 1990, pp. 49–52. Investing in a fast-rising fund that invests in a foreign country.

"How Risky Is Your Money Market Fund?" *Business Week,* March 26, 1990, p. 86. Warns against assuming that your money market fund is low-risk.

"How to Buy a Bond Fund." *Consumer Reports,* June 1990, pp. 428–435. Ratings of 125 bonds for safety and performance.

"Loads Vs. No-Loads: The Winner Is. . . . " *Changing Times,* February 1989. Hidden and back-end loads reduce the anticipated profits of investors in no-load mutual funds.

"Mutual Fund All-Stars." *Changing Times,* March 1990, pp. 25–32. Thirteen mutual funds that have done extremely well during market busts as well as boom times.

"Mutual Fund Hall of Shame." *Changing Times,* October 1990, pp. 77–82. Analysis of which funds have performed terribly in recent years and lost money for investors.

"Mutual Funds Demystified: Part 1." *Consumer Reports,* October 1989, p. 615. Why invest in mutual funds and how to sort out the types.

"Mutual Funds Demystified: Part 2." *Consumer Reports,* November 1989, p. 698. How fees can affect your yield on mutual funds.

"Mutual Funds, 1990: Part I." *Consumer Reports,* May 1990, pp. 330–341. Ratings of nearly 300 mutual funds for performance and safety.

"Our Top 20 Fund Champions." *Changing Times,* September 1990, pp. 116–126. The best performing mutual funds over the past five years listed according to six categories.

"Picking the Best Funds." *Money,* February 1990, pp. 126–175. *Money's* annual ranking of the performance of 960 mutual funds.

" 'Socially Conscious' Funds: A Fresh Look." *Changing Times,* August 1990, pp. 57–60. These funds do very well.

"Special Report: Mutual Funds." *Changing Times,* September 1990, pp. 29–79. Series of articles in *Changing Times* annual report of the best-performing mutual funds.

"The Case for Closed-End Funds." *Changing Times,* April 1990, pp. 49–57. The best-performing closed-end mutual funds.

"The Case of the Missing Champs." *Money,* April 1990, pp. 133–142. How both growth- and value-oriented mutual funds have been performing through the years.

"20 Superior Funds to Buy Now and Hold." *Money,* March 1990, pp. 135–139. Stock and bond funds that did well in the 1980s.

"Want a Winner? Look Here First." *Business Week,* February 19, 1990, pp. 70–106. *Business Week's* annual mutual fund scoreboard; repeated annually.

"Watch Out for Fee Grabbers!" *Money,* 1990, pp. 135–137. Mutual funds with the highest and lowest fees.

"Welcome to the Decade of the Mutual Funds." *Money,* December 1989, pp. 91–96. Five investment portfolios recommendations for a range of economic scenarios.

"What's Hot." *Money,* March 1990, pp. 113–124. Mutual fund investors looking for decency, the environment and Eastern Europe will like these choices.

19 Buying and Selling Securities and Managing Your Portfolio

OBJECTIVES

After reading this chapter, you should be able to

1. Explain the operation of primary and secondary securities markets, including reading newspaper quotations for stocks, bonds and mutual funds.

2. List the major sources of investment information about securities.

3. Discuss the factors to consider when selecting a brokerage firm.

4. Describe the elements in the actual process of buying and selling securities, such as stocks, bonds, and mutual funds.

5. Explain the twelve-step investment process.

6. Specify some investment approaches to portfolio management for long-term investors.

7. List three guidelines to use when deciding whether to sell securities.

• • • • • • • • • •

This chapter will give you specific information about how to buy and sell securities and manage your portfolio, especially if you are a long-term investor. The sequence of topics follows the investment process. You must first understand how the securities markets operate, including reading newspaper quotations for stocks, bonds, and mutual funds. Then you can begin to explore major sources of investment information, such as that available on general economic conditions, securities markets indexes, various industries, and specific companies. Then you need to choose a securities brokerage firm to perform your buying and selling transactions. Also provided are details about the actual process of buying and selling securities. A twelve-step process on how to invest is then presented. Finally, you need to select the long-term investment approaches to portfolio management that are most acceptable to you as well as anticipate the best times to consider selling your securities.

Securities Markets

Objective
To be able to explain the operation of primary and secondary securities markets including reading newspaper quotations for stocks, bonds, and mutual funds.

Securities markets exist to raise capital and arrange the buying and selling of stocks and bonds. Individual securities are bought and sold in primary and secondary markets. A **primary market** is where issuers and buyers of new offerings of stocks and bonds are brought together. For example, when Linda Webtek sold the original shares in Running Paws Catfood Company to her three friends, the primary market was her living room, where the transactions took place (see Chapter 16). More complex primary markets will be discussed below. A **secondary market** (also called the **aftermarket**) is where the trading of previously purchased securities occurs. Such markets include organized stock exchanges and over-the-counter markets. The activities of securities markets are regulated by the securities industry and by various government agencies.

Primary Markets

Securities markets exist to raise capital.

In the primary markets, companies that need capital to begin their operations sell new issues of stocks or bonds, or both, to the investing public. Later capital needs, perhaps for expansion, may be financed by using corporate profits or by selling additional securities. **Investment banking firms** are specialized sellers of new securities and serve as intermediaries between the issuing company and the investing public in the primary markets. (This task of raising money for corporations is called

FIGURE 19.1

Flow of Stocks and
Bonds in the Primary
Markets

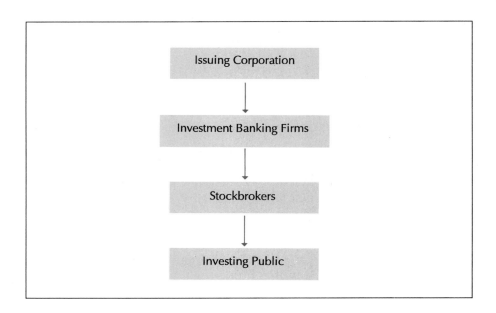

underwriting and is distinguished from insurance underwriting.) Investment banking firms, either individually or acting as a syndicate, typically purchase the entire new stock or bond issue of a corporation and then resell it to the investing public.

For example, assume that Running Paws, now a successful small corporation, wants to expand and sell its products nationally. The owners have calculated that they will need about $5 million. After careful analysis, they estimate that the likely per-share market value of their new 100,000 shares of stock is hopefully about $25. (The remainder of the needed funds will be raised by issuing long-term bonds and out of profits.) The underwriting firm, an investment banker, negotiates a purchase price, perhaps $24, after assessing the likely marketability of the stock and the anticipated expenses in selling it. The $1 difference between the purchase price and the expected resale price (the spread) is the potential profit for both the investment banker and the brokerage firm that eventually sells the stock to the investing public. The underwriter then publicly announces the availability of the stock as of a certain date. The underwriter sells blocks of shares to brokerage firms, which in this case will pay $24.50 per share, thus earning 50 cents for the investment banker. When the shares are sold to the investing public for $25, the other 50 cents represents the brokerage firms' per-share profit. Normally, brokerage firms charge no sales commissions on the sale of new securities. Figure 19.1 illustrates this flow of stocks and bonds in the primary markets.

Secondary Markets

After securities have been sold in the primary markets, they are further sold and bought in the secondary markets, composed of organized stock

FIGURE 19.2
Flow of Securities in
Secondary Markets

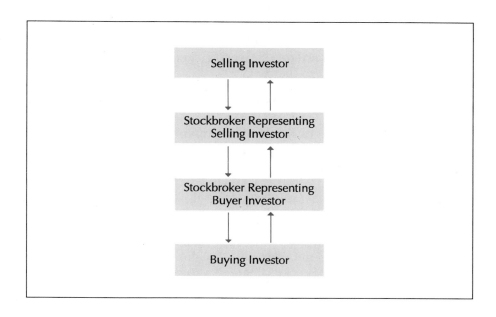

Selling Investor

Stockbroker Representing
Selling Investor

Stockbroker Representing
Buyer Investor

Buying Investor

exchanges and the over-the-counter market. These are commonly known as **securities markets** or **stock markets.**

You can buy or sell securities in the secondary markets through a **stockbroker** who works for a brokerage firm. This is a person who is licensed to buy and sell securities on behalf of clients, provides them with investment advice and information, and generally collects a commission on each purchase or sale of such securities. A stockbroker may be called an account executive, a customers' broker, or a registered representative and may work for a brokerage firm, broker/dealer, or brokerage house. The stockbroker may either buy securities for the firm's own account to then sell to investors or arrange the transactions between buyers and sellers. Stockbrokers must disclose when they are selling securities owned by the firm they work for. Figure 19.2 shows the flow of stocks, bonds, and other securities in secondary markets. Note that the issuing corporations are no longer involved.

Stockbrokers are also called account executives, customers' brokers, or registered representatives.

Organized Stock Exchanges An **organized stock exchange** is a market where agents of buyers and sellers meet and trade a specified list of securities, usually those of the larger, more well-known companies. More than three-fourths of all securities bought and sold are traded on one of the organized exchanges, such as the New York Stock Exchange, the American Stock Exchange, or a regional stock exchange (such as the Pacific Stock Exchange).

Securities are traded on the floor of each exchange only by members of the stock exchange, whose number is generally fixed. A **member firm** is an organization that has purchased a *seat on the exchange,* which gives the firm the legal right to buy and sell securities on the exchange. There are 1366 seats on the New York Stock Exchange. In recent years, the price of a seat sold on the New York Stock Exchange has ranged from $425,000 to over $1 million. The largest brokerage firm (Merrill, Lynch, Pierce, Fenner & Smith) owns more than 20 seats on the New York exchange.

Each exchange trades only **listed securities.** This is a designation by a stock exchange that the stock has been approved for sale on the exchange and that the issuing companies have met various criteria regarding number of stockholders, numbers of shares owned by the public (*outstanding shares*), market value of each share, and corporate earnings and assets. Such minimum requirements provide some assurance to investors that the stocks traded are issued by reputable companies.

The New York Stock Exchange is called the "Big Board."

The *New York Stock Exchange (NYSE),* founded in 1792, is by far the largest exchange in the world and has the most stringent requirements for listing. It also is called the "Big Board." Corporations must have minimum earnings of $2.5 million before taxes, net assets of at least $16 million, a minimum of 1.2 million shares publicly held, a market value of outstanding stocks of no less than $18 million (which varies according to market conditions), and a minimum number of 2000 shareholders owning at least 100 shares each. In addition, the company must be of interest to investors nationally, have stability in its industry, and be able to improve its competitive position within that industry. As with all exchanges, companies may be delisted if they later fail to meet the minimum requirements. Over 2400 common stock securities of the approximately 1450 companies on the NYSE account for about 97 percent of the market value of *all* listed stocks on the various exchanges. The average per-share price on the NYSE is $33. Note that the same stocks can be sold on more than one exchange.

The *American Stock Exchange (ASE or AMEX),* also located in New York City, represents the second largest exchange in the country, though it is a distant second, with only about 3 percent of the listed dollar volume traded. The AMEX was started in 1849 when people traded securities on a street corner on Wall Street, now the financial nerve center of the United States. Today the American Stock Exchange lists more than 940 stocks and 260 bonds. Its listing requirements are less stringent than those of the NYSE: $750,000 in earnings, $4 million in net assets, a minimum of 400,000 shares outstanding, $3 million in market value of outstanding shares, and a minimum of 800 shareholders owning a least 100 shares each. Thus the AMEX primarily lists smaller and younger companies than does the NYSE; the average per share price on the AMEX is $24. Note that these firms still have substantial investor interest.

Regional stock exchanges trade securities of interest primarily to investors living in certain areas of the country. Many stocks listed on the NYSE and the AMEX are also listed on some regional exchanges to encourage more trading. Smaller firms are also listed. For example, the Pacific Stock Exchange (PSE) requires, in addition to other criteria, net assets of only $1 million for listing. Another advantage of the PSE is that owing to the difference in time zones, it can stay open for trading for a couple of hours later than the New York-based exchanges. Other regional stock exchanges include the Boston, Cincinnati, Intermountain, Midwest, Philadelphia, and Spokane exchanges.

Over-the-Counter (OTC) Market   All publicly traded securities not sold on an organized exchange are traded on the **over-the-counter (OTC) market.** Securities sold "over the counter" are typically those of small firms that do not have many shares outstanding and/or do not have much trading interest. The OTC market has no listing requirements, and about 40,000 different securities are available to investors. The price per share for a typical stock is $11.

The OTC market has no listing requirements for companies.

In the OTC market, buyers and sellers negotiate transaction prices, often using a sophisticated telecommunications network connecting brokerage firms throughout the country. This National Association of Securities Dealers Automated Quotation (NASDAQ) system provides prices on over 4700 securities plus some foreign stocks. There is no central exchange floor for transactions.

An OTC sale occurs when a stockbroker at a brokerage firm representing a buyer communicates with another brokerage firm that has the desired securities. The second brokerage firm is more accurately known as a broker/dealer because besides offering the usual brokerage services, the firm also can "make a market" for one or more securities. **Broker/dealers** are engaged in the business of both buying and selling securities. **Market making** occurs in an effort to provide a continuous market as a broker/dealer maintains an inventory of specific securities to sell to other brokerage firms and stands ready to buy reasonable quantities of the same securities at market prices. When a stockbroker sells securities in which the brokerage firm has made a market, the buying investor must be informed that the firm made the market.

The investing OTC customer pays the asked price.

The transaction price is negotiated because there are two prices involved. The **bid price** is the amount a brokerage firm is willing to pay for a particular security, and the **asked price** is the amount for which a brokerage firm is willing to sell a particular security. The difference between bid and asked prices is called the **spread.** In addition to paying the asked price or one negotiated slightly lower, the investor also normally pays the broker a nominal sales commission. However, commissions are prohibited when a transaction is for securities for which the brokerage firm makes a market; in that event, the spread is the total profit earned by the brokerage firm.

Newspaper Stock, Bond, and Mutual Fund Quotations

The daily buying and selling transactions of stocks and bonds on secondary markets are summarized in the nation's most widely read financial newspaper, *The Wall Street Journal.* Additional detailed information on each company and trading transactions can be found in the weekly newspaper *Barron's,* which is available at many newsstands. Since a number of stocks and bonds may be traded on more than one exchange, the details are reported most often under the listings for the larger exchanges. Abbreviated information is also published in most daily newspapers but generally is confined to activities on the New York Stock Exchange, the American Stock Exchange, selected OTC stocks of local interest, and large mutual funds.

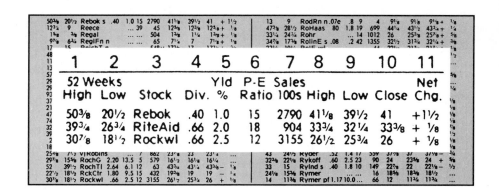

FIGURE 19.3
How Stocks Are Quoted

1	2	3	4	5	6	7	8	9	10	11
52 Weeks				Yld	P-E	Sales				Net
High	Low	Stock	Div.	%	Ratio	100s	High	Low	Close	Chg.
50⅜	20½	Rebok	.40	1.0	15	2790	41⅛	39½	41	+1½
39¾	26¾	RiteAid	.66	2.0	18	904	33¾	32¼	33⅜	+ ⅛
30⅞	18½	Rockwl	.66	2.5	12	3155	26½	25¾	26	+ ⅛

This section shows you how to read newspaper quotations for listed stocks, over-the-counter stocks, bonds, and mutual funds. Figure 19.3 gives quotations for listed stocks on the New York Stock Exchange on one particular day. The companies listed have an abbreviated trading symbol. Let's examine the listing for Rockwell Corporation, indicated by the *Rockwl* symbol. The listing is for Rockwell Corporation common stock. We will follow the quotations column by column.

1. *Columns 1 and 2: 52 Weeks, High/Low.* The first two columns show that Rockwell traded stock at a high price of 30⅞ and a low of 18½ during the past 52 weeks, not including the current trading day. Stock transactions are reported in eighths, with each eighth representing 12½ percent of the base price, dollars in this case. Thus, during the past 12 months, Rockwell stock ranged in price from $30.88 to $18.50.

2. *Column 3: Stock.* This column gives the name of the stock, in this example, Rockwell.

3. *Column 4: Div.* This dividend amount is based on the last quarterly declaration by the company. For example, Rockwell last paid a 16½ cents quarterly dividend, which was multiplied by 4 (quarters in a year) to obtain the estimate of 66 cents as an annual dividend.

4. *Column 5: Yld%.* The figure in this column is the yield of dividend income calculated by dividing the current price of the stock by the estimated annual dividend. The current price of the stock ($26) is in column 10; thus $0.66/$26 = 2.5 percent.

5. *Column 6: P-E Ratio.* This figure is the price earnings ratio based on the current price. The earnings figure used to calculate the *P/E* ratio is not published in the daily newspaper but is the latest available 12-month earnings amount published by the company. Since the *P/E* ratio is based on actual performance, it is known as a "trailing" *P/E.*

6. *Column 7: Sales 100s.* This figure indicates the trading activity of the stock in hundreds. Thus 315,500 shares of Rockwell were traded on this day.

7. *Columns 8, 9, and 10: High/Low/Close.* These three figures indicate the range of prices at which the stock traded on this day. *High* is the

660   *Part Five / Investment Planning*

FIGURE 19.4
How Over-the-Counter Stocks Are Quoted

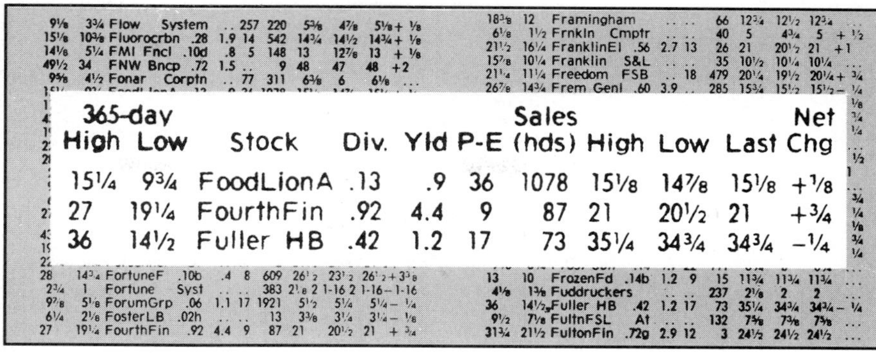

365-day High	365-day Low	Stock	Div.	Yld	P-E	Sales (hds)	High	Low	Last	Net Chg
15¼	9¾	FoodLionA	.13	.9	36	1078	15⅛	14⅞	15⅛	+⅛
27	19¼	FourthFin	.92	4.4	9	87	21	20½	21	+¾
36	14½	Fuller HB	.42	1.2	17	73	35¼	34¾	34¾	−¼

9⅛	3¾	Flow System		..	257	220	5⅜	4⅞	5⅛	+ ⅛
15⅛	10⅜	Fluorocrbn	.28	1.9	14	542	14¾	14½	14¾	+ ⅛
14⅛	5¼	FMI Fncl	.10d	.8	5	148	13	12⅞	13	+ ⅛
49½	34	FNW Bncp	.72	1.5	..	9	48	47	48	+2
9⅝	4½	Fonar Corptn		..	77	311	6⅜	6	6⅛	...
28	14¾	FortuneF	.10b	.4	8	609	26½	23½	26½	+3⅜
2¾	1	Fortune Syst		..	..	383	2⅛	2 1-16	2 1-16	−1-16
9⅞	5⅛	ForumGrp	.06	1.1	17	1921	5½	5¼	5¼	− ¼
6¼	2⅛	FosterLB	.02h	..	..	13	3⅜	3¼	3¼	− ⅛
27	19¼	FourthFin	.92	4.4	9	87	21	20½	21	+ ¾
18⅜	12	Framingham		..	..	66	12¾	12½	12¾	...
6⅛	1½	Frnkln Cmptr		..	..	40	5	4¾	5	+ ½
21½	16¼	FranklinEl	.56	2.7	13	26	21	20½	21	+1
15⅞	10¼	Franklin S&L		..	..	35	10½	10¼	10¼	...
21¼	11¼	Freedom FSB		..	18	479	20¼	19½	20¼	+ ¾
26⅞	14¾	Frem Genl	.60	3.9	..	285	15¾	15½	15½	− ¼
13	10	FrozenFd	.14b	1.2	9	15	11¾	11¾	11¾	...
4⅛	1⅜	Fuddruckers		..	..	237	2⅛	2	2	...
36	14½	Fuller HB	.42	1.2	17	73	35¼	34¾	34¾	− ¼
9½	7⅛	FultnFSL	At	..	..	132	7⅝	7⅜	7⅝	...
31¾	21½	FultonFin	.72g	2.9	12	3	24½	24½	24½	...

highest price at which it traded, *low* is the lowest price, and *close* is the last trade of the day before the market closed.

8. *Column 11: Net Chg.* The net change represents the difference between the closing price on this day and the closing price on the previous trading day. The Rockwell closing price of $26 was up 1/8 from the previous closing price, which thus must have been 25⅞.

Figure 19.4 shows recent over-the-counter stock quotations. We can see that Food Lion A stock paid a recent dividend of 13 cents. On one particular day, 107,800 shares were traded at prices between 14⅞ and 15⅛, and the price of the closing sale was up ⅛ from the last sale of the previous day.

Figure 19.5 shows corporate bond quotations for the Exxon Company for one particular day. The line for Exxon shows that 1000 Exxon bonds (volume of 10 × 100), due in the year 1998, with a coupon yield of 6½ percent, were sold. In bond quotations, the number quoted is the sales price expressed as a percentage of the bond's face value. Thus these Exxon bonds were sold at $838.75. The closing sale of the day also was $838.75, representing a 7/8 increase from the last sale of the previous day. Each bond pays 6½ percent interest, or $65 annually; thus the current yield (*Cur Yld*) is rounded to 7.7 percent ($65/$838.75 = 7.74).

An NL in the pricing column designates a no-load mutual fund.

Financial tables in newspapers list mutual fund prices and sales activity, as illustrated in Figure 19.6. An *NL* in the pricing column stands for no-load, meaning that there is no front-end sales charge. The Securities and Exchange Commission requires that listings show a **footnote p** to mark those which assess an annual 12b-1 fee for marketing expenses; mutual funds may be listed as NL even if they assess this fee. Funds that have authorized 12b-1 fees but are not currently using them are not required to put a *p* next to their names. The SEC further requires that **footnote r** be put after the names of mutual funds to identify those which assess redemption charges or exit fees. A redemption charge may be small and either permanent or temporary; it may be large, perhaps starting at 6 percent, and decline gradually until it disappears. A mutual fund can have a redemption charge and still be called no-load. A listing with both a *p* and an *r* means the fund levies both 12b-1 fees and redemption charges,

FIGURE 19.5
How Bonds Are Quoted

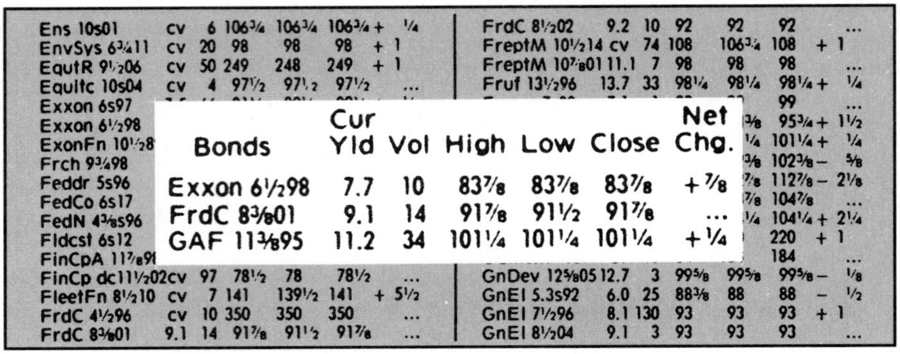

Bonds	Cur Yld	Vol	High	Low	Close	Net Chg.
Exxon 6½98	7.7	10	83⅞	83⅞	83⅞	+ ⅞
FrdC 8⅜01	9.1	14	91⅞	91½	91⅞	...
GAF 11⅜95	11.2	34	101¼	101¼	101¼	+ ¼

Ens 10s01	cv	6	106¾	106¾	106¾	+ ¼
EnvSys 6¾11	cv	20	98	98	98	+ 1
EqutR 9½06	cv	50	249	248	249	+ 1
Equitc 10s04	cv	4	97½	97½	97½	...
Exxon 6s97						
Exxon 6½98						
ExonFn 10½28						
Frch 9¾98						
Feddr 5s96						
FedCo 6s17						
FedN 4⅜s96						
Fldcst 6s12						
FinCpA 11⅞9						
FinCp dc11½02	cv	97	78½	78	78½	...
FleetFn 8½10	cv	7	141	139½	141	+ 5½
FrdC 4½96	cv	10	350	350	350	...
FrdC 8⅜01	9.1	14	91⅞	91½	91⅞	...
FrdC 8½02	9.2	10	92	92	92	...
FreptM 10½14	cv	74	108	106¾	108	+ 1
FreptM 10⅞01	11.1	7	98	98	98	...
Fruf 13½96	13.7	33	98¼	98¼	98¼	+ ¼
					99	...
				⅜	95¾	+ 1½
				¼	101¼	+ ¼
				⅜	102⅜	− ⅝
				⅞	112⅞	− 2⅛
				⅞	104⅞	...
				¼	104¼	+ 2¼
					220	+ 1
					184	...
GnDev 12⅝05	12.7	3	99⅝	99⅝	99⅝	− ⅛
GnEl 5.3s92	6.0	25	88⅜	88	88	− ½
GnEl 7½96	8.1	130	93	93	93	+ 1
GnEl 8½04	9.1	3	93	93	93	...

and such funds may not be listed as a no-load. Some newspapers use the **footnote t** to indicate mutual funds that charge both 12b-1 and redemption fees.

In Figure 19.6, Fidelity's *HiYld* fund has a net asset value (*NAV*) of $8.78. It is a load fund with an offering (*Offer*) price of $9.15, and the *NAV* has dropped $0.01 from the closing quotation of the previous day. In mutual funds, the *NAV* is also known as the *bid price* and is the amount per share that shareholders receive when they cash in (redeem) their shares. It is the amount the company is willing to pay to buy the shares back. Thus, on this day, Fidelity HiYield Fund is bidding $8.78 to repurchase any shares outstanding. For mutual funds, the *asked price* (or *offering price*) is the price at which a mutual fund's share can be purchased by investors; it is the current net asset value per share plus sales charges, if any. Thus, if you wanted to buy Fidelity's HiYield Fund, the company would offer to sell it to you for $9.15. The sales commission (load) may be calculated as a factor of the difference between the two prices ($9.15 − $8.78 = 0.37/$9.15 = 4.0 percent). By law, this load must be the same whether you purchase shares from a fund or through a brokerage firm. The footnote p indicates that the Fidelity HiYield Fund also assesses an annual 12b-1 fee.

The newspapers' quotations for no-load mutual funds are easier to comprehend. In Figure 19.6, the Fidelity Exchange Fund has a net asset value (*NAV*) of $73.89, is a no-load fund (*NL*), and had a change in the net asset value (*Chg*) of down $0.22 from the closing price of the previous trading day. Thus, if you wanted to buy *or* sell Financial Progress Dynam Fund on this day, the price would be $73.89 a share.

Regulation of Securities Markets

People must trust the market before they will invest.

Self-regulation is important in the securities industry because the public must trust the market before it will invest. Accordingly, organized exchanges have rules and regulations for listing and for trading. Similarly, the over-the-counter market is regulated by its self-regulatory organization (SRO), the National Association of Securities Dealers (NASD). The primary aims of SROs are to provide investors with accurate and reliable information

FIGURE 19.6
How Mutual Funds Are
Quoted

Evergrn	14.03	N.L.	+ .08		US Govt	9.22	N.L.	+ .02
Evrgrn TR	18.98	N.L.	+ .06		Fidelity Investments:			
Fairmnt	57					.05	N.L.	+ .07
Farm B Gr						.73	10.95	+ .02
Federated	Gro					.72	N.L.	+ .13
F B F	9					.72	12.98	+ .04
Fed Flt	9					.08	N L.	− .30
Fed StkB	x15					.64	N.L.	+ .02
Cash Tr	10					.54	N.L.	+ .03
Exch Fd	55					.51	N.L.	...
FIMT	9					.66	29.24	+ .04
FT Intl	24					.09	14.38	+ .04
GNMA	10.88	N.L.	+ .04		Exch Fd	73.89	N.L.	− .22
Grow Tr	17.67	N.L.	+ .04		Fidel Fd	17.87	N.L.	+ .01
Hi Yld	10.64	N.L.	+ .03		Flex B	6.89	N.L.	+ .03

Name	NAV	Offer	Chg.
Fidelity Investments:			
Cap App	12.72	12.98	+ .04
Eq Incm	28.66	29.24	+ .04
Europe	14.09	14.38	+ .04
Exch Fd	73.89	N.L.	− .22
Hi Yld$_P$	8.78	9.15	− .01

about securities, maintain ethical standards, and prevent fraud against investors.

State regulation of securities began in Kansas in 1911 with the passage of "blue sky laws." These were intended to prevent investors from being defrauded by companies selling securities about as valuable as "a piece of the blue sky." All states now require that securities to be sold within the state be registered and that brokerage firms and stockbrokers who give advice and/or buy and sell securities on behalf of clients be licensed.

Federal regulation of securities began in 1934 with the formation of the Securities and Exchange Commission (SEC). The SEC has focused on requiring disclosure of information about securities to the investing public and on approving the rules and regulations of the larger organized securities exchanges. The SEC requires registration of listed securities with appropriate and updated information. It also regulates all exchange members and prohibits manipulative practices, such as using insider information for illegal personal gain or falsely causing the price of a security to appear to rise or fall. The SEC regulates the advertising of securities and requires that proxies and proxy statements be mailed in a timely manner to all stockholders. The SEC possesses investigative police powers and has been characterized as a government agency that "strictly regulates the honesty and practices of the securities industry."

The SIPC insures investors against brokerage firm bankruptcy.

Investors' insurance is available to further protect the investing public. The Security Investors Protection Corporation (SIPC) is a government agency that safeguards the funds investors entrust to a brokerage firm in case the firm fails, providing the firm is registered with the Securities and Exchange Commission as required. As a matter of convenience, many investors prefer to leave securities certificates in the name of their brokerage firm rather than to take physical possession themselves. When securities certificates are kept in the brokerage firm's name instead of the name of the individual investor, this is known as the security's **street name.** This is a name other than that of the beneficial owner in which the stock may be listed, usually to facilitate resale. When securities are in the street name, each of an investor's accounts at a brokerage firm is protected against financial loss as a result of unreturned securities and cash up to a total of $500,000, but no more than $100,000 cash. Investment losses are not covered; the SIPC coverage only insures the return of the value of an investor's securities as of the date when the SIPC commences an audit of a bankrupt brokerage firm's accounts. Since this audit could take a few weeks, an uninsured decline in the value of your portfolio over that time period could occur.

Sources of Investment Information about Securities

Objective
To be able to list the major sources of investment information about securities.

To reduce investment risks and increase returns, the wise financial manager seeks out and utilizes investment information. By following your own hunches with research, you can build a portfolio of common stocks, bonds, mutual funds, and other securities that is superior to what you would end up with simply by relying on suggestions and tips from stockbrokers. Individual investors often have an edge over the more than 20,000 professional analysts working for large institutions, such as mutual funds and pension funds, because they can move more quickly to change the mix of their portfolio and have more choices than those trading big blocks of securities. This section takes a how-to approach to gathering investment information about general economic conditions, securities markets indexes, industry data, and company news. By spending a couple of hours with reference materials available in most public libraries and with documents from the companies themselves, you should be able to identify investments with profit potential as well as avoid those which suggest trouble.

General Economic Conditions

Knowing when to buy or sell securities requires an overview of general economic conditions. You need to know where the economy is in the business cycle (recession or prosperity) and what the current interest and inflation rates are. Also, you should know what economic conditions are to be expected in the next 12 to 18 months. (These topics were examined in Chapter 1.)

By reading a local daily newspaper or a weekly news magazine, you can gain insights into the economic conditions of the local community, state, region, country, and world. This is especially true for readers of cosmopolitan newspapers such as the *Los Angeles Times, Miami Herald,* and *Washington Post.* Many big city newspapers are available in smaller communities through libraries or by mail subscription. You can obtain specific economic news from *The Wall Street Journal* (published each weekday) and the weekly issues of *Barron's.* The two most popular financial newspapers in the country, they are also usually available at public and college libraries as well as at brokerage firm offices. *Business Week, U.S. News & World Report, Money,* and *Changing Times* also provide excellent information on economic conditions. An illustration of valuable information is provided in Figure 19.7. A good reference book

You must read to gain an understanding of general economic conditions.

FIGURE 19.7

Many Magazines and Newspapers Provide Useful Investment Information

Source: Reprinted from the September 10, 1990, issue of *Business Week* by special permission, copyright © 1990 by McGraw-Hill, Inc.

BusinessWeek Index

PRODUCTION

Change from last week: −0.3%
Change from last year: 2.5%

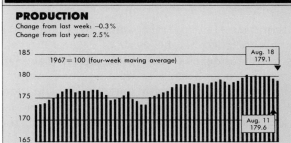

185 — 1967=100 (four-week moving average) — Aug. 18 179.1
180
175
170 — Aug. 11 179.6
165
Aug. 1989 — Dec. 1989 — Apr. 1990 — Aug. 1990

The production index declined for the week ended Aug. 18. On a seasonally adjusted basis, output of autos and trucks was down sharply, reflecting plant closings for model switchovers. Lumber, crude-oil refining, paperboard, and rail-freight traffic were also down. Electric power and steel output increased, and coal and paper production was unchanged for the week. Prior to calculation of the four-week moving average, the index dropped to 178.7, from 179.1 for the week before.
BW production index copyright 1990 by McGraw-Hill Inc.

LEADING

Change from last week: 0.0%
Change from last year: −1.1%

220 — Aug. 18 215.3
215
210
205 — Aug. 11 215.2r
200
Aug. 1989 — Dec. 1989 — Apr. 1990 — Aug. 1990

The leading index increased for the week ended Aug. 18, but it remains in a fairly narrow range indicating little pickup in economic growth. A sharp gain in materials prices, a drop in the number of business failures, and faster growth in real estate loans and M2 offset a small rise in bond yields. Stock prices were virtually unchanged for the week. Before calculation of the four-week moving average, the index rose to 216, from 214.9 posted in the previous week.
Leading index copyright 1990 by Center for International Business Cycle Research

PRODUCTION INDICATORS

	Latest week	Week ago	% Change year ago
STEEL (8/25) thous. of net tons	1,937	1,927 #	13.9
AUTOS (8/25) units	106,425	105,628r #	−18.7
TRUCKS (8/25) units	75,681	56,234r #	−4.7
ELECTRIC POWER (8/25) millions of kilowatt-hours	62,261	62,772 #	3.2
CRUDE-OIL REFINING (8/25) thous. of bbl./day	14,143	14,119 #	0.8
COAL (8/18) thous. of net tons	20,521 #	20,206	2.9
PAPERBOARD (8/18) thous. of tons	722.0 #	744.4r	−3.6
PAPER (8/18) thous. of tons	766.0 #	769.0r	2.8
LUMBER (8/18) millions of ft.	451.6 #	478.3	−11.6
RAIL FREIGHT (8/18) billions of ton-miles	20.6 #	20.5	4.6

Sources: American Iron & Steel Inst., *Ward's Automotive Reports*, Edison Electric Inst., American Petroleum Inst., Energy Dept., American Paper Inst., WWPA[1], SFPA[2], Association of American Railroads.

FOREIGN EXCHANGE

	Latest week	Week ago	Year ago
JAPANESE YEN (8/29)	144	146	145
GERMAN MARK (8/29)	1.56	1.55	1.97
BRITISH POUND (8/29)	1.95	1.93	1.56
FRENCH FRANC (8/29)	5.22	5.22	6.65
CANADIAN DOLLAR (8/29)	1.14	1.14	1.18
SWISS FRANC (8/29)	1.29	1.27	1.70
MEXICAN PESO (8/29)[3]	2,886	2,883	2,543

Sources: Major New York banks. Currencies expressed in units per U. S. dollar, except for British pound expressed in dollars.

PRICES

	Latest week	Week ago	% Change year ago
GOLD (8/29) $/troy oz.	384.300	408.750	6.3
STEEL SCRAP (8/28) # 1 heavy, $/ton	118.00	118.00	12.4
FOODSTUFFS (8/27) index, 1967=100	216.8	215.4	−0.2
COPPER (8/25) ¢/lb.	135.3	137.8	0.6
ALUMINUM (8/25) ¢/lb.	82.0	81.5	−1.2
WHEAT (8/25) # 2 hard, $/bu.	2.89	2.89	−32.0
COTTON (8/25) strict low middling 1-1/16 in., ¢/lb.	74.50	73.89	6.1

Sources: London Wed. final setting, Chicago mkt., Commodity Research Bureau, *Metals Week*, Kansas City mkt., Memphis mkt.

LEADING INDICATORS

	Latest week	Week ago	% Change year ago
STOCK PRICES (8/24) S&P 500	317.10	335.70	−8.3
CORPORATE BOND YIELD, Aaa (8/24)	9.50%	9.37%	5.3
INDUSTRIAL MATERIALS PRICES (8/24)	106.2	104.9	2.0
BUSINESS FAILURES (8/17)	276	290	7.4
REAL ESTATE LOANS (8/15) billions	$380.1	$378.9	10.3
MONEY SUPPLY, M2 (8/13) billions	$3,304.2	$3,295.5r	5.5
INITIAL CLAIMS, UNEMPLOYMENT (8/11) thous.	366	341	13.3

Sources: Standard & Poor's, Moody's, *Journal of Commerce* (index: 1980=100), Dun & Bradstreet (failures of large companies), Federal Reserve Board, Labor Dept. CIBCR seasonally adjusts data on business failures and real estate loans.

MONTHLY ECONOMIC INDICATORS

	Latest month	Month ago	% Change year ago
NEW HOME SALES (July) annual rate, thous.	548	561r	−26.0
12 LEADING INDICATORS COMPOSITE (July) index	146.1	146.1r	1.4
PERSONAL INCOME (July) annual rate, billions	$4,672.4	$4,646.1r	6.2
ORDERS FOR DURABLE GOODS: MFG. (July) billions	$128.3	$124.6r	5.1

Sources: Commerce Dept.

MONETARY INDICATORS

	Latest week	Week ago	% Change year ago
MONEY SUPPLY, M1 (8/13)	$814.4	$812.9r	5.1
BANKS' BUSINESS LOANS (8/15)	322.6	320.0r	1.4
FREE RESERVES (8/22)	−67	267r	NM
NONFINANCIAL COMMERCIAL PAPER (8/15)	146.0	147.2r	18.8

Sources: Federal Reserve Board (in billions, except for free reserves, which are expressed for a two-week period in millions).

MONEY MARKET RATES

	Latest week	Week ago	Year ago
FEDERAL FUNDS (8/28)	8.07%	8.00%	8.96%
PRIME (8/29)	10.00	10.00	10.50
COMMERCIAL PAPER 3-MONTH (8/28)	7.98	7.94	8.67
CERTIFICATES OF DEPOSIT 3-MONTH (8/29)	8.04	8.07	8.79
EURODOLLAR 3-MONTH (8/22)	8.13	7.93	8.83

Sources: Federal Reserve Board, First Boston

# Raw data in the production indicators are seasonally adjusted in computing the BW index (chart); other components (estimated and not listed) include machinery and defense equipment.
1 = Western Wood Products Assn. 2 = Southern Forest Products Assn. 3 = Free market value   NA = Not available   r = revised   NM = Not meaningful

is the second volume of *Value Line Investment Survey*, also found in many libraries. Select a few publications to read regularly to keep abreast of general economic conditions.

Securities Market Indexes

Securities market indexes measure the average value of a number of securities chosen as a sample to reflect the behavior of a general market of investments. Investors use the indexes to determine trends that might help guide them in investment decisions because short-run price movements may or may not be important compared with longer term situations. Ideally, for example, an investor would want to buy securities at low prices during the depths of a **bear market** (a protracted period when stock shares fall in value, perhaps with a 20 percent drop from the peak, or a 50 percent retracement of bull market gains) and sell at high prices during the height of a **bull market** (a protracted period when stock shares rise in value). The most popular indexes are described below.

A good time to invest is during a bear market.

Dow Jones Industrial Average (DJIA)   The DJIA is the most widely reported of all indexes, having been in continuous use since 1884. In determining the DJIA, the prices of only 30 huge industrial and service stocks are followed. These include well-known companies like American Express, American Telephone and Telegraph, DuPont, Exxon, General Motors, IBM, Sears, and Woolworth. When the evening newscaster reports that "the Dow rose three points today in heavy trading," realize that these "points" are changes in the index, not actual dollar changes in the value of the stocks. The average is calculated by adding the closing prices of the 30 stocks and dividing by a number adjusted for splits, spin-offs, and dividends. Figure 19.8 provides yearly highs and lows of the DJIA. The index has been respected for many years as a good barometer of daily activity of securities traded on the New York Stock Exchange, since the stocks chosen broadly represent the interests of the investing public. The Dow Jones Company also reports separate averages for transportation (20 stocks in the index) and utilities (15 stocks) to provide investors with information in these industries.

Standard & Poor's 500   S&P's 500 is an index that reports price movements of 500 top companies listed on the NYSE. It includes stocks of 400 industrial firms, 40 financial institutions, 40 public utilities, and 20 transportation companies. Although not as popularly reported as the DJIA, S&P's 500 is a more accurate index of daily transactions on the New York Stock Exchange.

New York Stock Exchange Composite   As the title suggests, this index includes all stocks traded on the NYSE (approximately 1600). Consequently, it provides a comprehensive measure of the price movements and value changes of those stocks.

FIGURE 19.8
Dow Jones Industrial Average

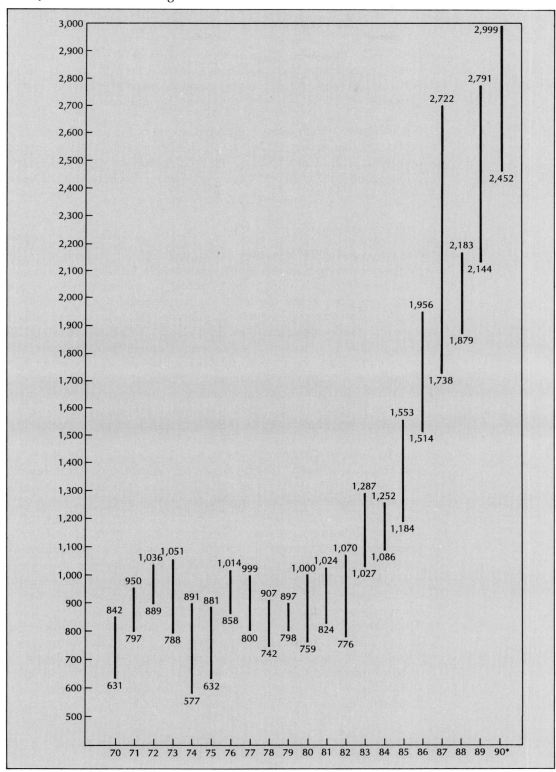

*Through September 25, 1990.

American Stock Exchange (AMEX)   This index is based on the market value of more than 1000 stocks in all industries traded on the American Stock Exchange (AMEX). It is a fair measure of **secondary stocks,** which are companies not as popular as those traded on the NYSE.

NASDAQ Composite   This index represents about 4700 over-the-counter stocks in the automated quotations system of the National Association of Securities Dealers. Most companies are young and relatively risky enterprises.

Nikkei Dow   Japan's best-known barometer of stock prices in that country represents the activity of 225 stocks. Because this market is open during nighttime in the United States, the Nikkei Dow is often looked at in the morning on U.S. exchanges as an indicator of what might happen that day.

Information about Industries

The current price of the securities of individual companies is often affected by the performance of the industry as a whole. Economic events can have considerable impact on an entire industry, such as aerospace, apparel, automotive, beverages, chemicals, construction, drugs, electronics, financial, foods, machinery, and metal industries, and depress the stock of even a very profitable company. For example, J. C. Penney could be having a most profitable year, but if a recession is anticipated and retail sales are expected to drop, the value of its stock is held down even if the company is enjoying a good year. Studying industries of interest to you will help *Select a few industries* you make intelligent buying and selling decisions. Industry information is *and study their prospects* reported in such publications as *Business Week* and *Forbes* (one issue of *for the future.* the latter per year analyzes the performance of all major industries). Excellent reference sources often found in large libraries include *Value Line Investment Survey* (Volume 1), *Standard and Poor's Industry Surveys,* and *Moody's Industry Review.* Figure 19.9 illustrates profitability data for selected industries. Specific information about industries is also available from trade associations and investment publications.

Trade Associations   A **trade association** is an organization representing the interests of companies in the same industry. For example, the American Council of Life Insurance is composed of representatives of life insurance companies, and the American Bankers Association represents the interests of the banking industry. Besides lobbying to present the views of the members, trade associations also have available a tremendous amount of detailed information on the history, current activities, and future prospects of the industry. Although their projections for the future are often optimistic, it is useful to know how an industry views its own prospects.

To contact the trade associations of interest to you, look up their names and addresses in the *Encyclopedia of Associations,* published by Gale Research Company, and the *National Trade and Professional Associations,*

FIGURE 19.9

Percentage Increase of Stocks of 71 Industries over Ten Years (January 1980 to January 1990).

Source: From page 30 in *Johnson's Charts* 1990, 42nd Annual Edition. Reprinted by permission of Johnson's Charts, 175 Bridle Path, Williamsville, NY 14221.

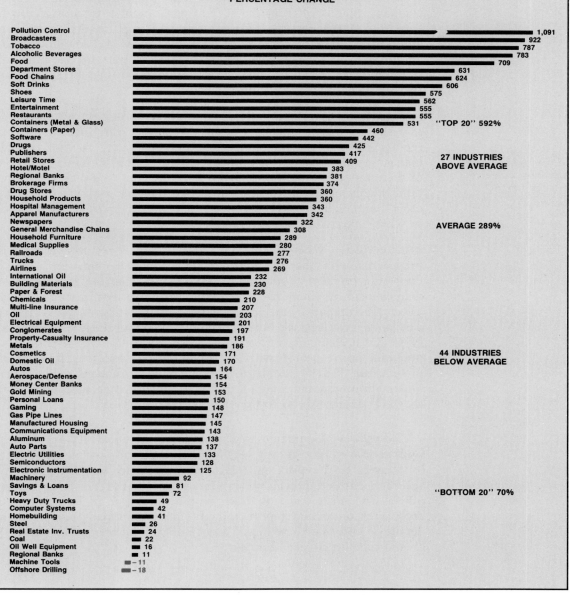

Selection

The wide range of investment results for the past 10 years of 71 different industries, as shown by Standard & Poor's, reveals the difficulty of selecting common stocks. During the period, 2 of the 71 industries shown below declined in value during a strongly rising market environment.
Investment of equal amounts in each industry would have resulted in a gain of 289% because of the broad diversification. However, the critical nature of careful selection is emphasized by the fact that investment in the top 20 industries would have shown a profit of 592%, while an investment in the bottom 20 would have shown a gain of only 70%.

STOCKS OF 71 INDUSTRIES
10 YEARS 1980-1989
PERCENTAGE CHANGE

Pollution Control	1,091
Broadcasters	922
Tobacco	787
Alcoholic Beverages	783
Food	709
Department Stores	631
Food Chains	624
Soft Drinks	606
Shoes	575
Leisure Time	562
Entertainment	555
Restaurants	555
Containers (Metal & Glass)	531
Containers (Paper)	460
Software	442
Drugs	425
Publishers	417
Retail Stores	409
Hotel/Motel	383
Regional Banks	381
Brokerage Firms	374
Drug Stores	360
Household Products	360
Hospital Management	343
Apparel Manufacturers	342
Newspapers	322
General Merchandise Chains	308
Household Furniture	289
Medical Supplies	280
Railroads	277
Trucks	276
Airlines	269
International Oil	232
Building Materials	230
Paper & Forest	228
Chemicals	210
Multi-line Insurance	207
Oil	203
Electrical Equipment	201
Conglomerates	197
Property-Casualty Insurance	191
Metals	186
Cosmetics	171
Domestic Oil	170
Autos	164
Aerospace/Defense	154
Money Center Banks	154
Gold Mining	153
Personal Loans	150
Gaming	148
Gas Pipe Lines	147
Manufactured Housing	145
Communications Equipment	143
Aluminum	138
Auto Parts	137
Electric Utilities	133
Semiconductors	128
Electronic Instrumentation	125
Machinery	92
Savings & Loans	81
Toys	72
Heavy Duty Trucks	49
Computer Systems	42
Homebuilding	41
Steel	26
Real Estate Inv. Trusts	24
Coal	22
Oil Well Equipment	16
Regional Banks	11
Machine Tools	−11
Offshore Drilling	−18

"TOP 20" 592%

27 INDUSTRIES ABOVE AVERAGE

AVERAGE 289%

44 INDUSTRIES BELOW AVERAGE

"BOTTOM 20" 70%

published by the U.S. Department of Commerce. Both are available in larger libraries.

Industry-Oriented Investment Publications You can spend a lot of money subscribing to investment publications and advisory services. The publications include *Industry Surveys* and *The Outlook* (published by Standard & Poor's), *Value Line Investment Survey* (Arnold Bernhard & Company), the *Monthly Economic Letter* (Citibank), and *Industrial Manual* (Moody's). Fortunately, many of these publications can be found in large libraries (especially at colleges) and in brokerage firm offices.

Information about Specific Companies

Of course, before buying any securities, you should learn about the company that is offering them. You can obtain this information from corporate annual reports, prospectuses, 10-K reports, investment ratings publications, research reports of brokerage firms and investment banks, and investment advisory newsletters. In your analysis, focus on the quality of management, the firm's financial stability, its earnings stream, and assess the company's competitive position.

Annual Reports Every public corporation publishes an annual report that summarizes its financial activities for the year. Investors use these reports to compare results from recent years and to find out about management's views of the immediate future. Keep in mind that the tone of these reports is often optimistic, since the company wants investors to think highly of the firm. Interesting information, sometimes negative, is often found in the footnotes. To receive an annual report, ask a stockbroker or write directly to the corporation.

Find out the views of company management about the future.

Prospectuses When a company issues any new security, it must file a **prospectus** with the Securities and Exchange Commission. This is a disclosure of facts about a corporation, including the experience of its management, its financial status, any anticipated legal matters that could affect the company, and potential risks of investing in the corporation. The language is legalese, but the details are there for the interested investor. Note that a company must issue a prospectus and make it public to any potential investor only when it issues a *new* security. Although many prospectuses are out of date, they might provide some needed background information; note that many firms update their prospectuses regularly and they are required to do so for each new securities offering.

10-K Reports Companies registered with the Securities and Exchange Commission must regularly report many financial particulars to the SEC by filing a **10-K report** once each year to ensure public availability of accurate, current information about the company. This comprehensive official document contains much of the same type of information as a prospectus or annual report and provides additional updated financial details on corporate activities. You can obtain these reports from the SEC or find them in college libraries.

What If You Want to Use the Personal Computer as a Source of Investment Information?

A variety of software is available to help the individual analyze and evaluate stocks, bonds, and other investments. In addition, software programs are available to help manage your investment portfolio as well.

Computers Can Help Analyze Investment Alternatives

The difficult task of looking over all the stock and bond alternatives in various industries can be made so much easier with the aid of a computer. Database systems exist that allow you to quickly sift through and screen hundreds of companies when trying to find those which best suit your investment objectives. A **financial database system** is a computer-based procedure that provides on-line access to information on 1500 or more stock and bond investments that can be screened by the investor by means of a personal computer. Some systems work using diskettes, while others offer on-line access by means of a modem and telephone. Historic information, current financial statements, current prices, and up-to-date news are available 24 hours a day.

Using a stock-screening program allows you to identify those which meet your specific imputed investment criteria.* You can rate companies according to a number of factors, such as price, earnings, sales, dividend, *P/E* ratio, current assets, and profits. Subscribers pay a modest hookup charge and a monthly usage fee. Many large public and college libraries subscribe to one or more financial database systems.

Computers Can Help Manage Your Portfolio

Keeping track of several stock, bond, and mutual fund investments, as well as buying and selling transactions, requires careful recordkeeping. These tasks can be performed using a computer software program. In addition, a stock portfolio manager program permits you to monitor and plan your investments by maintaining current values of the items in your portfolio. Some programs even allow you to trade securities through a brokerage firm by placing orders on your computer.†

---

* Popular financial diskette database systems include *Value/Screen* (Value Line Inc., 711 Third Avenue, New York, NY 10017) and *Stockpak II* (Standard and Poor's Corporation, 25 Broadway, New York,

NY 10004). On-line systems include *Compuserve* (5000 Arlington Centre Blvd., Columbus, OH 43220), *Dow Jones News/Retrieval* (P.O. Box 300, Princeton, NJ 08540), *The Source* (1616 Andern Road, McLean, VA 22102), and *Trade Plus* (82 Devonshire Street, Boston, MA 02109).

† Popular investment programs include *The Equalizer* (Charles Schwab and Company, 101 Montgomery Street, San Francisco, CA 94104), *Compustock* (A. S. Gibson and Sons, Inc., Box 130, Bountiful, UT 84010), *Market Analyzer Plus* (Dow Jones and Company, Inc., Box 300, Princeton, NJ 08540), and *Your Personal Investment Manager* (Timeworks, Inc., 444 Lake Cook Road, Deerfield, IL 60015).

Investment Ratings Publications You can also read about specific public corporations in this country in the following investment ratings publications: *Stock Reports, Stock Guide, Standard and Poor's Industry Surveys, Standard and Poor's Corporation Reports,* and *Standard and Poor's Stock Reports* (Standard & Poor's), *Moody's Manuals* and *Moody's Industry Review* (Moody's Investor Services), *Value Line Stock Picture* and Volume

3 of *Value Line Investment Survey* (M. C. Horsey & Company), *Trendline's Current Market Perspective* (Trendline), and the *Blue Book of 3-Trend Cycligraphs* (Securities Research Company). These publications all rank and rate corporations on performance.

A stock report for a corporation in an investment ratings publication typically contains a summary description and current outlook, important developments, comparisons with competitors, and tables with financial data going back 10 years. Figure 19.10 provides a sample stock report from *Value Line*. You can find these publications in larger libraries and in the offices of brokerage firms.

Research Reports   Basic investment research tries to separate companies that are on the way up financially from those on the way down. Hundreds of analysts produce research reports each day in the research departments of major brokerage firms (such as Paine Webber, Merrill Lynch, and Dean Witter) and investment banks (such as Kidder Peabody, Donaldson, Lufkin & Jenrette), and most of these are available through a general brokerage firm. The research reports usually recommend that investors buy "such and such," and they rarely recommend selling. Hence it is prudent to interpret their "hold" recommendations as a clear signal to sell. While the quality of advice is uneven, ranging from brilliant to pedestrian (there is a tendency to run with the herd and make similar recommendations), collectively this is the best research conducted on securities alternatives. Simply ask your stockbroker what reports can be made available to you.

Investment Advisory Newsletters   There are hundreds of *investment advisory newsletters,* which are specialized publications offering investment advice for a price. They are usually sold to a relatively small number of people. Investment advisory newsletters usually sell for $150 to $250 a year and are sold to perhaps 3000 to 30,000 individuals. Some of the better-known investment advisory newsletters are *Granville Market Letter* (P.O. Drawer 413006, Kansas City, MO 64141), *Turnaround Letter* (225 Friend Street, Suite 801, Boston, MA 02114), and *Prudent Speculator* (P.O. Box 1767, Santa Monica, CA 90406). Sample copies can be obtained by writing the companies involved; most public libraries subscribe to a few investment advisory newsletters.

Using a Brokerage Firm

The great majority of securities transactions in the primary and secondary markets are executed with the assistance of a brokerage firm that owns seats on the various organized exchanges. You can use a general brokerage firm or a discount brokerage firm; both will charge a commission for any trading they do for you. You should make clear to a brokerage firm, in writing, your investment objectives and your desired level of risk. References from friends or family members who invest, or possibly your lawyer, accountant, or financial planner, may help in assembling a list of prospects. You can check the background of a stockbroker by filling out an information request form obtained from the National Association of Securities Dealers (P.O. Box 9401, Gaithersburg, MD 20898). They will send you a summary of the education, employment history, and criminal or disciplinary record of any registered stockbroker.

General Brokerage Firms

General brokerage firms have someone available to give you personal advice.

The traditional **general brokerage firm** typically offers full services to customers, including a company investment newsletter that discusses general economic trends and offers investment recommendations, periodic reports that cover particular market trends and industries, capsule-written research analyses on hundreds of individual companies (available to customers just for the asking), and the personal advice and attention of one or more of the nation's 250,000 stockbrokers. The philosophy of general brokerage firms, such as Merrill Lynch or Shearson Lehman, is geared toward the value-added benefit of having someone personally advise you about investments. These firms maintain up-to-the-minute contact with the investment world through electronic equipment (usually including a **quotation board,** which is an electronic display of all security transactions on the major exchanges reported as they occur) and subscribe to an expensive but valuable newswire service that can keep customers apprised of world news affecting particular investments. Brokerage firms also maintain a reference library and provide custodial services for customers, since it is generally safer and more convenient for most investors to have a brokerage firm hold securities for them. Customers receive monthly statements summarizing all transactions and commissions, dividends, and interest. Of course, price quotations on securities are available over the telephone to the interested investor.

Discount Brokerage Firms

Some investors have an account with a general brokerage firm and another account at a discount brokerage firm.

In recent years, a number of investors have chosen to use a **discount brokerage firm,** such as Quick & Reilly or Charles Schwab. This is a brokerage firm that features especially low commission charges because it provides limited services to customers. It focuses on one function: efficiently executing orders to buy and sell securities. Discount brokerage firms do not normally conduct house research or provide specific investment advice to customers. Transactions usually are initiated by an investor who calls the discount brokerage firm at a toll-free telephone number. In 1991, the Charles Schwab discount brokerage firm expects to begin a TeleBroker computer system that permits customers to get price quotes, check their accounts, and buy and sell securities without talking to a human—and do it all on a Touch-Tone telephone. So-called *deep-discount brokerage firms,* such as Pacific Brokerage Services, Barry Murphy, K. Aufhauser and Company, or Brown and Company, charge even lower fees.

FIGURE 19.10

Sample Stock Report from *Value Line*

Source: From *Value Line Investment Survey.* Copyright © 1990 by Value Line Publishing, Inc. Used with permission of Value Line Publishing, Inc., 711 Third Avenue, New York, NY 10017-4064.

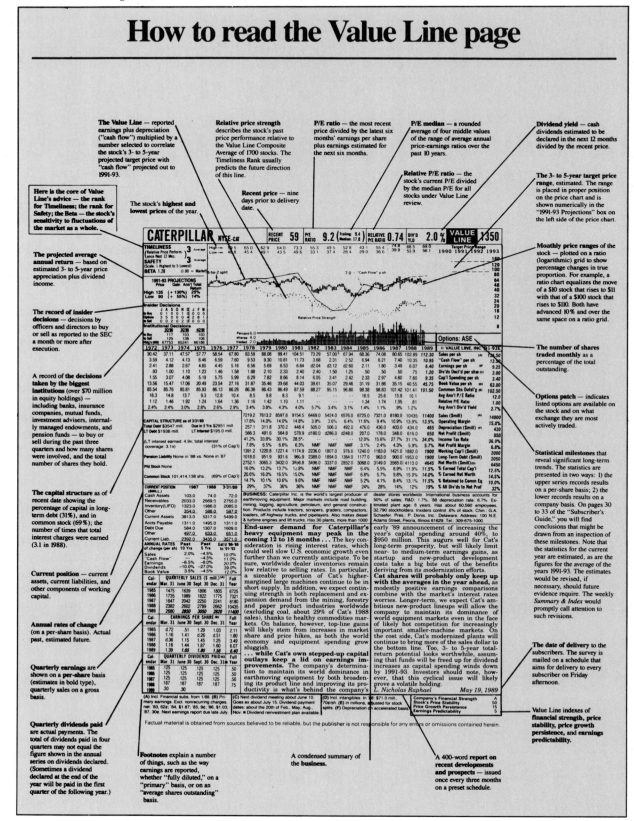

How to read the Value Line page

FIGURE 19.10   *(continued)*

How Value Line Suggests Building An Investment Portfolio

Building Your Portfolio

What Value Line Does	What You Do	Maintaining Your Portfolio

By Industry — Timeliness®

Value Line ranks groups in order of their Timeliness (Relative Performance in the Next 12 Months). You will find them listed on page 24 of the *Summary & Index*.

Read the latest Value Line reports on the 25 top-ranked industries. Select eight or more industry groups from among the 25 that Value Line ranks the most timely. See page 1 of the *Summary & Index* for the page numbers of these industry reports.

By Stock — Timeliness®

Value Line ranks 1700 (plus) stocks in five categories according to their Timeliness. The top 100 stocks are ranked 1 (Highest) for performance in the next 12 months; 300 are ranked 2 (Above Average); about 900, 3 (Average); 300, 4 (Below Average); and 100, 5 (Lowest).

Make up a list of those stocks included in your eight or more most timely industry groups that are also ranked 1 (Highest) or 2 (Above Average) for Performance in the Next 12 Months. You will find the latest full-page report on each stock in *Ratings & Reports*.

When and if a stock in your portfolio is found to be no longer a relatively timely investment—that is to say, it has fallen in rank to 4 or 5 for Timeliness—make that stock a candidate for sale. (See Post Script and Note at the bottom of this page.)

By Stock — Safety®

Value Line also ranks 1700 (plus) stocks according to their Safety in five categories with 1 (Highest) expected to be least volatile and financially most strong, and 5 (Lowest) most volatile and least strong financially.

Eliminate from this list of timely stocks in timely industries those that fall short of your Safety standard.

These safety ranks are significant and should not be ignored. (If you wish to rely on the Beta count please see page 49 of the "Subscriber's Guide.")

By Stock — Income

Value Line estimates the next 12 months' dividend yield of each stock at its most recent price. The expected yield is updated in the weekly *Summary & Index*. Value Line also shows, for comparative purposes, the median yield of all dividend-paying stocks on the first page of the weekly *Summary & Index*.

Eliminate from your list of timely stocks in timely indus-tries, which also have met your Safety standard or your Beta constraint, those that fall short of your current-income standard. For example, if your standard is 4%, eliminate stocks that yield less than 4%. Or if you accept a stock that yields less than 4%, see to it that other stocks you select yield enough more to bring the average up to 4%.

When a stock is sold, replace it with another stock ranked 1 or 2 for Timeliness that also meets your standards for Safety and current income. It would be best in the long run to maintain diversification through 15 or more stocks in more than eight different industries. (See Note below.)

Value Line Reports

Value Line reports on each stock and each industry once every three months, on a preset schedule, in the *Ratings & Reports* section. The page numbers on which the reports appear are shown in the weekly *Summary & Index*. When new evidence requires, a "Supplementary Report" is published as often as weekly. The "Supplemen-tary Reports" appear in the final pages of the *Ratings & Reports* section.

Read the latest Value Line reports on the industrial groups and stocks that have qualified according to all your standards.
   Make your final selection of 15 or more stocks from the list that has been refined through the above procedures. See to it that you have stock representation in at least eight different industry groups.

Selection & Opinion

Value Line's *Selection & Opinion* section provides a current appraisal of the economy and of the stock market. It recommends how much of one's capital should be invested in common stocks and how much set aside temporarily in cash reserves. Value Line will recommend the types of bonds or other safe haven for cash reserve investment when such a cash reserve seems timely. Value Line will also recommend, as a general strategy, investment in stocks with lower Beta counts if we believe that stocks in general are overvalued in the marketplace.

When the Value Line service in its *Selection & Opinion* section recommends building cash reserves because the general market seems temporarily to be too high, sell stocks and invest instead in short-term government bonds or other safe instruments, which will be recom-mended in the *Selection & Opinion* section. In selling, dispose of stocks ranked 5 or 4 or 3, in that order.

Post Script: Aggressive accounts may follow a policy of switching out of stocks when they fall to rank 3 for Timeliness and replacing them with others ranked 1. This strategy, of course, will result in a higher turnover rate. Tests have shown that, if followed consistently year in and year out, such a strategy will give an even higher return than the less aggressive policy of switching only when stocks have fallen to ranks 4 and 5.

Note: There can be no assurance that every one of the 1700-odd stocks will always perform in accordance with its rank for Timeliness. But it can be said that such a high percentage have done so in the past that you place the odds strongly in your favor if you keep your portfolio lined up with the Timeliness Ranks. Note that diversification is essential to this strategy.
   Of the Safety Ranks it can be said that stocks ranked high for Safety have held up better than average during significant market declines in the past. In strongly rising markets, however, Safety could prove to be a restraining influence upon performance. For example, in the case of two stocks, both

ranked 1 (Highest) for Timeliness, the stock ranked 1 for Safety will tend to go up less than another ranked 5 for Safety during a rising phase in the market. Conversely, in a down market, a high Safety Rank would help the stock ranked 1 (Highest) for Timeliness hold up better than another stock ranked 1 for Timeliness but rated low for Safety.
   In the case of well diversified portfolios—those consisting of 15 or more stocks in more than eight different industries—we recommend that risk be controlled by applying Beta counts instead of the Safety grades. (See page 48 of the "Subscriber's Guide.")
Explanation: In a widely diversified portfolio, the variations in individual stock prices in response to their individual characteristic risks tend to cancel each other out, leaving the general market fluctuation as the main influence. The Beta measures the individual stock's sensitivity to the general market. The Safety Rank, on the other hand, is a measure of the stock's total risk, i.e., sensitivity to the market plus sensitivity to all other factors affecting the individual stock's price.

TABLE 19.1
Typical Commission Charges of Brokerage Firms
(Commissions on $50 stock)

Broker	Number of Shares			
	50	100	500	5,000
Deep-discount	$29	$ 32	$ 65	$ 400
Discount	50	50	130	390
Full-service	75	100	430	2000

As Table 19.1 shows, you can save considerably by using the services of a discount brokerage firm. Reductions in actual commissions of up to 75 percent are possible. Many investors, however, may prefer to pay more for the full services of a general brokerage firm.

Commissions and Fees

Brokerage firms receive a commission on each securities transaction in order to cover the direct expenses of executing the transaction and other overhead expenses. At one time, commissions were fixed by the SEC, but now the SEC permits negotiation of commissions between brokerage firms and investors. In actuality, most brokerage firms have an established fee schedule that they use when dealing with any but the largest investors. These fees represent a declining commission rate as the total value of the transaction increases. For example, in lieu of a minimum commission charge of $25, a brokerage firm might charge 2.8 percent more on a transaction amounting to less than $800, 1.8 percent on transactions between $800 and $2500, 1.6 percent on amounts between $2500 and $5000, and 1.2 percent on amounts over $5000.

These transaction costs are based on sales of **round lots,** which are blocks of stock in units of 100 shares, or one $1000 bond. **Odd lots** are in units of more or less than 100 shares. When brokerage firms buy or sell shares in odd lots, they often charge a fee of 12.5 cents (called an *eighth*) per share on the odd-lot portion of the transaction. For example, an order for 140 shares at $25 each (total value $3500) could carry a round-lot commission fee of $40 (100 shares × $25 = $2500 × 0.016) plus an odd-lot fee of $5 (40 shares × 0.125) for a total of $45.00.

The payment of commissions can quickly reduce the return on any investment. A purchase commission of 2 percent added to a sales commission of another 2 percent means that the investor must earn a 4 percent yield just to pay the transaction costs. Although abuses in the securities industry are kept to a minimum, a small minority of unethical stockbrokers practice **churning** of investors' accounts by encouraging investors to frequently buy and sell securities in an effort to earn lots of commissions for themselves. Recall that mutual fund sales commissions can range up to 8.5 percent. You should carefully consider transaction costs when making securities investments.

Opening an Account with a Brokerage Firm

If you decide not to buy and sell securities through a discount brokerage firm, you must select a suitable general brokerage firm and a specific stockbroker at that firm to best represent your interests. Make these decisions with care. The brokerage firm should be **exchange registered,** meaning that it must comply with the rules and regulations of the exchange. The New York Stock Exchange has the highest standards of conduct. About 500 brokerage firms are registered with it; nonregistered firms go through exchanged-registered firms to conduct trades. Most brokerage firms emphasize fundamental analysis in their approach to investments (see Chapter 16). As a result, investors should be very interested in the quality of the firm's research analysis. Since not all firms carefully research each industry, you need to obtain research reports from various brokerage firms and compare them. The firm you select should be responsive to the needs of both large and small investors and should have a policy of automatically investing customers' idle monies in a money market account, where it will earn interest before being reinvested. And certainly, the reputation of the firm for fairness and honesty is paramount. Avoid brokerage firms with even a slightly suspect reputation.

Most brokerage firms emphasize fundamental analysis.

All individual stockbrokers at each brokerage firm must go through an extensive training program before taking licensing examinations. Ask for the recommendations of your banker, lawyer, financial planner, and knowledgeable friends and choose a stockbroker with an investment philosophy similar to yours. Your stockbroker should be willing to discuss your finances thoroughly and follow your particular investment objectives. If the stockbroker seems interested in short-term profits when you are a long-term investor, seek help elsewhere. Similarly, make sure your stockbroker has a lengthy record of success in your areas of interest and will be available to you when you want advice. If after a while the stockbroker or brokerage firm no longer suits your needs, by all means change. A new stockbroker at another brokerage firm can have your account transferred almost immediately.

When you open an account with a general brokerage firm or a discount brokerage firm, or both, you must supply them with your Social Security number and fill out a statement of personal financial worth. Although interested in earning commissions, the brokerage firm is required by the SEC to refuse orders that exceed a customer's financial capability. Often stockbrokers will review investment limits with new customers. If you submit a buy or sell order over the limit, your stockbroker will likely telephone you to discuss and confirm it.

You can open three kinds of accounts with a brokerage firm: cash account, margin account, and discretionary account. A **cash account** requires an initial deposit (perhaps as little as $50) and specifies that full settlement is due the brokerage firm within 5 business days (or 7 calendar days) after a buy or sell order has been given. After sale transactions, your

The typical investor opens a cash account at a brokerage firm.

What If You Have a Dispute with Your Brokerage Firm? Arbitration Is Available

Most brokerage firms require customers to sign agreements when they open trading accounts to send disputes to **arbitration**. This is a method of having a dispute between two or more parties resolved by the judgment of an impartial person or persons knowledgeable in the areas of controversy. Virtually all brokerage firms have mandatory arbitration clauses for margin and discretionary accounts; few require arbitration for cash accounts. Disputes are settled by a number of self-regulatory organizations (SROs), such as the New York Stock Exchange and the National Association of Securities Dealers, as well as the American Arbitration Association.

Investors who have a dispute relating to or resulting from the activities of a broker/dealer need only to inform the brokerage firm of the complaint and then file the formal request for arbitration. Procedures typically require that three arbitrators be selected, one from the investment industry and two from the general public. After hearing evidence from both the brokerage firm and the investor, the arbitration panel votes its binding decision. Arbitration is meant to provide cheap and quick settlements; usually the process takes 9 to 12 months. As upheld by the U.S. Supreme Court, most investment industry arbitration agreements and decisions cannot be challenged in court.

account is quickly credited with the proceeds. You can place uninvested monies in the brokerage firm's money market account with interest credited to you.

A **margin account** is a type of account at a brokerage firm in which the brokerage firm agrees to lend the customer part of the amount due for the purchase of securities. A margin account requires a deposit of substantial cash or securities ($2000 or more) and permits you to buy other securities on credit using additional funds borrowed from the firm. The Federal Reserve Board and the brokerage firm establish rules on the maximum amount of credit that can be used to purchase other securities. (Buying on margin is discussed in Chapter 21, Speculative Investments.) A **discretionary account** gives the brokerage firm discretion to buy and sell securities or commodities, including selection, timing, amount, and price to be paid or received. Both margin and discretionary accounts require that the investor and the brokerage firm accept a specific set of guidelines under which both agree to operate.

Objective
To be able to describe the elements in the actual process of buying and selling securities.

Securities Transactions and the Investor

It is not unusual to have 50 million shares of stocks traded daily on the over-the-counter market and another 200 million shares traded on the New York Stock Exchange. Between 75 and 80 percent of the trading is done by large investment banks and mutual funds. For every trade there must be a buyer and a seller to conclude the transaction at a given price.

How to Reduce Certain Investment Costs

There are ways to reduce investment costs.

In general, there are three types of investment costs: (1) sales commissions, such as when you buy and sell stocks, bonds, and some mutual funds, (2) management/administrative expenses for mutual funds, some real estate and precious metals investments, and relatively inactive accounts at brokerage firms, and (3) the *spread,* which is the difference between the retail, or ask, price at which dealers sell securities and the lower wholesale, or bid, price at which they buy them back. The bigger the spread, the harder it is for you to make money buying and selling. Spreads can be quite expensive and seriously cut into your anticipated return, particularly if you are purchasing zero-coupon bonds and over-the-counter stocks. To reduce costs, investors can use discount brokerage firms, avoid thinly traded issues and odd-lot purchases, refrain from buying front-load mutual funds, check projected charges and fees in the fee tables in prospectuses, avoid mutual funds with expense ratios above 0.67 percent and 12b-1 fees above 0.50 percent, buy Treasury securities through a Federal Reserve Bank, and comparison shop among brokerage firms for the amount of transaction costs. Sometimes you can negotiate spread costs too.

The Trading Process

Figure 19.11 illustrates the process of trading securities. Say you instruct brokerage firm A to purchase a certain number of shares of Running Paws Catfood Company at a specific price. Brokerage firm A relays the buy order to representative A, who coordinates brokerage firm A's trading around the country. Since brokerage firm A has a seat on the exchange, the buy order is then given to *floor broker* A, the brokerage firm's contact person at the exchange, who in turn contacts a **specialist.** This is a person on the floor of the exchange who specializes in handling trades of the particular stock ordered in an effort to maintain a fair and orderly market. The buy order is filled with shares, from the specialist's own inventory and/or by matching another investor's sell order. In Figure 19.11, your stock is purchased from the seller who contacted brokerage firm B.

Matching or Negotiating Prices

On the organized exchanges, there must be a *match* between the buyer's price and the seller's price for a sale to take place. Therefore, a specialist could hold a specific order for a few minutes, a couple of hours, or even a week before a match is made. With actively traded issues, a transaction normally is completed in just a few minutes. A slower-selling security can be traded more quickly if an investor is willing to accept the current market price (discussed below under Types of Orders).

On the over-the-counter market, the bid and asked prices represent *negotiation* of a final price. If a buyer does not want to pay the asking

FIGURE 19.11
The Process of Trading
Securities

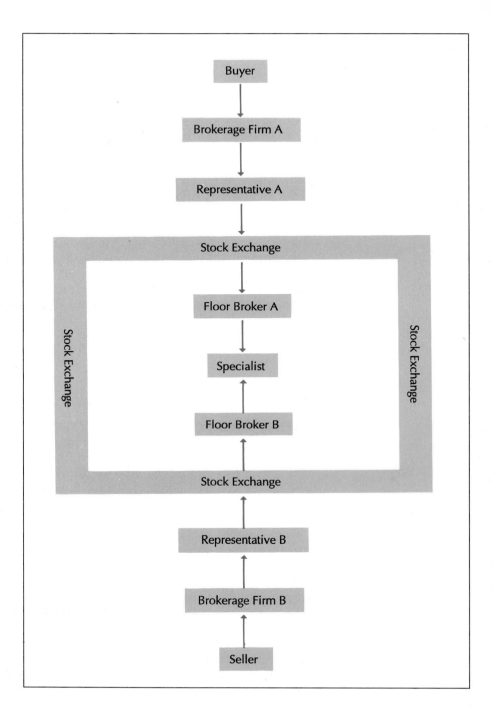

price, he or she instructs the stockbroker to offer a lower bid price, which may or may not be accepted. If it is not, the buyer might want to cancel the first order and raise the bid slightly in a second order in the hope that the seller will let the shares go at that price. Otherwise, the buyer may have to pay the full asked price in order to complete the picture. Generally, OTC trades occur at prices between the bid and asked figures.

Types of Orders

There are actually only two types of orders, buy and sell. When a stockbroker buys or sells securities according to prescribed instructions, it is called *executing an order*. The constraints that can be placed on the price of those orders are called *market, limit,* and *stop orders*.

Market Order   A **market order** instructs the stockbroker to execute an order at the best possible price. The best price to a seller, of course, is a high one; the buyer desires the lowest possible price. The stockbroker can generally secure a transaction within a few minutes at the *prevailing market price,* which is the current selling price of a security. In reality, the floor broker tries to match the instructions from the investor (getting the best price) with the narrow range of prices available from the specialist. The behavior of traders on the floor of the stock market shouting and signaling back and forth is this effort to obtain the best price.

Most stock trades are market orders.

Limit Order   A **limit order** instructs the stockbroker to buy at the best possible price but not above a specified limit or to sell at the best possible price but not below a specified limit. It provides some protection against buying a security at a price higher than wanted or selling at too low a price. The stockbroker transmits the limit order to the specialist. The order is executed if and when the specified price or better is reached and all other previously received orders on the specialist's book have been considered.

A disadvantage for a buyer who places a limit order is that the investor might miss an excellent opportunity. Assume that you put a limit order in with your stockbroker to buy 100 shares of Running Paws common stock at 60½ or lower, since you've seen in the newspaper that it has recently been selling at 61 and 61¼. You hope to save $0.50 to $1.00 on each share. That same day the company announces publicly that it plans to expand into the dog food area for the first time. Investor confidence in the new sales effort pushes the price up to 70. If you had given your stockbroker a market order instead, you would have gotten 100 shares of Running Paws at perhaps 61¼ or 61½, which would have given you an immediate profit of about $850 (70 − 61½ = 8½ × 100 shares) on an initial investment of $6150 (61½ × 100).

A disadvantage for a seller placing a limit order is that it could result in no sale if the price drops because of some news. Assume that you bought stock at 50 that is currently selling at 58 and that you have placed a limit order at a price of no less than 60. You hope to take your profit if and when it sells at that price. However, the price could creep up to 59 and then fall back to 48. In this event, you still own securities that you did not sell because the limit order was priced too high. Now they are worth less than what you originally paid for them. A limit order is best used when you expect great fluctuations in the price of a stock and when you buy or sell infrequently traded securities on the over-the-counter market.

Stop Order A **stop order** is an instruction telling a stockbroker to sell your shares at the market price if a stock declines to or goes below a specified price. It is often called a **stop-loss order** because the investor uses it to protect against a sharp drop in price and thus to stop a loss. The specialist executes the recorded order as soon as the stop-order price is reached and a buyer is matched at the next market price.

Let's consider an example of how to stop a loss. Assume that you bought 100 shares of Running Paws stock at 70. You are nervous about its entry into the competitive dog food business and feel the company might lose money. Therefore, you place a stop order to sell your shares if the price drops to 56, thus limiting your potential loss to 20 percent ($70 − $56 = $14/$70). Sure enough, some months later you read in the financial section of your newspaper that even after 6 months the newest competitor in the dog food industry, Running Paws, still has less than 1 percent of the market. You call your stockbroker, who informs you that Running Paws stock dropped in price drastically in response to the article, which was published the previous day in *The Wall Street Journal*. He reports that all your shares were sold at 55, that the current price is 49, and the sales transaction notice is already in the mail to your home. The stop order cut your losses to a little over 20 percent ($70 − $55 = $15/$70 = 21.4 percent) and saved an additional loss of $6 ($55 − $49) a share. Thus the stop order reduced your loss to $1500 [(100 × $70 = $7000) − (100 × $55 = $5500)] instead of $2100 [(100 × $70 = $7000) − (100 × $49 = $4900)].

You can use a stop order to protect profits, too. Assume that you bought 100 shares of Alpo Dog Food Company at $60 per share and the current selling price is $75. This gives you a paper profit of $1500 ($75 − $60 = $15 × 100 shares) less commissions. To protect part of that profit, you place a stop order with your stockbroker to sell at $65 should the price drop that low. If your stock is sold, you still have a real profit of $500 ($65 − $60 = $5 × 100 shares). If Alpo Dog Food stock climbs in price instead, perhaps in response to the bad news about Running Paws, the stop order would have cost you nothing. If the price does climb, you might replace the stop order with one priced a bit higher to try to lock in an even greater amount of profit.

Time Limits

Investors have several ways to place time limits on their orders. A **fill-or-kill order** instructs the stockbroker to buy or sell at the market price immediately or else the order is canceled. A **day order** is valid only for the remainder of the trading day during which it was given to the brokerage firm. Unless otherwise indicated, any order received by a stockbroker is assumed to be a day order. A **week order** is valid until the close of trading on Friday of the current week. A **month order** is good until the close of trading on the last business day of the current month. An **open order,** also called a **good-till-canceled** (GTC) **order,** is good until executed by the stockbroker or canceled by the investor. If you give a stockbroker an order longer than a week in duration, you must carefully monitor events to be sure you can alter the order if the situation changes substantially.

Special Factors Affecting Price

One factor that affects the market price of a stock is whether or not it is selling *ex dividend*. A factor that affects the selling price of a bond is how the interest is calculated. Both topics are discussed below.

Ex Dividend   If stock is selling **ex dividend,** it means that investors buying the stock will not receive the next dividend that has been recently declared by the company. Since it usually takes 4 or 5 business days to record a new buyer's name on the list of registered stockholders, stock exchanges list stocks as *ex div* for 4 to 5 days before the **record date.** This is the day companies take note of which shareholders are the legal owners and therefore should receive dividends. Since the company's declared dividend has been anticipated by investors, the price of the stock should drop accordingly when the stock is listed as ex dividend.

Calculation of Bond Interest   If you purchase an interest-paying bond in the secondary market, remember that it has been paying interest since the day it was issued. Specifically, it has been earning interest since the last payment was made to the previous owner. For example, an 8 percent $1000 bond that pays interest semiannually pays the original owner $40 on the first days of January and July. If you purchase it on September 1, the original owner deserves the amount of interest earned between July 1 and August 31, and so this interest is added to the sales price you pay for the bond. You later receive the full interest payment.

Purchasing Mutual Funds

There are three ways of buying open-end mutual funds: direct purchase, voluntary accumulation, and contractual accumulation.

Direct Purchase   A **direct purchase** is a method of acquiring shares in an open-end mutual fund where you simply order and pay for the shares, plus any commissions. Anyone can make a direct purchase, and each transaction is considered a one-time purchase. You generally would buy no-load shares directly from the mutual fund company, which would open an account for you and issue you a confirming statement shortly after it receives your payment.

You may buy load funds through a sales representative of the mutual fund, a financial planner, or a brokerage firm, which will open a regular account in your name to handle the transaction. Note that a minimum commission of perhaps $25 will be charged for each transaction. This means that the occasional mutual fund investor should make purchases of at least $300, since a typical commission rate of 8.5 percent times $300 equals $25.50, an amount just above the minimum fee.

The easiest way to buy mutual funds is with a direct purchase.

The amount of the commission, of course, reduces the number of shares purchased. For example, if you want shares of Conglomerate Cat and Dog Food Mutual Fund, which has a net asset value of $16.50 per share, a commission of 8 percent might be charged on the load fund. The 25 shares would cost $445.50: $412.50 for the stock (25 × $16.50) plus $33 in commission (0.08 × $412.50).

Voluntary Accumulation Plan   The most popular method of investing in open-end mutual funds is through a **voluntary accumulation plan.** Under this plan, you would open an account with a brokerage firm (for load funds) or the investment company itself and voluntarily invest money on a regular basis; periodic notices would be sent to you as reminders. Any commissions are deducted from each investment amount. The amount of your payment (less any sales charge) is invested, and your account is credited with ownership of fractional shares measured to three decimal places. The firm mails out a written confirmation for each transaction.

To open an account, you would fill out an application form and state the amount of the initial investment, which generally must be $100 to $500. Then you would indicate the amount you will invest regularly and the approximate dates of investment. The minimum amount for periodic investment is generally $25 to $50, and larger purchases are encouraged. Investments are generally monthly or quarterly. There is no requirement to stay with the voluntary plan; you may close it and redeem the shares at any time. Because of its flexibility, this plan is also called an **open account.** If your payments become irregular, the firm will usually notify you that future transactions will have to be handled through a direct purchase account. This type of mutual fund account is very similar to a monthly investment plan (MIP) account offered by brokerage firms to investors in stocks (discussed later in this chapter).

The concept behind a voluntary accumulation plan is twofold: (1) those with enough self-discipline to invest regularly will quickly accumulate holdings in a mutual fund and (2) those who invest on a regular basis are likely to achieve success because of the principle of dollar-cost averaging (discussed later in this chapter). Making regular purchases of shares without regard to price levels will ensure obtaining the maximum number of shares at the lowest average cost.

Contractual Accumulation Plans   A **contractual accumulation plan** is a formalized, long-term program to purchase shares in an open-end, load mutual fund. You would sign an agreement to invest a specific dollar amount periodically over a certain number of years, usually 10; commissions are paid as shares are purchased, although they are often accelerated and deducted during the first 2 years. This plan encourages you to establish a financial goal: a total amount of dollars that will be invested. It permits acquisition of mutual fund shares on a regular, budgeted schedule. To you it represents a type of forced-savings program.

The Investment Companies Amendments Act of 1970 protects mutual fund investors using contractual accumulation plans who change their minds and decide to liquidate. The law states that any investor is entitled to a full refund within 45 days. A partial refund, up to 85 percent in some instances, depending on the net asset value of the mutual fund, is available within 16½ months. Primarily because of the negative effect of the front-end load commission structure, some state legislatures (California, Illinois, and Wisconsin) have prohibited the sale of contractual accumulation plans. Fewer than 20 plans are now being sold to the investing public.

Contractual accumulation plans are generally not a good investment approach.

Contractual plans make up less than 2 percent of all mutual fund sales, primarily because they are such a bad deal for investors. They must be "sold" to investors, and salespersons have to earn commissions for their work. *Money* magazine says that contractual plans are a poor choice for most investors because "the up-front commissions and other charges are outrageously onerous and confiscatory."

Stock, Bond, and Mutual Fund Certificates

A *certificate* is a document that serves as evidence. **Bond certificates** are evidences of debt that are issued to investors who purchase them from corporations and governments. Corporations issue **stock certificates** to common and preferred shareholders as evidence of ownership.

Stock and bond certificates must be transferred to the new owners.

A bond certificate must be presented for payment when the bond is sold or when it reaches maturity and is redeemed. Similarly, when stocks are sold, the certificates must be transferred to the new owners. Holders of stocks and bonds might find it convenient to keep certificates in a safe-deposit box, but many investors who do a considerable amount of trading prefer to keep their certificates in the name of the brokerage firm. The securities are quite safe this way, and signatures are not needed when ownership is transferred upon sale. Mutual funds do not issue certificates but send quarterly statements instead.

Investors must pay a penalty for lost stock and bond certificates, generally a fee of 3 percent of the value of the securities. This money pays for an indemnification bond in the event that another person tries to make a wrongful financial claim with the certificates. If you hold your own certificates, it is wise to keep a list of the certificate numbers apart from the certificates.

Long-Term Investment Approaches to Portfolio Management

Objective
To be able to specify some investment approaches to portfolio management for long-term investors.

For some reason, it seems to be easy to lose money in the market fast, but it takes a long time to make big money. The losses of October 1987, when the Dow Jones Industrial Average dropped over 500 points in a single day, were losses only to people who took the losses. Long-term investors didn't lose a nickel because most stocks regained their prices, and then some, within 2 years. Long-term investment approaches (used by investors

The following twelve-step process will help you attain your investment goals.

1. *Identify your personal investment philosophy.* Before you make any investment, you must ascertain whether you are a speculative, moderate, or conservative investor. (This is discussed in Chapter 15.) All three types of investors can buy stocks (Chapter 16), bonds (Chapter 17), mutual funds (Chapter 18), and real estate (Chapter 20) to match their interest.

2. *Identify your desired total return.* It is important to identify the range of total return you desire, given the amount of risk you accept. For example, a conservative investor might be quite pleased with safe investments yielding 7 to 8 percent annually, a moderate investor might prefer a return of 9 to 12 percent, and a speculative investor could aim for a total annual return of 13 to 30 percent. Recall that the returns are relative, and they are better compared on a real return basis, after inflation and taxes. (This is discussed in Chapter 15.)

3. *Keep an eye on local situations.* Peter Lynch, former manager of the highly successful $9 billion Fidelity Magellan Fund, says that amateur investors have an advantage over the big investors because they can see things develop locally. About 3 to 5 years before analysts really start to follow such developments, local people can be among the first to see the industry in which they work start to turn around, and they can see nearby businesses with bright futures.

4. *Set a time horizon for your investing objectives.* Are you building up an amount for a down payment on a home, creating a college fund for a child, or putting money away for retirement? You should keep in mind why you are investing and proceed accordingly. An added bonus is that you need not worry about short-term ups and downs for long-term investments.

5. *Choose your preferred investment medium.* Whether speculative, moderate, or conservative, investors have many choices available. Study carefully and decide on the kind of investment you prefer to earn the desired total return. Some people love stocks and hate bonds, and others prefer real estate to either. Still others want to earn good yields using both mutual funds and real estate. It is crucial to remember that no matter how persuasive a stockbroker or salesperson may be, you should only invest in things you understand.

6. *Study available alternatives.* Study your specific investment alternatives and learn as much as you can about the one(s) you like. Take your time because you do not have to make a particular investment today, this week, or even this year. Carefully research the industry, the firm, and the competition. Look for firms that are leaders and that are efficient, and if you cannot find any that look attractive, do not invest.

7. *Choose an investment for its components of total return.* Your task is to choose an investment that will provide the desired potential total return through income and/or price appreciation in the proportions that you desire. For example, Willis Phillips of Nashville, Tennessee, has narrowed his investment selections to two rather comparable choices. The first is a well-known growth stock with an anticipated cash dividend of 3.5 percent and a projected annual price appreciation of 11 percent for an anticipated total return of 14.5

(continued)

percent. Willis' second choice is a lesser-known growth stock with an annual hoped-for cash dividend of 1.0 percent and capital gains of 14 percent for a projected total return of 15 percent. (This is discussed in Chapter 15.)

8. *Invest in companies that will out-earn competitors.* If you are interested in the long-term view, you should only consider the companies that will likely be the leaders in industry, not the largest, but the pacesetters in terms of profitability. You should not invest in a company because the price of its stock is rising. Instead, you should have good reasons related to profitability, such as a new division is turning around, certain competitors are losing ground, or product research is looking quite promising.

9. *Develop a plan for investing and stick to it by setting target prices and making a list of probable strategies, tactics, and actions.* A crucial step in the investment process requires you to carefully establish and write down a list of probable strategies, tactics, and actions you can take given certain investment conditions. Then you must become highly knowledgeable about the approaches you choose. This process begins with "setting target prices," both to buy and to sell. For example, Willis Phillips has determined that he wants to buy a certain stock currently selling at $37 when its price slips to $35 and then hold it for 5 years or a little longer. In addition, he has decided that if the price appreciates more than 20 percent during any given year after 2 years, he will sell to take his profits. Alternatively, if it loses more than 20 percent of its value over any 12-month time period, he will seriously consider selling

and investing his proceeds elsewhere. Also, Willis has decided that if the economy seems to be peaking out, with a probable recession forecast, he will immediately sell out and put the proceeds in bonds or a money market account.

10. *Diversify your portfolio.* It is critical that you not put all your eggs in one basket. For example, you might eventually buy three or even five stocks in an industry group instead of one. However, do not diversify into unknown companies just for the sake of diversification.

11. *Invest regularly.* Successful investing requires making investments over a long time period, preferably a lifetime.

12. *Reinvest your earnings.* This approach allows invested sums to grow rather than be spent, which will almost certainly boost your investment profits.

Unfortunately, many investors do not take a planned approach to investing. They begin by not doing the proper research. Then they avoid setting target prices and determining a list of strategic and tactical actions to take to obtain maximum gain. Instead of planning, many investors do one of two things. They follow their own speculative, moderate, or conservative nature and buy and sell investments as events occur; the resulting transaction costs eat substantially into potential profits. Or they simply invest their money and forget about it, hoping that when the time comes to sell the investment, the return and current market values will be positive. The wise investor decides in advance what investment strategies and tactics to follow and then maintains the necessary discipline to follow through on any decisions made. Good financial managers also review their investment strategies every few years as income and responsibilities change.

who buy and hold securities) are discussed below, and short-term approaches (used by investors who use a market-timing approach and frequently trade securities) are examined in Chapter 21, Speculative Investments.

A **long-term investor** is generally moderate or conservative in investment philosophy and wants to hold a security as long as it provides a return commensurate with its risk, usually for 5 years or more. Knowledgeable individuals can and do obtain long-term investment results that are superior to most professionals, but time and effort must be spent to make this happen.[1] It is not too late to begin when you are in your thirties or even older. Investment approaches for long-term investors are as follows: dollar-cost averaging; dividend reinvestment plans; business-cycle approach; portfolio diversification; asset allocation; monthly investment plans; rules, charts, and formulas; investment clubs; and employee stock purchase plans.

Dollar-Cost Averaging

Dollar-cost averaging may be boring but it works.

Dollar-cost averaging is a systematic program of investing equal sums of money at regular intervals regardless of the price of shares. It requires investing the same fixed dollar amount in the same stock or mutual fund at regular intervals over a long time with the result that you purchase more shares when the price is down and fewer shares when the price is high; therefore, most of the shares are accumulated at below-average costs. This approach avoids the risks and responsibilities of investment timing, since the stock purchases are made regularly (probably every month, rain or shine) regardless of the price. A periodic approach to investing filters out all the noise from Wall Street and provides the investor with a disciplined approach to buying.

Table 19.2 shows the results of systematic investments in a stock under varying market conditions. Commissions are excluded. Let's say that you put $300 into a stock every 3 months. To illustrate dollar-cost averaging, assume first that the funds were invested during the fluctuating market shown in Table 19.2. Since the initial price is $15 a share, you receive 20 shares. Then the market drops—an extreme but easy-to-follow example—and the price goes down to $10 a share. So you buy $300 worth and receive 30 shares. The market price rebounds to $15 three months later and you invest another $300, receiving 20 shares. Then it drops and rises again.

You now own 120 shares, with a total investment of $1500. The **average share price** is a simple calculation of the amounts paid for the investment, and it is calculated by dividing the share price total by the number of regular investments. It is $13.00 ($65/5) in this example. The **average**

---

[1] A useful source of information for do-it-yourself investors is the American Association of Individual Investors (625 North Michigan Avenue, Chicago, IL 60611). AAII is a 100,000-member nonprofit organization focusing on investor education, primarily in the areas of stocks and bonds. They publish the *AAII Journal,* which is aimed at overall investment strategies, not specific investments. Members can become involved in meetings of local chapters, attend seminars, and buy home-study courses.

TABLE 19.2
Dollar-Cost Averaging for a Stock Purchase

Fluctuating Market			Declining Market			Rising Market		
Regular Investment	Share Price	Shares Acquired	Regular Investment	Share Price	Shares Acquired	Regular Investment	Share Price	Shares Acquired
$ 300	$15	20	$ 300	$15	20	$ 300	$ 6	50
300	10	30	300	10	30	300	10	30
300	15	20	300	10	30	300	12	25
300	10	30	300	6	50	300	15	20
300	15	20	300	5	60	300	20	15
Total $1500	$65	120	Total $1500	$46	190	Total $1500	$63	140

Average share price: $13.00 ($65 ÷ 5)*	Average share price: $9.20 ($46 ÷ 5)*	Average share price: $12.60 ($63 ÷ 5)*
Average share cost: $12.50 ($1500 ÷ 120)†	Average share cost: $7.89 ($1500 ÷ 190)†	Average share cost: $10.71 ($1500 ÷ 140)†

* Sum of prices per share ÷ number of periods.
† Total amount invested ÷ total shares purchased.

The key of dollar-cost is the resulting low average share cost.

share cost is a more meaningful figure to the investor. This is the actual cost basis of the investment used for income tax purposes; it is calculated by dividing the total dollars invested by the total shares purchased. It is $12.50 ($1500/120) in this example. Note that since the recent price is $15 a share, your 120 shares are worth $300 more than you paid for them ($15 × 120 = $1800 − $1500).

Markets can decline for quite a long time period, as well as rise, and this affects dollar-cost averaging also. The "declining market" portion of Table 19.2 shows purchases of 190 shares for lower and lower prices, eventually reaching $5 a share at the bottom of that declining market. In a declining market, if you keep investing using dollar-cost averaging, you will purchase a lot of shares. Should you have to sell when the market is way down, you will not profit. In this example, you have purchased 190 shares at an average cost of $7.89, and they have a depressed recent price of $5. Selling now would result in a substantial loss of $550 [$1500 − (190 × $5)]. Dollar-cost averaging requires that you continue to invest should you believe the longer-term prospects suggest an eventual increase in price.

During a "rising market," as illustrated in Table 19.2, you continue to invest but buy fewer shares. The $1500 investment bought only 140 shares for an average cost of $10.71. In this rising market, you profit because your 140 shares have a recent market price of $20 a share for a total value of $2800 (140 × $20).

Almost anyone can profit in a rising market. If you use dollar-cost averaging over the long term, you will continue to buy in rising, falling, and fluctuating markets. The overall result is that you buy more shares when the cost is down, which lowers the average share cost to below-average prices. To illustrate, totaling in Table 19.2 reveals an overall investment of $4500 ($1500 + $1500 + $1500) used to purchase 450 shares (120 + 190 + 140) for an average cost of $10 a share ($4500/450). With the recent market price at $20, you will have a long-term gain of $4500 ($20 current market price × 450 shares = $9000 − $4500 amount invested). Note that the dollar-cost averaging method would still be valid if the time interval for investing were monthly, quarterly, or even semiannually; it is the regularity of investing that counts.

It should be clear that dollar-cost averaging produces two benefits. First, it reduces the average cost of shares of stock purchased over a relatively long period. Profits are made when stock market prices fluctuate and eventually go up. Although the possibility of loss is not eliminated, losses are limited during times of declining market prices. What is very important, profits are accelerated during rising market prices. The second benefit is investor discipline. This approach to investments is not particularly glamorous, but it is the only approach that is *almost guaranteed* to make a profit for the investor. It takes neither brilliance nor luck, just discipline.

Dividend Reinvestment Plans

Most large companies' stocks now permit reinvestment of dividends.

Instead of getting a check for dividends your shares earn, a **dividend reinvestment plan (DRIP)** automatically reinvests your money in additional shares, usually quarterly. A DRIP plan permits stockholders to reinvest dividends by purchasing additional shares directly from the corporation, usually at no commission, and sometimes at discounts of up to 5 percent. If you buy from a company that offers a 5 percent discount, you will get shares worth $105 for every $100 you reinvest. You receive regular statements for your purchases, and a small fee is charged if you want stock certificates. Many firms also allow additional cash purchases of stock free of commissions, and most will buy back the shares directly when you are ready to sell. More than 1000 companies now can credit you with whole and fractional shares of stock instead of sending dividend checks, but you'll have to ask, since companies seldom promote DRIPs. About one-third of AT&T's 3 million investors buy extra stock with their quarterly dividends. Company policies vary, and some allow investments of as little as $10 or as large as $5000 a month; some corporations allow an extra cash addition of perhaps no more than $3000 a quarter. Obviously, you should not participate in such a plan if you need the cash dividends for living expenses, but this is a conservative way to get more for your money and build capital over the long term.

DRIPs allow the long-term investor to purchase a small number of extra shares in the company in a convenient, systematic, and inexpensive way. Stocks with a track record of steadily rising dividends make the best choices. The December issue of *S&P's Quarterly Dividend Record* lists major companies that have DRIPs. Your first share must be purchased through a brokerage firm. Also, be sure to register a stock purchase in your name rather than in the brokerage firm's street name. If you are interested, telephone the company's shareholder relations department for a prospectus and application form.

The Internal Revenue Service has ruled that the value of administrative costs, fees, and brokerage commissions avoided through DRIPs is considered a taxable dividend to investors. Thus an investor with 200 shares receiving DRIP of 1.7 shares may have a taxable dividend of about $1. Note also that you must pay income tax on DRIP reinvested dividends each year just as if you had taken cash. And if the shares were bought at a discount, that amount too must be included in your taxable income in the year of the purchase. Still, dividend reinvestment plans are a bargain way to purchase shares of stock and get rich slowly. The DRIP concept in stock investments is basically the same thing as automatically reinvesting income dividends in mutual fund investments.[2]

The Business-Cycle Approach

Investors are frequently successful if they follow the **business-cycle approach,** which has as its object to have the investor participate in the rises while avoiding the declines. Figure 1.2, on page 16, illustrates various phases of the business cycle. This approach requires investing in securities when the general economy is in a **recession** (when reduced economic activity results in increasing unemployment, lower industrial production, and fewer retail sales) and prices of investment securities may have been declining over several months (a bear market). Then the investor must sell securities when the general economy is prospering and a bull market characterizes the investments scene. Selling when economic times are good is important; as Robert J. Farrell, chief market analyst at Merrill Lynch, says, "The better the economic news gets, the more cautious you should be."

The difficulty confronting the investor is to have the courage to buy during times of economic recession when most other investors are thinking about selling for fear that prices will drop even further. In fact, 6 months into the next recession will be the perfect time to buy more shares of common stock in top companies and shares in quality mutual funds. Recognize also that market averages almost always rebound before a recession ends in anticipation of better times ahead.

Also, it is difficult for most investors to sell during the peaks of prosperity when friends may be considering buying in the hope that prices will continue to climb. The stock market cycle of investor thinking goes through four stages: pessimism, skepticism, optimism, and euphoria. When interest rates rise and the economy is peaking, the investor should consider selling stocks and then consider buying bonds to lock in good returns.

The biggest challenge to the investor using the business-cycle approach

[2] A number of companies will sell their stock directly to the public, including American Recreation Centers, Central Vermont Public Utility, Citicorp, Control Data, W. R. Grace, Great Northern Nekoosa, Johnson Controls, Kroger, and Manufacturers Hanover.

is to know when to buy or sell. Accordingly, it is helpful to be able to make some estimate of the length and depth of each business cycle. Most important, an investor must choose securities that will appreciate in price along with generally rising markets. If you want to be a successful business-cycle investor, you probably will have six to eight full business cycles occur during your lifetime in which to act. During shifts in cycles, there definitely will be clear opportunities for substantial profit.

Almost anyone can make profits using the business-cycle approach.

Portfolio Diversification

With every market cycle, different investment alternatives become relatively attractive. For example, if the economy is growing and inflation is low (early months of recovery), common stock prices could be underpriced. Further along in the cycle, during times of economic prosperity, increasing inflation could have pushed interest rates up, making bonds more attractive than stocks. As an investor, you can either spend time trying to figure out how and when to move your money or have a diversified portfolio.

Portfolio diversification is the process of selecting alternatives that have dissimilar risk-return characteristics; this process provides a lower but acceptable overall potential return. Portfolio diversification offsets the riskiness of individual investments and it smoothes out the ups and downs of individual investment returns. A portfolio that is well balanced among stocks, bonds, cash equivalents, real estate, precious metals, collectibles, and other investments can limit the damage when the economy dips or collapses. Efforts to diversify can greatly reduce **random risk,** the risk associated with owning only one security that by chance may do very poorly in the future.

Portfolio diversification reduces random risk.

Investors in securities can diversify within an investment medium (such as different stocks in one industry) or across alternatives (such as in stocks, bonds, and mutual funds). Common stock investors can even diversify by the type of stock owned. For example, the moderate investor, instead of placing all funds into growth stocks or mutual funds (a prolonged recession would hold down values), might buy some growth stocks and some income stocks or similar mutual funds. The conservative investor could purchase some countercyclical income stocks or mutual funds. Securities investors also can diversify according to industry. For example, placing all your funds in a portfolio of transportation securities is riskier than diversifying into three economic industries, such as transportation, chemicals, and electronics. If transportation securities decline in value, your chemicals and electronics holdings may retain their values or even increase.

Investors in bonds can diversify by type of bond as well as by maturity. By purchasing bonds with maturities spaced out over several years, you minimize the risk that they would all come due at a time when interest rates were low. Of course, you should realize that an increasing diversification not only minimizes risk but is also likely to increase your brokerage costs. The extent of diversification you choose depends on your personal investment philosophy and the amount you have to invest. Table 19.3 shows guidelines for diversified investment portfolios, and Figure 19.12 shows some sample portfolios.

TABLE 19.3
Guidelines for Model Portfolios for Moderate-Philosophy Investors

Investment Alternatives	Average Investor	Single, Starting Out	Single, More Affluent	Working Couple, Childless	One-Income Couple with Two Young Children	One-Income Couple Nearing Retirement
					Types of Investors	
Fixed-dollar savings/ investments	5–15%	20–30%	10–20%	5–10%	10–20%	15–20%
Bonds	10–20	—	10–20	5–15	5–15	15–40
Common stock	10–20	10–20	10–30	10–30	10–20	10–15
Mutual funds	15–30	20–50	20–30	20–40	20–50	10–15
Speculative investments	0–10	5–20	0–5	5–10	5–10	0–5
Real estate (excluding private residence)	15–40	—	15–20	20–30	10–20	10–30

FIGURE 19.12
Illustrative Investment Portfolios

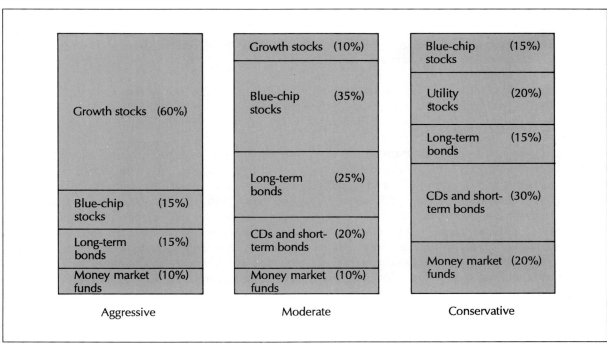

Aggressive	Moderate	Conservative
Growth stocks (60%)	Growth stocks (10%)	Blue-chip stocks (15%)
Blue-chip stocks (15%)	Blue-chip stocks (35%)	Utility stocks (20%)
Long-term bonds (15%)	Long-term bonds (25%)	Long-term bonds (15%)
Money market funds (10%)	CDs and short-term bonds (20%)	CDs and short-term bonds (30%)
	Money market funds (10%)	Money market funds (20%)

What If You Want to Use Beta to Calculate an Estimated Rate of Return?

Historical records indicate that prices in the overall securities market increase about 8 percent a year. Of course, in some years the market rises tremendously and in other years it dips precariously. These fluctuations are what we call **market risk**, the uncertainty of anticipated return an investor can have because of factors associated with fluctuations in the market owing to economic recessions, industrial restructurings, regional economic turmoil, and political upheavals.

The concept of **beta** (discussed in Chapter 15) has to do with statistically estimating the relative risk of a particular investment compared with the market for all investments by using historical data. A beta figure shows how responsive the price of an individual investment has been to overall market fluctuations. For example, if Running Paws Catfood Company stock has a historical performance beta of 1.5, it means that if the stock market as a whole goes up 10 percent, Running Paws stock will probably go up 15 percent. Should the market go down 10 percent, Running Paws will likely go down 15 percent.

The average for all securities is $+1.0$, and the price of an investment with a beta of $+1.0$ will move in the same direction as the market; the return and risk would be the same as the market. A beta of zero suggests that the price of the securities is independent of the market, similar to a risk-free U.S. Treasury security; return is guaranteed regardless of market performance. A negative beta, less than zero, means that the price of the security moves in the opposite direction as the market. A beta of from $+0.1$ to $+0.9$ means that the security price moves in the same direction as the general market but not to the same degree; these would be conservative investments. Higher betas mean greater risk relative to the market.

It is smart to use beta when calculating your estimated rate of return on an investment, be it stock, bonds, mutual funds, or whatever. Once a beta for a particular investment is known (these can be obtained from brokerage firms, mutual fund companies, realtors, and library reference books), you then need an estimate of both the market rate risk and the current Treasury-bill rate of return to calculate your total estimated return. The **total estimated return** on an investment is calculated by multiplying the beta value of an investment times an estimate for market risk (here we have used the historical average rate of 8 percent for securities) plus the current Treasury-bill rate (which is basically a risk-free return), as illustrated in the following equation. For example, if you are considering investing in Running Paws, which has a beta of 1.5, and you assume a market rate risk of 8 percent and today's T-bill rate, which at press time was 6.5, the total estimated return is 18.50 percent.

$$
\begin{aligned}
\text{Total estimated return} &= \text{beta value} \\
&\quad \times \text{market rate risk} \\
&\quad + \text{Treasury bill rate} \\
18.50 \text{ percent} &= 1.5 \times 0.08 \text{ percent} \\
&\quad + 0.065 \text{ percent}
\end{aligned}
$$

To sum up, the rate of return on the T-bill is risk-free, and that should be assumed as part of your anticipated return. Realize also that as the T-bill rate changes, so do other rates of return on investments. As an investor in something riskier than Treasury bills, you should expect an estimated return of at least what the market has historically offered. And since beta value estimates the market risk relative to one particular investment, you can calculate the total estimated return by multiplying the beta times the market rate risk and adding the rate of return for Treasury bills. The 8 percent estimate for market rate risk is fine for long-term investors.

Diversified Portfolios of Selected Investors

Tommy Jacobson, age 26	Money market fund	10 percent
Santa Monica, California	Mutual fund (aggressive growth)	20 percent
Annual income: $36,000	Mutual fund (income and equity)	30 percent
Current income needs: minimal	Growth stock (lesser known)	20 percent
Objectives: 15 to 17 percent annual growth	Growth stock (lesser known)	20 percent
Investment philosophy: moderate		
Net worth: $40,000		
Value of investments: $14,000		
Ronda and Ricardo Garcia,	Money market fund	5 percent
ages 41 and 43	Mutual fund (growth and income)	5 percent
Baltimore, Maryland	Mutual fund (growth and income)	10 percent
Annual income: $64,000	Mutual fund (growth and income)	20 percent
Current income needs: minimal	Bonds (high-quality corporate)	20 percent
Objectives: 12 to 14 percent annual return	Growth stock (well known)	5 percent
Investment philosophy: moderate	Growth stock (well known)	10 percent
Net worth: $130,000	Growth stock (lesser known)	10 percent
Value of investments: $48,000	Limited partnership	10 percent
	Gold	5 percent

Asset Allocation

Historical data suggest that at least 80 percent of the returns an investor earns are not obtained from specific investments; rather, they are derived from owning the right asset categories at the right time.[3] **Asset allocation** (also called **tactical asset allocation**) is a mathematical method of deciding what portion of one's total resources should be allocated to various types of assets. At the professional level, fund managers generally consider three classes of assets: stocks, bonds (or debts), and cash or cash equivalents. Asset allocation requires that for long time periods you keep your stock, bond, and money-market equivalents at a fixed ratio.[4] The objective, of course, is to increase return on assets while decreasing risk.

[3] A 1986 study published in the *Financial Analysts Journal* evaluated the 10-year performance of 91 pension funds. The authors concluded that 94 percent of the funds' returns were attributable to the way assets were allocated; the remaining 6 percent came from specific choices and market timing.

[4] Purists believe an asset allocation should be among five categories: (1) domestic stocks, (2) foreign stocks, (3) Treasury bonds, (4) real estate, and (5) cash equivalents. The percentages should remain at 20 percent forever.

You should divide your portfolio among (1) stocks, (2) bonds, and (3) cash equivalents.

The answer to how much a sample portfolio should be divided among stocks, bonds, and money-market instruments (such as T-bills) can be found in determining how much an investor is willing to lose in order to gain. Someone with no risk tolerance should invest only in money-market instruments. Those willing to accept a total return that is less than what stocks alone might provide, in hopes of a better return than money-market instruments offer, might divide their assets equally between money-market instruments and stocks. The apportionment also depends on the investor's time horizon. For long-term investors, a minimum time period of 5 years is appropriate for the asset-allocation approach. No two investors should allocate alike, because age, income, family situation, overall financial goals, and personal tolerance for risk vary.

Marshall Blume, professor of finance at the Wharton School and a principle in the money management firm of Prudent Management Associates (PMA), suggests that the investor's potential return can be projected given historical data for each group of assets.[5] The calculations assume the best expected return with the least amount of risk. Here *risk* is defined as the chance that events will turn out differently than expected, and the standard deviation statistic measures how different events might get. PMA calculates that over the next 5 years assuming good, fair, and poor markets, a high-risk strategy (100 percent stocks) might earn 30 percent, 13 percent, or minus 6 percent compounded annually. A moderate-risk strategy (50 percent stocks, 50 percent bonds) might yield 22 percent, 11 percent, and minus 1 percent, while the conservative strategy (20 percent stocks, 30 percent bonds, 50 percent equivalents) might return 14 percent, 9 percent, and 3 percent.

The appropriate allocations change with time and circumstances. Figure 19.13 illustrates decisions about how much to allocate to each type of security. A young investor might decide to keep most in equities, since they do better over the long term and younger investors have more time to make up any big losses. A middle-aged investor might decide on a more balanced portfolio, since stocks can be dangerous over a 5-year period and he or she may not want all his or her money there. A retired investor might decide to keep a small portion of the portfolio in equities. Once you decide how much to invest in each allocation, stick with it; you need not change your proportions until your broad investment goals change, probably another 5 or 10 years at least. Historically, asset allocation practiced by pension funds required that once invested, the funds be pretty much left alone.

[5] Roger Gibson, author of *Asset Allocation: Balancing Financial Risk,* notes that over the past 60 years or so stocks on the S&P 500 stock index have outpaced inflation by 6.9 percent; bonds have beat inflation by only 1.3 percent, and Treasury bills have beat inflation by 0.4 percent. *Money* magazine reports that for a variety of investments the historical average annual return after inflation is as follows: growth stocks, 9.7 percent; blue-chip stocks, 7.0 percent; utility stocks, 2.9 percent; long-term bonds, 0.2 percent; short-term debt, 0.7 percent; and money market funds and accounts, 0.1 percent.

FIGURE 19.13
Techniques of Asset Allocation

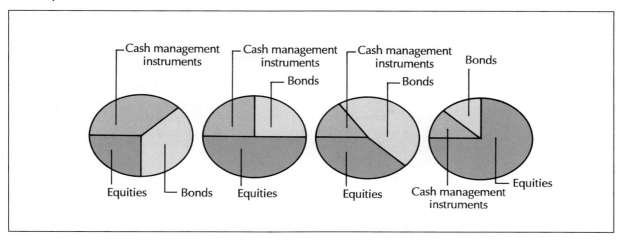

Individual investors practicing asset allocation now move funds as often as once a month, removing funds in the short term from less promising assets into others.[6] For example, when the bond market rises, you might cash in some of your profits and buy stocks, bringing your portfolio back to the originally determined split. Note, however, that moving funds once a year is sufficient to practice effective asset allocation, particularly if portions get out of line 10 to 15 percent. Note that when rebalancing you are always selling on the way up and buying on the way down. You try to win by not losing. Staying in balance is the key, since you cannot predict the future, but you can control your exposure to risk.

Asset allocation helps you win by preventing losses.

A number of mutual funds are organized to allocate assets. They gradually shift assets as market and economic conditions change in seeking to earn a high total return over the long term. The STAR Fund spreads your investment over six Vanguard funds, with 60 to 70 percent in stocks, 25 to 40 percent in bonds, and the remainder in money-market equivalents. Of course, it costs little or nothing to rebalance your portfolio with no-load mutual funds.[7]

Monthly Investment Plans

A **monthly investment plan** (**MIP**) is an arrangement you make with a brokerage firm to invest regularly (perhaps monthly or quarterly) a specified

---

[6] Some people call themselves asset allocators, although they resemble market timers as they move in and out of diversified investment opportunities when they believe a shift is warranted.

[7] The asset-allocation approach to investing is a form of diversification, since one constantly adjusts a diversified portfolio. A popular variation of dollar-cost averaging in a diversified portfolio is using a *constant-ratio formula,* which blends dollar-cost averaging with a formula for adjusting the mix of investments in a portfolio.

amount of funds ($40 to $1000) in a common stock listed on a major stock exchange. This plan provides you with the advantages of dollar-cost averaging. Additional features of MIPs offered by brokerage firms include the purchase of fractional shares, special low commission rates, automatic reinvestment of dividends, noncontractual agreements featuring no penalty should an investment payment be missed, and monthly statements evidencing ownership. Conservative or moderate investors are often quite satisfied with the results of a monthly investment plan. The primary drawbacks are the effect of commission charges on return rates and the lack of diversification. A monthly investment plan to invest in common stock operates in a manner similar to a voluntary accumulation plan for mutual funds.

Rules, Charts, Formulas, Technical Analysts, and Programmed Trading

Many investors set their own investment rules. "Sell whenever prices drop 15 percent or more" might be a good rule for the conservative investor. "Sell only when the loss exceeds 40 percent" could be a speculator's rule. "When the price drops sharply, double the investment" also could be used by the speculator. This latter rule is called **averaging down;** its merit is that the price need not rise to its original level to regain the investor's losses. For example, assume you have 1000 shares at $10 per share for an investment of $10,000. The price drops to $5 and you buy an additional 2000 shares for another investment of $10,000. Thus your total of $20,000 is invested in stock worth $15,000 (3000 shares at $5 each). Because of averaging down, the stock price need only reach 6¾ before you recoup losses and have a profit (3000 × 6¾ = $20,250). If the price rises to $8 before you sell, the gain is $4000, or 20 percent (3000 × 8 = $24,000 − $20,000 = $4000/$20,000).

Some people average down to recoup losses and try to make a profit.

Charts of different types help some investors decide when to buy or sell securities. Investors can do their own daily charting of stock activities (high, low, close, volume, and so on) and/or subscribe to advisory services that provide charting for a fee. *Technical investment analysts* or *theorists* often use complicated mathematical models on which to base their buy or sell recommendations. A sophisticated technical analyst might have charts of more than 1500 indicators, updated each day by hand, based on numbers "crunched" by computers. Large institutional investors use a form of technical analysis called **programmed trading.** This method uses specially designed computer software programs to monitor price fluctuations in the stock, options, and futures markets that contain built-in guidelines that instantly trigger and place buy and sell orders. They profit from small differences between the prices on stocks on the NYSE and the prices of futures contracts (discussed in Chapter 21) traded on the Chicago Mercantile Exchange.

Many long-term investors follow their own formula-timing guidelines and use a stock's *P/E* ratio as an indicator of buying low and selling high. For example, perhaps the price/earnings ratio of Running Paws Catfood Company common stock in recent years has ranged between 8 and 24.

An investor might decide to buy Running Paws when its *P/E* ratio is less than 10 and sell when it is greater than 20. A straightforward rule offered by growth stock specialist Elliott L. Schland is to buy stocks trading at three-fourths the company's projected growth rate and sell when the *P/E* ratio expands to equal the projected growth rate. To illustrate, if a company's earnings are estimated to rise 20 percent a year, using the Schland formula, you buy the stock when its *P/E* ratio is 15 (or less) and consider selling when it reaches 20.

One popular formula is to use a stock's P/E ratio as guide.

Investors also use formulas to manage their entire portfolio. These formulas are usually predicated on the belief that securities investments should include certain percentages of both an aggressive portfolio and a defensive portfolio. The concept is that securities in the aggressive portfolio should be more volatile (common stocks) than those in the defensive portfolio (usually bonds), and profits are made by varying the percentage of each in bull and bear markets. In a rising market, investors should shift more funds into the aggressive portfolio by selling some from the defensive portfolio; in a declining market, investors should increase funds in the defensive portfolio by selling securities from the aggressive portfolio. Hence the volatility of common stocks will reap profits in bull markets, and the values of bonds will increase in declining markets.

Investment Clubs

An **investment club** is an organization formed by individuals who want to share their investment knowledge and a limited amount of investment dollars both to learn about the securities market and to make a profit. These clubs usually meet monthly, have 5 to 15 members, and require a monthly contribution ranging from $10 to $50. The amounts collected are subsequently invested in securities based on decisions made by the entire group. Since trading typically involves substantial funds, commission charges represent a small proportion of each transaction. Generally, different members investigate particular investment alternatives and report their findings to the membership, which then votes on what actions to take according to the club's investment goals. All actions are governed by the bylaws of the club, and a legal partnership agreement protects members.

Investment clubs let you learn and profit.

Brokerage firms are usually happy to assist clubs, because members often will open individual accounts as well. The National Association of Investment Clubs (NAIC) provides a complete packet of information to help people establish investment clubs.[8] Included are guidelines for investing, a how-to manual on stock-study techniques, and a sample copy of *Better Investing,* a monthly magazine devoted to investment education that is available on subscription, and investment club startup and operating information. There are about 7000 NAIC investment clubs in the United States with 140,000 members and an estimated 20,000 unaffiliated clubs. The NAIC sponsors numerous regional and national meetings to improve investors' abilities.

[8] National Association of Investors Corporation, 1515 East Eleven Mile Road, Royal Oak, MI 48067.

Employee Stock Purchase Plans

Many corporations offer an **employee stock purchase plan** (**ESPP**) as a fringe benefit for employees. This plan permits employees to buy shares of stock in the company and gives them an extra incentive to do a good job, the hoped-for result being an increase in the profitability of the corporation and in the value of the stock. Generally, the purchase price of the stock is fixed and the amount that may be purchased is limited. In some cases, the employer will make a matching contribution of stock, which greatly accelerates the purchasing efforts of the individual investor-employee. For example, for every $100 of stock the employee purchases (perhaps up to a maximum of $2000 annually), the company might donate $50 of additional stock.

Knowing When It Is Best to Sell

Objective
To be able to list three guidelines to use when deciding whether to sell securities.

Don't you wish we could tell you precisely when to sell your stocks, bonds, and mutual funds to make lots of money? Although such certainty of knowledge is not available, following the three guidelines below will help you profit in the securities market.

Take Your Profits

The great financier Bernard Baruch was once asked how he made so much money in the securities market. He replied, "I always sold too soon!" Baruch suggested that one should not be too greedy. Sell when you have hit your goal. You also should sell when the venture is now the rage with other investors, such as when the biggest brokerage firms recommend the same investment, because the "smart money" gets out early. When you have earned a satisfactory profit, an amount that only you can determine, sell and take the real profit to avoid the risk of prices dropping later. Don't be paralyzed into missing modest and respectable profits in hopes of big ones.

The "smart money" gets out of the market early.

Cut Losses Quickly

Hindsight is sometimes much better than foresight, especially in securities transactions. When you have bought securities as a result of an error in judgment, sell them. Temporary shifts in prices of 10 to 15 percent happen all the time, but when the momentum has slowed and it is clear that an earlier decision to buy was incorrect, don't wait for a 10 percent loss to develop into a 20 or 30 percent loss some weeks or months later. Don't hold onto a loser. Accept your error, sell, and make a better investment with the proceeds. Also sell when there are changes in a company's products, market share, profit margins, or management strategy that soon may negatively affect prices.

Buying and Selling Advice for Conservative Stock Investors*

- When the market is retreating and the economy is deteriorating (a bear market), take profits and cut losses on most stocks; consider holding defensive stocks.
- As the bear market continues, plan ahead by being alert for low-priced stocks with high yields or undervalued issues that are likely to surge ahead when the market improves.

* Especially if you have some well-reasoned opinions on the direction of interest rates, inflation, and the economy for the next year or more.

- If the market is uncertain, lacks clear direction, and seesaws aimlessly, follow preceding suggestions or put your money into a money market fund.
- When the market is rising, buy on "corrections" if possible. These are brief time periods, a few days at most, when most market prices are depressed because of negative news.
- As the bull market continues, protect some of your profits by placing stop-loss orders with your stockbroker if prices fall back.
- As the bull market matures, consider taking some profits by selling half your stocks.

If You Wouldn't Buy It Now, Sell It

As you review your portfolio of securities investments, don't think about the price you originally paid and the possible income tax liability. Ask yourself, "If I had extra money to invest, would I put it into this investment?" and carefully analyze the individual investment, the industry, and the prospects for economic growth. If your answer is no, sell the investment and don't let a 2 or 3 percent commission stop you. Sell when the grass is greener and you have found a better investment.

Summary

1. After securities have been sold in the primary market, organized stock exchanges (such as the New York Stock Exchange) offer a secondary market.

2. Available information on general economic conditions and the securities markets indexes, along with industry data and news about corporations, can help reduce investment risks and increase returns.

3. To buy and sell securities, you need to open an account at a general brokerage firm or discount brokerage firm and pay specific fees on each transaction. A certificate will be provided to you as evidence of stock or bond ownership, while a statement is provided mutual fund investors.

4. The actual transaction to buy or sell securities involves brokers matching or negotiating the final price. Use of stop orders can help you reduce losses as well as protect gains in securities transactions. Mutual funds can best be purchased using a voluntary accumulation plan.

5. The 12-step investment process includes identifying your desired return as well as making a list of probable actions you can take during certain investment conditions.

6. There are several long-term investment approaches to portfolio management, such as dollar-cost averaging, dividend reinvestment plans, business-cycle approach, diversified portfolio, and asset allocation.

7. Guidelines on when to sell stocks and bonds include take your profits, cut losses quickly, and if you wouldn't buy it now, sell it.

Modern
Money
Management

The Johnsons Want to Invest in Stock

After reviewing several types of investment alternatives, Harry and Belinda have decided to invest $1200 now and then $200 to $400 a month for the next two years. All income from their investments will be automatically reinvested but they expect some price appreciation as well. Harry and Belinda are busy learning about different investments and generally "following the market."

1. Harry has been watching Rite Aid stock while Belinda is interested in Reebok. Which stock had the greatest volume of trading? Which stock reported the greatest net change in price? (See Figure 19.3.)

2. Based only on the *P/E* ratios for the two stocks, which is the better value?

3. If the Johnsons had a "windfall" and purchased 100 shares of Reebok stock, how much commission would they pay? On 100 shares of Reebok stock? Assume the purchases were made at the highest price of the day.

4. Briefly discuss the factors the Johnsons should consider in choosing a stock brokerage firm, particularly since they plan to invest regularly.

Key Words and Concepts

arbitration, 678
asked price, 659
asset allocation, 695
average share cost, 688

average share price, 688
averaging down, 698
bear market, 666
beta, 694

Review Questions

1. Explain why securities markets exist and the difference between primary and secondary markets.

2. Illustrate the role of an investment banking firm in the securities business.

3. Summarize the role of a brokerage firm in the process of trading securities in the secondary market.

4. Briefly explain how organized stock exchanges differ.

5. Explain the over-the-counter concepts of market making, bid price, and asked price.

6. What is meant by the following stock transaction terms: *stock, div, yld%, sales 100s, P/E ratio, high/low, close, net chg?*

7. Summarize what the newspaper quotations mean for open-end mutual funds.

8. What are the major factors in regulating in the securities market?

9. Summarize the insurance coverage provided investors by the Securities Investors Protection Corporation (SIPC).

10. Identify two popular stock indexes used by investors, and briefly distinguish between them.

11. Why is it important to obtain information about an industry in which you are considering investing?

12. Summarize the benefits to the investor of using a general brokerage firm.

13. Show what the commissions might be at a full-service general brokerage firm and a discount brokerage firm on a purchase of 350 shares of a stock priced at $10 a share.

14. Distinguish between a cash account and a margin account, and identify advantages of using each from an investor's point of view.

15. List five suggestions on how to reduce certain investment costs.

16. Explain when prices are matched or negotiated.

17. Give reasons why investors would want to use a market order, a limit order, and a stop order.

18. Distinguish among the three ways of buying mutual funds: direct purchase, voluntary accumulation, and contractual accumulation.

19. Choose 3 of the 12 steps in how to invest and summarize what they mean.

20. What two things does dollar-cost averaging achieve, and how does it work?

21. List some of the benefits of a dividend reinvestment plan (DRIP).

22. Give two examples of what an intelligent investor might do using a business-cycle approach to long-term investing.

23. Explain how portfolio diversification works, and give two examples of how to use it.

24. Summarize how to use beta in estimating rate of return on an investment.

25. Describe the logic behind the asset-allocation approach to long-term investing.

26. Give an example of using a formula plan to invest successfully.

27. Discuss one guideline that will help you know when to sell securities.

Case Problems

1. Mary Stephenson of College Park, Maryland, is trying to explain to her friend Charlotte Churaman how to read the newspaper financial data on

mutual funds. Mary turned to the financial section of the newspaper and located the part on mutual funds. Using Figure 19.6, help explain it all by responding to the following questions about the Fidelity Investments group of mutual funds.

a. How much would it cost to buy 100 shares of Fidelity Capital Appreciation?

b. What would be the commission charge in dollars and as a percent of the amount invested?

c. If Charlotte already owned 100 shares of Capital Appreciation, how much per share would she receive if she redeemed them?

d. Calculate the commission rates to buy shares in Fidelity Equity Income and Fidelity Europe.

e. How much would it cost to buy 100 shares of Fidelity Exchange Fund?

f. How much would it cost to sell 100 shares of Fidelity Exchange Fund? Explain why.

2. Linda Haag of New Egypt, New Jersey, has operated her own custom packaging business quite successfully for more than 5 years. She has decided to incorporate her business as Eagle Packaging Incorporated and seeks expansion funds. The total value of authorized stock is to be $450,000, and Linda plans to retain $250,000 of this authorization. Eagle common stock will have a par value of $50 per share. After her own purchase of 5000 shares, 4000 shares will be sold to the investing public.

a. Explain how the shares might be priced and how they will be marketed.

b. Explain why future trading of the 4000 shares will occur in the over-the-counter market after they are initially sold to the investing public.

c. Give an illustration of likely bid and asked prices of Eagle stock.

3. Harold Rubin of Shreveport, Louisiana, is interested in investing in Greenfield Computer Company. He notices that the market price for their common stock has been around $80 in recent months, and he wants to buy 100 shares. Give Harold advice as he ponders the following questions.

a. Should he use a general or discount brokerage firm for this purchase? Why?

b. Should he give the stockbroker a market order or a limit order? Why?

c. Should it be a day order or a good-till-canceled order? Why?

d. What would the discount brokerage firm's commission probably be if Harold bought Greenfield Computer for 79½?

e. Since Harold is an investor interested in cutting his losses and taking his gains, explain your advice to him to put in stop orders at 67 and 92.

4. Tommy Jacobson of Santa Monica, California, recently received an inheritance of more than $50,000. After paying off some bills and buying a new car, he has decided to invest the balance of $14,000 in the stock market. An investment advisor recommended a portfolio to include a

money-market fund, some mutual funds, and some stocks, as shown in the box, Diversified Portfolios of Selected Investors, on page 695.

Tommy is hesitant because he has never invested in stocks before, and he seeks your advice on selecting growth stocks. He says that cash dividends are of little concern to him because he earns enough money to live comfortably.

    a. Suggest to Tommy three industries that have had successful earnings in recent years (see Figure 19.9).

    b. Briefly tell Tommy how and when to obtain information about those industries and particular companies.

Suggested Readings

"A Cleaner Environment: Where to Invest." *Changing Times,* February 1990, pp. 32–39. How to profit by investing in companies that clean up the environment.

"A Dumb Way to Buy Mutual Funds." *Changing Times,* March 1989, pp. 59–63. Details on why contractual mutual fund purchasing methods are not the deal for many investors.

"Best of the Investment Software." *Changing Times,* June 1990, pp. 73–78. Suggestions for both general and technical investment software programs.

"Big Ideas for Little Money." *Changing Times,* August 1989, pp. 67–70. Where to put your money even if you only have $1000.

"Brokers' Statements: Close, But No Cigar." *Changing Times,* March 1989, pp. 47–51. Stockbrokers' statements are getting easier to understand.

"Cashing in on Cash-Rich Companies." *Changing Times,* July 1989, pp. 29–33. Techniques to invest in cash-rich companies.

"Does the Market Matter?" *Business Week,* October 30, 1989, pp. 24–26. Explores the meaning of fluctuations in the stock market.

"Drawing a Bead on Defense Stocks." *Changing Times,* June 1990, pp. 65–66. There is still money to be made in defense stocks.

"Funds That Cut the Risk . . . and the Reward." *Changing Times,* July 1989, pp. 43–48. Choosing the asset-allocation funds.

"Hitching a Ride on the Market." *Changing Times,* March 1989, pp. 93–97. The performance of thirteen mutual funds.

"How to Decode the Financial Pages." *Changing Times,* March 1990, pp. 83–87. Understanding the small type on the investment alternatives listed in newspapers.

"How to Do Even Better." *Money,* October 1989, pp. 82–83. Asset management portfolio recommendations for different stages of the life cycle.

"How to Launch an Investment Club." *Money,* May 1989, pp. 117–125. Details on how to start and run an investment club.

"If You're Getting Burned by 'Churning.' " *Business Week,* April 24, 1990, p. 124. How to tell if you are a victim of churning and what to do about it.

"Investing in a Perilous Market." *Changing Times,* October 1990, pp. 40–43. An historical look at past recessions and what to do if today's market continues to slide.

"Making the Most of a Bare Bones Broker." *Business Week,* April 9, 1990, pp. 86–87. How to choose and use a discount broker.

"Peter Lynch's Seven Money-Making Rules." *Money,* December 1990, pp. 74–75. Key suggestions from the most successful mutual fund investment manager.

"Prospering in Today's Manic Markets." *Money,* December 1990, pp. 72–87. Investment strategies for stocks, bonds, cash, and precious metals.

"Secrets of Successful Investment Clubs." *Changing Times,* February 1990, pp. 83–93. About 250 new investment clubs are formed each month, which continues a resurgence of this method of investing.

"Stockbrokers: When Discounts Don't Count." *Changing Times,* February 1989, pp. 50–56. Comparison of fees among brokerage firms shows that full-service brokers sometimes offer the best prices.

"Turning Your Desktop into a Personal Big Board." *Business Week,* March 27, 1989, p. 119. How to use your PC to monitor the New York Stock Exchange.

"Worryproof Your Investments." *Changing Times,* October 1989, pp. 75–77. Description of investment risks, how to hedge them, and which alternatives are the safest bets for the future.

20 Investing in Real Estate

OBJECTIVES

After reading this chapter, you should be able to

1. Identify the advantages of investing in real estate.
2. Describe the disadvantages of investing in real estate.
3. Explain ways to determine the proper price to pay for real estate.
4. Distinguish among the types of direct investments in real estate.
5. Describe the various types of indirect investments in real estate.
6. List the situations in which to consider selling real estate investments.

. . . .

Home owners know that the money used to buy their homes does more than just put a roof over their heads. Every home also has an investment aspect, since over several years it will probably increase in value. Profits on homes and other forms of real estate investments sometimes can be significant. This potential for profit encourages home owners and other investors to consider real estate as an alternative investment to stocks, bonds, or mutual funds.

Real estate is property consisting of land and all its permanently attached structures and accompanying rights and privileges, such as crops and mineral rights. People invest in real estate for economic and noneconomic reasons. One *noneconomic* reason is that most investors like the feeling of being closely involved with their investments and the pride and satisfaction in being owners of property. The ultimate goal of investing in real estate is *economic,* the maximization of after-tax returns. Real estate offers an investor an average yield of one and one-half to two times that of most common stocks. However, the investor must accept the corresponding increase in risk and also give up substantial liquidity.

This chapter begins with a discussion of the advantages and disadvantages of real estate investments. We then look at how to determine *value,* or the price that might be paid for a particular piece of property. Next we review the types of real estate investments, both direct and indirect. The chapter closes with a section on determining when to sell real estate.

Real Estate Investing

Objective
To be able to identify the advantages of investing in real estate.

All ownership investments offer a potential total return based on income received and/or price appreciation. The special benefits of real estate to the investor are an enhanced potential total return that comes from **leverage,** which is the use of borrowed funds to make investments, and special income tax provisions for real estate (such as deductions for depreciation) that often increase after-tax income. Thus there are four advantages of real estate investing: (1) the possibility of a positive cash flow, (2) potential for price appreciation, (3) availability of leverage, and (4) special tax treatments.

Positive Cash Flow

For an income-producing real estate investment, you pay operating expenses out of rental income. If the property has a mortgage, as is usual, payments toward the mortgage principal and loan interest also must be made out of rental income. The amount of rental income you have left after paying all operating expenses (including repairs) and mortgage expenses is called **cash flow.** The amount of cash flow depends on the amount of rent received, the amount of expenses paid, and the method you use to repay the mortgage debt. Most investors prefer a positive cash flow to a negative cash flow because any shortages have to be made up by the investors themselves. Many, however, can manage a negative cash flow by taking tax losses for a few years while hoping for profits to come in through substantial price appreciation in the value of the property.

A real estate investment need not generate a large cash flow to be successful. For example, assume that Mary Rupe, a free-lance writer from West Lafayette, Indiana, owns a small office building that cost $100,000. After subtracting expenses, she nets only $4000 annually in profits. This appears to be a yield of only 4 percent ($4000/$100,000). It could be much higher, depending on Mary's marginal income tax rate and whether she uses special tax treatments available to real estate investors.

Price Appreciation

Price appreciation is the amount above ownership costs that an investment is sold for. In real estate, the ownership costs include the original purchase price as well as expenditures for any capital improvements made to a property prior to sale. **Capital improvements** are costs incurred in making changes in real property that add to the value of the property. Paneling a living room, adding a new roof, and putting up a fence are capital improvements. In contrast, **repairs** are expenses—usually tax-deductible against an investor's cash-flow income—that are necessary to maintain the value of the property. Repainting, mending roof leaks, and fixing plumbing are repairs. For example, assume that Keith Martin, a school teacher from Grosse Pointe, Michigan, bought a duplex as an investment 3 years ago for $80,000. He fixed some roof leaks (repairs) for $1000 and then added a new shed and some kitchen cabinets (capital improvements) for a cost of $5000 before selling the property. When Keith sold the duplex this year for $105,000, he happily realized a price appreciation of $20,000 ($105,000 − $80,000 purchase price − $5000 capital improvements).

Leverage

Lenders normally permit real estate investors to borrow from 75 to 95 percent of the price of an investment property. As a result, leverage can increase the yield on an investment. Consider Keith Martin's property again. Suppose that instead of paying cash for the duplex, he had made a down payment of $25,000 and borrowed the remainder. What effect would this have on his yield? In the first instance he paid $80,000 cash for the building and thus earned a 25 percent yield on his investment ($20,000/$80,000) over the 3 years. In the second situation, using leverage, he would have an apparent yield of 80 percent ($20,000/$25,000). The true yield would be lower because of mortgage loan payments, interest expenses, capital improvements, and repairs, but still a substantial 60 to 65 percent. These details are illustrated later in this chapter.

The **loan-to-value ratio** measures the amount of leverage in an investment project. It is calculated by dividing the amount of debt by the value of the total original investment. For example, Keith Martin had a loan-to-value ratio of 68.75 percent (or 68.75 percent leverage), since his down payment was only $25,000 on the $80,000 property ($55,000/$80,000).

Beneficial Tax Treatments

The U.S. Congress, through provisions in the IRS Code, encourages real estate investments by permitting investors a variety of special tax treatments. These include depreciation, interest deductions, tax-free exchanges, and rental income tax regulations.

Depreciation May Be Deducted from Current Income   Investors in real estate become successful by understanding the "numbers" of real estate investing. For example, assume that Joanne Swiftson, a lawyer from Carbondale, Illinois, invests $115,000 in a residential building ($100,000) and land ($15,000) and rents it for $10,000 a year. The tenant pays all variable costs, such as real estate taxes, insurance, and maintenance. You may think that because the tenant pays all expenses Joanne must pay income taxes on the entire $10,000 in rental income, but the IRS allows her to deduct depreciation from this income amount. **Depreciation** is the decline in value of an asset over time due to normal wear and tear and obsolescence. A depreciated amount can be deducted from the cost of a capital asset over the asset's estimated life. Note that land cannot be depreciated. According to the straight-line method of depreciation, Joanne can deduct an equal part of the building's cost over the estimated life of the property. The IRS has a guideline of 27.5 years for depreciating residential properties and 31.5 years for commercial real estate. Thus Joanne calculates the amount she can annually deduct from income to be $3636 ($100,000/27.5). Table 20.1 shows the effects of depreciation on income taxes, assuming Joanne is in the 33 percent marginal tax bracket. In this example, the depreciation deduction lowers taxable income from $10,000 to $6364 and raises the yield on the investment from 5.8 percent to 6.9 percent, a 19 percent increase [(6.9 − 5.8 = 1.1)/5.8]. Note that this yield is based on the total investment of $115,000.

Interest Is Deductible from Current Income   Real estate investors incur several general business expenses in attempting to earn a profit: real estate taxes, repairs, insurance, utilities, capital improvements, and interest on mortgage loans. The largest of these costs is often the interest expense, since most properties are purchased with a substantial amount of borrowed money. Table 20.2 illustrates the effect of interest expenses on income taxes. Joanne Swiftson borrowed $64,000 to purchase her $100,000 building and $15,000 land. After she deducts interest expenses, her income flow is reduced to $3821, and after she deducts depreciation, her taxable income is reduced to $185. Since she thus has a minor income tax liability

Depreciation and mortgage interest can be used to reduce taxable rental income.

TABLE 20.1
Effect of Depreciation on Income Taxes and Yield

Cost of rental building		$100,000
Cost of land		15,000
Total amount invested		$115,000
Depreciation permitted for 27.5 years		$ 3,636

	Without Depreciation	With Depreciation
Gross rental income	$10,000	$10,000
Less annual depreciation expense	0	$ 3,636
Taxable income	$10,000	$ 6,364
Income taxes (33 percent marginal tax rate)	$ 3,300	$ 2,100
Return after taxes	$ 6,700	$ 7,900
Yield after taxes (divide by $115,000)	5.8 percent	6.9 percent

(only $61), the after-tax return on her leveraged investment increases to 7.4 percent. Note that this yield is based on an investment of $51,000 ($115,000 − $64,000).

Because the tax laws permit investors to deduct interest expenses, part of the real cost of financing investment property is shifted to the government. The amount of that transfer depends on the investor's marginal tax bracket. Joanne's interest deduction permits her to have an after-tax cash return of $3760. In essence, the $6179 in interest is paid with $2039 (33 percent tax bracket) of the money that was not sent to the government and $4140 ($6179 − $2039) of Joanne's money. Essentially, then, a major reason for using borrowed money to invest is that the government pays part of the loan costs for the investor.

Tax-Free Exchanges Defer Capital Gains Taxation   Another special tax treatment results when a real estate investor trades equity in one property for equity in another similar property. If none of the people involved in the trade receives any other form of property or money, the transaction is considered a **tax-free exchange.** If one person receives some money and/ or other property, only that person must report the extra proceeds as a taxable gain. For example, if you bought a duplex 5 years ago for $80,000 and now trade it with your friend, giving $5000 in cash for your friend's $135,000 commercial building, your friend need only report the $5000 as income this year. You need only report your long-term gains ($135,000 − $5000 − $80,000 = $50,000 to date) if and when you sell your new property.

Special Tax Regulations Apply to Rental Income   If the real estate is "business property," all expenses allocable to the rental use of the property are deductible—even if it produces a net loss to shelter other income from

TABLE 20.2
Additional Effect of Interest on Income Taxes and Yield

Gross rental income	$ 10,000
Less annual depreciation deduction	− 3,636
Subtotal	$ 6,364
Less interest expense ($64,000, 9 percent mortgage loan)	− 6,179
Taxable income	$ 185
Return after interest expense ($10,000–$6,179)	$ 3,821
Minus income taxes (0.33 × $185)	− 61
Return after taxes	$ 3,760
Yield after taxes [$3760/($115,000 − $64,000)]	7.4 percent

taxes. All real estate income and losses are classified for income purposes as "passive income" and "passive losses." Generally, passive losses can be used to offset only passive income.

For high-income people, passive losses cannot be used to shelter salary or other investment income. For those with more modest incomes who use a residence (such as a vacation home) for 14 or fewer days and "actively manage" the property (help make decisions on tenants, rents, and repairs), such passive losses may be valuable for tax purposes. When adjusted gross income (*AGI*) is under $100,000, up to $25,000 in passive losses may be used to shelter income from any source, such as salary or other investment income. The limit is gradually phased out as the *AGI* moves between $100,000 and $150,000. When personal use of a residence is for more than 14 days, income tax deductions are limited to the amount of rental income from the property. However, excess losses can be carried forward to offset future income generated by the vacation property.

Disadvantages of Real Estate Investing

The potential for a high total return from real estate investment carries with it a high degree of risk and uncertainty. Over the past 15 years, the average annual return (ignoring inflation) on real estate investments nationally has ranged from over 18 percent to just under 7 percent. This and other disadvantages of real estate investments are described below.

Financial Risk

It is quite possible to lose money in real estate investments. Unanticipated events can wreck your best estimates of expected income and expenses for an income-producing property. In times of economic recession, many investment properties just sit empty. Even if the general economy is robust, a large local industry fallen on hard times could force local real estate values to plunge. Other unforeseeable problems could be imposition of community rent controls and deterioration of a neighborhood owing to population shifts or a change in school-district boundaries. A great influx of college students into an area, for example, usually depresses the values of single-family dwellings and pushes up the prices of multiple-family dwellings.

Buying Real Estate Is More Involved Than Most Alternative Investments

Real estate investments require more study and careful investigation than do most other alternative investments. You must be able to analyze the real estate market and anticipate the impact of competition from other investment properties. To invest in commercial real estate, you need to consider location, traffic patterns, and demographics. To buy apartment buildings, you must investigate the income of the likely tenant population.

Real estate generally involves a large initial investment.

Investment in real estate generally requires many thousands of dollars, often $10,000 to $25,000 or more. In contrast, the average price of investment in stocks is less than $35 per share, and bonds can be purchased in units of $1000. In addition, appraisal and attorney fees and sales commissions can add to the cost of a real estate investment. For many investors, putting a large sum into real estate reduces the possibility of diversification. This disadvantage can be partially offset through real estate syndicates (limited partnerships) and real estate investment trusts, which are discussed later in the chapter.

The Management Required Is Often Time-Consuming

Managing a real estate investment requires time. You may need the services of both an accountant and an attorney to determine how much to spend for an investment property and when and at what price to sell it. If you are the landlord of your own property, your management time increases sharply. You must know how to advertise for new tenants, issue leases, perform repairs, handle delinquent payments, and, if necessary, legally evict tenants.

Current Income Is Often Low Most of the total return on real estate investments takes the form of price appreciation because income is used for mortgage payments, maintenance costs, occasional capital improvements, and other expenses. During times of relatively high mortgage interest rates, a real estate investor may find that interest expenses cut severely into income. Sometimes these expenses reduce cash-flow return to less than 2 percent or even cause an annual loss.

It Is Difficult to Accurately Estimate Costs Managing a real estate investment requires that you estimate the anticipated total return you expect on your investment based on expected income, expected expenses, and expected price appreciation. If you estimate any of these variables incorrectly, you could lose not only a great deal of money, but your investment property as well. There are many difficulties in estimating costs. Expenses might be greater because of high tenant turnover. Insurance costs might rise sharply while competition among rental units holds rent increases to a minimum. Rezoning could depress property values. Inaccurate estimates combined with limited reserve funds and unfortunate economic events could force you to sell at a loss and consider bankruptcy.

Selling a Real Estate Investment Can Be Difficult

Since real estate is expensive, the market for investment property is much smaller than the securities market. Thus you might receive comparatively few bids for a piece of real estate you want to sell. The nature of real estate is that every investment property is different and must be analyzed separately. Five different buyers might be interested in purchasing an income-producing duplex, but the one you have for sale may not meet their specific requirements. In such an individualized market, a lot of haggling over price also occurs.

Liquidity is a problem in real estate investing.

Liquidity is a problem in real estate investing, since it may take months to find a buyer, arrange the financing, and legally close the sale. You might have to accept some financial loss if you must convert your real estate into cash in a hurry. The liquidity of real estate investments is even worse during times of high mortgage interest rates, since most potential buyers cannot afford steep financing costs.

Substantial transfer costs also are incurred when real estate is bought or sold. Real estate brokers charge sales commissions of 6 to 7 percent of the property's sale price. Attorneys' fees usually amount to one-half of 1 percent or more. Add to this appraisal fees, title search fees, and accountant fees if special reports are to be shown to potential investors. Further, the lender might have a prepayment penalty of 1 or 2 percent. These costs can greatly reduce expected return and force the investor to keep the property for at least 3 or 4 years in order to spread out the expenses.

What Should You Pay for a Real Estate Investment?

Objective
To be able to explain ways to determine the proper price to pay for real estate.

Three methods are commonly used by investors to determine the price to pay for a piece of real estate property: the gross income multiplier, capitalization rate, and discounted cash flow.

The Gross Income Multiplier

The **gross income multiplier** (*GIM*) is a method of determining the price to pay for an income-producing property by dividing the asking price (or market value) of the property by the current annual gross rental income.

The gross income multiplier formula is

$$GIM = \frac{\text{asking price of property}}{\text{current gross rental income}} \qquad (20.1)$$

For example, if the advertised price on a small apartment complex is $240,000 and the gross rental income totals $40,000, the *GIM* is 6 ($240,000/$40,000). The *GIM* is much like a *P/E* ratio for common stocks. Real estate publications and local real estate investors can indicate the going *GIM* rate for various types of properties classed by age and community location. An investment with a *GIM* of more than 8 probably pays too low a return to be profitable. If you know the *GIM* rate for an area, you can rearrange Equation (20.1) to estimate the market value or likely asking price of the property as follows:

$$\text{Asking price} = \text{current gross rental income} \times GIM \qquad (20.2)$$

The *GIM* is limited, since it is only a rough guide to investment property values and the expenses for properties vary. If the *GIM* is too high, you might consider offering a lower price to the seller.

Capitalization Rate

The **capitalization rate** is widely used to determine the rate of return (yield) on a real estate investment. Also known as **income yield,** it is calculated by dividing the net operating income (first year) by the total investment, or asking price. The capitalization rate formula is

$$\text{Capitalization rate} = \frac{\text{net operating income (first year)}}{\text{total investment } or \text{ asking price}} \qquad (20.3)$$

Both the gross-income multiplier and the capitalization rate can be used to estimate the asking price of a property.

For example, if the **net operating income** (gross income less allowances for vacancies and operating expenses, except depreciation and debt repayments) were $18,000 on a property with a total investment of $240,000, the capitalization rate would be 7.5 percent (0.075 = $18,000/$240,000). Of course, this estimate of income yield is only a rough measure, since net operating income can be calculated in more than one way among comparable investment properties.

Note that the capitalization rate is the inverse of the price earnings ratio. Thus a capitalization rate of 12.5 percent is equivalent to a *P/E* ratio of 8 (100 percent divided by 12.5 percent), and conversely a price earnings ratio of 8 has a capitalization rate of 12.5 percent (8 divided by 100). The high price earnings ratios for growth stocks and low capitalization rate for growth properties (those bought primarily for their price appreciation potential rather than operating income) reflect this inverse relationship and allow a more direct comparison between real estate investments and stocks.

The capitalization rate is a popular method of determining the rate of return, since comparable data are available on other properties as well as

TABLE 20.3

Discounted Cash Flow Method Illustration (Asking Price of Property Is $80,000)

Number of Years	After-Tax Cash Flow	Present Value of $1 at 10 Percent*	Present Value of After-Tax Cash Flow
1	$ 4,000	0.909	$ 3,636
2	4,200	0.826	3,469
3	4,400	0.751	3,304
4	4,600	0.683	3,142
5	4,800	0.621	2,981
Sell Property	$100,000	0.621	62,100
Present value of property			$78,632

* From Appendix A2.

alternative investments. In addition, investors often estimate the market value or asking price of income-producing property by using an assumed capitalization rate and rearranging Equation (20.3) as

$$\text{Asking price} = \frac{\text{net operating income (first year)}}{\text{capitalization rate}} \qquad (20.4)$$

Thus, in this example, the asking price would equal $18,000/0.075 percent (assumed capitalization rate), or $240,000. Alternatively, if you require an income yield of 9 percent, you can conclude that the $240,000 asking price for this property is too high ($18,000/0.09 = $200,000). Although valuable, this method has two limitations: (1) it is based on only the first year's return, and (2) it ignores return through price appreciation.

Discounted Cash Flow

The **discounted cash flow** method of estimating the value or asking price of a real estate investment emphasizes after-tax cash flows and the return on the invested dollars discounted over time to reflect a discounted yield. Computer software programs are available to help calculate discounted cash flows. (You also can use Appendix A2 of this book, as shown in Table 20.3.) To illustrate, assume you require a rate of return of 10 percent on a piece of real estate property advertised for sale at $80,000. You estimate that rents can be increased each year for 5 years. You expect that after all expenses you would have an after-tax cash flow of $4000, $4200, $4400, $4600, and $4800 for the five years. Assuming some price appreciation, you expect to be able to sell the property for $100,000 after all expenses. How high a price should you pay *now* to buy the property?

Table 20.3 shows how to answer this question. Multiply the estimated after-tax cash flows and the expected proceeds of $100,000 to be realized on the sale of the property by the present value of a dollar at 10 percent,

What If You Are Considering an Income-Producing Real Estate Investment

When you are considering a real estate investment, you use your investment amount (purchase price or down payment) to estimate the likely rate of return. This allows comparisons with other investment alternatives. The following table shows 5-year estimates for a hypothetical income-producing property valued at $100,000. The gross income multiplier (*GIM*) is 10 ($100,000/ $10,000), so it is likely that the investment may be a poor one from the point of view of current income. The building will be purchased with a $75,000 mortgage loan, so the buyer has to make a $25,000 down payment and also pay $4000 in closing costs. The gross income is projected to rise at an annual rate of 5 percent, vacancies and unpaid rent at 10 percent, real estate taxes at 7 percent, insurance at 8 percent, and maintenance at 10 percent. Virtually the entire payment for the 30-year, $75,000, 12 percent fixed-rate mortgage loan is assumed to be interest during these early years. For income tax purposes, the land is valued at $10,000 and the building is depreciated over 27.5 years. Thus the amount of annual straight-line depreciation is calculated to be $3272 ($100,000 − $10,000 = $90,000/27.5). The buyer is in the 28 percent marginal tax bracket.

Estimates for a Successful Real Estate Investment

	Year				
	1	2	3	4	5
A. Gross possible income	$10,000	$10,500	$11,025	$11,576	$12,155
Less vacancies and unpaid rent	500	550	605	666	733
B. Projected gross income	$ 9,500	$ 9,950	$10,420	$10,910	$11,422
C. Less operating expenses					
Real estate taxes	$ 900	$ 963	$ 1,030	$ 1,103	$ 1,180
Insurance	400	432	467	504	544
Maintenance	1,200	1,320	1,452	1,597	1,757
Interest	9,261	9,261	9,261	9,261	9,261
Total operating expenses	$11,761	$11,976	$12,210	$12,465	$12,742
D. Total cash flow (negative)	$ (2,261)	$ (2,026)	$ (1,790)	$ (1,555)	$ (1,320)
E. Less depreciation expense	3,272	3,272	3,272	3,272	3,272
F. Taxable income (or loss) (D − E)	$ (5,533)	$ (5,298)	$ (5,062)	$ (4,827)	$ (4,592)
G. Annual tax savings (28 percent marginal rate)	1,549	1,483	1,417	1,352	1,286
H. Net cash flow income (or loss) after taxes (G − D)	$ (712)	$ (543)	$ (373)	$ (203)	$ (34)

Note how difficult it is to earn current income from rental properties when financing costs are relatively high. During the first year, the total cash flow loss is projected to be $2261. Further, because the income tax laws permit depreciation to be recorded as a real estate investment expense, even though it is not an out-of-pocket cost, the total taxable loss is projected to be $5533. This loss is deductible on the investor's income tax. Since the investor is in the 28 percent tax bracket, the loss of $5533 results in a first year annual tax savings of $1549 ($5,533 × 0.28). Instead of sending the $1549 to the government in taxes, the investor can use it to pay the operating expenses of the investment. Therefore, the cash-

(continued)

flow loss of $2261 can be reduced by $1549 for a net cash-flow loss after taxes of $712 ($2261 − $1549). During the first year of ownership, the investor will have to come up with the additional $712 (about $60 monthly) to make ends meet.

Assume the property appreciates in value at an annual rate of 6 percent and will be worth $133,823 in 5 years ($100,000 × 1.06 × 1.06 × 1.06 × 1.06 × 1.06). If it sold at this price, a 6 percent real estate sales commission would reduce the proceeds by $8029 to $125,794.

Now we can calculate crude annual rate of return on the property, as the following table shows. A **crude rate of return** is a rough measure of the yield on amounts invested that assumes that equal portions of the gain are earned each year. The total return in this example was substantial. There were out-of-pocket cash investments of $25,000 for the down payment, $4000 in closing costs, and $1865 in net cash-flow losses ($712 + $543 + $373 + $203 + $34), for a total investment of $30,865. The investor has a capital gain of $38,154, or a crude before-tax total return of 124 percent over 5 years, roughly 25 percent (124 percent/5) annually.

Crude Annual Rate of Return on a Successful Real Estate Investment

Amount invested

Down payment	$ 25,000
Closing costs	4,000
Accumulated net cash flow losses	1,865
Total invested	$ 30,865

Taxable cost (adjusted basis)

Purchase price	$100,000
Closing costs	4,000
Subtotal	$104,000
Less accumulated depreciation	16,360
Taxable cost (adjusted basis)	$ 87,640

Proceeds

Sale price	$133,823
Less sales commission	8,029
Net proceeds	$125,794
Less taxable cost	87,640
Taxable proceeds (capital gain)	$ 38,154
Income tax (28% marginal tax bracket)	$ 10,683
After-tax proceeds	$ 27,471

Crude annual rate of return

Total invested	$ 30,865
Taxable proceeds (capital gain)	$ 38,154
Before-tax total return ($38,154/$30,865)	124%
Crude before-tax annual rate of return (124 percent/5 years)	25%

the required rate of return. Add the present values together to find the total present value of the property, here $78,632. Thus the asking price of $80,000 is too high for you to earn an after-tax return of 10 percent. Your choices here are to negotiate the price down, accept less than a 10 percent return, or consider another investment. The discounted cash flow method is a superior and widely used way of estimating real estate values because it takes into account the selling price of the property, the effect of income taxes, and the time value of money.

Discounted cash flow calculations recognize the impact of the time value of money.

Direct Ownership

Objective
To be able to distinguish among the types of direct investments in real estate.

A real estate investment is referred to as **direct ownership** when an investor holds actual legal title to the property. You can invest directly as an individual, buying an apartment building, for example, or jointly with other investors. Joint direct ownership of real estate can take one of two forms, tenancy in common or joint tenancy. In **tenancy in common,** two or more people have control of the property regardless of whether they hold equal shares, and each person retains the right to dispose of (sell or give away) his or her undivided interest. Most unrelated individual investors prefer this kind of ownership. In **joint tenancy,** two or more people have an undivided interest in real estate held in equal or unequal shares; some states require that joint tenants always have a right of survivorship. **Joint tenancy with right of survivorship** requires that upon the death of a joint tenant (one owner), the remaining joint tenant or tenants assume full ownership of the property. Many husbands and wives own property in this kind of joint tenancy. You should decide what form of ownership you prefer before shopping for real estate investments with others.

Residential Units and Commercial Properties

Residential units are properties designed for residential living, such as houses, duplexes, apartments, mobile homes, and condominiums, with a potential to produce a profit. **Commercial properties** are properties designed for business uses, such as office buildings, medical centers, gasoline stations, and motels, that carry a potential to produce a profit. Making a good investment income from these properties normally requires you to take an active interest in their management.

Of all real estate investments, residential units are probably the easiest to begin with, the easiest to get out of, and the least profitable. One popular way to get a start in real estate investment is to purchase "sweat equity" property. Here, you would seek properties that have good underlying value and attempt to buy at a favorable price, perhaps because the seller is having financial difficulties. Once you acquire the property, you "sweat" by spending many hours painting, scrubbing, and fixing it up to sell it at a profit or to rent to tenants.

Commercial properties carry more risk of remaining unrented than residential units. Further, the services expected by business tenants are usually more extensive and costly, and the buildings have a greater risk of obsolescence. Accordingly, you can charge higher rents on commercial properties to offset the higher risks involved.

You need to consider several criteria in choosing successful income-producing rental property: good location, the dependability of income, the current value of the property, the condition of the property, the likely impact of future competition of similar real estate, the availability of reasonable financing, moderately priced utilities, stable real estate property taxes, and, of course, return on investment after taxes.

Second or Vacation Homes

Vacation home mortgage interest and property taxes are deductible.

Many people own a second or vacation home, usually a house, condominium, or mobile home located near a lake or a beach, in the mountains, or at some other resort area. The IRS generally considers a second or vacation home as just another piece of property. Thus owners can deduct only amounts spent for mortgage interest and real estate property taxes. For example, say Alice Skeller, a librarian from Durham, New Hampshire, buys vacation property with a $600 monthly payment on the west coast of Florida. Interest and taxes amount to $500. Since she is in the 28 percent tax bracket, she realizes tax savings of $140 monthly ($500 × 0.28). Thus it still costs Alice $460 ($600 − $140) a month, or $5520 annually, for the property.

Qualifying for a passive loss deduction is much more complicated.

Should she rent out her property, however, she can qualify for additional tax savings if her adjusted gross income is under $150,000. As mentioned earlier, Internal Revenue Service regulations allow you to take all or a portion of passive losses on your vacation home if used as rental property as long as (1) you "actively participate" in rental operations, (2) you rent it for 15 days or more, (3) you attempt to rent the property, either by listing it with a rental agent or advertising it, *and* (4) your personal use of it does not exceed the greater of 14 days or 10 percent of the total number of days the home is rented at a "fair rental value." Rental losses for depreciation, repair costs, utility bills, and so forth may be taken as tax deductions. For example, income for Alice could amount to $2000 for 20 days of rentals. Rental losses might total $3500 and result in a tax loss of $1500, but only if she did not personally use the property more than 4 days herself. Remember, too, that Alice stands to gain from long-term price appreciation.

A special provision in the tax law pertains to vacation properties that are rented out for fewer than 15 days during the year. It says that you cannot take any deductions, except for mortgage interest and property taxes, but the rental income you collect is *not* taxable. This tax-free income idea might work to your advantage.

Time Sharing and Interval Ownership

Time sharing and interval ownership are relatively new ways of obtaining vacation housing. For from $5000 to $10,000 buyers can purchase 1 week's use of luxury vacation housing furnished right down to the salt and pepper shakers. Vacationers also pay an annual maintenance fee for each week of ownership, perhaps $200 per year. The terms *time sharing* and *interval ownership* are not interchangeable, and their clarification requires distinguishing between the concepts of right to use and interval ownership. A **right-to-use purchase** of a limited, preplanned time-sharing period of use of a vacation property is actually only a vacation license. It does not grant legal real estate ownership interests to the purchaser, but instead provides a long-term lease permitting use of a hotel, suite, condominium, or other accommodation. This is also known as *nondeeded time sharing.* As in some other situations that involve leasing, should the true owner of the property (the developer) go bankrupt, the time share purchasers (actually renters) are locked out of the premises by the creditors. In contrast, an **interval ownership purchase** provides time-sharing buyers with actual titles and deeds to limited, preplanned use of real estate. Purchasers are thus secured creditors who are guaranteed continued use of the property throughout any bankruptcy proceedings. This is also known as *deeded time sharing.*

Time-sharing and interval ownership are not high quality investments.

Time sharing and interval ownership should be viewed as vacation plans not real estate investments. It is *very* difficult to sell a time-share investment, and people rarely get more than 50 percent of their original investment. If you are still interested in such property, you should be leery of gifts and awards often used to promote time-sharing units, consider interval ownership rather than right-to-use time sharing, demand a 15-day cancellation clause in the contract, and require that your money be placed in escrow until the construction of the time-sharing project is completed.

Raw Land and Residential Lots

Raw land and residential lots are the riskiest form of real estate investing.

Investing in raw land or residential lots on which you yourself do not intend to build is a speculative affair. No special tax advantages exist for this kind of investment. **Raw land** is undeveloped acreage, typically far from established communities, with no utilities and no improvements except perhaps a substandard access road. A **residential lot** is subdivided acreage with utilities (water, electricity, and sewerage) typically located within or adjacent to established communities. Do not buy acreage unless you firmly believe that (1) you will later build on the property, (2) the price paid today is substantially less than what it might be in the future, and (3) comparable acreage will not be available in the future when needed by buyers. Land speculators buy raw land and residential lots to sell to people who "think" they are certain they will build in the future.

Although they alone are not sufficient, "location, location, and location" are the first three rules of successful real estate investing. A corner lot is better than one in the middle of the block, and a waterfront lot is even better. A lot on the main street of a growing town is better than one on a nearby street. Beware of the speculative investment of buying unknown land in some distant place as part of a new city, retirement village, or resort. You should *always* see the land, hire an attorney to check out the deal, read the **property report** (a document legally required under the federal Interstate Land Sales Act for properties offered for sale across state lines), and obtain a private property appraisal.

Indirect Investment

Objective
To be able to describe the various types of indirect investments in real estate.

An **indirect investment in real estate** is one in which the investors do not hold actual legal title to the property. With real estate syndicates and real estate investment trusts, the actual title is held by a *trustee* (an individual or a financial institution) who manages the investment. Other forms of indirect real estate investment allow investors to buy an ownership stake in mortgages, thereby earning income from the mortgage interest paid by the property owner.

A **real estate syndicate** is an indirect form of real property investment often organized as a limited partnership in which a required minimum number of shares (often five) are sold to investors for as little as $500 each to raise capital for real estate projects. Syndicates finance the building of many office buildings, shopping centers, factories, apartment houses, supermarkets, and motels. The **limited partnership** form of real estate syndicate involves two classes of partners: the *general partner* (usually the organizer and initial investor), who operates the syndicate and has unlimited financial liability, and the *limited partners* (the outside investors), who receive part of the profits and the tax-shelter benefits but who are inactive in the management of the business and who have no personal liability for the operations of the partnership beyond their initial investment.

A **real estate investment trust (REIT)** is an unincorporated business that raises money by selling shares to the public, much like a closed-end mutual fund does, and owns property or makes mortgage and other loans to developers. REITs (pronounced "reets") were established under the Real Estate Investment Trust Act of 1960, which encourages small investors to place money indirectly into real estate. The goal was to offer the profit potential of real estate while maintaining the marketability of stock.

REITs include mortgage trusts and equity trusts.

There are two types of REITs, mortgage trusts and equity trusts. **Mortgage trusts** do not own property but provide short-term financing for construction loans or for permanent mortgage loans for large projects. **Equity trusts** concentrate on buying or building their own real estate properties, such as apartments, restaurants, nursing homes, condominiums, and office buildings, and hire management firms to run the properties.

The investor who wants some of the allure of real estate along with the advantages of common stock may simply purchase stocks of real estate investment corporations. Like any other public corporation, they are engaged in business to make a profit. Instead of building automobiles or computers, these firms specialize in financing large properties.

In Chapter 10 we discussed mortgage loans from the point of view of the borrower. However, somebody must play the role of lender/investor, earning the interest and taking the risk of default. Individual investors might find it advantageous to actually become a mortgage lender. Three alternatives are available. First is *seller financing* of a property, in which the buyer makes direct payments to the seller (who now becomes a lender/investor) as specified in the mortgage agreement. For example, Sid Margolius might personally finance the sale of his $125,000 home to Nancy Barclay by accepting $25,000 in cash as a down payment and taking back a $100,000 loan on which Nancy will make monthly payments for 25 years. A second is a *discount mortgage.* This is where an investor purchases the preceding type of mortgage from a seller who needs money now and is willing to let the mortgage go at a discount. For example, after 5 years, Margolius might find he needs cash, so he can sell Nancy's mortgage loan to a private investor at a slight discount to encourage the sale. The third alternative is a *shared-appreciation mortgage.* It is similar to seller financing, but the lender also will gain if the home goes up in value. In return for granting a lower than market interest rate or accepting a lower down payment, the seller receives the right to receive perhaps 20 to 25 percent of the equity in the home attributable to inflation when the home is ultimately sold by the buyer.

Participation certificates represent an investment in mortgage pools.

From the point of view of a lender, a mortgage is an asset because money will be repaid and interest earned. Like any other asset, mortgages can be sold. For example, a mortgage lending company might have a group of mortgage loans valued at $10 million on its books. It could sell 10,000 portions (or "slices") of this pool, or package, of mortgages for $1000 each ($10 million divided by 10,000 equals $1000) to investors who would then earn steady income from the interest and principal as the borrowers repay their individual mortgage loans. Each slice (sometimes called a **participation certificate**) represents the investor's share in the pooled mortgages. The lender could then take the $10 million proceeds of the sale and make another $10 million in mortgages to additional borrowers, and the pooling process could begin again.

Mortgage pools are very common and represent a special opportunity for the right investors. These investments are often referred to by acronyms such as Fannie Mae, Ginnie Mae, and Freddie Mac (discussed in Chapter 17) or REMIC (real estate mortgage investment conduit). A number of mutual funds also specialize in mortgage pool investments.

Summary

1. People invest in real estate to maximize after-tax returns and to experience the four advantages of real estate investing: the possibility of a positive cash flow, the potential for price appreciation, availability of high leverage, and special tax treatments that can enhance profits.

2. Disadvantages of real estate investing include the effort and cost of buying a real estate investment, the frequent need for management of the investment, and difficulties and costs of selling when necessary.

3. You can use three methods to determine the value of, or the price to pay for, a selected piece of real estate property: gross income multiplier, capitalization rate, and discounted cash flow.

Advice for the Conservative Real Estate Seller

The largest profits in real estate often are made when property is sold rather than while it is owned. So too are the biggest losses. Thus the conservative and careful real estate investor must know when and how to sell real estate. Investors who decide to sell should avoid doing so in an anxious moment; sellers, like buyers, should carefully analyze the best times to make a transaction. Even though the real estate investment alternatives described in this chapter are quite varied, we can still offer a few selling suggestions. Generally, you should sell in these situations:

1. *Your investments are unwise.* No matter how careful real estate investors are, some investments just do not work out. Perhaps the apartment building is located in the wrong neighborhood or the vacation property is deteriorating and actually declining in value. When troubles and expenses mount, it is time to consider selling.

2. *You are tired of ownership.* There may come a time when you no longer enjoy collecting rents, arranging maintenance, and making capital improvements. Or your vacation spot may lose its attractiveness. Sell the property and find another investment you like.

3. *Alternative investments pay more.* Some people buy a piece of real estate and feel they must hold onto it forever. You may have had a vacation property for many years and have paid off the mortgage in full. Or a rental building you bought years ago may still be bringing in a stream of income.

Could you make more money by selling or refinancing and investing the proceeds elsewhere? For example, a vacation home valued at $70,000 with no mortgage debt is a $70,000 asset earning no current income for the owner. An alternative would be to refinance it, perhaps obtaining $50,000, and to invest that amount.

4. *You need money.* Many owners of real estate go through crisis times when they simply need money. In these instances, you need not necessarily sell your property. When you refinance property instead of selling, perhaps at a higher interest rate, you may receive a substantial amount of cash in addition to a new mortgage.

5. *You want to invest "upward."* You can use leverage to enhance profits in real estate. If you sell your home and invest those proceeds (including price appreciation) into another more expensive property, you can avoid capital gains if you buy a home with the same or a higher value within 24 months. You can follow this procedure every few years, investing in increasingly more expensive dwellings, and pay no capital gains taxes until you choose not to reinvest. Recall from Chapters 8 and 10 that on a personal dwelling an individual has a once-in-a-lifetime capital gains exclusion of $125,000 beginning at age 55. Thus $125,000 of these gains may be tax exempt. Investors in real estate properties should consider selling when after-tax gains permit them to expand their real estate holdings.

4. Examples of types of direct investment in real estate include raw land and residential lots, income-producing properties, second or vacation homes, time sharing and interval ownership.

5. Examples of types of indirect investment in real estate include real estate syndicates, real estate investment trusts, and mortgage pools.

6. Suggestions for when to sell real estate include the following: sell unwise investments, sell when tired of ownership, and sell when an alternative investment will provide a better return.

Modern Money Management

The Johnsons Compare Real Estate Investments

Harry and Belinda Johnson are considering some residential income properties as investments. Respond to the following questions, given the financial data presented below on three properties.

	Property A	Property B	Property C
Asking price	$200,000	$220,000	$190,000
Gross rental income	30,000	34,000	27,000
Net operating income (first year)	15,000	16,500	15,000

1. Calculate the *GIM* for the three options.

2. Give the Johnsons your observations on which properties are the best and worst buys, given that the *GIM* for comparable residential rental properties in their community is 7.

3. What would the *GIM*s be if you successfully negotiated the prices downward to $190,000 for property *A*, $200,000 for property *B*, and $175,000 for property *C*?

4. Calculate the capitalization rates on the properties using the lower negotiated prices. Indicate which properties seem to be the best and the worst in terms of capitalization rate.

5. Recognize that the Johnsons desire an after-tax total return of 10 percent. Calculate the present value of after-tax cash flow for property *C*, assuming that the after-tax cash flow numbers are $8000 for the first year, $8400 for the second year, $8800 for the third year, $9200 for the fourth year, and $9600 for the fifth year and that the selling price of the property will be $220,000 in 5 years. Prepare your information in a format similar to Table 20.3. Use Appendix A2 or Personal Finance Cookbook (PFC) program PVSUM to discount the future after-tax cash flows to their present values.

6. Give the Johnsons your advice on whether or not they should invest in property *C* at its current price of $175,000.

Key Words and Concepts

capital improvements, 710
capitalization rate, 716
cash flow, 610
commercial properties, 720
crude rate of return, 719
depreciation, 711
direct ownership, 720
discounted cash flow, 717
equity trust, 723
gross income multiplier (*GIM*), 615
income yield, 716
indirect investment in real estate, 723
interval ownership purchase, 722
joint tenancy, 720
joint tenancy with right of survivor-ship, 720
leverage, 709

limited partnership, 723
loan-to-value ratio, 711
mortgage trust, 723
net operating income, 716
participation certificates, 724
price appreciation, 610
property report, 722
raw land, 722
real estate, 709
real estate investment trust (REIT), 723
real estate syndicate, 723
repairs, 610
residential lot, 722
residential units, 720
right-to-use purchase, 722
tax-free exchange, 612
tenancy in common, 720

Review Questions

1. List an economic and a noneconomic reason for investing in real estate.
2. Cite and briefly explain two advantages to investing in real estate.
3. Explain the difference between capital improvements and repairs, and give examples.
4. Explain how leverage can help a real estate investor.
5. Describe how a negative cash flow can occur in a real estate investment. Explain how a real estate investment can be successful while simultaneously having a negative cash flow.
6. Summarize how depreciation and interest costs can help the real estate investor.
7. Describe a circumstance in which a real estate investor might want a tax-free exchange with another real estate investor.
8. Cite five disadvantages to investing in real estate.
9. Describe how you would interpret a gross income multiplier of 7 on a piece of property with an asking price of $120,000.
10. Explain the usefulness of the capitalization rate method of determining the price to pay for real estate.
11. Illustrate the concept of discounted cash flow as a method of estimating the value of a real estate property.
12. What purpose does calculating a crude rate of return serve?
13. Name the two ways of having joint ownership, and distinguish between them.

14. Why might a first-time real estate investor choose residential units rather than commercial properties?

15. Briefly describe how a vacation home can provide tax benefits.

16. Distinguish between a right-to-use purchase and an interval-ownership purchase of vacation property.

17. Describe the differences between raw land and residential lots.

18. Define a real estate syndicate.

19. Explain the difference between limited and general partners in a limited partnership.

20. Describe a real estate investment trust (REIT), and identify the two major types of REITs.

21. Describe the ways an investor might invest in mortgage loans.

22. Describe three situations in which the conservative real estate investor might seriously consider selling a real estate investment.

Case Problems

1. Gerald Fitzpatrick of Scranton, Pennsylvania, is interested in the numbers of real estate investments. He reviews the figures in Table 20.2 and is impressed with the potential 7.4 percent yield after taxes. Since Gerald is only in the 15 percent marginal tax bracket, answer the following questions to help guide his investment decisions.
   a. Substitute Gerald's 15 percent marginal tax bracket in Table 20.2 and calculate his taxable income, his return after taxes, and his yield after taxes.
   b. Why does it appear to be a favorable investment for Gerald?
   c. Since the IRS allows only so much for depreciation expense, what other two factors might be changed in Table 20.2 in order to increase the yield for Gerald?
   d. Calculate the yield after taxes for Gerald, who is in the 15 percent tax bracket, assuming he bought the property and financed it with a $64,000, 8 percent mortgage loan with annual interest costs of only $5500.

2. Linda Berk of Menomonie, Wisconsin, is considering buying a vacation condominium apartment for $65,000 in Park City, Utah. Linda hopes to rent the condo to others in order to keep costs down. Respond to the following questions to help Linda with her decisions.
   a. If Linda's monthly payments are $580 ($500 goes for interest, $30 for principal, $30 for property taxes, and $20 for home owner's insurance) plus another $40 for the monthly home owner's association fee, which of these costs will be tax deductions? List the costs and total on an annualized basis.
   b. Since Linda is in the 28 percent marginal tax bracket, how much less in taxes will she pay if she buys this condo?
   c. Given that she would like to personally use the condo for vacations

10 to 12 days a year, how many days will she have to rent it out before she would be eligible to deduct rental losses from her taxes?

    d. Since Park City is mostly a winter ski resort and few condo renters can be found in the off season, Linda is concerned about qualifying to deduct rental losses. Assuming she could rent the condo for $120 a day, describe the rental IRS-approved alternative she could use to generate income, and then calculate the maximum amount of money Linda could obtain using that plan.

    e. Figure Linda's annual net out-of-pocket cost to buy the condominium and rent it out minimally for tax-free income. Start with her $7440 cost for monthly payments ($580) and home owner's association fees ($40). Then deduct the savings on income taxes as well as the presumed rental for 14 days.

    f. Using the figure derived in part e, how much out-of-pocket cost per day would it be for Linda to use the condo herself if she stayed there 10 days a year? Fifteen days a year?

Suggested Readings

"A Home Away from Home." *Changing Times*, April 1990, pp. 75–78. How to take advantage of tax-free exchanges when you want to sell vacation property.

"Backwater Bargains." *Forbes*, March 19, 1990, p. 200. Tips on investing in residential real estate in small towns.

"Honey, I Shrunk the Taxes." *Money*, May 1990, pp. 142–146. Suggestions on how to go about getting real estate taxes reduced.

"Going Once, Going Twice: Your Next Home?" *Consumer Reports*, June 1990, pp. 388–390. How to go about buying real estate at an auction.

"Now's the Time to Grab a Bargain Vacation Home." *Money*, October 1989, pp. 129–132. Tips on how to buy a vacation home since prices have dropped 10 to 50 percent on cottages and condos in recent years.

"Real Estate Deals That Really Work." *Money*, September 1989, pp. 115–120. Those satisfied with modest returns can succeed in real estate investing.

"Selling Rental Real Estate: Ways to Sweeten the Deal." *Changing Times*, July 1989, pp. 71–75. Some tax angles to help you sell the property.

"Still Like Real Estate? Try These Trusts." *Business Week*, February 26, 1990, pp. 110–111. Discusses the pros and cons of REITs in today's real estate investing market.

"Vacation Homes: It's a Buyer's Market." *Changing Times*, June 1989, pp. 37–43. Where and how to invest in vacation property.

"Vacation Properties for 40 Cents on the Dollar," *Changing Times*, August 1990, pp. 41–45. Bargains galore exist in timeshares because of a glut on the market.

"What's Ahead for Home Prices." *Changing Times*, January 1990, pp. 38–43. Analysis of the future of real estate prices.

21 Speculative Investments

OBJECTIVES

After reading this chapter, you should be able to

1. Identify the characteristics of speculative investments that make them both attractive and unattractive for investors.

2. Describe the speculative aspects of tangible investments.

3. Distinguish among ways of speculating in the securities markets.

4. Identify guidelines to use when deciding whether to sell speculative investments.

．．．．．．．．．
People who invest in stocks, bonds, mutual funds, and real estate instead of in low-risk government securities and certificates of deposit do so to obtain higher yields. Most are conservative or moderate-risk investors who generally avoid highly speculative investments. Speculative or high-risk investors seek very high returns and are willing to accept a greater degree of risk to achieve them. Speculative investments include tangible investments such as precious metals (gold, silver, and platinum), collectibles (such as stamps, art, and rare coins), and precious gems. It is also possible to speculate in securities markets by using short-term trading approaches and by speculating with rights, warrants, stock options, and futures contracts.

Are Speculative Investments for You?

Speculative investments, or high-risk investments, are investment transactions that carry considerable risk of loss for the chance of large gains. This means that in addition to the high potential profits, there is a clear danger of losing part or all of the dollars that have been invested. Accordingly, investment funds used for speculative purposes should be only those which you can afford to lose.

You can get a start in high-risk investments with a relatively small amount of capital, perhaps only $300 to $500. Sellers of speculative investments opportunities rarely screen customers to be sure that they can afford to take the risk. The decision as to whether you should become involved in high-risk investments is basically left to you, but the prudent investor limits high-risk investments to less than 15 percent of his or her total investment portfolio.

The high rewards from many speculative investments frequently come from the profits of short-term market fluctuations. To be successful, the speculator must act in a matter of hours, days, or weeks rather than years and must have a considerable amount of investment knowledge. To succeed in any area of investing, you have to research it carefully and make intelligent decisions. To succeed in high-risk investments, however, you need to remain constantly alert to developments, become thoroughly familiar with the intricacies of each type of investment, and act decisively to both ensure profits and cut losses.

Speculative investments can have a high return or a severe loss.

In most areas of high-risk investment, losers outnumber winners by three or four to one. Depending on your own investment philosophy, you may want to rule out high-risk investments entirely, consider speculative risks on an occasional basis, or seek out such opportunities regularly. The remainder of this chapter details the major types of high-risk investments.

To make speculative investments, you need an even temperament and a strong stomach. Since you will probably suffer several sharp short-term losses for every single super-successful investment, you must have sufficient resources to ride out losses and make high-risk investments only with dollars you can afford to lose. It is imperative for you to study a particular area of high-risk investments carefully and develop considerable technical expertise before actually investing; knowledge does not guarantee success, but it helps the odds somewhat. In addition, you should choose a brokerage firm that specializes in your particular area of high-risk investments and watch the investments daily to reduce losses and maximize gains.

Speculating with Tangible Investments

Objective
To be able to describe the speculative aspect of tangible investments.

Most of the investments we have discussed thus far, other than direct ownership of real estate, would be categorized as intangible investments because they involve the ownership of documents with a market value rather than ownership of a physical item. **Tangible investments** are physical items that are owned primarily for their investment value. They are often highly speculative in nature. Three tangible investments are discussed below: precious metals, collectibles, and precious gems.

Precious Metals

Gold, silver, and platinum are precious metals much in demand worldwide. Silver and platinum, unlike gold, have numerous industrial uses. Many people around the world invest in precious metals as a means of preserving capital in difficult economic times, reasoning that if their national economies experience difficulty, they themselves will be able to trade gold instead of devalued paper money. Using a similar rationale, some Americans invest 5 or 10 percent of their investment portfolio in precious metals as a hedge against political, military, and economic uncertainty.

The prices of precious metals tend to increase in times of economic and political turmoil, especially when there is high inflation. Fluctuating demand for precious metals also affects the market values. For example, over a recent 5-year period, gold rose from $200 to $600 per ounce. Silver rose from $5 to $50 an ounce in 2 years. Platinum jumped from $280 to over $800 an ounce in 3 years. Price drops are just as rapid. Silver, for example, declined from $50 to $10 an ounce in less than 1 year. Speculators can earn high profits on these sharp price swings over a period of months or weeks.

Note, however, that precious metals pay no dividends. Further, only the wealthy can afford to buy the actual product, which is referred to as bullion. Since gold bullion must be purchased in minimum amounts of 100 troy ounces, which is just over 8 pounds, an investor may need $40,000 or more. Those interested in smaller quantities turn to other ways of owning precious metal investments: coins, certificates, companies that mine metals, and metals futures. Bags of silver coins are sold on the New York Mercantile Exchange. Gold coins are generally available in minimum lots of five, although some banks will sell smaller amounts and, naturally, charge higher commissions. Gold coins that are easy to trade include the American "Eagle," and the Canadian "Maple Leaf." Silver coins include the American "Eagle" silver dollar. Some banks sell gold certificates, which evidence ownership of small amounts of gold kept by the institution for safety; of course, these banks charge commissions and storage fees. Stocks of gold-, silver-, and platinum-mining companies have done quite well in recent years. Such stocks are risky, but most pay small dividends, whereas the actual metals do not. The stocks also have a daily liquidity by wire or mail. Gold and silver futures, an extremely risky form of speculative investing, are discussed later in the chapter.

Collectibles

Collectibles are cultural artifacts that have value because of beauty, age, scarcity, or simply their popularity. Buying collectibles as investments can also become a relaxing hobby. People collect many types of assets that are not particularly liquid, such as stamps, art, coins (not for the metal but for the coin's scarcity), rare cars, baseball cards, and other items thought to have value. Stamps, art, and rare coins are collectibles with a sizable resale market. Like all tangible investments, the only return on collectibles is through price appreciation. Further, to profit you must sell.

The return on all tangible investments is due solely to price appreciation.

Stamps More than 30 million people in the United States engage in **philately,** the collection and study of stamps, envelopes, and similar material. You may have heard of the rare and valuable 24-cent 1918 "inverted Jenny" U.S. airmail stamp that was printed upside down or of the $1.60 brown Graf Zeppelin issue, which soared to a value of $10,000 for a very fine mint set of three. Recently, the 1918 stamp was valued above $30,000, but the Graf Zeppelin had slipped to $3000, reflecting changes in collector demand for each.

The former high school hobbyist needs to attain a high level of expertise before seriously considering stamps as an investment. Forgeries abound among unscrupulous traders. The wise buyer should deal only with the most reputable sellers, diversify stamp holdings, and purchase rare stamps of only the highest quality.

Art For the patient and knowledgeable investor who does not need current income from an investment, art may be an excellent alternative because prices for many types of works have risen steadily in recent decades. Increases in excess of 10 percent annually are not uncommon in art, and most paintings bought at auctions are purchased for less than $4000.

Items that have had good values in recent years are oil paintings, watercolors, and vintage prints by nineteenth- and twentieth-century artists. Strong demand exists for old masters (such as Rembrandt) and Western art. Works by contemporary artists also can be purchased for investment purposes but are even more speculative because they rise and fall on the likelihood that the artist will achieve a lasting reputation.

Rare Coins A **numismatist** collects coins, metals, and selected commemoratives. An investor in rare coins is more than just a hobbyist; there are some large profits to be made in this field. An uncirculated, quality 1829 Indian cent with large letters bought in 1948 for $11 has increased in value by over 3000 percent, since the price has risen to $350. Many other coins have risen in value by more than 10 or 15 percent a year in the past decade.

In all cases, the rarer the coin and the higher the quality, the better are the price and the likelihood of appreciation. A "type" collection consists of a set of one coin for each year of a specific coin design made over a period of years. A type-coin collection could include one each year from such issues as Morgan dollars minted between 1878 and 1921, Liberty walking half-dollars minted between 1907 and 1964, and Buffalo nickels minted between 1923 and 1956. The value of a complete type set is always higher than that of each individual coin taken together. Investors in rare coins should deal only with reputable sellers, obtain a written guarantee of genuineness from the dealer or auctioneer, and seek another professional opinion to corroborate the grade and value of rare coins.

Precious Gems

Precious gems used as investments include diamonds, rubies, emeralds, and sapphires. Investors most often purchase investment-grade gems as "loose stones" rather than as pieces of jewelry. The best-quality gems are sold by wholesale firms rather than jewelers. Most people buy precious gems at retail prices from jewelers and, if necessary, sell at wholesale prices; this is not investing. Deal only with reputable firms. Buying over the telephone is clearly unwise. A gem should be graded and appraised prior to purchase by a person certified by the Gemological Institute of America (GIA).

Speculating in the Securities Markets

Objective
To be able to distinguish among ways of speculating in the securities market.

Some speculative investments are available in the traditional securities markets through mechanisms such as **penny stocks** (these are stocks in new, untested companies selling for a dollar or two per share—most fail), junk bonds, and certain high-risk stocks and mutual funds. Speculation in these markets also occurs when people make use of short-term trading strategies and when they invest in specialized securities such as rights, warrants, stock options, and futures contracts.

Short-Term Investors

A **short-term investor** is speculative or moderately speculative and wants to earn quick profits (over a period of months, weeks, days, or even hours) on small but significant changes in the prices of securities. The two widely used investment approaches of short-term investors are buying on **margin** and selling short.

Margin Buying A *margin account* requires a deposit of substantial cash or securities ($2000 or more) and permits of other securities on credit granted by the brokerage firm. Using a margin account to purchase securities, or **margin buying,** is a method of applying leverages to magnify returns by borrowing money from a brokerage firm in order to buy securities. This credit account allows you to buy more stocks and/or bonds than you could with available cash. Use of credit to buy securities is regulated by both brokerage firms and the Federal Reserve Board. The **margin rate** is the percentage amount of the value (or equity) in an investment that is not borrowed. In recent years, the margin rate has ranged from 30 to 80 percent. Thus, if the margin rate is 40 percent, you can buy securities by putting up only 40 percent of the total price and borrowing the remainder from the brokerage firm. The securities purchased, as well as amounts in the margin account, are used as collateral. Interest is charged for the loan.

Buying on margin applies the concept of leverage.

Buying on margin is commonly used to increase return on investment, as Table 21.1 illustrates. For example, let's assume that Running Paws common stock is selling for $80 a share and you wish to buy 100 shares for a total of $8000. Using your margin account, you will make a cash payment of $3200 (40 percent × $8000), with the brokerage firm loaning you the difference of $4800 ($8000 − $3200). For the sake of simplicity, omit commissions and assume the brokerage firm loans the funds at 10 percent interest. Thus the equity (market value minus amount borrowed) you have in the investment is $3200. If Running Paws stock increases in price to $92 by the end of a year, you can sell for proceeds of $9200, minus the amount invested ($3200), minus the amount borrowed ($4800), and minus the cost of borrowing ($4800 × 0.10 = $480), for a yield of $720. Since you invested an equity of only $3200 for a profit of $720, you have earned a return of 22.5 percent ($720/$3200). If you had instead put up the entire $8000 and not bought on margin, your return on investment would have been only 15 percent ($9200 − $8000 = $1200/$8000). This illustrates the financial concept of **leverage,** using borrowed money to increase the rate of return on an investment higher than the cost of funds.

Speculative investors also like to buy on margin because leverage gives them the potential to make gains over short time periods. For example, assume the margin rate is 50 percent and you want to purchase 1000 shares of a $10 stock. Buying on margin, you need only put up $5000 (50 percent of $10,000). The price of the stock need rise to only $11 over the course of a month for you to make a handsome profit. The $1000 in proceeds ($11 × 1000 = $11,000 − $10,000) might be reduced by brokerage firm's interest charges of $100, for a return of $900. This represents a yield of 18 percent on the amount invested ($900/$5000) in only 1 month, which is well over 200 percent annually. By not buying on margin, the short-term investor just described would have had to wait until the price reached 11⅞ (almost a full point higher than the margin

TABLE 21.1
How Buying on Margin Affects the Return on Investment

	Cash Transaction	40% Margin Transaction
Price of stock rises (from $80 to $92 a share)		
Buy 100 shares @ $80 (amount invested)	−$8000	−$3200
Sell 100 shares @ $92 (proceeds)	9200	9200
Net proceeds	$1200	$6000
Minus amount borrowed	—	−4800
Net	$1200	$1200
Minus cost of borrowing	—	−480
Return	$1200	$ 720
Yield (return/amount invested)	+15.0%	+22.5%
Price of stock declines (from $80 to $70 a share)		
Buy 100 shares @ $80 (amount invested)	−$8000	−$3200
Sell 100 shares @ $70 (proceeds)	7000	7000
Net proceeds	−$1000	$3800
Minus amount borrowed	—	−4800
Net	−$1000	−$1000
Minus cost of borrowing	—	−480
Return	−$1000	−$1480
Yield (return/amount invested)	−12.5%	−46.25%
Price of stock declines (from $80 to $60 a share)		
Buy 100 shares @ $80 (amount invested)	−$8000	−$3200
Sell 100 shares @ $60 (proceeds)	6000	6000
Net proceeds	−$2000	$2800
Minus amount borrowed	—	−4800
Net	−$2000	−$2000
Minus cost of borrowing	—	−480
Return	−$2000	−$2480
Yield (return/amount invested)	−25.0%	−77.5%

investor) to realize a similar return ($11,875 − $10,000 = $1875/$10,000 = 18.75 percent).

Realize also that buying on margin can be dangerous as well. Should the price of a security bought on margin decline, leverage can work against you, as Table 21.1 illustrates. If the Running Paws stock bought at $80 dropped to $70 after a year, you would lose $10 a share on the 100 shares for a total of $1000. Proceeds would be only $7000. If you bought the stock on margin, against this amount goes the cost of the investment ($3200), the margin loan from the broker ($4800), and interest on the loan ($480), for a total of $8480 and a net loss of $1480 ($7000 − $8480). Thus a loss of $1480 on an investment of $3200 is a negative return of 46.25 percent ($1480/$3200). The same $10 loss per share ($80 to $70) would have been a negative loss of only 12.5 percent if the stocks were not bought on margin ($8000 − $7000 = $1000/$8000). When buying stocks on margin, leverage can enhance both profits and losses dramatically.

A margin call will require an immediate transmittal of cash to your broker.

A margin call also could hurt the financial position of the margin buyer. This is a requirement that the margin investor put up more funds if and when the value of the security declines to the point where the investor's equity is less than the required percentage (such as 25 percent) of the current market value. If additional cash or securities are not put up, the broker can and will legally sell the securities. The margin call concept protects the broker who has loaned money on securities. In Table 21.1 the 100 shares of Running Paws at $80 were originally valued at $8000, with investor's equity of $3200, or 40 percent ($3200/$8000), with $4800 borrowed from the brokerage firm. Assume that the stock price drops to $60 a share, which makes the current market value $6000. Since the investors still owes $4800, the equity has dropped to $1200/($6000 − $4800), which is only 20 percent of the value of the securities ($1200/$6000). The broker will immediately make a margin call, demanding that funds be added (perhaps within 72 hours) to the account to bring the equity up to a minimum of 25 percent. In this example, an additional $300 ($6000 × 25 percent = $1500 − $1200) would be required.

To determine at what price a margin call will occur, use the **margin call formula** [Equation (21.1)]. Substituting the figures from the preceding illustration, the investor will not receive a margin call unless the stock price drops below $64, since equity at this point is still 25 percent.

$$
\begin{aligned}
\text{Margin call price} &= \frac{\text{amount owed broker}/(1 - \text{margin call requirement})}{\text{number of shares bought}} \\
&= \frac{\$4800/(1 - 0.25)}{100} \\
&= \$64
\end{aligned}
\tag{21.1}
$$

Substantial losses can result when buying on margin.

If the investor can't meet the margin call, the broker will sell the securities as soon as possible (at whatever price is obtainable), and a sharp financial loss will result. Table 21.1 illustrates the magnitude of the loss as a negative return of 77.5 percent, compared with a negative of only 25 percent if you had not bought on margin.

Selling Short   When you buy a security in the hope that it will go up in value, this is called **buying long.** However, you might suspect that the price of a security is going to go down. You can earn profits when the price of a security drops by selling short. **Selling short** is a trading technique by which investors sell a security they do not own (borrowing it from a broker) and later buy a like amount of the same security at, it is hoped, a lower price (and return it to the broker), thus earning a profit on the transaction. Brokerage firms require an investor to have a margin account when selling short, since it provides some assurance that you can repay the value of the stock if necessary. Thus the investor's funds deposited in a margin account are effectively tied up during a short sale. Many brokers hold the proceeds of a short sale, without paying interest, until the customer "covers the position" by buying it back for delivery to the broker.

Selling short is advantageous when the price of a stock is expected to decline.

For example, assume that you have concluded that the price of Running Paws stock will drop substantially over the next several months. You have heard that some top managers of the company may resign and that competitors are expected to introduce newer products. Accordingly, you instruct your broker to sell 100 shares of Running Paws at $80 ($80 × 100 = $8000). In this illustration, assume you have a 40 percent margin requirement, which means you have $3200 (40 percent × $8000) committed. The shares are actually borrowed by the broker from another investor or another broker. Several months later Running Paws announces lower profits because of strong competition, and the price drops to $70 a share. Now you instruct your broker to buy 100 shares at that price. This gives you a profit of $1000 ($8000 − $7000), less commissions, providing a yield of 31.3 percent ($1000/$3200).

A very small price drop can provide big profits for the short-term investor who sells short *and* uses margin buying techniques. For example, assume you sell 100 shares of a $10 stock with a 40 percent margin requirement. The committed funds amount to $400 (40 percent × $1000). Even if the price of the stock declines only $1, you still earn a significant profit: 100 shares sold at $10 equals $1000, minus 100 shares bought at $9 equals $900, for a profit of $100 and a yield of 25 percent ($100/$400).

However, realize that almost unlimited losses can occur should the price rise instead of fall. If the $10 stock soars to $22 instead of falling, the loss will be more than the original investment: 100 shares sold at $10 equals $1000, minus 100 shares bought at $22 equals $2200, for a loss of $1200 and a negative yield of 550 percent ($2200/$400). In addition, when the price of a security rises, short sellers are subject to margin calls. Clearly, selling short and buying on margin are techniques to be used only by sophisticated investors.

Trading in Rights

Rights protect proportionate ownership and have a market rate.

When corporations raise additional capital by selling new shares of stock, current stockholders may experience dilution of their ownership position. For example, assume that Road Runners Shoe Company has 100,000 shares of stock outstanding and wants to sell an additional 100,000 shares. A stockholder who owns 10,000 shares would see his ownership in the company go from 10 percent (10,000 divided by 100,000) to 5 percent (10,000 divided by 200,000). The bylaws of many corporations and the statutes of most states require a **preemptive right** for existing stockholders, which is the legal right to be given the opportunity to purchase a proportionate share of any new stock issue to maintain their proportionate ownership share. To accomplish this, each current stockholder is issued a **right,** which is a legal instrument to purchase a number of shares of corporate stock at a specific price during a limited time period. Most rights lapse after 16 days, although some have a 1-month limit. The rights can be used to buy shares of the new stock offering or the holders of rights can sell their rights to other investors.

Rights normally allow purchase of the new shares at a price somewhat lower than the current market value of the stock. Consequently, there is a market for the buying and selling of rights, and once again, we enter the world of the speculator. A typical speculative investment is to use margin to buy rights with the hope that the value of the stock and hence the rights will rise.

For example, the right to buy one share of the new Road Runners stock at $18 is worth approximately $2 if the current selling price is $20 ($20 − $18 = $2). If other investors perceive this new stock offering as an indication that Road Runners will be more profitable in the future, the price of the stock might rise to perhaps $21 or $22 and the price of the right will rise as well. Say you purchase 1000 rights at $2 each and put up only $500 in cash, using margin for the remaining $1500. (Special margin rules exist for rights transactions.) If the price of the stock rises to $22, you will have a tremendous profit. The value of each right will have risen to about $4 ($22 − $18), and it may be higher if investor interest remains particularly strong. Selling the right or exercising it to purchase the shares at the specified price will bring you proceeds of $3500 ($4000 − $500) on an investment of only $500. This is a yield of 700 percent ($3500/$500) in just a matter of days or weeks. You should realize that the price of the stock could have dropped to below $18, forcing down the value of the right and possibly result in a total loss for the investor.

Buying and Selling Warrants

A **warrant** is a legal instrument accompanying a security (usually a bond) that gives the holder the opportunity to buy a certain number of shares of another security (usually common stock) at a specified price over a designated period of time (usually 5, 10, or 20 years, but sometimes in perpetuity). The distinction between a right and a warrant is that rights are issued to current stockholders, whereas warrants are issued attached to other securities (such as to bonds or preferred stock). Some of these warrants are detachable and some are not; a trading market exists for detachable warrants.

A company issues warrants along with another security to make the security offer more attractive. Further, a bond sold with a warrant may have an interest rate from 1 to 2 percentage points less than comparable bonds without warrants. Warrants are sometimes called *purchase warrants*, and each has a speculative value until the expiration date, at which time it may be worthless. To illustrate, assume that Road Runners common stock is selling for $22 and the company raises capital by selling bonds with detachable warrants. Each warrant provides that the bond purchaser or later holder of a detached warrant can buy one share of common stock at $30 for a period of 5 years. Five years is a long time, and the warrant could be worth only $0.50 at the onset. Technically, the warrant is worthless; what gives it value is "speculative hope." If the company continues to be successful and the price of the stock rises, the value of the warrant also will rise. During the five years, the value of the warrant will continue to increase as long as the common stock price is expected to rise.

Consider two scenarios that might occur. First, the warrant might have a value of $1 while Road Runners common stock is priced at $29. If the common stock price climbs above $30, the warrant value will soar. For every dollar climb in the stock price, the warrant increases a similar amount or more. A warrant bought for $1 will be worth at least $6 if the stock price moves to $35 per share, and the speculator would gain tremendously. If a warrant is actually exercised (which is rare), the company would issue new shares of common stock, which would raise more capital for the firm. In the second scenario, the warrant worth $1 when the price of the stock is $29 could drop in value to $0.50 or less if the common stock price declines to $28 or $27. This would cause the speculator to lose half or more of the amount invested. Figure 21.1 shows the **Swingers** over a given 1-week period. These are stocks and warrants that have gone up and down the most in the past *week* based on a percentage of change. To estimate the annual rate of return, multiply the percentage by 52 weeks. As you can see, warrants are truly speculative ventures.

Using Options

An **option** is a contract that gives the holder the right to buy or sell a specific asset, for example, real estate or common stock, at a specified price. Markets exist for options written for common stocks, debt instruments, foreign currencies, and stock indexes. The most common are stock options, although stock index options have become increasingly popular in recent years. A **stock option** is a contract giving the holder the right to buy or sell a specific number of shares (normally 100) of a certain stock at a particular price (the *striking price*) before a specified date (the *expiration date*). Buying options is a very speculative venture, but selling options is often a conservative investment decision.

Writing Options Options are created by option writers. Through a stock brokerage firm, an **option writer** issues an option contract promising either to buy or to sell a specified asset for a fixed striking price and receives an *option premium* (the price of the option itself) for standing ready to buy or sell the asset at the wishes of the person who has bought the option. Once written and sold, an option may change hands many times before its expiration. The **option holder** is the person who actually owns the option contract. It is always the original writer who is responsible for buying or selling the asset if requested by the holder of the option contract.

There are two types of options: puts and calls. A **call** is an option contract that gives the option holder the right to *buy* the optioned asset from the option writer at the striking price. A **put** is an option contract that gives the option holder the right to *sell* the optioned asset to the option writer at the striking price. The box, Making Sense of Options, illustrates the relationships between option writers and option holders for both puts and calls.

Most options expire without being exercised by the option holder, and the option writer is the only one to earn a profit, which results from the premium charged when the option was originally sold. However, an option

Options are created by an option writer.

FIGURE 21.1
Swingers

Source: From the *Washington Post,* July 2, 1990, p. 37. Reprinted by permission of the New York Stock Exchange.

SWINGERS

The following lists show stocks and warrants on the New York, American and over-the-counter markets that have gone up the most and down the most in the past week based on percent of change regardless of volume. No securities trading below $2 are included. Percentage changes are the difference between the previous week's closing price and last week's close. Footnotes: z-sales in full; x-ex-dividend; s-stock split or stock dividend of 25 percent or more in past 52 weeks; g-dividends or earnings in Canadian money.

New York Stock Exchange

UPS

Name	Sales	High	Low	Close	Chg.	Pct.
Foxboro	27334	51½	50¾	51⅜	+ 13¼	34.8
TacomaBt n	347	3⅝	2¾	3½	+ ¾	27.3
DavisWatr	896	12¾	10⅛	12⅝	+ 2⅝	26.3
Ferro s	10896	25¾	19⅞	25½	+ 4¾	22.9
MACOM	2780	5⅜	4⅛	5⅜	+ 1	22.9
vjSalant	2044	3½	2¾	3⅜	+ ⅝	22.7
MiltonRoy	7379	24¾	19¼	22⅞	+ 3¾	19.6
InspirRsc	4122	5½	4½	5½	+ ⅞	18.9
TexasInd	1380	23⅜	18⅝	23⅜	+ 3⅝	18.4
ArrowElec	2121	5⅞	5	5⅞	+ ⅞	17.5
SignalAprl	826	7¾	6⅜	7⅝	+ 1⅛	17.3
CMS Enhanc	645	6	5⅛	6	+ ⅞	17.1
Berlitz n	x3128	23¼	19⅞	23¼	+ 3⅜	17.0
Kysor	234	11¼	9½	11¼	+ 1⅝	16.9
NEstSvg pf	137	10⅝	9⅛	10½	+ 1½	16.7
Safeway wt	6684	3¾	2⅞	3½	+ ½	16.7
TucsonEP	7779	13	10⅞	12⅝	+ 1¾	16.1
GreenTree	6341	16½	13¾	16½	+ 2¼	15.8
RecognEq	2156	5½	4¾	5½	+ ¾	15.8
IntlTch	11622	11¼	9½	11¼	+ 1½	15.4
Gruman	5051	19⅛	16⅛	19	+ 2½	15.2
Safeway n	13874	14½	12⅜	14⅜	+ 1⅞	15.0
AydinCp	1352	14⅞	12⅝	14½	+ 1⅞	14.9
BenetonGp	2979	17½	15⅜	17½	+ 2¼	14.8
OnLine	966	8¾	7½	8¾	+ 1⅛	14.8

DOWNS

Name	Sales	High	Low	Close	Chg.	Pct.
AmSvBkNY pf	1261	5¾	3⅛	3½	− 2	36.4
CtytrstBcp	884	7¼	4⅝	4⅞	− 2⅛	30.4
FloatPnt	4554	3⅜	2¼	2½	− ⅞	25.9
HuntMfg	x4157	16¼	11¾	12	− 3⅞	24.4
Equimark	2674	7¼	5⅝	5⅞	− 1½	20.3
FtCtyBcp	4775	32½	25¼	26¼	− 6⅝	20.2
FairCom	2133	2¾	2	2¼	− ½	18.2
Caterpllr	99385	61⅜	51½	52⅝	− 10⅞	17.1
Sothbys	12292	18	15	15⅛	− 3⅛	17.1
AmreInc	4025	5⅜	3⅞	4½	− ⅞	16.3
WstUn pfB	533	5⅝	4	4⅝	− ⅞	15.9
ICN Pharm	691	4⅛	3½	3½	− ⅝	15.2
FtCtyBcp pf	657	60¾	51	52½	− 9	14.6
GaloobLew	2724	6⅜	5⅜	5½	− ⅞	13.7
Wellman	25975	31½	26⅝	27¼	− 4¼	13.5
Carolco wt	532	3⅝	3⅛	3¼	− ½	13.3
PatheComun	581	3⅞	3¼	3¼	− ½	13.3
AmSvBkNY	1801	3¼	2⅛	2½	− ⅜	13.0
CalFed	2955	19	16⅝	16¾	− 2⅜	12.4
Teledyne s	5391	27¼	23¾	23¾	− 3⅜	12.4
AlliedPrd	405	8	6⅝	7¼	− 1	12.1
EaglePch	1016	3¼	2¾	2¾	− ⅜	12.0
ArmcoInc	27186	8	7	7½	− 1	11.8
Quantum	7082	18⅝	16½	16⅝	− 2⅛	11.3
HadsonCp	4408	2¼	1⅞	2	− ¼	11.1

American Stock Exchange

UPS

Name	Sales	High	Low	Close	Chg.	Pct.
MatSci	6561	16⅝	12⅝	16½	+ 6⅛	59.0
ColumLab n	2410	10¾	7⅜	10¾	+ 2⅞	36.5
HeartIndPar n	1386	11	8½	10¾	+ 2½	30.3
LazareKap	274	27	20⅞	27	+ 6¼	30.1
PenrilCp s	2122	8⅜	6¼	8¼	+ 1⅞	29.4
Biomagnt	1629	6⅛	4¼	6⅛	+ 1⅜	28.9
LeePharm	508	2¾	2⅛	2½	+ ½	25.0
SystemInd	157	2	1⅝	2	+ ⅜	23.1
IncstarCp	2717	4⅞	3⅞	4¾	+ ⅞	22.6
Howtek	1885	13	10½	13	+ 2¼	20.9
GRI Corp	535	6⅝	4¾	5⅞	+ 1	20.5
Friedman	x121	4½	3¾	4½	+ ¾	20.0
DelElect	1163	9⅝	7¾	9⅜	+ 1½	19.0
SelasCp s	552	15¾	13	15¾	+ 2⅜	17.8
CashAmer s	1370	19¾	16½	19½	+ 2⅞	17.3
HlthConcpt n	1632	4¼	3¾	4¼	+ ⅝	17.2
GrahamFld	3070	4⅝	4	4⅝	+ ⅝	15.6
MarsGph	333	6½	5⅝	6½	+ ⅞	15.6
DevonEngy	453	13⅜	11½	13¼	+ 1¾	15.2
Thermedics	1451	16½	13¾	16⅜	+ 2⅛	14.9
CollinsInd	370	4	3¼	3⅞	+ ½	14.8
Spelling	1402	8¾	7	8¾	+ 1⅛	14.8
LawsonMard	136	8⅞	7⅞	8⅞	+ 1⅛	14.5
Harvey Gr	23	2	1¾	2	+ ¼	14.3
Telesphere	10588	5	3⅝	5	+ ⅝	14.3

DOWNS

Name	Sales	High	Low	Close	Chg.	Pct.
Baldwin Sec	51	2½	2	2	− ⅝	23.8
AT&E Cp	17462	23	15⅜	17½	− 5⅜	23.5
KV Phrm	1114	10	7	7¾	− 2⅜	23.5
FstConn SB	103	6⅞	5⅜	5⅜	− 1½	21.8
WichitaRvO	615	4⅞	3⅞	4	− 1	20.0
RichtonInt	246	2⅝	2⅛	2⅛	− ½	19.0
Sterl Electr	93	2⅝	2¼	2¼	− ½	18.2
AmTr-att2 sc	12171	15	11½	12⅜	− 2⅜	16.1
IncoOppor	119	3¼	2¾	2¾	− ½	15.4
AllouHlth n	645	3⅜	2¾	2⅞	− ½	14.8
Organog	946	12¼	10½	10⅝	− 1¾	14.1
FalconCbl	x374	14⅝	12¾	12⅞	− 2	13.4
Veronex	1288	3⅜	2⅞	2 15/16	− 7/16	13.0
StudLn wt93	139	6⅛	5¼	5¼	− ¾	12.5
SanMonicaBk	167	29	24¾	25⅝	− 3⅝	12.4
AmTr-hwp sc	272	3⅛	2¾	2¾	− ⅜	12.0
BambPly	219	3⅛	2⅞	2⅞	− ⅜	11.5
Compumat	111	3⅛	2⅝	2⅞	− ⅜	11.5
OEA s	696	34¾	30¼	30½	− 3⅞	11.3
AmTr-s sc	79	2¼	2	2	− ¼	11.1
Verit Ind	71	2¼	2	2	− ¼	11.1
AmTr-an sc	462	8	7	7⅛	− ⅞	10.9
DiagRet A	82	2¼	2⅛	2⅛	− ¼	10.5
GECa wtY	79	2½	2⅛	2⅛	− ¼	10.5
JonesPlmb	29	2¼	2⅛	2⅛	− ¼	10.5

Over the Counter

UPS

Name	Sales	High	Low	Close	Chg.	Pct.
SciAccess	762	2¾	1⅛	2¾	+ 1½	120.0
Bioject	5459	6⅜	3	6⅜	+ 3⅜	112.5
SciAcc un	67	4¼	2⅜	4¼	+ 1⅞	78.9
PolifyFn	1858	2¼	1¼	2⅛	+ ⅞	70.0
EnvrnMon un	437	3 3/16	1⅞	2 17/32	+ 25/32	44.6
MicroHlth	2956	16½	11⅝	16⅜	+ 4⅞	42.4
HomestdHld	107	13	8	12¼	+ 3½	40.0
Helionetic	622	7⅜	4¾	6⅝	+ 1⅞	39.5
GtAmComm	9286	5⅞	4	5⅝	+ 1½	36.4
MedicalSter	609	2⅜	1⅝	2⅜	+ ⅝	35.7
Novamtrx	1418	2⅞	1 15/16	2½	+ ⅝	33.3
GoldenEnt	2304	11½	8⅞	11¼	+ 2¾	32.4
CimmInc s	625	3¼	2	3⅛	+ ¾	31.6
InnoVet un	175	2 19/32	2	2 19/32	+ 19/32	29.7
TSS un	870	5⅞	4	5 3/16	+ 1 3/16	29.7
InvstFncl	3349	2⅞	1⅞	2¾	+ ⅝	29.4
RepubWaste	1961	18¼	13	16¾	+ 3¾	28.8
CimarronInv	10	18	14	18	+ 4	28.6
VenturEn wt	310	4½	3⅜	4½	+ 1	28.6
IntlMovie	889	2	1½	2	+ 7/16	28.0
AltosCptr	11591	8⅛	5⅝	7½	+ 1⅝	27.7
Dataimage	335	3½	2¾	3½	+ ¾	27.3
DesgnInc	474	4¾	4	4¾	+ 1	26.7
OSHAP un	258	13¼	10½	13¼	+ 2¾	26.2
USA Waste	2325	3 15/16	3⅛	3 15/16	+ 13/16	26.0

DOWNS

Name	Sales	High	Low	Close	Chg.	Pct.
MartnLaw	21319	7	4⅛	4⅜	− 2⅝	37.5
CedarGp wt	73	3⅝	2⅜	2⅜	− 1¼	34.5
Isramco	7380	3½	1½	2 5/16	− 1 3/16	33.9
EmpirFn	73	3	2	2	− 1	33.3
Keptel	430	7¼	5	5	− 2¼	31.0
Aquanut wtA	234	3⅞	2⅛	2 13/16	− 1 1/16	27.4
PowrSpec	679	3⅝	2⅝	2¾	− 15/16	25.4
McClain	117	4	3	3	− 1	25.0
RegentBnc	10	8	6	6	− 2	25.0
PlymthFive	405	2⅞	2	2	− ⅝	23.8
ViejoBncp	13	4	4	4	− 1¼	23.8
NwMilBcp	1330	5	3½	4	− 1⅛	22.0
MartechUSA	13206	16	12½	12½	− 3½	21.9
FstAmarilo	41	3	2¼	2¼	− ⅝	21.7
ChekRbt un	20	10½	7¾	8¼	− 2¼	21.4
HHOilTool	278	5¼	4⅛	4⅛	− 1⅛	21.4
Steves un	59	7	5½	5½	− 1½	21.4
CheckRobot	1851	4¾	3½	3¾	− 1	21.1
IntLse wt	1900	7¾	2⅛	6⅛	− 1⅝	21.0
FstFnCarb	42	8	6⅜	6⅜	− 1⅝	20.3
CoOpBnk	785	4⅝	3¾	4	− 1	20.0
MrchBcpCt	41	2½	2	2	− ½	20.0
ProspctPk	203	2½	2	2	− ½	20.0
FtNYBus	379	5	4¼	4 7/16	− 1 1/16	19.3
ThornAppV	91	6⅝	5⅛	5¼	− 1¼	19.2

Making Sense of Options

An option is a contract that gives its holder the right to buy or sell an asset at a specified price. The two principal players in the options game are the option writer and the option holder. Their relationship is summarized below.

Type of Option	Option Writer	Option Holder
Call	If requested by the option holder, the option writer must sell the asset to the option holder at the striking price.	Can force the option writer to sell him or her the asset at the striking price, or may sell the option through an options market, or may let the option expire.
Put	If requested by the option holder, the option writer must buy the asset from the option holder at the striking price.	Can force the option writer to buy the asset from him or her at the striking price, or may sell the option through an options market, or may let the option expire.

Option writers often write puts and calls for the same security.

writer can suffer considerable losses when options are exercised by a holder. The writer of a call may be forced to take a loss when the market price of the optioned asset rises above the striking price. If the writer owned the asset (a *covered option*), he or she might be forced to sell to the option holder at a price lower than the current market value. If the writer does not own the asset (a *naked option*), he or she might be forced to go into the market to buy the asset at its current price and then sell it at the lower striking price. Conversely, the writer of a put may be forced to take a loss when the market price of an optioned asset drops below the striking price. The writer probably would be forced to buy the asset from the option holder at a price above the market price. As you can see, writing options is highly speculative. This speculative risk can be offset by writing both puts and calls on an asset at the same striking price; this is called a **straddle**. The writer then simply makes money from the premiums charged for the options.

Options Markets The actual buying and selling of stock options and other forms of options take place in five major options markets: the Chicago Board Options Exchange (CBOE)—which is the largest—the American Stock Exchange (AMEX), the New York Stock Exchange (NYSE), the Philadelphia Exchange, and the Pacific Exchange. Note that these markets are dominated by professionals, yet data from the Securities and Exchange Commission reveal that four out of every five options traders lose money.

In reality, option holders rarely buy or sell the underlying asset. They simply buy and sell the options instead. The market price of puts goes down when the market price of the underlying asset goes down; it goes up when the market price of the underlying asset goes up. The market price of calls goes down when the market price of the underlying asset goes up; it goes up when the market price of the underlying asset goes down. As the option nears expiration, its value tends to fall. Actually, more than 90 percent of all options expire worthless. This should not be of grave concern, though, because the speculator-trader profits on rises and declines in the market prices of the options rather than in the expiration value of the options. The various classes of options (stock options, stock-index options, and so forth) each have specified expiration dates—usually at the close of the market on the third Friday of specified months. They may last up to 9 months.

Buying Calls   You might ask why someone would want to buy calls from a writer or holder. Remember that calls allow the holder of the contract to buy an asset at a specified price. The lure of calls is that the option holder can control a relatively large asset with a rather small amount of capital for a specified period of time. If the market price of the asset rises to exceed the striking price plus the premium, the holder could make a substantial profit. For example, assume Lillian Mohr of St. Petersburg, Florida, buys a March stock option call on Xerox when the stock is selling for $55 per share. The striking price is $60, the expiration date is the third Friday in March, and the price (premium) of the call is $2 per share. Thus the option contract costs her $200 ($2 × 100 shares under her control). Lillian hopes that the price of Xerox will rise. She prefers not to buy the stock outright because 100 shares of Xerox would cost her a great deal more—$5500 ($55 × 100).

The holder of a call hopes the price of the security will rise.

For Lillian to break even on the call option deal, the price of Xerox must rise to $62 before expiration, as the following formula shows:

$$\text{Break-even price for calls} = \text{striking price} + \frac{\text{contract cost}}{\text{number of shares under control}}$$

$$= \$60 + \frac{\$200}{100}$$

$$= \$62$$

(21.2)

If Lillian exercises the option, she can obtain the stock at $60 and sell it for the current market price of $62 (ignoring commissions). Thus she earns $2 per share ($62 − $60), which offsets the $2 per share purchase price of the option. If the price of Xerox stock rises to $65, Lillian would make a $3 profit per share on the stock for a total profit of $300. Based on her $200 investment, this amounts to a 150 percent yield ($300/$200) earned over a short period. On the other hand, if the Xerox stock price had failed to reach $60 by late March, Lillian's $200 in calls would have expired with no value at all and she would have lost her entire investment.

Selling Options   As mentioned earlier, most option holders never exercise their right to buy or sell the underlying asset. Instead, they simply let the

Advice for the Conservative Use of Put Options

Puts allow the holder of the contract to sell an asset at a specified striking price. Puts are a conservative investment and are used to reduce market risk. For example, if you purchase 100 shares of a common stock, you hope that the market price of the stock will go up. If it goes down instead, you may suffer a loss. To reduce this risk, you could buy a put for 100 shares at a striking price close to the purchase price of the stock. The total price of the option contract might be $200 ($2 per share). If the stock price went down, you could sell the stock at the striking price, thereby hedging a loss. If the stock price went up, you could let the option expire. Of course, you would lose the money spent on the option—but you would hope to offset it by the gain from the increased price of the stock. The break-even price on a put option is calculated according to the formula

Break-even price for puts

$$= \text{striking price} - \frac{\text{contract cost}}{\text{number of shares under control}} \quad (21.3)$$

If the striking price on a put option were $75 and the option contract provided for the control of 300 shares of stock at a total price of $450, the break-even price of a share of the stock would be $73.50, as illustrated below.

$$\text{Break-even price} = \$75 - \frac{\$450}{300}$$
$$= \$73.50$$

option expire, or they might sell the option to another party. You would want to sell a put or a call when its market price has risen sufficiently (due to changes in the market price of the underlying asset) to ensure you a profit. Or you might want to sell an option if its market price is dropping and you wish to prevent further losses.

Trading with Futures Contracts

Futures contracts have a specific delivery date.

Investors can profit from increases or decreases in the prices of various commodities (commercial products) by purchasing and selling **futures contracts.** These are marketable contracts that require the delivery of a specific amount of a commodity at a certain future date. These contracts for certain agricultural and mining products are standardized and traded on organized securities markets, such as the Chicago Mercantile Exchange (trading commodities such as pigs, pork bellies, eggs, potatoes, and cattle); the Chicago Board of Trade (corn, wheat, soybeans, soybean oil, oats, silver, and plywood); the New York Coffee and Sugar Exchange; the New York Cocoa Exchange; the International Monetary Market, which is part of the Chicago Mercantile Exchange (foreign currencies and U.S. Treasury bills); the New York Commodity Exchange (gold and silver); and the New York Mercantile Exchange (platinum). Stock futures are also traded on the New York Futures Exchange; in this case, the "commodity" is S&P's 500 or the index of another exchange.

An economic need creates futures markets. For example, a farmer planting a 10,000-bushel soybean crop might want to sell part of it now to ensure a certain price after the crop is harvested. Similarly, a food-processing company might desire to purchase corn or wheat now to protect itself against sharp price increases in the future. Or an orange juice manufacturer might want to make sure of a certain supply of oranges at a definite price now rather than take the chance of a winter freeze that could push up prices.

Future contracts lock in the price of a commodity.

The speculator who buys or sells a commodity contract is hoping not only that the price of the commodity will rise or fall, but also that it will move in the desired direction before the contract expires. Futures contracts have initial maturities of from 3 to 18 months.

The lure is the potential of extremely high profits. Depending on the commodity, the volatility of the market, and the brokerage house requirements, the speculator can put up as little as 5 to 15 percent of the total value of the contract. Some contracts require a deposit of only $300. Commissions average about $20 for each purchase and sale. To illustrate the use of leverage in buying futures contracts, assume that Ronald Edelman, a lawyer from Washington, D.C., purchases one July wheat contract (5000 bushels) at $3.80 per bushel. The contract value is $19,000 ($3.80 × 5000), but Ronald puts up only $2500. Each 1-cent increase in the price of wheat represents $50 ($3.81 × 5000/$19,050; $3.82 × 5000 = $19,100; and so forth). If the price rises $0.50, to $4.30, by late July, Ronald will make $2500 and double his investment.

However, the potential for loss exists, too. If the price drops $0.50, Ronald would be out $2500. As the price declines, the broker will make a margin call and ask Ronald to provide more money to back up the contract. If Ronald doesn't have these funds, the broker can legally sell Ronald's contract and "close out" his position, which results in a true, not a paper, cash loss. Because of the risks involved, most brokerage houses require their futures customers to have a minimum net worth of $50,000 to $75,000 exclusive of home and life insurance.

A speculator can make a large investment—perhaps $50,000 to $100,000—in futures contracts with only a small amount of capital, perhaps only several thousand dollars. The rest is borrowed. Thus it is a high-leverage game with lots of action. There are no interest charges because the credit is not technically extended until the commodity is actually delivered. Investors do not usually take possession of the commodity, since almost all contracts are just sold to someone else. Investors who have bought contracts normally sell identical contracts to close out their position.

In each commodity transaction there must be a winner and a loser. The buyer of a futures contract benefits if the price of the commodity increases, but the seller suffers. When prices decline, the reverse is true. Thus mathematicians describe futures trading as a **zero-sum game.** That is, the total wealth of all futures traders remains the same, since the trading simply redistributes the wealth among the traders. Thus the real rate of return on futures contracts would be zero if there were no transaction

Wealth simply changes hands from losers to winners in futures trading.

What If You Wish to Sell Your Speculative Investments?

Below are some suggestions on when to sell high-risk investments.

1. *Act when investment targets are reached.* You should set investment targets for gains and losses and always take actions to remain within them. For example, a purchaser of warrants might decide to sell when profits reach 30 percent (or when losses reach 20 percent). In a rising stock market, the price of a common stock could be pushing up the value of a warrant sharply, perhaps even 30 percent in a few days. The speculator should wisely avoid the greedy desire to hold the warrant and further increase profits by selling for the profits when the return reaches a preestablished goal. This approach keeps you from holding on too long only to watch the value of your investment drop dramatically.

2. *Cut losses short.* You should cut losses short by graciously and faithfully accepting losses when they occur. For example, an option you purchased at 3 that has now declined to 2 has caused you a loss of 33⅓ percent. If you had earlier decided to sell when losses reach 20 percent, the time to sell is now (or an hour ago). You are ill-served by "leveraging down" in high-risk markets, perhaps by buying another equal amount of options at 2 hoping that a climb in price to 2½ will recoup all losses.

3. *Consider using technical analysis.* Technical analysis is a tool that can help you make buying and selling decisions. We are not espousing a particular type of technical analysis or a single advisory service, but we recognize that technical analysis helps some investors make intelligent decisions. Indeed, the recommendations of some prominent technical analysts are so closely watched that market swings often occur because of their advice. This approach also may alert you to thinking of other speculators.

4. *Be patient.* You need to be patient before selling tangible assets such as rare coins,

(continued)

costs. An estimated 90 percent of investors in the futures market lose money; about 5 percent (mostly the professionals) make good profits from the losers and the remaining 5 percent break even.

The winning speculators in futures contracts study technical analyses, use the services of a good broker, keep informed, learn to sell short as well as buy long, trade only in active markets, trade only during major market moves, diversify their holdings into several commodities, cut losses short, keep accurate records, and hope. The losing speculators do the same.

Investors who want the glamour and high profit potential of commodities futures but fewer risks can invest in a public commodities fund, which operates much like a mutual fund. Losses cannot exceed the amount invested, and most funds close down if assets fall to 50 percent of the original capital. In recent years, more than three-fourths of such funds significantly outperformed S&P's 500 stock index.

stamps, art, and diamonds. The high sales commission costs on these assets can offset most of the paper gain achieved in a year or two. Such assets usually should be held about 5 years for maximum appreciation.

5. *Use contrarianism.* Consider practicing **contrarianism.** This investment approach suggests that once the general public has seized on an idea, its usefulness is over and the wise investor should take the opposite action. For example, if after a few days of notable rises in the stock market indexes the public thinks that the market is in for a sharp increase, then it is already too late to act and take advantage of rising prices. The contrarian would believe that a market correction is about to occur and would sell before the "herd" of other investors sells. The contrarian also might buy some put options, expecting the market to decline. This approach helps investors avoid the peaks and valleys of the market.

6. *Use arbitrage.* You might consider using **arbitrage.** This is the simultaneous purchase and sale of the same security, option, or futures contract in different markets to profit from unequal prices. For example, assume that silver futures for August delivery sell for $10.67 an ounce and silver slated for delivery in October of the following year (14 months later) sells for $11.67. The $1 spread partially represents the cost of storage and the cost of capital for the 14 months. To profit, you could purchase 1000 ounces of the August silver (taking delivery at that time) and simultaneously sell a contract for October of the next year. Come next October, you would simply deliver the silver purchased and take home a 9.4 percent ($100/$10.67) profit, less expenses. Arbitrage is used frequently by astute high-risk investors and is a technique often used by program traders.

Summary

1. Speculative investments are investment transactions involving considerable risk for the chance of large gains. Thus funds used for speculative purposes should be only those which one can afford to lose.

2. Tangible investments are often speculative investments. The prices of precious metals, such as gold, silver, and platinum, tend to increase in times of economic, military, and political turmoil, especially if inflation rises quickly. Buying collectibles, such as stamps, art, and rare coins, can provide hobby as well as investment benefits.

3. Certain securities can be speculative investments. Rights have an intrinsic financial value and if bought on margin can become quite a speculative investment. A warrant has a speculative value until the expiration date, after which it is worthless. The speculative investor can profit in both

buying and selling stock options, but buying puts can be a conservative move. Profit can be made in the volatile area of futures contracts as increases or decreases in the prices of various commodities occur.

4. Investors should consider selling high-risk investments when they have achieved their target for gains or losses or to cut losses short.

Modern Money Management

Belinda Johnson Invests in Commodity Futures

For months, Belinda Johnson has been cultivating a new and very wealthy customer for the stock brokerage firm where she works. Last week, her hard work paid off in the opening of a $500,000 account. In addition to her commission, Belinda was rewarded with a $3000 bonus by her boss. Since this money was totally unexpected, Harry suggested that Belinda do whatever she wished with the money. She has decided to invest in commodity futures, since she can do so through her employer without paying commission fees. For $3000 she purchased two corn futures contracts (5000 bushels each) at $2.40 per bushel.

1. What is the total value of Belinda's investment, and what percentage of the total investment is borrowed?

2. If the price of corn goes up $0.10 per bushel, what are the return and yield on Belinda's investment?

3. If the price of corn goes down $0.05 per bushel, calculate Belinda's paper loss in dollars and as a percentage.

4. Given the loss in number 3 and a margin requirement of 12.5 percent, how much more money would Belinda need to put up to meet the margin call?

Key Words and Concepts

arbitrage, 747
buying long, 737
call, 740
collectibles, 733

contrarianism, 747
futures contracts, 744
leverage, 735
margin buying, 735

Review Questions

1. What distinguishes speculative from other investments?
2. Distinguish intangible from tangible investments.
3. What seems to be the primary reason people invest in precious metals?
4. How is money made from an investment in precious metals?
5. What are the major forms of investment in collectibles?
6. Members of what organization have the responsibility of grading and certifying the authenticity of gems?
7. What are the benefits of using margin when investing?
8. Explain the negative impacts of a margin call.
9. Describe how money can be made by the trading technique called *selling short.*
10. What value is afforded stockholders who take advantage of their preemptive rights?
11. What two options are available to the holder of a right?
12. Distinguish between rights and warrants.
13. Why might a company attach a warrant to a security offer such as a bond?
14. Of what value are stock options for a holder of stock?
15. Identify the risks of writing a naked option.
16. Distinguish between a put and a call.
17. How are put options used as a conservative investment strategy?
18. What is a futures contract? Identify examples of the types of commodities that are traded with one.
19. How can an investor gain by investing in futures contracts?
20. Why is investing in futures contracts a high-risk investment?
21. What are the six criteria to use as guidelines when considering selling high-risk investments?

Case Problems

1. Anna Hall of University Park, Pennsylvania, inherited over $100,000 in cash from her deceased husband. She has a house almost paid for, a good life insurance plan for herself and her two children, and several thousand dollars in secure savings accounts. Also, she inherited over $150,000 in stocks and bonds that bring her more than $1000 a month in extra earnings. In addition, insurance guarantees her a monthly income of $1800 until her death. Anna talked to an investment counselor about making some high-risk investments. Since she has a steady income, she feels she can absorb any losses without detriment to herself or her children.
   a. Considering all the preceding information, do you feel that Anna is in a position to make high-risk investments?
   b. What precautions should Anna take before making high-risk investments?
   c. Assuming that Anna knows little about high-risk investments, advise her as to the most important positive and negative features of the major high-risk investments available today.
   d. Anna can't understand why she should pay $250 to borrow money for investments, when she clearly has funds available. Explain to her why buying 100 shares of stock for $50 per share and selling it at $65 per share offers less return than the same deal purchased at a 40 percent margin. Ignore commissions; show your calculations in tabular form like that of Table 21.1.
   e. Anna was also puzzled because a friend was elated that the price of a stock had fallen in a short selling deal. Anna thought a good deal required the stock price to rise. Help Anna understand who is right.

2. Gail Reichbach of Ypsilanti, Michigan, recently purchased 200 shares of Upjohn Pharmaceuticals common stock at $93 per share. She purchased the stock because the company is testing a new drug that may be a significant medical breakthrough. Already the stock's value has risen $8 in 3 months, in anticipation of the Food and Drug Administration's approval of the new drug. Many observers feel that the price of the stock could reach $100 if the drug is successful. If it is not the breakthrough anticipated, however, the price of the stock could drop back to the $85 range. Gail is optimistic but feels she should hedge her position a bit, so she has decided to purchase two 9-month Upjohn 100-share puts for $3 per share at a striking price of $93 per share. Ignore commissions when answering the following questions.
   a. What price would the Upjohn stock need to reach for Gail to break even on her investment?
   b. How much would Gail gain if she sold the stock for $102 six months from now?
   c. How much would Gail lose if the price of the stock dropped to $85 in 6 months?

Suggested Readings

"A Hard Truth About Partnerships." *Changing Times,* January 1990, pp. 59–63. If you do not know what you are doing you can lose a lot of money in limited partnerships.

"Big Loans for Small Businesses." *Changing Times,* April 1989, pp. 105–109. How to avoid the red tape when borrowing from the Small Business Administration.

"Cashing in on Old Coins." *Business Week,* June 5, 1989, pp. 140–141. The promises and pitfalls of numismatic investing.

"Coins: Heads You Lose, Tails You Lose." *Changing Times,* February 1989, pp. 71–76. It is difficult to make money in coins, particularly with so many swindlers and con artists around.

"Commodity Funds: An Investment for All Seasons." *Business Week,* July 24, 1989, p. 86. How to invest in the commodity markets via mutual funds.

"How Commodities Markets Fit Business Cycle Patterns." *Futures Magazine,* December 1989, pp. 34–38. Explores the relationship between the business cycle and commodities investment cycles.

"Investments You Can Live Without." *Changing Times,* November 1989, pp. 43–47. You need to think hard before investing in movie limited partnerships, new closed-end mutual funds, and some other investments.

"The 1980s: How Leaders Rate the Decade's Key Developments." *Futures Magazine,* December 1989, pp. 16–22. An analysis of changes in the futures and options markets in the 1980s.

"The Only Way to Invest in Coins." *Money,* April 1990, pp. 157–162. The proper way to invest in coins or face a good chance of getting ripped off.

"The Trouble with Stock Options." *Fortune,* January 1, 1990, pp. 93–95. Explains the growth in the number of companies offering stock options while warning that nonemployee stockholders may not be getting a fair shake.

"The War on Penny Stocks." *Newsweek,* April 10, 1989, p. 52. Exposes the high risk of penny stocks.

"Trade Metals! Little Money Down! Lose a Bundle Quick!" *Business Week,* January 29, 1990, pp. 87–88. Explores the pitfalls of investing in precious metals.

PART SIX

Retirement and Estate Planning

22 Developing and Implementing a Plan for a Secure Retirement

OBJECTIVES

After reading this chapter, you should be able to

1. Explain the procedures for estimating retirement expenses and the sources of income during retirement.
2. Explain and calculate the relative benefit of tax-sheltered versus non-tax-sheltered retirement plans.
3. Describe the types and characteristics of employer-sponsored pension plans.
4. Explain the purposes and benefits of personal retirement plans.
5. Describe how to qualify for the Social Security retirement program and the role Social Security plays in retirement planning.
6. Using a detailed example, estimate the dollar amount you should be putting away for retirement.
7. Discuss how investment strategies change during retirement.

· · · · · · · · · ·

Today's workers are healthier, will live longer, are better educated, and have higher expectations than those of earlier generations. When they retire, their goals will be much like their preretirement goals—they will want a comfortable, happy life. The time to begin planning for such a retirement is when you are young, although it is not easy. Young people have enough difficulty balancing their budgets, saving for a down payment on a home, buying furniture, and paying insurance premiums, so most postpone putting away money for their retirement years. Yet a beginning must be undertaken even if it means only putting a small amount away.

Your retirement may seem to be so far in the future that you needn't worry about it for a long time. However, you will have financial freedom and security during your retirement years only if you take specific steps early. This chapter first discusses retirement expenses and the sources of income available during your retirement years. Next we cover the benefits of using tax sheltering in retirement planning. Employer-sponsored pension plans are the next consideration in most people's retirement planning. Then we move on to the important topic of personal pension plans. A discussion of Social Security is also provided, since it is an important source of retirement funds. We cover Social Security after employer and personal pension plans because we want you to take charge of your own retirement planning and not assume that government programs, which are subject to change, will take care of you. To aid you in your planning, we provide an illustration of how you can determine the dollar amount you should be saving each year for your retirement. The final section of the chapter covers the need for changed investment strategies during retirement.

Exploring Retirement Expenses and Income Sources

Objective
To be able to explain the procedures for estimating retirement expenses and sources of income during retirement.

One of the roadblocks to an early start on retirement planning is motivation. People don't see the need and only see the difficulties in planning so far ahead. Actually, there are only two initial steps. First, you must estimate your expenses during retirement. Second, you must identify sources of income during retirement.

Estimating Retirement Expenses

Experts estimate that retirees need 65 to 80 percent of their preretirement income to live comfortably. This varies according to the desired retirement

TABLE 22.1
Sample Retirement Budget for a Couple

Items	Annual Expenditures 5 Years before Retirement	Expenditures If Retired (Ignoring Inflation)
Food	$ 3,600	$ 3,600
Housing (including $5000 in preretirement principal and interest mortgage payments)	8,400	3,600
Clothing	1,200	600
Transportation and related insurance	3,000	2,500
Savings	3,000	1,000
Life Insurance	500	0
Health insurance (out-of-pocket)	1,200	3,000
Medical expenses (out-of-pocket)	1,000	2,100
Leisure and travel	1,500	3,000
Charities and gifts	600	600
Social Security taxes	2,000	0
Income taxes	5,000	1,000
TOTALS	$31,000	$21,000

lifestyle, of course. Retirement in large cities costs more than in rural areas, and those who want to travel will need more than the average retirement income. Expenses may increase as a result of growing medical costs as well as financial responsibilities for children, parents, or other relatives and decrease for work-related transportation and clothes. By retirement age, most people will have paid off their home mortgages and will no longer need much, if any, life insurance coverage; in addition, income and Social Security taxes may be significantly reduced.

Table 22.1 shows a sample retirement budget for a couple. Expenditures in the fifth year preceding retirement amount to $31,000. If they were retired, these expenditures might drop to $21,000, primarily owing to the fact that their home mortgage would be paid and that taxes would be lower. Thus their expenditures would be only 67.7 percent of the preretirement amount ($21,000/$31,000). Note that some expenditure amounts could increase and others decrease.

People near retirement age can probably estimate expenditures quite accurately and develop a retirement budget with considerable confidence. People further than 5 years from retirement age have a harder time estimating needed expenditures because of potentially large changes in budget categories. Instead, they could estimate the current annual dollar amount that would be needed by a retired couple or individual to maintain a comfortable or desirable lifestyle. This figure, perhaps $25,000 in 1991, could then be used in the same way as the right column total from Table 22.1. Or one could use a figure equal to 75 percent of current income.

Regardless of how you estimate your annual retirement expenditures, you still only have an annual figure. Most Americans will live at least 20 years past their retirement age, so a fund must be established to provide for many years of retirement, not just the first. Assuming that the couple 5 years from retirement in Table 22.1 will live for 20 years past retirement and could earn an after-tax and after-inflation rate of return of 3 percent on their nest egg, what would their nest egg need to be? Calculations using Appendix A4 for 20 years at 3 percent reveal a nest egg of $312,438 ($21,000 × 14.878). For someone in his twenties, this figure could easily be $1 million to $2 million because of inflationary increases in the cost of living. The remainder of this chapter discusses various plans that can build your nest egg and culminates with an illustration of how one can save enough to retire comfortably.

People in their twenties today will need a retirement fund of $1 or $2 million at age 65.

Sources of Retirement Income

The days are gone (if they ever existed) when one could simply rely on Social Security to provide for retirement income needs. According to a report of the Social Security Administration, the average retired couple with income in excess of $20,000 receives income from the following sources: investments (34 percent), earnings (24 percent), Social Security (22 percent), company retirement plans (18 percent), and miscellaneous (2 percent). Most retirees in the next century will receive Social Security retirement benefits that are higher (even after adjusting for inflation) than those received by today's retirees. But because of increased costs and a higher standard of living, Social Security will represent only about 20 percent of a retiree's income needs. Further, the larger one's final salary amount, the smaller the percentage of retirement income composed of Social Security payments. The wise retirement planner views Social Security as the icing on the cake of a retirement plan. The foundation (or cake itself) is the employer-provided pension plan plus additional investment and personal retirement planning mechanisms. If one prepares adequately in these areas, whatever Social Security is received can serve as the difference between an adequate and affluent retirement lifestyle.

One source of income for many retirees is the equity in their home. By selling a home at retirement and moving into an apartment, a couple might be able to fund their rent for many years. For example, $80,000 in equity invested at 6 percent after taxes would provide $700 per month toward rent for almost 15 years (from Appendix A4). Or it might be advantageous to consider a reverse annuity mortgage (see Chapter 10, page 366), thereby allowing the couple to live in the home as well as use the equity as income.

Tax-Sheltered Retirement Plans

A **tax-sheltered (qualified) retirement plan** is one approved by the IRS for special tax advantages that reduce taxes and increase retirement benefits. The employer-sponsored retirement plans discussed below—pensions, 401(k) plans, and 403(b) plans—are tax-sheltered plans, as are personal retirement plans such as individual retirement accounts (IRAs), simplified employee pension (SEP) plans, Keogh plans (pronounced "key-oh"), and

TABLE 22.2
Tax Savings with Tax-Sheltered Retirement Plans
(Single Person, 1990 Tax Year)

	Person A	Person B
Without tax-sheltered plan		
Taxable income (after deductions and exemptions)	$17,000	$40,000
Final tax liability	2,550	8,672
Marginal tax rate	15 percent	28 percent
With tax-sheltered plan		
Taxable income (after deductions, and exemptions)	$17,000	$40,000
Less contribution to the plan (an adjustment to income)	−2,000	−2,000
Tax income with plan	15,000	38,000
Tax liability	2,250	8,112
Tax savings		
Tax liability without tax-sheltered plan	$ 2,550	$ 8,672
Tax liability with tax-sheltered plan	−2,250	−8,112
Tax savings	$ 300	$ 560

Tax-sheltering defers taxes on income earned on funds in a retirement plan and, possibly, the funds deposited into the plan.

certain annuity plans. Tax sheltering can occur in two ways. First, the contributions to such retirement plans might not be taxable until withdrawn and thus can be used to reduce current taxable income. Second, taxes on investment income from a retirement plan might be deferred until withdrawn. Plans that shelter contributions generally shelter investment income, but some plans only shelter the investment income from taxes.

First Benefit: Tax-Deductibility Allows Larger Contributions

The tax-deductibility aspects of tax-sheltered retirement plans are tremendous compared with ordinary savings and investment plans. Because all or at least a portion of contributions to IRS-approved plans are an adjustment to income, the current year's tax liability is lowered. In addition, the money saved in taxes also can be used to partially fund the contributions.

Table 22.2 illustrates how contributions to an IRA, Keogh, or most other tax-sheltered plans reduce current taxes. As shown, a single person with a taxable income of $17,000 who places $2000 into a tax-sheltered retirement plan saves $300 in taxes. In essence, the taxpayer puts $1700 ($2000 − $300) into the retirement plan, and the government puts in the remaining $300. The taxpayer in a higher tax bracket gains even more. A

FIGURE 22.1
How Tax-Sheltered
Money Grows ($3000
Invested Annually at
9 Percent)

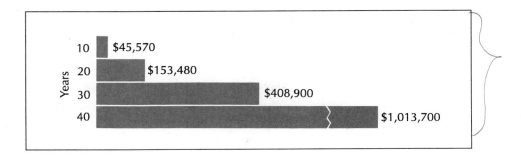

single person with taxable income of $40,000 can save $560 in taxes by making a $2000 contribution to a tax-sheltered retirement plan.

Second Benefit: Deferring Taxes Enhances Compounding

Tax-sheltered retirement plans also reduce taxes in the future. Because interest, dividends, and capital gains are not taxed until funds are withdrawn from the plan, the investments have more opportunity to grow and compound in value. When the funds are finally taxed on withdrawal some years later, the taxpayer may be in a lower tax bracket.

For example, if a regular savings account had interest income of $1200, a single person with a $30,000 taxable income would have to pay $336 in additional taxes (marginal tax rate 28 of percent × $1200); only $864 would be available for earnings the next year ($1200 − $336). A tax-sheltered retirement plan, however, permits the full $1200 to be retained and earn interest.

How to Be a Millionaire

A $1 million nest egg is achievable.

If you want to be a millionaire at retirement, you need only invest $3000 annually for 40 years at a 9 percent tax-free return. Figure 22.1 shows the totals earned with this investment plan for 10, 20, 30, and 40 years (calculations based on figures in Appendix A3). It is important to begin a tax-sheltered retirement plan at an early age. Investing $3000 a year in tax-sheltered plans for 20 years yields you a total of $153,480, but starting investments 10 years earlier (for a total of 30 years) yields $408,900.

Withdrawals from a Tax-Sheltered Plan

Deferred taxes are paid when the retirement funds are withdrawn.

The tax sheltering that results from setting aside monies in a qualified retirement plan is actually a deferment of taxes rather than a permanent avoidance of taxes. Income tax must be paid when the funds are withdrawn. If withdrawn prior to a certain age (usually 59½), a 10 percent penalty may be assessed as well. If you do a good job of saving for retirement, you may find yourself in the same tax bracket after retirement as before. Nonetheless, it is generally better to pay taxes later rather than sooner.

Regardless of your tax bracket, there are three things you can do to maximize the benefits you receive from a tax-sheltered retirement plan. First, begin your plan as soon as possible. The value of compounding increases with the length of time the funds are left to earn income. Second, if possible, contribute the maximum amount allowed by law. However, do not feel that you should wait to begin a plan until you can contribute the maximum amount annually. It is better to start early with reduced contributions than wait in order to make maximum contributions.

Third, choose investments for your plan that pay the highest earnings. The difference between an 8 percent and a 9 percent yield on an annual investment of $3000 over 30 years is $69,000, and over 40 years it is $236,400. A quick look at Appendix A3 will reveal the wisdom of obtaining the highest rates of return. The key is to pick out good mutual funds from the rubble of mediocre performers. (See Chapter 18). Focus on growth not current income, especially prior to age fifty.

Taxation of withdrawals from plans that sheltered both contributions and investment income are easiest to understand. Since no taxes were ever paid on any of the funds, all withdrawals are fully taxable. Taxation of withdrawals from plans that only sheltered a portion of contributions and/ or investment income can be very complicated. The IRS will assume that withdrawals consist of both previously taxed and previously untaxed funds and will use complicated formulas to determine the ratio for taxation purposes. To avoid such difficulties, never mix partially sheltered and fully sheltered funds in one retirement account. And make sure that you safely maintain adequate records even if for 40 years or more.

Employer-Sponsored Pension Plans

Objective
To be able to describe the types and characteristics of employer-sponsored pension plans.

About half of all workers in private firms are covered by an employer-sponsored pension plan, although over 85 percent of workers in medium to large firms are covered. If you are included in such a plan, it can serve as the cornerstone of your retirement planning. Table 22.3 illustrates the dollar amount you might receive from an employer-sponsored pension plan. If you are not included in an employer-sponsored plan, you should take immediate actions to prepare for retirement.

Because of the importance of employer-sponsored plans, Congress passed the Pension Reform Act of 1974, also called the Employee Retirement Income Security Act (ERISA). ERISA does not require companies to offer retirement plans but does regulate more than 350,000 existing plans. The law also established the Pension Benefit Guarantee Corporation (PBGC),

TABLE 22.3
Typical Monthly Benefits from Company Pension Plans (In Dollars and as a Percent of Final Year's Income)

Earnings in Last Year Prior to Retirement	Number of Years Worked for Firm			
	10	20	30	40
$20,000	$165	$314	$456	$ 571
	9.9 percent	18.8 percent	27.4 percent	34.3 percent
$30,000	242	462	662	814
	9.7 percent	18.5 percent	26.5 percent	32.6 percent
$40,000	326	623	886	1,075
	9.8 percent	18.7 percent	26.6 percent	32.2 percent

Source: From D. G. Schmitt, "Today's Pension Plans: How Much Do They Pay?" *Monthly Labor Review*, December 1985, pp. 19–25. Published by the U.S. Department of Commerce.

which provides an insurance program that guarantees certain benefits to eligible workers whose employer's plan is not financially sound enough to pay its obligations.

There are several important elements of company pension plans to consider: benefit determination, benefit participation, vesting, contributory or noncontributory, funded or unfunded plans, integration of benefits with Social Security, and distribution of benefits. Also, there are other types of employer-sponsored retirement plans. Each is discussed below.

Benefits Determination

Defined-benefit and defined-contribution are the two methods of pension benefits computation.

Retirement benefits are based on the benefit computation method utilized by the plan. Two methods predominate: the defined-benefit method and the defined-contribution method. Employer-sponsored pensions in the United States are about equally divided between the two, although most new plans are defined-contribution plans.

The **defined-benefit method** bases the level of retirement, survivors', or disability benefits on the income and/or years of employment of the worker. For example, an employee might have a defined annual benefit of 2 percent multiplied by the number of years of service multiplied by the average income during the last 5 years of employment. To illustrate, a worker with 30 years' service and an average income over the last 5 years of work of $28,000 would have an annual benefit of $16,800 (30 × 0.02 × $28,000), or $1400 a month. Crucial variables in defined-benefit plans are the number of years you work for the company and the number of years used to calculate the average income in the formula. Obviously, you would want a plan that includes your highest income years in the average and excludes your lowest.

With the **defined-contribution method,** also called the **money-purchase pension** or a **capital accumulation plan** the employer, and sometimes the employee, sets aside monies regularly during the working years in order to establish a fund for the payment of retirement benefits to the covered worker. Thus the money going into the plan is clearly specified, but the exact amount of the benefits is not fixed until the worker or survivor(s) begin drawing benefits. This is because the amount available depends greatly on the success of the investments made with the retirement funds.

There is a growing trend to shift from defined-benefit to defined-contribution pension plans among the nation's largest corporations. This helps the companies by eliminating any unfunded pension liability but presents more uncertainty for workers about the amount of benefits that actually will be received. On the plus side, defined-contribution plans generally permit earlier vesting and easy portability (discussed below). Additionally, in a defined-contribution plan, each employee's contribution is placed in a separate account, out of reach of corporate creditors should the company go bankrupt. Pension Benefit Guaranty Corporation collects compulsory premiums from all covered programs and pays out benefits to employees of firms that go bankrupt. There are limits to this coverage, however.

Benefit Participation

Employees must participate in a retirement plan to be eligible for any benefits. ERISA requires that employers choose one of two approaches in allowing full-time workers to participate in the retirement plan: (1) admitting every employee who has worked for the firm for 1 year and who is at least age 21, or (2) admitting every employee who has worked 3 years for the company.

Vesting

Vesting helps guarantee that you will receive benefits.

ERISA places stringent requirements on **vesting,** a process by which employees obtain during their working years nonforfeitable rights to their retirement benefits that cannot be taken away in case of dismissal or resignation. Retirement plans must offer government-approved vesting. Two alternatives are available. With 5-year (*cliff*) vesting, an employee is not vested during the first 5 years but becomes fully vested at the end of the fifth year. Seven-year (*graduated*) vesting calls for employees to be 20 percent vested after 3 years, 40 percent after 4 years, 60 percent after 5 years, 80 percent after 6 years, and 100 percent at the end of 7 years of service. All previous time worked for the business since age 18 must count toward vesting.

Contributory or Noncontributory Plans

Employees may put funds in a contributory plan.

In a *noncontributory retirement plan,* the employer puts all funds into the plan. Many companies offer noncontributory plans for employees. In a *contributory retirement plan,* both the employee and the employer place funds in the plan. Most government employees (local, state, and federal) are enrolled in contributory plans. Typically, employee and employer shares are equal. For example, each might contribute 5 percent of the employee's salary.

Corporations may establish various types of pension and profit-sharing plans. Since corporate contributions to the plans usually are not considered income to employees and are a tax deduction for the company, they may accumulate as tax-sheltered earnings. Contributions by employees to a contributory plan may or may not be used to reduce taxable income, depending on the type of plan. The big benefit comes when both the employer's and the employee's contributions are legally tax-sheltered, permitting all earnings to compound quickly. Taxes are finally due on the funds only as benefits are paid. For example, Judy Vogel, a single mother of two from Cincinatti, Ohio, earns a salary of $36,000 and is covered by a plan that has a company contribution of 5 percent and an employee contribution of 5 percent. Thus $3600 ($1800 + $1800) will be growing tax-free.

Employees have an absolute right to benefits based on their own contributions.

With contributory plans, employees have the right to receive benefits based on their own contributions no matter how long they worked for the firm. If Judy resigns after 4 years, she would be entitled to retirement benefits based on her $7200 (4 × $1800) contributions. Judy might have a right to contributions made by the company depending on the vesting plan used. If her employer uses 5-year vesting, Judy would receive nothing from the employer contributions. If her employer uses 7-year vesting, Judy would be entitled to receive benefits at retirement based on $2880 (4 × $1800 × 0.40). If available, Judy also might benefit from **portability,** which is a contract clause that permits workers to take pension money to another job or possibly withdraw the cash. Any of these funds that were deposited tax-free would be fully taxable upon withdrawal unless Judy transferred them into another tax-sheltered plan within specified time limits.

Funded or Unfunded Plans

Unfunded pension plans are risky.

Pension plans are either funded or unfunded. In a *funded pension plan,* the employer makes full formal payments annually to a trustee, who then places the funds in conservative and relatively safe investments (or annuities) so that full benefits will be available to all employees upon retirement. In an *unfunded pension plan,* retirement expenses are paid out of current earnings rather than from funds set aside to cover current and future liabilities. These are often called "owe-as-you-go" plans and are more risky should the employer go bankrupt. Defined-contribution plans are almost always funded. Defined-benefit plans may be unfunded. Most state and local government retirement plans are unfunded, as is Social Security. However, the "guarantee" of the government programs comes primarily from the political pressure of retirees and current workers who expect similar benefits.

Integration of Benefits with Social Security

Benefits from defined-benefit retirement plans are sometimes integrated with benefits from Social Security. This can be detrimental, since company benefits may be reduced by the amount of Social Security benefits received by the retiree. For example, assume you retire with a company pension of $900 a month and Social Security benefits of $600 a month. If your Social Security payments rise to $700, the company pension may drop to $800, thus offsetting the $100 increase in Social Security benefits. The net effect is that you lose ground to inflation despite raises in Social Security.

Methods of Distribution of Benefits

Three choices are available for the payment of retirement benefits.

Three payment methods are used to distribute funds from employer pension plans: (1) monthly benefits for the worker's (and usually a surviving spouse's) lifetime, (2) regular monthly benefits for a certain number of years, or a (3) lump-sum payment upon retirement. Choosing among these alternatives is an important decision that requires careful analysis of your tax situation and financial condition, your possibilities for earning a good return on a lump-sum investment, and the financial condition of the retirement plan and company. Two important factors affecting the distribution of benefits are your time of retirement and whether you have survivors' and disability benefits.

Early or Normal Retirement? The earlier you retire, the smaller your monthly retirement benefit will be because you are expected to live more years as a retired person. For example, refer to Table 14.1 on page 487, which lists average life expectancies. On average, a man retiring at age 62 has 16 years of life remaining to collect retirement benefits, whereas a man retiring at age 65 may collect benefits for only 14 years. Monthly benefits for the early retiree are reduced to give, in theory, the same total dollar amount of benefits as for the person who retires at age 65. Note that the U.S. Supreme Court has ruled that company retirement benefits must be the same for men and women who contribute equal amounts, even though their average life expectancies differ.

Benefits for early retirement are usually based on actuarial figures (calculations of insurance and pension risks) or a company formula. For example, the full benefit expected at age 65 could be reduced by 4 percent for each year a person retires before age 65 and an additional 2 percent for every year earlier than age 60. If you retire early—and about three-fourths of all working people currently approaching retirement do—your anticipated full monthly benefits could be cut sharply.

Early retirement reduces monthly benefits but may result in greater lifetime benefits.

Whether early retirement is financially beneficial will depend on life expectancy and the rate at which benefits are reduced. In the case illustrated in Table 22.4, retirement between ages 60 and 65 appears to have little impact on lifetime benefits received, but earlier retirement does have an impact. Of course, the general rule that funds obtained earlier are better than funds obtained later applies here. If you expect to live less than the average expectancy, you may be better off financially by retiring early. The opposite is true if your family history or health status indicates an extremely long life. Most employees are legally allowed to work for as long as they choose, but companies generally do not increase benefits to those who postpone retirement beyond age 65.

TABLE 22.4

Impact of Early Retirement on Monthly and Expected Lifetime Pension Benefits (Woman Retiree with a $1000 Monthly Benefit at Age 65)

Age at Retirement	Monthly Benefit	Life Expectancy in Months	Projected Lifetime Benefits
65	$1,000	208	$208,000
62	880	236	207,680
60	800	255	204,000
55	500	304	152,000

Most employee-sponsored retirement plans provide disability and survivors' benefits as well.

Disability and Survivors' Benefits The prospect of financial security during retirement is heartening, but disability and survivors' benefits are also of concern to workers who are married and/or parents. A retirement plan with disability benefits usually provides payments to employees if they become disabled while still working for the firm. The benefits are normally determined by a worker's present income, life expectancy, contributions to the retirement plan so far, and expected amount of income from Social Security.

A retirement plan with survivors' benefits must provide for retirement benefits to a surviving spouse in the event of the death of a fully vested worker. This can be waived if desired, however. For example, if you cancel your spousal benefit before retirement, your spouse will not receive any benefits upon your death, but during your retirement years your monthly benefit will be higher. This is because when a given benefit is changed to cover two people instead of one, the monthly payment must be less. Unless your spouse has his or her own retirement benefits, it is usually wise to keep the spousal benefit. Furthermore, federal law requires that a spouse or ex-spouse who qualifies for benefits under your plan *must* agree in writing to a waiver of the spousal benefit.

Other Types of Employer-Sponsored Retirement Plans

In addition to employer pension plans, many employers offer other benefit plans to employees that can be used to help with retirement expenses. Four such plans are salary-reduction plans, nonqualified deferred-compensation plans, employee stock-ownership plans (ESOPs), and profit-sharing plans.

401(k) and 403(b) plans are among the most effective retirement planning tools.

Salary-Reduction Plans A **salary reduction plan,** also known as a **401(k) plan** [and a similar 403(b) plan discussed below], is an employer-sponsored defined-contribution, contributory retirement savings plan in which employees divert a portion of their salary to a tax-sheltered savings account, where it accumulates tax-free. Some employers match money saved by employees dollar for dollar; an easy way to double your money. With the 401(k) plan (named after that section of the tax code), employees of

What If You Want to Know More about Your Employer-Sponsored Pension Plan?

As you plan for retirement, find out as much as you can about your company's pension plan by asking the following questions:

1. When is an employee eligible to participate in the plan? Is the plan optional or required?

2. Is the plan a defined-benefit or defined-contribution plan?

3. How do employees become vested?

4. Is the plan contributory or noncontributory? How much do the company and employee contribute?

5. Is the plan insured by the Pension Benefit Guaranty Corporation (PBGC)?

6. Can the plan be discontinued by the company? Can it be changed? How?

7. Are benefits calculated from final average pay or career earnings?

8. Are benefits integrated with Social Security benefits? How?

9. Where are the funds invested? Does the company publish investment reports?

10. What is the earliest retirement age, and what are the reductions for early retirement or increases for late retirement?

11. Are retirement benefits guaranteed for life once you are retired?

12. What are the survivors' and disability benefits?

13. What are the procedures for applying for benefits?

private corporations may contribute up to $7979 (in 1990 and adjusted for inflation thereafter) per year with the combined employee-employer contributions not to exceed $30,000 or 24 percent of income, whichever is less. Eligible employees of nonprofit organizations (schools, universities, hospitals, religious organizations, and others) may contribute up to $9500 to a similar 403(b) salary-reduction plan (also known as a *tax-sheltered annuity plan*) with the same $30,000 overall maximum. The funds contributed each year by the employee are in effect a reduction in income subject to tax and, along with any employer contributions, accumulate tax-free until they are withdrawn at retirement. The funds may be administered directly by the employer or be invested in annuities or mutual funds. Often the employee has several investment options from which to choose and is allowed to switch within a family of mutual funds.

You can accumulate substantial retirement funds by using a salary-reduction plan. For example, if your contribution of $1200 per year in such a fund was matched 100 percent by your employer for 25 years at an interest rate of 7 percent, it would amount to $151,800 (from Appendix A3, the calculation is $2400 × 63.25). Because early withdrawals (prior to age 59½) are subject to income tax and a 10 percent penalty, you should only place funds that you will not need until retirement in a

401(k) or 403(b) plan. These plans can provide substantial tax benefits when saving for retirement. Over one-third of the nation's full-time workers in medium-sized and large organizations are enrolled in 401(k) or 403(b) salary-reduction plans. And most employers match employee contributions to some extent.

Nonqualified Deferred-Compensation Plans   A **nonqualified deferred-compensation plan** is an approved process under ERISA regulations that permits an employee and employer to agree to defer large payments for services rendered to a later date when the employee expects to be in a lower marginal tax bracket. Highly paid athletes and executives often prefer such arrangements and frequently request that some funds be paid to them during retirement years. Deferred income is also tax-exempt until received by the taxpayer.

ESOPs and profit-sharing tie the adequacy of your retirement income to the success of your company.

ESOPs and Profit-Sharing Plans   Two employer-sponsored retirement plans allow employees to benefit personally when their company does well. These plans are often used to supplement a defined-benefit or defined-contribution pension plan or they can be the only retirement plan offered by an employer. An **employee stock-ownership plan** (**ESOP**) is a qualified retirement plan that invests the retirement funds in the stock of the employing corporation. In effect, your retirement fund is comprised of stock in the company. If that stock does well, your retirement nest egg will grow significantly. Of course, the opposite can occur as well. **Profit-sharing plans** are defined-contribution pension plans that base the level of contributions into the plan on the level of profits achieved by the employer. In high-profit years, contributions will be high; conversely in low-profit years. The quality of life during your retirement is certainly at risk if an ESOP or profit-sharing plan is the only retirement plan offered by your employer, therefore additional alternatives should be considered.

Personal Pension Plans

Objective
To be able to explain the purposes and benefits of personal retirement plans.

Employer-sponsored retirement plans are not available to all workers. And even if you can take advantage of an employer-sponsored pension plan and possibly a salary-reduction plan, you are likely to fall short of adequately preparing for retirement. In both cases, you can take advantage of other retirement planning mechanisms, most of which can provide tax-shelter advantages: annuities, individual retirement accounts (IRAs), Keogh plans, and simplified employee pension plans. These are all discussed below.

Annuities

Annuities provide a stream of income.

An **annuity** is a contract that provides for a series of payments to be received at stated intervals (usually monthly) for a fixed or variable time period. Annuities are usually sold by life insurance companies and are often described as being the opposite of life insurance because they provide funds during life, not after death. If you purchase an annuity, you deposit funds with an insurance company, where the funds grow as interest is earned and, possibly, more funds are deposited. Then, at a date specified in the contract, the annuity begins providing a stream of payments while you, the **annuitant** (the person receiving the annuity), are alive, often for the remainder of your life. For example, on his sixty-fifth birthday, Bob Fetsch, a retired tree farmer from Fort Collins, Colorado, purchased a "straight life" annuity for $10,000. The annuity pays him $95 per month and will do so for as long as he lives.

The annuitant is the person who receives the annuity benefits.

Classification of Annuities   As with life insurance, there are many varieties of annuities. Some will pay for the remainder of your life; others pay only for a specified time period. Some are purchased in installments, while others are paid for in a lump sum. With some the proceeds stay fixed, but with others the proceeds vary. There are five ways of classifying annuities: (1) by method of purchase, (2) by the variability of the rate of return and amount of the payments, (3) according to the plan for the payment of proceeds, (4) by the number of annuitants, and (5) by when benefits begin. Figure 22.2 provides a diagram of these classifications, and the following discussion expands on the diagram.

Method of Purchase   Annuities can be purchased with a single payment or with a series of payments. **Single-premium annuities** are purchased with a single lump-sum payment. **Installment-premium annuities** are purchased with a series of premium payments. Proceeds do not begin until installments cease, and proceeds may be deferred even longer if desired. Some installment-premium annuities allow premium payments to vary as the purchaser's ability to pay and desires change. The payout amounts under these annuities will depend on the dollar amount of premiums paid and the amount of time the funds were left to earn interest before being drawn upon. People often use installment-premium annuities in retirement planning, buying them during their working years.

Variability of Annuity Payment   The funds deposited in annuities may grow at a fixed rate of interest stated in the contract. Similarly, the payments received once the annuitant begins drawing proceeds are fixed. With the volatility in interest rates in recent years, however, new annuity instruments have been developed that reflect changes in interest rates in the economy. These **variable annuities** provide for variable rates of return while the funds are building and variable payments once proceeds begin. Such annuity contracts usually specify that the current interest rate never fall below some specified minimum (guaranteed) rate, such as 6 percent. Each year, while the funds are accumulating, the annuitant is notified of the rate of return paid during the year and the current balance of the account that results from the year's growth. Some annuity plans permit splitting the funds into various proportions between fixed and variable annuities and even among various investment programs (stocks, bonds, and so forth). Usually you may shift from fixed to variable and among

The rate of return and the monthly proceeds may change for a variable annuity.

FIGURE 22.2
Classifying Annuities

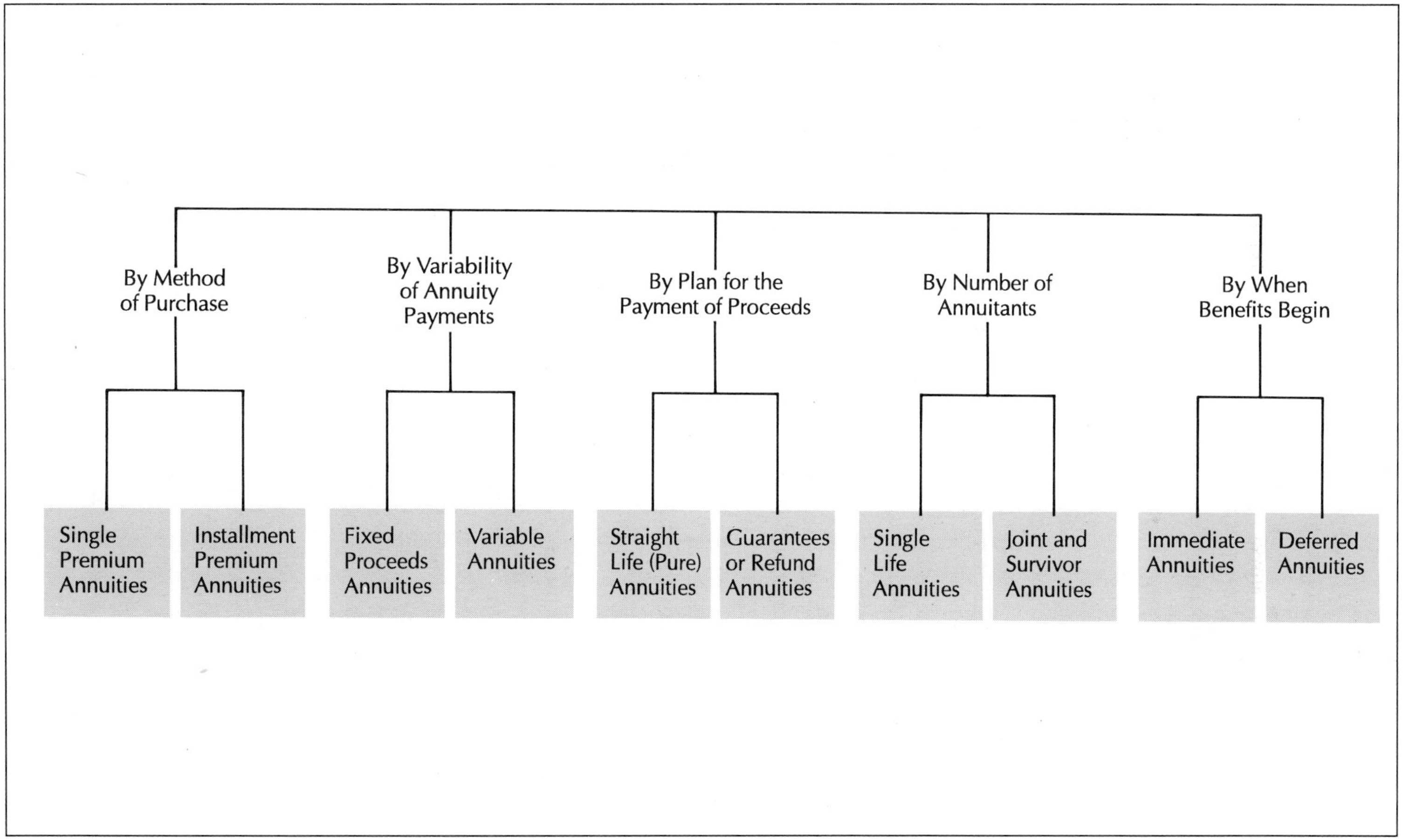

investment plans at your discretion. Once variable annuity payments begin, they will vary upward or downward according to the success of the insurance company's investments. For example, as an annuitant, you might receive $125 per month for the first year, and this amount might rise to $135 as the company's investments increase in value as a result of a bull market or drop to $115 in a bear market. Ideally, you would shift your annuity funds out of stocks and into bonds before a bear market proceeded too far to keep the payments up to perhaps $120.

Payment of Proceeds The simplest kind of annuity is a **straight life (pure) annuity,** which pays a fixed amount per month until the annuitant dies. The preceding example for Bob Fetsch illustrates a straight life annuity. Note that if Bob lived the average number of months (from Table 14.1 on page 487 we determine that a 65-year-old man has a life expectancy of 168 months) past age 65, he would collect $15,960 (168 × $95) in return for the payment of the $10,000 premium. The extra $5960 results from the interest earned on the premium paid while it is being held by the insurance company, since it pays out only $95 at a time.

Income payments cease at death with a straight life annuity.

With a straight life annuity, the annuitant will receive payments until death. If the annuitant dies after only 10 months, the contract ends and payments cease. If the annuitant lives well beyond the average life expectancy, payments will continue unaffected. The money the insurance company "saves" from those who die early is used to make the lifetime payments to those who live a long time. You can see, then, that an annuity can serve as protection against outliving your assets and can be an important retirement planning tool. The main problem with annuities is that, like cash-value life insurance, they often pay a low effective rate of return.

Straight life annuities are unattractive to many people because payments may cease well before all the money invested has been paid out to the annuitant. In response, several variations of *guaranteed* or *refund annuities* have been developed. An **installments-certain annuity** guarantees a minimum number of payments (installments) to the annuitant and/or to a beneficiary even if the annuitant dies before the minimum number of installments are paid. A **cash-refund annuity** pays the beneficiary a lump sum if the annuitant dies before collecting at least the premium paid. With both of these types of annuities, the annuitant would continue to receive payments for life. Because the insurance company must pay some minimum amount under each of these two variations, the monthly proceeds are lower than for an otherwise equivalent straight life annuity. A third variation, the **period-certain annuity,** provides payments to the annuitant, or a beneficiary if the annuitant should die early, for a fixed time period. At the end of the time period, the payments would cease even if the annuitant survives. If the time period specified is sufficiently short, the payments may be higher than for an equivalent straight life annuity.

A period-certain annuity pays benefits for a predetermined time period.

Number of Annuitants Most annuities are **single life annuities,** which cover the life of a single annuitant. Even annuities that provide proceeds to a beneficiary are single life annuities because everything hinges on the life span of the original annuitant. Several annuitants may be covered

Joint and survivor annu-
ities are designed for
married couples.

under one annuity contract, however. Most often, this involves a husband/
wife combination and the use of a **joint and survivor annuity,** which pays
proceeds until the death of both annuitants. Sometimes the payment is
reduced when the first annuitant dies (this allows for higher payments
while both are alive), but payments will continue throughout the life of
the second annuitant. When there are more than two annuitants, payments
will continue until the death of the last surviving annuitant.

When Benefits Begin   Annuities may be classified as either immediate
or deferred. An **immediate annuity** provides for payments to begin at the
end of the first month or year after final payment of the premium. For
example, an immediate annuity providing monthly payments of $400 for
life for a 65 year-old male will generate its first payment 30 days after
payment of the $40,000 premium. Immediate annuities are often used as
a means of distributing the proceeds of a life insurance policy (see Chapter
14) or a lump-sum pension plan distribution. Most annuities are **deferred
annuities,** which do not begin to pay off until a specified time period
elapses or an event, such as a sixtieth birthday or retirement, occurs.
People often use deferred annuities in retirement planning.

Using Annuities in Retirement Planning   Many people use annuities as
a means of saving for retirement. There are two tax advantages to using
an annuity as opposed to simply putting money in the bank. First, you
can buy annuities with the funds in a 401(k) or 403(b) supplemental
retirement plan. These **tax-sheltered annuities** can be used to shelter the
funds used to buy the annuity from taxation until the funds are withdrawn
during retirement. Second, the *earnings* from all annuity funds are sheltered
from taxation until they are withdrawn. This feature enhances the compounding aspect of annuities. Do not buy annuities simply to shelter
earnings until all other avenues for sheltering contributions [401(k), 403(b),
IRA, Keogh, and so on] have been exhausted.

Be careful when purchasing annuities because contract provisions can
be complicated as a result of the many ways of classifying annuities.
Further, the tax considerations make it difficult to compare the rate of
return you are being promised with that for other investment alternatives.
A final warning relates to the fact that many annuities have front-end and
back-end loads similar to those for some mutual funds. These loads will
affect the true rate of return you will receive. Federal regulations require
that every variable annuity prospectus include a table outlining costs
associated with purchase of the annuity.

Individual Retirement Accounts

If neither you nor your
spouse is covered by an
employer-sponsored plan,
you should use an IRA.

An **individual retirement account (IRA)** allows many people who earn
income to make tax-deductible payments (even if they do not itemize
deductions on their income tax returns) to their own personal investment
fund held by a bank, mutual fund, insurance company, or other trustee.
It is a special account created by Congress to encourage people with no
other pension to save for retirement. However, you may be able to open

one even if you participate in a retirement plan at your workplace. All employed people not covered by an employer-sponsored tax-sheltered (qualified) retirement plan (married workers are considered covered if the spouse is covered by such a plan) are eligible to make tax-deductible IRA contributions during any year in which they earn compensation. The maximum tax-deductible contribution is $2000 or the amount of compensation earned, whichever is less. A married couple may contribute up to $4000 annually if each of them earns $2000. The nonworking spouse of a working person can set up a spousal account as long as a combined maximum of $2250 for both spouses is not exceeded. The $2250 can be divided in any way as long as one account is not above $2000.

A worker who is considered covered by a tax-sheltered employer-sponsored retirement plan may or may not be able to shelter IRA contributions. The level of allowable tax-sheltered contributions depends on the amount of the adjusted gross income *(AGI)* for federal income tax purposes. Single workers with an *AGI* below $25,000 and married workers with a joint *AGI* below $40,000 may shelter IRA contributions up to $2000. For those with AGIs above these amounts, the allowable contribution is reduced $1 for each $5 increase in income until the allowable contribution is entirely phased out at $35,000 for single workers and $50,000 for married workers. For example, a single worker with an adjusted gross income of $30,000 would be able to shelter $1000 in IRA contributions [$2000 − ($30,000 − $25,000/5 × 1)].

Having an IRA is a tax bargain for two reasons. First, you may use the funds you deposit into the IRA account as a reduction in your taxable income. Second, the income generated by the account over the years is not subject to taxation until it is withdrawn during retirement, thereby enhancing the power of compounding as more money is left to generate income. This sheltering of IRA investment income from taxation exists whether the money deposited in the IRA is used as a tax deduction or not. Figure 22.3 illustrates the difference between taxable and nontaxable returns for investments earning the same return. After 30 years, the IRA account totals $297,200 (only $60,000 of which is the worker's contribution and the remainder is interest). A taxable account would total $183,300, having grown to only 61.7 percent of the IRA account. Note that the effects of compounding are small in the early years but quite large in later years, which demonstrates the importance of starting an IRA early.

The law sets no minimum amount for an IRA; further, you could contribute to an IRA account once and never contribute again. IRAs also can be used to shelter lump-sum pension plan distributions [from a company pension, a 401(k), or a Keogh plan, which is discussed below], which would be taxable if no tax had been paid as funds were deposited in the original pension plan. This type of deposit into an IRA is known as a **rollover IRA.** You can roll over all or part of the lump-sum distribution, although the portion not rolled over will be subject to income taxation.

If you withdraw funds before you turn 59½, you must pay a 10 percent tax penalty, and the amount of your withdrawal is considered ordinary income for tax purposes. You must begin withdrawing money from your IRA by April 1 of the year after you turn 70½ and withdraw at a rate

The tax deductibility of IRA contributions may be limited for those covered by an employer-sponsored plan, but contributions still grow tax free.

FIGURE 22.3

IRA vs. Taxable Returns (Assumes 9 Percent Annual Rate of Return and $2000 Annual Contribution)

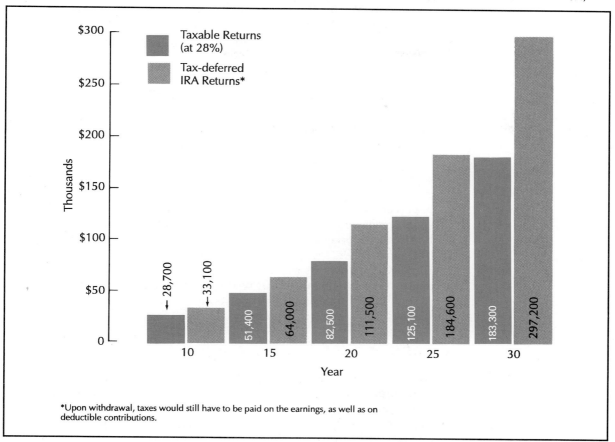

*Upon withdrawal, taxes would still have to be paid on the earnings, as well as on deductible contributions.

that will completely deplete the funds during your remaining life expectancy. This rule was set up to prevent people from using an IRA to pass funds tax-free to heirs.

You can simply place IRA funds in a savings account at a bank, savings and loan association, or credit union, or you can look for greater return in a money market fund, mutual fund, or insurance company annuity. You also can open a self-directed account with a brokerage firm and invest in stocks, bonds, and precious metals. Moving IRA funds from one type of account to another can be tax-free, but be sure to find out if your financial institution will charge you a fee for the transfer. Many experts advocate placing IRA funds in a family of no-load mutual funds (see Chapter 18), since this allows you to put dollars into a money market fund when interest rates are high and to transfer amounts to growth-focused mutual funds when interest rates decline and the values of stocks begin to go up. This kind of fund shifting does not take a particularly sophisticated investment approach, but it requires an alertness to broad economic events. This raises a final point: You should consider the management demands of your IRA investment vehicle. If you want to sock the money away and forget it, consider certificates of deposit and long-term zero-coupon bonds. If you want to manage your IRA more closely, consider stock and bond mutual funds.

Keogh Plans

A Keogh plan can be used to tax shelter self-employment income.

A **Keogh plan** (also called **HR-10**) allows self-employed people to make tax-deductible payments for themselves and their eligible employees to a pension plan fund held by a trustee who, in certain circumstances, could be the self-employed person. You may contribute up to the lower of 25 percent of earned income or $30,000 to a defined contribution plan. Earned income is net earnings from self-employment less the deductible Keogh contribution. Thus, the maximum Keogh contribution is reduced to 20 percent of net income before Keogh contributions. Both contributions to Keogh plans and earnings on assets are tax-free until withdrawal. Again, withdrawals before age 59½ are penalized; however, contributions can still be made after age 70½. Keogh investors face the same investment decisions as IRA owners but can also own real estate. Any income earned through self-employment such as writing, consulting, or child care qualifies for Keogh contributions and deductibility. It is possible for someone to have an IRA, a salary-reduction plan, and a Keogh.

Simplified Employee Pension Plans

A **simplified employee pension plan** (SEP) is a special retirement plan for the self-employed and their employees. With an SEP, a person can make tax-sheltered contributions of 15.0 percent of net self-employment income up to a maximum of $30,000. If the self-employed person also has employees, they too will be covered under the SEP. The reporting requirements for SEPs are less strict than for a Keogh plan. The investment alternatives for an SEP are more flexible than for a Keogh. It is possible for someone to have a salary-reduction plan, an IRA, and a SEP.

Understanding Social Security Retirement Benefits

Objective
To be able to describe how to qualify for the Social Security retirement program and the role Social Security plays in retirement planning.

In 1935, President Franklin D. Roosevelt signed the Social Security Act and commented that "we have tried to frame a law which will give some measure of protection to the average citizen and to his family . . . against poverty-ridden old age." The Social Security program continues today, with more than 45 million pension, survivor, and disability checks mailed monthly.

What If You Want to Use Your Qualified Retirement Funds Early?

Throughout this chapter we have mentioned that withdrawing tax-sheltered retirement funds prior to age 59½ exposes one to a potential 10 percent penalty as well as taxation of the funds as ordinary income. There is no way to avoid the taxation aspects. Funds that go into or grow in a retirement fund tax-free will be subject to income taxation whenever they are withdrawn. However, it may be possible to gain access to the funds and avoid the 10 percent penalty. This is almost always true if you become totally disabled. Three other mechanisms also are available under IRS rules. Note that even when IRS rules allow you to avoid a penalty, your employer may have rules that restrict withdrawals whether you pay a penalty or not.

1. *Borrow money from the retirement fund.* You may borrow money from your 401(k) or 403(b) plan without paying a penalty. Borrowing limits are $10,000 for accounts with $10,000 or less in them or 50 percent if the account has more than $10,000, with an overall maximum loan of $50,000. The money must be repaid in 5 years. You may borrow from a Keogh plan by paying a 5 percent rather than 10 percent penalty. You cannot borrow from an IRA or use an IRA account as collateral for a loan.

2. *Money may be withdrawn under certain hardship conditions.* You can withdraw money from a 401(k), 403(b), or Keogh for hardships such as a funeral, medical expenses, tuition, and a down payment on a home. However, you must prove that you have exhausted all other sources of funds and have been turned down for loans to meet the expense. Hard-ship withdrawals are not allowed from an IRA.

3. *Early retirement.* If you retire past age 55 but before age 59½, you may withdraw funds from a 401(k), 403(b), or Keogh plan without payment of a penalty. You will not avoid the penalty if you are under age 59½ and still working for the employer under whom the plan was established. You *must* be retired. If you are under age 55, rules of your employer's plan might allow you to take the money out of the plan and use the lump sum to establish a rollover IRA (see page 772), thereby qualifying for a special IRA early withdrawal opportunity. That is, you may withdraw funds from an IRA account without penalty prior to age 59½ *if* you take the money in substantially equal periodic payments designed to last the rest of your life. This concept is very similar to a straight life annuity. You must continue to receive the payments for a minimum of 5 years or until age 59½, whichever is longer. Once past the 5 years or age 59½, you can change the payout rate to fit your income needs.

As you can see, these penalty-free early uses of retirement funds are extremely complicated. And you cannot avoid the taxation aspects. In some cases, it might be advantageous to take monies out of an employer-sponsored account (if allowed under your employer's rules) or an IRA even if you have to pay the penalty. This is most likely to be true if the account has been in effect for more than 10 years. Always consult a qualified accountant, a financial planner, or tax specialist when considering such opportunities.

FIGURE 22.4
How Social Security Works

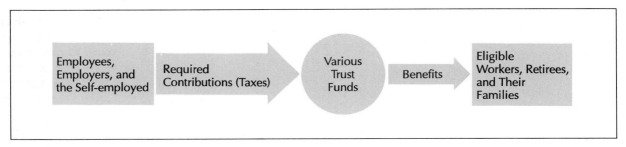

Numerous changes in the program and increases in benefits have occurred through the years, but the focus has remained the same: to provide Americans with minimum, not adequate, protection against the loss of income from retirement, disability, or death of a family wage earner. As the baby-boom generation moves into retirement, the ability of the Social Security system to meet Americans' retirement needs will be challenged. The modern Social Security program is a compilation of 11 social programs, including social insurance, public assistance, welfare services, and children's benefits. In this section we will examine Social Security from the perspective of retirement benefits.

Funding for Social Security benefits comes from a payroll tax split equally between employee and employer. It is a mandatory program, and the Social Security taxes withheld from your wages are called FICA taxes (for Federal Insurance Contributions Act). Amounts withheld are deposited in the Social Security trust fund accounts. Figure 22.4 illustrates how the Social Security system works. Social Security benefits constitute one of the most important assets in the life of a wage earner.

Making Contributions to Social Security

Social Security contributions are actually a tax not a deposit into a personal account.

Social Security "contributions," in reality, are taxes. In 1949 the maximum annual contribution by a worker was $30, in 1959 it was $120, in 1969 it was $374.40, and in 1979 it was $1403.77. Congress frequently raises both the tax rate and the earnings base. Wage earners pay Social Security taxes on wage income up to the **maximum taxable yearly earnings.** This is the base amount to which the full Social Security tax rate is applied, and it determines the maximum amount due for most wage earners. High-income taxpayers pay a 1.45 percent Medicare surcharge on the portion of wage income from $54,300 to $125.000. The maximum taxable yearly earnings figure is adjusted each year for inflation.

For example, the Social Security tax rate in 1991 is 7.65 percent. To illustrate, the law requires that a person earning $25,000 pay $1912.50 ($25,000 × 0.0765), and a person earning $54,300 pay a Social Security tax of $4153.95 ($54,300 × 0.0765). Each of these amounts is matched by contributions (taxes) paid by the employer. Self-employed workers pay a tax rate of 15.3 percent (7.65 × 2) because their contributions are not matched by an employer. Thus a self-employed person pays a tax of $8,307.90 on earnings of $54,300 ($54,300 × 0.153) in 1991. The Medicare surcharge for high-income self-employed persons is 2.9 percent. Self-employed persons may deduct a portion of their FICA taxes from their taxable income for federal income tax purposes, however.

Increases in the Social Security tax have been made in recent years to ensure that the system remains financially solvent. Increases have been needed because (1) people are living longer (22 percent of the population will be age 65 and over by the year 2025) and retiring earlier; (2) inflation has pushed up costs, since many benefits are legally tied to increases in the consumer price index; (3) greater and more liberal benefits have been granted by Congress to Social Security recipients; and (4) there have been stubborn problems in the economy. In addition, the ratio of people paying in to the system and people receiving benefits has changed dramatically over the years. In 1950, for example, there were 16 workers for every person receiving benefits; today there are only 3.2 workers. Projections suggest that in 2025 there will be only 2 workers for every person receiving benefits. In effect, the Social Security retirement system is an intergenerational contract that says that current workers support current retirees in return for a promise that the current workers will be supported when they retire by the workers of that day.

Social Security tax payments of future workers will fund the retirement benefits of today's workers.

Who Can Receive Social Security Retirement Benefits?

When a worker retires, various members of his or her family can receive benefits: the retiree; unmarried children under 18, or 19 if still in high school; unmarried children 18 or over who were severely disabled before age 22 and who are still disabled; retiree's spouse if aged 62 or over; and retiree's spouse under age 62 if caring for a child under 16 (or over 16 and disabled) who is receiving benefits. Electing to delay receipt of Social Security benefits beyond age 65 results in a monthly benefit adjustment of plus 3 percent for each year (one-quarter of 1 percent for each month). Starting in 1990, the adjustment will be gradually increased until it reaches a total of 8 percent per year in 2008.

Social Security retirement benefits can be received as early as age 62, but if you start receiving benefits before age 65, your benefit rate is permanently reduced to take account of the longer period of likely benefits. The size of the reduction depends on when you begin receiving benefits. For example, there is a reduction of 20 percent at age 62, 13⅓ percent at age 63, and 6⅔ percent at age 64. Thus someone who would be entitled to a monthly benefit of $800 at age 65 would only receive $640 ($800 − 20 percent) per month if he chose to start receiving benefits at age 62. Starting in 2000, the full-benefit age will be gradually increased until it reaches 67 in 2027. This change affects people born after 1937.

The Social Security full-benefit retirement age will be gradually increased beginning in the year 2000.

Qualifying for Social Security Benefits

Nine out of every 10 Americans employed in this country are covered by the Social Security program. Some federal, state, and local government employees are exempt because their employers have set up other plans. To qualify for benefits, you need credit for a certain amount of employment in any work covered by Social Security, including part-time and temporary employment, and the employment need not be consecutive. Military service also provides credits. **Quarters of coverage** are calendar units credited by the Social Security Administration (SSA) based on a minimum total earnings in a calendar year. For example, in 1990 workers received 1 quarter of coverage if they earned $515 and the annual maximum of 4 quarters of coverage if they earned $2060 (4 × $515). The dollar figure for each quarter is raised annually to keep up with inflation.

It is important that your earnings records with the Social Security Administration (SSA) be up to date and accurate. A **personal earnings and benefit estimate statement,** the SSA's record of your lifetime earnings covered under Social Security regulations, can be requested at any time from the SSA (Box 57, Baltimore, MD 21203). The information will help you calculate an estimate of benefits and enable you to compare it with your personal records for any discrepancies. You have only 3 years to correct errors.

The number of quarters of coverage determines your eligibility for benefits. The Social Security Administration has four statuses of eligibility (listed below), and Table 22.5 shows the length of work requirements for benefits.

1. *Fully insured.* This status requires 40 quarters of coverage for people born after 1929 and provides the worker and/or family with benefits under the retirement, survivors', and disability programs. Once obtained, this status cannot be lost even if the person never works again. Fully insured status is required to receive retirement benefits. Fully insured does not imply that full benefits will be received, since the dollar amount of benefits also depends on the level of earnings during the working years.

2. *Currently insured.* This status requires that 6 quarters of coverage be earned in the most recent 3 years and provides for some survivors' or disability benefits but no retirement benefits. To remain eligible for survivors' and disability benefits, workers must continue to earn at least 6 quarters every 3 years or meet a minimum number of covered years of work established by the Social Security Administration.

3. *Transitionally insured.* This status applies only to workers who reach the age of 72 without accumulating 40 quarters (10 years) of credit. They are eligible for limited benefits.

4. *Not insured.* This status applies to workers who have less than 6 quarters of credited work experience and are under age 72.

TABLE 22.5
Length of Work Requirements for Social Security Benefits

Type of Benefits	Payable to	Minimum Years of Work under Social Security
Retirement	You, your spouse, child, dependent spouse 62 or over	10 years (fully insured status) (If age 62 prior to 1991, you may need only 7¾ to 9¾ years.)
Survivors*		
Full	Widow(er) 60 or over, disabled widow(er) 50–59, widow(er) if caring for child 18 years or younger, dependent children, dependent widow(er) 62 or over, disabled dependent widow(er) 50–61, dependent parent at 62	10 years (fully insured status)
Current	Widow(er) caring for child 18 years or younger, dependent children	1½ years of last 3 years before death (currently insured status)
Disability	You and your dependents	If under age 24, you need 1½ years of work in the 3 years prior to disablement; if between ages 24 and 31, you need to work half the time between when you turned 21 and your date of disablement; if age 31 or older, you must have 5 years of credit during the 10 years prior to disablement.
Medicare		
Hospitalization (Part A: Automatic benefits)	Anyone 65 or over plus some others, such as the disabled	Anyone qualified for the Social Security retirement program is qualified for Medicare Part A at age 65; others may qualify by paying a monthly premium for Part A.
Medical expense (Part B: Voluntary benefits)	Anyone eligible for Part A and anyone else 65 or over (payment of monthly premiums required)	No prior work under Social Security is required.

Source: U.S. Department of Health and Human Services, 1990.

* A lump-sum death benefit no greater than $255 is also granted to dependents of those either fully or currently insured.

Calculating the Dollar Amount of Social Security Benefits

There are two methods of calculating Social Security benefits, the indexing method and the old method. Since 1984, laws require use of the **indexing method,** which revalues previous wage earnings in terms of current wage levels by multiplying each year's income by an index factor announced

Request a personal earnings and benefits statement every three to five years.

annually by the Social Security Administration. One result of indexing is that it is possible only to "guesstimate" retirement benefits, since the indexing formula for future years is unknown; in 1990, the maximum basic monthly benefit was $975 for those retiring at age 65 and $780 for those retiring at age 62. These dollar figures increase every year due to indexing for inflation. A current estimate for you can be obtained from the personal earnings and benefits statement. The amount of Social Security benefits subject to income tax is 50 percent of excess over the base amount ($25,000 for singles and $32,000 for marrieds) or 50 percent of benefits, which ever is less. Thus, for every dollar of extra earnings above the $25,000 or $32,000 base, 50 cents of Social Security benefits are taxable.

The second approach to determining Social Security benefits is the *old method*. This method, applicable for persons reaching age 62 prior to 1979 and optional for those reaching age 62 in 1979–1983, uses current dollars to determine Social Security monthly payments. Because the old method will eventually be phased out, we suggest you contact your local Social Security office if this method applies to you or someone of interest to you.

Supplemental Security Income Program

If you do not qualify for Social Security, if you have not been able to plan financially for retirement, or if you have had health problems that wiped out all your assets, the federal **supplemental security income (SSI)** program might provide you with limited monetary benefits. To qualify, you must have no more than $1500 in cash ($2250 for a couple), but you can own your home, automobile, and personal belongings of reasonable value. Most states pay a supplemental benefit in addition to the federal SSI payments.

Retirement Planning Illustrated

Objective
To be able to estimate the dollar amount you should be putting away for retirement utilizing a detailed example.

Knowing your annual retirement expenditures in current dollars (see Table 22.1) and being knowledgeable about the sources of income that might support these expenditures leads logically to the question of how much money must be set aside now to provide that support. Figure 22.5 provides a worksheet that can be used to arrive at this amount. The following steps use the worksheet to provide an example of how a worker might arrive at the amount that would need to be saved each year. Couples also could use the worksheet by simply combining their dollar amounts where appropriate. We will consider the case of William Handy, age 32 and single, who is a medical lab technician for a small firm in Taos, New Mexico. Bill currently earns $36,000 per year and has worked for his employer since age 24. He plans to retire at age 62.

1. Bill has chosen not to try to develop a retirement budget at this time. Instead, he multiplied his salary by 70 percent to arrive at an annual income (in current dollars) needed in retirement of $25,200 ($36,000 × 0.70). This amount was entered on line 1 of Figure 22.5.

Investment Advice for the Conservative Retiree

Investments during your retirement years should focus on a single objective: protection of income. No longer can you afford to make speculative investments, since you do not have the years left to recoup from poor investment decisions. Retirees would do well to review Table 15.2 on page 548, which describes eight types of risks of 10 different forms of investments. At this stage in their lives, retired investors need to reduce risks due to inflation and to market volatility. Taxes will be less important in investment choices because retirees generally pay somewhat lower income taxes.

You can take three specific actions to increase your income from investments during retirement: (1) convert non-income-producing or low-income-producing assets into investments with optimum yields (sell a rental property and put the proceeds into high-yielding corporate bonds), (2) convert tax-exempt earnings into higher-yield taxables (sell a municipal bond and put proceeds into a money-market fund, assuming interest rates are high), and (3) invade your capital assets to use the funds (cash a $10,000 certificate of deposit to pay living expenses). It also would be wise to own stocks with high dividend payouts and bonds with high coupons and to sell real estate for monthly installment payments. As a result of these moves, a conservative retiree might have an investment portfolio of cash and CDs (35 percent), real estate (25 percent), income stocks (25 percent), and bonds (15 percent).

2. Bill called the Social Security Administration to obtain his personal earnings and benefit estimate statement. The statement showed that at age 62 he could expect a monthly benefit in current dollars of $800. Multiplying by 12 gave him an expected annual Social Security benefit of $9600 in current dollars, which he entered on line 2 of Figure 22.5.

3. Line 3 of Figure 22.5 calls for Bill's expected pension benefit. This line is appropriate for defined-benefit plans and other employer-sponsored plans. Bill is covered by a plan through his employer that would provide 25 percent of his preretirement annual income. Because Figure 22.5 uses current dollars, Bill multiplied 0.25 times his $36,000 salary to arrive at a retirement benefit in current dollars of $9000 (0.25 × $36,000) and entered that figure on line 3.

4. Bill adds lines 2 and 3 to determine his expected income from retirement benefits. The amount on line 4 would be $18,600 ($9,600 + $9,000).

5. Subtracting line 4 from line 1 reveals that Bill would need an additional income of $6600 ($25,200 − $18,600) from a savings and investment plan in order to meet his annual retirement income needs.

6. So far Bill has only considered his annual needs and benefits. Yet, because he will retire at age 62, Bill will need income for over 16 years based on his life expectancy (from Table 14.1). And it is likely

ιunning the Numbers on Retirement," *Fall Money Guide*, p. 29. Reprinted from
ιagazine by special permission; copyright 1989 The Time Inc. Magazine Com-

Running the numbers on retirement

This worksheet will help you estimate how much you must save each year for retirement. It assumes that your investments will earn 3% after inflation, about the historical average for a conservative portfolio of stocks, bonds and cash. For extra safety, the worksheet also assumes that you will live 10 years beyond the life expectancy of a 65-year-old in 1989. All amounts are in today's dollars. If you are less than 10 years from leaving work, update your calculation annually. If retirement is further off, do so every two years.

1 Annual income needed in retirement (Transfer your estimated living costs in retirement from the worksheet on page 22. If you haven't completed that worksheet and want only a rough estimate, use 70% of your current income.) **$25,200**

2 Expected Social Security benefit (Call the Social Security Administration at 800-234-5772 for a projection of your benefit. Or use one of these ball park estimates: $10,788 if you make more than $48,000, or an amount between $9,300 and $10,788 if your earnings are between $25,000 and $48,000.) **$9,600**

3 Expected pension benefit (Ask your benefits counselor at work to estimate your future pension, assuming that your salary remains the same until you retire. For a rough estimate, multiply 1.5% of your salary by the number of years you plan to stay on the job and then subtract half your projected Social Security benefit.) **$9,000**

4 Expected income from retirement benefits (line 2 plus line 3) **$18,600**

5 Annual retirement income needed from savings and investments (line 1 minus line 4) **$6,600**

6 Amount you must save by retirement in today's dollars (line 5 times multiplier from line A below) **$133,320**

7 Amount you have saved already:

a IRAs and Keoghs	**b** Employer savings plans (Include vested amounts in 401(k)s, ESOPs, SEPs and profit-sharing plans.)	**c** Other investments (Include all CDs, mutual funds, bonds, stocks, investment real estate and any other assets available for retirement.)	**d** (Optional) If you wish to count a portion of your home's value as savings, enter its present value minus the anticipated cost of a new home in retirement.	**e** Total retirement savings (add lines a through d)
$0	**$3,300**	**$5,000**	**$0**	**$8,300**

8 Value of your retirement savings at the time you retire (line 7e times multiplier from line B below) **$20,169**

9 Amount of retirement capital still needed (line 6 minus line 8) **$113,151**

10 Total annual savings still needed (line 9 times multiplier from line C below) **$2,376.17**

11 Annual employer contributions to your company savings plans (Include 401(k)s, ESOPs, SEPs and profit-sharing plans.) **$720.00**

12 Annual amount you need to set aside in today's dollars (line 10 minus line 11) **$1,656.17**

Age at retirement	55	56	57	58	59	60	61	62	63	64	65	66	67
Multiplier A	22.8	22.5	22.1	21.8	21.4	21.0	20.6	20.2	19.8	19.3	18.9	18.4	17.9

Years until retirement	1	3	5	7	9	11	13	15	20	25	30
Multiplier B	1.03	1.09	1.16	1.23	1.30	1.38	1.47	1.56	1.81	2.09	2.43
Multiplier C	1.00	.324	.188	.131	.098	.078	.064	.054	.037	.027	.021

It is best to plan on living at least ten years beyond the average life expectancy for your current age and gender.

that Bill could live into his eighties, thereby needing the inflation-adjusted equivalent of his annual retirement expenditures for over 20 years. Multiplier A in Figure 22.5 can be used to adjust the annual figure arrived at on line 5 so that funds would be available 10 years beyond Bill's life expectancy. He would enter $133,320 ($6600 × 20.2) on line 6 to determine the amount he must save (in current dollars) by age 62.

7. Some of Bill's current savings can be used to offset the $133,320 he will need for retirement. These savings could include any personal pension plans (IRAs and Keogh plans), employer salary-reduction and savings plans [401(k), 403(b), ESOPs, SEPs, and profit sharing], investments, and the equity in a home if it is to be liquidated in retirement. Bill has no IRA and does not own a home. His employer offers a 401(k) plan that calls for a maximum 2 percent employer contribution if Bill also contributes 2 percent. Bill is allowed to contribute another 5 percent unmatched by his employer, but he has been contributing the minimum 2 percent for 2 years. The 401(k) plan has accumulated $3300. This amount is entered on line 7b. Bill also recently inherited stocks worth $5000, which he wants to hold until retirement, so he entered that amount on line 7c. Accordingly, he entered $8300 ($0 + $3300 + $5000 + $0) on line 7e of Figure 22.5.

8. The $8300 that Bill has built up thus far will continue to earn interest until he retires. Using multiplier B from Figure 22.5, Bill estimates that the value of his current retirement savings at the time he retires will be $20,169 ($8300 × 2.43), and this amount is entered on line 8.

9. Bill will need a nest egg of $133,320 (in current dollars) and will have $20,169. Subtracting these figures reveals that $113,151 in additional retirement capital will be needed at retirement.

10. Bill can use multiplier C from Figure 22.5 to determine how much annual savings he will need to reach his goal. The amount is $2376.17 ($113,151 × 0.021), and this figure is entered on line 10.

11. Part of the annual savings Bill needs will be provided through his employer's contributions to his 401(k) plan. Currently, the employer's 2 percent contribution amounts to $720 ($36,000 × 0.02), so this figure is entered on line 11.

12. Now for the moment of truth. How much should Bill be putting away in current dollars? Subtracting line 11 ($720) from line 10 ($2376.17) reveals that Bill should be saving $1656.17 toward his retirement. Unfortunately, he is not very close to doing this. Recall that Bill is also contributing 2 percent or $720 to his 401(k) plan. Thus he is $936.17 ($1656.17 − $720) short, a considerable amount, actually.

There are two reasons why Bill is in such bad shape as he considers his retirement plan. First, although he committed his inheritance to his retirement rather than spending it for current consumption, he still has very little in savings, although if he had spent the inheritance, his shortfall would have been $255.15 greater. Second, he started a little late to ensure that part of his salary would go into a retirement fund and the percentage (4 percent = 2 percent from his employer + 2 percent of his own) is low. Bill should begin to catch up by contributing an additional $936.17 per year into his 401(k) plan. For safety, he could contribute an additional 3 percent ($1080) of his salary for a total of 5 percent, below the 7 percent allowed with his plan. Or Bill could contribute to an IRA, but this opportunity may be limited, since Bill's adjusted gross income likely exceeds the $25,000 adjusted gross income limit for a full $2000 tax-sheltered IRA contribution allowed for a single taxpayer.

Note that Bill needs to set aside $1656.17 in *current dollars* and must rely on the $720 in *current dollars* that his employer is contributing. These figures must increase each year so that his retirement nest egg will keep up with inflationary increases in his expected retirement expenditures. Because he and his employer are contributing a percentage of his income rather than a fixed amount, his savings will grow with inflation along with his salary. This feature of defined-contribution plans should not be underestimated and is a principal reason why they are generally better than defined-benefit plans. Always plan on putting away a percentage of your income rather than a specific dollar amount if you want to help neutralize the negative impact of inflation.

Summary

1. Planning for retirement includes estimating retirement expenses and sources of income during retirement.

2. The two advantages of qualified retirement plans are that the contributions are tax-deductible and taxes are deferred on earnings.

3. Analyzing your employer-sponsored pension plan, if any, is the basis for retirement planning. Such plans are regulated by the Employee Retirement Income Security Act (ERISA). Other employer-sponsored plans include salary-reduction plans, nonqualified deferred-compensation plans, employee stock-ownership plans, and profit-sharing plans.

4. Personal pension plans include annuities, individual retirement accounts, Keogh plans, and simplified employee pension plans.

5. Social Security retirement benefits are funded by worker- and employer-paid taxes and may provide an important but insufficient portion of income needed during retirement years.

6. Planning now for retirement can help you avoid the difficulty of having to accumulate the money needed for retirement in a hurry. The process begins with estimating retirement expenses and sources of income and ends with an estimate of the additional dollar amount you should be setting aside for retirement each year of your working life.

7. Investment strategies change during retirement, with emphasis placed on protection of income.

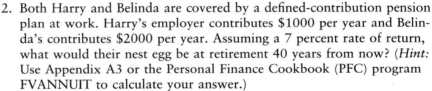

Modern Money Management

The Johnsons Consider Retirement Planning

Recently Harry Johnson's father, William, was forced into early retirement at age 63 because of poor health. In addition to the psychological impact of the unanticipated retirement, William's financial situation is not good because he had not planned for retirement. This has caused Harry and Belinda to take a look at their own retirement planning. They now make about $45,000 a year combined and would like to have a similar level of income when they retire. Harry and Belinda are both now 25 years old, and although retirement is a long way off, they know that the sooner they start a retirement plan, the larger their nest egg will be.

1. Belinda feels that they could maintain their current level of living if their retirement income represented 75 percent of their current income after adjusting for inflation. Assuming a 4 percent inflation rate, what would Harry and Belinda's income need to be at retirement at age 65? (*Hint:* Use Appendix A1 or the Personal Finance Cookbook (PFC) program FVSUM to calculate your answer.)

2. Both Harry and Belinda are covered by a defined-contribution pension plan at work. Harry's employer contributes $1000 per year and Belinda's contributes $2000 per year. Assuming a 7 percent rate of return, what would their nest egg be at retirement 40 years from now? (*Hint:* Use Appendix A3 or the Personal Finance Cookbook (PFC) program FVANNUIT to calculate your answer.)

3. For how many years would the nest egg provide the amount of income indicated in question 1? Assume a 4 percent after-tax and inflation return. (*Hint:* Use Appendix A4.)

4. Sometimes Harry likes to dream, and one of his dreams is to retire at age 55. What would the answers to questions 1, 2, and 3 be if he and Belinda were to retire at that age?

5. How would early retirement at age 55 affect their Social Security benefits?

6. What would you advise Harry and Belinda to do in order to meet their income needs for retirement?

Key Words and Concepts

annuitant, 768
annuity, 767
capital accumulation plan, 761

cash-refund annuity, 770
deferred annuities, 771
defined-benefit method, 761

Review Questions

1. Explain why it is important for people to begin planning for retirement when they are young.

2. Retirement expenses usually are about what percentage of preretirement expenses?

3. How might one go about estimating one's expenses during retirement?

4. What sources of income can retirees expect?

5. What is a tax-sheltered (qualified) retirement plan? In what two ways does such a plan help save on your income tax liability?

6. Describe how you can be a millionaire.

7. What federal law regulates company-sponsored retirement plans?

8. Distinguish between the defined-contribution method and the defined-benefit method as used in pension plans.

9. Why is vesting important to a person covered by a company-sponsored retirement plan? Distinguish between cliff vesting and graduated vesting.

10. Distinguish between contributory and noncontributory pension plans.

11. Define portability as a feature of pension plans.

12. What disadvantage arises when retirement benefits are integrated with Social Security benefits?

13. How might someone calculate the economic advantage or disadvantage of retiring early?

14. Explain why a salary-reduction plan may be an important part of the overall employee benefit program. What are the two types of salary-reduction plans?

15. Differentiate between an employee stock-ownership plan (ESOP) and a profit-sharing plan.

16. Describe how an annuity differs from life insurance. What are the five ways of classifying annuities?

17. Describe how annuities can be used in retirement planning?

18. What is an IRA, and how can it be used as a tax-sheltered retirement plan?

19. Who can make tax-sheltered contributions to an IRA?

20. Identify the special group of people for whom Keogh plans were devised.

21. Explain how one might qualify for an employer-sponsored retirement plan, an IRA, and a Keogh plan.

22. Describe how Social Security benefits are financed.

23. Besides the retired worker, which family members also can receive Social Security retirement benefits based on the retired worker's account?

24. How can you qualify to receive Social Security benefits? What are the four statuses of eligibility?

25. How can you get a statement of earnings from the Social Security Administration? Why is such a statement important?

26. What is the most important investment objective during retirement years?

Case Problems

1. Choosing a good job after finishing her formal education is a major objective for Marianna Kinard of Florence, South Carolina. She has many positions from which to select. Some are local, some within the state, and a few several hundred miles away. Marianna has been advised to choose a company that offers her not only a good salary, but also some good fringe benefits. Most of the companies that interviewed her offered similar salaries, but there was great variety in the type of pension plans available. Marianna was confused by terms such as *vesting, contributory, noncontributory, funded, unfunded,* and *defined benefit,* among others, and needs to spend time sorting them out so that she can decide where to take a job.

   a. Is Marianna overly concerned about the details of pension plans for her first job out of school? Why or why not?

   b. List some questions Marianna can ask to help her sort out the available plans.

c. What, in your opinion, are some characteristics that would make one pension plan more attractive than another? Justify each characteristic as a positive part of a pension plan.

2. Ben Dietrick of St. Louis, Missouri, age 35 and a confirmed bachelor, is busily making plans for his retirement. He is anxious to maintain his current lifestyle without "scrimping," yet he wants to actively start saving for his retirement to take advantage of compounding. Currently, Ben earns $40,000 a year with an adjusted gross income of $39,135 and an after-tax income of $28,750. He anticipates receiving $10,265 from Social Security annually, and another $12,865 in pension benefits upon retirement at age 65. At age 55, pension benefits are estimated at $9,500. To date, Ben has about $10,000 of investments.

   a. Using Figure 22.5, calculate the additional amount of annual savings that Ben needs to set aside to reach his goal of retiring at age 55 with 70 percent of his current income.
   b. What would Ben's savings for retirement need to be if he decided to work to age 65? Again, use Figure 22.5.
   c. Would you recommend Ben invest in an IRA? Why or why not?

Suggested Readings

"Annuities Reconsidered." *Newsweek,* July 17, 1989, p. 42. An analysis of the affects of fees on the returns of annuities.

"Annuities: What's in 'em for You." *Changing Times,* February 1990, pp. 65–75. How tax-sheltered annuities can be used effectively as an investment and which of the annuity mutual funds have done well.

"Caring for Your Aging Parents." *Money,* October 1989, pp. 136–145. Financial aspects of caring for parents and preparing yourself for retirement.

"Communities for the Elderly." *Consumer Reports,* February 1990, pp. 123–131. The ins and outs of what to look for when considering housing in communities for the elderly.

"Do Annuities Beat Mutual Funds." *Money,* November 1989, pp. 100–111. High fees and withdrawal penalties cause many annuities to earn less than mutual funds.

"Eight Myths of Retirement." *Money,* February 1990, pp. 111–116. A number of time-honored statements about retirement are simply not accurate anymore.

"Finally, the Good News About Social Security." *Money,* August 1990, pp. 90–94. This article projects that Social Security benefits will be higher for future retirees although they may represent a decreased share of retirement income.

"Five Sins to Avoid When Investing for Retirement." *Fortune,* March 27, 1989, p. 24. Explores the mistakes a typical person makes when saving for retirement.

"401K's: Adios to Those Bargain Loans." *Business Week,* October 9, 1989, p. 171. Outlines new rules on borrowing from 401(K) retirement accounts.

"Making up for Lost Time." *U.S. News & World Report,* July 30, 1990, pp. 61–63. Provides ideas on how to build retirement funds for those who have put it off until middle age.

"Partnerships with a Plus." *Changing Times,* October 1989, pp. 47–52. Master limited partnerships are one alternative for investing your IRA and Keogh funds.

"Pension Plans Pay Off for Small Business, Too." *Business Week,* January 29, 1990, pp. 98–99. Explains the most popular pension plans offered by small businesses.

"Retirement Plans—Part 1: 401(k) and 403(b) Programs." *Consumer Reports,* January 1990, p. 16. The tax advantages and basic regulations of these retirement plans.

"Retirement Plans—Part 2: Do IRAs Still Pay?" *Consumer Reports,* February 1990, p. 122. Who still benefits by investing in individual retirement accounts and why.

"Retirement Plans—Part 3: Keoghs and SEPs." *Consumer Reports,* March 1990, p. 150. Suggestions on choosing the right plan.

"Saying the Big Goodbye." *Newsweek,* October 9, 1989, p. 74. The joys and pitfalls of early retirement.

"Seeding, Feeding and Weeding Your IRA." *Money,* March 1990, pp. 138–144. Ways to improve your return on IRA accounts.

"The Best Ways to Help Financially." *Money,* October 1989, pp. 148–155. Cash handouts are only one way of helping parents and often not the best from a financial perspective.

"The Risk in Pension Maximization." *Newsweek,* May 7, 1990, p. 52. Explores the negative aspects of single-life annuities and single-life pension payout plans.

"Watchdogging Your Pension." *U.S. News & World Report,* July 30, 1990, pp. 64–65. Explains how and why you should go about monitoring your pension plan funds to protect them from misuse and fraud.

23 Planning and Protecting Your Estate

OBJECTIVES

After reading this chapter, you should be able to

1. Explain how an estate transfers to heirs.
2. Describe the types and characteristics of wills and other instruments designed to carry out your wishes related to estate planning.
3. Calculate estate taxes, given the dollar value of a gross estate.
4. Discuss the use of trusts for transferring and protecting an estate.

Your **estate** consists of the wealth you accumulate over your lifetime. While you are young, this wealth may be relatively modest, but as you get older, your estate can grow to an impressive size. College graduates who follow the basic tenants of this text will likely build an estate of well over $1 million by the time they reach retirement. The major components of such an estate will be a home, perhaps a vacation or second residence, retirement funds, investments in various securities and other assets, and personal property consisting of household furnishings, jewelry, and vehicles.

State laws require that one's estate must be disposed of at death by transferring it to survivors or, if none, to the state government itself. In addition, the value of the estate may be eroded by taxes and the cost of executing the transfers. **Estate planning** is the process of establishing, implementing, and revising plans to transfer an estate to heirs and to protect the estate from taxes and probate costs. The key words in this definition are *transfer* and *protect*. Effective estate planning will enable you to transfer the greatest amount of your hard-earned assets to your desired heirs. We examine the important steps in estate planning below and also recommend that you read further on the subject and consult with a lawyer before taking specific actions.

This chapter first discusses how state laws specify the transfer of assets when a person dies without a will. Details about using wills and other instruments to exert effective control over the transfer of one's estate are provided next. The chapter continues with a look at protecting an estate from a variety of taxes (estate, gift, and inheritance) that can erode its value. We finish with a look at trusts that can both transfer and protect an estate.

All Your Assets Will Transfer at Death

Objective
To be able to explain how an estate transfers to heirs.

After you die, your assets are distributed. If you die without leaving a valid will, you have died **intestate.** Dying intestate gives the state where you resided prior to death the complete right to determine how your estate is to be divided. This legal determination is rarely how you would want it done.

State Laws Governing Inheritance

Generally, when a single person dies intestate, state laws require that one-half of the estate go to each surviving parent; if only one parent survives, he or she receives the entire estate. If neither parent is alive, the estate would likely go to the brothers and sisters of the deceased. When a married person dies intestate, it is common for state laws to specify that half the estate goes to the surviving spouse and half to any surviving children. When a single parent dies intestate, the estate would likely be divided equally among his or her children. In such instances, the courts are required to appoint a guardian to supervise the children's finances and spend the money if needed until they reach the age of majority (18 in most states).

In several states the following guidelines apply: If a person with no surviving kin except a spouse dies without a will, the spouse gets the entire estate. If the deceased also had children, the spouse takes one-half and the other half is divided equally by the children. If there is a spouse and no children, but there are other kin, it becomes more complicated. When the estate is $50,000 or less, the spouse gets it all. In estates above $50,000, the spouse gets $50,000, plus one-half of all personal and real property, with the remainder going to the parents of the deceased or to the surviving parent. If parents are dead, their portion goes in equal shares to the deceased's brothers and sisters or to their children. If no brothers or sisters exist, the next of kin share the remainder in equal amounts. If there are no next of kin, the share goes to any surviving spouse of next of kin. If there is no such surviving spouse, the share goes to the state by right of **escheat.** This is the reverting of property to the state when there are no persons legally qualified to inherit or make claim to a deceased's property.

Legal heirs are defined by the laws of each state.

Are you confused yet? That's okay. It was our intention to expose you to the confusion of the complicated state laws governing who constitutes a legal heir. What seems least fair in the intestate distributions just described is that if you have no children, your spouse may be required by law to share your assets with a distant relative. The purpose of state intestacy guidelines is solely to distribute assets; it is your responsibility to make sure the distribution is fair and in accordance with your wishes by having a will.

Rights of Dower and Curtesy

The **right of dower** is a widow's lifetime legal right to a portion of her husband's property that he acquires during the marriage. The dower right is usually for one-third or one-half of the property. The **right of curtesy** (sometimes called *dower*) is a widower's lifetime legal right to a portion of his wife's property that she acquires during the marriage, again one-third or one-half. State laws provide that if a spouse leaves a will giving a surviving spouse less than the minimum required by the dower or curtesy rights, the survivor has the right to claim the legally allowed amount.

Community property laws assume that property acquired during marriage is jointly owned and equally shared.

Community property laws, which have been substituted for dower and curtesy rights in some states, distribute the property of deceased persons assuming that property acquired after marriage was jointly owned and equally shared by the spouses, no matter how much was actually contributed by either. (These states include Arizona, California, Idaho, Louisiana, Nevada, New Mexico, Texas, Washington, and Wisconsin.) **Separable**

property is a property wholly owned by one spouse, even in community property states. It is property that belonged to the spouse before marriage or was received as a gift or an inheritance. Thus separable property is typically not subject to disagreements in community property states. States that do not have community property laws often distribute property according to common law, which leaves a variety of options open to each court. For example, in some common-law situations, the husband owns the property entirely even if the wife helped to purchase it. You should learn about the property-distribution practices in your state as you begin to acquire property.

Property Can Be Transferred Quickly Outside of Probate

Probate is a legal procedure.

Probate is a court procedure for settling and disposing of an estate. This process occurs even when there is a will. Many people choose to bypass this sometimes slow process for at least a portion of their estate. To do so, one can transfer assets by contract or by law without going through probate. When this occurs, the property is referred to as **nonprobate property.** Such assets may be transferred by (1) contract or (2) by law.

Transferred by Contract   Life insurance is a common nonprobate property transferred by contract. Here the proceeds of the life insurance policy are transferred directly to the beneficiary by the life insurance company. The proceeds will not be included as part of the estate for federal estate tax computations unless the policy is payable to the estate or to a trust created in a will. Another example of transferring by contract is money in a corporate profit-sharing or pension plan that goes directly to the named beneficiary as nonprobate property. Assets transferred to a trust established prior to death are similarly forwarded contractually (the importance of trusts is discussed later in this chapter). Savings bonds also may be contractually assigned, and some assets in a business partnership may be transferred from a deceased partner without being probated.

Transferred by Law   The property interest of the deceased may or may not go to heirs without going through probate depending on how it is owned. Property owned by two or more persons provides an example. **Joint tenancy** provides that when two or more persons own property, the survivor(s) get the property. (Some states use other terms to designate similar legal rights, such as *joint tenancy with right of survivorship, tenancy by the entirety,* or *homestead.*) Most married couples have their checking and savings accounts in joint tenancy as well as automobiles and their home. Investors generally buy property with a **tenancy in common,** which provides that each investor retain control over his or her interest in the property and may dispose of it in any manner at any time; a tenant's survivors inherit the same rights. Tenancy-in-common assets are usually subject to probate.

Property owned by joint tenancy provides a right of survivorship for co-owners.

Wills

A **will** is a written document that directs the disposition of your assets at death, but only if the will is executed in accordance with statutory provisions. The major functions of a will are (1) to transfer assets to particular people; (2) to choose the executor, trustees, and other fiduciaries who will administer the estate; and (3) to reduce the tax liability on the estate of the deceased. In addition to a will, it is wise to draw up a letter of last instructions and a power of attorney to ensure that your wishes are carried out; these terms are discussed later in this chapter.

Legal Terms in a Will

The person who makes a will is called a **testator** and upon death is legally referred to as the **decedent.** A person who dies with a valid will has died **testate,** rather than intestate. Anyone at least 18 years old and of sound mind may make a legally valid will. A person receiving property identified in a will is referred to as a **beneficiary.**

Select your beneficiaries by having a will.

An **executor** or **executrix** (female executor) is named in a will to carry out the directions and requests in the will and is provided a certain amount of legal power by the state. Your executor needs to understand the personal aspects of your estate and have good business skills. The emotional difficulties of serving as executor for the estate of a loved one should not be underestimated. You might want to choose coexecutors: an intelligent relative or friend to watch over the personal aspects and serve as guardian for your children and a second person who has excellent business skills and savvy.

Dying Without a Will

About 75 percent of the adult population does not have a will. In most states, if you die without a will, an administrator (or conservator) is appointed by the court to liquidate your estate in accordance with the statutes of that state. A commission of perhaps 3 to 5 percent of the value of the estate is charged to cover the administrator's fee. If you have minor children, a guardian must be appointed for each, representing additional costs to the estate.

The powers given to an administrator by the court are limited, and as a result, the administrator must frequently seek the court's permission for specific legal actions, all of which cost money in court fees. In most states, for example, a court order is required to sell securities and real estate. If the heirs are of legal age, they all must agree on the sale of real estate or the method of current operations; such agreement is sometimes difficult to obtain.

Types of Wills

A **lawyer-prepared will** is a will drafted by an attorney and is least likely to be successfully challenged. A simple lawyer-prepared will can cost $75

What If You Are Chosen as an Executor?

It is quite possible that you will be named in the will of a parent or a sibling to be the executor of his or her estate. Will you know what duties to perform and how to do them? The following list outlines the basic tasks required of someone who has taken on this important duty.

1. Make the necessary funeral and burial arrangements in accordance with the wishes of the deceased.

2. Make the necessary provisions to ensure that dependent survivors of the deceased have adequate living arrangements until the estate has been settled.

3. Collect all amounts that are owed to the estate. These can include salary, pension, and insurance funds, as well as Social Security and other government benefits.

4. Pay all the debts of the estate. These will likely include the health care expenses for the period prior to death. Some of these may be covered by insurance and will need to be coordinated with item number 3.

5. Make arrangements for an assessment and appraisal of the value of the estate.

6. Take custody of all assets of the estate, including securities, real estate, and personal property. The trustees of any trusts established by the deceased will need to be contacted for information and further instructions.

7. Oversee the management of any business interests of the deceased.

8. Seek the help of accountants and lawyers in the preparation of all tax forms for income, inheritance, and gift and estate taxes.

9. Distribute the estate to heirs in accordance with the provisions of the will.

10. File the necessary reports with the court on your activities as executor.

---

to $100, and a more complex one more. A **nuncupative will** is an oral will spoken by a dying individual to another person or persons. It is legal in some states but difficult to verify. A **joint will** (also called a *mutual will*) is a will drawn up by a married couple who have made reciprocal provisions for each other. Experts suggest avoiding a joint will, since the surviving spouse may not be able to change the provisions of the will years later when circumstances differ.

Some people write their own wills. A **holographic will** is entirely in the handwriting of the person signing the will and is, as some states require, dated with the same hand. For the will to be valid in the decedent's state of residence, two witnesses' signatures may be needed. Since they are not written by an attorney and may be unclear, holographic wills are frequently not honored by courts, and the deceased is assumed to have died intestate.

A **California will** (or *do-it-yourself will*) is a blank-form document that people can fill out themselves. California was the first state to legally recognize these forms. Most do-it-yourself will forms are designed for the convenience of married couples with dependent children. Such forms generally do not effectively provide for tax planning considerations, the circumstances of those who were previously married and had children, or situations where a complex estate exists.

Major Provisions of a Will

1. *Identification* of the testator and places of residence.

2. *Introductory clause* to provide validity of the will, such as, "This is my will and testament . . ."

3. *Revocation of prior wills clause* if prior wills have been written.

4. *Final instructions* for the payment of taxes, debts, funeral, burial, and administrative costs of the estate.

5. *Specific bequests* for particular items, such as stamp collections or jewelry.

6. *General bequests* out of the general assets of the estate that usually provide for money to be given to individuals.

7. *Charitable gifts* to various organizations.

8. *Allocation of residual estate statement* explaining where the remaining portion of the estate goes after the preceding bequests.

9. *Survivorship clause* indicating the guardian(s) for children if both husband and wife die.

10. *Trust provisions* to create and/or give directions to trusts.

11. *Appointment clauses* to designate the executor of the estate and guardians to represent the interests of children (if any).

12. *Executive clauses* that add to the validity of the will, such as dating, witnessing, and signing.

Codicils

A codicil is used to amend a will.

Some circumstances that often cause people to consider changing a will are moving to another state, getting married or divorced, having children, having a substantial change in assets, or the death of heirs, executors, or guardians named in the will. You update a will either by writing a new will or by adding a **codicil,** which is a legal amendment to a will. A codicil should be drawn up by your attorney, witnessed, and signed.

The original copy of your will should be kept by your attorney in a safe-deposit box, and you should keep copies. Do not put the original of your will in your own safe-deposit box, since upon your death the box may be sealed (even if jointly held) until a court order is obtained to open it. This may take several days. Do, however, let your family know the location of your will.

Letters of Last Instructions

Many people prepare a **letter of last instructions** (also called a **letter precatory**), which is a letter often in their own handwriting, signed, and usually given to the executor that describes transfers of many odds and ends of personal property (both valuable and sentimental) without being made public in a formal will. Often people will put burial instructions and very sentimental items in their letter of last instructions. It is important to include information in the letter about the location of all your assets, such

A will and letter of last instructions are designed to allow you to exert control over your estate after your death. However, it is possible that you could lose such control before death. Many illnesses such as Alzheimer's disease, strokes, and cancer can result in a period of mental incompetence before death. Such a time period can be one of intense stress for your family and can jeopardize one's hard-earned estate. If you do not plan for the possibility of physical or mental incompetence, your family or business partners might find it necessary to seek to have you declared incompetent by the state and have a *guardian,* a person appointed by the court, manage your affairs. Of course, the guardian would be obligated to operate in your best interests, but he or she may not be fully cognizant of your intentions.

Therefore, you should consider establishing a **durable power of attorney**. This is a legal process to appoint a specific individual to control your affairs and give him or her the power to enter into and execute contracts on your behalf should you become mentally incapacitated. This power is an adaptation of the traditional *power of attorney,* which many people use when they are going to be out of the country or otherwise wishes to designate someone to manage their affairs. A power of attorney expires if the grantor is declared legally incompetent. In contrast, a durable power of attorney is designed to take effect *only* when the grantor is declared legally incompetent due to incapacitation. The durable power of attorney should be very specific about the aspects of your affairs that it covers and should even mention specific institutions (banks or brokerage firms, for example) and account numbers. Virtually absolute power to manage your affairs is given under a durable power of attorney, so choose a trusted individual who knows your wishes.

Note that most states have legalized the concept of a **living will**. This legal document can be used to direct that extraordinary life support and/or sustaining measures be terminated should you become terminally ill and mentally unable to make this decision for yourself. For example, if death is imminent, a living will could direct that life support measures, such as a respirator, be removed. This document differs from a durable power of attorney in two ways. First, no one else is given the legal right to make the life support decision. Second, a living will cannot address financial affairs. It is wise (though not necessary in all states) to have both a durable power of attorney and a living will drawn up by your lawyer.

as various checking and savings accounts, life insurance policies, and accounts at brokerage firms.

Protecting the Value of Your Estate by Avoiding Taxes at Death

Objective
To be able to calculate estate taxes, given the dollar value of a gross estate.

Mark Twain once said that "nothing is certain but death and taxes." Even after all the years of collecting income taxes from you during your life, state and federal governments still may collect taxes from your estate or on property inherited by your heirs after death. The **federal gift and estate tax** is a tax assessed on property owned and/or controlled by a deceased before it is transferred to heirs. (This definition immediately suggests a fundamental loophole in estate taxes—if property is not controlled, it will not be taxed—and we shall examine this subsequently when we discuss trusts.) Estate taxes are levied by the federal government and by four states (Massachusetts, Mississippi, New York, and Ohio), although for simplicity we will focus on the federal tax only. Note that the federal gift and estate tax is levied against the person who created the estate. In contrast, **inheritance taxes** are levied on inherited property when it is received by heirs. Only states levy inheritance taxes.

The Gift and Estate Tax

Making a will gives you confidence that your assets will be divided and transferred as you wish. However, without proper planning, a substantial portion of your estate may go for estate taxes. This will be true for anyone whose net taxable estate adds up to more than $600,000. Your **gross estate** includes just about everything you own and amounts owed to you at the time of your death. Any gift and estate taxes due will be paid on the net taxable estate. As illustrated in Figure 23.1, the **net taxable estate** is the gross estate *minus* liabilities (debts of the estate), expenses for settling the estate, charitable bequests, properties passed by law and contract, *plus* any taxable gifts (discussed below) given after 1976. Note further that federal tax laws permit an **unlimited marital deduction**, which allows everything left to a surviving spouse to transfer tax-free. This suggests that all federal gift and estate taxes could be avoided; however, the catch is that the estate may ultimately be taxed more heavily after the surviving spouse dies.

Spousal estate transfers are tax exempt.

Lifetime Gifts

Figure 23.1 illustrates that taxable gifts are added to one's taxable estate prior to the calculation of the gift and estate tax. To encourage both gift giving and building an estate, federal laws allow an initial portion of gifts to be tax-free. Gifts of $10,000 or less per recipient per year need not be included in the donor's net taxable estate when the gift and estate tax is calculated. Donors must report the portion of gifts in excess of $10,000 per person per year by filing IRS Form 709. These excess amounts will be subject to estate taxes at a later date when they are included in the donor's net taxable estate at death, as indicated in Figure 23.1. The government permits donors to give $10,000 tax-free gifts to as many people as they wish each year. Spouses may give $10,000 each for a total of $20,000 per married couple to each recipient.

Gifts over $10,000 per person per year must be reported to the IRS.

Consider the example of George Belton, co-owner of a construction company in Manhattan, Kansas, who several years ago gave $30,000 to his nephew Jeffrey for a down payment on a home. The first $10,000 of the gift is exempt from the gift and estate tax. The remaining $20,000 is subject to the tax, so George reported it to the IRS. In actuality, the tax

FIGURE 23.1

Steps in Determining a
Net Taxable Estate

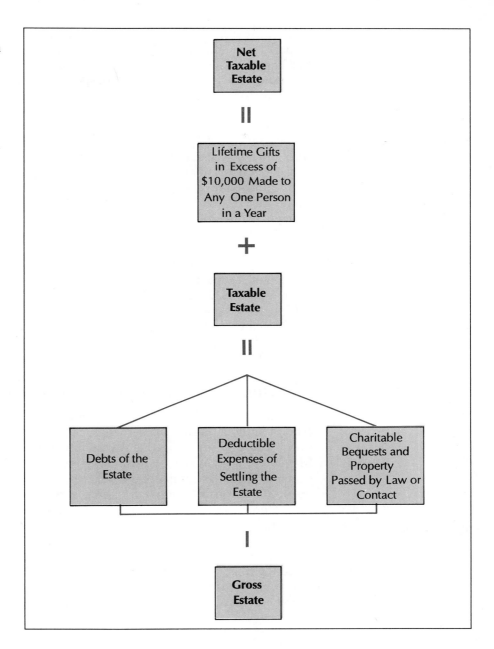

on the $20,000 is not payable until after George dies. At that point in time the $20,000 will be added to George's taxable estate for the calculation of gift and estate taxes. This is illustrated below.

To be defined as a gift by the IRS, the recipient must have a **present interest** in the money or property given, meaning that the recipient has an immediate and irrevocable right to the entire gift. *Gifts* as defined by the IRS may not be loans or payments for services rendered. Payments for services are classified as taxable income by the IRS, and income taxes must be paid by the recipient. Gifts of any amount are tax-free for the *recipient*, but any later income earned from the gift is subject to income taxation. For example, a gift of $10,000 worth of corporate stock is tax-free for both the donor and the recipient, but the recipient must pay income taxes on any dividends earned in the future as well as capital gains profits made between the date the stock was received and when it was sold.

Gifts can reduce the donor's taxable estate.

Gifts of $10,000 or less reduce the size of the donor's taxable estate, since the donated assets reduce the owner's gross estate and are not added back later. Thus the result of making gifts of $10,000 or less is a reduction of gift and estate tax liability. People also reduce taxes by giving gifts in excess of $10,000 because gifts for estate-tax purposes are valued at the time gifts were given, not later, at the death of the donor. For example, a gift of a $25,000 painting in 1991 is valued in 1991 dollars, not at its inflated value when the donor dies perhaps 8 years later. As a gift, the painting would add only $15,000 ($25,000 − $10,000) to the donor's net taxable estate at death. If not given as a gift, the value of the painting when transferred as part of the estate would be $53,600 ($25,000 × 2.144, from Appendix A1) in 1999, assuming 10 percent inflation, and would require payment of more taxes on the donor's estate. Gifts are valuable for estate-tax reduction, but there certainly are logical limitations on how much should be given away before death.

The Unified Gift and Estate Tax Credit

An understanding of the federal gift and estate tax is crucial to effective estate planning. Realize that theoretically a person might be tempted to avoid estate taxes altogether by simply giving away his or her estate $10,000 at a time prior to death, thereby depleting the estate to zero. To encourage people to maintain their estates, the law allows the initial $600,000 of one's combined taxable gifts and taxable estate to be tax-free. This is accomplished through the **unified gift and estate tax credit.** This credit, $192,800, is equivalent to the tax on an estate of $600,000, as can be seen in Table 23.1, which lists federal gift and estate tax rates. Because of this credit, over 90 percent of Americans probably will pay no federal gift and estate tax based on the current value of their estate. However, realize that inflation will push more of today's high-income people into the arena of estate taxes; and note how high the tax rates are.

The unified gift and estate tax credit has the effect of exempting the first $600,000 of a net taxable estate from tax.

Calculating Estate Taxes

Table 23.2 shows the tax calculation given for the $1,855,000 gross estate of George Belton, who is now deceased. The estate had debts of $135,000 for the mortgage on George's home plus several revolving credit accounts. There were $80,000 in deductible expenses, such as court and executor fees for the settlement of the estate. In addition, George willed a $100,000 bequest to the American Cancer Society, which also can be subtracted from the gross estate. George was a co-owner (joint tenancy with right of survivorship) of a construction company, and George's share in the

TABLE 23.1
Gift and Estate Tax Rates (Effective for 1991 and 1992)*

(1) Taxable Estate Plus Taxable Gifts	(2) Tax	(3) Rate of Tax on Excess over Amount in Column 1	(4) Unified Gift and Estate Tax Credit	(5) Federal Gift and Estate Tax
Under $10,000	18% of amount	—	$192,800	—
$ 10,000	$ 1,800	20%	192,800	—
20,000	3,800	22	192,800	—
40,000	8,200	24	192,800	—
60,000	13,000	26	192,800	—
80,000	18,200	28	192,800	—
100,000	23,800	30	192,800	—
150,000	38,800	32	192,800	—
200,000	54,800	32	192,800	—
250,000	70,800	34	192,800	—
300,000	87,800	34	192,800	—
500,000	155,800	37	192,800	—
600,000	192,800	37	192,800	—
700,000	229,800	37	192,800	$ 37,000
750,000	248,300	39	192,800	55,500
900,000	306,800	39	192,800	114,000
1,000,000	345,800	41	192,800	153,000
1,250,000	448,300	43	192,800	255,500
1,500,000	555,800	45	192,800	363,000
2,000,000	780,800	49	192,800	588,000
2,500,000	1,025,800	53*	192,800	833,000

Source: Internal Revenue Service.

* Beginning in 1993, the top rate will drop to 50 percent for taxable estates of $2,500,000 and above.

company of $800,000 passed directly by law to his business partner. (This would be unusual as most partners own assets by tenancy in common, although it results in higher estate taxes.) George was a widower, so there was no marital deduction. The result of these subtractions was a taxable estate of $740,000 ($1,855,000 − $135,000 − $80,000 − $100,000 − $800,000). After adding back the $20,000 taxable portion of Mr. Belton's gift to his nephew, Jeffrey, the Belton net taxable estate amounted to $760,000. Applying the tax rate from Table 23.1 results in a federal estate tax of $59,400 on the Belton estate. Better estate planning by using several $10,000 gifts and some trusts could have eliminated this liability and permitted most, if not all, of the $59,400 to transfer to heirs instead of going to the government.

Inheritance Taxes

State inheritance taxes also may be due on the value of an estate passed on to *heirs*. Recall, though, that inheritance taxes are assessed on the heirs,

TABLE 23.2
Calculation of Gift and Estate Tax Liability for George Belton

Gross estate	$1,855,000
Less debts of the estate	− 135,000
Less deductible estate settlement expenses	− 80,000
Less any charitable bequests	− 100,000
Less properties passed by law or contract	− 800,000
Less marital deduction	− 0
Taxable estate	$ 740,000
Plus taxable gifts (made after 1976)	+ 20,000
Net taxable estate	$ 760,000
Estate tax: $248,300 + 39 percent of $10,000*	$ 252,200
Unified tax credit	− 192,800
Gift and estate tax liability	$ 59,400

* From Table 23.1. Net taxable estate of $760,000 is closest to a tentative tax base of $750,000, corresponding to a base tax of $248,300. The difference of $10,000 is multiplied by 39 percent and added to the base amount to equal a total tax of $252,200 ($248,300 + $3900).

not on the estate. As a practical matter, inheritance taxes may be paid out of the funds remaining in an estate after all specific bequests have been distributed, but if insufficient funds remain, the heirs themselves must pay in proportion to their share of the total bequests. Tax rates and exemptions vary among the states and are complicated. Consider the case of Reggie Harmon of Hartford, Connecticut, who had an estate of $300,000 and who left one-half of his estate to his wife, $125,000 to his children, and $25,000 to his sister. Under Connecticut law, the $150,000 left to his wife was exempt. As required by Connecticut law, the $125,000 left to his children was taxed at 4.29 percent on the amount over $50,000 ($75,000). And the $25,000 left to his sister was taxed at 5.72 percent on the amount over $6000 ($19,000). Thus an inheritance tax of $4304.30 [(0.0429 × $75,000) + (0.0572 × $19,000)] was levied. Because of the variability among the 17 states that levy inheritance taxes,[1] details are omitted here. A tax attorney familiar with state inheritance taxes can be most helpful because state exemptions and deductions are much smaller than the federal allowances, and this can result in a substantial state inheritance tax on a relatively small estate.

About one third of the states levy inheritance taxes.

[1] Connecticut, Delaware, Indiana, Iowa, Kansas, Kentucky, Louisiana, Maryland, Michigan, Montana, Nebraska, New Hampshire, New Jersey, North Carolina, Pennsylvania, South Dakota, and Tennessee. Wisconsin's tax expires December 31, 1991.

Trusts

An alternative to paying large amounts of estate taxes is to create one or more **trusts,** which are legal instruments that place the control of some or all of your assets with a trustee. Trusts are an extremely flexible estate planning tool because they can both transfer the properties in an estate and protect the estate from taxation. This is because for certain types of trusts the assets held in trust are owned by the trust, not controlled by the estate, and therefore are exempt from federal estate taxes. Some of the important terms associated with trusts are defined below:

Trustee: Person, partnership, or corporation that manages the trust for the use and benefit of the beneficiary or beneficiaries (they normally charge an annual fee of less than one-half of 1 percent for the services)

Beneficiary: Person designated as the recipient of income funds under a trust

Remaindermen: Persons named in the trust who are to receive the assets upon termination of the trust agreement

Grantor: Person who makes a grant to set up a trust

Some grantors avoid having to manage assets by establishing a trust for themselves and receiving benefits from the trustee in the form of monthly income. This is an example of a **living trust** (or *inter vivos*), a trust created by a living grantor for the benefit of self or another. Politicians often establish a form of living trust called a *blind trust,* which prohibits the grantor from influencing the trustee's actions.

There are three forms of living trusts: irrevocable, revocable, and revisionary. An **irrevocable trust** is not subject to any modification by the grantor during his or her lifetime, thus bypassing probate and estate taxes. A **revocable trust** is subject to change, amendment, modification, or cancellation by the grantor. Thus the assets remain a part of the taxable estate, although they would pass through to the beneficiary without going through probate at the time of the grantor's death. A **revisionary trust** is irrevocable or unchangeable for at least 10 years (unless the beneficiary and/or remaindermen die), after which time it is revocable. During the irrevocable period, it is not part of the donor's taxable estate.

Irrevocable and revisionary living trusts are useful in estate planning.

Trusts used in connection with estate planning also can be **testamentary trusts** rather than living trusts. This form of trust is established and becomes effective upon the death of the grantor according to the terms written in the grantor's will. Such trusts can be designed to provide money or asset management after the grantor's death, to avoid probate, to reduce estate taxes, to provide income for a surviving spouse, to provide income for children, to give assets to grandchildren or great-grandchildren while providing income from the assets to the surviving spouse and/or children, to protect beneficiaries from creditors, and to prevent assets from being lured away from beneficiaries. These laudable objectives can be achieved only with the assistance of an experienced attorney who specializes in trusts.

Summary

1. If a person dies without a will (or intestate), the remaining assets are distributed according to state laws on the subject, including laws governing dower and curtesy rights. These distributions usually will not reflect what a person would actually prefer.
2. A well-prepared will is likely to include sections on revocation, final instructions, allocation of residual estate, and execution clauses.
3. Estate planning provides for the transfer of an estate and protects the estate from various taxes.
4. Trusts are legal instruments that place the control of assets with a trustee to administer in accordance with the agreement.

Modern Money Management

Belinda Johnson Helps Her Uncle Plan His Estate

Belinda Johnson has been approached by her uncle, David Lawrence, for some advice about planning his estate. She has been handling some of David's investments, and he trusts her judgment on financial matters. David has a net worth of $2,340,000 and at age 54 is concerned about preparing his finances in such a way that as much as possible goes to his heirs according to his wishes. David has no will but has set down on paper some of his ideas. He has no wife or children but wants to provide for his mother, four nephews, Belinda, and a disabled sister.

1. What is the first thing David should do in planning his estate? Why?
2. How might David use gifts to help reduce his estate taxes?
3. Why might a revisionary trust be a good idea for David in providing for his mother and sister?
4. What other types of trusts might David use in his estate planning?

Key Words and Concepts

beneficiary, 794
California will, 795
codicil, 796

community property laws, 792
decedent, 794
durable power of attorney, 797

Review Questions

1. Define estate planning, and explain its two major purposes.
2. What is one of the greatest disadvantages to survivors if a person dies intestate?
3. Explain how spousal transfers are controlled.
4. Distinguish between joint tenancy and tenancy in common.
5. What are the primary purposes of having a will?
6. Identify the parties who would be named in a will.
7. Why should you be careful in appointing an executor or executrix when making a will?
8. Describe the purposes of a letter of last instructions and a durable power of attorney.
9. Explain three ways you can reduce the federal gift and estate tax.
10. What is the effect of the unified gift and estate tax credit?
11. Distinguish between gross estate and net taxable estate.
12. Define trusts.
13. What two functions can trusts perform in estate planning?
14. How do a revocable trust, an irrevocable trust, and a revisionary trust differ?

Case Problems

1. Joe Michael of Sterling Heights, Michigan, is a 34-year-old police detective earning $45,000 per year. He and his wife, Doreen, have two children in elementary school. They jointly own a modestly furnished home and two late-model cars; along with a snowmobile, these are their principal physical assets. Each is covered by a $50,000 term life insurance policy. They have about $5000 in a joint savings account. Neither Joe nor Doreen has a will.

   a. List four possible negative things that could happen if either Joe or Doreen were to die without a will.

   b. What do you feel would be the most important negative consequence of not having a will if both Joe and Doreen were to die in some type of accident?

   c. Joe often mentions the cost of an attorney as a reason for not having a will. How might the problem of not having a will be solved at a lower cost?

2. Robert Alan of Fort Collins, Colorado, has been named executor of the estate of his aunt who has recently died. As executor, he wishes to determine the estate taxes that will need to be paid. Given the following information, answer the questions below for Robert: gross estate, $1,430,000; deductible expenses for settlement of the estate, $75,000; debts of the estate, $30,000; charitable contributions $75,000; irrevocable trusts of $100,000 to each of the five nieces and nephews. Not too long before her death, the aunt gave Robert an additional $10,000. Develop a table like Table 23.2 for Robert's information.

   a. What is the taxable estate?

   b. What is the net taxable estate?

   c. What is the unified estate tax credit for this estate?

   d. How much in estate taxes will be owed?

   e. Are there taxes to be assessed on the $10,000 gift to Robert?

Suggested Readings

"A Charitable Way to Provide for Heirs." *Business Week,* October 16, 1989, p. 139. Tips on using charitable trusts in estate planning.

"Confronting the Death of a Parent." *U.S. News & World Report,* May 22, 1989, pp. 74–75. Outlines the tasks to be performed in settling an estate.

"Dealing with Death in the Family." *Working Woman,* August 1989, pp. 47–50. How to help a surviving parent cope financially with the death of a spouse.

"How to Keep It All in the Family." *Money Guide,* 1989, pp. 104–127. A fully developed primer on estate planning.

"Keeping Down Estate Taxes." *Fortune, 1990 Investor's Guide,* pp. 189–199. The basics of practicing estate tax avoidance.

"Keeping the State Out of Your Estate." *Changing Times,* November 1989, pp. 73–78. A state-by-state analysis of inheritance taxes.

"Okay, Videotaping Buffs, Let's Get Real." *Money,* January 1989, pp. 117–124. Includes suggestions on how to make a living will.

"Passing the Bucks to Your Kids." *Changing Times,* March 1989, pp. 65–69. Latest ways to try to get money to your relatives without giving too much to the government along the way.

"Passing Wealth On Intact Takes a Will and a Way." *U.S. News & World Report,* July 17, 1989, pp. 60–64. Explains the hows and whys of writing a will.

"Protecting Your Estate." *Forbes,* October 23, 1989. Special issue of *Forbes* devoted entirely to estate planning.

"See a Lawyer Now to Save Your Heir Time and Taxes." *Money,* February 1989, p. 84. Advice for seeking legal assistance in estate planning.

"Tapping the Gifts of a Lifetime." *U.S. News & World Report,* July 30, 1990, pp. 67–69. Substantial tax and other benefits can be obtained from estate planning while you are alive.

"The Bad News about Estate Taxes." *Forbes,* June 26, 1989, pp. 238–239. Explains the ins and outs of estate taxes and the need for an up-to-date will to reduce them.

"The Gulag of Guardianship." *Money,* March 1990, pp. 141–152. The perils of guardianship and how to avoid them.

"The Windfalls Awaiting New Inheritances." *Fortune,* May 7, 1990, pp. 72–74. Estate planning from the point of view of the heirs.

"This Policy Takes the Sting Out of Inheritance Taxes." *Business Week,* June 12, 1989, p. 107. Explains how life insurance might be helpful in paying inheritance taxes in some situations.

"Trimming the Tax Bite on Gifts to Grandchildren." *Business Week,* October 23, 1989, p. 161. How to use gifts to grandchildren to lower estate taxes.

"When to Trust Living Trusts." *Money,* August 1990, pp. 118–120. Explains the benefits and costs of using living trusts in estate planning.

"When You're Asked to Be an Executor." *Changing Times,* April 1989, pp. 87–92. Suggestions on how to get an estate through probate.

"When Your Parents Need Help." *Changing Times,* May 1989, pp. 81–84. Tax angles on how to manage and protect the assets of elderly people.

"Your House's Hidden Problem." *Money,* November 1989, pp. 177–178. The effect of a large home equity on estate taxes owed.

APPENDIX

A Present and Future Value Tables

Many problems of personal finance involve decisions involving money values at different points in time. These values can be directly and fairly compared only when they are adjusted to a common point in time.

Four assumptions must be made to eliminate unnecessary complications: (1) each planning period is 1 year long; (2) only annual interest rates are considered; (3) interest rates are the same during each of the annual periods; and (4) interest is compounded and earns in subsequent periods.

Tables of present and future values can be constructed to make these adjustments. Future values are derived from the principles of compounding the dollar values ahead in time. Present values are derived from discounting (which is the inverse of compounding) the dollar values and transferring them to an earlier point in time.

For most of us it is unnecessary to have the precision of interest at the beginning of a period instead of the end of a period, or if interest compounds daily or quarterly instead of annually. (These require even more tables.) The following tables can be used to compute the mathematics of personal finance with high certainty and to confirm (or reject as inaccurate) what people tell you about financial matters.

The most significant task is to be certain that you are using the correct table. Accordingly, each table is clearly described and illustrations of use appear on the facing page where possible.

Illustrations: Using Appendix A1

1. You invest $500 at 15 percent for 12 years. How much will you have at the end of that 12-year period?

   The interest factor is 5.350; hence the solution is $500(5.350), or $2675.

2. Property values in your neighborhood are increasing at a rate of 5 percent per year. If your home is presently worth $90,000, what will its worth be in 7 years?

   The inflation factor is 1.407; hence the solution is $90,000(1.407), or $126,630.

3. You need to amass $40,000 in the next 10 years to meet a balloon payment on your home mortgage. You have $17,000 available to

invest. What annual interest rate must be earned to realize the $40,000? $40,000 ÷ $17,000 = 2.353.

Read down the "Periods" column to 10 years and across to 2.367 (close enough), which is under the 9 percent column. Hence the $17,000 invested at 9 percent for 10 years will grow to a future value of just over $40,000.

4. An apartment building is currently valued at $160,000, and it has been appreciating at 8 percent per year. If this rate continues, in how many years will it be worth $300,000? $300,000 ÷ $160,000 = 1.875.

   Read down the 8 percent column until you reach 1.851 (close enough to 1.875). Note that this number corresponds to a period of 8 years. Hence the $160,000 property appreciating at 8 percent annually will grow to a future value of $300,000 in just over 8 years.

5. You have the choice of receiving $15,000 today as a down payment from someone who wants to purchase your rental property or a personal note for $25,000 payable in 6 years. If you could expect to earn 8 percent on such funds, which is the better choice?

   The interest factor is 1.587; hence the future value of $15,000 at 8 percent is $15,000(1.587), or $23,805. Thus, it would be better to take the note for $25,000.

6. You want to know how much an automobile now priced at $20,000 will cost in 4 years, assuming an inflation rate of 5 percent annually.

   Read down the 5 percent column and across the row for 4 years to locate the factor 1.216. Hence the solution is $20,000(1.216), or $24,320.

7. You want to know how big a lump-sum investment you need now to have $20,000 available in 5 years assuming a 10 percent annual rate of return.

   The $20,000 future value is divided by 1.611 (10 percent at 5 years), resulting in a lump-sum investment now of $12,415.

8. You have $5000 now and need $10,000 in 9 years. What rate of return is needed to reach that goal?

   Divide the future value of $10,000 by the present value of the lump sum of $5000 to obtain a future value factor of 2.0. Look along the row for 9 years to locate the factor 1.999 (very close to 2.0). Read up the column to find that an 8 percent return on investment is needed.

9. You want to know how many years it will take your lump-sum investment of $10,000 to grow to $16,000 with an annual rate of return of 7 percent.

   Divide the future value of $16,000 by the present value of the $10,000 lump sum to compute a future value factor of 1.6; then look down the 7 percent column to find 1.606 (close enough). Read across the row to find that an investment period of 7 years is needed.

APPENDIX A1
Future Value of $1 (to Compute the Compounded Future Value of Some Given Present Lump-sum Investment)

Periods	1%	2%	3%	4%	5%	6%	7%	8%	9%	10%	12%	14%	15%
1	1.010	1.020	1.030	1.040	1.050	1.060	1.070	1.080	1.090	1.100	1.120	1.140	1.150
2	1.020	1.040	1.061	1.082	1.103	1.124	1.145	1.166	1.188	1.210	1.254	1.300	1.323
3	1.030	1.061	1.093	1.125	1.158	1.191	1.225	1.260	1.295	1.331	1.405	1.482	1.521
4	1.041	1.082	1.126	1.170	1.216	1.262	1.311	1.360	1.412	1.464	1.574	1.689	1.749
5	1.051	1.104	1.159	1.217	1.276	1.338	1.403	1.469	1.539	1.611	1.762	1.925	2.011
6	1.062	1.126	1.194	1.265	1.340	1.419	1.501	1.587	1.677	1.772	1.974	2.195	2.313
7	1.072	1.149	1.230	1.316	1.407	1.504	1.606	1.714	1.828	1.949	2.211	2.502	2.660
8	1.083	1.172	1.267	1.369	1.477	1.594	1.718	1.851	1.993	2.144	2.476	2.853	3.059
9	1.094	1.195	1.305	1.423	1.551	1.689	1.838	1.999	2.172	2.358	2.773	3.252	3.518
10	1.105	1.219	1.344	1.480	1.629	1.791	1.967	2.159	2.367	2.594	3.106	3.707	4.046
11	1.116	1.243	1.384	1.539	1.710	1.898	2.105	2.332	2.580	2.853	3.479	4.226	4.652
12	1.127	1.268	1.426	1.601	1.796	2.012	2.252	2.518	2.813	3.138	3.896	4.818	5.350
13	1.138	1.294	1.469	1.665	1.886	2.133	2.410	2.720	3.066	3.452	4.363	5.492	6.153
14	1.149	1.319	1.513	1.732	1.980	2.261	2.579	2.937	3.342	3.798	4.887	6.261	7.076
15	1.161	1.346	1.558	1.801	2.079	2.397	2.759	3.172	3.642	4.177	5.474	7.138	8.137
16	1.173	1.373	1.605	1.873	2.183	2.540	2.952	3.426	3.970	4.595	6.130	8.137	9.358
17	1.184	1.400	1.653	1.948	2.292	2.693	3.159	3.700	4.328	5.054	6.866	9.276	10.76
18	1.196	1.428	1.702	2.026	2.407	2.854	3.380	3.996	4.717	5.560	7.690	10.58	12.38
19	1.208	1.457	1.754	2.107	2.527	3.026	3.617	4.316	5.142	6.116	8.613	12.06	14.23
20	1.220	1.486	1.806	2.191	2.653	3.207	3.870	4.661	5.604	6.728	9.646	13.74	16.37
21	1.232	1.516	1.860	2.279	2.786	3.400	4.141	5.034	6.109	7.400	10.80	15.67	18.82
22	1.245	1.546	1.916	2.370	2.925	3.604	4.430	5.437	6.659	8.140	12.10	17.86	21.64
23	1.257	1.577	1.974	2.465	3.072	3.820	4.741	5.871	7.258	8.954	13.55	20.36	24.89
24	1.270	1.608	2.033	2.563	3.225	4.049	5.072	6.341	7.911	9.850	15.18	23.21	28.63
25	1.282	1.641	2.094	2.666	3.386	4.292	5.427	6.848	8.623	10.83	17.00	26.46	32.92
26	1.295	1.673	2.157	2.772	3.556	4.549	5.807	7.396	9.399	11.92	19.04	30.17	37.86
27	1.308	1.707	2.221	2.883	3.733	4.822	6.214	7.988	10.25	13.11	21.32	34.39	43.54
28	1.321	1.741	2.288	2.999	3.920	5.112	6.649	8.627	11.17	14.42	23.88	39.20	50.07
29	1.335	1.776	2.357	3.119	4.116	5.418	7.114	9.317	12.17	15.86	26.75	44.69	57.58
30	1.348	1.811	2.427	3.243	4.322	5.743	7.612	10.06	13.27	17.45	29.96	50.95	66.21
40	1.489	2.208	3.262	4.801	7.040	10.29	14.97	21.72	31.41	45.26	93.05	188.9	267.9
50	1.645	2.692	4.384	7.107	11.47	18.42	29.46	46.90	74.36	117.4	289.0	700.2	1,084

$FV_n = PV \times F$

FV_n = *future value* of interest at some future point in time (n)

PV = *present value* of investment

F = *factor* of future value (given a certain interest rate and n), which is located in the table, or determined by FV_n/PV

Illustrations: Using Appendix A2

1. You want to begin a college fund for your newborn child; you want $30,000 18 years from now. If a current investment opportunity yields 7 percent, how much must you invest in a lump sum to realize the $30,000 when needed?

   The interest factor is 0.296; hence the solution is $30,000 × 0.296, or $8800.

2. You hope to retire in 25 years and want to deposit one lump sum that will grow to $250,000 at that time. If you can now invest at 8 percent, how much must you invest to realize the $250,000 when needed?

   The interest factor is 0.146; hence the solution is $250,000 × 0.146, or $36,500. The present value of $250,000 received 25 years from now is $36,500 if the interest rate is 8 percent.

3. You have the choice of receiving $15,000 today as a down payment from someone who wants to purchase your rental property or a personal note for $25,000 payable in 6 years. If you could expect to earn 8 percent on such funds, which is the better choice?

   The interest factor is 0.630; hence the solution is $25,000 × 0.630, or $15,750. Thus, the present value of $25,000 received in 6 years is greater than $15,000 received now, and is the better choice.

4. You own a $1000 bond paying 8 percent annually until maturity in 5 years. You need to sell it now even though the market rate of interest on similar bonds has increased to 10 percent. What will be the lower discounted market price of the bond so that the buyer of your bond will earn a yield of 10 percent?

   The solution first involves computing the present value of the future interest payments of $80 per year for 5 years at 10 percent (using Appendix A4), $80 × 3.791, or $303.28. Second, compute the present value of the future principal repayment of $1000 after 5 years at 10 percent: $1000 × 0.621, or $621.00. Hence the market price is the sum of the two present values ($303.28 + $621.00), or $924.28.

APPENDIX A2
Present Value of $1 (to Compute the Present Value of Some Known Future Sum)

Periods	1%	2%	3%	4%	5%	6%	7%	8%	9%	10%	12%	14%	15%
1	0.990	0.980	0.971	0.962	0.952	0.943	0.935	0.926	0.917	0.909	0.893	0.877	0.870
2	0.980	0.961	0.943	0.925	0.907	0.890	0.873	0.857	0.842	0.826	0.797	0.769	0.756
3	0.971	0.942	0.915	0.889	0.864	0.840	0.816	0.794	0.772	0.751	0.712	0.675	0.658
4	0.961	0.924	0.888	0.855	0.823	0.792	0.763	0.735	0.708	0.683	0.636	0.592	0.572
5	0.951	0.906	0.883	0.822	0.784	0.747	0.713	0.681	0.650	0.621	0.567	0.519	0.497
6	0.942	0.888	0.837	0.790	0.746	0.705	0.666	0.630	0.596	0.564	0.507	0.456	0.432
7	0.933	0.871	0.813	0.760	0.711	0.665	0.623	0.583	0.547	0.513	0.452	0.400	0.376
8	0.923	0.853	0.789	0.731	0.677	0.627	0.582	0.540	0.502	0.467	0.404	0.351	0.327
9	0.914	0.837	0.766	0.703	0.645	0.592	0.544	0.500	0.460	0.424	0.361	0.308	0.284
10	0.905	0.820	0.744	0.676	0.614	0.558	0.508	0.463	0.422	0.386	0.322	0.270	0.247
11	0.896	0.804	0.722	0.650	0.585	0.527	0.475	0.429	0.388	0.350	0.287	0.237	0.215
12	0.887	0.788	0.701	0.625	0.557	0.497	0.444	0.397	0.356	0.319	0.257	0.208	0.187
13	0.879	0.773	0.681	0.601	0.530	0.469	0.415	0.368	0.326	0.290	0.229	0.182	0.163
14	0.870	0.758	0.661	0.577	0.505	0.442	0.388	0.340	0.299	0.263	0.205	0.160	0.141
15	0.861	0.743	0.642	0.555	0.481	0.417	0.362	0.315	0.275	0.239	0.183	0.140	0.123
16	0.853	0.728	0.623	0.534	0.458	0.394	0.339	0.292	0.252	0.218	0.163	0.123	0.107
17	0.844	0.714	0.605	0.513	0.436	0.371	0.317	0.270	0.231	0.198	0.146	0.108	0.093
18	0.836	0.700	0.587	0.494	0.416	0.350	0.296	0.250	0.212	0.180	0.130	0.095	0.081
19	0.828	0.686	0.570	0.475	0.396	0.331	0.277	0.232	0.194	0.164	0.116	0.083	0.070
20	0.820	0.673	0.554	0.456	0.377	0.312	0.258	0.215	0.178	0.149	0.104	0.073	0.061
21	0.811	0.660	0.538	0.439	0.359	0.294	0.242	0.199	0.164	0.135	0.093	0.064	0.053
22	0.803	0.647	0.522	0.422	0.342	0.278	0.226	0.184	0.150	0.123	0.083	0.056	0.046
23	0.795	0.634	0.507	0.406	0.326	0.262	0.211	0.170	0.138	0.112	0.074	0.049	0.040
24	0.788	0.622	0.492	0.390	0.310	0.247	0.197	0.158	0.126	0.102	0.066	0.043	0.035
25	0.780	0.610	0.478	0.375	0.295	0.233	0.184	0.146	0.116	0.092	0.059	0.038	0.030
26	0.772	0.598	0.464	0.361	0.281	0.220	0.172	0.135	0.106	0.084	0.053	0.033	0.026
27	0.764	0.586	0.450	0.347	0.268	0.207	0.161	0.125	0.098	0.076	0.047	0.029	0.023
28	0.757	0.574	0.437	0.333	0.255	0.196	0.150	0.116	0.090	0.069	0.042	0.026	0.020
29	0.749	0.563	0.424	0.321	0.243	0.185	0.141	0.107	0.082	0.063	0.037	0.022	0.017
30	0.742	0.552	0.412	0.308	0.231	0.174	0.131	0.099	0.075	0.057	0.033	0.020	0.015
40	0.672	0.453	0.307	0.208	0.142	0.097	0.067	0.046	0.032	0.022	0.011	0.005	0.004
50	0.608	0.372	0.228	0.141	0.087	0.054	0.034	0.021	0.013	0.009	0.003	0.001	0.001

$PV = FV_n \times F$
PV = present value
FV_n = future value of investment at some future point in time (n)
F = factor of present value (given a certain interest rate and n)

Illustrations: Using Appendix A3

1. You plan to retire after 16 years. To provide for that retirement, you initiate a savings program of $7000 per year in an investment yielding 8 percent. What will be the value of the retirement fund at the beginning of the seventeenth year?

   Your last payment into the fund will occur at the end of the sixteenth year, so scan down the periods column for period 16, and then across until you reach the 8 percent column. The interest factor is 30.32. Hence the solution is $7000(30.32), or $212,240.

2. What will be the value of an investment if you put $2000 into a retirement plan yielding 7 percent annually for 25 years?

   The interest factor is 63.250. Hence the solution is $2000(63.250), or $126,500.

3. You are trying to decide between putting $3000 or $4000 annually for the next 20 years into an investment yielding 7 percent for retirement purposes. What is the difference in the value of investing the extra $1000 for 20 years?

   The interest factor is 41.0 Hence the solution is $1,000(41.0), or $41,000.

4. You will receive an annuity payment of $1200 at the end of each year for 6 years. What will be the total value of this stream of income invested at 7 percent by the time you receive the last payment?

   The appropriate interest factor for 6 years at 7 percent is 7.153. Hence the solution is $1200(7.153), or $8584.

5. You want to know how many years of investing $1200 annually at 9 percent it will take to reach a goal of $11,000.

   Divide the future value of $11,000 by the lump sum of $1200 to find a factor of 9.17 and look down the 9 percent column to find 9.200 (close enough). Read across the row to find that an investment period of 7 years is needed.

6. You want to know what percent of return is needed if you plan to invest $12,000 annually for 9 years to reach a goal of $15,000.

   Divide the future value goal of $15,000 by $1200 to derive the factor 12.5 and look along the row for 9 years to locate the factor 12.49 (close enough). Read up the column to find that you need an 8 percent return.

APPENDIX A3
Future Value of an Annuity of $1 per year (to Compute the Future Value of a Stream of Annuity or Income Payments)

Periods	1%	2%	3%	4%	5%	6%	7%	8%	9%	10%	12%	14%	15%
1	1.000	1.000	1.000	1.000	1.000	1.000	1.000	1.000	1.000	1.000	1.000	1.000	1.000
2	2.010	2.020	2.030	2.040	2.050	2.060	2.070	2.080	2.090	2.100	2.120	2.140	2.150
3	3.030	3.060	3.091	3.122	3.153	3.184	3.215	3.246	3.278	3.310	3.374	3.440	3.473
4	4.060	4.122	4.184	4.246	4.310	4.375	4.440	4.506	4.573	4.641	4.779	4.921	4.993
5	5.101	5.204	5.309	5.416	5.526	5.637	5.751	5.867	5.985	6.105	6.353	6.610	6.742
6	6.152	6.308	6.468	6.633	6.802	6.975	7.153	7.336	7.523	7.716	8.115	8.536	8.754
7	7.214	7.434	7.662	7.898	8.142	8.394	8.654	8.923	9.200	9.487	10.09	10.73	11.07
8	8.286	8.583	8.892	9.214	9.549	9.897	10.26	10.64	11.03	11.44	12.30	13.23	13.73
9	9.369	9.755	10.16	10.58	11.03	11.49	11.98	12.49	13.02	13.58	14.78	16.09	16.79
10	10.46	10.95	11.46	12.01	12.58	13.18	13.82	14.49	15.19	15.94	17.55	19.34	20.30
11	11.57	12.17	12.81	13.49	14.21	14.97	15.78	16.65	17.56	18.53	20.65	23.04	24.35
12	12.68	13.41	14.19	15.03	15.92	16.87	17.89	18.98	20.14	21.38	24.13	27.27	29.00
13	13.81	14.68	15.62	16.63	17.71	18.88	20.14	21.50	22.95	24.52	28.03	32.09	34.35
14	14.95	15.97	17.09	18.29	19.60	21.02	22.55	24.21	26.02	27.98	32.39	37.58	40.50
15	16.10	17.29	18.60	20.02	21.58	23.28	25.13	27.15	29.36	31.77	37.28	43.84	47.58
16	17.26	18.64	20.16	21.82	23.66	25.67	27.89	30.32	33.00	35.95	42.75	50.98	55.72
17	18.43	20.01	21.76	23.70	25.84	28.21	30.84	33.75	36.97	40.54	48.88	59.12	65.08
18	19.61	21.41	23.41	25.65	28.13	30.91	34.00	37.45	41.30	45.60	55.75	68.39	75.84
19	20.81	22.84	25.12	27.67	30.54	33.76	37.38	41.45	46.02	51.16	63.44	78.97	88.21
20	22.02	24.30	26.87	29.78	33.07	36.79	41.00	45.76	51.16	57.28	72.05	91.02	102.4
21	23.24	25.78	28.68	31.97	35.72	39.99	44.87	50.42	56.76	64.00	81.70	104.8	118.8
22	24.47	27.30	30.54	34.25	38.51	43.39	49.01	55.46	62.87	71.40	92.50	120.4	137.6
23	25.72	28.85	32.45	36.62	41.43	47.00	53.44	60.89	69.53	79.54	104.6	138.3	159.3
24	26.97	30.42	34.43	39.08	44.50	50.82	58.18	66.76	76.79	88.50	118.2	158.7	184.2
25	28.24	32.03	36.46	41.65	47.73	54.86	63.25	73.11	84.70	98.35	133.3	181.9	212.8
26	29.53	33.67	38.55	44.31	51.11	59.16	68.68	79.95	93.32	109.2	150.3	208.3	245.7
27	30.82	35.34	40.71	47.08	54.67	63.71	74.48	87.35	102.7	121.1	169.4	238.5	283.6
28	32.13	37.05	42.93	49.97	58.40	68.53	80.70	95.34	113.0	134.2	190.7	272.9	327.1
29	33.45	38.79	45.22	52.97	62.32	73.64	87.35	104.04	124.1	148.6	214.6	312.1	377.2
30	34.78	40.57	47.58	56.08	66.44	79.06	94.46	113.34	136.3	164.5	241.3	356.8	434.7
40	48.89	60.40	75.40	95.03	120.8	154.8	199.6	259.1	337.9	442.6	767.1	1,342	1,779
50	64.46	84.58	112.8	152.7	209.3	290.3	406.5	573.8	815.1	1,164	2,400	4,995	7,218

$FV = A_n \times F$
$FV = $ future value
$A_n = $ amount (periodic payment) of the annuity for n periods
$F = $ factor of future value (given a certain interest rate and n)

Illustrations: Using Appendix A4

1. You are entering a contract that will provide you an income of $1000 at the end of the year for the next 10 years. If the annual interest rate is 7 percent, what is the present value of that stream of payments?

   The interest factor is 7.024; hence the solution is $1000 × 7.024, or $7024.

2. You expect to have $250,000 available in a retirement plan upon retirement. If the amount invested yields 8 percent and you hope to live an additional 20 years, how much can you withdraw each year so that the fund will just be liquidated after 20 years?

   The interest factor for 20 years at 8 percent is 9.818. Hence the solution is $250,000 ÷ 9.818, or $25,463.

3. You have received an inheritance of $60,000 and invest that sum earning 9 percent. If you withdraw $8000 annually to supplement your income, in how many years will the fund run out?

   Solving for n, $60,000 ÷ $8000 = 7.5. Scan down the 9 percent column until you find the interest factor nearest 7.5, which is 7.487. This is on the row indicating 13 years; thus the fund will be depleted in approximately 13 years with $8000 annual withdrawals.

4. A seller offers to finance the sale of a building to you as an investment. The mortgage loan of $280,000 will be for 20 years and requires an annual mortgage payment of $24,000. Should you finance the purchase through the seller or borrow the funds from a financial institution at a current rate of 10 percent?

   $280,000 ÷ $24,000 = 11.667. Scan down the periods column to 20 years and then read across to locate the figure closest to 11.667, which is 11.470. This is in the column indicating 6 percent; thus, seller financing offers a lower interest rate.

5. You have the opportunity to purchase an office building for $750,000 with an expected life of 20 years. Looking over the financial details, you see that the before-tax net rental income is $90,000. Since you want a return of at least 15 percent, how much should you pay for the building?

   The interest factor for twenty years at 15 percent is 6.259, and $90,000 × 6.259 = $563,310. Thus, the price is too high for you to earn a return of 15 percent.

Present Value of an Annuity of $1 per Year (to Compute the Present Value of a Stream of Annuity or Income Payments)

Periods	1%	2%	3%	4%	5%	6%	7%	8%	9%	10%	12%	14%	15%
1	0.990	0.980	0.971	0.962	0.952	0.943	0.935	0.926	0.917	0.909	0.893	0.877	0.870
2	1.970	1.942	1.913	1.886	1.859	1.833	1.808	1.783	1.759	1.736	1.690	1.647	1.626
3	2.941	2.884	2.829	2.775	2.723	2.673	2.624	2.577	2.531	2.487	2.402	2.322	2.283
4	3.902	3.808	3.717	3.630	3.546	3.465	3.387	3.312	3.240	3.170	3.037	2.914	2.855
5	4.853	4.713	4.580	4.452	4.329	4.212	4.100	3.993	3.890	3.791	3.605	3.433	3.352
6	5.795	5.601	5.417	5.242	5.076	4.917	4.767	4.623	4.486	4.355	4.111	3.889	3.784
7	6.728	6.472	6.230	6.002	5.786	5.582	5.389	5.206	5.033	4.868	4.564	4.288	4.160
8	7.652	7.325	7.020	6.733	6.463	6.210	5.971	5.747	5.535	5.335	4.968	4.639	4.487
9	8.566	8.162	7.786	7.435	7.108	6.802	6.515	6.247	5.995	5.759	5.328	4.946	4.772
10	9.471	8.983	8.530	8.111	7.722	7.360	7.024	6.710	6.418	6.145	5.650	5.216	5.019
11	10.368	9.787	9.253	8.760	8.306	7.887	7.499	7.139	6.805	6.495	5.938	5.453	5.234
12	11.255	10.575	9.954	9.385	8.863	8.384	7.943	7.536	7.161	6.814	6.194	5.660	5.421
13	12.134	11.348	10.635	9.986	9.394	8.853	8.358	7.904	7.487	7.103	6.424	5.842	5.583
14	13.004	12.106	11.296	10.563	9.899	9.295	8.745	8.244	7.786	7.367	6.628	6.002	5.724
15	13.865	12.849	11.938	11.118	10.380	9.712	9.108	8.559	8.061	7.606	6.811	6.142	5.847
16	14.718	13.578	12.561	11.652	10.838	10.106	9.447	8.851	8.313	7.824	6.974	6.265	5.954
17	15.562	14.292	13.166	12.166	11.274	10.477	9.763	9.122	8.544	8.022	7.120	6.373	6.047
18	16.398	14.992	13.754	12.659	11.690	10.828	10.059	9.372	8.756	8.201	7.250	6.467	6.128
19	17.226	15.678	14.324	13.134	12.085	11.158	10.336	9.604	8.950	8.365	7.366	6.550	6.198
20	18.046	16.351	14.878	13.590	12.462	11.470	10.594	9.818	9.129	8.514	7.469	6.623	6.259
21	18.857	17.011	15.415	14.029	12.821	11.764	10.836	10.017	9.292	8.649	7.562	6.687	6.312
22	19.660	17.658	15.937	14.451	13.163	12.042	11.061	10.201	9.442	8.772	7.645	6.743	6.359
23	20.456	18.292	16.444	14.857	13.489	12.303	11.272	10.371	9.580	8.883	7.718	6.792	6.399
24	21.243	18.914	16.936	15.247	13.799	12.550	11.469	10.529	9.707	8.985	7.784	6.835	6.434
25	22.023	19.523	17.413	15.622	14.094	12.783	11.654	10.675	9.823	9.077	7.843	6.873	6.464
26	22.795	20.121	17.877	15.983	14.375	13.003	11.826	10.810	9.929	9.161	7.896	6.906	6.491
27	23.560	20.707	18.327	16.330	14.643	13.211	11.987	10.935	10.027	9.237	7.943	6.935	6.514
28	24.316	21.281	18.764	16.663	14.898	13.406	12.137	11.051	10.116	9.307	7.984	6.961	6.534
29	25.066	21.844	19.189	16.984	15.141	13.591	12.278	11.158	10.198	9.370	8.022	6.983	6.551
30	25.808	22.396	19.600	17.292	15.373	13.765	12.409	11.258	10.274	9.427	8.055	7.003	6.566
40	32.835	27.355	23.115	19.793	17.159	15.046	13.332	11.925	10.757	9.779	8.244	7.105	6.642
50	39.196	31.424	25.730	21.482	18.256	15.762	13.801	12.234	10.962	9.915	8.305	7.133	6.661

$PV = A_n \times F$

PV = present value

A_n = amount (periodic payment) of annuity for n periods, or determined by $A_n = PV/F$

F = factor of present value (given a certain interest rate and n)

APPENDIX

B

Estimating Social Security Benefits

· · · · · · · · ·

The Social Security Administration (SSA) has a basic benefit credited to you right now for benefits for your retirement, for a period of disability, or for your survivors as long as you qualify based on the number of quarters of coverage you have attained. The level of benefits received from Social Security depends on your income in past years that was subject to Federal Insurance Contributions Act (FICA) taxes, commonly known as Social Security taxes. The tables that follow provide estimates of Social Security benefits for various ages, income levels, and benefit recipients. The tables are based on 1990 Social Security benefit levels, and you can estimate your own benefits by using your personal income data and age.

Social Security Retirement Benefits

To be eligible for Social Security retirement benefits, any worker born after 1928 must have attained 40 quarters of coverage. Remember from the text that it is possible to receive 4 quarters per year and that in 1990 a worker would receive 1 quarter for each $515 of income subject to Social Security taxes. Dependent children, spouses caring for dependent children, and retired spouses at age 62 (including former spouses if the marriage lasted more than 10 years) may also collect benefits based on the eligibility of the retired worker.

Use the table on page A-12 to estimate monthly retirement benefits from Social Security. The result will be the amount of likely monthly retirement benefits in today's dollars, assuming that you have worked steadily and received pay raises equal to the U.S. average throughout your working career. To calculate a more specific figure write William M. Mercer, Inc., to obtain the booklet cited in the table (for a nominal charge) or call the Social Security Administration for the pamphlet entitled "Estimating Your Social Security Retirement Check: Using the Indexing Method."

Social Security Disability Benefits

When a covered worker becomes disabled, Social Security will pay benefits to the worker, dependent children up to age eighteen (nineteen if still in high school), a spouse caring for a dependent child under age sixteen or disabled, and a spouse (even if divorced, but not remarried, provided the marriage lasted 10 years) age sixty-two and above. The dollar amount of

Monthly Retirement Benefits at Age 65

Your Age in 1990	Who Receives Benefits	Your Present Annual Earnings				
		$12,000	$20,000	$30,000	$40,000	$51,300 and Up
65	You	$ 491	$ 683	$ 886	$ 938	$ 975
	Spouse[a] or child	245	341	443	469	487
64	You	486	676	877	931	970
	Spouse[a] or child	243	338	438	465	485
63	You	496	690	896	952	995
	Spouse[a] or child	248	345	448	476	497
62	You	497	690	898	955	1,000
	Spouse[a] or child	248	345	449	477	500
61	You	497	692	899	958	1,006
	Spouse[a] or child	248	346	449	479	503
55	You	503	701	913	993	1,065
	Spouse[a] or child	251	350	456	496	532
50	You	491[b]	685[b]	892[b]	988[b]	1,077[b]
	Spouse or child[c]	254	354	461	511	557
45	You	478[b]	669[b]	868[b]	974[b]	1,079[b]
	Spouse or child[c]	256	358	465	522	578
40	You	483[b]	676[b]	873[b]	986[b]	1,109[b]
	Spouse or child[c]	258	362	467	528	594
35	You	481[b]	675[b]	867[b]	981[b]	1,109[b]
	Spouse or child[c]	261	366	470	532	601
30	You	456[b]	640[b]	819[b]	928[b]	1,050[b]
	Spouse or child[c]	263	369	473	535	606

Source: Table reprinted with permission from *1990: Guide to Social Security and Medicare,* William M. Mercer, Inc., Louisville, Kentucky, 40202-3415.

[a]Benefit at age 65 or at any age with eligible child in care.

[b]These amounts are reduced for retirement at age 65 because the Normal Retirement Age (NRA) is higher than age 65 for these persons.

[c]The amount shown is for the spouse at NRA or with eligible child in care, or for the child: the benefit for a spouse younger than NRA without a child in care would be reduced for early retirement.

the benefits will depend on two factors. The first is the eligibility of the disabled worker. Depending on year of birth workers need up to 39 quarters of coverage (maximum is 4 per year) under Social Security with at least 20 of the quarters attained in the last 10 years to be eligible for disability benefits. A worker under age thirty-one must have attained at least 6, or one more than one-half of the total quarters of coverage possible after age twenty-one, whichever is greater. (For example, a twenty-six-year-old worker would have 5 years, or 20 quarters, possible and would need 11 quarters of coverage.)

Use the table on page A-13 to estimate monthly disability benefits from Social Security. The result will be the amount of likely monthly disability

Monthly Benefits at Disability

Your Age in 1990	Who Receives Benefits	Your Present Annual Earnings				
		$12,000	$20,000	$30,000	$40,000	$51,300 and Up
64	You	$ 484	$ 673	$ 873	$ 922	$ 957
	Child (or children and spouse)	242	336	436	461	478
60	You	494	685	888	938	972
	Child (or children and spouse)	247	342	444	469	486
55	You	494	686	895	951	991
	Child (or children and spouse)	247	343	447	475	495
50	You	494	686	903	971	1,019
	Child (or children and spouse)	247	343	451	485	509
45	You	494	686	908	990	1,048
	Child (or children and spouse)	247	343	454	495	524
40	You	494	687	909	1,009	1,082
	Child (or children and spouse)	247	343	454	504	541
35	You	495	687	909	1,022	1,122
	Child (or children and spouse)	247	343	454	511	561
30	You	496	689	910	1,023	1,145
	Child (or children and spouse)	248	344	455	511	572

Table reprinted with permission from *1990: Guide to Social Security and Medicare*, William M. Mercer, Inc., Louisville, Kentucky, 40202-3415.

benefits in today's dollars assuming that you have worked steadily and received pay raises equal to the U.S. average throughout your working career. The maximum family benefit is 150 percent of the benefit for the covered worker (you). To calculate a more specific figure write William M. Mercer, Inc., to obtain the booklet cited in the table (for a nominal charge) or call the Social Security Administration.

Social Security Survivors' Benefits

When a covered worker dies, Social Security will pay benefits to surviving children under age eighteen (or nineteen if still in high school), to a surviving spouse (even if divorced from the deceased but not remarried, if the marriage lasted at least 10 years) caring for surviving children under age 16, and to a surviving spouse (even if divorced if the marriage lasted at least 10 years) age 60 or over. The amount of benefits will depend on two factors. The first is the eligibility of the covered worker. Depending on year of birth, a worker needs up to 39 quarters of coverage to be "fully insured." Those who have attained at least as many quarters of coverage as years since turning age 21 will also be fully insured. Others may be considered "currently insured" if they have 6 quarters of coverage in the previous 13 calendar quarters. The survivors of currently insured workers receive limited types of benefits compared to those of fully insured workers. The second factor is the covered worker's level of earnings.

Use the table below to estimate monthly survivors' benefits from Social Security for your eligible surviving family members. The result will be the amount of likely monthly benefits in today's dollars assuming that you have worked steadily and received pay raises equal to the U.S. average throughout your working career. To calculate a more specific figure write William M. Mercer, Inc., to obtain the booklet cited in the table below (for a nominal charge) or call the Social Security Administration.

Monthly Survivors' Benefits if You Died in 1990

Your Age in 1990	Who Receives Benefits	Your Present Annual Earnings				
		$12,000	$20,000	$30,000	$40,000	$51,300 and Up
65	Spouse, age 65	$ 491	$ 683	$ 886	$ 938	$ 975
	Spouse, age 60	351	488	634	670	697
	Child; spouse caring for child	368	512	665	703	731
	Maximum family benefit	789	1,262	1,551	1,641	1,705
60	Spouse, age 65	494	685	888	938	972
	Spouse, age 60	353	490	635	671	694
	Child; spouse caring for child	370	514	666	703	729
	Maximum family benefit	788	1,269	1,554	1,641	1,700
55	Spouse, age 65	494	686	895	951	991
	Spouse, age 60	353	490	640	680	708
	Child; spouse caring for child	370	514	671	713	743
	Maximum family benefit	788	1,269	1,566	1,664	1,733
50	Spouse, age 65	494	686	903	971	1,019
	Spouse, age 60	353	490	645	694	728
	Child; spouse caring for child	370	514	677	728	764
	Maximum family benefit	789	1,269	1,579	1,699	1,783
45	Spouse, age 65	494	686	908	996	1,057
	Spouse, age 60	353	491	649	712	756
	Child; spouse caring for child	370	515	681	747	793
	Maximum family benefit	789	1,270	1,589	1,742	1,849

Monthly Survivors' Benefits if You Died in 1990 (*continued*)

Your Age in 1990	Who Receives Benefits	Your Present Annual Earnings				
		$12,000	*$20,000*	*$30,000*	*$40,000*	*$51,300 and Up*
40	Spouse, age 65	494	687	909	1,015	1,100
	Spouse, age 60	353	491	650	726	786
	Child; spouse caring for child	371	515	681	761	825
	Maximum family benefit	790	1,270	1,590	1,776	1,924
35	Spouse, age 65	495	688	910	1,023	1,141
	Spouse, age 60	354	492	650	731	816
	Child; spouse caring for child	371	516	682	767	856
	Maximum family benefit	793	1,273	1,591	1,789	1,996
30	Spouse, age 65	499	694	914	1,028	1,157
	Spouse, age 60	356	496	653	735	827
	Child; spouse caring for child	374	520	685	771	868
	Maximum family benefit	802	1,280	1,599	1,799	2,025

Source: Table reprinted with permission from *1990: Guide to Social Security and Medicare*, William M. Mercer, Inc., Louisville, Kentucky, 40202-3415.

C

Personal Computers in Finance

Because personal computers manipulate numbers quickly, reliably, and impartially, they have had a tremendous impact on the field of financial analysis and money management. Either by choice or from competitive necessity, most financial advisors use personal computers to make projections, calculate payment schedules, compare investments, record transactions, write letters, and chart alternatives. Many people use financial programs on their home computers to design personal budgets, enter incomes and expenses into data files, generate cash flow statements, prepare tax returns, print checks, and construct graphs. More and more people are turning the clerical and analytical work of financial planning over to their personal computers; this leaves more time for thinking about alternatives and making decisions.

Software

To use personal computers effectively, you must select the right program, or software. Using the right software package for the job is just as important as using the right tools to build a house. Carpenters spend years learning how and when to use each tool. Many problems beginners have can be traced to using the wrong program. For example, you could maintain a home budget and expense-tracking system with a word processing program, but doing that makes as much sense as cutting a two-by-four in half with a hammer. A home finance management program would make it much easier to enter and update the budget and expense data and would have the added benefit of generating a wide range of reports and graphs from the data almost effortlessly.

You can choose from several general types of programs to help you with personal finance, depending on the kinds of calculations you're doing. After a brief discussion of each type, we'll cover spreadsheet, presentation graphics, and home finance programs in more detail.

Spreadsheet Programs

Spreadsheet programs are frequently used for financial modeling and forecasting because they make the power of a computer's numerical processing available to people who have no prior computer experience. One of the most common uses of spreadsheet programs is to construct

This appendix was prepared by David Sullivan, Assistant Professor of Information Systems, Oregon State University.

financial statements and budgets, but any repetitive task that you currently do with a pencil, paper, and calculator can probably be done quicker with a spreadsheet.

Presentation Graphics Programs

Sometimes called *business graphics programs,* presentation graphics programs convert numbers into histograms, bar charts, pie charts, and line graphs. Many finance programs can generate presentation-quality graphs from the numbers they manipulate, so for most personal finance needs it is not necessary to buy a separate "stand-alone" program.

Database Management Programs

This type of program makes it easy to store, retrieve, and manipulate lists of information. Most database systems have built-in functions for sorting records, printing simple reports, and designing on-screen forms to facilitate the entry of data. The simplest database programs are called "personal filing" programs; they can deal with only one file of information at a time and are ideal for mailing lists, personal inventories, and other light uses. More powerful database systems can merge information from one file into another, generate sophisticated reports, and manage millions of records. At the heart of many accounting and financial recordkeeping systems is a database program.

Telecommunications

You can use an ordinary telephone line to link your personal computer to any of thousands of other computers, from the largest scientific supercomputers to a friend's personal computer on the other side of the country. One of the most rapidly growing areas of communications is the linkage of personal computers to information utilities, which are time-shared mainframe computers that offer services ranging from electronic mail to news stories, investment services, biorhythms, and travel guides. Rates for using these services are based mostly on connect time, the time you are logged on to the utility, and go from a low of $5 an hour to well over $100 an hour. Here are some of the things you can do in a few minutes of connect time with an information utility:

Search the last few months of the *Wall Street Journal* for articles on a particular topic or company.

Order books, cameras, and other items at a substantial discount.

Capture detailed financial information for all the companies on a predetermined list. The information might include stock and bond prices, volumes sold, company revenues, earnings and financial ratios.

Send letters to be printed and delivered by the post office.

Read any of numerous "on-line" financial newsletters—even transcripts of Louis Rukeyser's *Wall Street Week* from the Public Broadcasting Service.

One unique service provided by information utilities is the ability to search quickly through large volumes of information and find all the items matching criteria you specify. Unfortunately, the commands used by some information utilities are rather hard to master. You can, however, use a communications program, such as Texas Instruments' NaturalLink, on your personal computer that allows you to construct queries that your communications program translates before it sends the queries to the utility.

Home Finance Programs

Also called *personal finance programs*, home finance programs help you monitor your financial health; they vary considerably in their capabilities. The simplest are little more than aids for balancing a checkbook. Most offer the ability to set up a database of income, expense, asset, and liability accounts and provide numerous financial reports along with simple graphs of the data. The high-end home finance programs would satisfy most of the accounting needs of a small business.

Tax-Planning and Preparation Programs

These programs compare alternative tax strategies and help prepare income tax returns. Tax-planning programs allow you to perform "what-if" calculations to explore the tax impact of various tax shelters, changes in income, depreciation methods, individual retirement accounts, estate plans, estimated tax payments, and the like. Tax-preparation programs help you through the maze of filling out your tax return. Often they can print directly on the IRS forms and schedules.

Real Estate Analysis Programs

Real estate analysis programs can provide guidance on real estate transactions that would take hours to calculate by hand. Typically these programs can perform a number of investment comparisons, such as comparing the cost of purchasing with renting, calculating an amortization schedule, making a cash flow projection, or determining if it is possible to qualify a buyer for a particular property. Both real estate analysis and tax preparation are activities that the average person does infrequently, usually no more than once a year. As a result, most of these programs are sold to professionals, who use them in consultation with their clients.

Stock and Bond Analysis Programs

These are tools for screening, evaluating, and selecting investments. Some of these packages focus on technical analysis, an analysis of the security's market price and volume statistics. Other programs stick to analyzing the fundamentals, such as facts from historical financial statements, expected earnings, or subjective evaluations of the company's management and products. Both types of programs allow you to establish a database of information on a list of securities you wish to track. Information can be entered into the database by hand, but most programs are also able to extract the necessary information automatically from an information utility such as the Dow Jones News/Retrieval service. Once the information is in the database, the program's analysis capabilities take over to create reports listing your investments, reports recommending purchase strategies, or charts plotting stock prices, among other things.

Spreadsheet Processing

A spreadsheet program transforms a personal computer into a number-crunching tool capable of solving problems you used to tackle with a pencil, scratch pad, and calculator. It is especially useful for time-consuming tasks, such as performing the same calculations repetitively with different starting assumptions or making decisions among several alternatives. These characteristics make spreadsheet processing ideal for ad hoc financial analysis.

The computer screen is broken into two areas: a program status and help information area, which helps you control the operation of the program much like a car's dashboard helps you drive a car; and a window into the worksheet, which shows you a processed version of the data in the worksheet.

The worksheet can be thought of as an enormous piece of multicolumn paper whose size depends on the program. A common size is 64 columns wide by 256 rows deep, although some worksheets have hundreds of columns and thousands of rows. Obviously only a small part of the entire worksheet can be visible on the screen at a time, so the screen acts like a window presenting a tiny part of the entire worksheet. It is possible to move the window through the worksheet by scrolling horizontally and vertically.

The real power of spreadsheet programs lies in their ability to store formulas for calculating numbers as well as storing the numbers themselves. Thus, when critical numbers are changed, the entire model is recalculated, updating any totals or other numbers as necessary to keep everything self-consistent and in balance. For example, if you changed the amount of January's food budget, the total budget for the month would be adjusted automatically.

This instantaneous "what-if" recalculation capability allows people to experiment with the relationships among numbers in a manner that was previously impractical. For example, changing the sales estimate in a business's typical five-year financial plan requires adjustments in manufacturing costs, overhead costs, warranty returns, and many other items. If the forecast is stored on a multicolumn paper worksheet, it can take an accountant hours of error-prone, tedious figuring to predict the implications of a specific set of changes in the forecast's basic assumptions. Such arduous work discourages experimentation and limits how many assumptions about the future are explored.

Presentation Graphics

A graph provides instant meaning to numbers in a manner that no table or paragraph can match. Trends and relationships that lie hidden in a collection of numbers are immediately exposed when the numbers are charted or graphed.

With the right combination of hardware and software, it takes only a few minutes to create graphs that would take hours to prepare by hand. Most programs allow you to preview the graphs on the screen. If you like what you see and have an appropriate output device, you can transfer the image onto paper, an overhead transparency, or 35-mm slides.

In addition to simple bar charts, pie charts, and line graphs, most stand-alone presentation graphics programs have numerous charting options, such as creating stacked bar charts, exploded pie charts, or stock market graphs with tick marks for each day's high, low, close, and open prices. Other features allow you to specify the size and placement of titles or to cross-hatch or color portions of the graph. However, the average person who just wants to graph personal expenses doesn't need the capabilities of a stand-alone graphics program.

Many of the advanced spreadsheet programs include a graphics module capable of generating a limited range of presentation graphics. Once you are familiar with the process, it takes no more than a few seconds to obtain a crude graph. The two major steps are to select the type of graph you want from a menu of options in the control panel and to point out what parts of the worksheet contain the numbers to be graphed.

Many home finance, stock and bond tracking, and other finance programs have very easy-to-use graphing capabilities. For example, a majority of the home finance programs will present a bar chart showing the monthly account balances of any income or expense category that you specify. Requesting one of these charts generally takes no more than a few keystrokes and can provide an immediate insight into your spending habits.

Home Finance Programs

A home finance management program helps record, summarize, print, and graph financial transactions. Basically, it is a miniature accounting system designed to be used by a family or a small business.

Like all accounting systems, a home finance program operates with the help of a chart of accounts. You must tell the program what accounts you want when you set up the system, but it should also be possible to modify the listing later.

Once the chart of accounts has been established, you can begin entering transactions. It is always possible to correct a transaction that you have entered in error. Also, most systems allow you to set up some transactions so that they can be posted automatically. This would make sense for a house payment that is the same amount each month.

A home finance program will record and enter transactions more slowly than you could write them down on paper, but this type of system really pays off when it comes to generating reports. You should be able to preview on the screen or send to the printer a cash flow statement, a personal net worth statement, and various types of transaction listings. In addition, most systems allow you to graph the activity in each account or account category. These graphs can be a real eye-opener and show you trends in your spending habits you hadn't noticed before.

A home finance program will not help you if the only accounting activity you do each month is to balance your checkbook—you can do that more quickly by hand. But if you are already recording your expenses, a home finance program can make the process more reliable and improve the quality of the information you receive from your efforts.

Finding Financial Software

Acquiring good financial software requires research, judgment, money, and luck. Searching for the "best" software package is often impractical because of the tremendous number of packages on the market—over 30,000 programs are available for personal computers.

The price of financial programs varies dramatically. A few excellent programs have been placed in the public domain by their authors; frequently these can be purchased from computer clubs for the cost of duplicating a disk (about $5). Most programs sold for use in the home cost from $30 to $300.

Finding information about financial programs can be difficult. Your local computer retailer is not likely to stock many financial programs; they sell slowly compared to programs like games and word processing. Also, nearly all software outlets are reluctant to lend copies of programs for evaluation because of the rampant software piracy problem in our society. Here are two basic sources to use to begin your search:

Personal computer magazines can be an excellent source of independent software reviews. You can consult either general personal computer magazines (such as *InfoWorld, Byte,* or *Personal Computing*) or magazines targeted to specific brands of machines (such as *PC World* for IBM PCs or *inCider* for Apple IIs).

Software catalogues and directories provide listings of programs organized by category. The boundaries between most categories are unclear; for finance programs you might check investment management, business, real estate, personal or home management, and graphics.

One such financial software program is *Managing Your Money* by Andrew J. Tobias, published by Micro Educational Corporation of America (MECA). This package is designed to allow individuals to organize their personal finances with the help of a microcomputer and to assist in budgeting, bank transactions, investments, taxes, and retirement planning. You can also use the Personal Finance Cookbook software that accompanies this text to create a budget, a balance sheet, and other of your own personal finance calculations.

D Common-Sense Principles of Success in Personal Finance

. . . .

1. Live within your income.
2. Set financial goals.
3. Save regularly.
4. Make realistic budgets.
5. Organize your financial records.
6. Use an interest-bearing checking account.
7. Open a money market account.
8. Comparison shop for more expensive products and services.
9. Do not borrow for the wrong things.
10. Avoid paying too much interest in installment credit purchases.
11. Drive used automobiles instead of buying new vehicles.
12. Avoid paying too much for monthly housing costs.
13. Buy a home for income tax reasons as soon as possible.
14. Reduce your income taxes so you will have more to spend, save, and invest.
15. Avoid paying too much for insurance.
16. Buy inexpensive term life insurance to protect earning power.
17. Open an individual retirement account (IRA) and contribute regularly.
18. Make a will for the security of your heirs.
19. Invest in what you understand and get started early.
20. Make your first investment in mutual funds.
21. Make your second investment in some good readings in personal finance and consider alternative investment opportunities.
22. Begin now to plan for a financially secure retirement.
23. Develop expertise in financial matters and heed your own advice, because ultimately you are responsible for your own financial success.
24. Take conservative actions to become more than a millionaire.

E

Careers in Personal Financial Planning and Counseling

. . . .

Personal financial planning and counseling is a professional field that addresses the financial concerns of individuals and families. Academic study in this field provides education and training for professionals who hope to provide counseling, education, and advice on personal and family financial matters. The need for sound counseling advice on financial matters is becoming more and more apparent to the public, and an increasing number of well-qualified persons are entering this important service profession.

Factors That Have Led to Growth in the Field of Personal Financial Planning and Counseling

Careers in personal financial planning and counseling focus on the evolving role of personal finances in the lives of American families. In short, they deal with how people should spend, save, manage, and invest their money. Times have changed and are continuing to transform the personal financial practices of the American family. Despite all the complexities in today's finances, family members remain the primary source of advice about financial matters, and most people know of no other source of help in their community other than banks. Not everyone is satisfied with their personal financial management practices, however. In fact, many people are quite dissatisfied. In response to these needs and opportunities, there has been a sharp demand for qualified professionals to enter the rapidly emerging field of personal financial planning and counseling.

Today the challenges and opportunities for professionals in personal financial planning and counseling can be overwhelming. Consumer choices among financial products and services have never been greater. Just 25 years ago, the average American consumer did not have any credit cards, seldom owned stocks, bonds, or life insurance, and either opened a non-interest-bearing checking account at the local bank or did not have a checking account at all.

In addition, a growing number of factors affect success in personal financial matters for today's families: the changing and increasingly deregulated personal financial marketplace, constant introduction of new financial products, wider availability of choices in products and services, increased impersonalization of marketplace transactions (automated teller machines, distant shopping malls, bill paying by computer, mail-order catalogs, home shopping via television, and so on), loss of real spendable income owing to inflation, higher costs for certain necessities (such as housing and transportation), substantial housing mobility, dislocations from regional economic instability and the resulting need for job retraining, and a growing dependence by families on two incomes to make financial ends meet to live a chosen lifestyle.

Although there truly are many opportunities for individuals and families in today's evolving financial marketplace, there also is a negative side, because everyone is not successful at handling personal finances. Mismanagement of credit and spending has serious results. Today there are over 800,000 personal bankruptcies annually, nearly 3 percent of homeowners with mortgages are delinquent by 90 days or more, and each year nearly one-half million people seek help from nonprofit consumer credit and budget counseling services. It is estimated that perhaps one-sixth of all middle-income families are currently experiencing difficulty in managing their finances. It is further estimated by one major American corporation that 10 percent of the time lost on the job is caused by financial problems. Also, the military cautions that the readiness of our armed forces is lessened by persons with financial difficulties who cannot perform their tasks properly. And, of course, money is consistently cited in research studies as the primary or secondary cause of divorce.

The Role of a Professional in Personal Financial Planning and Counseling

Professionals employed in personal financial planning and counseling careers may offer three types of advice: (1) budgeting advice (whether prescriptive or preventive), including suggestions on consumption and credit use, to people who may feel they are not handling their finances well, such as those who are spending excessively or overusing credit, (2) remedial advice and intervention to people experiencing severe financial difficulties, such as those with wage garnishments or with court judgments for defaulting on credit contracts, and (3) planning advice to clients who need to better manage their cash, build and protect assets, and develop personal and family financial plans for the future. The role of the personal financial planning and counseling professional is to work with clients in a proactive manner by causing or initiating actions and changes. People in such careers, of course, should have good communications and counseling skills.[1]

Career opportunities for professionals in financial planning and counseling historically have been divided into (1) financial planning and

---

[1] An excellent book on the subject is C. J. Pulvino, J. L. Lee, and C. Forman, *Communicating with Clients: A Guide for Financial Professionals* (Englewood Cliffs, N.J.: Prentice Hall, 1987).

(2) budget/credit counseling. Those in financial planning occupations usually sell financial products (such as life insurance or stocks) and offer planning suggestions to middle- and high-income clients. Those in budget/ credit counseling occupations generally advise clients of all income levels who are experiencing financial difficulties.

The definition of a *financial counselor* has evolved through the years. It now more accurately describes a professional who offers fundamental advice that the people who have historically called themselves financial planners and budget/credit counselors both have been offering. The prototype of this type of financial counselor is often employed in an employee assistance program (EAP), where he or she handles inquiries on all types of financial concerns. The well-educated financial counselor of today and tomorrow is an individual who can provide remedial and preventive advice to individuals and families regarding managing debts, budgeting finances, and fundamental financial planning opportunities. Their clients may or may not already be managing their personal finances effectively. Keep in mind, however, that most job opportunities today remain divided into the traditional financial planning or the budget/credit counseling occupations, where the financial planner offers suggestions on productive financial opportunities while the budget/credit counselor helps people resolve problems with overspending and poor budgeting techniques.

People today who graduate from academic programs and enter professional careers in personal financial planning and counseling should take a holistic perspective to financial concerns in helping clients resolve specific financial problems, take advantage of unique planning opportunities, and integrate all aspects of a client's finances into a comprehensive financial plan. This comprehensive approach to helping people manage their resources is what distinguishes today's personal financial planning counselors from credit counselors, insurance agents, and stockbrokers, each of whom might focus on one area of a client's finances rather than the client's total financial needs.

Today's professionally educated financial counselor should be able to provide counseling, education, and advice to families on financial matters, such as utilizing human and community assets, obtaining entitlements, resolving credit and budgeting problems, managing cash, and dealing with risk management, retirement planning, and capital accumulation. These financial counselors can present issues, alternatives, and possible courses of action for clients to consider, with the overall goal of empowering individuals and families to function in their own self-interest. Importantly, the financial counselor also tries to educate and empower clients to be able to achieve their goals themselves. The process encourages clients to clarify their personal values and goals as well as develop healthy attitudes toward financial matters.

Today's financial counselor is able to help individuals and families determine whether and how they can meet their life goals through proper management of financial and human resources. The immediate task is to help clients articulate goals and identify problems that may impede progress toward achievement of those goals. Then the financial counselor helps the client determine whether the goals are achievable and how to do so. Next, the financial counselor helps to coordinate the implementation of a financial plan to improve the likelihood that the client attains his or her immediate goals. In most circumstances, the financial counselor periodically reviews the progress of clients and, if needed, assists them in making revisions to help achieve their goals.

In advising clients, the financial counselor tries to help them understand how decisions and actions at one stage of life affect economic security at other stages of life and ultimately affect their long-term quality of life. If necessary, both remedial and preventive advice is offered, as well as productive planning suggestions. The broad purpose of the advice provided by a financial counselor is to help clients position their assets, debts, and income to efficiently and effectively meet their personal and family financial objectives.

In financial counseling, a number of sensitive issues may arise with clients, occasionally including unresolved conflicts, and these may result in the financial counselor making appropriate referrals to other specialized professionals as well as social services agencies. Thus, in addition to clients, financial counselors often interact with professionals employed in social service and government agencies, educational institutions, legal firms, and a variety of businesses.

Major activities of financial counseling professionals include responding to client inquiries, offering credit and budgeting advice, proposing a budgeting format, contacting creditors and public assistance organizations (if necessary), explaining provisions of an employee benefits package, preparing reports for and about clients, making productive financial planning suggestions (perhaps on how to provide for a child's education, reduce income taxes, or invest funds for a financially secure retirement), developing promotional and informational programs, writing news releases, informational brochures, and newsletters, attending seminars and workshops to update personal knowledge, and speaking to various consumer, employee, educational, government, business, and professional groups.

Professional Certifications

Professional certifications are obtained by many successful financial counselors who have voluntarily undergone training and met various qualifications. For those in financial planning occupations, these include Certified Financial Planner (CFP), Chartered Financial Consultant (ChFC), Certified Financial Analyst (CFA), Registry of Financial Planning Practitioners, Registered Investment Advisor (RIA), Certified Employee Benefits Specialist (CEBS), Certified Professional Insurance Woman (CPIW), and master of science (MS) degree in personal financial subjects. Forty-two academic programs across the country are registered with the International Board of Standards and Practices for Certified Financial Planners, Inc. Graduates of IBCFP-registered curricula are automatically entitled to sit for the Certified Financial Planner (CFP) examination. For those in budget/credit counseling occupations, the traditional certification is the Certified Consumer Credit Counselor (CCCS) or a master's degree in personal financial subjects.

Career Opportunities

The financial services industry, of which careers in budget/credit counseling and financial planning are a part, has been identified as one of the brighter career prospects in the 1990s and beyond. This expanding field offers career opportunities for well-educated financial counselors with social service agencies, governments, financial institutions, stock and insurance brokerage businesses, financial planning firms, and private businesses.

The financial counseling professional is sometimes the one member of a team with special expertise in financial matters and is relied on accordingly. A growing number of large organizations have such a financial counseling professional who informs, updates, and educates the firm's employees. In other employment situations, there may be three or four (or more) financial counselors in an office with similar backgrounds and job responsibilities.

Appropriate target entry-level employment positions for financial counseling graduates include credit counselor, budget counselor, consumer credit counseling service operations manager, employee assistance counselor, preretirement counselor, financial counselor, military financial educator, consumer relations coordinator, housing counselor, loan coordinator, loan officer, new accounts representative, debt collections coordinator, credit investigator, claims representative, bankruptcy court service worker, extension agent, coordinator of financial counseling volunteers, stockbroker, insurance broker, and financial planner.

Appropriate target entry-level positions for financial counseling graduates include a number of nonprofit and service-oriented employers: consumer credit counseling service, credit union, family service agency, armed forces family/community service agency, corporate and government employee assistance program, employee benefits counseling firm, college financial aid office, social welfare agency, hospital, credit grantor, corporate credit department, credit bureau, credit collection agency, juvenile and domestic relations court, marriage counseling firm, mental health association, community program for elderly/low income, ministerial organization, divorce mediation firm, cooperative extension service, labor union, bankruptcy attorney, U.S. bankruptcy court, Federal Home Administration, Farmers Home Administration, Housing and Urban Development office, bank, savings and loan association, insurance company, and financial counseling firm.

Of course, there are many potential entry-level positions and employers in the financial planning industry, including account representative at a brokerage firm, customer service agent at a mutual fund, accounts officer at a bank or savings and loan association, sales representative for a real estate agency or an insurance company, and junior associate at a financial planning firm.

Lifelong career development opportunities exist for financial counseling professionals. Advanced positions in middle management require several years of successful financial counseling experience. Such managers direct and train other financial counselors, represent the organization at meetings, work with advisory committees, monitor legislative and regulatory issues, address legislative hearings, and reasonably advocate the interests of personal financial planning and counseling clients.

Graduates from academic programs in personal financial planning and counseling are employed in government agencies and other nonprofit agencies as well as business firms. Financial counseling positions are likely to be found in both small and large organizations. Potential employers are located throughout the country, in both small and large communities.

Many employment positions are available in consumer credit counseling services, credit unions, and armed forces family/community services centers. Additional positions are anticipated in corporate and government employee assistance programs. Other employment positions involve sales of financial products and/or advice.

Job-satisfaction studies have found that financial counseling professionals are challenged and satisfied by their work. Pay for entry-level employment positions varies. Entry-level positions for those employed in nonprofit credit/budget counseling positions usually pay below $20,000 annually; those employed by government or business earn substantially higher salaries. Financial counselors typically feel that they are making a significant contribution to their clients' economic well-being.

F

How to Use the Personal Finance Cookbook (PFC) Software

• • • • • • • • •

The Personal Finance Cookbook (PFC) computer software accompanies the textbook *Personal Finance*, third edition, by E. Thomas Garman and Raymond E. Forgue, Houghton Mifflin Company, 1991. The software can be successfully used *without* any reference to the text; what appears on each screen is self-explanatory.[1]

The PFC disk contains sixteen spreadsheet models called "templates" for use with LOTUS 1-2-3 and other compatible spreadsheet programs. To use these spreadsheet templates with PFC, you will need a spreadsheet software program such as LOTUS 1-2-3. The following instructions allow you to:

1. Start your computer with DOS.
2. Get inside (load) the electronic PFC templates.
3. Select (retrieve) a template for use.
4. Enter work for calculations.
5. Save your work, if desired.
6. Print, if desired.
7. Quit—load another template or exit.

The PFC templates are stored as files on a disk. You retrieve a file by its filename as listed below:

Filename	Template
BALANCE	Balance Sheet
BUDGET	Annual Budget Estimates
FVANNUIT	Future Value (Compounding) of an Annuity
FVSUM	Future Value of Some Given Lump Sum Investment
INCOME	Income and Expense Statement
INSTALL	Monthly Installment Payment to Repay a Loan
INSURANC	Amount of Life Insurance Needed
MORTLOAN	Monthly Installment Payments to Repay a Mortgage Loan
PVSTREAM	Present Value (Discounting) of a Stream of Income Payments
PSVUM	Present Value (Discounting) of Some Known Future Sum
QUALIFY	Income and Monthly Payment Needed to Qualify for a Home Loan
REALRATE	Real Rates of Return after Taxes and Inflation (*continued*)

[1] Since many college teachers and extension specialists need to create instructions to hand out to people desiring to learn to use computers, permission is hereby given to those wanting to modify these instructions for such nonproprietary educational and informational purposes.

Filename	Template
RETURN	Projection of an Investment's Potential Total Return
TAXEQUIV	Tax-Equivalent Yields (in Percent) for Investments
TAXLIAB	Calculating Federal Income Tax Liability
YTM	Yield to Maturity for Bond Investments

Each file includes a template and instructions for its use. When you retrieve a file, a "help screen" appears first. Carefully read the instructions on the help screen for individual templates. Use the directional keys ($\leftarrow \updownarrow \rightarrow$) to move about the template. Then you need only to type in the numbers or words where needed. Finally you press the ENTER ($\leftarrow\!\!\dashv$) key to put your data onto the screen.

Tips for Using This Software

1. You can use UPPER CASE (CAPITAL LETTERS) or lower case letters or a combination of both.
2. Press the **BACKSPACE** ($\leftarrow$) key to erase any typing or keystroke mistakes.
3. Some things to remember when entering your work in a spreadsheet:
   a. When entering number, enter *without* commas.

   > correct: 8000   incorrect: 8,000

   b. When entering percentages, enter *as a decimal*.

   > correct: .07   incorrect: 7 or 7%

   c. When entering the date (for example, the date a balance sheet is prepared), enter it as words or begin by typing a space before numbers so that the number will not be calculated.

   > correct: _5/12/91 or May 12, 1991
   > incorrect: 5/12/91 or 4/1–5/1

   d. If you receive a "protected cell" error messsage when entering information, check the position of the inverse bar that is highlighting where you are on the screen. You are trying to type over protected parts of your template, so move off that position by using the directional keys.
   e. Calculations are automatic. You do not need to enter totals. They will automatically appear on the screen as you work through the template because that is what the spreadsheet program does.
4. If you ever run into a problem, pressing the **ESCAPE** (**Esc**) key usually remedies the situation and allows you to continue.

5. If you are in one of the templates and would like to switch to another, just type **/FR** and select from the menu using the directional keys.

6. To save the data you are putting on a template simply type **/FS** and the computer will automatically save the information in a file called (**name of file.WK1**) that you can retrieve later. (If you ever get an "insufficient space" message simply remove the PFC disk and insert a blank disk upon which to save the data.)

7. Printing the templates is easy, assuming a printer is connected to your computer. Proceed as follows:

   a. Turn the printer on.

   b. Adjust the perforated line on the paper in the printer so that it is even with the paper holder roller bar.

   c. In some computer labs you may have to turn a switch on a central switching device to connect the computer you are using to the printer.

Instructions on How to Use the PFC Software on Laboratory Computers That Have the LOTUS Spreadsheet Software Program on the Hard Disk

1. Turn on a computer.
2. **C:\>** appears on the screen.
3. Insert your Personal Finance Cookbook disk into drive A.
4. Type **123** and push the **RETURN** (↵) key. This brings up a blank LOTUS spreadsheet on the screen.
5. Type **/FD**
6. Type **A:** and push the **RETURN** (↵) key.
7. Type **/FR** to obtain the menu (list) of templates.
8. Use the directional keys (←↕→) to highlight the specific template desired and push the **RETURN** (↵) key to activate the specific program that is highlighted.
9. Follow the instructions on the screen.

How to Copy the PFC Software onto a Blank Disk to Use on Your Personal Computer

Locate a microcomputer in your computer lab that has the PFC software stored on its hard disk and available for copying.

1. Turn the computer on. There should be no floppy disks in any disk drive when the switch is being turned on. A DOS (called a "disk operating system") is probably already on the hard drive C of the computer(s). If not, you will need to inquire about borrowing a DOS disk and "booting up" a computer. When the machine comes on **C:\>** will appear on the screen.

2. a. If you have a formatted 5¼ inch blank disk, insert it into disk drive A or B as appropriate and type **cd\pfc** and then type **copy** *.* **a:** or **b:** as appropriate.

   b. If you have a formatted 3½ inch blank disk, insert it into disk drive A or B as appropriate and type **cd\pfc** and then type **copy** *.* **a:** or **b:** as appropriate.

3. The Personal Finance Cookbook program in the hard drive will be copied to your floppy disk, assuming the instructor used "PFC" to name the hard disk directory containing the template files.

How to Use PFC on a Personal Computer at Home

Because the configurations of computers are varied, these instructions can only be used as general reference material. The commercial software program LOTUS 1-2-3, or another spreadsheet program, is required to retrieve and use the PFC program.

1. If necessary, insert a DOS disk and turn on the computer.

2. After getting the DOS system activated, remove the DOS disk and insert a spreadsheet program disk (such as LOTUS 1-2-3) into drive A and the PFC disk into drive B.

3. Type **123** for LOTUS 1-2-3 (or use the proper command for an alternative software program) and push the **RETURN** (↵) key to activate the program.

4. Type **/FD**

5. Type **B:** and push **RETURN** (↵) key.

6. Type **/FR** to obtain the menu (list) of templates.

7. Use the directional keys (←↑↓→) to highlight the specific template desired and push the **RETURN** (↵) key to activate the specific program that is highlighted.

How to Format a Blank Disk

Before a new blank disk is used, it has to be formatted to prepare it to use the type of computer available. Instructions for disk formatting are as follows:

1. If necessary, insert a DOS disk and turn on the computer.

2. A prompt, **A:\\>** or **C:\\>**, appears on the screen.

3. Type **format A:** or **B:,** depending on which disk drive the blank disk will be inserted into.

4. Insert the blank disk into the appropriate disk drive for the prompt shown.

5. Press the **RETURN** (⏎) key and follow the instructions shown on the screen.

6. Press the **RETURN** (⏎) key. The formatting procedure may take about 30 seconds. When the formatting is finished, you will see this message on the screen:

Format another (Y/N)?

7. Type **N** (or if you want to format another disk, insert a new disk and type **Y**).

Glossary

Abilities Actions that a person is capable of performing either physically, mentally, artistically, mechanically, financially, or legally.

Acceleration clause A clause that requires that after one loan payment is late (and therefore defaulted) all remaining installments are due and payable at once or at the demand of the lender.

Accident insurance A type of health insurance plan designed to pay a specific amount per day (for example, $100) for a hospital stay that results from an accident, and/or a specific amount for the loss of certain limbs or body parts (for example, $2000 for the loss of an arm).

Account exceptions The costs and penalties frequently assessed on savings accounts by savings institutions.

Accrual-basis budgeting Financial recordkeeping that recognizes earnings and expenditures when money is earned and expenditures are incurred, regardless of when money is actually received or paid.

Actual cash value The purchase price of property less depreciation.

Actual-cash-value formula A mathematical method for determining reimbursement for lost or stolen property under a home owner's insurance policy.

Actuaries People employed to calculate the probability of losses and to establish the rates individuals must pay for insurance.

Add-on loan A second loan taken out for a larger amount before the first loan is repaid. Taking out add-on loans is called *flipping*.

Adjustable life insurance A life insurance policy that allows the policyholder to change the premium, the face amount, or the rate of cash value accumulation.

Adjustable rate certificate of deposit See *Variable rate certificate of deposit*.

Adjustable rate mortgage A type of mortgage loan for which the interest rate can fluctuate up or down according to an index of interest rates.

Adjusted gross income (AGI) Total income minus legal adjustments to income when calculating income tax.

Adjustments to income A selected group of legal reductions to gross income, used when determining income taxes, that are generally related to employment.

Aftermarket See *Secondary market*.

Agency issues Bonds, notes, and certificates issued by various federal agencies that often pay a yield one-quarter of 1 percent higher than Treasury securities.

Aggregate limits Clauses in health insurance policies that place an *overall* maximum on the total amount of reimbursement that can be made under a policy.

All-risk policy A property insurance or other type of policy that covers all perils except those specifically listed.

Alternative cost See *Opportunity cost*.

Alternative investment A type of investment in which monies are placed in assets that are riskier than savings investments, as neither principal nor earnings are guaranteed.

Amortization The process of gradually paying off the principal and interest of a mortgage loan through a series of periodic payments to a lender.

Annual average dividend The sum of dividends paid by a company over a number of years divided by the number of years.

Annual percentage rate (APR) An annualized measure of a finance charge stated as a percentage of the unpaid balance of a debt.

Annual renewable term (ANT) Term life insurance with a guaranteed renewability option.

Annuitant A person who receives an annuity.

Annuity A contract (generally with a life insurance company) that provides for a series of payments to be received at stated intervals for a fixed or variable time period in return for the payment of a premium or premiums.

Appraisal fee A fee required for a professionally prepared estimate of the value of property by an independent party.

Appreciation Increase in value of a home or other property.

Approximate compound yield (ACY) A mathematical measure of the annualized compound growth of a long-term investment.

Arbitrage The simultaneous purchase and sale of the same security, option, or futures contract in different markets, to profit from unequal prices.

Asked price The price at which a broker is willing to

For text locations of glossary terms and definitions, see the index.

sell a particular security; for mutual funds it is the current net asset value per share plus sales charges, if any. Also called *offering price*.

Assessed value The taxable value of a real estate property.

Asset allocation A mathematical method for deciding what portion of one's total resources should be allocated to various types of assets.

Assets Items owned, usually measured in terms of their fair market value.

Attitude A persistent, learned predisposition to behave in a consistent way toward given objects, not necessarily as they are, but as they are conceived to be.

Automated teller machine (ATM) A terminal provided by a financial institution enabling cash to be withdrawn by consumers.

Automatic funds transfer (AFT) An agreement with a bank that permits customers to write checks in amounts larger than the funds in their checking account with needed funds automatically transferred from their savings account.

Automatic income reinvestment A provision of a mutual-fund agreement that allows for the automatic reinvestment of earned dividends and capital gains distributions in more shares of the fund.

Automatic overdraft loan An agreement with a bank that permits customers to write checks in amounts larger than the funds in their checking account with needed funds automatically borrowed from their VISA or MasterCard account.

Automatic premium loan A provision in a life insurance policy that states that any premium not paid by the end of the grace period will be paid automatically with a policy loan, provided sufficient cash value or dividends have accumulated.

Automobile bodily injury liability Liability that occurs when a driver or car owner is legally responsible for bodily injury losses suffered by others.

Automobile insurance Insurance that combines liability and property insurance coverage needed by automobile owners and drivers into a single-package policy.

Automobile insurance plan (AIP) An insurance program that assigns a proportional share of the uninsurable drivers to each company writing auto insurance coverage in a state.

Automobile medical payments insurance Insurance that will pay for the personal injury losses suffered by the driver of the insured vehicle and any passengers regardless of who is at fault.

Automobile property damage liability Liability that occurs when a driver or car owner is legally responsible for damages to the property of others.

Average-balance account A bank account that assesses a service fee only if the average daily balance of funds in the account drops below a certain amount.

Average daily balance The sum of the outstanding credit-card balances owed each day during the billing period divided by the number of days in the period.

Average share cost The actual cost basis of an investment as used for income tax purposes. It is calculated by dividing the total dollars invested by the total shares purchased.

Average share price A simple calculation of the amounts paid for an investment, determined by dividing the total of the share prices at each investment by the number of periodic investments made.

Average tax rate A calculated figure showing a person's tax liability as a percentage of total, gross, adjusted gross, or taxable income.

Back-end load (insurance) The deduction of a fee when cash value is withdrawn under a universal life insurance policy.

Back-end load (investing) A charge paid when withdrawing money from a mutual fund.

Bad check A check for which there are insufficient funds in the account.

Balanced fund A mutual fund that includes various amounts of bonds, preferred stocks, and common stocks in its portfolio.

Balance sheet A statement describing an individual's or family's financial condition at a particular time, showing assets, liabilities, and net worth.

Balloon automobile loan A loan whereby the buyer takes the title to the car, and the last monthly payment is equal to the projected resale value of the vehicle at the end of the loan period.

Balloon clause A clause that permits the last payment to be abnormally large in comparison to the other installment payments. Such a payment is called a *balloon payment*.

Bank A common term for the type of financial institution that offers various forms of both checking and savings accounts.

Bank credit card account A form of option account in which the user of a credit card (such as VISA or MasterCard) has the option of paying the bill in full when it arrives or repaying over several months.

Basic banking See *Lifeline banking*.

Basic calculation method A way of determining future value by a series of multiplications.

Basic math method A way of determining future value by using simple arithmetic operations.

Bearer bond A bond whose owner is unknown to the corporation; possession of a series of post-dated coupons attached to the bond represents ownership. Also called a *coupon bond*.

Bear market A market in which stock prices are generally declining.

Belief The mental acceptance of or conviction about the truth or actuality of some statement or some thing based on what one implicitly considers adequate grounds.

Beneficiary (insurance) The person or organization that will receive the life insurance or other benefit payment upon the death of the insured.

Beneficiary (will) A person receiving property identified in a will.

Beneficiary designation clause A clause that provides that a mutual fund shareholder can name a beneficiary in a separate legal trust agreement; in the event of death the proceeds go to the beneficiary without going through probate.

Benefit period In a disability income insurance policy, the maximum period of time for which benefits will be paid.

Best buy A product or service that, in one's opinion, represents acceptable quality at a fair or low price for that level of quality.

Beta A statistically determined measure of the relative risk of a common stock compared to the market for all stocks.

Bid price The amount a broker is willing to pay, or "bid," for a particular security; also the amount per share that shareholders receive when they cash in (redeem) their shares.

Billing date The last day of the month for which any transactions will be reported on a credit card statement.

Binder A temporary insurance contract, effective until its expiration or until a permanent policy is issued, whichever occurs first.

Blue-chip stock Stock of a company with a well-regarded reputation and a long history of both good earnings and consistent cash dividends.

Bond An interest-bearing negotiable certificate of long-term debt issued by corporations and governments.

Bond and preferred stock fund A mutual fund that concentrates its holdings on senior securities: bonds and preferred stocks.

Bond certificates Evidence of debt issued to investors who purchase bonds.

Bond selling price formula A way of estimating the selling price of an old bond: the annual interest income in dollars divided by the current interest rate.

Book-entry form A method of registering bonds in which records are held electronically by a depository.

Book value The net worth of a company, determined by subtracting the total of a company's liabilities (including preferred stock) from its assets. In automobile insurance, the value of a car based on the average current selling price of cars of the same make, model, and age.

Book value per share The book value of a company divided by the number of shares of common stock outstanding.

Broker (real estate) A person licensed by a state to provide advice and assistance, usually for a fee, to both buyers and sellers of real estate.

Broker-dealer (investing) A stock brokerage firm that is engaged in the business of both buying and selling securities on the over-the-counter market.

Brokered certificates of deposit Certificates of deposit bought in volume by stockbrokers and resold to individuals.

Budget A document or set of documents used to plan and record estimated and actual income and expenditures for a period of time.

Budget account A somewhat limited charge account in which users must repay a specific amount of the charge within thirty days, then pay the remainder over a period of months.

Budget controls Methods and techniques intended to keep income and expenditures within the planned budget totals.

Budget estimates The recorded amounts in a budget that are planned and expected to be received or spent during a certain period of time.

Budget exceptions The difference between budget estimates in various classifications and the actual expenditures.

Budgeting A process of financial planning and controlling that involves using a budget to set and achieve short-term goals that are in harmony with long-term goals.

Bull market A market in which stock prices are generally increasing.

Bunching deductions The process of prepaying some deductible items in order to qualify for the tax advantage of having excess deductions.

Business cycle A wavelike pattern of economic activity that includes four phases: expansion, recession, depression, and recovery. Also called *economic cycle*.

Business cycle approach An approach by which an investor intends to participate in the rises of the stock market and avoid its declines by investing when the general economy is in a recession.

Buying long A trading technique in which an investor buys a security in the hope that it will go up in value.

Cafeteria plan An employee's benefit plan that lets employees choose from a menu of various benefits.

Calculator method A way of determining future values using any type of calculator.

California will A blank-form will that people can fill

in themselves; it is legally valid if completed properly on a form that has been codified in state law.

Call An option contract that gives the option holder the right to buy the optioned asset from the option writer at the striking price.

Callable A feature of a bond or preferred stock that permits a company to prematurely redeem its preferred stocks or bonds by paying a slight premium during a certain period if the price reaches a certain amount. If interest rates decline substantially, the issuing agency can pay off the debt before the maturity date.

Callable bonds Bonds that can be bought back by the issuer before the maturity date.

Capital Funds invested in a business enterprise.

Capital accumulation plan See **money-purchase pension**.

Capital asset Property owned by a taxpayer for pleasure or as an investment.

Capital gain Income received from the sale of a capital asset above the costs incurred to purchase and sell the asset.

Capital gains distribution Income for investors resulting from net long-term profits of a mutual fund realized when portfolio securities are sold at a gain.

Capital growth An increase in the market value of a mutual fund's securities, usually reflected in the net asset value of fund shares.

Capital improvements Costs incurred from making changes in real property that add to the value of the property.

Capitalization rate A widely used method of determining the rate of return on a real estate investment, found by dividing the net operating income (first year) by the total investment. Also known as *income yield*.

Capital loss A financial loss on an investment that occurs when the selling price (plus expenses) is lower than the original amount invested (plus commissions).

Career planning A process involving evaluation of one's aptitudes and interests, gathering information about various occupations, setting career goals, and developing a plan to achieve one's goals.

Carrying forward balances The noting of residual positive or negative balances from a completed budgeting time period onto the budget of the next budgeting time period.

Cash account An investor account that requires a modest initial deposit with a stockbroker and specifies that full settlement is due the broker within five business days (or seven calendar days) after a buy or sell order has been given.

Cash advance A small loan amount secured by charging the amount to certain debit or credit cards.

Cash-basis budgeting Financial recordkeeping that recognizes earnings and expenditures when money is actually received or paid out.

Cash dividends Distributions in cash by a corporation, usually paid out of earnings to holders of preferred and common stock.

Cash flow (real estate) The amount of income available to a real estate investor after subtracting all operating expenses and mortgage payments from rental income.

Cash-flow calendar A budgeting device on which annual estimated income and expenses are recorded for each budgeting time period in an effort to ascertain surplus or deficit situations.

Cash-flow management A set of activities performed by individuals and family members focused on allocating the family's flow of income toward the immediate goal of meeting tacit or explicit financial needs.

Cashier's check A check made out to a specific payee and drawn on the financial institution itself and thus backed by its finances.

Cash loan A loan that gives a person cash to make purchases or to pay off other debts.

Cash management The task of earning maximum interest on all one's funds, regardless of the type of account in which they are kept, while having sufficient funds available for living expenses, emergencies, and savings and investment opportunities.

Cash management account (CMA) A multipurpose account, offered through brokerage firms and other financial institutions, that combines a checking account, money market fund, stock brokerage account, credit card, and debit card.

Cash refund annuity An annuity that pays the beneficiary a lump sum if the annuitant dies before collecting the original invested money.

Cash surrender value A savings amount within an insurance policy that the policyholder receives upon request if the policy is canceled.

Cash value The savings/investing element of certain types of life insurance policies.

Cash value life insurance A type of life insurance contract that pays benefits on the death of the insured and has a savings element that allows the payment of benefits prior to death.

Certificate of deposit (CD) A form of fixed-time-period savings that pays much greater interest rates because financial institutions can count on having the funds for a fixed period and can make longer-term investments accordingly.

Certificate of insurance A document that outlines the benefits and policy provisions for individuals covered by group insurance.

Certificate of title A legal opinion (not a guarantee) of the status of a title, which is often provided when an abstract is unavailable or lost.

Certified check A personal check written on an account, on which the financial institution imprints the word *certified*, guaranteeing payment of funds in the proper amount to cover the check.

Certified financial planner (CFP) A person who has been approved by the International Board of Standards and Practices for Certified Financial Planners (IBCFP).

Charge-back The withholding of payment to a third-party lender such as a credit-card company for defective products or services.

Chartered financial consultant (ChFC) A person who takes correspondence courses in investments, real estate, and tax shelters given by American College in Bryn Mawr, Pennsylvania.

Check clearing The process of transferring funds from the bank, savings and loan association, or credit union upon which the check was drawn to the financial institution that accepted the deposit.

Checking account An account technically known as a *demand deposit*; the bank withdraws funds and makes payment whenever demanded by the depositor, which is typically done in the form of writing a check.

Check truncation A practice whereby a financial institution does not return actual checks unless specifically requested and with payment of a fee.

Churning A stockbroker's unethical encouragement of an investor to frequently buy and sell securities in an effort to earn large commissions for the broker.

Civil court A state court in which numerous civil and criminal matters are resolved and a written record is made of the happenings; the proceedings are completed with the assistance of attorneys, witnesses, a judge, and often a jury.

Claims adjuster A person designated by an insurance company to assess whether a loss is covered and the dollar amount the company will pay.

Claims ratio The percentage of premiums collected by an insurance company that are subsequently paid out to reimburse the losses of insureds.

Claims ratio formula The mathematical formula for determining an insurance company's claims ratio: losses paid divided by premiums collected.

Closed-end lease A leasing arrangement in which there is no charge at the end of the lease period.

Closed-end mutual fund A type of investment company that issues a limited and fixed number of shares of stock and does not buy them back (*redeem* them), so that after the original issue is sold the price of a share is established by supply and demand in the secondary market.

Closing The process of financially and legally transferring a home to a new buyer, which usually takes place in the office of the lender or an attorney.

Club account A regular savings account that is used to deposit money for a special purpose, such as a vacation.

Codicil A legal amendment to a will.

Coinsurance A method by which the insured and insurer share proportionately in the payment for a loss.

Coinsurance cap A stipulation in a health insurance plan that establishes a maximum loss beyond which the coinsurance requirement is not applied.

Collateral An asset a borrower pledges to back up a debt.

Collateralized mortgage obligations (CMOs) Bonds secured by mortgage securities that pass interest and principal payments on to investors.

Collectibles Cultural artifacts that have value because of beauty, age, scarcity, or popularity.

Collision insurance A type of automobile insurance designed to reimburse the insured for losses to his or her vehicle resulting from a collision with another car or object or from a rollover.

Commercial bank A financial institution offering various forms of checking and savings accounts that is chartered under federal and state regulations.

Commercial property Property designed for business uses, such as an office building, medical center, gasoline station, or motel, that carries a potential for profit.

Common stock The most basic form of ownership of a corporation. The owner has a residual claim on the assets of the firm after those made by bondholders and preferred stockholders.

Common stock fund A mutual fund that includes only common stocks among its portfolio of holdings.

Community property Property that is jointly owned and equally shared by spouses.

Community property laws Laws that distribute the property of deceased persons in a manner that assumes that property acquired during marriage is jointly owned and equally shared by the spouses no matter how much each contributed.

Community property states States in which all money and property acquired during a marriage are legally considered the joint property of both spouses (Arizona, California, Idaho, Louisiana, Nebraska, New Mexico, Texas, Washington, Wisconsin).

Comparison shopping A process of comparing products or services to determine the best buy.

Complete audit An IRS audit of a return that requires the taxpayer to prove each deduction to the satisfaction of the auditor.

Compound interest The calculation of interest on reinvested interest as well as on the original amount invested.

Comprehensive automobile insurance Insurance that provides payment for property damage losses caused by perils other than collision and rollover.

Comprehensive health insurance A health insurance plan that combines the protection provided by hospital insurance, surgical insurance, medical expense insurance, and major medical expense insurance into one policy.

Comprehensive personal liability insurance Insurance that provides the insured protection from liability losses that might arise out of any activity.

Computer-chip card A plastic card in which a silicon memory chip is embedded, used for various financial transactions.

Computer money management Banking by means of a home computer linked to a financial institution through the telephone system.

Conditional sales contract A credit agreement (also called a *financing lease*) under which the title to the property being financed does not pass to the buyer until the last installment payment has been made.

Conditions Statements in an insurance policy that impose obligations on both the insured and the insurer by establishing the ground rules of the agreement.

Condominium A home ownership arrangement in which the owner holds title to a housing unit within a building or project and a proportionate interest in the common grounds and facilities.

Consumer credit Nonbusiness debt used by consumers for purposes other than home mortgages.

Consumer price index (CPI) A broad measure of the cost of living for consumers, published monthly by the U.S. Bureau of Labor Statistics.

Contents replacement-cost protection An optional feature available in some home owners' insurance policies that pays the replacement cost of any personal property.

Contingency clause A stipulation in an offer to purchase that the earnest money will be refunded by the seller of the home if the buyer cannot obtain satisfactory financing.

Contingent beneficiary The person or organization that will become the beneficiary if the original beneficiary dies before the insured.

Contingent deferred sales charges Sales commissions of 1 to 6 percent levied on the mutual fund investor if shares are redeemed within a certain period after purchase.

Contract A legally binding agreement between two or more parties.

Contrarianism An investment philosophy suggesting that once the general public has seized upon an idea its usefulness is over and the wise investor should take the opposite action.

Convertibility privilege The right to exchange preferred stock for common stock for a specified time period.

Convertible bond A bond that the owner can exchange during a specified time period before maturity for a predetermined number of shares of stock in the same corporation.

Convertible security Preferred stock or bond that may be exchanged by the owner for common stock or another security.

Convertible term insurance A type of life insurance policy that allows the policyholder to convert a term policy to a cash value policy.

Cooperative A corporation that owns housing units and whose tenants purchase shares of ownership in the corporation equivalent to the value of their particular housing unit.

Coordination-of-benefits clause A clause in an insurance contract that prevents an insured from collecting more than 100 percent of a loss and designates the order in which policies will pay benefits if multiple policies are applicable to a loss.

Copayment clause A stipulation in a health insurance contract requiring that the insured pay a specific dollar portion of specifically covered expense items.

Corporation A state-chartered legal entity that can conduct business operations in its own name and be totally responsible for its actions as well as its debts.

Correspondence audit An IRS audit of a return conducted by mail in which the IRS questions a particular deduction and wants documentation.

Cosigner A person who agrees to pay a loan should the borrower fail to do so.

Cost index A numerical method to compare the costs of similar plans of life insurance.

Countercyclical (defensive) stocks Stocks of companies that maintain substantial earnings during a general decline in economic activity because their products are needed.

Coupon The interest rate printed on the bond certificate when it is issued. Also called *coupon yield*.

Coupon bond See *Bearer bond*.

Coupon rate See *Stated interest rate (bonds)*.

Coupon yield See *Coupon*.

Court not of record See *Small claims court*.

Cover letter A letter to a prospective employer expressing the writer's interest in obtaining an interview.

Credit A form of trust established between a lender and a borrower.

Credit agreement A contract signed when an installment loan is made.

Credit application A form used to record information regarding a credit applicant's ability and willingness to repay debts.

Credit bureau An agency that gathers information on individuals from merchants, creditors, and court records and provides reports of this information to credit grantors for a fee.

Credit card A plastic card identifying the holder as a

participant in the credit plan of a lender, such as a department store, oil company, or bank.

Credit card liability A liability for unauthorized use of a credit card that occurs only if the cardholder received notification of potential liability, accepted the card when it was first mailed, the company provided a self-addressed form to be used to notify them if the card disappeared, *and* the card was illegally used before the cardholder notified the company of its loss.

Credit controlsheet A form used to monitor the use of credit, amounts owed, and to whom money is owed.

Credit investigation The process of investigating or checking out an applicant's credit history to compare it with information provided on the credit application.

Credit life insurance A life insurance policy that will pay the remaining balance of a loan if the insured dies before repaying the debt.

Credit limit The maximum outstanding debt on a credit account.

Creditor A person or institution to whom money is owed.

Credit overextension A condition under which excessive personal debts cause extreme difficulty and possible inability to repay.

Credit rating A rating to help the lender determine if a credit applicant should be granted credit.

Credit receipt Written evidence of merchandise returned and the sales price.

Credit risk See *Default risk.*

Credit statement A monthly report of the charges, payments, finance charges, and other activity on a charge account. Also called a *periodic statement.*

Credit term life insurance Insurance that will pay the remaining balance of a loan if the insured dies before repaying the debt.

Credit union A financial institution developed to serve members/owners that have some common bond, such as the same employer, religion, union, or fraternal association.

Credit union share An investment (savings) in a credit union in minimum amounts of $5 or $10, upon which interest is earned.

Crop insurance Insurance that provides all-risk protection from losses to crops between planting and harvest.

Crude rate of return A rough measure of the yield on amounts invested that assumes that equal portions of the gain were earned each year.

Cumulative preferred stock A type of stock for which prior dividends must be paid before distributing any future dividends to the common stockholders if the board of directors had voted to skip paying prior cash dividends to preferred stockholders.

Current income Money received from an investment, usually on a regular basis, in the form of interest, dividends, rent, or other such payment.

Current liabilities See *Short-term liabilities.*

Current rate The rate of return recently paid by the company to policyholders under a universal life policy (cf. *guaranteed minimum rate*).

Current yield A measure of the current annual return expressed as a percentage when divided by its current market price.

Current yield formula A measure of the current annual income of a bond expressed as a percentage when divided by the bond's current market price.

Cyclical stock A stock whose price movements typically follow the general state of the economy and the various phases of the business cycle.

Data base An electronic filing cabinet suitable for checkbook and budgeting information.

Day of deposit to day of withdrawal (DDDW) method A method of determining savings account balance whereby each deposit earns interest for the total number of days it was actually in the institution.

Day order Instructions to a stockbroker that are valid only for the remainder of the trading day during which they were given to the broker.

Death benefit The amount that will be paid under a life insurance policy upon the death of the insured person.

Death rate The term used for the probability that an individual will die at a given age.

Debenture Any unsecured bond.

Debit card A card that permits the holder to make immediate deductions from or additions to accounts through an automatic teller machine.

Debt-consolidation loan A type of credit in which a borrower obtains a new loan to pay off several smaller debts with varying due dates and interest rates and instead has one monthly payment which is usually lower in amount than the payments on the other debts combined.

Debt limit A limit set by a lender on the amount that a loan applicant may borrow.

Debt ratio The ratio of liquid assets to total debt.

Debt service ratio The ratio of annual debt repayments for interest and principal for all consumer and mortgage debts to a person's annual take-home pay.

Decedent A person who has died with a valid will in effect.

Declaration A section of an insurance policy that provides basic descriptive information about the insured person or property, the premium to be paid, the time period of the coverage, and the policy limits.

Decreasing term insurance A type of term life insurance

contract in which the face amount declines annually and the premiums remain constant.

Deductible Requirement in an insurance policy that an insured pay an initial portion of any loss before receiving insurance benefits.

Deed A written document used to convey real estate ownership.

Deep discount bonds See *Zero-coupon bonds.*

Default A failure to meet legal financial obligations.

Default risk The likelihood that a bondholder will not receive the promised interest and bond redemption when due. Also called *credit risk.*

Defendant In a court of law, the person who allegedly committed a wrong deed and is the subject of litigation.

Deferred annuity An annuity that does not begin to pay off until a specified time period elapses or an event, such as a sixtieth birthday or retirement, occurs.

Deferred premium life insurance A type of insurance in which a modest amount of insurance is purchased with an interest-bearing loan that is repaid through a series of postponed payments.

Defined-benefit method A method of calculating retirement benefits that fixes the level of retirement, survivors', or disability benefits based on the income and/or years of employment of the worker.

Defined-contribution method See *Money-purchase pension.*

Demand deposit An account for which the financial institution must withdraw funds and make payments whenever demanded by the depositor.

Dental expense insurance. A type of health insurance plan designed to provide reimbursement for dental care expenses.

Depreciation The decline in value of an asset over time due to normal wear and tear and obsolescence.

Depression A period of severely reduced economic activity characterized by high unemployment, lowered prices, and sharply decreasing purchasing power.

Direct ownership A type of ownership in which one or more investors have legal title to real estate.

Direct purchase A method of acquiring shares in an open-end mutual fund where the investor simply orders and pays for the shares ordered, plus any commissions.

Direct seller An insurance company that sells its policies directly through salaried employees, mail-order marketing, newspapers, and even vending machines.

Disability income insurance A type of health insurance that replaces a portion of the income lost when the insured cannot work due to illness or injury.

Discount A selling price for a bond that is below its face value.

Discount brokerage firm A brokerage firm that features especially low commission charges because it provides limited services to customers.

Discounted cash flow A method of estimating the value or asking price of a real estate investment, which emphasizes after-tax cash flows and the return on the invested dollars discounted over time to reflect a discounted yield.

Discount rate Interest rate paid by financial institutions when they borrow funds from Federal Reserve banks.

Discount yield The rate of return on investments that are sold below face value, with the gain at sale or maturity representing the interest for federal income-tax purposes.

Discretionary account An investor account that gives the brokerage firm discretion to buy and sell securities or commodities.

Discretionary income The money people have left over when they have paid for the necessities of living.

Disposable income See *Disposable personal income.*

Disposable personal income The amount of take-home pay after all deductions are withheld for taxes, insurance, union dues and the like; in other words, gross pay minus payroll deductions. Also called *disposable income.*

Diversification The process of reducing risk by spreading investment monies among several alternative investments.

Dividend payout ratio The percentage of the total earnings of a company paid out to stockholders as cash dividends.

Dividend reinvestment plan (DRP) An investment plan that permits stockholders to reinvest stock dividends by purchasing additional shares directly from the corporation.

Dividends Cash profits distributed to shareholders of corporations.

Dividends per share A per-share figure of cash dividends paid out by a company.

Dividend yield The relationship between the current cash dividend and the current market value of a security. It is determined by dividing the dollar amount of a recent annual dividend by the current market value of the stock or by the purchase price if the stock is already owned.

Document matching notice A request by the IRS for an explanation of a tax-return discrepancy and photocopies of missing documentation.

Dollar-cost averaging An investment approach that requires investing the same fixed dollar amount in the same stock at regular intervals over a long time with the result that more shares are purchased when the price is low and fewer shares when the price is high.

Drawee The financial institution at which an account is held and upon which a check is drawn.

Drawer A person who opens a checking account and writes checks. Also called a *payer*.

Dread disease insurance A form of health insurance plan designed to provide reimbursement for medical expenses arising out of the occurrence of a specific disease.

Dual-earner household Two people living together, married or unmarried, with each providing earnings on a regular basis.

Due date The date by which any payment owed must be paid.

Due-on-sale clause A clause that requires that a mortgage loan be paid in full if the home is sold and effectively prohibits a new buyer from assuming the loan.

Dunning letters Notices from creditors that insistently demand repayment of debts.

Durable power of attorney A legal process to appoint a specific individual to control another person's affairs should that person become mentally incapacitated.

Earned income Salaries, wages, fringe benefits, and income from sole proprietorships that is taxed in a normal manner.

Earned income credit A form of negative income tax available to those with income under $19,340 who have a child living with them the whole year.

Earnest money A deposit in advance of the down payment on a real estate purchase.

Earnings per share (EPS) A measure of the profitability of a firm on a per-share basis: it is a dollar figure determined by dividing the corporation's total after-tax annual earnings (before cash dividends) by the total number of shares held by investors.

Economic cycle See *Business cycle.*

Economic growth A condition of increasing production and consumption in the economy; increasing national income.

Economy A system of managing the productive and employment resources of a country, community, or business.

Effective marginal tax rate The tax rate at which the last dollar earned is *effectively* taxed—that is, including Social Security tax, state income tax, and city income tax.

Effective personal finance management The planning, analyzing, and controlling of financial resources to meet personal financial goals.

Effective rate of interest The actual rate at which deposits earn interest after consideration of all interest calculation variables, costs, and penalties.

Electronic funds transfer (EFT) The use of computers and electronic means to transfer funds from one party to another.

Electronic funds transfer point of sale system (EFT-POS) A system that transfers funds by electronic means directly from a customer's bank account to a retailer's bank account.

Elimination period (waiting period) In a disability income insurance policy, the time period between the onset of the disability and the date the disability benefits begin.

Employee stock-ownership plan A retirement plan that invests the retirement funds in the stock of the employing corporation.

Employee stock purchase plan (ESPP) A fringe benefit for employees that permits them to buy shares of stock in the company and gives them an extra incentive to do a good job, with the hoped result of an increase in the profitability of the corporation and in the value of the stock.

Employment register A computer-based information-sharing system that lists resume information about job seekers in an effort to facilitate employment. Also called a *job bank* or *job clearinghouse operation.*

Endorsement In banking, the process by which checks are transferred from one person to another; when a person signs, or endorses, the back of a check written to him or her, it can then be either cashed or deposited. In insurance, amendments and additions to a basic insurance policy; also known as *riders.*

Endowment date The date of payment for endowment life insurance, commonly 20 or 30 years after issuance of the policy or at a specified age.

Endowment life insurance A type of life insurance that provides payment of the face amount at the death of the insured or at some previously agreed-upon date, whichever occurs first.

Entrepreneur A person who organizes, operates, and assumes the risk for a business venture.

Envelope system A method of strict budgetary control whereby exact amounts of money are placed into envelopes for specific purposes.

Episode limits Clauses in health insurance policies that specify the maximum payment for health-care expenses arising from a single episode of illness or injury.

Equity The dollar value of a home in excess of what is owed on it.

Equity trusts Real estate investment trusts that concentrate on buying or building their own real estate properties, such as apartments, restaurants, nursing homes, condominiums, and office buildings and hire management firms to run the properties.

Escheat The right of the state to take property when no persons are legally qualified to inherit or make claim to a deceased's property.

Escrow account A special reserve account used to pay

third parties and often used in conjunction with real estate loans.

Estate   The wealth that a person accumulates over his or her lifetime.

Estate planning   The process of planning, reviewing, and revising efforts to reduce the tax liability on an estate and to keep probate costs low.

Exchange privilege   See *Switching privilege.*

Exchange registered   An adjective describing a brokerage firm that is a member of an organized stock exchange.

Exclusions (insurance)   Clauses in an insurance policy that narrow the focus and eliminate specific coverages broadly stated in the insuring agreements.

Exclusions (tax)   Sources of income that are not considered as income for federal tax purposes; such income is tax exempt.

Exclusive insurance agent   A person who represents only one insurance company.

Ex dividend   A term that means that investors buying a particular stock will not receive the next dividend that the company has recently declared.

Executive search firm   A firm that attempts to recruit personnel, especially executive personnel, for vacant positions in corporations. Also called a *headhunter.*

Executor   A male named in a will (a female is known as an *executrix*) to carry out the directions and requests in the will and provided a certain amount of legal power by the state.

Executrix   See *Executor.*

Exemption   The legally permitted reduction in the taxpayer's taxable income based on the number of persons supported by that income.

Exit fees   Charges assessed upon redemption of mutual fund shares regardless of the length of time the investor has owned the shares.

Expansion   A phase of the business cycle in which production is at high capacity, there is little unemployment, and retail sales are high.

Expenditure   An amount of money that has been spent.

Exposures   Items owned and behaviors engaged in that expose one to the risk of financial loss.

Express warranty   A written warranty that accompanies many products and is offered by manufacturers on a voluntary basis to induce customers to buy.

Eye care insurance   A health insurance plan designed to provide reimbursement for the expenses related to the purchase of glasses and contact lenses.

Face amount   In life insurance, the amount of money stated in the policy that will be paid on the death of the insured party.

Face value   The value of a bond as stated on the certificate; also, the amount the investor receives when the bond matures.

Fair market value   The price that a willing buyer would pay a willing seller for an asset.

Family automobile policy (FAP)   An insurance policy designed for autos owned by families in which there are several persons who might drive the car.

Family financial management   The dynamic and active process of planning, implementing, and evaluating done by individuals and family members in allocating their income and wealth to meet the family's implicit and explicit goals.

Family of funds   A group of mutual funds under the same management company.

Federal Deposit Insurance Corporation (FDIC)   An agency of the federal government that insures bank accounts.

Federal gift and estate tax   A tax assessed on property owned or controlled by a deceased before it is transferred to heirs.

Federal Housing Administration (FHA)   A subdivision of the Department of Housing and Urban Development that insures mortgage loans that meet its standards.

FIFO (first-in, first-out) method   A method of determining savings account balances whereby withdrawals are first deducted from the balance at the start of the interest period and then, if the balance is not sufficient, from later deposits.

Fill-or-kill order   Instructions to the stockbroker to buy or sell at the market price immediately or else the order is canceled.

Final expenses   Outlays occurring just prior to or after a death.

Final tax liability   The resulting tax liability for a taxpayer after deducting the last legally allowable tax credits. It is the amount actually owed the government.

Finance charge   The lender's charge for borrowing money.

Financial goals   The long-term objectives that one's financial planning and management efforts are intended to attain.

Financial loss   Any decline in value of income or assets in the present or future.

Financial planner   A person who advises clients about personal finances. He or she has usually undergone training and has met the qualifications for particular professional certifications.

Financial planning   The process of developing and implementing plans to achieve financial objectives.

Financial planning advice   Information and counseling concerning taxation, credit, money management, investments, estate planning, and other financial matters.

Financial ratios   Objective yardsticks designed to simplify making judgmental analytical measurements of financial strength and change over time.

Financial security The comfortable feeling that one's financial resources will be enough to fulfill any needs as well as most wants.

Financial services company National or regional corporation that offers a great number of financial services to consumers, including checking, savings, credit, and advice on investments and other financial matters.

Financial services industry The institutions that offer checking, banking, and/or savings services.

Financial skills The techniques of decision making in personal financial management.

Financial statement A compilation of personal financial data designed to communicate information on money matters.

Financial strategies Plans of action to be taken in certain situations that help guide one's actions.

Financial success The achievement of financial aspirations that are desired, planned, or attempted.

Financial tools The forms and charts used in making personal financial management decisions.

Fixed-asset investments Investments of a specific amount of funds for a certain amount of time.

Fixed expenses Expenditures that are the same amount each time period.

Fixed income A characteristic of lending investment in which the borrower agrees to pay a specific rate of return for the use of the principal.

Fixed interest rate A constant interest rate on a credit card or any credit arrangement.

Fixed maturity A characteristic of lending investment in which the borrower agrees to repay the principal on a specific date.

Fixed-time deposit A time deposit with a specific time period during which the savings must be left on deposit.

Flexible spending account A salary-reduction program that sets aside up to $5000 of an employee's pretax income for dependent-care expenses.

Flipping Taking out a second loan for a larger amount before repaying the first loan. This type of additional loan is called an *add-on loan*.

Float The time the check writer actually has the funds in his or her account until the check finally clears.

Floater policy Property insurance that provides all-risk protection for accident and theft losses to movable personal property regardless of where in the world the loss occurs.

Floating-rate bonds Long-term corporate or municipal bond issues, redeemable after two or three years with an interest rate fixed for six to eighteen months, after which it varies according to an index or government interest rate. Also called *variable rate bonds*.

Flood insurance Insurance that protects property from losses caused by floods and mud slides provided that

the property is located in areas eligible under the National Flood Insurance Act of 1968.

Footnote p In a newspaper's financial tables, *p* indicates that a mutual fund assesses a 12b-1 fee.

Footnote r In a newspaper's financial tables, *r* indicates that a mutual fund assesses redemption charges.

Footnote t In some newspapers' financial tables, *t* indicates that a mutual fund charges both 12b-1 and redemption fees.

Forecasting The ability to predict, estimate, or calculate in advance.

Foreclosure The process of suing a borrower to prove default and asking the court to order the sale of the mortgaged property to pay the debt.

Form 1099 An IRS form that reports income of all kinds, including interest, consulting income, and stock dividends.

401(k) plan See *Salary reduction plan.*

Franchising Authorization granted by a manufacturer to a distributor or dealer to sell products.

Fringe benefit Any payment for employment that is not provided in the form of wages or commissions.

Front-end load (investing) An arrangement in the purchase of mutual funds specifying that total commissions and other fees will be deducted on an accelerated basis from the amounts invested (usually in the first two years). See also *Load fund.*

Front-end load (insurance) The deduction of a fee from each annual premium under a universal life insurance policy.

Full warranty As defined in the Magnuson-Moss Warranty Act, an express warranty that includes stringent requirements such as free repair or replacement of covered components.

Futures contract A marketable contract that requires the delivery of a specific amount of a commodity at a certain future date.

Future value The valuation of an asset projected to the end of a particular time period in the future.

Garnishment A legal attachment to one's wages directed by a court.

General brokerage firm The traditional type of stock brokerage firm, which offers full services to customers, including a newsletter, periodic reports, and personal advice.

General obligation bond A common type of municipal bond that is backed by the full taxing authority of the issuing agency.

Good-till-canceled order See *Open order.*

Grace period In banking, the time period in days in which savings deposits or withdrawals can be made and still earn interest from a given day of the interest period. In credit, a period after receipt of a credit bill during which no finance charges are assessed. In insurance, a period after the insurance premium due date, usually 31 days, during which late payment may be made without a lapse of the policy.

Gross estate The gross value in dollars of an estate, which includes just about everything owned by and amounts owed to the estate owner.

Gross income All income received in the form of money, property, and services that is not legally exempt from tax.

Gross income multiplier (GIM) A method of determining the price to pay for an income-producing property by dividing the asking price (or market value) of the property by the current gross rental income.

Gross national product (GNP) The value of all goods and services produced and bought for final use in the United States.

Group insurance Insurance sold collectively to an entire group under one policy.

Group legal insurance plan Insurance that provides reimbursement for legal expenses to eligible members of a group.

Growth stock Stock of a company with a record of growth in earnings at a relatively rapid rate.

Growth stocks (lesser known) Stocks of companies that have had higher-than-average earnings in recent years and have good prospects for the future but may not be the industry giants or industry leaders.

Growth stocks (well known) Stocks of companies that are leaders in their fields and have several consecutive years of above-average earnings.

Guaranteed insurability option An option that allows a cash value life insurance policyholder to buy additional life insurance coverage without proving insurability.

Guaranteed minimum rate The rate which the company is obligated by contract to pay the insured under a universal life policy (cf. *current rate*).

Guaranteed renewability option An option available with term life insurance policies that eliminates the need to prove insurability when the policy is to be renewed.

Hazard Any condition that increases the probability that a peril will occur.

Hazard reduction Action by the insured to reduce the probability of a loss occurring.

Headhunter See *Executive search firm.*

Health insurance Insurance that provides protection against financial losses resulting from illness, injury, and disability.

Health insurance coinsurance clause A provision that requires the insured to pay a percentage of health care expenses once the deductible is paid.

Health maintenance organization (HMO) A group of health-care providers who operate on a prepaid basis.

Hidden load An annual undeclared charge by a mutual fund of 1 to 1.25 percent annually, which pays for marketing and distribution fees.

Holder-in-due-course doctrine Legal protection for a merchant that states that if a merchant sells a product on credit to a consumer and then sells the credit contract to a sales finance company, the legally binding contract exists between the consumer and the finance company and the consumer no longer has the right to withhold payment for faulty merchandise. In 1976 federal law was changed so that today, in the great majority of cases, the ruling does not apply.

Holographic will A will that is entirely in the handwriting of the person signing the will and, as some states require, dated with the same hand.

Home-equity credit line loan A form of second mortgage whereby the lender offers a line of credit up to a maximum loan value of perhaps 75 percent of the home's value minus what is owed on the first mortgage. Money can then be tapped from this account by check, debit card, or credit card.

Home owner's fee An amount established by the (condominium) home owner's association that pays for such things as maintenance of common areas and facilities, repairs to the outside of any unit (paid for by all), real estate taxes on the common areas, and fire insurance covering the exterior of the building(s).

Home owner's general liability protection Insurance that covers situations where the home owner or renter is legally liable for the losses of another.

Home owner's insurance Insurance that combines liability and property insurance coverage needed by home owners and renters into a single-package policy.

Home owner's no-fault medical payments protection Insurance that will pay for injuries to visitors regardless of who was at fault for the loss.

Hospital insurance A health insurance plan designed to protect the insured from the costs arising out of a period of hospitalization (also called *hospitalization insurance*).

Housing ownership record A record that shows the dates and amounts spent to improve, but not maintain, the home.

Human capital The abilities, skills, and knowledge people have that permit them to perform work or services.

Immediate annuity An annuity that provides for payments to begin at the end of the first month or year after final payment of the premium.

Implied warranty A legal right based in state law that provides that products sold are warranted to be suitable for sale and will work effectively whether there is an express warranty or not.

Impulsive buying An emotional, almost reckless buying of goods and services with little regard to planning or need.

Income and expense statement A summary of a person's or family's income and expense transactions that have taken place over a specific period of time.

Income fund A mutual fund whose primary objective is current income and which seeks a portfolio of bonds, preferred stocks, and some select blue-chip stocks.

Income insurance Insurance that provides protection against the loss of future income.

Income splitting A process that takes place when one person with a high marginal tax rate shifts income to another person who is in a lower tax bracket.

Income stock A stock that pays a cash dividend that is high year after year because the company has fairly high earnings and chooses to declare high cash dividends regularly and retain only a small portion of the earnings.

Income yield See *Capitalization rate.*

Incontestability clause A clause that places a time limit, usually two years, on the right of the life insurance company to deny a claim after the death of the insured.

Indenture A legally written agreement between a group of bondholders and the debtor as to the terms of the debt.

Independent insurance agent A person who represents two or more insurance companies.

Index of leading economic indicators A composite index that represents eleven components of economic growth; it is reported monthly by the U.S. Department of Commerce.

Indexing Annual modification of income-tax brackets to reduce the effects of inflation.

Indexing method A technique of calculating Social Security benefits that revalues previous wage earnings in terms of current wage levels by multiplying each year's income by an index factor announced annually by the Social Security Administration.

Indirect investment in real estate A type of investment in which the investors do not hold actual legal title to the property.

Individual account An account with one owner who is solely responsible for the account and its activity.

Individual Retirement Account (IRA) An account that allows people earning income to make tax-deductible payments to their own private investment fund held by a bank, mutual fund, insurance company, or other trustee.

Inflation A condition of across-the-board increases in the prices of goods and services.

Inheritance taxes Taxes levied on inherited property when it is received by heirs.

Insolvent An adjective describing a person with a negative net worth.

Installment credit A type of consumer credit in which the consumer pays the amount owed in equal payments, usually monthly.

Installment-premium annuity An annuity purchased with a series of premium payments.

Installment purchase agreement A credit agreement (also called a *collateral installment loan* or *chattel mortgage*) in which the title of the property passes to the buyer as the document is signed.

Installments-certain annuity An annuity that guarantees a minimum number of payments (installments) to the annuitant or a beneficiary even if the annuitant dies before the minimum number of installments are paid.

Institute of Certified Financial Planners The professional association of certified financial planners (CFPs).

Insurable interest A situation that exists when a person or organization stands to suffer a financial loss resulting directly from a peril.

Insurance A mechanism for reducing risk by having a large number of individuals share in the financial losses suffered by members of the group.

Insurance agent A person who sells, modifies, and terminates contracts of insurance between the insured and insurers.

Insurance agreement A legal agreement by the borrower to purchase credit and/or disability insurance that would pay the lender the balance of the loan in full should the borrower die or become seriously disabled.

Insurance claim A formal request to an insurance company for reimbursement for a covered loss.

Insurance dividends Payments made by stock insurance companies to their policyholders as partial refunds of premiums.

Insurance policy The written agreement between a person buying insurance and an insurance company.

Insurance rate The cost to the insured for each unit of insurance coverage.

Insured The person buying or covered by insurance.

Insurer Any individual or organization that provides insurance coverage.

Insuring agreements Broadly defined coverages provided under an insurance policy.

Interest An expression of curiosity or concern about something.

Interest The payment one receives for allowing a

financial institution (sometimes just an individual) to use and invest one's money.

Interest-adjusted cost index (IACI) A measure of the cost of life insurance that takes into account the interest that would have been earned had the premiums been invested rather than used to buy insurance.

Interest-adjusted net payment index (IANPI) A measure of the cost of cash value life insurance to be held until death.

Interest inventory A pencil-and-paper psychological examination that assists in assessing and profiling a person's overall interest trends by indicating which personality types enter certain occupations.

Interest rate The price of money, expressed as a percentage; what it costs to borrow and what may be earned by lending.

Interest-rate risk The uncertainty of the market value of an asset resulting from possible interest rate changes.

Interval ownership purchase Purchase of vacation property through time sharing, which provides for actual titles and deeds to limited, preplanned use of the real estate and which legally makes the purchaser a secured creditor, thus guaranteeing continued use of property throughout any bankruptcy proceedings.

Intestate Adjective describing someone who dies without leaving a valid will.

Investment assets Tangible and intangible items acquired for generating additional income and in anticipation of increases in their value.

Investment banking firm A specialized seller of new securities that serves as middleman between the issuing company and the investing public.

Investment club An organization formed by individuals who want to share their investment knowledge and a limited amount of investment dollars to learn about the securities market and to make a profit.

Investment company A corporation, trust, or partnership in which investors with similar financial goals pool their funds to utilize professional management and to achieve diversification of their investments.

Investment manager A specialist who takes almost complete charge of one's investment portfolio and gives periodic reports.

Investment philosophy A personal investment strategy that anticipates specific returns and risks and contains tactics for accomplishing one's investment goals.

Irrevocable trust A trust that is not subject to any modification by the grantor during his or her lifetime and thus bypasses probate and estate taxes.

IRS private letter rulings IRS advisory opinions on individual tax-management proposals, issued annually to several hundred individuals and corporations.

IRS regulations Interpretations of the tax laws passed by Congress and having the force and effect of law.

IRS rulings Decisions based on the IRS interpretation of both the tax laws and their regulations, which provide guidance to how the IRS will act in certain general situations.

Item limits Provisions in a health insurance policy that specify the maximum reimbursement for particular health-care expenses.

Itemized deductions Specific expenses that can be deducted from adjusted gross income.

Job bank See **Employment register.**

Job clearinghouse operation See **Employment register.**

Job search A process that involves listing potential employers, preparing a resume and letters of application, filling out applications, taking tests, interviewing, and negotiating.

Joint account See **Joint tenancy account with right of survivorship.**

Joint and survivor annuity An annuity that pays proceeds until the death of both annuitants.

Joint tenancy A type of direct ownership in which two or more people have an undivided interest in real estate held in equal or unequal shares. In the event that an owner dies, the survivor(s) gets the property.

Joint tenancy account with right of survivorship A bank account that is held by two or more people, each of whom has access to it and responsibility for it, and that gives the survivor immediate access to funds in case of death. Also called a *joint account.*

Joint tenancy with right of survivorship Joint tenancy that requires that upon the death of a joint tenant (one owner) the remaining joint tenant or tenants assume full ownership of the property.

Joint will A will drawn by a married couple who have made reciprocal provisions for each other. Also called a *mutual will.*

Junk bonds Unsecured bonds of low quality with high default risk that pay two to five more interest points than quality bonds.

Keogh plan A pension plan that allows self-employed persons to make large tax-deductible payments for themselves and their eligible employees; the fund is held by a trustee who, in certain circumstances, could be the self-employed person.

Kiddie tax Tax on unearned income received by a child in excess of $1000.

Lapsed policy An insurance policy that has been terminated due to the policyholder's failure to pay the required premium.

Law of large numbers A statistical concept stating that as the number of units in a group increases, predictions about the group become increasingly accurate.

Lawyer-prepared will A will drafted by an attorney; the least likely of all wills to be successfully challenged.

Lease A legal contract specifying the responsibilities of both the tenant and the landlord.

Letter of last instructions A letter written in one's own handwriting, signed, and usually given to the executor, which can include transfers of any odds and ends of personal property (both valuable and sentimental) without being made public in the formal will. Also called a *letter precatory*.

Letter precatory See *Letter of last instructions*.

Letter stock A security that has not yet been registered with the Securities and Exchange Commission for sale to the public.

Leverage The use of borrowed money to make an investment that, it is hoped, will earn a rate of return greater than the after-tax costs of borrowing.

Leveraged buy-out A takeover of a company financed with the assets of the corporation pledged as security for the debt.

Liabilities The dollar value of items owed.

Liability insurance Insurance that provides protection against losses suffered by others for which the insured party is responsible.

Lien A legal right to hold property or to sell it for payment of a claim.

Life cycle A description of the progress of human life along a continuous sequence of family-status periods and stages.

Life insurance Insurance that reduces the risk of financial loss resulting from death.

Lifeline banking Certain minimal financial services needed to function in society, offered by banks to low-income consumers. Also called *lifeline financial services* or *basic banking*.

Lifestyle One's particular way of living.

LIFO (last-in, first-out) method A method of determining savings account balances whereby withdrawals are first deducted from the most recent deposits and then from the less recent ones, and so on.

Limited partnership A form of owning real estate investment property involving two classes of partners, the general partner (usually the organizer), who operates the syndicate and has unlimited financial liability, and the limited partners (the investors), who receive part of the profits and the tax-shelter benefits but who have no voice in the management of the business and have no personal liability for the operations of the partnership beyond their initial investment.

Limited-pay life insurance Whole life insurance that allows premium payments to cease sometime prior to the age of one hundred.

Limited warranty A warranty that offers less than a full warranty as defined in the Magnuson-Moss Warranty Act.

Limit order An instruction to the stockbroker to buy at the best possible price but not above a specified limit or to sell at the best possible price but not below a specified limit.

Linton yield A mathematical measure of the true rate of return on cash value insurance.

Liquid assets See *Monetary assets*.

Liquidity The speed and ease with which an asset can be converted to cash.

Liquidity ratio The ratio of liquid assets (basic liquidity ratio) or liquid assets and other financial assets (expanded liquidity ratio) to monthly expenses.

Listed securities A security designation given by a stock exchange to securities issued by member companies that meet various criteria regarding number of stockholders, numbers of shares owned by the public, market value of each share, and corporate earnings and assets.

Listing agreement A contract permitting a realtor to list a property exclusively or with a multiple listing service and specifying the commission rate and time period of the agreement.

Living trust A trust created by a living grantor for the benefit of self or another. Also called *inter vivos*.

Living will A legal document that can be used to direct that extraordinary life support measures be terminated if a person becomes terminally ill.

Load (sales charge) A commission earned for selling a mutual fund.

Load fund A mutual fund sold to the public that charges a sales commission, usually called a *front-end load* when purchased.

Loan origination fee The lender's charge to the borrower for doing all the paperwork and setting up the mortgage loan.

Loan-to-value ratio A measure of the amount of leverage in an investment project; determined by dividing the amount of debt by the value of the total of the original investment.

Long-term capital gain or loss A gain or loss occurring after a capital asset has been owned for more than six months at the time of sale.

Long-term goals or objectives Targets or ends that an individual or family desires to achieve using financial resources one or more years in the future.

Long-term investor An investor who is generally moderate or conservative in investment philosophy and wants to hold securities as long as they provide a return commensurate with their risk, usually for a number of years.

Long-term liabilities Debts that must be paid over a period greater than one year.

Loss control An effort to reduce both the frequency and severity of losses.

Loss reduction Action by an insured to lessen the severity of loss should a peril occur.

Low-balance method A method of determining savings account balance whereby interest is paid only on the least amount of money that was in the account during the interest period.

Low par A one- or two-dollar par value for a common stock.

Major medical expense insurance A type of health insurance plan designed to provide reimbursement for a broad range of medical expenses (including hospital, surgical, and medical expenses) with policy limits as high as $1 million and deductibles as high as $1000.

Manufactured housing Partially factory-assembled housing units designed to be transported in portions to the home site, where finishing of the building requires another two to six weeks.

Margin account An investor account with a brokerage firm that requires a deposit of substantial cash or securities ($2000 or more) and permits the investor to buy other securities on credit using funds borrowed from the firm.

Marginal cost An aid to decision making that compares the additional (marginal) price or cost of something with the additional (marginal) value received.

Marginal tax bracket (MTB) An income range shown in the tax rate schedules for which there is a marginal tax rate.

Marginal tax rate The tax rate at which the last dollar earned is taxed.

Marginal utility The extra satisfaction derived from having one more incremental unit of a good or service.

Margin buying A method of reducing an investor's equity in an investment in order to magnify returns by borrowing money from a broker.

Margin call A regulation imposed by the broker that requires the margin investor to put up more funds if the value of the security declines to the point where the investor's equity is less than the required percentage of the current market value, or the broker can legally sell the securities.

Margin call formula A formula to determine the price of a share of stock at which a broker will sell securities bought on margin if the investor does not put up more funds.

Margin rate The percentage amount of the value (or equity) in an investment that an investor may not borrow from the stockbroker.

Market interest rates The current interest rates charged on various types of corporate and government debts that have similar risks.

Market making A process designed to provide a continuous market for over-the-counter stocks, in which a broker/dealer maintains an inventory of specific securities to sell to other brokers and stands ready to buy reasonable quantities of the same securities at market prices.

Market order A process that instructs the stockbroker to execute an order immediately at the best possible price.

Market price See *Market value.*

Market rate for savings bonds The rate that series EE and HH savings bonds will pay if held to maturity. The rate is 85 percent of the latest six-month average rate on five-year treasury securities.

Market value The current price that a willing buyer would pay a willing seller for an asset. Also called *market price.*

Marriage tax penalty A result of the progressive tax system that may require married couples to pay more in taxes than couples living together without being married, even though both couples have similar combined taxable incomes.

Maximum taxable yearly earnings The base amount to which the full Social Security tax rate is applied and which determines the maximum amount due for most wage earners.

Medicaid A jointly financed program of the federal government and the states that pays some medical expenses of the poor.

Medical expense insurance A health insurance plan designed to provide reimbursement for physicians' services other than those for surgery.

Medicare A program administered by the Social Security Administration that provides payment for hospital and medical expenses of persons age sixty-five and over and some others.

Medicare supplement insurance A form of health insurance plan designed to supplement the protection provided by Medicare. Also called *Medigap insurance.*

Member firm A brokerage firm that has purchased a seat on the exchange (the legal right to buy and sell securities on the exchange) with the approval of the board of directors of the exchange.

Memory card A plastic card with an embedded microchip or magnetic strip containing information that is changed when the card is used. Also called a *"smart" card.*

Minimum-balance account An account that requires the customer to keep a certain amount in the account throughout the month to avoid a flat service charge or fee.

Minor's account An account owned by a minor, who is ultimately responsible for the activity of the account.

Mobile homes Fully factory-assembled housing units built to a certain size and designed to be towed on a frame with a trailer hitch.

Modified life insurance A whole life insurance policy with reduced premiums in the early years and higher premiums thereafter.

Monetary assets Cash or near-cash items than can be readily converted into cash. Primarily used for living expenses, emergencies, and savings. Also called *liquid assets*.

Money income Income measured in current dollars. Also called *nominal income*.

Money market See *Money market mutual fund*.

Money market account The generic term for a variety of high-interest earning accounts that have limited checkwriting privileges.

Money market deposit account A government-insured money market account offered through a depository institution, such as a bank, credit union, or savings and loan association.

Money market mutual fund (MMMF) A mutual fund that pools the cash of thousands of investors and specializes in earning a relatively safe and high return by buying securities that have very short-term maturities, generally less than one year.

Money order A form of cash bought for a particular amount and signed over by the purchaser to the payee.

Money-purchase pension A method in which the employer, and sometimes the employee, sets aside monies regularly during the working years to establish a fund for the payment of retirement benefits. Also called *defined-contribution method*.

Monitoring unexpended balances A method to control overspending that uses a budget design showing declining balance.

Month order Instructions to a stockbroker that are good until the close of trading on the last business day of the current month.

Monthly investment plan (MIP) An arrangement with a brokerage firm that permits regular investment (monthly or quarterly) of a specified amount of funds ($40 to $1000) in a common stock listed on a major stock exchange.

Mortality table A statistical table showing the death rate (probability of death) at each age.

Mortgage The legal right of the lender to sell the property purchased (the security) in the event the borrower defaults on the loan.

Mortgage loan An amount loaned to a borrower by a lender for the purchase of a home.

Mortgage rate Interest rate paid by individuals on their home loans.

Mortgage trust A real estate investment trust that does not own property but provides short-term financing for construction loans or for permanent mortgage loans for large projects.

Multiple-earnings approach An approach that involves estimating the funds needed to replace the income lost due to a premature death by multiplying the annual income of the person involved by the number of years the income will be needed by dependent survivors.

Multiple indemnity clause A clause in a life insurance contract that provides for a doubling or tripling of the face amount if death results from certain specified causes.

Multiple-listing service An information and referral network among real estate brokers allowing properties listed with a particular realtor to be shown by all other realtors as well.

Municipal bonds (munies) Long-term debts issued by local governments and their agencies.

Municipal bond (tax-exempt) fund A mutual fund that seeks to earn current tax-exempt income by investing solely in municipal bonds issued by cities, states, and various districts and political subdivisions.

Mutual fund An investment company that combines the funds of investors who have purchased shares of ownership in the investment company and invests those monies in a diversified portfolio of securities issued by other corporations or governments.

Mutual insurance company A company that is owned by its policyholders and operates on a nonprofit basis.

Mutual savings bank (MSB) Similar to a savings and loan association, but in an MSB the depositors of savings are technically the owners of the institution.

Named perils policy An insurance policy that covers only losses caused by perils specifically listed.

National Association of Personal Financial Advisors (NAPFA) The largest U.S. organization of fee-only financial planners, prohibited from receiving sales commissions.

Needs Those items that people find are necessary to survive and live in society.

Needs approach An approach for determining life insurance needs that involves estimating the total dollar loss due to a premature death.

Negotiable order of withdrawal (NOW) account An account offered by savings and loan associations, mutual savings banks, and banks, in which money deposited in the account goes to a savings account, where it earns interest income and can be withdrawn by a check.

Negotiating The step in the buying process when the buyer discusses the actual terms of an agreement with the seller.

Net asset value The current worth of the underlying securities in a mutual fund minus company liabilities.

Net gain Total income minus total expenses where income exceeds expenses.

Net loss Total income minus total expenses where expenses exceed income.

Net operating income Gross income of a rental property less allowances for vacancies and operating expenses, except depreciation and debt repayments.

Net surplus The amount of money remaining after all budget classification deficits are subtracted from those with a surplus.

Net taxable estate The gross value of an estate minus marital deductions, liabilities, charitable bequests, properties passed by law and contract, and the basic inheritance tax exemption.

Net worth The dollar value remaining when liabilities are subtracted from assets.

New issue A bond or stock sold by a corporation or government for the first time.

No-fault automobile insurance Insurance that allows an insured to collect directly from his or her insurance company for losses resulting from an auto accident without regard to who was at fault.

No-load fund A mutual fund that does not have a sales charge.

No-load insurance Life insurance that does not involve payment of a commission by the insurer to the insurance agent.

Nominal income See **Money income.**

Nominal rate See **Stated interest rate.**

Nominal rate of interest The apparent interest rate that is applied to deposits before consideration of the time period. Also called *stated rate of interest.*

Nonbank bank A new kind of financial institution that either makes commercial loans or accepts consumer deposits, but not both.

Noncumulative preferred stock A type of stock for which the stockholder would have no claim to previously unpaid dividends.

Nonforfeiture values Clauses in an insurance contract that protect the value, either in cash or in another form of insurance, available to insureds upon failure to pay the required premiums.

Noninstallment credit A type of consumer credit that includes single-payment loans and open-ended credit.

Nonparticipating An adjective used to describe preferred stock that permits the owner to receive only the fixed amount per share, no extra dividends.

Nonparticipating policies. Insurance policies that do not provide for the payment of dividends to policyholders.

Nonprobate property An asset that is transferred by law or by contract without going through probate.

Nonqualified deferred-compensation plan An approved process under ERISA regulations that permits an employee and employer to agree to defer large payments for services rendered to a later date, when the person is expected to be in a lower tax bracket.

No par An adjective describing common stock issued at zero par value.

Note The formal promise of the borrower to repay the lender as detailed in the loan contract.

Numismatist One who collects coins, medals, and selected commemoratives.

Nuncupative will An oral will spoken by a dying individual to another person or persons.

Odd lot A block of stock of more or less than one hundred shares.

Offer to purchase A written offer to purchase real estate, specifying a price and conditions.

Offering price See **Asked price.**

Office audit An IRS audit of a return that requires the taxpayer to visit the nearest IRS office to document all items in a section of the form.

Old method A technique of benefits calculation that uses current dollars to determine specific Social Security monthly payments.

On a register Having on file at the Office of Personnel Management a completed application and a satisfactory test score on an appropriate examination in a particular geographic area where certain types of positions might become available.

Open-ended credit A type of consumer credit whereby the consumer may choose to repay the debt in a single payment or to make a series of equal or unequal payments. Most credit cards operate in this manner. Also called *revolving credit.*

Open-end lease A lease in which one must pay any difference between the projected resale value of a car and its true market value at the end of the lease period.

Open-end mutual fund An investment company that continuously stands ready to sell new shares and to redeem old ones at net asset value.

Open order Instructions to a stockbroker that are good until executed by the broker or canceled by the investor. Also called a *good-till-canceled order.*

Opportunity cost The cost of giving up one financial option for another. Also called *alternative cost.*

Option A contract that gives the holder the right to buy or sell a specific asset—e.g., real estate or common stock—at a specified price.

Option account A credit account permitting either payment in full when the bill arrives (with no credit costs) or partial payment spread over several months.

Option holder The person who actually owns a stock or other option contract.

Option writer A person who issues an option contract promising either to buy or to sell a specified asset for a fixed striking price and receives an option premium for standing ready to buy or sell.

Ordinary income dividend distribution Payment that is made when a mutual fund distributes dividend or interest income (plus some short-term capital gains).

Organized stock exchange A market where agents of buyers and sellers meet and trade a specified list of securities, which are usually those of larger, well-known companies.

Original source records Formal documents that record personal financial activities.

Over-the-counter (OTC) market A market for trading securities outside the organized stock exchanges, where buyers and sellers negotiate the prices of transactions, often using a sophisticated telecommunications network connecting brokers throughout the country.

Overwithholding The withholding by an employer of more payroll withholding taxes than the actual tax liability due the government.

Paid up An adjective describing a life insurance policy for which the time period for premium payment has ended.

Paper profit (paper loss) An unrealized profit or loss on an investment still held.

Partial disability An injury or illness that prevents a worker from performing one or more functions of his or her regular occupation.

Participating policy An insurance policy that has a provision for the payment of dividends to the policyholder.

Participating preferred stock A stock that allows the preferred stockholder to receive extra dividends above the stated amount after the common stockholders have received a certain amount.

Participation certificate An investor's share in a pool of mortgages.

Partnership A business owned by two or more persons operated in the interests of all partners.

Par value The dollar amount assigned to a share of stock by a corporation when issued. Also, the face value of a bond.

Passive activities Rental operations and all other businesses in which a taxpayer does not actively participate. Losses on passive activities may not be used to offset ordinary income.

Pawnbroker A specialized business offering single-payment loans to individuals in amounts based on the value of personal property left in possession of the lender.

Payee The persons or firms to which a check is made out.

Payer The person who opens the checking account and writes checks. Also called a *drawer*.

Payroll withholding A method of prepaying income taxes in which an employer withholds a portion of each of an employee's paychecks an an estimate of taxes owed and forwards those funds to the government.

Penny stocks Stocks in new, untested companies selling for a dollar or two per share, most of which fail.

Peril Any event that causes a financial loss.

Period-certain annuity An annuity that provides payments to the annuitant—or a beneficiary if the annuitant should die early—for a fixed time period.

Periodic rate Annual percentage rate for a charge account divided by the number of billing periods per year, usually 12.

Personal automobile policy (PAP) An insurance policy designed for automobiles owned by an individual driver.

Personal earnings and benefit estimate statement The Social Security Administration's record of covered earnings during a person's lifetime.

Personal finance The study of personal and family resources considered important in achieving financial success.

Personal financial planning The process of developing and implementing long-range plans to achieve financial success.

Personal identification number (PIN) A four- to seven-digit access number issued to each customer by a financial institution for use with a particular debit or credit card.

Personal inflation rate The rate of increase in prices of items purchased by a person or household.

Personal line of credit A lending arrangement that allows the borrower access to loans much like cash advances on a credit card.

Personal spending style An individual's way of spending money, which is influenced by the person's values, attitudes, emotions, and other factors shaped through the experiences of his or her life.

Philately The collection and study of stamps, envelopes, and similar material.

PITI Abbreviation for "principal, interest, taxes, and insurance," the components of many monthly mortgage loan payments.

Plaintiff A person who has filed a small claims or civil court case and is suing the defendant.

Pocket money A sum of coins and paper currency used daily and weekly to pay for marketplace transactions that generally require cash.

Point A fee equal to one percent of the amount of the

total mortgage loan, which must be paid in full when a home is bought.

Policy   The written contract between an insurer and a policyholder.

Policyholder   The person who pays for an insurance policy and retains all rights and privileges granted by the policy, including the right to amend the policy and the right to designate who shall receive the proceeds (also called the *owner*).

Policy limit   The maximum dollar amount that will be paid under an insurance policy.

Portability   A retirement plan contract clause that permits workers to take pension money to another job.

Portfolio   A collection of securities and other investment instruments.

Portfolio diversification   In investment practice, the process of selecting alternatives that have dissimilar risk-return characteristics; this process provides a lower but acceptable overall potential return.

Postnuptial agreement   A contractual agreement signed after marriage to spell out each spouse's financial responsibilities.

Postponing income   The process of delaying paycheck(s) to avoid being pushed into a higher marginal tax rate. This method is useful only if the expected income for the following year is lower than usual.

Potential total return   A figure estimating the potential value of a stock, determined by adding its anticipated dividend income and price appreciation over a period of five years or more.

Preemptive right   The right of current common stockholders to purchase additional shares of any new stock issue: this allows them to maintain their proportionate ownership interest.

Preexisting condition   A medical condition that becomes evident and for which treatment is received before the issuance of a health insurance policy.

Preferred provider organization (PPO)   A group of medical providers (doctors, hospitals, etc.) who contract with a health insurance company to provide services at a discount to policyholders if the policyholders choose to be served by PPO members.

Preferred stock   A fixed-income ownership security of a corporation with the right to assets and earnings before the claims of common stockholders but after those of bondholders.

Premium   The fee paid for insurance protection; the difference that results when a bond is sold above its face value; the fee received by an option writer.

Premium-quote service   Service offered by a profit-oriented firm that makes computer-aided comparisons among 20 to 80 life insurance companies to help individuals select the least expensive policy.

Prenuptial agreement   A contract specifying what, if any, share of each person's assets the other will be entitled to during marriage and in case of divorce.

Prepayment fee   A fee charged by a mortgage lender designed to discourage people from refinancing a mortgage loan every time interest rates drop.

Present interest   The immediate, irrevocable, and complete right of a recipient of a tax-free gift to the property or money given.

Present value   The current value of an asset that is to be received in the future.

Preshopping research   The process of gathering information about products or services before buying them.

Price appreciation   Net income received from the sale of capital assets beyond the expenses incurred in the purchase, capital improvements (if any), and sale of those assets.

Price/earnings ratio (P/E ratio, P/E multiple)   A ratio of the current market value (price) of a common stock to its earnings per share (EPS) that shows how the market is valuing the stock.

Price-sales ratio (PSR)   A ratio obtained by dividing the total current market value of a stock by the total sales over the past year.

Price-to-book ratio   The ratio of the price of a share of common stock to its book value per share.

Primary market   A market that exists when issuers and buyers of new offerings of stocks and bonds are brought together.

Prime rate   The short-term interest rate charged by banks on loans to large business customers with the highest credit rating.

Principal   The original amount borrowed in a real estate or other loan, or the amount placed in an investment.

Principle of indemnity   A philosophy and practice followed by insurance companies, holding that insurance will pay no more than the actual financial loss suffered.

Private employment agency   A firm that specializes in locating positions for certain types of employees, such as executives, secretaries, or computer personnel.

Private mortgage insurance   Insurance sold by a company that insures the first 20 percent of a mortgage loan in case of default.

Probate   A court procedure for settling and disposing of an estate.

Producer cooperatives   Insurance operations owned by individuals or organizations that have come together to provide insurance coverage.

Professional liability insurance   Insurance designed to protect individuals and organizations that provide professional services when they are held liable for the losses of their clients.

Profit-sharing plan   A defined-contribution pension plan that bases the level of contributions on the level of profits achieved by the employer.

Programmed trading The use of computer software programs to generate investment activity.

Progressive tax A tax that demands a higher percentage of a person's income as income increases.

Property insurance. Insurance that provides protection against losses resulting from the damage to or destruction of property or possessions.

Property report A document legally required under the federal Interstate Land Sales Act for real estate properties offered for sale across state lines.

Prospectus A corporation's disclosure of facts regarding its operations, including the experience of its management, its financial status, any anticipated legal matters that could affect the company, and potential risks of investing in the corporation.

Proxy A legal procedure used by a common stockholder to assign voting rights to another.

Purchase contract A formal legal document that conveys the dollar offer and any list of conditions the buyer might want in a real estate or other sale/purchase transaction. Also known as a *sales contract.*

Purchase (sales credit) loan A consumer loan to make a purchase on credit with no cash passing from lender to borrower. Cash passes instead from lender to seller (or the seller may be the lender).

Purchase warrant See *Warrant.*

Purchasing power The dollar amount of goods and services an income can buy after adjusting for inflation.

Pure risk Risk that exists when there is no potential for gain, but a possibility of loss.

Put An option contract that gives the option holder the right to sell an optioned asset to the option writer at the striking price.

Quality of life That which people strive for, including love, self-esteem, good health, achievement, and a general feeling of security.

Random risk The risk associated with owning only one security that by chance may do very poorly in the future.

Rate of return See *Yield.*

Raw land Undeveloped acreage, typically located far from established communities, with no utilities and no improvements except perhaps a substandard access road.

Real estate Property consisting of land and all its permanently attached structures and accompanying rights and privileges, such as crops and mineral rights.

Real estate investment trust (REIT) A type of closed-end investment company in which the proceeds from the sale of the original shares are invested by trust managers in a diversified group of income-producing properties, such as apartments and office buildings.

Real estate property taxes Local (town, city, country, township, parish) taxes based on the assessed value of buildings and land.

Real estate syndicate An indirect form of real property investment often organized as a limited partnership in which a required number of shares (often five) are sold to investors for as little as $500 each to raise capital for local, regional, or national projects.

Real income Income measured in constant prices relative to some base period.

Real return on investment The yield after subtracting the effects of inflation and taxes.

Realtor See *Broker (real estate).*

Rear-end load See *Back-end load.*

Reasonableness tests Computer tests conducted by the IRS on every tax return to help decide which ones will be audited, based on overage amounts for each category of deductions.

Rebate A return to the customer of part of the purchase price of an automobile or other product.

Recession A several-month period during which reduced economic activity results in increasing unemployment, lower industrial production, and declining prices of investment securities.

Reciprocal exchanges Self-insurance mechanisms through which the insureds share in the provision of insurance.

Reconciling budget estimates Reconciling conflicting needs and wants as one revises one's budget until total expenses do not exceed income.

Record date The official day when companies take note of which shareholders deserve dividends.

Recordkeeping The process of recording the sources and amounts of dollars earned and spent.

Recovery A phase of the economic cycle in which levels of production, employment, and retail sales are improving rapidly.

Recurring clause A clause in a health insurance policy that clarifies whether a recurrence of an illness is considered a continuation of the first episode or a separate episode.

Redemption charges Charges levied when mutual-fund shares are redeemed regardless of the length of time the investor has owned the shares. Also called *exit fees.*

Redress To right a wrong.

Registered bond A bond that calls for recording the bondholder's name so that checks for interest and principal can be safely mailed when due.

Registered financial planner A person who meets the qualifications of the International Association of Registered Financial Planners.

Registered investment advisor (RIA) A person giving investment advice to more than five people a year who is required to register with the U.S. Securities and Exchange Commission. Many states also permit the designation "registered investment advisor."

Registry of Financial Planners A designation by the International Association for Financial Planning indicating that a person has passed a day-long examination and met other requirements.

Regressive tax A tax that demands a decreasing proportion of a person's income as income increases.

Regular checking account A non-interest-bearing account that does not assess fees so long as a minimum balance is maintained.

Regular savings account A savings account that permits frequent deposit or withdrawal of funds.

Rehabilitation The retraining of disabled persons for their previous, or a new, occupation.

Reissue rate The charge for a title insurance policy that has lower premiums because the property history has been checked in recent years.

Release An insurance document affirming that the insured accepts the dollar amount of the loss settlement as full and complete reimbursement and that no further claims for the loss will be made against the insurance company.

Rent The payment received in return for the use of property (particularly housing space) such as land or a building.

Repairs Expenses, usually tax-deductible for the investor, that are necessary to maintain the value of a property.

Replacement-cost-requirement formula A mathematical method for determining the reimbursement payable under a home owner's insurance policy when less than 80 percent of a home's replacement value is insured.

Repossession The act of physically seizing the secured property as described in the contract after a loan is defaulted.

Residential lot Subdivided acreage with utilities (including water, electricity, and sewerage) typically located within or adjacent to established communities.

Residential unit A property designed for residential living—such as a house, duplex, apartment, mobile home, or condominium—with a potential to produce a profit.

Residual value The projected value of an automobile at the end of the time period of a lease.

Resume A summary record of one's personal history and experience submitted with a job application.

Retail installment contract A credit agreement used when financing the purchase of a product through the seller or a sales finance company.

Retained earnings Amounts of past and current earnings not paid to shareholders but instead left to accumulate and finance the goals of the company.

Retired (bonds) Bonds paid off at the maturity date stated on the indenture.

Return The total income from an investment, including current income plus capital gains or minus capital losses. Also called *total return*.

Revenue bond A type of municipal bond backed by the revenues from the projects built or maintained by the bond's proceeds, such as dormitories, sewers, waterworks, and toll roads.

Revisionary trust A trust that is irrevocable for at least ten years (unless the beneficiary and/or remaindermen die), after which time it is revocable; during the irrevocable period, it is not part of the donor's estate.

Revocable trust A trust subject to change, amendment, modification, or cancellation by the grantor; the assets remain a part of the donor's taxable estate but pass through to the beneficiary without going through probate at the time of the grantor's death.

Revolving charge account Any charge account where the user has the option to pay the bill in full or spread repayment over several months.

Revolving savings fund A variable expense classification in budgeting into which funds are allocated; done to create a savings amount that can be used to balance the budget in months when expenses exceed income and prohibit the individual or family from running out of money.

Rider See **Endorsement**.

Right A legal instrument to purchase a number of shares of company stock at a specific price during a limited time period.

Right of curtesy A widower's lifetime right to a portion of his wife's property that she acquires during the marriage, usually one-third.

Right of dower A widow's lifetime right to a portion of her husband's property that he acquires during the marriage, usually one-third.

Right-to-use purchase A purchase of limited, pre-planned time to use a vacation property, which is actually a vacation license as it does not grant true legal real estate ownership interests to the purchaser but instead provides a long-term lease or other contract permitting use of a hotel, suite, condominium apartment, or other housing accommodation.

Risk In insurance, the uncertainty about whether a financial loss will occur; in an investment, the uncertainty that the yield will deviate from what is expected.

Risk-averse Opposed to risk; efforts are made to avoid it wherever possible.

Risk management A process of identifying and analyzing each risky situation to determine the best means available to manage it.

Risk-neutral Adjective describing persons who neither fear nor enjoy risk but view it in an objective rational manner with an eye toward its control when beneficial and feasible.

Risk takers People who are not upset by uncertainty and may even enjoy risky situations.

Rollover IRA An individual retirement account into which a lump-sum pension plan distribution has been deposited.

Round lot A block of stock of one hundred shares.

Rule of 78s A method of calculating rebates of finance charges and the prepayment penalty charged the borrower who pays off an installment loan early.

Rule of 72 A formula for figuring the number of years it takes to double principal using compound interest; the interest rate is divided into 72, the result being the number of years it will take to double.

Safe-deposit box Secured lock box available for rent in banks and used for keeping valuables.

Safety Freedom from financial risk.

Salary-reduction plan An employer-sponsored retirement savings plan in which employees divert a portion of their salary to a tax-sheltered savings account, where it accumulates interest tax-free. Also called a *401(k) plan.*

Sales contract See *Purchase contract.*

Sales finance companies Seller-related lenders who are primarily engaged in financing the sales of their parent companies.

Savings and loan association (S&L) A financial institution whose primary purpose is to accept savings and to provide home loans.

Savings investment A type of investment in which the saver expects virtually no risk for either the principal or the interest.

Savings ratio The percentage of disposable income that is saved annually.

Secondary market A market in which the trading of previously purchased securities occurs. Also called *aftermarket.*

Secondary stocks Companies that are not as popular as those traded on the New York Stock Exchange.

Second mortgage A loan on a residence in addition to the original mortgage; in case of default, what is owed on the original mortgage is paid first.

Secured bond A bond for which the issuing corporation pledges specific assets as collateral in the indenture or has the principal and interest guaranteed by another corporation or government agency.

Secured loan A loan that requires that certain assets (collateral) be pledged to secure the debt or the assurance of another person (cosigner), who will agree to pay the loan should the borrower fail to do so.

Securities Negotiable instruments of ownership or debt.

Securities market indexes Indexes that measure the value of a number of securities chosen as a sample to reflect the behavior of the general market of investments.

Security agreement The section of a retail installment contract or other credit agreement that gives the lender a legally secure interest in the item being financed.

Security deposit An amount paid in advance to a landlord to pay for refurbishing the unit beyond what would be expected from normal wear and tear; sometimes charged in addition to prepayment of the last month's rent.

Security interest A lender's control over property: when a loan is secured with collateral, security interest gives the creditor the right to go to court to obtain possession of the property in the event the borrower defaults.

Seller financing Arrangements under which the seller of a home agrees to lend the buyer some or all of the purchase price.

Selling short A trading technique by which investors sell a security they do not own (by borrowing it from a broker) and later buy a like amount of the same security at, it is hoped, a lower price (and return it to the broker), thus earning a profit on the transaction.

Senior debenture A type of bond giving all holders a right to all assets not pledged to secured bondholders.

Separable property Property wholly owned by one spouse, even in community property states, which belonged to the spouse before marriage or was received as a gift or an inheritance.

Series EE savings bond A U.S. government bond purchased for 50 percent of its face value. At maturity, it is worth its face value.

Series HH savings bond A U.S. government bond purchased at face value that pays semiannual interest until maturity five years later.

Service contract An agreement between the contract seller and the buyer of a product to provide free or nearly free repair services to covered components of the product for a specified time period.

Service credit Credit extended by professionals such as doctors, dentists, and lawyers, who expect full payment soon after the service is performed.

Settlement options The choices available to the life insurance beneficiary or the insured concerning the form of payment of the death benefit of a life insurance policy.

Share draft A document, much like a check, used by credit unions to process withdrawals from an interest-bearing share account.

Shareholder See *Stockholder.*

Short-term capital gain (or loss) A gain or loss occurring when the capital asset has been held for six months or less at the time of sale.

Short-term goals or objectives Needs and wants requiring financial resources that can be satisfied within one year.

Short-term investor An investor who is speculative or moderately speculative and wants to earn quick profits (over a period of months, weeks, days, or even hours) on small but significant changes in prices of securities.

Short-term liabilities Debts that must be paid within one year. Also called *current liabilities*.

Signature card A document that provides verification of an account holder's signature when withdrawals are made.

Simple interest Interest earned each period that is withdrawn from an account and not reinvested.

Simplified employee pension plan (SEP) A special retirement plan for the self-employed and their employees that permits contributions from each.

Single-balance, single-fee checking account See **Regular checking account**.

Single-family dwelling A housing unit detached from others.

Single life annuity An annuity that covers the life of a single annuitant.

Single-premium annuity An annuity purchased with a single lump-sum payment.

Sinking fund A requirement in a bond indenture that monies be set aside each year to repay the debt.

Skill A proficiency, dexterity, or technique, particularly one that requires use of the hands or body.

Small claims court A state court with no written record of testimony, where civil matters are often resolved without the assistance of attorneys, providing that the legal amount claimed is less than a generally low maximum set in each state. Also called *court not of record*.

"Smart" card See **Memory card**.

Social Security blackout period Period of ineligibility for Social Security benefits; it begins when the youngest child reaches age 18 and ends when the surviving spouse reaches 60.

Social Security disability income insurance Insurance that provides benefits that will help replace the lost income of eligible disabled workers during a period of disability that is expected to last twelve full months or until death.

Social Security survivors' benefits Payments by the Social Security Administration to the family of the deceased; the level of benefits is based on the amount of Social Security taxes paid by the deceased.

Sole proprietorship A business owned by one person who is responsible for and has control over all aspects of the operation.

Solvency ratio The ratio of total assets to total debt.

Special checking account A non-interest-bearing account that has no minimum balance but may charge various fees.

Specialist A person on the floor of a stock exchange who specializes in handling trades of a particular stock in an effort to maintain a fair and orderly market.

Specialty fund A mutual fund created for just about any investment need that requires both concentration and diversification in a field.

Speculative bonds See **Junk bonds**.

Speculative investment An investment transaction involving considerable risk of loss for the chance of large gains.

Speculative risk Risk that exists when there is potential for gain as well as loss.

Speculative stock A stock whose earnings record has been spotty but apparently has a potential for substantial earnings sometime in the future, even though such earnings may or may not be realized.

Spread The difference between the purchase price paid by an investment banking firm and expected resale price of a new issue of stock.

Spreadsheet A computer capability that permits calculating the effects of a variety of transactions.

Standard deduction The amount all taxpayers, except some dependents, may deduct when filing an income tax return; the government's legally permissible estimate of a person's tax-deductible expenses.

Stated interest rate (bonds) A fixed interest rate printed on the bond certificate. Also called *coupon* or *nominal rate*.

State rate (credit) The rate of interest quoted by lenders when asked the rate of interest on a loan or charge account. By law, this rate must be the same as the annual percentage rate (APR).

State rate of interest (savings) The apparent interest rate that is applied to savings deposits before consideration of the time period. Also called *nominal rate of interest*.

Sticker price The manufacturer's suggested price for a new car and its options as listed on the window sticker.

Stockbroker A person who acts as a middleman in buying and selling securities and who collects a commission on each purchase or sale. Also known as an *account executive* or a *registered representative*.

Stock brokerage firm A licensed financial service institution that specializes in selling and buying securities.

Stock certificate Evidence of a common or preferred shareholder's ownership of a company in which he or she has invested.

Stock dividend An issuance of new stock certificates to existing stockholders on the basis of current proportional ownership.

Stockholder The owner of common stock. Also called a *shareholder*.

Stock insurance companies Companies owned by stockholders that provide insurance coverage in return for the opportunity to earn a profit for their owners.

Stock option A contract giving the holder the right to buy or sell a specific number of shares (normally one hundred) of a certain stock at a particular price (the *striking price*) before a specified date (the *expiration date*).

Stocks Shares of ownership in the assets, earnings, and future direction of a corporate form of business.

Stock split A trade of a given number of old shares of stock for a certain number of newly issued shares.

Stop-loss order See **Stop order.**

Stop order Instructions to the stockbroker to sell at the next available opportunity when a stock reaches or drops below a specified price. Also called a *stop-loss order*.

Stop-payment order A notice assuring that a check will not be honored and cashed when presented to the drawer's financial institution.

Straddle The act of writing both puts and calls on an asset at the same striking price in order to offset speculative risk.

Straight bankruptcy A type of bankruptcy in which all debts are wiped out once the designated bankruptcy trustee has listed the debts and determined that it would be highly unlikely that substantial repayment could be made.

Straight life (pure) annuity An annuity that pays a fixed amount every month until the annuitant's death.

Street name A name other than that of the individual investor who owns securities. Certificates are kept in the brokerage firm's name.

Subleasing Leasing of property by the original tenant to another tenant.

Subordinate budgets A method of budget control that requires explicit details for particular expense categories within the budget.

Subordinated debenture A bond that gives holders a lesser claim to assets perhaps similar to those of the stockholders.

Subrogation rights Rights that allow an insurer to take action against a negligent third party (and that party's insurance company) to obtain reimbursement for payments made to an insured.

Suicide clause A clause that allows the life insurance company to deny coverage if the insured commits suicide within the first few years after issuance of the policy.

Super NOW account A government-insured high-interest NOW account offered through depository institutions. The initial minimum deposit ranges from $1000 to $2500, and yields are calculated weekly or monthly.

Supplemental health insurance A form of health insurance designed to fill the gaps in coverage of the standard health insurance plans or provide reimbursement in addition to that provided by the standard plans.

Supplemental security income (SSI) A federal program to provide limited monetary benefits for those of very little financial means.

Surgical insurance A health insurance plan designed to protect the insured from the expenses of surgical procedures.

Sweep account An account that combines a regular NOW account with a money market fund and is offered through various institutions. An investor's money flows between the NOW account and the money market fund, depending on the balance in the account, with a goal of maximizing interest earnings.

Swingers Stocks and warrants that have gone up and down the most in the past week based on a percentage of change.

Switching privilege A privilege for mutual fund shareholders that permits them, if their needs or objectives change, to swap shares on a dollar-for-dollar basis for shares in another mutual fund managed by the same corporation. Also called *exchange privilege*.

Table method A way of determining future value using a table (such as Table 1.1).

Tactical asset allocation See **Asset allocation.**

Tangible assets Physical items that have fairly long life spans and could be sold to raise cash but whose primary purpose is to provide maintenance of a lifestyle.

Tangible investments Physical items that are owned primarily for their investment value.

Taxable income The amount of income upon which taxes are finally assessed after subtracting a variety of adjustments, deductions, and exemptions from a total gross income.

Taxable yield (TY) A percentage yield on a tax-exempt investment, determined by a formula, that equals what would have to be earned on a taxable investment to achieve the same gain.

Taxable-yield formula A mathematical method for determining what would have to be earned on a tax-exempt investment to equal the yield from a taxable one.

Tax attorney An attorney who specializes in income tax laws and regulations.

Tax audit   A formal examination of a taxpayer's tax forms for accuracy and completeness conducted by the IRS.

Tax avoidance   An attempt to avoid paying taxes by reducing tax liability through legal techniques.

Tax credits   A group of items that can be deducted dollar for dollar against one's tax liability.

Tax-deductible expenditure record   The written record of all income tax-deductible expenditures by date, amount paid and to whom, and tax classification.

Taxes   Compulsory charges imposed by a government on citizens and property.

Tax evasion   An illegal process that involves deliberately hiding income, falsely claiming deductions, or otherwise cheating the government out of taxes owed.

Tax-exempt investment   An investment free from federal taxation.

Tax-exempt yield (TEY)   A percentage yield on a taxable investment, determined by a formula, that equals what would have to be earned on a tax-exempt investment to achieve the same gain.

Tax-exempt yield formula   A mathematical method for determining what would have to be earned on a taxable investment to equal the yield from a tax-exempt one.

Tax Form 1040   "Long form" for taxpayers who itemize deductions and utilize a number of other tax-saving deductions and credits.

Tax Form 1040-A   Intermediate-length form that permits reporting of salaries, wages, nontraditional sources of income (up to $50,000), and tax-saving credits.

Tax Form 1040-ES   Declaration of Estimated Tax for Individuals: form used by taxpayers who are required to make quarterly payments because they do not have payroll withholding.

Tax Form 1040-EZ   "Very short form" for single people with uncomplicated tax information.

Tax Form 1040-X   Amended U.S. Individual Tax Return: form used to make corrections and obtain deserved refunds for previous three years.

Tax-free exchange   A transaction in which none of the people involved in a trade of property receives any other form of property or money.

Tax liability   The actual tax owed on income earned during the previous year.

Tax loss   A "paper" loss, created when deductions generated from an investment exceed the income from an investment.

Tax-preparation services   Companies that help individuals or businesses list appropriate deductions, compute accurately, and determine proper tax liability when preparing tax forms.

Tax shelter   A high-risk investment that is attractive to a high-income taxpayer because losses may be used to offset other income.

Tax-sheltered annuity   An annuity used to defer income subject to taxation until the funds in the annuity are withdrawn.

Tax-sheltered (qualified) retirement plan   A financial plan approved by the IRS for special tax advantages that reduces taxes and increases retirement benefits.

Tax swap   The selling of a depressed stock for a tax loss and purchase of a similar security, permitting the investor to register a tax loss while upgrading his or her portfolio.

Tenancy in common   A type of direct ownership in which two or more people have control of a property regardless of whether they hold equal shares, and each person retains the right to dispose of his or her undivided interest.

Tenancy in common account   A bank account held by two persons that requires both owners to sign a withdrawal slip before it can be honored.

10-K report   A comprehensive document filed with the SEC by a corporation; it contains much of the same type of information as a prospectus or annual report and provides additional updated financial details about corporate activities.

Term life insurance   A type of life insurance contract that pays benefits only if the insured party dies within the time period of the contract.

Testamentary trust   A trust that is established and becomes effective upon the death of the grantor according to the terms written in the grantor's will.

Testate   An adjective describing a person who dies with a valid will in effect.

Testator   A person who makes a will.

Thirty-day acount   An account in which debts incurred are expected to be paid in full within thirty days.

Three-month Treasury bill   A U.S. government security that matures and is payable in 91 days.

Time deposit   A savings account deposit in an institution that is expected to remain on deposit for an extended period and is a legal debt upon which the institution must pay interest as specified.

Time period limits   Clauses in health insurance policies that specify the maximum payment to be made for covered expenses occurring within a specified time period, usually one year.

Time value of money   The concept applied in the comparison and prediction of the present and future values of an asset.

Title   The legal right of ownership interest in real property.

Title insurance   Insurance required of home buyers by lenders, to protect against the possibility that the title later will be found faulty.

Title search   An attorney's examination of the abstract and other documents in order to establish the status of a title of real estate.

Total disability An injury or illness that prevents a worker from performing any of the tasks of his or her previous occupation or any other occupation.

Total return The combination of the dividend yield and the potential capital gains on an investment. Also called *return*.

Total return (of a mutual fund) Overall change in value, including changes in share price and assuming all dividends and capital gain distributions are reinvested (defined by SEC regulations).

Trade association An organization representing the interests of companies in the same industry.

Tradeoff See *Opportunity cost.*

Trailing edge The area of the back of a check where endorsements may legally be placed. It extends 1½ inches from the left edge as seen from the front.

Transaction costs Fees charged by the broker and the seller to pay for the expenses of transferring ownership of an investment.

Transfer payments Payments by governments and individuals for which no goods or services are expected in return, such as welfare payments.

Travel and entertainment account A special type of charge account used primarily by business people for food and lodging expenses while traveling, generally requiring the entire balance charged to be repaid within thirty days.

Traveler's checks Checks issued as a cash substitute by large financial institutions and sold through smaller institutions such as a local bank or credit union.

Treasury bill (T-bill) A U.S. government security that matures in 91 days, 6 months, 9 months, or 360 days. It is sold on a "discount basis," with the gain at maturity representing interest for federal income-tax purposes.

Treasury bond A U.S. government security that is sold in $1000 and $10,000 denominations, with a maturity of more than ten years and a semiannual fixed interest rate higher than a Treasury note because it is a longer-term issue.

Treasury Direct A plan under which sales of U.S. Treasury issues are recorded on a book-entry basis and all interest is deposited directly into the bondholder's bank account.

Treasury note A U.S. government security sold in $1000 and $10,000 denominations, with a maturity of one to ten years, and a semiannual fixed interest rate slightly higher than a Treasury bill.

Trust A legal instrument that places control of one's assets with a trustee.

Trustee A person or institution that manages the financial assets of another.

Trustee account An account that restricts a child from withdrawing money from the account without a responsible adult's signature.

12b-1 fee An annual charge assessed to shareholders that pays for advertising, marketing, and distribution costs of a mutual fund.

Underinsured motorist insurance Automobile insurance that protects the insured driver and passengers from bodily injury losses (and, in some cases, property damage losses) when the at-fault driver carries insufficient liability insurance.

Underwriting The insurer's process of deciding which insurance applicants to accept.

Unearned income Income from rents, dividends, interest, royalties, and transfer payments.

Unified gift and estate tax credit A credit of $192,800, equivalent to the tax on an estate of $600,000.

Uninsured motorist insurance Automobile insurance that protects the insured driver and passengers from bodily injury losses (and, in a few states, property damage losses) resulting from an auto accident caused by an uninsured motorist.

Units of coverage Calendar units accredited by the Social Security Administration based on minimum total earnings in a year.

Universal life insurance A type of life insurance that provides both the pure protection and cash value build-up of whole life insurance but with variability in the face amount, rate of cash value accumulation, premiums, and rate of return.

Unlimited marital deduction A provision of federal tax laws that allows everything left to a surviving spouse to transfer tax-free.

Unsecured bond A bond that has no collateral named as security for the debt and is backed only by the good faith and reputation of the issuing agency.

Unsecured loan A loan that has the assurance of neither collateral nor a cosigner.

U.S. Treasury note See *Treasury note.*

Usury laws Legal interest-rate maximums that can be charged by lenders.

Utility The ability of a good or service to satisfy a human want.

Values Principles, standards, or qualities considered worthwhile or desirable that provide criteria for goals, thereby giving continuity to decisions.

Values clarification The process of determining values by searching and selecting one over another.

Variable annuity An annuity for which the payments to an individual vary upward or downward according to the success of the insurance company's investments.

Variable expenses Expenditures over which an individual has considerable control.

Variable interest rate An interest rate on a credit card or other instrument that moves up or down monthly according to changes in an index of the lender's cost of funds.

Variable life insurance A cash value insurance policy that allows policyholders to choose the investments made with their cash value accumulations and to share in the gains and losses of those investments.

Variable rate bonds See *Floating-rate bonds.*

Variable rate certificate of deposit A financial instrument that pays an interest rate which is adjusted monthly and that allows savers to "lock in" the rate at any time.

Variable rate loan A loan for which the periodic interest rate fluctuates according to some measure of interest rates in the economy as a whole.

Variable-universal life insurance A form of universal life insurance that allows the policyholder to choose the investments made with the cash value accumulated by the policy.

Variance analysis The comparison of actual expenditures with budgeted estimates.

Vesting A process by which employees obtain during their working years a legal claim on retirement benefits that cannot be taken away if they resign or are dismissed.

Veterans Administration (VA) A federal government agency that promotes home ownership among veterans by providing the lender with a guarantee against buyer default.

Veterans Administration hospitals Medical care facilities designed exclusively to provide care to veterans.

Voting rights The proportionate authority of common stock owners to express an opinion or choice in matters affecting the company.

Wage-earner plan A plan designed for those filing bankruptcy who might be able to pay off their debts given certain protections of the court.

Waiver-of-premium A provision that sets certain conditions, such as disability, under which an insurance policy would be kept in force without the payment of premiums.

Wants Items people would like to have to improve their comfort and satisfaction.

Warrant A legal option that gives the holder the opportunity to buy a certain number of shares of a bond, preferred stock, or some issues of common stock at a specified price over a designated period. Also called a *purchase warrant.*

Warranty An assurance by a seller to a buyer that goods are as promised.

Warranty insurance Insurance sold through builders and real estate brokers to provide warranty protection for home buyers.

Wealth An abundance of money, property, investments, and other resources.

Week order Instructions to a stockbroker that are valid until the close of the trading on Friday of the current week.

Whole life insurance A type of cash value life insurance that provides life insurance protection for the lifetime of the insured and requires the payment of premiums for life.

Will A written instrument that directs the disposition of an individual's assets at death, but only if it is executed in accordance with statutory provisions.

Work style The unique set of ways in which a person works with and responds to his or her job surroundings and associates.

Workers' compensation insurance Insurance that protects employers from liability for any injury or disease suffered by employees and resulting from employment-related causes.

Yield (of a mutual fund) The rate of income the fund earns on its investments as a percentage of the fund's share price (defined by SEC regulation).

Yield (rate of return) The profitability of an investment described as a percentage over a certain time period, usually a year.

Yield to maturity (YTM) The total annual rate of return earned by a bondholder on a bond when it is held to maturity; it reflects both the current income and any difference if the bond was purchased at a price other than face value.

Yield to maturity (YTM) formula A mathematical method for determining the total annual rate of return on a bond held to maturity.

Zero-coupon bonds Municipal or corporate bonds issued at prices far lower than their face value; they pay no interest income. The return to the investor comes solely from redeeming them at their face value or selling them for a price higher than what was paid. Also called *deep discount bonds.*

Zero-sum game An investment situation in which the total wealth of all traders remains the same, as the trading simply redistributes the wealth among the traders.

Index

Key terms and the numbers of pages on which they are defined are set in boldface italic type.

Flipping, 256
Float, 183
   using, to your advantage, 183
Floater policies, 438–439
Floating-rate bonds, 609
Flood insurance, 439
Floor broker, 679
Food Additives Amendment, 337
Footnote p, 661
Footnote r, 661
Footnote t, 662
Forbes, 640, 668
Forecasting, 10
Foreclosure, 357
Form 1099, 279, *305*
Formulas, investors' use of, 699
Fortuitous losses, 391
403(b) salary-reduction plan, 766–767
   borrowing from, 775
   and early retirement, 775
   hardship withdrawals from, 775
401(k) plan, 765–767
   borrowing from, 775
   and early retirement, 775
   hardship withdrawals from, 775
Franchising, 58
Freddie Mac. *See* Federal Home
   Loan Mortgage Corporation
Friends, as source of loans, 243–244
Fringe benefit, 55, 469
   value of, 55
Front-end load, 633
FSB, 171
FTC Used Car Rule, 337
Full warranties, 327
Fundamental theory, of stock
   prices, 584–585
Fundscope, 640
Futures contracts, 744
   trading, 744–746
Future value, 20
   determination of
      basic calculation method, 20
      basic math method, 20
      calculator method, 20
      table method, 20–21
      tables of, A-1–A-3, A-6–A-7

Garnishment, 256
Gender, and income, 40–41
General brokerage firm, 673

General obligation bonds, 608
Generic products, buying, 320
Geographic region, and income, 37
Gift and estate tax, 798
Gifts
   as defined by IRS, 799–800
   lifetime, 798–800
GIM. See Gross income multiplier
Ginnie Mae. *See* Government National Mortgage Association
Givers, 119
GNP. *See* Gross national product
Good-till-canceled (GTC) order, 683
Government, employment with, 52–53
Government National Mortgage Association, 607
Government securities, 606
Grace period, 192
   on credit card purchases, 222
Graduated-payment mortgage, 364
Grantor, of trust, 803
Granville Market Letter, 672
Gross estate, 798
Gross income, 279
   determination of, 279–280
Gross income multiplier, 715–716
Gross national product, 16
Group insurance, 410
   advantages of, 410–412
Group legal insurance plan, 441–442
Group term life insurance, 497–498
Growing-equity mortgage, 365
Growth and income fund, 630
Growth fund, 630
Growth stock, 581
Growth stocks (lesser known), 581–582
Growth stocks (well known), 581
Guardian, 797

Hazard, 390
Hazard reduction, 411
Headhunters, 53
Health care expenditures, in United States, 452–453
Health insurance, 399, 452, 455, 534
   application for, 463

   cancelable policies, 467
   claims procedures for, 477
   continuation provisions of, 467–468
   convertibility of, 468
   copayment clause in, 466
   cost of, 475
   coverage limitations of, 466–467
   government, 473–474
   grace period, 468
   group vs. individual, 469–470
   guaranteed renewable policies, 468
   needs, determining, 453–455
   noncancelable policies, 468
   optionally renewable policies, 468
   policy
      criteria to use in judging, 476–477
      definitions of, 464
      general exclusions of, 467
      general terms and provisions of, 462–464
      limitations based on timing of loss, 466–467
      limits of, 465
      maternity benefits of, 466–467
      nonmedical provisions of, 467–468
      payment limitations of, 464–466
      and preexisting condition, 466
      time period of, 464
      who is covered by, 464
   shopping for, 468–477
   sources of, 470–474
   types of, 455–456
   waiver-of-premium option, 468
Health insurance coinsurance clause, 457
Health insurance coverage, 455
Health maintenance organizations, 470–472
Health-related losses, 453–455
Hidden loads, 634
HMOs. *See* Health maintenance organizations
Holder-in-due-course doctrine, 226–227
Holographic will, 796